Income Tax Fundamentals 2025

Gerald E. Whittenburg

Steven L. Gill

San Diego State University

Australia • Brazil • Canada • Mexico • Singapore • United Kingdom • United States

Income Tax Fundamentals, **43rd Edition**
Gerald E. Whittenburg and Steven L. Gill

SVP, Product: Cheryl Costantini

Portfolio Product Director: Joe Sabatino

Portfolio Product Manager: Jonathan Gross

Product Assistant: Flannery Cowan

Senior Learning Designer: Kristen Meere

Senior Content Manager: Sheila Moran

Content Project Manager: Pradhiba Kannaiyan

Product Marketing Manager: Danielle Dornbusch

Digital Project Manager: Steven McMillian

Production Service: MPS Limited

Senior Designer: Chris Doughman

Cover Images: alexsl/E+/Getty Images

Special page images:

Zhukov Oleg/Shutterstock.com;
ILYA AKINSHIN/Shutterstock.com

Intellectual Property

Content Acquisition Analyst: Rida Syed

Project Manager: Subashini Mohan

Copyright © 2025 Cengage, Inc. ALL RIGHTS RESERVED.
WCN: 01-100-496

No part of this work covered by the copyright herein may be reproduced or distributed in any form or by any means, except as permitted by U.S. copyright law, without the prior written permission of the copyright owner.

Unless otherwise noted, all content is Copyright © Cengage, Inc.

Previous edition(s): © 2024, © 2023, © 2022

> For product information and technology assistance, contact us at
> **Cengage Customer & Sales Support, 1-800-354-9706**
> **or support.cengage.com.**
>
> For permission to use material from this text or product, submit all requests online at **www.copyright.com**.

Tax forms reproduced courtesy of the Internal Revenue Service (**www.irs.gov**).

Library of Congress Control Number: 2024923612

Student Edition:
ISBN: 978-0-357-98857-2

Cengage
5191 Natorp Boulevard
Mason, OH 45040
USA

Cengage is a leading provider of customized learning solutions. Our employees reside in nearly 40 different countries and serve digital learners in 165 countries around the world. Find your local representative at: **www.cengage.com.**

To learn more about Cengage platforms and services, register or access your online learning solution, or purchase materials for your course, visit **www.cengage.com.**

Printed in the United States of America
Print Number: 04   Print Year: 2025

Concise, Current, & Practical!

Income Tax Fundamentals' Winning Forms Approach Is Time-Tested

Income Tax Fundamentals 2025 Edition is designed as a self-contained book for an introductory course in individual income taxation. We take pride in the concise, current, and practical coverage of the income tax return preparation process. *Income Tax Fundamentals* continues to be the **market-leading textbook** with a tax forms-based approach that is a reliable choice, with an experienced author team that offers a commitment to accuracy. The workbook format of the textbook presents materials in practical sections with multiple examples and review problems. The presentation of the material does not assume that the reader has taken a course in accounting, making it appropriate for use as a self-study guide to federal income tax. *Income Tax Fundamentals* adopters tell us:

> Great text. I have used it for years mostly because of its simple and straightforward approach to the basic income tax elements.
> — Jerold K. Braun, Daytona State College

> This text provides an excellent overview for community tax classes. The software gives these students good hands-on experience with the concepts.
> — Jay Wright, New River Community College

> I love this book with all its comprehensive problems that progress from easy to difficult.
> — LoAnn Nelson, PhD, CPA, Lake Region State College

> The layout of the chapters is well-thought out.
> — James Hromadka, San Jacinto College

> I enjoy using the Whittenburg text...it is the best I have found.
> — Jana Hosmer, Blue Ridge Community College

Whittenburg and Gill's hallmark **"Forms Approach"** allows students to practice filling out tax returns, with the option to download tax forms online or complete tax returns in ProConnect Tax software. *Income Tax Fundamentals* follows the Form 1040 and supporting Schedules 1 through 3, A through E, and many more. Every attempt to align the concepts with the schedules has been made so students can follow from the detailed form or worksheet to the schedule and eventually to Form 1040.

ProConnect™ Tax Each individual tax form required to complete the problems in the textbook is included within *Income Tax Fundamentals* and within the complimentary ProConnect Tax software. ProConnect Tax is an industry-leading tax preparation software that is hosted on the cloud and provides robust tax content and easy navigation. The ProConnect Tax website offers community and knowledge-based content, view alerts, and FAQ articles. All of the 2024 individual income tax return problems in the textbook may be solved using the ProConnect Tax software, or students may prepare the tax returns by hand.

Income Tax Fundamentals

Evolves Each Year to Benefit You

New to This Edition

Plenty to Consider in a Slow Legislative Year

Legislation was particularly quiet with no significant tax laws enacted since the previous edition. This edition of Income Tax Fundamentals includes new content for the following items:

- Section 199A (real estate investment trust) dividends and the impact on the qualified business income deduction.
- The rollover of Section 529 plan funds into a Roth IRA for the plan beneficiary.
- The Public Safety Officer health insurance exclusion from pension income.
- Coverage of the new Form 1099-LS and Form 1099-SB for reporting the sale of a life insurance policy.
- Filing Form 8815 to exclude the proceeds of U.S. Savings Bond interest when used for qualified education expenses.
- Discussion of the tax treatment of charitable contributions made by a Schedule C business.
- Introduction to the deferred loss associated with wash sales on securities.
- The special tax treatment for sales of Section 1202 and Section 1244 small business stock.
- A discussion of the exclusion of the gain on sale of a primary residence by a surviving spouse.
- Introduction of new Form 172 for reporting net operating losses.
- Introduction of new Form 461 for reporting excess business losses.
- Introduction to the tax treatment of subscription-based health care.
- The tax treatment of the self-employed health insurance deduction for partners and S corporation shareholders.
- Introduction of Form 5329 to report the 10-percent penalty tax on early distributions from an IRA or similar qualified plan.
- The form of tax reporting of distributions from qualified plans.
- The tax treatment of jury duty pay and repayments of jury duty pay to an employer.
- Introduce Form 4952 for reporting the investment interest expense deduction.
- Added discussion of a basic allocation of the premium tax credit when the tax family and the coverage family are not the same.
- Significantly expanded coverage of the foreign income and foreign housing exclusion.
- The computation of depreciation related to asset disposals.
- Coverage of Form 2210 and the penalty calculation of taxpayer failure to make estimated tax payments, using the annualized income method.
- New requirements for beneficial ownership interest (BOI) reporting.

This edition also includes updates and expanded coverage of:

- Detailed support calculation for determining dependency.
- Update of artificial intelligence (AI) related tax research.
- A revision of the discussion on annuities to better explain how annuities in a qualified retirement plan are treated.
- The unique rules for the deduction of international business travel.
- The allocation of expenses for a home office including classifying taxes and interest on Form 8829 based on whether the taxpayer itemizes or not.
- An improved discussion on reporting passive income and losses on Form 8582.
- Form 7206 used to report the deduction for self-employed health insurance.
- IRA deduction limitations (both traditional and Roth) including use of worksheets from IRS Publication 590A and expanded definition of modified adjusted gross income for these limits.
- The 5-year rule for excluding distributions from a Roth IRA.
- Early distributions that are eligible for exclusion from the 10-percent penalty tax.

- The Small Employer Pension Plan Start-up Costs credit, including the credit for employer contributions made to the plan.
- Qualified student loan payment treatment as qualified plan contributions eligible for an employer match.
- Mortgage interest reporting on Form 1098.
- Enhancement of the charitable contribution limitation worksheet for easier use.
- Changes in accounting methods and reporting on Form 3115.
- Deletion of foreign adoption (adoption of foreign children by U.S. citizens is at record low levels).
- The new and used clean vehicle credits, including transfer of the credit to a dealer.
- Bonus depreciation change in percentage.
- Large employer qualified retirement plans, including governmental employee plans.
- Common IRS notices received by taxpayers.

Content has been compared to the state requirements that regulate the training and education of tax preparers and also compared to content included in Volunteer Income Tax Assistance (VITA) training, in an effort to provide as much overlap in coverage as possible.

Introduction of Additional Real-life Source Documents

Income Tax Fundamentals continues to include commonly used source documents in the exercises and tax return problems, such as Form W-2, a myriad of Forms 1099, Form 1095-A, payroll documents, and additional accounting schedules, such as trial balances and income statements, in an effort to replicate the tax return preparation process. Information that is extraneous to the problem is included to encourage students to use analytical and critical-thinking skills to deal with less-structured problems.

Updated Cumulative Software Problem

The cumulative software problem included as Group 5 questions at the end of Chapters 1–8 has been updated to include additional source documents (Forms W-2, 1099, etc.) and extraneous information to encourage students to think more critically about the relevance of certain items when preparing tax returns.

A Complete Learning System—CNOWv2

CNOWv2 for Taxation takes students from motivation to mastery. It elevates thinking by providing superior content designed with the entire student workflow in mind. Students learn more efficiently with a variety of engaging assessments and learning tools. For instructors, CNOWv2 provides ultimate control and customization with a clear view into student performance that allows for the opportunity to tailor the learning experience to improve outcomes.

Motivation

Many instructors find that students come to class unmotivated and unprepared. To help with engagement and preparedness, CNOWv2 for Income Tax Fundamentals offers **Self-Study Questions** for each learning objective throughout the chapters to help students prepare for class lectures or review prior to an exam. Self-Study Questions provide ample practice for the students as they read the chapters, while providing them with valuable feedback and checks along the way, as the solutions are provided conveniently in Appendix E of the textbook.

Application

Students need to learn problem-solving skills in order to complete taxation problems on their own. However, as students try to work through homework problems, sometimes they need additional guidance. To help reinforce concepts and keep students on the right track, CNOWv2 for Income Tax Fundamentals offers the following:

- **End-of-chapter homework:** Group 1 and 2 problems
- **Algorithmic versions:** End-of-chapter homework is available for at least 20–30 problems per chapter.
- **Detailed feedback for each homework question:** Homework questions include enhanced, immediate feedback so students can learn as they go. Levels of feedback include an option for "check my work" prior to submission of an assignment. Then, after submitting an assignment, students receive even more extensive feedback explaining why their answers were incorrect. Instructors can decide how much feedback their students receive and when, including providing the full solution, if desired.

- Built-in **Test Bank:** Provides online assessment.
- CNOWv2's **Adaptive Study Plan:** Complete with quizzes, an eBook, and more, the Adaptive Study Plan is designed to provide assistance for students who need additional support and prepare them for the exam.

Mastery

Finally, students need to make the leap from memorizing concepts to critical thinking. They need to be able to connect multiple topics and master the material. To help students grasp the big picture of taxation, tax return preparation, and achieve the end goal of mastery, CNOWv2 for Income Tax Fundamentals offers **Comprehensive Problems:** allowing students to complete the tax return problems by entering the relevant information on tax forms and schedules in the ProConnect Tax software or by manually preparing the tax forms and schedules provided in an online appendix.

Cengage Learning Testing Powered by Cognero®

Cognero® is a flexible, online system that allows instructors to:

- author, edit, and manage test bank content from multiple Cengage Learning solutions.
- create multiple test versions in an instant.
- deliver tests from instructors' LMS, instructors' classrooms or wherever convenient.

Cognero® possesses the features necessary to make assessment fast, efficient, and effective:

- **Simplicity at every step:** A desktop-inspired interface features drop-down menus and familiar, intuitive tools.
- **Full-featured test generator:** Choose from various question types. Multi-language support, an equation editor, and unlimited metadata help ensure instructors' tests are complete and compliant.
- **Cross-compatible capability:** Import and export content into other systems.

CL Testing Powered by Cognero® is accessible through the instructor companion site, **www.cengage.com/login**.

Key Terms

Key Terms with page references are located at the end of all of the chapters and reinforce the important tax terms introduced and covered in each chapter.

Key Points

Following the Key Terms is a brief summary of the learning objective highlights for each chapter to allow students to focus quickly on the main points of each chapter.

Reliable Instructor Resources Are Convenient

Solutions Manual

The manual, located on the instructor companion website: **www.cengage.com/login**, contains detailed solutions to the end-of-chapter problems in the textbook.

Comprehensive Instructor Companion Website

This password-protected site contains instructor resources: the Solutions Manuals, the Test Banks, Cognero® testing tools, Solutions to the Cumulative Tax Return Problems, ProConnect Tax software solutions and instructions, PowerPoints, and more: **www.cengage.com/login**.

As We Go to Press

To access tax law information after the publication of this textbook, please visit **www.cengage.com**. At the home page, input the ISBN of your textbook (from the back cover of your book). The link to the Cengage website will take you to the product page where free companion resources are located.

Step-by-Step Format Builds Student Confidence

The practical, step-by-step format in **Income Tax Fundamentals 2025 Edition** builds from simple to complex topics. The authors are careful to lead students down a path of understanding rather than overwhelming them with excessive detail and multiple Internal Revenue Code references.

- Helpful examples within each chapter provide realistic scenarios for students to consider.

Example Glenn owns a lake home. During the year he rented the home for $1,800 for two weeks, lived in the home for three months, and left the home vacant during the remainder of the year. The expenses for the lake home included $5,000 in mortgage interest, $700 in property taxes, $2,100 in utilities and maintenance, and $3,000 in depreciation. Since the lake home was rented for fewer than 15 days, Glenn would not report the $1,800 of income and may deduct only the interest and property taxes as itemized deductions on Schedule A. The other expenses are nondeductible personal expenses. ◆

- The short Learning Objective sections within each chapter offer numerous examples, supported by the "Self-Study Problems" throughout. The Self-Study Problems encourage students to answer a series of relevant questions in a short-answer format. The solutions to the Self-Study Problems are provided at the end of the textbook in Appendix E, offering immediate feedback to students to help build confidence.

- The Quick Tax Reference Guide on the inside of the back cover of the textbook and included in the ebook with this edition shows the Tax Equation and federal tax rate schedule.

2024 Federal Tax Rate Schedule

If Taxable Income Is Over:	But Not Over:	The Tax Is:
Single Individual		
$0	$11,600	10% of taxable income *
$11,600	$47,150	$1,160.00 + 12% of the excess over $11,600 *
$47,150	$100,525	$5,426.00 + 22% of the excess over $47,150 *
$100,525	$191,950	$17,168.50 + 24% of the excess over $100,525 *
$191,950	$243,725	$39,110.50 + 32% of the excess over $191,950 *
$243,725	$609,350	$55,678.50 + 35% of the excess over $243,725 *
$609,350		$183,647.25 + 37% of the excess over $609,350 *
Married Filing Jointly or Surviving Spouse		
$0	$23,200	10% of taxable income *
$23,200	$94,300	$2,320.00 + 12% of the excess over $23,200 *
$94,300	$201,050	$10,852.00 + 22% of the excess over $94,300 *
$201,050		$34,337.00 + 24% of the excess over $201,050 *

Learning Objectives
After completing this chapter, you should be able to:

- LO 2.1 Apply the definition of gross income.
- LO 2.2 Describe salaries and wages income reporting and inclusion in gross income.
- LO 2.3 Explain the general tax treatment of health insurance.
- LO 2.4 Determine when meals and lodging may be excluded from taxable income.
- LO 2.5 Identify the common employee fringe benefit income exclusions.
- LO 2.6 Determine when prizes and awards are included in income.

- Learning Objectives help organize information and are referenced in the end-of-chapter exercises.

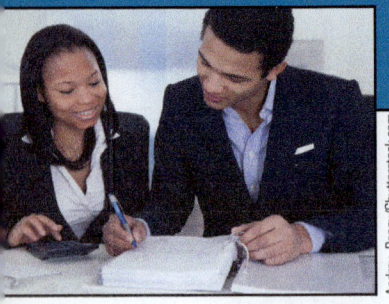

Real-World Applications Keep Students Engaged

- The "Would You Sign This Tax Return?" feature places readers in the office of a tax preparer with interesting and sometimes humorous real-world tax ethics questions that will intrigue students. Many of these features are inspired by the authors' own experiences working with various clients in tax preparation. As part of each scenario, students decide if they would sign the tax return. The instructor can use the cases to spark group discussions on basic tax preparation ethics.

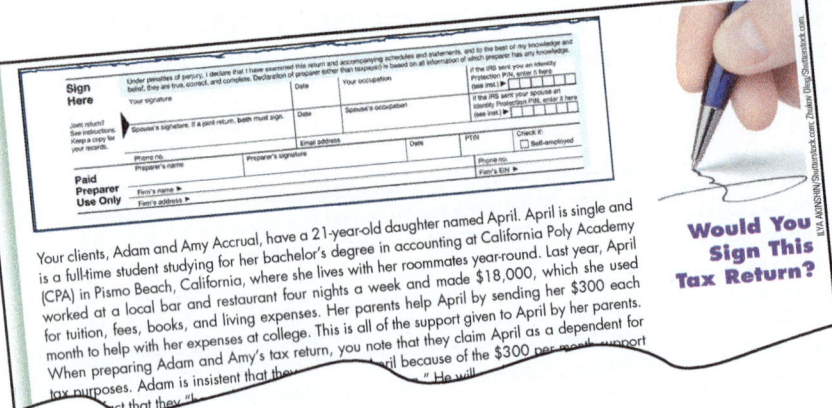

Your clients, Adam and Amy Accrual, have a 21-year-old daughter named April. April is single and is a full-time student studying for her bachelor's degree in accounting at California Poly Academy (CPA) in Pismo Beach, California, where she lives with her roommates year-round. Last year, April worked at a local bar and restaurant four nights a week and made $18,000, which she used for tuition, fees, books, and living expenses. Her parents help April by sending her $300 each month to help with her expenses at college. This is all of the support given to April by her parents. When preparing Adam and Amy's tax return, you note that they claim April as a dependent for tax purposes. Adam is insistent that the... April because of the $300 per month support...

- Real-world examples within Tax Break segments provide actual, effective examples of tax-planning strategies that clearly illustrate the concepts discussed throughout the book and cover nearly every basic tax-planning technique used by tax preparers.

Tax Break

Head of Household is a filing status that can be difficult to understand but comes with some substantial tax benefits if a taxpayer qualifies. Single parents should carefully analyze their situation since Head of Household provides lower tax rates and a higher standard deduction than Single filing status. This benefit is not just limited to single parents. All unmarried taxpayers that maintain a household and provide support for another person should consider whether they qualify for this tax-advantageous filing status.

- Interesting tax facts within "Would You Believe?" sections grab students' attention with interesting asides, including captivating facts, quotations, and stories about tax laws and preparation.

In 2017, about 69 percent of individual taxpayers selected the standard deduction. After the expansion of the standard deduction amounts, the percentage jumped to over 88 percent. Recall that the expanded standard deduction is scheduled to expire at the end of 2025.

- New Tax Law boxes throughout the textbook draw students' attention to specific areas affected by new tax legislation.

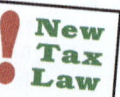

Starting after December 29, 2025, distributions for long-term care be excluded from the 10-percent penalty tax on early distributions. As a reminder, the exclusion is for the 10-percent penalty tax on early distributions; ordinary income tax will still apply.

viii

Income Tax Fundamentals
Delivers Proven End-of-Chapter Tools

- Several question types ensure a variety of assignment options:
  - Multiple-Choice Questions
  - Short-Answer Problems
  - Writing Assignments
  - Comprehensive Problems
- The Cumulative Software Problem provided in Chapters 1–8 gives students the flexibility to use multiple resources, such as the tax forms within the book, ProConnect Tax or alternative tax preparation software. The problem evolves with each succeeding chapter's content, allowing students to build on their comprehension of various tax topics.
- Additional Comprehensive Tax Return Problems are located in Appendix D.

Digital Tools Enhance Student Understanding

CNOWv2 is a powerful online homework tool. This online resource includes an interactive eBook, end-of-chapter homework, detailed student feedback and interactive quizzing, that covers the most challenging topics, a lab guide for using the ProConnect Tax software, and much more. The student companion website offers—*at no additional cost*—study resources for students. Go to **www.cengage.com**, and input the ISBN number of your textbook (from the back cover of your book). The link to the Cengage website will take you to the product page where free companion resources are located.

ProConnect™ Tax ProConnect Tax access is included with each textbook at no additional cost. A detailed reference Lab Guide will help the student use the tax software for solving end-of-chapter problems.

For students who are new to the ProConnect Tax software product, tips have been placed throughout the textbook to provide guidance to assist with the transition from a paper form to using the tax software.

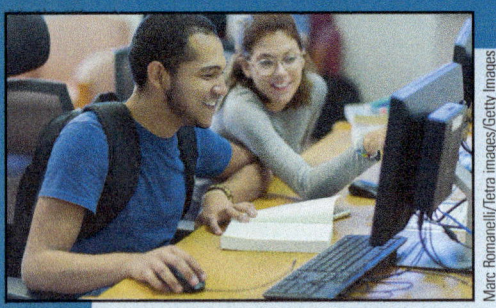

Note to Students: Maximize Your Reading Experience

This textbook includes many examples to help demonstrate learning objectives. After reviewing each section, including the examples, complete the corresponding Self-Study Problems. Solutions to the Self-Study Problems are located at the end of the textbook in Appendix E to check for accuracy. Use your performance to measure your understanding, and re-read the Learning Objectives section if needed. Many key tax terms are defined in each chapter, which will help improve your overall comprehension.

Using Tax Software

Numerous tax return problems in the textbook can be solved using either the online tax preparation software or hand preparation. The popular software, ProConnect Tax, is available at no additional cost with the textbook. Helpful tips for using ProConnect Tax have been placed throughout the book so that students can more easily train on the software and prepare the tax returns included in each of the first eleven chapters. A student tax preparation lab guide to ProConnect Tax is provided on the companion website. Your college may offer additional tax preparation software, but remember that you can always prepare the solutions manually on the textbook-provided tax forms, schedules and worksheets located conveniently in one place in Appendix F, which can be found online with student and instructor resources.

Using the "Would You Sign This Tax Return?" Feature

A practitioner who knows when to say "I cannot sign this tax return," even if it means losing a client, is exercising the most basic ethical wisdom. Most chapters contain a "Would You Sign This Tax Return?" case reflecting a common client issue. Each issue corresponds to an obvious concept illustrated in the previous section. However, the approach to advise the client is not always obvious nor easy. The art of explaining tax rules to a client who does not understand them, or worse, wants to break them, requires not only a good understanding of the rules, but also good interpersonal skills and sometimes the gift of persuasion. The news in the last several years has shown reports of respected CPA firms with members who failed to say the simple words, "I cannot sign this tax return," demonstrating that simple ethical practice is not always easy. We hope instructors will use these cases to spark group discussions or contemplation, and, perhaps, add examples from their own experience.

Using the Cumulative Software Problem

The Cumulative Software Problem can be found at the end of Chapters 1–8. The case information provided in each chapter builds on the information presented in previous chapters, resulting in a lengthy and complex tax return by the conclusion of the problem in Chapter 8. Your instructor may have you work in groups to prepare each of the tax returns. The groups can follow the real-world accounting firm model using a preparer, a reviewer, and a firm owner who takes responsibility for the accuracy of the return and signs it. All of the issues in the problem are commonly seen by tax preparers and are covered in the textbook. The full return is difficult to prepare by hand, so tax software is recommended. If the problem is prepared using tax software, the data should be saved so the additional information in the succeeding chapters can be added without duplicating input from previous chapters.

About the Authors

Gerald E. Whittenburg In 2015, we unexpectedly lost our dear friend and co-author Gene Whittenburg. As the original author of *Income Tax Fundamentals*, Gene was critical in designing the forms-based approach that the book has used successfully for over four decades. Gene started his life in a small town in Texas, entered the Navy, served his country in Vietnam, earned a Bachelor's, Master's, and PhD degrees, and served as a distinguished faculty at San Diego State University for almost 40 years. We intend to continue to honor Gene by committing to uphold his standard of publishing excellence.

Steven L. Gill is an associate professor of accounting and taxation in the Charles W. Lamden School of Accountancy and Assistant Dean of Graduate Studies at San Diego State University. He also served as the Director of Graduate Programs and the Director of Assessment at the Fowler College of Business at SDSU. Steve received a BS in Accounting from the University of Florida, an MS in Taxation from Northeastern University, and a PhD in Accounting from the University of Massachusetts. Prior to entering academia, he worked in the field of tax and accounting, including roles in public accounting, internal audit, corporate accounting, and ultimately, vice president of finance. Steve holds a Certified Public Accountant designation in the State of Massachusetts. He has published a wide variety of articles in various academic and practitioner journals, and has taught at both the undergraduate and graduate levels, including taxation and financial and management accounting. Steve also serves as an author on Cengage's Federal Tax Research series.

Acknowledgments

Many people have been involved in shaping this product through all of its editions. We thank every one of them for their contributions. The authors particularly wish to thank all of the instructors who provided feedback for the 2025 edition via surveys as well as the following supplement authors and verifiers for their most valuable suggestions and support:

D. Elizabeth Stone Atkins—*High Point University, High Point, NC*
Pennie Eddy—*Appalachian Technical College, Jasper, GA*
David Candelaria—*Mt. San Jacinto College, Menifee, CA*
Paul Shinal—*Cayga Community College, Auburn, NY*
Jim Clarkson—*San Jacinto College South, Houston, TX*

The authors would like to thank Susan Gill, Doug Kelley, Jill Kelley, Nicole Doherty, and Richard Price for their time and attention in reviewing chapters. We would also like to thank Tracy Newman and Wendy Shanker for their work of reviewing and verifying the content in CengageNOWv2, including the end-of-chapter items. We would also like to extend our thanks to the Tax Forms and Publications Division of the Internal Revenue Service for their assistance in obtaining draft forms each year.

We appreciate your continued support in advising us of any revisions or corrections you feel are appropriate.

Steve Gill

The Annotated 1040 Map

The annotated 1040 map is an expanded tax formula, illustrating where each piece of the tax formula is covered in the textbook. The 1040 map helps you understand how all of the elements of the textbook and the tax formula fit together. Use this as a reference and bookmark this page.

Form 1040 — Department of the Treasury—Internal Revenue Service
U.S. Individual Income Tax Return — 2024 — OMB No. 1545-0074 — IRS Use Only—Do not write or staple in this space.

For the year Jan. 1–Dec. 31, 2024, or other tax year beginning _____, 2024, ending _____, 20 ____ See separate instructions.

Your first name and middle initial | Last name | Your social security number

If joint return, spouse's first name and middle initial | Last name | Spouse's social security number

Home address (number and street). If you have a P.O. box, see instructions. | Apt. no.

City, town, or post office. If you have a foreign address, also complete spaces below. | State | ZIP code

Foreign country name | Foreign province/state/county | Foreign postal code

Presidential Election Campaign
Check here if you, or your spouse if filing jointly, want $3 to go to this fund. Checking a box below will not change your tax or refund.
☐ You ☐ Spouse

Filing Status — Check only one box. — **LO 1.5**
☐ Single
☐ Married filing jointly (even if only one had income)
☐ Married filing separately (MFS)
☐ Head of household (HOH)
☐ Qualifying surviving spouse (QSS)
If you checked the MFS box, enter the name of your spouse. If you checked the HOH or QSS box, enter the child's name if the qualifying person is a child but not your dependent: _____
☐ If treating a nonresident alien or dual-status alien spouse as a U.S. resident for the entire tax year, check the box and enter their name (see instructions and attach statement if required): _____

Digital Assets — At any time during 2024, did you: (a) receive (as a reward, award, or payment for property or services); or (b) sell, exchange, or otherwise dispose of a digital asset (or a financial interest in a digital asset)? (See instructions.) ☐ Yes ☐ No — **LO 4.1**

Standard Deduction — Someone can claim: ☐ You as a dependent ☐ Your spouse as a dependent
☐ Spouse itemizes on a separate return or you were a dual-status alien — **LO 1.7**

Age/Blindness You: ☐ Were born before January 2, 1960 ☐ Are blind Spouse: ☐ Was born before January 2, 1960 ☐ Is blind

Dependents (see instructions): If more than four dependents, see instructions and check here ☐
(1) First name Last name — **LO 1.6**
(2) Social security number
(3) Relationship to you
(4) Check the box if qualifies for (see instructions):
Child tax credit — **LO 1.6, 7.1**
Credit for other dependents

Income

Attach Form(s) W-2 here. Also attach Forms W-2G and 1099-R if tax was withheld.
If you did not get a Form W-2, see instructions.

Line	Description			LO
1a	Total amount from Form(s) W-2, box 1 (see instructions)		1a	LO 2.2
1b	Household employee wages not reported on Form(s) W-2		1b	LO 6.6
1c	Tip income not reported on line 1a (see instructions)		1c	LO 9.2
1d	Medicaid waiver payments not reported on Form(s) W-2 (see instructions)		1d	LO 2.1
1e	Taxable dependent care benefits from Form 2441, line 26		1e	LO 2.5
1f	Employer-provided adoption benefits from Form 8839, line 29		1f	LO 7.7
1g	Wages from Form 8919, line 6		1g	LO 9.2
1h	Other earned income (see instructions)		1h	
1i	Nontaxable combat pay election (see instructions)	1i		LO 6.9
1z	Add lines 1a through 1h		1z	
2a	Tax-exempt interest	2a	LO 2.9	
2b	Taxable interest		2b	LO 2.9
3a	Qualified dividends	3a	LO 2.10	
3b	Ordinary dividends		3b	LO 2.10
4a	IRA distributions	4a	LO 5.3	
4b	Taxable amount		4b	LO 5.3
5a	Pensions and annuities	5a	LO 2.7	
5b	Taxable amount		5b	LO 2.7
6a	Social security benefits	6a	LO 2.16	
6b	Taxable amount		6b	LO 2.16
6c	If you elect to use the lump-sum election method, check here (see instructions) ☐			
7	Capital gain or (loss). Attach Schedule D if required. If not required, check here ☐		7	LO 4.1 to 4.6
8	Additional income from Schedule 1, line 10		8	Sch. 1
9	Add lines 1z, 2b, 3b, 4b, 5b, 6b, 7, and 8. This is your **total income**		9	
10	Adjustments to income from Schedule 1, line 26		10	Sch. 1
11	Subtract line 10 from line 9. This is your **adjusted gross income**		11	
12	Standard deduction or itemized deductions (from Schedule A)		12	LO 1.7, 5.6 to 5.10
13	Qualified business income deduction from Form 8995 or Form 8995-A		13	LO 4.11
14	Add lines 12 and 13		14	
15	Subtract line 14 from line 11. If zero or less, enter -0-. This is your **taxable income**		15	

Attach Sch. B if required.

Standard Deduction for—
- Single or Married filing separately, $14,600
- Married filing jointly or Qualifying surviving spouse, $29,200
- Head of household, $21,900
- If you checked any box under Standard Deduction, see instructions.

For Disclosure, Privacy Act, and Paperwork Reduction Act Notice, see separate instructions. Cat. No. 11320B Form **1040** (2024)

Form 1040 (2024) Page 2

Tax and Credits	16	Tax (see instructions). Check if any from Form(s): 1 ☐ 8814 2 ☐ 4972 3 ☐ _____			16	LO 1.5, 2.10, 4.4, 6.4
	17	Amount from Schedule 2, line 3			17	Sch. 2
	18	Add lines 16 and 17			18	
	19	Child tax credit or credit for other dependents from Schedule 8812			19	LO 7.1
	20	Amount from Schedule 3, line 8			20	Sch. 3
	21	Add lines 19 and 20			21	
	22	Subtract line 21 from line 18. If zero or less, enter -0-			22	
	23	Other taxes, including self-employment tax, from Schedule 2, line 21			23	Sch. 2
	24	Add lines 22 and 23. This is your **total tax**			24	
Payments	25	Federal income tax withheld from:				
	a	Form(s) W-2		25a		LO 2.2, 9.2
	b	Form(s) 1099		25b		LO 9.1, 9.2
	c	Other forms (see instructions)		25c		
	d	Add lines 25a through 25c			25d	
If you have a qualifying child, attach Sch. EIC.	26	2024 estimated tax payments and amount applied from 2023 return			26	LO 9.4
	27	Earned income credit (EIC)		27		
	28	Additional child tax credit from Schedule 8812		28		LO 7.1
	29	American opportunity credit from Form 8863, line 8		29		LO 7.5
	30	Reserved for future use		30		
	31	Amount from Schedule 3, line 15		31		Sch. 3
	32	Add lines 27, 28, 29, and 31. These are your **total other payments and refundable credits**			32	
	33	Add lines 25d, 26, and 32. These are your **total payments**			33	
Refund	34	If line 33 is more than line 24, subtract line 24 from line 33. This is the amount you **overpaid**			34	
	35a	Amount of line 34 you want **refunded to you**. If Form 8888 is attached, check here ☐			35a	
Direct deposit? See instructions.	b	Routing number ____ c Type: ☐ Checking ☐ Savings				
	d	Account number ____				
	36	Amount of line 34 you want **applied to your 2025 estimated tax**		36		
Amount You Owe	37	Subtract line 33 from line 24. This is the **amount you owe**. For details on how to pay, go to *www.irs.gov/Payments* or see instructions			37	
	38	Estimated tax penalty (see instructions)		38		

Third Party Designee

Do you want to allow another person to discuss this return with the IRS? See instructions ☐ **Yes.** Complete below. ☐ **No**

Designee's name ____ Phone no. ____ Personal identification number (PIN) ____

Sign Here

Under penalties of perjury, I declare that I have examined this return and accompanying schedules and statements, and to the best of my knowledge and belief, they are true, correct, and complete. Declaration of preparer (other than taxpayer) is based on all information of which preparer has any knowledge.

Joint return? See instructions. Keep a copy for your records.

Your signature	Date	Your occupation	If the IRS sent you an Identity Protection PIN, enter it here (see inst.)
Spouse's signature. If a joint return, **both** must sign.	Date	Spouse's occupation	If the IRS sent your spouse an Identity Protection PIN, enter it here (see inst.)
Phone no.		Email address	

Paid Preparer Use Only

Preparer's name	Preparer's signature	Date	PTIN	Check if: ☐ Self-employed
Firm's name			Phone no.	
Firm's address			Firm's EIN	

Go to *www.irs.gov/Form1040* for instructions and the latest information. Form **1040** (2024)

**SCHEDULE 1
(Form 1040)**

Department of the Treasury
Internal Revenue Service

Additional Income and Adjustments to Income

Attach to Form 1040, 1040-SR, or 1040-NR.
Go to *www.irs.gov/Form1040* for instructions and the latest information.

OMB No. 1545-0074

2024

Attachment
Sequence No. **01**

Name(s) shown on Form 1040, 1040-SR, or 1040-NR | Your social security number

For 2024, enter the amount reported to you on Form(s) 1099-K that was included in error or for personal items sold at a loss ....

Note: The remaining amounts reported to you on Form(s) 1099-K should be reported elsewhere on your return depending on the nature of the transaction. See *www.irs.gov/1099k*.

Part I   Additional Income

Line	Description	Box	Reference
1	Taxable refunds, credits, or offsets of state and local income taxes	1	LO 5.7
2a	Alimony received	2a	LO 2.13
b	Date of original divorce or separation agreement (see instructions):		
3	Business income or (loss). Attach Schedule C	3	Chapter 3
4	Other gains or (losses). Attach Form 4797	4	LO 8.7, 8.8
5	Rental real estate, royalties, partnerships, S corporations, trusts, etc. Attach Schedule E	5	LO 4.7, 4.8
6	Farm income or (loss). Attach Schedule F	6	LO 6.8
7	Unemployment compensation	7	LO 2.15
8	Other income:		
a	Net operating loss	8a (	LO 4.9)
b	Gambling	8b	LO 2.1, 2.6
c	Cancellation of debt	8c	LO 2.18
d	Foreign earned income exclusion from Form 2555	8d (	LO 7.6)
e	Income from Form 8853	8e	
f	Income from Form 8889	8f	
g	Alaska Permanent Fund dividends	8g	
h	Jury duty pay	8h	LO 2.1
i	Prizes and awards	8i	LO 2.6
j	Activity not engaged in for profit income	8j	LO 3.12
k	Stock options	8k	LO 2.1
l	Income from the rental of personal property if you engaged in the rental for profit but were not in the business of renting such property	8l	LO 4.7
m	Olympic and Paralympic medals and USOC prize money (see instructions)	8m	LO 2.6
n	Section 951(a) inclusion (see instructions)	8n	
o	Section 951A(a) inclusion (see instructions)	8o	
p	Section 461(l) excess business loss adjustment	8p	LO 4.9
q	Taxable distributions from an ABLE account (see instructions)	8q	
r	Scholarship and fellowship grants not reported on Form W-2	8r	LO 2.12
s	Nontaxable amount of Medicaid waiver payments included on Form 1040, line 1a or 1d	8s (	LO 2.1)
t	Pension or annuity from a nonqualifed deferred compensation plan or a nongovernmental section 457 plan	8t	
u	Wages earned while incarcerated	8u	
v	Digital assets received as ordinary income not reported elsewhere. See instructions	8v	
z	Other income. List type and amount: _____	8z	Chapter 2
9	Total other income. Add lines 8a through 8z	9	
10	Combine lines 1 through 7 and 9. This is your **additional income**. Enter here and on Form 1040, 1040-SR, or 1040-NR, line 8	10	

For Paperwork Reduction Act Notice, see your tax return instructions.   Cat. No. 71479F   Schedule 1 (Form 1040) 2024

Schedule 1 (Form 1040) 2024 — Page **2**

Part II — Adjustments to Income

Line	Description		Ref
11	Educator expenses	11	LO 5.5
12	Certain business expenses of reservists, performing artists, and fee-basis government officials. Attach Form 2106	12	LO 5.5
13	Health savings account deduction. Attach Form 8889	13	LO 5.1
14	Moving expenses for members of the Armed Forces. Attach Form 3903	14	LO 6.9
15	Deductible part of self-employment tax. Attach Schedule SE	15	LO 4.10
16	Self-employed SEP, SIMPLE, and qualified plans	16	LO 5.4
17	Self-employed health insurance deduction	17	LO 5.2
18	Penalty on early withdrawal of savings	18	LO 2.9
19a	Alimony paid	19a	LO 2.13
b	Recipient's SSN		
c	Date of original divorce or separation agreement (see instructions):		
20	IRA deduction	20	LO 5.3
21	Student loan interest deduction	21	LO 5.8
22	Reserved for future use	22	
23	Archer MSA deduction	23	LO 5.1
24	Other adjustments:		
a	Jury duty pay (see instructions)	24a	LO 5.5
b	Deductible expenses related to income reported on line 8l from the rental of personal property engaged in for profit	24b	LO 4.7
c	Nontaxable amount of the value of Olympic and Paralympic medals and USOC prize money reported on line 8m	24c	LO 2.6
d	Reforestation amortization and expenses	24d	
e	Repayment of supplemental unemployment benefits under the Trade Act of 1974	24e	
f	Contributions to section 501(c)(18)(D) pension plans	24f	
g	Contributions by certain chaplains to section 403(b) plans	24g	
h	Attorney fees and court costs for actions involving certain unlawful discrimination claims (see instructions)	24h	
i	Attorney fees and court costs you paid in connection with an award from the IRS for information you provided that helped the IRS detect tax law violations	24i	
j	Housing deduction from Form 2555	24j	LO 7.6
k	Excess deductions of section 67(e) expenses from Schedule K-1 (Form 1041)	24k	
z	Other adjustments. List type and amount: _____	24z	
25	Total other adjustments. Add lines 24a through 24z	25	
26	Add lines 11 through 23 and 25. These are your **adjustments to income**. Enter here and on Form 1040, 1040-SR, or 1040-NR, line 10	26	

SCHEDULE 2 (Form 1040)
Department of the Treasury
Internal Revenue Service

Additional Taxes
Attach to Form 1040, 1040-SR, or 1040-NR.
Go to *www.irs.gov/Form1040* for instructions and the latest information.

OMB No. 1545-0074

2024
Attachment Sequence No. **02**

Name(s) shown on Form 1040, 1040-SR, or 1040-NR | Your social security number

Part I Tax

1	Additions to tax:		
a	Excess advance premium tax credit repayment. Attach Form 8962	1a	LO 7.4
b	Repayment of new clean vehicle credit(s) transferred to a registered dealer from Schedule A (Form 8936), Part II. Attach Form 8936 and Schedule A (Form 8936)	1b	LO 7.8
c	Repayment of previously owned clean vehicle credit(s) transferred to a registered dealer from Schedule A (Form 8936), Part IV. Attach Form 8936 and Schedule A (Form 8936)	1c	LO 7.8
d	Recapture of net EPE from Form 4255, line 2a, column (l)	1d	
e	Excessive payments (EP) from Form 4255. Check applicable box and enter amount. (i) ☐ Line 1a, column (n) (ii) ☐ Line 1c, column (n) (iii) ☐ Line 1d, column (n) (iv) ☐ Line 2a, column (n)	1e	
f	20% EP from Form 4255. Check applicable box and enter amount. See instructions. (i) ☐ Line 1a, column (o) (ii) ☐ Line 1c, column (o) (iii) ☐ Line 1d, column (o) (iv) ☐ Line 2a, column (o)	1f	
y	Other additions to tax (see instructions): _____	1y	
z	Add lines 1a through 1y	1z	
2	Alternative minimum tax. Attach Form 6251	2	LO 6.5
3	Add lines 1z and 2. Enter here and on Form 1040, 1040-SR, or 1040-NR, line 17	3	

Part II Other Taxes

4	Self-employment tax. Attach Schedule SE	4	LO 4.10
5	Social security and Medicare tax on unreported tip income. Attach Form 4137	5	LO 9.2
6	Uncollected social security and Medicare tax on wages. Attach Form 8919	6	LO 9.2
7	Total additional social security and Medicare tax. Add lines 5 and 6	7	
8	Additional tax on IRAs or other tax-favored accounts. Attach Form 5329 if required. If not required, check here ☐	8	LO 5.3
9	Household employment taxes. Attach Schedule H	9	LO 6.6
10	Repayment of first-time homebuyer credit. Attach Form 5405 if required	10	
11	Additional Medicare Tax. Attach Form 8959	11	LO 6.7
12	Net investment income tax. Attach Form 8960	12	LO 6.7
13	Uncollected social security and Medicare or RRTA tax on tips or group-term life insurance from Form W-2, box 12	13	
14	Interest on tax due on installment income from the sale of certain residential lots and timeshares	14	
15	Interest on the deferred tax on gain from certain installment sales with a sales price over $150,000	15	
16	Recapture of low-income housing credit. Attach Form 8611	16	

(continued on page 2)

For Paperwork Reduction Act Notice, see your tax return instructions.   Cat. No. 71478U   Schedule 2 (Form 1040) 2024

Schedule 2 (Form 1040) 2024   Page **2**

Part II   Other Taxes *(continued)*

17	Other additional taxes:		
a	Recapture of other credits. List type, form number, and amount: _____	**17a**	
b	Recapture of federal mortgage subsidy, if you sold your home see instructions	**17b**	
c	Additional tax on HSA distributions. Attach Form 8889	**17c**	LO 5.1
d	Additional tax on an HSA because you didn't remain an eligible individual. Attach Form 8889	**17d**	LO 5.1
e	Additional tax on Archer MSA distributions. Attach Form 8853	**17e**	LO 5.1
f	Additional tax on Medicare Advantage MSA distributions. Attach Form 8853	**17f**	LO 5.1
g	Recapture of a charitable contribution deduction related to a fractional interest in tangible personal property	**17g**	
h	Income you received from a nonqualified deferred compensation plan that fails to meet the requirements of section 409A	**17h**	
i	Compensation you received from a nonqualified deferred compensation plan described in section 457A	**17i**	
j	Section 72(m)(5) excess benefits tax	**17j**	
k	Golden parachute payments	**17k**	
l	Tax on accumulation distribution of trusts	**17l**	
m	Excise tax on insider stock compensation from an expatriated corporation	**17m**	
n	Look-back interest under section 167(g) or 460(b) from Form 8697 or 8866	**17n**	
o	Tax on non-effectively connected income for any part of the year you were a nonresident alien from Form 1040-NR	**17o**	
p	Any interest from Form 8621, line 16f, relating to distributions from, and dispositions of, stock of a section 1291 fund	**17p**	
q	Any interest from Form 8621, line 24	**17q**	
z	Any other taxes. List type and amount: _____	**17z**	
18	Total additional taxes. Add lines 17a through 17z	**18**	
19	Recapture of net EPE from Form 4255, line 1d, column (l)	**19**	
20	Section 965 net tax liability installment from Form 965-A	**20**	
21	Add lines 4, 7 through 16, and 18. These are your **total other taxes**. Enter here and on Form 1040 or 1040-SR, line 23, or Form 1040-NR, line 23b	**21**	

Schedule 2 (Form 1040) 2024

SCHEDULE 3
(Form 1040)
Department of the Treasury
Internal Revenue Service

Additional Credits and Payments

Attach to Form 1040, 1040-SR, or 1040-NR.
Go to *www.irs.gov/Form1040* for instructions and the latest information.

OMB No. 1545-0074

2024

Attachment Sequence No. **03**

Name(s) shown on Form 1040, 1040-SR, or 1040-NR | Your social security number

Part I Nonrefundable Credits

1	Foreign tax credit. Attach Form 1116 if required	1	LO 7.6
2	Credit for child and dependent care expenses from Form 2441, line 11. Attach Form 2441	2	LO 7.3
3	Education credits from Form 8863, line 19	3	LO 7.5
4	Retirement savings contributions credit. Attach Form 8880	4	LO 7.9
5a	Residential clean energy credit from Form 5695, line 15	5a	LO 7.8
b	Energy efficient home improvement credit from Form 5695, line 32	5b	LO 7.8
6	Other nonrefundable credits:		
a	General business credit. Attach Form 3800 . . . . . . 6a		LO 7.8
b	Credit for prior year minimum tax. Attach Form 8801 . . 6b		
c	Adoption credit. Attach Form 8839 . . . . 6c		LO 7.7
d	Credit for the elderly or disabled. Attach Schedule R . . 6d		LO 7.8
e	Reserved for future use 6e		
f	Clean vehicle credit. Attach Form 8936 . . . . 6f		LO 7.8
g	Mortgage interest credit. Attach Form 8396 . . . . . 6g		
h	District of Columbia first-time homebuyer credit. Attach Form 8859 6h		
i	Qualified electric vehicle credit. Attach Form 8834 . . . 6i		
j	Alternative fuel vehicle refueling property credit. Attach Form 8911 6j		
k	Credit to holders of tax credit bonds. Attach Form 8912 . 6k		
l	Amount on Form 8978, line 14. See instructions . . . 6l		
m	Credit for previously owned clean vehicles. Attach Form 8936 6m		LO 7.8
z	Other nonrefundable credits. List type and amount: _____ 6z		
7	Total other nonrefundable credits. Add lines 6a through 6z	7	
8	Add lines 1 through 4, 5a, 5b, and 7. Enter here and on Form 1040, 1040-SR, or 1040-NR, line 20	8	

Part II Other Payments and Refundable Credits

9	Net premium tax credit. Attach Form 8962	9	LO 7.4
10	Amount paid with request for extension to file (see instructions)	10	LO 9.4
11	Excess social security and tier 1 RRTA tax withheld	11	LO 9.3
12	Credit for federal tax on fuels. Attach Form 4136	12	
13	Other payments or refundable credits:		
a	Form 2439 . . . . 13a		
b	Section 1341 credit for repayment of amounts included in income from earlier years 13b		
c	Net elective payment election amount from Form 3800, Part III, line 6, column (j) 13c		
d	Deferred amount of net 965 tax liability (see instructions) . 13d		
z	Other refundable credits (see instructions): _____ 13z		
14	Total other payments or refundable credits. Add lines 13a through 13z	14	
15	Add lines 9 through 12 and 14. Enter here and on Form 1040, 1040-SR, or 1040-NR, line 31	15	

For Paperwork Reduction Act Notice, see your tax return instructions. Cat. No. 71480G Schedule 3 (Form 1040) 2024

Table of Contents

Chapter 1 — The Individual Income Tax Return

LO	1.1	History and Objectives of the Tax System	1-2
LO	1.2	Reporting and Taxable Entities	1-3
LO	1.3	The Tax Formula for Individuals	1-5
LO	1.4	Who Must File	1-7
LO	1.5	Filing Status and Tax Computation	1-10
LO	1.6	Qualifying Dependents	1-17
LO	1.7	The Standard Deduction	1-28
LO	1.8	A Brief Overview of Capital Gains and Losses	1-30
LO	1.9	Tax and the Internet	1-32
LO	1.10	Electronic Filing (E-filing)	1-36
		Questions and Problems	1-39

Chapter 2 — Gross Income and Exclusions

LO	2.1	The Nature of Gross Income	2-2
LO	2.2	Salaries and Wages	2-4
LO	2.3	Accident and Health Insurance	2-7
LO	2.4	Meals and Lodging	2-8
LO	2.5	Employee Fringe Benefits	2-10
LO	2.6	Prizes and Awards	2-17
LO	2.7	Annuities	2-18
LO	2.8	Life Insurance	2-23
LO	2.9	Interest Income	2-25
LO	2.10	Dividend Income	2-34
LO	2.11	Gifts and Inheritances	2-38
LO	2.12	Scholarships	2-39
LO	2.13	Alimony	2-39
LO	2.14	Educational Incentives	2-42
LO	2.15	Unemployment Compensation	2-46
LO	2.16	Social Security Benefits	2-46
LO	2.17	Community Property	2-51
LO	2.18	Cancellation of Debt Income	2-53
		Questions and Problems	2-59

Chapter 3 — Business Income and Expenses

LO	3.1	Schedule C	3-2
LO	3.2	Inventories	3-10
LO	3.3	Transportation	3-13
LO	3.4	Travel Expenses	3-15
LO	3.5	Meals and Entertainment	3-19
LO	3.6	Educational Expenses	3-20
LO	3.7	Dues, Subscriptions, and Publications	3-22
LO	3.8	Special Clothing and Uniforms	3-23

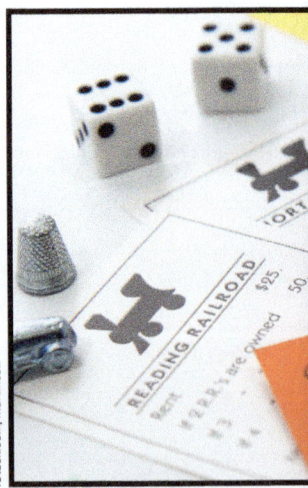

iStock.com/martinez2

LO	3.9	Business Gifts	3-24
LO	3.10	Bad Debts	3-25
LO	3.11	Office in the Home	3-27
LO	3.12	Hobby Losses	3-32
		Questions and Problems	3-36

Chapter 4 Additional Income and the Qualified Business Income Deduction

LO	4.1	What Is a Capital Asset?	4-2
LO	4.2	Holding Period	4-3
LO	4.3	Calculation of Gain or Loss	4-4
LO	4.4	Net Capital Gains	4-9
LO	4.5	Net Capital Losses	4-12
LO	4.6	Sale of a Personal Residence	4-23
LO	4.7	Rental Income and Expenses	4-27
LO	4.8	Passive Loss Limitations	4-31
LO	4.9	Net Operating Losses	4-36
LO	4.10	Self-Employment Tax	4-44
LO	4.11	Qualified Business Income (QBI) Deduction	4-49
		Questions and Problems	4-61

Chapter 5 Deductions For and From AGI

LO	5.1	Health Savings Accounts	5-2
LO	5.2	Self-Employed Health Insurance Deduction	5-6
LO	5.3	Individual Retirement Accounts	5-9
LO	5.4	Small Business and Self-Employed Retirement Plans	5-20
LO	5.5	Other for AGI Deductions	5-32
LO	5.6	Medical Expenses	5-34
LO	5.7	Taxes	5-37
LO	5.8	Interest	5-44
LO	5.9	Charitable Contributions	5-50
LO	5.10	Other Itemized Deductions	5-57
		Questions and Problems	5-65

Chapter 6 Accounting Periods and Other Taxes

LO	6.1	Accounting Periods	6-2
LO	6.2	Accounting Methods	6-3
LO	6.3	Related Parties (Section 267)	6-7
LO	6.4	Unearned Income of Minor Children and Certain Students	6-9
LO	6.5	The Individual Alternative Minimum Tax (AMT)	6-14
LO	6.6	The Nanny Tax	6-19
LO	6.7	Special Taxes for High-Income Taxpayers	6-23
LO	6.8	Special Taxpayer Situations	6-29
LO	6.9	Military Taxpayers	6-42
		Questions and Problems	6-52

Chapter 7 Tax Credits

LO	7.1	Child Tax Credit	7-2
LO	7.2	Earned Income Credit	7-10
LO	7.3	Child and Dependent Care Credit	7-14
LO	7.4	The Affordable Care Act	7-16
LO	7.5	Education Tax Credits	7-28
LO	7.6	Foreign Exclusion and Tax Credit	7-35
LO	7.7	Adoption Expenses	7-43
LO	7.8	Other Credits	7-47
LO	7.9	Low-Income Retirement Plan Contribution Credit	7-60
		Questions and Problems	7-66

Chapter 8 Depreciation and Sale of Business Property

LO	8.1	Capitalization and Depreciation	8-2
LO	8.2	Modified Accelerated Cost Recovery System (MACRS) and Bonus Depreciation	8-6
LO	8.3	Election to Expense (Section 179)	8-17
LO	8.4	Listed Property	8-19
LO	8.5	Limitation on Depreciation of Luxury Automobiles	8-20
LO	8.6	Intangibles	8-23
LO	8.7	Section 1231 Gains and Losses	8-24
LO	8.8	Depreciation Recapture	8-26
LO	8.9	Business Casualty Gains and Losses	8-29
LO	8.10	Installment Sales	8-33
LO	8.11	Like-Kind Exchanges	8-36
LO	8.12	Involuntary Conversions	8-39
		Questions and Problems	8-46

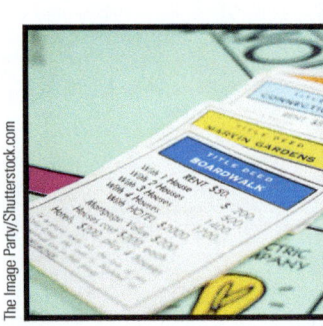

Chapter 9 Employment Taxes, Estimated Payments, and Retirement Plans

LO	9.1	Employee Versus Independent Contractor	9-2
LO	9.2	Income Tax Withholding Methods	9-5
LO	9.3	The FICA Tax	9-25
LO	9.4	Estimated Payments	9-28
LO	9.5	Federal Tax Deposit System	9-37
LO	9.6	Employer Reporting Requirements	9-41
LO	9.7	The FUTA Tax	9-47
LO	9.8	Qualified Retirement Plans	9-51
LO	9.9	Rollovers	9-55
		Questions and Problems	9-59

Chapter 10 Partnership Taxation

LO	10.1	Nature of Partnership Taxation	10-2
LO	10.2	Partnership Formation	10-4
LO	10.3	Partnership Income Reporting	10-6
LO	10.4	Current Distributions	10-17

LO	10.5	Tax Years	10-18
LO	10.6	Transactions Between Partners and the Partnership	10-19
LO	10.7	Qualified Business Income Deduction for Partners	10-20
LO	10.8	The At-Risk Rule	10-22
LO	10.9	Limited Liability Companies	10-23
		Questions and Problems	10-26

Chapter 11 The Corporate Income Tax

LO	11.1	Corporate Tax Rates	11-2
LO	11.2	Corporate Gains and Losses	11-2
LO	11.3	Special Deductions and Limitations	11-4
LO	11.4	Schedule M-1	11-7
LO	11.5	Filing Requirements and Estimated Tax	11-8
LO	11.6	S Corporations	11-19
LO	11.7	Corporate Formation	11-22
LO	11.8	Corporate Accumulations	11-32
		Questions and Problems	11-35

Chapter 12 Tax Administration and Tax Planning

LO	12.1	The Internal Revenue Service	12-2
LO	12.2	The Audit Process	12-6
LO	12.3	Interest and Penalties	12-11
LO	12.4	Statute of Limitations	12-15
LO	12.5	Preparers, Proof, and Privilege	12-16
LO	12.6	The Taxpayer Bill of Rights	12-22
LO	12.7	Tax Planning	12-22
		Questions and Problems	12-30

Appendices

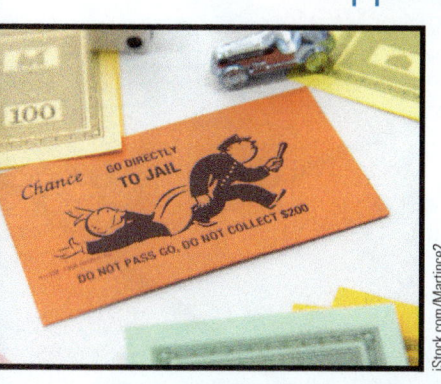

Appendix A Tax Rate Schedules and Tax Table	A-1
Appendix B Earned Income Credit Table	B-1
Appendix C 2024 Withholding Tables	C-1
Appendix D Additional Comprehensive Tax Return Problems	D-1
Appendix E Solutions to Self-Study Problems	E-1
Appendix F Blank Forms	Located Online
Glossary of Tax Terms	G-1
Index	I-1

Questions

Please contact the Cengage Taxation publishing team if you have any questions:

Jonathan Gross, Portfolio Product Manager: jonathan.gross@cengage.com
Danielle Dornbusch, Product Marketing Manager: danielle.dornbusch@cengage.com
Sheila Moran, Senior Content Manager: sheila.moran@cengage.com

Chapter 1

The Individual Income Tax Return

Learning Objectives

After completing this chapter, you should be able to:

- **LO 1.1** Explain the history and objectives of U.S. tax law.
- **LO 1.2** Describe the different entities subject to tax and reporting requirements.
- **LO 1.3** Apply the tax formula for individuals.
- **LO 1.4** Identify individuals who must file tax returns.
- **LO 1.5** Determine filing status and understand the calculation of tax according to filing status.
- **LO 1.6** Define qualifying dependents.
- **LO 1.7** Calculate the correct standard or itemized deduction amount for taxpayers.
- **LO 1.8** Compute basic capital gains and losses.
- **LO 1.9** Access and use various Internet tax resources.
- **LO 1.10** Describe the basics of electronic filing (e-filing).

Overview

This chapter introduces the U.S. individual income tax system. Important elements of the individual tax formula are covered, including the tax calculation, who must file, filing status, and the interaction of itemized deductions and the standard deduction. The chapter illustrates all of the steps required for completion of a basic Form 1040. There is also a discussion of reporting and taxable entities.

An introduction to capital gains and losses is included to provide a basic understanding of capital transactions prior to the detailed coverage in Chapter 4. An overview of tax information available at the Internal Revenue Service (IRS) website and other helpful tax websites is also provided. A presentation of the process for electronic filing (e-filing) of an individual tax return completes the chapter.

Learning Objective 1.1

Explain the history and objectives of U.S. tax law.

1-1 History and Objectives of the Tax System

1-1a Tax Law History and Objectives

The U.S. income tax was established in 1913, by the Sixteenth Amendment to the Constitution. Prior to the adoption of this amendment, the U.S. government had levied various income taxes for limited periods of time. For example, an income tax was used to help finance the Civil War. The finding by the courts that the income tax law enacted in 1894 was unconstitutional eventually led to the adoption of the Sixteenth Amendment. Since adoption of the amendment, the constitutionality of the income tax has not been questioned by the federal courts.

Many people inaccurately believe the sole purpose of the income tax is to raise sufficient revenue to operate the government. The tax law has many goals other than raising revenue. These goals fall into two general categories—economic goals and social goals—and it is often unclear which goal a specific tax provision was written to meet. Tax provisions have been used for such economic motives as reduction of unemployment, expansion of investment in productive (capital) assets, and control of inflation. Specific examples of economic tax provisions are the limited allowance for expensing of capital expenditures and the bonus depreciation provisions. In addition to pure economic goals, the tax law is used to encourage certain business activities and industries. For example, an income tax credit encourages businesses to engage in research and experimentation activities, the energy credits encourage investment in solar and wind energy businesses, and a special deduction for soil and water conservation expenditures related to farm land benefits farmers.

Social goals have also resulted in the adoption of many specific tax provisions. The child and dependent care credit, the earned income credit, and the charitable contributions deduction are examples of tax provisions designed to meet social goals. Social provisions may influence economic activities, but they are written primarily to encourage taxpayers to undertake activities to benefit themselves and society.

An example of a provision that has both economic and social objectives is the provision allowing the gain on the sale of a personal residence up to $250,000 ($500,000 if married) to be excluded from taxable income. From a social standpoint, this helps a family afford a new home, but it also helps achieve the economic goal of ensuring that the United States has a mobile workforce.

The use of the income tax as a tool to promote economic and social policies has increased in recent years. Considering these objectives, the beginning tax student can better understand how and why the tax law has become so complex.

The United States (U.S.) tax law is often considered complex. A count in 2014 puts the entire Internal Revenue Code at over 2,500 pages, and that is just the code itself. The regulations add an additional 9,000 pages. Jointly, the Code and regulations are well over two million words. In their 2020 Tax Complexity Index, taxcomplexity.org ranks the U.S. forty-third out of sixty-four countries in the index. Countries considered less complex than the U.S. include Estonia (2), Kazakhstan (22), and France (35). Refer to **www.taxcomplexity.org** for a complete list.

Self-Study Problem 1.1
Refer to Appendix E for Solutions to Self-Study Problems

Which of the following is not a goal of the income tax system?

a. Raising revenue to operate the government.

b. Providing incentives for certain business and economic goals, such as higher employment rates, through business-favorable tax provisions.

c. Providing incentives for certain social goals, such as charitable giving, by allowing tax deductions, exclusions, or credits for selected activities.

d. All the above are goals of the income tax system.

1-2 Reporting and Taxable Entities

1.2 Learning Objective
Describe the different entities subject to tax and reporting requirements.

Under U.S. tax law, there are five basic tax reporting entities: individuals, corporations, partnerships, estates, and trusts. The taxation of individuals is the major topic of this textbook; an overview of the taxation of partnerships and corporations is presented in Chapters 10 and 11, respectively. Taxation of estates and trusts is a specialized area not covered in this textbook.

1-2a The Individual

The most familiar taxable entity is the individual. Taxable income for individuals generally includes income from all sources such as wages, salaries, self-employment earnings, rents, interest, and dividends. Most individual taxpayers file either Form 1040, or for taxpayers ages 65 or older, Form 1040-SR. The Forms 1040 and 1040-SR are organized so that most taxpayers may only need to use that specific form. Items such as wages, certain interest and dividends, and common deductions and credits are reported directly on the Forms 1040 and 1040-SR. Less common items are reported on a series of supplemental schedules first and then totals from those schedules are carried to the Forms 1040 and 1040-SR.

As presented in Table 1.1, three supplemental schedules, Schedules 1, 2 and 3, are used for additional income and deductions, supplemental taxes, and other credits.

Table 1.1 Supplemental Schedules 1–3 for Form 1040

Schedule	Primary Purpose
1	Additional forms of income other than wages, interest, dividends, distributions from qualified retirement plans such as IRAs and pensions, Social Security benefits, and capital gains and losses, along with many of the deductions for adjusted gross income
2	Additional taxes beyond the basic income tax such as the alternative minimum tax, repayments of excess advance premium tax credit, self-employment taxes, and household employment taxes
3	Credits and payments other than withholding including education credits, the credit for child and dependent care expenses, residential energy credit, estimated tax payments, excess Social Security taxes withheld, and the net premium tax credit

In addition to Schedules 1–3, certain types of income and deductions must be reported on specific schedules that are included with the Forms 1040 or 1040-SR as presented in Table 1.2.

Table 1.2 Supplemental Schedules A–F for Form 1040

Schedule	Primary Purpose
A	Itemized deductions such as medical expenses, certain taxes, certain interest, charitable contributions, and other miscellaneous deductions
B	Interest income and/or ordinary dividend income (over $1,500)
C	Net profit or loss from a sole proprietor trade or business, other than farm or ranch activities
D	Capital gains and losses
E	Rental, royalty, and pass-through income from partnerships, S corporations, estates, and trusts
F	Farm or ranch income

These tax forms and schedules and some less common forms are presented in this textbook.

> The origin of the Form 1040 has been rumored to be associated with the year 1040 B.C. when Samuel warned his people that if they demanded a king, the royal leader would require them to pay taxes. However, in the early 1980s, the then-Commissioner of the IRS, Roscoe Eggers indicated that the number was simply the next one in the control numbering system for federal forms in 1914 when the form was issued for taxpayers for the tax year 1913. About 350,000 people filed a 1040 for 1913. All the returns were audited. Less than 1 percent of the approximately 164 million 2020 individual tax returns were audited.

1-2b The Corporation

Corporations are subject to the U.S. income tax and must report income annually on Form 1120. All corporations are taxed at a flat rate of 21 percent regardless of income level.

Some corporations may elect S corporation status. An S corporation does not generally pay regular corporate income taxes; instead, the corporation's income passes through to the shareholders and is included on their individual returns. S corporations must report tax information annually on Form 1120-S. Chapter 11 covers the basics of corporate taxation, including an explanation of S corporations.

1-2c The Partnership

The partnership is not a taxable entity; instead it is a reporting entity. Generally, all income or loss of a partnership is included on the tax returns of the partners. However, a partnership must file Form 1065 annually to report the amount of the partnership's total income or loss and show the allocation of the income or loss to the partners. The partners, in turn, report their share of ordinary income or loss on their tax returns. Other special gains, losses, income, and deductions of the partnership are reported and allocated to the partners separately, since these items are given special tax treatment at the partner level. Capital gains and losses, for example, are reported and allocated separately, and the partners report their share on Schedule D of their income tax returns. Refer to Chapter 10 for coverage of partnerships, including limited partnerships and limited liability companies.

A summary of some of the more important tax forms is presented in Table 1.3.

Table 1.3 Summary of Major Tax Forms and Schedules

Form or Schedule	Description
1040	Individual income tax return
1040-SR	Individual income tax return for taxpayers aged 65 or older
Schedule 1	Additional income and adjustments to income
Schedule 2	Additional taxes
Schedule 3	Additional credits and payments
Schedule A	Itemized deductions
Schedule B	Interest and ordinary dividends
Schedule C	Profit or loss from business (sole proprietorship)
Schedule D	Capital gains and losses
Schedule E	Supplemental income and loss (rent, royalty, and pass-through income from Forms 1065, 1120-S, and 1041)
Schedule F	Profit or loss from farming
1041	Fiduciary (estates and trusts) tax return
1120	Corporate tax return
1120-S	S corporation tax return
1065	Partnership information return
Schedule K-1 (Form 1065)	Partner's share of partnership results

All of the forms listed here, and more, are available at the IRS website (**www.irs.gov**).

Self-Study Problem 1.2   Refer to Appendix E for Solutions to Self-Study Problems

Determine which is the most appropriate form or schedule(s) for each of the following items. Unless otherwise indicated in the problem, assume the taxpayer is an individual.

1. Bank interest income of $1,600 received by a taxpayer who itemizes deductions
2. Capital gain on the sale of Meta stock
3. Income from a farm
4. Estate income of $850
5. Partnership reporting of an individual partner's share of partnership income
6. Salary of $70,000 for a taxpayer under age 65 who itemizes deductions
7. Income from a sole proprietorship business
8. Income from rental property
9. Ordinary dividends of $2,000 received by a taxpayer who does not itemize deductions
10. Income of a corporation
11. Partnership's loss
12. Charitable contributions deduction for an individual who itemizes deductions
13. Single individual, age 67, with no dependents whose only income is $18,000 (all from Social Security) and who does not itemize deductions or have any credits

1-3 The Tax Formula for Individuals

1.3 Learning Objective
Apply the tax formula for individuals.

Individual taxpayers calculate their tax in accordance with a tax formula. Understanding the formula is important, since income tax determinations are based on the result. The formula is:

    Gross Income
− Deductions for Adjusted Gross Income
= Adjusted Gross Income
− Greater of Itemized Deductions or the Standard Deduction
− Qualified Business Income Deduction
= Taxable Income
× Tax Rate (using appropriate tax tables or rate schedules)
= Gross Income Tax Liability and Additional Taxes
− Tax Credits and Prepayments
= Tax Due or Refund

1-3a Gross Income

The calculation of taxable income begins with gross income. Gross income includes all income, unless the tax law provides for a specific exclusion. The exclusions from gross income are covered in Chapter 2. Gross income from wages, interest, dividends, pensions, Social Security, and capital gains and losses are reported directly on Form 1040 (interest and dividends and capital gains and losses may first flow through Schedules B and D, respectively). Most other forms of income are reported on Schedule 1.

1-3b Deductions for Adjusted Gross Income

The first category of deductions includes the deductions *for* adjusted gross income. These deductions include certain trade or business expenses, certain reimbursed employee business expenses paid under an accountable plan, pre-2019 alimony payments, student loan interest, the penalty on early withdrawal from savings, contributions to qualified retirement plans, and certain educator expenses. Later chapters explain these deductions in detail. Deductions for gross income are reported on Schedule 1.

1-3c Adjusted Gross Income (AGI)

The amount of adjusted gross income is sometimes referred to as the "magic line," since it is the basis for several deduction limitations, such as the limitation on medical expenses. A taxpayer's adjusted gross income is also used to determine limits on certain charitable contributions and contributions to certain individual retirement accounts.

1-3d Standard Deduction or Itemized Deductions

Itemized deductions are personal expense items that Congress has allowed as tax deductions. Included in this category are medical expenses, certain interest expenses, certain taxes, charitable contributions, certain casualty losses, and a small number of miscellaneous items. Taxpayers should itemize their deductions only if the total amount exceeds their standard deduction amount as presented in Table 1.4.

Table 1.4 Standard Deduction Amounts 2024

Filing Status	Standard Deduction
Single	$ 14,600
Married filing jointly	29,200
Married filing separately	14,600
Head of household	21,900
Surviving spouse [qualifying widow(er)]	29,200

Taxpayers who are 65 years of age or older or blind are entitled to an additional standard deduction amount. For 2024, the additional standard deduction amount is $1,950 for unmarried taxpayers and $1,550 for married taxpayers and surviving spouses. Taxpayers who are both 65 years of age or older and blind are entitled to two additional standard deduction amounts. A complete explanation of the basic and additional standard deduction amounts is found later in this chapter.

1-3e Qualified Business Income Deduction

The qualified business income (QBI) deduction is available to individual taxpayers. The QBI deduction is generally 20 percent of the taxpayer's qualified business income from flowthrough businesses such as a sole proprietorship, partnership, or S-corporation. The QBI deduction is covered in Chapter 4. The standard or itemized deductions plus the QBI deduction are considered *from* AGI deductions.

1-3f Exemptions

Prior to the Tax Cuts and Jobs Act of 2017 (TCJA), taxpayers received a deduction called an exemption for themselves, spouse (if married filing jointly), and dependents. Exemptions were suspended by the TCJA starting in 2018. The suspension is scheduled to expire at the end of 2025. The exemption amount, which is still used for some limitations such as the gross income test for a qualifying relative, is $5,050 for 2024.

1-3g The Gross Tax Liability

A taxpayer's gross tax liability is calculated by referencing the tax table or by using a tax rate schedule. Tax credits and prepayments are subtracted from gross tax liability to calculate the net tax payable to the government or the refund to the taxpayer.

Defining "total tax" is not a simple task. The tax liability calculated for Line 16 of Form 1040 is only the income tax associated with taxable income. Total tax (Line 24) also considers a number of additional taxes, such as alternative minimum tax, any repayment of the premium tax credit for that year, and many other taxes from Schedule 2 such as self-employment tax, household employment taxes, and the net investment income tax, just to name a few. Total tax also considers non-refundable credits such as the child tax credit, the other dependent credit, and other credits from Schedule 3, including the foreign tax credit and the child and dependent care expense credit.

Self-Study Problem 1.3 Refer to Appendix E for Solutions to Self-Study Problems

Bill is a single taxpayer, age 27. In 2024, his salary is $37,000 and he has interest income of $1,500. In addition, he has deductions for adjusted gross income of $2,000 and he has $9,300 of itemized deductions. Calculate the following amounts:

1. Gross income
2. Adjusted gross income
3. Standard deduction or itemized deduction amount
4. Taxable income

1-4 Who Must File

1.4 Learning Objective

Identify individuals who must file tax returns.

Several conditions must exist before a taxpayer is required to file a U.S. income tax return. These conditions primarily relate to the amount of the taxpayer's income and the taxpayer's filing status. Figures 1.1 through 1.3 summarize the filing requirements for taxpayers in 2024. If a taxpayer has any nontaxable income, the amount should be excluded in determining whether the taxpayer must file a return.

Taxpayers are also required to file a return if they have net earnings from self-employment of $400 or more, or owe taxes such as Social Security taxes on unreported tips. When a taxpayer is not required to file but is due a refund for overpayment of taxes, a return must be filed to obtain the refund.

A taxpayer who is required to file a return should electronically file the return or mail the return to the appropriate IRS Campus Processing Site listed on the IRS website (**www.irs.gov**). Generally, individual returns are due on the fifteenth day of the fourth month of the year following the close of the tax year. For a calendar year individual taxpayer, the return due date is generally April 15. If the fifteenth falls on a weekend or holiday, returns are due the next business day. However, there are two exceptions: (1) In Maine and Massachusetts, Patriots' Day is celebrated on the third Monday of April. When Patriots' Day is on April 15 or the first business day after April 15, the tax filing deadline is deferred for an additional day for residents of Maine and Massachusetts. (2) The second exception is a result of Emancipation Day, a holiday observed in the District of Columbia. Emancipation Day is observed on April 16; however, when the sixteenth is a Saturday, the holiday is celebrated on the prior Friday and when the sixteenth is Sunday, the holiday is celebrated on the following Monday. In 2025, April 15 is a Tuesday, Patriots' Day is Monday, April 21, and Emancipation Day is Wednesday, April 16; thus, the filing deadline will be Monday, April 15.

> In an effort to avoid paying federal income taxes, a variety of schemes have been mounted over the years by "tax protestors." One of the more popular themes is that the Sixteenth Amendment was never ratified and therefore, the income tax is unconstitutional. In spite of numerous court cases that have debunked this "strategy," this claim remains popular. In a 1989 court case, *Miller v. U.S.*, the court noted, "As best we can surmise [Miller]... has followed the advice of those associated with the 'tax protester movement.' The leaders of this movement conduct seminars across the country in which they attempt to convince taxpayers that the Sixteenth Amendment and assorted enforcement provisions of the tax code are unconstitutional." The court continues, "We find it hard to understand why the long and unbroken line of cases upholding the constitutionality of the Sixteenth Amendment generally, *Brushaber v. Union Pacific Railroad Company*, 36 S. Ct. 236 (1916)...have not persuaded Miller and his compatriots to seek a more effective forum for airing their attack on the federal income tax structure." The IRS maintains a web page designed to address common tax protest myths at **www.irs.gov/businesses/small-businesses-self-employed/anti-tax-law-evasion-schemes**.

A six-month extension of time to file may be requested on Form 4868 by the April due date. Regardless of the original filing deadline, the extension is until October 15 unless that day falls on a weekend or holiday, in which case the extended due date is the following business day. However, all tax due must be paid by the April due date or penalties and interest will apply.

Example Mohamed is a resident of Massachusetts. Mohamed's 2023 individual income tax return was due April 16, 2024. If Mohamed filed for a six-month extension, the return was due Tuesday, October 15, 2024 (not October 16, 2024). ♦

Figure 1.1 Who Must File

Chart A—For Most People

IF your filing status is ...	AND at the end of 2024 you were* ...	THEN file a return if your gross income** was at least ...
Single	under 65 65 or older	$14,600 16,550
Married filing jointly***	under 65 (both spouses) 65 or older (one spouse) 65 or older (both spouses)	$29,200 30,750 32,300
Married filing separately	any age	$5
Head of household	under 65 65 or older	$21,900 23,850
Qualifying surviving spouse	under 65 65 or older	$29,200 30,750

*If you were born on January 1, 1960, you are considered to be age 65 at the end of 2024. (If your spouse died in 2024 or if you are preparing a return for someone who died in 2024, see Pub. 501.)

Gross income means all income you received in the form of money, goods, property, and services that isn't exempt from tax, including any income from sources outside the United States or from the sale of your main home (even if you can exclude part or all of it). Don't include any social security benefits unless (a) you are married filing a separate return and you lived with your spouse at any time in 2024, or (b) one-half of your social security benefits plus your other gross income and any tax-exempt interest is more than $25,000 ($32,000 if married filing jointly). If (a) or (b) applies, see the instructions for lines 6a and 6b to figure the taxable part of social security benefits you must include in gross income. Gross income includes gains, but not losses, reported on Form 8949 or Schedule D. Gross income from a business means, for example, the amount on Schedule C, line 7, or Schedule F, line 9. But, in figuring gross income, don't reduce your income by any losses, including any loss on Schedule C, line 7, or Schedule F, line 9.

***If you didn't live with your spouse at the end of 2024 (or on the date your spouse died) and your gross income was at least $5, you must file a return regardless of your age.

Figure 1.2 For Children and Other Dependents

Chart B—For Children and Other Dependents (See *Who Qualifies as Your Dependent*, later.)

If your parent (or someone else) can claim you as a dependent, use this chart to see if you must file a return.
In this chart, **unearned income** includes taxable interest, ordinary dividends, and capital gain distributions. It also includes unemployment compensation, taxable social security benefits, pensions, annuities, and distributions of unearned income from a trust. **Earned income** includes salaries, wages, tips, professional fees, and taxable scholarship and fellowship grants. **Gross income** is the total of your unearned and earned income.

Single dependents. Were you **either** age 65 or older **or** blind?

☐ **No.** You must file a return if **any** of the following apply.
- Your unearned income was over $1,300.
- Your earned income was over $14,600.
- Your gross income was more than the **larger** of—
  - $1,300, or
  - Your earned income (up to $14,600) plus $450.

☐ **Yes.** You must file a return if **any** of the following apply.
- Your unearned income was over $3,250 ($5,200 if 65 or older **and** blind).
- Your earned income was over $16,550 ($18,500 if 65 or older **and** blind).
- Your gross income was more than the **larger** of—
  - $3,250 ($5,200 if 65 or older **and** blind), or
  - Your earned income (up to $14,150) plus $2,400 ($4,350 if 65 or older **and** blind).

Married dependents. Were you **either** age 65 or older **or** blind?

☐ **No.** You must file a return if **any** of the following apply.
- Your unearned income was over $1,300.
- Your earned income was over $14,600.
- Your gross income was at least $5 and your spouse files a separate return and itemizes deductions.
- Your gross income was more than the **larger** of—
  - $1,300, or
  - Your earned income (up to $14,150) plus $450.

☐ **Yes.** You must file a return if **any** of the following apply.
- Your unearned income was over $2,850 ($4,400 if 65 or older **and** blind).
- Your earned income was over $16,150 ($17,700 if 65 or older **and** blind).
- Your gross income was at least $5 and your spouse files a separate return and itemizes deductions.
- Your gross income was more than the **larger** of—
  - $2,850 ($4,400 if 65 or older **and** blind), or
  - Your earned income (up to $14,150) plus $2,000 ($3,550 if 65 or older **and** blind).

Figure 1.3 Other Situations When You Must File

Chart C—Other Situations When You Must File

You must file a return if any of the conditions below apply for 2024.

1. You owe any special taxes, including any of the following (see the instructions for Schedule 2).
   a. Alternative minimum tax.
   b. Additional tax on a qualified plan, including an individual retirement arrangement (IRA), or other tax-favored account.
   c. Household employment taxes.
   d. Social security and Medicare tax on tips you didn't report to your employer or on wages you received from an employer who didn't withhold these taxes.
   e. Write-in taxes, including uncollected social security and Medicare or RRTA tax on tips you reported to your employer or on group-term life insurance and additional taxes on health savings accounts.
   f. Recapture taxes.
2. You (or your spouse, if filing jointly) received health savings account, Archer MSA, or Medicare Advantage MSA distributions.
3. You had net earnings from self-employment of at least $400.
4. You had wages of $108.28 or more from a church or qualified church-controlled organization that is exempt from employer social security and Medicare taxes.
5. Advance payments of the premium tax credit were made for you, your spouse, or a dependent who enrolled in coverage through the Marketplace. You or whoever enrolled you should have received Form(s) 1095-A showing the amount of the advance payments.
6. You are required to include amounts in income under section 965 or you have a net tax liability under section 965 that you are paying in installments under section 965(h) or deferred by making an election under section 965(i).

Self-Study Problem 1.4 — Refer to Appendix E for Solutions to Self-Study Problems

Determine whether the following taxpayers are *required* to file a return for 2024 in each of the following independent situations:

1. Taxpayer (age 45) is single with income of $12,000.
2. Husband (age 67) and wife (age 64) have an income of $30,000 and file a joint return.
3. Taxpayer is a college student with a salary from a part-time job of $6,500. She is claimed as a dependent by her parents.
4. Taxpayer has net earnings from self-employment of $2,000.
5. Taxpayers are married with income of $27,000 and file a joint return. They expect a refund of $600 from excess withholding.
6. Taxpayer has only self-employment income of $650.
7. Taxpayer is a surviving spouse (age 48) with a dependent son (age 18) and income of $27,000.

1-5 Filing Status and Tax Computation

Learning Objective 1.5
Determine filing status and understand the calculation of tax according to filing status.

An important step in calculating the amount of a taxpayer's tax liability is the determination of the taxpayer's correct filing status. The tax law has five different filing statuses: single; married filing jointly; married filing separately; head of household; and surviving spouse. A tax table that must be used by most taxpayers, showing the tax liability for all five filing statuses, is provided in Appendix A. The tax table must be used unless the taxpayer's taxable income is $100,000 or more or the taxpayer is using a special method to calculate the tax liability. If taxpayers cannot use the tax table to determine their tax, a tax rate schedule is used. Each filing status has a separate tax rate schedule as presented in Appendix A except surviving spouse, which uses the married filing jointly table.

1-5a Single Filing Status

A taxpayer who does not meet the definition of married, surviving spouse, or head of household status must file as single. Any taxpayer who is unmarried or legally separated from their spouse by divorce or separate maintenance decree as of December 31 of the tax year does not generally meet the definition of married. State law governs whether a taxpayer is married, divorced, or legally separated.

Example After ten years of marriage, Ana divorced their spouse on December 15, 2024. Ana and their ex-spouse stopped living in the same household in October of 2024. They have no children or other dependents. Ana is considered unmarried without dependents at the end of 2024 and will file as a single taxpayer. ♦

1-5b Married Filing Jointly

Taxpayers are considered married for tax purposes if they are married as of December 31 of the tax year. Also, in the year of one spouse's death, the spouses are considered married for the full year. If a taxpayer remarries in the same year their spouse dies, they will be treated as married with the new spouse and the deceased spouse's tax return will be filed as married filing separately. In most situations, married taxpayers pay less tax by filing jointly than by filing separately. Married taxpayers may file a joint return even if they did not live together for the entire year.

Example Elan and Justice divorced in March 2024. Elan married Tabbouleh in September 2024 but unfortunately, Tabbouleh passed away in a car accident in December 2024. Elan did not remarry prior to December 31, 2024. Elan may file either married filing jointly (with Tabbouleh) or married filing separately for 2024. ♦

> **Tax Break**
>
> Head of Household is a filing status that can be difficult to understand but comes with some substantial tax benefits if a taxpayer qualifies. Single parents should carefully analyze their situation since Head of Household provides lower tax rates and a higher standard deduction than Single filing status. This benefit is not just limited to single parents. All unmarried taxpayers that maintain a household and provide support for another person should consider whether they qualify for this tax-advantageous filing status.

1-5c Married Filing Separately

Married taxpayers may file separate returns and should do so if it reduces their total tax liability. They may file separately if one or both had income during the year. If separate returns are filed, both taxpayers must compute their tax in the same manner. For example, if one spouse itemizes deductions, the other spouse must also itemize deductions. Each taxpayer reports their income, deductions, and credits and is responsible only for the tax due on their return. If the taxpayers live in a community property state, they must follow state law to determine community income and separate income. The community property states include Arizona, California, Idaho, Louisiana, Nevada, New Mexico, Texas, Washington, and Wisconsin. Refer to Chapter 2 for additional explanation of income and losses from community property.

A legally married taxpayer may file as head of household (based on the general filing status rules) if they qualify as an abandoned spouse. A taxpayer qualifies as an abandoned spouse only if *all* of the following requirements are met:

1. A separate return is filed,
2. The taxpayer paid more than half the cost (rent, utilities, etc.) to maintain their home during the year,
3. The spouse did not live with the taxpayer at any time in the last six months of the year, and
4. For over six months during the year the home was the principal residence for a dependent child, stepchild, or adopted child. Under certain conditions, a foster child may qualify as a dependent.

In certain circumstances, married couples may be able to reduce their total tax liability by filing separately. For instance, since some itemized deductions, such as medical expenses and casualty losses, are reduced by a percentage of adjusted gross income (Chapter 5), a spouse with a casualty loss and low separate adjusted gross income may benefit from filing separately.

Example In May 2024, Joe left Teresa (his spouse) and returned to his ancestral home in Italy. Teresa was left to support herself and her dependent daughter (Teresa and Joe's son went with Joe to Italy) in her home for the remainder of 2024. Teresa and Joe did not file for legal separation or divorce until 2025. Teresa is an abandoned spouse and may file as head of household. If both children had moved to Italy with Joe, Teresa would not meet the requirement of having a dependent child living with her and would have to file jointly or, more likely, married filing separately. ♦

1-5d Head of Household

If an unmarried taxpayer can meet special tests or if a married taxpayer qualifies as an abandoned spouse, they are allowed to file as head of household. Head of household tax rates are lower than rates for single or married filing separately. A taxpayer qualifies for head of household status if the following conditions exist:

1. The taxpayer was an unmarried or abandoned spouse as of December 31 of the tax year,
2. The taxpayer paid more than half of the cost of keeping a home for the year, and
3. A qualifying person lived with the taxpayer in the home for more than one-half of the year; however, if the qualifying person is a dependent parent, they are not required to live with the taxpayer.

The requirements to be a qualifying person are similar, but not identical to the requirements to be a dependent as either a qualifying child or qualifying relative (qualifying person, child, and relative are all covered in the next section).

Example Andrew is a single taxpayer with no children. In 2024, he pays to keep up the home he lives in and also the home in which his mother, Gammie, lives for the entire year. Although Gammie did not live with Andrew during 2024, because she is Andrew's parent, Andrew may file as head of household in 2024. ♦

Because head of household status provides greater tax benefits than that of single filing status, tax preparers that complete an individual income tax return for a head of household taxpayer are required to complete Form 8867 Preparer's Due Diligence Checklist (Pages 1-13 and 1-14). Form 8867 is also used if the taxpayer is claiming the earned income credit, the American Opportunities credit, the child tax credit, or the other dependent credit. For purposes of head of household due diligence, the emphasis is on inquiries surrounding the three required conditions covered above and documenting what responses or information the taxpayer is able to provide related to the requirements. The Form 8867 is filed with the taxpayer's return like any other form.

Tax Break Divorcing couples may save significant taxes if one or both of the spouses qualify as an "abandoned spouse" and can use the head of household filing status. The combination of head of household filing status for one spouse with married filing separately filing status for the other spouse is commonly used in the year (or years) leading up to a divorce. In cases where each spouse has custody of a different child, the separated taxpayers may each claim head of household status.

1-5e Surviving Spouse with Dependent Child

A taxpayer may continue to benefit from the married filing jointly filing status rates for two years after the year of the death of a spouse. To qualify to use married filing jointly status, the surviving spouse (or sometimes called qualifying widow(er)) must pay over half the cost of maintaining a household where a dependent child, stepchild, or adopted child lives. After the two-year period, these taxpayers often qualify for the head of household filing status.

Example Grace's spouse, Joe, died in 2024. Grace has two dependent children ages 6 and 8 that she continues to claim as dependents for at least the next ten years. Grace may file married filing jointly in 2024, the year of her spouse's death. Grace may continue to file as a surviving spouse (using married filing jointly rates) for both 2025 and 2026. Starting in 2027, assuming Grace meets the other requirements, she may file as head of household (or less likely, single). ♦

Form **8867**
(Rev. November 2024)
Department of the Treasury
Internal Revenue Service

Paid Preparer's Due Diligence Checklist
Earned Income Credit (EIC), American Opportunity Tax Credit (AOTC),
Child Tax Credit (CTC) (including the Additional Child Tax Credit (ACTC) and
Credit for Other Dependents (ODC)), and Head of Household (HOH) Filing Status
To be completed by preparer and filed with Form 1040, 1040-SR, 1040-NR, or 1040-SS.
Go to *www.irs.gov/Form8867* for instructions and the latest information.

OMB No. 1545-0074

For tax year
20____

Attachment
Sequence No. **70**

Taxpayer name(s) shown on return | Taxpayer identification number

Preparer's name | Preparer tax identification number

Part I	**Due Diligence Requirements**

Please check the appropriate box for the credit(s) and/or HOH filing status claimed on the return and complete the related Parts I–V for the benefit(s) claimed (check all that apply). ☐ EIC ☐ CTC/ACTC/ODC ☐ AOTC ☐ HOH

		Yes	No	N/A
1	Did you complete the return based on information for the applicable tax year provided by the taxpayer or reasonably obtained by you?	☐	☐	
2	If credits are claimed on the return, did you complete the applicable EIC and/or CTC/ACTC/ODC worksheets found in the Form 1040, 1040-SR, 1040-NR, 1040-SS, or Schedule 8812 (Form 1040) instructions, and/or the AOTC worksheet found in the Form 8863 instructions, or your own worksheet(s) that provides the same information, and all related forms and schedules for each credit claimed?	☐	☐	☐
3	Did you satisfy the knowledge requirement? To meet the knowledge requirement, you must do both of the following. • Interview the taxpayer, ask questions, and contemporaneously document the taxpayer's responses to determine that the taxpayer is eligible to claim the credit(s) and/or HOH filing status. • Review information to determine that the taxpayer is eligible to claim the credit(s) and/or HOH filing status and to figure the amount(s) of any credit(s)	☐	☐	
4	Did any information provided by the taxpayer or a third party for use in preparing the return, or information reasonably known to you, appear to be incorrect, incomplete, or inconsistent? (If "**Yes**," answer questions 4a and 4b. If "**No**," go to question 5.)	☐	☐	
a	Did you make reasonable inquiries to determine the correct, complete, and consistent information?	☐	☐	
b	Did you contemporaneously document your inquiries? (Documentation should include the questions you asked, whom you asked, when you asked, the information that was provided, and the impact the information had on your preparation of the return.)	☐	☐	
5	Did you satisfy the record retention requirement? To meet the record retention requirement, you must keep a copy of your documentation referenced in question 4b, a copy of this Form 8867, a copy of any applicable worksheet(s), a record of how, when, and from whom the information used to prepare Form 8867 and any applicable worksheet(s) was obtained, and a copy of any document(s) provided by the taxpayer that you relied on to determine eligibility for the credit(s) and/or HOH filing status or to figure the amount(s) of the credit(s)	☐	☐	
	List those documents provided by the taxpayer, if any, that you relied on: _____ _____			
6	Did you ask the taxpayer whether he/she could provide documentation to substantiate eligibility for the credit(s) and/or HOH filing status and the amount(s) of any credit(s) claimed on the return if his/her return is selected for audit?	☐	☐	
7	Did you ask the taxpayer if any of these credits were disallowed or reduced in a previous year? **(If credits were disallowed or reduced, go to question 7a; if not, go to question 8.)**	☐	☐	☐
a	Did you complete the required recertification Form 8862?	☐	☐	
8	If the taxpayer is reporting self-employment income, did you ask questions to prepare a complete and correct Schedule C (Form 1040)?	☐	☐	☐

For Paperwork Reduction Act Notice, see separate instructions. Cat. No. 26142H Form **8867** (Rev. 11-2024)

Form 8867 (Rev. 11-2024) Page **2**

Part II	Due Diligence Questions for Returns Claiming EIC (If the return does not claim EIC, go to Part III.)	Yes	No	N/A
9a	Have you determined that the taxpayer is eligible to claim the EIC for the number of qualifying children claimed, or is eligible to claim the EIC without a qualifying child? **(If the taxpayer is claiming the EIC and does not have a qualifying child, go to question 10.)**	☐	☐	
b	Did you ask the taxpayer if the child lived with the taxpayer for over half of the year, even if the taxpayer has supported the child the entire year?	☐	☐	
c	Did you explain to the taxpayer the rules about claiming the EIC when a child is the qualifying child of more than one person (tiebreaker rules)?	☐	☐	☐

Part III	Due Diligence Questions for Returns Claiming CTC/ACTC/ODC (If the return does not claim CTC, ACTC, or ODC, go to Part IV.)	Yes	No	N/A
10	Have you determined that each qualifying person for the CTC/ACTC/ODC is the taxpayer's dependent who is a citizen, national, or resident of the United States?	☐	☐	
11	Did you explain to the taxpayer that he/she may not claim the CTC/ACTC if the child has not lived with the taxpayer for over half of the year, even if the taxpayer has supported the child, unless the child's custodial parent has released a claim to exemption for the child?	☐	☐	☐
12	Did you explain to the taxpayer the rules about claiming the CTC/ACTC/ODC for a child of divorced or separated parents (or parents who live apart), including any requirement to attach a Form 8332 or similar statement to the return?	☐	☐	☐

Part IV	Due Diligence Questions for Returns Claiming AOTC (If the return does not claim AOTC, go to Part V.)	Yes	No
13	Did the taxpayer provide substantiation for the credit, such as a Form 1098-T and/or receipts for the qualified tuition and related expenses for the claimed AOTC?	☐	☐

Part V	Due Diligence Questions for Claiming HOH (If the return does not claim HOH filing status, go to Part VI.)	Yes	No
14	Have you determined that the taxpayer was unmarried or considered unmarried on the last day of the tax year and provided more than half of the cost of keeping up a home for the year for a qualifying person?	☐	☐

Part VI   Eligibility Certification

You will have complied with all due diligence requirements for claiming the applicable credit(s) and/or HOH filing status on the return of the taxpayer identified above if you:

- A. Interview the taxpayer, ask adequate questions, contemporaneously document the taxpayer's responses on the return or in your notes, review adequate information to determine if the taxpayer is eligible to claim the credit(s) and/or HOH filing status and to figure the amount(s) of the credit(s);
- B. Complete this Form 8867 truthfully and accurately and complete the actions described in this checklist for any applicable credit(s) claimed and HOH filing status, if claimed;
- C. Submit Form 8867 in the manner required; **and**
- D. Keep all five of the following records for 3 years from the latest of the dates specified in the Form 8867 instructions under *Document Retention*.
    1. A copy of this Form 8867.
    2. The applicable worksheet(s) or your own worksheet(s) for any credit(s) claimed.
    3. Copies of any documents provided by the taxpayer on which you relied to determine the taxpayer's eligibility for the credit(s) and/or HOH filing status and to figure the amount(s) of the credit(s).
    4. A record of how, when, and from whom the information used to prepare this form and the applicable worksheet(s) was obtained.
    5. A record of any additional information you relied upon, including questions you asked and the taxpayer's responses, to determine the taxpayer's eligibility for the credit(s) and/or HOH filing status and to figure the amount(s) of the credit(s).

If you have not complied with all due diligence requirements, you may have to pay a penalty for each failure to comply related to a claim of an applicable credit or HOH filing status (see instructions for more information).

		Yes	No
15	Do you certify that all of the answers on this Form 8867 are, to the best of your knowledge, true, correct, and complete?	☐	☐

Form **8867** (Rev. 11-2024)

1-5f Tax Computation

For 2024, there are seven income tax brackets (10 percent, 12 percent, 22 percent, 24 percent, 32 percent, 35 percent, and 37 percent). Individuals with taxable income below $100,000 are required to use the tax tables presented in Appendix A. Taxpayers with income equal to or more than $100,000 use the tax rate schedules (also presented in Appendix A). An example of the single tax rate schedule is presented below. Certain high-income taxpayers are subject to additional taxes covered in Chapter 6.

Figure 1.4 Tax Rate Schedule

If taxable income is:	The tax is:
Not over $11,600	10% of the taxable income
Over $11,600 but not over $47,150	$1,160 + 12% of the excess over $11,600
Over $47,150 but not over $100,525	$5,426 + 22% of the excess over $47,150
Over $100,525 but not over $191,950	$17,168.50 + 24% of the excess over $100,525
Over $191,950 but not over $243,725	$39,110.50 + 32% of the excess over $191,950
Over $243,725 but not over $609,350	$55,678.50 + 35% of the excess over $243,725
Over $609,350	$183,647.25 + 37% of the excess over $609,350

Example Guadalupe, a single taxpayer, has adjusted gross income of $120,000 and taxable income of $105,000 for 2024. Her tax is calculated using the 2024 tax rate schedule from Appendix A as follows:

$18,242.50 = $17,168.50 + [24% × ($105,000 − $100,525)] ♦

Example Yao is a single taxpayer during 2024. Their taxable income for the year is $43,362. Using the tax table in Appendix A, their gross tax liability for the year is found to be $4,973. ♦

The tax tables and the tax rate schedules provide the tax rates associated with an individual taxpayer's ordinary income. Most wages, salaries, interest, self-employment income, and rental income is ordinary income. The tax law contains different tax rates depending on the *character* of the income being recognized. For example, the tax rates applicable to net long-term capital gains currently range from 0 percent to 31.8 percent depending on the taxpayer's tax bracket and the type of capital asset. The calculation of the tax on capital gains is covered in detail in Chapter 4, and the applicable tax rates are covered in this chapter. The tax rates for qualifying dividends, presented in detail in Chapter 2, range from 0 percent to 23.8 percent in 2024.

Example Arisa has wages of $30,000, long-term capital gains of $500, qualified dividends of $300, interest income on a savings account of $35, and short-term capital gains of $660. The wages, interest, and short-term gains are likely to be treated as ordinary income and taxed at ordinary tax rates per the tax tables. The long-term capital gains and qualified dividends are likely to enjoy preferential tax rates as explained later in this chapter. ♦

Tax Break

If filing a tax return for an individual that passed away, the IRS offers an interactive tax assistant to provide step-by-step instructions (**https://www.irs.gov/help/ita/how-do-i-file-a-deceased-persons-tax-return**). For example, if filing jointly, be sure and enter the deceased spouse's name on the tax return and write "deceased" along with the spouse's name at the top of the return. If using Intuit's ProConnect, enter the date of death of the deceased spouse (or taxpayer if not filing jointly) in the General/Client Information input screen.

Self-Study Problem 1.5
Refer to Appendix E for Solutions to Self-Study Problems

Indicate the generally preferred filing status (or statuses) and other filing status (or statuses) that are available in each of the following independent cases, using this legend:

- **A** – Single
- **B** – Married, filing a joint return
- **C** – Married, filing separate returns
- **D** – Head of household
- **E** – Surviving spouse

1. The taxpayers are married on December 31 of the tax year.
2. The taxpayer is single, with a dependent child living in her home.
3. The taxpayer is unmarried and is living with their girlfriend.
4. The taxpayer is married and their spouse left midyear and has disappeared. The taxpayer has no dependents.
5. The unmarried taxpayer supports her dependent mother, who lives in her own home.
6. The taxpayer's spouse died last year. His 15-year-old dependent son lives with him.

ProConnect™ Tax TIP

In ProConnect, much of the input is controlled by the left-hand margin. Filing status is part of Client Information under the General heading. By clicking on Filing Status, a dropdown appears in the main window to allow the preparer to select the taxpayer's filing status. For married filing jointly and separately statuses, the Live With Spouse box should be checked if it applies.

1-6 Qualifying Dependents

1-6a Dependents

Prior to 2018, taxpayers were able to deduct an exemption amount of approximately $4,000 each for themselves, their spouse (if married filing jointly), and any dependents. The Tax Cuts and Jobs Act of 2017 (TCJA) eliminated the personal and dependency exemptions in lieu of a larger standard deduction; however, dependents remain important for other reasons. For example, head of household filing status, the child tax credit, and the earned income tax credit require or provide a greater benefit with a qualified dependent. Lastly, the suspension of personal and dependency exemptions is scheduled to expire after 2025 which means standard deduction amounts may be reduced and exemptions may yet return. All dependents must meet the following tests:

1. The taxpayer (and the taxpayer's spouse, if filing jointly) may not be claimed as a dependent by another taxpayer.
2. The potential dependent may not be a married person that files jointly unless that joint return is only filed to claim a refund of income tax withheld or estimated payments made.
3. The potential dependent must be a U.S. citizen, a U.S. resident alien, a U.S. national, or a resident of Canada or Mexico. A U.S. national is a person born in American Samoa or in the Commonwealth of the Northern Mariana Islands or those born outside of U.S. territory to two U.S. national parents, or those born abroad to one alien parent and one U.S. national parent.
4. The potential dependent must have a taxpayer identification number (in most cases, a Social Security number).
5. The potential dependent must be either a qualifying child or a qualifying relative.

> 1.6 Learning Objective
> Define qualifying dependents.

The IRS started requiring the disclosure of Social Security numbers for each dependent claimed by a taxpayer to stop dishonest taxpayers from claiming extra dependents or even claiming pets. Before this change, listing phony dependents was one of the most common forms of tax fraud. Reportedly, seven million dependents disappeared from the tax rolls after Congress required taxpayers to include dependents' Social Security numbers on tax returns.

Example Joanna is an 18-year-old single mother who can be claimed as a dependent by her parents. Joanna will be unable to claim her infant son as a dependent on her own tax return. ♦

Example Diego and Paola are a married couple that file jointly. Diego works part-time and Paola is a full-time student and has no income. Diego and Paola's gross income is $8,800, all of which is wages earned by Diego. Angelo is Paolo's single father and provides all other support for Diego and Paola, which is more than half. Assuming Diego and Paola meet the other dependency tests, they can be claimed as dependents since although they are married and plan to file jointly, they would only need to do so to claim a refund. ♦

1-6b Qualifying Child

To be a qualifying child, the potential dependent must meet all of the four following tests:

1. **Relationship Test**
   The potential qualifying child must be the taxpayer's child, stepchild, or adopted child, or the taxpayer's brother or sister, half-brother or half-sister, or stepsibling, or a descendant of any of these. Under certain circumstances, a foster child can also qualify.

Example Jon and Kate, a married filing jointly couple, have eight children living in their home with them all year. Five of the children are the biological children of Jon and Kate. One child is Jon's from a previous relationship. Another child was adopted in the previous tax year and another is the child of Kate's brother. The five biological children, the stepchild, the adopted child, and the nephew (son of Kate's brother) all meet the relationship test for a qualifying child. ♦

2. **Domicile or Abode Test**
   The potential qualifying child must have the same principal place of abode as the taxpayer for more than half of the taxable year. There are exceptions for temporary absences from the household due to special circumstances such as illness, education, and vacation; birth and death of a child within the tax year; children of divorced or separated parents, or parents that live apart; and kidnapped children.

Example Aseel, a single taxpayer, sent her 15-year-old child away to boarding school for eight months during the tax year. The child lived at home during the summer and returned home for most school holidays. Because being away for school is generally considered a temporary absence, Aseel's child meets the domicile or abode test for the tax year. ♦

If the potential qualifying child's parents are divorced or legally separated, the custodial parent (the parent whom the child lived with for the greater number of nights during the year) typically claims the potential qualifying child. The custodial parent can agree to allow the noncustodial parent to claim the potential qualifying child by providing a signed Form 8332 (or if a pre-2009 divorce, the divorce decree provides for such assignment of the dependent).

Example Caesar and Cleopatra were divorced in 2015. Cleo has primary custody of their eight-year-old son, Marcus. Cleo provides Caesar with a signed Form 8832 allowing Caesar to claim Marcus despite Cleo being the custodial parent. ♦

3. **Age Test**
   The potential qualifying child must be under age 19 or a full-time student under the age of 24. A potential qualifying child is considered a full-time student if enrolled full-time for at least five months of the year. Thus, a college senior graduating in May or June can qualify in the year of graduation. The taxpayer must be older than the potential qualifying child unless the potential qualifying child is permanently disabled.

Example Rodolfo and Felicia, a married couple filing jointly, have three children: Gustav, a 26-year-old that is a full-time medical student; Bella Rose, a 23-year-old full-time graduate student in business; and Juan, a 15-year-old high school student. Juan is under age 19 and meets the age test. Bella Rose is under the age of 24 and a full-time student and meets the age test. Gustav, although a full-time student, is not under the age of 24 and thus, does not meet the age test. Gustav could possibly meet the qualifying relative test (covered in the next section) and thus, may qualify as a dependent. ♦

4. **Self-Support Test**
   A potential qualifying child who provides more than one-half of their own support cannot be claimed as a dependent of someone else. Support includes expenditures for items such as food, lodging, clothes, medical and dental care, and education. In many

instances, the level of support provided by the potential qualifying child will be zero or close thereto.

Example   Horace is a single father of a 4-year-old child that has no income and is solely supported by Horace. The child does not provide more than one-half of their own support. ♦

For more complex situations, the IRS provides a support calculation worksheet in IRS Publication 17. An abridged version of the worksheet is presented as follows:

Worksheet for Determining Support

Funds Belonging to the Potential Qualifying Child

1. Savings or Funds belonging to the person at the start of the year plus any income earned (taxable and tax-exempt) or borrowed by that person during the year   1. _____

2. The amount of line 1 used for that person's support   2. _____

3. The amount of line 1 used for any other purposes plus savings at the end of the year   3. _____

4. Add lines 3 and 4 (should agree to line 1)   4. _____

Total Household Expenses

5a. If renting, total rent paid   5a. _____

5b. If a homeowner, the fair market value of rent if the home were rented   5b. _____

6. Total amount spent for food, utilities (not included in lines 5a or 5b), repairs (not included in lines 5a or 5b), and other household expenses (not including mortgage interest, property taxes, or insurance)   6. _____

7. Total of line 5a or 5b plus line 6   7. _____

8. Total number of persons living in the home   8. _____

Expenses for the Person Supported

9. Divide line 7 by line 8 for the person's share of household expenses   9. _____

10. The person's clothing, education, out-of-pocket medical and dental, travel, recreation, and other expenses   10. _____

11. Total lines 9 and 10   11. _____

Percentage of Support Provided by Person

12. Multiply line 11 by 50 percent   12. _____

13. Enter the amount from line 2 plus line 5b if the person supported is the homeowner   13. _____

14. If line 13 is greater than line 12, the person provided more than 50% of their own support and does not meet the support test to be a qualifying child.   14. _____

Taxpayer Provides Greater Than 50 Percent of Support

15. Support provided to the person from other sources   15. _____

16. Add Line 13 and Line 15   16. _____

17. Subtract Line 16 from Line 11   17. _____

18. If Line 17 is greater than Line 12 then the taxpayer provided more than one-half of the person's support and the person is a qualifying relative   18. _____

To calculate support, the taxpayer uses the actual cost of the above items, except lodging. The value of lodging is calculated at its fair rental value. Funds received by students as scholarships are excluded from the support test.

Example   Hien is a single mother and has an 18-year-old daughter, Anh. Hien and Anh are the only persons living in their apartment for the entire year with a rental cost of $24,000 per year. Hien estimates the following expenditures:

- Food, utilities, and other household expenses are $7,200 for the year
- Clothing, education, medical costs, and recreation expenses for Anh are $2,000 for the year

Anh works full-time during the tax year and starts the tax year with $4,000 in savings and generates income of $22,000 (after withholding) during the year. Of the $26,000 in funds Anh had available to her, she spent $10,000 on her own support for items like clothing, recreation, and transportation.

The household expenses total $31,200 ($24,000 for rent and $7,200 for other household expenses). Since the household has two members, one-half ($15,600) is Anh's share of household expenses provided by Hien. To that amount, add Hien's $2,000 of additional support to calculate total support of $17,600. Half of Hien's total support provided to Anh is $8,800. Since Anh's support ($10,000) for herself is greater than 50 percent of Hien's support of Anh ($8,800), Anh does not meet the support test. ♦

1-6c Tiebreaker Rules

In some instances, more than one person may be eligible to claim a person as a qualifying child.

Example   Paul is 27 years old and a single father of a 4-year-old daughter, Anna. Both Paul and Anna live with Brittney, Paul's younger sister, who provides all the support for both Paul and Anna. All are U.S. citizens and have Social Security numbers. Anna is a qualifying child of both Paul and Brittney. Note that for the support test for a qualifying child, it is not relevant that Paul provides no support for Anna. To pass the support test, Anna must not provide more than one-half of her own support. ♦

If more than one person can claim a qualifying child, a series of tiebreaker rules exist:

- If only one of the persons that can claim the qualifying child is the child's parent, then the parent claims the qualifying child.
- If the married parents do not file jointly, the parent with whom the child lived the longer period of time during the year will claim the qualifying child. If the child lived with each parent for the same number of days, the parent with the higher AGI will claim the qualifying child (note that for divorced parents, refer to the Domicile/Abode test above).

- If no parent can claim the qualifying child, then the child will be treated as the qualifying child of the individual with the highest AGI.
- If a parent can claim the qualifying child but does not, the individual with the highest AGI can claim the qualifying child but only if that individual's AGI is higher than the AGI of any parent that could have claimed the child.

Example In the previous example, assume Paul's AGI is $50,000 and Brittney's AGI is $60,000. Since Paul is the qualifying child's parent, he would normally be entitled to claim Anna but he may elect to allow Brittney to claim her. If Brittney's AGI were lower than Paul's, Brittney would be unable to claim Anna as a qualifying child. ♦

1-6d Qualifying Relative

A person who is not a qualifying child may be a qualifying relative and thus, claimed as a dependent. The potential qualifying relative must meet the first four tests for all dependents outlined earlier: (1) the taxpayer cannot be claimed as a dependent and the potential qualifying relative, (2) cannot file jointly, (3) must be a U.S. citizen or resident alien, and (4) must have a taxpayer identification number. The potential qualifying relative may not be a qualifying child of any taxpayer. For purposes of being a qualifying child, if the potential claimant of the qualifying child is not required to file a tax return (or files only to claim a refund), then the qualifying child is not considered a qualifying child of that person.

Example Howard, a single father, and his child, Pat, live with Howard's parents for the entire year and the parents provide all the support for both Howard and Pat. Howard's parents meet all the other tests to claim Pat as a qualifying child. Pat cannot be Howard's qualifying relative. ♦

Example Joan and her 6-year-old daughter live with Joan's friend, Marcelle. Joan has no income and is not required to file a tax return. Although Joan could claim her daughter as a qualifying child, because she is not required to file a tax return, Marcelle could claim both Joan and the daughter, if the other qualifying relative tests are met. ♦

To be a qualifying relative, the following tests must be met:

1a. Relationship Test
With some exceptions the potential qualifying relative must be a relative of the taxpayer. The list of qualifying relatives is larger than that of the relationship test for a qualifying child, and includes:
- children, stepchildren, adopted children, foster children, or a descendant of any of these (e.g., grandchildren);
- sibling, stepsibling, or a child of one of these (e.g., nieces and nephews);
- parents or an ancestor or sibling of them (e.g., grandparents, aunts and uncles, and "in-laws").

Note that cousins (a descendant of an aunt or uncle) do not meet the relationship test. However, an individual does not have to meet the relationship test if they meet the domicile/abode test for a qualified relative.

1b. Domicile/Abode Test
If the potential qualifying relative does not meet the relationship test, that person must live as a member of the taxpayer's household for the entire year. As with the domicile/adobe test for qualifying child, absences that stem from temporary

circumstances such as illness, education, business trips, vacation, and military service are excluded. A person is not considered a member of the household if at any time during the year the relationship between the taxpayer and the dependent was in violation of local law.

Example Iana and Castro are a married couple that file jointly and provide support for Castro's unmarried mother, who does not live with them. Castro dies unexpectedly in the current year but Iana continues to support Castro's mother. Castro's mother meets the relationship test and is not required to live with Iana. ♦

Example Paula is a single taxpayer and provides all the support for two individuals: Paula's cousin that lives in a nearby nursing home and Paula's childhood friend that lives in Paula's home. Neither of these individuals are a qualifying child of any taxpayer. Paula's friend does not meet the relationship test but does meet the domicile/abode test and may be a qualifying relative. Paula's cousin meets neither the relationship nor the domicile/abode test and cannot be a qualifying relative. ♦

2. **Gross Income Test**

    The qualifying relative cannot have gross income equal to or above the exemption amount ($5,050 in 2024). Although the deduction for exemptions is suspended until after 2025, the exemption amount will continue to be updated by the IRS. Gross income does not include any income exempt from tax (for example, tax-exempt interest or exempt Social Security benefits) but does include unemployment compensation and the taxable portion of Social Security benefits.

Example In 2024, Eesha and Paul are a married couple that file jointly. They have two children, Paul, Jr., a 26-year-old medical student and Nita, a 17-year-old high school student. Paul, Jr. works during the summer and earns $5,500. Both live at home. Nita also works and has earnings of $5,200. Paul, Jr. does not meet the requirements to be a qualifying child as he fails the age test (although he is a full-time student, he is not under age 24). He also fails the gross income test since his income exceeds $5,050; thus, Paul, Jr. cannot be claimed as a qualifying relative. Nita probably meets the requirements to be a qualifying child and the gross income test will not apply. ♦

3. **Support Test**

    The dependent must receive over half of their support from the taxpayer or under certain circumstances, a group of taxpayers. Unlike the gross income test, income exempt from tax and earned by the potential dependent is considered for the support test. If a dependent is supported by two or more taxpayers, a multiple support agreement may be filed. To file the agreement, the taxpayers (as a group) must provide over one-half of the support of the dependent. Assuming that all other dependency tests are met, the group may give the dependent to any member of the group who provided over 10 percent of the dependent's support by executing a signed Form 2120 Multiple Support Declaration.

Example Gina and Lola are sisters and share in the support of taking care of their mother, Raquel. In the current tax year, Raquel provides 10 percent of her own support, Gina provides 30 percent and Lola provides the remaining 60 percent. Only Lola meets the support test for claiming the mother as a qualifying relative because Lola provides more than one-half of the support to Raquel. ♦

Example In the previous example, if Raquel provides 30 percent of her own support, Gina provides 30 percent, and Lola provides 40 percent. No single person provides more than one-half of Raquel's support but as a group Gina and Lola provide over half of Raquel's support (70 percent). Both Gina and Lola individually provide more than 10 percent of Raquel's support and as a group must execute a multiple support agreement that permits one of them the right to claim Raquel as a qualifying relative. ♦

Figure 1.5 illustrates the dependency tests for both a qualifying child and a qualifying relative.

1-6e Qualifying Person for Head of Household

As explained previously in the filing status section, head of household is generally preferable to single filing status for an unmarried taxpayer (including an abandoned spouse) with dependents. To claim head of household, the taxpayer must pay more than one-half the cost of keeping up a home for the year and a "qualifying person" lives with the taxpayer in the home for more than one-half of the year. The rules for being a qualifying person for head of household filing status are not identical to the rules for being a qualifying child or qualifying relative.

A person can be a qualifying person by meeting any one of three tests:

1. The taxpayer paid over half the cost of maintaining a home that was the main home of a parent that can be claimed as a qualifying relative (note: the parent is not required to live with the taxpayer). If the parent is claimed under a multiple support agreement, the parent is not a qualifying person.

Example Jalen is a single taxpayer who provides a household for himself and a separate household for his mother, who meets the definition of a qualifying relative. No other person provides support for his mother. Jalen has a qualifying person and may file head of household. ♦

Example Gina and Lola are sisters and share in the support of taking care of their mother, Raquel. In the current tax year, Raquel provides 30 percent of her own support, Gina provides 30 percent, and Lola provides 40 percent. Gina claims Raquel as a qualifying relative under the multiple support agreement that she and Lola have agreed to. Although Raquel is a qualifying relative, she is not a qualifying person to Gina because Gina can claim her as a dependent only though a multiple support agreement. Gina may not file under head of household status. ♦

2. The taxpayer paid over half the cost of maintaining a home that was the main home of a qualifying child of the taxpayer. Recall that to be a qualifying child, the potential qualifying person must meet the relationship, domicile/abode, age, and support tests. If the qualifying child is unmarried, then that child is not required to meet the overall "citizenship" test to be considered a dependent. That is, the child need not be a U.S. citizen, resident alien, or resident of Canada or Mexico. In addition, if the taxpayer is a non-custodial divorced parent, the child is not a qualifying person for head of household. The custodial parent may claim the qualifying child for head of household despite not claiming the child as a dependent.

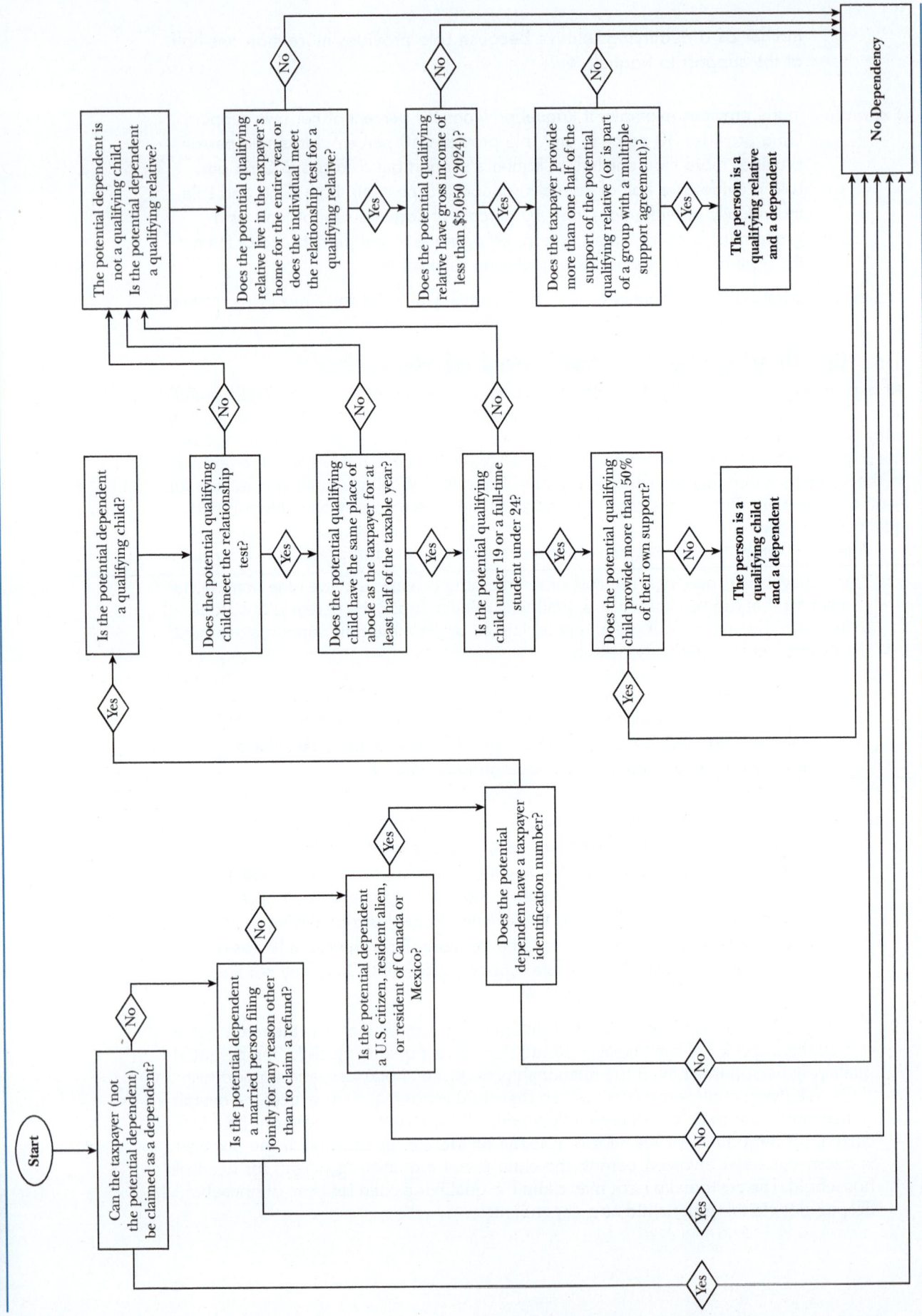

Figure 1.5 Dependency Tests Flow Chart for Qualifying Child and Qualifying Relative

3. The taxpayer paid to maintain the home of a qualifying relative other than the taxpayer's parent and the qualifying relative lived in the taxpayer's home for more than half of the year. In order to qualify as a qualifying person for purposes of head of household, this qualifying relative must be one of the following:
   - child, stepchild, adopted child, foster child, or a decedent of any of them
   - sibling, half-sibling, or a son or daughter of any of them
   - an ancestor or sibling of the taxpayer's parent
   - stepsibling, stepparent, son-in-law, daughter-in-law, father-in-law, mother-in-law, brother-in-law, sister-in-law

Example Howard is a single taxpayer and lives with his girlfriend, Gloria. Gloria lives with Howard all year and meets all of the qualifying relative tests. Because she is not related to Howard in one of the ways presented in test 3 above, Gloria is not a qualifying person. ♦

Example Assuming the same facts as the previous example, Gloria has a 3-month-old child, Esther, for whom Howard is not the father. Esther lives with Howard and Gloria all year. Esther cannot be Howard's qualifying child because she does not meet the relationship test. Esther cannot be a qualifying relative because she is Gloria's qualifying child. Esther is a not a qualifying person. ♦

The rules that define qualifying persons are complex and thus, the IRS makes available several different publications and aids to assist taxpayers and tax preparers with this determination. IRS Publication 501 describes qualifying child, relative, and person in detail with considerable examples. IRS Publication 4012, the resource guide for volunteers in the Volunteer Income Tax Assistance (VITA) program contains a decision tree, interview tips, and a chart to assist with determining head of household filing status. Lastly, the IRS website (**www.irs.gov/help/ita/what-is-my-filing-status**) offers an online Interactive Tax Assistant that uses interview questions to assist in determining filing status. Tax preparers that use these aids responsibly should be able to meet the due diligence requirements of Form 8867.

ProConnect™ Tax TIP

Spouse information is entered under Client Information and is just under Taxpayer Information on the left-hand margin. Dependents are a category under General. Be sure and input date of birth and other fields. Typically, the Child Tax Credit and the Earned Income Credit should be set to When Applicable to permit the software to make the correct determination based on input. New dependents can be added by clicking the [+] tab at the top of the main window for Dependents.

1-6f Credits for Children and Other Dependents

Although deductions for personal exemptions are no longer permitted from 2018 through 2025, dependent status is important for claiming a number of individual tax credits such as the child tax credit, the credit for other dependents, the credit for child and dependent care expenses, and the earned income tax credit. Many of these tax credits are covered in Chapter 7; however, due to the relatively large number of taxpayers that are eligible for the child tax credit and the credit for other dependents, an overview is provided here.

A tax credit differs from a tax deduction. A tax deduction serves to lower the taxable income of the taxpayer.

Example Emily's adjusted gross income is $52,000. She is eligible for a $14,600 standard deduction. This deduction lowers her taxable income to $37,400. If Emily is single, her 2024 tax liability is $4,259. ♦

A tax credit lowers the tax liability dollar for dollar. A credit is generally more advantageous than a deduction.

Example Emily (from the previous example) is also eligible for a $500 tax credit. Rather than reduce her taxable income, the tax credit reduces the tax itself to $3,759 ($4,259 − $500). ♦

For 2024, the child tax credit is $2,000 for a child under 17 years of age. To qualify for the credit, this child must be a qualifying child and have a Social Security number at the time the tax return is filed.

The credit for other dependents is $500 per dependent. An "other dependent" need not be a child but must qualify as either a qualifying child or qualifying relative. Additional requirements are covered in Chapter 7.

Example Bruce and Demi Mehr have two children, Anna (age 12) and Clark (age 18). Both Anna and Clark qualify as qualifying children under the dependent rules. Assuming all other requirements are met, the Mehrs may claim a $2,000 child tax credit for Anna and a $500 other dependent credit for Clark (as Clark is not under age 17). ♦

ProConnect™ Tax TIP ProConnect is designed to automatically compute the child tax credit and other dependent credit based on the information input in the Dependent window. If no such credit is being reported, it could be due to missing information (for example, birthdate) or the credits were inadvertently suppressed in the Dependent window. The child tax credit and other dependent credit can be overridden under Credits/EIC, Residential Energy, Oth Credits in the left-hand margin, but overriding the system is generally not a good idea.

Self-Study Problem 1.6 Refer to Appendix E for Solutions to Self-Study Problems

Indicate in each of the following situations whether the taxpayer has a dependent in 2024. In each situation you can assume the taxpayer cannot be claimed as a dependent, that all individuals are U.S. citizens, and that all have valid Social Security numbers, unless otherwise indicated.

1. Paris and Calijah, a married couple filing jointly, had a new baby in December 2024. Can the baby be claimed as a dependent?
2. Quentin, age 25, supports his 26-year-old brother, who is not a full-time student. His brother lives with Quentin all year. His brother's gross income is $5,100 from a part-time job. Can Quentin claim his brother as a dependent?
3. Donna and her sister support their mother and together provide 60 percent of her support. If Donna provides 25 percent of her mother's support and her sister signs a multiple support agreement, can Donna claim the mother as a dependent?
4. Keion is single and supports his son and his son's wife, both of whom lived with Keion for the entire year. The son (age 20) and his wife (age 19) file a joint return to get a refund, reporting $2,500 ($2,000 earned by the son) of gross income. Both the son and daughter-in-law are full-time students. Can Keion claim his son and daughter-in-law as dependents?
5. Gary is single and provides $5,000 toward his 19-year-old daughter's college expenses. The remainder of her support is provided by a tax-exempt $9,500 tuition scholarship. The daughter is a full-time student. Can Gary claim his daughter as a dependent?
6. Ruthy is 50 years old and supports her 72-year-old mother, who is blind and has $5,000 of Social Security benefits that are not taxable. Can Ruthy claim her mother as a dependent?

Would You Sign This Tax Return?

Your clients, Adam and Amy Accrual, have a 21-year-old daughter named April. April is single and is a full-time student studying for her bachelor's degree in accounting at California Poly Academy (CPA) in Pismo Beach, California, where she lives with her roommates year-round. Last year, April worked at a local bar and restaurant four nights a week and made $18,000, which she used for tuition, fees, books, and living expenses. Her parents help April by sending her $300 each month to help with her expenses at college. This is all of the support given to April by her parents. When preparing Adam and Amy's tax return, you note that they claim April as a dependent for tax purposes. Adam is insistent that they can claim April because of the $300 per month support and the fact that they "have claimed her since she was born." He will not let you take April off his return as a dependent. Would you sign the Paid Preparer's declaration (refer to example above) on this return? Why or why not?

1-7 The Standard Deduction

The standard deduction was placed in the tax law to provide relief for taxpayers with few itemized deductions. The amount of the standard deduction is subtracted from adjusted gross income by taxpayers who do not itemize their deductions. If a taxpayer's gross income is less than the standard deduction amount, the taxpayer has no taxable income. The 2024 standard deduction amounts are presented in Table 1.5.

Table 1.5 Standard Deduction Amounts 2024

Filing Status	Standard Deduction
Single	$ 14,600
Married filing jointly	29,200
Married filing separately	14,600
Head of household	21,900
Surviving spouse [qualifying widow(er)]	29,200

The standard deduction amounts were increased significantly by the TCJA. The temporary increases are scheduled to expire after 2025.

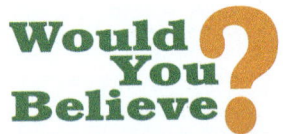

In 2017, about 69 percent of individual taxpayers selected the standard deduction. After the expansion of the standard deduction amounts, the percentage jumped to over 88 percent. Recall that the expanded standard deduction is scheduled to expire at the end of 2025.

1-7a Additional Amounts for Old Age and Blindness

Taxpayers who are 65 years of age or older or blind are entitled to an additional standard deduction amount. For 2024, the additional standard deduction amount is $1,950 for unmarried taxpayers and $1,550 for married taxpayers and surviving spouses. The additional standard deduction amounts are also available for the taxpayer's spouse, but not for dependents. Taxpayers who are both at least 65 years old and blind are entitled to two additional standard deduction amounts. An individual is considered blind for purposes of receiving an additional standard deduction amount if:

1. Central visual acuity does not exceed 20/200 in the better eye with correcting lenses, or
2. Visual acuity is greater than 20/200 but is limited to a field of vision not greater than 20 degrees.

Example Erling is single and 70 years old in 2024. His standard deduction is $16,550 ($14,600 plus an additional $1,950 for being 65 years of age or older). ♦

Example Takehiro and Mary are married in 2024 and file a joint return. Takehiro is age 68 and Mary is age 63 and meets the test for blindness. Their standard deduction is $32,300 ($29,200 plus $1,550 for Takehiro being 65 years or older and another $1,550 for Mary's blindness). ♦

1-7b Individuals Not Eligible for the Standard Deduction

The following taxpayers cannot use the standard deduction, but must itemize instead:

1. A married individual filing a separate return, whose spouse itemizes deductions
2. Most nonresident aliens
3. An individual filing a short-period tax return because of a change in the annual accounting period

Example Sika and Granite are married individuals who file separate returns for 2024. Sika itemizes her deductions on her return. Granite's adjusted gross income is $12,000, and he has itemized deductions of $900. Granite's taxable income is calculated as follows:

Adjusted gross income	$ 12,000
Itemized deductions	(900)
Taxable income	$ 11,100

Since Sika and Granite file their taxes separately and Sika itemizes her deductions, Granite must also itemize deductions and is not entitled to use the standard deduction amount. ♦

1-7c Special Limitations for Dependents

The standard deduction is limited for the tax return of a dependent. The total standard deduction may not exceed the greater of $1,300 or the sum of $450 plus the dependent's earned income up to the basic standard deduction amount in total (e.g., $14,600 for single taxpayers), plus any additional standard deduction amount for old age or blindness. The standard deduction amount for old age and blindness is only allowed when a dependent files a tax return. It is not allowed to increase the standard deduction of the taxpayer claiming the dependent.

Example Penzer, who is 8 years old, earned $17,000 as a child model during 2024. Penzer is claimed as a dependent by his parents on their tax return. Penzer is required to file a tax return, and his taxable income will be $2,400 ($17,000 less $14,600, the standard deduction amount). If Penzer had earned only $9,000, his standard deduction would be $9,450 [the greater of $1,300 or $9,450 ($9,000 + $450)], and he would not owe any tax or be required to file a return. ♦

Example Geoffrey, who is 4 years old and claimed as a dependent on his parents' tax return, earned $6,500 of interest income on a large bank account left to him by his grandmother. He had no earned income. His standard deduction is $1,300 (the greater of $1,300 or $450). His taxable income will be $5,200 ($6,500 less $1,300, the standard deduction amount). Dependent children may be taxed at their parents' tax rates when their taxable income is made up of unearned income, such as interest. The special "kiddie tax" calculations are covered in Chapter 6. ♦

Self-Study Problem 1.7

Refer to Appendix E for Solutions to Self-Study Problems

Indicate in each of the following independent situations the amount of the standard deduction the taxpayers should claim on their 2024 income tax returns.

1. Adam is 45 years old, in good health, and single.
2. Bill and Betty are married and file a joint return. Bill is 66 years old, and Betty is 60.
3. Charlie is 70, single, and blind.
4. Debbie qualifies for head of household filing status, is 35 years old, and is in good health.
5. Elizabeth is 9 years old, and her only income is $3,600 of interest on a savings account. She is claimed as a dependent on her parents' tax return.
6. Frank and Frieda are married with two dependent children. They file a joint return, are in good health, and both of them are under 65 years of age.

1-8 A Brief Overview of Capital Gains and Losses

Learning Objective 1.8
Compute basic capital gains and losses.

When a taxpayer sells an asset, there is normally a gain or loss on the transaction. Depending on the kind of asset sold, this gain or loss will have different tax consequences. Chapter 4 of this textbook has detailed coverage of the effect of gains and losses on a taxpayer's tax liability. Because of the importance of gains and losses to the understanding of the calculation of an individual's tax liability, a brief overview will be presented here.

The amount of gain or loss realized by a taxpayer is determined by subtracting the *adjusted basis* of the asset from the *amount realized*. Generally, the adjusted basis of an asset is its cost less any depreciation (covered in Chapter 8) taken on the asset. The amount realized is generally what the taxpayer receives from the sale (e.g., the sales price less any cost of the sale). The formula for calculating the gain or loss can be stated as follows:

$$\text{Gain (or loss) realized} = \text{Amount realized} - \text{Adjusted basis}$$

Most gains and losses realized are also recognized for tax purposes. Recognized gains and losses are those that are included in the taxpayer's taxable income. The exceptions to this general tax recognition rule are covered in Chapter 4.

Example Lisa purchased a rental house a few years ago for $100,000. Total depreciation to date on the house is $25,000. In the current year she sells the house for $155,000 and receives $147,000 after paying selling expenses of $8,000. Her gain on the sale is $72,000, calculated as follows:

Amount realized ($155,000 − $8,000)	$147,000
Adjusted basis ($100,000 − $25,000)	(75,000)
Gain realized	$72,000

This gain realized will be recognized as a taxable gain. ♦

1-8a Capital Gains and Losses

Gains and losses can be either *ordinary* or *capital*. Ordinary gains and losses are treated for tax purposes just like other items of income such as salaries and interest, and they are taxed at ordinary rates. Capital gains and losses receive special tax treatment.

A capital gain or loss arises from the sale or exchange of a capital asset. In general, a capital asset is any property (either personal or investment) held by a taxpayer, with certain exceptions as listed in the tax law (Chapter 4). Examples of capital assets held by individual taxpayers include stocks, bonds, land, cars, boats, and other items held as investments or for personal use. Typical assets that are not capital assets are inventory and accounts receivable.

The tax rates on long-term (held more than twelve months) capital gains are summarized in Table 1.6.

Table 1.6 Long-term Capital Gains and Qualified Dividends Rates 2024

Income Level	Tax Rate
Married Filing Jointly & Surviving Spouse	
$0–$94,050	0%
$94,051–$583,750	15%
>$583,750	20%
Single	
$0–$47,025	0%
$47,026–$518,900	15%
>$518,900	20%
Head of Household	
$0–$63,000	0%
$63,001–$551,350	15%
>$551,350	20%
Married Filing Separately	
$0–$47,025	0%
$47,026–$291,850	15%
>$291,850	20%

Special higher rates for "high-income" taxpayers are covered in Chapter 6.

Gain from property held twelve months or less is deemed to be short-term capital gain and is taxed at ordinary income rates. Capital gains from the sale of assets that have been depreciated, or capital gains from "collectibles," may be taxed at higher rates as covered in Chapter 4 and Chapter 8.

Example In the current year, DeWanna, a single taxpayer, sells Meta stock for $25,000. The stock was purchased five years ago for $15,000, providing for an adjusted basis of $15,000 and a long-term gain of $10,000. DeWanna's taxable income without the sale of the stock is $140,000, which is in the 24-percent ordinary tax bracket. The tax due on the long-term capital gain would be $1,500 (15% × $10,000) instead of $2,400 (24% × $10,000) if the gain on the stock were treated as ordinary income. ♦

When calculating capital gain or loss, the taxpayer must net all capital asset transactions to determine the amount of the net capital gain or loss. If an individual taxpayer ends up with a net capital loss (short-term or long-term), up to $3,000 per year can be deducted against ordinary income. The net loss not used in the current year may be carried forward and used to reduce taxable income in future years. Losses from capital assets held for personal purposes, such as a nonbusiness auto or a personal residence, are not deductible, even though gains on personal assets are taxable.

Example Natisha purchased gold coins as an investment. She paid $50,000 for the coins. This year she sells the coins to a dealer for $35,000. As a result, Natisha has a $15,000 capital loss. She may deduct $3,000 of the loss against her other income this year. The remaining unused loss of $12,000 ($15,000 − $3,000) is carried forward and may be deducted against other income in future years. Of course, the carryover is subject to the $3,000 annual limitation in future years. ♦

Example Zelimkhan, a married filing jointly taxpayer, sold two automobiles this year. The first was sold at a loss of $4,000. The second auto was unique and sold for a gain of $1,000. Because both autos were for personal use, Zelimkhan must recognize the gain of $1,000 but may not recognize the loss. ♦

Tax Break

Volunteer Income Tax Assistance (VITA) Program

The VITA program offers free tax help to people who report income of $64,000 or less, persons with disabilities, the elderly, and limited English-speaking taxpayers who need assistance in preparing their own tax returns. IRS-certified volunteers provide free basic income tax return preparation with electronic filing to qualified individuals. VITA sites are generally located at community and neighborhood centers, libraries, schools, shopping malls, and other convenient locations across the country.

Many universities and colleges operate VITA sites in conjunction with their accounting programs. This is a small but vital part of the VITA program run by the IRS. The majority of the VITA sites are not run by schools, but rather by community groups, such as churches, senior groups (AARP), military bases, etc. If a student has a chance to participate in a VITA program, they should do so if at all possible. The experience provides valuable insight into preparing tax returns for others. Please refer to the IRS website **https://irs.treasury.gov/freetaxprep/** to locate the nearest VITA site and for more information.

Self-Study Problem 1.8 *Refer to Appendix E for Solutions to Self-Study Problems*

Erin purchased stock in JKL Corporation several years ago for $9,000. In the current year, she sold the same stock for $13,100. She paid a $25 sales commission to her stockbroker.

1. What is Erin's amount realized?
2. What is Erin's adjusted basis?
3. What is Erin's *realized* gain or loss?
4. What is Erin's *recognized* gain or loss?
5. Describe how the gain or loss may be treated for tax purposes?

Learning Objective 1.9

Access and use various Internet tax resources.

1-9 Tax and the Internet

Taxpayers and tax practitioners can find a substantial amount of useful information on the Internet. Government agencies, businesses, organizations, and groups (e.g., the IRS, AICPA, and Cengage) maintain sites that contain information of interest to the public.

The information available on various websites is subject to rapid change. Presented on the following pages are some current Internet sites that are of interest to taxpayers. Taxpayers should be aware that the locations and information provided on the Internet are subject to change by the site organizer without notice.

1-9a The IRS Website, www.irs.gov

One of the most useful websites containing tax information is the one maintained by the IRS. The IRS site has a search function to assist users in locating information. A number of common tasks are available at the home page such as refund status or making a tax payment. The Forms and Publications search function is particularly useful and allows the user to locate and download almost any tax form, instructions, or publication available from the IRS. A Help function is available to aid users of the IRS website. Online and telephone assistance from the IRS is provided for users who have questions or want to communicate with the IRS. The IRS also has a YouTube channel, an X (formerly known as Twitter) account, and a LinkedIn, Instagram, and Facebook page. The YouTube channel has numerous educational videos covering a number of tax-related topics, including how to check on a refund and how to file a tax return extension. The IRS offers various news feeds on X, including @IRSnews, which are good sources of tax information. In addition, the IRS offers IRS2GO—a mobile phone application. The IRS also offers access to an online account where a taxpayer can access their tax records, make payments, and view certain balances.

A 2024 screenshot of the IRS website (**www.irs.gov**) is presented in Figure 1.6.

Figure 1.6 IRS Website

Source: Internal Revenue Service

1-9b Intuit's ProConnect Tax Online

Intuit offers a line of tax preparation products such as ProConnect Tax, Lacerte, and the well-known Turbo Tax. Many of the Intuit products have training and support available online at no charge. You can find ProConnect help at **https://accountants.intuit.com/support/en-us?product=proconnect-tax**.

1-9c Tax Notes

Tax Notes is a portfolio of publications offered by Tax Analysts, a nonprofit tax publisher. Founded in 1970, Tax Analysts was created to foster free, open, and informed discourse about taxation. Recently, Tax Notes has made their entire library of federal tax research information available at no cost. For a taxpayer or tax preparer looking for just about any source of tax federal law, the Tax Notes Research library probably has it. The entire Internal Revenue Code and all the related regulations, revenue rulings, revenue procedures, and an extensive repository of tax-related court cases are available. A 2024 screenshot of the Tax Notes Research home page is presented in Figure 1.7.

1-9d ChatGPT and Artificial Intelligence

The advent of new artificial intelligence (AI) technology is likely to change the way tax preparers find answers to client tax questions in ways that cannot yet be imagined. One such technology, ChatGPT sprang into cultural popularity in recent years. Large language models (LLMs), like ChatGPT, are trained using copious amounts of data, most often by scraping data from the internet. The data is processed through a neural network (often called a transformer), made up of many nodes and layers, that continuously adjust and

Figure 1.7 **Tax Notes Website**

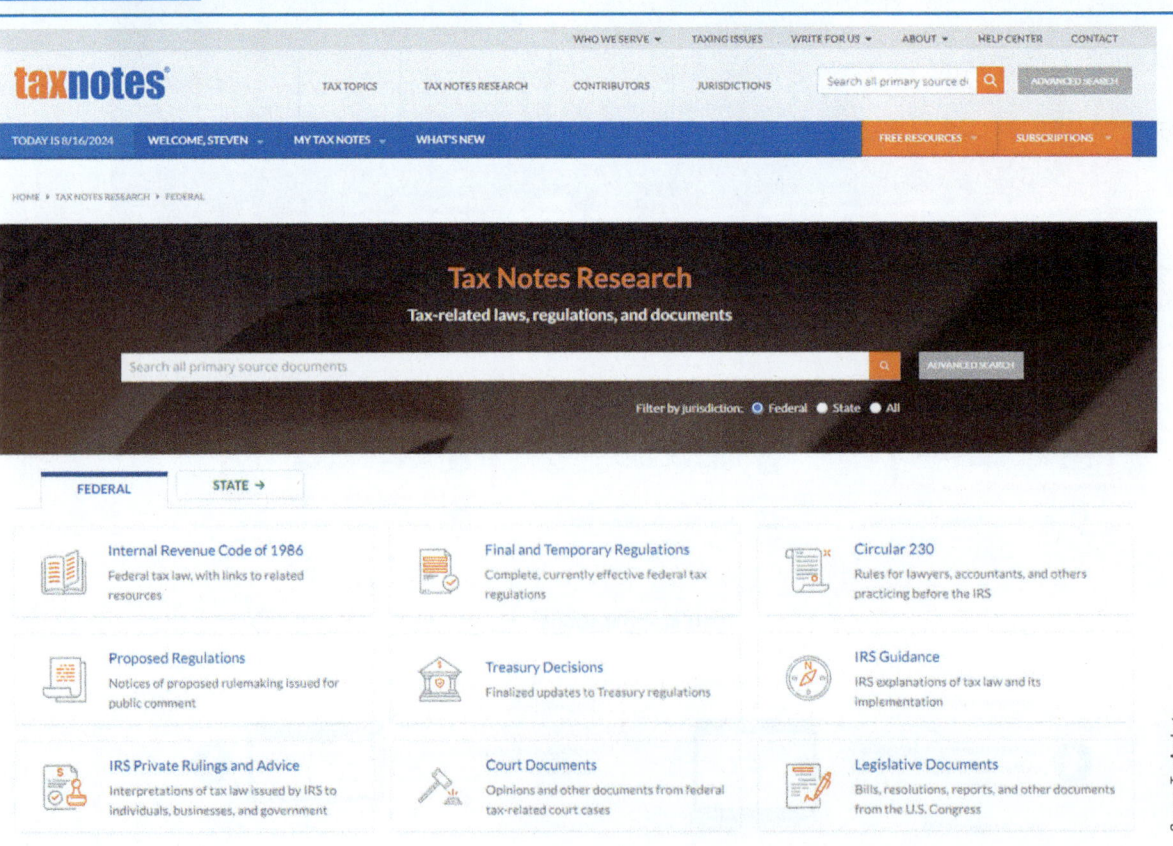

Source: Tax Analysts

interpret the data. Humans help modify the LLM by evaluating its responses to queries and ranking those that are the most accurate or otherwise considered the best. This allows LLMs to predict what words and responses best match future queries after the training has been completed.

Since the last edition of this textbook (one year ago), ChatGPT has made significant improvements. When asked about an alimony deduction in the prior year, ChatGPT provided an incorrect response; however, when asked currently, ChatGPT provides an accurate response. Figure 1.8 presents the ChatGPT results for a question associated with the standard deduction for a taxpayer that can be claimed as a dependent. The response provided is incorrect as the deduction is $1,300 not $1,350 as reported by ChatGPT. In addition, when queried a short time later, ChatGPT responded with a different and incorrect amount (not shown). Bear in mind that all ChatGPT responses should be confirmed using primary sources of tax law before advising clients.

Figure 1.8 ChatGPT

ChatGPT

> what is the standard deduction for a taxpayer that can be claimed as dependent for united states tax purposes

For the tax year 2024, if you are a taxpayer who can be claimed as a dependent on someone else's return, your standard deduction is limited. The standard deduction for a dependent is the greater of:

1. **$1,350**, or
2. **Your earned income plus $450** (but not more than the standard deduction for your filing status, which for a single filer is $14,600 in 2024).

Examples:

- **Example 1**: If you have no earned income, your standard deduction would be $1,350.
- **Example 2**: If you have $3,000 in earned income, your standard deduction would be $3,000 + $450 = $3,450.
- **Example 3**: If you have $14,000 in earned income, your standard deduction would be $14,000 + $450 = $14,450 (which is less than the single filer standard deduction of $14,600, so you would take $14,450).

This rule helps ensure that dependents with little or no income don't have a large standard deduction, while still allowing those who do earn income to reduce their taxable income.

Would you like more details or examples on how this works?

Source: OpenAI

Self-Study Problem 1.9 Refer to Appendix E for Solutions to Self-Study Problems

Indicate whether the following statements are true or false.

1. Taxpayers can download tax forms and IRS publications from the IRS website.
2. A help function is available to aid users of the IRS website.
3. The IRS has a mobile phone app.
4. The Tax Notes Research website does not contain tax-related court cases.

Learning Objective 1.10

Describe the basics of electronic filing (e-filing).

1-10 Electronic Filing (E-filing)

Electronic filing (e-filing) is the process of transmitting federal income tax return information to the IRS Service Center using a device with Internet access. For the taxpayer, electronic filing offers faster processing and generally a faster refund. The fastest refund can be obtained through a direct deposit to the taxpayer's bank account (however, the taxpayer may also choose to be paid by check). IRS statistics show an error rate of less than 1 percent on electronically-filed returns, compared with more than 20 percent on paper returns.

The e-filing process often involves a number of different parties starting with the Electronic Return Originator (ERO). The ERO either prepares the return or collects the completed return from a taxpayer. Most preparers using software like Intuit ProConnect will be EROs. When the return is prepared, the ERO either sends the electronic return to a Transmitter (that transmits the return to the IRS), acts as the Transmitter themselves, or uses an Intermediate Service Provider (ISP) to process the e-filing. EROs must identify the paid preparer's name, identifying number, and PTIN.

As with a paper-filed return, e-filed tax returns must be signed by the taxpayer. Taxpayers are also required to sign and date the Declaration of Taxpayer which authorizes the origination of the electronic submission to the IRS and includes the declaration under penalties of perjury that the return is true, correct, and complete. Tax returns are electronically signed through the use of a personal identification number or PIN. PINs can be either generated by the taxpayer or by the ERO. Self-selected PINs generated by the taxpayer also require the prior year AGI or PIN to authenticate the taxpayer. Before a PIN can be created by the ERO, the preparer must obtain a signed copy of an IRS E-file signature authorization (Form 8878 or 8879). Preparer-generated PINs do not require prior year AGI.

Once the return is e-filed, the IRS recommends that the ERO keep the following items until the end of the calendar year:

- Form 8453 U.S. Individual Income Tax Transmittal for an IRS e-file Return (if required)
- Copies of Forms W-2, W-2G, and 1099-R
- A copy of the consent to disclose form
- A copy of the electronic return that could be retransmitted
- An acknowledgment file for IRS accepted return

Forms 8878 and 8879 must be kept for approximately three years.

A copy of the return must be provided to the taxpayer and can be in any media as long as acceptable to the taxpayer.

The IRS website contains detailed information on this process as the IRS is constantly working to make e-filing more user-friendly and widely available. The IRS provides free tax preparation and e-filing software to individuals with income below certain thresholds. Individuals with higher income may still e-file free, using IRS fill-in forms. The fillable forms program performs calculations but will not provide the tax preparation guidance that standard commercial tax software programs provide. Refer to **www.irs.gov/filing/free-file-do-your-federal-taxes-for-free** for the latest free methods to file income taxes.

Electronic filing represents a significant growth area in computerized tax services. More than 90 percent of all individual taxpayers now e-file. Mandatory electronic filing is required for nearly the entire professional tax return preparation industry.

Self-Study Problem 1.10
Refer to Appendix E for Solutions to Self-Study Problems

Indicate whether the following statements are true or false.

1. Compared to paper returns, electronic filings significantly reduce the error rate for tax returns filed.
2. Individuals must sign the tax return whether filing electronically or paper.
3. Taxpayers who e-file generally receive faster refunds.
4. Taxpayers who e-file can only request their refund in the form of a check.

Key Terms

individual, 1-3
Form 1040, 1-3
Form 1040-SR, 1-3
corporation, 1-4
S corporation, 1-4
partnership, 1-4
gross income, 1-5
for adjusted gross income deduction, 1-5
adjusted gross income, 1-6
standard deduction, 1-6
itemized deductions, 1-6
qualified business income (QBI) deduction, 1-6
exemptions, 1-6
filing deadline, 1-7
extension, 1-8
single filing status, 1-10
married filing jointly, 1-10
married filing separately, 1-11
abandoned spouse, 1-11
head of household, 1-12
Form 8867, 1-12
surviving spouse, 1-12
qualifying widow(er), 1-12
tax table, 1-15
tax rate schedule, 1-15
character, 1-15
dependent, 1-17
qualifying child, 1-17
support, 1-18
qualifying relative, 1-21
qualifying person, 1-23
tax deduction, 1-26
tax credit, 1-26
child tax credit, 1-26
other dependent credit, 1-26
adjusted basis, 1-30
amount realized, 30
capital assets, 1-31
ordinary gains and losses, 1-31
capital gains and losses, 1-31
e-filing, 1-36

Key Points

Learning Objectives	Key Points
LO 1.1: Explain the history and objectives of U.S. tax law.	• The income tax was established in 1913 by the Sixteenth Amendment to the U.S. Constitution. • In addition to raising money to run the government's programs, the income tax is used as a tool for enacting economic and social policies. • Examples of economic tax provisions are the limited allowance for expensing capital expenditures and bonus depreciation provisions. The child and dependent care credit, earned income credit, and the charitable contributions deduction are examples of social tax provisions.
LO 1.2: Describe the different entities subject to tax and reporting requirements.	• Individual taxpayers file Form 1040 or 1040-SR (if age 65 or older) and any supplemental schedules required. • Corporations must report income annually on Form 1120 and pay taxes at a flat rate of 21 percent. • An S corporation generally does not pay regular corporate income taxes; instead, the corporation's income or loss passes through to its shareholders and is included in their individual tax returns. S corporations file on Form 1120-S. • A partnership files Form 1065 to report the amount of partnership income or loss and to allocate the items of income, loss, deduction, and credit to the partners. Generally, all income or loss of a partnership is included in the tax returns of the partners.
LO 1.3: Apply the tax formula for individuals.	• Adjusted gross income (AGI) is gross income less deductions for adjusted gross income. • AGI less the larger of itemized deductions or the standard deduction and less the qualified business income deduction equals taxable income. • Appropriate tax tables or rate schedules are applied to taxable income to calculate the gross tax liability. • The gross income tax liability plus additional taxes less credits and prepayments equals the tax due or refund.

LO 1.4: Identify individuals who must file tax returns.	• Conditions relating to the amount of the taxpayer's income must exist before a taxpayer is required to file a U.S. income tax return. • Taxpayers are also required to file a return if they have net earnings from self-employment of $400 or more, or owe taxes such as Social Security taxes on unreported tips.
LO 1.5: Determine filing status and understand the calculation of tax according to filing status.	• There are five filing statuses: single; married filing jointly; married filing separately; head of household; and surviving spouse [qualifying widow(er)]. • Tax is calculated using the appropriate tax table or tax rate schedule for the taxpayer's filing status.
LO 1.6: Define qualifying dependents.	• Personal and dependency exemptions were suspended by the TCJA for tax years 2018–2025. • Dependents are still important for determining filing status and certain credits. • A dependent is an individual who is either a qualifying child or qualifying relative.
LO 1.7: Calculate the correct standard or itemized deduction amount for taxpayers.	• The standard deduction was placed in the tax law to provide relief for taxpayers with few itemized deductions. • For 2024, the standard deduction amounts are: Single $14,600; Married, filing jointly $29,200; Married, filing separately $14,600; Head of household $21,900; Surviving spouse $29,200. • Taxpayers who are 65 years of age or older or blind are entitled to additional standard deduction amounts of $1,950 for unmarried taxpayers and $1,550 for married taxpayers and surviving spouses in 2024.
LO 1.8: Compute basic capital gains and losses.	• The amount of gain or loss realized by a taxpayer is determined by subtracting the adjusted basis of the asset from the amount realized. • Gains and losses can be either ordinary or capital. • Ordinary gains and losses are treated for tax purposes like other items such as salary and interest. • Capital gains and losses result from the sale or exchange of capital assets. • Common capital assets held by individual taxpayers include stocks, bonds, land, cars, boats, and other items held as investments. Typical assets that are not capital are inventory and accounts receivable. • Gain from property held twelve months or less is deemed to be short-term capital gain and is taxed at ordinary income tax rates. • Gain from property held more than twelve months is deemed to be long-term capital gain and is taxed at preferential income tax rates. • The long-term capital gain rates vary between 0, 15, and 20 percent, depending on the taxpayer's income. • If an individual taxpayer ends up with a net capital loss (short-term or long-term), up to $3,000 per year can be deducted against ordinary income. Any excess capital loss is carried forward to subsequent tax years. Losses from personal-use assets are not deductible.
LO 1.9: Access and use various Internet tax resources.	• Taxpayers and tax practitioners can find a substantial amount of useful information on the Internet. • Useful websites containing tax information include the IRS (**www.irs.gov**) and the Intuit websites. • The Tax Notes website offers free access to a library of federal tax law.
LO 1.10: Describe the basics of electronic filing (e-filing).	• Electronic filing (e-filing) is the process of transmitting federal income tax return information to the IRS Service Center using a device with Internet access. • Electronic filing offers a faster refund through a direct deposit to the taxpayer's bank account or the taxpayer can request the refund be sent by check.

Questions and Problems

Group 1:
Multiple Choice Questions

LO 1.1 1. The current income tax system is:
   a. Designed solely to raise money for the government
   b. Authorized by the founding fathers when the government was formed
   c. Not designed with social objectives in mind
   d. Used as a tool to promote social and economic policies as well as raise revenue
   e. None of the above

LO 1.1 2. The amendment to the United States Constitution that authorized the federal income tax is the:
   a. Thirteenth Amendment in 1865
   b. Fourteenth Amendment in 1868
   c. Sixteenth Amendment in 1913
   d. Twenty-first Amendment in 1933

LO 1.2 3. Which of the following tax forms are used by individuals in 2024?
   a. 1040
   b. 1040-EZ
   c. 1065
   d. 1120

LO 1.2 4. Typically, a corporation reports its taxable income or loss on:
   a. Form 1040
   b. Form 1120
   c. Form 1040X
   d. Form 1065

LO 1.2 5. On which of these schedules would capital gain income be reported?
   a. Schedule B
   b. Schedule 2
   c. Schedule 3
   d. Schedule D

LO 1.2 6. Which of the following entities is *not* likely to be a tax-paying entity?
   a. A single taxpayer over the age of 65
   b. A single taxpayer under the age of 65
   c. A corporation
   d. A partnership

LO 1.3 7. Which of the following is a deduction for adjusted gross income in 2024?
   a. Personal casualty losses
   b. Medical expenses
   c. Student loan interest
   d. Mortgage interest

LO 1.3 8. All of the following are itemized deductions in 2024 *except*:
   a. Charitable contributions
   b. Mortgage interest expense
   c. State and local taxes
   d. Certain educator's expenses
   e. All of the above are itemized deductions

LO 1.3 9. Ramon, a single taxpayer with no dependents, has adjusted gross income for 2024 of $98,000 and his itemized deductions total $13,000. What taxable income will Ramon show in 2024?
   a. $83,400
   b. $84,150
   c. $84,000
   d. $85,000
   e. $89,000

LO 1.3 10. To arrive at adjusted gross income (AGI), deduct _____ from gross income.
   a. from AGI deductions
   b. the greater of the standard deduction or itemized deductions
   c. The qualified business income deduction
   d. for AGI deductions

LO 1.3 11. Which of the following statements related to standard and itemized deductions is correct?
   a. A taxpayer may only deduct the lower of itemized deductions or the standard deduction.
   b. A taxpayer may deduct the greater of itemized deductions or the standard deduction.
   c. The standard deduction is the same for all tax filing statuses but itemized deductions may differ.
   d. Itemized deductions are only available to corporate taxpayers.

LO 1.3 12. Which of the following is a from AGI deduction?
   a. The exclusion of an item of gross income
   b. Moving expenses
   c. One-half of self-employment taxes
   d. The qualified business income deduction

LO 1.4 13. The gross income threshold to require a federal income tax return for a single taxpayer is generally equal to:
   a. The sum of the taxpayer's itemized deductions.
   b. The same as the current year standard deduction ($14,600 in 2024).
   c. Any amount over zero.
   d. An amount that cannot be determined without knowing if any for AGI deductions will be claimed.

LO 1.4 14. Ben is a single taxpayer with no dependents and is 32 years old. What is the minimum amount of income that he must have to be required to file a tax return for 2024?
   a. $1
   b. $1,300
   c. $13,850
   d. $14,600
   e. $15,050

LO 1.4 15. Abed and Anahita are married filing jointly. Abed is 64 and Anahita is 63 and they also care for Anahita's 83-year-old mother and claim her as a dependent. What is the 2024 filing threshold for Abed and Anahita?
   a. $0
   b. $19,400
   c. $27,300
   d. $27,700
   e. $29,200

LO 1.4 16. Valary is single, 82 years old, and blind. She is claimed as a dependent by her daughter and spouse, who file jointly. Valary has no earned income but did receive $3,800 of investment (unearned) income in 2024. What is Valary's filing threshold for the current year and is she required to file a tax return?
   a. $5,200 of unearned income and thus, not required to file
   b. $1,300 of unearned income and thus, required to file
   c. $4,950 of earned income and thus, not required to file
   d. $400 of self-employment income and thus, required to file

LO 1.5 17. Joan, who was divorced in 2024, had filed a joint tax return with her husband in 2023. During 2024, she did not remarry and continued to maintain her home and has no dependents. In the preparation of her tax return for 2024, Joan should file as:
   a. A single individual
   b. A surviving spouse
   c. Head of household
   d. Married, filing separately
   e. None of the above

LO 1.5 18. Glenda, a single taxpayer from Kansas, paid for more than one-half of the support for her cousin, Dorothy. Dorothy did not live with Glenda in Kansas, but rather has lived in a nursing home in an adjacent state since Dorothy's husband died three years ago. Glenda's filing status should be:
   a. Single
   b. Married filing separately
   c. Surviving spouse
   d. Head of household
   e. Parental dependent

LO 1.5 19. Angela's spouse died in 2024. She has no dependent children, but she pays the entire cost to maintain her home. What is Angela's most advantageous filing status in 2024?
   a. Single
   b. Head of household
   c. Surviving spouse
   d. Married filing jointly

LO 1.5 20. Angela's spouse died in 2021. She has two dependent children, and she pays the entire cost to maintain her home. What is Angela's most advantageous filing status in 2024?
   a. Single
   b. Head of household
   c. Surviving spouse
   d. Married filing jointly

LO 1.5 21. When completing a tax return for a client claiming head of household filing status, a tax preparer must:
   a. Obtain and keep copies of the taxpayer and any dependents state issued ID or birth certificate
   b. Complete Form 8867 and attach to the tax return
   c. Observe the existence of the dependent either in-person or over a video-conferencing platform
   d. Both a. and b.

LO 1.6 22. Margaret and her sister support their mother and together provide 45 percent of their mother's support. If Margaret provides 40 percent of her mother's support:
   a. Her sister is the only one who can claim their mother as a dependent.
   b. Neither Margaret nor her sister may claim their mother as a dependent.
   c. Both Margaret and her sister will claim their mother as a dependent.
   d. Margaret and her sister may split the dependency exemption.
   e. Margaret may claim her mother as a dependent if her sister agrees in a multiple support agreement.

LO 1.6 23. Kardi, age 65, and Kanye, age 62, are married with a 23-year-old daughter who lives in their home. They provide over half of their daughter's support, and their daughter earned $5,100 this year from a part-time job. Their daughter is not a full-time student. With regard to their daughter's dependency status:
   a. She can be claimed because she lived in their household for twelve months.
   b. She can be claimed because she is a qualifying child.
   c. She can be claimed because she is a qualifying relative.
   d. She cannot be claimed because she fails the age and gross income test.

LO 1.6 24. Yasmine and her spouse Carlos, who file married filing jointly with 2024 AGI of $130,000, provide all the support for their 16-year-old son, Miguel. If Miguel qualifies as a qualifying child under the dependent rules, Yasmine and Carlos will be able to claim a 2024 child tax credit of:
   a. $0
   b. $500
   c. $1,000
   d. $2,000
   e. $3,000

LO 1.6 25. In 2024, Lakota and Dominique file married filing jointly and have a 13-year-old daughter. They also provide 75 percent of the support for Lakota's 82-year-old mother, who lives in a nursing home nearby and has no taxable income. The amount of the combined child tax credit and other dependent credit for Lakota and Dominique is:
   a. $0
   b. $2,000
   c. $2,500
   d. $3,500
   e. $4,000

LO 1.6 26. In 2024, Alexandria is a single mother with a 17-year-old dependent child. Alexandria's adjusted gross income in 2024 is $78,000. What is the total amount of Alexandria's child tax credit and other dependent credit?
   a. $0
   b. $500
   c. $2,000
   d. $2,500

LO 1.7 27. Morgan is 65 years old and single. He supports his father, who is 90 years old, blind, and has no income. What is Morgan's standard deduction?
   a. $23,850
   b. $21,900
   c. $22,400
   d. $16,550
   e. $22,650

LO 1.7 28. Taxpayers who are 65 or older get the benefit of:
   a. An additional exemption
   b. An additional amount added to their child tax credit
   c. An additional amount added to their itemized deductions
   d. None of the above

LO 1.7 29. Taxpayers who are blind get the benefit of:
   a. An additional exemption
   b. An additional amount added to their standard deduction
   c. An additional amount added to their itemized deductions
   d. None of the above

LO 1.7 30. Marta, a single, 19-year-old, full-time student, is claimed as a dependent by her parents in 2024. She has earned income of $15,000 and unearned income of $130. What is Marta's 2024 standard deduction?
a. $0
b. $1,300
c. $1,750
d. $14,600
e. $15,050

LO 1.7 31. Myrtle, a single, 19-year-old, full-time student, is claimed as a dependent by her parents in 2024. She has earned income of $5,000 and unearned income of $130. What is Myrtle's 2024 standard deduction?
a. $0
b. $1,300
c. $3,000
d. $5,450
e. $14,600

LO 1.8 32. Which of the following is *not* a capital asset to an individual taxpayer?
a. Stocks
b. A 48-foot sailboat
c. Raw land held as an investment
d. Inventory in the taxpayer's business
e. All of these responses are capital assets

LO 1.8 33. Joyce purchased General Electric stock four months ago for $10,000. In the current year, she sells the stock for $25,000. What is Joyce's gain or loss?
a. $15,000 long-term gain
b. $15,000 short-term gain
c. $15,000 ordinary loss
d. $15,000 extraordinary gain
e. No gain or loss is recognized on this transaction

LO 1.8 34. Alex purchased a rental house four years ago for $270,000. Their depreciation at the time of the sale is $40,000. Due to a decrease in real estate prices, they sell the house for only $240,000 in 2024. What is their gain or loss for tax purposes?
a. $0
b. $10,000 loss
c. $10,000 gain
d. $35,000 loss
e. $25,000 gain

LO 1.8 35. Dorit, a single taxpayer, has a long-term capital loss of $7,000 on the sale of bonds in 2024 and no other capital gains or losses. Her taxable income without this transaction is $46,000. What is her taxable income considering this capital loss?
a. $40,000
b. $39,000
c. $43,000
d. $46,000
e. Some other amount

LO 1.9 36. Access the Internet and go to **www.irs.gov** and select the Forms & Instructions tab. Enter "1040" into the search box. What is Line 12 of the 2024 Form 1040?
a. Other income
b. Multiply Line 6 by $500
c. Capital gain or (loss)
d. Standard deduction or itemized deductions
e. Qualified business income deduction

Chapter 1 • The Individual Income Tax Return

LO 1.10 37. If a tax preparer provides a PIN for the taxpayer:
   a. The taxpayer must also provide prior year AGI
   b. The tax preparer must obtain a signed Form 8878 or 8879
   c. The e-filing must go directly to the IRS
   d. Preparers may not provide PINs, only taxpayers.

LO 1.10 38. Electronically-filed tax returns:
   a. May not be transmitted from a taxpayer's home computer
   b. Constitute over 90 percent of the returns filed with the IRS
   c. Have error rates similar to paper returns
   d. Offer larger refunds than paper returns

Group 2: Problems

LO 1.1 1. List three major purposes of the tax system.

LO 1.2 2. Match each type of transaction with the form on which it is most likely reported

Transaction	Form
a. Wages and salaries	Schedule 1
b. Interest income over $1,500	Schedule 2
c. Capital gains from the sale of stock	Schedule 3
d. Deduction for charitable contributions	Schedule A
e. Self-employment taxes	Schedule B
f. Rental income	Schedule C
g. Credit for child and dependent care expenses	Schedule D
h. Net profit from sole proprietorship	Schedule E
i. Deductions for gross income	Form 1040

LO 1.3 3. Rahul and Ruby are married taxpayers. They are both under age 65 and in good health. For 2024, they have a total of $73,000 in wages and $500 in interest income. Rahul and Ruby's deductions for adjusted gross income amount to $7,000 and their itemized deductions equal $28,000. They have two children, ages 32 and 28, that are married and provide support for themselves.
   a. What is the amount of Rahul and Ruby's adjusted gross income?
   b. What is the amount of their itemized deductions or standard deduction?
   c. What is their taxable income?

LO 1.3 4. Xialu is a single taxpayer who is under age 65 and in good health. For 2024, she has a salary of $45,000 and itemized deductions of $5,200. Xialu allows her mother to live with her during the winter months (3–4 months per year), but her mother provides all of her own support otherwise.
   a. How much is Xialu's adjusted gross income?
   b. What amount of itemized or standard deduction(s) should she claim?
   c. What is the amount of Xialu's taxable income?

LO 1.3
LO 1.5
LO 1.7 5. Diego, age 28, married Dolores, age 27, in 2024. Their salaries for the year amounted to $54,000. They had dividend income of $3,000. Diego and Dolores' deductions for adjusted gross income amounted to $2,600, their itemized deductions were $30,000, and they have no dependents.
   a. What is the amount of their adjusted gross income?
   b. What is the amount of their itemized deductions or standard deduction?
   c. What is the amount of their taxable income?
   d. Assuming no tax credits apply, what is their tax liability for 2024?

LO 1.3
LO 1.5
LO 1.7

6. Marco and Tatiana are married and file separate returns for 2024. Tatiana itemizes her deductions on her return. Marco's adjusted gross income was $19,000, his itemized deductions were $2,600. Neither have any dependents. Calculate Marco's income tax liability assuming the couple does not live in a community property state.

LO 1.3
LO 1.5
LO 1.7

7. Alicia, age 27, is a single, full-time college student. She earns $14,200 from a part-time job and has taxable interest income of $1,300. Her itemized deductions are $925. Calculate Alicia's taxable income for 2024.

LO 1.3
LO 1.5
LO 1.6
LO 1.7

8. Jonathan is a 35-year-old single taxpayer with adjusted gross income in 2024 of $51,000. He uses the standard deduction and has no dependents.
   a. Calculate Jonathan's taxable income. Please show your work.
   b. When you calculate Jonathan's tax liability are you required to use the tax tables or the tax rate schedules, or does it matter?
   c. Assuming no tax credits, what is Jonathan's tax liability?

LO 1.3
LO 1.5
LO 1.6
LO 1.7

9. Brock, age 50, and Erin, age 49, are married with three dependent children. They file a joint return for 2024. Their income from salaries totals $63,000, and they received $800 in taxable interest, $1,200 of short-term gains, and $3,000 in other ordinary income. Brock and Erin's deductions for adjusted gross income amount to $3,500, and they have itemized deductions totaling $29,000. Calculate the following amounts:
   a. Gross income
   b. Adjusted gross income
   c. Itemized deduction or standard deduction amount
   d. Taxable income
   e. Income tax liability (Do not consider the alternative minimum tax covered in Chapter 6 or any credits.)
   f. Assume that two of the children are eligible for the child tax credit and one is eligible for the other dependent credit. What is the total amount of eligible child and other dependent credits (ignore any tax liability limitation)?

LO 1.3
LO 1.5
LO 1.7

10. Jackson, age 35, and Peggy, age 34, are married and file a joint income tax return for 2024. Their salaries for the year total $87,000 and they have dividend income of $3,200. They have no deductions for adjusted gross income. Their itemized deductions are $25,000. Jackson and Peggy do not have any dependents.
    a. What is the amount of their adjusted gross income?
    b. What is their deduction for personal exemptions?
    c. What is the amount of their taxable income?

LO 1.3
LO 1.5
LO 1.7

11. Wanda is a single 50-year-old taxpayer with no dependents. Her only 2024 income is $43,333 of wages. Calculate her taxable income and her tax liability assuming no tax credits. Please show your work.

LO 1.4

12. Griffin is a server at a California restaurant. Griffin received $1,200 in unreported tips during 2024 and owes Social Security and Medicare taxes on these tips. His total income for the year, including the tips, is $4,300. Is Griffin required to file an income tax return for 2024? Why or why not?

LO 1.4

13. For each of the following situations (none of the taxpayers claim dependents), indicate whether the taxpayer(s) is (are) required to file a tax return for 2024. Explain your answer.
    a. Helen is a head of household taxpayer with wage income of $16,000 and interest income of $5,000.
    b. Joan is a single college student who is claimed as a dependent by her parents. She earned $1,600 from a part-time job and has $1,400 in interest income.
    c. Leslie, age 64, and Mark, age 66, are married and file a joint return. They received $30,000 in interest income from a savings account.
    d. Ray, age 60, and Jean, age 57, are married and file a joint tax return. Their only income is $28,000 in interest income.
    e. Harry, a 19-year-old single taxpayer, had net earnings from self-employment of $1,500.

LO 1.5

14. Each of the following taxpayers has 2024 taxable income before the standard deduction as presented below. Determine the income tax liability (before any credits) for each taxpayer using the Tax Tables in Appendix A.

Taxpayer(s)	Filing Status	Taxable Income Before the Standard Deduction
a. Allen	Single	$37,000
b. Boyd	MFS	39,000
c. Caldwell	MFJ	65,040
d. Dell	H of H	51,570
e. Evans	Single	61,056

LO 1.5

15. Melissa and Whitney are married taxpayers with taxable income of $108,000 and one dependent.
    a. When you calculate their tax liability, are you required to use the tax tables or the tax rate schedules, or does it matter?
    b. What is their 2024 pre-credit tax liability?

LO 1.5
LO 1.6

16. For each of the following taxpayers, indicate the filing status for the taxpayer(s) for 2024 using the following legend:

    A—Single
    B—Married filing a joint return
    C—Married filing separate returns
    D—Head of household
    E—Surviving spouse [qualifying widow(er)]

    a. Linda is single and she supports her friend, Kayla (who has no income), including paying all the costs of Kayla's housing in an apartment across town.
    b. Frank is single and claims his unrelated significant other as a qualifying relative as the significant other lives in the home paid for by Frank. The significant other has no income.
    c. Arthur is single and he supports his 30-year-old brother, who lives in Arthur's home. The brother has no income and is not disabled.
    d. Leslie's spouse died in 2024. She has no dependents and did not remarry.
    e. Lester's spouse dies in 2023. He has one 17-year-old dependent child that lives with him in the home Lester pays for.

LO 1.5
LO 1.6

17. Karl is a single taxpayer and has listed his brother, Jonas, as a dependent (qualifying relative). Head of household filing status seems preferable for Karl. What questions should you ask Karl to confirm his filing status? What Form should be filed with Karl's tax return if he files as head of household?

LO 1.5
LO 1.6

18. Maggie is single and supports her 85-year-old parents who have no income and live in a home rented for them by Maggie. What is Maggie's filing status and why?

LO 1.5

19. List each alternative filing status available to unmarried individual taxpayers and the circumstances under which the alternatives can be used.

LO 1.5
LO 1.6

20. Marquez is single and supports his 30-year-old son, who has income of $2,000 and lives in his own apartment.
    a. Can Marquez claim his son as a dependent?
    b. Can Marquez claim head of household filing status? Why or why not?

LO 1.6

21. In each of the following situations, determine whether the taxpayer(s) has/have a dependent and if so, the total amount of child tax credit and other dependent credit for 2024 (assuming no credit limitations apply).
    a. Donna, a 20-year-old single taxpayer, supports her mother, who lives in her own home. Her mother has income of $1,350.
    b. William, age 43, and Mary, age 45, are married and support William's 19-year-old sister, who is not a student. The sister's income from a part-time job is $5,100.

c. Devi was divorced in 2022 and receives child support of $250 per month from her ex-husband for the support of their 8-year-old son, John, who lives with her. Devi is 45 and provides more than half of her son's support.

d. Wendell, an 89-year-old single taxpayer, supports his son, who is 67 years old, lives with him, and earns no income.

e. Wilma, age 65, and Morris, age 66, are married. They file a joint return.

LO 1.6 22. What is the total dollar amount of personal and dependency exemptions a married couple with two children (ages 11 and 17, both of which are qualified children) and $80,000 of adjusted gross income would deduct in 2024? What is the total child and other dependent credit that could be claimed (before any advance payments or limitations)?

LO 1.6 23. If Charles, a 16-year-old child model, earns $50,000 a year and is completely self-supporting even though he lives with his parents, can his parents claim him as a dependent? Why or why not?

LO 1.6 24. Marc's brother, Phillip, who is a 20-year-old French citizen, lives in France for the full year. Marc supports Phillip while he attends college. Can Marc claim Phillip as a dependent? Why or why not?

LO 1.7 25. Describe the difference between the standard deduction and itemized deductions. How should a taxpayer decide whether to take the standard deduction or claim itemized deductions?

LO 1.7 26. Describe the three possible limits that can be used to compute the standard deduction for a taxpayer that can be claimed as a dependent.

LO 1.7 27. List the three types of individual taxpayers that are not eligible for the standard deduction.

LO 1.3
LO 1.8 28. In 2024, Manon earns wages of $58,000. She also has dividend income of $7,000. Manon is single, under age 65, and has no dependents. During the year, Manon sold silver coins held as an investment for a $5,000 loss. Calculate the following amounts for Manon:
a. Adjusted gross income
b. Standard deduction
c. Taxable income

LO 1.8 29. Compute the realized and recognized gain or loss for each of the following transactions and classify as short-term or long-term:
a. Marge, a single taxpayer, receives $8,000 for the sale of stock she purchased six years ago for $3,000.
b. Lisa, a single taxpayer, receives $3,000 for the sale of stock she purchased six months ago for $8,000.
c. Bart and Maggie, married filing jointly taxpayers, receive $3,000 for the sale of stock they purchased three years ago for $10,000.
d. Homer, a single taxpayer, receives $12,000 on the sale of his personal-use motorcycle. He purchased the motorcycle four months ago for $16,000.
e. Mo, a single taxpayer, receives $16,000 on the sale of his personal-use motorcycle. He purchased the motorcycle four years ago for $12,000.

LO 1.9 30. Go to the IRS website (**www.irs.gov/newsroom**) and note the name of the most recent news release.

LO 1.9 31. Go to the IRS website (**www.irs.gov**) and select the Forms & Instructions tab. Search for Form 4868 and provide the title of this form.

LO 1.9 32. Go to the Turbo Tax Blog (**http://blog.turbotax.intuit.com/**) and search the blog for an article on Alston awards. What are Alston awards and are they generally taxable?

LO 1.9   33. Go to the Tax Notes website (**www.taxnotes.com**) and find the Tax Notes Research library. What is the title of Section 10.34 of Circular 230?

LO 1.9   34. What response does ChatGPT (or Google Gemini) provide for the question, "Can I claim head of household filing status if I support my brother and he lives with me?" Note that access to ChatGPT or Google Gemini may require an existing or creation of a username and password.

LO 1.10   35. Describe how a tax preparer can obtain a taxpayer signature on an electronically-filed tax return.

LO 1.10   36. List the documents the IRS recommends a tax preparer retain when electronically filing a taxpayer's return.

Group 3: Writing Assignments

Research

1. Jerry, age 23, a full-time student and not disabled, lives with William and Sheila Carson. Jerry is William's older brother. Jerry is single, a U.S. citizen, and does not provide more than one-half of his own support. William and Sheila are both 21 years old and file a joint return. Can William and Sheila claim Jerry as a qualifying child?
   Required: Go to the IRS website (**www.irs.gov**) and review Publication 501. Write a letter to William and Sheila stating if they can claim Jerry as a qualifying child.

Ethics

2. Jason and Mary Wells, friends of yours, were married on December 30, 2024. They know you are studying taxes and have sent you an e-mail with a question concerning their filing status. Jason and Mary would each like to file single for tax year 2024. Jason has prepared their taxes both as single and married filing jointly, and he has realized that the couple will get a larger combined refund if they each file single. Jason argues "that it's not as if we were married for very long in 2024." Prepare an e-mail to respond to the couple's inquiry.

Group 4: Comprehensive Problems

> **Instructions for working all Group 4 Comprehensive Tax Return Problems in this textbook are as follows:**
>
> **Birthdays:** If using the tax software, create birthdates for taxpayers and dependents. Adult taxpayers should have ages between 25 and 64 unless a different age is specified.
>
> **Wages:** Assume the wages subject to income tax in the problems are the same as Social Security wages and Medicare wages unless presented otherwise. Create employer names and other information which may be required by your tax software package.
>
> **Missing Data:** Please make realistic assumptions about any missing data. Decide whether taxpayers contribute to the Presidential Election Campaign, which does not affect tax liability. No taxpayers will have traded digital assets unless specific details are provided. All taxpayers request a refund of any overpaid tax unless otherwise indicated.
>
> **Child and Dependent Credits:** You are not required to complete Form 8812 unless instructed to do so.
>
> **Tax Forms:** Tax forms to complete the problems are found in Appendix F. Additional copies can be found on the IRS website (**www.irs.gov**).

1A. Amonute Tallbear is a single taxpayer (birthdate May 18, 1997) living at 1919 Barker Cypress Road, Cypress, TX 77433. Her Social Security number is 466-33-1234. For 2024, Amonute has no dependents, and her W-2, from her job at a local restaurant where she is a cashier, contains the following information:

a Employee's social security number 466-33-1234		
b Employer identification number (EIN) 33-1235672	1 Wages, tips, other compensation 24,478.44	2 Federal income tax withheld 1,250.66
c Employer's name, address, and ZIP code Kuutsu Burger 1990 Barker Cypress Road Cypress, TX 77433	3 Social security wages 24,478.44	4 Social security tax withheld 1,517.66
	5 Medicare wages and tips 24,478.44	6 Medicare tax withheld 354.94

Form W-2 Wage and Tax Statement 2024

These wages are Amonute's only income for 2024.

Required: Complete Form 1040 for Amonute Tallbear for the 2024 tax year.

1B. Using the information from Problem 1A, assume Amonute's birthdate is May 18, 1957, and complete Form 1040-SR for Amonute Tallbear for the 2024 tax year.

2A. Richelle and Dallas Land are married and file a joint return for 2024. Richelle's Social Security number is 312-44-7788 and her birthdate is January 4, 1978. Dallas' Social Security number is 367-12-8972 and her birthday is July 7, 1979. They live at 2300 Walnut Street, Apt. F2, Dallas, TX 75243. For 2024, Richelle did not work, and Dallas' W-2 from her teaching job showed the following:

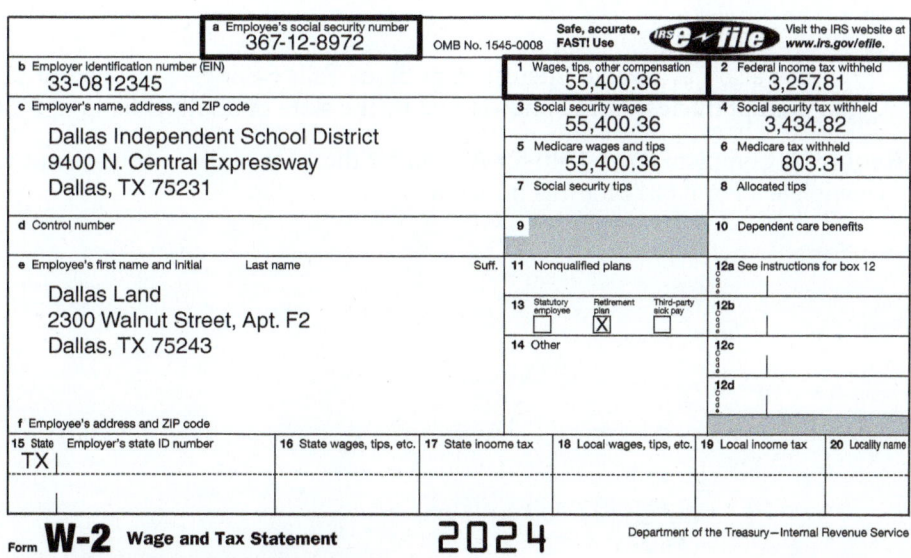

a Employee's social security number 367-12-8972		
b Employer identification number (EIN) 33-0812345	1 Wages, tips, other compensation 55,400.36	2 Federal income tax withheld 3,257.81
c Employer's name, address, and ZIP code Dallas Independent School District 9400 N. Central Expressway Dallas, TX 75231	3 Social security wages 55,400.36	4 Social security tax withheld 3,434.82
	5 Medicare wages and tips 55,400.36	6 Medicare tax withheld 803.31

Form W-2 Wage and Tax Statement 2024

Richelle and Dallas have a son they provide more than half of the support for named Legolas (birthdate December 21, 2004, Social Security number 712-34-4315), who is living with them, is not a full-time student, and generates $4,700 of gross income for himself. If Legolas qualifies as a dependent, the taxpayers will qualify for the other dependent credit of $500.

Required: Complete Form 1040 for Richelle and Dallas for the 2024 tax year. You are not required to complete a Form 8812 for this problem.

2B. Abigail (Abby) Gandt is a single mother (birthdate April 28, 1986) working as a civilian accountant for the U.S. Army. Her Social Security number is 676-73-3311 and she lives at 3456 S Career Avenue, Sioux Falls, SD 57107. Susan Gandt, Abby's 18-year-old daughter (Social Security number 676-73-3312 and birthdate April 16, 2006), is a dependent child living with her mother, and although she does not qualify for the child tax credit due to age, she does qualify for the other dependent credit of $500. Abby's Form W-2 from the U.S. Department of Defense shows the following:

Form W-2 Wage and Tax Statement — 2024

Box	Description	Amount
a	Employee's social security number	676-73-3311
b	Employer identification number (EIN)	31-1575142
c	Employer's name, address, and ZIP code	DFAS Cleveland Center, PO Box 998002, Cleveland, OH 44199
e/f	Employee's name and address	Abigail Gandt, 3456 S. Career Avenue, Sioux Falls, SD 57107
1	Wages, tips, other compensation	63,004.86
2	Federal income tax withheld	4,612.90
3	Social security wages	63,004.86
4	Social security tax withheld	3,906.30
5	Medicare wages and tips	63,004.86
6	Medicare tax withheld	913.57
15	State	SD

Abby also has taxable interest from Sioux Falls Savings and Loan of $200 and tax-exempt interest from bonds issued by the state of South Dakota of $250.

Required: Complete Form 1040 for Abigail for the 2024 tax year. You are not required to complete a Form 8812 for this problem.

Group 5:
Cumulative Software Problem

1. Albert Gaytor and his wife Allison are married and file a joint return for 2024. The Gaytors live at 4100 SE Lincoln Street, Stuart, FL 34997. Captain Albert Gaytor is a charter fishing boat captain but took six months off from his job in 2024 to train and study for his Master Captain's License.

    In 2024, Albert received a Form W-2 from his employer:

Form W-2 Wage and Tax Statement — 2024

Box	Description	Amount
a	Employee's social security number	266-51-1966
b	Employer identification number (EIN)	60-3456788
c	Employer's name, address, and ZIP code	Sport Fishing of Stuart, 4247 SE Anchor Ave., Stuart, FL 34997
e/f	Employee's name and address	Albert T. Gaytor, 4100 SE Lincoln Street, Stuart, FL 34997
1	Wages, tips, other compensation	70,706.12
2	Federal income tax withheld	5,502.33
3	Social security wages	70,706.12
4	Social security tax withheld	4,383.78
5	Medicare wages and tips	70,706.12
6	Medicare tax withheld	1,025.24
15	State	FL

Name	Social Security Number	Date of Birth
Albert T. Gaytor	266-51-1966	09/22/1975
Allison A. Gaytor	266-34-1967	07/01/1976
Crocker Gaytor	261-55-1212	12/21/2006
Cayman Slacker	261-11-4444	03/13/2005
Sean Slacker	344-23-5656	05/01/2004

The Gaytors have an 18-year-old son, Crocker, who is a full-time freshman at Jupiter State University. The Gaytors also have a 19-year-old daughter, Cayman, who is a full-time student at Tribal River Community College (TRCC). Cayman is married to Sean Slacker, who is 20 years old and a part-time student at TRCC. Sean and Cayman have a 1-year-old child, Wanda Slacker (Social Security number 648-99-4306). Sean, Cayman, and Wanda all live in an apartment up the street from Albert and Allison during the entire current calendar year.

At the start of the year, neither Sean nor Cayman had any savings. Through their part-time work, Cayman earned $4,000 and Sean earned $23,000 of wages in 2024. Cayman also received a $1,000 scholarship that was paid directly toward her 2024 college tuition. Cayman and Sean incurred the following household expenses in 2024 for themselves and Wanda:

- Apartment rent $25,200
- Food   4,800
- Utilities   1,000

Amounts spent by Cayman for clothing, education, travel, and other personal support was $9,300 (after considering the $1,000 scholarship that Cayman received toward her tuition). Also, $6,000 of Sean's income was spent on Cayman. The rest of Sean's income was spent on himself and Wanda. Any other support for Cayman was provided by Albert and Allison. Sean and Wanda did not receive support from any other sources.

Albert's cousin, Jeff (everyone calls him Swampy) Gaytor is 25 years old (birthdate 4/16/1999, Social Security number 542-11-5562). Swampy lost his job and in 2024, received $3,200 of unemployment compensation. The remainder (well above 50 percent) of Swampy's support was provided by the Gaytors, including the rent on Swampy's apartment in Palm City, FL, about 7 miles from the Gaytors' home.

Albert and Allison have a savings account and received the following Form 1099-INT for 2024:

Form 1099-INT — Interest Income (2024)

- PAYER: Jensen Beach Bank, 1000 NE Jensen Beach Blvd, Jensen Beach, FL 34957
- PAYER'S TIN: 61-7654321
- RECIPIENT'S TIN: 266-51-1966
- RECIPIENT: Albert T. Gaytor, 4100 SE Lincoln Street, Stuart, FL 34997
- Box 1 Interest income: $312.69
- Box 4 Federal income tax withheld: $0.00

Required: Use a computer software package such as Intuit ProConnect to complete Form 1040 for Albert and Allison Gaytor for 2024. Be sure to save your data input files since this case will be expanded with more tax information in each succeeding chapter. Make assumptions regarding any information not given.

Chapter 2

Gross Income and Exclusions

Learning Objectives

After completing this chapter, you should be able to:

LO 2.1	Apply the definition of gross income.
LO 2.2	Describe salaries and wages income reporting and inclusion in gross income.
LO 2.3	Explain the general tax treatment of health insurance.
LO 2.4	Determine when meals and lodging may be excluded from taxable income.
LO 2.5	Identify the common employee fringe benefit income exclusions.
LO 2.6	Determine when prizes and awards are included in income.
LO 2.7	Calculate the taxable and nontaxable portions of annuity payments.
LO 2.8	Describe the tax treatment of life insurance proceeds.
LO 2.9	Identify the tax treatment of interest income.
LO 2.10	Identify the tax treatment of dividend income.
LO 2.11	Identify the general rules for the tax treatment of gifts and inheritances.
LO 2.12	Describe the elements of scholarship income that are excluded from tax.
LO 2.13	Describe the tax treatment of alimony and child support.
LO 2.14	Explain the tax implications of using educational savings vehicles.
LO 2.15	Describe the tax treatment of unemployment compensation.
LO 2.16	Apply the rules governing inclusion of Social Security benefits in gross income.
LO 2.17	Distinguish between the different rules for married taxpayers residing in community property states when filing separate returns.
LO 2.18	Describe the inclusion and exclusion of cancellation of debt income.

Overview

This chapter starts with the definition of gross income. Detailed coverage is provided for inclusions and exclusions that may present unique issues for taxpayers. The coverage includes the special tax treatment for interest and dividends, alimony, prizes and awards, annuities, life insurance proceeds, gifts, inheritances, community property, and cancellation of debt. Coverage of exclusions from gross income includes scholarships, accident and health insurance benefits, certain meals and lodging, municipal bond interest, and the special treatment of Social Security benefits. The elements of gross income discussed here represent much of what is included in the first line of the individual tax formula.

Learning Objective 2.1

Apply the definition of gross income.

2-1 The Nature of Gross Income

Gross income is the starting point for calculating a taxpayer's tax liability. The tax law states that gross income is:

> … all income from whatever source derived, including (but not limited to) the following items:

- Compensation for services, including fees, commissions, fringe benefits, and similar items
- Gross income derived from business
- Gains derived from dealings in property
- Interest
- Rents
- Royalties
- Dividends
- Annuities
- Income from life insurance and endowment contracts
- Pensions
- Income from discharge of indebtedness
- Distributive share of partnership gross income
- Income in respect of a decedent
- Income from an interest in an estate or trust

The definition of gross income as **"all income from whatever source derived"** is perhaps the most well-known definition in the tax law. Under this definition, unless there is an exception in the law, the U.S. government considers all income taxable. Therefore, prizes and awards, cash and noncash payments for goods and services, payments made in trade or *barter* (such as car repairs traded for tax preparation services), and illegal income are all still taxable income.

An expanded list of items that are included in gross income is included in Table 2.1. When in doubt, the general rule is that everything a taxpayer receives must be included in gross income unless specifically excluded. Any noncash items must be included in gross income at the fair market value of the items received.

The tax law provides that certain items of income are exempt from taxation; these items are referred to as *exclusions*. The exclusions include items such as life insurance proceeds, gifts, and veterans' benefits. A more complete list of exclusions from gross income is provided in Table 2.2.

Table 2.1 Inclusions in Gross Income

Accrued leave pay	Awards
Alimony (for divorce before 2019)	Back pay
Amounts recovered after being deducted in prior years	Bargain purchase from employer
	Bonuses
Annuities	Breach of contract damages

Table 2.1 Inclusions in Gross Income (*Continued*)

Business/self-employment income
Cash income
Cancellation of debt income
Clergy fees
Commissions
Compensation for services
Contributions received by members of the clergy
Damages for nonphysical personal injury
Death benefits
Debts forgiven
Differential wage payments
Directors' fees
Dividends
Embezzled funds
Employee awards (except certain service awards)
Employee benefits (except certain fringe benefits)
Employee bonuses
Employee stock options and stock appreciation rights
Estate and trust income
Farm income
Fees
Gains from illegal activities
Gains from sale of property or securities
Gambling winnings
Group term life insurance premiums paid by employer for coverage over $50,000
Hobby income
Incentive awards
Income in respect of a decedent
Interest income
IRA distributions (most)
Jury duty fees
Living quarters, meals (unless furnished for employer's convenience, etc.)
Military pay (unless combat pay)
Nonemployee compensation
Notary fees
Outplacement services
Partnership and S Corporation income (taxpayer's share from K-1)
Pensions (including military)
Prizes
Professional fees
Punitive damages
Rents
Retirement pay
Rewards
Royalties
Salaries
Scholarships (room and board)
Severance pay
Sick pay
Strike and lockout benefits
Supplemental unemployment benefits
Tips and gratuities
Unemployment compensation
Virtual currency (such as Bitcoin) paid for services
Wages

Table 2.2 Exclusions from Gross Income

Accident insurance proceeds
Alimony (excluded after 2018)
Annuities (to a limited extent)
Bequests
Casualty insurance proceeds
Child support payments
Damages for physical personal injury or sickness
Disability benefits (generally, but not always)
Federal income tax refunds
Foster care payments
Gifts
Government cost-of-living allowances
Group term life insurance premiums paid by employer (coverage not over $50,000)
Health insurance proceeds
Inheritances
Insurance payments for living expenses after casualty loss to home
Interest on tax-free securities
Interest on certain U.S. savings bonds if used for higher education
Life insurance proceeds
Meals and lodging (furnished for employer's convenience, etc.)
Military allowances (including G.I. bill benefits)
Minister's dwelling rental value allowance
Municipal bond interest
Olympic and Paralympic medals and cash awards given to athletes
Qualified Medicaid waiver payments
Qualified retirement planning services paid by employer
Reimbursements by employers or volunteer organizations for actual expenses under an accountable plan
Relocation payments
Rental income for less than 15 days
Reverse mortgage
Scholarships (tuition and books)
Social Security benefits (with limits)
Student loan forgiveness (through 2025)
Supplemental Security Income (SSI)
Veterans' benefits
Welfare payments (including TANF and food stamps)
Workers' compensation
Wrongful incarceration awards

Example Alec and Jamison are a married couple that operate a licensed foster home in their residence. In 2024, Alec and Jamison received $54,000 in home-based family care payments from the social services department of their state. In addition, Alec and Jamison received $15,000 in Medicaid waiver payments for taking care of Alec's disabled older brother. Lastly, Alec did some part-time work as an actor and was paid $25,000. The foster care and Medicaid waiver payments can be excluded from gross income but the acting compensation is included. ♦

Example Aspen Wood, a carpenter, agrees to perform home repairs for Mario Carte in exchange for driving lessons. Normally Mario would charge $400 for the same lessons. In this barter transaction, Aspen and Mario must both include the fair market value ($400) of the bartered exchange in gross income. ♦

Self-Study Problem 2.1 *Refer to Appendix E for Solutions to Self-Study Problems*

Determine whether each of the items listed below should be included in gross income or excluded from gross income in 2024.

1. Prizes and awards
2. Embezzled funds
3. Child support payments
4. Alimony received from a 2022 divorce
5. Pension payments received
6. Inheritances received
7. Welfare payments received
8. Bequests received
9. Reasonable housing allowance provided to a clergy
10. Royalties received
11. Life insurance proceeds paid at death
12. Hobby income
13. Legal settlement related to physical injury
14. Partnership income allocated
15. Casualty insurance proceeds
16. G.I. Bill benefits
17. Scholarships for tuition and fees
18. Qualified Medicaid waiver payments
19. Gifts received

2-2 Salaries and Wages

Learning Objective 2.2
Describe salaries and wages income reporting and inclusion in gross income.

Serving as an employee of a business is the most common way to earn income in the United States. Just under 80 percent of all individual income tax returns include some amount of wage income, and wages represent approximately 66 percent of the adjusted gross income reported. Payments in almost any form, including salaries and wages, from an employer to an employee are considered income. The primary form of reporting wages to an employee is through Form W-2. An employee should receive a Form W-2 from an employer providing information about the wages paid to that employee during the year (the employer's responsibilities with Form W-2 are examined in Chapter 9). Figure 2.1 presents a Form W-2 for 2024.

Figure 2.1 Form W-2

Box	Field	Amount
a	Employee's social security number	791-51-4335
b	Employer identification number (EIN)	12-3456789
c	Employer's name, address, and ZIP code	Ivy Technologies, Inc., 436 E. 35 Avenue, Gary, IN 46409
e	Employee's name and address	Robert Rothschild, 555 E 81st Street, Merrillville, IN 46410
1	Wages, tips, other compensation	156,512.00
2	Federal income tax withheld	19,267.34
3	Social security wages	168,600.00
4	Social security tax withheld	10,453.20
5	Medicare wages and tips	170,112.00
6	Medicare tax withheld	2,466.62
10	Dependent care benefits	5,000.00
12a	C	112.00
12b	D	13,600.00
12c	DD	13,108.43
13	Retirement plan	X
15	State	IN
16	State wages, tips, etc.	156,512.00
17	State income tax	5,841.23
18	Local wages, tips, etc.	156,512.00
19	Local income tax	1,262.00
20	Locality name	LAKE

Form W-2 Wage and Tax Statement 2024
Copy B—To Be Filed With Employee's FEDERAL Tax Return.
This information is being furnished to the Internal Revenue Service.
Department of the Treasury—Internal Revenue Service

Box 1 of Form W-2 is where employers report taxable wages, salary, bonuses, awards, commissions, and almost every other type of taxable compensation. The amount in Box 1 is reported directly on Line 1a of Form 1040. If a taxpayer receives more than one Form W-2 or is jointly filing with a spouse having their own Form W-2, the amounts in Box 1 are combined before entering on Line 1a of Form 1040.

Example Bonnie and Clyde are married and file jointly. In 2024, Bonnie received two Form W-2s from two separate employers reporting $34,000 of wages on one and $16,500 on the other. In addition, Clyde also received a Form W-2 reporting wages of $23,000 in Box 1. Bonnie and Clyde should report $73,500 ($34,000 + $16,500 + $23,000) on Line 1a of Form 1040 (or Form 1040-SR, if Bonnie or Clyde are age 65 or older and choose to use that form). ♦

Box 2 of Form W-2 reports the amount of federal income tax withheld from the taxpayer's wages by the employer for the year. This amount is reported on Line 25a of Forms 1040 and 1040-SR.

Boxes 3 through 6 report information related to the amount of wages subject to Social Security and Medicare (employment) taxes and the related taxes withheld. The amounts generally do not impact the income tax reporting by a taxpayer, although as covered in Chapter 9, when a taxpayer has multiple employers and the amount of Social Security tax withheld exceeds the annual limits of Social Security taxable wages, the excess is treated as an additional tax payment. Note that the amounts in Box 1 and Boxes 3 and 5 often agree but they are not always the same for all taxpayers.

For example, if an employee contributes part of their salary to a qualified retirement plan such as a 401k plan, the contribution is not generally subject to income tax but is subject to employment taxes. The amount of taxable wages in Box 1 would be lower than the amounts reported in Boxes 3 and 5 by the retirement plan contribution amount. In addition, wages are subject to Social Security tax up to a limit ($168,600 in 2024) and therefore, Box 3 will not exceed the annual limit.

Box 8 reports allocated tips for amounts not included in Box 1 taxable wages. Box 10 is where flexible spending contributions to a dependent care program are reported (refer to LO 2.5 for more information). Box 12 is for reporting a variety of different forms of compensation such as reimbursed parking, health care premiums paid by the employer, and other fringe benefits. The type of compensation is identified by the code provided adjacent to the amount in Box 12, as described in the instructions to the Form W-2 as shown below in Figure 2.2.

The retirement plan box in Box 13 will be checked if the taxpayer is eligible to participate in a retirement plan [and thus, may limit the amount of deductible IRA (individual retirement account) contributions]. Box 14 is designated to report other forms of compensation as needed.

State and local tax information is reported at the bottom of Form W-2 in Boxes 15 through 20. This includes the taxable wages for state tax purposes and the amount of state income tax withheld, which is generally part of the state and local tax itemized deduction (covered in Chapter 5).

Figure 2.2 Form W-2 Reference Guide for Box 12 Codes

Code	Description	Code	Description	Code	Description
A	Uncollected social security or RRTA tax on tips	L	Substantiated employee business expense reimbursements	Y	Deferrals under a section 409A nonqualified deferred compensation plan
B	Uncollected Medicare tax on tips (but not Additional Medicare Tax)	M	Uncollected social security or RRTA tax on taxable cost of group-term life insurance over $50,000 (former employees only)	Z	Income under a nonqualified deferred compensation plan that fails to satisfy section 409A
C	Taxable cost of group-term life insurance over $50,000	N	Uncollected Medicare tax on taxable cost of group-term life insurance over $50,000 (but not Additional Medicare Tax) (former employees only)	AA	Designated Roth contributions under a section 401(k) plan
D	Elective deferrals under a section 401(k) cash or deferred arrangement plan (including a SIMPLE 401(k) arrangement)	P	Excludable moving expense reimbursements paid directly to members of the Armed Forces	BB	Designated Roth contributions under a section 403(b) plan
E	Elective deferrals under a section 403(b) salary reduction agreement	Q	Nontaxable combat pay	DD	Cost of employer-sponsored health coverage
F	Elective deferrals under a section 408(k)(6) salary reduction SEP	R	Employer contributions to an Archer MSA	EE	Designated Roth contributions under a governmental section 457(b) plan
G	Elective deferrals and employer contributions (including nonelective deferrals) to a section 457(b) deferred compensation plan	S	Employee salary reduction contributions under a section 408(p) SIMPLE plan	FF	Permitted benefits under a qualified small employer health reimbursement arrangement
H	Elective deferrals to a section 501(c)(18)(D) tax-exempt organization plan	T	Adoption benefits	GG	Income from qualified equity grants under section 83(i)
J	Nontaxable sick pay	V	Income from exercise of nonstatutory stock option(s)	HH	Aggregate deferrals under section 83(i) elections as of the close of the calendar year
K	20% excise tax on excess golden parachute payments	W	Employer contributions (including employee contributions through a cafeteria plan) to an employee's health savings account (HSA)	II	Medicaid waiver payments excluded from gross income under Notice 2014-7

Self-Study Problem 2.2
Refer to Appendix E for Solutions to Self-Study Problems

Form W-2 Wage and Tax Statement — 2024

Box	Description	Amount
a	Employee's social security number	232-11-4444
b	Employer identification number (EIN)	12-9876543
c	Employer's name, address, and ZIP code	Luminary Dollars Inc., 3338 Little River Turnpike, Annandale, VA 22003
e/f	Employee's name and address	Virginia Nova, 202 Wheatstone Drive, Fairfax, VA 22032
1	Wages, tips, other compensation	53,580.00
2	Federal income tax withheld	3,798.77
3	Social security wages	57,000.00
4	Social security tax withheld	3,534.00
5	Medicare wages and tips	57,000.00
6	Medicare tax withheld	826.50
12a	D	3,420.00
12b	DD	8,453.12
13	Retirement plan	X
15	State / Employer's state ID number	VA / 1899012A
16	State wages, tips, etc.	53,580.00
17	State income tax	1,816.22

Based on Virginia's Form W-2, determine the following amounts:

a. Taxable wages to report on Line 1a of Form 1040
b. Federal tax payments withheld to report on Line 25a of Form 1040
c. The amount that Virginia contributed to her company's 401k plan
d. The amount to report as state income taxes paid if Virginia itemizes her deductions

---

ProConnect™ Tax TIP

Entering wages from a Form W-2 is one of the most common data entry points for a tax preparer. Predictably, wages are entered under the Income section, more specifically, under Wages, Salaries, Tips (W-2). When selecting the Wages subheading, the entire entry screen for the W-2 is presented in the main window. The subheadings on the left-hand margin slide the entry form up and down for easier entry. Any additional Forms W-2 can be added using the [+] tab at the top of the main window. Although the fictional textbook employers do not have import access, using ProConnect Tax, many Forms W-2 can be imported directly from an employer's payroll system. Enter the employer's identification number and click the circular arrow to import wages data.

2-3 Accident and Health Insurance

2.3 Learning Objective: Explain the general tax treatment of health insurance.

Many taxpayers are covered by accident and health insurance plans through their employer. These plans pay for the cost of medical care of the taxpayer and any dependents who are insured under the plan. The taxpayer may pay the total premiums of the plan, or their employer may pay part or all of the premiums. Taxpayers are allowed liberal exclusions for payments received from these accident and health plans. Generally, as long as the plan is nondiscriminatory, the taxpayer may exclude the total amount received for payment of medical care. This exclusion applies to any amount paid for the medical care of the taxpayer, their spouse, or dependents and can also apply to a retired employee, the surviving spouse of a deceased employee, or a former employee if the coverage is based on the employment relationship (for example, COBRA). The payment may be made to the doctor, the hospital, or the taxpayer as reimbursement for the payment of the expenses. In addition, any premiums paid by a taxpayer's employer are excluded from the taxpayer's income, and the premium payments may be deducted by the employer. Although it will not generally affect income taxes, the cost of employer-provided healthcare is reported in Box 12 of the Form W-2 under code DD.

Most accident and health care policies also pay fixed amounts to the insured for loss of the use of a member or function of the body. These amounts may also be excluded from income. For example, a taxpayer who receives $25,000 because they are blinded in one eye may exclude the $25,000 from income.

Example Bob is a married taxpayer. His employer pays a $750 per month premium on a policy covering Bob and his family. Jean, Bob's wife, is sick during the year, and her medical bills amount to $6,500; the insurance company paid $6,000 for the bills. Bob and Jean may exclude from income the $750 per month premium paid by Bob's employer and the $6,000 paid by the insurance company. The $500 not paid by the insurance company may be deductible on Bob and Jean's return, subject to the medical expense deduction limitations (covered in Chapter 5). ♦

Self-Study Problem 2.3 — Refer to Appendix E for Solutions to Self-Study Problems

Martin Dean, a single taxpayer, is an employee of Wiretonne Steel Inc. Wiretonne pays premiums of $3,000 on Martin's health insurance for the current year. Also, during the current year, Martin has an operation for which the insurance company pays $5,000 to the hospital and doctor. Of the above amounts, how much must Martin include in gross income?

2-4 Meals and Lodging

Learning Objective 2.4
Determine when meals and lodging may be excluded from taxable income.

The value of meals provided to an employee may be excluded from the employee's gross income in two situations: (1) when meals are provided on the business premises and (2) when meals are considered de minimis. Meals provided on the business premises must be furnished to the employee on the business premises and must also be for the convenience of the employer. The term "for the convenience of the employer" is based on the facts and circumstances; however, the meals must be provided for a substantial noncompensatory business reason.

Example Ace is a security guard at a casino. In order to limit Ace's lunch break to only 30 minutes, the casino furnishes his lunch at no charge in one of the casino restaurants because the job requires that the security guards watch the casino floor continuously to identify suspicious activity. Ace may exclude the value of the meals provided by the casino. ♦

If more than half of the employees are furnished meals for the convenience of the employer, the employer may treat all meals as furnished for the convenience of the employer. Meals furnished so employees can be available for emergency calls are considered for the employers' convenience.

Example A hospital maintains a cafeteria and employees receive meals at no charge. Over half of the employees at the hospital at any time are on call to respond to emergencies, which the hospital can confirm. Although the hospital does not require employees to eat in the cafeteria, most do. Because the hospital provides meals to over half of the employees for the convenience of the hospital, the value of meals provided at the hospital to all employees may be excluded. ♦

Meals furnished to food service employees during, immediately before, or immediately after the employee's working hours are considered for the convenience of the employer and may be excluded.

Example Up and Down Burger (UDB) furnishes free meals to employees. Brad, a UDB employee, has a meal during his break and also has one at the end of his shift. Generally, the value of these meals can be excluded. If Brad stops by UDB on his day off for a free meal, the value of the meal provided to him by UDB would be taxable. ♦

Meals are considered de minimis if provided occasionally and provide so little value that accounting for such value would be unreasonable or administratively impractical. Examples of de minimis meals might include:

- Coffee, doughnuts, and soft drinks
- Occasional overtime meals
- Occasional parties or picnics for employees

Example Winchell provides bagels and doughnuts to all employees in the breakroom of her business every third Friday of the month. Winchell also hosts an employee holiday party in December each year and has food catered at a nearby park for employees and their families. The value of these meals would be considered de minimis and excludable from the employee's wages. ♦

The value of subsidized meals provided to employees at an on-premise employer-operated eating facility (i.e., a company cafeteria) are considered de minimis meals if the annual revenue of the facility exceeds the direct operating costs of the facility.

Example Cysco Company operates a company cafeteria for its employees. The employees are charged an amount for the meals that is equal to the cost of the meals to Cysco (that is, the meals are subsidized). Because the facility is on the business premises and operates at break-even, the value of the meals may be excluded from the employees' income. ♦

As explained in Chapter 3, the deductions for de minimis meals can be limited.

The value of lodging provided to an employee is excludable if it meets three requirements:
1. The lodging is furnished on the business premises,
2. The lodging is for the convenience of the employer, and
3. The lodging must be accepted as a condition of the employment

Lodging is a condition of employment if the employee must live on the business premises to be able to properly perform their duties.

Example Harry Stamper works on an oil rig in the Gulf of Mexico 120 miles from the Louisiana coast. Due to the inaccessibility of the work site, lodging is provided by his employer on the rig. Harry is required to agree to lodging as a condition of his employment. Harry's employer may exclude the value of his lodging. ♦

Example Pat Schneider works as the superintendent of a large apartment building in Indianapolis. In order to make emergency repairs and provide on-call service to the tenants of the building, Schneider is required to live in the building. Their employer provides an apartment to Schneider at no cost. The value of Schneider's lodging may be excluded. ♦

The exclusion for lodging also includes the value of utilities such as electricity, water, heat, gas, and similar items that make the lodging habitable. The value of meals or lodging provided by the employer in other situations, and cash allowances for meals or lodging, must be included in the employee's gross income (consider also business and travel meals and lodging in Chapter 3).

Example Greta receives an all-expenses paid trip to Cancun, Mexico, for achieving her sales quotas for the year. The cost of the airfare, lodging, and meals would be included in Greta's gross income. ♦

> **Self-Study Problem 2.4** *Refer to Appendix E for Solutions to Self-Study Problems*
>
> In each of the following independent cases, indicate whether the value of the meals or lodging should be included in or excluded from the taxpayer's income.
>
> 1. A waiter is required to eat lunch, furnished by his employer, on the premises during a busy lunch hour.
> 2. A police officer receives a cash allowance to pay for meals while on duty.
> 3. A worker receives lodging at a remote construction site in Alaska.
> 4. A taxpayer manages a motel and, although the owner does not require it, she lives at the motel rent free.
> 5. A bank teller is furnished meals on the premises to limit the time she is away during busy hours.

2-5 Employee Fringe Benefits

Learning Objective 2.5
Identify the common employee fringe benefit income exclusions.

Fringe benefits are generally included in the employee's gross income, unless specifically excluded by law. The primary types of fringe benefits that may be excluded from gross income are described below.

2-5a Flexible Spending Accounts (FSAs)

One way in which an employer may provide qualified nontaxable benefits to employees is through the use of a cafeteria plan. A cafeteria plan is a written plan that permits employees to choose between two of more benefits consisting of cash or some qualified nontaxable benefit.

Example Jersey Manufacturing Inc. operates a cafeteria plan that allows employees to choose among three options: (1) cash compensation, (2) health insurance for the employee and family, and (3) contributions to a 401k plan. As qualified benefits, payments for health insurance and 401k contributions will be excluded from the employees' gross income; whereas, the cash payments are included. ♦

A popular form of cafeteria plan is to offer a flexible spending arrangement or flexible spending account (FSA) as part of the plan. FSAs permit employees to contribute pre-tax money from their wages to a special account to pay for health care, dependent care, or adoption expenses. If all of the requirements of the plan are met, and the employee provides receipts for the expenses incurred, the full amount of expenses reimbursed out of the employee's account will be treated as a tax-free reduction in salary. These accounts may provide significant tax savings for employees, with only a small administrative cost to employers. The two most popular types of FSAs are those for health care costs and those for dependent care costs.

Example In 2024, Dina has wage income of $43,000 and elects to defer $2,000 into a health care flexible spending account. She uses all $2,000 of the deferred funds to pay for qualifying medical expenses in 2024. Dina's taxable wage income will be $41,000. The $2,000 is excluded from her income if she uses the funds for qualifying medical expenses. ♦

Health Care Flexible Spending Accounts

Employers may offer health care flexible spending accounts in which employees can set aside up to $3,200 (2024) from their salary to cover medical expenses that they anticipate incurring during the year. These expenses may include eyeglasses, laser-eye surgery, necessary dental work, and health insurance copayments. Amounts used from a health care FSA may not be deducted as an itemized deduction for medical expenses (refer to Chapter 5). Health care FSAs should not be confused with Archer medical spending accounts (MSAs) or health savings accounts (HSAs) which are covered in Chapter 5.

Dependent Care Flexible Spending Accounts

Employers may offer dependent care flexible spending accounts (FSAs) in which employees may set aside up to $5,000 of their salary each year to cover the costs of caring for a dependent child or aging parent. Such costs may include day care, day camp, in-home care, and preschool. A dependent care FSA is separate from dependent care assistance programs presented later in this section.

Employees should be aware, however, of the "use-it-or-lose-it" rule for FSAs (i.e., any balance remaining in the employee's account at December 31 is lost). For health care flexible spending accounts, employers generally have the option to allow $640 (in 2024) of the unused medical spending account to carry over to 2025 or to offer a 2 ½-month grace period after year-end to incur additional medical expenses before the employee loses the balance in the account. The plan may not offer both types of relief from use-it-or-lose-it.

Example Allie contributed $3,200 to her employer's FSA for health care, expecting to use the funds for orthodontics in 2024. Unfortunately, she was unable to have the dental work done until February of 2025. If Allie's employer has a 2 ½ month policy for the health care FSA, then Allie will be able to access the 2024 funds to cover the cost of her dental care. If her employer follows a carryover balance policy, then she can only access up to $640 of her 2024 funds in 2025. ♦

2-5b Transportation (Commuting) Benefits

The value of transportation or commuting benefits can be excluded from an employee's gross income under two circumstances: (1) they are qualified transportation benefits and (2) they are de minimis transportation benefits.

Qualified transportation benefits often apply to parking but can also apply to use of a commuter highway vehicle (such as an employer-operated van pool) or a mass-transit pass (such as bus, rail, or ferry). Employees can exclude from gross income payments from employers of up to $315 per month in 2024 (the maximum exclusion is adjusted for inflation) to cover the cost of public transportation to, or parking for, work. However, employers *may not* deduct these payments to the extent they are excluded from the employee's income; thus, effectively limiting the benefit from employer-paid transportation and parking.

Example Portnoy Company provides parking for the executive management team at their headquarters building located in downtown. In 2024, the parking costs $340 per month for each parking space. Portnoy will be able to exclude $315 of the value of the provided parking from the employees' gross income. Portnoy will be unable to deduct the transportation costs when computing its own taxable income. ♦

A de minimis transportation benefit is any local transportation benefit provided to an employee that has little value (taking into account frequency) and accounting for such cost would be unreasonable or administratively impracticable. An occasional cab or ride-share fare provided to an employee for working overtime would likely qualify. Providing mass transit passes to employees at a discount is also a de minimis transportation benefit if the discount does not exceed $21 in any month.

Transportation costs can also be provided to employees under a compensation reduction agreement that operates in a fashion similar to FSAs. This type of program allows the employee to use pre-tax compensation to pay for a form of a qualified transportation benefit up to the monthly exclusion amount.

Example Portnoy Company also provides a compensation reduction arrangement whereby non-executives may have anywhere from $80 to $315 (depending on the actual cost of the public transit pass) deducted from their pay each month to pay for a monthly transit pass to accommodate the employee's daily commute. Helen has $200 per month deducted from her pay to cover the cost of her light rail pass into downtown. Her wages subject to income tax will be reduced by $2,400 ($200 × 12) and thus, she will use pre-tax dollars to pay for her commute. ♦

Similar to qualified transportation fringe benefits, amounts used as part of a compensation reduction agreement for transportation are also not deductible. The bicycle commuter fringe is suspended through 2025.

2-5c Dependent Care Assistance Programs

Under a dependent care assistance program (DCAP), an employer may pay directly or indirectly up to $5,000 for dependent care services that allow the employee to work. The amount excluded cannot be more than the employee's earned income. The value of the dependent care assistance is reported in Box 10 of the Form W-2 of the employee. One method of offering a DCAP is through an FSA. The total amount of dependent care benefits may not exceed $5,000.

Example Fizzy Bottling Company operates a dependent care assistance program for employees in which Fizzy pays for sudden or unexpected child care for employees at a nearby child care center. Charlie uses the child care center a number of times in 2024 when his regular day care was unavailable. The value of child care paid by Fizzy Bottling was $700. Charlie also participates in the dependent care FSA and had $4,500 withheld from his pay. Charlie's Form W-2 will reflect $5,200 ($4,500 + $700) of dependent care assistance and $200 will be included in his taxable wages. ♦

Dependent care expenses paid through an FSA may not be used toward the child and dependent care credit (Chapter 7).

2-5d Group Term Life Insurance

Employers may pay for up to $50,000 of group term life insurance for employees as a tax-free fringe benefit. Providing group term life insurance to employees must not favor officers, shareholders, or highly-compensated personnel. Amounts paid for employee term life insurance coverage above $50,000 are subject to an income inclusion for the cost of the insurance above $50,000 based on amounts provided by the IRS as presented in Table 2.3

Table 2.3 Monthly Cost of Life Insurance per $1,000 of Coverage

Age	Cost
Under 25	$ 0.05
25 through 29	0.06
30 through 34	0.08
35 through 39	0.09
40 through 44	0.10
45 through 49	0.15
50 through 54	0.23
55 through 59	0.43
60 through 64	0.66
65 through 69	1.27
70 and older	2.06

Source: Adapted from IRS Publication 15-B.

Example Terri's employer provides her with a $100,000 group term life insurance coverage. Terri is 45 and contributes $0 annually for the policy. Terri's employer will include $90 [($50,000 ÷ $1,000) × $0.15 × 12 months] of taxable income with her taxable wages and enter $90 and Code C in Box 12 of her Form W-2. ♦

Internal Revenue Code §79 was first passed in 1964 and provided the exclusion of employer paid group term life insurance premiums up to $50,000. The $50,000 limit has not been adjusted since originally passed into law. In today's dollars, you would need over $475,000 to equal $50,000 in 1964. The National Funeral Directors Association estimated the median cost of a funeral in 1965 as $790 and $8,300 in 2023.

2-5e Education Assistance Plans and Tuition Reduction

Employers may provide up to $5,250 of excludable annual tuition assistance under an educational assistance plan. The exclusion requires an employer to have a written plan and the educational assistance can be paid to an employee or former employee. Assistance over $5,250 is included in the taxpayer's wages unless otherwise excludable as a working condition benefit that would have been deductible as a business expense (covered in Chapter 3). Through 2025, payments from an education assistance plan can also be excluded if paid to an employee or lender if the payments are applied toward the employee's student loans.

Example Ahmaud's employer offers an education plan that Ahmaud had been taking advantage of every year. Unfortunately, the cost of Ahmaud's college education exceeded $5,250 each year, and he was required to take out student loans. Ahmaud graduated in 2023. After graduation but before 2026, Ahmaud's employer may pay his student loan debt up to $5,250 each year, and Ahmaud is not required to include the payment in his income. ♦

Employees of educational institutions may exclude from their income the value of a tuition reduction, if the plan is for an undergraduate education and available to all employees. The exclusion applies to the employees, their spouses, and their dependents. The value of a graduate education tuition reduction plan may only be excluded by graduate students of the institution who are teaching or doing research at that institution.

Example Dale is a faculty affairs administrator for Vermont State University (VSU). One of the VSU benefits available to all VSU employees is a 50-percent discount on the tuition for any employee, spouse, or dependent. Dale's daughter, Pam, is a freshman at VSU and Dale saves $4,500 on her 2024 tuition and fees due to the employee discount. The discount is excluded from Dale's gross income. ♦

2-5f No-Additional-Cost Services and Qualified Employee Discounts

No-additional-cost services are services that are provided to employees and their families at little or no additional cost to the employer, and which would otherwise have remained unused. An airline employee who is allowed to fly at no cost on a standby basis is an example. The value of the airfare may be excluded from the employee's gross income.

Employees are only allowed to receive tax-free services in the major line of business in which they are employed. For example, if an airline company also owns a rental car agency, the employees working in the airline division would not be entitled to the tax-free use of rental cars. Different companies may enter into reciprocal agreements and provide no-additional-cost services to the other company's employees.

Example BlueStar Airlines (BSA) permits employees and their spouses to fly for free on flights when seats are available. In addition, BSA has a written reciprocity agreement with TransAmerican Airlines (TAA) that allows flight crews to fly TAA and vice versa. In 2024, Yonah, a flight attendant for BSA, flies to Hawaii on BSA for free using available seats on the flight. On the return flight, BSA has no seats available so Yonah flies for free on TAA's flight with open seats. The value of the flights is excludable from Yonah's income. ♦

The value of employee discounts may be excluded from gross income if the discounts are available on a nondiscriminatory basis. That is, the discounts must be available to substantially all full-time employees. The item being discounted must be from the line of business in which the employee is engaged. The discount exclusion also does not apply to discounts on real estate or personal property held for investment. For services provided at a discount, the exclusion is limited to 20 percent of the typical customer price. For merchandise, the exclusion is limited to the employer's gross markup on the goods.

Example R.J. works for an auto parts store chain. R.J. purchases a new water pump for her car at the employee discounted price of $26. Normally, the part would be sold for $41. R.J.'s employer's cost for the part is $26. Because R.J.'s cost is not less than the cost of the part to her employer, the discount is within the exclusion and is not taxable to R.J. ♦

Example Megan Zane is an administrative assistant at a law firm. Megan hires one of the lawyers at the firm to assist with her personal divorce proceedings. The firm provides a 15-percent employee discount on legal services provided to employees. Megan can exclude the value of the discount from her gross income. ♦

2-5g Working Condition Fringe Benefits

An employee may exclude the value of property or services provided by an employer to the extent that the cost of the property or services would be a deductible expense of the employee and the property or services are necessary for the employee to perform their job. Examples of this type of exclusion include the use of a company car for business (not personal) purposes and a subscription to a tax journal paid for by a CPA firm. The working condition fringe benefit rules also allow several expenses which would not be deductible if paid by the employee. These include the value of certain employer-provided education and certain use of demonstrator autos by automobile salespeople.

Example Slick Tyre is a full-time salesperson for Lemon Autos, a local car dealer. Lemon provides Slick with a new model vehicle each year for customer test drives during Slick's business hours and personal use otherwise. Slick's use of the demonstrator car is considered a working condition fringe and the value of his personal use may be excluded from his gross income. ♦

2-5h De Minimis Fringe Benefits

The value of small fringe benefits may be excluded from an employee's gross income if the value of the item or service (taking into account the frequency) is small and accounting for it would be unreasonable or administratively impractical. Examples of this type of exclusion include occasional personal use of an office copy machine, personal letters typed by a company administrative assistant, small non-cash holiday gifts provided to employees (e.g., a holiday turkey), occasional tickets (not season tickets) for theatre or sporting events, and the de minimis meals and transportation described earlier in this section.

Cell phones provided to employees primarily for business purposes are considered tax-free de minimis fringe benefits. Examples of cell phones which qualify include those provided to allow employees to communicate with clients, or to allow employers to contact employees in the field or at home.

Cash and cash equivalent fringe benefits (gift certificates, gift cards, the use of a business credit card for personal expenses) are almost never de minimis regardless of how small the amount.

Example Prestige Global provides each employee with a modest fruit basket on their birthday. One year, the normal supplier of fruit baskets was short of inventory and so Prestige gave employees a gift card to purchase a basket later. The employees that received the fruit baskets may exclude the value as a de minimis fringe; however, the employees that received the gift card will include the value of the card in their gross income. ♦

2-5i Athletic Facilities

Employees may exclude from gross income the value of the use of an athletic facility (gym). The facility must be used primarily by employees, their spouses, and dependent children. The facility does not need to be on the business premises, but must be located on premises that the employer owns or leases and must be operated by the employer.

2-5j Retirement Planning Fringe Benefit

Qualified retirement planning services constitute a fringe benefit that is excluded from income. This change was made to encourage employers to provide retirement planning services for their employees to assist them in preparing for retirement. Qualified retirement planning services are any retirement planning services provided to an employee and their spouse by an employer maintaining a "qualified employer plan." The exclusion also applies to advice and information on retirement income planning for an individual and their spouse, including how the employer's plan fits into the individual's overall retirement income plan. The exclusion, however, does not apply to services that may be related to tax preparation, accounting, legal, or brokerage services.

Example As part of its qualified plan, Lizzo's employer provides retirement planning services. Lizzo has a meeting with a financial planner to review her retirement plan. The $600 cost of the meeting is paid for by her employer's qualified plan. The $600 is not income to Lizzo and is deductible by the employer. ♦

2-5k Fringe Benefits and Eligibility

To be excluded from gross income, many fringe benefits must not discriminate in favor of highly-compensated employees. Failure to do so can result in the fringe being taxable to such highly-compensated employees or in some instances, taxable to all employees.

Table 2.4 presents the classification of each fringe benefit on the issue of discrimination for highly-compensated or key employees.

Table 2.4 Fringe Benefits and Highly-Compensated Employees

Fringe	Discrimination Prohibited
Accident and health insurance benefits	Y
Achievement awards under a qualified plan	Y
Adoption assistance	Y
Athletic facilities	N
De minimis (not including meals offered at an employee-operated eating facility)	N
Dependent care assistance	Y
Education assistance	Y
Employee discount	Y
Group term life insurance	Y
Health savings account (unless employer makes contributions or through a cafeteria plan)	N
Lodging for convenience of employer	N
Meals for convenience of employer	N
Meals (offered at an employer-operated eating facility)	Y
Moving expense benefits	N
No-additional-cost services	Y
Retirement planning services	Y
Transportation	N
Tuition reduction	Y
Working condition fringe	N

Example The law offices of Ginsberg and Scalia offer $350 per month in paid parking to the top eight partners in the firm. No other employees are provided with paid parking. Because the transportation fringe is not required to conform to the discrimination rules, $315 a month (the transportation fringe limit for 2024) may be excluded from the partners' taxable compensation. ♦

A summary of various fringe benefits is provided in Table 2.5.

Table 2.5 Fringe Benefits Summary

Type of Fringe	Summary of Treatment	Learning Objective
Accident and health benefits	Exempt except for long-term care provided through a flexible spending arrangement	2.3, 2.5
Achievement awards	Exempt up to $1,600 for qualified plan awards ($400 for nonqualified)	2.6
Adoption assistance	Exempt up to $16,810 (adjusted each year)	7.7
Athletic facilities	Exempt is use is by employees and families and operated on employer's premises	2.5
De minimis (not including meals offered at an employer-operated eating facility)	Exempt if property or service has minimal value making accounting administratively impractical (does not apply to cash and cash equivalents)	2.5
Dependent care assistance	Exempt up to $5,000	2.5
Educational assistance	Exempt up to $5,250	2.5
Employee discounts	Exempt within certain limits	2.5
Employee stock options	Outside the scope of the textbook	
Employer-provided cell phone	Exempt if primarily for business	2.5
Group-term life insurance	Exempt up to $50,000 coverage	2.5
Health savings accounts (HSA)	Exempt up to certain limits for qualifying plans	5.1
Lodging on business premises	Exempt if for convenience and as a condition of employment	2.4
Meals	Exempt if furnished on premises for convenience or de minimis	2.4
Moving expenses	Exempt if otherwise deducible and related to military service	5.5, 6.9

Table 2.5 Fringe Benefits Summary (*Continued*)

Type of Fringe	Summary of Treatment	Learning Objective
No-additional-cost services	Exempt	2.5
Retirement planning services	Exempt	2.5
Transportation benefits	Exempt up to $315 (adjusted annually) for parking and transit passes are exempt if de minimis	2.5
Tuition reduction	Exempt if undergraduate or graduate and student performs teaching or research	2.5
Working condition benefits	Exempt	2.5

Source: Adapted from IRS Publication 15-B.

Self-Study Problem 2.5   Refer to Appendix E for Solutions to Self-Study Problems

Indicate in each of the following cases whether the value of the employee fringe benefit is included in or excluded from the employee's gross income.

1. An employee of a railroad receives a free train-trip ticket.
2. An employee of a department store receives a 25-percent discount on a shirt. The department store's markup is 15 percent.
3. An employee attends her employer's New Year's party paid for by her employer.
4. An employee of a stock brokerage firm receives a subscription to a financial newsletter paid for by his employer.
5. An employee's spouse regularly uses a company car to go shopping.
6. An employer sets aside $4,500 for an employee's dependent care costs.
7. An employee uses the company's on-site employee fitness room.

2-6 Prizes and Awards

2.6 Learning Objective
Determine when prizes and awards are included in income.

Prizes and awards are taxable income to the recipient. Winnings from television or radio shows, door prizes, lotteries, and other contest winnings are income to taxpayers. In addition, most other awards are generally taxable, even if they are awards given for accomplishments and with no action on the part of the taxpayer. If the prize or award is received in tangible personal property instead of cash, the fair market value of the property is included in the taxpayer's income. Taxpayers may refuse a prize and exclude its value from income.

Example Tanya has a streak of luck in 2024. She wins a radio quiz and is awarded tickets to a concert worth $250. She is also a contestant on the Press Your Fortune game show and wins cash and prizes worth $13,500. Tanya is required to include the $13,750 of prizes in her gross income. ♦

Winnings from online sports betting are included in gross income. This is true whether the winnings are from fantasy sports, or betting on the Superbowl, or some other event. Winnings are generally reported on Line 8b of Schedule 1 of Form 1040. Unfortunately, losses are only deductible if the taxpayer itemizes and only to the extent of winnings (no net gambling losses).

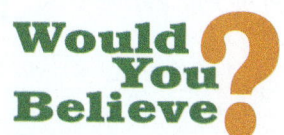

An exception is provided for certain employee achievement awards in the form of tangible personal property, such as a gold watch for 25 years of service. If the award is made in recognition of length of service or safety achievement, the value of the property may be excluded from income. Generally, the maximum amount excludable is $400. However, if the award is a "qualified plan award," the maximum exclusion is increased to $1,600. The definition of tangible personal property with respect to employee achievement awards excludes cash, cash equivalents, gift cards, gift coupons, gift certificates, vacations, meals, lodging, tickets to theater or sporting events, stocks, bonds, other securities, and other similar items.

Example   Van enters a drawing and wins a new automobile. The automobile has a sticker price of $20,200. The fair market value of the prize should be included in Van's gross income, but the fair market value is probably not the sticker price; instead, it is the price at which a similar car normally would be sold. ♦

There are two other awards or prizes that can be excluded from gross income under certain conditions. The first is an award received for accomplishment in religious, charitable, scientific, artistic, educational, literary, or civic fields (such as a Nobel or Pulitzer prize) which can be excluded only if:

- The taxpayer took no action to enter the contest,
- No substantial future services are required to be performed as a condition of the award, and
- The prize or award is transferred directly to a charitable organization or governmental unit.

The second excluded prize is a medal or prize money paid to Olympic or Paralympic athletes by the US Olympic Committee. The exclusion does not apply if the athlete's AGI exceeds $1 million.

Self-Study Problem 2.6   Refer to Appendix E for Solutions to Self-Study Problems

For each of the following independent cases, indicate the amount of gross income that should be included on the taxpayer's return.

1. Helen enters a radio contest and wins $2,000.
2. Professor Deborah wins an award of $10,000 for a book on literature she published four years ago. The award was presented in recognition of her past literary achievements.
3. Bill is a professional baseball player. Because he has hit 50 home runs this season, he was given a new wrist watch worth $2,500.
4. John is an employee of Big Corporation. He is awarded $5,000 for a suggestion to improve the plant layout.
5. Martha received a desk clock worth $350 from her employer in recognition of her fifteen years of loyal service as an employee.

Learning Objective 2.7

Calculate the taxable and nontaxable portions of annuity payments.

2-7 Annuities

An annuity is a type of investment in which the taxpayer purchases the right to receive periodic payments for the remainder of their life or for a fixed period of years. The amount of each periodic payment is based on the annuity purchase price, the life expectancy of the annuitant, or the life of the annuity contract. Qualified annuities are purchased as part of a qualified retirement plan (Individual Retirement Account [IRA], pension, 401k, 403(b), and 457 plans). Nonqualified annuities are sold outside of a retirement plan. Life insurance companies are the primary seller of annuities. Annuities have two characteristics that make them attractive to potential buyers: (1) the opportunity to defer income taxes until distributed and (2) the ability to extend payments over an individual's lifetime, providing income security. The number and types of annuities are extensive, but the taxation can be classified into annuities that use the simplified method and those that use the general rule.

Many annuities are part of qualified retirement plans. These plans are funded by either before-tax or after-tax contributions. "Before-tax" means that the employee did not pay taxes on the money at the time it was contributed.

Example Eugene is a retired taxpayer. While he was working, his employer withheld contributions from Eugene's pay to invest in the company pension fund. The amounts withheld were not subject to taxation (excluded from his gross income in the year earned). At retirement, all of the amounts paid to Eugene will be taxable. ♦

"After-tax" means the employee paid taxes on the money when it was contributed, and thus the taxpayer has cost basis in the annuity investment. If the taxpayer made all contributions to a plan with before-tax dollars, the entire distribution will be fully taxable as is common with 401k plans.

Example Eugene is a retired taxpayer. While he was working, his employer withheld contributions from Eugene's pay to invest in the company pension fund. The amounts withheld were subject to taxation at the time earned and thus Eugene paid taxes on the amount contributed. At retirement, Eugene will receive a monthly pension payment from the fund for the rest of his life. Eugene will use the simplified or general rule (depending on annuity starting date) to determine the tax-free part of monthly payments. ♦

If the taxpayer made contributions to a plan with after-tax dollars, then the distributions will be partially taxable. The portion of the distribution that is considered a return of the after-tax dollars will not be taxed again. It is considered a return of the taxpayer's cost basis (an amount for which taxes have already been paid). The portion of the distribution that represents the earnings/investment gains is taxable since it has not been previously taxed. This treatment is common in employer retirement plans. A summary of the tax treatment of before and after-tax contributions and distributions is presented in Figure 2.3.

Figure 2.3 Treatment of Contributions and Distributions from Qualifed Plans

Employee Contributions	Contributions		Taxability of Distributions		
	Before-Tax	After-Tax	Fully	Partially	Nontaxable
No	n/a	n/a	Yes	—	—
Yes	Yes	—	Yes	—	—
Yes	—	Yes	—	Yes	—
Yes, Roth	—	Yes	—	—	Yes

Source: IRS Publication 4491.

Under both the simplified and general methods, the annuitant is entitled to receive a portion of their investment back tax-free.

2-7a The Simplified Method

Individual taxpayers generally must use the "simplified" method to calculate the taxable amount from a qualified annuity for annuities starting after November 18, 1996. Nonqualified plan annuities and certain annuitants age 75 or older must still use the general rule discussed below. Under the simplified method, standard mortality tables, based on the current age of the annuitant, are used to calculate the taxable annuity amount.

To calculate the excluded amount, the IRS provides the worksheet shown in Figure 2.4.

Figure 2.4 Simplified Method Worksheet

1. Enter total amount received this year.   1. _____
2. Enter cost in the plan at the annuity starting date.   2. _____
3. Age at annuity starting date

	Enter
55 or under	360
56–60	310
61–65	260
66–70	210
71 or older	160

    3. _____

4. Divide line 2 by line 3.   4. _____
5. Multiply line 4 by the number of monthly payments this year. If the annuity starting date was before 1987, also enter this amount on line 8, and skip lines 6 and 7. Otherwise, go to line 6.   5. _____
6. Enter the amount, if any, recovered tax free in prior years.   6. _____
7. Subtract line 6 from line 2.   7. _____
8. Enter the smaller of line 5 or 7.   8. _____
9. Taxable amount this year: Subtract line 8 from line 1. Do not enter less than zero.   9. _____

Note 1: The denominators provided in line 3 above are effective for annuity starting dates after November 18, 1996. For annuity starting dates prior to November 18, 1996, refer to the IRS website.

Note 2: When annuity benefits with starting dates after 1997 are paid over two lives (joint and survivor annuities), a different set of denominators must be used in line 3.

Combined Age of Annuitants	Number of Payments
110 or under	410
111–120	360
121–130	310
131–140	260
141 or older	210

Example   Joey, age 67, began receiving benefits under a qualified joint and survivor annuity to be paid over the joint lives of himself and his wife Jody, who is 64. He received his first annuity payment in March of the current year (10 payments this year). Joey contributed $38,000 after-tax to the annuity and he had no distributions from the plan before the current year. The monthly payment to Joey is $1,700.

Joey must use the simplified method to calculate his taxable amount. Using the worksheet, Joey's taxable amount for the current year would be:

Simplified Method Worksheet

1. Enter total amount received this year.   1. $17,000
2. Enter cost in the plan at the annuity starting date.   2. $38,000
3. Combined age at annuity starting date

	Enter	
110 or under	410	
111–120	360	
121–130	310	3. 260
131–140	260	
141 or older	210	

4. Divide line 2 by line 3.   4. $ 146
5. Multiply line 4 by the number of monthly payments this year.   5. $ 1,460
6. Enter the amount, if any, recovered tax free in prior years.   6. $ 0
7. Subtract line 6 from line 2.   7. $38,000
8. Enter the smaller of line 5 or 7.   8. $ 1,460
9. Taxable amount this year: Subtract line 8 from line 1. Do not enter less than zero. ♦   9. $15,540

The exclusion ratio (the result on line 4 of the Simplified Method Worksheet) is calculated at the start of the annuity and remains constant. For annuities starting after 1986, the maximum amount excludable is limited to the taxpayer's investment in the annuity. After the taxpayer's investment is recovered, all additional amounts received are fully taxable. If the taxpayer dies before the entire investment is recovered, any unrecovered amount is permitted as a miscellaneous itemized deduction (not subject to the 2-percent floor) at the time of the annuitant's death. For annuities starting before 1987, the exclusion ratio is used for the life of the annuitant, even after full recovery of the investment. For these earlier annuities, if the annuitant dies prior to recovering the entire investment, the unrecovered portion is lost.

2-7b The General Rule

Prior to implementation of the Simplified Method covered above, the General Rule was used for most annuities and is still used for nonqualified annuities. Rather than use the denominators provided in line 3 of the Simplified Method Worksheet, the life expectancy of the annuitant was determined based on mortality tables provided by the IRS. The excluded amount under the general rule can be calculated as follows:

$$\text{Amount Excluded} = \frac{\text{Investment in Contract}}{\text{Annual Payment} \times \text{Life Expectancy}} \times \text{Amount Received}$$

2-7c Reporting Annuities

Both annuities and pensions are reported to taxpayers on Form 1099-R (refer to Figure 2.5). Much of the information necessary to compute the taxable portion of the annuity distribution will be reported on Form 1099-R including the total distributions made during the year (Box 1), the taxable portion if determined by the payor (Box 2a), and total annuitant contributions made to the annuity (Box 9b). As with other reporting forms, any tax withheld (Box 4) should be reported on the tax return. If the taxable portion is not included on the 1099-R then the simplified method or general rule must be employed to determine the taxable portion.

Figure 2.5 Form 1099-R

2-7d Exclusion for Public Safety Officers

An eligible retired public safety officer (law enforcement officer, firefighter, chaplain, or member of a rescue squad or ambulance crew who is retired because of disability or because of reaching normal retirement age), can elect to exclude up to $3,000 from income distributions made from an eligible retirement plan that are used to pay the premiums for coverage by an accident or health plan or a long-term care insurance contract. The premiums can be for coverage for the retired public safety officer, their spouse, or dependents. The distribution must be from the plan maintained by the employer from which the public safety officer retired.

To make the election, reduce the otherwise taxable amount of the pension or annuity by the amount paid for accident or health insurance up to $3,000. The taxable amount shown in box 2a of Form 1099-R will not reflect the exclusion. Total distributions from pensions are reported on Form 1040 (and SR), line 5a. Reduce the taxable amount by the exclusion and report on Form 1040, line 5b. Enter "PSO" next to the appropriate line on which the taxable amount is reported.

The amount excluded from your income can't be used to claim a medical expense deduction.

Example Ed Frock is a retired Federal Bureau of Investigation (FBI) agent. He receives a Form 1099-R from the FBI reporting distributions of $56,000 in 2024. Using the simplified method, Ed computes the taxable amount as $53,222. Although Ed is covered by Medicare, he pays the supplemental insurance (Medigap) premiums of $3,400 in 2024. Ed elects to exclude $3,000 of the Medigap premiums and reports a taxable pension amount of $50,222 on line 5b of his Form 1040. ♦

Self-Study Problem 2.7
Refer to Appendix E for Solutions to Self-Study Problems

Phil retired in January 2024 at age 63. His pension is $2,400 per month and this year he received 10 payments. Phil's remaining life expectancy is 21 years. He received the following Form 1099-R:

PAYER'S name, address: Pierce Corporation Pension Plan, 6200 Winnetka Avenue, Woodland Hills, CA 91371	**1 Gross distribution:** $24,000.00	**Form 1099-R (2024)**
PAYER'S TIN: 24-7654567	**RECIPIENT'S TIN:** 120-66-4377	
2a Taxable amount: (blank)	**2b Taxable amount not determined:** X	
4 Federal income tax withheld: $2,400.00		
RECIPIENT'S name: Phillip Ventura	**Street address:** 1001 Chawareewong Blvd.	**City:** Sharman Oaks, CA 91403
7 Distribution code(s): 7	**9b Total employee contributions:** $47,880.00	

a. Calculate Phil's taxable income from the annuity in the current year, using the general rule.

b. Calculate Phil's taxable income using the Simplified Method Worksheet found on Page 2-20.

2-8 Life Insurance

2.8 Learning Objective: Describe the tax treatment of life insurance proceeds.

A major exclusion from gross income is provided for life insurance proceeds. To be excluded, the proceeds must be paid to the beneficiary by reason of the death of the insured. If the proceeds are taken over several years instead of a lump sum, the insurance company pays interest on the unpaid proceeds. The interest is generally taxable income.

Early payouts of life insurance, also called accelerated death benefits or viatical settlements, are excluded from gross income for certain terminally or chronically ill taxpayers. The taxpayer may either collect an early payout from the insurance company or sell or assign the policy to a viatical settlement provider. A terminally ill individual must be certified by a medical doctor to have an illness which is reasonably expected to cause death within 24 months. A chronically ill individual must be certified by a medical doctor as unable to perform daily living activities without assistance. Chronically ill taxpayers may only exclude gain on accelerated death benefits to the extent proceeds are used for long-term care.

If an insurance policy is transferred to another person for valuable consideration, all or a portion of the proceeds from the life insurance policy may be taxable to the recipient. For example, taxable proceeds result when a policy is transferred to a creditor in payment of a debt. When a transfer for value occurs, the proceeds at the death of the insured are taxable to the extent they exceed the cash surrender value of the policy at the time it was transferred, plus the amount of the insurance premiums paid by the purchaser. There is an exception to the rule for policies transferred for valuable consideration resulting in taxable proceeds. Transfers to a partner of the insured, a partnership in which the insured is a partner, or a corporation in which the insured is an officer or a shareholder do not cause the policy proceeds to be taxable. The sale of the insurance policy will also generally trigger a gain to the original holder of the policy in the amount of the proceeds over the total premiums paid by the original holder of the policy.

The sale or transfer of an insurance policy will generally generate two reporting forms. The acquirer of the life insurance policy is required to file Form 1099-LS to report the amount paid for the contract and the date of sale. The life insurance company associated with the policy is required to file Form 1099-SB which reports the investment in the contract made by the owner and the cash surrender value at the time of sale.

Example Howard dies on January 15, 2020, and leaves Wanda, his wife, a $50,000 insurance policy, the proceeds of which she elects to receive as $10,000 per year plus interest for five years. In the current year, Wanda receives $10,500 ($10,000 + $500 interest). She must include the $500 of interest as income. ♦

Example Monique owns a life insurance policy at the time she is diagnosed with a terminal illness. After her diagnosis, she sells the policy to Viatical Settlements, Inc., for $100,000. Monique is not required to include the gain on the sale of the insurance in her gross income. ♦

Example Kalani transfers to Bill an insurance policy with a face value of $40,000 and a cash surrender value of $10,000 for the cancellation of a $10,000 debt owed to Bill. The total amount of premiums paid by Kalani is $6,000. Kalani will recognize a gain of $4,000 ($10,000 proceeds less $6,000 premiums paid). Bill continues to make payments, and after two years Bill has paid $2,000 in premiums. Kalani dies and Bill collects the $40,000. Since the transfer was for valuable consideration, Bill must include $28,000 in taxable income, which is equal to the $40,000 total proceeds less $10,000 value at the time of transfer and $2,000 of premiums Bill paid. If Kalani and Bill were partners in the same partnership, the entire proceeds ($40,000) would be tax-free. ♦

Self-Study Problem 2.8
Refer to Appendix E for Solutions to Self-Study Problems

a. On March 19, 2017, Alysha dies and leaves Giannis an insurance policy with a face value of $100,000. Alysha is Giannis' sister, and Giannis elects to take the proceeds over 10 years ($10,000 plus interest each year). This year Giannis receives $11,250 from the insurance company. How much income must Giannis report for the current year?

b. Kamala transfers her life insurance policy to Tim (not a viatical settlement) and received the following Forms 1099-LS and 1099-SB.

```
☐ CORRECTED (if checked)
ACQUIRER'S name, street address, city or town, state or province, country,    1 Amount paid to payment    OMB No. 1545-2281
ZIP or foreign postal code, and telephone no.                                   recipient
    Timothy Waltz                                                              $ 12,000.00               Form 1099-LS           Reportable Life
    260 W Bridge St                                                            2 Date of sale            (Rev. December 2019)   Insurance Sale
    West Point, NE 68788                                                          01/06/2024             For calendar year
                                                                                                         20 24
ACQUIRER'S TIN           PAYMENT RECIPIENT'S TIN           Issuer's name                                                         Copy B
123-77-8888              244-21-5193                       Washington Mutual Life Ins. Co.                                       For Payment
                                                                                                                                 Recipient
PAYMENT RECIPIENT'S name                                   Acquirer's information contact name, street address, city or
    Kamala Charis                                          town, state or province, country, ZIP or foreign postal code,         This is important tax
                                                           and telephone no. (if different from ACQUIRER)                        information and is being
                                                                                                                                 furnished to the IRS. If
Street address (including apt. no.)                                                                                              you are required to file a
    288 E 18th Street                                                                                                            return, a negligence
City or town, state or province, country, and ZIP or foreign postal code                                                         penalty or other
    Oakland, CA 94606                                                                                                            sanction may be
                                                                                                                                 imposed on you if this
Policy number                                                                                                                    item is required to be
                                                                                                                                 reported and the IRS
                                                                                                                                 determines that it has
                                                                                                                                 not been reported.
Form 1099-LS (Rev. 12-2019)       (keep for your records)       www.irs.gov/Form1099LS    Department of the Treasury - Internal Revenue Service
```

Self-Study Problem 2.8, continued
Refer to Appendix E for Solutions to Self-Study Problems

	☐ CORRECTED (if checked)	
ISSUER'S name, street address, city or town, state or province, country, ZIP or foreign postal code, and telephone no. Washington Mutual Life Insurance Co. 11299 Illinois St Suite 200 Carmel, IN 46032	1 Investment in contract $ 8,564.00 2 Surrender amount $ $10,000.00	OMB No. 1545-2281 Form **1099-SB** (Rev. December 2019) For calendar year 20 **24**	Seller's Investment in Life Insurance Contract
ISSUER'S TIN 54-1245678	SELLER'S TIN 244-21-5193	Issuer's information contact name, street address, city or town, state or province, country, ZIP or foreign postal code, and telephone no. (if different from ISSUER)	Copy B For Seller This is important tax information and is being furnished to the IRS. If you are required to file a return, a negligence penalty or other sanction may be imposed on you if this item is required to be reported and the IRS determines that it has not been reported.
SELLER'S name Kamala Charis			
Street address (including apt. no.) 288 E 18th Street			
City or town, state or province, country, and ZIP or foreign postal code Oakland, CA 94606			
Policy number			

Form **1099-SB** (Rev. 12-2019) (keep for your records) www.irs.gov/Form1099SB Department of the Treasury - Internal Revenue Service

What is the amount of gain that Kamala will recognize on the transfer?

2-9 Interest Income

2.9 Learning Objective
Identify the tax treatment of interest income.

Any interest a taxpayer receives or that is credited to their account is taxable income, unless it is specifically exempt from tax such as state or municipal bond interest. If the interest totals more than $1,500, the taxpayer is required to file Schedule B of Form 1040, which instructs the taxpayer to list the amounts and sources of the income.

The fair market value of gifts or services a taxpayer receives for making long-term deposits or opening accounts in savings institutions is also taxable interest income. Interest is reported in the year it is received by a cash-basis taxpayer.

> **Tax Break**
>
> Taxpayers may defer reporting interest income on a bank certificate of deposit (CD) if the CD has a maturity of one year or less and there is a substantial penalty for early withdrawal. For example, assume an investor purchases a six-month CD on September 1, 2023, which matures on March 1, 2024, and the bank charges a penalty equal to two months of interest in the event of early withdrawal. In this case, the four months of interest earned on the account during 2023 will not have to be reported until the investor's 2024 tax return is filed.
>
> When a taxpayer withdraws funds early from a CD and must pay a penalty as described above, the full amount of the interest is reported as income and the penalty may be deducted on Form 1040 as a deduction for adjusted gross income.

2-9a U.S. Savings Bonds

The U.S. government issues three basic types of savings bonds to individuals: Series I Bonds, Series EE Bonds, and Series HH Bonds.

Series I Bonds can be purchased directly up to $10,000 per person or through an income tax refund for up to $5,000. I bonds are issued with a fixed interest rate component and an inflation-adjusted interest rate component that is reset every six months. In late 2024, I bonds were paying an interest rate of 4.3 percent. I Bonds can be sold after five years with no penalty or after 12 months with a three-month interest penalty. Interest is paid to the I Bond holder when the bond is redeemed.

Example Zelda purchases $10,000 of I Bonds on January 1, 2024, when the rate is 6 percent. On July 1, 2024, the I Bond rate resets to 5 percent. She earns interest of $557.50 in 2024. Zelda elects to defer interest recognition and therefore has no taxable interest income from I Bonds in 2024. In 2030, Zelda sells the I Bonds and receives $13,946. She will recognize $3,946 of interest income in 2030. ♦

Series EE Bonds, whether purchased at a discount (before 2012) or at face value, increase in value over their life at a fixed rate of interest for the first 20 years of the bond's life. In late 2024, EE Bonds are paying 2.7 percent. After 20 years, the bond's value is doubled from the original purchase price with a one-time adjustment. EE Bonds pay interest when the bond is redeemed and have the same restrictions on redemptions as I bonds.

Cash-basis taxpayers report the increase in redemption value (interest) on an I or EE Bond using one of the following methods:

(1) The interest may be reported in the year the bonds are cashed or in the year they mature, whichever is earlier (no election is required to use this method), or
(2) The taxpayer may elect to report the increase in redemption value each year.

If the taxpayer wants to change from method (1) to method (2), they may do so without the permission of the IRS. In the year of change, all interest earned to date and not previously reported must be reported on all I and EE Bonds held by the taxpayer. Once method (2) is selected, the taxpayer must continue to use it for all I and EE Bonds currently held or acquired in the future. Taxpayers cannot change back to method (1) without permission of the IRS.

If the taxpayer uses the interest from I or EE Bonds to pay for higher education costs, the interest can be excluded from gross income. To exclude the savings bond interest under this provision, the I and EE bonds must have been redeemed in the same tax year as the payment of the higher education expenses for the taxpayer, spouse, or dependent. The I or EE Bonds must have been purchased when the taxpayer was at least 24 years of age. Married filing separately taxpayers are not eligible for the exclusion. In 2024, the exclusion is phased out for taxpayers with adjusted gross income (excluding the bond interest and without a deduction for student loan interest) of over $145,200 for married filing jointly and $96,800 for all others. The phase-out range is $30,000 for married filing jointly and $15,000 for all others.

Example Jorge, a married filing jointly taxpayer, cashes out Series EE Bonds that qualify for the higher education costs exclusion, for a value of $45,000 in 2024. He purchased the bonds for $37,000 and thus has $8,000 of potentially excludable interest. He pays $16,000 in qualified higher education expenses for his son to attend college. Jorge's 2024 AGI not including the bond interest or any student loan interest deduction is $154,200. Form 8815 on Page 2-27 presents Jorge's $1,994 exclusion for Series EE bond interest associated with higher education. ♦

Form 8815 is used to report the higher education exclusion of interest from EE or I bonds.

Series HH Bonds were last issued in August 2004 and have a 20-year maturity. HH Bonds were issued at face value and pay interest twice a year. Interest on Series HH Bonds is reported in the year received by a cash-basis taxpayer.

Form **8815**	**Exclusion of Interest From Series EE and I U.S. Savings Bonds Issued After 1989** (For Filers With Qualified Higher Education Expenses) Attach to Form 1040 or 1040-SR. Go to *www.irs.gov/Form8815* for the latest information.	OMB No. 1545-0074
Department of the Treasury Internal Revenue Service		**2024** Attachment Sequence No. **167**

Name(s) shown on return	Your social security number
Jorge and Araceli Gomez	131-31-3131

1
(a) Name of person (you, your spouse, or your dependent) who was enrolled at or attended an eligible educational institution	(b) Name and address of eligible educational institution
Oscar Gomez	Southern California State University
	1000 Wilshire Blvd, Santa Monica, CA 90401

If you need more space, attach a statement.

2	Enter the total qualified higher education expenses you paid in 2024 for the person(s) listed in column (a) of line 1. See the instructions to find out which expenses qualify.	**2**	16,000
3	Enter the total of any nontaxable educational benefits (such as nontaxable scholarship or fellowship grants) received for 2024 for the person(s) listed in column (a) of line 1. See instructions	**3**	0
4	Subtract line 3 from line 2. If zero or less, **stop.** You **cannot** take the exclusion	**4**	16,000
5	Enter the total proceeds (principal and interest) from all series EE and I U.S. savings bonds **issued after 1989** that you **cashed during 2024**	**5**	45,000
6	Enter the interest included on line 5. See instructions	**6**	8,000
7	If line 4 is equal to or more than line 5, enter "1.000." If line 4 is less than line 5, divide line 4 by line 5. Enter the result as a decimal (rounded to at least three places)	**7** ×	.356
8	Multiply line 6 by line 7	**8**	2,848
9	Enter your modified adjusted gross income. See instructions **9** 154,200		
	Note: If line 9 is $111,800 or more if single, head of household, or qualifying surviving spouse; or $175,200 or more if married filing jointly, **stop.** You **cannot** take the exclusion.		
10	Enter $96,800 if single, head of household, or qualifying surviving spouse; or $145,200 if married filing jointly **10** 145,200		
11	Subtract line 10 from line 9. If zero or less, skip line 12, enter -0- on line 13, and go to line 14 . . . . **11** 9,000		
12	Divide line 11 by $15,000 if single, head of household, or qualifying surviving spouse; or $30,000 if married filing jointly. Enter the result as a decimal (rounded to at least three places)	**12** ×	.300
13	Multiply line 8 by line 12	**13**	854
14	**Excludable savings bond interest.** Subtract line 13 from line 8. Enter the result here and on Schedule B (Form 1040), line 3	**14**	1,994

For Paperwork Reduction Act Notice, see your tax return instructions. Cat. No. 10822S Form **8815** (2024)

Source: Department of the Treasury—Internal Revenue Service

2-9b Bond Interest

A common source of interest income is from the ownership of bonds. The traditional definition of a bond is a fixed-income debt instrument that represents a loan made by an investor to a borrower. The return paid for the use of the money is interest and is generally gross income. Bonds are issued by a wide variety of sources including corporations, federal and state governments, and related agencies.

U.S. Treasury Bills, Notes, and Bonds

Treasury bills, notes, and bonds are direct debts of the United States government. Unlike municipal bonds, interest earned on U.S. government debt is subject to federal income tax but has the advantage of being exempt for individual state income taxes. Treasury bills (T-bills) are debt issued at a discount (a price lower than the face or par value) by the government typically in durations of one year or less. At maturity, the T-bill owner is paid the full par value. The difference between the purchase price and the maturity value is generally interest income. Treasury notes have a fixed rate for durations of two, three, five, seven, and 10 years and pay interest every six months. Treasury bonds are similar to notes but have 20 and 30-year durations.

Corporate Bonds

Many large corporations issue bonds of varying maturities to provide capital to operate or expand their business. Corporate bonds generally pay interest every six months, although the terms of any specific bond can vary. Corporations can also issue zero coupon bonds at a deep discount, which do not have any "coupon" interest rate. Instead, as the bond matures, interest is added to the principal value of the bond until reaching par value at maturity. As a result, these bonds pay no interest until maturity (much like T-bills). The tax rules classify that discount as original issue discount or OID. The details of OID are outside the scope of this textbook but generally, a portion of OID is included in the bond holder's taxable income. OID is reported to the bond holder on Form 1099-OID.

State and Local Bonds (Municipals)

In 1913 when the Sixteenth Amendment was enacted, Congress questioned the constitutionality of taxing the interest earned on state and local government obligations. Congress provided an exclusion from taxpayers' income for the interest on such bonds. To qualify for the exclusion, the interest must be from an obligation of a state, territory, or possession of the United States, a political subdivision of the foregoing, or of the District of Columbia. For example, Puerto Rico bonds qualify for the exclusion. Federal obligations, such as treasury bills and treasury bonds, do not qualify.

The interest exclusion allows high-income taxpayers to lend money to state and local governments at lower interest rates (discounts).

Example Rigby is considering two different bond investments. This first option is a corporate taxable bond that yields a pre-tax return of 8.4 percent. The second option is a tax-exempt municipal bond that yields 6.5 percent. If Rigby is in the 35-percent tax bracket, the after-tax return of the taxable bonds can be computed as:

$$\text{After-tax return} = \text{Pre-tax return} \times (1 - \text{tax rate})$$
$$5.46\% = 8.4\% \times (1 - 0.35)$$

Since the tax-exempt bond is not subject to tax, the after-tax return is 6.5 percent and thus, is preferable. Using a re-arranged version of the same formula can determine what the equivalent yield on a taxable bond would need to be to make Rigby indifferent between the two bonds (all other terms being equal):

$$\text{After-tax return} = \text{Tax-free return} / (1 - \text{tax rate})$$
$$10.0\% = 6.5\%/(1 - 0.35) \blacklozenge$$

Typically, interest rates on municipal bonds reflect the after-tax return that compensates for higher income tax rates (35 or 37 percent) and thus tax-exempt bonds will often have a lower after-tax yield than a taxable bond in the hands of a lower-income investor.

Example Mordecai is also considering the same bonds as Rigby in the previous example; however, Mordecai is in the 22-percent tax bracket. The after-tax return on the corporate bond is 6.55 percent [8.4% × (1 − 0.22)]. In Mordecai's situation, the after-tax return on the taxable corporate bond is greater than the tax-exempt return of 6.5 percent on the municipal bond. $\blacklozenge$

> **Tax Break**
>
> Taxpayers in low tax brackets are likely to find that they earn a higher overall return investing in taxable bonds rather than comparable tax-free municipal bonds. This is because the smaller tax benefit from the municipal bonds does not make up for the reduced interest rate paid on municipal bonds. Municipal bonds are also generally not appropriate investments for IRAs or other retirement accounts since income on these accounts is excluded from tax until withdrawn.

Bond Discount and Premium

For the most part, bonds of all types can be bought and sold on the secondary market at just about any time. This creates two challenges for taxpayers to consider: (1) the accrual of interest when bonds are purchased and sold between interest payment dates and (2) fluctuations in bond price creating market discount and premiums.

If a taxpayer sells a bond between interest payment dates, part of the sales price represents interest accrued to the date of sale. The interest portion of the sales price must be reported as interest income for the year of sale.

Example Helga purchases at issuance a $10,000 bond that pays 5 percent annually on December 31. On January 31, she sells the bond for $10,042 to Hagar. The proceeds include $42 of interest accrued from the date of the last interest payment ($10,000 × 5% ÷ 365 × 31 days). Because on December 31, the holder of the bond is going to receive the entire coupon amount of $500 ($10,000 × 5%), Helga includes her share of the interest in her sales proceeds but treats the $42 as interest income, not as a gain on the sale of the bond. ♦

Example Continued from the previous example, Hagar will receive $500 of interest on December 31; however, he must deduct $42 to reflect only the interest he earned. The IRS recommends reporting the full $500 on Line 1 of Schedule B (if required) and then reporting the reduction as "Accrued Interest" on the last line above Line 2 of Schedule B. ♦

Bonds that are issued at a fixed rate of interest will often change in price when prevailing interest rates more broadly increase or decrease.

Example Mabel owns a $10,000 30-year bond with a 4-percent annual interest rate, that matures in 28 years. Due to economic and market fluctuations, prevailing interest rates increase and thus bonds similar to Mabel's are now paying interest rates of 6 percent. If Mabel wishes to sell a 4-percent bond to investors that are seeking a 6 percent return, since the interest rate on the bond is fixed, Mabel will have to sell the bond at a discount (a price lower than the par value of the bond) for only $7,319. In this way, the purchaser will collect the 4-percent coupon rate as well as the increase in value to maturity of $2,681, and thus a 6-percent yield. ♦

The price of bonds has an inverse relationship with prevailing interest rates. If prevailing interest rates increase, bond prices decrease and if interest rates decrease bond prices increase. The resulting market discount and premium must be reflected as an addition to or a reduction of interest income by the bond holder. The mechanics of bond discount and premium are outside the scope of this textbook but in general, discount can be included in income each year or included at the sale or maturity of the bond. Market premium is generally amortized each year as a reduction of interest income and a commensurate reduction of basis in the bond. For tax-exempt state and local bonds, premium must be amortized. The rules for market discount and premium are complex. Refer to IRS Publication 550 for additional details.

2-9c Below Market Loans

Individuals may often make smaller loans to one another with interest rates that are below prevailing market rates. Common below-market loans are between friends or family (gift loans), between a business and its employee, or between a business and an owner.

Example   Chuck loans his daughter, Elaine, $15,000 to help with the purchase of a new car. Out of affection for his daughter, Chuck charges no interest on the loan (the loan is a bona fide loan in all other respects). Elaine benefits from the use of $15,000 and is not required to compensate Chuck through the payment of interest. ♦

The tax law requires the lender in a gift loan to recognize foregone interest income that reflects the applicable federal rate of interest on similar loans. The applicable federal rates are issued by the IRS each month.

Example   Continuing with the previous example, the applicable federal rate for Chuck's loan to Elaine is 4 percent. If the balance of the loan is $15,000 for the entire year, Chuck will recognize deemed interest income of $600 ($15,000 × 4%). Since Chuck does not actually receive $600 from Elaine, he is treated as having gifted the $600 back to Elaine. ♦

The borrower in a gift loan is treated as having deemed interest expense based on the applicable federal rate. In many situations, the deemed interest expense is personal interest expense and not deductible by the borrower (refer to Chapter 5).

Below market gift loans and loans from an employer to an employee are not subject to the deemed interest rules if the loan amount is $10,000 or less.

Example   Jon loans his daughter Angelina $1,000 at a zero-percent interest rate. The gift loan is not subject to the below market loan rules and Jon is not required to recognize deemed interest income. ♦

The rules that apply to below market loans between a business and its employees or owners are outside the scope of this textbook.

2-9d Reporting Interest Income

Generally, interest amounts of at least $10 must be reported by the payor to the recipient on a Form 1099-INT. On the Form 1099-INT, most taxable interest is reported in Box 1. The penalty for early withdrawal from a deposit account is reported in Box 2 and if paid is generally deductible as a for adjusted gross income (AGI) or "above-the-line" deduction (refer to Chapter 5). Because states may not tax interest from U.S. government obligations such as Treasury Bills, Treasury Bonds, and U.S. savings bonds, interest from these items is reported in Box 3. Tax-exempt interest is reported in Box 8 and to the extent the payor withheld income tax, that amount is reported in Box 4 and should be included on Line 25b of Form 1040. Taxable interest from each payor is reported on Schedule B (presented on Page 2-32) if interest totals more than $1,500 or is simply totaled on Line 2b of Form 1040 if less than $1,500. Tax-exempt interest is reported on Line 2a of Form 1040 (but not on Schedule B). Payments on deposits held by cooperative banks, credit unions, domestic savings and loan associations, and federal savings and loan associations are often described as "dividends;" however, these payments represent interest and will generally be reported on a Form 1099-INT.

Self-Study Problem 2.9

Refer to Appendix E for Solutions to Self-Study Problems

Christy and John Harris-Thomas received the following Form 1099-INTs during 2024:

Form 1099-INT (Rev. January 2024) — Interest Income

- CORRECTED (if checked): ☐
- PAYER'S name, street address, city or town, state or province, country, ZIP or foreign postal code, and telephone no.:
  Lake Osbourne Savings and Loan
  4400 S. Congressional Avenue
  Lake Worth, FL 33461
- Payer's RTN (optional):
- OMB No. 1545-0112
- Box 1 Interest income: $1,217.78
- For calendar year: 2024
- PAYER'S TIN: 13-2122333
- RECIPIENT'S TIN: 313-44-5454
- Box 2 Early withdrawal penalty:
- Box 3 Interest on U.S. Savings Bonds and Treasury obligations:
- Box 4 Federal income tax withheld:
- Box 5 Investment expenses:
- RECIPIENT'S name: Christy Harris-Thomas
- Street address: 1112 Constitution Avenue, NW
- City, state, ZIP: Washington, DC 20224
- Box 6 Foreign tax paid:
- Box 7 Foreign country or U.S. territory:
- Box 8 Tax-exempt interest:
- Box 9 Specified private activity bond interest:
- Box 10 Market discount:
- Box 11 Bond premium:
- Box 12 Bond premium on Treasury obligations:
- Box 13 Bond premium on tax-exempt bond:
- Box 14 Tax-exempt and tax credit bond CUSIP no.:
- Box 15 State: Box 16 State identification no.: Box 17 State tax withheld:

2024 Combined Forms 1099

This is important tax information and is being furnished to the IRS (except as indicated). If you are required to file a return, a negligence penalty or other sanction may be imposed on you if this income is taxable and the IRS determines that it has not been reported.

Copy B For Recipient
OMB No. 1545-0110

Friar Tuck Investments
38 Wall Street, 8th Floor
New York, NY 10005

John and Christy Harris-Thomas
1112 Constitution Ave., NW
Washington DC 20224

Account Number: 3100987765
Tax ID: ***-**-5454
Payer's Federal Tax ID: 33-1357246
Financial Adviser/Phone: Will Scarlett 888-555-1212

Form 1099-INT — Interest Income

Box 1 Interest income	Box 2 Early withdrawal penalty	Box 3 Interest on U.S. Savings Bonds and Treasury obligations
365.12		700.00

Box 4 Federal income tax withheld	Box 5 Investment expenses	Box 6 Foreign Tax Paid

Box 7 Foreign country or U.S. possession	Box 8 Tax-exempt interest	Box 9 Specified private activity bond interest
	350.00	

Box 10 Market Discount	Box 11 Bond Premium

Box 12 Bond premium on Treasury obligations	Box 13 Bond premium on tax-exempt bond

According to Christy and John's records, they purchased US Treasury bonds between interest payments and paid accrued interest of $105.67 to the seller.

Complete Part I of Schedule B of Form 1040 on Page 2-32 for the Harris-Thomas' 2024 tax year.

Self-Study Problems 2.9 and 2.10

SCHEDULE B (Form 1040)
Department of the Treasury
Internal Revenue Service

Interest and Ordinary Dividends
Attach to Form 1040 or 1040-SR.
Go to www.irs.gov/ScheduleB for instructions and the latest information.

OMB No. 1545-0074

Attachment Sequence No. 08

Name(s) shown on return | Your social security number

Part I — Interest

(See instructions and the Instructions for Form 1040, line 2b.)

Note: If you received a Form 1099-INT, Form 1099-OID, or substitute statement from a brokerage firm, list the firm's name as the payer and enter the total interest shown on that form.

1. List name of payer. If any interest is from a seller-financed mortgage and the buyer used the property as a personal residence, see the instructions and list this interest first. Also, show that buyer's social security number and address: **Amount**

2. Add the amounts on line 1 . . . . **2**

3. Excludable interest on series EE and I U.S. savings bonds issued after 1989. Attach Form 8815 . . . . **3**

4. Subtract line 3 from line 2. Enter the result here and on Form 1040 or 1040-SR, line 2b **4**

Note: If line 4 is over $1,500, you must complete Part III.

Part II — Ordinary Dividends

(See instructions and the Instructions for Form 1040, line 3b.)

Note: If you received a Form 1099-DIV or substitute statement from a brokerage firm, list the firm's name as the payer and enter the ordinary dividends shown on that form.

5. List name of payer: **Amount**

6. Add the amounts on line 5. Enter the total here and on Form 1040 or 1040-SR, line 3b **6**

Note: If line 6 is over $1,500, you must complete Part III.

Part III — Foreign Accounts and Trusts

You must complete this part if you **(a)** had over $1,500 of taxable interest or ordinary dividends; **(b)** had a foreign account; or **(c)** received a distribution from, or were a grantor of, or a transferor to, a foreign trust.

Caution: If required, failure to file FinCEN Form 114 may result in substantial penalties. Additionally, you may be required to file Form 8938, Statement of Specified Foreign Financial Assets. See instructions.

		Yes	No

7a. At any time during 2024, did you have a financial interest in or signature authority over a financial account (such as a bank account, securities account, or brokerage account) located in a foreign country? See instructions . . . .

If "Yes," are you required to file FinCEN Form 114, Report of Foreign Bank and Financial Accounts (FBAR), to report that financial interest or signature authority? See FinCEN Form 114 and its instructions for filing requirements and exceptions to those requirements . . . . . .

b. If you are required to file FinCEN Form 114, list the name(s) of the foreign country(-ies) where the financial account(s) is (are) located:

8. During 2024, did you receive a distribution from, or were you the grantor of, or transferor to, a foreign trust? If "Yes," you may have to file Form 3520. See instructions . . . .

For Paperwork Reduction Act Notice, see your tax return instructions. Cat. No. 17146N Schedule B (Form 1040) 2024

Source: Department of the Treasury—Internal Revenue Service

Self-Study Problem 2.10

Qualified Dividends and Capital Gain Tax Worksheet—Line 16

Keep for Your Records

Before you begin:
- ✓ See the earlier instructions for line 16 to see if you can use this worksheet to figure your tax.
- ✓ Before completing this worksheet, complete Form 1040 or 1040-SR through line 15.
- ✓ If you don't have to file Schedule D and you received capital gain distributions, be sure you checked the box on Form 1040 or 1040-SR, line 7.

1. Enter the amount from Form 1040 or 1040-SR, line 15. However, if you are filing Form 2555 (relating to foreign earned income), enter the amount from line 3 of the Foreign Earned Income Tax Worksheet ..... **1.** _____
2. Enter the amount from Form 1040 or 1040-SR, line 3a* ..... **2.** _____
3. Are you filing Schedule D?*
   - ☐ **Yes.** Enter the **smaller** of line 15 or 16 of Schedule D. If either line 15 or 16 is blank or a loss, enter -0-.
   - ☐ **No.** Enter the amount from Form 1040 or 1040-SR, line 7. ..... **3.** _____
4. Add lines 2 and 3 ..... **4.** _____
5. Subtract line 4 from line 1. If zero or less, enter -0- ..... **5.** _____
6. Enter:
   $47,025 if single or married filing separately,
   $94,050 if married filing jointly or qualifying widow(er),
   $63,000 if head of household. ..... **6.** _____
7. Enter the smaller of line 1 or line 6 ..... **7.** _____
8. Enter the smaller of line 5 or line 7 ..... **8.** _____
9. Subtract line 8 from line 7. This amount is taxed at 0% ..... **9.** _____
10. Enter the smaller of line 1 or line 4 ..... **10.** _____
11. Enter the amount from line 9 ..... **11.** _____
12. Subtract line 11 from line 10 ..... **12.** _____
13. Enter:
    $518,900 if single,
    $291,850 if married filing separately,
    $583,750 if married filing jointly or qualifying widow(er),
    $551,350 if head of household. ..... **13.** _____
14. Enter the smaller of line 1 or line 13 ..... **14.** _____
15. Add lines 5 and 9 ..... **15.** _____
16. Subtract line 15 from line 14. If zero or less, enter -0- ..... **16.** _____
17. Enter the smaller of line 12 or line 16 ..... **17.** _____
18. Multiply line 17 by 15% (0.15) ..... **18.** _____
19. Add lines 9 and 17 ..... **19.** _____
20. Subtract line 19 from line 10 ..... **20.** _____
21. Multiply line 20 by 20% (0.20) ..... **21.** _____
22. Figure the tax on the amount on line 5. If the amount on line 5 is less than $100,000, use the Tax Table to figure the tax. If the amount on line 5 is $100,000 or more, use the Tax Computation Worksheet ..... **22.** _____
23. Add lines 18, 21, and 22 ..... **23.** _____
24. Figure the tax on the amount on line 1. If the amount on line 1 is less than $100,000, use the Tax Table to figure the tax. If the amount on line 1 is $100,000 or more, use the Tax Computation Worksheet ..... **24.** _____
25. **Tax on all taxable income.** Enter the **smaller** of line 23 or 24. Also include this amount on the entry space on Form 1040 or 1040-SR, line 16. If you are filing Form 2555, don't enter this amount on the entry space on Form 1040 or 1040-SR, line 16. Instead, enter it on line 4 of the Foreign Earned Income Tax Worksheet ..... **25.** _____

* If you are filing Form 2555, see the footnote in the Foreign Earned Income Tax Worksheet before completing this line.

This worksheet adapted from the 2023 worksheet.

Learning Objective 2.10

Identify the tax treatment of dividend income.

2-10 Dividend Income

2-10a Dividends

Dividends are a type of distribution paid to a shareholder by a corporation. Taxpayers may receive the following types of distributions from a corporation, mutual fund, or similar investment that owns corporate stocks:

1. Ordinary and qualified dividends
2. Nontaxable distributions
3. Capital gain distributions

Ordinary dividends are by far the most common type of corporate distribution. They are paid from the earnings and profits of the corporation. Ordinary dividends are also qualifying dividends if the stock is held for a certain amount of time (generally sixty days) and the dividend is issued by a U.S. corporation. If the ordinary dividends are not qualifying dividends, then instead of being taxed at the lower long-term capital gains rate, they will be taxed at the ordinary income rate. Corporations issuing dividends and brokerage companies holding stock investments for taxpayers are required to classify and report the amount of qualifying dividends to investors.

Nontaxable distributions are a return of invested capital and are not paid from the earnings and profits of the corporation. They are considered a return of the taxpayer's investment in the corporation and are not included in the taxpayer's income. Instead, the taxpayer's basis in the stock is reduced by nontaxable distributions until the basis reaches zero.[1] After the stock has reached a zero basis, distributions that represent a return of capital are taxed as capital gains. Capital gain distributions are reported on Line 7 of Forms 1040 or 1040-SR or, if required, Schedule D, Line 13.

2-10b Current Tax Rates for Dividends

For years, experts have argued that corporate dividends are taxed twice, once when the corporation pays tax on profits, and once when the dividend is received by the shareholder. As presented in Table 2.6, to provide some tax relief for individual taxpayers who receive corporate dividends, the tax rates on qualifying dividends are the same as long-term capital gains, which are lower than the rates for ordinary income.

Table 2.6 Long-Term Capital Gains and Qualified Dividend Tax Rates 2024

Income Level	Tax Rate
Married Filing Jointly & Surviving Spouse	
$0–$94,050	0%
$94,051–$583,750	15
>$583,750	20
Single	
$0–$47,025	0%
$47,026–$518,900	15
>$518,900	20
Head of Household	
$0–$63,000	0%
$63,001–$551,350	15
>$551,350	20
Married Filing Separately	
$0–$47,025	0%
$47,026–$291,850	15
>$291,850	20

Special higher rates for "high-income" taxpayers are covered in

---

[1] A taxpayer's basis in an investment is usually the cost of the investment. The basis is used to determine the gain or loss when the investment is sold.

Note that the break points between 0 and 15 percent for qualified dividends and long-term capital gains rates are similar to but not the same as the ordinary rate brackets (presented in Appendix A) for the same filing status. For example, the single ordinary income rate bracket breaks between 12 and 22 percent at $47,150; whereas the dividend/capital gain rate breaks at $47,025.

Example Sandra is a single taxpayer with wage income of $47,000 and qualified dividends of $1,000 in 2024. Assume Sandra has no other deductions or income except the standard deduction. Sandra's taxable income is:

Wage income	$47,000
Qualified dividends	1,000
Standard deduction	(14,600)
Exemption (suspended by TCJA)	0
Taxable income	$33,400

Sandra's income now must be separated into the ordinary and qualified dividends portions:

Taxable income	$33,400
Qualified dividends	(1,000)
Ordinary income	$32,400

The 2024 tax on $32,400 of ordinary income of a single taxpayer is $3,659 (from the tax tables in Appendix A). As Sarah's taxable income of $33,400 including the qualified dividend is below $47,025, the threshold for 0 percent qualified dividend and long-term capital gains for a single taxpayer in 2024 (Table 2.6), her qualified dividend tax rate is 0 percent and thus her total tax liability is $3,659. ♦

Example Dee is a single taxpayer with wage income of $54,000 and qualified dividends of $9,000 in 2024. Assume Dee has no other deductions or income except the standard deduction. Dee's taxable income is

Wage income	$54,000
Qualified dividends	9,000
Standard deduction	(14,600)
Taxable income	$48,400

Dee's income now must be separated into the ordinary and qualified dividend and long-term capital gain portions:

Taxable income	$48,400
Qualified dividends	(9,000)
Ordinary income	$39,400

The 2024 tax on $39,400 of ordinary income of a single taxpayer is $4,499 (from the tax tables in Appendix A). Dee's taxable income without the qualified dividends is below the 15 percent threshold of $47,025 for a single taxpayer in 2024 (Table 2.6), but her taxable income with qualified dividends of $48,400 is above the threshold; thus, a part of the qualified dividend will be taxed at 0 percent and a part at 15 percent. Of her $9,000 qualified dividends, $7,625 is below the $47,025 threshold and is taxed at 0 percent while $1,375 is above the $47,025 threshold and is taxed at 15 percent for an additional tax of $206.25 to bring Dee's total tax liability to $4,705.25. The treatment of Dee's ordinary and qualified dividend income is presented in Figure 2.6. ♦

Figure 2.6 Tax Rates for Qualified Dividends and Long-Term Capital Gains

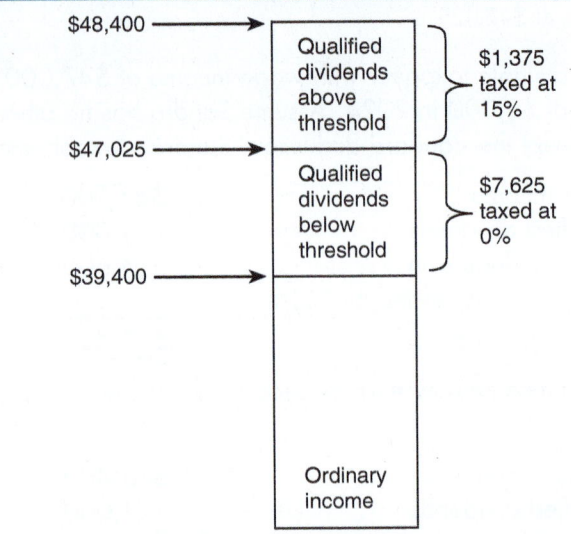

In order to assist with the calculation of preferential taxes on qualified dividends and long-term capital gains, the IRS provides the Qualified Dividends and Capital Gain Tax Worksheet as part of the Form 1040 instructions. This worksheet is on Page 2-33.

2-10c Section 199A Dividends

The qualified business income (QBI) deduction (covered in Chapter 4) permits a deduction of 20 percent of QBI. One of the components of QBI is certain dividends received from a real estate investment trust (REIT). A REIT is an investment instrument that holds almost exclusively real estate (as opposed to a traditional mutual fund which is likely to hold stock or bonds). Individual taxpayers that receive qualified dividends from a REIT should receive a Form 1099-DIV that reports these as Section 199A dividends in Box 5 as well as including the amount in Box 1a. These dividends are income like other dividends but should also be included in the QBI total used to compute the QBI deduction.

2-10d Reporting Dividend Income

Generally, dividend income in amounts of at least $10 must be reported by the payor to the recipient on a Form 1099-DIV. Form 1099-DIV reports total ordinary dividends in Box 1a. Box 1b reports the amount of qualified dividends included in Box 1a. These amounts are entered on Schedule B (if more than $1,500 in total) or directly on Lines 3a and 3b of Form 1040. Mutual fund investments, and to a lesser degree, corporate stock investments, can also distribute capital gain dividends, which are reported in Box 2a of Form 1099-DIV. Unlike ordinary and qualified dividends, which are reported by the taxpayer on Schedule B or Form 1040 as described above, capital gain dividends are reported on Schedule D of Form 1040 (refer to Chapter 4). If a taxpayer has *only* capital gain dividend distributions reported on Form 1099-DIV, the amount can be reported on Line 7 of Form 1040.

Self-Study Problem 2.10

Refer to Appendix E for Solutions to Self-Study Problems

Christy and John Harris-Thomas received the following Form 1099-DIVs during 2024:

☐ CORRECTED (if checked)

Form 1099-DIV (Rev. January 2024) — Dividends and Distributions — For calendar year 2024 — OMB No. 1545-0110 — Copy B For Recipient

Field	Value
PAYER'S name, address	Tangerine Equity Fund, PO Box 1001, Kansas City, MO 64108
PAYER'S TIN	41-5982262
RECIPIENT'S TIN	513-17-7711
RECIPIENT'S name	John Harris-Thomas
Street address	1112 Constitution Ave., NW
City, state, ZIP	Washington, DC 20224
1a Total ordinary dividends	$975.00
1b Qualified dividends	$975.00
2a Total capital gain distr.	
2b Unrecap. Sec. 1250 gain	
2c Section 1202 gain	
2d Collectibles (28%) gain	
2e Section 897 ordinary dividends	
2f Section 897 capital gain	
3 Nondividend distributions	
4 Federal income tax withheld	
5 Section 199A dividends	
6 Investment expenses	
7 Foreign tax paid	
8 Foreign country or U.S. possession	
9 Cash liquidation distributions	
10 Noncash liquidation distributions	
11 FATCA filing requirement	☐
12 Exempt-interest dividends	
13 Specified private activity bond interest dividends	
14 State	
15 State identification no.	
16 State tax withheld	

Form 1099-DIV (Rev. 1-2024) (keep for your records) www.irs.gov/Form1099DIV Department of the Treasury - Internal Revenue Service

---

2024 Combined Forms 1099

This is important tax information and is being furnished to the IRS (except as indicated). If you are required to file a return, a negligence penalty or other sanction may be imposed on you if this income is taxable and the IRS determines that it has not been reported.

Copy B For Recipient
OMB No. 1545-0110

Friar Tuck Investments
38 Wall Street, 8th Floor
New York, NY 10005

John and Christy Harris-Thomas
1112 Constitution Ave., NW
Washington DC 20224

Account Number	Tax ID
3100987765	***-**-5454

Payer's Federal Tax ID: 33-1357246
Financial Adviser/Phone: Will Scarlett 888-555-1212

Form 1099-DIV — Dividend Income

Box 1a Total ordinary dividends	Box 1b Qualified dividends	Box 2a Total capital gain distr.
1,650.00	1,550.00	190.00

Box 2b Unrecap Sec 1250 gain	Box 2c Section 1202 gain	Box 2d Collectibles (28%) gain

Box 2e Section 897 ordinary dividends	Box 2f Section 897 capital gain	Box 3 Nondividend distributions

Box 4 Federal income tax withheld	Box 5 Section 199A dividends	Box 6 Investment expenses

Box 7 Foreign taxes paid	Box 8 Foreign country or possession	Box 9 Cash liquidation distributions

The Harris-Thomases file jointly, take the standard deduction, and have taxable income, including interest and dividends, of $95,000. Complete Part II of Schedule B of Form 1040 on Page 2-32. Using the information from this problem and Self-Study Problem 2-9, complete the Qualified Dividends and Capital Gains Tax Worksheet on Page 2-33 for the 2024 tax year.

ProConnect™ Tax TIP

Interest and dividends are both common forms of income in addition to wages. The way the two items are reported is slightly different and not always intuitive. Tax-exempt interest (which is entered on Line 2a of Form 1040) is not included as part of taxable interest (Line 2b). Qualified dividends (line 3a) however, are included as part of ordinary dividends (Line 3b). Interest and Dividends are both located in ProConnect Tax under Income and have a Quick Entry and a 1099 entry screen (with Box numbers presented) available. Quick Entry handles most Form 1099-INTs and Form 1099-DIVs; however, should one wish to use the detailed entry screens, they will appear in the left-hand margin when Quick Entry is open. One can always return to Quick Entry using the link at the top of the detail entry form (especially if there is a need to enter additional Form 1099s).

Learning Objective 2.11

Identify the general rules for the tax treatment of gifts and inheritances.

2-11 Gifts and Inheritances

Taxpayers are allowed to exclude from income the fair market value of gifts and inheritances received, but income received from the property after such a transfer is generally taxable. Normally, the gift tax or estate tax is paid by the donor or the decedent's estate; such property is, therefore, usually tax-free to the person receiving the gift or inheritance.

One tax problem that may arise concerning a gift is the definition of what constitutes a gift. The courts define a gift as a voluntary transfer of property without adequate consideration. Gifts made in a business setting are suspect since they may be disguised payments for goods or services. The courts are likely to rule that gifts in a business setting are taxable income, even if there was no obligation to make the payment. Also, if the recipient renders services for the gift, it will be presumed to be income for the services performed.

Example In January of the current year, Richard inherits shares of Birch Corporation stock worth $22,000. After receiving the stock, he is paid $1,300 in dividends during the current year. His gross income from the inheritance in the current year would be $1,300. The $22,000 fair market value of the stock is excluded from gross income. ♦

Example Lorela worked for the Milano Corporation during a difficult economic period. As a token of their appreciation, the Milano Board of Directors voted to give Lorela a new Alfa Romeo Tonale automobile with a fair market value of $50,000. Although the Board may have classified the auto as a "gift," because Lorela is an employee, $50,000 will be included in her compensation. ♦

Tax Break

Although the recipient of a gift generally excludes the value of the gift from income tax, the person that makes the gift might be subject to the unified transfer tax, more commonly known as the estate and gift tax. The lifetime exclusion amount increased to $13.61 million per person in 2024 (decreases to $5 million after 2025) and thus, most gifts will remain untaxed.

Self-Study Problem 2.11   Refer to Appendix E for Solutions to Self-Study Problems

Consider how much income each of the following taxpayers should recognize from the described transaction and describe the reason.

a. Don is an attorney who supplied a list of potential clients to a new attorney, Lori. This list aided in the success of Lori's practice. Lori was very pleased and decided to do something for Don. In the current year, Lori gives Don a new car worth $40,000. Lori was not obligated to give this gift to Don, and she did not expect Don to perform future services for the gift.

b. Napheesa gives her son, Jahmyr, a gift of $25,000 for graduating college as a congratulations and to provide seed money to help him get started.

2-12 Scholarships

2.12 Learning Objective

Describe the elements of scholarship income that are excluded from tax.

A scholarship is an amount paid or awarded to, or for the benefit of, a student to aid in the pursuit of his or her studies. Scholarships granted to degree candidates are taxable income, with the exception of amounts spent for tuition, fees, books, and course-required supplies and equipment. Therefore, scholarship amounts received for items such as room and board are taxable to the recipient.

Example In 2024, Diane receives a $5,000 scholarship to study accounting at Big State University. Diane's expenses for tuition and books amount to $3,200 during the fall semester; therefore, she would have taxable income of $1,800 ($5,000 − $3,200) from the scholarship. ♦

Payments received by students for part-time employment are not excludable; they are taxable as compensation. For example, students in work–study programs must include their compensation in gross income. Some scholarships will be reported on Form 1098-T. This form is presented in Chapter 7.

Self-Study Problem 2.12   Refer to Appendix E for Solutions to Self-Study Problems

Indicate whether each item below would be included in or excluded from the income of the recipient in 2024.

1. A $2,000 National Merit Scholarship for tuition
2. A basketball scholarship for room and board
3. Payments under a work–study program
4. Salary for working at Beech Research Laboratory
5. A scholarship for $10,000 to cover tuition, fees, and required textbooks of $7,600.
6. Payment received from an employer while on leave working on a research project

2-13 Alimony

2.13 Learning Objective

Describe the tax treatment of alimony and child support.

The term alimony, for income tax purposes, includes separate maintenance payments or similar periodic payments made to a spouse or former spouse. Payments must meet certain requirements to be considered alimony:

1. The payments must be in cash and must be received by the spouse (or former spouse).
2. The payments must be made under a decree of divorce, a separate maintenance agreement, or under a written instrument incident to the divorce.
3. The payor must have no liability to make payments for any period following the death of the spouse receiving the payments.

4. The payments must not be designated in the written agreement as anything other than alimony.
5. If the parties are divorced or legally separated, they must not be members of the same household at the time the payments are made.

Disguised child support payments may not be treated as alimony. Payments contingent on the status of a child, such as the age or marital status of the child, are not considered alimony.

Example Under a 2016 divorce agreement, Sam has agreed to pay his former spouse, Silvia, $1,000 per month. The payments meet all the tests for classification as alimony, but they will be reduced to $600 per month when their child, in Silvia's custody, becomes 18 years of age. In this situation, $400 of each payment must be treated as nondeductible child support and cannot be considered alimony. ♦

Under previous tax law, alimony was deductible by the payor and includable in income by the recipient. For alimony paid pursuant to a divorce or separation instrument executed on or before December 31, 2018, alimony is deductible by the payor and included by the recipient unless the agreement is modified and the modification expressly provides that the new tax law applies to such modification. However, the alimony provisions were repealed and these amounts are neither includable nor deductible for divorce and separation agreements entered into after December 31, 2018.

Example Brad and Jen were married in 2015. The relationship did not work out and they divorced in 2016. The divorce decree required Brad to pay Jen alimony of $1,000 per month. Because this divorce was effective prior to 2019, the alimony is deductible by Brad and is gross income to Jen. ♦

Example Miley and Liam were married in 2017. The relationship did not work out and they divorced in 2022. Miley is required to pay Liam alimony of $1,000 per month. The alimony is neither deductible to Miley nor included in Liam's gross income. ♦

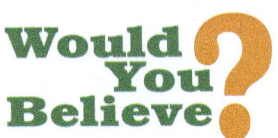

Claiming an alimony deduction may very well be an audit "red flag." Confirm any deductions are associated with a pre-2019 divorce and are per the terms of the divorce decree or written separation agreement. Of course, be certain and enter the taxpayer identification number of the alimony recipient and the date of the divorce on the face of Schedule 1.

2-13a Property Transfers

A spouse who transfers property in settlement of a marital obligation is not required to recognize any gain as a result of the property's appreciation. Thus, if in a divorce settlement, a wife transfers property with a fair market value of $10,000 and a tax basis of $3,000 to her husband, she will not be required to recognize the gain of $7,000 ($10,000 − $3,000). Of course, the husband would be required to assume the wife's tax basis ($3,000) in the property. The transfer of property in settlement of a divorce is not considered alimony and there is no deduction by the spouse who transfers the property, nor is it income to the recipient.

2-13b Child Support

Payments made for child support are not deductible by the taxpayer making them, nor are they income to the recipient. However, they may be an important factor in determining which spouse is entitled to claim the dependent child (refer to Chapter 1). Child support payments must be up to date before any amount paid may be treated as alimony. That is, if a taxpayer is obligated to pay both child support and alimony, they must first meet the

> **ProConnect™ Tax TIP**
>
> Income from alimony, when applicable, is reported in the Income section under SS Benefits, Alimony, Misc. Income (SS Bene., Misc. Inc.). Once this heading is selected, Alimony and Other Income will be presented as a subheading. Deductible alimony paid, when applicable, is reported under Deductions. Once Adjustments to Income is selected, a series of subheadings is presented, including Alimony Paid.

child support obligation before obtaining a deduction for alimony payments (for divorce agreements prior to 2019). Payments for child support include payments designated as such in the marital settlement agreement, plus any alimony payments that are contingent upon the status of a child.

Example Jim is required under a 2015 divorce decree to pay $400 in alimony and $250 in child support per month. Since the decree separately states that $250 is child support, only $400 per month is deductible by Jim and counts as income to his ex-wife. ♦

Self-Study Problem 2.13 *Refer to Appendix E for Solutions to Self-Study Problems*

A taxpayer (payor ex-spouse) is required to pay an ex-spouse (recipient ex-spouse) alimony of $12,000 per year. Determine how much alimony is deductible by the payor ex-spouse and how much alimony is recognized as income by the recipient ex-spouse based on the following information:

a. The payments are made in 2024 as part of a divorce decree executed in 2018. The divorce decree is modified in 2021 to explicitly apply the provisions of the TCJA.
b. The payments are made in 2024 as part of a divorce decree executed in 2016.
c. The payments are made in 2024 as part of a divorce decree executed in 2021.

Would You Sign This Tax Return?

For the last 10 years, you prepared the joint tax returns for Dominic (husband; age 40) and Dulce (wife; age 35) Divorcio. In 2018, they divorced and remained as your separate tax clients. Under the dissolution decree, Dominic has to pay Dulce $2,500 per month alimony, which he does for the current year. You have completed Dominic's tax return for the current year, and you deducted the required alimony payments to Dulce on Dominic's Form 1040. Dulce came in to have you prepare her tax return and refused to report her alimony received as income. She stated, "I am not going to pay tax on the $30,000 from Dominic." She views the payments as "a gift for putting up with him for all those years of marriage." Dulce will not budge on excluding this alimony from income. Would you sign the Paid Preparer's declaration (refer to example above) on this return? Why or why not?

Learning Objective 2.14

Explain the tax implications of using educational savings vehicles.

2-14 Educational Incentives

2-14a Qualified Tuition Programs (QTP)

A Qualified Tuition Program (more commonly referred to as a Section 529 tuition plan) allows taxpayers (1) to buy in-kind tuition credits or certificates for qualified higher education expenses (a prepaid tuition plan) or (2) to contribute to an account established to meet qualified higher education expenses (a savings-type plan). Such Section 529 plans may be sponsored by a state government or a private institution of higher learning. Section 529 plans permit tax-free distributions if the distribution is used for qualified higher education expenses. Qualified higher education expenses include tuition, fees, books, supplies, and equipment required for the enrollment or attendance at an eligible educational institution. In addition, reasonable room and board costs, subject to certain limitations, are also qualified expenses allowed to be paid from the Section 529 tuition plan. Qualified higher education expenses also include tuition in connection with enrollment or attendance at an elementary or secondary public, private, or religious school. The use of the specific term "tuition" excludes other types of qualifying education expenses such as books, supplies, and equipment for elementary or secondary students. The maximum exclusion for elementary or secondary education (i.e., K-12) is $10,000 per beneficiary per year.

Example Walt and Skyler Blanco have two children, Jesse and Jane, and established 529 plans for both of them many years ago. Jesse is now in his second year of college at Albuquerque Community College and Jane is a junior at Albuquerque High School for Math and Science, a private high school. In 2024, $3,500 is distributed from the 529 plan with Jesse as the named beneficiary to pay for his community college tuition, books, and course-related supplies. Jane's private school tuition is more expensive and $12,000 is distributed from the 529 plan for which she is the beneficiary. $11,000 of Jane's distribution is used to pay for tuition, $550 for books, and $450 for her private school uniforms. The Blancos may exclude $13,500 of the distributions. Jesse's $3,500 distribution meets the definition of qualified higher education expenses. Only $10,000 of Jane's distribution meets the definition of qualified higher education expenses. The remaining $1,000 of Jane's tuition would be included in gross income as the amount is in excess of the annual limit and her books and uniform costs do not qualify. ♦

The definition of qualified higher education costs that are eligible for exclusion from income when distributed from a Section 529 plan was expanded to include distributions of up to $10,000 used to pay student loan principal or interest for the plan beneficiary, a sibling, or both. However, the $10,000 limit related to student loan principal or interest payments is a lifetime limit for any single beneficiary.

Example Breonna graduated college in 2023 and has a remaining student loan debt balance in 2024 of $13,000. Breonna's brother Christian is a current college student and is the beneficiary of Section 529 qualified tuition plan. In 2024, a $16,000 distribution is made to Christian to pay for his qualified higher education expenses. In addition, the same plan makes a $10,000 distribution to Breonna to pay her student loans. Neither Breonna nor Christian will be required to include the distribution in income. Breonna will not be eligible for any additional exclusion on Section 529 distributions for loans in the future as she has met her lifetime limit; however, if Christian finishes college with student loan debt, his $10,000 lifetime limit remains available. ♦

> Only nine states currently have a prepaid college savings plan: Florida, Massachusetts, Maryland (no new entrants), Michigan, Mississippi, Nevada, Pennsylvania, Texas, and Washington. These programs generally allow an individual to pay for the college tuition of a young child, locking in at today's tuition rates. Some programs offer the flexibility for the child to select an out-of-state university as well as the in-state options. Many states closed their prepaid plans when the returns in the stock market did not match with the rate in tuition inflation.

Taxpayers may not exclude a distribution for student loan interest under these provisions and also deduct the same interest as a for AGI student loan interest deduction (Chapter 5). In an additional expansion of qualified higher education costs, 529 distributions used to pay for costs for apprenticeship programs which are registered and certified are now eligible to be excluded from income. The U.S. Department of Labor certifies such programs.

The earnings portion of 529 plan distributions that are not used for qualified tuition expenses are includable in the distributee's gross income under the annuity income rules and are subject to a 10-percent early withdrawal penalty.

Unlike Educational Savings Accounts, discussed later in this section, there is no income limit on the amount of contributions to a Section 529 plan. Like an Educational Savings Account, however, the contributions are not deductible. Any contributions are considered gifts, and thus, subject to the gift tax rules. In addition, most programs impose some form of overall maximum contribution for each beneficiary based on estimated future higher education expenses.

Example Bill has AGI of $275,000 and has two children. He chooses to contribute $9,000 (he is allowed to contribute any amount up to the limit imposed by his state's law) to a QTP for each of his children in 2024, even with his high AGI. The $18,000 is not deductible to Bill. Any earnings on the contribution accumulate tax free and are excluded from gross income if used for future qualified higher education expenses. ♦

A taxpayer may claim an American Opportunity credit or lifetime learning credit (covered in detail in Chapter 7) for a tax year and exclude from gross income amounts distributed (both the principal and the earnings portions) from a qualified tuition program on behalf of the same student. This is true as long as the distribution is not used for the same expenses for which a credit was claimed. However, the amount of qualified higher education expenses for a tax year for purposes of calculating the exclusion from income must be reduced by scholarships, veterans' benefits, military reserve benefits, employer-provided educational assistance amounts, and the tuition amounts used to generate the American Opportunity and lifetime learning credits.

Example In 2024, Sammy receives $15,000 from a qualified tuition program. He uses the funds to pay for his college tuition and other qualified higher education expenses. Sammy also claims an American Opportunity credit of $1,500 for the year, using the expenses paid from the Section 529 plan funds. For purposes of the Section 529 plan exclusion calculation, the $15,000 must be reduced to $13,500 ($15,000 − $1,500). ♦

The tax law provides that if the total distributions from a Section 529 plan and from an educational savings account exceed the total amount of qualified higher education expenses, the taxpayer will have to allocate the expenses among the distributions for purposes of determining how much of each distribution is excludable.

Tax Break

If Section 529 funds are used to pay for qualified higher education expenses that are then refunded because of classes being canceled or university housing closing, those funds may be redeposited within 60 days of the refund, and avoid the tax and 10-percent penalty.

Starting in 2024, amounts held in a 529 account may be rolled over to a Roth IRA (covered in Chapter 5) of the same beneficiary and excluded from gross income. To qualify for the exclusion, all of the following requirements must be met:

- The 529 account must have been open and in the beneficiary's name for at least 15 years
- The amounts must have been held in the 529 plan for at least 5 years
- The rollover distribution cannot exceed the amount contributed to the 529 account (including earnings) made in the previous five years
- There is a lifetime limit of $35,000 on such rollover distributions with respect to any designated beneficiary

The rollover distribution counts toward the annual Roth IRA contribution limit and the beneficiary of the Roth must have earned income to cover the amount of the rollover (more in Chapter 5).

Example Fiero and Glenda Wycked give birth to their daughter, Alfaba, in 2006. On April 28, 2006, they contribute $3,000 to a 529 naming Alfaba as beneficiary. The Wyckeds make an additional $3,000 contribution on the 28th of April each year through April 28, 2017 and then stop making contributions. The 529 account would not be eligible for a Roth IRA rollover until April 29, 2021 (15 years from inception with the same beneficiary). The maximum amount eligible for a rollover on April 29, 2021 would be the balance in the account less the $3,000 contribution in 2017 (within the five-year period) and any earnings attributable to the 2017 contribution. ♦

Example Continuing the previous example, in fall 2024, when Alfaba starts college, the account is worth $84,000. Fortunately, Alfaba receives a partial scholarship and makes distributions of only $50,000 from the 529 account over the next 4 years until graduation. In 2028, when Alfaba graduates and generates adequate earned income, the account is worth $41,000 and $7,000 (the maximum Roth contribution in 2024) is rolled over to a Roth IRA for Alfaba. Note that no contributions are now within the 5 year window since the last contribution was in 2017. The Wyckeds can roll over the maximum amount each year until the lifetime maximum of $35,000 is reached. Any balance remaining in the 529 account above the $35,000 maximum could be rolled over to a new beneficiary (e.g., a younger sibling, grandchild or other individual) or distributed to Alfaba and subject to both a 10-percent penalty tax and regular income taxes. ♦

2-14b Educational Savings Accounts

Taxpayers are allowed to set up educational savings accounts, also known as Coverdell Education Savings Accounts, to pay for qualified education expenses. The maximum amount a taxpayer can contribute annually to an educational savings account for a beneficiary is $2,000. Contributions are not deductible and are subject to income limits. Contributions cannot be made to an educational savings account after the date on which the designated beneficiary becomes 18 years old. A contribution can be made to both a Coverdell account and a qualified state tuition program for the same beneficiary during the year, subject to the limitations of each program. The educational savings account exclusion for distributions of income is available in any tax year in which the beneficiary claims the American Opportunity credit or the lifetime learning credit (Chapter 7), provided the distribution is not used for the same expenses for which the credit was claimed.

Contributions to educational savings accounts are phased out between AGIs of $95,000 and $110,000 for single taxpayers and $190,000 and $220,000 for married couples who file a joint return (these limits are not adjusted annually for inflation). Like regular and Roth IRAs, contributions applied to the current tax year must be made by April 15 (or the next business day, if April 15 falls on a weekend or holiday) of the following year.

Example Joe, who is single, would like to contribute $2,000 to an educational savings account for his 12-year-old son. However, his AGI is $105,000, so his contribution is limited to $667, calculated as follows:

$$\frac{(\$110,000 \text{ upper limit} - \$105,000 \text{ AGI})}{\$15,000} \times \$2,000 = \$667 \text{ contribution}$$

$15,000 is the difference between the upper ($110,000) and lower ($95,000) phase-out limits. ♦

Tax Break

For parents with income above the allowable limit, a gift may be made to a child and the child may make the contribution to an educational savings account. There is no requirement that the contributor have earned income as there is for IRAs.

Amounts received from an educational savings account are tax-free if they are used for qualified education expenses. Qualified education expenses include tuition, fees, books, supplies, and related equipment for private, elementary, and secondary school expenses as well as for college. Room and board also qualify if the student's course load is at least 50 percent of the full-time course load. If the distributions during a tax year exceed qualified education expenses, part of the excess is treated as a return of capital (the contributions), and part is treated as a distribution of earnings. The distribution is presumed to be pro rata from each category. The exclusion for the distribution of earnings is calculated as follows:

$$\frac{\text{Qualified education expenses}}{\text{Total distribution}} \times \text{Earnings} = \text{Exclusion}$$

Example Amy receives a $2,000 distribution from her educational savings account. She uses $1,800 to pay for qualified education expenses. Immediately prior to the distribution, Amy's account balance is $5,000, $3,000 of which are her contributions. Because 60 percent ($3,000/$5,000) of her account balance represents her contributions, $1,200 ($2,000 × 60%) of the distribution is a tax-free return of capital and $800 ($2,000 × 40%) is a distribution of earnings. The excludable amount of the earnings is calculated as follows:

$$\frac{\$1,800}{\$2,000} \times \$800 = \$720 \text{ is excludable (thus, the amount taxable is \$80, or \$800} - \$720).$$

Amy's adjusted basis for her educational savings account is reduced to $1,800 ($3,000 − $1,200). ♦

Chapter 2 • Gross Income and Exclusions

> **Self-Study Problem 2.14** — See Appendix E for Solutions to Self-Study Problems
>
> a. Abby has a distribution of $10,000 from a qualified tuition program, of which $3,000 represents earnings. The funds are used to pay for her daughter's qualified higher education expenses. How much of the $10,000 distribution is taxable to the daughter?
>
> b. During 2024, Henry (a single taxpayer) has a salary of $85,000 and interest income of $4,000. Henry has no other income or deductions. Calculate the maximum contribution Henry is allowed for an educational savings account.

Learning Objective 2.15
Describe the tax treatment of unemployment compensation.

2-15 Unemployment Compensation

Unemployment compensation payments are generally fully taxable. Unemployment compensation is generally reported on a Form 1099-G.

Example Genny was unemployed for several months during the current year and received unemployment compensation of $4,000. The $4,000 is included in Genny's taxable income for the current year. ♦

> **Self-Study Problem 2.15** — Refer to Appendix E for Solutions to Self-Study Problems
>
> Bear was unemployed during part of 2024 and received the following Form 1099-G:
>
> **Form 1099-G (Rev. 3-2024)** — Certain Government Payments — For calendar year 2024
>
> PAYER'S name: North Carolina Division of Employment Security, PO Box 25900, Raleigh, NC 27611
> PAYER'S TIN: 21-4321234
> RECIPIENT'S TIN: 239-03-0045
> RECIPIENT'S name: Bear Shaw
> Street address: 118 E. North Street, Unit 7
> City: Raleigh, NC 27601
>
> Box 1 Unemployment compensation: $3,250.00
> Box 4 Federal income tax withheld: $295.00
>
> How much unemployment compensation is included in Bear's gross income?

Learning Objective 2.16
Apply the rules governing inclusion of Social Security benefits in gross income.

2-16 Social Security Benefits

Some taxpayers may exclude all of their Social Security benefits from gross income. However, most middle-income and upper-income Social Security recipients may have to include up to 85 percent of their benefits in gross income. The formula to determine taxable Social Security income is based on *modified adjusted gross income* (MAGI). Generally, MAGI is the taxpayer's adjusted gross income (without Social Security benefits) plus any tax-free interest income. On rare occasions, taxpayers will also have to add back unusual items such as the foreign earned income exclusion, employer-provided adoption benefits, or interest on education loans. If MAGI plus 50 percent of Social Security benefits is less than the base amount shown in Table 2.7 (base amounts are not adjusted for inflation), benefits are excluded from income.

Table 2.7 Social Security Benefits Base Taxable Thresholds

Base Amounts	Applies to
$32,000	Married filing jointly
0	Married taxpayers who did not live apart for the entire year and still filed separate returns
25,000	All other taxpayers

The formula for calculating the taxable amount of Social Security is complex and time-consuming. Many taxpayers rely on tax-preparation software to perform the calculation. For preparation by hand, the Form 1040 instructions include a full-page worksheet that takes taxpayers through the calculation one step at a time.

The Social Security Administration reports Social Security benefits to recipients on Form SSA-1099 each year. Net benefits are typically reported in Box 5 and federal income tax withholding is reported in Box 6. Some Social Security beneficiaries will pay for certain types of Medicare health insurance through withholding from benefits, which are reported in the box labeled Description of Amounts in Box 3 on the Form SSA-1099. The amounts withheld for Medicare can often be deducted as either self-employment health insurance or an itemized deduction for medical expenses (refer to Chapter 5).

Originally, Social Security benefits were not taxed; however, starting in 1984, a portion of Social Security benefits became taxable using the now familiar $25,000 and $32,000 base amounts. At the time, the explanation used to support the change was that one-half of the tax was paid by employers and employees were not taxed on that benefit. The base amounts have not changed since 1984. Using the Consumer Price Index Inflation Calculator (**www.bls.gov/data/inflation_calculator.htm**), one would need about $77,000 more to equal the purchasing power of $25,000 in 1984. As a result, a much larger percentage of taxpayers are paying tax on their Social Security benefits.

Example For the 2024 tax year, Nancy, a single taxpayer, receives $7,000 in Social Security benefits. She has adjusted gross income of $20,000, not including any Social Security income, and receives $10,000 of tax-exempt municipal bond interest. Nancy must include $3,500 of her Social Security benefits in gross income as determined as follows:

Simplified Taxable Social Security Worksheet (for most people)

1. Enter the total amount of Social Security income.	1. $ 7,000
2. Enter one-half of line 1.	2. 3,500
3. Enter the total of taxable income items on Form 1040 except Social Security income.	3. 20,000
4. Enter the amount of tax-exempt interest income.	4. 10,000
5. Add lines 2, 3, and 4.	5. 33,500
6. Enter all adjustments for AGI except for student loan interest deduction.	6. -0-
7. Subtract line 6 from line 5. If zero or less, stop here, none of the Social Security benefits are taxable.	7. 33,500
8. Enter $25,000 ($32,000 if married filing jointly; $0 if married filing separately and living with spouse at any time during the year).	8. 25,000

9. Subtract line 8 from line 7. If zero or less, enter –0–. 9. 8,500

Note: *If line 9 is zero or less, stop here;* **none of your benefits are taxable.** *Otherwise, go on to line 10.*

10. Enter $9,000 ($12,000 if married filing jointly; $0 if married filing separately and living with spouse at any time during the year). 10. 9,000
11. Subtract line 10 from line 9. If zero or less, enter –0–. 11. –0–
12. Enter the **smaller** of line 9 or line 10. 12. 8,500
13. Enter one-half of line 12. 13. 4,250
14. Enter the **smaller** of line 2 or line 13. 14. 3,500
15. Multiply line 11 by 85% (.85). If line 11 is zero, enter –0–. 15. –0–
16. Add lines 14 and 15. 16. 3,500
17. Multiply line 1 by 85% (.85). 17. 5,950
18. **Taxable benefits.** Enter the **smaller** of line 16 or line 17. 18. $ 3,500

♦

Example Dulcy, a widow, is retired and receives Social Security benefits of $14,000 in 2024. She has MAGI of $47,000. Dulcy must include $11,900 of her Social Security benefits in gross income as determined as follows:

Simplified Taxable Social Security Worksheet (for most people)

1. Enter the total amount of Social Security income. 1. $14,000
2. Enter one-half of line 1. 2. 7,000
3. Enter the total of taxable income items on Form 1040 except Social Security income. 3. 47,000
4. Enter the amount of tax-exempt interest income. 4. –0–
5. Add lines 2, 3, and 4. 5. 54,000
6. Enter all adjustments for AGI except for student loan interest deduction. 6. –0–
7. Subtract line 6 from line 5. If zero or less, stop here, none of the Social Security benefits are taxable. 7. 54,000
8. Enter $25,000 ($32,000 if married filing jointly; $0 if married filing separately and living with spouse at any time during the year). 8. 25,000
9. Subtract line 8 from line 7. If zero or less, enter –0–. 9. 29,000

Note: *If line 9 is zero or less, stop here;* **none of your benefits are taxable.** *Otherwise, go on to line 10.*

10. Enter $9,000 ($12,000 if married filing jointly; $0 if married filing separately and living with spouse at any time during the year). 10. 9,000
11. Subtract line 10 from line 9. If zero or less, enter –0–. 11. 20,000
12. Enter the **smaller** of line 9 or line 10. 12. 9,000

13. Enter one-half of line 12.	13.	4,500
14. Enter the **smaller** of line 2 or line 13.	14.	4,500
15. Multiply line 11 by 85% (.85). If line 11 is zero, enter –0–.	15.	17,000
16. Add lines 14 and 15.	16.	21,500
17. Multiply line 1 by 85% (.85).	17.	11,900
18. **Taxable benefits.** Enter the **smaller** of line 16 or line 17.	18.	$11,900

♦

A summary of the tax treatment of Social Security benefits is presented in Table 2.8.

Table 2.8 Social Security Income Inclusion Formulas

Filing Status	MAGI + 50% SS	Amount of SS That Is Included in Taxable Income
Single, Head of Household, Surviving Spouse, Married Filing Separately (Living Apart)	Under $25,000	No SS benefits included in taxable income
	$25,000–$34,000	The lesser of: 50% of SS benefits, or 50% of (MAGI + 50% SS, over $25,000)
	Over $34,000	The lesser of: 85% of SS benefits, or (lesser of box above or $4,500) + 85% of (MAGI + 50% SS, over $34,000)
Married Filing Jointly	Under $32,000	No SS benefits included in taxable income
	$32,000–$44,000	The lesser of: 50% of SS benefits, or 50% of (MAGI + 50% SS, over $32,000)
	Over $44,000	The lesser of: 85% of SS benefits, or (lesser of box above or $6,000) + 85% of (MAGI + 50% SS, over $44,000)

Note: The Social Security income inclusion formulas in the table above are shown for information only. No problems in the textbook will require the use of these formulas.

Social Security benefits are entered under the same heading in Income as alimony discussed in LO 2.13.

ProConnect™ Tax TIP

Self-Study Problem 2.16

Refer to Appendix E for Solutions to Self-Study Problems

For the 2024 tax year, Linnae and Edward Cartman are married and file a joint tax return. Not including any Social Security benefits, they have adjusted gross income of $20,000 and also have $30,000 in tax-exempt municipal bond interest. They received the following Forms SSA-1099 for 2024:

FORM SSA-1099 – SOCIAL SECURITY BENEFIT STATEMENT

2024
- Part of your social security benefits shown in box 5 may be taxable income
- See reverse side for more information

Box 1 Name	Box 2 Beneficiary's Social Security Number
Linnae Cartman	812-90-9095

Box 3 Benefits Paid in 2024	Box 4 Benefits Repaid to SSA in 2023	Box 5 Net Benefits for 2024
$7,700.00		$7,700.00

Description of Amount in Box 3	Description of Amount in Box 4
Paid by direct deposit $6,200.00	
Medicare Part B premiums deducted from benefits $1,200	**Box 6 Voluntary Federal Income Tax Withheld** $300.00
	Box 7 Address 6716 W Colfax Ave Lakewood, CO 80214
	Box 8 Claim Number
Form SSA-1099-SM (1-2023)	DO NOT RETURN THIS FORM TO SSA OR IRS

FORM SSA-1099 – SOCIAL SECURITY BENEFIT STATEMENT

2024
- Part of your social security benefits shown in box 5 may be taxable income
- See reverse side for more information

Box 1 Name	Box 2 Beneficiary's Social Security Number
Edward Cartman	762-12-0007

Box 3 Benefits Paid in 2024	Box 4 Benefits Repaid to SSA in 2023	Box 5 Net Benefits for 2024
$5,300.00		$5,300.00

Description of Amount in Box 3	Description of Amount in Box 4
Paid by direct deposit $3,900.00	
Medicare Part B premiums deducted from benefits $1,200	**Box 6 Voluntary Federal Income Tax Withheld** $200.00
	Box 7 Address 6716 W Colfax Ave Lakewood, CO 80214
	Box 8 Claim Number
Form SSA-1099-SM (1-2023)	DO NOT RETURN THIS FORM TO SSA OR IRS

Using the worksheet below, determine the amount of Social Security benefits that the Cartmans should include in gross income.

Self-Study Problem 2.16, continued
Refer to Appendix E for Solutions to Self-Study Problems

Simplified Taxable Social Security Worksheet (for most people)

1. Enter the total amount of Social Security income.   1. $_____
2. Enter one-half of line 1.   2. _____
3. Enter the total of taxable income items on Form 1040 except Social Security income.   3. _____
4. Enter the amount of tax-exempt interest income.   4. _____
5. Add lines 2, 3, and 4.   5. _____
6. Enter all adjustments for AGI except for student loan interest deduction.   6. _____
7. Subtract line 6 from line 5. If zero or less, stop here, none of the Social Security benefits are taxable.   7. _____
8. Enter $25,000 ($32,000 if married filing jointly; $0 if married filing separately and living with spouse at any time during the year).   8. _____
9. Subtract line 8 from line 7. If zero or less, enter –0–.   9. _____

Note: *If line 9 is zero or less, stop here;* **none of your benefits are taxable.** *Otherwise, go on to line 10.*

10. Enter $9,000 ($12,000 if married filing jointly; $0 if married filing separately and living with spouse at any time during the year).   10. _____
11. Subtract line 10 from line 9. If zero or less, enter –0–.   11. _____
12. Enter the **smaller** of line 9 or line 10.   12. _____
13. Enter one-half of line 12.   13. _____
14. Enter the **smaller** of line 2 or line 13.   14. _____
15. Multiply line 11 by 85% (.85). If line 11 is zero, enter –0–.   15. _____
16. Add lines 14 and 15.   16. _____
17. Multiply line 1 by 85% (.85).   17. _____
18. **Taxable benefits.** Enter the **smaller** of line 16 or line 17.   18. $_____

2-17 Community Property

2.17 Learning Objective

Distinguish between the different rules for married taxpayers residing in community property states when filing separate returns.

When married couples file separate income tax returns, income derived from property held by a married couple, either jointly or separately, as well as wages and other income earned by a husband and wife, must be allocated between the spouses. State law becomes important in making this allocation.

The law in nine states is based on a community property system of marital law. In these states, the property rights of married couples differ from the property rights of married couples residing in the remaining common law states. The nine states that are community property states are:

- Arizona
- California
- Idaho
- Louisiana
- Nevada
- New Mexico
- Texas
- Washington
- Wisconsin

Note: In Alaska South Dakota, and Tennessee, spouses may elect to treat income as community income.

Under the community property system, all property is deemed to be either separate property or community property. Separate property includes property acquired by a spouse before marriage or received after marriage as a gift or inheritance. All other property owned by a married couple is presumed to be community property. For federal income tax purposes, each spouse is automatically taxed on half of the income from community property.

The tax treatment of income from separate property depends on the taxpayer's state of residence. In Idaho, Louisiana, Texas, and Wisconsin, income from separate property produces community income. Thus, just as each spouse is taxed on half of the income from community property, each spouse is also taxed on half of the income from separate property. In the other five community property states, income on separate property is separate income and is reported in full on the tax return of the spouse who owns the property. Income from capital gains, nontaxable dividends, royalties from mineral rights, and similar forms of income is generally classified as separate or community income based on the classification of the underlying property as separate or community property.

Example Luka and Annamaria are married and live in Texas. Luka owns, as his separate property, stock in Grape Corporation. During the year, Luka receives Grape dividends of $4,000. Assuming Luka and Annamaria file separate returns, each of them must report $2,000 of the dividends. If Luka and Annamaria lived in California, Luka would report the entire $4,000 of the dividends on his tax return and Annamaria would not include any of the dividend income on her tax return. ◆

In all of the community property states, income from salary and wages is generally treated as having been earned one-half by each spouse.

Example Robert and Linda are married but file separate tax returns. Robert receives a salary of $30,000 and has interest income of $500 from a savings account which is in his name. The savings account was established with salary earned by Robert since his marriage. Linda collects $20,000 in dividends on stock she inherited from her father. The amount of income which Linda must report on her separate income tax return depends on the state in which Robert and Linda reside. Three different assumptions are presented below:

State of Residence

Linda's Income	Texas	California	Common Law States
Salary	$15,000	$15,000	$ 0
Dividends	10,000	20,000	20,000
Interest	250	250	0
Total	$25,250	$35,250	$20,000

◆

2-17a Spouses Living Apart

To simplify problems that could arise when married spouses residing in a community property state do not live together, the tax law contains an exception to the above community property rules. Under this special provision, a spouse will be taxed only on his or her actual earnings from personal services. For this provision to apply, the following conditions must be satisfied:

1. The individuals must live apart for the entire year,
2. They must not file a joint return, and
3. No portion of the earned income may be transferred between the spouses.

Example Andre and Steffi, both residents of Nevada, are married but live apart for the entire year. Andre has a salary of $30,000 and Steffi has a salary of $35,000. Normally, Andre and Steffi would each report $32,500. However, if the required conditions are met, Andre and Steffi would each report their own salary. If Andre and Steffi had any unearned income, such as dividends or interest, the income would be reported under the general community property rules. The special provision applies only to earned income of the spouses. ♦

Another provision addresses the problem of spouses who fail to qualify for the above special exception because they do not live apart for the entire year. In certain cases, a spouse who fails to include in income his or her share of community income, as required by the community property laws, may be relieved of any liability related to this income. To be granted relief, the taxpayer must not know of or have reason to know of the omitted community property income.

Self-Study Problem 2.17
Refer to Appendix E for Solutions to Self-Study Problems

George and Talia are married and living together in California. Their income is as follows:

George's salary	$40,000
Talia's salary	30,000
Dividends (George's property)	5,000
Dividends (Talia's property)	3,000
Interest (community property)	4,000
Total	$82,000

a. If Talia files a separate tax return, what should Talia report as income?
b. If George and Talia lived in Texas, what should Talia report as income?

2-18 Cancellation of Debt Income

2.18 Learning Objective
Describe the inclusion and exclusion of cancellation of debt income.

The cancellation of debt represents an economic benefit to the taxpayer that receives the debt relief. Unsurprisingly, the broad definition of gross income generally treats the amount forgiven as income to the taxpayer. This can also be referred to as forgiveness of debt income or discharge of indebtedness income.

Example Uta borrowed funds from Usury National Bank so he could start a small business. Unfortunately, Uta's business failed and he was unable to pay back the entire loan balance. Uta and the bank agreed to settle Uta's $50,000 outstanding debt for only $40,000. Uta has $10,000 of cancellation of debt income. ♦

There are a number of provisions provided to exclude forgiveness of debt from gross income including:

- The taxpayer is bankrupt or insolvent at the time the debt is cancelled or reduced.
- The debt is qualified real property business debt.
- The debt is qualified principal residence debt.
- The debt is certain types of student loan debt that is forgiven under certain conditions.

If a taxpayer's debt has been discharged in a bankruptcy, the tax law recognizes that requiring a bankrupt individual to pay taxes on debt that was required to be forgiven because the taxpayer lacks the ability to repay the debt would not make economic sense. As a result, cancellation of debt income due to bankruptcy is generally excluded from gross income.

Example Sharon borrowed funds from Usury National Bank so she could start a small business. Unfortunately, Sharon's business failed and her entire debt was discharged in a bankruptcy proceeding. Sharon may exclude the debt discharged. ♦

Often times debt is associated with the acquisition of real property, for example, land, a building used in business, or a house; and that property serves as collateral on the debt. If that property is qualified business property or the taxpayer's principal residence, an exclusion of the cancellation of debt income may apply. In the case of business property, the debt generally must have been incurred with respect to the acquisition, construction, or a substantial improvement to real property used in a trade or business.

Example Jonquel's small business purchased a warehouse to store inventory. The acquisition was funded by a loan from a local bank. The loan is secured by the building. Jonquel found herself unable to make the loan payments and the bank agreed to cancel $15,000 of the loan. Jonquel will be able to exclude the cancellation of debt income under the qualified real property business debt provisions. ♦

Similarly, debt incurred by a taxpayer to purchase, build, or substantially improve the taxpayer's principal residence is afforded similar treatment when forgiven. To qualify, the debt must be secured by the principal residence. The provision to exclude qualified principal residence debt forgiven is scheduled to expire at the end of 2025.

Example Tyra acquired a new principal residence for $250,000 using a $200,000 mortgage that was secured by the home. In 2024, when the balance of the loan was $190,000, Tyra lost her job and was struggling to continue to make mortgage payments. The bank agreed to lower Tyra's loan principal to $160,000. Tyra may exclude the $30,000 of cancellation of debt income. ♦

When cancellation of debt income is excluded under the qualified business property and principal resident provisions, the basis in the underlying property is adjusted to reflect that exclusion amount.

Example Muffy purchased her principal residence for $160,000 in 2013. In 2024, Muffy was required to renegotiate the mortgage on her principal residence. Although Muffy was solvent at the time, she was unable to make mortgage payments due to losing her job. The mortgage balance was $100,000 and she was able to reduce the balance to $75,000, which in turn reduced her monthly mortgage payments. The $25,000 cancellation of mortgage debt will be excluded from Muffy's gross income. Accordingly, Muffy will need to reduce her basis in the home to $135,000 ($160,000 − $25,000 debt forgiven). ♦

The amount of excludable income under the qualified principal residence exception is limited to $750,000 ($375,000 for married taxpayers filing separately).

Because taxpayers that exclude cancellation of debt income under any of these provisions are often bankrupt, insolvent, or both, the tax rules require that the cancellation be attributed first to bankruptcy, if that applies and next to insolvency, if that applies.

In order to encourage students to pursue careers in certain occupations or locations that have unmet needs, the cancellation of certain student loans is also excluded from income. The student loan generally must be issued by a university or government agency.

Example Yousef attended Grays Medical University to become a pediatrician. Due to the cost of medical education, Yousef incurred substantial student loan debt. When Yousef graduated, he entered Grays Native American Loan Repayment Program. This program will refinance Yousef's existing student loans and then cancel Yousef's debt if he agrees to serve as a pediatrician for 5 years at a Native American reservation hospital. ♦

More broadly, student loans discharged before 2026 for any reason are also excluded from income.

The rules related to the exclusion of cancellation of debt can be complex and this section provides only a basic overview. Taxpayers report exclusions from bankruptcy, insolvency, and qualified business or principal residence property on Form 982.

Self-Study Problem 2.18 *Refer to Appendix E for Solutions to Self-Study Problems*

In 2024, Bogdan loses his job when his employer closes. Because Bogdan is struggling to pay his monthly expenses, he arranges a decrease in his mortgage from $160,000 to $120,000 with his mortgage lender. His basis in the home is $200,000 and the fair market value at the time of the mortgage reduction is $250,000. Bogdan also has $10,000 of student loan debt forgiven in 2024 under a federal program to forgive students loans for lower-income individuals.

a. What amount of the cancellation of debt must Bogdan include in his income in 2024?

b. What is Bogdan's basis in his home after applying exclusion provisions (if any)?

Key Terms

gross income, 2-2
barter, 2-2
Form W-2, 2-5
health insurance, 2-7
convenience of employer, 2-8
de minimis meals, 2-8
qualified fringe benefits, 2-10
cafeteria plan, 2-10
flexible spending accounts (FSA), 2-10
qualified transportation benefits, 2-11
de minimis transportation benefits, 2-11
dependent care assistance programs (DCAP), 2-12
group term life insurance, 2-12
education assistance plans, 2-13
tuition reduction, 2-13
no-additional-cost services, 2-13
employee discounts, 2-14
working condition fringe benefits, 2-14
de minimis fringe benefits, 2-14

athletic facilities, 2-15
retirement planning fringe benefit, 2-15
prizes, 2-17
awards, 2-17
qualified plan award, 2-18
annuities, 2-18
simplified method, 2-19
the general rule, 2-21
Form 1099-R, 2-22
life insurance proceeds, 2-23
viatical settlements, 2-23
interest income, 2-25
U.S. savings bonds, 2-25
U.S. Treasury Bills, 2-27
corporate bonds, 2-28
original issue discount (OID), 2-28
state and local bonds (municipals), 2-28
market discount and premium, 2-29
gift loans, 2-30
Form 1099-INT, 2-30
ordinary and qualified dividends, 2-34

Form 1099-DIV, 2-36
Section 199A dividends, 2-36
gift, 2-38
inheritance, 2-38
scholarship, 2-39
alimony, 2-39
property transfers, 2-40
child support, 2-40
qualified tuition programs (Section 529 tuition plan), 2-42
educational savings account (Coverdell), 2-44
unemployment compensation, 2-46
Social Security benefits, 2-46
Form SSA-1099, 2-47
community property, 2-51
separate property, 2-51
cancellation of debt income, 2-53
qualified real property business debt, 2-54
qualified principal residence debt, 2-54

Key Points

Learning Objectives	Key Points
LO 2.1: Apply the definition of gross income.	• Gross income means "all income from whatever source derived." • Gross income includes everything a taxpayer receives unless it is specifically excluded from gross income by the tax law.
LO 2.2: Describe salaries and wages income reporting and inclusion in gross income.	• The primary form of reporting wages to an employee is through Form W-2. • Employers should report the employee's taxable wages, salary, bonuses, awards, commissions, and almost every other type of taxable compensation in Box 1 of the Form W-2. • If a taxpayer receives more than one Form W-2 or is jointly filing with a spouse having their own Form W-2, the amounts in Box 1 are combined before entering the total on Line 1a of the Form 1040. • Other Form W-2 information such as federal and state income taxes withheld will also be reported by the taxpayer on the Form 1040.
LO 2.3: Explain the general tax treatment of health insurance.	• Taxpayers may exclude health insurance premiums paid by their employer. • Taxpayers are allowed an exclusion for payments received from accident and health plans. The taxpayer may exclude the total amount received for payment of medical care, including any amount paid for the medical care of the taxpayer, their spouse, or dependents.
LO 2.4: Determine when meals and lodging may be excluded from taxable income.	• Meals and lodging are excluded from gross income provided they are for the convenience of the employer and they are furnished on the business premises. Lodging must be a condition of employment to be excluded.
LO 2.5: Identify the common employee fringe benefit income exclusions.	• Certain fringe benefits provided to employees may be excluded from the employees' gross income. These include dependent care and health care flexible spending accounts, transportation (commuter) benefits, dependent care assistance programs, group term life insurance (up to $50,000), education assistance plans, and others.
LO 2.6: Determine when prizes and awards are included in income.	• Amounts received from prizes and awards are normally taxable income unless refused by the taxpayer. • Certain small prizes of tangible personal property (generally under $400) for length of service and safety achievement are excluded from gross income. If the award is a "qualified plan award," up to $1,600 of the value of the award may be excluded.
LO 2.7: Calculate the taxable and nontaxable portions of annuity payments.	• Under both the simplified method and the general rule, annuity payments received by a taxpayer may have an element of taxable income and an element of tax-free return of the original purchase price. • Individual taxpayers generally must use the "simplified" method to calculate the taxable amount from a qualified annuity starting after November 18, 1996. • The part of the payment that is excluded from income is the ratio of the investment in the contract to the total return. • The total return is the annual payment multiplied by the life expectancy of the annuitant, based on mortality tables provided by the IRS.

LO 2.8: Describe the tax treatment of life insurance proceeds.	• Life insurance proceeds are generally excluded from gross income. If the proceeds are taken over several years instead of in a lump sum payment, any interest on the unpaid proceeds is generally taxable income. • Early payouts of life insurance are excluded from gross income for certain terminally or chronically ill taxpayers. • All or a portion of the proceeds from a life insurance policy transferred to another person for valuable consideration may be taxable to the recipient.
LO 2.9: Identify the tax treatment of interest income.	• Interest income is taxable except for certain state and municipal bond interest. • Interest income exceeding $1,500 per year must be reported in detail on Schedule B of Form 1040. • Series EE and Series I Savings Bond interest is taxable in the year the bonds are cashed unless a taxpayer elects to report the interest each year as it accrues. • Under certain circumstances, interest income from EE and I Savings Bonds can be excluded if used for higher education expenses. • Interest must be adjusted for purchases and sales between interest payments, and at times, for market discount and premium. • Interest from an obligation of a state, territory, or possession of the United States, a political subdivision of the foregoing, or the District of Columbia, is excluded from gross income.
LO 2.10: Identify the tax treatment of dividend income.	• Ordinary dividends are also qualifying dividends if the stock is held for a certain length of time (usually 60 days) and is issued by a U.S. corporation. • If ordinary dividends are not qualifying dividends, they are taxed as ordinary income, which is generally a higher rate than the long-term capital gains rate. • Qualified dividends are taxed at rates ranging from 0 percent to 20 percent and possibly included in the 3.8 percent net investment income tax for high-income taxpayers. • Like interest income, ordinary dividend income exceeding $1,500 per year must be reported in detail on Schedule B of Form 1040. Ordinary dividends of $1,500 or less and qualified dividends of any amount are reported on Lines 3a and 3b of Form 1040.
LO 2.11: Identify the general rules for the tax treatment of gifts and inheritances.	• The receipt of gifts and inheritances is usually excludable from gross income. Income received from the property after the transfer may be taxable to the recipient.
LO 2.12: Describe the elements of scholarship income that are excluded from tax.	• Scholarships granted to degree candidates are excluded from gross income if spent for tuition, fees, books, and course-required supplies and equipment. Amounts received for items such as room and board are taxable to the recipient.
LO 2.13: Describe the tax treatment of alimony and child support.	• Alimony paid in cash is taxable to the person who receives it and is deductible to the person who pays it, for divorce agreements dated prior to January 1, 2019. • Alimony is neither included in nor deducted from taxable income beginning with divorce or separation agreements after December 31, 2018. • Child support is not alimony and is not taxable when received, nor deductible when paid. • A spouse who transfers property in settlement of a marital obligation is not required to recognize any gain as a result of the property's appreciation. The receiving spouse assumes the tax basis of the property.

LO 2.14: Explain the tax implications of using educational savings vehicles.	• A Qualified Tuition Program (Section 529 plan) allows taxpayers (1) to buy in-kind tuition credits or certificates for qualified higher education expenses (a prepaid tuition plan) or (2) to contribute to an account established to meet qualified higher education expenses (a savings-type plan). Distributions from the account are not taxable if the proceeds are used for qualified higher education expenses. • Qualified higher education expenses include tuition, fees, books, supplies, and equipment required for the enrollment or attendance at an eligible educational institution. In addition, taxpayers are allowed reasonable room and board costs, subject to certain limitations. • The maximum exclusion for elementary or secondary education (K-12) for tuition only, is $10,000 per beneficiary per year. • Distributions from a Section 529 plan may be used for student loan payments up to a lifetime limit of $10,000 per beneficiary or beneficiary's siblings. • Under certain circumstances, excess 529 account balances can be rolled over into Roth IRA accounts for the beneficiary. • Taxpayers can annually contribute $2,000 to an educational savings account (Coverdell) for a beneficiary, subject to income and other limitations.
LO 2.15: Describe the tax treatment of unemployment compensation.	• Unemployment compensation is taxable.
LO 2.16: Apply the rules governing inclusion of Social Security benefits in gross income.	• Taxpayers with income under $25,000 ($32,000 for married filing jointly) exclude all of their Social Security benefits from gross income. • Middle-income and upper-income Social Security recipients, however, may have to include up to 85 percent of their benefits in gross income. • Calculating the taxable amount of Social Security is complex and most easily performed using a worksheet, such as the one provided in this textbook, or by using a tax program such as ProConnect Tax.
LO 2.17: Distinguish between the different rules for married taxpayers residing in community property states when filing separate returns.	• Income derived from community property held by a married couple, either jointly or separately, as well as wages and other income earned by a married couple, must be allocated between the spouses, if filing separately. • Nine states use a community property system of marital law. These states are Arizona, California, Idaho, Louisiana, Nevada, New Mexico, Texas, Washington, and Wisconsin. • In general, in a community property state, income is split one-half (50 percent) to each spouse. There are exceptions for certain separate property (e.g., property owned prior to marriage, inherited property, etc.).
LO 2.18: Describe the inclusion and exclusion of cancellation of debt income.	• Generally, cancellation of debt results in taxable income. • Income from the cancellation of debt due to bankruptcy, insolvency, associated with qualified real business property or a qualified primary residence, and certain student loan debt can be excluded from gross income.

Questions and Problems

Group 1: Multiple Choice Questions

LO 2.1 1. The definition of gross income in the tax law is:
   a. All items specifically listed as income in the tax law
   b. All cash payments received for goods provided and services performed
   c. All income from whatever source derived
   d. All income from whatever source derived unless the income is earned illegally

LO 2.1 2. Which of the following is excluded from gross income for income tax purposes in 2024?
   a. Commissions
   b. Student loan forgiveness
   c. Qualified dividends
   d. Unemployment compensation
   e. Bonus pay

LO 2.1 3. In 2024, all of the following items are gross income to the taxpayer receiving them, *except*:
   a. Damages for personal injury
   b. Hobby income
   c. Embezzled funds
   d. Gains from illegal activities
   e. Gambling winnings

LO 2.1 4. In 2024, which of the following types of income is excluded from gross income?
   a. Unemployment compensation
   b. Income earned illegally
   c. Dividends from foreign corporations
   d. Corporate bond interest income
   e. Qualified Medicaid waiver payments

LO 2.1 5. Which of the following is included in gross income?
   a. Loans
   b. Scholarships for room and board
   c. Gifts
   d. Health insurance proceeds
   e. Rental allowance received by clergy

LO 2.1 6. Pastor Ize is a minister at a local church. Which of the following payments made to her by the church will be excluded from income?
   a. Her monthly salary/wages
   b. Fees she receives for performing marriages
   c. The rental allowance that covers reasonable rent
   d. Compensation paid by other churches when she serves as a visiting pastor

LO 2.1 7. Kay Nein is a dentist and provides Rusty Clutch with $800 of dental services in exchange for Rusty repairing Kay's car. Kay will recognize how much gross income on this exchange?
   a. $0
   b. The out-of-pocket cost of the car repair (parts)
   c. The out-of-pocket costs for the dental work
   d. The market value of the services exchanged ($800)

Chapter 2 • Gross Income and Exclusions

LO 2.2
8. Annual wages subject to income tax are reported:
   a. On Form W-4
   b. On Form W-2 in Box 1
   c. On Form W-2 in Boxes 1, 3, and 5
   d. On Form 1099-W in Box 1

LO 2.2
9. State income tax withholding is reported on:
   a. Form W-2S
   b. Form W-4
   c. Each state has a unique reporting form
   d. Form W-2 in Box 17

LO 2.3
10. In 2024, Jonah's employer pays $8,700 for health insurance premiums for Jonah, Jonah's spouse, and Jonah's three dependent children. Jonah has $100 per month withheld from his pay toward the cost as well. Jonah's employer covers the entire cost ($1,400 for the year) of Jonah's dental plan for his household. How much gross income will Jonah report from his employer's payments for his health and dental plan premiums?
    a. $0
    b. $1,400
    c. $8,700
    d. $10,100

LO 2.3
11. Taylor's 2024 health insurance premiums of $7,800 are paid by her employer. During 2024, Taylor requires surgery on her vocal chords. The cost of the surgery is $10,000 and Taylor's insurance covers all but $500, which Taylor pays herself. How much is Taylor's gross income from these health-related transactions?
    a. $0
    b. $7,800
    c. $9,500
    d. $10,000
    e. $17,800

LO 2.4
12. Homer works at the Springfield Nuclear Plant as a nuclear technician. The plant is located 15 miles from the town of Springfield. Homer eats his lunch at the plant's cafeteria because he is required to be available for nuclear emergencies during his shift. No other eating establishments are located near the plant. Homer estimates the value of the meals he was provided during the current year to be $1,300. He estimates the cost for him to have prepared those lunches for himself to be about $560. The cost of the meals to the power company was $470. How much income does Homer need to recognize from the meals?
    a. $1,300
    b. $560
    c. $470
    d. $830 ($1,300 − $470)
    e. Some other amount

LO 2.4
13. In which of the following situations is the value of employer-provided meals included in gross income?
    a. An employee that is not required to eat at the company cafeteria but often does. The majority of other employees at this location are required to eat in the cafeteria for business reasons.
    b. An employee of a quick-service restaurant that eats a meal at the end of his work shift each day.
    c. An employee that eats two to three doughnuts on Doughnut Day (the third Friday of each month) while most employees eat one or none.
    d. An employee who occasionally receives a free meal when working overtime
    e. None of these meals are included in gross income.

LO 2.5 14. Which of the following is a fringe benefit excluded from income?
   a. A mechanic at Denise's employer, a car rental company, provides $1,000 of repair services to Denise's personal car for free
   b. Alfa-Bet, a high-tech corporation, pays for each employee's membership at the 24 Hour Biceps Gym closest to each Alfa-Bet office
   c. Quickchat Inc. gives each employee a $10 giftcard to the local coffee shop on National Coffee Day
   d. Hedaya, a doctoral student at Ivy University, receives a full tuition waiver while serving as research assistant

LO 2.5 15. Which of the following will result in the recognition of gross income?
   a. Gail's employer allows her to set aside $4,000 from her wages to cover the cost of daycare for Gail's 4-year-old daughter. Gail's daycare costs are $4,300 for the year.
   b. Hannah purchases a new sofa from her employer, Sofas-R-Us, for $1,200. The cost of the sofa to the furniture store is $1,100 and the sofa normally sells for $1,700.
   c. Jayden's employer purchases his commuting pass for the subway at a cost of $350 per month.
   d. Havana is a lawyer. The law firm they work for pays their subscription to Lawyer's Weekly, a trade magazine for attorneys.
   e. None of the items listed will result in recognition of gross income.

LO 2.5 16. In 2024, the limit for contributions to a health care flexible spending account is:
   a. $500
   b. $2,850
   c. $3,050
   d. $3,200

LO 2.5 17. Veruca's employer offers both a dependent care flexible spending account (FSA) and a dependent care assistance program in which employees can receive occasional dependent care at no cost. In 2024, the maximum total amount Veruca can exclude from her gross income for both dependent care programs is:
   a. $0
   b. $5,000
   c. $5,250
   d. $10,000

LO 2.5 18. Which of the following transportation-related costs paid by an employer to or on behalf of an employee cannot be excluded from gross income?
   a. Providing bus passes to employees at a $20 discount.
   b. Paying for the parking of only senior executives at a cost of $285 per month.
   c. Paying the occasional ride-sharing fare for an employee that has worked overtime late into the evening.
   d. Paying $10 per month for bicycle storage for employees that bike to work.

LO 2.5 19. Air Suppliers Inc. provides group term insurance to all its employees for policies up to $250,000. Michelle, an Air Suppliers employee, has a $100,000 policy. The cost of the policy is $50 per month, all of which is paid by Air Suppliers. Which of the following best describes how much gross income Michelle will recognize for this employee benefit?
   a. Michelle will recognize no gross income.
   b. Michelle will recognize gross income for the estimated cost of the premiums of the life insurance above $50,000.
   c. Michelle must recognize the annual cost of the policy ($600) as gross income.
   d. Michelle will recognize no gross income but if she dies, the beneficiary will pay taxes on the life insurance benefits paid.

Chapter 2 • Gross Income and Exclusions

LO 2.5

20. Which of the following fringe benefits can be offered to only executives and remain excluded from employee gross income?
    a. Parking
    b. Group term life insurance up to $50,000
    c. De minimis cafeteria provided meals
    d. Employee discounts

LO 2.6

21. Which of the following prizes or awards is *not* taxable?
    a. A crystal paperweight worth $125 given to an employee for achieving 10 years of service to the company
    b. Prizes from a television game show
    c. Awards for superior performance on the job
    d. A $100 gift card received as a prize in a raffle run by the local school parent-teacher organization
    e. All of the prizes or awards listed are taxable

LO 2.6

22. Huihana receives four tickets to the local professional football game for achieving twenty years of employment with her employer. The tickets cost the employer $390 and have a market value of the same on the date awarded. Huihana is in the highest tax bracket for single taxpayers. How much gross income will Huihana recognize on the receipt of the tickets?
    a. $390
    b. $200
    c. $25
    d. $0
    e. $50 or $59.50 including the net investment income tax

LO 2.7

23. A 67-year-old taxpayer retires this year and receives the first payment on a qualified annuity that was purchased several years ago. The taxpayer's investment in the annuity is $94,500, and the annuity pays $1,000 per month for the remainder of the taxpayer's life. Based on IRS mortality tables, the taxpayer is expected to live another twenty years. If the taxpayer receives $4,000 in annuity payments in the current year, the nontaxable portion calculated using the simplified method is:
    a. $0
    b. $1,500
    c. $1,800
    d. $4,000
    e. Some other amount

LO 2.7

24. Amara has an annuity and over time has recovered her entire investment but it continues to pay her $450 per month. Amara should recognize how much of each monthly payment as gross income?
    a. $0
    b. Some amount greater than $450
    c. Some amount between $0 and $450
    d. $450

LO 2.7

25. In 2024, Georgia, a single taxpayer, contributes a portion of her wages to her employer's qualified retirement plan. In addition, her employer contributes an amount as well. Georgia's 2024 taxable wage amount does not include either of these contributions. As a result, distributions from the plan to Georgia after her retirement age will:
    a. Be taxed on the total amount.
    b. Be taxed, but only to the extent of income earned since the contribution.
    c. Not be taxed.
    d. Be taxed, but only to the extent of the amount contributed.

LO 2.7

26. McGarrett is a retired police officer with the city of Honolulu and receives a pension of $66,000 per year. All of the contributions to the pension on McGarrett's behalf were made by the city of Honolulu. As part of his retiree health insurance, McGarrett is required to contribute $400 per month. Based on this information, what is the taxable amount of McGarrett's pension?
    a. $0 (pensions are not taxable)
    b. $66,000
    c. $63,000
    d. $61,200

LO 2.8

27. Which of the following might result in life insurance proceeds that are taxable to the recipient?
    a. A life insurance policy in which the insured is the son of the taxpayer and the beneficiary is the taxpayer
    b. A life insurance policy transferred by a partner to the partnership
    c. A life insurance policy transferred to a creditor in payment of a debt
    d. A life insurance policy purchased by a taxpayer insuring his or her spouse
    e. A life insurance policy purchased by a corporation insuring an officer

LO 2.8

28. Lupita dies in 2024 but has a $1 million life insurance policy that lists her spouse, M'Baku as the beneficiary. M'Baku elects to receive all $1 million in a lump sum and spends $200,000 immediately on a new yacht. M'Baku's gross income from the life insurance is:
    a. $0
    b. $200,000
    c. $800,000
    d. $1,000,000

LO 2.9

29. Rebecca, a single taxpayer, owns a Series I U.S. Savings Bond that increased in value by $46 during the year. She makes no special election. How much income must Rebecca recognize this year?
    a. $0
    b. $46
    c. $23
    d. $0 if in first 5 years or $46 thereafter

LO 2.9

30. Interest from which of the following types of bonds is included in federal taxable income?
    a. State of California bond
    b. City of New Orleans bond
    c. Bond of the Commonwealth of Puerto Rico
    d. U.S. Treasury Bond
    e. All of the bonds listed are excluded from income

LO 2.9

31. Which of the following best describes the treatment of U.S. obligation interest income?
    a. Excluded from federal and state gross income
    b. Excluded from federal gross income but included for most states
    c. Included in federal gross income but excluded for most states
    d. Included in gross income for federal and state purposes

LO 2.9

32. In 2024, Yui, a single mother, redeems Series EE bonds and uses the total proceeds ($6,700 par value and $1,300 interest) to pay for her daughter's college education. If Yui's 2024 AGI is $75,000, how much of the proceeds from the redemption of the EE bonds must she include in gross income?
    a. $0
    b. $1,300
    c. $6,700
    d. $8,000

LO 2.9
33. On September 22, 2024, Jerry purchases a corporate bond. The bond pays interest each sixth months on June 30 and December 31 of each year. On December 31, 2024, Jerry receives an interest payment of $400. The amount of interest Jerry will need to include in gross income is:
   a. None
   b. Exactly $400
   c. More than $400
   d. Less than $400

LO 2.9
34. A bond is issued in 2022 at its face value of $10,000 with an interest rate of 5 percent. In 2024, the bond is sold when prevailing interest rates have increased. When recognizing gross income from the interest on the bond, the buyer of the bond in 2024 will have to consider:
   a. market bond discount
   b. original issue discount
   c. market bond premium
   d. in-kind dividends

LO 2.9
35. Helen loans her son Ricky, $25,000 to help with the purchase of investments and personal expenses. Due to her affection for her son, Helen charges Ricky zero interest. Which of these statements best describes the result of this below-market loan?
   a. Ricky will have interest income.
   b. Helen will have interest income and an offsetting gift to Ricky.
   c. Helen will have interest expense since she is out the interest she could have earned.
   d. Ricky will have interest income since he is better off by not having to pay interest.

LO 2.10
36. Nomi is in the highest individual tax bracket (37 percent) and receives $375 in qualified dividends from Omega Corp. Nomi's tax liability (not including any net investment income tax) with respect to these dividends is:
   a. $0
   b. $277.20
   c. $100.00
   d. $75.00
   e. $50.00

LO 2.10
37. The distinction between qualified dividends and ordinary dividends is:
   a. There is no distinction.
   b. Ordinary dividends are taxed at preferential rates.
   c. Qualified dividends are taxed at preferential rates and are a subset of ordinary dividends.
   d. Qualified dividends are excluded from gross income.

LO 2.11
38. Which of the following gifts would probably be taxable to the person receiving the gift?
   a. One thousand dollars given to a taxpayer by his or her father
   b. An acre of land given to a taxpayer by a friend
   c. A car given to a retiring loyal employee to recognize her faithful service
   d. A Mercedes-Benz given to a taxpayer by his cousin
   e. An interest in a partnership given to a taxpayer by his or her uncle

LO 2.12
39. Kelly receives a $40,000 scholarship to Ivy University. She uses $35,000 on tuition and books and $5,000 for rent while at school. How much gross income will Kelly recognize, if any?
   a. $0
   b. $5,000
   c. $10,000
   d. $30,000
   e. $40,000

LO 2.13 40. Hillary gets divorced in 2020 and is required to pay her ex-spouse $200 per month until her son reaches 18 years of age in seven years and $120 per month thereafter. How much of her 2024 payments are deductible as alimony?
a. $0
b. $2,400
c. $1,440
d. $960

LO 2.13 41. Donald and Michelle are divorced in the current year. As part of the divorce settlement, Michelle transfers a plot of land in Long Island, NY to Donald. Michelle's basis in the property was $20,000 and the market value of the property was $250,000 when transferred. Donald holds the property through the end of the year in hopes of building a residence on it. How much income do Michelle and Donald recognize in the current year?
a. $0 for Michelle and $20,000 for Donald
b. $230,000 for Michelle and $20,000 for Donald
c. $230,000 for Michelle and $0 for Donald
d. $0 for both Michelle and Donald
e. $0 for Michelle and $250,000 for Donald

LO 2.14 42. Gina receives a $2,900 distribution from her educational savings account. She uses $1,500 to pay for qualified higher education expenses and $1,400 on a vacation. Immediately prior to the distribution, Gina's account balance is $5,000, $3,000 of which are her contributions. What is Gina's taxable income (after any exclusion) from the distribution?
a. $1,400
b. $560
c. $840
d. $0
e. Some other amount

LO 2.14 43. Which of the following is correct for Qualified Tuition Programs (Section 529 plans)?
a. Contributions are deductible, and qualified educational expense distributions are tax-free.
b. Contributions are not deductible, and qualified educational expense distributions are tax-free.
c. Contributions are deductible, and qualified educational expense distributions are taxable.
d. Contributions are not deductible, and qualified educational expense distributions are taxable.

LO 2.14 44. In 2024, Amy receives $8,000 (of which $3,000 is earnings) from a qualified tuition program. She uses the funds to pay for tuition and other qualified higher education expenses. What amount is taxable to Amy?
a. $0
b. $8,000
c. $3,000
d. $11,000

LO 2.14 45. For married taxpayers filing a joint return in 2024, at what AGI level does the phase-out limit for contributions to Section 529 plans start?
a. $110,000
b. $190,000
c. $220,000
d. There is no phase-out limit on Section 529 plan contributions

LO 2.14 46. Which of the following is true with respect to education incentives?
a. The contributions to qualified tuition programs (Section 529 plans) are deductible.
b. The contributions to educational savings accounts (Coverdell) are deductible.

c. Tuition paid by a taxpayer earning $300,000 of income is deductible.
d. Married taxpayers have no income limit to contribute to a qualified tuition program (Section 529 plan).

LO 2.14
47. During 2024, Carl (a single taxpayer) has a salary of $91,500 and interest income of $11,000. Calculate the maximum contribution Carl is allowed for an educational savings account (Coverdell).
    a. $0
    b. $400
    c. $1,000
    d. $2,000
    e. Some other amount

LO 2.15
48. Alicia loses her job part way through 2024. Her employer paid her wages of $15,450 up through her date of termination. After that, she received $1,600 of unemployment compensation from the state until she started a new job for which she is paid wages of $1,400 through year-end. Based on this information, Alicia's gross income for 2024 is:
    a. $15,450
    b. $16,850
    c. $17,050
    d. $18,450
    e. $21,850

LO 2.16
49. For 2024, the maximum percentage of Social Security benefits that could be included in a taxpayer's gross income is:
    a. 0%
    b. 25%
    c. 50%
    d. 75%
    e. 85%

LO 2.16
50. Generally, when calculating the taxable portion of Social Security benefits, modified adjusted gross income (MAGI) is adjusted gross income (without Social Security benefits):
    a. Plus tax-exempt interest
    b. Less personal and dependency exemptions
    c. Less itemized deductions
    d. Less tax-exempt interest plus any foreign income exclusion
    e. Less tax-exempt interest income

LO 2.17
51. Dana and Larry are married and live in Texas. Dana earns a salary of $45,000 and Larry has $25,000 of rental income from his separate property. If Dana and Larry file separate tax returns, what amount of income must Larry report?
    a. $0
    b. $22,500
    c. $25,000
    d. $47,500
    e. None of the above

LO 2.17
52. Which of the following conditions need *not* be satisfied in order for a married taxpayer, residing in a community property state, to be taxed only on their separate salary?
    a. The spouses must live apart for the entire year.
    b. A minor child must be living with the spouse.
    c. The spouses must not file a joint income tax return.
    d. The spouses must not transfer earned income between themselves.
    e. All of the above must be satisfied.

LO 2.18 53. Jack borrows $13,000 from Sawyer Savings and Loan and uses the proceeds to acquire a used car. When the loan balance is $12,000, Jack loses his job and is unable to make payments for three months. When Jack gets a new job, the bank agrees to forgive the missed principal payments and reduces his loan to $11,500. Jack remains solvent even when unemployed. How much cancellation of debt income does Jack have?
   a. $0
   b. $500
   c. $1,500
   d. $2,000

LO 2.18 54. Kate acquires a principal residence in 2018 for $200,000 secured by a $180,000 mortgage. In 2024, Kate misses work for three months. Her employer stops paying her after ten days. In 2024, when the mortgage balance is $170,000, Kate and the bank revise her terms and lower the loan balance to $150,000. The market value of the home remains above $200,000. How much cancellation of debt income will Kate recognize?
   a. $0
   b. $20,000
   c. $10,000
   d. $150,000
   e. $170,000

LO 2.18 55. Mike, a single taxpayer, has $10,000 of student loans forgiven in 2024 under a federal student loan forgiveness program. His total student loan balance was $34,000. His 2024 AGI is $55,000. How much cancellation of debt income will Mike need to recognize in 2024?
   a. $0
   b. $10,000
   c. $5,000
   d. $24,000

Group 2: Problems

LO 2.1 1. Indicate whether each of the items listed below would be included in or excluded from gross income for the 2024 tax year.
   a. Welfare payments
   b. Wrongful incarceration awards
   c. Hobby income
   d. Scholarships for room and board
   e. $300 set of golf clubs, an employee award for length of service
   f. Nonemployee compensation
   g. Cancellation of debt income
   h. Accident insurance proceeds received for personal bodily injury
   i. Inheritances
   j. Gifts
   k. Tips and gratuities

LO 2.1 2. Jane is a roofing contractor. Jane's friend needed a new roof but did not have the cash to pay. Jane's friend instead paid with a used truck that Jane could use in her roofing business. The truck had originally cost the friend $17,500 but it was gently used and only worth $6,000. Jane did not actually need the truck and ended up selling it to a used car dealer for $5,200 a few months later. Explain what amount of gross income Jane must recognize as a result of the truck payment and why.

LO 2.1

3. Larry is a tax accountant and Sheila is a hairdresser. Larry prepares Sheila's tax return for free and Sheila agrees to style Larry's hair six times for free in return for the tax return. The value of the tax return is approximately $300 and the hair styling work is approximately $300.
   a. How much of the $300 is includable income to Larry? Why?
   b. How much of the $300 is includable income to Sheila? Why?

LO 2.1

4. Kerry and Jim have a successful marijuana farm in the woods around Humboldt County, California. Growing marijuana is illegal for federal purposes. Are Kerry and Jim required by law to report the income from their farm on their tax return? Why?

LO 2.2

5. Kristen, a single taxpayer, receives two 2024 Form W-2s from the two employers she worked for during the year. One Form W-2 lists her wages in Boxes 1, 3, and 5 as $19,000. Her other employer's Form W-2 has $47,000 in Box 1 but $48,410 in both Box 3 and Box 5. Kristen participated in the second employer's 401k plan. She also received health care from her second employer. Lastly, her second employer provided $30,000 of group term life insurance to Kristen.
   a. What amount should Kristen report as taxable wages in 2024?
   b. What could explain the difference between Box 1 wages and Boxes 3 and 5 on her second employer's W-2?

LO 2.2

6. Use the Form W-2 below to answer the following questions:
   a. Explain the $7,000 difference between wages reported in Box 1 and Box 5.
   b. Explain why Box 3 reports only $168,600.
   c. Which boxes are likely to be reported on the taxpayer's Form 1040? What do those amounts represent and what line of the 1040 or supplemental schedule are they likely to be reported on?

a Employee's social security number 451-78-9001	OMB No. 1545-0008	Safe, accurate, FAST! Use e-file	Visit the IRS website at www.irs.gov/efile.
b Employer identification number (EIN) 31-1122334		1 Wages, tips, other compensation 171,000.00	2 Federal income tax withheld 42,867.23
c Employer's name, address, and ZIP code Chaffey Corporation 100 Panther Drive Rancho Cucamonga, CA 91737		3 Social security wages 168,600.00	4 Social security tax withheld 10,453.20
		5 Medicare wages and tips 178,000.00	6 Medicare tax withheld 2,581.00
		7 Social security tips	8 Allocated tips
d Control number		9	10 Dependent care benefits
e Employee's first name and initial Last name Suff. Fontana Chino 8800 Highland Ave Rancho Cucamonga, CA 91737		11 Nonqualified plans	12a See instructions for box 12 D 7,000.00
		13 Statutory employee ☐ Retirement plan ☒ Third-party sick pay ☐	12b DD 9,876.56
		14 Other	12c
			12d
f Employee's address and ZIP code			
15 State Employer's state ID number CA 00341156	16 State wages, tips, etc. 171,000.00	17 State income tax 15,634.50	18 Local wages, tips, etc. 19 Local income tax 20 Locality name

Form **W-2** Wage and Tax Statement **2024** Department of the Treasury—Internal Revenue Service
Copy B—To Be Filed With Employee's FEDERAL Tax Return.
This information is being furnished to the Internal Revenue Service.

LO 2.3

7. Skyler is covered by his company's health insurance plan. The health insurance costs his company $9,500 a year. During the year, Skyler is diagnosed with a serious illness and health insurance pays $100,000 for surgery and treatment. How much of the insurance and treatment payments are taxable to Skyler?

LO 2.3

8. Malin is a married taxpayer and has three dependent children. Malin's employer offers health insurance for employees and Malin takes advantage of the benefit for her entire family (her spouse's employer also offers health insurance but they opt out).

During the year, Malin paid $1,200 toward her family's health insurance premiums through payroll deductions while the employer paid the remaining $9,200. Malin's family visited health care professionals numerous times during the year and made total co-payments toward medical services of $280. Malin's daughter had knee surgery due to a soccer injury and the insurance company paid the hospital $6,700 directly and reimbursed Malin $400 for her out-of-pocket health care expenses related to the surgery. Explain how much gross income should Malin recognize related to her health insurance and why?

LO 2.4

9. For each of the following, explain whether the value of the meals provided to the taxpayer are part of the taxpayer's gross income and why:
   a. Milton is a nurse whose employer provided meals for him on the employer's premises, since he is given only 30 minutes for lunch.
   b. Mary is a San Diego ambulance driver. The city provides Mary with meals while she is working so she will be available for emergencies.
   c. Indigo is the head of security at a casino. The casino operator frequently provides meals from the casino buffet to Indigo as a gesture of goodwill for the great job she is doing. The casino does not provide meals to other employees.
   d. Kerrie works at Sante Fe Memorial Hospital as an administrative assistant. Sante Fe operates a heavily subsidized on-site cafeteria because the majority of Sante Fe employees are required to eat lunch on the premises to be available for emergencies. Kerrie's job description has no such requirement and she is free to eat anywhere during a typical lunch hour. Kerrie likes the cafeteria and generally eats her meals there anyway. Kerrie estimates the value of her 2024 meals at the cafeteria as $2,750. Her records show she paid $400 for these meals.

LO 2.5

10. Linda and Richard are married and file a joint return for 2024. During the year, Linda, who works as an accountant for a national airline, flew stand-by on her employer's flights with a value of $2,100; Richard used the same amount. Linda and Richard also used $850 worth of employee vouchers for hotel rooms at the hotel chain that is also owned by the airline. Richard is employed at State University as an accounting clerk. Under a tuition reduction plan, Richard saved $4,000 in tuition fees during 2024. He is taking classes toward a master's degree in business at night while still working full-time. Richard also had $30 worth of personal typing done by his administrative assistant at the University. What is the amount of fringe benefits that should be included in Linda and Richard's gross income on their 2024 tax return?

LO 2.5

11. Ellen's tax client, Tom, is employed at a large company that offers health care flexible spending accounts to its employees. Tom must decide at the beginning of the year whether he wants to put as much as $3,200 of his salary into the health care flexible spending account. He expects that he will have to pay for at least $8,000 of medical expenses for his family during the year since his wife is seeing a psychiatrist every week and his daughter and son are both having orthodontic work. Tom does not itemize deductions. Should Ellen recommend that Tom put the maximum amount in his health care flexible spending account, and if so, why?

LO 2.6

12. How much of each of the following is included in gross income?
    a. Cheline, an actor, received a $7,600 gift bag for attending the Academy Awards Ceremony during 2024.
    b. Jon received a gold watch worth $700 for twenty-five years of service to his accounting firm (not a qualified award).
    c. Kerry won $1,000,000 in her state lottery.
    d. Deborah is a professor who received $30,000 as an award for her scientific research from the university that employs her.

Chapter 2 • Gross Income and Exclusions

LO 2.6
LO 2.12

13. For each of the following independent cases, indicate the amount of gross income that must be included on the taxpayer's 2024 income tax return.
    a. Malchia won a $4,000 humanitarian award.
    b. Rob won a new automobile (with a sticker price of $15,700 and a market value of $14,500) for being the best junior tennis player in 2024.
    c. George received a $3,500 tuition and fees scholarship to attend Western University.

LO 2.7

14. Lola, age 67, began receiving a $1,000 monthly annuity in the current year upon the death of her husband. She received seven payments in the current year. Her husband contributed $48,300 to the qualified employee plan. Use the Simplified Method Worksheet below to calculate Lola's taxable amount from the annuity.

Simplified Method Worksheet

1. Enter total amount received this year.   1. _____
2. Enter cost in the plan at the annuity starting date.   2. _____
3. Age at annuity starting date

	Enter
55 and under	360
56–60	310
61–65	260
66–70	210
71 and older	160

                                                                                    3. _____

4. Divide line 2 by line 3.   4. _____
5. Multiply line 4 by the number of monthly payments this year. If the annuity starting date was before 1987, also enter this amount on line 8, and skip lines 6 and 7. Otherwise, go to line 6.   5. _____
6. Enter the amount, if any, recovered tax free in prior years.   6. _____
7. Subtract line 6 from line 2.   7. _____
8. Enter the smaller of line 5 or 7.   8. _____
9. Taxable amount this year: Subtract line 8 from line 1. Do not enter less than zero.   9. _____

LO 2.8

15. Sharon transfers to Russ a life insurance policy with a cash surrender value of $30,000 and a face value of $100,000 in exchange for real estate worth $30,000. Russ continues to pay the premiums on the policy until Sharon dies seven years later. At that time, Russ has paid $12,000 in premiums, and he collects the $100,000 face value. Explain how much of the life insurance proceeds are taxable to Russ and why?

LO 2.8

16. Deandre died on July 1, 2024, and left Lea, his spouse, a $45,000 life insurance policy which she elects to receive at $9,000 per year plus interest for five years. In the current year, Lea receives $9,500. How much should Lea include in her gross income?

LO 2.8

17. David is certified by his doctor as terminally ill with liver disease. His doctor certifies that he cannot reasonably be expected to live for more than a year. He sells his life insurance policy to Viatical Settlements, Inc., for $250,000. He has paid $20,000 so far for the policy. How much of the $250,000 must David include in his taxable income?

LO 2.8

18. Amandine receives a $200,000 lump sum life insurance payment when her friend Clarisse dies. How much of the payment is taxable to Amandine?

LO 2.9

19. Describe the methods that an individual taxpayer that holds Series I Bonds can use to recognize interest.

LO 2.9 20. Yorick purchases a bond with a $10,000 face value and a 5 percent interest rate from Hamlet on March 31, 2024. The bond pays interest semiannually on June 30 and December 31. Prevailing interest rates have risen since Hamlet first purchased the bond for $10,000 at issuance and so Yorick pays $9,561 for the bond. Explain what two items are affecting the price that Yorick pays for the bond. Explain how these items will impact Yorick's gross income (if at all). The adjustment amounts need not be calculated.

LO 2.9 21. Vandell is a taxpayer in the 24-percent tax bracket. He invests in Otay Mesa Water District Bonds that pay 4.5 percent interest. What interest on a taxable bond would provide the same after-tax return to Vandell?

LO 2.9 22. Karen is a wealthy retired investment advisor who is in the 35-percent tax bracket. She has a choice between investing in a high-quality municipal bond paying 5 percent or a high-quality corporate bond paying 7 percent. What is the after-tax return of each bond and in which one should Karen invest? Explain your answer.

LO 2.10 23. How are qualified dividends taxed in 2024? Please give the rates of tax which apply to qualified dividends, and specify when each of these rates applies.

LO 2.9
LO 2.10 24. Sally and Charles Colonel received the following Form 1099-DIV in 2024:

Form 1099-DIV (Rev. January 2024) — **Dividends and Distributions** — For calendar year 2024

PAYER'S name, street address, city or town, state or province, country, ZIP or foreign postal code, and telephone no.:
Kentucky East Corporation
500 Lancaster Avenue
Richmond, KY 40475

- 1a Total ordinary dividends: $850.00
- 1b Qualified dividends: $775.00
- 2a Total capital gain distr.: $165.00
- 2b Unrecap. Sec. 1250 gain:
- 2c Section 1202 gain:
- 2d Collectibles (28%) gain:
- 2e Section 897 ordinary dividends:
- 2f Section 897 capital gain:
- 3 Nondividend distributions:
- 4 Federal income tax withheld: $0.00
- 5 Section 199A dividends:
- 6 Investment expenses:
- 7 Foreign tax paid:
- 8 Foreign country or U.S. possession:
- 9 Cash liquidation distributions:
- 10 Noncash liquidation distributions:
- 11 FATCA filing requirement: ☐
- 12 Exempt-interest dividends:
- 13 Specified private activity bond interest dividends:
- 14 State:
- 15 State identification no.:
- 16 State tax withheld:

PAYER'S TIN: 45-6067473
RECIPIENT'S TIN: 313-13-1313
RECIPIENT'S name: Sally Colonel
Street address: 1045 Gibson Bay Drive
City, state, ZIP: Richmond, KY 40475

Copy B For Recipient

The Colonels also received the following statement from the broker:

2024 Combined Forms 1099

This is important tax information and is being furnished to the IRS (except as indicated). If you are required to file a return, a negligence penalty or other sanction may be imposed on you if this income is taxable and the IRS determines that it has not been reported.

Copy B For Recipient
OMB No. 1545-0110

Friar Tuck Investments
38 Wall Street, 8th Floor
New York, NY 10005

Sally and Charles Colonel
1045 Gibson Bay Drive
Richmond, KY 40475

Account Number: 3100987765
Tax ID: ***-**-1313
Payer's Federal Tax ID: 33-1357246
Financial Adviser/Phone: Sherrie Nottingham 888-555-1212

Form 1099-DIV — Dividend Income

Box 1a Total ordinary dividends	Box 1b Qualified dividends	Box 2a Total capital gain distr.
5,450.00	4,850.00	
Box 4 Federal income tax withheld	**Box 5 Section 199A dividends**	**Box 6 Investment expenses**

Form 1099-INT — Interest Income

Box 1 Interest income	Box 2 Early withdrawal penalty	Box 3 Interest on U.S. Savings Bonds and Treasury obligations
1,700.00		250.00
Box 4 Federal income tax withheld	**Box 5 Investment expenses**	**Box 6 Foreign Tax Paid**
Box 7 Foreign country or U.S. possession	**Box 8 Tax-exempt interest**	**Box 9 Specified private activity bond interest**
	300.00	
Box 10 Market Discount	**Box 11 Bond Premium**	
Box 12 Bond premium on Treasury obligations	**Box 13 Bond premium on tax-exempt bond**	

Details provided by Friar Tuck Investments:

Dividends

Security	CUSIP	Date	Amount	Type
Micron Corp	909343566	03/15/2024	$1,000.00	Qualified dividend
		06/15/2024	1,000.00	Qualified dividend
		09/15/2024	1,000.00	Qualified dividend
		12/15/2024	1,000.00	Qualified dividend
Cucuko Rubber Corp	412309111	09/15/2024	600.00	Nonqualified dividend
Lectrowash Inc.	867001267	01/31/2024	425.00	Qualified dividend
		07/31/2024	425.00	Qualified dividend
Total Dividends			**$5,450.00**	

Interest

Security	Account Type	Account #	Amount	Type
Porcine Bank	MMKT	BGT334567	$ 600.00	Interest
River Bank	Preferred Savings	11000567	1,100.00	Interest
U.S. Treasury Bond	US Govt. Obligation		250.00	US Gov't interest
City of Richmond, KY Muni Bonds	Muni Bond		300.00	Muni interest
Total Interest			**$2,250.00**	

a. Assuming the Colonels file a joint tax return, complete Schedule B of Form 1040 (Appendix F) for them for the 2024 tax year.
b. What amounts are reported on Lines 2a and 2b of Form 1040?
c. What amounts are reported on Lines 3a and 3b of Form 1040?
d. Are any other amounts reportable on the Colonel's federal income tax return?

LO 2.11 25. In June of 2024, Thembi inherits stock worth $125,000. During the year, they collect $5,600 in dividends from the stock. Explain how much of these amounts, if any, should Thembi include in gross income for 2024 and why?

LO 2.11 26. Gwen is a tax accountant who works very hard for a large corporate client. The client is pleased and gives her a gift of $10,000 at year-end. How much of the gift is taxable to Gwen?

LO 2.11 27. Charlene receives a gift from her boyfriend of $10,000. He knows she is having financial problems and wants to help her. How much of the gift is taxable to Charlene?

LO 2.12 28. Bismack receives a scholarship of $20,000 to an elite private college. $12,000 of the scholarship is earmarked for tuition, and $8,000 covers his room and board. How much of the scholarship, if any, is taxable to Bismack?

LO 2.13 29. Answer the following questions:
   a. Under a 2017 divorce agreement, Britney is required to pay her ex-husband, Sam, $700 a month until their daughter is 18 years of age. At that time, the required payments are reduced to $450 per month.
      1. How much of each $700 payment may be deducted as alimony by Britney?
      2. How much of each $700 payment must be included in Sam's taxable income?
      3. How much would be deductible/included if the divorce agreement were dated 2024?
   b. Under the terms of a property settlement executed during 2024, Ariana transferred property worth $450,000 to her ex-husband, Dalton. The property has a tax basis to Ariana of $425,000.
      1. How much taxable gain must be recognized by Ariana at the time of the transfer?
      2. What is the amount of Dalton's tax basis in the property he received from Ariana?

LO 2.13 30. Arlen is required by his 2024 divorce agreement to pay alimony of $2,000 a month and child support of $2,000 a month to his ex-wife Nahomi. What is the tax treatment of these two payments for Arlen? What is the tax treatment of these two payments for Nahomi?

LO 2.13 31. As part of the property settlement related to their divorce, Bebe must give Keyon the house that they have been living in, while she gets 100 percent of their savings accounts. The house in southern California was purchased 20 years ago for $90,000 and is now worth $700,000. How much gain must Bebe recognize on the transfer of the house to Keyon? What is Keyon's tax basis in the house for calculating tax on any future sale of the house?

LO 2.14 32. Jose paid the following amounts for his son to attend Big State University in 2024:

Tuition	$6,400
Room and board	4,000
Books	800
A car to use at school	1,932
Student football tickets	237
Spending money	4,775

How much of the above is a qualified higher education expense for purposes of his Section 529 plan?

LO 2.14 33. In 2024, Van receives $16,000 (of which $4,000 is earnings) from a Section 529 plan. He uses the funds to pay for his college tuition and other qualified higher education expenses. How much of the $16,000 is taxable to Van?

LO 2.15 34. Lydia, a married individual, was unemployed for a few months during 2024. During the year, she received $2,250 in unemployment compensation payments. How much of her unemployment compensation payments must be included in gross income?

LO 2.16 35. During the 2024 tax year, Dalano, a single taxpayer, received $7,600 in Social Security benefits. Their adjusted gross income for the year was $16,000 (not including the Social Security benefits) and they received $28,000 in tax-exempt interest income and has no for AGI deductions. Calculate the amount of the Social Security benefits that Dalano must include in his gross income for 2024.

Simplified Taxable Social Security Worksheet (for most people)

1. Enter the total amount of Social Security income. 1. _____
2. Enter one-half of line 1. 2. _____
3. Enter the total of taxable income items on Form 1040 except Social Security income. 3. _____
4. Enter the amount of tax-exempt interest income. 4. _____
5. Add lines 2, 3, and 4. 5. _____
6. Enter all adjustments for AGI except for student loan interest deduction. 6. _____
7. Subtract line 6 from line 5. If zero or less, stop here, none of the Social Security benefits are taxable. 7. _____
8. Enter $25,000 ($32,000 if married filing jointly; $0 if married filing separately and living with spouse at any time during the year). 8. _____
9. Subtract line 8 from line 7. If zero or less, enter –0–. 9. _____

Note: *If line 9 is zero or less, stop here;* **none of your benefits are taxable.** *Otherwise, go on to line 10.*

10. Enter $9,000 ($12,000 if married filing jointly; $0 if married filing separately and living with spouse at any time during the year). 10. _____
11. Subtract line 10 from line 9. If zero or less, enter –0–. 11. _____
12. Enter the **smaller** of line 9 or line 10. 12. _____
13. Enter one-half of line 12. 13. _____
14. Enter the **smaller** of line 2 or line 13. 14. _____
15. Multiply line 11 by 85% (.85). If line 11 is zero, enter –0–. 15. _____
16. Add lines 14 and 15. 16. _____
17. Multiply line 1 by 85% (.85). 17. _____
18. **Taxable benefits.** Enter the **smaller** of line 16 or line 17. 18. _____

LO 2.16 36. Please answer the following questions regarding the taxability of Social Security:

a. A 68-year-old taxpayer has $20,000 in Social Security income and $100,000 in tax-free municipal bond income. Does the municipal bond income affect the amount of Social Security the taxpayer must include in income?

b. A 68-year-old taxpayer has $20,000 in Social Security income and no other taxable or tax-free income. How much of the Social Security income must the taxpayer include in taxable income?

c. A 68-year-old taxpayer has $20,000 in Social Security income and has significant other taxable retirement income. What is the maximum percentage of Social Security that the taxpayer might be required to include in taxable income?

LO 2.17 37. In 2024, Kelly and Kerry live in California and are married and live together but plan to file separately. Their income for the year is as follows:

Kelly and Kerry Income

Income Item	Kelly	Kerry	Joint
Wages	$40,000	$30,000	
Investment income from Kelly's family inheritance			$8,000
Investment income from joint brokerage account			1,600

a. Compute the separate gross income for Kelly and Kerry.
b. Assume they live in Texas instead of California. Compute the separate gross income for Kelly and Kerry.

LO 2.18 38. In 2024, Son loses his job and he is able to reduce his mortgage debt on his principal residence by $30,000 and remains solvent. Explain how much cancellation of debt income Son will recognize and what exception provision might apply, if any.

Group 3:
Writing Assignment

Research

Vanessa Lazo was an amazing high school student and so it was no great surprise when she was accepted into Prestige Private University (PPU). To entice Vanessa to attend PPU, the school offered her a reduced tuition of $13,000 per year (full-time tuition would typically be $43,000 per year). PPU also has a scholarship program thanks to a large donation from William Gatos. Vanessa was the Gatos Scholarship winner and will receive a scholarship for $20,000. Vanessa is required to use the scholarship first to pay her $13,000 tuition and the remainder is to cover room and board at PPU. Lastly, PPU also offered Vanessa a part-time job on the PPU campus as a student lab assistant in the Biology Department of PPU for which she is paid $1,500.

Required: Go to the IRS website (www.irs.gov) and locate Publication 970. Review the section on Scholarships. Write a letter to Vanessa Lazo stating how much of the PPU package is taxable.
(An example of a client letter is available at the website for this textbook, located at **www.cengage.com**.)

Group 4: Comprehensive Problems

1. Donna and Chris Hoser have been married for three years. Donna works as nurse at Dade University Hospital. Chris is a full-time student at Wolfson University and also works part-time during the summer at Dade University Hospital. Chris' birthdate is January 12, 1998, and Donna's birthdate is November 4, 2000. Donna and Chris' earnings and income tax withholdings are reported on the following Form W-2s:

Form W-2 — Donna Hoser (2024)

- a Employee's social security number: 465-74-3322
- b Employer identification number (EIN): 31-1238977
- c Employer's name, address, and ZIP code: Dade University Hospital, 1925 NW 15th Street, Miami, FL 33125
- e Employee: Donna Hoser, 1001 Wren Avenue, Miami Springs, FL 33166
- 1 Wages, tips, other compensation: 53,147.00
- 2 Federal income tax withheld: 4,209.87
- 3 Social security wages: 53,147.00
- 4 Social security tax withheld: 3,295.11
- 5 Medicare wages and tips: 53,147.00
- 6 Medicare tax withheld: 770.63
- 12a C: 47.00
- 12b DD: 5,945.12
- 14 Other: FSA $3,200.00
- 15 State: FL

Form W-2 — Chris Hoser (2024)

- a Employee's social security number: 465-57-9935
- b Employer identification number (EIN): 31-1238977
- c Employer's name, address, and ZIP code: Dade University Hospital, 1925 NW 15th Street, Miami, FL 33125
- e Employee: Chris Hoser, 1001 Wren Avenue, Miami Springs, FL 33166
- 1 Wages, tips, other compensation: 3,780.00
- 2 Federal income tax withheld: 200.30
- 3 Social security wages: 3,780.00
- 4 Social security tax withheld: 234.36
- 5 Medicare wages and tips: 3,780.00
- 6 Medicare tax withheld: 54.81
- 15 State: FL

Donna and Chris received the following Forms 1099-INT and 1099-DIV:

Form 1099-INT — Interest Income (Rev. January 2024), For calendar year 2024

- CORRECTED (if checked): ☐
- PAYER'S name, street address, city or town, state or province, country, ZIP or foreign postal code, and telephone no.: Dade County Credit Union, 3440 NE 2nd Ave, Miami, FL 33137
- Payer's RTN (optional):
- OMB No. 1545-0112
- 1 Interest income: $671.23
- 2 Early withdrawal penalty:
- PAYER'S TIN: 33-1234556
- RECIPIENT'S TIN: 465-74-3322
- 3 Interest on U.S. Savings Bonds and Treasury obligations:
- RECIPIENT'S name: Donna and Chris Hoser, TBE
- Street address: 1001 Wren Avenue
- City, state, ZIP: Miami Springs, FL 33166
- 4 Federal income tax withheld:
- 5 Investment expenses:
- 6 Foreign tax paid:
- 7 Foreign country or U.S. territory:
- 8 Tax-exempt interest:
- 9 Specified private activity bond interest:
- 10 Market discount:
- 11 Bond premium:
- 12 Bond premium on Treasury obligations:
- 13 Bond premium on tax-exempt bond:
- 14 Tax-exempt and tax credit bond CUSIP no.:
- 15 State:
- 16 State identification no.:
- 17 State tax withheld:

Copy B — For Recipient

Form 1099-OID — Original Issue Discount (Rev. January 2024), For calendar year 2024

- CORRECTED (if checked): ☐
- PAYER'S name, street address, city or town, state or province, country, ZIP or foreign postal code, and telephone no.: Miami-Dade Public Schools, 1540 NE 2nd Avenue, Miami, FL 33132
- 1 Original issue discount for the year*:
- 2 Other periodic interest:
- OMB No. 1545-0117
- * This may not be the correct figure to report on your income tax return. See instructions on the back.
- PAYER'S TIN: 13-3229985
- RECIPIENT'S TIN: 465-74-3322
- 3 Early withdrawal penalty:
- 4 Federal income tax withheld:
- 5 Market discount:
- 6 Acquisition premium:
- RECIPIENT'S name: Donna Hoser
- Street address: 1001 Wren Avenue
- City, state, ZIP: Miami Springs, FL 33166
- 7 Description: Miami-Dade Pub School CUSIP 859128HW3 0% DUE 2/15/25
- 8 Original issue discount on U.S. Treasury obligations*:
- 9 Investment expenses:
- 10 Bond premium:
- 11 Tax-exempt OID: $134.00
- 12 State:
- 13 State identification no.:
- 14 State tax withheld:

Copy B — For Recipient

Form 1099-DIV

PAYER'S name: Hialeah Corporation, 11000 SW 104th Street, Miami, FL 33176

PAYER'S TIN: 33-1122335
RECIPIENT'S TIN: 465-57-9935

RECIPIENT'S name: Chris Hoser
Street address: 1001 Wren Ave.
City, state, ZIP: Miami Springs, FL 33166

- **1a Total ordinary dividends:** $377.00
- **1b Qualified dividends:** $322.00

Form 1099-DIV (Rev. January 2024), For calendar year 2024

Chris is an excellent student at Wolfson University. He was given a $1,750 scholarship by the university to help pay educational expenses. The scholarship funds were used by Chris for tuition and books.

Chris entered the Compositors Exonerating Dwelling (CED) sweepstakes and ended up winning $10,000. Chris took advantage of the no-purchase-required option and paid nothing to join the sweepstakes. He received a 1099-MISC (not shown) reporting the $10,000 prize.

Donna is a valued employee at the hospital. Her supervisor gave her two tickets to a single game of the nearby professional football team that were worth $45 each. The hospital also sent Donna flowers valued at $40 when her mother passed away during 2024.

Chris has a 4-year-old son, Robert R. Hoser, from a prior marriage that ended in divorce in 2019. During 2024, he paid his ex-wife $300 per month in child support. Robert is claimed as a dependent by Chris's ex-wife.

During 2024, Chris' aunt died. The aunt, in her will, left Chris $15,000 in cash. Chris deposited this money in the Lone Star State Bank savings account.

Required: Complete the Hoser's federal tax return for 2024 on Form 1040, Schedule 1, and the Qualified Dividends and Capital Gain Tax Worksheet.

2A. Terry and Maria Redlin have been married for eight years. Terry is an oil rig maintenance supervisor for Holyann Corporation and Maria works as a cashier for Mynards. Terry's birthdate is February 21, 1991, and Maria's is December 30, 1993. Terry and Maria have a 9-year-old son named Jaime Redlin, born March 22, 2015 (Social Security number 721-34-1134). Terry and Maria's earnings are reported on the following Form W-2s:

W-2 (Form 1 — Terry Redlin)

- a Employee's social security number: 432-21-2253
- b Employer identification number (EIN): 21-5432117
- c Employer's name, address, and ZIP code: Holyann Corporation, 800 21st Street SW, Watertown, SD 57201
- e Employee's name and address: Terry Redlin, 1300 33rd Street SE, Watertown, SD 57201
- 1 Wages, tips, other compensation: 46,366.00
- 2 Federal income tax withheld: 3,931.81
- 3 Social security wages: 47,800.00
- 4 Social security tax withheld: 2,963.60
- 5 Medicare wages and tips: 47,800.00
- 6 Medicare tax withheld: 693.10
- 10 Dependent care benefits: 600.00
- 12a D: 1,434.00
- 12b DD: 9,173.36
- 13 Retirement plan: X
- 14 Other: FSA Health $3,200.00
- 15 State: SD
- Form W-2 Wage and Tax Statement 2024

W-2 (Form 2 — Maria Redlin)

- a Employee's social security number: 444-65-8801
- b Employer identification number (EIN): 23-3333123
- c Employer's name, address, and ZIP code: Mynards, 1200 9th Ave SE, Watertown, SD 57201
- e Employee's name and address: Maria Redlin, 1300 33rd Street SE, Watertown, SD 57201
- 1 Wages, tips, other compensation: 34,250.00
- 2 Federal income tax withheld: 2,098.45
- 3 Social security wages: 34,250.00
- 4 Social security tax withheld: 2,123.50
- 5 Medicare wages and tips: 34,250.00
- 6 Medicare tax withheld: 496.63
- 14 Other: Educ. Asst. Plan $5,250.00
- 15 State: SD
- Form W-2 Wage and Tax Statement 2024

Terry took advantage of his employer-provided dependent care assistance program on a small number of days when Jaime was sick and unable to go to school. The value of dependent care assistance was $600.

Once each week, Terry is required to work at the site of an oil drilling rig for a 24-hour period to provide on-call maintenance on the rig. On those days, Holyann requires Terry to stay in an apartment building that sits on the oil rig site. Because different maintenance workers stay each night, the building has a cook and dining room that prepares meals for the crew. All crew members must take their meals in the dining room when staying the night. The value of the lodging provided to Terry is $6,000 and the value of the meals provided to Terry is $750.

Maria frequently takes advantage of the 10-percent employee discount on merchandise from Mynards. The discount is available to all employees of Mynards and the company still makes a small profit on the items after the discount. Maria estimates her employee discounts in 2024 total $780.

Terry and Maria have investment income from a money market account, U.S. Treasury bonds, and municipal bonds as reported on the following Form 1099-INT and brokerage statements:

Form 1099-INT — Interest Income (Rev. January 2024), For calendar year 2024

PAYER'S name, street address, city or town, state or province, country, ZIP or foreign postal code, and telephone no.:
Big Western Bank
426 5th St SE
Watertown, SD 57201

PAYER'S TIN: 34-8121888
RECIPIENT'S TIN: 444-65-8801

RECIPIENT'S name: Maria Redlin
Street address: 1300 33rd Street SE
City, state, ZIP: Watertown, SD 57201

OMB No. 1545-0112

Box 1 Interest income: $835.13
Box 2 Early withdrawal penalty:
Box 3 Interest on U.S. Savings Bonds and Treasury obligations:
Box 4 Federal income tax withheld:
Box 5 Investment expenses:
Box 6 Foreign tax paid:
Box 7 Foreign country or U.S. territory:
Box 8 Tax-exempt interest:
Box 9 Specified private activity bond interest:
Box 10 Market discount:
Box 11 Bond premium:
Box 12 Bond premium on Treasury obligations:
Box 13 Bond premium on tax-exempt bond:
Box 14 Tax-exempt and tax credit bond CUSIP no.:
Box 15 State:
Box 16 State identification no.:
Box 17 State tax withheld:

Copy B For Recipient

2024 Combined Forms 1099

This is important tax information and is being furnished to the IRS (except as indicated). If you are required to file a return, a negligence penalty or other sanction may be imposed on you if this income is taxable and the IRS determines that it has not been reported.

Copy B For Recipient
OMB No. 1545-0110

Friar Tuck Investments
38 Wall Street, 8th Floor
New York, NY 10005

Terry and Maria Redlin
1300 33rd Street SE
Watertown, SD 57201

Account Number	Tax ID
4500881661	***-**-2253

Payer's Federal Tax ID
33-1357246
Financial Adviser/Phone
May Marion 888-555-1212

Form 1099-INT — Interest Income

Box 1 Interest income	Box 2 Early withdrawal penalty	Box 3 Interest on U.S. Savings Bonds and Treasury obligations
44.22		500.00

Box 4 Federal income tax withheld	Box 5 Investment expenses	Box 6 Foreign Tax Paid

Box 7 Foreign country or U.S. possession	Box 8 Tax-exempt interest	Box 9 Specified private activity bond interest
	400.00	

Box 10 Market Discount	Box 11 Bond Premium

Box 12 Bond premium on Treasury obligations	Box 13 Bond premium on tax-exempt bond

Form 1099-DIV — Dividend Income

Box 1a Total ordinary dividends	Box 1b Qualified dividends	Box 2a Total capital gain distr.
1,235.00	1,235.00	80.00

Box 2b Unrecap Sec 1250 gain	Box 2c Section 1202 gain	Box 2d Collectibles (28%) gain

Box 2e Section 897 ordinary dividends	Box 2f Section 897 capital gain	Box 3 Nondividend distributions

Box 4 Federal income tax withheld	Box 5 Section 199A dividends	Box 6 Investment expenses

Box 7 Foreign taxes paid	Box 8 Foreign country or possession	Box 9 Cash liquidation distributions

Terry has an ex-wife named Judy Redlin. Pursuant to their January 27, 2016, divorce decree, Terry pays her $210 per month in alimony. All payments were made on time in 2024. Judy's Social Security number is 566-74-8765.

During 2024, Terry was in the hospital for a successful operation. His health insurance company reimbursed Terry $4,732 for all of his hospital and doctor bills.

In June of 2024, Maria's father died. Under a life insurance policy owned and paid for by her father, Maria was paid death benefits of $25,000. She used $7,800 to cover a portion of the funeral costs for her father.

Maria bought a South Dakota lottery ticket on impulse during 2024. Her ticket was lucky and she won $1,000. The winning amount was paid to Maria in November 2024 with no income tax withheld.

Maria is pursuing a Masters of Business Administration from Lakes Region University. Mynards operates an employee assistance plan that she takes full advantage of. She is also the beneficiary of the $1,000 Mynards Adult Learner Scholarship. All of the scholarship is used to pay for tuition and books.

Terry and Maria are eligible for a $2,000 child tax credit in 2024.

Required: Complete the Redlin's federal tax return for 2024 on Form 1040, Schedule 1, Schedule B, and Qualified Dividends and Capital Gains Tax worksheet. Form 8812 for the child tax credit does not need to be completed.

2B. Carl Conch and Mary Duval are married and file a joint return. Carl is retired US Army but likes to stay busy, and so he works as a part-time baker at the Key Lime Pie Company. Mary is unemployed since losing her job in 2023. Carl's birth date is June 14, 1959, and Mary's is October 2, 1969.

Carl and Mary help support an old Army friend of Carl's named Buster Crabbe. Buster is 72 years old and lives in an over-55 community in Key West near Carl and Mary's apartment. Buster has a small Social Security benefit of $6,000 per year, and so Carl and Mary provide for more than half of his support. Buster's birth date is June 12, 1952, and his Social Security number is 454-11-1719.

Carl's W-2, 1099-R (Army pension), and Social Security benefits statement are presented below.

Form W-2 Wage and Tax Statement (2024)

- a. Employee's social security number: 835-21-5423
- b. Employer identification number (EIN): 61-7651234
- c. Employer's name, address, and ZIP code: Key Lime Pie Company, 223 Key Deer Blvd., Big Pine Key, FL 33043
- e. Employee's name and address: Carl Conch, 1234 Mallory Square, Apt #64, Key West, FL 33040
- 1. Wages, tips, other compensation: 24,800.00
- 2. Federal income tax withheld: 2,048.00
- 3. Social security wages: 24,800.00
- 4. Social security tax withheld: 1,537.60
- 5. Medicare wages and tips: 24,800.00
- 6. Medicare tax withheld: 359.60
- 15. State: FL

Form 1099-R (2024) – Distributions From Pensions, Annuities, Retirement or Profit-Sharing Plans, IRAs, Insurance Contracts, etc.

- PAYER'S name: Defense Finance and Accounting Service, U.S. Military Retired Pay, 8899 E 56th Street, Indianapolis IN 46249-1200
- PAYER'S TIN: 22-4564561
- RECIPIENT'S TIN: 835-21-5423
- RECIPIENT'S name: Carl Conch
- Street address: 1234 Mallory Square #64, Key West, FL 33040
- 1. Gross distribution: 13,800.00
- 2a. Taxable amount: 13,800.00
- 4. Federal income tax withheld: 1,100.00
- 7. Distribution code(s): 7
- 9b. Total employee contributions: 0.00

FORM SSA-1099 – SOCIAL SECURITY BENEFIT STATEMENT

2024
- Part of your social security benefits shown in box 5 may be taxable income
- See reverse side for more information

Box 1 Name	Box 2 Beneficiary's Social Security Number
Carl Conch	835-21-5423

Box 3 Benefits Paid in 2024	Box 4 Benefits Repaid to SSA in 2023	Box 5 Net Benefits for 2024
$7,800.00		$7,800.00

Description of Amount in Box 3	Description of Amount in Box 4
Paid by direct deposit $7,500.00 Benefits for 2024: $7,800.00	
	Box 6 Voluntary Federal Income Tax Withheld $300.00
	Box 7 Address 1234 Mallory Square, Apt #64 Key West, FL 33040
	Box 8 Claim Number

Form SSA-1099-SM (1-2023) — DO NOT RETURN THIS FORM TO SSA OR IRS

Mary is divorced, and she pays her ex-husband (Tom Tortuga, Social Security number 722-81-8620) child support. Pursuant to their January 12, 2021, divorce decree, Mary pays Tom $500 per month in child support. All payments were made on time in 2024.

In early 2024, when Mary was struggling financially due to the loss of her job, she was able to renegotiate her auto loan and had the balance reduced. The Form 1099-C is presented below:

Form 1099-C — Cancellation of Debt (Rev. January 2022)

☐ CORRECTED (if checked)

CREDITOR'S name, street address, city or town, state or province, country, ZIP or foreign postal code, and telephone no.
Tesla Finance LLC
4500 Deer Creek Road
Palo Alto, CA 94304

OMB No. 1545-1424

1 Date of identifiable event	03/15/2024
2 Amount of debt discharged	$ 3,900.00
3 Interest, if included in box 2	$
For calendar year	20 24

CREDITOR'S TIN	DEBTOR'S TIN
46-3896777	633-65-7912

4 Debt description: Auto loan 2021 Tesla Model S

DEBTOR'S name: Mary Duval
Street address (including apt. no.): 1234 Mallory Square, Apt #64
City or town, state or province, country, and ZIP or foreign postal code: Key West, FL 33040

5 If checked, the debtor was personally liable for repayment of the debt ☒

6 Identifiable event code: F

7 Fair market value of property: $

Copy B — For Debtor

Sadly, in June 2024, Mary's father passed away. Her father left her $75,000.

Mary also received unemployment compensation as shown on the following Form 1099-G:

PAYER'S name: Florida Dept. of Economic Opportunity, 107 E. Jefferson Blvd., Tallahassee, FL 32399
PAYER'S TIN: 21-5556666
RECIPIENT'S TIN: 633-65-7912
RECIPIENT'S name: Mary Duval
Street address: 1234 Mallory Sq. Apt 64
City: Key West, FL 33040

Box 1 Unemployment compensation: $2,400.00
Box 4 Federal income tax withheld: $220.00
Form 1099-G (Rev. March 2024), For calendar year 2024

The Key Lime Pie Company provides all employees with a gym on the premises of the pie factory that Carl works at. Carl uses the gym at least three days a week. The value of a similar gym membership would be $1,200.

Required: Complete Carl and Mary's federal tax return for 2024 on Form 1040-SR and Schedule 1. If not using software, consider completing the Simplified Taxable Social Security Worksheet found in Chapter 2 to determine the taxable portion of Social Security benefits.

Group 5:
Cumulative Software Problem

1. The following additional information is available for the family of Albert and Allison Gaytor.

   In 2024, Albert received a Form W-2 from his employer, Sport Fishing of Stuart (note: slightly modified from Chapter 1):

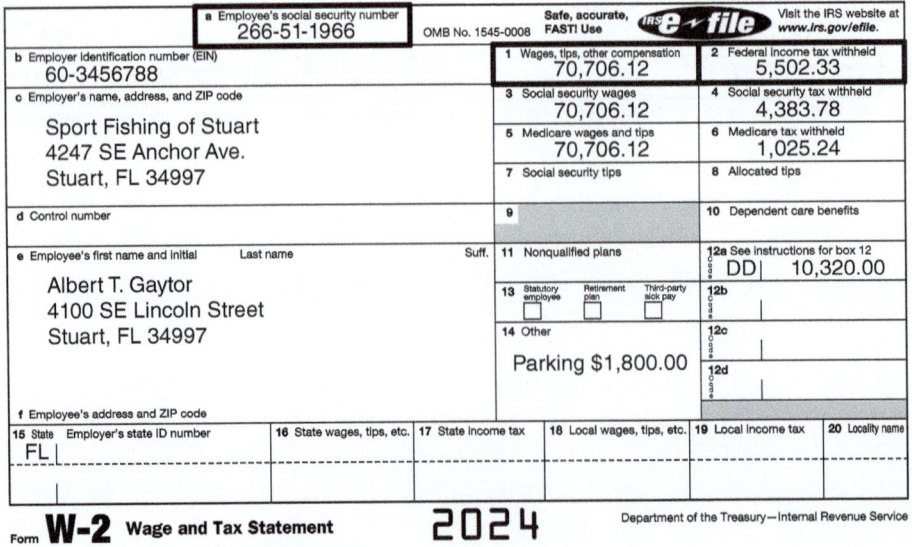

Form W-2 Wage and Tax Statement 2024

- a Employee's social security number: 266-51-1966
- b Employer identification number (EIN): 60-3456788
- c Employer's name, address, and ZIP code: Sport Fishing of Stuart, 4247 SE Anchor Ave., Stuart, FL 34997
- e Employee's first name and initial, Last name: Albert T. Gaytor, 4100 SE Lincoln Street, Stuart, FL 34997
- 1 Wages, tips, other compensation: 70,706.12
- 2 Federal income tax withheld: 5,502.33
- 3 Social security wages: 70,706.12
- 4 Social security tax withheld: 4,383.78
- 5 Medicare wages and tips: 70,706.12
- 6 Medicare tax withheld: 1,025.24
- 12a DD 10,320.00
- 14 Other: Parking $1,800.00
- 15 State: FL

In addition to the interest from Chapter 1, Albert and Allison also received four Form 1099s:

Form 1099-INT (Rev. January 2024) — Interest Income — Copy B For Recipient

- CORRECTED (if checked): ☐
- PAYER'S name, street address, city or town, state or province, country, ZIP or foreign postal code, and telephone no.: Department of Treasury, Bureau of the Fiscal Service, PO Box 7105, Minneapolis, MN 55480
- Payer's RTN (optional):
- OMB No. 1545-0112
- For calendar year: 2024
- PAYER'S TIN: 53-0247776
- RECIPIENT'S TIN: 266-51-1966
- 1 Interest income: $
- 2 Early withdrawal penalty: $
- 3 Interest on U.S. Savings Bonds and Treasury obligations: $985.33
- 4 Federal income tax withheld: $
- 5 Investment expenses: $
- 6 Foreign tax paid: $
- 7 Foreign country or U.S. territory:
- 8 Tax-exempt interest: $
- 9 Specified private activity bond interest: $
- 10 Market discount: $
- 11 Bond premium: $
- 12 Bond premium on Treasury obligations: $
- 13 Bond premium on tax-exempt bond: $
- 14 Tax-exempt and tax credit bond CUSIP no.:
- 15 State:
- 16 State identification no.:
- 17 State tax withheld: $
- FATCA filing requirement: ☐
- RECIPIENT'S name: Albert T. Gaytor
- Street address: 4100 SE Lincoln Street
- City, state, ZIP: Stuart, FL 34997
- Account number (see instructions):

Form 1099-INT (Rev. 1-2024) (keep for your records) www.irs.gov/Form1099INT Department of the Treasury - Internal Revenue Service

Form 1099-DIV (Rev. January 2024) — Dividends and Distributions — Copy B For Recipient

- CORRECTED (if checked): ☐
- PAYER'S name, street address, city or town, state or province, country, ZIP or foreign postal code, and telephone no.: Everglades Boating Corp., 1500 S. Krome Avenue, Homestead, FL 33034
- OMB No. 1545-0110
- For calendar year: 2024
- 1a Total ordinary dividends: $1,250.00
- 1b Qualified dividends: $1,000.00
- 2a Total capital gain distr.: $
- 2b Unrecap. Sec. 1250 gain: $
- 2c Section 1202 gain: $
- 2d Collectibles (28%) gain: $
- 2e Section 897 ordinary dividends: $
- 2f Section 897 capital gain: $
- PAYER'S TIN: 57-4443344
- RECIPIENT'S TIN: 266-34-1967
- 3 Nondividend distributions: $
- 4 Federal income tax withheld: $0.00
- 5 Section 199A dividends: $
- 6 Investment expenses: $
- 7 Foreign tax paid: $
- 8 Foreign country or U.S. possession:
- 9 Cash liquidation distributions: $
- 10 Noncash liquidation distributions: $
- 11 FATCA filing requirement: ☐
- 12 Exempt-interest dividends: $
- 13 Specified private activity bond interest dividends: $
- 14 State:
- 15 State identification no.:
- 16 State tax withheld: $
- RECIPIENT'S name: Allison Gaytor
- Street address: 4100 SE Lincoln Street
- City, state, ZIP: Stuart, FL 34997
- Account number (see instructions):

Form 1099-DIV (Rev. 1-2024) (keep for your records) www.irs.gov/Form1099DIV Department of the Treasury - Internal Revenue Service

Form 1099-DIV — Dividends and Distributions

PAYER: Grapefruit Mutual Fund
1500 S. Orange Blossom Trail
Orlando, FL 32809

PAYER'S TIN: 51-3332215
RECIPIENT'S TIN: 266-34-1967

RECIPIENT: Allison Gaytor
4100 SE Lincoln Street
Stuart, FL 34997

- 1a Total ordinary dividends: $500.00
- 1b Qualified dividends: $500.00
- 2a Total capital gain distr.: $180.00
- 4 Federal income tax withheld: $0.00

Form 1099-DIV (Rev. 1-2024) — For calendar year 2024

Form 1099-INT — Interest Income

PAYER: Miami-Dade County Airport Department
General Revenue Bonds
111 NW 1st Street, 25th Floor
Miami, FL 33128

PAYER'S TIN: 24-6767888
RECIPIENT'S TIN: 266-51-1966

RECIPIENT: Albert T. Gaytor
4100 SE Lincoln Street
Stuart, FL 34997

- 8 Tax-exempt interest: $850.00

Form 1099-INT (Rev. 1-2024) — For calendar year 2024

The interest from US Treasury notes was from bonds purchased between interest payments. Included in the purchase price was $164.70 of accrued interest. There is no market discount or bond premium on the bonds.

Albert went to the casino on his birthday and won big, as reflected on the following Form W-2G:

☐ CORRECTED (if checked)

PAYER'S name, street address, city or town, state or province, country, and ZIP or foreign postal code	1 Reportable winnings	2 Date won	OMB No. 1545-0238	Form W-2G
Triumph Casino Cruises 200 Columbia Drive Terminal B-12 Port Canaveral, FL 32920	$ 5,750.00			Certain Gambling Winnings
	3 Type of wager Slot machine	4 Federal income tax withheld $ 1,600.00		(Rev. December 2023)
	5 Transaction	6 Race		For calendar year 20 24
	7 Winnings from identical wagers $	8 Cashier		
PAYER'S TIN 22-7778877	PAYER'S telephone no. 855-555-1212	9 WINNER'S TIN 266-51-1966	10 Window		This information is being furnished to the IRS.
WINNER'S name Albert T. Gaytor		11 First identification no.	12 Second identification no.		
Street address (including apt. no.) 4100 SE Lincoln Street		13 State/Payer's state identification no.	14 State winnings $		Copy B Report this income on your federal tax return. If this form shows federal income tax withheld in box 4, attach this copy to your return.
City or town, state or province, country, and ZIP or foreign postal code Stuart, FL 34997		15 State income tax withheld $	16 Local winnings $		
		17 Local income tax withheld $	18 Name of locality		

Form **W-2G** (Rev. 12-2023) www.irs.gov/FormW2G Department of the Treasury - Internal Revenue Service

Albert had no other gambling income or losses for the year.

In February, Allison received $50,000 in life insurance proceeds from the death of her friend, Sharon.

In July, Albert's uncle Ivan died and left him real estate (undeveloped land) worth $72,000.

Six years ago, Albert and Allison divorced. Albert married Iris, but the marriage did not work out, and they divorced a year later. Under the July 1, 2017 divorce decree, Albert pays Iris $12,000 per year in alimony. All payments were on time in 2024 and Iris' Social Security number is 667-34-9224. Three years ago, Albert and Allison were remarried.

Sport Fishing of Stuart pays Albert's captain's license fees and membership dues to the Charter Fisherman's Association. During 2024, Sport Fishing paid $1,300 for such dues and fees for Albert.

Allison was laid off from her job on January 2, 2024. She received a Form 1099-G for unemployment benefits:

☐ CORRECTED (if checked)

PAYER'S name, street address, city or town, state or province, country, ZIP or foreign postal code, and telephone no.	1 Unemployment compensation	OMB No. 1545-0120	Form **1099-G**	Certain Government Payments
Florida Dept. of Economic Opportunity 107 E. Jefferson Blvd. Tallahassee, FL 32399	$ 4,000.00		(Rev. March 2024)	
	2 State or local income tax refunds, credits, or offsets $		For calendar year 2024	
PAYER'S TIN 21-5556666	RECIPIENT'S TIN 266-34-1967	3 Box 2 amount is for tax year	4 Federal income tax withheld $ 400.00		Copy B For Recipient
RECIPIENT'S name Allison A. Gaytor		5 RTAA payments $	6 Taxable grants $		This is important tax information and is being furnished to the IRS. If you are required to file a return, a negligence penalty or other sanction may be imposed on you if this income is taxable and the IRS determines that it has not been reported.
Street address (including apt. no.) 4100 SE Lincoln Street		7 Agriculture payments $	8 If checked, box 2 is trade or business income ☐		
City or town, state or province, country, and ZIP or foreign postal code Stuart, FL 34997		9 Market gain $			
Account number (see instructions)		10a State	10b State identification no.	11 State income tax withheld $ $	

Form **1099-G** (Rev. 3-2024) (keep for your records) www.irs.gov/Form1099G Department of the Treasury - Internal Revenue Service

Albert and his family are covered by an employee-sponsored health plan at his work. Sport Fishing pays $860 per month in premiums for Albert and his family. During the year, Allison was in the hospital for appendix surgery. The bill for the surgery was $10,100 of which the health insurance reimbursed Albert the full $10,100.

Sport Fishing also paid for Albert's parking at the marina for the six months he worked there. The monthly cost is $300.

Required: Combine this new information about the Gaytor family with the information from Chapter 1 and complete a revised 2024 tax return for Albert and Allison. Be sure to save your data input files since this case will be expanded with more tax information in each succeeding chapter.

Chapter 3

Business Income and Expenses

Learning Objectives

After completing this chapter, you should be able to:

- **LO 3.1** Complete a basic Schedule C (Profit or Loss from Business).
- **LO 3.2** Describe the tax treatment of inventories and cost of goods sold.
- **LO 3.3** Identify the requirements for deducting transportation expenses.
- **LO 3.4** Identify the requirements for deducting travel expenses.
- **LO 3.5** Determine the requirements for deducting meals.
- **LO 3.6** Identify the requirements for claiming business education expenses.
- **LO 3.7** Identify the tax treatment of dues and subscriptions.
- **LO 3.8** Determine which clothing and uniforms may be treated as tax deductions.
- **LO 3.9** Explain the special limits for business gift deductions.
- **LO 3.10** Explain the tax treatment of bad debt deductions.
- **LO 3.11** Ascertain when a home office deduction may be claimed and how the deduction is computed.
- **LO 3.12** Apply the factors used to determine whether an activity is a hobby, and understand the tax treatment of hobby losses.

Overview

This chapter covers Schedule C, "Profit or Loss from Business (Sole Proprietorship)," and many of the common business expenses allowed as deductions in arriving at net taxable business income. Schedule C is filed by self-employed taxpayers, such as accountants, doctors, lawyers, architects, consultants, small manufacturers, restaurateurs, store owners, gardeners, event planners, bookkeepers, and other small businesses. This form is one of the most commonly used tax forms and, for many taxpayers, the net income reported on Schedule C is the primary component of their adjusted gross income. With the qualified business income (QBI) deduction, the sole proprietorship, along with income from rental properties (refer to Chapter 4), partnerships (refer to Chapter 10), and S corporations (refer to Chapter 11), may enjoy a reduction in tax rate in an attempt to match the 21-percent corporate tax rate. The QBI deduction is covered in detail in Chapter 4.

The business expenses discussed in this chapter include travel, transportation, bad debts, inventory, home office, meals and entertainment, business education, dues, subscriptions, publications, special clothing, uniforms, and business gifts. While these expenses are often associated with Schedule C (sole proprietorship income), they may also be reported with rental and royalty income on Schedule E, or farm and ranch income on Schedule F. Employee business expenses are covered in Chapter 5.

Learning Objective 3.1

Complete a basic Schedule C (Profit or Loss from Business).

3-1 Schedule C

A taxpayer who operates a trade or business or practices a profession as a sole proprietorship must file a Schedule C with the Form 1040 (or 1040-SR), reporting their taxable income or loss from the activity. Schedule C is similar to the income statement in financial accounting. Taxable income from a business or profession is reported on either Schedule C or Schedule F (a specialized version of Schedule C for farmers and ranchers).

3-1a Trade or Business

The term *trade or business* is not formally defined, although the term is used often in the Internal Revenue Code (the Code). For example, Section 162 of the Code states that a taxpayer is allowed to deduct all the ordinary and necessary expenses in carrying on a trade or business. Generally, a "trade or business" for tax purposes is any activity engaged in for profit. Note that a taxpayer does not have to actually make a profit, but they should be seeking to make a profit through regular and continual effort. Intermittent activities (e.g., casual craft sales) or leisure pursuits (e.g., wine making) do not always rise to the level of a trade or business and may require reporting under the hobby loss rules discussed later in this chapter.

3-1b Tests for Deductibility

Expenses must meet several general tests to qualify as a tax deduction. Listed below are three common tests for deductibility. These tests give guidelines for deductibility, but often in practice it is a matter of judgment as to whether an expense is considered a deductible business expense. Taxpayers and IRS agents frequently disagree as to whether specific expenses pass the following tests, and many court cases have been devoted to resolving these disagreements. The tests below overlap and an expense may fail more than one test.

- **The Ordinary and Necessary Test:** Under the tax law, for trade or business expenses to be deductible they must be ordinary and necessary. Generally, this means that the expense is commonly found in the specific business, and is helpful and appropriate in running the business.

Example Rob is a CPA who goes to a "tax boot camp" which offers intensive training on tax return preparation every year. Rob also hires a trainer at his local gym to work out with him to help him maintain the strength and endurance needed to handle the rigors of tax season. The cost of the "tax boot camp" would be deductible. The cost of the personal trainer is not a common or ordinary expense of CPA firms and is not necessary for preparing tax returns, and therefore, would not be deductible. ♦

- **The Business Purpose Test:** Expenses must have a legitimate business purpose to be considered deductible.

Example Larry is an independent consultant who maintains an office in his home, although he always meets with clients at their place of business. He spent $75,000 upgrading his office to include a large attached glass sunroom and a display area for his orchid collection. This home office upgrade would likely be considered to serve no business purpose, so the expenses related to the improvements would not be deductible. ♦

- **The Reasonableness Test:** The tax law requires that deductions be reasonable to be deducted.

Example Derek owns a small business and takes one of his clients, who is also a friend, to an expensive business dinner every week. They enjoy a variety of restaurants and fine wines, and always spend some time talking about their joint business interests. The yearly cost of the meetings and meals is $20,000, and Derek generates $15,000 of fees from his friend each year. This lavish and extravagant business entertainment would likely not be considered reasonable given the circumstances. If they had met for a modest lunch and a business discussion every week, the expense would likely be considered reasonable and deductible. ♦

The IRS and courts have taken a fairly permissive perspective on the deduction of business expenses; however, the Code does restrict the deduction of certain expenses such as the following:

- Personal, living, and family expenses (refer to itemized deductions in Chapter 5)
- Capital expenditures (refer to Chapter 8)
- Expenses related to tax-exempt income
- Expenditures related to the sale of illegal drugs
- Illegal bribes and kickbacks
- Fines, penalties, and other payments to governments related to the violation of law
- Lobbying and political expenditures
- Settlement or attorney fees related to sexual abuse or harassment if subject to a nondisclosure agreement

Taxes are specifically excepted from the nondeductibility of fines and penalties, as are payments made to bring the taxpayer into compliance with the law or as restitution.

Example Maria owns and operates a small pizza shop in the city. The City Council is considering new zoning laws that would permit the creation of a large hotel and theme park next to Maria's restaurant which she expects would increase her business significantly. She pays $10,000 to have a study prepared to show the economic benefits of the new zoning to the City Council at a future meeting. Maria also has been a member of the GOP since she was old enough to vote and makes a $1,000 contribution to the Republican National Committee (RNC). The $10,000 fee and her contribution to the RNC are lobbying and political expenditures and are not deductible. ♦

3-1c Schedule C

Schedule C is used by sole proprietors to report profit or loss from their businesses. The first section (lines A to J) of Schedule C requires disclosure of basic information such as the business name and location, the accounting method (cash, accrual, or other, as covered in Chapter 6), material participation in the business (for passive activity loss classification purposes, refer to Chapter 4), and whether the business was started or acquired during the year.

Schedule C requires the taxpayer to provide a principal business or professional activity code (refer to Figure 3.1). These codes are used to classify sole proprietorships by the type of business activity. For example, a full-service restaurant is code 722511, as shown in Figure 3.1.

In 2024, the Department of Justice proposed to move marijuana from a Schedule I class drug to a Schedule III. The Drug Enforcement Agency decided to defer hearings until after November elections. Should marijuana be rescheduled, most cannibis businesses would be eligible to deduct typical business expenses like rent, advertising expenses, wages and salaries, travel, and other normal overhead expenses, which are currently nondeductible.

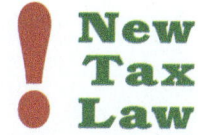

Figure 3.1 Principal Business or Professional Activity Codes Excerpt

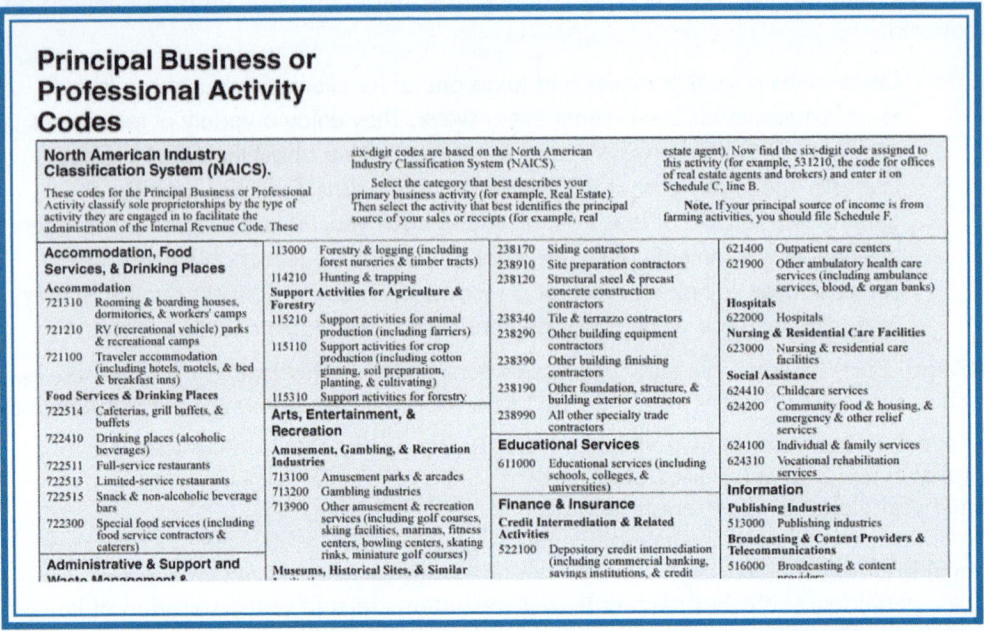

3-1d Schedule C Income (Part I)

Part I of Schedule C (Figure 3.2) contains the calculation of the taxpayer's gross income from the business or profession. The calculation starts with gross receipts or sales (line 1). Returns and allowances (line 2) and cost of goods sold (line 4) are subtracted to arrive at the gross profit from the activity. Other related income from the business (line 6) is added to the gross profit to produce the Schedule C gross income (line 7). Schedule C, line 7 is included in the amount of gross income used to determine whether a taxpayer must file a tax return (Figure 1.3 in Chapter 1).

Figure 3.2 Schedule C Income (Part I)

Part I	Income		
1	Gross receipts or sales. See instructions for line 1 and check the box if this income was reported to you on Form W-2 and the "Statutory employee" box on that form was checked ☐	1	
2	Returns and allowances	2	
3	Subtract line 2 from line 1	3	
4	Cost of goods sold (from line 42)	4	
5	**Gross profit.** Subtract line 4 from line 3	5	
6	Other income, including federal and state gasoline or fuel tax credit or refund (see instructions)	6	
7	**Gross income.** Add lines 5 and 6	7	

3-1e Schedule C Expenses (Part II)

The taxpayer reports the expenses from their business or profession in Part II of Schedule C (Figure 3.3). Expenses such as advertising, insurance, interest, rent, travel, wages, and utilities are reported on lines 8 through 27. Some expenses such as depreciation may require additional supporting information from another schedule. The expenses are totaled on line 28 and subtracted from gross income (line 7) to arrive at the tentative profit or loss from the activity (line 29). An expense for business use of a taxpayer's home (LO 3.11) is computed on Form

Figure 3.3   Schedule C Expenses (Part II)

Part II	Expenses. Enter expenses for business use of your home **only** on line 30.					
8	Advertising	8		18	Office expense (see instructions)	18
9	Car and truck expenses (see instructions)	9		19	Pension and profit-sharing plans	19
				20	Rent or lease (see instructions):	
10	Commissions and fees	10		a	Vehicles, machinery, and equipment	20a
11	Contract labor (see instructions)	11		b	Other business property	20b
12	Depletion	12		21	Repairs and maintenance	21
13	Depreciation and section 179 expense deduction (not included in Part III) (see instructions)	13		22	Supplies (not included in Part III)	22
				23	Taxes and licenses	23
				24	Travel and meals:	
14	Employee benefit programs (other than on line 19)	14		a	Travel	24a
				b	Deductible meals (see instructions)	24b
15	Insurance (other than health)	15		25	Utilities	25
16	Interest (see instructions):			26	Wages (less employment credits)	26
a	Mortgage (paid to banks, etc.)	16a		27a	Other expenses (from line 48)	27a
b	Other	16b		b	Energy efficient commercial bldgs deduction (attach Form 7205)	27b
17	Legal and professional services	17				
28	Total expenses before expenses for business use of home. Add lines 8 through 27b					28
29	Tentative profit or (loss). Subtract line 28 from line 7					29
30	Expenses for business use of your home. Do not report these expenses elsewhere. Attach Form 8829 unless using the simplified method. See instructions. **Simplified method filers only:** Enter the total square footage of (a) your home: _____ and (b) the part of your home used for business: _____. Use the Simplified Method Worksheet in the instructions to figure the amount to enter on line 30					30
31	Net profit or (loss). Subtract line 30 from line 29. • If a profit, enter on both **Schedule 1 (Form 1040), line 3**, and on **Schedule SE, line 2**. (If you checked the box on line 1, see instructions.) Estates and trusts, enter on **Form 1041, line 3**. • If a loss, you **must** go to line 32.					31
32	If you have a loss, check the box that describes your investment in this activity. See instructions. • If you checked 32a, enter the loss on both **Schedule 1 (Form 1040), line 3**, and on **Schedule SE, line 2**. (If you checked the box on line 1, see the line 31 instructions.) Estates and trusts, enter on **Form 1041, line 3**. • If you checked 32b, you **must** attach **Form 6198**. Your loss may be limited.				32a ☐ All investment is at risk. 32b ☐ Some investment is not at risk.	

8829 or using the simplified method. The deductible portion of home office expenses is entered on line 30 and subtracted from tentative profit, resulting in the net profit or loss (line 31) from the activity. Common business expenses are covered in detail later in this chapter. The deduction for one-half of self-employment tax, self-employed health insurance, and self-employed retirement contributions are uniquely deducted on Schedule 1 of Form 1040, and not on Schedule C. These additional business deductions are often considered when calculating limitations based on business income, for example, qualified business income. These deductions are covered in detail in subsequent chapters of this textbook.

3-1f Schedule C Cost of Goods Sold (Part III)

The calculation of cost of goods sold is reported in Part III (Figure 3.4) of Schedule C. In Part III lines 33 and 34, taxpayers must answer questions about the methods used to calculate inventory. Cost of goods sold (line 42) is equal to the beginning inventory (line 35) plus purchases (line 36), labor (line 37), materials and supplies (line 38), and other costs (line 39) less ending inventory (line 41). LO 3.2 has a more detailed discussion of inventories.

3-1g Schedule C Vehicle Information (Part IV)

If a taxpayer uses a car or truck in their sole proprietorship, then Part IV of Schedule C (Figure 3.5) must be completed to provide the IRS with supplemental vehicle information. In Part IV, a taxpayer should provide the date the vehicle was placed in service for business use (line 43), the business miles driven (line 44a), the commuting miles driven (line 44b), and other miles driven (line 44c). On lines 45 to 47 of Part IV, taxpayers must answer questions relevant to obtaining a deduction for business use of a vehicle.

Tax Break According to the Small Business Administration, almost 50 percent of small businesses fail in the first five years and about two-thirds fail within 10 years. To assist small business owners with winding up their tax affairs, the IRS provides a website devoted to this unenviable task. Go to **www.irs.gov/businesses/small-businesses-self-employed/closing-a-business** and select the type of entity (sole proprietor, corporation, etc.).

Figure 3.4 — Cost of Goods Sold (Part III)

Part III Cost of Goods Sold (see instructions)

33 Method(s) used to value closing inventory: **a** ☐ Cost   **b** ☐ Lower of cost or market   **c** ☐ Other (attach explanation)

34 Was there any change in determining quantities, costs, or valuations between opening and closing inventory? If "Yes," attach explanation . . . . ☐ Yes   ☐ No

35 Inventory at beginning of year. If different from last year's closing inventory, attach explanation . . . | 35 |
36 Purchases less cost of items withdrawn for personal use . . . . | 36 |
37 Cost of labor. Do not include any amounts paid to yourself . . . . | 37 |
38 Materials and supplies . . . . | 38 |
39 Other costs . . . . | 39 |
40 Add lines 35 through 39 . . . . | 40 |
41 Inventory at end of year . . . . | 41 |
42 **Cost of goods sold.** Subtract line 41 from line 40. Enter the result here and on line 4 . . . . | 42 |

Figure 3.5 — Vehicle Information (Part IV)

Part IV Information on Your Vehicle. Complete this part **only** if you are claiming car or truck expenses on line 9 and are not required to file Form 4562 for this business. See the instructions for line 13 to find out if you must file Form 4562.

43 When did you place your vehicle in service for business purposes? (month/day/year) _____ / _____ / _____

44 Of the total number of miles you drove your vehicle during 2024, enter the number of miles you used your vehicle for:

   a Business _____   **b** Commuting (see instructions) _____   **c** Other _____

45 Was your vehicle available for personal use during off-duty hours? . . . . ☐ Yes   ☐ No
46 Do you (or your spouse) have another vehicle available for personal use? . . . . ☐ Yes   ☐ No
47a Do you have evidence to support your deduction? . . . . ☐ Yes   ☐ No
   b If "Yes," is the evidence written? . . . . ☐ Yes   ☐ No

3-1h Schedule C Other Expenses (Part V)

The expenses section of Schedule C (Part II), line 27a contains an entry for other miscellaneous expenses. These other expenses must be itemized in Part V of Schedule C and include deductible items which do not have specific lines already assigned in the expenses section (Part II). Expenses for business gifts, education, professional dues, and consulting fees are commonly listed.

3-1i Self-Employment Tax

Self-employed taxpayers, sole proprietors, and independent contractors with net earnings of $400 or more, many of whom report income on Schedule C, must pay self-employment tax calculated on Schedule SE with their Form 1040. For new business owners, the self-employment tax may come as a particularly unpleasant and costly surprise if they are not aware of its existence.

The self-employment tax is made up of two taxes, the Social Security tax, which is meant to fund old age and disability insurance payments, and the Medicare tax. For 2024, the Social Security tax rate of 12.4 percent applies to the first $168,600 of net self-employment income, while the Medicare tax rate of 2.9 percent applies to all net self-employment income, with no income ceiling. Half of the self-employment tax is allowed as a deduction on line 15 of Schedule 1 of Form 1040 in arriving at adjusted gross income. Self-employment taxes are similar to FICA taxes, which are levied on employees partly through payroll withholding and partly through employer contributions. FICA taxes are not paid with Form 1040 as self-employment taxes are. Self-employed Social Security and Medicare taxes are covered in detail in Chapter 4.

ProConnect™ Tax TIP

To report profits from a sole proprietorship in ProConnect Tax, under Income, use Business Income (Schedule C) to enter information. Additional businesses can be added using the [+] tab at the top of the main window.

Self-Study Problem 3.1
Refer to Appendix E for Solutions to Self-Study Problems

Shelly Wie is self-employed as a professional golf instructor. She uses the cash method of accounting, and her Social Security number is 466-47-8833. Her principal business code is 812990. Shelly's business is located at 96-540 Ala `Ike, Pearl City, HI 96782. During 2024, Shelly had the following income and expenses:

Fees from golf lessons	$48,000
Expenses:	
Car expenses (5,000 business miles)	3,350
Business liability insurance	500
Office expense	600
Rent on office space	10,000
City business license	300
Travel expense	1,300
Meals (deductible portion)	700
Utilities	515
Membership in professional golfers' association	750

Shelly bought her car on January 1, 2024. In addition to the business miles listed above, she commuted 1,200 miles and she drove 4,500 miles for nonbusiness purposes.

Complete Schedule C on Pages 3-8 and 3-9 for Shelly showing her net income from self-employment. Make realistic assumptions about any missing data.

Self-Study Problem 3.1

SCHEDULE C (Form 1040)
Department of the Treasury
Internal Revenue Service

Profit or Loss From Business
(Sole Proprietorship)
Attach to Form 1040, 1040-SR, 1040-SS, 1040-NR, or 1041; partnerships must generally file Form 1065.
Go to www.irs.gov/ScheduleC for instructions and the latest information.

OMB No. 1545-0074
2024
Attachment Sequence No. 09

Name of proprietor | Social security number (SSN)

- **A** Principal business or profession, including product or service (see instructions)
- **B** Enter code from instructions
- **C** Business name. If no separate business name, leave blank.
- **D** Employer ID number (EIN) (see instr.)
- **E** Business address (including suite or room no.)
  City, town or post office, state, and ZIP code
- **F** Accounting method: (1) ☐ Cash (2) ☐ Accrual (3) ☐ Other (specify)
- **G** Did you "materially participate" in the operation of this business during 2024? If "No," see instructions for limit on losses . ☐ Yes ☐ No
- **H** If you started or acquired this business during 2024, check here . ☐
- **I** Did you make any payments in 2024 that would require you to file Form(s) 1099? See instructions . ☐ Yes ☐ No
- **J** If "Yes," did you or will you file required Form(s) 1099? . ☐ Yes ☐ No

Part I Income

1	Gross receipts or sales. See instructions for line 1 and check the box if this income was reported to you on Form W-2 and the "Statutory employee" box on that form was checked . ☐	1
2	Returns and allowances	2
3	Subtract line 2 from line 1	3
4	Cost of goods sold (from line 42)	4
5	**Gross profit.** Subtract line 4 from line 3	5
6	Other income, including federal and state gasoline or fuel tax credit or refund (see instructions)	6
7	**Gross income.** Add lines 5 and 6	7

Part II Expenses. Enter expenses for business use of your home **only** on line 30.

8	Advertising	8	18	Office expense (see instructions)	18
9	Car and truck expenses (see instructions)	9	19	Pension and profit-sharing plans	19
10	Commissions and fees	10	20	Rent or lease (see instructions):	
11	Contract labor (see instructions)	11	a	Vehicles, machinery, and equipment	20a
12	Depletion	12	b	Other business property	20b
13	Depreciation and section 179 expense deduction (not included in Part III) (see instructions)	13	21	Repairs and maintenance	21
			22	Supplies (not included in Part III)	22
			23	Taxes and licenses	23
			24	Travel and meals:	
14	Employee benefit programs (other than on line 19)	14	a	Travel	24a
			b	Deductible meals (see instructions)	24b
15	Insurance (other than health)	15	25	Utilities	25
16	Interest (see instructions):		26	Wages (less employment credits)	26
a	Mortgage (paid to banks, etc.)	16a	27a	Other expenses (from line 48)	27a
b	Other	16b	b	Energy efficient commercial bldgs deduction (attach Form 7205)	27b
17	Legal and professional services	17			
28	**Total expenses** before expenses for business use of home. Add lines 8 through 27b				28
29	Tentative profit or (loss). Subtract line 28 from line 7				29
30	Expenses for business use of your home. Do not report these expenses elsewhere. Attach Form 8829 unless using the simplified method. See instructions.
Simplified method filers only: Enter the total square footage of (a) your home: _____ and (b) the part of your home used for business: _____. Use the Simplified Method Worksheet in the instructions to figure the amount to enter on line 30				30
31	**Net profit or (loss).** Subtract line 30 from line 29.
• If a profit, enter on both **Schedule 1 (Form 1040), line 3,** and on **Schedule SE, line 2.** (If you checked the box on line 1, see instructions.) Estates and trusts, enter on **Form 1041, line 3.**
• If a loss, you **must** go to line 32.				31
32	If you have a loss, check the box that describes your investment in this activity. See instructions.
• If you checked 32a, enter the loss on both **Schedule 1 (Form 1040), line 3,** and on **Schedule SE, line 2.** (If you checked the box on line 1, see the line 31 instructions.) Estates and trusts, enter on **Form 1041, line 3.**
• If you checked 32b, you **must** attach **Form 6198.** Your loss may be limited.			32a ☐ All investment is at risk.
32b ☐ Some investment is not at risk.	

For Paperwork Reduction Act Notice, see the separate instructions. | Cat. No. 11334P | Schedule C (Form 1040) 2024

Schedule C (Form 1040) 2024 Page **2**

Part III Cost of Goods Sold (see instructions)

33 Method(s) used to
    value closing inventory: **a** ☐ Cost   **b** ☐ Lower of cost or market   **c** ☐ Other (attach explanation)

34 Was there any change in determining quantities, costs, or valuations between opening and closing inventory?
    If "Yes," attach explanation . . . . ☐ Yes   ☐ No

35 Inventory at beginning of year. If different from last year's closing inventory, attach explanation . . | 35 |

36 Purchases less cost of items withdrawn for personal use . . . . | 36 |

37 Cost of labor. Do not include any amounts paid to yourself . . . . | 37 |

38 Materials and supplies . . . . | 38 |

39 Other costs . . . . | 39 |

40 Add lines 35 through 39 . . . . | 40 |

41 Inventory at end of year . . . . | 41 |

42 **Cost of goods sold.** Subtract line 41 from line 40. Enter the result here and on line 4 . . . . . . | 42 |

Part IV Information on Your Vehicle. Complete this part **only** if you are claiming car or truck expenses on line 9 and are not required to file Form 4562 for this business. See the instructions for line 13 to find out if you must file Form 4562.

43 When did you place your vehicle in service for business purposes? (month/day/year) ____/____/____

44 Of the total number of miles you drove your vehicle during 2024, enter the number of miles you used your vehicle for:

    a Business _____ **b** Commuting (see instructions) _____ **c** Other _____

45 Was your vehicle available for personal use during off-duty hours? . . . . ☐ Yes   ☐ No

46 Do you (or your spouse) have another vehicle available for personal use? . . . . ☐ Yes   ☐ No

47a Do you have evidence to support your deduction? . . . . ☐ Yes   ☐ No

  b If "Yes," is the evidence written? . . . . ☐ Yes   ☐ No

Part V Other Expenses. List below business expenses not included on lines 8–26, line 27b, or line 30.

_____	_____
_____	_____
_____	_____
_____	_____
_____	_____
_____	_____
_____	_____
_____	_____
_____	_____

48 **Total other expenses.** Enter here and on line 27a . . . . | 48 |

Learning Objective 3.2

Describe the tax treatment of inventories and cost of goods sold.

3-2 Inventories

Inventory is the stock of goods or materials that a business holds for the purpose of resale to generate a profit. The purchase or sale of merchandise is almost always an income-producing factor for manufacturers, retailers, and wholesalers, and cost of goods sold is often the largest expense for these types of businesses.

Example Yashida operates a small business that sells crafts over the Internet. The crafts are manufactured in her small factory. The purchase and sale of merchandise is clearly an income-producing factor for this business. ♦

Example Alan is a lawyer that specializes in consumer class-action lawsuits against large corporations. Because his primary product is legal services, inventory is not a significant income-producing factor for Alan's business. ♦

When a business supplies goods in conjunction with providing services to customers, it is not always clear whether providing goods is an income-producing factor that requires the business to keep inventories.

Accounting for inventory can be complex. One of the primary steps in accrual-based inventory accounting is to measure ending inventory at the end of the accounting period (usually at year-end). To do so often requires a physical inventory, which is a process by which the actual count of goods is taken. An additional step is to assign an inventory flow method such as first-in, first-out (FIFO) or last-in, first-out (LIFO). Once ending inventory is established, cost of goods sold can be computed as follows:

Beginning inventory	$ 75,000
Add: purchases	250,000
Costs of goods available for sale	325,000
Less: ending inventory	(100,000)
Cost of goods sold	$ 225,000

Because of the time and effort associated with tracking inventory, the tax law permits small businesses to use the cash method for accounting for inventory. For purposes of this tax provision, a business with three-year average gross receipts of less than $30 million (in 2024) is considered a small business. Under the cash method, the taxpayer has three options:

1. treat inventory as non-incidental materials and supplies,
2. treat inventory the same as on the applicable financial statements of the business, or
3. for taxpayers without applicable financial statements, treat inventory as it conforms with the business books and records.

Non-incidental materials and supplies (NIMS) are deducted either in the year that the merchandise is sold or the year in which the inventory is paid for, whichever is later.

Example Geoff purchases unique goods from a variety of manufacturers and then sells those items over the Internet. Geoff's business is small and he treats inventory as NIMS. He will include the cost of the goods in his cost of goods sold when the items are sold. ♦

The treatment of inventory as NIMS does not differ considerably from typical inventory accounting, which generally also recovers the cost of inventory when the inventory is sold.

The second option is to treat inventory the same as that of applicable financial statements (or AFS) of the business. AFS are generally financial statements that have been prepared in accordance with generally accepted accounting principles (GAAP). Since GAAP is going to require proper inventory accounting, this option provides no significant relief from accrual-based inventory accounting.

The last option is to use the same accounting for inventory as is used on the books and records of the business. Under this option, if a business chooses to expense inventory when purchased, the business would be permitted to deduct the costs in the same year for tax purposes.

Example Debinha operates a garage that repairs European-made automobiles. As part of the service, the garage purchases and eventually sells a variety of car parts, including oil filters, brake pads, various belts, and motors (such as alternators). Debinha expenses any part as it is purchased, in spite of the item not yet being sold. For example, Debinha may purchase five oil filters (when only one is needed for a current repair) with the expectation that the remaining four filters will be sold in the near future. Debinha does not prepare applicable financial statements for her business. Debinha will be able to conform her tax accounting for inventory with her books and records, and thus, will deduct inventory when purchased. ◆

However, the regulations surrounding this tax law appear to increase the likelihood that *any* use of typical inventory accounting may preclude deducting the cost of inventory at any time except when sold.

Example Sasha is engaged in the retail business of selling beer, wine, and liquor. Sasha has average annual gross receipts for the prior three taxable years of less than $30 million and thus, uses the cash method of accounting. Sasha treats all merchandise costs paid during the taxable year as expensed on the bookkeeping software. However, as part of its regular business practice, Sasha takes a physical count of inventory of merchandise on hand at year end. Sasha also makes representations to its creditor of the amount of inventory on hand. Because Sasha's books and records do not accurately reflect the inventory records used for non-tax purposes in its regular business activity, Sasha must use the physical inventory count to determine its ending inventory, and thus, will deduct only the cost of inventory sold based on that count. ◆

The above examples of the three options for cash-basis inventory accounting show that only a small business that pays very little attention to inventory, can use the cash-basis method of inventory. To the extent that the purchase or sale of merchandise is a significant income-producing activity, recommended business practices would not permit such transactions without some form of tracking and accounting controls. Tax law generally requires the capitalization of certain indirect costs into inventory under Section 263A, sometimes known as the Uniform Capitalization (UNICAP) rules. Businesses with gross receipts of no more than $30 million are not required to apply the UNICAP rules. The details of the UNICAP rules are beyond the scope of this textbook.

As a result of the current interpretation of inventory tax law, most businesses must calculate cost of goods sold by determining the value of the beginning and ending inventories of the business. This involves determining the cost of the items on hand, which is complicated by the taxpayer often having paid different prices during the year for the same inventory item. There are two common methods of inventory valuation used by taxpayers: first in, first out (FIFO) and last in, first out (LIFO). The FIFO method is based on the assumption that the first merchandise acquired is the first to be sold. Accordingly, the inventory on hand consists of the most recently acquired goods. Alternatively, when the taxpayer uses the LIFO method, it is assumed that the most recently acquired goods are sold first and the inventory on hand consists of the earliest purchases. FIFO and LIFO are simply calculation assumptions; the goods that are actually on hand do not have to correspond to the assumptions of the method selected. In addition to the LIFO and FIFO methods, which are commonly used by taxpayers in valuing beginning and ending inventories, taxpayers may specifically identify the goods that are sold and the goods that are in ending inventory. However, the process of specifically identifying items sold and on hand is not a practical alternative for most taxpayers.

Example Yuki made the following purchases of a particular inventory item during the current year:

March 1	50 units at $120 per unit	$ 6,000
August 1	40 units at $130 per unit	5,200
December 1	25 units at $140 per unit	3,500
Total		$14,700

If the ending inventory is 60 units, it is valued under the FIFO method as illustrated below:

35 units at $130 each	$4,550
25 units at $140 each	3,500
Ending inventory	$8,050

Assuming that Yuki had no beginning inventory of the item, the same ending inventory (60 units) would be valued using the LIFO method as follows:

50 units at $120 each	$6,000
10 units at $130 each	1,300
Ending inventory	$7,300

The cost of goods sold for both the FIFO and LIFO methods are presented below:

	FIFO	LIFO
Beginning inventory	$ 0	$ 0
Add: purchases	14,700	14,700
Cost of goods available for sale	14,700	14,700
Less: ending inventory	(8,050)	(7,300)
Cost of goods sold	$ 6,650	$ 7,400

Notice that taxable income will be $750 more when the FIFO method is used instead of the LIFO method. During periods of rising inventory prices, taxpayers have lower taxable income and pay less tax if they use the LIFO inventory valuation method. ♦

A taxpayer may adopt the LIFO method by using it in a tax return and attaching Form 970 to make the election. Once the election is made, the method may be changed only with the consent of the IRS. Also, if the LIFO election is made for reporting taxable income, taxpayers must use the same method for preparing their financial statements. In other words, a taxpayer may not use LIFO for their tax return and use FIFO for financial statements presented to a bank. This rule is strictly enforced by the IRS.

> **Self-Study Problem 3.2** Refer to Appendix E for Solutions to Self-Study Problems
>
> Amirah owns a small retail store. During the year, Amirah purchases $200,000 worth of inventory. Her beginning inventory is $75,000 and her ending inventory is $88,000. Use Part III of Schedule C below to calculate Amirah's cost of goods sold for the year.
>
> | Part III | Cost of Goods Sold (see instructions) | |
> |---|---|---|
> | 33 | Method(s) used to value closing inventory: a ☐ Cost b ☐ Lower of cost or market c ☐ Other (attach explanation) | |
> | 34 | Was there any change in determining quantities, costs, or valuations between opening and closing inventory? If "Yes," attach explanation . . . . ☐ Yes ☐ No | |
> | 35 | Inventory at beginning of year. If different from last year's closing inventory, attach explanation | 35 |
> | 36 | Purchases less cost of items withdrawn for personal use . . . . | 36 |
> | 37 | Cost of labor. Do not include any amounts paid to yourself . . . . | 37 |
> | 38 | Materials and supplies . . . . | 38 |
> | 39 | Other costs . . . . | 39 |
> | 40 | Add lines 35 through 39 . . . . | 40 |
> | 41 | Inventory at end of year . . . . | 41 |
> | 42 | **Cost of goods sold.** Subtract line 41 from line 40. Enter the result here and on line 4 . . . . . | 42 |

3-3 Transportation

3.3 Learning Objective

Identify the requirements for deducting transportation expenses.

Certain transportation expenses for business purposes are deductible by self-employed taxpayers and employers. Deductible expenses include travel by airplane, rail, and bus, and the cost of operating and maintaining an automobile. Meals and lodging are *not* included in the transportation expense deduction; those expenses may be deducted as travel expenses (LO 3.4). Transportation expenses may be deducted even if the taxpayer is not away from their tax home.

Deductible transportation costs do not include the normal costs of commuting. Commuting includes the expenses of buses, subways, taxis, and operating a private car between home and the taxpayer's principal place of work, and is generally a nondeductible personal expense. The cost of transportation between the taxpayer's home and a work location is generally not deductible, but nevertheless, may be deductible in circumstances described below:

1. A taxpayer is allowed to deduct daily transportation expenses incurred in going between the taxpayer's residence and work locations outside the metropolitan area where the taxpayer lives and normally works.
2. If the taxpayer has a regular place of business, daily expenses for transportation between the taxpayer's home and temporary work locations are deductible.
3. A taxpayer may deduct daily expenses for transportation between the taxpayer's home and other regular or temporary work locations if the taxpayer's residence is the taxpayer's principal place of business, based on the home office rules, which are discussed later in this chapter.

In all cases, the additional costs of hauling tools and instruments are deductible. For example, the cost of renting a trailer to haul tools to a job site is deductible.

If the taxpayer works at two or more jobs during the same day, they may deduct the cost of going from one job to the other or from one business location to another. The deductible expense is based on the cost of travel by the shortest, most normally traveled route, even if the taxpayer uses another route. If the taxpayer works at a second job on a day that they do not work at the first job, the commuting expenses to the second job are not deductible.

Example Luca Pacioli is a self-employed CPA working full time Monday through Friday. On Tuesday night he teaches an accounting class at a local university. Luca leaves the office at 5:30 p.m. on his class day and, after dinner at a local cafe, teaches his class from 7:00 p.m. to 10:00 p.m. The distance from Luca's home to his office is 12 miles, the distance from his office to the university is 15 miles, and the distance from the university to his home is 18 miles. If Luca teaches the class 32 times a year, his mileage deduction is based on 480 miles (32 × 15 miles). While he is traveling from home to the office (12 miles) and from the university to home (18 miles), he is commuting and the mileage is not deductible. If Luca taught the class in the afternoon and returned to his regular job before going home, he could claim a deduction based on the round-trip mileage from his office to and from the university, 30 miles (2 × 15 miles). Alternatively, if he taught the course on a day (Saturday) when he did not work at his full-time job, Luca would not be entitled to any mileage deduction. ♦

Taxpayers may deduct the actual expenses of transportation, or they may be entitled to use a standard mileage rate to calculate their deduction for transportation costs. The standard mileage rate for 2024 is 67 cents per mile. Most costs associated with the operation of an automobile, such as gasoline, oil, insurance, repairs, and maintenance, as well as depreciation, are built into the standard mileage rate. The deduction for parking and toll fees related to business transportation (not commuting) and the deduction for interest on car loans and state and local personal property taxes on the automobile are determined separately. Self-employed taxpayers deduct the business portion of the state and local personal property taxes and interest on automobile loans on Schedule C or F. To use the standard mileage method, the taxpayer must:

1. own or lease the automobile,
2. not operate a fleet of automobiles, using five or more at the same time,
3. not have claimed depreciation on the automobile using any method other than straight-line depreciation, and
4. not have claimed Section 179 (expense election) depreciation or bonus depreciation on the automobile (Chapter 8 has a complete explanation of depreciation).

If the taxpayer is entitled to use either the actual cost or the standard mileage method, they may select the method that results in the largest tax deduction for the first year. If the taxpayer does not use the standard mileage method in the first year, the method is no longer available for any subsequent year. A change to the actual cost method can be made any year. If, after using the standard mileage method, the taxpayer uses actual costs to determine the automobile expense deduction, depreciation on the automobile must be calculated using straight-line depreciation (Chapter 8). The standard mileage method may be used for a car for hire, such as a taxi, if the automobile meets the other requirements for use of this method.

Taxpayers who use the actual cost method to calculate their transportation deductions must keep adequate cost records. The deductible portion of the total automobile expenses is based on the ratio of the number of business miles driven during the year to the total miles driven during the tax year multiplied by the total automobile expenses for the year. The business-use percentage is applied to the total automobile expenses for the year, including depreciation, but excluding any expenses which are directly attributable to business use of the automobile, such as business parking fees and tolls. The deduction for interest and personal property taxes is also separately computed.

Example T.J. is a self-employed salesperson who drove their new automobile 20,000 total miles during the 2024 tax year. The business use of the automobile was 80 percent of the total miles driven. The actual cost of gasoline, oil, repairs, depreciation, and insurance for the year was $10,000. The automobile expense deduction is calculated as follows:

1. Standard mileage method:
   Business mileage = 16,000 miles (20,000 miles × 80%)
   16,000 × 67 cents/mile $10,720

2. Actual cost method:
   80% × $10,000 (total actual cost) $ 8,000

   T.J. is permitted to deduct the larger amount. ♦

ProConnect™ Tax TIP

Vehicle expenses are reported on Form 2106 and are carried over to Schedule C or other forms. To enter deductions associated with a business vehicle, go to Vehicle/Employee Business Expense (2106) under the general Deductions item in the left margin. The deduction can be connected to the appropriate Schedule C or other business using a dropdown box.

Self-Study Problem 3.3
Refer to Appendix E for Solutions to Self-Study Problems

Marc Lusebrink, sole proprietor of Oak Company, bought a used automobile that was driven 13,000 miles during 2024 for business purposes. Total miles (including business miles) is 16,000. His total expenses for his automobile for the year are:

Gasoline	$2,061
Oil changes	92
Insurance	1,030
Tires	225
Repairs	620
Total	$4,028

The automobile cost $40,000 on January 1, and total depreciation for the year, including personal use, was $8,000. His business parking and toll fees for business amount to $327. Calculate Marc's transportation expense deduction for the year.

3-4 Travel Expenses

3.4 Learning Objective
Identify the requirements for deducting travel expenses.

Travel expenses are defined as ordinary and necessary expenses incurred when traveling away from home in pursuit of the taxpayer's trade or business. These expenses are deductible as long as they can be substantiated and are not lavish or extravagant. Other business expenses incurred while not away from home such as business gifts are not included as travel expenses, although these items may be separately deductible, subject to certain limitations. Expenses included as part of the travel deduction include the cost of such items as meals, lodging, taxis, tips, and laundry. Most travel expenses are fully deductible, but Congress decided that a portion of the cost of meals is a personal expense. Therefore, only 50 percent of the cost of meals is deductible. If an employer reimburses an employee for the cost of meals, then the 50 percent limitation applies to the employer so that the employer can deduct only 50 percent of the expense.

To deduct travel expenses, a taxpayer must be away from home "overnight." Overnight does not literally mean 24 hours; it is a period of time longer than an ordinary work day in which rest or relief from work is required. Also, the taxpayer must be away from their "tax home" to be on travel status. A tax home is the taxpayer's principal place of business or employment, and not necessarily the same location as their family residence. If the taxpayer has two or more places of business, the taxpayer's tax home is at the principal place of business. Factors that determine the principal place of business include total time spent in each location, the degree of business activity, and the relative amount of income from each location.

Example Randolph is an independent salesperson for an electronics distributor (not an employee). Randolph lives and his primary work office is in Asheboro, NC. During 2024, Randolph drives to High Point, NC (30 miles each way), to meet with a customer. He spends the day at the customer's facility and then returns to Asheboro in the early evening. Under these circumstances, Randolph can return to his work home on the same day and his workday is not longer than an ordinary workday. Randolph can deduct his transportation costs (e.g., mileage) but this trip is not considered away from home. ♦

Example Continuing from the previous example, later in 2024, Randolph is required to travel to meet with a customer in Asheville, NC (180 miles each way). There are no efficient ways to fly between Asheboro and Asheville, so Randolph drives. The meeting is expected to last all day and so Randolph leaves Asheboro at 5:00 am and stays in Asheville until the meeting ends at 6:00 pm. Although Randolph could drive home and likely be home by 9:00 pm, he elects to stay the night in Asheville, as his workday has already been 13 hours long (including the drive to Asheville in the morning). Returning to home on the same day is neither reasonable nor safe, and thus, this trip qualifies as travel away from home. Randolph's transportation and travel costs should be deductible. ♦

Expenses of a temporary assignment are deductible if it is not practical to return home at the end of each day's work or if the employer requires the employee's attendance at a business meeting, training activity, or other overnight business function. If the assignment is for a long period of time or indefinite (generally more than one year), the new location may be considered the taxpayer's new tax home and they may lose the travel deduction. If the travel costs are not deductible, an employee must include as income any reimbursements of non-deductible travel expenses.

Example Cleavon Lakeshore is the Assistant Manager of Team Travel and Logistics for the Las Vegas Raiders professional football team. Cleavon and family live in Austin, TX, but starting in August, Cleavon lives and works in Las Vegas, NV, until the end of the regular season (five months) or perhaps into the playoffs and Super Bowl (as many as seven months) if the team is successful. During the duration of the season, he rents a small apartment in Las Vegas while his spouse and children remain in Austin. Managing the team travel of the Raiders is Cleavon's only job. Cleavon's tax home is in Las Vegas, and thus, his living expenses while in Las Vegas are not deductible. ♦

Example Clodagh Walsh is a new restaurant team manager for the Pie Plant chain of upscale family restaurants. Her primary job is to travel to locations where a new Pie Plant is opening and work to hire and train local management and staff until the restaurant is operating well. She is then redeployed to the next new restaurant to open. Normally, Clodagh lives in Detroit, MI, and has an office in the Pie Plant corporate headquarters building. When not traveling, she works in the Pie Plant test kitchen. In 2024, Clodagh spent 3 months opening a new restaurant in Marietta, GA, and three months in Hayward, CA. The rest of the year was spent in Detroit. Clodagh's travel away from home is for a temporary assignment and her lodging, meals, laundry, and incidentals while on the road will be deductible. ♦

Taxpayers who make a combined business and pleasure trip within the United States may deduct all of the costs incurred in traveling to and from the business destination (for example, airfare) provided the trip is primarily for business. Once at the destination, only the business portion of the travel costs for meals, lodging, local transportation, and incidental expenses may be deducted; any costs which are not associated with the taxpayer's business are not deductible. If a taxpayer makes a trip which is primarily for pleasure, the travel expenses to and from the destination are not deductible even though the taxpayer engages in some business activity while at the destination. Although the traveling expenses to and from the destination are not deductible, any expenses incurred while at the destination that are related to the taxpayer's business are deductible.

Example During 2024, Susan travels from Los Angeles to Hawaii for an eight-day business trip and pays $900 for the airfare. While in Hawaii, Susan spends five days on business and an additional three days on vacation. The lodging and meal costs are $1,200 and $200, respectively, for the business portion of the trip. The total cost of meals and lodging for the personal portion of the trip is $1,100. Susan may deduct $900 for the airfare, $1,200 for the business lodging, and $100 (50 percent of $200) for the business meals. None of the $1,100 of personal expenses is deductible. ♦

Special rules and limitations apply to combined business and pleasure travel outside the United States. Even though a trip is primarily for business, if the trip has any element of pleasure, the cost of traveling to and from the destination must be allocated between the business and personal portions of the trip. The travel expenses for transportation to and from the destination must be allocated based on the number of business days compared to the total number of days outside the United States. The rules for travel costs to and from the destination where the trip is primarily for pleasure are the same as the rules for travel within the United States; none of the travel costs are deductible. Under certain circumstances, the entire foreign travel expense can be deducted (i.e., the total trip is for one week or less or less than 25 percent of the trip is for nonbusiness reasons). Once at the destination, the taxpayer's expenses directly related to the taxpayer's business are deductible. For a complete explanation of travel outside the United States, see IRS Publication 463.

Example During 2024, Susan travels from Los Angeles to Singapore for an eight-day business trip and pays $900 for the airfare. While in Singapore, Susan spends five days on business and an additional three days on vacation. The lodging and meal costs are $1,200 and $200, respectively, for the business portion of the trip. The total cost of meals and lodging for the personal portion of the trip is $1,100. Susan may deduct $562.50 ($900 × 5 days ÷ 8 days) for the airfare, $1,200 for the business lodging, and $100 (50 percent of $200) for the business meals. None of the $1,100 of personal expenses is deductible. If Susan's trip to Singapore was five days business and two days personal, because the trip does not exceed one week (7 consecutive days), the airfare need not be prorated and all $900 can be deducted. The lodging and meals remain the same. ♦

No deduction for travel expenses is allowed unless the taxpayer keeps proper expense records. Taxpayers must substantiate the following:

1. The amount of each separate expenditure, such as airfare and lodging. Expenses such as meals and taxi fares may be accumulated and reported in reasonable categories. As an alternative to reporting actual expenses, a per diem method may be used in certain circumstances.
2. The dates of departure and return for each trip and the number of business days on the trip.
3. The destination or locality of the travel described by the name of the city or town.
4. The business reason for the travel or the business benefit expected to be gained from the travel.

3-4a Per Diem Substantiation

Instead of requiring actual expense records, employers who reimburse employees for travel expenses can choose a per diem method of substantiation. Per diem is a daily allowance used for business travel expenses while away from an employee's tax home. The primary advantage of using a per diem method to substantiate expenses is that it eliminates much of the record keeping usually associated with travel expenses. The IRS has approved two per diem methods to substantiate travel expenses: (1) the standard per diem method and (2) the high-low per diem method. Employers can use per diem for all travel expenses including lodging, meals, and incidentals or an employer can use per diem for only meals and incidentals. Self-employed taxpayers may only use per diem for meals and incidentals.

1. *The Standard Federal Rate Method.* Under this method, the employee is allowed a per diem amount for travel equal to the current federal per diem rate which varies based on the travel location. A complete list of the regular per diem rates in effect for each area of the United States is available at the U.S. General Services Administration website (**www.gsa.gov**). The GSA also offers a mobile app.
2. *The High-Low Method.* The high-low method provides a simplified way of computing the federal per diem rate for travel within the United States. This method avoids the need to keep a current list of the per diem rates for all localities in the United States. Under this method a small number of locations are designated as high-cost localities and all other locations are deemed to be low-cost areas. Starting in October 2024, the high-cost allowance is $319 per day and the low-cost amount is $225 per day. If an employer uses this method to reimburse an employee at any time during a calendar year, this method must be used for all travel for that employee in the same calendar year.

Under either the standard method or the high-low method, the employee can use a current per diem amount for meals and incidental expenses (M&IE) only. Actual cost records are required for lodging expenses. The M&IE rate may be taken from the standard per diem rate tables or the high-low method may be used. For 2024, the M&IE allowance using the high-low method is $86 per day for high-cost localities and $74 per day for low-cost localities. Employees and self-employed taxpayers who do not incur meal expenses when traveling are allowed an incidental expense allowance of $5 per day.

Per diem rates are revised on October 1 every year with additional revisions made for specific locations throughout the year. For purposes of illustration and problems, the rates above are assumed to be chosen for the full year. Different rates than those shown above may apply.

Self-Study Problem 3.4   Refer to Appendix E for Solutions to Self-Study Problems

Byron is a certified public accountant who is self-employed. He is required to make a five-day business trip to Salt Lake City for an audit. Since he is going to be in Utah, Byron decides to stay for the weekend and go skiing. His expenses for the trip are as follows:

Airfare to Salt Lake City and return	$ 480
Hotel while on the audit (five nights at $165 per night)	825
50 percent of meals while on the audit	168
Laundry in Salt Lake City	22
Taxi fares in Salt Lake City	72
Transportation from Salt Lake City to and from Park City ski resort	100
Lodging at Park City ski resort	380
Lift tickets	99
Ski rental	89
Meals at Park City	182
Total	$2,417

If Byron has proper records to substantiate the above expenses, how much may he deduct as travel expenses for the seven-day trip?

3-5 Meals and Entertainment

3.5 Learning Objective
Determine the requirements for deducting meals.

There is no deduction for (1) an activity generally considered to be entertainment, amusement, or recreation, (2) membership dues for any club organized for business, pleasure, recreation, or other social purposes, or (3) a facility used in connection with any of the previous items. Entertainment costs related to a recreation, social, or similar activities for the benefit of employees remain deductible.

Example Dee Skotech operates a small business and hosted two parties at a local night club during 2024. The first was a party for all of her clients to celebrate a great year and to thank them for their loyalty. The second party was a holiday celebration for all the employees in Dee's company. The costs associated with the client party are nondeductible entertainment costs. The costs for the employee holiday party are 100-percent deductible. ♦

Because meals and entertainment are often closely aligned, taxpayers should be cautious in attempting to deduct meals associated with an entertainment event. Client meals in which business is conducted (and the taxpayer or taxpayer's employee is present) and which are not lavish or extravagant are typically 50-percent deductible. An entertainment-related meal such as one associated with a cocktail party, theatre, golf outing, or other entertainment event is only deductible if the meal is purchased or invoiced separately. Deductible business meal expenses must be substantiated in the same manner as deductible business gift expenses, covered later in this chapter.

Example Beau Gee is a salesperson for Hamilton Company. Beau has a meeting with an important customer at a local diner. Business is conducted at the meal as Beau and the customer discuss pricing, delivery dates, and other particulars, although no sale is actually closed. After the meal, Beau suggests they play a round of golf at the local golf course. After playing a round of golf, Beau and the customer stop in the golf club's restaurant and have a drink or two and some appetizers. Because business was conducted at the diner, the cost of the first meal is 50-percent deductible; however, the golf is entertainment and is not deductible. If the drinks and appetizers are separately purchased, the cost is 50-percent deductible. ♦

Celebratory meals such as holiday parties and company picnics are 100-percent deductible. Other types of meals can be either 50- or 100-percent deductible, as shown in Table 3.1:

Table 3.1 Deductibility of Certain Meal Expenses

Type of meal	Deductible
Meals for the convenience of the employer	50-percent until 2025. Thereafter, nondeductible
Water, coffee, and other office snacks	50-percent deductible
Restaurant meals provided for in-office meetings with employees	50-percent deductible
Restaurant meals during business travel	50-percent deductible
Meals offered for free to the public (e.g., a free seminar)	100-percent deductible
Food and beverages from a grocery store or liquor store	50-percent deductible

Although entertainment-related club dues are nondeductible, dues paid to business-related professional organizations, such as legal or medical organizations, are deductible. Dues paid to civic or public organizations, such as Chambers of Commerce, Kiwanis, and Rotary, are also allowed as legitimate business deductions. These clubs do public service work and are not organizations like country clubs which are entertainment or pleasure driven. Many business people belong to clubs such as Kiwanis or Rotary to network, meet potential clients, and increase their visibility in the community, but the club must do significant service work for the members' dues to qualify as deductions.

Self-Study Problem 3.5 — Refer to Appendix E for Solutions to Self-Study Problems

Laeticia operates a small business and incurs the following expenses:

Annual dues Tampa Bay Golf Club	$2,000
Restaurant meals with clients after golf	500
Meals with clients at the Club's dining room where business was conducted	600
Greens fees (personal and with clients)	700
Meals (personal)	250
Total	$4,050

Calculate the portion of the $4,050 that Laeticia can deduct.

Learning Objective 3.6

Identify the requirements for claiming business education expenses.

3-6 Educational Expenses

Please note: Educational incentives such as qualified tuition programs and educational savings accounts are covered in Chapter 2. The deduction for education loan interest is covered in Chapter 5. Education tax credits are covered in Chapter 7. Because there are numerous education incentives, the tax law in this area has become very complex. There may be more than one tax option for treating a particular education expense. This section deals primarily with the deduction of continuing education expenses incurred by self-employed taxpayers. The suspension of the deduction for miscellaneous expenses subject to 2 percent of AGI has effectively eliminated the deduction of unreimbursed educational costs for employees.

> **Tax Break**
>
> Taxpayers have been able to manage a handful of wins against the IRS when it comes to claiming a deduction for the cost of an MBA degree. In *Zuo v. Comm.* (2021), an entrepreneur was permitted an unreimbursed employee business deduction after demonstrating that the MBA did not prepare him for a new job since he was already an entrepreneur before starting the degree. This follows a series of cases such as *Blair v. Comm.* (1980), *Beatty v. Comm.* (1980), *Allemeier v. Comm.* (2005), *Singleton-Clarke v. Comm.* (2009), *Long v. Comm.* (2016) in which the court held that the MBA did not qualify an already experienced businessperson for a new job and permitted a deduction. In *Zhao Creigh v. Comm.*; however, the court held the opposite view since the taxpayers' role prior to the MBA differed substantially from her role afterward. Note that the temporary repeal of unreimbursed employee business expenses limits this deduction to self-employed taxpayers only through 2025.

There are two tests related to the deduction of educational expenses, at least one of which must be met to deduct the expenses. The tests are:

1. the educational expenses must be paid to meet *the requirements of the taxpayer's employer or the requirements of law or regulation* for keeping the taxpayer's salary, status, or job, or
2. the educational expenses must be paid to *maintain* or *improve existing skills* required in performing the duties of the taxpayer's present work.

Educational expenses meeting one of the above tests, which have a bona fide business purpose, may be deducted even if the education leads to a college degree.

Educational expenses are not deductible, even if one of the above tests is met, if (1) the education is required to meet the minimum requirements for the taxpayer's current job, or (2) the education is part of a program that will lead to a new trade or business even if the taxpayer does not intend to enter that new trade or business.

3-6a Education Required by Employer or Law

Taxpayers who are required to meet educational standards beyond minimum requirements may deduct the expenses of the education. However, the expenses must be paid for education to maintain the taxpayer's current job, not to meet the minimum requirements for that job. If the education qualifies the taxpayer for a new trade or business, the expenses are not deductible.

Example Jenny is a high school teacher working under a temporary teaching certificate. The state in which she teaches requires a master's degree to receive a permanent certificate, and Jenny only has a bachelor's degree. Her expenses to obtain a master's degree are not deductible even though the degree is required by her school district, since she has not yet met the minimum educational requirements to be a permanent teacher. However, Jenny may qualify for the lifetime learning credit as covered in Chapter 7. ♦

3-6b Maintaining or Improving Existing Skills

Expenses that are paid by a taxpayer for education to maintain or improve existing skills are deductible. Expenses deductible under this category include the costs of continuing education courses and academic work at a college or university. However, the education must not lead to qualification in a new trade or business. The deduction of a review course for the CPA exam and bar exam is consistently disallowed by the IRS.

Example John is a certified public accountant (CPA) in practice with a CPA firm. He decides a law degree would be helpful to him in his present job since he does a lot of trust and estate tax planning for clients. He enrolls in a night program at a local law school. John's educational expenses are not deductible since the program leads to a new trade or business, the practice of law. Whether or not John plans to practice law is not relevant. However, John may qualify for the lifetime learning credit covered in Chapter 7. ♦

Example Kenzie recently completed her degree in accounting and went to work for a local CPA firm. She spends $1,000 for a CPA exam review course to help her pass the exam. The $1,000 is not deductible since passing the CPA exam leads to a new trade or business, that of being a licensed CPA as opposed to an accountant. Depending on whether Kenzie takes this course at a qualified institution of higher education, and other circumstances, she may qualify for the lifetime learning credit covered in Chapter 7. ♦

3-6c Expenses of Travel for Educational Purposes

Travel expenses incurred while away from home for trips that are primarily to obtain qualifying education are also deductible. For example, a taxpayer may deduct travel expenses for attending a continuing education course in a distant city. Whether a trip is primarily personal or primarily educational depends on the relative amount of time devoted to each activity. If the trip qualifies as primarily for educational purposes, the cost of transportation to and from the destination is fully deductible. The lodging and meal expenses directly connected with the educational activity are also deductible. As is the case with other travel expenses, the cost of meals is only 50-percent deductible. Expenses for "travel as a form of education" are not deductible.

Example Jay is a self-employed doctor who attended a continuing education seminar in New York. His expenses related to attendance at the program are as follows:

Lodging in New York	$ 350
Transportation	700
Restaurant meals	150
Fee for the course	250
Total	$1,450

Jay's educational expense deduction for the seminar would be $1,375 including lodging of $350, transportation of $700, meals of $75, and the course fee of $250. ♦

Example Natalie is an instructor of Japanese at Big State University. She spends the summer traveling in Japan to improve her understanding of the Japanese language and culture. Although Natalie arranges her trip to improve her ability to teach the Japanese language, the trip is travel as a form of education and no deduction is allowed for the travel expenses. ♦

Self-Study Problem 3.6
Refer to Appendix E for Solutions to Self-Study Problems

Nadine is a self-employed attorney. Her expenses for continuing legal education are as follows:

Lodging in Tempe, Arizona	$1,200
Transportation	350
Snacks and drinks purchased at a convenience store	30
Meals purchased at restaurants	170
Books	175
Tuition	550
Weekend trip to the Grand Canyon	175
Total	$2,650

Calculate Nadine's educational expense deduction for the current year. Assume Nadine's household income is too high for her to qualify for the lifetime learning credit covered in Chapter 7.

3-7 Dues, Subscriptions, and Publications

Learning Objective 3.7

Identify the tax treatment of dues and subscriptions.

Doctors, lawyers, accountants, engineers, teachers, and other professionals who are self-employed or are employers may deduct certain dues and the costs of certain subscriptions and publications. Included in this category of deductions are items such as membership to the local bar for a lawyer, dues to the American Institute of Certified Public Accountants (AICPA) for an accountant, and the cost of subscriptions to any journal that is directly related to the taxpayer's profession. Due to the suspension of miscellaneous deductions subject to 2 percent of AGI through 2025, only self-employed taxpayers can deduct dues and subscriptions. Employees can no longer deduct these costs; however, if the dues or subscription costs are reimbursed by the employer, the employer can deduct those costs.

Example Hal is a federal law enforcement officer who pays $200 per year for a subscription to the official agency work manual. The agency provides a manual in the office for its employees, but Hal spends a lot of time on the road away from the office. As an employee, Hal may not deduct the cost of the subscription. If Hal's employer reimbursed Hal for the manual, the employer could deduct the cost. If Hal were self-employed, the cost would be deductible. ♦

Self-Study Problem 3.7   Refer to Appendix E for Solutions to Self-Study Problems

Indicate which of the following dues, subscriptions, and publications are deductible and which are not deductible.

1. Dues to the American Medical Association paid by a self-employed physician.
2. A subscription to a tax journal paid for by an accounting professor.
3. Dues to a health spa paid by a lawyer.
4. Union dues paid by a carpenter that works for a large construction company.
5. Subscription to *Motor Trend* magazine paid for by a registered nurse.

3-8 Special Clothing and Uniforms

3.8 Learning Objective

Determine which clothing and uniforms may be treated as tax deductions.

Self-employed individuals and employers are allowed a deduction for the costs of special work clothing or uniforms. The deduction is not allowed for the general cost and upkeep of normal work clothes; the clothing must be specialized. To be deductible, the clothing or uniforms must (1) be required as a condition of employment, and (2) not be suitable for everyday use. Both conditions must be met for the deduction to be allowed. It is not enough that the taxpayer is required to wear special clothing if the clothing can be worn while the taxpayer is not on the job. The costs of protective clothing, such as safety shoes, hard hats, and rubber boots, required for the job are also deductible. If the clothing or uniforms qualify, the costs of purchase, alterations, laundry, and their maintenance are deductible. Any uniforms purchased by an employer for its employees are deductible by the employer.

The suspension of miscellaneous deductions subject to 2 percent of AGI has severely limited the deduction of uniforms and related costs by employees. In the past, uniforms worn by police officers, firefighters, nurses, and letter carriers would have qualified as an unreimbursed employee business expense. Because of the suspension of many miscellaneous deductions, taxpayers that serve in these roles as an employee are no longer permitted to deduct uniform costs. To the extent they serve as an independent contractor or are self-employed, qualifying uniform costs may be deducted. Similar to dues and subscriptions, if the employer reimburses the employee for qualifying uniform costs, the employer may deduct the costs. Self-employed taxpayers deduct special clothing and uniforms on Schedule C.

Self-Study Problem 3.8   Refer to Appendix E for Solutions to Self-Study Problems

Steve has his own business as an installer for the light company, and he wears clothes suitable for everyday use that cost $400 during the year. Also, Steve must wear safety shoes and an orange neon vest on the job that cost $650 this year, and he purchased pole-climbing equipment, spikes, and a safety belt that cost $275. What is Steve's deduction on Schedule C for these items?

Learning Objective 3.9

Explain the special limits for business gift deductions.

3-9 Business Gifts

Within limits, taxpayers are allowed a deduction for business gifts. Salespersons and other taxpayers may deduct up to $25 per year per donee. For purposes of this limitation, spouses count as one donee. Thus, the maximum that a taxpayer could deduct for gifts to a client or potential client and their spouse is a total of $25 per year, unless the spouse is also a client, in which case the spouse may receive a separate $25 gift. Incidental expenses such as gift wrapping and shipping may be excluded from the limitation and are fully deductible. Recall from Chapter 2 that transfers of value to employees are rarely going to be classified as a gift that can be excluded from gross income.

There is no limitation for small business gifts costing up to $4 each that have the taxpayer's name or company name imprinted on them, such as pencils and calendars, and no limitation on promotional materials, such as signs and display racks. Also, the cost of gifts of tangible personal property made to employees for length of service on the job and safety achievement may be deducted up to a limit of $400 per employee per year. If the gift is made in conjunction with a "qualified plan," the limit is raised to $1,600. Gifts made to a taxpayer's supervisor (or individuals at a higher employment level) are not deductible. Those gifts are considered nondeductible personal expenses.

Example Marc is a salesperson who gives gifts to his clients. During the year, Marc gives Mr. Alford a gift costing $20 and Mrs. Alford (not a client) a gift costing $15. He also gives Ms. Bland a gift that cost $24 plus $2 for wrapping. Marc may deduct a total of $25 for the two gifts to Mr. and Mrs. Alford, and $26 for the gift to Ms. Bland. The $2 gift-wrapping charge is not included as part of the $25 limitation on the gift to Ms. Bland. ♦

A Schedule C reporting business such as a sole proprietor may make charitable contributions to a qualifying organization; however, the contributions are not considered gifts. Nevertheless, business charitable contributions are not reported as a business expense, but rather as an itemized deduction (Chapter 5) on Schedule A, and thus, do not appear on Schedule C. Payments to a charitable organization to place an advertisement in a newsletter or event program are generally considered advertising expenses and are deductible on Schedule C as business expenses.

3-9a Substantiation Requirement

Consistent with the substantiation requirement for business meals, in order to deduct business gifts, taxpayers must be able to substantiate the deduction. The four items that must be substantiated to deduct business meals expenses and business gifts are the:

1. amount of the expense,
2. date and description,
3. business purpose, and
4. business relationship.

If any of the above information is unavailable, the IRS will disallow the deduction for business meals expenses or business gifts.

> **Self-Study Problem 3.9** Refer to Appendix E for Solutions to Self-Study Problems
>
> Carol makes the following business gifts during the tax year:
>
> | Donee | Amount |
> |---|---|
> | 1. Mr. Jones (a client) | $ 20 |
> | 2. Mr. Brown (a client) | 32 |
> | 3. Mrs. Green (a client) received a $15 gift while her husband, Mr. Green (a non-client) received an $18 gift | 33 |
> | 4. Ms. Gray (Carol's supervisor) | 45 |
> | 5. Mr. Edwards (a client) receiving a display rack with Carol's company name on it | 75 |
> | 6. Various customers (receiving ball point pens with the company name on them) | 140 |
>
> Calculate Carol's allowed deduction for each business gift and her total allowed deduction.

3-10 Bad Debts

3.10 Learning Objective

Explain the tax treatment of bad debt deductions.

When a taxpayer sells goods or services on credit and the accounts receivable subsequently become worthless (uncollectible), a bad debt deduction is allowed to the extent that income arising from the sales was previously included in gross income. Taxpayers must use the specific charge-off method and are allowed deductions for bad debts only after the debts are determined to be partially or completely worthless.

A taxpayer who uses the specific charge-off method must be able to satisfy the IRS requirement that the debt is worthless and demonstrate the amount of the worthlessness. For a totally worthless account, a deduction is allowed for the entire amount of the taxpayer's basis in the account in the year the debt becomes worthless. The taxpayer's basis in the debt is the amount of income recognized from the recording of the debt, or the amount paid for the debt if it was purchased.

Example Mia operates a computer network and support consulting business in which other small businesses hire Mia to assist with technology issues. Mia operates on the cash basis of accounting for tax purposes. Mia provided $10,000 of services to a customer on a credit basis and the customer has run into financial difficulty and can only pay $8,000. As a cash-basis business, Mia does not recognize gross income until the cash is received and so she will recognize $8,000 when paid and will not have a bad debt deduction. If Mia were an accrual-based taxpayer, she would recognize the $10,000 at the time the services were provided. Later, when she was only paid $8,000, the remaining $2,000 would be deducted as bad debt expense. ♦

3-10a Business and Nonbusiness Bad Debts

Bad debts fall into two categories, business bad debts and nonbusiness bad debts. Debts that arise from the taxpayer's trade or business are classified as business bad debts, while all other debts are considered nonbusiness bad debts. The distinction between the two types of debts is important, since business bad debts are ordinary deductions and nonbusiness bad debts are short-term capital losses. Short-term and long-term capital gains may be offset by short-term capital losses. If there are net capital losses, only $3,000 of net capital losses may be deducted against ordinary income in any one tax year. Unused short-term capital losses are carried forward and may be deductible in future years, subject to the $3,000 annual limitation. The treatment of capital gains and losses is covered in Chapter 4.

Example Robert loaned his friend, Calvin, $5,000 to start a business. In the current year, Calvin went bankrupt and the debt became completely worthless. Since the debt is a nonbusiness debt, Robert may claim only a $3,000 short-term capital loss deduction this year (assuming no other capital transactions). The $2,000 unused deduction may be carried forward to the next year. This is not a business bad-debt deduction, because Robert is not in the business of loaning funds. ♦

ProConnect™ Tax TIP

Nonbusiness bad debts are treated as short-term capital losses. To report these items, use the Schedule D/4797/etc., item under Income. Drill down into the Schedule D entry form and select the Nonbusiness Bad Debt button after entering the other relevant information.

Self-Study Problem 3.10 Refer to Appendix E for Solutions to Self-Study Problems

Indicate whether the debt in each of the following cases is a business or nonbusiness debt and determine the deductible loss for the current year and describe the character of the loss if the debt becomes worthless.

1. Accounts receivable of a doctor from patients of $16,000
2. A father loans his son $2,000 to buy a car
3. A corporate president with no other capital gains personally loans another corporation $100,000
4. Loans of $100,000 by a bank to its customers
5. A taxpayer loans her sister $15,000 to start a business

Would You Sign This Tax Return?

Your clients, Tom (age 48) and Teri (age 45) Trendy, have a son, Tim (age 27). Tim lives in Hawaii, where he studies the effects of various sunscreens on his ability to surf. Last year, Tim was out of money and wanted to move back home and live with Tom and Teri. To prevent this, Tom lent Tim $20,000 with the understanding that he would stay in Hawaii and not come home. Tom had Tim sign a formal note, including a stated interest rate and due date. Tom has a substantial portfolio of stocks and bonds and has generated a significant amount of capital gains in the current year. He concluded that Tim is unlikely to repay the loan and the $20,000 note is worthless. Consequently, Tom wants to report Tim's bad debt on his and Teri's current tax return and net it against his other capital gains and losses. Tom is adamant about this. Would you sign the Paid Preparer's declaration (refer to example above) on this return? Why or why not?

3-11 Office in the Home

3.11 Learning Objective

Ascertain when a home office deduction may be claimed and how the deduction is computed.

Some taxpayers operate a trade or business in their homes and qualify for home office deductions. The tax law imposes strict limits on the availability of the deduction. In fact, the deduction for an office in the home is allowed by exception. The general rule for a home office deduction states that a taxpayer will not be allowed a deduction for the use of a dwelling unit used by the taxpayer as a residence. The law provides four exceptions to the general rule under which a deduction may be allowed.

Under the first exception, a deduction is allowed if the home office is used on a regular basis and exclusively as the self-employed taxpayer's principal place of business. To meet the exclusive use test, a specific area of the home must be used only for the trade or business. If the area is used for both business and personal purposes, no home office deduction is allowed.

Example Moussa is a self-employed home inspector. He maintains a business office in a specific room in his home. On holidays, when Moussa's extended family visits, he uses his office as a guest bedroom for his family. Because Moussa's use of the space is not exclusively for the business, no home office deduction is permitted. ♦

A second exception states that a deduction is allowed if the home office is used exclusively and on a regular basis by patients, clients, or customers in meetings or dealings with the taxpayer in the normal course of a trade or business. This exception allows doctors and salespeople to deduct home office expenses even though they maintain another office away from their residence, and even though the office is not the self-employed taxpayer's principal place of business.

Example Dr. Phil McCaw is a licensed psychotherapist. He meets with most of his clients in his office located near the hospital and medical group he serves. Dr. Phil also has several high-profile clients (actors and professional athletes) that prefer to keep their meetings as confidential as possible. Dr. Phil meets with these clients in his home office in a gated community. Because Dr. Phil's home office is used exclusively and on a regular basis, he is eligible for the home office deduction. ♦

Under the third exception, the deduction of home office expenses is allowed if the home office is a separate structure not attached to the dwelling unit and is used exclusively and on a regular basis in the taxpayer's trade or business.

The fourth and final exception to the rule allows a deduction of a portion of the cost of a dwelling unit if it is used on a regular basis for the storage of business inventory or product samples held for use in the self-employed taxpayer's trade or business of selling products. Under this fourth exception, the taxpayer's home must be the taxpayer's sole place of business.

Example Mabel operates a small business in which she sells fruitcakes during the holiday season (roughly November 1 to December 31) each year. Each October she places an order for approximately 1,000 fruit cakes and stores these in the basement of her home. She has no other storage space or office. Once the holiday season is over and all the fruitcakes are sold, she returns to using her basement for personal activities. Although Mabel does not use the basement exclusively for her business, the space is used regularly for the storage of inventory and she has no other business location. Mabel is eligible for a home office deduction. ♦

3-11a The Income Limitation

The home office deduction may not reduce the net income from the business below zero, except for mortgage interest and property taxes allocable to the office, which are generally tax deductible as an itemized deduction anyway. The other costs of operating a home, which are included in the home office allocation, include rent, home insurance, repairs, cleaning, utilities and other services, homeowners' association dues, and depreciation on the cost of the home. Depreciation expense is considered only after all other expenses have been allowed. These expenses are typically allocated to the home office on the basis of the square footage of the office to the total square footage of the home. Any unused deductions may be carried over to offset income in future years.

Example Jane, an accounting professor, maintains an office in her apartment where she conducts a small tax practice. Jane properly allocates $1,500 in rent to the home office, and during the year she collects $1,400 in fees from various clients. Assuming Jane has no other expenses associated with her practice, only $1,400 of the rent may be claimed as a home office deduction, since she may not show a loss from the practice due to the gross income limitation. The $100 unused portion of the deduction is carried over to the next taxable year. ♦

Example Assume the same facts as those in the previous example, except Jane owns her home. She has real estate taxes of $100, mortgage interest of $600, maintenance expenses of $200, and depreciation of $1,000 attributable to the home office. Her deduction for home office expenses is calculated as follows:

Gross income from tax practice	$1,400
Less: mortgage interest and real estate taxes	(700)
Balance	700
Less: maintenance expense	(200)
Balance	500
Depreciation (maximum allowed)	(500)
Net income from tax practice	$ 0

Note that the only way the home office can generate an overall business loss for Jane is if her home office mortgage interest and taxes exceed her gross business income. The unused portion of depreciation is carried over to the next taxable year. ♦

If a home office is used for both business and personal purposes, no deduction is allowed. For example, Professor Jane in the previous example would not be allowed a deduction for any expenses associated with the office in her home if the office was also used for personal activities, such as watching television or as a guest room.

3-11b The Home Office Allocation

The calculation of home office expenses involves the allocation of the total expenses of a self-employed taxpayer's dwelling between business and personal use. This allocation is usually made on the basis of the number of square feet of business space as a percentage of the total number of square feet in the residence, or on the basis of the number of rooms devoted to business use as a percentage of the total number of rooms in the dwelling. Expenses that are directly related to only the office portion of the home, such as repairs or painting made directly to the home office, do not require allocation.

Example Lois operates a hair-styling salon in her rental home. The salon occupies 400 square feet of her residence, which has a total of 1,600 square feet. Her expenses for her residence are presented below and allocated as shown.

Expenses	Total Amount	Business Percentage*	Business Portion
Rent	$10,000	25%	$2,500
Utilities	4,000	25%	1,000
Cleaning	2,000	25%	500
Repairs to salon chair located in home office	400	100%	100

*400 sq. ft./1,600 sq. ft.

♦

Self-employed taxpayers filing Schedule C and claiming a deduction for home office expenses are required to file Form 8829, Expenses for Business Use of Your Home. The Form 8829 segregates reporting of mortgage interest and real estate taxes depending on whether the taxpayer is claiming the standard deduction or itemizes deductions and also captured the portion of interest and real property taxes associated with the home office.

Example Ja'keem has a home office (10 percent of the square footage of his home) and also itemizes their deductions on Schedule A. Ja'Keem incurs $6,000 of mortgage interest and $5,000 of property taxes on his home that includes his home office. Ja'Keem will report his interest and property taxes on lines 10 and 11 of Form 8829 as shown below:

			(a) Direct expenses	(b) Indirect expenses		
7	Business percentage. For daycare facilities not used exclusively for business, multiply line 6 by line 3 (enter the result as a percentage). All others, enter the amount from line 3				7	10 %
Part II	**Figure Your Allowable Deduction**					
8	Enter the amount from Schedule C, line 29, **plus** any gain derived from the business use of your home, **minus** any loss from the trade or business not derived from the business use of your home. See instructions.				8	13,000
	See instructions for columns (a) and (b) before completing lines 9–22.					
9	Casualty losses (see instructions)	9				
10	Deductible mortgage interest (see instructions)	10		6,000		
11	Real estate taxes (see instructions)	11		5,000		
12	Add lines 9, 10, and 11	12		11,000		
13	Multiply line 12, column (b), by line 7		13	1,100		
14	Add line 12, column (a), and line 13				14	1,100
15	Subtract line 14 from line 8. If zero or less, enter -0-				15	11,900

♦

Example Continuing the prior example, if Ja'keem does not itemize, he will report the interest and property taxes on lines 16 and 17 of Form 8829 as shown below:

14	Add line 12, column (a), and line 13				14	0
15	Subtract line 14 from line 8. If zero or less, enter -0-				15	13,000
16	Excess mortgage interest (see instructions)	16		6,000		
17	Excess real estate taxes (see instructions)	17		5,000		
18	Insurance	18				
19	Rent	19				
20	Repairs and maintenance	20				
21	Utilities	21				
22	Other expenses (see instructions)	22				
23	Add lines 16 through 22	23		11,000		
24	Multiply line 23, column (b), by line 7		24	1,100		
25	Carryover of prior year operating expenses (see instructions)		25			
26	Add line 23, column (a), line 24, and line 25				26	1,100
27	Allowable operating expenses. Enter the **smaller** of line 15 or line 26				27	1,100

♦

Lines 16 and 17 are also used if a taxpayer that itemizes deductions has interest or property taxes that exceed the deduction limitations (mortgage balance greater than $750,000 or total state and local taxes in excess of $10,000). These items may be limited for purposes of itemizing deductions (Chapter 5), but the home office portion of these deductions is not limited in the same way.

Tax Break
If business is structured as a corporation (refer to Chapter 11), the corporation can deduct rent paid to an owner or employee as long as the expenses are ordinary and necessary. Be sure and document the lease arrangement as support for the deduction.

3-11c Optional Safe Harbor Method

In an effort to reduce the complexity of the home office deduction, the IRS has introduced a simplified method. Under the simplified method, the self-employed taxpayer may deduct home office expenses at the applicable rate ($5) multiplied by the number of square feet used in the home office, up to a maximum of 300 square feet, thus limiting the home office deduction under the safe harbor to $1,500. The deduction is still limited to the net profit from the business. Any deduction in excess of the income limit may not be carried forward. The same home office qualifications apply but no allocations are required. A taxpayer that uses the simplified method may deduct mortgage interest and property taxes as itemized deductions (refer to Chapter 5) without having to allocate a portion to the home office.

Example Martha operates a business that generates $6,700 of income before the home office deduction. She has a qualifying home office of 350 square feet in her home. She properly allocates $1,200 of household expenses to her home office. Under the safe harbor method, Martha's home office deduction is $1,500 ($5 per square foot × maximum 300 square feet). Martha should elect the larger safe harbor home office deduction. ♦

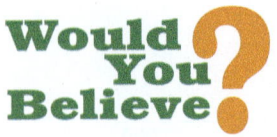

In 2013, when the safe harbor was introduced at $5 per square foot, the IRS notice stated "The Service and the Treasury Department may update this rate from time to time as warranted." According to data provided by the Federal Reserve Bank of St. Louis, at the start of 2013, the median cost of a home in the US was about $258,400. In the second quarter of 2024, the median price was $412,300, an increase of 60 percent. An increase above $5 is probably warranted.

ProConnect™ Tax TIP
Similar to auto expenses, the home office deduction is not entered into Schedule C directly, but rather under Deductions and then Business Use of the Home. The interaction between the cap on taxes (refer to Chapter 5) and the allocation of property taxes can create complexity in this area for certain taxpayers.

> **Tax Break**
>
> The safe harbor method may hold advantages that extend beyond ease of use. One possible advantage is that no depreciation is deducted from the basis of a taxpayer's home, and thus, "depreciation recapture" (refer to LO 8.8) can be avoided and the exclusion of the gain on the sale of a principal residence (refer to LO 4.6) can still apply. A second advantage is that the property taxes and interest allocated to the small business can still be deducted on Schedule A as an itemized deduction (refer to Chapter 5).

3-11d Home Office Deduction for an Employee

Prior to 2018, under certain circumstances, an employee was eligible to take a home office deduction. One of the most important requirements was that the use of the home office was for the convenience of the employer. The deduction of unreimbursed employee business expenses is suspended through 2025, and thus, a home office deduction for an employee is not currently available.

Example Sam is an employee of Fox Valley Graphic Design. Sam was able to negotiate a part-time work from home arrangement with three days at the office in Menasha, WI and two days at her home in Appleton, WI. She rearranged one of the rooms in her house to serve as her home office exclusively. Despite meeting the requirements of a home office, Sam will be unable to deduct any costs due to the suspension of the unreimbursed employee expense deduction. ♦

Self-Study Problem 3.11 *Refer to Appendix E for Solutions to Self-Study Problems*

Terry Cruz (Social Security number 712-12-9002) is a self-employed lawyer who maintains an office in their home. The office is used exclusively for client work, and clients regularly visit the home office. The home office represents 150 square feet of 1,000 square feet for the entire dwelling. Terry incurs the following expenses:

Expense	Total Amount
Mortgage interest	$7,000
Property taxes	5,000
Insurance	3,000
Utilities	2,000
Cleaning	1,000
Repairs to only home office space	200

Terry's home has a depreciable basis of $560,000 (not including land) and their depreciation rate for the current year is 3.636 percent. Terry itemizes deductions and their state and local tax deduction is over $10,000 before considering property taxes on the home. Assume Terry's business generates $46,000 in income before considering the home office deduction.

a. Prepare Form 8829 to calculate the home office deduction.

b. Assume that Terry does not itemize deductions and that their business generates $4,600 of income before considering the home office deduction. Prepare Form 8829 to calculate the home office deduction.

Learning Objective 3.12

Apply the factors used to determine whether an activity is a hobby, and understand the tax treatment of hobby losses.

3-12 Hobby Losses

If a taxpayer enters into an activity without a profit motive, the tax law limits the amount of tax deductions available. Under the hobby loss provisions, a taxpayer may not show a loss from an activity that is not engaged in for profit.

Example The breeding of race horses is an activity which might not be considered a trade or business when carried on by a full-time dentist. The IRS might contend that the activity was for personal enjoyment and disallow any loss for tax purposes. ♦

Despite the limitation on losses, any profits from hobbies must be included in taxable income. Hobby income is reported on line 8j, Other income on Schedule 1 of Form 1040.

3-12a Operational Rules

Individual taxpayers (or S corporations) can avoid the hobby loss rules if they can show that the activity was conducted with the intent to earn a profit. To determine whether the activity was engaged in for profit, the IRS will look at the following factors:

1. carrying on the activity in a businesslike manner,
2. the time and effort put into the activity indicate an intent to make it profitable,
3. dependence on the income for the taxpayer's livelihood,
4. whether the losses are due to circumstances beyond the taxpayer's control (or are normal in the startup phase of this type of business),
5. attempts to change methods of operation to improve profitability,
6. the taxpayer or advisors have the knowledge needed to carry on the activity as a successful business,
7. success in making a profit in similar activities in the past,
8. the activity makes a profit in some years, and
9. the activity is expected to make a future profit from the appreciation of the assets used in the activity.

The tax law provides a rebuttable presumption that if an activity shows a profit for three of the five previous years (two of the seven previous years for activities involving horses), the activity is engaged in for profit. For example, if an activity shows a profit for three of the previous five years, it is presumed to be a trade or business, and the IRS has the burden to prove that it is a hobby.

Example Dean McCopper is an auto mechanic but also likes to create sculptures from scrap iron materials. Dean's sculpting business turned a small profit in 2019, 2020, and 2022 but had modest losses in 2021 and 2023. Because Dean's sculpting activity has profits in three of the previous five years, the presumption is that the activity is not a hobby. ♦

3-12b Loss Limitations

Historically, the deduction of hobby expenses have been limited. Hobby expenses were deductible to the extent of hobby income (unless otherwise deductible such as mortgage interest and property taxes) and claimed as a miscellaneous itemized deduction subject to 2 percent of AGI floor. Thus, hobby expenses were only available to deduct if the taxpayer itemized deductions.

The miscellaneous expense deduction for items subject to the 2 percent of AGI floor is suspended through 2025; thus, no miscellaneous hobby expenses are currently deductible. Hobby expenses associated with other allowable itemized deductions (e.g., taxes or interest) are deductible subject to the limitations on those items (refer to Chapter 5). The income, net of cost of goods sold, must still be reported as other income on Schedule 1, line 8j.

Example Owen, a professional football player, decides that he wants to be a famous wine maker. He has the following expenses related to this activity:

Costs of the wine sold	$2,000
Personal property taxes on equipment	2,500
Advertising costs	4,600

During the year, Owen sells 200 cases of wine for $7,500. The tax consequences of Owen's wine operations will differ depending on whether the activity is treated as a hobby or as a trade or business.

	Business	Hobby
Sales	$ 7,500	$ 7,500
Cost of goods sold	(2,000)	(2,000)
Property taxes	(2,500)	n/a
Advertising	(4,600)	n/a
Income/(Loss) reported for tax	$ (1,600)	$ 5,500

Under the hobby classification, Owen might be able to deduct the property taxes as an itemized deduction. ♦

ProConnect™ Tax TIP

Hobby income can be entered under Income and then Alimony and Other Income. Be sure and net the cost of goods sold against gross income when reporting this amount. Other hobby expenses are not deductible.

Self-Study Problem 3.12 Refer to Appendix E for Solutions to Self-Study Problems

Kana is a CPA who loves chinchillas. She breeds chinchillas as pets (she currently owns 13 of them) and every so often sells a baby chinchilla to a suitable family to keep as a pet. In the current year, she sells $250 worth of chinchillas and incurs the following expenses:

Chinchilla cages	$ 300
Advertising for chinchilla sales	2,500

This activity is considered a hobby. Kana has adjusted gross income of $72,000 before considering any impact from the hobby. What is the amount of income and expense Kana recognizes (assume she itemizes deductions) associated with her chinchilla hobby?

Key Terms

Schedule C, 3-2
trade or business, 3-2
ordinary and necessary, 3-2
cost of goods sold, 3-5
self-employment tax, 3-7
inventory, 3-10
non-incidental materials and
  supplies (NIMS), 3-10
first in, first out (FIFO), 3-10

last in, first out (LIFO), 3-10
transportation expense, 3-13
commuting, 3-13
standard mileage rate, 3-14
travel expense, 3-15
tax home, 3-15
per diem, 3-17
meals expense, 3-19
entertainment expense, 3-19

dues, 3-22
subscriptions, 3-22
uniforms, 3-23
business gifts, 3-24
business and nonbusiness bad
  debts, 3-25
home office, 3-27
simplified method, 3-30
hobby losses, 3-32

Key Points

Learning Objectives	Key Points
LO 3.1: Complete a basic Schedule C (Profit or Loss from Business).	• Taxpayers who operate a business or practice a profession as a sole proprietorship must file a Schedule C to report the net profit or loss from the sole proprietorship. • Deductions taken on Schedule C must be ordinary and necessary, reasonable, and have a business purpose. • Schedule C filers such as sole proprietors and independent contractors with net earnings of $400 or more must pay a self-employment tax calculated on Schedule SE with their Form 1040.
LO 3.2: Describe the tax treatment of inventories and cost of goods sold.	• Inventory is the stock of goods or materials that a business holds for the purpose of resale to generate a profit. • Cost of goods sold, which is the largest single deduction for many businesses, is calculated as follows: beginning inventory + purchases − ending inventory. • Small businesses are permitted to use the cash method to account for inventory; however, in many instances, typical inventory accounting is still used. • There are two common methods of inventory valuation used by taxpayers: first in, first out (FIFO) and last in, first out (LIFO).
LO 3.3: Identify the requirements for deducting transportation expenses.	• Deductible transportation expenses include travel by airplane, rail, bus, and automobile. Normal commuting costs to and from the taxpayer's place of regular employment are not deductible. • If the taxpayer works at two or more jobs during the same day, they may deduct the cost of going from one job to the other or from one business location to another. • The standard mileage rate for 2024 is 67 cents per mile.
LO 3.4: Identify the requirements for deducting travel expenses.	• Travel expenses are defined as ordinary and necessary expenses incurred when traveling away from home in pursuit of the taxpayer's trade or business. • Deductible travel expenses include the cost of such items as meals, lodging, taxis, tips, and laundry. • A taxpayer must be away from home "overnight" in order to deduct travel expenses. Overnight is a period of time longer than an ordinary work day in which rest or relief from work is required. Also, the taxpayer must be away from their "tax home" to be on travel status. • Taxpayers must substantiate the following: the amount of each separate expenditure, the dates of departure and return for each trip and the number of business days on the trip, the destination or locality of the travel, and the business reason for the travel. • As an alternative to reporting actual expenses, a per diem method may be used in certain circumstances.

LO 3.5: Determine the requirements for deducting meals.	• Business meals are generally subject to a 50-percent limitation. • Generally, entertainment costs are not deductible. • Certain meals and entertainment costs are deductible in full when celebratory for all employees.
LO 3.6: Identify the requirements for claiming business education expenses.	• To be deductible as a business expense, educational expenditures must be paid to meet the requirements of the taxpayer's employer or the requirements of law or regulation for keeping the taxpayer's salary, status, or job, or the expenses must be paid to maintain or improve existing skills required in performing the duties of the taxpayer's present work.
LO 3.7: Identify the tax treatment of dues and subscriptions.	• Self-employed professionals may deduct dues and the costs of subscriptions and publications. Employees may no longer deduct these costs due to the suspension of miscellaneous deductions subject to 2 percent of AGI through 2025.
LO 3.8: Determine which clothing and uniforms may be treated as tax deductions.	• Self-employed individuals and employers are allowed a deduction for the costs of special work clothing or uniforms. • In order to be deductible, clothing or uniforms must: (1) be required as a condition of employment, and (2) not be suitable for everyday use.
LO 3.9: Explain the special limits for business gift deductions.	• Taxpayers are allowed a deduction for business gifts up to $25 per year per donee. For purposes of this limitation, a husband and wife count as one donee, unless the husband and wife are both clients. • To deduct business meals and business gifts, taxpayers must be able to substantiate the deduction with the expense amounts, the dates and descriptions, the business purposes, and the business relationships.
LO 3.10: Explain the tax treatment of bad debt deductions.	• Bad debts are classified as either business bad debts or nonbusiness bad debts. Debts arising from a taxpayer's trade or business are classified as business bad debts, while all other debts are considered nonbusiness bad debts. • Business bad debts are treated as ordinary deductions and nonbusiness bad debts are treated as short-term capital losses, of which only $3,000 can be deducted against ordinary income each year.
LO 3.11: Ascertain when a home office deduction may be claimed and how the deduction is computed.	• A home office is generally not deductible, allowed only by exception. There are four exceptions to the general rule. • A home office deduction is allowed if the home office is used on a regular basis and exclusively as the self-employed taxpayer's principal place of business. • A home office deduction is allowed if the home office is used exclusively and on a regular basis by patients, clients, or customers in meetings or dealings with the self-employed taxpayer in the normal course of a trade or business. • The deduction of home office expenses is allowed if the home office is a separate structure not attached to the dwelling unit and is used exclusively and on a regular basis in the self-employed taxpayer's trade or business. • A home office deduction of a portion of the cost of a dwelling unit is allowed if it is used on a regular basis for the storage of business inventory or product samples and the home is the sole place of business. • The home office deduction is limited by the amount of net income from the associated trade or business. • A simplified home office deduction is also available at $5 per square foot up to an annual maximum of $1,500. • Employees may no longer deduct a home office, even when at the convenience of their employer, due to the suspension of the miscellaneous business expense deduction.

LO 3.12:
Apply the factors used to determine whether an activity is a hobby, and understand the tax treatment of hobby losses.

- Under the hobby loss provisions, a taxpayer may not show a loss from an activity that is not engaged in for profit.
- To determine whether the activity was engaged in for profit, the IRS will look at numerous factors including whether the activity is conducted like a business.
- Hobby expenses are no longer deductible due to the TCJA suspension of miscellaneous itemized deductions subject to the 2 percent of AGI floor.

Questions and Problems

Group 1:
Multiple Choice Questions

LO 3.1
1. Which of the following is *not* a test for the deductibility of a business expense?
    a. Ordinary and necessary test
    b. Sales generation test
    c. Reasonableness test
    d. Business purpose test

LO 3.1
2. Which of the following taxpayers will file a Schedule C with their Form 1040?
    a. A small business owner that operates as a corporation
    b. A general partner with an interest in a business partnership
    c. A limited partner with an interest in a business partnership
    d. An individual taxpayer that operates a business through a sole proprietorship

LO 3.1
3. In the current year, Mary started a profitable housekeeping business as a sole proprietor. She has ten housekeepers working for her and spends her time selling their services and coordinating her employees' time. Mary made $50,000 in her first year of operations. In addition to filing a Schedule C to report her business earnings, Mary *must* also file
    a. Schedule A
    b. Schedule F
    c. Schedule B
    d. Schedule SE
    e. None of the above

LO 3.1
LO 3.3
LO 3.4
LO 3.5
4. Kade just became a self-employed consultant. Prior to this year, Kade had always worked as an employee. He comes to discuss his new business with you. As his tax accountant, you should:
    a. Discuss setting up a good record-keeping system for his new business
    b. Discuss the substantiation requirements for meals
    c. Discuss the self-employment tax, as well as the income tax, on business earnings in order to help Daniel estimate what he might owe in taxes for the year
    d. Discuss the rules for deducting automobile expenses
    e. Discuss all of the above

LO 3.1
5. Which of the following expenses is generally deductible in the year incurred?
    a. Capital expenditures for land and buildings
    b. Illegal bribes or kickbacks
    c. Continuing legal training for a practicing professional attorney
    d. Political contributions

LO 3.1
6. Which of the following expenses is generally deductible in the year incurred?
    a. Payments to remediate the contaminated ground water surrounding an oil refinery
    b. Interest expense associated with debt incurred to purchase municipal bonds
    c. A speeding fine paid by an express delivery company for one of its drivers
    d. Rent for a retail store in which medical marijuana is sold

LO 3.2   7. A small business that qualifies for the cash method may use which method to account for inventory?
   a. Treat as non-incidental materials and supplies
   b. Treat the same as in the applicable financial statements
   c. Treat the same as books and records if no applicable financial statements
   d. Under the accrual method
   e. All of these choices are suitable for accounting for inventory

LO 3.2   8. If a taxpayer has beginning inventory of $45,000, purchases of $175,000, and ending inventory of $25,000, what is the amount of the cost of goods sold for the current year?
   a. $155,000
   b. $180,000
   c. $175,000
   d. $195,000
   e. None of the above

LO 3.2   9. Which of the following is *not* true about a taxpayer making a LIFO election?
   a. Form 970 is used to make a LIFO election.
   b. LIFO can only be used when inventory prices are increasing.
   c. Once LIFO is elected, the taxpayer will require IRS approval to change from LIFO.
   d. A taxpayer that uses LIFO must also use LIFO for their financial statements.

LO 3.3   10. Which of the following taxpayers may use the standard mileage method of calculating transportation costs?
   a. A taxi driver who owns a fleet of six cars for hire
   b. A taxpayer who used accelerated depreciation on their automobile
   c. A business executive who claimed bonus depreciation in the first year she used the car
   d. An attorney who uses their European sports car for calling on clients
   e. None of the above

LO 3.3   11. Heather drives her minivan 792 miles for business purposes in 2024. She elects to use the standard mileage rate for her auto expense deduction. Her deduction will be
   a. $506
   b. $515
   c. $519
   d. $531
   e. $560

LO 3.3   12. Which of the following is *not* considered commuting miles?
   a. The miles from a taxpayer's home to their regular place of work
   b. The miles to a taxpayer's home from a regular second job
   c. The miles from a taxpayer's main job to a temporary work location
   d. The miles from a temporary work location to a taxpayer's home (and the taxpayer has a main work location)

LO 3.3   13. Helen drives her car 4,000 miles, including 3,000 miles for business purposes. Her actual costs to operate the vehicle (gas, maintenance, depreciation, etc.) are $3,500. She also incurs tolls of $100 and pays $300 for parking while on business trips and another $50 for parking during personal use. Using the actual cost method, what is Helen's deduction for car expenses?
   a. $2,010
   b. $3,075
   c. $3,025
   d. $2,410

LO 3.4 14. In which of the following cases is the employer entitled to a travel expense deduction?
   a. An employee, who worked in the Salt Lake City plant of a company, who is assigned to the Denver plant of the company for four years
   b. An employee who travels between several business locations within the same city each day
   c. A manager of a chain of department stores who works in the main store three weeks out of every month and visits distant branch locations on overnight trips during the remainder of the month
   d. An employee who resigns from his current job and accepts a new job in a city 500 miles away from his current residence
   e. A bank employee who travels to a branch office for a couple of hours of work and decides to stay overnight to attend a play

LO 3.4 15. Which of the following expenses incurred while the taxpayer is away from home "overnight" is *not* included as a travel expense?
   a. Laundry expenses
   b. Transportation expenses
   c. Meal expenses
   d. Business gifts
   e. Lodging expenses

LO 3.4 16. Under the high-low method, the federal per diem amount is
   a. The same in every city in the U.S.
   b. Different for every city in the U.S.
   c. The same for most cities but higher in certain locations
   d. An average of the highest and lowest costs for that city
   e. The boundary for expenses incurred in a city (never higher than the high amount but never lower than the low amount)

LO 3.4 17. Joe is a self-employed information technology consultant from San Francisco. He takes a week-long trip to Chicago primarily for business. He takes two personal days to go to museums and see the sights of Chicago. How should he treat the expenses related to this trip?
   a. One hundred percent of the trip should be deducted as a business expense since the trip was primarily for business.
   b. Half of the trip should be deducted as a business expense since the IRS limits such business expenses to 50 percent of the actual cost.
   c. The cost of all of the airfare and the business days should be deducted, while the cost of the personal days are not deductible.
   d. None of the expenses are deductible since there was an element of personal enjoyment in the trip.

LO 3.4 18. Which of the following self-employed business travelers will need to prorate the cost of their airfare between business and nonbusiness in computing the deduction for such costs?
   a. A domestic trip in which the taxpayer spends 5 days on business and 1 personal day.
   b. A domestic trip in which the taxpayer spends 1 day on business and 5 personal days.
   c. An international trip in which the taxpayer spends 5 days on business and 3 personal days.
   d. An international trip in which the taxpayer spends 3 days on business and 2 personal days.

LO 3.5 19. Which of the following expenses is deductible as an entertainment expense?
   a. The depreciation on an airplane used to entertain customers
   b. The cost of a hunting camp used to entertain customers
   c. The dues of a racquet club used to keep in shape
   d. The cost of a paintball party for clients paid for by a computer salesman at a computer fair
   e. None of these are deductible

LO 3.5 20. Which of the following is *not* likely to be a deductible expense?
   a. The cost of tickets to a stage play for a client and the taxpayer.
   b. The cost for Rosa to take a potential customer to lunch to describe a new service Rosa's company is offering. Unfortunately, the customer explains that they are not interested in the service.
   c. The cost of a party for all of Dan's employees to celebrate a record-breaking profits year.
   d. The dues for Charles Coke to join the City Chamber of Commerce to generally improve the reputation of his business in the community.
   e. None of the above are deductible expenses.

LO 3.5 21. In 2024, Values R Us, a real estate appraising firm, incurs the following meals expenses:
   - $1,200 restaurant meals with business clients
   - $1,600 for an end-of-year celebratory company dinner for all employees
   - $400 for bagels once a month for all employees
   - $300 for pre-packaged snacks offered to potential clients at a business fair
   - $40 for non-restaurant travel snacks consumed by employees while on business travel
   - $800 of restaurant meals consumed by employees while on business travel

   What is Values R Us' deductible meals expense in 2024?
   a. $2,770
   b. $3,120
   c. $4,120
   d. $4,340

LO 3.6 22. Which of the following taxpayers may *not* deduct their educational expense?
   a. A CPA who attends a course to review for the real estate agents' exam
   b. An independent sales representative who attends a customer relations course at a local university
   c. A self-employed attorney who attends a course on computing legal damages
   d. An independent real estate broker who attends a college course on real estate law
   e. All of the above are deductible

LO 3.6 23. Which of the following is likely a deductible business educational expense?
   a. Leah is a self-employed tax preparer. The State Board of Taxation requires Leah to attend federal and state taxation training each year to maintain her tax preparation licence.
   b. Mike is an auto mechanic. He decides he wants to be a high school math teacher but the state Department of Education requires Mike to earn a bachelor's degree in education.
   c. John teaches European History at Ridgemont High School. In order to better understand the material he teaches, John takes a summer trip with *American Geographic* magazine to tour Western Europe.
   d. Becca is a marketing manager. She has always wanted to obtain an MBA degree in hopes of getting promoted to an executive position.
   e. None of these are deductible educational expenses.

LO 3.7 24. Which of the following is *not* deductible by the self-employed taxpayer?
   a. A subscription to *The CPA Journal* by a CPA
   b. A subscription to *The Yale Medical Journal* by a doctor
   c. A subscription to *Financial Management* by a financial planner
   d. A subscription to *The Harvard Law Review* by a lawyer
   e. All of the subscriptions listed are deductible

LO 3.8 25. Which of the following self-employed taxpayers are most likely permitted to deduct the cost of their work apparel?
   a. A lawyer who wears a business suit
   b. A furnace repairman who must wear overalls while on the job
   c. A nurse who can wear casual clothes while on duty
   d. A butcher who wears stainless steel safety gloves

LO 3.8 26. Which of the following characteristics are *not* required to deduct the cost of apparel?
   a. It must be business-related.
   b. The apparel is required as a condition of employment.
   c. The employer's name must appear on the apparel.
   d. The apparel is not suitable for everyday use.

LO 3.9 27. Which of the following business gifts are fully deductible?
   a. A gift to a client that cost $35
   b. A gift to an employee, for 10 years of continued service, that cost $250
   c. A gift to a client and her nonclient spouse that cost $45
   d. A gift to an employee paid under a qualified plan, for not having an on-the-job injury for 25 years, that cost $1,650
   e. None of the above are fully deductible

LO 3.9 28. Which of the following statements about business gift deductions is *not* true?
   a. A taxpayer can provide two gifts to a client during the year and the maximum deduction is $50.
   b. Reasonable shipping costs do not count toward the $25 business gift limit.
   c. Employee gifts for a significant number of years of service can exceed $25 and remain deductible.
   d. A holiday gift from an employee to their supervisor is a non-deductible personal expense.

LO 3.10 29. Grady operates a lawn maintenance business using the accrual method. He estimates that 5 percent, or about $2,500 of his 2024 year-end customers' invoices will never be paid. During 2024, he wrote off $13,500 of his receivables as uncollectible. Grady's bad debt expense deduction is:
   a. $0
   b. $2,500
   c. $13,500
   d. $16,000

LO 3.10 30. Grady operates a lawn maintenance business using the cash method. He estimates that 5 percent, or about $2,500 of 2024 year-end customers' invoices will never be paid. During 2024, he wrote off $13,500 of his invoices as uncollectible. Grady's bad debt expense deduction is:
   a. $0
   b. $2,500
   c. $13,500
   d. $16,000

LO 3.10 31. Loren loaned a friend $9,000 as financing for a new business venture. In the current year, Loren's friend declares bankruptcy and the debt is considered totally worthless. What amount may Loren deduct on his individual income tax return for the current year as a result of the worthless debt, assuming he has no other capital gains or losses for the year?
   a. $9,000 ordinary loss
   b. $9,000 short-term capital loss
   c. $3,000 short-term capital loss
   d. $3,000 ordinary loss
   e. $6,000 short-term capital loss

LO 3.11 32. Kathy is a self-employed taxpayer working exclusively from her home office. Before the home office deduction, Kathy has $3,000 of net income. Her allocable home office expenses are $5,000 in total (includes $2,000 of allocated interest and property taxes). How are the home office expenses treated on her current year tax return?
   a. All home office expenses may be deducted, resulting in a business loss of $2,000.
   b. Only $3,000 of home office expenses may be deducted, resulting in net business income of zero. None of the extra $2,000 of home office expenses may be carried forward or deducted.
   c. Only $3,000 of home office expenses may be deducted, resulting in net business income of zero. The extra $2,000 of home office expenses may be carried forward and deducted in a future year against home office income.
   d. None of the home office expenses may be deducted since Kathy's income is too low.

LO 3.11 33. Which of the following taxpayers qualifies for a home office deduction?
   a. An attorney who is employed by a law firm and has a home office in which to read case briefs
   b. A doctor who has a regular office downtown and a library at home to store medical journals
   c. An accounting student who maintains a home office used exclusively for her business preparing tax returns
   d. A nurse who maintains a home office to pay bills and read nursing journals
   e. A corporate president who uses his home office to entertain friends and customers

LO 3.11 34. Kahleeah maintains an office in her home where she conducts a dressmaking business. During the year she collects $4,000 from sales, pays $1,300 for various materials and supplies, and properly allocates $2,500 of rent expense and $500 of her utilities expense to the use of her home office. What amount of the rent and utilities expense may Kahleeah deduct in the current year in computing her net income or loss from the dressmaking business?
   a. $0
   b. $500
   c. $2,500
   d. $2,700
   e. $3,000

LO 3.12 35. Which of the following factors is *not* considered by the IRS in determining whether an activity is a hobby?
   a. Whether the activity is conducted like a business
   b. The time and effort expended by the taxpayer
   c. Whether there have been changes in the methods of operation in an attempt to improve profitability
   d. Income and loss history of the activity
   e. All of the above are considered to determine if an activity is a hobby

LO 3.12 36. Stewie, a single taxpayer, operates an activity as a hobby. Brian operates a similar activity as a bona fide business. Stewie's gross income from his hobby activity is $5,000 and his expenses are $6,000. Brian's gross income and expenses are coincidentally the same as Stewie. Neither Stewie nor Brian itemize, but both have other forms of taxable income. What is the impact on taxable income for Stewie and Brian from these activities?
   a. Stewie will report $0 income and Brian will report a $1,000 loss.
   b. Stewie will report $5,000 income and $0 deduction and Brian will report a $1,000 loss.
   c. Stewie and Brian will report $0 taxable income.
   d. Stewie and Brian will report a $1,000 loss.
   e. Stewie will report a $1,000 loss and Brian will report $5,000 income.

Group 2: Problems

LO 3.1
LO 3.3
LO 3.5
LO 3.7

1. Scott Butterfield is self-employed as a CPA. He uses the cash method of accounting, and his Social Security number is 644-47-7833. His principal business code is 541211. Scott's CPA practice is located at 678 Third Street, Riverside, CA 92860. Scott's income statement for the year shows the following:

Income Statement

Scott Butterfield, CPA
Income Statement
31/12/24

	Current Period 1/1/2024 to 12/31/2024	Prior Period 1/1/2023 to 12/31/2023
REVENUES		
Tax Services	$ 77,000	$ 75,067
Accounting Services	49,400	48,860
Other Consulting Services	10,095	10,115
TOTAL REVENUES	1,36,495	1,34,042
COST OF SERVICES		
Salaries	35,000	30,100
Payroll Taxes	3,098	2,387
Supplies	1,300	1,548
TOTAL COST OF SERVICES	39,398	34,035
GROSS PROFIT (LOSS)	97,097	1,00,007
OPERATING EXPENSES		
Advertising and Promotion	200	350
Business Licenses and Permits	300	250
Charitable Contributions	450	275
Continuing Education	500	300
Dues and Subscriptions	2,700	3,500
Insurance	900	875
Meals and Entertainment	4,300	5,500
Office Expense	300	150
Postage and Delivery	100	50
Printing and Reproduction	50	100
Office Rent	12,000	14,000
Owner's health insurance premiums	7,000	6,700
Travel	800	865
Utilities	2,800	2,978
TOTAL OPERATING EXPENSES	32,400	35,893
NET INCOME (LOSS)	$ 64,697	$ 64,114

Scott provides the following additional information:

- The expenses for dues and subscriptions were his country club membership dues for the year.
- $350 of the charitable contributions were made to a political action committee and $100 was made to the Red Cross.
- Scott does not generate income from the sale of goods and therefore, does not record supplies and wages as part of cost of goods sold.
- Scott placed a business auto in service on January 1, 2021 and drove it 3,800 miles for business, 3,250 miles for commuting, and 4,100 miles for nonbusiness purposes. No business expenses for the car are included above. Scott wishes to use the standard mileage method. His wife has a car for personal use.

- Meals and Entertainment expense includes $2,500 related to golf greens fees for entertaining clients, $1,200 for business meals provided by restaurants, and $600 for the bagels and doughnuts once a month for all employees.
- Owner's health insurance of $7,000 is for Scott's health insurance only.

Complete Schedule C from Appendix F for Scott showing the net taxable profit from self-employment.

LO 3.1
LO 3.3
LO 3.4
LO 3.5
LO 3.9
LO 3.11

2. Margaret started her own business in the current year and will report a profit for her first year. Her results of operations are as follows:

Gross income	$45,000
Travel	1,000
Contribution to Presidential Election Campaign	100
Transportation 5,303 miles, using standard mileage method	?
Entertainment in total	4,200
Nine gifts at $50 each	450
Rent and utilities for apartment in total (25 percent is used for a home office)	10,500

What is the net income Margaret should show on her Schedule C? Show the calculation of her gross income, expenses, and taxable business income.

LO 3.2

3. Lawrence owns a small candy store that sells one type of candy. His beginning inventory of candy was made up of 10,000 boxes costing $1.50 per box ($15,000), and he made the following purchases of candy during the year:

March 1	10,000 boxes at $1.60	$16,000
August 15	20,000 boxes at $1.65	33,000
November 20	10,000 boxes at $1.75	17,500

At the end of the year, Lawrence's inventory consisted of 16,000 boxes of candy.
a. Calculate Lawrence's ending inventory and cost of goods sold using the FIFO inventory valuation method.
b. Calculate Lawrence's ending inventory and cost of goods sold using the LIFO inventory valuation method.

LO 3.2

4. Torrey owns a retail store, and during the current year purchased $585,000 worth of inventory. Torrey's beginning inventory was $63,000, and ending inventory is $82,000. During the year, Torrey withdrew $800 in inventory for personal use. Use Part III of Schedule C from Appendix F to calculate Torrey's cost of goods sold for the year.

LO 3.2

5. Dyson owns an auto repair shop that serves a particular model of auto and he tends to purchase parts in bulk. Dyson is eligible to treat inventory as non-incidental materials. In December of 2023 he purchases 24 oil filters. He uses one filter to service an auto in January 2024, and then about two filters per month and ends 2024 with 14 filters. Dyson's business has gross receipts of around $1.2 million per year. Dyson expenses oil filters when he purchases them on his books and records (Dyson does not have financial statements other than for taxes). Explain how Dyson could treat his oil filter inventory.

LO 3.3

6. Teresa is a self-employed civil engineer who uses her automobile for business. Teresa drove her automobile a total of 12,800 miles during 2024, of which 10,240 were business miles. The actual cost of gasoline, oil, depreciation, repairs, and insurance for the year was $8,000. Teresa is eligible to use the actual cost or standard mileage method.
   a. How much is Teresa's transportation deduction based on the standard mileage method?
   b. How much is Teresa's transportation deduction based on the actual cost method?
   c. Which method should Teresa use to calculate her transportation deduction? Why?

LO 3.3

7. Art is a self-employed installer of home entertainment systems, and he drives his car frequently to installation locations. Art drove his car 15,000 miles for business purposes and 20,000 miles in total. His actual expenses, including depreciation, for operating the auto are $10,000 since he had to have the car repaired several times. Art has always used the actual cost method in the past. How much is Art's deductible auto expense for the year?

LO 3.3

8. Martha is a self-employed tax accountant who drives her car to visit clients on a regular basis. In 2024, she drives her car 4,000 miles for business and 10,000 miles for commuting and other personal use. Assuming Martha uses the standard mileage method, how much is her auto expense for the year? Where on her tax return should Martha claim this deduction?

LO 3.4

9. Joan is a self-employed attorney in New York City. Joan took a trip to San Diego, CA, primarily for business, to consult with a client and take a short vacation. On the trip, Joan incurred the following expenses:

Airfare to and from San Diego	$ 500
Hotel charges while on business	450
Restaurant meals while on business	260
Car rental while on business (she drove 240 miles)	110
Hotel charges while on vacation	475
Restaurant meals while on vacation	300
Car rental while on vacation	180
Total	$2,275

Calculate Joan's travel expense deduction for the trip, assuming the trip was made in 2024.

LO 3.4

10. Go to the U.S. General Services Administration (GSA) website (**www.gsa.gov**). For the month of September 2024, what is the lodging per diem rate for each of the following towns:
    a. Hartford, CT
    b. Chicago, IL
    c. San Francisco, CA

LO 3.4
LO 3.5
LO 3.6

11. Ruth is a self-employed lawyer and is required to take a week of continuing legal education every year to maintain her license. This year she paid $1,400 in course fees for her continuing legal education in a different city. She also paid $600 for airfare and a hotel room and paid $280 for meals, all of which were provided by the hotel's restaurant. Ruth also spent $40 for a taxi to the airport and $38 for parking at the airport. What is the total amount she can deduct on her Schedule C related to these expenses?

LO 3.5 12. Grace is a self-employed sales consultant who spends significant time entertaining potential customers. She keeps all the appropriate records to substantiate her entertainment. She has the following expenses in the current year:

Meals where business was conducted	$4,000
Greens fees (all business)	500
Tickets to baseball games (all business)	500
Country Club dues (50-percent business use)	6,000

What are the tax-deductible meals and entertainment expenses Grace may claim in the current year? On which tax form should she claim the deduction?

LO 3.5 13. Marty is a sales consultant. Marty incurs the following expenses related to the entertainment of his clients in the current year:

Dues to a country club (The country club was used for business 25 days of the total 75 days that it was used.)	$4,500
Business meals at the country club restaurant not associated with golf or tennis	1,600
Dues to a tennis club (The club was used 75 percent for directly related business.)	1,200
Tennis fees (personal use)	300
Business meals at various restaurants	2,000

a. How much is Marty's deduction for meals and entertainment expenses for the current year?
b. For each item listed above that you believe is not allowed as a deduction, explain the reason it is not allowed.

LO 3.6 14. a. Loren is a secretary in a lawyer's office. Since they often deals with legal matters, Loren feels that a law degree will be beneficial to them. Explain whether Loren may deduct their educational expenses for law school?
b. Alicia is an employee in the sales department for an international firm. She wishes to learn Spanish to improve her ability to communicate with foreign clients. Explain whether Alicia may deduct her educational expenses for language school as a miscellaneous itemized deduction?
c. Joan is a practicing lawyer. She enrolls in a local medical school and works toward a medical degree in her spare time. Explain whether Joan may deduct her educational expenses for the medical classes?

LO 3.7 15. Carey opens a law office in Chicago on January 1, 2024. On January 1, 2024, Carey purchases an annual subscription to a law journal for $240 and a one-year legal reference service for $3,500. Carey also subscribes to *Chicago Magazine* for $60 so she can find great places to take clients to dinner and review the "Best 50 Lawyers in Chicago" list published each year. Calculate Carey's deduction for the above items for the 2024 tax year.

LO 3.8 16. Cooper and Brandy are married and file a joint income tax return with two separate Schedule Cs. Cooper is an independent security specialist who spent $400 on uniforms during the year. The uniforms are orange overalls with bright florescent safety reflectors and the company logo. His laundry expenses for the uniforms were $160 for this year, plus $85 for altering them. Brandy works as a drill press operator and wears jeans and a t-shirt on the job, which cost $175 this year. Her laundry costs

were $50 for the work clothes. Brandy is also required by state regulators to wear safety glasses and safety shoes when working, which cost a total of $125.
  a. How much is Cooper's total deduction on his Schedule C for special clothing and uniforms?
  b. How much is Brandy's total deduction on her Schedule C for special clothing and uniforms?

17. Sam owns an insurance agency and makes the following business gifts during the year. Calculate Sam's deduction for business gifts.

Donee	Amount
Ms. Sears (a client)	$35, plus $4 shipping
Mr. Williams (a tennis partner, not a business prospect or client)	55
Mr. Sample (a client) received $22 and Mrs. Sample (spouse of Mr. Sample and also a client) received a gift valued at $20	42
Various customers (calendars costing $3 each with the company name on them)	300
Mr. Shiver (an employee gift, a watch, for 25 years of continuous service)	175

18. Steinar loaned a friend $9,500 to buy some stock three years ago. In the current year the debt became worthless when his friend declared bankruptcy.
  a. How much is Steinar's deduction for the bad debt for this year? (Assume he has no other capital gains or losses.)
  b. What is the tax treatment of any amount that Steiner is unable to deduct in the current tax year?
  c. What is the tax treatment of the forgiven debt by Steiner's friend?

19. Sharon is an orthopedic surgeon. She performed a surgery two years ago and billed $10,000 to her patient. After two years of attempting to collect the money, it is clear that Sharon will not be able to collect anything. Sharon reports income on her tax return on the cash basis, so she only reports the income she actually receives in cash each year. Can she claim a bad debt deduction for the $10,000?

20. Carrie loaned her friend $4,500 to buy a used car. She had her friend sign a note with repayment terms and set a reasonable interest rate on the note because the $4,500 was most of her savings. Her friend left town without a forwarding address and nobody Carrie knows has heard from the friend in the last year. How should Carrie treat the bad loan for tax purposes?

21. Cindy operates a computerized engineering drawing business from her home. Cindy maintains a home office and properly allocates the following expenses to her office:

Depreciation	$3,500
Utilities	1,500
Real estate taxes	1,325
Mortgage interest (100-percent deductible)	2,500

  a. Assume that Cindy earns income of $4,400 from her business for the year before deducting home office expenses. She has no other expenses associated with the business. Calculate Cindy's deduction for home office expenses.

b. Assume that Cindy earns income of $12,600 from her business during the year before deducting home office expenses. Calculate Cindy's deduction for home office expenses.

LO 3.11 22. DeAndre qualifies for a home office deduction. The amount of space devoted to business use is 175 square feet of the total 1,400 square feet in his apartment. DeAndre's total rent for the year is $14,400, and he pays utilities (other than telephone) of $2,600 for the year. Calculate DeAndre's deduction for home office expenses (rent and utilities, other than telephone) before the gross income limitation.

LO 3.11 23. Randi qualifies for a home deduction. The amount of space devoted to business use is 400 square feet of the total 2,000 square feet of her home. Randi's mortgage interest and property taxes in total are $1,600. Other deductions properly allocated to the home office total $300. In addition, Randi purchases and uses business supplies costing $200 during the year. Assume Randi earns income of $3,400 for the year before deducting any home office or supplies deduction. Calculate the largest deduction Randi can take for her home office (ignore self-employment taxes).

LO 3.11 24. Ann is a self-employed restaurant critic who does her work exclusively from a home office. Ann's income is $25,000 before the home office deduction this year. Her office takes up 200 square feet of her 1,000-square-foot apartment. The total expenses for her apartment are $6,000 for rent, $1,000 for utilities, $200 for renter's insurance, and $800 for pest control and other maintenance. What is Ann's home office deduction? Please show your calculations.

LO 3.12 25. Lew is a practicing CPA who decides to raise bonsai as a business. Lew engages in the activity and has the following revenue and expenses:

Sales	$ 5,000
Depreciation on greenhouse	10,000
Advertising	1,500

a. What are the factors that the IRS will consider when evaluating whether the activity is a business or a hobby?
b. If the activity is deemed to be a regular business, what is the amount of Lew's loss from the activity?
c. If the activity is deemed to be a hobby, what is the amount of Lew's expenses (if any) from the activity that may be deducted?

Group 3:
Writing Assignment

Ethics

1. Bobby Reynolds, a new client of yours, is a self-employed caterer in Santa Fe, New Mexico. Bobby drives his personal van when delivering catered meals to customers. You have asked him to provide the amount of business miles driven using his vehicle. You are planning on using the standard mileage method to calculate Bobby's deduction for transportation costs. Bobby has responded by saying, "Well, I don't really keep track of my miles. I guess I drove around 3,000 miles last year for the business." What would you say to Bobby?

Research

2. Your supervisor has asked you to research a potential tax deduction for a client, Randall Stevens. Randall is a self-employed loan agent who lives in Portland, Maine. His specialty is marine loans; in particular, loans for the renovation of classic boats. Over the years, Randall has developed a very unique expertise in valuation of classic boats and is considered a global expert in the field. In 2024, Randall is hoping to attend the North American Classic Marine Boat Show that takes place in Zihuatanejo, Mexico. Randall attends the show more or less every year in order to stay current on classic boat valuations. Interested parties from around the world attend the show in the quaint Mexican coastal town. Randall's costs to attend are $800 for show registration, $1,750 for airfare from Portland to Zihuatanejo, $2,400 for lodging. Meals are estimated at $600. Please prepare a letter for Randall that describes the issues he will face when attempting to deduct the cost of attending the show. Use IRS Publication 463 (available at **www.irs.gov**) to assist you.

(An example of a client letter is available at the website for this textbook located at **www.cengage.com**.)

Group 4:
Comprehensive Problems

1. Gordon Temper is a single taxpayer (birthdate July 1, 1987 and Social Security number 242-11-6767) who operates a food truck that specializes in food from South Africa. His business is named "Mobile Peri Peri" and although the truck moves around quite a bit, he generally parks it in an office park where he maintains an office and a supply of inventory. The business address is 150 Erie Street, Laramie, WY 82070. The principal business code is 722300.

Gordon's food truck business is fairly new, so he also works part-time as a cook at a steak house restaurant in Laramie. His Form W-2 follows:

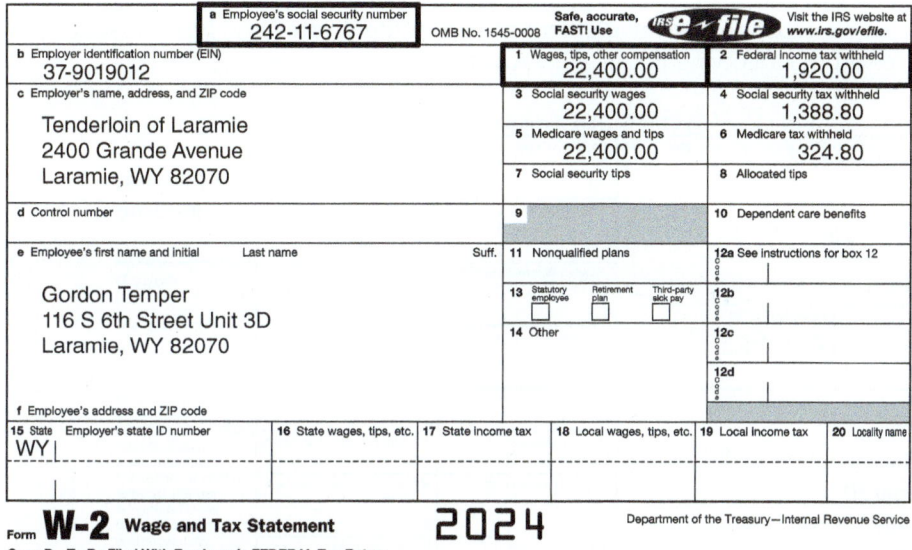

Gordon provided the following financial information related to Mobile Peri Peri:

Revenues	$81,000	Insurance	3,400
Beginning Inventory	5,600	Food license	500
Purchases	43,000	Uniforms	200
Ending inventory	5,000	Dues	100
Truck rental	24,000	Travel	1,600
Office rental	8,600	Office expense	400
Advertising	1,000		

Mobile Peri Peri uses the cash method of accounting and the cost method for inventory.

Gordon also provided a transportation log that shows that the truck drove 5,600 business miles in 2024. Gordon's log also listed total mileage of 680 miles for his drive in his personal car from the Mobile Peri Peri office to his second job at the steak house. He did not provide mileage from his apartment to or from either work location.

Dues are for a subscription to *Food Truck Monthly*, a trade magazine.

His travel expense of $1,600 is for a trip to Steamboat Springs, CO, for a one-day seminar on South African cuisine. He spent the day at the seminar and then went snow-skiing for two days before returning to Laramie. His airfare to Steamboat Springs was $400, his lodging was $300 per night for three nights, and his meals cost $100 per day. The uniforms are white chef's coats and puffy chef's hats embroidered with the South African flag and the Mobile Peri Peri logo on front and back.

Gordon was divorced in 2017. His ex-spouse, Tanya Ramsey, pays him alimony of $300 per month. She also has custody of their five children. One of the Ramsey's children, Buffy, age 17, lived with Gordon for five months during 2024 and he estimates he provided more than one-half of her support. Buffy has a part-time job at Taco Shell quick service restaurant and made $5,500 in 2024.

Gordon received a sizable property settlement as part of the divorce and has invested wisely. He received the following Forms 1099 for 2024:

Form 1099-INT — Interest Income (Rev. January 2024), For calendar year 2024

- PAYER: Investcorp Bond Fund, PO Box 11234, Valley Forge, PA 19481
- PAYER'S TIN: 43-9871236
- RECIPIENT'S TIN: 242-11-6767
- RECIPIENT: Gordon Temper, 116 S. 6th Street 3D, Laramie, WY 82070
- Box 1 Interest income: $3,190.04

Form 1099-DIV — Dividends and Distributions (Rev. January 2024), For calendar year 2024

- PAYER: Investcorp Small Cap Equity Fund, PO Box 11234, Valley Forge, PA 19481
- PAYER'S TIN: 42-1313445
- RECIPIENT'S TIN: 242-11-6767
- RECIPIENT: Gordon Temper, 116 S. 6th St. #3D, Laramie, WY 82070
- Box 1a Total ordinary dividends: $5,800.00
- Box 1b Qualified dividends: $5,500.00
- Box 2a Total capital gain distr.: $1,000.00

Required: Complete Gordon's federal income tax return for 2024 on Form 1040, Schedule 1, Schedule B, Schedule C, and the Qualified Dividends and Capital Gains Tax Worksheet.

2A. Russell (birthdate February 2, 1973) and Linda (birthdate August 30, 1978) Long have brought you the following information regarding their income and expenses for the current year. Russell owns and operates a landscaping business called Lawns and Landscapes Unlimited (EIN: 32-1456789). The business is operated out of their home, located at 1234 Cherry Lane, Nampa, ID 83687. The principal business code is 561730. Russell's bookkeeper provided the following income statement from the landscaping business:

Lawns and Landscapes
Income Statement
12/31/2024

	Current Period 1/1/2024 to 12/31/2024	Prior Period 1/1/2023 to 12/31/2023
REVENUES		
Lawn maintenance	$ 85,000	$ 71,998
Lawn and plant installation	35,000	48,576
Other	17,200	8,001
TOTAL REVENUES	137,200	128,575
COST OF SERVICES		
Salaries	85,300	78,445
Payroll Taxes	6,800	6,432
Equipment Rental	12,500	10,651
Maintenance (Equipment)	8,300	8,435
Special Clothing and Safety Shoes	700	200
Contract Labor	7,800	6,790
TOTAL COST OF SERVICES	121,400	110,953
GROSS PROFIT (LOSS)	15,800	17,622
OPERATING EXPENSES		
Advertising and Promotion	1,400	700
Donations	600	500
Insurance	3,800	870
Meals and Entertainment	1,800	2,100
Subscriptions	110	120
Business Gifts	790	600
Telephone	2,525	1,956
Training	1,975	-
Travel	865	750
Other	1,700	2,724
TOTAL OPERATING EXPENSES	15,565	10,320
NET INCOME (LOSS)	$ 235	$ 7,302

The bookkeeper provided the following additional information:
- Donations expense is a $600 donation to the Campaign to Re-Elect Senator Ami Dahla.
- Training includes $575 for an educational seminar on bug control. It also includes the cost for Russell to attend an online certificate program in landscaping in order to improve his skills and advertise his designation as a certified landscaper. The tuition, fees, and books cost $1,400.
- No business gift exceeded $22 in value.
- The subscription is for a trade magazine titled *Plants Unlimited*.
- Meals and entertainment expense is $1,000 of business meals and $800 for season tickets to Boise State University that Russell uses to entertain potential clients.

- Russell drove his pickup truck (purchased 3/14/2023) 970 business miles in 2024. He also drove the truck 2,300 commuting miles and 3,000 other miles. The Longs have another car available for personal use. Truck business mileage is not reflected in the income statement.

The business uses the cash method of accounting and has no accounts receivable or inventory held for resale.

In addition to the above expenses, the Longs have set aside one room of their house as a home office. The room is 192 square feet and their house has a total of 1,600 square feet. They pay $13,200 per year rental on their house, and the utilities amount to $1,800 for the year.

The Longs inherited a large number of acres of farm land from Linda's father in 2023 and sold it immediately for its market value of $1,000,000. They invested the proceeds in the Potato Dividend High Yield Fund and received the following Form 1099-DIV.

Form 1099-DIV — Dividends and Distributions (Rev. January 2024), For calendar year 2024

PAYER: Potato Dividend High Yield Fund, 1100 W. Front Street, 8th Fl., Boise, ID 83702
PAYER'S TIN: 12-3144562
RECIPIENT'S TIN: 554-98-3946
RECIPIENT: Linda Long, 1234 Cherry Lane, Nampa, ID 83687

- 1a Total ordinary dividends: $29,000.00
- 1b Qualified dividends: $29,000.00

Linda lost her job in late 2023 and collected unemployment in 2024 as shown on the following Form 1099-G.

Form 1099-G — Certain Government Payments (Rev. March 2024), For calendar year 2024

PAYER: Idaho Department of Labor, 317 W. Main Street, Boise, ID 83735
PAYER'S TIN: 11-2456871
RECIPIENT'S TIN: 554-98-3946
RECIPIENT: Linda Long, 1234 Cherry Lane, Nampa, ID 83687

- 1 Unemployment compensation: $1,100.00
- 4 Federal income tax withheld: $120.00

Russell was divorced on April 1, 2021 and pays his ex-spouse, Lois Long (SSN 313-29-3133) alimony of $200 per month in 2024.

Russell's Social Security number is 664-98-5678 and Linda's is 554-98-3946. The Longs elected to apply the prior year income tax overpayment of $326 to this years taxes in lieu of a refund.

Required: Complete the Longs' federal tax return for 2024 on Form 1040, Schedule 1, Schedule B, Schedule C, Form 8829, and the Qualified Dividends and Capital Gain Tax Worksheet. Do not complete Form 4562 (depreciation).

2B. Christopher Crosphit (birthdate April 28, 1982, Social Security number 565-12-6789) and Traynor Crosphit (birthdate July 17, 1981) are married filing jointly in 2024. They have a dependent son, Arnold (Social Security number 276-23-3954). Arnold (birthdate July 1, 2006) is a high school student; he does not qualify for the child tax credit but does qualify for the $500 other dependent credit.

Chris owns and operates a health club called "Catawba Fitness." The business is located at 4321 New Cut Road, Spartanburg, SC 29303. The principal business code is 812190 and the EIN is 12-3456789. Chris had the following income and expenses from the health club:

Income	$ 215,000
Expenses	
Business insurance	3,500
Office supplies	3,300
Payroll	99,000
Payroll taxes	8,900
Travel	2,550
Meals	2,100
Business gifts	800
Equipment maintenance	10,500
Cleaning service	8,800
Equipment rent	22,500
Utilities	13,700
Telephone	2,700
Rent	32,000
Advertising	3,700
Special workout clothes and boxing gloves	800
Subscription to Biceps Monthly magazine	100
Online educational seminar on gym safety	900
Other expenses	1,800

The business uses the cash method of accounting and has no accounts receivable or inventory held for resale.

Travel includes a trip to a weight-lifting seminar in Miami, FL. The one-day seminar cost $450. Chris took Traynor and Arnold with him. Airfare was $400 for each of them. The seminar started early in the morning, so they flew down the night before and then left the following morning since the seminar ended late in the day. Traynor and Arnold went to Miami Beach for the day. Lodging was $250 per night for two nights and meals were $100 for each of the three of them ($300 total). They also paid $100 for ground transportation from the airport to the hotel hosting the seminar.

Meals includes $1,000 for a staff party for all employees of Catawba Fitness, $800 in restaurant meals, and $300 in non-restaurant meals.

Chris purchased business gifts for 20 customers at a cost of $40 each.

The Crosphits live next door to the health club at 4323 New Cut Road. Chris does all the administrative work for the health club out of an office in their home because the gym lacks any suitable space. The room is 171 square feet and the house has a total of 1,800 square feet. The Crosphits pay $20,000 per year in rent and $4,000 in utilities. Chris would prefer to use the simplified method to deduct his home office if possible.

Traynor works as a sales representative for an online manufacturer and distributor of exercise bicycles. Her W-2 follows:

Form W-2 Wage and Tax Statement (2024)

- a Employee's social security number: 712-22-9881
- b Employer identification number (EIN): 47-3533716
- c Employer's name, address, and ZIP code: Pack of Bikes, Inc., 120 East 25th Street, 10th Floor, New York, NY 10001
- e Employee's name and address: Traynor Crosphit, 4323 New Cut Road, Spartanburg, SC 29303
- 1 Wages, tips, other compensation: 52,550.00
- 2 Federal income tax withheld: 2,794.29
- 3 Social security wages: 52,550.00
- 4 Social security tax withheld: 3,258.10
- 5 Medicare wages and tips: 52,550.00
- 6 Medicare tax withheld: 761.98
- 12a C 50.00
- 12b DD 6,500.00
- 14 Other: FSA Health $3,200.00
- 15 State: SC; Employer's state ID number: 10008723
- 16 State wages, tips, etc.: 52,550.00
- 17 State income tax: 660.00

Chris ran up credit card debt in 2024 and was able to negotiate a reduction of his balance. He received the following 1099-C:

Form 1099-C Cancellation of Debt

- CREDITOR: Explorer Card Services, 100 N. Phillips Avenue, Sioux Falls, SD 57104
- 1 Date of identifiable event: 3/19/2024
- 2 Amount of debt discharged: $4,300.00
- CREDITOR'S TIN: 31-4543431
- DEBTOR'S TIN: 565-12-6789
- 4 Debt description: Consumer credit card debt
- DEBTOR'S name: Christopher Crosphit
- Street address: 4323 New Cut Road
- Spartanburg, SC 29303
- 5 If checked, the debtor was personally liable for repayment of the debt: [X]
- 6 Identifiable event code: F
- For calendar year 2024

Chris also dabbles as a broker of antique and rare books. He acquires and scavenges for books and then sells them on the Internet. He generated $4,000 of sales in 2024 and the books he sold cost $3,300. He also incurred $7,600 in travel and other expenses related to this activity. Chris has never turned a profit in the book business, but he loves books and book selling and does not mind losing money doing it.

The Crosphits withdrew $2,000 from the health care flexible account with Traynor's employer to pay for Arnold's orthodontic work.

Chris made an estimated tax payment to the IRS of $200 on April 15, 2024.

Required: Complete the Crosphit's federal tax return for 2024 on Form 1040, Schedule 1, and Schedule C. Do not complete Form 4562 (depreciation).

Group 5:
Cumulative Software Problem

1. The following additional information is available for the Albert and Allison Gaytor family from Chapters 1 and 2.

   On September 1, Allison opened a retail store that specializes in sports car accessories. The name of the store is "Toge Pass." The store is located at 1966 SE Federal Hwy, Stuart, FL 34994. The store uses the cash method of accounting for everything except inventory, which is kept on an accrual basis. The store's EIN is 98-7321654. Allison purchased inventory in August and then started her business on September 1 with $40,100 of inventory. The Toge Pass accountant provided the following financial information:

Income Statement

Toge Pass Auto Parts
Calendar Year 2024

Financial Statements in U.S. Dollars

Revenue			
Gross Sales		64,800	
Less: Sales Returns and Allowances		500	
Net Sales			64,300
Cost of Goods Sold			
Beginning Inventory		40,100	
Add: Purchases		37,900	
Inventory Available		78,000	
Less: Ending Inventory		38,000	
Cost of Goods Sold			40,000
Gross Profit (Loss)			24,300
Expenses			
Advertising		3,000	
Dues and Subscriptions		-	
Gifts		210	
Insurance		1,000	
Interest		1,600	
Legal and Professional Fees		400	
Licenses and Fees		800	
Miscellaneous		100	
Office Expense		1,300	
Payroll Taxes		500	
Postage		-	
Rent		7,500	
Repairs and Maintenance		400	
Supplies		600	
Telephone		775	
Travel		900	
Uniforms		400	
Utilities		1,050	
Vehicle Expenses		-	
Wages		3,500	
Total Expenses			24,035
Net Operating Income			265
Other Income			
Gain (Loss) on Sale of Assets			
Interest Income			
Total Other Income			-
Net Income (Loss)			265

A review of the expense account detail reveals the following:

- The travel expense includes the costs Allison incurred to attend a seminar on sports car accessories. She spent $300 on airfare, $400 on lodging, $100 on a rental car, and $100 on meals. Allison has proper receipts for these amounts.
- The gift account details show that Allison gave a $30 gift to each of her seven best suppliers.

- The supplies expense account detail reflects the purchase of 250 pens with the "Toge Pass" logo inscribed on each pen. Allison gave the pens away to suppliers, customers, and other business contacts before the end of the year.
- Uniforms expense reflects the cost to purchase polo shirts Allison provided for each employee (but not herself). The shirts have the Toge Pass logo printed on the front and back and are the required apparel while working but otherwise are just like any other polo shirts.
- The license and fee account includes a $650 fine Toge Pass paid to the state of Florida for environmental damage resulting from an oil spill.

Allison drove her 2016 Ford Explorer 1,651 miles in 2024 for business related to Toge Pass. The Explorer was driven a total of 11,450 miles for the year. Included in the total 11,450 miles is 5,000 miles spent commuting to the store. Allison has the required substantiation for business mileage. She uses the standard mileage method.

In July, Albert loaned a friend $7,000 so he could buy a car. Albert's friend lost his job in 2024 and stopped making payments on the loan. He plans to start making payments again, however, with additional interest as soon as he has new employment.

In late 2024, Albert started to mount and stuff some of his trophy fish to display in his "man cave" at the Gaytor's home. Some of his friends liked Albert's taxidermy work and asked him to prepare a couple of trophy fish for them as well. Although he doubts he will ever sell any more stuffed fish, he received $175 and had no expenses related to this activity in 2024.

Required: Combine this new information about the Gaytor family with the information from Chapters 1 and 2 and complete a revised 2024 tax return for Albert and Allison. Be sure to save your data input files since this case will be expanded with more tax information in each succeeding chapter.

Chapter 4

Additional Income and the Qualified Business Income Deduction

Learning Objectives

After completing this chapter, you should be able to:

- **LO 4.1** Define the term "capital asset."
- **LO 4.2** Apply the holding period for long-term and short-term capital gains and losses.
- **LO 4.3** Calculate the gain or loss on the disposition of an asset.
- **LO 4.4** Compute the tax on capital gains.
- **LO 4.5** Describe the treatment of capital losses.
- **LO 4.6** Apply the exclusion of gain from personal residence sales.
- **LO 4.7** Apply the tax rules for rental property and vacation homes.
- **LO 4.8** Explain the treatment of passive income and losses.
- **LO 4.9** Describe the basic tax treatment of deductions for net operating losses.
- **LO 4.10** Calculate and report the self-employment tax (both Social Security and Medicare portions) for self-employed taxpayers.
- **LO 4.11** Compute the qualified business income (QBI) deduction.

Overview

Chapter 4 covers additional important elements of income and expense which enter into the calculation of adjusted gross income (AGI). The first part of this chapter includes capital gains and other items reported through Schedule D. The second part covers the tax rules for rental properties and other business activities including limitations on passive activities reported through Schedule E. This chapter concludes with the self-employment tax and the qualified business income deduction. The business income and expenses included in this chapter are all part of the calculation of a taxpayer's AGI.

Learning Objective 4.1

Define the term "capital asset."

4-1 What Is a Capital Asset?

When taxpayers dispose of property, they must calculate any gain or loss on the transaction and report the gain or loss on their tax returns. The gain or loss realized is equal to the difference between the amount realized on the sale or exchange of the property and the taxpayer's adjusted basis in the property. How gains and losses are reported is dependent on the nature of the property and the length of time the property has been owned. Gains and losses on the sale of capital assets are known as capital gains and losses and are classified as either short-term or long-term. For a gain or loss on the sale of a capital asset to be classified as a long-term capital gain or loss, the taxpayer must have held the asset for the required holding period.

The tax law defines a capital asset as any property, whether used in a trade or business or not, other than:

1. Stock in trade, inventory, or property held primarily for sale to customers in the ordinary course of a trade or business;
2. Depreciable property or real property used in a trade or business (Section 1231 assets);
3. A patent, invention, model or design (whether or not patented), a secret formula or process, a copyright, a literary, musical, or artistic composition, a letter or memorandum, or similar property, if the property is created by the taxpayer;
4. Accounts or notes receivable; and
5. Certain U.S. government publications.

The definition of a capital asset is a definition by exception. All property owned by a taxpayer, other than property specifically noted as an exception, is a capital asset. Depreciable property and real estate used in a trade or business are referred to as Section 1231 assets and will be covered in Chapter 8 because special rules apply to such assets.

4-1a Virtual Currency

Virtual currency is a digital representation of value that functions as a medium of exchange, a unit of account, or a store of value. Cryptocurrency is a type of virtual currency that utilizes blockchain to validate and secure transactions that are digitally recorded on a distributed ledger.

Some virtual currencies, such as Bitcoin, have an equivalent value in real currency. For example, Bitcoin can be digitally traded between users and can be purchased for, or exchanged into, U.S. dollars, Euros, and other real currencies.

Example Micah, a cash-basis single taxpayer, has a customer that paid him 0.75 units of Bitcoin worth $60,000 per unit for the services he provided as part of his business. Later in the year, Micah exchanged 0.50 units of his Bitcoin for an automobile when the value of the Bitcoin was $62,000 per unit. ♦

In general, virtual currency is treated the same as property. For most taxpayers, the rules will follow those laid out in this chapter.

Example Continuing with the previous example, Micah will be required to recognize the fair market value of the Bitcoin ($60,000 per unit times 0.75 units or $45,000 total) received as gross income in payment for his services. His basis in the Bitcoin will be $60,000 per unit. When he exchanges 0.50 units of Bitcoin for an auto, the value has increased to $62,000 per unit. As a result, Micah will recognize a gain of $1,000 (amount realized of $31,000 less adjusted basis of $30,000). The character of the gain depends on the character of the virtual currency to Micah, which appears to be a capital asset. ♦

In the world of cryptocurrency, a hard fork occurs when a cryptocurrency undergoes a protocol change resulting in a permanent diversion from the legacy distributed ledger. A hard fork may result in the creation of a new cryptocurrency on a new distributed ledger in addition to the legacy cryptocurrency on the legacy distributed ledger. If a cryptocurrency goes through a hard fork, but the taxpayer did not receive any new cryptocurrency, whether through an airdrop (a distribution of cryptocurrency to multiple taxpayers' distributed ledger addresses) or some other kind of transfer, there is no taxable income. A soft fork does not result in income.

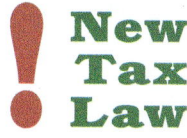

Self-Study Problem 4.1

Refer to Appendix E for Solutions to Self-Study Problems

Determine whether each of the following properties is a capital asset.
1. Shoes held by a shoe store
2. A taxpayer's personal residence
3. A painting held by the artist
4. Accounts receivable of a dentist
5. A copyright purchased from a company
6. A truck used in the taxpayer's business
7. IBM stock owned by an investor
8. AT&T bonds owned by an investor
9. Land held as an investment
10. A taxpayer's television
11. Automobiles for sale owned by a car dealer
12. A taxpayer's investment in virtual currency

4-2 Holding Period

Assets must be held for more than one year for the gain or loss to be considered long-term. A capital asset sold before it is owned for the required holding period results in a short-term capital gain or loss. A net short-term capital gain is treated as ordinary income for tax purposes. In calculating the holding period, the taxpayer excludes the date of acquisition and includes the date of disposition.

4.2 Learning Objective

Apply the holding period for long-term and short-term capital gains and losses.

Example Glen purchased stock as an investment on March 27, 2023. The first day the stock may be sold for long-term capital gain treatment is March 28, 2024. ♦

To satisfy the long-term holding period requirement, a capital asset acquired on the last day of a month must not be disposed of before the first day of the thirteenth month following the month of purchase.

Example If Elwood purchases a painting on March 31, 2023, the first day the painting may be sold for long-term capital gain treatment is April 1, 2024. ♦

For inherited property, the holding period is deemed to be over one year, regardless of actual holding period. For property received as a gift, the holding period from the donor will "tack on" if the basis carries over; otherwise, the holding period starts at the date of the gift. Refer to the basis rules in the next section for additional details.

Self-Study Problem 4.2

Refer to Appendix E for Solutions to Self-Study Problems

Determine whether a gain or loss realized in each of the following situations would be long-term or short-term.

	Date Acquired	Date Sold
1.	October 16, 2023	May 30, 2024
2.	May 2, 2023	October 12, 2024
3.	July 18, 2023	July 18, 2024
4.	August 31, 2022	March 1, 2024

Learning Objective 4.3

Calculate the gain or loss on the disposition of an asset.

4-3 Calculation of Gain or Loss

A taxpayer must calculate the amount realized and the adjusted basis of property sold or exchanged to arrive at the amount of the gain or loss realized on the disposition. The taxpayer's gain or loss is calculated using the following formula:

Amount realized − Adjusted basis = Gain or loss realized

4-3a Sale or Exchange

The realization of a gain or loss requires the "sale or exchange" of an asset. The term "sale or exchange" is not defined in the tax law, but a sale generally requires the receipt of money or the relief from liabilities in exchange for property. An exchange is the transfer of ownership of one property for another property.

Example Maggie sells virtual currency for $8,500 that she purchased two years ago for $6,000. Maggie's adjusted basis in the virtual currency is its cost, $6,000; therefore, she realizes a long-term capital gain of $2,500 ($8,500 − $6,000) on the sale. ♦

Example Art owns a home which has increased in value during the tax year. If Art does not sell the home, there is no realized gain during the tax year. ♦

4-3b Amount Realized

The amount realized from a sale or other disposition of property is equal to the sum of the money received, plus the fair market value of other property received, less the costs paid to transfer the property. If the taxpayer is relieved of a liability, the amount of the liability is added to the amount realized.

Amounts Realized = Cash + FMV of property received + Liabilities relieved − Selling costs

Example During the tax year, Ted sells real estate held as an investment for $75,000 in cash, and the buyer assumes the mortgage on the property of $120,000. Ted pays real estate commissions and other transfer costs of $11,000. The amount realized on the sale is calculated as:

Cash received	$ 75,000
Liabilities transferred	120,000
Total sales price	195,000
Less: transfer costs	(11,000)
Amount realized	$ 184,000

♦

4-3c Adjusted Basis

The adjusted basis of property is equal to the original basis adjusted by adding capital (major) improvements and deducting depreciation allowed or allowable, as illustrated by the following formula:

Adjusted basis = Original basis + Capital improvements − Accumulated depreciation

The original basis of property is usually its cost. The cost is the amount paid in cash, debt obligations, other property, or services. The original basis also includes amounts you pay for the sales tax, freight, installation and testing, excise taxes, revenue stamps, recording fees, and real estate taxes if you assume the liability of the seller. If the acquired asset is real property, certain fees and other expenses are part of the cost basis in the property such as the settlement fees and closing costs paid for buying the property but does not include fees and costs for getting a loan on the property.

The following are some of the settlement fees or closing costs included in the basis of real property:

- Charges for installing utility services
- Legal fees (including the title search and preparation of the sales contract and deed)
- Recording fees
- Survey fees
- Transfer taxes
- Owner's title insurance
- Any amounts the seller owes that the buyer agrees to pay, such as back taxes or interest, recording or mortgage fees, charges for improvements or repairs, and sales commissions

The following are some of the settlement fees and closing costs that cannot be included in the basis of property:

- Amounts placed in escrow for the future payment of items such as taxes and insurance
- Casualty insurance premiums
- Rent for occupancy of the property before closing
- Charges for utilities or other services related to occupancy of the property before closing
- Charges connected with obtaining a loan, such as points (discount points, loan origination fees), mortgage insurance premiums, loan assumption fees, cost of a credit report, and fees for an appraisal required by a lender

Capital improvements are major expenditures for permanent improvements to or restoration of the taxpayer's property. These expenditures include amounts which result in an increase in the value of the taxpayer's property or substantially increase the useful life of the property, as well as amounts which are spent to adapt property to a new use. For example, architect fees paid to plan an addition to a building, as well as the cost of the addition, must be added to the original basis of the asset as capital improvements. Ordinary repairs and maintenance expenditures are not capital expenditures.

Example Alan and his spouse purchased a house on September 15, 2024. Their closing statement for the purchase is illustrated on Pages 4-6 and 4-7. Their original tax basis in the house is equal to the purchase price of $130,000 plus the incidental costs of the owner's title insurance (not lender's), government recording fees, and transfer taxes. Therefore, their original basis is $130,740 ($130,000 + $500 + $50 + $190). The loan origination fee represents "points" on the mortgage loan. If the house is their principal residence, the points are deductible as interest in the year of payment. The prorated interest and taxes affect their deductions for interest and taxes, as described in Chapter 5. The homeowners' insurance is a nondeductible personal expense, assuming the house is their personal residence. ♦

OMB Approval No. 2502-0265

A. Settlement Statement (HUD-1)

B. Type of Loan

1. ☐ FHA 2. ☐ RHS 3. ☒ Conv. Unins. 6. File Number: 7. Loan Number: 8. Mortgage Insurance Case Number:
4. ☐ VA 5. ☐ Conv. Ins.

C. Note: This form is furnished to give you a statement of actual settlement costs. Amounts paid to and by the settlement agent are shown. Items marked "(p.o.c.)" were paid outside the closing; they are shown here for informational purposes and are not included in the totals.

D. Name & Address of Borrower:	E. Name & Address of Seller:	F. Name & Address of Lender:
Alan and Julie Jung 66 W. 2nd Street, Apt. 3F Peru, IN 46926	Chris and Fiona Evert 89 Payson Street Denver, IN 46926	2nd Farmers Bank 120 N. Broadway Peru, IN 46970

G. Property Location:	H. Settlement Agent:	I. Settlement Date:
68 W. Canal Street Peru, IN 46970	Place of Settlement:	

J. Summary of Borrower's Transaction

100. Gross Amount Due from Borrower

101. Contract sales price	$130,000.00 *
102. Personal property	
103. Settlement charges to borrower (line 1400)	$4,354.40
104.	
105.	
Adjustment for items paid by seller in advance	
106. City/town taxes to	
107. County taxes 10/01/2024 to 12/31/2024	$1,000.00
108. Assessments to	
109.	
110.	
111.	
112.	
120. Gross Amount Due from Borrower	**$135,354.40**

200. Amount Paid by or in Behalf of Borrower

201. Deposit or earnest money	$1,000.00
202. Principal amount of new loan(s)	$104,000.00
203. Existing loan(s) taken subject to	
204.	
205.	
206.	
207.	
208.	
209.	
Adjustments for items unpaid by seller	
210. City/town taxes to	
211. County taxes to	
212. Assessments to	
213.	
214.	
215.	
216.	
217.	
218.	
219.	
220. Total Paid by/for Borrower	**$105,000.00**

300. Cash at Settlement from/to Borrower

301. Gross amount due from borrower (line 120)	$135,354.40
302. Less amounts paid by/for borrower (line 220)	( )
303. Cash ☒ From ☐ To Borrower	$30,354.40

K. Summary of Seller's Transaction

400. Gross Amount Due to Seller

401. Contract sales price	$130,000.00
402. Personal property	
403.	
404.	
405.	
Adjustment for items paid by seller in advance	
406. City/town taxes to	
407. County taxes 10/01/2024 to 12/31/2024	$1,000.00
408. Assessments to	
409.	
410.	
411.	
412.	
420. Gross Amount Due to Seller	**$131,000.00**

500. Reductions In Amount Due to seller

501. Excess deposit (see instructions)	
502. Settlement charges to seller (line 1400)	$8,240.00
503. Existing loan(s) taken subject to	
504. Payoff of first mortgage loan	
505. Payoff of second mortgage loan	
506.	
507.	
508.	
509.	
Adjustments for items unpaid by seller	
510. City/town taxes to	
511. County taxes to	
512. Assessments to	
513.	
514.	
515.	
516.	
517.	
518.	
519.	
520. Total Reduction Amount Due Seller	**$8,240.00**

600. Cash at Settlement to/from Seller

601. Gross amount due to seller (line 420)	$131,000.00
602. Less reductions in amounts due seller (line 520)	($8,240.00)
603. Cash ☒ To ☐ From Seller	$122,760.00

The Public Reporting Burden for this collection of information is estimated at 35 minutes per response for collecting, reviewing, and reporting the data. This agency may not collect this information, and you are not required to complete this form, unless it displays a currently valid OMB control number. No confidentiality is assured; this disclosure is mandatory. This is designed to provide the parties to a RESPA covered transaction with information during the settlement process.

*Included in buyer's basis.

L. Settlement Charges

700. Total Real Estate Broker Fees $7,800				Paid From Borrower's Funds at Settlement	Paid From Seller's Funds at Settlement
Division of commission (line 700) as follows:					
701. $ 3,900.00 to Max/Re					
702. $ 3,900.00 to Century 22					
703. Commission paid at settlement					$7,800.00
704.					

800. Items Payable in Connection with Loan				
801. Our origination charge incl. origination points (1.000%)	$ 1,040.00	(from GFE #1)		
802. Your credit or charge (points) for the specific interest rate chosen	$	(from GFE #2)		
803. Your adjusted origination charges		(from GFE #A)	$1,040.00	
804. Appraisal fee to Appraisers R Us		(from GFE #3)	$400.00	
805. Credit report to Equifacts		(from GFE #3)	$50.00	
806. Tax service to		(from GFE #3)		
807. Flood certification to		(from GFE #3)		
808.				
809.				
810.				
811.				

900. Items Required by Lender to be Paid in Advance				
901. Daily interest charges from 09/15/2024 to 10/31/2024 @ $ 11.40 /day		(from GFE #10)	$524.40	
902. Mortgage insurance premium for months to		(from GFE #3)		
903. Homeowner's insurance for 1 years to ($600 P.O.C.)		(from GFE #11)		
904.				

1000. Reserves Deposited with Lender					
1001. Initial deposit for your escrow account			(from GFE #9)	$250.00	
1002. Homeowner's insurance	1	months @ $ 50.00	per month $ 50.00		
1003. Mortgage insurance		months @ $	per month $		
1004. Property Taxes	2	months @ $ 100.00	per month $ 200.00		
1005.		months @ $	per month $		
1006.		months @ $	per month $		
1007. Aggregate Adjustment			-$		

1100. Title Charges			
1101. Title services and lender's title insurance	(from GFE #4)	$1,350.00	
1102. Settlement or closing fee $			$250.00
1103. Owner's title insurance Title Company, Inc.	(from GFE #5)	$500.00	*
1104. Lender's title insurance $ 500.00			
1105. Lender's title policy limit $ 130,000.00			
1106. Owner's title policy limit $ 130,000.00			
1107. Agent's portion of the total title insurance premium to Title Company, Inc. $ 300.00			
1108. Underwriter's portion of the total title insurance premium to Underwriter $ 75.00			
1109.			
1110.			
1111.			

1200. Government Recording and Transfer Charges			
1201. Government recording charges	(from GFE #7)	$50.00	*
1202. Deed $ 25.00 Mortgage $ 25.00 Release $ 15.00			$15.00
1203. Transfer taxes	(from GFE #8)	$190.00	*
1204. City/County tax/stamps Deed $ 130.00 Mortgage $			
1205. State tax/stamps Deed $ 60.00 Mortgage $			
1206.			

1300. Additional Settlement Charges			
1301. Required services that you can shop for	(from GFE #6)		
1302. Pest Inspection	$ 75.00		$75.00
1303. Home warranty	$ 100.00		$100.00
1304.			
1305.			
1400. Total Settlement Charges (enter on lines 103, Section J and 502, Section K)		$4,354.40	$8,240.00

*Included in buyer's basis.

Example Paul acquired a rental house four years ago for $91,000. Depreciation claimed on the house for the four years totals $14,000. Paul installed a new patio at a cost of $2,500. The adjusted basis of the house is $79,500, as calculated below:

Adjusted basis = original basis + capital improvements − accumulated depreciation
$79,500 = $91,000 + $2,500 − $14,000 ♦

If property is received from a decedent (as an inheritance), the original basis is generally equal to the fair market value at the decedent's date of death.

Example Ron received Alphabet stock upon the death of his grandfather. The stock cost his grandfather $6,000, 40 years ago and was worth $97,000 on the date of his grandfather's death. Ron's basis in the stock is $97,000. ♦

For property acquired as a gift, the general rule is that the donee's basis is the donor's basis at the time of the gift. In this way, the donee steps into the shoes of the donor and the built-in gain is preserved.

Example Jane received a gift of stock from her mother. The stock cost her mother $9,000 five years ago and was worth $12,000 on the date of the gift (appreciated property). If the stock is sold by Jane for $13,000, her gain would be $4,000 ($13,000 − $9,000). Jane's basis is $9,000 regardless of the selling price ♦

However, only if the property's fair market value is less than the donor's basis at the time of the gift (depreciated property), the basis at the time of sale depends on the selling price. If sold for less than the fair market value at the time of the gift, the basis is the fair market value at the time of the gift (loss basis).

Example Jane received a gift of stock from her mother. The stock cost her mother $12,000 five years ago and was worth $9,000 on the date of the gift (depreciated property). If the stock is sold by Jane for $8,000, her loss would be $1,000 ($8,000 − $9,000). ♦

If sold for more than the donee's basis at the time of the gift, the basis is the donee's basis (gain basis).

Example Jane received a gift of stock from her mother. The stock cost her mother $12,000 five years ago and was worth $9,000 on the date of the gift (depreciated property). If the stock is sold by Jane for $13,000, her gain would be $1,000 ($13,000 − $12,000). ♦

Lastly, if sold for a price that is between gain basis and loss basis, the basis is deemed to be equal to the selling price and no gain or loss is realized.

Example Jane received a gift of stock from her mother. The stock cost her mother $12,000 five years ago and was worth $9,000 on the date of the gift (depreciated property). If the stock is sold by Jane for $10,000, her gain would be $0 ($10,000 − $10,000). ♦

Note that the basis for gain and the basis for loss will be different only where the gifted property has a fair market value, on the date of the gift, that is less than the donor's adjusted basis in the property. To the extent that the donor's sale of the property would result in a deductible loss, the donor is generally better off selling the property and transferring the proceeds to the donee.

Example Rather than gift the property in the previous example, the grandmother elects to sell the stock at a deductible loss of $3,000. The proceeds of the sale can be gifted to Jane, and she will have cash (and basis) of $9,000. ♦

> **Self-Study Problem 4.3** — Refer to Appendix E for Solutions to Self-Study Problems
>
> For each of the following situations, determine the basis of the property:
>
> 1. Jakobi purchased equipment at a cost of $15,000, made capitalizable improvements of $1,000 and depreciated the equipment $5,000. What is the basis of the equipment?
> 2. Kristian purchased a new home for $200,000. He put down $50,000 in cash and took out a mortgage for the rest. At the time of closing, he also paid $1,000 for title insurance, $500 in recording fees, and the bank required that he place $2,500 in an escrow account for property taxes. What is the basis of the home?
> 3. When Barry's grandmother passed away, she gave Barry a diamond ring that was worth $6,000 at the time of death. Barry's grandmother had purchased the ring for $5,400. What is Barry's basis in the ring if he sells it for $7,000? What if he sells it for $5,000? What is he sells it for $5,800?
> 4. On Robin's birthday, his grandmother gave him a ring that was worth $6,000 at the time of the gift. Robin's grandmother had purchased the ring for $5,400. What is Robin's basis in the ring if he sells it for $7,000? What if he sells it for $5,000? What if he sells it for $5,800?
> 5. On Maurice's birthday, his grandmother gave him a ring that was worth $5,400 at the time of the gift. Maurice's grandmother had purchased the ring for $6,000. What is Maurice's basis in the ring if he sells it for $7,000? What if he sells it for $5,000? What is he sells it for $5,800?

4-4 Net Capital Gains

4.4 Learning Objective

Compute the tax on capital gains.

In recent years, the tax rates on long-term and short-term capital gains have become complex. Short-term capital gains are taxed as ordinary income, while there are various different preferential long-term capital gains tax rates. A summary of the 2024 capital gains tax rates are presented in Table 4.1:

Table 4.1 Capital Gains Tax Rates

Type of Gains	Tax Rate*
Short-Term Capital Gains	Taxed at ordinary income rates consistent with filing status
Typical Long-Term Capital Gains	Taxed at 0, 15, or 20 percent depending on level of other taxable income (refer to Chapter 2)
Long-Term Unrecaptured Section 1250 Gain (refer to Chapter 8)	Capped at 25 percent
Long-Term Collectibles Gains (Art, Gems, Coins, Stamps, etc.)	Capped at 28 percent

*The 3.8 percent Medicare tax on net investment income, including qualified dividends, applies to high-income taxpayers with income over certain thresholds. Please refer to Chapter 6 for further details.

The application of the typical long-term capital gains rates of 0, 15, or 20 percent depends on the taxable income and filing status of the taxpayer. Formerly, the different rates applied to a taxpayer depending on which ordinary tax bracket the taxpayer was in (e.g., a taxpayer in the 12-percent tax bracket would pay tax on long-term gains at 0 percent since 15 percent is not preferential). The current long-term capital gains tax rates do not align perfectly with the existing ordinary income tax rates. For 2024, typical long-term capital gains (and dividends as covered in Chapter 2) are taxed as presented in Table 4.2:

Table 4.2 Long-Term Capital Gains and Qualified Dividends Rates 2024

Income level	Tax Rate*
Married Filing Jointly & Surviving Spouse	
$0–$94,050	0%
$94,051–$583,750	15%
>$583,750	20%
Single	
$0–$47,025	0%
$47,026–$518,900	15%
>$518,900	20%
Head of Household	
$0–$63,000	0%
$63,001–$551,350	15%
>$551,350	20%
Married Filing Separately	
$0–$47,025	0%
$47,026–$291,850	15%
>$291,850	20%

*Special higher rates for "high-income" taxpayers are covered in Chapter 6.

The 2024 break points between the ordinary rates and the typical long-term capital gains rates differ by minor amounts. For example, a single taxpayer moves from an ordinary income tax rate of 12 percent to 22 percent at $47,150; whereas the same taxpayer moves from a 0 percent to 15 percent long-term capital gains tax rate at $47,025.

Example Dee is a single taxpayer with wage income of $53,500 and long-term capital gains of $9,000 in 2024. Assume Dee has no other deductions or income except the standard deduction. Dee's taxable income is

Wage income	$53,500
Long-term capital gains	9,000
Standard deduction	(14,600)
Taxable income	$47,900

Dee's income now must be separated into the ordinary and long-term capital gain portions:

Taxable income	$47,900
Long-term capital gains	(9,000)
Ordinary income	$38,900

The 2024 tax on $38,900 of ordinary income is $4,439. Dee's taxable income without the long-term gain is below the 15-percent threshold of $47,025 for a single taxpayer in 2024, but her taxable income with the long-term gain is above the threshold; thus, a portion of the long-term gain will be taxed at 0 percent and a portion at 15 percent. Of her $9,000 long-term capital gain, $8,125 is below the threshold and taxed at 0 percent while $875 is above the threshold and is taxed at 15 percent for an additional capital gains tax of $131 to bring Dee's total tax liability to $4,570. The Qualified Dividends and Capital Gain Tax Worksheet introduced in Chapter 2 may be used to calculate the ordinary and long-term capital gains tax. ♦

4-4a Ordering Rules for Capital Gains

Since there are multiple kinds of capital gains on which to calculate tax, an ordering system is necessary to know which capital gains to tax at what rates. The various kinds of gains are included in taxable income in the following order:

1. Short-term capital gains
2. Unrecaptured Section 1250 gains on real estate
3. Gains on collectibles
4. Long-term capital gains

If taxpayers (or tax practitioners) have several different types of capital gains that interact with each other, the calculation may become very complex. A good tax preparation software will provide the calculation along with supporting worksheets for further review. The rules for the taxation of capital gains are exceptionally complex, and coverage of them is beyond the scope of this textbook.

4-4b Calculation of a Net Capital Position

If a taxpayer has a "net long-term capital gain" (net long-term capital gain in excess of net short-term capital loss), the gain is subject to a preferential tax rate as presented above. Thus, a taxpayer has to net all of the long-term and short-term capital transactions that take place during a year to calculate tax liability. In calculating a taxpayer's net capital gain or net capital loss, the following procedure is followed:

1. Capital gains and losses are classified into two groups, long-term and short-term.
2. Long-term capital gains are offset by long-term capital losses, resulting in either a net long-term capital gain or a net long-term capital loss.
3. Short-term capital gains are offset by short-term capital losses, resulting in a net short-term capital gain or a net short-term capital loss.
4. If Step 2 above results in a net long-term capital gain, it is offset by any net short-term capital loss (Step 3), resulting in either a net long-term capital gain (net long-term capital gain exceeds net short-term capital loss) or a net short-term capital loss (net short-term capital loss exceeds net long-term capital gain). If Step 2 above results in a net long-term capital loss, it is offset against any net short-term capital gain (Step 3), resulting in either a net long-term capital loss (net long-term capital loss exceeds net short-term capital gain) or ordinary income (net short-term capital gain exceeds net long-term capital loss).

Example The net capital gain computation is illustrated in the following table:

Taxpayer	Net LT Capital Gain or (Loss)	Net ST Capital Gain or (Loss)	Net Capital Position	Taxable LT Gain	Taxable ST Gain
A.	$10,000	$ 0	$ 10,000	$10,000	$ 0
B.	10,000	(4,000)	6,000	6,000	0
C.	0	20,000	20,000	0	20,000
D.	0	(20,000)	(20,000)	0	0
E.	10,000	8,000	18,000	10,000	8,000
F.	(8,000)	12,000	4,000	0	4,000
G.	(8,000)	(6,000)	(14,000)	0	0

Self-Study Problem 4.4

Refer to Appendix E for Solutions to Self-Study Problems

In October 2024, Jackie, a single taxpayer, sold IBM stock for $12,000, which she purchased four years ago for $4,000. She also sold GM stock for $14,000, which cost $17,500 three years ago, and she had a short-term capital loss of $1,800 on the sale of land. If Jackie's other ordinary income after the standard deduction is $46,000, what is the amount of Jackie's tax on these capital transactions?

Learning Objective 4.5
Describe the treatment of capital losses.

4-5 Net Capital Losses

4-5a Calculation of Net Capital Losses

The computation of an individual taxpayer's net capital loss is accomplished in a manner similar to the computation of a net capital gain. A net capital loss is incurred when the total capital losses for the period exceed the total capital gains for the period.

Example Connie has net long-term capital gains of $6,500 and a short-term capital loss of $8,000. The net short-term capital loss is $1,500 ($6,500 − $8,000). ♦

Example Delvin has net long-term capital losses of $8,000 and a short-term capital gain of $4,500. The net long-term capital loss is $3,500 ($4,500 − $8,000). ♦

4-5b Treatment of Net Capital Losses

Individual taxpayers may deduct up to $3,000 of net capital losses against ordinary income per year. Unused capital losses in a particular year may be carried forward indefinitely. Capital losses and capital loss carryovers first offset capital gains using the ordering rules presented below. Any remaining net capital loss may be used to offset ordinary income, subject to the $3,000 annual limitation.

Example Carter has a net long-term capital loss of $15,000 and other taxable income for the year of $25,000. He may deduct $3,000 of the loss against the $25,000 of other taxable income. The remaining capital loss of $12,000 ($15,000 − $3,000) is carried forward to future years. ♦

When unused capital losses are carried forward, they maintain their character as either long-term or short-term. If an individual taxpayer has both net long-term losses and net short-term losses in the same year, the net short-term losses are deducted first.

Example Frances has a long-term capital loss of $7,000 and a $2,000 short-term capital loss in Year 1. For that year, Frances may deduct $3,000 in capital losses, the $2,000 short-term capital loss, and $1,000 of the long-term capital loss. Her carryforward would be a $6,000 long-term capital loss. If Frances has no capital gains or losses in Year 2, she would deduct $3,000 in long-term capital losses and carry forward $3,000 ($6,000 − $3,000) to Year 3. Assuming she has no other capital gains and losses, the deduction of losses by year can be summarized as follows:

	Year 1	Year 2	Year 3
Long-term capital loss	$7,000	$6,000	$3,000
Short-term capital loss	2,000	0	0
Deduction, limited to $3,000	3,000	3,000	3,000
Short-term capital loss used	2,000	0	0
Long-term capital loss used	1,000	3,000	3,000
Carryforward, long-term capital loss	6,000	3,000	0	♦

> **Tax Break**
>
> Taxpayers who have recognized a large capital loss during the year may wish to sell appreciated stock or other property to generate enough capital gains prior to year-end to use up all but $3,000 of the capital loss. This way, the capital loss in excess of $3,000 will be used in the current period rather than carried forward, and the capital gains will be fully sheltered from tax.

4-5c Ordering Rules for Capital Losses

When a taxpayer ends up with net capital losses, the losses offset capital gains using the following ordering rules:

- Net short-term capital losses first reduce 28-percent gains, then 25-percent gains, then regular long-term capital gains.
- Net long-term capital losses first reduce 28-percent gains, then 25-percent gains, then any short-term capital gains.

As with the ordering rules for capital gains, the ordering calculation may become quite complex when different classes of capital assets are present. A detailed presentation is beyond the scope of this textbook.

4-5d Personal Capital Losses

Losses from the sale of personal capital assets are not allowed for tax purposes. For instance, the sale of a personal automobile at a loss or the sale of a personal residence at a loss does not generate a tax-deductible capital loss for individual taxpayers.

Example Rosa moved to a nursing home in 2024 and sold both her personal auto and her principal residence. She originally purchased her auto for $20,000 and sold it for $10,000. She originally purchased her residence for $125,000 and sold it for $100,000. The losses on these sales are not tax deductible to Rosa because the assets were personal-use assets. ♦

4-5e Wash Sales

Because capital losses offset capital gains, taxpayers may be tempted to engage in a tax strategy known as "loss harvesting."

Example Robert has significant capital gains during the year. To reduce the tax on those gains, on December 28, 2024, he sells 100 shares of Ghost Inc. for $50,000. His basis in the shares sold was $60,000, generating a capital loss of $10,000. He uses these losses to offset the previously recognized gains. ♦

Loss harvesting is an acceptable tax strategy; however, the tax law denies a loss on the sale of a security if a substantially identical security is purchased either 30 days before or 30 days after the sale at a loss.

Example Robert has significant capital gains during the year. To reduce the tax on those gains, on December 28, 2024, he sells 100 shares of Ghost Inc. for $50,000. His basis in the shares sold was $60,000, generating a capital loss of $10,000. Robert also acquires 100 shares of Ghost on December 28, 2024 for $52,000. Because Robert sold securities at a loss and repurchased substantially identical securities within 30 days, the loss is not recognized. ♦

The loss associated with a wash sale is deferred and the amount of the loss is added to the basis of the substantially identical securities purchased. In addition, the holding period "tacks on" to the substantially identical securities.

Example Robert has significant capital gains during the year. To reduce the tax on those gains, on December 28, 2024, he sells 100 shares of Ghost Inc. for $50,000 that were purchased on March 15, 2021. His basis in the shares sold was $60,000, generating a capital loss of $10,000. Robert also acquires 100 shares of Ghost on December 28, 2024 for $52,000 creating a wash sale. The loss of $10,000 is not recognized and added to the basis of the 100 new shares, bringing the total basis to $62,000. The holding period for the new shares starts when the original shares were purchased on March 15, 2021. ♦

The loss associated with the wash sale can be recognized if the shares are sold and no purchase of substantially identical securities is made.

Example Continuing from the previous example, Robert sells the new shares of Ghost on January 15, 2025 for $52,000 and does not repurchase any shares for 31 days. Although he purchased the shares for $52,000, the basis of the shares, due to the previous wash sale, is $62,000 and he recognizes the $10,000 loss that was previously deferred under the wash sale rules. Because the holding period is tacked on, the loss is a long-term loss. ♦

4-5f Special Rules for Small Company Stock

There are two special rules that govern the sale of small company stock, and both are generally referred to by the Internal Revenue Code section that governs the treatment: (1) §1202 stock and (2) §1244 stock. The rules for both of these provisions are somewhat complex and beyond the scope of this textbook; however, a brief overview is provided.

§1202 Stock

§1202 stock is qualified small business corporate stock. Generally, individuals are permitted to exclude an applicable percentage of the gain of up to (1) $10 million or (2) ten times the basis of qualified stock disposed of. For qualified stock acquired after September 27, 2010, the applicable percentage is 100 percent. To qualify, the stock must have been held by the individual for five years and as part of the original issue. The corporation issuing the stock must have basis in its assets that does not exceed $50 million when the stock was issued.

Example Quinn owns qualifying §1202 stock that he purchased at issuance in 2015 and has a basis of $1 million when he sells the shares for $20 million. Quinn may exclude the greater of $10 million or $100,000 (10 x $10,000 basis). Quinn will recognize the remaining $9 million as long-term capital gain. ♦

§1244 Stock

§1244 allows an individual taxpayer to treat a loss on the sale of qualifying corporate stock as ordinary (not capital, as would be typical) of up to $50,000 ($100,000 if married filing jointly) annually. Only the first $1 million of shares issued by the corporation can qualify as §1244 stock and the shares must be owned by the individual to whom they were issued at the creation of the shares.

Example Gregg, a single taxpayer, sells qualifying §1244 stock at a loss of $130,000 in 2024. Gregg can treat $50,000 of that loss as ordinary and the remaining $80,000 will be a capital loss. If Gregg was married filing jointly in 2024, he could treat $100,000 as ordinary and the remaining $30,000 will be a capital loss. ♦

4-5g Reporting Capital Gains and Losses

Capital gains and losses are frequently reported in a two-step process. First, report each item on Form 8949 and then report aggregated data from Form 8949 onto Schedule D. If reporting each trade, the first step is to list each sale on Form 8949. Part I of Form 8949 is used to report the details of short-term capital gains and losses and Part II (the opposite side of the form) is used to report long-term capital gains and losses. Generally, each sale will be listed and the acquisition date, sale date, sale proceeds (amount realized) and cost basis (adjusted basis) will be reported along with the resulting capital gain or loss. Form 8949 also requires the taxpayer to indicate an explanation code (column f) and an exclusion or adjustment to the gain or loss amount (column g). Common codes are H for the exclusion of gain on the sale of a principal residence; Q for the exclusion of gain on the sale of small business stock (§1202 stock); W for a nondeductible wash sale; and L for a nondeductible loss such as a disallowed related party loss. The complete set of codes can be found in the Form 8949 instructions. The ordinary loss from sale of §1244 stock is reported on Form 4979, which is covered in Chapter 8.

Example Maria sells her primary residence for a gain of $270,000. She is eligible to exclude $250,000 of that gain. On Form 8949, Maria will report the dates of acquisition and sale, the proceeds from the sale, and the basis, as is typical. Because she is excluding a part of the gain, she will also enter code H in column f and $250,000 in column g to adjust the gain recognized to $20,000, the amount in excess of the exclusion. ♦

Form 8949 also requires that the taxpayer indicate whether the sales were reported on Form 1099-B and if so, whether the Form 1099-B reported the basis to the IRS. This information is indicated with boxes in Part I (short-term) and Part II (long-term) as presented in Table 4.3:

Table 4.3 Codes for Reporting Sales on Form 1099-B

Box	Part I (short-term)	Part II (long-term)
Sales reported on Form 1099-B and basis provided to IRS	A	D
Sales reported on Form 1099-B and basis not reported to IRS	B	E
Sales not reported on Form 1099-B	C	F

If a taxpayer has capital transactions classified in more than one box, a separate Form 8949 should be completed.

Example Greta traded a number of stocks in the current year. Her broker sent her a 1099-B with the following activity:

- Two short-term trades for which basis was provided to the IRS (A)
- One short-term trade for which no basis was provided to the IRS (B)
- Three long-term trades for which basis was reported to the IRS (D)

Greta also made one short-term trade that was not reported on a Form 1099-B (C).

Greta will need to complete three different Parts I of Form 8949 since she has three different types of short-term trades, all of which require a different box. She can use the reverse side of any of the Forms 8949 to report her one type of long-term trading activity. ♦

To save taxpayers' time and effort, under certain circumstances, the capital gains and losses can be aggregated and reported directly on Schedule D. In order to aggregate either short-term or long-term trades into a single amount, all the trades must be of either Type A for short-term or Type D for long-term and require no adjustments, for example, such as a wash sale deferral. Figure 4-1 presents line 1a on Part I of Schedule D where aggregated data can be reported.

Figure 4.1

SCHEDULE D (Form 1040)	Capital Gains and Losses	OMB No. 1545-0074
Department of the Treasury Internal Revenue Service	Attach to Form 1040, 1040-SR, or 1040-NR. Use Form 8949 to list your transactions for lines 1b, 2, 3, 8b, 9, and 10. Go to *www.irs.gov/ScheduleD* for instructions and the latest information.	2024 Attachment Sequence No. 12

Name(s) shown on return — Your social security number

Did you dispose of any investment(s) in a qualified opportunity fund during the tax year? ☐ Yes ☐ No
If "Yes," attach Form 8949 and see its instructions for additional requirements for reporting your gain or loss.

Part I — Short-Term Capital Gains and Losses—Generally Assets Held One Year or Less (see instructions)

See instructions for how to figure the amounts to enter on the lines below.
This form may be easier to complete if you round off cents to whole dollars.

	(d) Proceeds (sales price)	(e) Cost (or other basis)	(g) Adjustments to gain or loss from Form(s) 8949, Part I, line 2, column (g)	(h) Gain or (loss) Subtract column (e) from column (d) and combine the result with column (g)
1a Totals for all short-term transactions reported on Form 1099-B for which basis was reported to the IRS and for which you have no adjustments (see instructions). However, if you choose to report all these transactions on Form 8949, leave this line blank and go to line 1b .				
1b Totals for all transactions reported on Form(s) 8949 with Box A checked				

Example

Gunter spent a fair amount of his time trading stocks in 2024. As a result, he has 24 short-term gain transactions for which the basis was reported to the IRS and two short-term transactions for which no basis was reported to the IRS. Gunter will report the two trades for which no basis was reported on Forms 8949 and select Box B and carry the totals to line 2 of Part I of Schedule D. The aggregate data for the 24 trades can all be reported directly on line 1a of Part I of Schedule D and no reporting on Form 8949 is required. ♦

ProConnect™ Tax TIP

When entering capital gains and losses in ProConnect, whether using the Quick Entry or Detail screen, if the box for Basis Reported to the IRS is left blank, ProConnect will automatically aggregate those items and report them directly on Schedule D and bypass Form 8949 as permitted. If aggregated data is entered with no date acquired or disposed, the classification of short-term or long-term can be selected by using the 1=short-term, 2=long-term [Override] box.

Self-Study Problem 4.5

Refer to Appendix E for Solutions to Self-Study Problems

During 2024, Louis Winthorpe, who is single, received the following Form 1099-B:

Form 1099-B (2024) — Duke Brothers Brokerage

PAYER'S name, street address, city or town, state or province, country, ZIP or foreign postal code, and telephone no.
Duke Brothers Brokerage
135 S. Broad Street
Philadelphia, PA 19103

Applicable checkbox on Form 8949: **D**

OMB No. 1545-0715
Form 1099-B
Proceeds From Broker and Barter Exchange Transactions

Field	Value
PAYER'S TIN	34-9876543
RECIPIENT'S TIN	123-44-3214
1a Description of property	100 shs. Second Maid Juice Corp.
1b Date acquired	06/12/2015
1c Date sold or disposed	08/15/2024
1d Proceeds	$18,000.00
1e Cost or other basis	$12,500.00
2 Type of gain or loss	Long-term gain or loss ☒
6 Reported to IRS	Net proceeds ☒
12 If checked, basis reported to IRS	☒

RECIPIENT'S name: Louis Winthorpe
Street address: 2014 Delancey Street
City: Philadelphia, PA 19103

Copy B For Recipient

He also received the following 1099-B from a different broker:

2024 Combined Forms 1099 — Friar Tuck Investments

Friar Tuck Investments
38 Wall Street, 8th Floor
New York, NY 10005

Louis Winthorpe
2014 Delancey Street
Philadelphia, PA 19103

Account Number: 5600911452
Tax ID: ***-**-3214
Payer's Federal Tax ID: 33-1357246
Financial Adviser/Phone: Marion Maide 888-555-1212

Form 1099-B — Proceeds from Broker and Barter Exchange Transactions

Box 6: Gross Proceeds | Box 5: Not checked | Box 3: Basis reported to IRS | Box 2: Type of Gain or Loss: Short Term

Box 1 Security description (CUSIP)	Quantity sold	Box 1b Date acquired	Box 1c Date sold or disposed	Box 1d Proceeds	Box 1e Cost or other basis	Box 1g Wash sale loss disallowed	Gain/(Loss) amount
Sargent Corp	100	04/18/2024	12/07/2024	12,000	19,200	(7,200)	(7,200)
Mullin, Inc.	50	05/16/2024	12/16/2024	3,000	9,000		(6,000)

Box 6: Gross Proceeds | Box 5: Not checked | Box 3: Basis reported to IRS | Box 2: Type of Gain or Loss: Long Term

Box 1 Security description (CUSIP)	Quantity sold	Box 1b Date acquired	Box 1c Date sold or disposed	Box 1d Proceeds	Box 1e Cost or other basis	Box 1g Wash sale loss disallowed	Gain/(Loss) amount
Reynolds Corp	50	12/18/2015	10/02/2024	25,000	21,000	-	4,000

On January 3, 2025, Louis purchased 100 shares of Sargent Corp. for $13,000.

Louis' taxable income is $50,000 (including gains and losses from above). Calculate Louis' net capital gain or loss and tax liability using Schedule D of Form 1040, Parts I, II, and III; Form 8949, Parts I and II; and the Qualified Dividends and Capital Gain Tax Worksheet on Pages 4-18 to 4-22.

Self-Study Problem 4.5

SCHEDULE D
(Form 1040)

Department of the Treasury
Internal Revenue Service

Capital Gains and Losses

Attach to Form 1040, 1040-SR, or 1040-NR.
Use Form 8949 to list your transactions for lines 1b, 2, 3, 8b, 9, and 10.
Go to *www.irs.gov/ScheduleD* for instructions and the latest information.

OMB No. 1545-0074

2024

Attachment Sequence No. **12**

Name(s) shown on return | Your social security number

Did you dispose of any investment(s) in a qualified opportunity fund during the tax year? ☐ Yes ☐ No
If "Yes," attach Form 8949 and see its instructions for additional requirements for reporting your gain or loss.

Part I — Short-Term Capital Gains and Losses—Generally Assets Held One Year or Less (see instructions)

See instructions for how to figure the amounts to enter on the lines below.

This form may be easier to complete if you round off cents to whole dollars.

	(d) Proceeds (sales price)	(e) Cost (or other basis)	(g) Adjustments to gain or loss from Form(s) 8949, Part I, line 2, column (g)	(h) Gain or (loss) Subtract column (e) from column (d) and combine the result with column (g)
1a Totals for all short-term transactions reported on Form 1099-B for which basis was reported to the IRS and for which you have no adjustments (see instructions). However, if you choose to report all these transactions on Form 8949, leave this line blank and go to line 1b .				
1b Totals for all transactions reported on Form(s) 8949 with **Box A** checked				
2 Totals for all transactions reported on Form(s) 8949 with **Box B** checked				
3 Totals for all transactions reported on Form(s) 8949 with **Box C** checked				

4 Short-term gain from Form 6252 and short-term gain or (loss) from Forms 4684, 6781, and 8824 .	**4**	
5 Net short-term gain or (loss) from partnerships, S corporations, estates, and trusts from Schedule(s) K-1	**5**	
6 Short-term capital loss carryover. Enter the amount, if any, from line 8 of your **Capital Loss Carryover Worksheet** in the instructions	**6**	( )
7 **Net short-term capital gain or (loss).** Combine lines 1a through 6 in column (h). If you have any long-term capital gains or losses, go to Part II below. Otherwise, go to Part III on the back	**7**	

Part II — Long-Term Capital Gains and Losses—Generally Assets Held More Than One Year (see instructions)

See instructions for how to figure the amounts to enter on the lines below.

This form may be easier to complete if you round off cents to whole dollars.

	(d) Proceeds (sales price)	(e) Cost (or other basis)	(g) Adjustments to gain or loss from Form(s) 8949, Part II, line 2, column (g)	(h) Gain or (loss) Subtract column (e) from column (d) and combine the result with column (g)
8a Totals for all long-term transactions reported on Form 1099-B for which basis was reported to the IRS and for which you have no adjustments (see instructions). However, if you choose to report all these transactions on Form 8949, leave this line blank and go to line 8b .				
8b Totals for all transactions reported on Form(s) 8949 with **Box D** checked				
9 Totals for all transactions reported on Form(s) 8949 with **Box E** checked				
10 Totals for all transactions reported on Form(s) 8949 with **Box F** checked				

11 Gain from Form 4797, Part I; long-term gain from Forms 2439 and 6252; and long-term gain or (loss) from Forms 4684, 6781, and 8824	**11**	
12 Net long-term gain or (loss) from partnerships, S corporations, estates, and trusts from Schedule(s) K-1	**12**	
13 Capital gain distributions. See the instructions	**13**	
14 Long-term capital loss carryover. Enter the amount, if any, from line 13 of your **Capital Loss Carryover Worksheet** in the instructions	**14**	( )
15 **Net long-term capital gain or (loss).** Combine lines 8a through 14 in column (h). Then, go to Part III on the back	**15**	

For Paperwork Reduction Act Notice, see your tax return instructions. Cat. No. 11338H Schedule D (Form 1040) 2024

Schedule D (Form 1040) 2024   Page **2**

Part III   Summary

16   Combine lines 7 and 15 and enter the result **16**

- If line 16 is a **gain**, enter the amount from line 16 on Form 1040, 1040-SR, or 1040-NR, line 7. Then, go to line 17 below.
- If line 16 is a **loss**, skip lines 17 through 20 below. Then, go to line 21. Also be sure to complete line 22.
- If line 16 is **zero**, skip lines 17 through 21 below and enter -0- on Form 1040, 1040-SR, or 1040-NR, line 7. Then, go to line 22.

17   Are lines 15 and 16 **both** gains?
     ☐ **Yes.** Go to line 18.
     ☐ **No.** Skip lines 18 through 21, and go to line 22.

18   If you are required to complete the **28% Rate Gain Worksheet** (see instructions), enter the amount, if any, from line 7 of that worksheet **18**

19   If you are required to complete the **Unrecaptured Section 1250 Gain Worksheet** (see instructions), enter the amount, if any, from line 18 of that worksheet **19**

20   Are lines 18 and 19 both zero or blank and you are not filing Form 4952?
     ☐ **Yes.** Complete the **Qualified Dividends and Capital Gain Tax Worksheet** in the instructions for Form 1040, line 16. **Don't** complete lines 21 and 22 below.

     ☐ **No.** Complete the **Schedule D Tax Worksheet** in the instructions. **Don't** complete lines 21 and 22 below.

21   If line 16 is a loss, enter here and on Form 1040, 1040-SR, or 1040-NR, line 7, the **smaller** of:

- The loss on line 16; or
- ($3,000), or if married filing separately, ($1,500)

     21 (   )

Note: When figuring which amount is smaller, treat both amounts as positive numbers.

22   Do you have qualified dividends on Form 1040, 1040-SR, or 1040-NR, line 3a?

     ☐ **Yes.** Complete the **Qualified Dividends and Capital Gain Tax Worksheet** in the instructions for Form 1040, line 16.

     ☐ **No.** Complete the rest of Form 1040, 1040-SR, or 1040-NR.

Self-Study Problem 4.5

Form 8949
Department of the Treasury
Internal Revenue Service

Sales and Other Dispositions of Capital Assets

File with your Schedule D to list your transactions for lines 1b, 2, 3, 8b, 9, and 10 of Schedule D.
Go to *www.irs.gov/Form8949* for instructions and the latest information.

OMB No. 1545-0074
2024
Attachment Sequence No. **12A**

Name(s) shown on return | Social security number or taxpayer identification number

Before you check Box A, B, or C below, see whether you received any Form(s) 1099-B or substitute statement(s) from your broker. A substitute statement will have the same information as Form 1099-B. Either will show whether your basis (usually your cost) was reported to the IRS by your broker and may even tell you which box to check.

Part I — **Short-Term.** Transactions involving capital assets you held 1 year or less are generally short-term (see instructions). For long-term transactions, see page 2.

Note: You may aggregate all short-term transactions reported on Form(s) 1099-B showing basis was reported to the IRS and for which no adjustments or codes are required. Enter the totals directly on Schedule D, line 1a; you aren't required to report these transactions on Form 8949 (see instructions).

You *must* check Box A, B, *or* C below. Check only one box. If more than one box applies for your short-term transactions, complete a separate Form 8949, page 1, for each applicable box. If you have more short-term transactions than will fit on this page for one or more of the boxes, complete as many forms with the same box checked as you need.

☐ **(A)** Short-term transactions reported on Form(s) 1099-B showing basis was reported to the IRS (see **Note** above)
☐ **(B)** Short-term transactions reported on Form(s) 1099-B showing basis **wasn't** reported to the IRS
☐ **(C)** Short-term transactions not reported to you on Form 1099-B

1 (a) Description of property (Example: 100 sh. XYZ Co.)	(b) Date acquired (Mo., day, yr.)	(c) Date sold or disposed of (Mo., day, yr.)	(d) Proceeds (sales price) (see instructions)	(e) Cost or other basis See the **Note** below and see *Column (e)* in the separate instructions.	(f) Code(s) from instructions	(g) Amount of adjustment	(h) Gain or (loss) Subtract column (e) from column (d) and combine the result with column (g).
2 Totals. Add the amounts in columns (d), (e), (g), and (h) (subtract negative amounts). Enter each total here and include on your Schedule D, **line 1b** (if **Box A** above is checked), **line 2** (if **Box B** above is checked), or **line 3** (if **Box C** above is checked) . .							

Note: If you checked Box A above but the basis reported to the IRS was incorrect, enter in column (e) the basis as reported to the IRS, and enter an adjustment in column (g) to correct the basis. See *Column (g)* in the separate instructions for how to figure the amount of the adjustment.

For Paperwork Reduction Act Notice, see your tax return instructions. Cat. No. 37768Z Form **8949** (2024)

4-5 Net Capital Losses   4-21

Form 8949 (2024)   Attachment Sequence No. **12A**   Page **2**

Name(s) shown on return. Name and SSN or taxpayer identification no. not required if shown on other side | Social security number or taxpayer identification number

Before you check Box D, E, or F below, see whether you received any Form(s) 1099-B or substitute statement(s) from your broker. A substitute statement will have the same information as Form 1099-B. Either will show whether your basis (usually your cost) was reported to the IRS by your broker and may even tell you which box to check.

Part II **Long-Term.** Transactions involving capital assets you held more than 1 year are generally long-term (see instructions). For short-term transactions, see page 1.

Note: You may aggregate all long-term transactions reported on Form(s) 1099-B showing basis was reported to the IRS and for which no adjustments or codes are required. Enter the totals directly on Schedule D, line 8a; you aren't required to report these transactions on Form 8949 (see instructions).

You *must* **check Box D, E,** *or* **F below. Check only one box.** If more than one box applies for your long-term transactions, complete a separate Form 8949, page 2, for each applicable box. If you have more long-term transactions than will fit on this page for one or more of the boxes, complete as many forms with the same box checked as you need.

☐ **(D)** Long-term transactions reported on Form(s) 1099-B showing basis was reported to the IRS (see **Note** above)
☐ **(E)** Long-term transactions reported on Form(s) 1099-B showing basis **wasn't** reported to the IRS
☐ **(F)** Long-term transactions not reported to you on Form 1099-B

1 (a) Description of property (Example: 100 sh. XYZ Co.)	(b) Date acquired (Mo., day, yr.)	(c) Date sold or disposed of (Mo., day, yr.)	(d) Proceeds (sales price) (see instructions)	(e) Cost or other basis See the **Note** below and see *Column (e)* in the separate instructions.	Adjustment, if any, to gain or loss If you enter an amount in column (g), enter a code in column (f). See the separate instructions.		(h) Gain or (loss) Subtract column (e) from column (d) and combine the result with column (g).
					(f) Code(s) from instructions	(g) Amount of adjustment	
2 Totals. Add the amounts in columns (d), (e), (g), and (h) (subtract negative amounts). Enter each total here and include on your Schedule D, **line 8b** (if **Box D** above is checked), **line 9** (if **Box E** above is checked), or **line 10** (if **Box F** above is checked) . . .							

Note: If you checked Box D above but the basis reported to the IRS was incorrect, enter in column (e) the basis as reported to the IRS, and enter an adjustment in column (g) to correct the basis. See *Column (g)* in the separate instructions for how to figure the amount of the adjustment.

Form **8949** (2024)

Self-Study Problem 4.5

Qualified Dividends and Capital Gain Tax Worksheet—Line 16 *Keep for Your Records*

Before you begin: ✓ See the earlier instructions for line 16 to see if you can use this worksheet to figure your tax.
✓ Before completing this worksheet, complete Form 1040 or 1040-SR through line 15.
✓ If you don't have to file Schedule D and you received capital gain distributions, be sure you checked the box on Form 1040 or 1040-SR, line 7.

1. Enter the amount from Form 1040 or 1040-SR, line 15. However, if you are filing Form 2555 (relating to foreign earned income), enter the amount from line 3 of the Foreign Earned Income Tax Worksheet .... **1.** _____
2. Enter the amount from Form 1040 or 1040-SR, line 3a* .... **2.** _____
3. Are you filing Schedule D?*
   ☐ **Yes.** Enter the **smaller** of line 15 or 16 of Schedule D. If either line 15 or 16 is blank or a loss, enter -0-.
   ☐ **No.** Enter the amount from Form 1040 or 1040-SR, line 7. .... **3.** _____
4. Add lines 2 and 3 .... **4.** _____
5. Subtract line 4 from line 1. If zero or less, enter -0- .... **5.** _____
6. Enter:
   $47,025 if single or married filing separately,
   $94,050 if married filing jointly or qualifying widow(er),
   $63,000 if head of household. .... **6.** _____
7. Enter the smaller of line 1 or line 6 .... **7.** _____
8. Enter the smaller of line 5 or line 7 .... **8.** _____
9. Subtract line 8 from line 7. This amount is taxed at 0% .... **9.** _____
10. Enter the smaller of line 1 or line 4 .... **10.** _____
11. Enter the amount from line 9 .... **11.** _____
12. Subtract line 11 from line 10 .... **12.** _____
13. Enter:
    $518,900 if single,
    $291,850 if married filing separately,
    $583,750 if married filing jointly or qualifying widow(er),
    $551,350 if head of household. .... **13.** _____
14. Enter the smaller of line 1 or line 13 .... **14.** _____
15. Add lines 5 and 9 .... **15.** _____
16. Subtract line 15 from line 14. If zero or less, enter -0- .... **16.** _____
17. Enter the smaller of line 12 or line 16 .... **17.** _____
18. Multiply line 17 by 15% (0.15) .... **18.** _____
19. Add lines 9 and 17 .... **19.** _____
20. Subtract line 19 from line 10 .... **20.** _____
21. Multiply line 20 by 20% (0.20) .... **21.** _____
22. Figure the tax on the amount on line 5. If the amount on line 5 is less than $100,000, use the Tax Table to figure the tax. If the amount on line 5 is $100,000 or more, use the Tax Computation Worksheet .... **22.** _____
23. Add lines 18, 21, and 22 .... **23.** _____
24. Figure the tax on the amount on line 1. If the amount on line 1 is less than $100,000, use the Tax Table to figure the tax. If the amount on line 1 is $100,000 or more, use the Tax Computation Worksheet .... **24.** _____
25. **Tax on all taxable income.** Enter the **smaller** of line 23 or 24. Also include this amount on the entry space on Form 1040 or 1040-SR, line 16. If you are filing Form 2555, don't enter this amount on the entry space on Form 1040 or 1040-SR, line 16. Instead, enter it on line 4 of the Foreign Earned Income Tax Worksheet .... **25.** _____

If you are filing Form 2555, see the footnote in the Foreign Earned Income Tax Worksheet before completing this line.

This worksheet adapted from the 2023 worksheet.

4-6 Sale of a Personal Residence

4-6a Sales After May 6, 1997

For gains on the sale of a personal residence after May 6, 1997, a seller who has owned and used a home as a principal residence for at least two of the last five years before the sale can exclude from income up to $250,000 of gain ($500,000 for joint and surviving spouse return filers). In general, this personal residence exclusion can be used only once every two years. A personal residence includes single-family homes, mobile homes, houseboats, condominiums, cooperative apartments, duplexes, or row houses.

> **4.6 Learning Objective**
> Apply the exclusion of gain from personal residence sales.

Example Hassan, a single taxpayer, bought his home 22 years ago for $25,000. He has lived in the home continuously since he purchased it. In November 2024, he sells his home for $300,000. Therefore, his realized gain on the sale of his personal residence is $275,000 ($300,000 − $25,000). Hassan's recognized taxable gain on this sale is $25,000, which is his total gain of $275,000 less the exclusion of $250,000. ♦

A seller otherwise qualified to exclude gain on a principal residence who fails to satisfy the two-year ownership and use requirements may calculate the amount of excluded gain by prorating the exclusion amount if the residence sale is due to an employment-related move, health, or unforeseen circumstances. Unforeseen circumstances includes death, divorce or separation, a change in employment that leaves the taxpayer unable to pay the mortgage, multiple births from the same pregnancy, and becoming eligible for unemployment compensation. The $250,000 or $500,000 exclusion amount is prorated by multiplying the exclusion amount by the length of time the taxpayer owned and used the home divided by two years.

Example Luis is a single taxpayer who owns and uses his principal residence for one year. He then sells the residence due to an employment-related move at a $100,000 gain. Because he may exclude up to one-half (one year divided by two years) of the $250,000 exclusion amount, or $125,000, none of his gain is taxable. ♦

4-6b Married Taxpayers

Taxpayers who are married and file a joint return for the year of sale may exclude up to $500,000 of gain realized on the sale of a personal residence. The full $500,000 for a married couple can be excluded if all three tests are met:

1. Either spouse owned the home for at least two of the five years before the sale,
2. Both spouses used the home as a principal residence for at least two of the last five years, and
3. Neither spouse has used the exclusion during the prior two years.

Example Sean and Fatima have been married for 20 years. At the time they were married, they purchased a home for $200,000 and have lived in the home since their marriage. Sean and Fatima sell their home for $800,000 and retire to Arizona. Their realized gain on the sale is $600,000 ($800,000 − $200,000), of which only $100,000 is taxable because of the $500,000 exclusion. ♦

A surviving spouse who doesn't meet the 2-year ownership and residence requirements and has not remarried, may include any time when the late spouse owned and lived in the home, even if without the surviving spouse, to meet the ownership and residence requirements.

Also, the surviving spouse may be able to increase your exclusion amount from $250,000 to $500,000 if all of the following conditions are met:

1. The home is sold within 2 years of the death of the spouse;
2. The surviving spouse has not remarried at the time of the sale;
3. Neither the surviving nor the late spouse took the exclusion on another home sold less than 2 years before the date of the current home sale; and

4. The surviving spouse meets the 2-year ownership and residence requirements (including the late spouse's times of ownership and residence, if applicable).

4-6c Reporting the Sale of a Personal Residence

If a portion of the sale of a residence is taxable, then it should be reported on Form 8949 using Code H and Schedule D. Generally, the sale of a home requires the preparation of Form 1099-S by the party responsible for the closing of the sale (typically, a bank, escrow company, or real estate attorney). Form 1099-S reports the gross proceeds of the sale of the property, the location of the property, and the name of the transferor (typically, the seller). Because the gross proceeds are reported, the taxpayer will typically need to make an adjustment to reflect selling costs. Selling costs should be reported as a negative adjustment in column (f) of Form 8949 using code E. If the sale is also eligible for an exclusion, the exclusion amount and the selling costs are reported together in column (g) and both Codes E and H are reported in column (f).

Example Jenni and Alexia sell their primary residence and receive the following Form 1099-S:

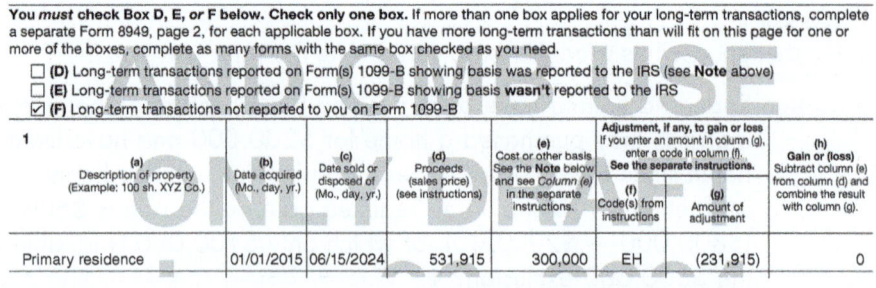

Their basis in the home was $300,000 at the time of the sale and they are eligible for the maximum gain exclusion. They incurred selling costs of $31,915. The recognized gain on the sale of the home is $0 ($531,915 gross proceeds − $31,915 selling costs − $300,000 basis − $200,000 exclusion on sale of primary residence) and is reported on Form 8949 as follows:

(a) Description of property (Example: 100 sh. XYZ Co.)	(b) Date acquired (Mo., day, yr.)	(c) Date sold or disposed of (Mo., day, yr.)	(d) Proceeds (sales price) (see instructions)	(e) Cost or other basis See the Note below and see Column (e) in the separate instructions.	(f) Code(s) from instructions	(g) Amount of adjustment	(h) Gain or (loss) Subtract column (e) from column (d) and combine the result with column (g).
Primary residence	01/01/2015	06/15/2024	531,915	300,000	EH	(231,915)	0

Beginning in 2009, Congress closed a loophole in the residence gain exclusion laws, which was used effectively by some owners of multiple rental properties. Under the residence gain exclusion laws in operation prior to 2009, taxpayers with multiple rental properties could move into a previously rented property, reside in the property for the required two-year period, and then sell the property using the $250,000 or $500,000 gain exclusion. Over a period of 10 years, a married couple could theoretically exclude $2.5 million of taxable gain on five separate properties. Beginning in 2009, taxpayers who rent their residence prior to their two years of personal use are generally limited to an exclusion smaller than the full $250,000 or $500,000 amounts. For details, examples, and exceptions to the law, refer to IRS Publication 523.

The exclusion of the gain on the sale of a principal residence in its current form was introduced in 1997. The $250,000 and $500,000 (married filing jointly) exclusions were certainly considered generous at the time. A married filing jointly taxpayer with a 15-percent capital gains rate can save up to $75,000 ($500,000 × 15%) in taxes with this provision. Amazingly, the 25-year-old provision is finally starting to show its age. The median value of a home in 2000 was just under $120,000. According to data provided by the S&P/Case-Shiller U.S. National Home Price Index, that value has tripled since 2000. Unsurprisingly, homes in cities such as San Francisco, Los Angeles, and Miami have increased more than $500,000 since 2000 but more modest cities such as Denver, Phoenix, and Boston have also seen values increase by more than the exclusion amount. For example, a home in Denver valued at $350,000 in 2000 is now estimated to be worth just over $946,000.

4-6d Sales Before May 7, 1997

Please note: The law below no longer applies to sales of principal residences. However, because many taxpayers still own residences with "rollover" basis determined under this law, it is important to understand how the law operated.

For sales of a personal residence before May 7, 1997, taxpayers did not have to recognize gain on the sale if they rolled the gain into a new house with a cost as high as the adjusted sales price of the old residence. The adjusted sales price was the amount realized on the sale less any qualified fixing-up expenses. Fixing-up expenses must have been incurred within 90 days prior to the date of sale and paid within 30 days after the date of sale. In addition, the purchase of the new residence had to be within two years of the date of sale of the old residence to qualify for nonrecognition of the gain. The adjusted basis of the new residence was reduced by any gain not recognized on the sale of the old residence.

Example Mary sold her personal residence for $60,000 in 1994 and paid selling expenses of $3,600. Mary had fixing-up expenses of $1,400, and the basis of her old residence was $40,000. If Mary purchased a new residence within two years for $85,000, her recognized gain and the basis of the new residence was calculated as follows:

1. Sales price	$ 60,000
Less: selling expenses	(3,600)
Amount realized	56,400
Adjusted basis of the old residence	(40,000)
Gain realized on the sale	$ 16,400
2. Amount realized	$ 56,400
Less: fixing-up expenses	(1,400)
Adjusted sales price	55,000
Less: cost of the new residence	(85,000)
Gain recognized	$ 0
3. Gain realized	$ 16,400
Less: gain recognized	(0)
Gain not recognized (deferred)	$ 16,400
4. Cost of the new residence	$ 85,000
Less: gain deferred	(16,400)
Basis of the new residence	$ 68,600

♦

Example Assume instead that Mary paid only $50,000 for a new residence. The gain and basis of the new residence are calculated as follows:

1. Adjusted sales price (from above)	$ 55,000
Less: cost of new residence	(50,000)
Gain recognized	$ 5,000
2. Gain realized (from above example)	$ 16,400
Less: gain recognized	(5,000)
Gain not recognized (deferred)	$ 11,400
3. Cost of the new residence	$ 50,000
Less: gain deferred	(11,400)
Basis of the new residence	$ 38,600

♦

The calculations on the previous page show that a taxpayer who sold one or more principal residences over a period of years and has a "rollover" basis under the old law may have a principal residence basis that is far lower than the cost of the taxpayer's residence. Because the current law does not require rollover treatment, taxpayers receive a fresh basis in a newly purchased residence which is equal to the purchase price.

Self-Study Problem 4.6
Refer to Appendix E for Solutions to Self-Study Problems

Ryuji, a single taxpayer, purchased a house 20 years ago for $30,000. He sells the house in December 2024 for $350,000. He has always lived in the house.

a. How much taxable gain does Ryuji have from the sale of his personal residence?

b. Assume Ryuji married Mary three years ago and she has lived in the house since their marriage. If they sell the house in December 2024 for $350,000, what is their taxable gain on a joint tax return?

c. Assume Ryuji is not married and purchased the house only one year ago for $200,000, and he sells the house for $350,000 due to an employment-related move. What is Ryuji's taxable gain?

Would You Sign This Tax Return?

Ivy Tower (age 45), a history professor at Coastal State University, recently purchased a house near the beach. In the current year, she accepted an offer from a buyer who wants to make the house into a bed and breakfast. Ivy sold her personal residence for a $100,000 gain. She owned the house 11 months as of the date of sale. After the sale closed, she discovered that the $100,000 is taxable as a short-term taxable gain (i.e., ordinary income) because she had not lived in her home for the two years required for exclusion of gain on the sale of a residence. She is upset that she will have to pay substantial tax on the sale. Her best friend's husband is a physician who signed a letter that Ivy had to move due to the dampness and humidity at the beach. She is not a regular patient of the doctor, and Ivy has no history of respiratory problems. Ivy claims she meets the medical extraordinary circumstances exception, and therefore, refuses to report the gain on her Form 1040. If Ivy were your tax client, would you sign the Paid Preparer's declaration (refer to example above) on her return? Why or why not?

4-7 Rental Income and Expenses

The net income from rental property is taxable income to the taxpayer. In most cases, rental income is reported with the related expenses on Part I of Schedule E. If services are provided to the tenant beyond those customarily provided, such as cleaning and maid services, the income is reported on Schedule C and is subject to the self-employment tax. Expenditures deductible as rental expenses include real estate taxes, mortgage interest, insurance, commissions, repairs, and depreciation.

4.7 Learning Objective

Apply the tax rules for rental property and vacation homes.

Example June Sanchez owns a house that she rents to a tenant for $600 per month. The following are June's expenses for the year:

Real estate taxes	$ 800
Mortgage interest	2,000
Insurance	200
Rent collection commissions	432
General repairs	350

June bought the property on July 1, 2008, and her original basis for depreciation of the house is $55,000. She uses straight-line depreciation with a 27.5 year life.

In 2024, June bought a new stove for the rental house that cost $500. The stove has a five-year life, and 20 percent of the stove's cost is depreciated this year. June's net rental income for the year is calculated as follows:

Rental income ($600 × 12)		$ 7,200
Less expenses:		
Real estate taxes	$ 800	
Mortgage interest	2,000	

Insurance	200
Commissions	432
General repairs	350
Depreciation:	
House ($55,000/27.5 years)	2,000
Stove ($500 × 20%)	100
Total expenses	(5,882)
Net rental income	$ 1,318

Please note that depreciation is an advanced topic which will be covered in detail in Chapter 8. ♦

4-7a Vacation Homes

Many taxpayers own residences which they use personally as part-year residences and rent during the remainder of the year. Such part-year rental properties are often referred to as "vacation homes." The tax law limits the deduction of expenses associated with the rental of vacation homes.

Example Jean owns a condo in Vail, Colorado. The condo is rented for three months during the year and is used by Jean for one month. If there were no vacation home limitations, Jean could deduct eleven months' worth of depreciation, maintenance, and other costs associated with the property. The resulting loss could then be deducted against Jean's other taxable income. ♦

To prevent taxpayers from claiming a deduction for expenses that are effectively personal in nature (associated with a personal residence), the tax law limits the deductions a taxpayer can claim for expenses associated with a vacation home. Deductions attributable to vacation homes used primarily as personal residences are limited to the income generated from the rental of the property. In general, only profit or breakeven (no loss) tax situations are allowed on the rental of vacation homes.

The expenses associated with the rental of a residence used for both personal and rental purposes are subject to three possible tax treatments. The tax treatment depends on the period of time the residence is used for personal versus rental purposes.

1. **Primarily Personal Use**

   If a residence is rented for fewer than 15 days during the year, the rental period is disregarded and it is treated as a personal residence for tax purposes. The rental income is not taxable and the mortgage interest and real estate taxes may be allowed as itemized deductions. Other expenses, such as utilities and maintenance, are considered nondeductible personal expenses.

   Example Glenn owns a lake home. During the year he rented the home for $1,800 for two weeks, lived in the home for three months, and left the home vacant during the remainder of the year. The expenses for the lake home included $5,000 in mortgage interest, $700 in property taxes, $2,100 in utilities and maintenance, and $3,000 in depreciation. Since the lake home was rented for fewer than 15 days, Glenn would not report the $1,800 of income and may deduct only the interest and property taxes as itemized deductions on Schedule A. The other expenses are nondeductible personal expenses. ♦

2. **Primarily Rental Use**

   If the residence is rented for 15 days or more and is used for personal purposes for not more than *fourteen days or 10 percent of the days rented, whichever is greater*, the residence is treated as rental property. The expenses must then be allocated between the personal and rental days. If this is the case, the rental expenses may exceed the rental income, and the resulting loss would be deducted against other income, subject to the passive loss rules. (LO 4.8 for further details.)

Example Assume the same facts as in the preceding example except that the $1,800 rental fee is for 20 days and Glenn uses the lake home for only 10 days during the year. Since the lake home is now rented for 15 days or more and Glenn's use of the home is not more than 14 days (or 10 percent of the days rented, if greater), the property is treated as primarily a rental property. Allocation of expenses associated with the home is based on the number of days of rental or personal use compared to the total number of days of use. Glenn's personal use percentage is 33.33 percent (10 days/30 days) and the rental portion is 66.67 percent (20 days/30 days). For tax purposes, the rental income or loss is calculated as follows:

	Rental (66.67%)	Personal (33.33%)
Income	$ 1,800	$ 0
Interest and taxes	(3,800)	(1,900)
Utilities and maintenance	(1,400)	(700)
Depreciation	(2,000)	(1,000)
Rental loss	$(5,400)	$ 0

The interest and taxes allocable to Glenn's personal use of the property may be deductible as itemized deductions on Schedule A (refer to Chapter 5). The personal portion of utilities, maintenance, and depreciation are nondeductible personal expenses. ◆

3. **Rental/Personal Use**
   If the residence is rented for 15 days or more and is used for personal purposes for more than *fourteen days or 10 percent of the days rented, whichever is greater*, allocable rental expenses are allowed only to the extent of rental income. Allocable rental expenses are deducted in three separate steps: first, the direct costs, interest, and taxes are deducted; second, utilities, maintenance, and other expenses are deducted; and third, depreciation expense is deducted. For utilities, maintenance, and depreciation expenses to be deductible, there must be positive income following the deduction of items in the preceding step(s). In addition, the expenses, other than interest and taxes, are only deductible to the extent of that positive income. Expenses are allocated between the rental and personal days before the limits are applied. The IRS requires that the allocation be on the basis of the total days of rental use or personal use divided by the total days of use.

Example Assume Glenn rents the lake home for $2,500 for 20 days and uses it for personal purposes for 60 days. Assume Glenn has the same operating expenses as in the previous examples. Since the lake home is rented for 15 days or more and Glenn uses the home for personal purposes for more than 14 days (or 10 percent of the days rented, if greater), the property is subject to the vacation home limitations. Glenn's personal use percentage is 75 percent (60 days/80 days) and the rental portion is 25 percent (20 days/80 days). The IRS requires that the rental income or loss be calculated as follows:

Gross rental income	$ 2,500
Less: interest and taxes ($5,700 × 25%)	(1,425)
Balance	1,075
Less: utilities and maintenance ($2,100 × 25%)	(525)
Balance	550
Less: depreciation ($3,000 × 25%, limited to $550)	(550)
Net rental income	$ 0

The interest and taxes allocable to Glenn's personal use of the property may be deductible as itemized deductions on Schedule A (refer to Chapter 5). The personal portion of utilities, maintenance, and depreciation are nondeductible personal expenses. The depreciation that is limited by income can be carried forward to the next tax year. ♦

It should be noted that the U.S. Tax Court has allowed taxpayers to use 365 days for the allocation of interest and taxes. Under the Tax Court rules, the interest and taxes allocable to the rental use of the property in the above example would be 5.5 percent (20 days/365 days) instead of 25 percent (20 days/80 days). The allocation of utilities and maintenance would remain unchanged, while the full $750 of depreciation (25% of $3,000) would be allowed. The remaining interest and taxes (345 days/365 days) may be included in itemized deductions on Schedule A.

The donation of the right to use your vacation home does not result in a charitable contribution deduction. For example, if a one-week stay in a vacation home is donated as a prize at a school fundraiser, no deduction arises and the days used by the winner count as personal days toward the taxpayer.

ProConnect™ Tax TIP

Rental activity is entered under Income and then Rental and Royalty Income (Schedule E). Key fields to consider are the Type of Property (dropdown), the number of days rented, the number of days of personal use (located below the expenses fields), and the number of days owned (if the Tax Court method is to be used).

4-7b Other Rental Issues

Many rental property owners collect deposits up front from tenants. If the deposit is a security deposit to be returned at the end of the lease (assuming no damage), that amount should generally not be included in the taxpayer's gross rental income. Any amount kept during or at the end of the lease is rental income at the time the deposit will no longer be returned. Collections of rent in advance are generally rental income at the time of collection, regardless of what time period the rent is intended to apply to.

Example Sadie rents an apartment to Brendan for $2,000 per month for 12 months starting July 1, 2024. The terms of the lease require Brendan to provide Sadie with the first and last months' rent, and a security deposit of one month's rent at the start of the lease. Brendan pays Sadie $6,000 when he signs the lease. Sadie will include $4,000 of rental income in 2024 for the first and last month's rent that was collected; however, the deposit is not rental income. In 2025, at the end of the lease, Sadie determines that Brendan has caused $800 of damage to the unit and under the terms of the security deposit clause in the lease, she will keep $800 and return the remaining $1,200 deposit to him. Sadie will include the $800 of the security deposit in her 2025 rental income. ♦

Occasionally, a tenant will pay expenses on behalf of the rental property owner. Generally, these must be included in rental income.

Example Hugo rents a condominium to Caroline. During the lease, the condo has a plumbing issue and because Hugo was out of town, Caroline contacted a plumber directly and had the $300 of repairs made. Caroline then deducted $300 from her next monthly rent payment. Hugo is required to include $300 in rental income, but, assuming the repairs are deductible, may deduct the repairs as a rental expense. ♦

> **Self-Study Problem 4.7** — Refer to Appendix E for Solutions to Self-Study Problems
>
> Nancy Kapiolani lives in a duplex that she owns at 1218 Park Ave S., Tacoma, WA 98447. Nancy rents one-half of her duplex and lives in the other half. In 2024, her existing tenant's lease expires and the tenant moves out. The tenant paid $2,500 in rent during 2024. Nancy had collected first and last months' rent from the tenant in 2023. Due to the condition of the unit, Nancy keeps $200 of the security deposit to make repairs. Her new tenant moves in and pays $1,000 per month for a one-year lease starting July 1, 2024. The new tenant is also required to pay Nancy first and last months' rent plus a $500 security deposit. The unit is rented for 365 days during 2024.
>
> Nancy's basis for depreciation on the rental portion is $120,000, and she uses straight-line depreciation with a 27.5 year useful life. Repairs to the rental half of the unit are $400 (including the $200 from the security deposit). On the whole duplex, real estate taxes are $2,200, interest on the mortgage is $3,400, utilities are $1,800, and insurance is $450. Use Part I of Schedule E on Page 4-32 to report Nancy's income from the rental of part of the duplex.

4-8 Passive Loss Limitations

4.8 Learning Objective

Explain the treatment of passive income and losses.

Because of past abuses primarily involving tax shelters and loss deductions from rental real estate, Congress enacted legislation limiting the deduction of certain "passive" losses from other taxable income. A passive activity is a trade or business in which the taxpayer does not materially participate and includes most rental real estate activity. Because the most common passive loss seen on tax returns is from ordinary real estate rental activities, many taxpayers with an investment in a real estate rental property are affected by these rules. In establishing the limitations, the tax law classifies individual income into three categories. These categories are (1) active income (e.g., wages, self-employment income, and salaries), (2) portfolio income (e.g., dividends and interest), and (3) passive income and losses (e.g., rental real estate income and loss, and income and loss passed through from limited partnerships and other ventures in which the taxpayer has minimal or no involvement).

Generally, passive losses cannot be used to offset either active or portfolio income. Also, any tax credits derived from passive activities can only offset income taxes attributable to passive income. Any unused passive losses and credits are carried over and may be used to offset future passive income or taxes attributable to such income, respectively. Generally, losses remaining when the taxpayer disposes of their entire interest in the passive activity may be used in full; however, the taxpayer can only use remaining credits to offset the income tax arising from any gain recognized on the disposition of the activity.

Example Shelby's income and loss items for 2024 are:

Salary	$40,000
Sales commissions	15,000
Dividends on Microsoft stock	2,000
Rental income from real estate	5,000
Loss from limited partnership	(9,000)
Interest on savings account	4,000

Shelby's active income for the year is $55,000 ($40,000 + $15,000), their portfolio income is $6,000 ($2,000 + $4,000), and their passive loss is $4,000 ($5,000 − $9,000). Shelby must report gross income of $61,000 ($55,000 + $6,000), since the passive loss cannot be used to offset their active or portfolio income. The net passive loss of $4,000 will be carried over to 2025. ♦

Self-Study Problem 4.7

SCHEDULE E
(Form 1040)
Department of the Treasury
Internal Revenue Service

Supplemental Income and Loss
(From rental real estate, royalties, partnerships, S corporations, estates, trusts, REMICs, etc.)
Attach to Form 1040, 1040-SR, 1040-NR, or 1041.
Go to *www.irs.gov/ScheduleE* for instructions and the latest information.

OMB No. 1545-0074
2024
Attachment Sequence No. **13**

Name(s) shown on return | Your social security number

Part I — Income or Loss From Rental Real Estate and Royalties

Note: If you are in the business of renting personal property, use **Schedule C**. See instructions. If you are an individual, report farm rental income or loss from **Form 4835** on page 2, line 40.

A Did you make any payments in 2024 that would require you to file Form(s) 1099? See instructions. ☐ Yes ☐ No
B If "Yes," did you or will you file required Form(s) 1099? ☐ Yes ☐ No

1a Physical address of each property (street, city, state, ZIP code)

A	
B	
C	

1b Type of Property (from list below)

A	
B	
C	

2 For each rental real estate property listed above, report the number of fair rental and personal use days. Check the QJV box only if you meet the requirements to file as a qualified joint venture. See instructions.

	Fair Rental Days	Personal Use Days	QJV
A			☐
B			☐
C			☐

Type of Property:
1 Single Family Residence
2 Multi-Family Residence
3 Vacation/Short-Term Rental
4 Commercial
5 Land
6 Royalties
7 Self-Rental
8 Other (describe) _____

			Properties:		
			A	B	C
Income:					
3	Rents received	3			
4	Royalties received	4			
Expenses:					
5	Advertising	5			
6	Auto and travel (see instructions)	6			
7	Cleaning and maintenance	7			
8	Commissions	8			
9	Insurance	9			
10	Legal and other professional fees	10			
11	Management fees	11			
12	Mortgage interest paid to banks, etc. (see instructions)	12			
13	Other interest	13			
14	Repairs	14			
15	Supplies	15			
16	Taxes	16			
17	Utilities	17			
18	Depreciation expense or depletion	18			
19	Other (list) _____	19			
20	Total expenses. Add lines 5 through 19	20			
21	Subtract line 20 from line 3 (rents) and/or 4 (royalties). If result is a (loss), see instructions to find out if you must file **Form 6198**	21			
22	Deductible rental real estate loss after limitation, if any, on **Form 8582** (see instructions)	22	( )	( )	( )

23a	Total of all amounts reported on line 3 for all rental properties	23a		
b	Total of all amounts reported on line 4 for all royalty properties	23b		
c	Total of all amounts reported on line 12 for all properties	23c		
d	Total of all amounts reported on line 18 for all properties	23d		
e	Total of all amounts reported on line 20 for all properties	23e		
24	**Income.** Add positive amounts shown on line 21. **Do not** include any losses		24	
25	**Losses.** Add royalty losses from line 21 and rental real estate losses from line 22. Enter total losses here		25	( )
26	**Total rental real estate and royalty income or (loss).** Combine lines 24 and 25. Enter the result here. If Parts II, III, and IV, and line 40 on page 2 do not apply to you, also enter this amount on Schedule 1 (Form 1040), line 5. Otherwise, include this amount in the total on line 41 on page 2		26	

For Paperwork Reduction Act Notice, see the separate instructions. Cat. No. 11344L Schedule E (Form 1040) 2024

Under the passive loss rules, real estate rental activities are specifically defined as passive, even if the taxpayer actively manages the property and even if the activity is not conducted as a partnership. Individual taxpayers, however, may deduct up to $25,000 of rental property losses against other income, if they are actively involved in the management of the property and their income does not exceed certain limits. The $25,000 loss deduction is phased out when the taxpayer's modified adjusted gross income (adjusted gross income before passive losses and Individual Retirement Account deductions) exceeds $100,000. The $25,000 is reduced by 50 cents for each $1.00 the taxpayer's modified adjusted gross income exceeds that amount. Therefore, no deduction is allowed when the taxpayer's modified adjusted gross income reaches $150,000 (this threshold is not adjusted for inflation). Special limitations apply to taxpayers filing as married filing separately and claiming a deduction for real estate rental losses under this special rule.

Example Liu has modified AGI before passive losses of $120,000. In addition, she has a rental house that she actively manages which shows a loss of $18,000 for the year. She may deduct only $15,000 ($25,000 − 50% × $20,000) of the loss because of the phase-out of the $25,000 allowance for passive rental losses where modified AGI is over $100,000. ♦

ProConnect™ Tax TIP

ProConnect Tax assumes that a rental property is actively managed and will apply the appropriate phase-out based on the modified AGI information entered elsewhere. There is a box to check on the General Information page of the rental property section to indicate otherwise.

4-8a Real Estate Rental as Trade or Business

Taxpayers heavily involved in real estate rental activities may qualify as having an active business rather than a passive activity. If so, the income and losses from qualified rental activities are not subject to passive loss limitations. For a real estate rental to be considered an active business, the taxpayer must materially participate in the activity. An individual will satisfy this requirement if both of the following are met:

1. More than 50 percent of the individual's personal service during the tax year is performed in real property trades or businesses, and
2. The individual performs more than 750 hours of service during the tax year in the real property trade or business in which they claim material participation.

Example In 2024, Allan owns 18 rental houses and spends 100 percent of his personal service time (1,800 hours in 2024) managing them. Allan spends his 1,800 hours of time doing repairs, landscaping, collecting rents, cleaning and painting vacant houses, advertising for and interviewing new tenants, doing bookkeeping, and purchasing/installing new appliances, drapes, carpets, and toilets. He keeps a log to prove how many hours he works on his property. Since both the above tests are met, Allan's real estate rental activity is not a passive activity. If Allan has an overall loss of $40,000 on the real estate rentals, he can deduct the entire loss on his tax return as an active business, not a passive loss. ♦

Tax Break

Real estate professionals who report large losses tend to attract the attention of the IRS. The real estate professional exception to the passive loss rules considers a two-step hurdle for deducting losses: (1) the real estate professional exception is used to overcome the presumption that a rental real estate activity is a passive activity but that does not guarantee treatment as non-passive; (2) the taxpayer is still going to have to demonstrate material participation. When multiple properties are owned, electing to treat them as a single activity can be useful for meeting the material participations rules.

Income from passive activities can be used by taxpayers to absorb passive losses that would otherwise be disallowed. The interaction between passive activities with losses and with income can become very complex, but in general, if a taxpayer has multiple loss activities and an income activity, the disallowed loss is required to be allocated across the loss activities.

Example Hana has two rental properties (A and B) and a limited partnership investment (C) with the following results for the year:

A	$(10,000)
B	5,000
C	(3,000)

Assume that Hana is not eligible for the $25,000 active management passive loss deduction due to her income. Hana's net passive loss is $8,000 ($10,000 + $3,000 − $5,000), all of which is disallowed. The $8,000 disallowed loss must be allocated between the two loss activities (A and C) based on their pro-rata share of losses:

A	$10,000	76.9% (10/13)
B	3,000	23.1% (3/13)
Total	$13,000	

The disallowed loss for activity A is $6,152 ($8,000 × 76.9%) and the disallowed loss for activity C is $1,848 ($8,000 × 23.1%). ♦

Rental activities are generally reported in Part 1 of Schedule E while other investments in partnerships and S corporations are reported in Part II of Schedule E. Any passive activities from Schedule E are also reported on Form 8582 to compute the net loss allowed and the loss suspended (disallowed).

Form 8582 (presented on Pages 4-39 and 4-40) has different parts that may need to be completed under certain circumstances. Per Form 8582 instructions, generally Parts IV and V must be completed first. Part IV is used to report income and losses from rental real estate activities. Part V is used to report all other passive activities. That information is transferred to Parts I through III. To the extent the taxpayer has more than one loss activity, Parts VI, VII, and VIII are used to compute the allocation of disallowed losses to each loss activity. Specifically, Part VI accumulates all loss activities and computes the total disallowed loss after considering the actively managed real estate exception. Part VII computes the ratio for each loss and the disallowed portion and Part VII computes the allowed loss. Form 8582 has some unique conventions that must be used to complete the form. In Part II and Part III of Form 8582, all the amounts, including the loss amounts, are entered as positive numbers. In Parts IV through VIII, all amounts are entered as positive amounts. Given that those parts of the forms are used for reporting losses, this convention is not obvious.

Taxpayers with several passive activities can find the complexity of their reporting quite daunting. Certain oil and gas investments are not subject to the passive loss limitations, and special rules apply to investments in qualified low-income housing.

ProConnect™ Tax TIP

Rental real estate is a common form of passive income and is input through the Rental and Royalty Income (Schedule E) window. Another source of passive income is from partnerships, LLCs or S corporations. As discussed in Chapters 10 and 11, these entities report income to individual owners through a Schedule K-1. K-1 income is input under Income in the left margin and the applicable Partnership K-1 or S Corporation K-1 input.

Self-Study Problem 4.8

Refer to Appendix E for Solutions to Self-Study Problems

Part A. This part includes only loss properties, and thus, the allocation of losses between activities does not affect an activity's deductible loss amount.

Louise Jefferson, a single taxpayer (Social Security number 112-67-1234), owns two investments in 2023. The first is a condominium rental property located at 185 E 85th St, New York, NY 10028. The condo was actively managed by Louise and rented for the entire year and has the following income and expenses:

Gross rental income	$20,000	Condo HOA fees	4,000
Mortgage interest	6,000	Utilities	2,000
Property taxes	8,000	Depreciation	9,000

Louise also owns a limited partner investment in Bunker Dry Cleaners LP (EIN 13-3434347). Bunker allocated a $15,000 loss to Louise in 2024.

Louise has adequate basis and at-risk amount to cover each loss. Louise has no passive loss carryover from the prior year and $138,000 of modified adjusted gross income before considering the losses.

1. Complete Part I of Schedule E on Page 4-37 through line 21.
2. Complete Form 8582 on Pages 4-39 and 4-40. Remember to start with Parts IV and V. Some of the information has been provided to assist in completion and required fields are also marked.
3. Complete the rest of Schedule E on Pages 4-37 and 4-38 as applicable, using the information from Form 8582 completed in the previous part.

Part B. This part includes both income and loss properties, and thus, the allocation of losses affects an activity's deductible loss amount making Parts VII and VIII of Form 8582 more complex.

Jorge Jefferson, a single taxpayer (Social Security number 656-76-4321), owns three investments in 2024. The first is a condominium rental property located at 186 E 85th St, New York, NY 10028. The condo was rented for the entire year.

Jorge also owns a single-family rental home located at 8970 Cooper Ave., Queens, NY 11374 that is rented the entire year. The rentals had the following results for the year:

	186 E 85th St	8970 Cooper Ave.
Gross rental income	$20,000	$20,000
Mortgage interest	6,000	5,000
Property taxes	8,000	6,000
Utilities	2,000	2,000
Condo HOA fees	4,000	—
Depreciation	9,000	5,000

Jorge actively manages both properties. Jorge also owns a limited partner investment in Bunker Dry Cleaners LP (EIN 13-3434347). Bunker allocated a $15,000 loss to Jorge in 2024.

> **Self-Study Problem 4.8, continued** *Refer to Appendix E for Solutions to Self-Study Problems*
>
> Jorge has adequate basis and at-risk amount to cover each loss. Jorge has no passive loss carryover from the prior year and $138,000 of modified adjusted gross income before considering the passive activities.
>
> 1. Complete Part I of Schedule E from Appendix F through line 21 for both rental properties.
> 2. Complete Form 8582 from Appendix F. Remember to start with Parts IV and V.
> 3. Complete the rest of Schedule E from Appendix F as applicable, using the information from Form 8582 completed in the previous step.

4-9 Net Operating Losses

Learning Objective 4.9
Describe the basic tax treatment of deductions for net operating losses.

Most taxpayers are required to file an annual tax return. The pattern of a taxpayer's income, however, can lead to inequities among taxpayers with the same total amount of taxable income over a number of years. To alleviate this problem, Congress enacted the Net Operating Loss (NOL) provision.

The NOL provision is primarily designed to provide relief for trade or business losses. Generally, only losses from the operation of a trade or business and casualty and theft losses can generate a net operating loss. Thus, individual taxpayers with only wages, itemized deductions (except casualty losses), and personal exemptions (although currently suspended) cannot generate a net operating loss.

The tax law is designed to permit individuals to deduct business NOLs and prevent the deductions of nonbusiness NOLs. Thus, the NOL computation for individual taxpayers requires the categorization of items of income, deductions, gains, and losses as either business or nonbusiness related. The NOL is not simply the total taxable loss shown at the bottom of page 1 of Form 1040. In general, when calculating a current net operating loss, the following tax items should be considered:

- No personal or dependency exemptions (exemptions are suspended after 2017)
- No deduction for an NOL from a different year
- Capital losses in excess of capital gains are not allowed
- "Nonbusiness" capital losses (those arising outside of a trade or business, or employment) can only be used against "nonbusiness" capital gains. Excess capital losses cannot increase the NOL
- "Business" capital losses can only be used against "business" capital gains, except that they can be used to offset a net nonbusiness capital gain if one exists
- "Nonbusiness" deductions (e.g., charitable donations, deductible medical expenses, mortgage interest, pre-2019 alimony, etc.) can only be used against "nonbusiness" income (interest, dividends, etc.). However, if nonbusiness capital gains exceed nonbusiness capital losses (see above), "excess" nonbusiness deductions can be offset against these gains. (Note that casualty losses are treated as "business deductions" for NOL purposes.)

Self-Study Problem 4.8 Part A

SCHEDULE E
(Form 1040)

Department of the Treasury
Internal Revenue Service

Supplemental Income and Loss
(From rental real estate, royalties, partnerships, S corporations, estates, trusts, REMICs, etc.)
Attach to Form 1040, 1040-SR, 1040-NR, or 1041.
Go to www.irs.gov/ScheduleE for instructions and the latest information.

OMB No. 1545-0074

2024

Attachment Sequence No. **13**

Name(s) shown on return | Your social security number

Part I — Income or Loss From Rental Real Estate and Royalties

Note: If you are in the business of renting personal property, use **Schedule C**. See instructions. If you are an individual, report farm rental income or loss from **Form 4835** on page 2, line 40.

A Did you make any payments in 2024 that would require you to file Form(s) 1099? See instructions ☐ Yes ☐ No
B If "Yes," did you or will you file required Form(s) 1099? ☐ Yes ☐ No

1a Physical address of each property (street, city, state, ZIP code)
A
B
C

1b	Type of Property (from list below)	2 For each rental real estate property listed above, report the number of fair rental and personal use days. Check the QJV box only if you meet the requirements to file as a qualified joint venture. See instructions.		Fair Rental Days	Personal Use Days	QJV
A			A			☐
B			B			☐
C			C			☐

Type of Property:
1 Single Family Residence 3 Vacation/Short-Term Rental 5 Land   7 Self-Rental
2 Multi-Family Residence   4 Commercial   6 Royalties   8 Other (describe) _____

			Properties:		
			A	B	C
Income:					
3	Rents received	3			
4	Royalties received	4			
Expenses:					
5	Advertising	5			
6	Auto and travel (see instructions)	6			
7	Cleaning and maintenance	7			
8	Commissions	8			
9	Insurance	9			
10	Legal and other professional fees	10			
11	Management fees	11			
12	Mortgage interest paid to banks, etc. (see instructions)	12			
13	Other interest	13			
14	Repairs	14			
15	Supplies	15			
16	Taxes	16			
17	Utilities	17			
18	Depreciation expense or depletion	18			
19	Other (list) _____	19			
20	Total expenses. Add lines 5 through 19	20			
21	Subtract line 20 from line 3 (rents) and/or 4 (royalties). If result is a (loss), see instructions to find out if you must file **Form 6198**	21			
22	Deductible rental real estate loss after limitation, if any, on **Form 8582** (see instructions)	22	( )	( )	( )

23a	Total of all amounts reported on line 3 for all rental properties	23a	
b	Total of all amounts reported on line 4 for all royalty properties	23b	
c	Total of all amounts reported on line 12 for all properties	23c	
d	Total of all amounts reported on line 18 for all properties	23d	
e	Total of all amounts reported on line 20 for all properties	23e	
24	**Income.** Add positive amounts shown on line 21. **Do not** include any losses	24	
25	**Losses.** Add royalty losses from line 21 and rental real estate losses from line 22. Enter total losses here	25	( )
26	**Total rental real estate and royalty income or (loss).** Combine lines 24 and 25. Enter the result here. If Parts II, III, and IV, and line 40 on page 2 do not apply to you, also enter this amount on Schedule 1 (Form 1040), line 5. Otherwise, include this amount in the total on line 41 on page 2	26	

For Paperwork Reduction Act Notice, see the separate instructions. Cat. No. 11344L   Schedule E (Form 1040) 2024

Schedule E (Form 1040) 2024 Attachment Sequence No. **13** Page **2**

Name(s) shown on return. Do not enter name and social security number if shown on other side. Your social security number

Caution: The IRS compares amounts reported on your tax return with amounts shown on Schedule(s) K-1.

Part II — Income or Loss From Partnerships and S Corporations

Note: If you report a loss, receive a distribution, dispose of stock, or receive a loan repayment from an S corporation, you **must** check the box in column (e) on line 28 and attach the required basis computation. If you report a loss from an at-risk activity for which **any** amount is **not** at risk, you **must** check the box in column (f) on line 28 and attach **Form 6198**. See instructions.

27 Are you reporting any loss not allowed in a prior year due to the at-risk or basis limitations, a prior year unallowed loss from a passive activity (if that loss was not reported on Form 8582), or unreimbursed partnership expenses? If you answered "Yes," see instructions before completing this section . . . . ☐ Yes ☐ No

28

	(a) Name	(b) Enter **P** for partnership; **S** for S corporation	(c) Check if foreign partnership	(d) Employer identification number	(e) Check if basis computation is required	(f) Check if any amount is not at risk
A			☐		☐	☐
B			☐		☐	☐
C			☐		☐	☐
D			☐		☐	☐

	Passive Income and Loss		Nonpassive Income and Loss		
	(g) Passive loss allowed (attach **Form 8582** if required)	(h) Passive income from **Schedule K-1**	(i) Nonpassive loss allowed (see **Schedule K-1**)	(j) Section 179 expense deduction from **Form 4562**	(k) Nonpassive income from **Schedule K-1**
A					
B					
C					
D					

29a Totals
  b Totals

30 Add columns (h) and (k) of line 29a 30
31 Add columns (g), (i), and (j) of line 29b . . . . 31 ( )
32 **Total partnership and S corporation income or (loss).** Combine lines 30 and 31 32

Part III — Income or Loss From Estates and Trusts

33

	(a) Name	(b) Employer identification number
A		
B		

	Passive Income and Loss		Nonpassive Income and Loss	
	(c) Passive deduction or loss allowed (attach **Form 8582** if required)	(d) Passive income from **Schedule K-1**	(e) Deduction or loss from **Schedule K-1**	(f) Other income from **Schedule K-1**
A				
B				

34a Totals
  b Totals

35 Add columns (d) and (f) of line 34a 35
36 Add columns (c) and (e) of line 34b . . . . 36 ( )
37 **Total estate and trust income or (loss).** Combine lines 35 and 36 37

Part IV — Income or Loss From Real Estate Mortgage Investment Conduits (REMICs) — Residual Holder

38

	(a) Name	(b) Employer identification number	(c) Excess inclusion from **Schedules Q,** line 2c (see instructions)	(d) Taxable income (net loss) from **Schedules Q,** line 1b	(e) Income from **Schedules Q,** line 3b

39 Combine columns (d) and (e) only. Enter the result here and include in the total on line 41 below . 39

Part V — Summary

40 Net farm rental income or (loss) from **Form 4835.** Also, complete line 42 below 40
41 **Total income or (loss).** Combine lines 26, 32, 37, 39, and 40. Enter the result here and on Schedule 1 (Form 1040), line 5 41
42 **Reconciliation of farming and fishing income.** Enter your **gross** farming and fishing income reported on Form 4835, line 7; Schedule K-1 (Form 1065), box 14, code B; Schedule K-1 (Form 1120-S), box 17, code AN; and Schedule K-1 (Form 1041), box 14, code F. See instructions . 42
43 **Reconciliation for real estate professionals.** If you were a real estate professional (see instructions), enter the net income or (loss) you reported anywhere on Form 1040, Form 1040-SR, or Form 1040-NR from all rental real estate activities in which you materially participated under the passive activity loss rules 43

Schedule E (Form 1040) 2024

Self-Study Problem 4.8 Part A

Form 8582
Department of the Treasury
Internal Revenue Service

Passive Activity Loss Limitations
See separate instructions.
Attach to Form 1040, 1040-SR, or 1041.
Go to www.irs.gov/Form8582 for instructions and the latest information.

OMB No. 1545-1008

2024
Attachment Sequence No. **858**

Name(s) shown on return | Identifying number

Part I — 2024 Passive Activity Loss
Caution: Complete Parts IV and V before completing Part I.

Rental Real Estate Activities With Active Participation (For the definition of active participation, see *Special Allowance for Rental Real Estate Activities* in the instructions.)

1a	Activities with net income (enter the amount from Part IV, column (a))	1a
b	Activities with net loss (enter the amount from Part IV, column (b))	1b ( )
c	Prior years' unallowed losses (enter the amount from Part IV, column (c))	1c ( )
d	Combine lines 1a, 1b, and 1c	1d

All Other Passive Activities

2a	Activities with net income (enter the amount from Part V, column (a))	2a
b	Activities with net loss (enter the amount from Part V, column (b))	2b ( )
c	Prior years' unallowed losses (enter the amount from Part V, column (c))	2c ( )
d	Combine lines 2a, 2b, and 2c	2d

3   Combine lines 1d and 2d and subtract any prior year unallowed CRD. See instructions. If this line is zero or more, stop here and include this form with your return; all losses are allowed, including any prior year unallowed losses entered on line 1c or 2c. Report the losses on the forms and schedules normally used **3**

If line 3 is a loss and: • Line 1d is a loss, go to Part II.
 • Line 2d is a loss (and line 1d is zero or more), skip Part II and go to line 10.

Caution: If your filing status is married filing separately and you lived with your spouse at any time during the year, **do not** complete Part II. Instead, go to line 10.

Part II — Special Allowance for Rental Real Estate Activities With Active Participation
Note: Enter all numbers in Part II as positive amounts. See instructions for an example.

4	Enter the **smaller** of the loss on line 1d or the loss on line 3	4
5	Enter $150,000. If married filing separately, see instructions	5
6	Enter modified adjusted gross income, but not less than zero. See instructions	6

Note: If line 6 is greater than or equal to line 5, skip lines 7 and 8 and enter -0- on line 9. Otherwise, go to line 7.

7	Subtract line 6 from line 5	7
8	Multiply line 7 by 50% (0.50). **Do not** enter more than $25,000. If married filing separately, see instructions	8
9	Enter the **smaller** of line 4 or line 8. If line 3 includes any CRD, see instructions	9

Part III — Total Losses Allowed

10	Add the income, if any, on lines 1a and 2a and enter the total	10
11	**Total losses allowed from all passive activities for 2024.** Add lines 9 and 10. See instructions to find out how to report the losses on your tax return	11

Part IV — Complete This Part Before Part I, Lines 1a, 1b, and 1c. See instructions.

Name of activity	Current year		Prior years	Overall gain or loss	
	(a) Net income (line 1a)	**(b)** Net loss (line 1b)	**(c)** Unallowed loss (line 1c)	**(d)** Gain	**(e)** Loss
Total. Enter on Part I, lines 1a, 1b, and 1c					

For Paperwork Reduction Act Notice, see instructions.   Cat. No. 63704F   Form **8582** (2024)

Form 8582 (2024) Page **2**

Part V — Complete This Part Before Part I, Lines 2a, 2b, and 2c. See instructions.

Name of activity	Current year		Prior years	Overall gain or loss	
	(a) Net income (line 2a)	**(b)** Net loss (line 2b)	**(c)** Unallowed loss (line 2c)	**(d)** Gain	**(e)** Loss
Total. Enter on Part I, lines 2a, 2b, and 2c ▶					

Part VI — Use This Part if an Amount Is Shown on Part II, Line 9. See instructions.

Name of activity	Form or schedule and line number to be reported on (see instructions)	**(a)** Loss	**(b)** Ratio	**(c)** Special allowance	**(d)** Subtract column (c) from column (a).
Total ▶			1.00		

Part VII — Allocation of Unallowed Losses. See instructions.

Name of activity	Form or schedule and line number to be reported on (see instructions)	**(a)** Loss	**(b)** Ratio	**(c)** Unallowed loss
Total ▶			1.00	

Part VIII — Allowed Losses. See instructions.

Name of activity	Form or schedule and line number to be reported on (see instructions)	**(a)** Loss	**(b)** Unallowed loss	**(c)** Allowed loss
Total ▶				

Form **8582** (2024)

Example Yujian, a single taxpayer, has completed her 2024 Schedule C and her net loss is $70,000. She also has wages of $45,000 and interest income from her savings of $500. Her business sold property during the year and generated a $3,000 ordinary gain and a separate $5,000 long-term capital gain. Yujian also had several capital gains and losses from the sale of stock investments. Her net results are a $17,000 short-term capital gain and a $6,000 long-term capital loss from these stock sales. Yujian itemizes her deductions and her Schedule A reports the following:

Taxes paid	$ 8,500
Mortgage interest	6,000
Charitable gifts	500
Casualty loss (federal disaster area loss)	2,500
Total itemized deductions	$ 17,500

Yujian calculates her taxable income as follows:

Wages	$ 45,000
Interest income	500
Business loss	(70,000)
Capital gains[1]	16,000
Other gains	3,000
Total income (loss) and AGI	(5,500)
Itemized deductions	(17,500)
Taxable income (loss)	$(23,000)

To compute Yujian's NOL, we need to categorize business and nonbusiness items:

	Business	Nonbusiness
Wages	$ 45,000	$ —
Interest income	—	500
Business loss	(70,000)	—
Capital gains	5,000	11,000
Other gains	3,000	—
Itemized deductions	(2,500)	(15,000)
Total loss	$(19,500)	$ (3,500)

Using the above information, we can modify taxable income to compute the NOL.

Step 1: Excess nonbusiness capital losses cannot exceed nonbusiness capital gains.

Since the $6,000 nonbusiness capital losses do not exceed $17,000 of nonbusiness capital gains, no adjustment is required. In addition, we can use the $11,000 "excess" nonbusiness capital gain to absorb any nonbusiness deductions in the next step.

Step 2: Nonbusiness deductions cannot exceed nonbusiness income.

Nonbusiness deductions $15,000 − Nonbusiness income $500 = Net nonbusiness deductions $14,500

However, as previously mentioned, net nonbusiness deductions can also offset any net nonbusiness capital gains. Thus, $11,000 of the nonbusiness

---

[1] $1,000 long-term capital loss ($5,000 long-term capital gain from business less $6,000 long-term capital loss from stocks) netted against $17,000 short-term capital gain from stocks.

deductions can be used; however, the remaining $3,500 ($14,500 − $11,000) are not deductible and must be added back to the taxable loss $(23,000) + $3,500 = $(19,500).

Step 3: The business capital (casualty) loss of $2,500 can only be offset by business capital gains of $5,000. There is no excess loss, and thus, no adjustment is needed.

The calculated NOL of $19,500 agrees to the business category total loss of $19,500 above which is consistent with the NOL representing only business losses.

Yujian may carryforward the NOL of $19,500 to offset future income. ♦

4-9a NOL Carryforward and Carryback

The rules related to NOLs have changed three times in recent years and with each change, NOLs are treated slightly differently. The three periods are: (1) the pre-2018 period, (2) the 2018–2020 period (due to COVID-19 provisions), and (3) the post-2020 period. Since the NOLs from the COVID-19 period are almost certainly either exhausted or are being treated as post-2020 NOLs, loss carryforwards from that period will not be covered in this textbook.

In the pre-2018 period, NOLs were eligible to be carried back two years and forward for 20 years. Any NOL carryforward or carryback could be used to offset 100 percent of the income generated in the carryback or carryforward period. NOLs generated in this period can continue to be utilized in the same manner.

Example Henri generated a loss in 2017 of $45,000. His business income was $2,000 and $5,000 in 2015 and 2016, respectively. Henri will first carryback the NOL to offset the income generated in 2015 and 2016. The remaining NOL of $38,000 can be carried forward for 20 years and offset any income generated in those years. ♦

The TCJA of 2017 changed the treatment of NOLs to permit only the indefinite carryforward of NOLs generated after 2017. In addition, the use of an NOL generated after December 31, 2017, is limited to 80 percent of the current year's taxable income (without regard to the NOL deduction) when used. The same post-2017 NOL rules are effective after 2020. NOLs generated in 2021 and after may only be carried forward and any post-2017 NOLs are limited to 80 percent.

Example Lionel generated an NOL in 2023 of $14,000. He is unable to carry the NOL back and must carry it forward only. In 2024, Lionel generates $15,000 of business income. Lionel may only offset up to 80 percent or $12,000 of the 2024 income ($15,000 × 80%). The remaining $2,000 NOL can be carried forward indefinitely. ♦

Previously, individual taxpayer NOLs were generally filed on Schedule A of Form 1045. The IRS has released a new Form 172 that appears to be designed to capture individual NOLs starting for tax year 2024. The structure of Form 172 is very much like the previous used Schedule A of Form 1045.

4-9b Excess Business Loss Limitation

To reduce the potential for large business losses being claimed in a single year, starting in 2018, the tax law places an annual limitation on noncorporate business losses for taxpayers. After adjusting for inflation, the 2024 limits were set to be $610,000 for married filing jointly and $305,000 for all other returns. The business loss limitation is in place through the end of 2028.

4-9 Net Operating Losses

Example In 2024, Bettina Graziani is a single taxpayer with wages of $20,000, a sole proprietorship business with income of $5,000, investment capital losses of $6,000, and nonpassive partnership losses of $317,000. Bettina had no other capital gains. Bettina's excess business loss is $7,000 as calculated on Form 461 presented below. Should Bettina have an NOL in 2024, this amount will become part of Bettina's NOL and subject to the NOL limitation and carryforward rules. ♦

Form **461**	**Limitation on Business Losses**	OMB No. 1545-2283
Department of the Treasury Internal Revenue Service	Attach to your tax return. Go to www.irs.gov/Form461 for instructions and the latest information.	**2024** Attachment Sequence No. **64**

Name(s) shown on return: Bettina Graziani

Identifying number:

Part I — Total Income/Loss Items
See instructions if you are filing a tax return other than Form 1040 or 1040-SR.

Line	Description		Amount
1	Reserved for future use	1	
2	Enter amount from Schedule 1 (Form 1040), line 3	2	5,000
3	Enter amount from Form 1040 or 1040-SR, line 7. See instructions	3	(3,000)
4	Enter amount from Schedule 1 (Form 1040), line 4	4	
5	Enter amount from Schedule 1 (Form 1040), line 5	5	(317,000)
6	Enter amount from Schedule 1 (Form 1040), line 6	6	
7	Reserved for future use	7	
8	Enter other income, gain, or losses from a trade or business not reported on lines 1 through 7	8	
9	Combine lines 1 through 8	9	(315,000)

Part II — Adjustment for Amounts Not Attributable to Trade or Business
See instructions if you are filing a tax return other than Form 1040 or 1040-SR.

Line	Description		Amount
10	Enter any income or gain reported on lines 1 through 8 that is not attributable to a trade or business	10	
11	Enter any losses or deductions reported on lines 1 through 8 that are not attributable to a trade or business. See instructions	11	3,000
12	Subtract line 11 from line 10	12	(3,000)

Part III — Limitation on Losses

Line	Description		Amount
13	If line 12 is a negative number, enter it here as a positive number. If line 12 is a positive number, enter it here as a negative number	13	3,000
14	Add lines 9 and 13	14	(312,000)
15	Enter $305,000 (or $610,000 if married filing jointly)	15	305,000
16	Add lines 14 and 15. If less than zero, enter the amount from line 16 as a positive number on Schedule 1 (Form 1040), line 8p. See instructions if you are filing a tax return other than a Form 1040 or 1040-SR. If zero or greater, do not attach this form to your tax return	16	(7,000)

For Privacy Act and Paperwork Reduction Act Notice, see the separate instructions. Cat. No. 16654I Form **461** (2024)

> **ProConnect™ Tax TIP**
>
> When a taxpayer creates a net operating loss (NOL), no specific entry is required by the preparer. Instead, supplemental schedules that track the NOL will be created automatically by the software.

Self-Study Problem 4.9
Refer to Appendix E for Solutions to Self-Study Problems

A. Silja Buoy is a single taxpayer. Her 2024 income tax return is almost complete and includes the following information:

Wages of $7,000
Standard deduction of $14,600
Nonbusiness short-term capital gains of $3,000
Nonbusiness long-term capital losses of $8,000
Business capital gains of $1,000
Nonbusiness interest income $200
Business loss $18,000

Using the first page of Form 172 on Page 4-45, compute Silja's NOL carryforward (if any) into 2024.

B. Using the NOL carryforward from Part A, if Silja has taxable income of $12,000 in 2025, how much NOL will she carryforward to 2026?

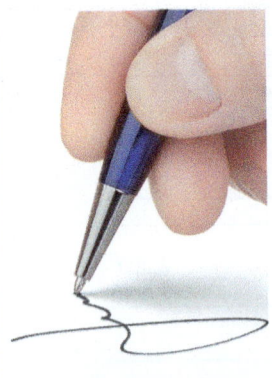

Would You Sign This Tax Return?

Mark (age 44) and Mary (age 41) Mower are your tax clients. They have two children, Matthew (age 20) and Mindy (age 17), who live at home. Mindy is a senior in high school and Matthew commutes to a local college where he is studying soil management. Mark owns and operates a successful lawn maintenance and landscaping business. He has six employees and three pick-up trucks used for transportation to the job sites. The business has a credit card in its name for use by the employees and Mark, who fills the trucks with gas almost daily. Mark gave a business credit card to Mary, Matthew, and Mindy and told them to use it to buy gas for their automobiles used for shopping, going to school, and short trips. In the current year, his wife and children put $5,210 of gasoline in their automobiles using the business credit card. Mark is adamant that the $5,210 be deducted on his Schedule C. He feels the amount is small compared to the business gas purchases of approximately $28,000. Mark says the amounts charged are spread throughout the credit card statements and would be very difficult for the IRS to detect in an audit. Would you sign the Paid Preparer's declaration (refer to example above) on this return? Why or why not?

4-10 Self-Employment Tax

Learning Objective 4.10
Calculate and report the self-employment tax (both Social Security and Medicare portions) for self-employed taxpayers.

The Federal Insurance Contributions Act (FICA) imposes Social Security (Old Age, Survivors, and Disability Insurance (OASDI)) and Medicare taxes. As discussed in Chapter 9, employees and their employers are both required to pay FICA taxes. Employers withhold a specified percentage of each employee's wages up to a maximum base amount, match the amount withheld with an equal amount, and pay the total to the IRS.

Self-Study Problem 4.9, Part A

Form 172 (January 2025)
Department of the Treasury
Internal Revenue Service

Net Operating Losses (NOLs)
For Individuals, Estates, and Trusts.
Go to www.irs.gov/Form172 for instructions and the latest information.

OMB No. 1545-0074

For calendar year _____, or other tax year beginning _____ and ending _____

Name(s) shown on return

Social security or employer identification number

Address (number and street). If you have a P.O. box, see instructions.   Apt. or suite no.

Spouse's social security number (SSN)

City, town, or post office. If you have a foreign address, also complete spaces below.   State   ZIP code

Daytime phone number

Foreign country name   Foreign province/county   Foreign postal code

Part I — NOL (see instructions)

1. For individuals, subtract your standard deduction or itemized deductions from your adjusted gross income (AGI) and enter it here. For estates and trusts, enter taxable income increased by the total of the charitable deduction, income distribution deduction, and exemption amount **1**
2. Nonbusiness capital losses before limitation. Enter as a positive number . . **2**
3. Nonbusiness capital gains (without regard to any section 1202 exclusion) . . **3**
4. If line 2 is more than line 3, enter the difference. Otherwise, enter -0- . . . **4**
5. If line 3 is more than line 2, enter the difference. Otherwise, enter -0- . . . **5**
6. Nonbusiness deductions (see instructions). Enter as a positive number . . **6**
7. Nonbusiness income other than capital gains (see instructions) . . . **7**
8. Add lines 5 and 7 . . . . **8**
9. If line 6 is more than line 8, enter the difference. Otherwise, enter -0- . . . **9**
10. If line 8 is more than line 6, enter the difference. Otherwise, enter -0-. **But don't enter more than line 5** . . **10**
11. Business capital losses before limitation. Enter as a positive number . . . **11**
12. Business capital gains (without regard to any section 1202 exclusion) . . **12**
13. Add lines 10 and 12 . . . . **13**
14. Subtract line 13 from line 11. If zero or less, enter -0- **14**
15. Add lines 4 and 14 . . . . **15**
16. Enter, if any, the combined net short-term and long-term capital loss from your Schedule D (Form 1040). Estates and trusts, enter, if any, the total net short-term and long-term loss from Schedule D (Form 1041). Enter as a positive number. If you don't have a loss on that line (and don't have a section 1202 exclusion), skip lines 16 through 21 and enter on line 22 the amount from line 15 . . . . **16**
17. Section 1202 exclusion. Enter as a positive number **17**
18. Subtract line 17 from line 16. If zero or less, enter -0- **18**
19. If line 16 is a loss, enter, as a positive number, the smaller of:
    - The loss on line 16; or
    - $3,000 (If filing Form 1040, $1,500 when married filing separately) . . . **19**
20. If line 18 is more than line 19, enter the difference. Otherwise, enter -0- . . **20**
21. If line 19 is more than line 18, enter the difference. Otherwise, enter -0- . . **21**
22. Subtract line 20 from line 15. If zero or less, enter -0- **22**
23. NOL deduction for losses from other years. Enter as a positive number . . **23**
24. **NOL.** Combine lines 1, 9, 17, and 21 through 23. If the result is less than zero, enter it here. If the result is zero or more, you don't have an NOL **24**

For Paperwork Reduction Act Notice, see the instructions.   Cat. No. 16545W   Form **172** (1-2025)

Self-employed individuals pay self-employment taxes instead of FICA taxes. Since these individuals have no employers, the entire tax is paid by self-employed individuals. Like the FICA taxes to which employees and their employers are subject, the self-employment tax also consists of two parts, Social Security and Medicare. The maximum base amount of earnings subject to the Social Security portion of the self-employment tax is $168,600 in 2024. All earnings are subject to the Medicare portion of the self-employment tax. The Social Security tax rate is 12.4 percent and the Medicare tax rate is 2.9 percent. The self-employment tax rates and the maximum base amounts for five years are illustrated in Table 4.4:

Table 4.4 Self-Employment Tax Maximum Base Amounts

Year	Maximum $ Base for 12.4%	Maximum $ Base for 2.90%*
2020	137,700	Unlimited
2021	142,800	Unlimited
2022	147,000	Unlimited
2023	160,200	Unlimited
2024	168,600	Unlimited

*A 0.9 percent additional Medicare tax on self-employment income over $250,000 for married filing jointly filing status, $200,000 for single, head of household and surviving spouse, and $125,000 for married filing separately. Refer to Chapter 6 for more information.

If a self-employed individual also receives wages subject to FICA taxes during a tax year, the Social Security tax maximum base amount for self-employment taxes is reduced by the amount of wages. Therefore, the total amount of earnings subject to the Social Security tax portion of both FICA and self-employment tax for 2024 cannot exceed $168,600.

The self-employment tax is imposed on net earnings of $400 or more from self-employment. Net earnings from self-employment include gross income from a trade or business less trade or business deductions, the distributive share of nonpassive partnership business income, and net income earned as an independent contractor. Gains and losses from property transactions, except inventory transactions, and other unearned income are not considered self-employment income. In arriving at net earnings for purposes of computing the self-employment tax, self-employed taxpayers are allowed a deduction for AGI of one-half of the otherwise applicable self-employment tax. A shortcut to arriving at the self-employment income subject to self-employment tax is to multiply the net earnings from self-employment by 92.35 percent. This shortcut is used on Schedule SE as illustrated below.

Example Norman is a self-employed accountant in 2024. From his practice, Norman earns $161,001, and has wages subject to FICA from a part-time job of $21,000. Norman's self-employment tax is calculated as follows:

Step 1:

Net earnings from self-employment, before the self-employment tax deduction	$161,001
	× 92.35%
Tentative net earnings from self-employment after deduction for self-employment tax	$148,684

Step 2:

	Social Security	Medicare
Maximum base for 2024	$168,600	Unlimited
Less: FICA wages	(21,000)	Not Applicable
Maximum self-employment tax base	$147,600	Unlimited
Lesser of net earnings from self-employment after deduction for self-employment tax or maximum base	$147,600	$148,684
Self-employment tax rate	12.4%	2.9%
Self-employment tax for 2024	$ 18,302	$ 4,312

Norman's total self-employment tax for 2024 is $22,614 ($18,302 + $4,312). On his 2024 income tax return, Norman will report net earnings from self-employment of $161,001, a deduction for adjusted gross income of $11,307 (50% × $22,614), and a self-employment tax liability of $22,614. ♦

The calculation of self-employment tax is reported on page 1 of Schedule SE, Part I, and must be included with a taxpayer's Form 1040.

Self-Study Problem 4.10

Refer to Appendix E for Solutions to Self-Study Problems

Joanne Plummer is self-employed in 2024. Her Schedule C shows the following:

28	Total expenses before expenses for business use of home. Add lines 8 through 27b	28	35,670
29	Tentative profit or (loss). Subtract line 28 from line 7	29	172,000
30	Expenses for business use of your home. Do not report these expenses elsewhere. Attach Form 8829 unless using the simplified method. See instructions. **Simplified method filers only:** Enter the total square footage of (a) your home: _____ and (b) the part of your home used for business: _____ . Use the Simplified Method Worksheet in the instructions to figure the amount to enter on line 30	30	
31	**Net profit or (loss).** Subtract line 30 from line 29. • If a profit, enter on both **Schedule 1 (Form 1040), line 3**, and on **Schedule SE, line 2.** (If you checked the box on line 1, see instructions.) Estates and trusts, enter on **Form 1041, line 3.** • If a loss, you **must** go to line 32.	31	172,000

Joanne also has a part-time job and received the following Form W-2:

1 Wages, tips, other compensation	2 Federal income tax withheld
10,400.00	998.00
3 Social security wages	4 Social security tax withheld
10,400.00	644.80
5 Medicare wages and tips	6 Medicare tax withheld
10,400.00	150.80
7 Social security tips	8 Allocated tips

Joanne also received taxable dividends of $1,110 during the year and has a capital gain on the sale of stock of $9,100. Calculate Joanne's self-employment tax using Schedule SE of Form 1040 on Page 4-48.

Self-Study Problem 4.10

SCHEDULE SE
(Form 1040)

Department of the Treasury
Internal Revenue Service

Self-Employment Tax

Attach to Form 1040, 1040-SR, 1040-SS, or 1040-NR.
Go to www.irs.gov/ScheduleSE for instructions and the latest information.

OMB No. 1545-0074

2024

Attachment Sequence No. **17**

Name of person with self-employment income (as shown on Form 1040, 1040-SR, 1040-SS, or 1040-NR) | Social security number of person with **self-employment** income

Part I Self-Employment Tax

Note: If your only income subject to self-employment tax is **church employee income**, see instructions for how to report your income and the definition of church employee income.

A If you are a minister, member of a religious order, or Christian Science practitioner **and** you filed Form 4361, but you had $400 or more of **other** net earnings from self-employment, check here and continue with Part I . . . . ☐

Skip lines 1a and 1b if you use the farm optional method in Part II. See instructions.

1a Net farm profit or (loss) from Schedule F, line 34, and farm partnerships, Schedule K-1 (Form 1065), box 14, code A **1a**

b If you received social security retirement or disability benefits, enter the amount of Conservation Reserve Program payments included on Schedule F, line 4b, or listed on Schedule K-1 (Form 1065), box 20, code AQ **1b** (   )

Skip line 2 if you use the nonfarm optional method in Part II. See instructions.

2 Net profit or (loss) from Schedule C, line 31; and Schedule K-1 (Form 1065), box 14, code A (other than farming). See instructions for other income to report or if you are a minister or member of a religious order **2**

3 Combine lines 1a, 1b, and 2 . . . . **3**

4a If line 3 is more than zero, multiply line 3 by 92.35% (0.9235). Otherwise, enter amount from line 3 . **4a**
Note: If line 4a is less than $400 due to Conservation Reserve Program payments on line 1b, see instructions.

b If you elect one or both of the optional methods, enter the total of lines 15 and 17 here **4b**

c Combine lines 4a and 4b. If less than $400, **stop**; you don't owe self-employment tax. **Exception:** If less than $400 and you had **church employee income**, enter -0- and continue **4c**

5a Enter your **church employee income** from Form W-2. See instructions for definition of church employee income **5a**

b Multiply line 5a by 92.35% (0.9235). If less than $100, enter -0- **5b**

6 Add lines 4c and 5b **6**

7 Maximum amount of combined wages and self-employment earnings subject to social security tax or the 6.2% portion of the 7.65% railroad retirement (tier 1) tax for 2024 . . . . **7** | 168,600

8a Total social security wages and tips (total of boxes 3 and 7 on Form(s) W-2) and railroad retirement (tier 1) compensation. If $168,600 or more, skip lines 8b through 10, and go to line 11 . . . . **8a**

b Unreported tips subject to social security tax from Form 4137, line 10 . . . **8b**

c Wages subject to social security tax from Form 8919, line 10 . . . . . . **8c**

d Add lines 8a, 8b, and 8c **8d**

9 Subtract line 8d from line 7. If zero or less, enter -0- here and on line 10 and go to line 11 . . . . **9**

10 Multiply the **smaller** of line 6 or line 9 by 12.4% (0.124) **10**

11 Multiply line 6 by 2.9% (0.029) **11**

12 Self-employment tax. Add lines 10 and 11. Enter here and on **Schedule 2 (Form 1040), line 4**, or Form 1040-SS, Part I, line 3 . . . . **12**

13 Deduction for one-half of self-employment tax.
Multiply line 12 by 50% (0.50). Enter here and on **Schedule 1 (Form 1040), line 15** **13**

For Paperwork Reduction Act Notice, see your tax return instructions.   Cat. No. 11358Z   Schedule SE (Form 1040) 2024

4-11 Qualified Business Income (QBI) Deduction

4.11 Learning Objective
Compute the qualified business income (QBI) deduction.

The Qualified Business Income (QBI) deduction was introduced in 2018 and applies to tax years through 2025. The QBI deduction is a deduction for individual taxpayers reporting business income from a passthrough entity such as a sole proprietorship, partnership, limited liability company, or S corporation. It is also referred to as the Section 199A deduction, the passthrough deduction, or the QBI deduction. The QBI deduction requires no additional outlay or investment of funds but is simply granted as a function of legislative grace. A discussion of the QBI deduction related specifically to partnerships and S corporations is covered in Chapters 10 and 11, respectively.

The QBI deduction is available to individual taxpayers as a "below the line" deduction (after adjusted gross income) and is also available to taxpayers who take the standard deduction. The deduction is generally 20 percent of a taxpayer's qualified business income (QBI) from a partnership (including LLC if so treated), S corporation, or sole proprietorship.

4-11a Definition of Qualified Business Income

Qualified business income for a tax year is the net amount of qualified items of income, gain, deduction, and loss relating to any qualified trade or business of the taxpayer in the United States (foreign income is not considered). QBI excludes the following:

- Short-term capital gain, short-term capital loss, long-term capital gain, or long-term capital loss
- Dividend income
- Interest income
- Commodity transaction income or foreign currency gain or loss
- Any item of income, gain, deduction, or loss relating to certain notional principal contracts
- Amounts received from an annuity that is not received in connection with the trade or business
- Any item of deduction or loss properly allocable to an amount described in any of the preceding items in this list (e.g., interest expense associated with investment income)

Reasonable employee compensation paid to the taxpayer by the qualified trade or business and guaranteed payments to a partner are not QBI, and therefore, the QBI deduction is not applicable to such income. For a sole proprietor, QBI is often the net profit reported on line 31 less any for AGI deductions associated with the business such as one-half of self-employment taxes. As presented in Chapter 2, certain qualified dividends from real estate investment trusts (REITs) are also treated as QBI income.

Example Princess is a single taxpayer and operates a small business as a sole proprietor. In 2024, her business generates $80,000 of gross business income, $50,000 of business expenses, $3,000 of interest income, and a $2,000 capital gain. Her deduction for one-half of self-employment taxes is $2,120. Princess' QBI is $27,880 ($80,000 − $50,000 − $2,120). The interest and capital gains are excluded from QBI. ♦

With respect to the QBI deduction, the term "*qualified* trade or business" means any trade or business other than a specified service trade or business, or the trade or business of performing services as an employee. Unfortunately, "trade or business" is not defined in the tax law. The regulations interpret trade or business to be consistent with the same phrase in Internal Revenue Code Section 162 related to the deduction of trade or business expenses. This does not provide an exceptional level of guidance for many businesses, but certainly hobby activities (Chapter 3) would not qualify. The tax law provides a safe-harbor under which income from rental real estate (even if treated as passive) can qualify as qualified business income. The requirements are:

1. 250 hours or more are spent by the taxpayer with respect to the rental activity
2. Contemporaneous records of the time spent are maintained
3. Separate books and records for the rental activity are maintained

Note that 250 hours per year amounts to an average of over 20 hours per month. Time spent related to the rental activity on advertising, negotiating with tenants, verifying applications, daily operation, repair and maintenance, purchase of materials, and supervision of employees all count toward the required 250 hours. Time spent purchasing or financing the acquisition of the property and time spent traveling to and from the property do not generally qualify.

As presented in Chapter 2, certain dividends from REITs are treated as QBI income.

4-11b QBI Deduction Taxable Income Limitation

The QBI deduction is subject to a number of limitations and exceptions. A limitation that applies to all taxpayers is that the QBI deduction cannot exceed 20 percent of the taxpayer's taxable income (excluding net long-term capital gains and qualified dividend income).

Example Alice operates a small accounting business that generates $60,000 of qualified business income. She also operates a separate investment advising business that focuses on providing crypto-currency investment advice that lost $20,000. Both of Alice's businesses are sole proprietorships. Her pre-limitation QBI deduction is $8,000 [($60,000 − $20,000) × 20%]. Alice also earned $5,000 in net capital gains but had no other forms of income and elects the standard deduction. In 2024, Alice's taxable income subject to the 20-percent limit is $25,400 ($40,000 of business income less her standard deduction of $14,600; capital gains are excluded from this calculation). Her QBI deduction is limited to $5,080 ($25,400 × 20%). ♦

4-11c Wage Limitation

The two additional limitations on the QBI deduction are (1) the wage limitation and (2) the specified service business limitation. These limitations apply to taxpayers that have taxable income (*total* taxable income not just *business* income, including long-term capital gains or qualified dividends) above the threshold amounts, which in 2024 are $383,900 for married filing jointly and $191,950 for all other taxpayers. These threshold amounts are indexed for inflation each year. The limitations are computed before considering the QBI deduction.

For taxpayers with income below the thresholds, the QBI deduction is as described above. For taxpayers with taxable income above the threshold amounts, the two limitations apply and subject to a complex phase-out.

The wage limitation is the greater of:

- 50 percent of the allocable share of W-2 wages with respect to the business (the "wage limit") or
- 25 percent of the allocable share of W-2 wages with respect to the business plus 2.5 percent of the unadjusted basis of all qualified business property (the "wage and capital limit")

W-2 wages are defined as wages paid to employees (not independent contractors) including deferrals into Section 401(k) plans and the like. The term allocable share pertains to the allocation of wages similar to that associated with the allocation of partnership income (see further coverage of allocation of wages in Chapter 10). Because the tax law was designed to encourage investment in employees and business capital, the wage and capital limit includes a percentage of the unadjusted basis immediately after acquisition (UBIA) of business property.

Example Pat operates a sole proprietorship which generates $210,000 of qualified business income that includes the deduction for wages of $66,000 that Pat pays to employees. Pat's business has invested $20,000 in qualified business property. Pat has no other sources of income and files as a single taxpayer and elects the standard deduction. Pat's initial QBI deduction is $210,000 × 20% or $42,000 which is limited to 20 percent of Pat's taxable income [$195,400 ($210,000 − standard deduction of $14,600) × 20% = $39,080]. Furthermore, since Pat's income exceeds the $191,950 threshold, the wage limit applies. The wage limit is the greater of 50 percent of the wages ($66,000 × 50% = $33,000) or the wage and capital limit of 25 percent of the wages ($66,000 × 25% = $16,500) plus 2.5 percent of the unadjusted basis of qualified business property ($20,000 × 2.5% = $500) which totals $17,000. The greater of the two wage-limit amounts applies, and thus, Pat's QBI deduction is limited to $33,000. Pat's final taxable income will be $162,400 ($210,000 − $33,000 − $14,600). Recall that the wage limit applies if the taxpayer's taxable income *before* the QBI deduction exceeds the threshold. ♦

Qualified business property for purposes of the wage and capital limit is defined as tangible property subject to depreciation (i.e., not inventory or land) for which the depreciable period has not ended before the close of the taxable year, held by the business at year end, and used at any point during the year in the production of QBI. If the "depreciation period" for a property ended in any prior tax year, that property is not included in the calculation of tangible property. The depreciable period is defined as starting when the property was placed in service and ending on the later of (1) 10 years or (2) the last day in the last year of the property's regular depreciation.

Example Josh, a single taxpayer, operates a sole proprietorship. He qualifies for the QBI deduction and his taxable income subjects him to the wage and capital limitations. Josh has purchased and placed in service the following property (all of which is currently being used in 2024):

Year	5-year recovery period	39-year recovery period
2013	$20,000	$600,000
2014	0	0
2015	4,000	0
2016	0	0
2017	0	0
2018	0	0
2019	25,000	0
2020	0	0
2021	10,000	0
2022	2,000	0
2023	50,000	0
2024	13,000	0
Total	$124,000	$600,000

☐ Qualified business property still within recovery period

In determining qualified business property for purposes of the QBI wage limit in 2024, Josh's property must still be within the depreciable period which ends on the later of the last full year of the recovery period or ten years. The 2013–2019 five-year property is fully depreciated BUT only the property placed in service before 2015 is no longer qualified; thus, Josh has $104,000 of qualified five-year property. In spite of being placed in service more than ten years ago, all of the building in the 39-year category is qualified as it is still being depreciated. Josh's total qualified property under the wage and capital limit for the QBI deduction is $704,000 ($104,000 + $600,000). ♦

Recall that the wage limitation applies only if the taxpayer's taxable income exceeds the threshold amount ($383,900 for married filing jointly and $191,950 for all others). As is typical in the tax law, a taxpayer's opportunity to use the QBI deduction does not cease entirely if the threshold is exceeded. Instead, the QBI deduction is subject to a phase-out up to an excess of $100,000 for married filing jointly taxpayers and $50,000 for all others. First, the QBI deduction is computed as if no wage limitation applies. The next step is to compute the QBI deduction including the wage limitation. The excess of the QBI deduction with no limitation over the QBI deduction with limitation is known as the "excess amount." The excess amount is subject to a pro rata phase-out based on the taxpayer's income over the threshold amount.

Example Phil is a single taxpayer with a QBI-eligible small business and his taxable income as measured for the QBI deduction is $204,950, and thus, exceeds the $191,950 threshold. Phil's QBI is $150,000 and the business paid wages of $42,000 in 2024 and has qualified business property of $660,000.

Phil's QBI deduction with no limitation = $30,000 ($150,000 × 20%)
The wage limitation is $27,000, which is the greater of:

$21,000 ($42,000 wages × 50%) or

$27,000 [($42,000 × 25%) + ($660,000 × 2.5%)]

Phil's QBI deduction is limited to $27,000; however, Phil is not subject to the entire wage limitation as his income is not $50,000 or more over the threshold amount. Thus, the wage limitation is "phased-in."

Phil's taxable income for QBI deduction purposes	$204,950
Phil's threshold amount (single taxpayer)	191,950
Excess	$ 13,000
Excess divided by the phase-out range	$13,000/$50,000 = 26%

Thus Phil will lose 26 percent of his "excess amount" of $3,000 ($30,000 QBI deduction without limit less $27,000 QBI deduction with limit) or $780. Phil's QBI deduction is $29,220 ($30,000 − $780). ♦

To summarize thus far, the QBI deduction is 20 percent of qualified business income, which is the income of a business held in any form but the corporate form. QBI excludes forms of "portfolio" income such as interest, dividends, and gains. For taxpayers below the income thresholds ($383,900 for married filing joint returns, $191,950 for all other returns), there are no explicit limitations other than the taxable income limit. For those with taxable income above the thresholds, the QBI deduction is limited by the wage limitation and also by the specified service business limitation (which is covered in the following section).

4-11d Specified Service Business Limitation

For taxpayers with income in excess of the threshold, certain types of businesses are not eligible for the QBI deduction:

1. a taxpayer whose business is being an employee, and
2. a specified service trade or business.

A specified service trade or business is defined as any trade or business involving the performance of services in the fields of health, law, accounting, actuarial science, performing arts, consulting, athletics, financial services, brokerage services, or any trade or business where the principal asset of such trade or business is the reputation or skill of one or more of its owners or employees. Also, specified service businesses include those involved in investing and investment management, trading, or dealing in securities, partnership interests, or commodities.

To be clear, recall that a taxpayer in a specified service business is not necessarily prohibited from the QBI deduction but rather is not eligible for the QBI deduction if the taxpayer's taxable income exceeds the thresholds presented previously. The same phase-out for the wage limitation also applies to a specified service business (i.e., the with and without comparison of the QBI deduction and pro-rata reduction of the excess amount). However, the phase-out applies in a two-step process that is almost certainly better left to tax software.

Example Jenny and Jason file jointly in 2024. Jenny is a physician and works for her pass-through business that has QBI of $310,000 in 2024. The S corporation paid Jenny wages of $80,000 and her employee wages of $40,000 in 2024. Jenny and Jason's taxable income before any QBI deduction is $400,000. Jenny's S corporation has qualified business property of $300,000.

Jenny's QBI without any limits would be $62,000 ($310,000 × 20%). However, Jenny and Jason exceed the threshold income by $16,100 ($400,000 − $383,900). The excess income of $16,100 is 16.1 percent of the phase-out range of $100,000 for married filing jointly taxpayers, and thus, Jenny is eligible for only 83.9 percent of the benefits from the deduction. This eligible share is applied to each of the limits as follows:

QBI is $310,000 × 83.9% = $260,090
W-2 wages of $120,000 × 83.9% = $100,680
Qualified business property $300,000 × 83.9% = $251,700

Using this information, Jenny's tentative QBI deduction under the general rules is:

20% of QBI: $52,018 ($260,090 × 20%)
Or the greater of
Wages limit: $50,340 ($100,680 × 50%) or
Wages and capital limit: $31,463 [($100,680 × 25%) + $251,700 × 2.5%]

Under the first step, the QBI deduction would be limited to $50,340. But now, the phase-out associated with income over the threshold must be applied based on these amounts. Jenny's QBI would be $52,018 with no limitation and $50,340 with limitation or an excess QBI deduction of $1,678. As previously calculated, Jenny and Jason's income exceeds the threshold by $16,100 or 16.1 percent of the phase-out range of $100,000. Thus, Jenny is going to lose $270 of the QBI deduction (16.1 percent of the excess QBI deduction of $1,678).

As a result of the above steps, Jenny's QBI deduction for 2024 is $51,748 ($52,018 − $270). ◆

If a taxpayer has net QBI from one or more businesses that is less than zero, no QBI deduction is permitted and the QBI loss is carried over to the following year.

Example Alice operates a small business that generates $20,000 of qualified business income. She also operates a separate business that lost $60,000. Both of Alice's businesses are sole proprietorships. Alice's total net QBI is less than

$0 ($40,000 net loss). As a result, Alice is not permitted a QBI deduction in the current year and will carry the QBI loss forward to next year. ♦

The regulations that cover the QBI deduction are complex and the calculation of the QBI deduction can become unwieldy when a taxpayer subject to the limitations has multiple businesses eligible for the QBI deduction and some of these businesses operate at a loss and others generate income. These computations are beyond the scope of this textbook.

4-11e Reporting the QBI Deduction

Forms 8995 and 8995-A are used for reporting the QBI deduction. Form 8995 is for taxpayers whose taxable income before the QBI deduction does not exceed the phase-out thresholds ($383,900 for married filing joint returns, $191,950 for all other returns in 2024). Otherwise, taxpayers must use Form 8995-A. As the complexity of the QBI deduction increases, taxpayers may also need to use four accompanying schedules (A–D) that are part of Form 8995-A. These additional schedules are beyond the scope of this textbook.

Self-Study Problem 4.11 *Refer to Appendix E for Solutions to Self-Study Problems*

Determine whether the following taxpayers are eligible for the QBI deduction and the deduction amount, if any.

a. Aretha is a married taxpayer filing jointly and a shareholder in Soul Corporation (not an S corporation). She owns 10 percent of the outstanding stock and the corporation generates $700,000 of taxable income from its business operations and distributes a $70,000 dividend to Aretha. Her total taxable income before the QBI deduction is $92,000.

b. Terri Jones is a single taxpayer and sole proprietor who operates a small chain of hair salons called The Bee Hive that specializes in obscure hair colors. Her business has no employees since all the stylists operate as independent contractors. The taxpayer identification number of the Bee Hive is 317-65-4321. Terri's business generated business income of $120,000 in 2024. Her taxable income before any QBI deduction is $133,000. Use Form 8995 on Page 4-55 to determine her QBI deduction.

c. Alice Delvecchio is married and files a joint return with her spouse, Chris Delvecchio. Alice operates a small family restaurant called D's Pizza as a sole proprietor (taxpayer identification number 565-22-4321). She pays wages of $36,000, has qualified property with a basis of $67,000, and the QBI from the restaurant is $100,000. Chris has wages of $290,000 and their joint taxable income before the QBI deduction is $406,000 and includes $12,000 of qualified dividends. Use Form 8995-A on Pages 4-56 and 4-57 to determine their QBI deduction amount.

ProConnect™ Tax TIP

All of the different entry points for information for a tax return are located on the left-hand margin of ProConnect Tax. At the top of that list are two tabs: All and In Use. The All tab shows all of the possible data entry points and aids in the prevention of overlooking a tax item while preparing the return. For reviewing a return, the In Use tab hides the areas not in use and can be very helpful.

Self-Study Problem 4.11, Part B

Form 8995
Department of the Treasury
Internal Revenue Service

Qualified Business Income Deduction Simplified Computation

Attach to your tax return.
Go to www.irs.gov/Form8995 for instructions and the latest information.

OMB No. 1545-2294
2024
Attachment Sequence No. 55

Name(s) shown on return

Your taxpayer identification number

Note: You can claim the qualified business income deduction **only** if you have qualified business income from a qualified trade or business, real estate investment trust dividends, publicly traded partnership income, or a domestic production activities deduction passed through from an agricultural or horticultural cooperative. See instructions.

Use this form if your taxable income, before your qualified business income deduction, is at or below $191,950 ($383,900 if married filing jointly), and you aren't a patron of an agricultural or horticultural cooperative.

1	(a) Trade, business, or aggregation name	(b) Taxpayer identification number	(c) Qualified business income or (loss)
i			
ii			
iii			
iv			
v			

2	Total qualified business income or (loss). Combine lines 1i through 1v, column (c)	2	
3	Qualified business net (loss) carryforward from the prior year	3 ( )	
4	Total qualified business income. Combine lines 2 and 3. If zero or less, enter -0-	4	
5	Qualified business income component. Multiply line 4 by 20% (0.20)		5
6	Qualified REIT dividends and publicly traded partnership (PTP) income or (loss) (see instructions)	6	
7	Qualified REIT dividends and qualified PTP (loss) carryforward from the prior year	7 ( )	
8	Total qualified REIT dividends and PTP income. Combine lines 6 and 7. If zero or less, enter -0-	8	
9	REIT and PTP component. Multiply line 8 by 20% (0.20)		9
10	Qualified business income deduction before the income limitation. Add lines 5 and 9		10
11	Taxable income before qualified business income deduction (see instructions)	11	
12	Enter your net capital gain, if any, increased by any qualified dividends (see instructions)	12	
13	Subtract line 12 from line 11. If zero or less, enter -0-	13	
14	Income limitation. Multiply line 13 by 20% (0.20)		14
15	Qualified business income deduction. Enter the smaller of line 10 or line 14. Also enter this amount on the applicable line of your return (see instructions)		15
16	Total qualified business (loss) carryforward. Combine lines 2 and 3. If greater than zero, enter -0-		16 ( )
17	Total qualified REIT dividends and PTP (loss) carryforward. Combine lines 6 and 7. If greater than zero, enter -0-		17 ( )

For Privacy Act and Paperwork Reduction Act Notice, see instructions. Cat. No. 37806C Form **8995** (2024)

Self-Study Problem 4.11, Part C

Form 8995-A
Department of the Treasury
Internal Revenue Service

Qualified Business Income Deduction

Attach to your tax return.
Go to www.irs.gov/Form8995A for instructions and the latest information.

OMB No. 1545-2294

2024
Attachment Sequence No. **55A**

Name(s) shown on return _____ Your taxpayer identification number _____

Note: You can claim the qualified business income deduction **only** if you have qualified business income from a qualified trade or business, real estate investment trust dividends, publicly traded partnership income, or a domestic production activities deduction passed through from an agricultural or horticultural cooperative. See instructions.

Use this form if your taxable income, before your qualified business income deduction, is above $191,950 ($383,900 if married filing jointly), or you're a patron of an agricultural or horticultural cooperative.

Part I — Trade, Business, or Aggregation Information

Complete Schedules A, B, and/or C (Form 8995-A), as applicable, before starting Part I. Attach additional worksheets when needed. See instructions.

1	(a) Trade, business, or aggregation name	(b) Check if specified service	(c) Check if aggregation	(d) Taxpayer identification number	(e) Check if patron
A		☐	☐		☐
B		☐	☐		☐
C		☐	☐		☐

Part II — Determine Your Adjusted Qualified Business Income

			A	B	C
2	Qualified business income from the trade, business, or aggregation. See instructions	2			
3	Multiply line 2 by 20% (0.20). If your taxable income is $191,950 or less ($383,900 if married filing jointly), skip lines 4 through 12 and enter the amount from line 3 on line 13	3			
4	Allocable share of W-2 wages from the trade, business, or aggregation	4			
5	Multiply line 4 by 50% (0.50)	5			
6	Multiply line 4 by 25% (0.25)	6			
7	Allocable share of the unadjusted basis immediately after acquisition (UBIA) of all qualified property	7			
8	Multiply line 7 by 2.5% (0.025)	8			
9	Add lines 6 and 8	9			
10	Enter the greater of line 5 or line 9	10			
11	W-2 wage and UBIA of qualified property limitation. Enter the smaller of line 3 or line 10	11			
12	Phased-in reduction. Enter the amount from line 26, if any	12			
13	Qualified business income deduction before patron reduction. Enter the greater of line 11 or line 12	13			
14	Patron reduction. Enter the amount from Schedule D (Form 8995-A), line 6, if any. See instructions	14			
15	Qualified business income component. Subtract line 14 from line 13	15			
16	Total qualified business income component. Add all amounts reported on line 15	16			

For Privacy Act and Paperwork Reduction Act Notice, see separate instructions.   Cat. No. 71661B   Form **8995-A** (2024)

Form 8995-A (2024) Page **2**

Part III Phased-in Reduction

Complete Part III only if your taxable income is more than $191,950 but not $241,950 ($383,900 and $483,900 if married filing jointly) and line 10 is less than line 3. Otherwise, skip Part III.

			A	B	C
17	Enter the amounts from line 3	17			
18	Enter the amounts from line 10	18			
19	Subtract line 18 from line 17	19			
20	Taxable income before qualified business income deduction	20			
21	Threshold. Enter $191,950 ($383,900 if married filing jointly)	21			
22	Subtract line 21 from line 20	22			
23	Phase-in range. Enter $50,000 ($100,000 if married filing jointly)	23			
24	Phase-in percentage. Divide line 22 by line 23	24 %			
25	Total phase-in reduction. Multiply line 19 by line 24	25			
26	Qualified business income after phase-in reduction. Subtract line 25 from line 17. Enter this amount here and on line 12, for the corresponding trade or business	26			

Part IV Determine Your Qualified Business Income Deduction

27	Total qualified business income component from all qualified trades, businesses, or aggregations. Enter the amount from line 16	27
28	Qualified REIT dividends and publicly traded partnership (PTP) income or (loss). See instructions	28
29	Qualified REIT dividends and PTP (loss) carryforward from prior years	29 ( )
30	Total qualified REIT dividends and PTP income. Combine lines 28 and 29. If less than zero, enter -0-	30
31	REIT and PTP component. Multiply line 30 by 20% (0.20)	31
32	Qualified business income deduction before the income limitation. Add lines 27 and 31	32
33	Taxable income before qualified business income deduction	33
34	Enter your net capital gain, if any, increased by any qualified dividends (see instructions)	34
35	Subtract line 34 from line 33. If zero or less, enter -0-	35
36	Income limitation. Multiply line 35 by 20% (0.20)	36
37	Qualified business income deduction before the domestic production activities deduction (DPAD) under section 199A(g). Enter the smaller of line 32 or line 36	37
38	DPAD under section 199A(g) allocated from an agricultural or horticultural cooperative. Don't enter more than line 33 minus line 37	38
39	Total qualified business income deduction. Add lines 37 and 38	39
40	Total qualified REIT dividends and PTP (loss) carryforward. Combine lines 28 and 29. If zero or greater, enter -0-	40 ( )

Form **8995-A** (2024)

Key Terms

capital asset, 4-2
virtual currency, 4-2
holding period, 4-3
short-term, 4-3
long-term, 4-3
sale or exchange, 4-4
amount realized, 4-4
adjusted basis, 4-5
capital improvement, 4-5
inherited property basis, 4-8
gift property basis, 4-8
net capital gains, 4-11
net capital losses, 4-12
personal loss, 4-13
wash sales, 4-13

Section 1202 stock, 4-14
Section 1244 stock, 4-14
Form 8949, 4-14
Schedule D, 4-14
Form 1099-B, 4-15
principal residence, 4-23
Form 1099-S, 4-24
net rental income, 4-27
Schedule E, 4-27
vacation home, 4-28
deposit, 4-30
passive activity, 4-31
Form 8582, 4-34
net operating loss (NOL), 4-36
NOL carry forward/back, 4-42

Form 172, 4-42
excess business loss, 4-42
Form 461, 4-43
self-employment tax, 4-44
Schedule SE, 4-46
qualified business income, 4-49
qualified business income
    deduction, 4-49
wage limitation, 4-50
unadjusted basis immediately after
    acquisition (UBIA), 4-50
qualified business property, 4-51
specified service trade or business
    (SSTB), 4-53
Form 8995, 4-54

Key Points

Learning Objectives	Key Points
LO 4.1: Define the term "capital asset."	• A capital asset is any property, whether or not used in a trade or business, except: (1) inventory, (2) depreciable property or real property used in a trade or business, (3) patents, inventions, models or designs, secret formulas or processes, copyrights, literary, musical, or artistic compositions, letters or memorandums, or similar property, if the property is created by the taxpayer, (4) accounts or notes receivable, and (5) certain U.S. government publications. • Virtual currency is a digital representation of value that functions as a medium of exchange, a unit of account, or a store of value. In general, virtual currency is treated as property. • Cryptocurrency is a type of virtual currency that utilizes blockchain to validate and secure transactions that are digitally recorded on a distributed ledger.
LO 4.2: Apply the holding period for long-term and short-term capital gains and losses.	• Assets must be held for more than one year for the gain or loss to be considered long-term. • A capital asset held one year or less results in a short-term capital gain or loss. • A net short-term capital gain is treated as ordinary income. • In calculating the holding period, the taxpayer excludes the date of acquisition and includes the date of disposition.

LO 4.3:
Calculate the gain or loss on the disposition of an asset.

- The taxpayer's gain or loss is calculated using the following formula:
  Amount realized − Adjusted basis = Gain or loss realized
- The amount realized from a sale or other disposition of property is equal to the sum of the money received, plus the fair market value of other property received, plus any liabilities relieved, less the costs paid to transfer the property.
- The adjusted basis of property is equal to:
  Original basis + Capital improvements − Accumulated depreciation
- In most cases, the original basis is the cost of the property at the date of acquisition, plus any costs incidental to the purchase, such as title insurance, escrow fees, and inspection fees (but not fees or costs for getting a loan on the property).
- Capital improvements are major expenditures for permanent improvements to or restoration of the taxpayer's property.
- Basis of property received from inheritance is equal to the fair market value at the date of the decedent's death.
- Basis of property acquired as a gift depends on whether the property is sold for a gain or loss by the donee.

LO 4.4:
Compute the tax on capital gains.

- Short-term capital gains are taxed as ordinary income, while there are various different preferential long-term capital gains tax rates.
- Net long-term capital gains may be subject to rates ranging from 0 percent to 28 percent (an additional 3.8 percent Medicare tax on net investment income applies to high-income individuals).
- Special rates apply to long-term gains on collectibles (e.g., art, stamps, gems, coins, etc.) and depreciation recapture on the disposition of certain Section 1250 assets.

LO 4.5:
Describe the treatment of capital losses.

- Individual taxpayers may deduct net capital losses against ordinary income in amounts up to $3,000 per year with any unused capital losses carried forward indefinitely.
- When a taxpayer ends up with net capital losses, the losses offset capital gains as follows: (1) net short-term capital losses first reduce 28-percent gains, then 25-percent gains, then regular long-term capital gains, and (2) net long-term capital losses first reduce 28-percent gains, then 25-percent gains, then any short-term capital gains.
- Personal capital losses are not deductible for tax purposes.
- A wash sale occurs when a substantially identical security has been purchased either 30 days before or 30 days after the sale of a security at a loss. Wash sale losses are deferred until substantially identical security is sold.

LO 4.6:
Apply the exclusion of gain from personal residence sales.

- Taxpayers who have owned their personal residence and lived in it for at least two of the five years before the sale can exclude from income up to $250,000 of gain ($500,000 for joint return filers).

LO 4.7:
Apply the tax rules for rental property and vacation homes.

- Rental income and related expenses are reported on Schedule E.
- Rental expenses include real estate taxes, mortgage interest, insurance, commissions, repairs, and depreciation.
- If a residence is rented for fewer than 15 days during the year, the rental income is disregarded and the property is treated as a personal residence for tax purposes.
- If the residence is rented for 15 days or more and is used for personal purposes for not more than 14 days or 10 percent of the days rented, whichever is greater, the residence is treated as a rental property.
- If the residence is rented for 15 days or more and is used for personal purposes for more than 14 days or 10 percent of the days rented, whichever is greater, allocable rental expenses are allowed only to the extent of rental income.

LO 4.8:
Explain the treatment of passive income and losses.

- The tax law defines three categories of income: (1) active income, (2) portfolio income, and (3) passive income and losses.
- Normally, passive losses cannot be used to offset either active or portfolio income. Passive losses not used to offset passive income are carried forward indefinitely.
- Generally, losses remaining when the taxpayer disposes of their entire interest in a passive activity may be used in full.
- Under the passive loss rules, real estate rental activities are specifically defined as passive, even if the taxpayer actively manages the property.
- Individual taxpayers may deduct up to $25,000 of rental property losses against other income, if they are actively involved in the management of the property and their modified adjusted gross income does not exceed certain limits.
- Taxpayers heavily involved in real estate rental activities may qualify as running an active trade or business rather than a passive activity and may fully deduct all rental losses.

LO 4.9:
Describe the basic tax treatment of deductions for net operating losses.

- Computation of an individual taxpayer NOL requires classification of income and deductions as business and nonbusiness.
- An NOL generated in 2017 or before may be carried back two years and forward twenty years.
- An NOL generated after 2017 may be carried forward only and may only offset up to 80 percent of a future year's income.
- Total business losses generated between 2021 and 2028 are limited.

LO 4.10:
Calculate and report the self-employment tax (both Social Security and Medicare portions) for self-employed taxpayers.

- Self-employed individuals pay self-employment (SE) taxes instead of FICA taxes and, since these individuals have no employers, the entire tax is paid by the self-employed individuals.
- For 2024, the Social Security (OASDI) tax rate is 12.4 percent, with a maximum base amount of earnings subject to the Social Security portion of $168,600. The Medicare tax rate is 2.9 percent with all earnings subject to the Medicare portion, without limitation.
- If an individual, subject to SE taxes, also receives wages subject to FICA taxes during a tax year, the individual's maximum base amount for SE taxes is reduced by the amount of the wages when calculating the SE taxes.
- Net earnings from self employment include gross income from a trade or business less trade or business deductions, the distributive share of partnership income from a trade or business, and net income earned as an independent contractor.
- Self-employed taxpayers are allowed a deduction for AGI of one-half of the SE tax.

LO 4.11:
Compute the qualified business income (QBI) deduction.

- Flow-through entities are eligible for a deduction of 20 percent of QBI, subject to limitations.
- QBI is business income only and generally does not include interest, dividends, or capital gains.
- Tax law provides a safe-harbor under which income from rental real estate can qualify as QBI if it meets the necessary requirements.
- The QBI deduction may not exceed 20 percent of taxable income.
- If taxable income exceeds $383,900 for married filing joint returns, $191,950 for all other returns, the QBI deduction is limited by the wage limitation, which is the greater of the wage limit (50 percent of wages) or the wage and capital limit [(25 percent of wages) plus (2.5 percent of qualified business property)].
- QBI from service-related business may also be subject to limitation if income thresholds are surpassed.

Questions and Problems

Group 1:
Multiple Choice Questions

LO 4.1
1. All of the following assets are capital assets, *except*:
   a. A personal automobile
   b. IBM stock
   c. A child's bicycle
   d. Personal furniture
   e. Used car inventory held by a car dealer

LO 4.1
2. Which of the following is a capital asset?
   a. Accounts receivable
   b. Copyright created by the taxpayer
   c. Copyright (held by the writer)
   d. Business inventory
   e. A taxpayer's residence

LO 4.1
3. In 2024, Aryna receives 0.50 units of Bahtcoin, a virtual currency as payment for services provided when the market value of Bahtcoin is $1,200 per unit. Later during 2024, she later uses 0.25 units to purchase goods for personal use when the value of Bahtcoin is $1,500 per unit. What is the tax consequence of the use of the Bahtcoin?
   a. No effect
   b. Deduction for $375
   c. Capital gain of $75
   d. Gross income of $375

LO 4.2
4. Yasmeen purchases stock on January 30, 2023. If she wishes to achieve a long-term holding period, what is the first date that she can sell the stock as a long-term gain?
   a. January 30, 2024
   b. January 31, 2024
   c. February 1, 2024
   d. July 31, 2023
   e. July 30, 2023

LO 4.2
5. To calculate the number of days in the holding period, a taxpayer should:
   a. Include the date of acquisition
   b. Exclude the date of disposition
   c. Exclude the date of acquisition
   d. Include the date of acquisition and disposition

LO 4.3
6. Vijay sells land and receives $5,000 cash, a motorcycle worth $1,600, and two tickets to the Super Bowl with a total face value (cost) of $800 but worth $1,200. In addition, the buyer assumes the mortgage on the land of $12,000. What is Vijay's amount realized in this transaction?
   a. $5,000
   b. $7,800
   c. $8,200
   d. $19,800
   e. $20,200

LO 4.3   7. Jaye purchased a building for $100,000. After deducting depreciation of $12,000 through the date of sale, Jaye sells the building for $120,000. What is Jaye's adjusted basis for computing realized gain or loss?
   a. $100,000
   b. $120,000
   c. $88,000
   d. $108,000

LO 4.3   8. Agnes passes away in 2024 and leaves her child, Sam, 100 shares of stock. Agnes purchased the stock for $2,000 over 15 years ago. It was worth $8,000 on the date of Agnes' death. Sam sells the stock a short time later for $9,500. What is the basis of the stock for computing Sam's realized gain or loss?
   a. $2,000
   b. $8,000
   c. $9,500
   d. Some other amount

LO 4.3   9. Grady gives a watch to his nephew, Fred. Grady's original basis in the watch is $100 and the value of the watch on the date of the gift is $1,000. Fred keeps the watch for a year or two and then sells it for $1,200. What is Fred's basis in the watch for computing his realized gain or loss?
   a. $0. It's a gift so Fred has no basis.
   b. $100. Grady's basis carries over to Fred.
   c. $1,000. Fred takes basis as the market value on the date of the gift.
   d. $1,200. Fred's basis should result in no gain or loss on a gift property.

LO 4.3   10. Bob sells a stock investment for $35,000 cash, and the purchaser assumes Bob's $32,500 debt on the investment. The basis of Bob's stock investment is $55,000. What is the gain or loss realized on the sale?
   a. $10,000 loss
   b. $10,000 gain
   c. $12,500 gain
   d. $22,500 loss
   e. $22,500 gain

LO 4.4   11. In 2024, what is the top tax rate for individual long-term capital gains and the top tax rate for long-term capital gains of collectible items assuming that the net investment income tax does not apply.
   a. 10; 20
   b. 20; 28
   c. 15; 25
   d. 25; 28

LO 4.4   12. In November 2024, Ben and Betty (married, filing jointly) have a long-term capital gain of $54,000 on the sale of stock. They have no other capital gains and losses for the year. Their ordinary income for the year after the standard deduction is $72,500, making their total taxable income for the year $126,500 ($72,500 + $54,000). In 2024, married taxpayers pay 0 percent on long-term gains up to $94,050. What will be their 2024 total tax liability assuming a tax of $8,239 on the $72,500 of ordinary income?
   a. $8,100
   b. $13,107
   c. $8,239
   d. $13,851
   e. $0

LO 4.4

13. Harold, a single taxpayer, has $35,000 of ordinary income after the standard deduction, and $10,000 in long-term capital gains, for total taxable income of $45,000. For 2024, single taxpayers pay 0 percent on long-term gains up to $47,025. Assuming a tax of $3,971 on the $35,000 of ordinary income, what is Harold's total income tax?
    a. $3,383
    b. $3,971
    c. $1,500
    d. $4,094
    e. $5,471

LO 4.4

14. In 2024, Mina, a single taxpayer, has $12,000 in short-term capital gains, long-term capital losses of $10,000, and long-term capital gains of $4,000. What is Mina's net capital gain or loss?
    a. $6,000 short-term gain
    b. $13,000 short-term gain
    c. $22,000 long-term gain
    d. $13,000 long-term gain and $3,000 loss carryover

LO 4.4
LO 4.5

15. In 2024, Hagos, a single taxpayer, has ordinary income of $33,000. In addition, he has $2,000 in short-term capital gains, long-term capital losses of $10,000, and long-term capital gains of $4,000. What is Hagos' AGI for 2024?
    a. $27,000
    b. $29,000
    c. $30,000
    d. $33,000

LO 4.5

16. Angela sold her personal auto in 2024 for $8,000. She purchased the car for $26,000 in 2017. She has long-term capital gains of $4,000 from the sale of stock in 2024. What is Angela's net recognized capital gain or loss in 2024?
    a. Gain of $4,000
    b. Gain of $1,000
    c. Loss of $14,000
    d. Loss of $3,000

LO 4.5

17. If an individual taxpayer generates a net capital loss in excess of $3,000 in 2024:
    a. The loss can be carried back for three years and forward for five years
    b. The loss can be carried back for two years and forward for 20 years
    c. The loss can be carried forward indefinitely
    d. The loss can be carried forward indefinitely but only offset 80 percent of a future year's capital gains

LO 4.5

18. Serena, a married filing jointly taxpayer, has the following capital gains and losses in 2024:

    - $4,000 short-term capital gain
    - $2,000 short-term capital loss
    - $2,000 long-term capital gain
    - $8,000 long-term capital loss

    What is the amount and nature of Serena's net capital loss carryforward into 2025?
    a. $1,000 long-term loss carryforward
    b. $3,000 long-term loss carryforward
    c. $4,000 long-term loss carryforward
    d. $6,000 long-term loss carryforward

Chapter 4 • Additional Income and the Qualified Business Income Deduction

LO 4.6

19. Oscar, a single taxpayer, sells his residence of the last 10 years in January of 2024 for $190,000. Oscar's basis in the residence is $45,000, and his selling expenses are $11,000. If Oscar does not buy a new residence, what is the taxable gain on the sale of his residence?
    a. $0
    b. $9,000
    c. $45,000
    d. $134,000
    e. $145,000

LO 4.6

20. Jim, a single taxpayer, bought his home 25 years ago for $25,000. He has lived in the home continuously since he purchased it. In 2024, he sells his home for $325,000. What is Jim's taxable gain on the sale?
    a. $0
    b. $25,000
    c. $50,000
    d. $300,000

LO 4.6

21. Kemi, a single taxpayer, bought her home 25 years ago for $30,000. She has lived in the home continuously since she purchased it. In 2024, she sells her home for $200,000. What is Kemi's taxable gain on the sale?
    a. $0
    b. $20,000
    c. $250,000
    d. $170,000

LO 4.6

22. Roshawn purchased a house 20 years ago for $100,000 and he has always lived in the house. Three years ago Roshawn married Karen, and she has lived in the house since their marriage. If they sell Roshawn's house in December 2024 for $425,000, what is their taxable gain on a joint tax return?
    a. $0
    b. $75,000
    c. $125,000
    d. $250,000

LO 4.6

23. Peruth, a single taxpayer, purchased a house 18 months ago for $350,000. If Peruth sells their house due to unforeseen circumstances for $550,000 after living in it for a full 18 months, what is their taxable gain?
    a. $0
    b. $12,500
    c. $50,000
    d. $200,000

LO 4.6

24. Monoghan and her spouse own and lived in their home for 15 years until the spouse died in 2023. In 2024, Monoghan appropriately files as a surviving spouse and also sells the family home at a gain of $367,000 after considering selling expenses. How much of this gain will Monoghan include in taxable income in 2024?
    a. $0
    b. $117,000
    c. $250,000
    d. $367,000

LO 4.7

25. Which of the following is *true* about the rental of real estate?
    a. Depreciation and maintenance expenses for an apartment complex are deductible.
    b. The expense deductions for a home rented for 100 days and used for personal use for 17 days will be limited to the gross rental income.
    c. If a home is rented for less than 15 days a year, the rent is not taxable.
    d. Repairs on rental property are deductible by the taxpayer.
    e. All of the above.

LO 4.7 26. Jonathan rents his home for twelve days during the 2024 USA Cup of Soccer. Due to the popularity of the event, he earns $4,000 in rent. He spends $150 on a cleaning service immediately after the rental. He does not rent the home otherwise during the year. What is Jonathan's rental income and deductions from this short-term rental?
   a. $0 income and $0 deduction
   b. $4,000 income and $150 deduction
   c. $4,000 income and $0 deduction
   d. $4,000 income and $5 (12/365 × $150)

LO 4.7 27. Juanita rents her vacation condo for 120 days and uses the condo for herself for 20 days. What allocation percentage will Juanita apply to the condo's operating expenses (for example, insurance, utilities, etc.) to compute the rental portion under the IRS allocation method?
   a. 32.9 percent (120/365)
   b. 5.5 percent (20/365)
   c. 85.7 percent (120/140)
   d. 38.4 percent (140/365)

LO 4.7 28. John owns a second home in Palm Springs, CA. During the year, he rented the house for $5,000 for 56 days and used the house for 14 days during the summer. The house remained vacant during the remainder of the year. The expenses for the home included $5,000 in mortgage interest, $850 in property taxes, $900 for utilities and maintenance, and $3,500 of depreciation. What is John's deductible rental loss, before considering the passive loss limitations?
   a. $0
   b. $200
   c. $875
   d. $2,500
   e. $3,200

LO 4.8 29. Helen, a single taxpayer, has modified adjusted gross income (before passive losses) of $124,000. During the tax year, Helen's rental house generated a loss of $15,000. Assuming Helen is actively involved in the management of the property, what is the amount of Helen's passive loss deduction from the rental house?
   a. $0
   b. $3,000
   c. $12,000
   d. $13,000
   e. $15,000

LO 4.8 30. Which of the following types of income is passive income?
   a. Net rental income from real estate limited partnership investments
   b. Dividends from domestic corporations
   c. Wages
   d. Interest income from certificates of deposit
   e. None of the above

LO 4.8 31. Which of the following is classified as active income?
   a. Self-employment income from a small business
   b. Interest income
   c. Limited partnership income
   d. Ordinary dividend income
   e. a. and d.

LO 4.8

32. Nancy has active modified adjusted gross income before passive losses of $75,000. She has a loss of $5,000 on a rental property she actively manages. How much of the loss is she allowed to take against the $75,000 of other income?
    a. None
    b. $2,500
    c. $5,000
    d. $25,000

LO 4.8

33. Ned has active modified adjusted gross income before passive losses of $250,000. He has a loss of $15,000 on rental property he actively manages. How much of the loss is he allowed to take against the $250,000 of other income?
    a. $15,000
    b. $10,000
    c. $5,000
    d. None

LO 4.8

34. Norm is a real estate professional with a real estate trade or business as defined in the tax law. He has $80,000 of business income and $40,000 of losses from actively managed real estate rentals. How much of the $40,000 in losses is he allowed to claim on his tax return?
    a. $40,000
    b. $25,000
    c. $20,000
    d. None

LO 4.9

35. Bonita earns $31,000 from her job, and she has $1,000 of interest income. She has itemized deductions of $35,000. There are no casualty or theft losses in the itemized deductions. What is Bonita's net operating loss for the current year?
    a. $0
    b. $1,000
    c. $3,000
    d. $4,000
    e. Some other amount

LO 4.9

36. Jim has a net operating loss in 2023. If he does not make any special elections, what is the first year to which Jim carries the net operating loss?
    a. 2024
    b. 2022
    c. 2021
    d. 2020
    e. 2019

LO 4.10

37. For 2024, Roberta is a self-employed truck driver with earnings of $50,414 from her business. During the year, Roberta received $2,500 in interest income and dividends of $500. She also sold investment property and recognized a $1,500 gain. What is the amount of Roberta's self-employment tax (Social Security and Medicare taxes) liability for 2024?
    a. $3,857
    b. $6,641
    c. $6,358
    d. $7,123
    e. $7,713

LO 4.10

38. Which of the following is *not* subject to self-employment tax?
    a. Gain on the sale of real estate held for investment
    b. Net earnings of a self-employed lawyer
    c. Distributive share of earnings of a partnership
    d. Net earnings of the owner of a shoe store
    e. Net earnings of the owner of a dry cleaner

LO 4.10 39. Katrina has wages of $169,000 in 2024. She also operates a small business that generated net profits of $8,000. What is Katrina's total self-employment tax?
  a. $0
  b. $214.25
  c. $232.00
  d. $1,224.00

LO 4.11 40. The qualified business income deduction is unavailable to which of the following businesses:
  a. A sole proprietor dental practice that generates about $70,000 in income each year
  b. A shareholder of an incorporated small tools manufacturer
  c. A partner in a partnership operated by spouses that sells wood carvings over the Internet
  d. A shareholder in an S corporation that owns and operates a restaurant. The S corporation has six different owners.
  e. The QBI deduction is available to all of the above.

LO 4.11 41. Qualified business income does not include which of the following:
  a. Income from sales of goods
  b. Deductions related to cost of goods sold
  c. Deductions for business expenses such as rent
  d. Interest income from an investment in bonds

LO 4.11 42. In 2024, Tracy generates a $10,000 loss from an otherwise qualified business activity. Fortunately, she also works as an employee and has taxable wages of $40,000. Tracy's 2024 QBI deduction is
  a. $0
  b. $2,000
  c. $8,000
  d. $6,000

Group 2: Problems

LO 4.1
LO 4.2
LO 4.3
1. Martin sells a stock investment for $26,000 on August 2, 2024. Martin's adjusted basis in the stock is $15,000.
   a. If Martin acquired the stock on November 15, 2022, calculate the amount and the nature of the gain or loss.
   b. If Martin had acquired the stock on September 10, 2023, calculate the amount and nature of the gain or loss.

LO 4.1
LO 4.2
LO 4.3
LO 4.5
2. During 2024, Tom sold GM stock for $10,000. The stock was purchased four years ago for $13,000. Tom also sold Ford Motor Company bonds for $35,000. The bonds were purchased two months ago for $30,000. Home Depot stock, purchased two years ago for $1,000, was sold by Tom for $2,500. Calculate Tom's net gain or loss, and indicate the nature of the gain or loss.

3. Charu Khanna received a Form 1099-B showing the following stock transactions and basis:

2024 Combined Forms 1099

This is important tax information and is being furnished to the IRS (except as indicated). If you are required to file a return, a negligence penalty or other sanction may be imposed on you if this income is taxable and the IRS determines that it has not been reported.

Copy B For Recipient
OMB No. 1545-0110

Friar Tuck Investments
38 Wall Street, 8th Floor
New York, NY 10005

Charu Khanna
206 Commonwealth Ave, Apt 3B.
Boston, MA 02116

Account Number: 5612311789   Tax ID: ***-**-4023
Payer's Federal Tax ID: 33-1357246
Financial Adviser/Phone: John Little 888-555-1212

Form 1099-B — Proceeds from Broker and Barter Exchange Transactions

Box 1 Security description (CUSIP)	Box 6: Gross Proceeds / Box 5: Not checked — Quantity sold	Box 1b Date acquired	Box 1c Date sold or disposed	Box 3: Basis reported to IRS — Box 1d Proceeds	Box 1e Cost or other basis	Box 2: Type of Gain or Loss: Short Term — Box 1g Wash sale loss disallowed	Gain/(Loss) amount
Gold Corp	500	02/12/2024	09/05/2024	42,000	52,500	-	(10,500)
Orange Corp	100	11/15/2023	07/12/2024	20,500	19,200	-	1,300

Box 1 Security description (CUSIP)	Box 6: Gross Proceeds / Box 5: Not checked — Quantity sold	Box 1b Date acquired	Box 1c Date sold or disposed	Box 3: Basis reported to IRS — Box 1d Proceeds	Box 1e Cost or other basis	Box 2: Type of Gain or Loss: Long Term — Box 1g Wash sale loss disallowed	Gain/(Loss) amount
Green Corp	4,000	06/04/2013	08/05/2024	9,000	3,200	-	5,800
Blue Corp	50	02/04/2014	10/01/2024	15,000	19,700	-	(4,700)

None of the stock is qualified small business stock. The stock basis was reported to the IRS. Calculate Charu's net capital gain or loss using Schedule D in Appendix F.

4. Jocasta owns an apartment complex that she purchased six years ago for $705,000. Jocasta has made $45,000 of capital improvements on the complex, and her depreciation claimed on the building to date is $120,000. Calculate Jocasta's adjusted basis in the building.

5. Chrissy receives 200 shares of Chevron stock as a gift from her father. The father purchased the stock for $8,000 ten years ago and it is worth $10,000 at the date of the gift.
   a. If Chrissy sells the stock for $11,200, calculate the amount of the realized gain or loss on the sale.
   b. If Chrissy sells the stock for $7,500, calculate the amount of the realized gain or loss on the sale.

6. John receives 200 shares of Chevron stock worth $8,000 as a gift from his mother. The mother purchased the stock for $10,000 eight years ago.
   a. If John sells the stock for $11,000, calculate the amount of the realized gain or loss on the sale.
   b. If John sells the stock for $7,800, calculate the amount of the realized gain or loss.
   c. If John sells the stock for $9,200, calculate the amount of the realized gain or loss.

7. In 2024, Michael has net short-term capital losses of $1,700, a net long-term capital loss of $17,000, and other ordinary taxable income of $45,000.
   a. Calculate the amount of Michael's deduction for capital losses for 2024.
   b. Calculate the amount and nature of his capital loss carryforward.
   c. For how long may Michael carry forward the unused loss?

LO 4.6 8. Larry Gaines, a single taxpayer, age 42, sells his personal residence on November 12, 2024, for $170,000. He lived in the house for seven years. The expenses of the sale are $10,000, and he has made capital improvements of $9,000. Larry's original cost basis in his residence is $88,000. On November 30, 2024, Larry purchases and occupies a new residence at a cost of $155,000. Calculate Larry's realized gain, recognized gain, and the adjusted basis of his new residence.

LO 4.6 9. On July 1, 2024, Ted, age 73 and single, sells his personal residence of the last thirty years for $370,000. Ted's basis in his residence is $64,000. The expenses associated with the sale of his home total $22,000. On December 15, 2024, Ted purchases and occupies a new residence at a cost of $225,000. Calculate Ted's realized gain, recognized gain, and the adjusted basis of his new residence.

LO 4.6 10. Kendra and Lloyd get married on July 1, 2024 and will file jointly in 2024. Both of them owned a home prior to marriage, but they agree that they wish to live together in one of the homes. Kendra's home was purchased on September 1, 2023 for $270,000 and is now worth $290,000. Lloyd's home was purchased in 2020 for $170,000 and is now worth $215,000. Both believe that the housing market in their area will remain strong (and maybe prices will increase). They also plan to start having children in two or three years and expect to have to move into a larger home than either of their existing homes now. Describe the possible alternatives available to Kendra and Lloyd with respect to excluding the gain on the sale of the homes.

LO 4.7 11. Dick owns a house that he rents to college students. Dick receives $9,600 for annual rent and incurs the following expenses during the year:

Real estate taxes	$1,250
Mortgage interest	1,500
Insurance	425
Repairs	562
Association dues	1,500

Dick purchased the house in 1989 for $48,000. The house is fully depreciated. Calculate Dick's net rental income for the year, assuming the house was rented for a full twelve months.

LO 4.7 12. Sherry rents her vacation home for six months and lives in it for six months during the year. Her gross rental income during the year is $6,000. Total real estate taxes for the home are $2,200, and interest on the home mortgage is $4,000. Annual utilities and maintenance expenses total $2,000, and depreciation expense is $4,500. Calculate Sherry's deductible depreciation, the net income or loss from the vacation home, and the loss carryforward, if any.

LO 4.7 13. On May 1, 2024, Ella leases her condo to Fitz for a 12-month lease period starting May 1 for $1,000 per month. Ella requires that Fitz pay first month's rent, last month's rent and a $1,000 security deposit (total $3,000) prior to turning over the keys to Fitz. The security deposit is refundable as long as Fitz abides by the terms of the lease agreement. Compute the amount of gross rental income Ella will recognize in 2024.

LO 4.8 14. Walter, a single taxpayer, purchased a limited partnership interest in a tax shelter in 1997. He also acquired a rental house in 2024, which he actively manages. During 2024, Walter's share of the partnership's losses was $30,000, and his rental house generated $20,000 in losses. Walter's modified adjusted gross income before passive losses is $130,000.
   a. Calculate the amount of Walter's allowable loss for rental house activities for 2024.
   b. Calculate the amount of Walter's allowable loss for the partnership activities for 2024.
   c. What may be done with the unused losses, if anything?

LO 4.8   15. Clifford Johnson has a limited partnership investment and a rental condominium. Clifford actively manages the rental condominium. During 2024, his share of the loss from the limited partnership was $18,000, and his loss from the rental condo was $17,000. Assuming Clifford's modified adjusted gross income is $132,000 for 2024, and he has no prior year unallowed losses from either activity, complete pages 1 and 2 Form 8582 in Appendix F.

LO 4.9   16. Tyler, a single taxpayer, generates business income of $3,000 in 2021. In 2022, he generates an NOL of $5,000. In 2023, he generates business income of $1,000. In 2024, his business generates income of $1,100. What is Tyler's NOL carryforward into 2025, if any?

LO 4.9   17. Julie, a single taxpayer, has completed her 2024 Schedule C and her net loss is $40,000. Her only other income is wages of $30,000. Julie takes the standard deduction of $14,600 in 2024.
     a. Calculate Julie's taxable income or loss.
     b. Calculate the business and nonbusiness portions of her taxable income or loss.
     c. Determine Julie's NOL carryforward.

LO 4.10   18. Tommy Staples is a self-employed surfboard maker in 2024. His Schedule C net income is $137,100 for the year. He also has a part-time job and earns $38,000 in wages subject to FICA taxes. Calculate James' self-employment tax for 2024 using Schedule SE in Appendix F.

LO 4.11   19. Sanjay is a single taxpayer that operates a curry cart on the streets of Baltimore. The business is operated as a sole proprietorship with no employees (Sanjay does everything). Sanjay's Schedule C reports income of $90,000. His taxable income is $76,000 and includes no capital gains. Compute Sanjay's QBI deduction.

LO 4.11   20. Rob Wriggle operates a small plumbing supplies business as a sole proprietor. In 2024, the plumbing business has gross business income of $421,000 and business expenses of $267,000, including wages paid of $58,000. The business sold some land that had been held for investment generating a long-term capital gain of $15,000. The business has $300,000 of qualified business property in 2024. Rob's wife, Marie, has wage income of $250,000. They jointly sold stocks in 2024 and generated a long-term capital gain of $13,000. Rob and Marie have no dependents and in 2024, they take the standard deduction of $29,200.
     a. What is Rob and Marie's taxable income before the QBI deduction?
     b. What is Rob and Marie's QBI?
     c. What is Rob and Marie's QBI deduction?
     d. Complete Form 8995-A in Appendix F to report Rob's QBI deduction.

Group 3:
Writing Assignment

Research

You recently received the following e-mail from a client and friend:

Hey Great Student,

I cannot believe it is almost year-end! Only a few days before it's 2025.

As you recall, I was lucky enough to win big at the casino back on New Year's Day earlier this year (thanks for celebrating with me). I took the $3,000 I won and bought 100 shares of stock in that cool new smartphone app company, Regal Equal. I just love playing that game. Anyway, the stock has done well, and I am thinking of selling before year-end now that the price has reached $240 per share. Since you are my tax adviser, I thought I'd ask a couple of questions:

1. Is there any reason to wait and sell later?
2. If I don't sell, the price might go down (OligopolyGo seems to be replacing Regal Equal as the "hot" new game). I'm thinking the price might be as low as $220 by early next year.

My taxable income this year and next year is expected to be $46,000 (not including the stock sale). I think that puts me in the 12-percent tax bracket? Any suggestions on what I should do?

Thanks!

Sue

Prepare an e-mail to your friend Sue addressing her questions. Be certain to include estimates of the different after-tax outcomes she is suggesting. Sue is a single taxpayer and not a tax expert and so your language should reflect her limited understanding of tax law and avoid technical jargon. Although Sue is your friend, she is also a client and your e-mail should maintain a professional style.

Group 4:
Comprehensive Problems

1. Theodore E. Lariat is a single taxpayer born on September 22, 1976. He was appointed the new coach of the Nashville Country Stars soccer team in January 2024. His address, Social Security number and wages are reported on his Form W-2:

Form W-2 Wage and Tax Statement — 2024

- a Employee's social security number: 775-89-9532
- OMB No. 1545-0008
- b Employer identification number (EIN): 36-1389676
- c Employer's name, address, and ZIP code: Nashville Country Stars Soccer Club, 501 Interstate Blvd. S. 10th Floor, Nashville, TN 37210
- e Employee's name: Theodore E. Lariat, 140 Whitsett Road, Nashville, TN 37210
- 1 Wages, tips, other compensation: 130,000.00
- 2 Federal income tax withheld: 21,740.00
- 3 Social security wages: 135,000.00
- 4 Social security tax withheld: 8,370.00
- 5 Medicare wages and tips: 135,000.00
- 6 Medicare tax withheld: 1,957.50
- 12a D: 5,000.00
- 12b DD: 6,234.12
- 13 Retirement plan: X
- 15 State: TN

Theodore was previously the coach at a different soccer club in a different state. He sold his previous home before moving to Nashville (refer to 1099-S below). His only selling expense was sales commissions of $28,000. His basis in the home was $400,000. Theodore purchased his previous home on January 5, 2023, and sold it on January 6, 2024. Obviously, he would not have sold the home if it were not for the new job. He is currently renting the home he lives in.

Form 1099-S — Proceeds From Real Estate Transactions (Rev. January 2022) — For calendar year 2024

- FILER'S name: Troy Title and Escrow, Inc., 40700 Woodward Ave #150, Bloomfield Hills, MI 48304
- FILER'S TIN: 45-1331787
- TRANSFEROR'S TIN: 775-89-9532
- TRANSFEROR'S name: Theodore E. Lariat
- Street address: 140 Whitsett Rd.
- City: Nashville, TN 37210
- 1 Date of closing: 01/06/2024
- 2 Gross proceeds: $557,000.00
- 3 Address of property: 8383 Livernois Rd., Troy, MI 48083

Theodore was welcomed back to the Nashville area as he was formerly a star player on the Country Stars team. During his playing time he had purchased a modest home in Nashville but did not sell it, instead choosing to rent the home over the years. His rental home is located at 2300 Bransford Ave., Nashville, TN 37204 and was rented all year to his tenant. The tenant occupied the home on January 1, 2024, and pays rent of $1,500 per month for each month of 2024 (the lease is a two-year lease). Theodore required first and last months' rent and a security deposit of $500 and all were paid on January 1, 2024. Theodore's rental expenses for the year are:

Mortgage interest	$16,000
Real estate taxes	10,000
Insurance	3,000
Depreciation (fully depreciated)	0
Repairs	1,000
Lawn and other maintenance	3,000

Now that Theodore is back in Nashville, he actively manages the rental home. He probably spends about ten hours per month on the rental.

Theodore received the following 1099-B from his broker:

2024 Combined Forms 1099

This is important tax information and is being furnished to the IRS (except as indicated). If you are required to file a return, a negligence penalty or other sanction may be imposed on you if this income is taxable and the IRS determines that it has not been reported.

Copy B For Recipient
OMB No. 1545-0110

Richman Investments
40 Wall Street, 24th Floor
New York, NY 10005

Theodore Lariat
140 Whitsett Road
Nashville, TN 37210

Account Number: 56-12232556
Tax ID: ***-**-9532
Payer's Federal Tax ID: 32-9863145
Financial Adviser/Phone: Leroy Khent 888-555-1212

Form 1099-B — Proceeds from Broker and Barter Exchange Transactions

Box 6: Gross Proceeds | Box 5: Not checked | Box 3: Basis reported to IRS | Box 2: Type of Gain or Loss: Short Term

Box 1 Security description (CUSIP)	Quantity sold	Box 1b Date acquired	Box 1c Date sold or disposed	Box 1d Proceeds	Box 1e Cost or other basis	Box 1g Wash sale loss disallowed	Gain/(Loss) amount
Tart Corp	100	04/27/2024	12/15/2024	3,500	3,000	-	500
Sam-O Inc	50	10/01/2023	04/28/2024	5,600	5,900	-	(300)

Box 6: Gross Proceeds | Box 5: Not checked | Box 3: Basis reported to IRS | Box 2: Type of Gain or Loss: Long Term

Box 1 Security description (CUSIP)	Quantity sold	Box 1b Date acquired	Box 1c Date sold or disposed	Box 1d Proceeds	Box 1e Cost or other basis	Box 1g Wash sale loss disallowed	Gain/(Loss) amount
Beard Corp	130	01/17/2013	08/21/2024	11,550	11,000	-	550
Nate Inc	50	03/25/2020	06/01/2024	1,200	6,200	-	(5,000)

Form 1099-INT — Interest Income

Box 1 Interest income	Box 2 Early withdrawal penalty	Box 3 Interest on U.S. Savings Bonds and Treasury obligations
135.98		

Box 4 Federal income tax withheld	Box 5 Investment expenses	Box 6 Foreign Tax Paid

Box 7 Foreign country or U.S. possession	Box 8 Tax-exempt interest	Box 9 Specified private activity bond interest

Box 10 Market Discount	Box 11 Bond Premium

Box 12 Bond premium on Treasury obligations	Box 13 Bond premium on tax-exempt bond

Required: Complete Theodore's federal tax return for 2024. Determine if Form 8949 and Schedule D are required. If so, use those forms and Form 1040, Schedule E (page 1 only), and Form 8582 (page 1 only) to complete this tax return. Do not complete Form 4562 for reporting depreciation.

2A. Skylar and Walter Black have been married for 25 years. They live at 883 Scrub Brush Street, Unit 52B, Las Vegas, NV 89125. Skylar is self-employed and Walter is a high school teacher. Skylar's Social Security number is 222-43-7690 and Walter's is 700-01-0002. Walter's birthdate is January 21, 1969, and Skylar's is February 14, 1982. The Blacks provide all the support for Skylar's mother, Rebecca Backin (Social Security number 411-66-2121), who lives in a nursing home in Reno, NV, and has no income. Walter's father, Alton Black (Social Security number 343-22-8899), lives with the Blacks in Las Vegas. Although Alton received Social Security benefits of $7,600 in 2024, the Blacks provide more than half of Alton's support. If Rebecca or Alton qualify as dependents, Skylar and Walter can claim a $500 other dependent credit for each.

Walter's earnings from teaching are:

Form W-2 (2024) — Wage and Tax Statement

- a. Employee's social security number: 700-01-0002
- b. Employer identification number (EIN): 31-1239876
- c. Employer's name, address, and ZIP code: Las Vegas School District, 2234 Vegas Valley Drive, Las Vegas, NV 89169
- e. Employee's name and address: Walter Black, 883 Scrub Brush Street, 52B, Las Vegas, NV 89125
- 1. Wages, tips, other compensation: 58,000.00
- 2. Federal income tax withheld: 4,200.00
- 3. Social security wages: 58,000.00
- 4. Social security tax withheld: 3,596.00
- 5. Medicare wages and tips: 58,000.00
- 6. Medicare tax withheld: 841.00
- 12a: DD 7,976.31
- 13: Retirement plan — X
- 15. State: NV

The Blacks moved from New Hampshire to Nevada. As a result, they sold their house in New Hampshire on January 4, 2024 (refer to 1099-S below). They originally paid $80,000 for the home on July 3, 1998. They spent $16,000 on improvements over the years and paid $31,500 in selling costs.

Form 1099-S — Proceeds From Real Estate Transactions

- FILER'S name: Dartmouth Title and Escrow, 43 S Main St, Hanover, NH 03755
- FILER'S TIN: 44-1233211
- TRANSFEROR'S TIN: 700-01-0002
- TRANSFEROR'S name: Walter and Skylar Black
- Street address: 883 Scrub Brush Street, 52B
- City, state, ZIP: Las Vegas, NV 89125
- 1. Date of closing: 01/04/2024
- 2. Gross proceeds: $632,000.00
- For calendar year: 2024
- 3. Address or legal description of property: 34 Maple Street, Hanover, NH 03755

The Blacks own a ski condo located at 123 Buncombe Lane, Brian Head, UT 84719. The condo was rented for 176 days during 2024 and used by the Blacks for 24 days. The rental activity does not rise to the level to qualify for the QBI deduction. Pertinent information about the condo rental is as follows:

Rental income	$25,000
Mortgage interest reported on Form 1098	12,000
Homeowners' association dues	4,200
Utilities	4,400
Maintenance	4,600
Depreciation (assume fully depreciated)	0

The above amounts do not reflect any allocation between rental and personal use of the condo. The Blacks are active managers of the condo.

Skylar runs a small car wash in Las Vegas as a sole proprietor. The business name is A1A Car Wash and is located at 4900 Cutler Ave NE, Las Vegas, NV 89146. The employer identification number is 19-3451234. She uses the cash method of accounting and does not track inventory of the sundries she sells (air fresheners, etc.). She therefore does not have beginning or ending inventories and recognizes the cost as supplies expense. The business code for a car wash is 811190. Her financial results for 2024 were as follows:

Revenues:	
Car Wash	$ 33,200
Sundries	3,200
Total	$ 36,400
Expenses:	
Payroll	$ 22,400
Utilities	1,987
Depreciation	0
Taxes	1,034
Licenses	300
Sundries cost	800
Insurance	1,100
Advertising	200
Total	$ 27,821
Net profit	$ 8,579

The business office at the car wash is not conducive to any type of work. It is basically a glorified broom closet. As a result, Skylar has a home office in their primary residence (which they rent). The office is 200 square feet in their 2,500 square foot apartment. They pay rent of $20,000 per year and their 2024 utilities are $2,200.

In 2019, Walter loaned his friend, Hank Shorter $5,000. In 2024, Hank declared bankruptcy and Walter is certain he will never get paid.

Walter is attending the Las Vegas Polytechnical University, pursuing a master's degree in chemistry. His employer has an education assistance program that paid Walter $5,250 in 2024. His total 2024 tuition was $10,000. The remaining tuition was paid for through the Los Gatos Hermanos Foundation scholarship for adult learners.

Walter has been experimenting with a new candy formula in his garage chemistry lab. He has been working on a new blueberry flavor that tastes more like real blueberries. For the past few years, he has spent between $1,000 and $2,000 per year on this venture but has never made any money. In 2024, a bakery in town bought some of Walter's formula for $850 to try a new blueberry muffin formula but did not purchase any additional formula after the first attempt. Walter spent $1,000 on advertising during 2024. Walter does not realistically expect to ever turn a profit, he just does not care for the existing artificial blueberry flavors.

Required: Complete the Black's federal tax return for 2024. Use Form 1040, Schedule 1, Schedule 2, Schedule C, Schedule D, Form 8949, Schedule E (page 1 only), Schedule SE, Form 8995, and Form 8829 to complete their tax return.

2B. Ryan and Blake Lovely are married filing jointly taxpayers. Ryan's birthdate is August 10, 1984 and Social Security number is 434-14-4448. Blake's birthdate is March 19, 1985 and Social Security number is 763-16-1562. They live at 22 Thornton Road, Nashua, NH 03063. Both are self-employed.

The Lovelys received the following statement from their brokerage account:

2024 Combined Forms 1099

This is important tax information and is being furnished to the IRS (except as indicated). If you are required to file a return, a negligence penalty or other sanction may be imposed on you if this income is taxable and the IRS determines that it has not been reported.

Copy B For Recipient
OMB No. 1545-0110

Pooled Investments
40 Wall Street, 24th Floor
New York, NY 10005

Ryan and Blake Lovely
22 Thornton Road
Nashua, NH 03063

Account Number	Tax ID
2345660009	***-**-4448
Payer's Federal Tax ID	
32-9863145	
Financial Adviser/Phone	
Monty Cook 888-555-1212	

Form 1099-B — Proceeds from Broker and Barter Exchange Transactions

Box 6: Gross Proceeds   Box 5: Not checked   Box 3: Basis reported to IRS   Box 2: Type of Gain or Loss: Long Term

Box 1 Security description (CUSIP)	Quantity sold	Box 1b Date acquired	Box 1c Date sold or disposed	Box 1d Proceeds	Box 1e Cost or other basis	Box 1g Wash sale loss disallowed	Gain/(Loss) amount
Green Lantern Inc	1,000	04/21/2019	03/22/2024	35,200	3,100	-	32,100

Form 1099-INT — Interest Income

Box 1 Interest income	Box 2 Early withdrawal penalty	Box 3 Interest on U.S. Savings Bonds and Treasury obligations
89.12		610.00

Box 4 Federal income tax withheld	Box 5 Investment expenses	Box 6 Foreign Tax Paid

Box 7 Foreign country or U.S. possession	Box 8 Tax-exempt interest	Box 9 Specified private activity bond interest

Box 10 Market Discount	Box 11 Bond Premium
46.23	

Box 12 Bond premium on Treasury obligations	Box 13 Bond premium on tax-exempt bond

Form 1099-DIV — Dividend Income

Box 1a Total ordinary dividends	Box 1b Qualified dividends	Box 2a Total capital gain distr.
2,900.00	2,900.00	

Box 2b Unrecap Sec 1250 gain	Box 2c Section 1202 gain	Box 2d Collectibles (28%) gain

Box 2e Section 897 ordinary dividends	Box 2f Section 897 capital gain	Box 3 Nondividend distributions

Box 4 Federal income tax withheld	Box 5 Section 199A dividends	Box 6 Investment expenses
	2,900.00	

Box 7 Foreign taxes paid	Box 8 Foreign country or possession	Box 9 Cash liquidation distributions

The U.S. Treasury interest is associated with bonds that also have market discount. The accrued market discount in 2024 was $46.23. The Lovelys elect to recognize market discount in the year earned.

Blake started a new life coach business in 2024 as a sole proprietor. The business office is located at 4 Townsend W, Suite 8, Nashua, NH 03063. The business code is 812990. The financial results are:

Client revenue	$ 5,200
Office rent expense	14,000
Supplies	1,000
Utilities	500
Telephone	400

During 2024, Ryan invested in Vaporcoin, a virtual currency. He purchased 40 units of Vaporcoin for $3,000 on February 2, 2024. On May 15, 2024, he exchanged the Vaporcoin into dollars when the value was $3,500. He did not receive a Form 1099-B or Form 1099-DA from the Vaporcoin account broker.

Ryan also operates a small business teaching fitness classes in a park near their house. The business code is 812190. Ryan has a loyal clientele, and the books and records show the following:

Exercise class receipts	$5,100
Exercise clothes	1,000
Various exercise supplies	1,600

The exercise clothes that Ryan purchased are not dissimilar to any other type of workout clothing.

Neither business has employees, an EIN or inventory. Both businesses are accounted for using the cash basis of accounting.

Ryan and Blake own a rental property located at 52 Charlotte Ave, Nashua, NH 03064. The condo was rented all year but is in need of an update. The condo's finances are as follows:

Rent	$ 8,000
Interest	10,000
Property taxes	4,000
Utilities	1,400
Maintenance	500

Ryan and Blake made a $500 estimated payment on September 15, 2024.

Required: Complete the Lovelys' federal tax return for 2024. Use Form 1040, Schedule 1, Schedule 2, Schedule B, Schedule C (two of them), Schedule D, Form 8949, Schedule E, Schedule SE, Form 8995, Form 8582 (page 1 only) to complete this tax return. Also, to compute the Lovelys' net operating loss carryforward, using Form 172.

Group 5:
Cumulative Software Problem

1. The following additional information is available for the Albert and Allison Gaytor family.

    The Gaytors own a rental beach house in Hawaii. The beach house was rented for the full year during 2024 and was not used by the Gaytors during the year. The Gaytors were active participants in the management of the rental house but the activity is not eligible for a QBI deduction. Pertinent information about the rental house is as follows:

Address: 1237 Pineapple St., Lihue, HI 96766

Gross rental income	$21,000
Mortgage interest	9,100
Real estate taxes	2,800
Utilities	1,500
Cleaning	2,600
Repairs	1,000

The house is fully depreciated so there is no depreciation expense.

Albert and Allison received the following combined statements from their investment manager:

2024 Combined Forms 1099

This is important tax information and is being furnished to the IRS (except as indicated). If you are required to file a return, a negligence penalty or other sanction may be imposed on you if this income is taxable and the IRS determines that it has not been reported.

Copy B For Recipient
OMB No. 1545-0110

Fortress Securities
40 Wall Street, 24th Floor
New York, NY 10005

Albert & Allison Gaytor
4100 SE Lincoln Road
Stuart, FL 34997

Account Number	Tax ID
2345661234	***-**-1966
Payer's Federal Tax ID	
32-9863145	
Financial Adviser/Phone	
George Edmonson 888-555-1212	

Form 1099-B — Proceeds from Broker and Barter Exchange Transactions

Box 6: Gross Proceeds   Box 5: Not checked   Box 3: Basis reported to IRS

Box 1 Security description (CUSIP)	Quantity sold	Box 1b Date acquired	Box 1c Date sold or disposed	Box 1d Proceeds	Box 1e Cost or other basis	Box 1g Wash sale loss disallowed	Gain/(Loss) amount
Orange Corp	100	02/11/2024	04/16/2024	3,000.00	2,300.00	-	700.00
Banana Company	100	07/17/2023	07/31/2024	2,200.00	4,200.00	W	(2,000.00)
Grape Corp	100	12/18/2023	09/01/2024	9,000.00	10,500.00	-	(1,500.00)
Bonds	5	12/13/2014	01/02/2024	5,100.00	5,415.00	-	(315.00)
Peach Fund	5,011.23	05/30/2015	08/22/2024	60,300.00	56,000.00	-	4,300.00
Banana Company	100	08/01/2024	12/31/2024	1,000.00	2,100.00	-	(1,100.00)

Form 1099-INT — Interest Income

Box 1 Interest income	Box 2 Early withdrawal penalty	Box 3 Interest on U.S. Savings Bonds and Treasury obligations
289.12		

Box 4 Federal income tax withheld	Box 5 Investment expenses	Box 6 Foreign Tax Paid

Box 7 Foreign country or U.S. possession	Box 8 Tax-exempt interest	Box 9 Specified private activity bond interest

Box 10 Market Discount	Box 11 Bond Premium

Box 12 Bond premium on Treasury obligations	Box 13 Bond premium on tax-exempt bond

Form 1099-DIV — Dividend Income

Box 1a Total ordinary dividends	Box 1b Qualified dividends	Box 2a Total capital gain distr.
350.00	350.00	500.00

Box 2b Unrecap Sec 1250 gain	Box 2c Section 1202 gain	Box 2d Collectibles (28%) gain

Box 2e Section 897 ordinary dividends	Box 2f Section 897 capital gain	Box 3 Nondividend distributions

Box 4 Federal income tax withheld	Box 5 Section 199A dividends	Box 6 Investment expenses
	350.00	

Box 7 Foreign taxes paid	Box 8 Foreign country or possession	Box 9 Cash liquidation distributions

The Gaytors sold 100 shares of Banana Company on July 31, 2024 and the following day purchased 100 shares at a cost of $2,100. The Gaytors held no shares of Banana Company at year end.

On January 12, 2024, Albert and Allison sold their personal residence and purchased a new house for $725,000 (refer to 1099-S below). Selling costs totaled $54,000. The house they sold was their personal residence before and after the divorce (they have lived in it together for three years since remarrying). The sold house cost $120,200 back in January of 2011 and the Gaytors added on a new bedroom and bathroom a few years ago for a cost of $20,300. They also built a pool for a cost of $61,400. They moved into their new house on January 19, 2024.

CORRECTED (if checked)	
FILER'S name, street address, city or town, state or province, country, ZIP or foreign postal code, and telephone number Jensen Beach Bank 1000 NE Jensen Beach Blvd Jensen Beach, FL 34957	1 Date of closing: 01/12/2024 OMB No. 1545-0997 Form **1099-S** (Rev. January 2022) For calendar year 20 **24** **Proceeds From Real Estate Transactions** 2 Gross proceeds: $ 770,500.00
FILER'S TIN: 61-7654321	TRANSFEROR'S TIN: 266-51-1966
TRANSFEROR'S name Albert and Allison Gaytor Street address (including apt. no.) 4100 SE Lincoln Street City or town, state or province, country, and ZIP or foreign postal code Stuart, FL 34997	3 Address (including city, state, and ZIP code) or legal description 12860 79th Ave. Sebastian, FL 32958 4 Transferor received or will receive property or services as part of the consideration (if checked) ☐ 5 If checked, transferor is a foreign person (nonresident alien, foreign partnership, foreign estate, or foreign trust) ☐
Account number (see instructions)	6 Buyer's part of real estate tax: $

Form **1099-S** (Rev. 1-2022)   (keep for your records)   www.irs.gov/Form1099S   Department of the Treasury - Internal Revenue Service

Required: Combine this new information about the Gaytor family with the information from Chapters 1–3 and complete a revised 2024 tax return for Albert and Allison. Be sure to save your data input files since this case will be expanded with more tax information in each succeeding chapter.

Chapter 5

Deductions For and From AGI

Learning Objectives

After completing this chapter, you should be able to:

LO 5.1 Explain how Health Savings Accounts (HSAs) can be used for tax-advantaged medical care.

LO 5.2 Describe the self-employed health insurance deduction.

LO 5.3 Explain the treatment of Individual Retirement Accounts (IRAs), including Roth IRAs.

LO 5.4 Explain the general contribution rules for small business and self-employed retirement plans.

LO 5.5 Describe other adjustments for adjusted gross income.

LO 5.6 Calculate the itemized deduction for medical expenses.

LO 5.7 Calculate the itemized deduction for taxes.

LO 5.8 Apply the rules for an individual taxpayer's interest deduction.

LO 5.9 Determine the charitable contributions deduction.

LO 5.10 Describe other itemized deductions.

Overview

Deductions related to a business (for example, Schedule C in Chapter 3) or the production of income or investment (for example, Schedules D and E in Chapter 4) represent deductions that are for AGI (above-the-line). The business deductions are generally reported on the separate schedules. However, the tax law permits additional for AGI deductions that may be associated with business activity or, in some instances unrelated to business activity, such as the student loan interest deduction, as simply a matter of legislative grace for individual taxpayers. These additional deductions are reported on Part II of Schedule 1 of Form 1040. Included among the more common for AGI deductions is:

- Individual retirement account (IRA) contributions,
- One-half of self-employment taxes,
- Student loan interest, and
- Self-employed health care and qualified retirement plan contributions.

Deductions that occur after AGI (from AGI deductions, or below-the-line) include the standard deduction covered in Chapter 1, the qualified business income deduction covered in Chapter 4, and Schedule A itemized deductions, introduced in this chapter. Itemized deductions fall into six categories: medical and dental expenses, state and local taxes, interest expenses, charitable contributions, casualty and theft losses, and other itemized deductions.

Recall from Chapter 1, that when calculating taxable income, individuals determine their standard deduction and their allowable itemized deductions and use the larger of the two, in order to minimize taxable income. For example, if a taxpayer's standard deduction is $14,600 and her itemized deductions are $18,100, she would use her itemized deductions in calculating taxable income. On the other hand, if her itemized deductions were $9,500, she would use the larger standard deduction of $14,600 in computing taxable income.

A number of limitations are placed on itemized deductions. One example is the $10,000 limit on state and local taxes. Many limitations are scheduled to end after 2025. As a result, brief explanations of the pre-limitation deductions are provided.

5-1 Health Savings Accounts

Learning Objective 5.1

Explain how Health Savings Accounts (HSAs) can be used for tax-advantaged medical care.

There are four types of tax-favored medical spending plans available to taxpayers:

1. Health care flexible spending arrangements or FSAs (covered in Chapter 2) allow employees to set aside money to cover medical expenses and exclude the funds from gross income.
2. Health Reimbursement Arrangements (HRAs) are funded solely by the employer (not part of a cafeteria plan) to reimburse the employee, spouse, and dependents for medical expenses, up to a maximum dollar amount for a coverage period, and provide that any unused portion is carried forward to increase the maximum reimbursement amount in later coverage periods. Coverage and reimbursements of medical care expenses of an employee, spouse, and dependents are generally excluded from gross income in a qualifying HRA.
3. Medical Savings Accounts (MSAs or Archer MSAs) permit (limited) deductions for amounts contributed to an account established to cover medical expenses for small business and self-employed individuals. As of January 1, 2008, no new MSA accounts were to be established, and thus, are not covered in detail in this textbook. Note that an Archer MSA can be rolled over into an HSA.
4. Health Savings Accounts (HSAs) are a type of savings account which may be established for the purpose of paying unreimbursed medical expenses by taxpayers who carry qualifying high-deductible medical insurance.

Contributions to HSAs are a deduction for AGI and are limited to certain dollar amounts depending on age and whether the high-deductible insurance covers an individual or a family. Earnings and unused contributions accumulated in an HSA are not taxed, and distributions to cover medical expenses are not taxed or penalized.

Health insurance with a high deductible is less expensive than standard health insurance since the issuing insurance company does not have to pay any of the taxpayer's medical expenses until a certain threshold (the deductible plus any other required out-of-pocket medical costs) is reached. The funds contributed to the HSA may then be used by the taxpayer to pay medical expenses not covered by health insurance. This popular combination of tax benefits and less expensive insurance is designed to encourage taxpayers to carry health insurance.

5-1a Deductions for Contributions to HSAs

Table 5.1 shows the contribution limits for HSA deductions for 2024. The table also shows the additional "catch-up" contributions allowed for individuals beginning at age 55 and ending at age 65, the age for Medicare eligibility. Individuals are not allowed to make contributions to HSAs once they attain the age of 65 and qualify for Medicare coverage. Finally, Table 5.1 shows the lower and upper deductible and out-of-pocket medical expense limits (excluding the actual cost of insurance) required for insurance to qualify as a high-deductible health plan.

Table 5.1   2024 Limits for HSA

	Family	Self-Only
Contribution limit	$ 8,300	$ 4,150
Additional catch-up contribution for taxpayer age 55 or older	1,000 per qualifying spouse	1,000
Minimum health insurance deductible	3,200	1,600
Maximum health insurance out-of-pocket	16,100	8,050

Although the out-of-pocket limits under the Affordable Care Act (ACA) are slightly higher than those listed above, the IRS limits determine tax compliance for HSAs. Contributions to HSAs must generally be made by April 15 of the year following the year for which the contribution is made. IRS Form 8889 is used to provide information to the IRS regarding HSA deductions claimed on line 13 of Schedule 1 of Form 1040 and to compute the deduction amount.

Example Gary is 35 years old and carries self-only coverage in a qualifying high-deductible health insurance plan during 2024. Gary may contribute up to $4,150 to his HSA account and deduct this amount for AGI. Gary may use some or all of the contributions to pay medical expenses he has incurred. Any amount he leaves in the HSA account will accumulate earnings tax-free and carry forward to be available for payment of qualifying medical expenses in the future. ♦

5-1b Distributions

Distributions from HSAs are excluded from income when used to pay for qualified medical expenses. Distributions which are not used to pay for qualified medical expenses are subject to both income tax and a 20-percent penalty. Once a taxpayer is 65 years old, distributions may be taken for nonmedical expenses and will be subject to income tax, but not the 20-percent penalty. Distributions from an HSA are reported on Form 1099-SA. The amount of the distribution is reported in Box 1 and codes indicating the proper treatment are provided in Box 3. A normal distribution is coded 1.

To report HSA information and complete a Form 8889, the input area can be found in the left-hand margin under Deductions/Adjustments to Income. The input area is conveniently called Health Savings Account (Form 8889).

ProConnect™ Tax TIP

Example Debbie is 66 years old and has $30,000 in her HSA. She can withdraw the $30,000 to purchase a new car, but will have to pay income tax on the distribution. If she takes the distribution to pay medical expenses, no income tax will be due. If Debbie was under age 65 and took a distribution from her HSA to buy a car, she would owe both income tax and a 20-percent penalty on the distribution. ♦

5-1c Guidance

The rules governing HSAs are more detailed and lengthy than the summaries above. IRS Publication 969 is a good source of information on a range of additional issues related to HSAs and their operation.

New Tax Law

Most healthcare in the United States is provided on a fee-for-services basis. If a taxpayer visits a doctor, the taxpayer (or in many instances, the taxpayer's health insurer) is charged for the cost of whatever services are provided. Subscription-based healthcare is a fairly new healthcare model where taxpayers pay a fixed amount every month, quarter, or year and all the services the medical practitioner provides are covered. Although nothing has yet passed, a number of congressional bills have addressed using HSAs with this type of healthcare model. Considering the cost of healthcare, HSAs are a ripe target for congressional action. Through July 2024, the 118th Congress has proposed almost 50 bills that would amend the operation of HSAs in some way.

Self-Study Problem 5.1 *Refer to Appendix E for Solutions to Self-Study Problems*

a. Determine the deductible HSA amount for each of the following taxpayers for 2024:
   1. Amy is 40 years old, has a qualifying high-deductible health plan, carries family coverage, and contributes the maximum amount to her family HSA.
   2. Cary is 60 years old, has self-only health insurance with no deductible, and contributes $1,200 to an HSA.
   3. Annabelle is 52 years old and contributes $2,000 to her HSA. She has qualifying self-only coverage in a high-deductible health plan.
   4. Lucille is 70 years old and is covered by Medicare. She contributes $3,050 to her HSA.

b. Alex Morton is a single taxpayer, age 34, and uses the pronouns they/them. They are part of a qualifying high-deductible health plan. In 2024, Alex made contributions of $4,000 to their HSA. Alex's employer reported making $150 of contributions to their HSA in Box 12 of their Form W-2 (code W). Alex spent $2,000 on qualified medical expenses. Alex received the following Form 1099-SA from their HSA administrator:

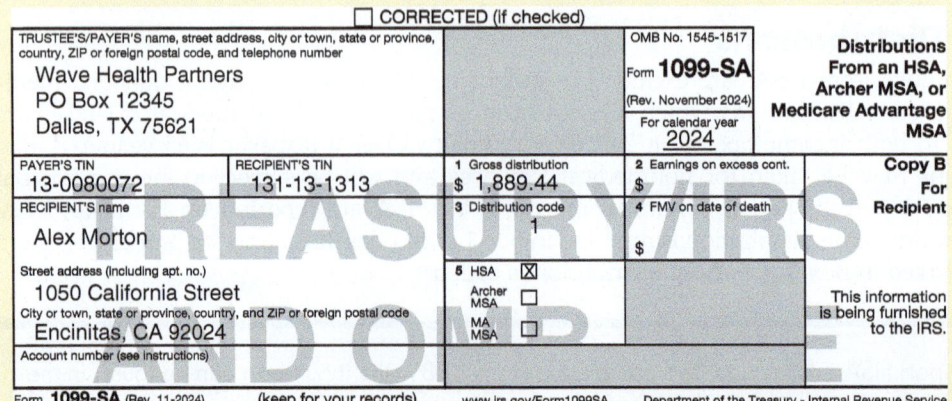

Prepare Form 8889 on Page 5-5 to determine Alex's HSA deduction and taxable HSA distribution.

Self-Study Problem 5.1

Form 8889
Department of the Treasury
Internal Revenue Service

Health Savings Accounts (HSAs)

Attach to Form 1040, 1040-SR, or 1040-NR.
Go to *www.irs.gov/Form8889* for instructions and the latest information.

OMB No. 1545-0074
2024
Attachment Sequence No. **52**

Name(s) shown on Form 1040, 1040-SR, or 1040-NR

Social security number of HSA beneficiary. If both spouses have HSAs, see instructions.

Before you begin: Complete Form 8853, Archer MSAs and Long-Term Care Insurance Contracts, if required.

Part I — HSA Contributions and Deduction. See the instructions before completing this part. If you are filing jointly and both you and your spouse each have separate HSAs, complete a separate Part I for each spouse.

1. Check the box to indicate your coverage under a high-deductible health plan (HDHP) during 2024. See instructions . . . . ☐ Self-only ☐ Family

2. HSA contributions you made for 2024 (or those made on your behalf), including those made by the unextended due date of your tax return that were for 2024. **Do not** include employer contributions, contributions through a cafeteria plan, or rollovers. See instructions **2**

3. If you were under age 55 at the end of 2024 and, on the first day of **every** month during 2024, you were, or were considered, an eligible individual with the **same** coverage, enter $4,150 ($8,300 for family coverage). **All others**, see the instructions for the amount to enter **3**

4. Enter the amount you and your employer contributed to your Archer MSAs for 2024 from Form 8853, lines 1 and 2. If you or your spouse had family coverage under an HDHP at any time during 2024, also include any amount contributed to your spouse's Archer MSAs **4**

5. Subtract line 4 from line 3. If zero or less, enter -0- **5**

6. Enter the amount from line 5. But if you and your spouse each have separate HSAs and had family coverage under an HDHP at any time during 2024, see the instructions for the amount to enter . . **6**

7. If you were age 55 or older at the end of 2024, married, and you or your spouse had family coverage under an HDHP at any time during 2024, enter your additional contribution amount. See instructions . **7**

8. Add lines 6 and 7 . . . . **8**

9. Employer contributions made to your HSAs for 2024 . . . . . . **9**

10. Qualified HSA funding distributions **10**

11. Add lines 9 and 10 . . . . **11**

12. Subtract line 11 from line 8. If zero or less, enter -0- **12**

13. **HSA deduction** (see instructions) **13**

Part II — HSA Distributions. If you are filing jointly and both you and your spouse each have separate HSAs, complete a separate Part II for each spouse.

14a. Total distributions you received in 2024 from all HSAs (see instructions) **14a**

b. Distributions included on line 14a that you rolled over to another HSA. Also include any excess contributions (and the earnings on those excess contributions) included on line 14a that were withdrawn by the due date of your return. See instructions **14b**

c. Subtract line 14b from line 14a **14c**

15. Qualified medical expenses paid using HSA distributions (see instructions) **15**

16. **Taxable HSA distributions.** Subtract line 15 from line 14c. If zero or less, enter -0-. Also, include this amount in the total on Schedule 1 (Form 1040), Part I, line 8f **16**

17a. If any of the distributions included on line 16 meet any of the **Exceptions to the Additional 20% Tax** (see instructions), check here . . . . ☐

b. **Additional 20% tax** (see instructions). Enter 20% (0.20) of the distributions included on line 16 that are subject to the additional 20% tax. Also, include this amount in the total on Schedule 2 (Form 1040), Part II, line 17c **17b**

Part III — Income and Additional Tax for Failure To Maintain HDHP Coverage. See the instructions before completing this part. If you are filing jointly and both you and your spouse each have separate HSAs, complete a separate Part III for each spouse.

18. Last-month rule **18**

19. Qualified HSA funding distribution **19**

20. **Total income.** Add lines 18 and 19. Include this amount on Schedule 1 (Form 1040), Part I, line 8f . **20**

21. **Additional tax.** Multiply line 20 by 10% (0.10). Include this amount in the total on Schedule 2 (Form 1040), Part II, line 17d **21**

For Paperwork Reduction Act Notice, see your tax return instructions. Cat. No. 37621P Form **8889** (2024)

Learning Objective 5.2

Describe the self-employed health insurance deduction.

5-2 Self-Employed Health Insurance Deduction

Self-employed taxpayers are allowed an above-the-line deduction for the cost of providing health insurance for themselves and their families. This deduction is meant to give self-employed taxpayers the same tax treatment available to employees who are offered health insurance as a tax-free benefit of employment. The deduction of self-employed healthcare is not reported on Schedule C with most other business expenses, but is instead reported as a for AGI deduction on line 17 of Part II of Schedule 1 to Form 1040. Deductible insurance includes the following:

- Medical and dental insurance paid to cover the self-employed taxpayer, spouse, and dependents;
- Medical and dental insurance paid for children under the age of 27 who are not dependents;
- Medicare premiums;
- Long-term care insurance paid for the taxpayer and the family of the taxpayer within certain dollar limitations, presented in Table 5.2.

Example Tre has a barbershop and earns $60,000 in 2024, which he reports on Schedule C. Tre pays $10,000 in health and dental insurance costs for himself, his unemployed wife, and his 10-year-old daughter. The full $10,000 is a deduction on Tre's Schedule 1 of Form 1040 (not Schedule C). ♦

5-2a Special Rules

The following special rules limit the treatment of health insurance as a deduction for AGI:

- Other health care plan available: The self-employed health insurance deduction is not allowed for any months in which the taxpayer is eligible to participate in a subsidized health care plan offered by an employer of either the taxpayer or the spouse of the taxpayer.
- Definition of self-employment: Taxpayers with income reportable on Schedule C are generally considered self-employed. However, taxpayers with earnings from certain partnerships, S corporations, limited liability corporations (LLCs), and farm businesses may also be considered self-employed and may be allowed the above-the-line deduction for self-employed health insurance.
- The self-employed health insurance deduction is available for partners, but if a partner performs services for the partnership and the partnership pays health insurance premiums on behalf of that partner, the premiums are deductible by the partnership and includable in the recipient-partner's gross income. The partner then takes the self-employed insurance deduction.
- Any taxpayer who is a two-percent or more shareholder of an S corporation is treated like a partner of a partnership. Health insurance premiums paid by an S corporation on behalf of a two-percent shareholder-employee are deductible by the corporation, and includable in the recipient shareholder-employee's income. The shareholder-employee may deduct the cost of the premium using the self-employment insurance deduction.
- Deductible portion: Self-employed taxpayers who receive advance premium tax credits under the ACA may deduct only the portion paid out of pocket, not the portion covered by the premium tax credit.
- Earned income limitation: The deduction for self-employed health insurance is only allowed to the extent of the taxpayer's net self-employed earned income. For example, a taxpayer with a Schedule C business loss would not be allowed to claim a self-employed health insurance deduction even though they paid for health insurance. The deduction may instead be allowed as an itemized medical deduction subject to the limits discussed in LO 5.6.
- Long-term care premium limitation: The individual limitations on the deduction of long-term care premiums are presented in Table 5.2.

Table 5.2 2024 Long-Term Care Premium Deduction Limitations

Age Before Year-End	Limitation on Premiums
40 or less	$ 470
More than 40 but not more than 50	880
More than 50 but not more than 60	1,760
More than 60 but not more than 70	4,710
More than 70	5,880

ProConnect™ Tax TIP

To enter self-employed health insurance and many of the other for AGI deductions, go to Deductions/Adjustments to Income. There is a long input page, and a number of subheadings are available in the left-hand margin.

Example Candace is a 55-year-old massage therapist who earns $40,000 of net self-employment income in 2024. She pays $6,000 for medical insurance and $1,790 for long-term care insurance. Candace can take $7,760 ($6,000 + $1,760) as a deduction for AGI. ♦

Self-Study Problem 5.2
Refer to Appendix E for Solutions to Self-Study Problems

During the 2024 tax year, Gwen Eyeful operates a small business as a physical therapist. They report $90,000 of net earned income on their Schedule C, reported a deduction of $6,358 for one-half of their self-employment tax, and paid the following insurance premiums:

- Family health insurance: $15,000
- Family dental insurance: $2,000
- Health insurance for their 24-year-old son who is not a dependent: $3,000
- Long-term care insurance for their 49-year-old spouse: $900

Use Form 7206 on Page 5-8 to determine Gwen's self-employed health insurance deduction for 2024.

Self-Study Problem 5.2

Form 7206
Department of the Treasury
Internal Revenue Service

Self-Employed Health Insurance Deduction

Attach to Form 1040, 1040-SR, or 1040-NR.
Go to *www.irs.gov/Form7206* for instructions and the latest information.

OMB No. 1545-0074
2024
Attachment Sequence No. **206**

Name(s) shown on return | Your taxpayer identification number

Note: Use a separate Form 7206 for each trade or business under which an insurance plan is established.

1. Enter the total amount paid in 2024 for health insurance coverage established under your business (or the S corporation in which you were a more-than-2% shareholder) for 2024 for you, your spouse, and your dependents. But **don't** include the following. See instructions **1**

   • Amounts for any month you were eligible to participate in a health plan subsidized by your employer or your spouse's employer or the employer of either your dependent or your child who was under the age of 27 at the end of 2024.

   • Any amounts paid, not to exceed $3,000, from retirement plan distributions that were **nontaxable** because you are a retired public safety officer. See instructions.

   • Any payments for qualified long-term care insurance (see line 2).

2. For coverage under a qualified long-term care insurance contract, enter for each person covered the **smaller** of (a) or (b).
   (a) Total payments made for that person during the year.
   (b) The amount shown below. Use the person's age at the end of the tax year.
      $470— if that person is age 40 or younger
      $880— if age 41 to 50
      $1,760— if age 51 to 60
      $4,710— if age 61 to 70
      $5,880— if age 71 or older

   Note: The amount of long-term care premiums that can be included as a medical expense is limited by the person's age. **Don't** include payments for any month you were eligible to participate in a long-term care insurance plan subsidized by your employer or your spouse's employer, or the employer of either your dependent or your child who was under the age of 27 at the end of 2024. If more than one person is covered, figure separately the amount to enter for each person. Then enter the total of those amounts **2**

3. Add lines 1 and 2 . . . . **3**

4. Enter your net profit* and any other earned income** from the trade or business under which the insurance plan is established. Don't include Conservation Reserve Program payments exempt from self-employment tax. If the business is an S corporation, skip to line 11 . . . . **4**

5. Enter the total of all net profits* from Schedule C (Form 1040), line 31; Schedule F (Form 1040), line 34; or Schedule K-1 (Form 1065), box 14, code A, plus any other income allocable to the profitable businesses. Don't include Conservation Reserve Program payments exempt from self-employment tax. See the Instructions for Schedule SE (Form 1040). **Don't** include any net losses shown on these schedules **5**

6. Divide line 4 by line 5 . . . . **6**

7. Multiply Schedule 1 (Form 1040), line 15, deductible part of self-employment tax, by the percentage on line 6 . . . . **7**

8. Subtract line 7 from line 4 . . . . **8**

9. Enter the amount, if any, from Schedule 1 (Form 1040), line 16, self-employed SEP, SIMPLE, and qualified plans, attributable to the same trade or business in which the insurance plan is established **9**

10. Subtract line 9 from line 8 . . . . **10**

11. Enter your Medicare wages (box 5 of Form W-2) from an S corporation in which you are a more-than-2% shareholder and in which the insurance plan is established **11**

12. Enter any amount from Form 2555, line 45, attributable to the amount entered on line 4 or 11 above **12**

13. Subtract line 12 from line 10 or 11, whichever applies **13**

14. **Self-employed health insurance deduction.** Enter the **smaller** of line 3 or line 13 here and on Schedule 1 (Form 1040), line 17. **Don't** include this amount when figuring any medical expense deduction on Schedule A (Form 1040) **14**

* If you used either optional method to figure your net earnings from self-employment from any business, don't enter your net profit from the business. Instead, enter the amount attributable to that business from Schedule SE (Form 1040), Part I, line 4b.

** **Earned income** includes net earnings and gains from the sale, transfer, or licensing of property you created. However, it doesn't include capital gain income.

For Privacy Act and Paperwork Reduction Act Notice, see separate instructions. Cat. No. 56399C Form **7206** (2024)

5-3 Individual Retirement Accounts

The two principal types of individual retirement accounts (IRAs) are the *traditional IRA* and the *Roth IRA*. Generally, annual contributions to a traditional IRA are deductible, and retirement distributions are taxable. Annual contributions to a Roth IRA are not deductible, but retirement distributions are nontaxable. Earnings in both types of IRAs are not taxable in the current year.

5.3 Learning Objective
Explain the treatment of Individual Retirement Accounts (IRAs), including Roth IRAs.

Example Thayer has $30,000 in his IRA in 2024. The earnings for the year on this IRA are $1,600. These earnings are not taxed to Thayer in the current year. ♦

5-3a IRA Annual Contributions and Deductions

There are annual contribution limits for both traditional and Roth IRAs. In 2024, the total maximum annual contribution that may be made to both types of IRAs combined is equal to the lesser of (1) 100 percent of the taxpayer's compensation or self-employment income (earned income) or (2) $7,000. For example, a taxpayer with earned income of over $7,000 may contribute $4,000 to a traditional IRA and $3,000 to a Roth IRA, or any other combination that does not exceed $7,000. If married filing jointly, the maximum amount increases to $14,000 if an additional $7,000 is contributed to a spouse's IRA, even if the spouse has no earned income. The maximum contribution to a spouse's IRA may not exceed $7,000. In 2024, an additional $1,000 annual "catch-up" contribution is allowed for taxpayers and spouses age 50 and over, increasing the maximum contribution to $8,000.

Example Quincy, age 31, works for Big Corporation and has a salary of $40,000 for 2024. Quincy is eligible to contribute the maximum $7,000 to his traditional or Roth IRA for 2024. If Quincy has a spouse who does not work, he could also contribute $7,000 into her IRA or Roth IRA. If Quincy is 55 years old instead of 31 years old, he could contribute $8,000 to his traditional or Roth IRA, and $7,000 or $8,000 for his spouse, depending on whether she is old enough to qualify for the $1,000 "catch-up" contribution. ♦

The annual deduction maximums may be reduced for traditional IRAs if the taxpayer is an active participant in another qualified retirement plan. The annual contribution allowed for a Roth IRA is reduced for all taxpayers over certain income levels, but is not affected by whether the taxpayer or spouse is an active participant in another retirement plan. In each case, the maximum annual contribution is phased out proportionately between certain modified adjusted gross income ranges, as shown in Table 5.3.

Table 5.3 PHASE-OUT AGI Limits for Contributions to IRAs

	Roth IRA	Traditional IRA		
		No Active Participant	**One Active Participant**	**Both Active Participants**
Single or Head of Household	$146,000–$161,000	No phase-out	$77,000–$87,000	N/A
Married Filing Jointly	$230,000–$240,000	No phase-out	Active spouse $123,000–$143,000 Nonactive spouse $230,000–$240,000	$123,000–$143,000
Married Filing Separately	$0–$10,000 for all			

When one spouse is an active participant in a retirement plan and the other is not, two separate income limitations apply but both measure the joint income of the married couple.

A nondeductible traditional IRA contribution may be made by taxpayers with income over the phase-out ranges shown above. Although the taxpayer cannot deduct the contribution, all income earned in the IRA account is sheltered from tax until the earnings are withdrawn. When there have been nondeductible IRA contributions, the taxable portion of the withdrawn IRA money is calculated similar to the treatment of annuities covered in Chapter 2. Many high-income taxpayers make nondeductible traditional IRA contributions each year because of the deferral of tax on the earnings of the IRA.

Example Wayde, age 31, is single and is covered by a retirement plan. If his adjusted gross income is $77,500 and includes a student loan deduction of $2,500 but does not include any deduction for an IRA contribution. Worksheet 1-1 from IRS Publication 590A can be used to compute Wayde's modified adjusted gross income for purposes of the IRA deduction limitation:

Worksheet 1-1. Figuring Your Modified AGI

Keep for Your Records

Use this worksheet to figure your modified AGI for traditional IRA purposes.

1.	Enter your adjusted gross income (AGI) from Form 1040, 1040-SR, or Form 1040-NR, line 11, figured without taking into account the amount from Schedule 1 (Form 1040), line 20	1.	77,500
2.	Enter any student loan interest deduction from Schedule 1 (Form 1040), line 21	2.	2,500
3.	Enter any foreign earned income exclusion and/or housing exclusion from Form 2555, line 45	3.	
4.	Enter any foreign housing deduction from Form 2555, line 50	4.	
5.	Enter any excludable savings bond interest from Form 8815, line 14	5.	
6.	Enter any excluded employer-provided adoption benefits from Form 8839, line 28	6.	
7.	Add lines 1 through 6. This is your **modified AGI** for traditional IRA purposes	7.	80,000

Wayde wishes to make the maximum contribution of $7,000. The deductible portion of the traditional IRA contribution can be computed using Worksheet 1-2 from IRS Publication 590A presented on Page 5-11.

Worksheet 1-2. Figuring Your Reduced IRA Deduction for 2024

Keep for Your Records

(Use only if you or your spouse are covered by an employer plan and your modified AGI falls between the two amounts shown below for your coverage situation and filing status.)

Note. If you were married and both you and your spouse contributed to IRAs, figure your deduction and your spouse's deduction separately.

IF you...	AND your filing status is...	AND your modified AGI is over...	THEN enter on line 1 below...
are **covered** by an employer plan	single or head of household	$77,000	$87,000
	married filing jointly or qualifying surviving spouse	$123,000	$143,000
	married filing separately	$0	$10,000
aren't covered by an employer plan, but your spouse is **covered**	married filing jointly	$230,000	$240,000
	married filing separately	$0	$10,000

1. Enter applicable amount from table above .... **1.** _87,000_

2. Enter your *modified AGI* (that of both spouses, if married filing jointly) .... **2.** _80,000_

   Note. If line 2 is equal to or more than the amount on line 1, **stop here**. Your IRA contributions aren't deductible. See *Nondeductible Contributions*, earlier.

3. Subtract line 2 from line 1. **If line 3 is $10,000 or more ($20,000 or more if married filing jointly or qualifying surviving spouse and you are covered by an employer plan), stop here.** You can take a full IRA deduction for contributions of up to $7,000 ($8,000 if you are age 50 or older) or 100% of your (and if married filing jointly, your spouse's) compensation, whichever is less .... **3.** _7,000_

4. Multiply line 3 by the percentage below that applies to you. If the result isn't a multiple of $10, round it to the next highest multiple of $10. (For example, $611.40 is rounded to $620.) However, if the result is less than $200, enter $200.
   - Married filing jointly or qualifying surviving spouse **and** you are covered by an employer plan, multiply line 3 by 35% (0.35) (by 40% (0.40) if you are age 50 or older).
   - All others, multiply line 3 by 70% (0.70) (by 80% (0.80) if you are age 50 or older). ...... **4.** _4,900_

5. Enter your compensation minus any deductions on Schedule 1 (Form 1040), line 15 (deductible part of self-employment tax), and Schedule 1 (Form 1040), line 16 (self-employed SEP, SIMPLE, and qualified plans). If you are filing a joint return and your compensation is less than your spouse's, include your spouse's compensation reduced by his or her traditional IRA and Roth IRA contributions for this year. If you file Form 1040, 1040-SR, or 1040-NR, don't reduce your compensation by any losses from self-employment .... **5.** _77,500_

6. Enter contributions made, or to be made, to your IRA for 2024, but **don't** enter more than $7,000 ($8,000 if you are age 50 or older). If contributions are more than $7,000 ($8,000 if you are age 50 or older), see *Excess Contributions*, later .... **6.** _7,000_

7. **IRA deduction.** Compare lines 4, 5, and 6. Enter the smallest amount (or a smaller amount if you choose) here and on your Schedule 1 (Form 1040), line 20. If line 6 is more than line 7 and you want to make a nondeductible contribution, go to line 8 .... **7.** _4,900_

8. **Nondeductible contribution.** Subtract line 7 from line 5 or 6, whichever is smaller. Enter the result here and on line 1 of your Form 8606 .... **8.** _2,100_

Wayde may choose to contribute the $7,000 maximum to a traditional IRA, but the phased-out $2,100 will not be deductible. Alternatively, he may contribute the remaining $2,100 to a Roth IRA since his income is below the phase-out range for Roth IRA contributions. He could also choose to ignore the allowed $4,900 traditional IRA contribution and contribute the full nondeductible $7,000 to a Roth IRA. ♦

Example Iryna, who is 36 and single, would like to contribute the maximum $7,000 to her Roth IRA. Her modified AGI is $156,000 which is greater than the 2024 threshold of $146,000. Her maximum contribution to a Roth IRA can be computed using Worksheet 2-2 from IRS Publication 590A:

Worksheet 2-2. Determining Your Reduced Roth IRA Contribution Limit

Before using this worksheet, check Table 2-1 to determine whether or not your Roth IRA contribution limit is reduced. If it is, use this worksheet to determine how much it is reduced.

1. Enter your modified AGI for Roth IRA purposes (Worksheet 2-1, line 10) .... 1. _____156,000_
2. Enter:
   - $230,000 if filing a joint return or qualifying surviving spouse,
   - $-0- if married filing a separate return and you lived with your spouse at any time in 2024, or
   - $146,000 for all others .... 2. _____146,000_
3. Subtract line 2 from line 1 .... 3. _____10,000_
4. Enter:
   - $10,000 if filing a joint return or qualifying surviving spouse or married filing a separate return and you lived with your spouse at any time during the year, or
   - $15,000 for all others .... 4. _____15,000_
5. Divide line 3 by line 4 and enter the result as a decimal (rounded to at least three places). If the result is 1.000 or more, enter 1.000 .... 5. _____0.667_
6. Enter the lesser of:
   - $7,000 ($8,000 if you are age 50 or older), or
   - Your taxable compensation .... 6. _____7,000_
7. Multiply line 5 by line 6 .... 7. _____4,669_
8. Subtract line 7 from line 6. Round the result up to the nearest $10. If the result is less than $200, enter $200 .... 8. _____2,340_
9. Enter contributions for the year to other IRAs .... 9. _____0_
10. Subtract line 9 from line 6 .... 10. _____7,000_
11. Enter the lesser of line 8 or line 10. This is your **reduced Roth IRA contribution limit** .... 11. _____2,340_

◆

Example Paul and Lonah are married and are both 36 years old. Lonah is covered by a retirement plan and earns $80,000. Paul is not covered by a retirement plan and earns $66,000. Lonah cannot make a deductible contribution to a traditional IRA since the income on their joint tax return is greater than the $143,000 maximum phase-out range for married couples. Paul, however, can make a fully deductible IRA contribution of $7,000 since Paul and Lonah's AGI is below the $230,000 phase-out threshold used when one spouse is an active participant in a plan and the other is not. Lonah could still choose to make a $7,000 contribution to a Roth IRA since their joint income is below the Roth IRA phase-out range for married couples. Paul would have a choice between making a $7,000 deductible contribution to a traditional IRA or a contribution of $7,000 to a Roth IRA or some combination thereof, not greater than $7,000 in total. ♦

Contributions made above the maximum permitted for that year are subject to a 6-percent excise tax for each year the excess amount has not been withdrawn.

An IRA contribution may be made at any time before the original due date of the tax return for the year in which the deduction is to be claimed. This means, for example, that an individual can contribute to an IRA as late as the filing deadline of April 15, 2025, and still deduct the amount on the 2024 tax return.

5-3b Roth IRA Conversions

Taxpayers may benefit from a rule allowing conversions of traditional IRAs into Roth IRAs. Although the income generated by the conversion is subject to current income tax, taxpayers with certain factors in their favor such as number of years to retirement, a low current tax bracket, or a high expected tax bracket in retirement, may wish to convert. Also, taxpayers with negative taxable income due to large personal deductions may wish to convert enough of their regular IRAs to Roth IRAs to bring taxable income to zero. This way the conversion can be done with no tax cost since deductions which would otherwise be lost are used to offset the taxable IRA income.

5-3c Traditional IRA Distributions

Money removed from a traditional IRA is taxable as ordinary income and may be subject to a 10-percent penalty for early withdrawal.

Example Ben Zima is 63 years old and decides he will take a cruise around the world. He withdraws $35,000 from his traditional IRA to purchase the cruise. All of Ben's contributions to the IRA were deductible. The $35,000 is taxable to Ben as ordinary income. Because Ben is older than 59½, he meets the age requirement to avoid any penalty for early withdrawal. ♦

Example Tomas is 48 years old and decides he must have a red sports car. He withdraws $35,000 from his traditional IRA to purchase the car. Tomas does not qualify for any of the penalty-free withdrawals listed in Table 5.4 on Page 5-15. The $35,000 is taxable to Tomas as ordinary income and he is subject to a $3,500 (10% × $35,000) penalty for removing the funds before age 59½. ♦

5-3d Roth IRA Distributions

Unlike a traditional IRA, distributions from a Roth IRA are not generally subject to tax and a Roth IRA does not have required minimum distributions. If the funds have been in the Roth IRA for a five-year holding period, distributions will be tax-free if any of the following requirements are satisfied:

1. The distribution is made on or after the date on which the participant attains age 59½.
2. The distribution is made to a beneficiary (or the participant's estate) on or after the participant's death.
3. The participant becomes disabled.
4. The distribution is used to pay for up to $10,000 in qualified first-time home-buyer's expenses.

Example Shunsuke establishes a Roth IRA at age 50 and contributes to the Roth each year for 10 years. The account is now worth $61,000, consisting of $50,000 of nondeductible contributions and $11,000 in earnings that have not been taxed. Shunsuke may withdraw the $61,000 tax-free from the Roth IRA because he is over age 59½ and has met the five-year holding period requirement. ♦

The distributions may be taxable if the taxpayer receives distributions from a Roth IRA and does not satisfy the above requirements. The part of the distributions that represents a return of capital is tax-free, and the part that represents a payout of earnings is taxable and subject to the 10-percent early withdrawal penalty. Under the ordering rules for Roth IRA distributions, distributions are treated as first made from contributions (return of capital) and then from earnings.

Example Assume the same facts in the previous example, except that Shunsuke is age 56 and receives distributions of $10,000. Assume his adjusted basis for the Roth IRA is $35,000 (contributions made of $5,000 × 7 years). The distribution is tax-free and his adjusted basis is reduced to $25,000 ($35,000 − $10,000). ♦

Tax Break The five-year holding period for tax-free distributions for a Roth IRA is measured in a taxpayer-favorable manner. The five-year clock starts when funds are first deposited into the Roth account. For example, if a taxpayer contributes to a Roth IRA annually starting in 2019. Once the five-year timeframe has been completed on the first contribution, all the subsequent contributions are also deemed to meet the five-year rule. Remember, however, the taxpayer also must be age 59½ at the time of the distribution to avoid the 10-percent penalty tax.

5-3e Early Distributions

The 10-percent penalty that applies to early withdrawals from a traditional IRA and the earnings of a Roth IRA can most easily be avoided by waiting until the taxpayer has reached age 59½. Under certain circumstances, the 10-percent penalty tax is waived. Many of these waiver provisions also apply to other forms of qualified retirement plans covered later in this chapter, so details are provided for all types of plans in Table 5.4 on Page 5-15.

Example Juanita, a single taxpayer under age 55, is stricken with a serious illness in 2024 that results in out-of-pocket medicals costs of $23,000. Her 2024 AGI is $50,000 and she will use the standard deduction. To help pay for her medical bills, Juanita takes a distribution from her IRA in the amount of $20,000. Her medical expenses in excess of 7.5 percent of AGI are $19,250 [$23,000 − (50,000 × 7.5%)]. Although she will pay ordinary income tax on the entire $23,000 distribution, she may exclude $19,250 from the additional 10-percent penalty tax. ♦

Example Nozomi, a single taxpayer under age 55, purchases a new home in 2024 for $230,000. To provide funds for the down payment, she takes a $15,000 distribution from her IRA. Nozomi has not owned a home in the last two years, and thus, qualifies as a first-time home buyer. Although Nozomi will pay ordinary income tax on the entire $15,000 distribution, she may exclude $10,000 from the 10-percent penalty tax. Nozomi has used her entire lifetime exclusion under the first-time home buyer exclusion. ♦

An early distribution is generally reported to the taxpayer on Form 1099-R using the distribution codes 1 (for early distributions for which the taxable amount may not be known) or 2 (for early distributions for which the payor knows the specific exception to the 10-percent penalty tax). The taxpayer reports early distributions from an IRA (along with several other distributions subject to the 10-percent penalty tax) on Form 5329. Form 5329 has a series of codes that are used to identify an exception to the 10-percent penalty tax as presented in Table 5.4. Form 5329 is presented on Page 5-19.

Table 5.4 Exceptions to 10-percent Tax on Early Distributions

Exception	The distribution will NOT be subject to the 10% additional early distribution tax in the following circumstances:	IRA, SEP, SIMPLE IRA(a) and SARSEP Plans	Qualified Plans (401(k), etc.)	Form 5329 Code
Adoption	up to $5,000 within a year of a qualified birth or adoption	yes	yes	19
Age	after participant/IRA owner reaches age 59½	yes	yes	n/a
Death	distributions to beneficiaries after death of the participant/IRA owner	yes	yes	04
Disability	total and permanent disability of the participant/IRA owner	yes	yes	03
Qualified disaster	participant/IRA owner lives in a federally declared disaster area, up to $22,000 lifetime maximum	yes	yes	(b)
Domestic abuse victim	victim of domestic abuse by a spouse or domestic partner, up to the lesser of $10,000 or 50% of account	yes	yes	22
Domestic Relations	to an alternate payee under a Qualified Domestic Relations Order	n/a	yes	06
Education	qualified higher education expenses (includes tuition, fees, books, and room and board for owner, spouse, children, or grandchildren)	yes	no	08
Emergency personal expense	one distribution per calendar year for personal or family emergency expenses, up to the lesser of $1,000 or vested account balance over $1,000	yes	yes	23
Equal Payments	series of substantially equal payments	yes	yes	02
Heath Insurance	health insurance premiums paid while unemployed (minimum 12 weeks of unemployment compensation)	yes	no	07
Homebuyers	qualified first-time homebuyers, up to $10,000 lifetime maximum	yes	no	09
Levy	because of an IRS levy of the plan	yes	yes	10
Medical	amount of unreimbursed medical expenses (>7.5% AGI)	yes	yes	05
Military	certain distributions to qualified military reservists called to active duty	yes	yes	11
Rollovers	in-plan Roth rollovers or eligible distributions contributed to another retirement plan or IRA within 60 days	yes	yes	n/a
Separation from Service	the employee separates from service during or after the year the employee reaches age 55 (age 50 for a variety of public safety employees)	no	yes	01
Terminally ill	participant/IRA owner has been certified as terminally ill by a physician	yes	yes	20

(a) SIMPLE IRA distributions incur a 25% additional tax instead of 10% if made within the first 2 years of participation.
(b) Report on Form 8915-F.

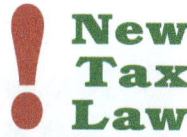

Starting after December 29, 2025, distributions for long-term care be excluded from the 10-percent penalty tax on early distributions. As a reminder, the exclusion is for the 10-percent penalty tax on early distributions; ordinary income tax will still apply.

5-3f Required Minimum Distributions

Taxpayers that participate in a qualified retirement plan or own an IRA must start taking required minimum distributions (RMDs) from that plan starting at an applicable age. This prevents taxpayers from extending the tax benefit of deferring income using a qualified plan for a period beyond what lawmakers intended. Under previous law, RMDs were required to begin the year the taxpayer turns age 72; however, the initial distribution may be deferred to no later than April 1 of the year after turning age 72.

Example Mildred turned age 72 on September 22, 2022. Mildred is required to start taking RMDs in 2022 but may elect to defer the first RMD until no later than April 1, 2023. Under either circumstance, Mildred is also required to take her 2023 RMD by December 31, 2023. ♦

Starting in 2023, the applicable age is increased to 73 for individuals that turn 72 after 2022 but before 2033. In the case of an individual who turns age 74 after December 31, 2032, the applicable age is 75. Under certain circumstances, a taxpayer that is still working can delay RMDs from their employer-sponsored 401k plan; however, that delay does not apply to IRAs.

Example Pat turns 72 in 2024. Pat's beginning year for RMDs is 2025 (when they turn 73); however, Pat can defer the initial RMD until April 1 of 2026. ♦

The excise tax on failure to take RMDs is 25 percent. For taxpayers that correct the failure to take adequate RMDs and file a corrected return, the excise tax may be reduced to 10 percent if the correction is made by the earlier of the mailing of a notice of deficiency, the date the tax is assessed, or the last day of the second year of the year in which the tax is imposed.

Example Zia is a 75-year old single taxpayer subject to the required minimum distribution rules. In 2024, she fails to take RMDs and does not report the failure or the excise tax on her timely-filed return. In late 2025, she realizes the error, takes the RMD, and files an amended 2024 tax return, reporting the income and the 10-percent excise tax. By filing the corrected return within the required time limits, Zia can avoid the 25-percent excise tax. ♦

A taxpayer over age 70½ may also elect to make a charitable contribution directly from their IRA. If made before RMDs have started, the taxpayer may exclude up to $105,000 (in 2024) from gross income. If made after RMDs have started, then the amount (up to $105,000) is also counted toward any RMDs for the year.

Example Jurgen is 75 years of age and has RMDs for 2024 from his IRA in the amount of $105,000. Jurgen elects to make a qualified charitable distribution from his IRA in 2024 in the amount of $90,000. Jurgen may exclude $90,000 from his gross income and also count the same $90,000 toward his 2024 RMDs. Jurgen will be required to include only $15,000 of his 2024 RMDs in his gross income. ♦

If a taxpayer contributes more than $105,000 or in excess of the annual RMDs, no carryforward to a future year is permitted. Qualifying charitable distributions (QCDs) are not counted toward the charitable itemized deduction limits covered later in this chapter. The $105,000 limit is annually adjusted for inflation.

New Tax Law The SECURE 2.0 Act requires that the U.S. Department of Labor develop a retirement savings "lost and found" by the end of 2024. This solution to finding owners of unknown retirement accounts is largely expected to be an online searchable database. By some estimates, over $1 trillion of 401k accounts alone have been "forgotten."

5-3g Inherited IRAs

Unlike many other types of inherited property, when a beneficiary inherits an IRA (both traditional and Roth) from a deceased taxpayer, the beneficiary does not receive a step-up in basis to the market value of the IRA. A series of complex tax rules are intended to prevent the infinite deferral of taxes on the underlying IRA by generally requiring mandatory distributions, regardless of the age of the beneficiary. These rules have also evolved over time so the date of death of the original taxpayer is important in determining what rules may apply. A modest overview of the current rules is:

- If the beneficiary is the deceased taxpayer's spouse, the surviving spouse can elect to treat the IRA as their own (a spousal rollover) and RMDs are based on the age of the surviving spouse. The surviving spouse can also elect to treat the IRA as an inherited IRA.
- If the spouse elects to treat the IRA as an inherited IRA, the RMDs begin with reference to the deceased spouse's age but the RMD amounts are based on the surviving spouse's life expectancy.
- If the beneficiary is any individual other than an eligible designated beneficiary, the RMDs are based on the life expectancy of the beneficiary but limited to a 10-year period (the balance of the account must be distributed annually by the end of 10 years).
- Eligible designated beneficiaries may use their own life expectancy for RMDs. Eligible designated beneficiaries are defined as the deceased taxpayer's spouse, minor children, individuals that are disabled or chronically ill, and any individual that is no more than 10 years younger than the deceased owner. For a minor child, once the child reaches the age of majority, the 10-year rule starts.

Example Ernesto dies at age 76 after naming his spouse, Chingching, as primary beneficiary of his traditional IRA. In the year that Ernesto dies, Chingching performs a spousal rollover. Chingching is not required to take RMDs until her required beginning date. ♦

This is merely an overview of a challenging area of the tax law. For more information refer to IRS Publication 590-B.

5-3h Prohibited Transactions

IRA owners and family members of the owner are not generally permitted to engage in certain transactions with the IRA account itself. Most IRAs are held by large financial institutions and invest overwhelmingly in publicly-traded investments and the risk of a prohibited transaction is extremely low. Self-directed IRAs that are controlled directly by the IRA owner and invest in non-publicly-traded assets are far more likely to be at risk for a prohibited transaction. The following are likely to be prohibited transactions:

- Borrowing money from the IRA
- Selling property to the IRA
- Using the funds in the IRA as security for a loan
- Buying property for personal use (present or future) with IRA funds

If an IRA engages in a prohibited transaction, it ceases to be an IRA at that time and is treated as having distributed all of the assets of the IRA to the beneficiary at fair market value on the first day of the year, triggering tax on any amounts in excess of basis.

Example Cliven's self-directed IRA invests in a small corporation over which Cliven or a member of his family has significant influence (for example, greater-than-50-percent ownership). This is a prohibited transaction. All of Cliven's contributions to the IRA were deductible and he therefore, has no basis. The IRA is deemed to have made a taxable distribution of the market value of the IRA to Cliven. ♦

Example Ammon's self-directed IRA has a 98-percent ownership of an LLC. The LLC pays Ammon a salary as compensation. The investment is a prohibited transaction due to the salary payment. ♦

If an IRA invests in collectibles such as artworks, antiques, metals, gems, and certain coins, the amount invested is considered to have been distributed to the owner as of the date of the investment.

> **Tax Break**
>
> A gift of a contribution to a Roth IRA for a child or grandchild with a summer job can grow into a very large gift over time. The amount that may be contributed to a child's Roth IRA is the lesser of $7,000 or the child's earnings. A child with $7,000 in a Roth IRA at age 16 will have almost $180,000 at age 65 if the Roth IRA investment earns 7 percent annually.

Self-Study Problem 5.3 — Refer to Appendix E for Solutions to Self-Study Problems

a. During 2024, Neeraj (a 24-year-old single taxpayer) has a salary of $62,000, dividend income of $14,000, and interest income of $4,000. In addition, he has rental income of $1,000. Neeraj is covered by a qualified retirement plan. Calculate the maximum regular IRA deduction that Neeraj is allowed using the IRA contribution limitation Worksheets 1-1 and 1-2 from Appendix F (if needed).

b. During 2024, Irene (a single taxpayer, over age 50) has a salary of $132,000 and dividend income of $20,000. Calculate Irene's maximum contribution to a Roth IRA using the Roth IRA contributions limitation Worksheet 2-2 from Appendix F.

c. Kalpana, a single taxpayer age 63, takes a $10,000 distribution from her traditional IRA to purchase furniture for her home. Over the years she has contributed $36,000 to the IRA which she deducted. The IRA has a $50,000 balance at the time of the distribution. Determine how much of Kalpana's distribution is taxable.

d. Same as part c., except the distribution is from a Roth IRA.

e. Tiffani Hicks, a single taxpayer age 43, took an early distribution from her IRA as reported on the 1099-R below. She used the entire amount of the distribution for the purchase of her first home. Complete Part I of Form 5329 on Page 5-19 to determine the amount of the 10-percent penalty tax on the distribution.

Form 1099-R (2024)

PAYER: Hifidelity Investments, 344 Harbor Drive, Boston, MA 02110
PAYER'S TIN: 23-9088123
RECIPIENT'S TIN: 312-34-4445
RECIPIENT: Tiffani Hicks, 101 Rolando Drive, San Diego, CA 92118

- Box 1 Gross distribution: $24,000.00
- Box 2a Taxable amount: (blank)
- Box 2b Taxable amount not determined: X
- Box 4 Federal income tax withheld: $2,400.00
- Box 7 Distribution code(s): 1; IRA/SEP/SIMPLE: X

Self-Study Problem 5.3, Part E.

Form 5329
Department of the Treasury
Internal Revenue Service

Additional Taxes on Qualified Plans (Including IRAs) and Other Tax-Favored Accounts
Attach to Form 1040, 1040-SR, 1040-NR, or 1041.
Go to www.irs.gov/Form5329 for instructions and the latest information.

OMB No. 1545-0074
2024
Attachment Sequence No. **29**

Name of individual subject to additional tax. If married filing jointly, see instructions.

Your social security number

Fill in Your Address Only if You Are Filing This Form by Itself and Not With Your Tax Return

Home address (number and street), or P.O. box if mail is not delivered to your home

Apt. no.

City, town or post office, state, and ZIP code. If you have a foreign address, also complete the spaces below. See instructions.

If this is an amended return, check here ☐

Foreign country name | Foreign province/state/county | Foreign postal code

If you **only** owe the additional 10% tax on the full amount of the early distributions, you may be able to report this tax directly on Schedule 2 (Form 1040), line 8, without filing Form 5329. See instructions.

Part I — Additional Tax on Early Distributions.
Complete this part if you took a taxable distribution (other than a qualified disaster distribution) before you reached age 59½ from a qualified retirement plan (including an IRA) or modified endowment contract (unless you are reporting this tax directly on Schedule 2 (Form 1040)—see above). You may also have to complete this part to indicate that you qualify for an exception to the additional tax on early distributions or for certain Roth IRA distributions. See instructions.

1	Early distributions includible in income (see instructions). For Roth IRA distributions, see instructions.	1
2	Early distributions included on line 1 that are not subject to the additional tax (see instructions). Enter the appropriate exception number from the instructions: _____	2
3	Amount subject to additional tax. Subtract line 2 from line 1	3
4	**Additional tax.** Enter 10% (0.10) of line 3. Include this amount on Schedule 2 (Form 1040), line 8	4

Caution: If any part of the amount on line 3 was a distribution from a SIMPLE IRA, you may have to include 25% of that amount on line 4 instead of 10%. See instructions.

Part II — Additional Tax on Certain Distributions From Education Accounts and ABLE Accounts.
Complete this part if you included an amount in income, on Schedule 1 (Form 1040), line 8z, from a Coverdell education savings account (ESA) or a qualified tuition program (QTP), or on Schedule 1 (Form 1040), line 8q, from an ABLE account.

5	Distributions included in income from a Coverdell ESA, a QTP, or an ABLE account	5
6	Distributions included on line 5 that are not subject to the additional tax (see instructions)	6
7	Amount subject to additional tax. Subtract line 6 from line 5	7
8	**Additional tax.** Enter 10% (0.10) of line 7. Include this amount on Schedule 2 (Form 1040), line 8	8

Part III — Additional Tax on Excess Contributions to Traditional IRAs.
Complete this part if you contributed more to your traditional IRAs for 2024 than is allowable or you had an amount on line 17 of your 2023 Form 5329.

9	Enter your excess contributions from line 16 of your 2023 Form 5329. See instructions. If zero, go to line 15		9
10	If your traditional IRA contributions for 2024 are less than your maximum allowable contribution, see instructions. Otherwise, enter -0-	10	
11	2024 traditional IRA distributions included in income (see instructions)	11	
12	2024 distributions of prior year excess contributions (see instructions)	12	
13	Add lines 10, 11, and 12		13
14	Prior year excess contributions. Subtract line 13 from line 9. If zero or less, enter -0-		14
15	Excess contributions for 2024 (see instructions)		15
16	Total excess contributions. Add lines 14 and 15		16
17	**Additional tax.** Enter 6% (0.06) of the **smaller** of line 16 **or** the value of your traditional IRAs on December 31, 2024 (including 2024 contributions made in 2025). Include this amount on Schedule 2 (Form 1040), line 8		17

Part IV — Additional Tax on Excess Contributions to Roth IRAs.
Complete this part if you contributed more to your Roth IRAs for 2024 than is allowable or you had an amount on line 25 of your 2023 Form 5329.

18	Enter your excess contributions from line 24 of your 2023 Form 5329. See instructions. If zero, go to line 23		18
19	If your Roth IRA contributions for 2024 are less than your maximum allowable contribution, see instructions. Otherwise, enter -0-	19	
20	2024 distributions from your Roth IRAs (see instructions)	20	
21	Add lines 19 and 20		21
22	Prior year excess contributions. Subtract line 21 from line 18. If zero or less, enter -0-		22
23	Excess contributions for 2024 (see instructions)		23
24	Total excess contributions. Add lines 22 and 23		24
25	**Additional tax.** Enter 6% (0.06) of the **smaller** of line 24 **or** the value of your Roth IRAs on December 31, 2024 (including 2024 contributions made in 2025). Include this amount on Schedule 2 (Form 1040), line 8		25

For Privacy Act and Paperwork Reduction Act Notice, see your tax return instructions. Cat. No. 13329Q Form **5329** (2024)

5-4 Small Business and Self-Employed Retirement Plans

Learning Objective 5.4
Explain the general contribution rules for small business and self-employed retirement plans.

The tax law provides employees, employers, and the self-employed with an incentive to plan for retirement through qualified retirement plans. Under the tax law, favorable tax treatment is granted to contributions by or for employees, to qualified retirement plans. Employers may claim a deduction in the current year for contributions to qualified retirement plans on the employees' behalf, while the employees do not include the employer contributions in income until the contributed amounts are distributed (generally during their retirement years). Tax on earnings on the amounts contributed to the plan is also deferred. This deferral of income taxation is a significant benefit to most taxpayers.

Example In the current year, Polly's employer makes a $2,000 contribution to a qualified plan for Polly's retirement. The $2,000 is deductible to the employer in the current year and is not taxable to Polly until she withdraws the money from the plan. Any earnings on the money contributed to the plan are also taxable only upon withdrawal from the plan. ♦

Many plans also offer the option for an employee to defer compensation under an elective deferral.

Example Continuing from the previous example, Polly also elects to defer 4 percent of her $40,000 wages into the qualified plan. Her employer will withhold $1,600 ($40,000 × 4%) from her pay and contribute that amount to the plan for her benefit. Typically, the $1,600 will be excluded from her gross income for that year. The employer will generally deduct the $1,600 contribution as compensation expense. ♦

The tax law provides for several different types of plans for taxpayers to save for retirement. Most retirement plans must meet certain requirements to be classified as "qualified," thereby extending the tax benefits described previously:

- Eligibility requirements: Most plans require that the benefit be extended to all employees and not favor only the highly-compensated (nondiscriminatory).
- Fiduciary responsibility: Most plans require a separate account to hold the retirement assets, typically handled by a bank or financial institution.
- Early withdrawals: Most plans penalize or prohibit early distributions from the plan with limited hardship exceptions (discussed in the previous section).
- Vesting requirement: Some plans require immediate "vesting" of contributions (i.e., the contributions are immediately set aside for an employee and will not be returned to the employer even if the employee leaves the company).

The retirement plan area has become one of the most complex areas of the tax law. Many tax accountants refer taxpayers to a specialist for help in choosing a plan and for guidance with the ongoing employee coverage, tax reporting, and contribution requirements. The coverage in this textbook is meant to give an overview of several common options available to taxpayers for tax-deferred retirement plans, which remain some of the best completely legal tax shelters available. Retirement plans for small businesses are covered here while large retirement plans, which are generally operated by larger employers, are covered in Chapter 9.

5-4a Self-Employed and Small Business Retirement Plan Options

Although available to small businesses, complex retirement plans such as defined-benefit plans or employee stock ownership plans are generally used by only large companies due to their complexity and cost to operate (refer to Chapter 9). However, over time, the tax law has created several retirement plans directed at the small business owner or even a self-employed sole proprietor. These include:

- Payroll deduction IRAs
- SEP plans
- SIMPLE plans
- 401k plans

Each of these different types of plans involves a different plan creation and approval process, and different contribution and deduction limits.

Qualified plans such as 403(b), 457(c), profit-sharing, money purchase, and employee stock ownership plans are generally used by large employers and are presented in Chapter 9.

5-4b Payroll Deduction Plans

A payroll deduction plan is probably the simplest way for a business to give employees a way to save for retirement. The employer sets up a payroll deduction IRA with a financial institution(s) and employees have the option to participate. Employees open the IRA or Roth IRA and choose how much to deduct from their pay and contribute to a traditional IRA or Roth IRA, depending on what options have been made available by the employer. The employer makes no contributions (other than withholding) to the accounts but is responsible for publishing employee contributions limits, which are the same as if the employee contributed to an IRA or Roth IRA on their own (maximum $7,000 or $8,000, if catch up, in 2024). The taxpayer income limits apply to Roth IRA contributions and the deduction of traditional IRA contributions. This type of program has no requirements for minimum employee coverage and employees can elect how much they want directed to the IRA at any time. The employer receives no additional deduction in a payroll deduction plan because the employer makes no contributions.

Example Thobias establishes an IRA payroll deduction program for his employees. Rene, one of Thobias' employees, opens a traditional IRA account with the selected financial institution and elects to have $100 withheld from his weekly paycheck to contribute to the IRA in 2024. Thobias withholds the funds each pay period and transfers them to Rene's IRA account. At year-end, Rene can claim a for AGI deduction for his $5,200 IRA contribution assuming his income does not exceed the threshold for deductibility. ♦

5-4c Simplified Employee Pension (SEP) Plans

A SEP is an IRA-based retirement plan available to any employer (including a self-employed-individual). These plans are simple to establish; the IRS even provides a one-page Form 5305-SEP that can be used to set up the plan. The selected financial institution handles most of the SEP paperwork. SEPs have flexible funding requirements in the event funding the plan with consistent contribution amounts might be an issue for the employer. The amount of employer contributions can change from year-to-year and can be zero. Only employers contribute to a SEP. Employees that meet the SEP requirements for minimum age (21) and years of service (employed by the employer for at least three of the last five years), and make at least $750 in annual compensation in 2024 (this amount is adjusted for inflation each year), *must* be offered an opportunity to participate in the SEP. If the employer makes a contribution, it must be as an equal percentage of compensation made for all eligible employees for that year. SEP contributions immediately vest to the employee.

SEP contributions are limited under slightly different rules for employees versus a self-employed business owner. The maximum contribution made for an employee cannot exceed the lesser of 25 percent of the employee's compensation or $69,000 and may not be based on more than $345,000 of compensation in 2024. The employee is permitted to exclude qualified contributions from their gross income.

Example Talitha operates a small business with employees and has a SEP plan in place. Talitha's business is very profitable in 2024 and she elects to contribute the maximum 25 percent of each eligible employee's compensation for the tax year. Greg, Horace, and Bonita are all employees of Talitha and have 2024 wages of $30,000, $100,000, and $300,000, respectively. Talitha will make a contribution to the SEP for Greg, Horace, and Bonita of $7,500 ($30,000 × 25%), $25,000 (100,000 × 25%), and $69,000 ($300,000 × 25% but limited to $69,000), respectively. ♦

For the self-employed business owner, the contribution limit considers the net self-employment income after consideration of the deduction for the contribution to the SEP. As a result, the maximum contribution (and deduction) available for the self-employed taxpayer will be slightly lower than that of an employee and is derived by taking the plan contribution rate and dividing by one plus the contribution rate; thus, effectively lowering the maximum contribution rate to 20 percent (0.25 ÷ 1.25).

Example Talitha, from the previous example, has net earned income (Schedule C net income less one-half of self-employment tax) from her business of $500,000. Under the terms of the SEP plan, Talitha contributed 25 percent of compensation (up to the maximum allowable) to the plan. Talitha's maximum contribution percentage is 20 percent (0.25 ÷ 1.25 = 0.20 or 20 percent). Her maximum contribution is $69,000, which is the lesser of $69,000 (20% × $345,000, which is the maximum eligible compensation) or $69,000. ♦

The 2024 employer's deduction for SEP contributions paid is limited to 25 percent of the aggregate total of participating employees' compensation up to $345,000, not to exceed $69,000 per participant. The same adjusted limitation applies to the deduction for a self-employed individual as applied to the contribution. The contribution can be made up through the filing date of the employer's tax return (including extension) to be deducted for that tax year.

Example Continuing the previous examples, as long as Talitha makes the contribution prior to timely filing the 2024 tax return (including extensions), she may deduct the contributions in 2024. ♦

Note that a SEP does not permit catch-up contributions. A SEP plan can also be structured as a Roth account. Both employee deferrals and employer contributions can be characterized as non-deductible Roth IRA contributions. The contributions must vest immediately and qualified distributions from these contributions, as well as the earnings thereon, are excluded from taxable income.

Prior to 1997, businesses could open a Salary Reduction SEP (SARSEP) in which employees could elect to defer a portion of their salary into the SEP. The employer could make nonelective contributions as well. Although no longer available as a new plan, existing SARSEPs may remain active but must meet three requirements: (1) at least 50 percent of eligible employees participate, (2) the business has 25 or fewer employees, and (3) the plan contributions do not discriminate in favor of highly-compensated employees.

5-4d Savings Incentive Match Plan for Employees (SIMPLE) IRA

A SIMPLE IRA is available to any employer with 100 or fewer employees (including a self-employed individual). SIMPLE IRAs are also easy to establish (Form 5304-SIMPLE or 5305-SIMPLE) and administer. An employer with a SIMPLE IRA may not offer any other retirement plan. The SIMPLE IRA must be offered to employees with compensation of at least $5,000 in any prior two years and are expected to have compensation of $5,000 in the current year. Unlike a SEP, a SIMPLE IRA requires certain contributions *must* be made by the employer. Employees decide how much they would like to contribute, and the employer must match contributing employees for the first 3 percent of compensation (with some flexibility) or 2 percent of each eligible employee's compensation (up to $345,000 for any employee in 2024) regardless of the employee's contributions. Employees immediately vest in both the employee and employer contributions.

Example Flat Stone Company offers its employees a SIMPLE IRA plan in which they match 3 percent of the employee's contribution to the plan. One employee, Barnaby, elects to defer 5 percent of his $50,000 compensation. Another employee, Freddy, does not elect any deferred contribution on his $40,000 compensation. Flat Stone will match up to 3 percent ($1,500) of Barnaby's 5-percent elective contribution ($2,500) for a total contribution of $4,000. Flat Stone will make no contributions to Freddy's SIMPLE IRA. ♦

Example Slate Rock Company offers its employees a SIMPLE IRA in which they match 2 percent of the employee's compensation. One employee, Elizabeth, elects to defer 5 percent of her $50,000 compensation. Another employee, Wilhelmina, does not elect any contribution of her $40,000 compensation. Slate Rock will make a 2-percent contribution ($1,000), plus Elizabeth's elective 5-percent contribution ($2,500), for a total contribution of $3,500. Slate Rock will also make a 2 percent contribution of Wilhelmina's compensation ($800) to Wilhelmina's SIMPLE IRA. ♦

The employer and employee contribution are excluded from gross income if within the annual limits. The employee contribution limit is $16,000 (plus catch-up contributions of $3,500 for taxpayers aged 50 or older) in 2024. The employer's contribution limit is the same as the required contributions for a SIMPLE IRA

Example If in the previous Slate Rock example, a third employee, Stony (who is under age 50), elected to contribute 10 percent of her $150,000 salary and Slate Rock makes a 2-percent nonelective contribution, Stony's elective contribution would be limited. The 2-percent nonelective contribution of $3,000 plus the 10-percent elective deferral of $15,000 exceeds the 2024 limit of $16,000. Stony will need to reduce her elective contribution to no more than $13,000 or risk excess contributions which creates a host of issues for the plan and the employee. ♦

The employer's deduction limitation for a SIMPLE IRA is the same as the employer contribution requirements. If the plan allows, contributions to a SIMPLE IRA can be treated as Roth IRA contributions, similar to SEP plans covered previously. The tax law also permits a SIMPLE 401k plan, which is discussed in the next section.

Example DeWayne Incorporated operates a SIMPLE IRA plan for its employees. Starting in 2024, DeWayne amends the plan to permit employees to treat their accounts as Roth IRAs. In 2024, Travis, an employee of DeWayne, decides future contributions will be treated as Roth contributions. His existing SIMPLE IRA account will continue to be treated as a traditional SIMPLE IRA with taxable distributions (unless Travis also decides to do a Roth conversion). His new contributions will be nondeductible Roth contributions held in a separate SIMPLE Roth IRA account and qualified distributions from that account will be excluded from gross income. ♦

SIMPLE Plan Contribution Changes

Starting in 2024, employers will be permitted to make additional nonelective contributions of a uniform percentage up to the lesser of 10 percent of compensation or $5,000.

Example Hamaya Corporation operates a SIMPLE IRA plan for its employees in which the plan matches employee contributions up to 3 percent of the employees' compensation. Starting in 2024, the company has elected to expand its contributions to include an additional nonelective contribution of 4 percent of the employees' compensation. In 2024, Bruno contributes 2 percent of their $30,000 salary and Christina contributes 5 percent of her $100,000 salary. Hamaya will be required to match Bruno's 2 percent contribution ($600) and up to 3 percent of Christina's salary ($3,000). Because Hamaya's plan includes an additional nonelective contribution of 4 percent, an additional 4 percent contribution will be made to Bruno's account ($1,200) and Christina's account ($4,000). ♦

5-4e 401k Plans

The 401k plan, named after §401(k) of the Internal Revenue Code, is one of the more popular choices of retirement plans today. Its popularity has bred a number of variations of the plan such as the SIMPLE 401k, the Safe Harbor 401k, and the Automatic Enrollment 401k.

401k plans must meet certain requirements in addition to the general qualification requirements for all qualified plans. Generally, any employee who is at least 21 years old with at least 1,000 hours of work performed in a previous year, must be permitted to participate. An employee with over 500 hours in each of three consecutive years must also be permitted to participate. The amount deferred must be 100-percent vested and may be distributed only upon retirement, death, disability, or other separation from service, attainment of age 59½, or hardship.

Traditional 401k

The traditional 401k plan permits an employee to choose to receive a payment of compensation in cash or to defer the amount through an employer contribution on behalf of the employee to the 401k plan using a salary reduction agreement. The agreement may allow the employee to reduce their compensation or forgo an increase in compensation, with the amount contributed to the qualified retirement plan, thereby deferring tax on the compensation ("elective contributions"). Employees choose the percentage of their pay which will be withheld and contributed to the plan. Some employers match employee contributions up to a certain percentage to encourage participation ("nonelective contributions").

Example In 2023, Margo elects to defer 5 percent of her next year's salary into her company's 401k plan. Margo's 2024 salary is $50,000, and thus, $2,500 ($50,000 × 5%) will be contributed to the 401k plan. Her taxable wages for 2024 will be $47,500. ♦

Any matching amount contributed to the plan by the employer on behalf of the employee is also excluded from the employee's gross income. The contributions and the earnings on the amounts invested in the plan are taxable when withdrawn.

Example In the previous example, Margo's employer matches contributions up to 4 percent, and thus, contributes an additional $2,000 ($50,000 × 4 percent) to Margo's 401k plan. The $2,000 is also excluded from Margo's taxable wages. ♦

Employment taxes (covered in Chapter 9) apply to the employee's contribution but do not apply to the employer's match.

For most 401k plans, contributions are limited in two ways: (1) an employee may elect to make an annual contribution up to $23,000 (in 2024) plus a catch-up contribution of $7,500 (in 2024) for taxpayers aged 50 or older; and (2) the total contributions (employee plus employer) made to the 401k plan are also subject to the limitations applicable to all qualified plans of 100 percent of compensation up to $345,000, subject to a limit of $69,000 (in 2024), not including catch-up contributions if over age 50.

Example Jundong, a 42-year-old employee, elects to defer 20 percent of his $100,000 salary into his employer's 401k plan for 2024. His employer will match up to the first 8 percent of compensation contributed. Jundong's elective contributions are $20,000. which is less than the $23,000 limit. His employer contributes an additional $8,000. His total contributions of $28,000 are less than $69,000 and are not limited. ◆

Example If Jundong's salary in the previous example were $200,000, his elective contribution of $40,000 ($200,000 × 20%) would be limited to $23,000. The employer match of a maximum of $16,000 ($200,000 × 8%) brings Jundong's total contributions to $39,000 ($23,000 + $16,000), which is less than the 2024 limit of $69,000. ◆

Example Marisol's salary in 2024 is $360,000 and she elects to contribute 5 percent of her 2024 salary into her employer's 401k plan. Marisol's employer matches up to the first 5 percent of elective contributions. Marisol's elective contributions of $18,000 ($360,000 × 5%) are under the 2024 limit of $23,000. Marisol's employer is not permitted to consider contributions on compensation above $345,000 in 2024, and thus, the employer's contribution is limited to $17,250 ($345,000 × 5%). The total contributions of $35,250 are less than the 2024 limit of $69,000. ◆

Example If Marisol in the previous example elects a 15-percent contribution of her salary, her elective contributions of $54,000 ($360,000 × 15%) will be limited to $23,000. Marisol's employer matches up to the first 15 percent of elective contributions. Marisol's employer is not permitted to consider contributions on compensation above $345,000 in 2024, and thus, the employer's contribution is limited to $51,750. The total contributions of $74,750 ($23,000 + $51,750) are more than the 2024 limit of $69,000 and Marisol's employer will need to return excess contributions above the limit or pay an excise tax. ◆

The annual maximum is reduced dollar for dollar by amounts contributed as a result of the employee's participation in other salary reduction plans of any employer. Contributions in excess of the maximum allowed may be subject to a 10-percent excise tax imposed on the employer.

The employer's deduction for contributions to a traditional 401k plan is limited to 25 percent of the total compensation (up to $345,000 for any individual employee in 2024) of all participating employees. Contributions must be paid by the end of the year to be deductible.

SIMPLE 401k

A SIMPLE 401k has some of the characteristics of a SIMPLE IRA plan and some of a traditional 401k. A SIMPLE 401k is available to employers with 100 or fewer employees (like a SIMPLE IRA) but must have a plan document and meet the qualification rules of a traditional 401k. The one unique aspect of the SIMPLE 401k is that this plan is not required to meet the nondiscrimination testing required of a traditional 401k. The employer of a SIMPLE 401k permits employees to make an elective deferral of their salary and is also required to make either a matching 3 percent contribution or a nonelective contribution of 2 percent. Currently, no other nonelective contributions are permitted.

The limits on employee contributions, employer contributions, and the employer deduction are the same as for SIMPLE IRAs discussed previously.

Other 401k Plans

A safe harbor 401k plan operates like other 401k plans with one important distinction: it must provide for mandatory employer contributions that are fully vested when made. If the required contributions are made, the safe harbor 401k plan is not subject to the complex annual nondiscrimination tests that apply to traditional 401k plans. The contributions can be either a matching contribution or a nonelective contribution. If a matching contribution, all non-highly-compensated employees must be matched up to 3 percent and the same group of employees must be matched at 50 percent for any elective deferrals from 3 to 5 percent. The rate of matching for non-highly compensated must be equal to or greater than that on highly compensated. If the employer elects nonelective contributions in a safe-harbor 401k plan, the contribution is mandatory and may be no less than 3 percent of the employee's wages.

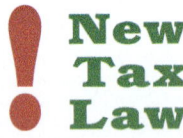

Effective after 2024, auto enrollment will become mandatory on a number of retirement plans including 401k plans. To provide incentive to employers to create auto-enroll plans, there is an annual $500 Small Employer Automatic Enrollment credit which can be claimed for up to three years for certain qualified small employers.

Example Gazu Industries wishes to adopt a safe-harbor 401k plan. Bam is a non-highly compensated employee that elects to contribute 5 percent of his $30,000 salary. To qualify, Gazu must match Bam's first 3 percent of contributions ($900 contributed by both Bam and Gazu) and also match one-half of his contributions from 3 to 5 percent ($600 contributed by Bam and $300 by Gazu). If instead Gazu opted for nonelective contributions, then Bam would contribute $1,500 (5 percent of $30,000) and Gazu would contribute $900 (3 percent of $30,000). ♦

Safe-harbor 401k plans have the same contribution and deduction limits as a traditional 401k plan.

Employers can also choose a Roth 401k plan for their employees. The amounts allowed to be set aside are the same as for traditional 401k plans ($23,000 in 2024), but the contributions do not reduce the employees' taxable income, same as contributions to a Roth IRA. Withdrawals, including earnings, are generally tax-free based on rules similar to those for Roth IRA withdrawals. Roth 401k plans are popular because they allow a significantly larger Roth contribution than a non-plan Roth IRA and, because there is no AGI limitation, a high-income taxpayer may contribute to a Roth 401k plan.

A self-employed 401k or solo 401k plan is designed for self-employed individuals with no employees (spouse is permitted). Setup and maintenance of the plan are relatively inexpensive and easy. Elective deferral limits are the same as for traditional 401k plans ($23,000 in 2024) and the nonelective deferral limit functions much like that of a SEP (the 25 percent is mathematically limited to 20 percent for self-employed).

5-4f Small Employer Pension Plan Startup Costs Credit

To encourage small businesses to create qualified retirement plans for employees, the tax law permits a credit for plan start-up costs for certain smaller eligible employers and a credit for employer contributions made to the plan.

For the first three years of plan operation, a new small employer pension plan (100 or fewer employees) is eligible to claim a credit for 50 percent of the plan start-up costs up to a maximum credit of the greater of (1) $500 or (2) the lesser of (A) $250 per eligible employee (non-highly compensated) or (B) $5,000.

Example Howie Company is starting a new qualified retirement plan for its 70 employees in 2024. Howie incurred administrative costs of $1,600 to start the plan and paid a financial adviser $2,000 to educate the employees on how the plan operates and the benefits of retirement savings. Howie Company's credit before any limitations is $1,800 ($3,600 × 50%). The credit is limited to the greater of (1) $500 or (2) the lesser of $17,500 ($250 × 70 employees) or $5,000. Since $5,000 is less than $17,500, the limit is the greater of $500 or $5,000. Since 50 percent of the actual expenses ($1,800) is below the limit, the credit allowed is $1,800. ♦

For employers with 50 or fewer employees, the credit for start-up costs is increased to 100 percent.

Example Marion Company is starting a new qualified retirement plan for its 40 employees in 2024. Marion incurred administrative costs to start the plan of $3,600 and paid a financial adviser $2,000 to educate the employees on how the plan operates and the benefits of retirement savings. Marion Company's credit before any limitations is $5,600 ($5,600 × 100%). This is limited to the greater of (1) $500 or (2) the lesser of $10,000 ($250 × 40 employees) or $5,000. Since $5,000 is less than $10,000, the limit is the greater of $500 or $5,000. Since 100 percent of the actual expenses ($5,600) exceeds the limit, the credit allowed is $5,000. ♦

Qualified start-up costs are ordinary and necessary costs associated with the establishment or administration of an eligible employer plan, or the retirement-related education of employees with respect to such plan.

There is an additional credit of an applicable percentage of the total amount of eligible employer contributions to the plan during the year. The amount of contribution that is eligible for the credit is $1,000 after applying the applicable percentage for the year. The applicable percentages presented in Table 5.5 are based on the year in which the employer plan is established:

Table 5.5 Applicable Percentages and Eligible Contributions for the Small Employer Pension Plan Startup Costs Credit

Year	Applicable Percentage	Maximum Eligible Contribution
Year plan is established	100%	$1,000
First year after year plan is established	100%	1,000
Second year	75%	1,333
Third year	50%	2,000
Fourth year	25%	4,000

The applicable percentage is zero percent for every year thereafter.

Example In 2023, Maradonna Company starts business and a new qualified retirement plan. For the next four years (2024-2027) Maradonna's entire workforce is the same five employees, all of which receive a $1,500 nonelective contribution to the plan and none have compensation in excess of $100,000. The amount of contribution that is eligible for the credit is as follows:

Year	Applicable percentage	Limit ($1,000 divided by the applicable percentage)	Contribution pre applicable percentage	Base amount to include for eligible contribution credit (line 6b of Form 8881)	Additional amount of eligible contribution due to applicable percentage (line 6c of Form 8881)
2023	100	$1,000	$1,500	1,000	0
2024	100	1,000	1,500	1,000	0
2025	75	1,333	1,500	1,000	333
2026	50	2,000	1,500	1,000	500
2027	25	4,000	1,500	1,000	500

In 2023, the amount of eligible contributions for the credit is $5,000 ($1,000 × 5 × 100%). In 2025, the amount of eligible contributions is $5,000 ($1,333 × 5 × 75%). In 2026, the amount of eligible contributions is $3,750 ($1,500 × 5 × 50%). ♦

For employers with more than 50 employees for which the credit was claimed in the prior year, the contribution credit is phased out 2 percent for each employee over 50. The contributions which are taken into account for the credit may not include any contributions for an employee with wages over $100,000 (this amount is adjusted for inflation each year).

Example In 2023, Ritchie Company started a new qualified plan for their 60 employees. In 2024, Ritchie made contributions of $1,500 per employee to the same 60 employees. In 2023 and 2024, five of Ritchie's employees earned wages in excess of $100,000. Ritchie's employer contributions for purposes of the credit are $82,500 (55 eligible employees × $1,500 per employee). The applicable percentage is 100 percent since this is the first year after the plan was established; thus, the pre-limit credit is $82,500. The first limit to apply is the $1,000 per employee reducing the eligible credit to $55,000 (55 × $1,000). Since Ritchie claimed a credit in the prior year for 55 employees, a phase-out of 10 percent [(55 − 50) × 2%] also applies, reducing the eligible credit to $49,500 [$55,000 − (10% × $55,000)]. ♦

Example Continuing the previous example, in 2025, the second year after the plan was established, Ritchie has only 40 employees and makes a contribution of $1,500 per employee to a qualified retirement plan. Eight of the employees earned wages in excess of $100,000 in 2025. The applicable percentage is 75 percent and the eligible contribution amount is $1,333. The credit is $31,992 (32 eligible employees × $1,333 per employee × 75%). Ritchie previously had 55 employees for which the credit was claimed in the prior year and will apply a 10-percent phase-out of $3,199 reducing the credit to $28,793. ♦

An employee that has compensation of less than $5,000 does not count toward the 100 employee limit. The amount taken as a credit may not also be deducted by the employer. The start-up cost and contribution credits are claimed by the employer on Form 8881. The credit is also part of the General Business Credit which could limit the amount of the credit that can be claimed (beyond the scope of this textbook).

5-4g Qualified Student Loan Payments

After 2023, qualified plans may treat an eligible employee's qualified student loan payments (QSLPs) as an elective deferral (contribution) to qualified 401k plans and SIMPLE plans. The employer is permitted to provide a match on the QSLP. These provisions are designed to permit an employee to make a payment on their student loan in lieu of the contribution to the plan but continue to receive a match. Contributions, including the QSLP, are subject to the typical annual contribution limitations. Note that the contribution due to the QSLP is not considered as part of the nondiscrimination rules.

Example Brenda is an employee of Hughes Corp. In 2024, Brenda elects to contribute $2,000 to the Hughes Corp 401k plan. Brenda also makes a QSLP of $4,000. Hughes Corp's 401k plan includes a dollar for dollar match on up to $5,000 of contributions. Given that the 2024 401k plan contribution limit is $23,000, Hughes may match the $2,000 deferral contribution and $3,000 of the QSLP. ♦

5-4h Reporting Qualified Plan Contributions and Distributions

Self-employed taxpayers report deductible contributions for themselves as a for AGI deduction on line 16 of Schedule 1. Like the deduction for self-employed healthcare and the deductible portion of self-employment tax covered previously in this textbook, these deductions are not reported on Schedule C for a sole proprietor or Schedule E for a partner. For the taxpayers that are making contributions as an employee, generally the employer is responsible for reporting the excludable amount on the employee's Form W-2 and, as necessary, providing the proper code in Box 12 as covered in Chapter 2. In general, the retirement plan in Box 13 should be checked.

Example Angus, a single taxpayer, is an employee of Young Electrical Contractors (YEC). YEC has a SIMPLE IRA plan for employees in which Angus participates. During 2024, Angus contributes 5 percent of his salary ($2,000) and YEC matches the first 3 percent ($1,200). Assuming no other excluded benefits or additional compensation, Angus' 2024 Form W-2 should be completed as follows:

Box	Field	Value
a	Employee's social security number	XXX-XX-XXXX
b	Employer identification number (EIN)	XX-XXXXXXX
c	Employer's name, address, and ZIP code	Young Electrical Contractors
e	Employee's first name and initial	Angus
1	Wages, tips, other compensation	38,000.00 (a)
2	Federal income tax withheld	X,XXX.XX
3	Social security wages	40,000.00 (b)
4	Social security tax withheld	2,480.00
5	Medicare wages and tips	40,000.00
6	Medicare tax withheld	580.00
12a	See instructions for box 12	S 2,000.00 (c)
13	Retirement plan	[X] (d)

Form **W-2** Wage and Tax Statement 2024
Copy B—To Be Filed With Employee's FEDERAL Tax Return.
This information is being furnished to the Internal Revenue Service.
Department of the Treasury—Internal Revenue Service

(a) Taxable wages are reduced by the $2,000 employee contribution by Angus. Note that Angus will not report a separate contribution to an IRA deduction on line 20 of Schedule 1.

(b) Employee contributions to qualified plans are subject to employment taxes and included in Boxes 3 and 5.

(c) The employee contribution is reported in Box 12 using the code S to indicate SIMPLE plan contribution.

(d) Box 13 Retirement Plan is checked to indicate Angus is eligible to participate in the SIMPLE plan. ♦

Distributions from qualified retirement plans are generally reported on Form 1099-R and included on Form 1040 as covered in Chapter 2

Self-Study Problem 5.4 — Refer to Appendix E for Solutions to Self-Study Problems

a. Lewis, a self-employed individual, has net earned income of $50,000 in 2024. If Lewis has no employees, calculate the maximum contribution to a SEP plan that he may deduct from his adjusted gross income.

b. During 2024, Linda, age 32, has a salary of $40,000. She participates in a 401k plan and chooses to defer 25 percent of her compensation.

   i. What is the maximum amount Linda can contribute to the 401k plan on a tax-deferred basis?

   ii. If Linda's salary was $125,000, instead of $40,000, what is the maximum amount that she could contribute to the 401k plan on a tax-deferred basis?

c. Laura contributed $78,000 (including employer match) of pre-tax salary to her 401k plan over the years. In 2024, at age 62, she retires and takes a distribution of $25,000 when the 401k has an account balance of $164,000. Compute the taxable portion of Laura's distribution.

d. Malcolm Company started business in 2024 and also started a new auto-enrollment SIMPLE plan. Malcolm has 70 employees in 2024, all of which were eligible to participate in the plan and had compensation in excess of $5,000. Malcolm incurred administrative costs of $4,600 to start the plan and paid a financial adviser $3,000 to educate the employees on how the plan operates and the benefits of retirement savings. In 2024 Malcolm made nonelective contributions of $52,000 for 65 employees, none of which was over $1,000 for any employee. Malcolm also made nonelective contributions of $12,000 for 5 employees, all of whom earned wages in excess of $100,000. Use Form 8881 on Page 5-31 to determine the amount of the Credit for Small Employer Pension Plan Startup Costs (including Employer Contributions) and the Small Employer Auto-Enrollment Credit.

Form 8881
(Rev. December 2023)
Department of the Treasury
Internal Revenue Service

Credit for Small Employer Pension Plan Startup Costs, Auto-Enrollment, and Military Spouse Participation

Attach to your tax return.
Go to *www.irs.gov/Form8881* for instructions and the latest information.

OMB No. 1545-1810

Attachment Sequence No. **130**

Name(s) shown on return

Identifying number

Part I — Credit for Small Employer Pension Plan Startup Costs (Including Employer Contributions)

A Enter the number of qualifying employees. See instructions _____

1 Qualified startup costs incurred during the tax year . . . . | **1** |

2 Employers with 1-50 employees enter the amount from line 1. Employers with 51-100 employees enter 50% (0.50) of line 1 . . . . | **2** |

3 Enter the number of employees eligible to participate in the pension plan. See instructions.
_____ X $250 . . . . | **3** |

4 Enter the greater of $500 or the amount from line 3 (Do not enter more than $5,000) . . . . . . | **4** |

5 Enter the smaller of line 2 or line 4 . . . . | **5** |

6a Enter the number of employees from the preceding tax year. See instructions . . . . | **6a** |

b Enter employer contributions made to the plan, but don't include (i) elective deferrals, (ii) contributions made to employees whose wages paid to the employee were in excess of $100,000 and (iii) any amount of contributions to an employee to whom you made contributions of more than $1,000 . . | **6b** |

c For employees for whom you made matching and nonelective contributions of more than $1,000, (and who are not disqualified because they meet 6b(ii) above), see the instructions for information on how to determine the amount to enter on line 6c. If you did not make this type of contributions, enter -0- . | **6c** |

d Add lines 6b and 6c . . . . | **6d** |

If the number of employees entered on line 6a is 50 or less, enter the amount from line 6d on line 6f. If the number of employees entered on line 6a is 51-100, continue to line 6e(1).

e (1) Subtract 50 (50.0) from the number of employees entered on line 6a . . . . . . | **6e(1)** |
   (2) Multiply line 6e(1) by 2% (0.02) . . . . | **6e(2)** |
   (3) Multiply line 6e(2) by line 6d . . . . | **6e(3)** |
   (4) Subtract line 6e(3) from line 6d . . . . | **6e(4)** |

f If you did NOT complete line 6e, enter the amount from line 6d. If you completed line 6e, enter the amount from line 6e(4) . . . . | **6f** |

g Applicable percentages. See instructions . . . . | **6g** |
   • If this is treated as the first or second year of the plan, enter the amount from line 6f.
   • If this is treated as the third year of the plan, multiply line 6f by 75% (0.75).
   • If this is treated as the fourth year of the plan, multiply line 6f by 50% (0.50).
   • If this is treated as the fifth year of the plan, multiply the amount on line 6f by 25% (0.25).

7 Credit for small employer pension plan startup costs from partnerships and S corporations . . . . | **7** |

8 Add lines 5, 6g, and 7. Partnerships and S corporations, report this amount on Schedule K. All others, report this amount on Form 3800, Part III, line 1j . . . . | **8** |

Part II — Small Employer Auto-Enrollment Credit

9 Enter $500 if an auto-enrollment option is provided for retirement savings . . . . | **9** |

10 Small employer auto-enrollment credit from partnerships and S corporations . . . . | **10** |

11 Add lines 9 and 10. Partnerships and S corporations, report this amount on Schedule K. All others, report this amount on Form 3800, Part III, line 1dd . . . . | **11** |

Part III — Military Spouse Participation Credit

Caution: You can't claim the credit if you had more than 100 employees in the preceding tax year.

12 Enter the number of military spouse employees participating in an eligible plan. See instructions.
_____ X $200 . . . . | **12** |

13 Amount of contributions paid by employer for each eligible military spouse employee. Do not enter more than $300 per employee. See instructions . . . . | **13** |

14 Credit for small employer military spouse retirement plan from partnerships and S corporations . . | **14** |

15 Add lines 12, 13, and 14. Partnerships and S corporations, report this amount on Schedule K. All others, report this amount on Form 3800, Part III, line 1ee . . . . | **15** |

For Paperwork Reduction Act Notice, see separate instructions.   Cat. No. 33435N   Form **8881** (Rev.12-2023)

Learning Objective 5.5

Describe other adjustments for adjusted gross income.

5-5 Other for AGI Deductions

There are a number of other deductions for AGI available under the tax law. Because of the limited nature of these deductions, a less detailed description is provided. The deduction for one-half of self-employment tax, which affects almost all self-employed taxpayers, is described in Chapter 4.

5-5a Educator Expenses

Eligible educators may deduct up to $300 for the unreimbursed cost of classroom materials such as books, supplies, computer equipment, supplementary materials, and personal protective equipment and supplies used for the prevention of the spread of COVID-19 as a deduction in arriving at AGI. An eligible educator is a K-12 teacher, instructor, counselor, principal, or aide who works at least 900 hours a school year in a school that provides elementary or secondary education. If a married couple filing jointly are both eligible educators, the total deduction is up to $600 but not more than $300 for either spouse.

Example Glen and Iris Holland are a married couple that files jointly, and both are high school teachers. In 2024, Glen and Iris spent $320 and $120 on various school supplies, respectively. The Hollands are eligible for a $420 ($300 + $120) educator expense for AGI deduction. ♦

5-5b Unreimbursed Business Expenses for Performing Artists and Others

As discussed later in this chapter, employees who incur business expenses are no longer permitted to deduct those costs as an itemized deduction subject to a 2 percent of AGI floor. Certain employee taxpayers, however, are eligible to take a for AGI deduction for unreimbursed employee costs, and thus, are not required to itemize to deduct these costs.

There are three different types of taxpayers eligible for this deduction (and the rules are different for each one):

1. Performing artists who worked for two or more employers during the year
2. National Guard or Reserve member
3. Fee-basis government officials

Performing artists may deduct employee business expenses as a for AGI deduction if they meet the following qualifications:

1. The taxpayer was paid for providing performing arts as an employee for at least two employers.
2. The taxpayer received at least $200 each from any two of these employers.
3. The related performing-arts business expenses are more than 10 percent of gross income from the performance of those services, and
4. AGI is not more than $16,000 before deducting these business expenses.

The performing-artist deduction for business expenses has an extremely low AGI cap of $16,000 as a requirement, rendering the deduction virtually useless for most taxpayers. The cap was instituted in 1986 and has not been adjusted since. Over time, this has become known as the "starving artists" deduction with good reason.

Members of a reserve component of the Armed Forces of the United States that travel more than 100 miles away from home in connection with services in the reserves can deduct travel expenses. The travel expense deduction is limited to the regular federal per diem rate (for lodging, meals, and incidental expenses) and the standard mileage rate (for car expenses) plus any parking fees, ferry fees, and tolls. Per diems are described in Chapter 3.

Certain fee-basis officials can claim their employee business expenses. Fee-basis officials are persons who are employed by a state or local government and who are paid in whole or in part on a fee basis.

Example Sally is a building inspector for the city of Hickory, Indiana. Sally is compensated solely from fees paid directly to her by clients and is not considered an employee of Hickory. Sally's travel and other business expenses can be deducted as a for AGI deduction. ♦

Unreimbursed business expenses that are deductible are claimed on Form 2106.

5-5c Moving Expenses

In the past, the tax law provided a deduction for moving expenses to help relieve taxpayers of a portion of the financial burden of moving from one job location to another. The deduction for moving expenses is currently suspended (through 2025) for all taxpayers except members of the Armed Forces of the United States on active duty whose move is pursuant to a military order and incident to a permanent change of station.

Reimbursements to an employee from an employer for qualified moving costs are no longer excluded from the employee's income.

Under the former law, taxpayers (except for those in the Armed Forces) had to meet three tests in order to deduct moving costs:

1. The taxpayer must change job sites.
2. The taxpayer must move so that the distance from the taxpayer's former residence to the new job location must be at least 50 miles more than the distance from the former residence to the former job location.
3. The taxpayer must remain at the new job location for a certain period of time, generally, 39 weeks. Taxpayers who were self-employed had to work at least 78 weeks at the new location.

Taxpayers in the Armed Forces are not required to meet the time or distance tests.

For the members of the military that qualify, moving expenses are reported on Form 3903.

5-5d Jury Duty

As noted in Chapter 2, jury duty pay is taxable income. Some employees that receive jury duty pay from the court are required to repay the amount to their employer, generally because their employer is also paying them for that time. To avoid including the jury pay for which the employee had to reimburse their employer in taxable income, taxpayers are permitted to deduct the jury pay reimbursed.

Example Kato, an individual taxpayer, served on a jury in his home state and was paid $25 a day in jury pay by the court for 10 days ($250). Kato's employer follows a policy of paying employees normal wages during jury duty and requires that the employee reimburse the employer for the jury duty pay received from the court. Kato will report the jury duty pay on line 8h of Schedule 1 and report the reimbursement on line 24a of Schedule 1. ♦

Self-Study Problem 5.5   Refer to Appendix E for Solutions to Self-Study Problems

For each of the following situations, determine the amount of the for AGI deduction for each taxpayer:

a. Professor Hill teaches at Bunker Hall Community College. In 2024, he spent $307 on supplies for his classroom and was not reimbursed. He was also required to reimburse Bunker Hall $175 for jury duty pay received from the court.

b. Jackie Rights played the lead role in two different plays in 2024 in the local community theatre. Two different production companies sponsored the plays and so she was an employee of both in 2024 and was paid the same by both employers: $4,000 per play. Jackie spent $1,100 in business expenses such as new business cards, personal management fees, and new head-shots for her portfolio. Her 2024 AGI was $15,200 (she also generated income as a shared-ride vehicle driver).

c. Lieutenant Dan of the U.S. Army was stationed in Fort Liberty, NC. In 2024, his permanent post was moved from Fort Liberty to Fort Jackson. The unreimbursed moving costs for Dan and his wife are $4,500.

5-6 Medical Expenses

Learning Objective 5.6
Calculate the itemized deduction for medical expenses.

Medical expenses are the first itemized deduction listed on Schedule A. Taxpayers are allowed a deduction for the medical expenses paid for themselves, their spouse, and dependents. Unreimbursed medical expenses can only be deducted to the extent that they exceed 7.5 percent of the taxpayer's AGI. The formula for calculating a taxpayer's medical expense deduction is as follows:

Prescription medicines and drugs, insulin, doctors, dentists, hospitals, medical insurance premiums	$ xxx
Other medical and dental expenses, such as lodging, transportation, eyeglasses, contact lenses, etc.	xxx
Less: insurance reimbursements	(xxx)
Subtotal	xxx
Less: 7.5 percent of adjusted gross income	(xxx)
Excess expenses qualifying for the medical deduction	$ xxx

5-6a What Qualifies as a Medical Expense?

Expenses that are deductible as medical expenses include the cost of items for the diagnosis, cure, mitigation, treatment, and prevention of disease. Also included are expenditures incurred that affect any structure or function of the body. Therefore, amounts for all of the following categories of expenditures qualify as medical expenses:

- Prescription medicines and drugs and insulin
- Fees for doctors, dentists, nurses, and other medical professionals
- Hospital fees
- Hearing aids, dentures, prescription eyeglasses, and contact lenses
- Medical transportation and lodging
- Medical aids, such as crutches, wheelchairs, and guide dogs
- Birth control prescriptions
- Acupuncture
- Psychiatric care
- Medical, dental, and vision insurance premiums, including Medicare premiums
- Certain capital expenditures deemed medically necessary by a doctor
- Nursing home care for the chronically ill (e.g., Alzheimer's disease care)

The IRS has allowed a deduction for:	The courts upheld an IRS denial of deduction for:
• Long-distance phone calls made to a psychological counselor • Hair transplants for premature baldness • A wig prescribed by a psychiatrist for a taxpayer upset by hair loss • A mobile phone for a taxpayer who may need instantaneous medical help • Treatments provided by a Native American medicine man	• Aromatic oils • The cost of heating and air conditioning a home • Shampoo, toothpaste and dental floss • Lawn maintenance service • Ti leaves used for apparel • Medicare tax paid

The IRS and taxpayers have a long history of battling over what is a medical expense for purposes of an itemized deduction.

Certain medical expenses are not deductible. For example, the cost of travel for the general improvement of the taxpayer's health is not deductible. The expense of a swimming pool is not deductible unless the pool is designed specially for the hydrotherapeutic treatment of the taxpayer's illness. No deduction is allowed for the cost of weight-loss programs (unless prescribed by a doctor; diet foods do not qualify) or marriage counseling. Medical expenses for unnecessary cosmetic surgery or similar procedures are not deductible. Cosmetic surgery is considered unnecessary unless it corrects (1) a congenital abnormality, (2) a personal injury resulting from an accident or trauma, or (3) a disfiguring disease. In general, unnecessary cosmetic surgery is any procedure which is directed at improving the patient's appearance and does not meaningfully promote the proper function of the body or prevent or treat illness or disease.

Tax Break

Taxpayers that do not spend medical expenses greater than 7.5 percent of AGI can still enjoy the tax benefit associated with the deduction by using the medical flexible spending account discussed in Chapter 2. By excluding up to $3,200 from gross income, the after-tax savings is basically identical to taking the medical expense deduction for the same amount.

5-6b Medical Insurance

Medical insurance includes standard health policies (including dental and vision), whether the benefits are paid to the taxpayer or to the provider of the services directly. In addition, the premiums paid for membership in health maintenance plans are deductible as medical insurance, as are supplemental payments for optional Medicare coverage. Insurance policies that pay a specific amount each day or week the taxpayer is hospitalized (coverage for lost wages) are not considered medical insurance and the premiums are not deductible. Premiums paid for qualified long-term care insurance policies are also deductible medical expenses up to specified limits which change each year and are based on the age of the taxpayer.

Self-employed taxpayers are allowed, subject to certain limitations, a deduction for adjusted gross income for the medical insurance premiums paid for themselves and their families. Long-term care insurance premiums, up to a specified amount based on the taxpayer's age, are considered health insurance for this purpose. These deductions are covered earlier in this chapter. If a deduction is taken for these items in arriving at AGI, then these same expenses are excluded from the medical expense deduction on Schedule A. However, if the self-employed insurance deduction is limited by net self-employment income, the excess medical insurance expenses can be included on Schedule A.

5-6c Medicines and Drugs

Prescription medicines and drugs and insulin are the only drugs deductible as medical expenses. No deduction is allowed for drugs imported illegally from abroad, including Canada and Mexico. Nonprescription medicines such as over-the-counter antacids, allergy medications, and pain relievers, even if recommended by a physician, are not deductible as a medical expense.

5-6d Capital Expenditures

Payments for capital improvements purchased and installed in the taxpayer's home for medical reasons may also be deductible. Examples include support railings, lowering kitchen cabinets, and medically necessary swimming pools. Unlike other capital expenditures, allowable amounts are deducted fully in the year the item is purchased. If the expenditure is for an improvement that increases the value of the taxpayer's property, the deduction is limited to the amount by which the expenditure exceeds the increase in the value of the property. If the value of the property does not increase as a result of the expenditure, the entire cost is deductible. The cost of upkeep and operation of an item, the cost of which qualified as a medical expense, is also deductible, provided the medical reason for the improvement or special equipment still exists. To take advantage of this deduction, the taxpayer must show the improvement is used primarily for and directly related to medical care. A doctor's recommendation is an important factor in supporting the deduction.

Example A taxpayer has a heart condition and installs an elevator in his home at a cost of $6,000. The value of the home is increased by $4,000 as a result of the improvement. The taxpayer is allowed a deduction of $2,000 ($6,000 − $4,000), the excess of the cost of the equipment over the increase in the value of the taxpayer's home. ♦

5-6e Transportation

Transportation expenses primarily and necessary for medical care are deductible, including amounts paid for taxis, trains, buses, airplanes, and ambulances. Taxpayers may also claim a deduction for the use of their personal automobile for medical transportation. However, only out-of-pocket expenses such as the cost of gas and oil are deductible. Maintenance, insurance, general repair, and depreciation expenses are not deductible. If the taxpayer does not wish to deduct actual costs of transportation by personal automobile, the standard mileage rate for medical care purposes is 21 cents per mile in 2024. In addition to the deduction for actual automobile costs or the standard mileage amount, parking and toll fees for medical transportation are deductible medical expenses. If the transportation expenses are for the medical care of a dependent child, the amounts are deductible by the parent.

5-6f Lodging for Medical Care

Taxpayers may deduct the cost of lodging up to $50 per night, per person, on a trip primarily for and essential to medical care provided by a physician or a licensed hospital. The deduction is allowed for the patient and an individual accompanying the patient, such as the parent of a child. However, no deduction is allowed if the trip involves a significant element of recreation or vacation. No deduction is allowed for meal costs.

Tax Break The cost of buying, training, and maintaining a service animal to assist a visually impaired person, a hearing disabled person, or a person with other physical disabilities, qualifies as a medical expense.

> Itemized deductions are located under Deductions/Itemized Deductions (Schedule A). Subheadings for each of the itemized deductions will be found in tabs near the top of the page.

ProConnect™ Tax TIP

Self-Study Problem 5.6
Refer to Appendix E for Solutions to Self-Study Problems

During the 2024 tax year, Kiran (age 65) and Demi (age 63) paid the following medical expenses:

Medical insurance	$ 450
Prescription medicines and drugs	375
Nutribiotic grapefruit seed supplements	67
Hospital bills	2,550
Health club dues	725
Prescription eyeglasses for Kiran's dependent mother	180
Doctor bills for Kiran's dependent mother	200

In addition, during 2024, they drove 534 miles for medical transportation in their personal automobile. Their insurance company reimbursed Kiran and Demi $1,100 during the year for the medical expenses. If their adjusted gross income for the year is $26,000, calculate their medical expense deduction. Use the Medical and Dental Expenses section of Schedule A of Form 1040 on Page 5-38.

5-7 Taxes

5.7 Learning Objective
Calculate the itemized deduction for taxes.

Taxpayers are allowed to deduct certain state, local, and foreign taxes paid during the year. The purpose of the deduction for taxes is to relieve the burden of multiple taxation of the same income. However, the tax law distinguishes between a "tax" and a "fee." A tax is imposed by a government to raise revenue for general public purposes, and a fee is a charge with a direct benefit to the person paying the fee. Taxes are generally deductible; fees are not deductible. For example, postage, fishing licenses, and dog tags are considered fees that are not deductible as taxes.

Prior to the enactment of the TCJA, tax law provided for an itemized deduction for the following taxes:

- State, local, and foreign income taxes
- Sales taxes (in lieu of state and local income taxes)
- State, local, and foreign real property taxes
- State, local, and foreign personal property taxes

After the TCJA, these taxes largely remain deductible; however, foreign property taxes are only deductible if incurred in carrying on a business or for the production of income (e.g., rental activity). In addition, the aggregate amount of the deduction for state and local real property taxes, state and local personal property taxes, state and local, and foreign, income taxes, and general sales taxes (if elected) for any tax year is limited to $10,000 ($5,000 for married filing separately). But, the $10,000 aggregate limitation rule does not apply to (i) foreign income taxes; (ii) state and local, and foreign real property taxes; and (iii) state and local personal property taxes, if these taxes are paid or accrued in carrying on a business or for the production of income. In other words, taxes deductible on an individual's Schedule C, Schedule E, or Schedule F remain fully deductible and are not subject to the limitation. Note that state and local *income* taxes are not included in the business-related exclusion from the limitation as these taxes have always been deductible as an itemized deduction on an individual's Schedule A. These provisions (the loss of the foreign property tax deduction and $10,000 deduction limitation) apply through 2025.

Self-Study Problems 5.6, 5.7, 5.8, 5.9, and 5.10

SCHEDULE A (Form 1040)
Department of the Treasury
Internal Revenue Service

Itemized Deductions
Attach to Form 1040 or 1040-SR.
Go to www.irs.gov/ScheduleA for instructions and the latest information.
Caution: If you are claiming a net qualified disaster loss on Form 4684, see the instructions for line 16.

OMB No. 1545-0074
2024
Attachment Sequence No. 07

Name(s) shown on Form 1040 or 1040-SR | Your social security number

Medical and Dental Expenses

Caution: Do not include expenses reimbursed or paid by others.
1. Medical and dental expenses (see instructions) ... **1**
2. Enter amount from Form 1040 or 1040-SR, line 11 ... **2**
3. Multiply line 2 by 7.5% (0.075) ... **3**
4. Subtract line 3 from line 1. If line 3 is more than line 1, enter -0- ... **4**

Taxes You Paid

5. State and local taxes.
   a. State and local income taxes or general sales taxes. You may include either income taxes or general sales taxes on line 5a, but not both. If you elect to include general sales taxes instead of income taxes, check this box ☐ ... **5a**
   b. State and local real estate taxes (see instructions) ... **5b**
   c. State and local personal property taxes ... **5c**
   d. Add lines 5a through 5c ... **5d**
   e. Enter the smaller of line 5d or $10,000 ($5,000 if married filing separately) ... **5e**
6. Other taxes. List type and amount: _____ ... **6**
7. Add lines 5e and 6 ... **7**

Interest You Paid

Caution: Your mortgage interest deduction may be limited. See instructions.

8. Home mortgage interest and points. If you didn't use all of your home mortgage loan(s) to buy, build, or improve your home, see instructions and check this box ☐
   a. Home mortgage interest and points reported to you on Form 1098. See instructions if limited ... **8a**
   b. Home mortgage interest not reported to you on Form 1098. See instructions if limited. If paid to the person from whom you bought the home, see instructions and show that person's name, identifying no., and address _____ ... **8b**
   c. Points not reported to you on Form 1098. See instructions for special rules ... **8c**
   d. Reserved for future use ... **8d**
   e. Add lines 8a through 8c ... **8e**
9. Investment interest. Attach Form 4952 if required. See instructions ... **9**
10. Add lines 8e and 9 ... **10**

Gifts to Charity

Caution: If you made a gift and got a benefit for it, see instructions.

11. Gifts by cash or check. If you made any gift of $250 or more, see instructions ... **11**
12. Other than by cash or check. If you made any gift of $250 or more, see instructions. You **must** attach Form 8283 if over $500 ... **12**
13. Carryover from prior year ... **13**
14. Add lines 11 through 13 ... **14**

Casualty and Theft Losses

15. Casualty and theft loss(es) from a federally declared disaster (other than net qualified disaster losses). Attach Form 4684 and enter the amount from line 18 of that form. See instructions ... **15**

Other Itemized Deductions

16. Other—from list in instructions. List type and amount: _____ ... **16**

Total Itemized Deductions

17. Add the amounts in the far right column for lines 4 through 16. Also, enter this amount on Form 1040 or 1040-SR, line 12 ... **17**
18. If you elect to itemize deductions even though they are less than your standard deduction, check this box ☐

For Paperwork Reduction Act Notice, see the Instructions for Form 1040. Cat. No. 17145C Schedule A (Form 1040) 2024

Example Britney and Brad are married taxpayers filing jointly. In 2024, Britney has $7,800 in state income taxes withheld by her employer from her wages. Brad operates a sole proprietorship that owns a building and pays property taxes of $2,300. Brad also pays estimated state income tax payments on his business of $4,000. Lastly, in 2024 Brad and Britney pay property taxes on their home of $1,600. The $2,300 of property taxes associated with the business building are deductible on Schedule C as a business deduction. The $13,400 of itemized deduction for taxes includes Britney's state income taxes ($7,800), Brad's estimated tax payments ($4,000), and the property taxes on their home ($1,600). However, the itemized deduction for taxes is limited to $10,000 in 2024. ♦

The following taxes are not deductible:
- Federal income taxes
- Employee portion of Social Security taxes
- Estate, inheritance, and gift taxes (except in unusual situations not discussed here)
- Excise taxes and gasoline taxes (except when business-related)
- Foreign income taxes if the taxpayer elects a foreign tax credit

5-7a Income Taxes and Sales Taxes

Taxpayers may elect to deduct either state and local sales and use taxes or state and local income taxes as itemized deductions. The election to deduct state and local sales tax instead of income tax primarily benefits taxpayers in states with no income taxes or low income tax rates.

For taxpayers electing to deduct state and local income taxes paid during 2024, the amount of the deduction is the total amount of state and local taxes withheld from wages plus any amounts actually paid during the year, even if the tax payments are for a prior year's tax liability. If the taxpayer receives a refund of taxes deducted in a previous year, the refund must generally be included in gross income (e.g., line 1 on Schedule 1 of the Form 1040) in the year the refund is received. Taxes which did not provide any tax benefit (reduction in taxes) in the year paid are not required to be included in income in the year received as a refund. For example, a taxpayer claiming the standard deduction in the year taxes are paid does not receive a tax benefit for the payment and is not required to include in income a tax refund received the following year.

Example For 2024, Mary's total itemized deductions are $4,500, including state income tax withheld of $1,800. As a result, Mary uses the standard deduction of $14,600. When Mary prepares her 2024 state income taxes, she realizes that she overpaid state income tax through withholding by $200 and receives a refund in 2025. In early 2026, she receives a Form 1099-G reporting her $200 state income tax refund. Because Mary did not benefit from the state tax deduction since she used the standard deduction, she is not required to include the $200 refund in income. ♦

Example Damone paid state income and property taxes of $10,250 in 2024. Damone claimed total itemized deductions of $15,100, including the $10,000 limit on state and local taxes. In 2025, Damone received a state income tax refund of $1,000. If Damone had deducted the actual amount of state taxes in 2024, he would have deducted on $9,250 ($10,250 paid in 2024 less $1,000 refund). His adjusted total itemized deductions would have been $14,350. As a result, Damone would have elected the standard deduction of $14,600 in 2024. The difference between his 2024-claimed itemized deductions ($15,100) and his properly adjusted standard deduction ($14,600) is $500. Thus, he received a $500 benefit from the overpayment of taxes, and Damone must include $500 in his 2025 income. ♦

For taxpayers electing to deduct sales taxes in 2024, the deduction is calculated by using either (a) actual sales taxes paid or (b) estimated sales taxes from IRS tables. Actual sales and use tax expenses are based on a "general sales tax," which is a tax imposed at one rate with respect to the retail sale of a broad range of classes of items. To the extent a higher sales tax rate than the general rate applies to motor vehicles, that excess amount is specifically excluded from the deduction amount.

The actual sales taxes paid method requires a taxpayer to maintain extensive records to substantiate the sales and use taxes paid during the year. To ease the burden on taxpayers, the tax law also permits taxpayers to use estimated state sales tax tables to calculate the deduction. Taxpayers using the estimation tables may add the sales taxes paid on items that include motor vehicles (car, truck, van, motor home, recreational vehicle), aircraft, boats, a home or a substantial addition or renovation to a home. The estimated state sales tax tables are based on the taxpayer's adjusted gross income modified by adding back certain tax-exempt sources of income such as tax-exempt interest, workers compensation, and the nontaxable parts of Social Security or qualified retirement plan distributions. The estimated sales tax also differs by the number of dependents a taxpayer has. The following is a portion of the sales tax estimation table:

2023 Optional State Sales Tax Tables

Income		Family Size						Family Size						Family Size					
At least	But less than	1	2	3	4	5	Over 5	1	2	3	4	5	Over 5	1	2	3	4	5	Over 5
Income		Alabama			2		4.0000%	Arizona			2		5.6000%	Arkansas			2		6.5000%
$0	$20,000	365	436	485	523	555	600	382	428	458	480	498	522	470	532	572	603	628	662
$20,000	$30,000	490	583	646	696	738	796	547	612	654	686	711	746	667	755	812	855	890	938
$30,000	$40,000	551	654	725	780	826	891	630	705	753	790	819	859	766	867	932	981	1021	1076
$40,000	$50,000	602	714	790	850	899	970	701	784	837	878	910	955	850	961	1033	1088	1132	1193
$50,000	$60,000	646	765	847	910	963	1038	763	853	911	955	990	1039	923	1044	1122	1181	1229	1295
$60,000	$70,000	685	811	897	964	1020	1098	818	915	977	1024	1062	1114	989	1118	1202	1265	1316	1387
$70,000	$80,000	721	852	942	1012	1070	1153	869	972	1038	1087	1127	1182	1049	1186	1274	1341	1395	1470
$80,000	$90,000	753	890	983	1056	1117	1203	916	1024	1093	1145	1188	1245	1104	1248	1341	1411	1468	1547
$90,000	$100,000	783	925	1022	1097	1160	1249	959	1073	1145	1200	1244	1304	1156	1306	1403	1477	1536	1619
$100,000	$120,000	823	971	1072	1151	1217	1309	1017	1137	1214	1272	1318	1382	1223	1382	1485	1563	1626	1713
$120,000	$140,000	874	1030	1137	1220	1289	1387	1092	1220	1302	1364	1414	1483	1311	1481	1591	1674	1742	1835
$140,000	$160,000	920	1084	1196	1283	1355	1457	1160	1296	1384	1449	1503	1575	1392	1572	1688	1776	1848	1947
$160,000	$180,000	963	1134	1250	1340	1415	1522	1223	1366	1458	1528	1584	1660	1465	1655	1777	1870	1945	2049
$180,000	$200,000	1002	1179	1300	1393	1471	1581	1282	1432	1528	1601	1659	1740	1534	1733	1861	1958	2037	2145
$200,000	$225,000	1043	1227	1351	1448	1529	1643	1343	1500	1601	1677	1738	1822	1606	1813	1947	2048	2131	2244
$225,000	$250,000	1086	1277	1406	1506	1590	1708	1408	1573	1678	1757	1822	1910	1682	1899	2039	2145	2231	2349
$250,000	$275,000	1127	1323	1456	1560	1647	1769	1469	1640	1750	1833	1900	1992	1753	1979	2125	2235	2325	2448
$275,000	$300,000	1165	1367	1504	1611	1700	1826	1527	1705	1819	1905	1974	2070	1820	2055	2206	2321	2414	2542
$300,000	or more	1384	1620	1780	1905	2008	2154	1863	2080	2219	2323	2407	2523	2212	2496	2679	2818	2930	3085
Income		California			3		7.2500%	Colorado			2		2.9000%	Connecticut			4		6.3500%
$0	$20,000	490	561	607	643	672	712	197	228	248	264	277	295	405	449	477	498	514	537
$20,000	$30,000	679	776	839	887	926	981	275	317	345	366	384	409	578	640	680	710	734	767
$30,000	$40,000	774	883	954	1008	1053	1114	314	362	393	417	437	465	665	737	783	817	845	882
$40,000	$50,000	853	972	1050	1110	1158	1226	347	399	434	460	482	513	738	819	869	907	938	980
$50,000	$60,000	923	1051	1135	1199	1251	1324	376	432	469	498	521	554	803	890	946	987	1020	1066

*The 2024 version of the Optional State Sales Tax Tables was not available as we went to print. Please check the IRS website (**www.irs.gov**) for updates to the instructions for Form 1040 Schedule A.

Because a number of states permit localities to also charge a general sales tax, a local sales tax table for some of the states is provided to assist with that calculation. Because the estimation method is fairly complex, the IRS provides a worksheet to assist with the deduction calculation (refer to Page 5-41) and most tax preparation software will compute the amounts as well. The IRS also provides an online sales tax deduction calculator at **www.irs.gov**.

ProConnect™ Tax TIP

When it comes to entering state tax deduction information, much of the work will be done elsewhere. For example, income taxes withheld are generally input as part of the Form W-2 input. Estimated payments are input under the primary heading Payments, Penalties, and Extensions. Lastly, ProConnect Tax has the state sales tax calculator built in and does not require the manual completion of the state and local sales tax worksheet.

State and Local General Sales Tax Deduction Worksheet—Line 5a*

Keep for Your Records

Instead of using this worksheet, you can find your deduction by using the Sales Tax Deduction Calculator at IRS.gov/SalesTax.

Before you begin: See the instructions for line 1 of the worksheet if you:
- ✓ Lived in more than one state during 2024, or
- ✓ Had any **nontaxable** income in 2024.

1. Enter your **state** general sales taxes from the 2024 Optional State Sales Tax Table .... 1. $ _____

   Next. If, for all of 2024, you lived only in Connecticut, the District of Columbia, Indiana, Kentucky, Maine, Maryland, Massachusetts, Michigan, New Jersey, or Rhode Island, skip lines 2 through 5, enter -0- on line 6, and go to line 7. Otherwise, go to line 2.

2. Did you live in Alaska, Arizona, Arkansas, Colorado, Georgia, Illinois, Louisiana, Mississippi, Missouri, New York, North Carolina, South Carolina, Tennessee, Utah, or Virginia in 2024?

   ☐ **No.** Enter -0-.

   ☐ **Yes.** Enter your base **local** general sales taxes from the 2024 Optional Local Sales Tax Tables.
   .... 2. $ _____

3. Did your locality impose a **local** general sales tax in 2024? Residents of California and Nevada, see the instructions for line 3 of the worksheet.

   ☐ **No.** Skip lines 3 through 5, enter -0- on line 6, and go to line 7.

   ☐ **Yes.** Enter your **local** general sales tax rate, but omit the percentage sign. For example, if your local general sales tax rate was 2.5%, enter 2.5. If your local general sales tax rate changed or you lived in more than one locality in the same state during 2024, see the instructions for line 3 of the worksheet .... 3. _____ . _____

4. Did you enter -0- on line 2?

   ☐ **No.** Skip lines 4 and 5 and go to line 6.

   ☐ **Yes.** Enter your **state** general sales tax rate (shown in the table heading for your state), but omit the percentage sign. For example, if your state general sales tax rate is 6%, enter 6.0 .... 4. _____ . _____

5. Divide line 3 by line 4. Enter the result as a decimal (rounded to at least three places) .... 5. _____ . _____

6. Did you enter -0- on line 2?

   ☐ **No.** Multiply line 2 by line 3.

   ☐ **Yes.** Multiply line 1 by line 5. If you lived in more than one locality in the same state during 2024, see the instructions for line 6 of the worksheet.
   .... 6. $ _____

7. Enter your state and local general sales taxes paid on specified items, if any. See the instructions for line 7 of the worksheet .... 7. $ _____

8. **Deduction for general sales taxes.** Add lines 1, 6, and 7. Enter the result here and the total from all your state and local general sales tax deduction worksheets, if you completed more than one, on Schedule A, line 5a. Be sure to check the **box** on that line .... 8. $ _____

*Download the latest version of this worksheet from the Schedule A instructions available at www.irs.gov. The 2024 worksheet was not available as we went to print. This worksheet is adapted from the 2023 version.

Example Jason and Tina Sterling are married filing jointly taxpayers and residents of Brentwood, Tennessee (Davidson County, zip code 37027). They have no dependents and their AGI for 2024 is $85,000. Brentwood has a 9.25 percent sales tax that includes 7 percent for the state portion and 2.25 percent for the local portion. The Sterlings paid no sales tax on specified items during the year.

The state sales tax table for Tennessee provides a general sales tax amount for income between $80,000 and $90,000 for married filing jointly as $1,463. Tennessee permits a local general sales tax, and thus, the Sterlings use the Local Sales Tax Table for income between $80,000 and $90,000 with two family members to derive a local sales tax estimate of $200. Using the sales tax deduction worksheet, the local amount of $200 is multiplied by 2.25 to yield a total local sales tax amount of $450. Thus, the total sales tax deduction is $1,913. ♦

This example uses 2023 state and local general sales tax estimates as the 2024 amounts were not available as we went to print.

When a married couple files separately, if one spouse uses the optional sales tax tables, the other spouse must use the optional sales tax tables as well.

5-7b Property Taxes

Taxes that are levied on state and local real property for the general public welfare are deductible. However, special assessments charged to provide local benefit to property owners are not deductible; these amounts increase the basis of the taxpayer's property. Also, service fees, such as garbage fees and homeowner association fees, are not deductible as property taxes.

If real estate is sold during the year, the taxes must be allocated between the buyer and the seller, and the division must be made according to the number of days in the year that each taxpayer held the property. The seller is generally responsible for the property taxes up to, but not including, the date the house was sold.

Example Sally sells her home to Patty on March 3, 2024. The taxes for 2024 are paid by Patty and they total $1,830, or $5.00 per day ($1,830/366 days). The purchaser is treated as the owner on the day of sale. Sally is entitled to deduct 62 days of real property taxes or $310 (62 days × $5.00 per day). Patty deducts $1,520 (304 days × $5.00 per day). ♦

Generally, the escrow company or closing agent handling the sale of the property will make the allocation of taxes between the buyer and the seller and the result will be reflected in the settlement charges on the transfer of the title. These amounts are itemized on closing statements for the sale, which are provided to the buyer and the seller (refer to Chapter 4 for an example).

Example William purchased a residence from John in 2024. William's closing statement shows that he receives a credit for $299.80 in taxes that he will pay later in the year on behalf of the seller. Assuming that William pays $525.00 in total taxes on the property later in 2024, his property tax deduction for 2024 would be $225.20 ($525.00 − $299.80). John, the seller, would be allowed a deduction for $299.80 plus any other taxes he paid during the year prior to selling the property. Both of these deductions may be subject to the $10,000 cap. ♦

5-7c Personal Property Taxes

To be deductible as an itemized deduction, personal property taxes must be levied based on the value of the property. Taxes of a fixed amount, or those calculated on a basis other than value, are not deductible. For example, automobile fees that are calculated on the basis of the automobile's weight are not deductible.

Example Rich lives in a state that charges $20 per year plus 2 percent of the value of the automobile for vehicle registration. If Rich pays $160 [$20 + (2% × $7,000)] for his automobile registration, he may deduct only $140, the amount that is based on the value of the automobile. ♦

5-7d Passthrough Entity Tax

The $10,000 aggregate limit on the itemized deduction for state and local taxes ("SALT cap") limits the deduction for many taxpayers in high-tax states such as California, New York, and New Jersey. It also limits the deduction for many high-income earners regardless of state of residence.

Example Walt and Marge Boogewah are a married couple filing jointly in 2024. They live in Darien, CT. Connecticut is a relatively high-tax state and in 2024, the Boogewahs paid state income taxes of $8,600 and state and local property taxes of $8,800. Because of the SALT cap, the Boogewahs' total state and local tax deduction is limited to $10,000. ♦

To provide a workaround to the SALT cap, several states enacted a passthrough entity tax (PTE tax) that either permits or requires taxpayers to remit an income tax at the entity level and then the taxpayer reflects an income tax credit on the individual state income tax return. By shifting the tax off the individual taxpayer and on to the passthrough entity, the tax is an ordinary and necessary business expense of the entity for federal tax purposes and is no longer limited by the SALT cap. The equal and offsetting credit for the individual state income tax return mitigates double taxation at the state level.

Example Marge Boogewah, from the previous example, operates a business as a passthrough entity that generates about $100,000 of the Boogewah's taxable income. The state of Connecticut requires a passthrough entity tax of 6.99% (or about $7,000) on Marge's business. Connecticut also permits Marge and Walt to take an equal $7,000 tax credit on their state income tax return. The Boogewahs' individual state income tax is reduced to $1,600 via the credit ($8,600 − $7,000) and the total itemized deduction for state taxes is $10,400, reducing most of the lost deduction from the SALT cap. ♦

As of June 2024, 36 states and the City of New York have enacted some form of passthrough entity tax with a related credit. Although similar, each state has a slightly different version and so care should be taken to follow local tax law.

Self-Study Problem 5.7 — Refer to Appendix E for Solutions to Self-Study Problems

Sharon is single, lives in Idaho, and has adjusted gross income of $130,000 for 2024. Sharon deducts state income tax rather than state sales tax. The tax withheld from her salary for state income taxes in 2024 is $6,600, and in May of 2024 she received a $225 refund on her state income tax return for the prior year. Sharon paid real estate taxes on her house of $3,400 for the year and an automobile registration fee of $140, of which $120 is based on the weight of the automobile and the balance on the value of the property. Use the Taxes You Paid section of Schedule A on Page 5-38 to report Sharon's deduction for state and local taxes.

5-8 Interest

Learning Objective 5.8
Apply the rules for an individual taxpayer's interest deduction.

Taxpayers are allowed a deduction for certain interest paid or accrued during the tax year. Interest is defined as an amount paid for the use of borrowed funds. The type and amount of the deduction depend on the purpose for which the money is borrowed. Interest on loans for business, rent, and royalty activities is deducted for adjusted gross income. Certain interest on personal loans is deductible as an itemized deduction. The following types of personal interest are deductible:

- Qualified residence interest (mortgage interest)
- Mortgage interest prepayment penalties
- Investment interest
- Certain interest associated with a passive activity

Interest on other loans for personal purposes which do not fall into one of the above categories is generally referred to as consumer interest and is not deductible. Consumer interest includes interest on any loan, the proceeds of which are used for personal purposes, such as credit card interest, finance charges, and automobile loan interest. Interest on loans used to acquire assets generating tax-exempt income is also not deductible.

The following items are not considered "interest," and therefore, are not deductible as an itemized deduction for interest:

- Service charges
- Credit investigation fees
- Loan fees other than "points" discussed later under Prepaid Interest
- Interest paid to carry single premium life insurance
- Premium on convertible bonds

Many lenders require that home mortgage borrowers purchase private mortgage insurance (PMI) to protect the lender. The deduction for PMI expired at the end of 2021.

5-8a Taxpayer's Obligation

To deduct interest on a debt, the taxpayer must be legally liable for the debt. No deduction is allowed for payments made for another's obligation, where the taxpayer is not liable for payment. Also, both the lender and the borrower must intend for the loan to be repaid.

Example Bill makes a payment on his son's home mortgage since his son is unable to make the current payment. The interest included in the mortgage payment is not deductible by Bill since the mortgage is not his obligation. Bill's son cannot deduct the interest since he did not make the payment. ♦

Example Mary loans her daughter $50,000 to start a business. The daughter is 19 years old and unsophisticated in business. No note is signed and no repayment date is mentioned. Mary would be surprised if the daughter's business venture is a success. In all likelihood, a true debtor-creditor relationship is not created. ♦

A taxpayer who assumes the benefits and burdens of ownership, and is considered to essentially be an owner under state law, may be allowed to deduct mortgage interest on a residence even if not directly liable on the mortgage. This situation is not typical and the deduction is allowed only on a case-by-case basis.

5-8b Prepaid Interest

Cash-basis taxpayers are required to use the accrual basis for deducting prepaid interest. Prepaid interest must be capitalized and the deduction spread over the life of the loan. This requirement does not apply to points paid on a mortgage loan for purchasing or improving a taxpayer's principal residence, provided points are customarily charged and they do not exceed the normal rate. Such points paid on a mortgage for the purchase or improvement of a personal residence may be deducted in the year they are paid. Points paid to refinance a home mortgage are not deductible when paid, but must be capitalized and the deduction spread over the life of the loan. Points charged for specific loan services, such as the lender's appraisal fee and other settlement fees, are not deductible.

Example On November 1, 2024, Allen, a cash-basis taxpayer, obtains a six-month loan of $500,000 on a new apartment building. On November 1, Allen prepays $36,000 interest on the loan. He must capitalize the prepaid interest and deduct it over the six-month loan period. Therefore, his interest deduction for 2024 is $12,000 ($36,000/6 months × 2 months). ♦

5-8c Qualified Residence, Home Equity, and Consumer Interest

No deduction is available for consumer (personal) interest, such as interest on credit cards and loans for personal automobiles. Qualified residence interest, however, is a type of personal interest specifically allowed as a deduction. The term "qualified residence interest" is the interest paid on "qualified residence acquisition debt." The term "qualified residence acquisition debt" is defined as debt secured by the taxpayer's principal or second residence in acquiring, constructing, or substantially improving that residence. Qualified residence acquisition debt can include the original mortgage, home equity debt, or refinanced debt. Refinanced debt is treated as acquisition debt only to the extent it does not exceed the principal amount of acquisition debt immediately before the refinancing.

For mortgage debt incurred on or before December 15, 2017, interest is deductible on the first $1 million ($500,000 for married filing separately) of debt. After December 15, 2017, interest related to the first $750,000 of mortgage debt is deductible.

After 2025, the qualified mortgage debt limit returns to $1 million, regardless of the date of the mortgage. Refinancing of pre-TCJA qualified mortgage debt retains the $1 million limit as long as the refinanced debt does not exceed the debt balance at the time of the refinancing.

Tax Break

In order to take a home mortgage interest deduction, debt must be secured by a qualified home (primary residence or second home). A "home" includes a house, condominium, cooperative, and mobile home. A home also includes house trailer, recreational vehicle, boat, or similar property that has sleeping, cooking, and toilet facilities.

Example Klaus and Len file jointly in 2024. They purchased their primary residence in New Jersey in January 2016 using a 30-year mortgage of $1,000,000. In 2024, Klaus and Len decide to refinance the full amount of their $950,000 mortgage balance. Because the refinanced amount is the same or less than the mortgage balance at the time of the refinancing, the interest on the entire $950,000 balance will remain deductible. ♦

Example Meredith and Scott file jointly in 2024. They purchase their primary residence in Palo Alto, CA, in January 2024 using a 30-year mortgage of $1,000,000. In 2024, Meredith and Scott pay interest of $38,000 and make no payments toward loan principal, and thus, the average loan balance is $1,000,000. Because Meredith and Scott's 2024 mortgage exceeds $750,000, the interest deduction will be limited to $28,500 ($38,000 × $750,000/$1,000,000). ♦

The previously permitted deduction of interest on up to $100,000 of home equity debt has been suspended through 2025 (unless the home equity debt is qualified acquisition debt). Interest on home equity loans originated prior to 2018 is also not deductible.

Example Michael and Jeanette Stern file jointly in 2024. In 2007, the Sterns purchased a home using a mortgage of $400,000. In 2016, when the mortgage balance was $50,000, the Sterns used a $300,000 home equity loan to build a substantial addition to their home. The home equity loan is treated as acquisition financing and thus, is treated as qualified mortgage debt and the interest remains deductible. The Sterns could also have used the home equity to refinance the original mortgage debt and retained the deduction of interest. ♦

Example Barb is a single taxpayer. In 2024, she uses a home equity loan of $46,000 to pay for a new car and part of her nephew's college tuition. Barb may not deduct any of the interest on the home equity loan. ♦

In certain circumstances, when the debt balance exceeds the purchase price or the fair market value of the home, the amount of deductible interest can be further limited. If loan proceeds are used in part for a qualified residence and part for other purposes, the amount of debt attributable to the residence will need to be determined using tracing rules. Refer to IRS Publication 936 for more information.

Mortgage interest paid to financial institutions is generally reported on Form 1098. Box 1 reports the amount of interest paid during the year. Box 5 reports PMI, and Box 6 reports any points paid. Some financial institutions will report property taxes paid through escrow in Box 10; however, property taxes are not required to be reported on Form 1098 and taxpayers should review their escrow statement or property tax bills if paid directly.

> **Tax Break** If the sum of mortgage interest and other itemized deductions is less than the standard deduction, no tax benefit is received from the mortgage interest payments. In this case, a taxpayer may wish to pay the mortgage off as quickly as possible if the taxpayer believes its investments will generate an after-tax rate of return greater than the interest rate on the home mortgage.

5-8d Student Loan Interest

Taxpayers are allowed a deduction for adjusted gross income (above-the-line) for certain interest paid on qualified education loans. The deduction is limited to $2,500 for 2024, and is phased out for single taxpayers with modified AGI of $80,000 to $95,000 and for married taxpayers with modified AGI of $165,000 to $195,000. Qualified higher education expenses include tuition, room and board, and related expenses.

Example Sam graduated from college in 2022, taking a job with a salary of $55,000 per year. During 2024, he pays $2,500 interest on qualified education loans. Because his income is below the $80,000 phase-out amount for individual taxpayers, he can deduct the full $2,500 of the interest in arriving at adjusted gross income on his 2024 tax return. If he had paid more than $2,500 in interest, the excess would be considered nondeductible consumer interest. ◆

If the interest is paid through the use of funds from a Section 529 program or through an employer's education assistance program, the interest may not also be deducted as an itemized deduction.

5-8e Investment Interest

To prevent abuses by taxpayers, the Internal Revenue Code includes a provision limiting the deduction of investment interest expense. This provision limits the amount of deductible interest on loans to finance investments. The investment interest deduction is limited to the taxpayer's net investment income. Net investment income is income such as dividends and interest, less investment expenses other than interest. Special rules apply to dividends and capital gains included as investment income due to their preferential tax rates. The general rule is that they may only be included as investment income if the taxpayer chooses to calculate tax on them at ordinary income rates. Any disallowed interest expense is carried over and may be deducted in succeeding years, but only to the extent that the taxpayer's net investment income exceeds investment interest expense for the year. Investment interest expense is commonly reported to the taxpayer as a disclosure on Form-1099B or as a separately stated item on Schedule K-1 when incurred through a partnership or S corporation. The taxpayer will use Form 4952 (refer to Page 5-48) to report the deductible amount of investment interest expense.

Example Gillian borrows $150,000 at 12-percent interest on January 1, 2024. The proceeds are used to purchase $100,000 worth of land and a $50,000 Certificate of Deposit (CD). During 2024, the CD pays interest of $1,700. Gillian incurs expenses (for example, property taxes) attributable to the investment property of $500. Of the $18,000 (12% × $150,000) interest expense incurred in 2024, only $1,200 is deductible due to being limited by the total net investment income in 2024. The deduction is computed as follows:

Investment income	$1,700
Less: investment expenses	(500)
Net investment income	$1,200
Interest deductible in 2024	$1,200

The unused deduction of $16,800 ($18,000 − $1,200) is carried forward and may be used as an interest deduction in future years, subject to the net investment income limitation. ◆

Form 4952 — Investment Interest Expense Deduction (2024)

Form 4952
Department of the Treasury
Internal Revenue Service

Investment Interest Expense Deduction
Attach to your tax return.
Go to www.irs.gov/Form4952 for the latest information.

OMB No. 1545-0191
2024
Attachment Sequence No. 51

Name(s) shown on return | Identifying number

Part I — Total Investment Interest Expense

1	Investment interest expense paid or accrued in 2024 (see instructions)	1
2	Disallowed investment interest expense from 2023 Form 4952, line 7	2
3	**Total investment interest expense.** Add lines 1 and 2	3

Part II — Net Investment Income

4a	Gross income from property held for investment (excluding any net gain from the disposition of property held for investment)	4a
b	Qualified dividends included on line 4a	4b
c	Subtract line 4b from line 4a	4c
d	Net gain from the disposition of property held for investment	4d
e	Enter the **smaller** of line 4d or your net capital gain from the disposition of property held for investment. See instructions	4e
f	Subtract line 4e from line 4d	4f
g	Enter the amount from lines 4b and 4e that you elect to include in investment income. See instructions	4g
h	Investment income. Add lines 4c, 4f, and 4g	4h
5	Investment expenses (see instructions)	5
6	**Net investment income.** Subtract line 5 from line 4h. If zero or less, enter -0-	6

Part III — Investment Interest Expense Deduction

7	Disallowed investment interest expense to be carried forward to 2025. Subtract line 6 from line 3. If zero or less, enter -0-	7
8	**Investment interest expense deduction.** Enter the **smaller** of line 3 or line 6. See instructions	8

For Paperwork Reduction Act Notice, see page 4.   Cat. No. 13177Y   Form **4952** (2024)

Self-Study Problem 5.8
Refer to Appendix E for Solutions to Self-Study Problems

Jordin Clapper, a single taxpayer, received the following Form 1098 related to her primary residence:

Form 1098 — Mortgage Interest Statement (Rev. January 2022) — For calendar year 2024
OMB No. 1545-1380
Copy B — For Payer/Borrower

RECIPIENT'S/LENDER'S name, street address, city or town, state or province, country, ZIP or foreign postal code, and telephone no.:
Kalamazoo Savings and Loan
355 E Kalamazoo Ave.
Kalamazoo, MI 49007

RECIPIENT'S/LENDER'S TIN: 42-7654123
PAYER'S/BORROWER'S TIN: 332-17-9111

PAYER'S/BORROWER'S name: Jordin Clapper
Street address: 211 E Water Street
City, state, ZIP: Kalamazoo, MI 49007

1. Mortgage interest received from payer(s)/borrower(s): $9,250.00
2. Outstanding mortgage principal: $180,000.00
3. Mortgage origination date: 05/28/2013
4. Refund of overpaid interest: $
5. Mortgage Insurance premiums: $
6. Points paid on purchase of principal residence: $
7. [X] If address of property securing mortgage is the same as PAYER'S/BORROWER'S address, the box is checked, or the address or description is entered in box 8.
8. Address or description of property securing mortgage:
9. Number of properties securing the mortgage: 1
10. Other:
11. Mortgage acquisition date:

Caution: The amount shown may not be fully deductible by you. Limits based on the loan amount and the cost and value of the secured property may apply. Also, you may only deduct interest to the extent it was incurred by you, actually paid by you, and not reimbursed by another person.

Self-Study Problem 5.8, continued

Refer to Appendix E for Solutions to Self-Study Problems

The 1099-B she received from her broker reported the following:

VANWILDER MARKETING CORPORATION
VANWILDER BROKERAGE
2024
Summary Information (continued)
Account XXXX293
01/20/2025

INTEREST INCOME — 2024 1099-INT — OMB No. 1545-0112

This is important tax information and is being furnished to the Internal Revenue Service. If you are required to file a return, a negligence penalty or other sanction may be imposed on you if this income is taxable and the IRS determines that it has not been reported.

	Amount
1- Interest income (not included in line 3)	1,000.00
2- Early withdrawal penalty	0.00
3- Interest on US Savings Bonds & Treasury obligations	0.00
4- Federal income tax withheld	0.00
5- Investment expenses	0.00
7- Foreign country or US possession: 6- Foreign tax paid:	0.00
8- Tax-exempt interest (includes line 9)	0.00
9- Specified private activity bond interest (AMT)	0.00
10- Market discount (covered lots)	0.00
11- Bond premium (covered lots)	0.00
12- Bond premium on Treasury obligations (covered lots)	0.00
13- Bond premium on tax-exempt bonds (categorized below)	
Tax-exempt obligations (covered lots)	0.00
Tax-exempt private activity obligations (AMT, covered lots)	0.00
14- Tax-exempt and tax credit bond CUSIP number	
FATCA filing requirement [ ]	

RECONCILIATIONS, FEES, EXPENSES AND EXPENDITURES

The amounts in this section are not reported to the IRS. They are presented here for your reference when preparing your income tax return(s).

	Amount
Other Receipts & Reconciliations- Partnership distributions	0.00
Other Receipts & Reconciliations- Foreign tax paid- partnership	0.00
Other Receipts & Reconciliations- Return of principal	0.00
Other Receipts & Reconciliations- Deferred income payment	0.00
Other Receipts & Reconciliations- Deemed premium	0.00
Other Receipts & Reconciliations- Income accrual- UIT	0.00
Other Receipts & Reconciliations- Basis adjustments	0.00
Other Receipts & Reconciliations- Foreign tax pd beyond treaty	0.00
Fees & Expenses- Margin interest	1,600.30
Fees & Expenses- Dividends paid on short position	0.00
Fees & Expenses- Interest paid on short position	0.00
Fees & Expenses- Non reportable distribution expense	0.00
Fees & Expenses- Other expenses	0.00
Fees & Expenses- Severance tax	0.00
Fees & Expenses- Organizational expense	0.00
Fees & Expenses- Miscellaneous fees	0.00
Fees & Expenses- Tax-exempt investment expense	0.00
Foreign Exchange Gains & Losses- Foreign currency gain/loss	0.00

Jordin had no other investment income or expenses.

Other interest paid during the year:

- Service charges on her checking account $ 48
- Credit card interest   168
- Auto loan interest   675
- Interest from a home equity line of credit (HELOC)   2,300
- Interest from a loan used to purchase stock   1,600
- Credit investigation fee for loan   75

Jordin's residence has a fair market value of $250,000. Jordin used the same home to secure her HELOC with a balance of $50,000. Jordin used the proceeds of her HELOC to pay for college and to buy a new car. Compute Jordin's interest deduction in the following scenarios:

a. Complete Form 4952 on Page 5-48 to compute deductible investment interest and then complete the Interest You Paid section of Schedule A on Page 5-38 to calculate Jordin's interest deduction for 2024.

b. Same as part a, except that Jordin instead used the HELOC proceeds to add a new bedroom to her home.

c. Same as part a, but Jordin's home is valued at $1.2 million and her mortgage balance is $900,000.

Learning Objective 5.9

Determine the charitable contributions deduction.

5-9 Charitable Contributions

To encourage individuals to be socially responsible, the Internal Revenue Code allows a deduction for charitable contributions. To be deductible, the donation must be made in cash or property; the value of free use of the taxpayer's property by the charitable organization does not qualify.

Example Lucille allows the Red Cross to use her building rent-free for 8 months. The building normally rents for $600 per month. There is no deduction allowed for the free use of the building. ♦

In addition, out-of-pocket expenses related to qualified charitable activities are deductible as charitable contributions.

Example Jerry drives his car 200 miles during 2024 to take a church group to a meeting out of town. Jerry is permitted a charitable deduction of $28 (200 miles × 14 cents per mile). ♦

To be deductible, donations must be made to a qualified recipient as listed in the tax law, including:

1. the United States, a state, or political subdivision thereof, if the donation is made for exclusively public purposes (such as a contribution to pay down the federal debt);
2. domestic organizations operated exclusively for charitable, religious, educational, scientific, or literary purposes, or for the prevention of cruelty to children or animals;
3. church, synagogue, or other religious organizations;
4. war veterans' organizations;
5. civil defense organizations;
6. fraternal societies operating under the lodge system, but only if the contribution is used for one or more of the charitable purposes listed in (2) above;
7. certain nonprofit cemetery companies; and
8. under the tax treaties with Mexico, Canada, and Israel, payments to charities in those countries may be deductible but you must also have income sourced from the country.

The following contributions are not deductible:

1. gifts to nonqualified recipients, for example, needy individuals, social clubs, labor unions, international organizations, and political parties;
2. contributions of time, service, the use of property, or blood;
3. contributions where benefit is received from the contribution, for example, tuition at a parochial school; and
4. wagering losses, such as church bingo and raffle tickets.

If a taxpayer has doubt as to the deductibility of a payment to a specific organization, they should review the IRS's online search tool called "Tax Exempt Organization Search."

If cash is donated, the deduction is equal to the amount of the cash. For donated property other than cash, the general rule is that the deduction is equal to the fair market value of the property at the time of the donation. The fair market value is the price at which the property would be sold between a willing buyer and seller. There is an exception to this general rule for property that would have resulted in ordinary income or short-term capital gain had it been sold on the date of the contribution. In that situation, the deduction for the contribution is equal to the property's fair market value less the amount of the ordinary income or short-term capital gain that would have resulted from sale of the property. If the sale of the property would have produced a long-term capital gain, the deduction is generally equal to the fair market value of the property. However, the fair market value is reduced by the amount of the potential long-term capital gain, if the donation is made to certain private nonoperating foundations or the donation is a contribution of tangible personal property to an organization that uses the property for a purpose unrelated to the organization's primary purpose.

Example Jeano donates a painting acquired five years ago at a cost of $4,000 to a museum for exhibition. The painting's fair market value is $12,000. If Jeano had sold the painting, the difference between the sales price ($12,000) and its cost ($4,000) would have been a long-term capital gain. The deduction is $12,000, and it is not reduced by the amount of the appreciation, since the painting was put to a use related to the museum's primary purpose. If the painting had been donated to a hospital, the deduction would be $4,000, which is $12,000 less $8,000 ($12,000 − $4,000), the amount of the long-term capital gain that would have resulted if the painting had been sold. ♦

5-9a Percentage Limitations

Different limits apply to different types of charitable contributions and depend on to whom the contribution is made. The rules for charitable contributions classify organizations as either: (1) a "50-percent organization" or (2) any other charitable organization (a "non-50-percent organization"). Public charities, churches, most educational institutions, hospitals, the United States or any state or local government, all private operating foundations, and private nonoperating foundations if they distribute their contributions to public charities within a specified time period, are all 50-percent charities. Any other qualified organization is a non-50-percent organization.

There are currently four different limitations, all of which represent a percentage of the taxpayer's AGI:

1. 60-percent limitation
2. 50-percent limitation
3. 30-percent limitation
4. 20-percent limitation

Given the complexity of the charitable contribution limits, the IRS provides a worksheet in Publication 526 which has been adapted and presented in Figure 5.1 on Page 5-52.

60-percent Limitation

For tax years from 2022 to 2025, the limit for cash contributions to 50-percent organizations is 60 percent of AGI.

Example In 2024, Doug, a single taxpayer, donates $25,000 in cash to a public charity (a 50-percent organization). Doug's 2024 AGI is $30,000. Doug may deduct only $18,000 ($30,000 × 60%) of the donation. The remaining contribution of $7,000 may be carried forward for up to 5 years. ♦

50-percent Limitation

For noncash contributions to a 50-percent organization, the limit is 50 percent of AGI less any deductions that were subject to the 60-percent limit.

Example In 2024, Jill, a single taxpayer with AGI of $30,000, makes the following donations:

Amount	Organization
$10,000 cash	50-percent organization
$7,000 non-cash (not capital gain property)	50-percent organization

- The $10,000 is below the 60-percent limit of $18,000 ($30,000 × 60%), and thus, is deductible.

- The non-cash donation is subject to a limit of 50-percent of AGI decreased by any deductions taken at the 60-percent level. The $7,000 donation is limited to $5,000 [($30,000 × 50%) − $10,000 previous deduction].
- The excess contribution of $2,000 may be carried forward for up to five years. ♦

Figure 5.1 Charitable Contributions Limits Worksheet

Step 1. Enter charitable contributions made during the year

1. Enter contributions of capital gain property to non-50-percent qualified organizations.   1._____
2. Enter other contributions to qualified organizations that are non-50-percent organizations. Do not include any contributions entered Line 1   2._____
3. Enter contributions of capital gain property to 50-percent-limit organizations deducted at fair market value. Do not include any contributions entered on a previous line.   3._____
4. Enter noncash contributions to 50-percent-limit organizations other than capital gain property deducted at fair market value. Be sure to include contributions of capital gain property to 50-percent-limit organizations if electing to deduct at basis. Do not include any contributions entered on a previous line.   4._____
5. Enter cash contributions to 50-percent-limit organizations. Do not include any contributions entered on a previous line   5._____

Step 2. Figure the deduction for the year (if any result is zero or less, enter -0-)

6. Enter adjusted gross income (AGI)   6._____

Cash contributions subject to 60% limit (if line 5 is zero, enter -0- on lines 7 through 9)

7. Multiply line 6 by 0.6   7._____
8. Deductible amount. Enter the smaller of line 5 or line 7   8._____
9. Carryover. Subtract line 8 from line 5   9._____

Noncash contributions subject to 50% limit (if line 4 is zero, enter -0- on lines 10 through 13)

10. Multiply line 6 by 0.5   10._____
11. Subtract line 8 from line 10   11._____
12. Deductible amount. Enter the smaller of line 4 or line 11   12._____
13. Carryover. Subtract line 12 from line 14   13._____

Contributions (other than capital gain property) subject to 30% limit (if line 2 is zero, enter -0- on lines 14 through 20)

14. Multiply line 6 by 0.5   14._____
15. Add lines 3, 4, and 5   15._____
16. Subtract line 15 from line 14   16._____
17. Multiply line 6 by 0.3   17._____
18. Enter line 2   18._____
19. Deductible amount. Enter the smallest of Line 16, 17, or 18   19._____
20. Carryover. Subtract line 19 from line 18   20._____

Contributions of capital gain property subject to 30% limit (if line 3 is zero, enter -0- on lines 21 through 26)

21. Multiply line 6 by 0.5   21._____
22. Add lines 4 and 5   22._____
23. Subtract line 22 from line 21   23._____
24. Multiply line 6 by 0.3   24._____
25. Deductible amount. Enter the smallest of Line 3, 23, or 24   25._____
26. Carryover. Subtract line 25 from line 3   26._____

Contributions subject to 20% limit (of line1 is zero, enter -0- on lines 27 through 36)

27. Multiply line 6 by 0.5   27._____
28. Add lines 8, 12, 19, and 25   28._____
29. Subtract line 28 from line 27   29._____
30. Multiply line 6 by 0.3   30._____
31. Subtract line 19 from line 30   31._____
32. Subtract line 25 from line 30   32._____
33. Multiply line 6 by 0.2   33._____
34. Enter line 1   34._____
35. Deductible amount. Enter the smallest of lines 29, 31, 32, 33, or 34   35._____
36. Carryover. Subtract line 35 from line 34   36._____
37. Deduction for the year. Add lines 8, 12, 19, 25, and 35   37._____

This worksheet has been adapted from Worksheet 2 of IRS Publication 526.

30-percent Limitation

The 30-percent limit applies to cash donations made to a non-50-percent organization. The 30-percent limit also applies to capital gain property donated to a 50-percent organization for which the taxpayer is taking a deduction for the fair market value of the property. The 50-percent limit also applies in that the total deduction cannot exceed 50 percent of AGI less any previously deducted donations.

Example In 2024, Nicole, a single taxpayer with AGI of $36,000, makes the following donations:

Amount	Organization
$10,000 cash	50-percent organization
$7,000 non-cash (not capital gain property)	50-percent organization
$4,000 cash	Non-50-percent organization

- The $10,000 is below the 60-percent limit of $21,600 ($36,000 × 60%), and thus, is deductible.
- The non-cash donation is subject to a limit of 50 percent of AGI decreased by any deductions taken at the 60-percent level. The $7,000 donation is less than $8,000 ($36,000 × 50% less the previous deduction of $10,000) and can be deducted.
- The cash donation of $4,000 to a non-50-percent organization is subject to the 30 percent of AGI limit ($10,800) but also may not exceed $1,000 [50% of AGI ($18,000) less any deductible contributions previously made to a 50-percent organization ($17,000)].
- Nicole may carryforward the excess $3,000 donation for up to 5 years. ♦

If a taxpayer donates both types of 30-percent-limitation property (capital gains property to a 50-percent organization and cash to a non-50-percent organization), one deduction does not reduce the 30-percent limitation of the other; however, neither may exceed 50 percent of AGI less deductible contributions previously made to a 50-percent organization.

Example In 2024, Darby, a single taxpayer with AGI of $46,000, makes the following donations:

Amount	Organization
$10,000 cash	50-percent organization
$7,000 non-cash (not capital gain property)	50-percent organization
$5,000 capital gain property (basis $2,000)	50-percent organization
$4,000 cash	Non-50-percent organization

- The $10,000 cash donation is below the 60-percent limit of $27,600 ($46,000 × 60%) and thus, is deductible.
- The non-cash donation of $7,000 is subject to a limit of 50 percent of AGI decreased by any deductions taken at the 60-percent level. The $7,000 donation is less than $13,000 ($46,000 × 50% less the previous deduction of $10,000) and can be deducted.

- The $5,000 capital gain property donation can be deducted as it is less than the 30-percent of AGI limit ($13,800) and also less than $6,000, which is the 50-percent limitation of $23,000 less $17,000 ($10,000 + $7,000) of other donations subject to the 50-percent limitation.
- The $4,000 cash donation to a non-50-percent organization is less than the 30-percent limitation ($13,800) but is not less than the 50-percent limitation of $23,000 less all other donations subject to the 50-percent limitation of $22,000 ($10,000 + $7,000 + $5,000), leaving only $1,000 available against which to deduct the $4,000.
- The remaining $3,000 is carried forward for up to 5 years.

As a result, Darby's total deduction is $23,000 ($10,000 + $7,000 + $5,000 + $1,000) or 50 percent of AGI, with an excess of $3,000 remaining that can be carried forward for up to 5 years. ♦

A taxpayer that donates capital gains property to a 50-percent organization can elect to deduct their basis in the property rather than fair market value. If this election is made, the 50-percent limit would apply instead of the 30-percent limit.

Example If in the previous example, Darby instead elects to deduct his $2,000 basis in the capital gain property, rather than the $5,000 market value.

- The $10,000 cash donation is below the 60-percent limit of $27,600 ($46,000 × 60%), and thus, is deductible.
- The non-cash donation of $7,000 plus the capital gain property basis of $2,000 are subject to a limit of 50 percent of AGI decreased by any deductions taken at the 60-percent level. The $9,000 donation is less than $13,000 ($46,000 × 50% less the previous deduction of $10,000) and can be deducted.
- The $4,000 donation to a non-50-percent organization is subject to the 30-percent limit ($13,800) and 50 percent of AGI ($23,000) less all donations to 50-percent organizations, which is now only $19,000 ($10,000 + $7,000 + $2,000) leaving $4,000 against which to deduct the $4,000. No amount is carried forward. ♦

20-percent Limitation

The final limit of 20 percent of AGI applies to non-cash contributions of capital gain property to other non-50-percent charitable organizations. The deductible amount of 20-percent contributions is subject to the same cascading effect of previous limits as shown with the 60, 50, and 30-percent limits.

In practice, there are additional contribution limitations such as donations for the use of an organization (as opposed to directly to the organization), qualified conservation contributions, and qualified disaster relief donations. These more complex limitations are beyond the scope of this textbook.

In general, any contributions not allowed due to the adjusted gross income limitations may be carried forward for up to five years. The contributions may be deducted in the carryover years subject to the same percentage of income limitations which were applicable to the contributions in the year they originated. Contribution carryovers are allowed only after taking into account the current year contributions in the same category.

In summary, if a taxpayer's total contributions total 20 percent or less of their AGI, then none of these limits apply.

No charitable contribution deduction is permitted for a payment to a college or university in exchange for the right to purchase tickets or seating at an athletic event. Pre-2018 law permitted an 80-percent deduction for such contributions.

Example In 2024, Marco donates $5,000 to Big State University in exchange for the right to purchase 2024 season tickets to Big State football games. Marco may not deduct any of the $5,000 payment. ♦

> **Tax Break**
>
> In most instances, a sole proprietor cannot deduct a charitable contribution on Schedule C, and thus, must itemize for a corresponding tax deduction. If the payment qualifies as a business expense, however, it could be deductible. For example, a payment to a football boosters club for an advertisement at the field or in the program is likely to be deductible. The key element to the deduction is the payment must be an ordinary and necessary business expense as covered in Chapter 3.

5-9b Substantiation Rules

Taxpayers should keep records, receipts, canceled checks, and other proof of charitable contributions. For gifts of property, such as clothes and household goods given to the Salvation Army, totaling over $500, the taxpayer must attach a Form 8283 to their return giving the name and address of the donee, the date of the contribution, a description of the property, the approximate date of acquisition of the property, and certain other required information. For large gifts of property worth $5,000 or more, the donor must also obtain and submit an appraisal.

No charitable deduction is allowed for contributions of $250 or more unless the taxpayer substantiates the contributions with written acknowledgments from the recipient charitable organizations. The acknowledgments must contain this information:

- The amount of cash and a description (but not the value) of property other than cash contributed.
- Whether the charitable organization provided any goods or services in consideration, in whole or in part, for any property contributed. (If a payment is partly a gift and partly in consideration for goods or services provided to the donor, it is a "quid pro quo contribution" and special rules apply.)
- A description and good-faith estimate of the value of any goods or services provided by the donor, or, if the goods and services consist solely of intangible religious benefits, a statement to that effect. Intangible religious benefits are any benefits provided by organizations formed exclusively for religious purposes and not generally sold in a commercial setting. For example, attendance at church is considered an intangible religious benefit while attendance at a private religious school is not. Therefore, a donation made at a church service is generally considered a charitable contribution while tuition paid to a private religious school is not considered a charitable contribution.

Taxpayers donating amounts of cash smaller than the $250 limit are required to keep a bank record (canceled check) or a written communication from the charity. Taxpayers who itemize deductions should use checks or a credit card instead of cash for church and similar cash donations.

Gifts of clothing and household items (including furnishings, electronics, appliances, and linens) must be in "good" condition or better to qualify for a deduction. Also, charitable deductions may be denied for contributions of items with minimal value, such as used socks and undergarments. The rules for noncash contributions were enacted because some taxpayers significantly overstated the value of noncash contributions deducted.

No particular form is prescribed for the written acknowledgment, nor does the donor's tax identification number have to be contained on the acknowledgment. It may be a receipt, letter, postcard, or computer form. The acknowledgment must be obtained on or before the date on which the tax return for the tax year of the contribution is filed, or by the due date (plus extensions) if it is earlier than the actual filing date.

Taxpayers donating used vehicles to charity cannot claim a deduction greater than the amount for which the charity actually sells the vehicle. The charity is required to provide the resale information on Form 1098-C to taxpayers donating vehicles. The same rule also applies to boats and planes donated to charity. Taxpayers must attach Form 1098-C to their tax return to substantiate the deduction. Taxpayers may claim an estimated value for the automobile if the charity does not sell it but rather uses it or gives it to a needy individual. The charity must certify that an exception applies if no resale amount is provided on Form 1098-C.

For quid pro quo contributions (donations involving the receipt of goods or services by the donee), written statements (disclosures) are required from the charitable organization to donors making contributions of more than $75. The disclosures need not be individual letters to donors; they simply need to provide the donors with good-faith estimates of the value of the goods or services and inform the donors that only the amounts of the contributions in excess of the value of the goods or services are deductible for federal income tax purposes.

A charitable organization knowingly providing false written acknowledgments is subject to penalty (generally $1,000) for aiding and abetting in the understatement of tax liability. A penalty of $10 per contribution per event, capped at $5,000, may be imposed on charities failing to make the required disclosures for quid pro quo contributions.

Tax Break

A cash-basis taxpayer may charge year-end expenses on a credit card and still deduct the expenses even when payment on the credit card is not made until the next year. Instead of paying medical bills, charitable contributions, or even property taxes by check at year-end, the taxpayer may prefer to charge the expense. Note however, that the credit card may not be one issued by the company supplying the deductible goods or services, but must be a card issued by a third party.

Self-Study Problem 5.9
Refer to Appendix E for Solutions to Self-Study Problems

In 2024, Jon makes the following donations:

a. $8,000 cash to his church
b. $500 check to the Guayaquil Soup Kitchen, a charity based in Ecuador
c. 100 shares of stock with a fair market value of $11,000 and a cost basis of $2,000 to a local university
d. $1,500 to Rhode Island State University (his alma mater) for the right to purchase season tickets to the Fightin' Nutmeggers basketball games
e. $3,200 cash to the Stonecutters, a fraternal benefit society (a non-50-percent charitable organization)
f. Clothing and household items valued at $1,000 donated to a public charity.
g. 10 shares of stock with a value of $1,500 (basis of $100) donated to a non-50-percent organization

Jon's 2024 AGI is $45,000. Use the worksheet on Page 5-52 to determine the charitable contribution deduction and then report that amount in the Gifts to Charity section of Schedule A on Page 5-38. You are not required to complete Form 8283.

5-10 Other Itemized Deductions

The final portion of this chapter discusses casualty and theft losses, other miscellaneous deductions, and the phase-out of itemized deductions for high-income taxpayers (the "Pease" phase-out).

5.10 Learning Objective

Describe other itemized deductions.

5-10a Casualty and Theft Losses

Taxpayers are allowed deductions for certain casualty and theft losses. The deductions may be itemized deductions or, if related to a business, deductions for adjusted gross income. A casualty is a complete or partial destruction of property resulting from an identifiable event of a sudden, unexpected, or unusual nature. Examples of casualties include property damage from storms, floods, shipwrecks, fires, automobile accidents, and vandalism. For damage from weather conditions to be deductible, the condition must be unusual for the particular region. To qualify as a casualty, an automobile accident must not be caused by the taxpayer's willful act or willful negligence.

Example A taxpayer has an automobile that he decides is a lemon, and he wants to get rid of it. He drives the automobile to the top of a cliff and pushes it off. There is no casualty loss deduction since the act is willful. ♦

Many events do not qualify as casualties. For example, progressive deterioration from rust or corrosion and disease or insect damage are usually not "sudden" enough to qualify as casualties. The IRS has held that termite damage is not deductible as a casualty; however, several courts have in the past allowed the deduction. Indirect losses, such as losses in property value due to damage to neighboring property, also are not deductible.

If the taxpayer can establish that theft occurred, certain theft losses are deductible. It is important to show that the item was not simply misplaced. Theft losses are deductible in the year the theft is discovered, not in the year the theft took place. This is important in cases of embezzlement, where the theft has gone on for many years and the statute of limitations has run out on earlier years, otherwise preventing the taxpayer from amending returns for those years.

As a general rule, casualty losses are deductible in the year of occurrence, but there is an exception for federally declared disaster area losses. Taxpayers may elect to treat the losses in a disaster area as a deduction in the year prior to the year the casualty occurred. If a return has already been filed for the prior year, an amended return may be filed and a refund claimed for the prior year's taxes paid. This provision is designed to provide taxpayers with cash on a more timely basis when they have suffered severe casualties.

Example In May of 2024, Amy's house is damaged by flooding. Shortly thereafter, the president of the United States declared the region a disaster area. The damage to the house is $6,000 and the loss may be deducted in 2023 or 2024, even if the 2023 return has already been filed. If Amy elects to take the deduction in 2023, she may immediately file an amended tax return for that year and collect a refund of previously paid taxes. ♦

5-10b Measuring the Loss

The amount of the casualty or theft loss is measured by one of the following two rules:

Rule A—The deduction is based on the decrease in fair market value of the property, not to exceed the adjusted basis of the property.

Rule B—The deduction is based on the adjusted basis of the property.

Rule A applies to the partial destruction of business or investment property and the partial or complete destruction of personal property, while Rule B applies to the complete destruction of business and investment property. The cost of repairs is usually used for the measurement of loss from automobile damage. Repair costs may also be used to measure losses involving other types of property, but it is not a controlling factor. Indirect costs, such as cleanup costs, are part of the loss, provided the payments do not restore the property to better than its previous condition.

Example A taxpayer purchased their house 15 years ago for $25,000. Today it is worth $160,000, and heavy rains cause the house to slide into a canyon and be completely destroyed. The taxpayer's casualty loss deduction under Rule A is the decrease in fair market value ($160,000 − $0) not to exceed the taxpayer's basis ($25,000). Thus, the deduction is limited to $25,000. ♦

> **Tax Break**
>
> The IRS recognizes that measuring the decrease in the fair market value of your property can be difficult for most taxpayers. To provide some assistance, the IRS has generally agreed to follow a set of safe-harbor approaches to measuring losses including safe harbors based on estimated repair costs, insurance estimates, contractor repairs estimates, disaster loan estimates, and de minimis estimates. Not all types of safe harbors can be used with all losses. Refer to Revenue Procedure 2018-08 for details.

5-10c Deduction Limitations

Personal casualty losses are only deductible if associated with a federally declared disaster. The restriction to a federally declared disaster applies to tax years 2018 to 2025. Such losses are subject to a $100 floor per casualty and must exceed 10 percent of AGI to be deducted. If a taxpayer has a net casualty gain, the declared disaster restriction does not apply to the extent of the gain. If related to business property, there is no federally declared disaster restriction, no adjusted gross income limitation or dollar reduction applicable to casualty and theft losses; such losses are deductions for adjusted gross income.

Example In 2024, Wanda incurs a loss due to a complete destruction of her personal-use car due to a casualty event not attributable to a federally declared disaster. Her adjusted basis in the car was $19,000 and the fair market value at the time of the loss was $8,000. Wanda's AGI is $55,000. Wanda was not insured for this type of loss and received no reimbursement. Wanda will not be able to deduct any of her loss as it was not attributable to a federally declared disaster.

If instead Wanda's loss was attributable to a federally declared disaster, she can deduct $8,000 less the $100 floor and also less 10 percent of her AGI:

$$\$2,400 = \$8,000 - \$100 - \$5,500$$ ♦

Example Cosmo incurs two personal losses during 2024. His car was stolen and destroyed by the thieves. His basis in the car was $22,000 and the fair market value at the time of the theft was $16,000. Cosmo also lost a family heirloom watch with a basis of $4,000 in a different theft. Neither of these losses is attributable to a federally declared disaster. Cosmo's insurance covered the auto and reimbursed him $22,000 but the loss of the watch was not covered. Cosmo's casualty gain on the auto is $6,000 ($22,000 − $16,000) and his loss on the watch is $3,900 ($4,000 − $100 floor). Because Cosmo experienced a net casualty gain of $2,100, he may offset the casualty loss against the gain despite the loss not being attributable to a federally declared disaster. ♦

Certain disasters can be deemed "qualified" federally declared disasters and were eligible for additional relief. For example, certain areas affected by Hurricanes Harvey, Irma, and Maria as well as the 2017 California wildfires, were declared qualified federal disaster areas. The rules for qualified federally declared disasters require the taxpayer to use a $500 floor (instead of $100) but do not subject the casualty loss to the 10 percent AGI limitation. In addition, taxpayers who do not itemize were permitted to add the qualified federally declared disaster area loss to the standard deduction. At the time we go to print, no events in 2024 have been declared a qualified federal disaster.

A casualty or theft loss is reported on Form 4684 and then the deductible amount is generally taken as an itemized deduction on Schedule A.

> **ProConnect™ Tax TIP**
>
> Entering the loss from a casualty is input on the left navigation menu. Select Income and then Schedule D/4797/etc. Select Detail entry and then the 4684, 6781, 8824, 4255 tab. Casualty and thefts are entered at the top of the screen.

5-10d Miscellaneous Expenses

Miscellaneous itemized deductions are categorized into two types: (1) those subject to the 2 percent of AGI floor and (2) those not subject to the 2 percent of AGI floor.

Miscellaneous itemized deductions subject to the 2 percent of AGI rule have been suspended through 2025. The most common deductions subject to the 2 percent of AGI rule are:

- Unreimbursed employee business expenses and employee expenses reimbursed under a nonaccountable plan
- Investment expenses
- Other miscellaneous expenses including the all-important tax preparation fees

The most common unreimbursed employee expenses are included in the following list:

- Business bad debt of an employee
- Business liability insurance premiums
- Damages paid to a former employer for breach of an employment contract
- Depreciation on a computer your employer requires you to use in your work
- Dues to a chamber of commerce if membership helps you do your job
- Dues to professional societies
- Educator expenses
- Home office or part of your home used regularly and exclusively in your work
- Job search expenses in your present occupation
- Laboratory breakage fees
- Legal fees related to your job
- Licenses and regulatory fees
- Malpractice insurance premiums
- Medical examinations required by an employer
- Occupational taxes
- Passport for a business trip
- Repayment of an income aid payment received under an employer's plan
- Research expenses of a college professor
- Rural mail carriers' vehicle expenses
- Subscriptions to professional journals and trade magazines related to your work
- Tools and supplies used in your work
- Travel, transportation, meals, entertainment, gifts, and local lodging related to your work
- Union dues and expenses
- Work clothes and uniforms, if required and not suitable for everyday use
- Work-related education

The repeal of miscellaneous deductions subject to the 2-percent floor could result in an employee being subject to additional tax liability when receiving reimbursement from an employer without an accountable plan. Since changing from an employee to an independent contractor is generally not possible without a significant change in the relationship between the individual and the business (this is a matter of law, not a choice by

Chapter 5 • Deductions For and From AGI

either the employee or employer), taxpayers that are employees in this situation may want to inquire if an accountable plan can be implemented by their employer going forward.

Miscellaneous itemized deductions not subject to the 2-percent floor were not affected by the TCJA. This category of expenses includes the following items:

- Amortizable premium on taxable bonds
- Casualty and theft losses from income-producing property
- Federal estate tax on income in respect of a decedent
- Gambling losses up to the amount of gambling winnings
- Impairment-related work expenses of persons with disabilities
- Excess deductions for a trust or estate's final return
- Losses from Ponzi-type investment schemes
- Repayments of more than $3,000 under a claim of right
- Unrecovered investment in an annuity

Gambling losses are not subject to the 2-percent limitation and are not directly limited, but gambling losses are only deductible for taxpayers that itemize deductions. Gambling winnings must be reported as other income on Schedule 1 and losses may be deducted on Schedule A only to the extent of winnings.

5-10e Phase-out of Itemized Deductions

Prior to 2018, certain high-income taxpayers were subject to limits on the amount of itemized deductions. Certain AGI limits for different filing status triggered a reduction in itemized deductions by the lesser of 3 percent of the excess of the taxpayer's AGI over the threshold amount or 80 percent of itemized deductions excluding the deductions for medical expenses, investment interest expense, casualty and theft losses, and gambling losses to the extent of gambling income. The so-called "Pease" phase-out is suspended through 2025.

Self-Study Problem 5.10   *Refer to Appendix E for Solutions to Self-Study Problems*

During 2024, Roberto (a single taxpayer) is an employee and has AGI of $35,000. He lives in Cedar Key, FL in Levy County (zip code 32625).

a. Roberto's community was struck by Hurricane Idalia. During the flood, his car was destroyed. The flood was declared a federal disaster (FEMA Code DR-3596-EM). The market value of the car on the date of destruction was $14,000. Roberto purchased the car in July 2021 at a cost of $18,500. Roberto's car was only partially covered for this type of loss and his insurance paid him $5,000. Calculate Roberto's casualty or theft loss on Form 4684 on Page 5-61 and carry any deductible amount to the Casualty and Theft Losses section of the Schedule A on Page 5-38.

b. Roberto also incurs the following expenses:

Safe-deposit box rental (for investments)	$ 25
Tax return preparation fees	450
Professional dues	175
Trade journals	125
Bank trust fees	1,055
Qualifying job hunting expenses	1,400
Total	$3,230

Roberto also had a big day at the casinos and won $1,400. Over the year, he had substantiation for $1,700 in gambling losses. Assuming Roberto is not self-employed, calculate any miscellaneous deductions and enter them in the Other Itemized Deductions section of Schedule A on Page 5-38.

Self-Study Problem 5.10

Form 4684
Department of the Treasury
Internal Revenue Service

Casualties and Thefts
Attach to your tax return.
Use a separate Form 4684 for each casualty or theft.
Go to www.irs.gov/Form4684 for instructions and the latest information.

OMB No. 1545-0177

2024
Attachment Sequence No. **26**

Name(s) shown on tax return

Identifying number

SECTION A—Personal Use Property (Use this section to report casualties and thefts of property **not** used in a trade or business or for income-producing purposes. For tax years 2018 through 2025, if you are an individual, casualty or theft losses of personal-use property are deductible only if the loss is attributable to a federally declared disaster. You must use a separate Form 4684 (through line 12) for each casualty or theft event involving personal-use property. **If reporting a qualified disaster loss, see the instructions for special rules that apply before completing this section.**)

If the casualty or theft loss is attributable to a federally declared disaster, check here ☐ and enter the DR- _____ or EM- _____ declaration number assigned by FEMA. (See instructions.)

1. Description of properties (show type, location (city, state, and ZIP code), and date acquired for each property). Use a separate line for each property lost or damaged from the same casualty or theft. If you checked the box and entered the FEMA disaster declaration number above, enter the ZIP code of property most affected on the line for Property **A**.

	Type of Property	City and State	ZIP Code	Date Acquired
Property **A**				
Property **B**				
Property **C**				
Property **D**				

			Properties		
		A	B	C	D
2	Cost or other basis of each property				
3	Insurance or other reimbursement (whether or not you filed a claim) (see instructions) . **Note:** If line 2 is **more** than line 3, skip line 4.				
4	Gain from casualty or theft. If line 3 is **more** than line 2, enter the difference here and skip lines 5 through 9 for that column. See instructions if line 3 includes insurance or other reimbursement you did not claim, or you received payment for your loss in a later tax year				
5	Fair market value **before** casualty or theft				
6	Fair market value **after** casualty or theft				
7	Subtract line 6 from line 5				
8	Enter the **smaller** of line 2 or line 7				
9	Subtract line 3 from line 8. If zero or less, enter -0-				

10. Casualty or theft loss. Add the amounts on line 9 in columns A through D **10**
11. Enter $100 ($500 if qualified disaster loss rules apply; see instructions) **11**
12. Subtract line 11 from line 10. If zero or less, enter -0- **12**

Caution: Use only one Form 4684 for lines 13 through 18.

13. Add the amounts on line 4 of all Forms 4684 . . . . **13**
14. Add the amounts on line 12 of all Forms 4684. If you have losses not attributable to a federally declared disaster, see the instructions **14**

Caution: See instructions before completing line 15.

15. • If line 13 is **more** than line 14, enter the difference here and on Schedule D. **Do not** complete the rest of this section.
    • If line 13 is **equal** to line 14, enter -0- here. **Do not** complete the rest of this section.
    • If line 13 is **less** than line 14, and you have no qualified disaster losses subject to the $500 reduction on line 11 on any Form(s) 4684, enter -0- here and go to line 16. If you have qualified disaster losses subject to the $500 reduction, subtract line 13 from line 14 and enter the smaller of this difference or the amount on line 12 of the Form(s) 4684 reporting those losses. Enter that result here and on Schedule A (Form 1040), line 16; or Schedule A (Form 1040-NR), line 7. If you claim the standard deduction, also include on Schedule A (Form 1040), line 16, the amount of your standard deduction (see the Instructions for Form 1040). Do not complete the rest of this section if all of your casualty or theft losses are subject to the $500 reduction. **15**

16. Add lines 13 and 15. Subtract the result from line 14 . . . . **16**
17. Enter 10% of your adjusted gross income from Form 1040, 1040-SR, or 1040-NR, line 11. Estates and trusts, see instructions **17**
18. Subtract line 17 from line 16. If zero or less, enter -0-. Also, enter the result on Schedule A (Form 1040), line 15; or Schedule A (Form 1040-NR), line 6. Estates and trusts, enter the result on the "Other deductions" line of your tax return **18**

For Paperwork Reduction Act Notice, see instructions.   Cat. No. 12997O   Form **4684** (2024)

Key Terms

for AGI deduction, 5-2
health reimbursement arrangement (HRA), 5-2
medical savings account (MSA), 5-2
health savings account (HSA), 5-2
Form 8889, 5-3
Form 1099-SA, 5-3
self-employed health insurance deduction, 5-6
long-term care, 5-6
traditional individual retirement account (IRA), 5-9
Roth IRA, 5-9
nondeductible traditional IRA, 5-10
early distribution, 5-14
Form 5329, 5-14
Required minimum distribution (RMD), 5-15
prohibited transaction, 5-17

Simplified Employee Pension (SEP), 5-21
Savings Incentive Match Plan for Employees (SIMPLE), 5-22
SIMPLE IRA, 5-22
401k plan, 5-24
SIMPLE 401k, 5-25
small employer pension plan startup cost credit, 5-26
qualified student loan payments, 5-29
educator's expense, 5-32
unreimbursed employee business expense, 5-32
moving expense, 5-33
Schedule A, 5-34
medical expense, 5-34
medical transportation, 5-36
medical lodging, 5-36

state and local tax expense, 5-37
state and local sales and use tax, 5-39
property tax expense, 5-42
passthrough entity (PTE) tax, 5-43
interest expense, 5-44
mortgage interest expense, 5-44
consumer interest expense, 5-45
home equity loan interest expense, 5-46
student loan interest expense, 5-46
investment interest expense, 5-47
Form 4952, 5-47
charitable contributions, 5-50
50-percent organization, 5-51
casualty and theft loss, 5-57
federally declared disaster, 5-58
Form 4684, 5-59
miscellaneous expense, 5-59

Key Points

Learning Objectives	Key Points
LO 5.1: Explain how Health Savings Accounts (HSAs) can be used for tax-advantaged medical care.	• Health Savings Accounts (HSAs) are used for the purpose of paying unreimbursed medical expenses. • HSAs have an annual age-based contribution dollar limitation for deductions for individuals ($4,150) and families ($8,300). There is an additional $1,000 "catch-up" contribution allowed for individuals beginning at age 55 and ending at age 65, the age for Medicare eligibility. • Distributions from HSAs are tax-exempt when used to pay for qualified medical expenses. Distributions which are not used to pay for qualified medical expenses may be subject to income tax and a 20-percent penalty. • Once a taxpayer is 65 years old, distributions may be taken for nonmedical expenses and will be subject to income tax, but not the 20-percent penalty.
LO 5.2: Describe the self-employed health insurance deduction.	• Deductible health insurance includes: (1) medical and dental insurance paid to cover the self-employed taxpayer, spouse, and dependents; (2) medical and dental insurance paid for children under the age of 27 who are not dependents; (3) Medicare premiums; and (4) long-term care insurance paid for the taxpayer and the family of the taxpayer. • Taxpayers with income reportable on Schedule C are generally considered self-employed. • Taxpayers with earnings from certain partnerships, S corporations, LLCs, and farm businesses may also be considered self-employed and may be allowed the deduction for self-employed health insurance. • The deduction for self-employed health insurance is only allowed to the extent of the taxpayer's net self-employed income.

LO 5.3:
Explain the treatment of Individual Retirement Accounts (IRAs), including Roth IRAs.

- Generally, annual contributions to a traditional IRA are deductible and retirement distributions are taxable; whereas, annual contributions to a Roth IRA are not deductible and retirement distributions are nontaxable.
- Earnings in both types of IRAs are not taxable in the current year.
- In 2024, the maximum annual contribution that may be made to either type of IRA is equal to the lesser of (1) 100 percent of the taxpayer's compensation or self-employment income (earned income) or (2) $7,000 (plus an additional $7,000 which may be contributed on behalf of a spouse with no earned income). An additional catch-up $1,000 annual contribution is allowed for taxpayers age 50 and over.
- The tax deduction for contributions to traditional IRAs is limited for taxpayers who are active participants in qualified retirement plans and have income over certain limits. Contributions to Roth IRAs are limited for taxpayers with income over certain limits; however, they are not affected by taxpayer participation in other retirement plans.
- Taxpayers may benefit from a rule allowing conversions of traditional IRAs into Roth IRAs.
- Generally, money distributed from a traditional IRA is taxable as ordinary income and may be subject to a 10-percent penalty for early withdrawal (before age 59½). Some types of early withdrawals may be made without penalty.
- A taxpayer can make tax-free withdrawals from a Roth IRA after a 5-year holding period if the distribution is made on or after the date on which the participant attains age 59½. Other tax-free withdrawals may also apply.

LO 5.4:
Explain the general contribution rules for small business and self-employed retirement plans.

- Employers may claim a deduction in the current year for contributions to qualified retirement plans on employees' behalf. The employees do not include the employer contributions in income until the contributed amounts are distributed generally in retirement years.
- For 2024, the maximum contribution to a SEP is the lesser of 25 percent of compensation or $69,000.
- For 2024, contributions to retirement plans by self-employed taxpayers are generally limited to the lesser of 20 percent of their net earned income before the contribution deduction or $69,000.
- For 2024, an employee may elect to make an annual contribution up to $23,000 to a 401k plan. In addition, any matching amount contributed to the plan by the employer on behalf of the employee is excluded from the employee's gross income.

LO 5.5:
Describe other adjustments for adjusted gross income.

- Eligible educators may deduct up to $300 for the unreimbursed cost of classroom materials as a for AGI deduction.
- Certain performing artists, reservists, and fee-basis government officials can deduct unreimbursed employee expenses as a for AGI deduction.
- Starting in 2018, moving expenses are only deductible for members of the Armed Forces pursuant to a military order and permanent change of station.

LO 5.6:
Calculate the itemized deduction for medical expenses.

- Taxpayers are allowed an itemized deduction on Schedule A for medical expenses paid for themselves, their spouse, and their dependents.
- Qualified medical expenses are deductible only to the extent they exceed 7.5 percent of a taxpayer's adjusted gross income.
- Qualified medical expenses include such items as prescription medicines and drugs, insulin, fees for doctors, dentists, nurses, and other medical professionals, hospital fees, hearing aids, dentures, prescription eyeglasses, contact lenses, medical transportation and lodging, crutches, wheelchairs, guide dogs, birth control prescriptions, acupuncture, psychiatric care, medical and Medicare insurance premiums, and various other listed medical expenses.

LO 5.7:
Calculate the itemized deduction for taxes.

- The following taxes are deductible on Schedule A: state and local income taxes or state and local sales taxes, real property taxes (state and local), and personal property taxes (state and local).
- The itemized deduction for taxes is limited to $10,000.
- Nondeductible taxes include the following: federal income taxes, employee portion of Social Security taxes, estate, inheritance, and gift taxes (except in unusual situations), gasoline taxes, excise taxes, and foreign taxes if the taxpayer elects a foreign tax credit.
- If real estate is sold during the year, the taxes must be allocated between the buyer and seller based on the number of days in the year that each taxpayer held the property to determine each party's deductible amount.
- To be deductible, personal property taxes must be levied based on the value of the property. Personal property taxes of a fixed amount, or those calculated on a basis other than value, are not deductible.
- Some states permit a passthrough entity tax and offsetting state income tax credit to allow the federal deduction of income taxes on certain business income.

LO 5.8:
Apply the rules for an individual taxpayer's interest deduction.

- Deductible personal interest includes qualified residence interest (mortgage interest), mortgage interest prepayment penalties, investment interest, and certain interest associated with a passive activity.
- Nondeductible consumer interest includes interest on any loan, the proceeds of which are used for personal purposes, such as credit card interest, finance charges, and automobile loan interest.
- "Qualified residence interest" is the sum of the interest paid on "qualified residence acquisition debt."
- Taxpayers are allowed a deduction for AGI for certain interest paid on qualified education loans.
- Deductible investment interest is limited to the taxpayer's net investment income, which is investment income such as dividends and interest, less investment expenses other than interest.

LO 5.9:
Determine the charitable contributions deduction.

- To be deductible, the donation must be made in cash or property.
- For donated property other than cash, the general rule is that the deduction is equal to the fair market value of the property at the time of the donation.
- Donations are limited to 60, 50, 30, or 20 percent of AGI in certain cases.
- Excess contributions due to the limitations may be carried forward up to five years.

LO 5.10:
Describe other itemized deductions.

- A loss from a personal casualty such as property damage from storms, floods, shipwrecks, fires, automobile accidents, and vandalism is only deductible if associated with a federally declared disaster.
- For the partial destruction of business or investment property and the partial or complete destruction of personal property, the deduction is based on the decrease in fair market value of the property, not to exceed the adjusted basis of the property.
- For the complete destruction of business and investment property, the deduction is based on the adjusted basis of the property.
- The amount of each personal casualty loss attributable to a federally declared disaster, is reduced by $100 and only the excess over 10 percent of the taxpayer's AGI is deductible.
- The deduction for miscellaneous expenses subject to the 2 percent of AGI limit is suspended through 2025.
- Miscellaneous expenses not subject to the 2 percent of AGI limit such as gambling losses to the extent of gambling winnings, impairment-related work expenses of persons with disabilities, certain estate taxes, amortizable bond premiums, and unrecovered annuity costs at death remain deductible.
- The phase-out of itemized deductions for high-income taxpayers has been suspended.

Questions and Problems

Group 1:
Multiple Choice Questions

LO 5.1 1. Which of the following is a *false* statement about Health Savings Accounts (HSAs)?
   a. Taxpayers who contribute to an HSA must carry qualifying high-deductible health insurance.
   b. HSAs are available to any taxpayer using any health plan purchased through the state or federal exchange under the Affordable Care Act.
   c. Distributions from HSAs are not taxable when used to pay qualifying medical expenses.
   d. Taxpayers must contribute to the HSA by April 15 of the year following the tax year for which they want the deduction.
   e. Distributions from HSAs which are not used to pay qualifying medical expenses are generally subject to a 20-percent penalty as well as income taxes for taxpayers under age 65.

LO 5.1 2. Charlene has family coverage in a qualifying high-deductible health insurance plan. She is 47 years old and wishes to contribute the maximum amount to her HSA. How much is she allowed to contribute and deduct in 2024?
   a. $16,100
   b. $8,300
   c. $4,150
   d. $3,850
   e. $0

LO 5.1 3. In 2024, Estelle, a 67-year old single taxpayer, took a distribution of $4,000 from her HSA. She used $1,200 toward qualifying medical expenses and used the rest for other personal expenses. What is/are the tax consequences of the excess distribution?
   a. None
   b. Typical income taxes
   c. A 20-percent additional tax
   d. Both typical income taxes and a 20-percent additional tax

LO 5.2 4. Kidd is a self-employed single taxpayer in 2024 that files Schedule C for his sole proprietorship. He pays for his own health insurance and the premiums are less than his net profits. Kidd will deduct his self-employed health insurance on which form?
   a. Schedule C
   b. Form 1040 as a from AGI deduction
   c. Form 1040 as a for AGI deduction
   d. Self-employed health care insurance is not deductible

LO 5.2 5. Which type of insurance is *not* deductible as self-employed health insurance?
   a. Medical insurance
   b. Disability insurance
   c. Dental insurance
   d. Long-term care insurance
   e. Spousal medical insurance

LO 5.2 6. Which of the following is *true* about the self-employed health insurance deduction?
a. The deduction cannot be claimed when a subsidized employer health insurance plan is also available.
b. The deduction can be claimed if the taxpayer has an overall business loss from self-employment.
c. Long-term care premiums may not be deducted.
d. The self-employed health insurance deduction is a from AGI deduction.
e. Dental insurance is not included as deductible self-employed health insurance.

LO 5.2 7. In 2024, Yasmin is a single self-employed taxpayer with net profits of $36,000 before considering a deduction for self-employed health insurance. She pays $7,700 for health insurance coverage for the entire 2024 tax year. In 2024, she is eligible for a premium tax credit of $4,000. Her 2024 deduction for self-employed health insurance will be:
a. $0
b. $7,700
c. $4,000
d. $3,700

LO 5.3 8. Lyndon, age 24, has a nonworking spouse and earns wages of $36,000 for 2024. He also received rental income of $5,000 and dividend income of $900 for the year. Assuming Lyndon's employer does not offer a retirement plan, what is the maximum amount Lyndon can deduct for contributions to his and his spouse's individual retirement accounts for the 2024 tax year?
a. $36,000
b. $14,000
c. $13,000
d. $7,000
e. $6,500

LO 5.3 9. Merel and Samir, a married couple under 50 years of age, have adjusted gross income and taxable income on their 2024 joint income tax return of $45,000 and $15,800, respectively, before considering any IRA deduction. Included in AGI is earned income of $11,000 and $0 for Samir and Merel, respectively. What is the amount of Merel's maximum deductible IRA contribution?
a. $0
b. $6,500
c. $7,000
d. $14,000
e. $15,800

LO 5.3 10. Donna, age 42 and a single taxpayer, has a salary of $133,500 and interest income of $20,000. What is the maximum amount Donna can contribute to a Roth IRA for 2024?
a. $0
b. $3,250
c. $3,500
d. $6,500
e. $7,000

LO 5.3 11. Mary has a Roth IRA held more than five years to which she has contributed $30,000. The Roth IRA has a current value of $62,000. Mary is 62 years old and she takes a distribution of $40,000 to take a world cruise. How much of the distribution will be taxable to Mary?
a. $0
b. $8,000
c. $10,000
d. $40,000
e. Some other amount

LO 5.3   12. Marge has a Roth IRA held more than five years to which she has contributed $38,000. The IRA has a current value of $62,000. Marge is 55 years old and she takes a distribution of $40,000. How much of the distribution will be taxable to Marge?
   a. $2,000
   b. $10,000
   c. $22,000
   d. $40,000
   e. Some other amount

LO 5.3   13. Mindy has a Roth IRA held longer than five years to which she has contributed $30,000. The IRA has a current value of $62,000. Mindy is 55 years old and she takes a distribution of $40,000 after retiring on disability. How much of the distribution will be taxable to Mindy?
   a. $0
   b. $8,000
   c. $30,000
   d. $40,000
   e. Some other amount

LO 5.3   14. What is the deadline for making a contribution to a traditional IRA or a Roth IRA for the 2024 tax year?
   a. April 15, 2025
   b. July 15, 2024
   c. December 31, 2024
   d. October 15, 2025

LO 5.3   15. Which of the following would *not* be considered a prohibited transaction between an IRA and its owner?
   a. The owner taking a loan from the IRA
   b. The owner selling property to the IRA
   c. Investing in foreign stocks
   d. Buying property for personal use with IRA funds

LO 5.3   16. In 2024, Estelle, a 47-year old single taxpayer, took a distribution of $10,000 from her traditional IRA. She used all $10,000 toward the purchase of her first home. What is/are the tax consequences of the early distribution?
   a. None.
   b. Typical income taxes
   c. A 10-percent additional tax
   d. Both typical income taxes and a 10-percent additional tax

LO 5.4   17. Which of the following statements with respect to a qualified retirement plan is accurate?
   a. Self-employed individuals are not eligible to be members of a SEP.
   b. Contributions to SIMPLE IRAs are limited to 15 percent of the taxpayer's net earned income or $100,000, whichever is greater.
   c. Employer matching of employee contributions to a 401k plan is not taxable in the year contributed.
   d. Taxpayers must begin receiving distributions from a qualified plan by the age of 65.
   e. None of these statements are accurate.

LO 5.4   18. What is the maximum tax-deferred contribution that can be made to a 401k plan by an employee under age 50 in 2024?
   a. $19,000
   b. $19,500
   c. $22,500
   d. $23,000
   e. $69,000

LO 5.4

19. Paul, age 37, participates in a 401k plan which allows employees to contribute up to 15 percent of their salary. His annual salary is $130,000 in 2024. What is the maximum he can contribute, on a tax-deferred basis under a salary reduction agreement, to this plan?
    a. $24,000
    b. $20,500
    c. $18,500
    d. $19,500
    e. None of the above

LO 5.4

20. Which of the following is a requirement to claim the small employer pension plan startup cost credit?
    a. The employer must have 100 or fewer employees.
    b. The plan must include an auto-enrollment feature.
    c. The plan must have been in existence for at least three years.
    d. The employer must report a taxable loss for each year the credit is claimed.

LO 5.5
LO 5.10

21. Eliza is a kindergarten teacher for Alexander Hamilton Elementary School. Eliza decorates her classroom with new artwork, posters, bulletin boards, etc. In 2024, she spends $470 on materials and supplies for her classroom. The school reimburses her $100 (the annual reimbursement limit). Eliza can deduct _____ for AGI and _____ from AGI.
    a. $0 for and $0 from AGI
    b. $370 for and $0 from AGI
    c. $250 for and $0 from AGI
    d. $300 for and $0 from AGI
    e. $0 for and $370 from AGI

LO 5.5

22. Jessica is a U.S. Army Reservist and in 2024 traveled 130 miles each way to serve duty at a local military installation. She was required to report four times in 2024. Her normal route from home to the base included a $1.75 toll each way. Jessica's for AGI deduction for these costs is:
    a. $0
    b. $695.20
    c. $710.80
    d. $696.80
    e. $643.20

LO 5.5

23. J.R. Ayte served on a jury for 6 days and was paid $180 for his jury service by the court system. J.R.'s employer pays employees for days off due to jury duty but requires that the employee reimburse the company for any jury pay received, which J.R. does promptly. What is the impact of jury duty on J.R's taxable income?
    a. None. Jury duty is excluded.
    b. Jury duty pay is included in gross income only.
    c. J.R. receives a from AGI deduction for the reimbursement of jury duty pay.
    d. Jury duty pay is included in gross income but is offset by a for AGI deduction for the jury duty reimbursement.

LO 5.6

24. The cost of which of the following expenses is *not* deductible as a medical expense on Schedule A, before the 7.5 percent of adjusted gross income limitation?
    a. A psychiatrist
    b. Botox treatment to reduce wrinkles around eyes
    c. Acupuncture
    d. Expense to hire and train a guide dog for a visually-impaired taxpayer

LO 5.6

25. The cost of which of the following is deductible as a medical expense?
    a. Travel to a warm climate
    b. Birth control pills
    c. A disability insurance policy that pays $200 for each day the taxpayer is in the hospital
    d. Liposuction to reduce waist size

LO 5.6

26. Which of the following is not considered a deductible medical expense?
    a. Once daily multivitamin
    b. Prescription eyeglasses
    c. Acupuncture
    d. Filling a tooth cavity

LO 5.7

27. Which of the following taxes may be deducted as an itemized deduction?
    a. State gasoline taxes
    b. Local property taxes
    c. Federal income taxes
    d. Social Security taxes
    e. Medicare taxes

LO 5.7

28. In April 2024, Linton paid $40 of state income tax that was due when he filed his 2023 income tax return. During 2024, Linton's employer withheld $1,200 of state income tax from his pay. In April 2025, Linton determined that his 2024 state tax liability was $1,100 and received his state income tax refund of $100 in May 2025. Assuming Linton itemizes, how much state income tax deduction should he report on his 2024 federal income tax return?
    a. $1,200
    b. $1,240
    c. $1,100
    d. $1,140
    e. $1,000

LO 5.7

29. Antonio is a small business owner and files jointly with his spouse. In 2024, he generates $100,000 of net profits from his business. His spouse, Maria, has $4,000 of state income tax withheld from her wages in 2024. They also pay $4,500 in property taxes on their home. Antonio determines that their state income taxes associated with his business are about $5,600 and makes estimated state income tax payments of that amount in 2024. How much should Antonio and Maria deduct for state taxes?
    a. Itemized deductions of $9,500 and deduct $5,600 for taxes on Antonio's Schedule C for his business
    b. Itemized deductions of $10,000 and deduct $5,100 for taxes on Antonio's Schedule C for his business
    c. Itemized deductions of $10,000
    d. Itemized deductions of $4,000 and deduct $5,600 for taxes on Antonio's Schedule C for his business

LO 5.7

30. Antonio is a small business owner and files jointly with his spouse. In 2024, he generates $100,000 of net profits from his passthrough business. His spouse, Maria, has $4,000 of state income tax withheld from her wages in 2024. They also pay $4,500 in property taxes on their home. The state in which Antonio and Maria live requires that Antonio pay a passthrough entity tax (PTE) of $5,600, which Antonio does through estimated payments of that amount in 2024. Antonio and Maria receive a tax credit on their individual state income tax return for the PTE they paid. How much should Antonio and Maria deduct for state taxes?
    a. Itemized deductions of $14,100 and deduct $5,600 for taxes on Antonio's business tax return
    b. Itemized deductions of $10,000 and deduct $4,100 for taxes on Antonio's business tax return
    c. Itemized deductions of $10,000
    d. Itemized deductions of $8,500 and deduct $5,600 for taxes on Antonio's business tax return

5-70 Chapter 5 • Deductions For and From AGI

LO 5.7 31. The itemized deduction for state and local taxes in 2024 is
  a. Total taxes less 10 percent of AGI
  b. Limited to no more than $10,000
  c. Unlimited
  d. Only deductible if the taxes are business related
  e. Deductible if your home value is less than $750,000

LO 5.8 32. Which of the following is deductible as interest on Schedule A?
  a. Fees for having the home's value assessed by the bank for purposes of getting a mortgage
  b. Purchase mortgage insurance paid in 2024
  c. Interest on a credit card balance from the purchase of home furnishings.
  d. Interest on loans to finance tax-exempt bonds
  e. None of the above are deductible as interest

LO 5.8 33. Carrie, a single taxpayer, finished her undergraduate degree using money from a student loan. She earned $56,000 her first year and paid $2,600 in interest in 2024. She can take a deduction for student loan interest in the amount of:
  a. $2,600
  b. $2,500
  c. $1,500
  d. $0
  e. None of the above

LO 5.8 34. Which of the following interest expense amounts is *not* deductible in the current year?
  a. Education loan interest of $2,000, assuming the taxpayer has income of $30,000.
  b. Home equity loan interest of $6,000, on a loan of $90,000, the proceeds of which were used to add a new bedroom and bathroom to an existing primary residence.
  c. Investment interest expense of $1,200, assuming the taxpayer has no investment income.
  d. Qualified residence interest of $70,000 on a $730,000 loan used to purchase a luxury condominium in downtown San Diego.

LO 5.9 35. Which of the following donations are *not* deductible as a charitable contribution?
  a. A donation of clothing to Goodwill Industries
  b. A cash contribution to a church
  c. A contribution of stock to a public university
  d. A contribution of a taxpayer's time picking up trash on the beach
  e. A painting contributed to a museum

LO 5.9 36. Stanley donates a hotel to a university for use as a conference center. The building was purchased three years ago for $1,200,000 and has a fair market value of $1,500,000 on the date the contribution is made. If Stanley had sold the building, the $300,000 difference between the sales price and cost would have been a long-term capital gain. What is the amount of Stanley's deduction for this contribution, before considering any limitation based on adjusted gross income?
  a. $1,800,000
  b. $1,500,000
  c. $1,900,000
  d. $1,200,000
  e. $0

LO 5.9 37. Rico a single taxpayer, makes $5,000 of cash donations in 2024. His standard deduction exceeds his itemized deductions including the contribution. What amount will Rico deduct for charitable contributions? His AGI in 2024 is $48,000.
  a. $300
  b. $5,000
  c. $4,800
  d. $0
  e. $48,000

LO 5.9

38. Which of the following gifts is a deductible contribution?
    a. A gift of $100 to a homeless person
    b. A $500 gift to the Democratic National Committee
    c. $1,000 spent on church bingo games
    d. A $200 contribution to your child's public elementary school

LO 5.10

39. Which of the following would typically be deductible as a casualty loss in 2024?
    a. Long-term damage to a home from termites
    b. An automobile accident during the daily commute
    c. A theft of a big screen television
    d. Dropping your smartphone in the pool
    e. None of the above

LO 5.10

40. Which of the following is *not* a possible limitation on the deduction of a personal casualty loss in 2024?
    a. The lesser of the fair market value of the property or the adjusted basis at the time of the loss
    b. A $100 floor for each casualty event
    c. A 10 percent of AGI floor for all casualty losses during the year
    d. A personal casualty not associated with a federally declared disaster
    e. All of the above are possible limitations on a personal casualty loss

LO 5.10

41. Which of the following is deductible as an other itemized deduction in 2024?
    a. Tax preparation fees
    b. Gambling losses in excess of gambling winnings
    c. Losses from Ponzi-type schemes
    d. Job-hunting expenses subject to the 2 percent of AGI floor
    e. None of the above are deductible as a miscellaneous itemized deduction.

LO 5.10

42. Which of the following items is deductible as an other deduction on Schedule A?
    a. Investment expenses
    b. Gambling losses to the extent of gambling winnings
    c. Unreimbursed business expenses
    d. Subscriptions to professional publications
    e. Charitable contributions

Group 2: Problems

LO 5.1

1. Evan participates in an HSA carrying family coverage for himself, his spouse, and two children. In 2024, Evan has $200 per month deducted from his paycheck and contributed to the HSA. In addition, Evan makes a one-time contribution of $2,000 on April 15, 2025 when he files his tax return. Evan also receives a 2024 Form 1099-SA that reports distributions to Evan of $3,200 which Evan used for medical expenses. Compute the effect of the HSA transactions on Evan's adjusted gross income.

LO 5.2

2. Serena is a 48-year-old single taxpayer. She operates a small business on the side as a sole proprietor. Her 2024 Schedule C reports net profits of $15,000. Her employer does not offer health insurance. Serena pays health insurance premiums of $7,800 in 2024. Serena also pays long-term care insurance premiums of $1,200 in 2024. Calculate Serena's self-employed health care deduction.

Chapter 5 • Deductions For and From AGI

LO 5.3 3. Shyla, 28 years old and a single taxpayer, has a salary of $51,500 and rental income of $33,000 for the 2024 calendar tax year. Shyla is covered by a pension through her employer.
   a. What is the maximum amount that Shyla may deduct for contributions to her IRA for 2024?
   b. If Shyla is a calendar-year taxpayer and files her extended tax return on August 15, what is the last date on which she can make her contribution to the IRA and deduct it for 2024?

LO 5.3 4. Phil and Naoko are 25-year-old newlyweds and file a joint tax return. Naoko is covered by a retirement plan at work, but Phil is not.
   a. Assuming Phil's wages were $27,000 and Naoko's wages were $18,500 for 2024 and they had no other income, what is the maximum amount of Phil and Naoko's deductions for contributions to a traditional IRA for 2024?
   b. Assuming Phil's wages were $60,000 and Naoko's wages were $71,000 for 2024 and they had no other income, what is the maximum amount of Phil and Naoko's deductions for contributions to a traditional IRA for 2024?

LO 5.3 5. What is the maximum amount a 45-year-old taxpayer and 45-year-old spouse can put into a Traditional or Roth IRA for 2024 (assuming they have sufficient earned income, but do not have an income limitation and are not covered by another pension plan)?

LO 5.3 6. What is the maximum amount a 55-year-old taxpayer and 52-year-old spouse can put into a Traditional or Roth IRA for 2024, assuming they earn $70,000 in total and are not participants in pension plans?

LO 5.3 7. Kaylen is a single, 40-year-old software engineer earning $152,000 a year and is not covered by a pension plan at work. How much can they put into a Roth IRA in 2024?

LO 5.3 8. Andreas is a single, 40-year-old doctor earning $190,000 a year and is not covered by a pension plan at work. What is Andreas' maximum deductible contribution into a Traditional IRA in 2024?

LO 5.3 9. Dori is 58 years old and retired in 2024. She receives a pension of $25,000 a year and no other income. She wishes to put the maximum allowed into an IRA. How much can she contribute to her IRA?

LO 5.4 10. During 2024, Pencho is a self-employed therapist, and his net earned income is $160,000 from his practice. Pencho's SEP-IRA Plan, a defined contribution plan, states that he will contribute the maximum amount allowable. Calculate Pencho's contribution.

LO 5.4 11. Eligio is a 45-year-old self-employed psychiatrist who has net earned income of $360,000 in 2024. What is the maximum amount he can contribute to his SEP for the year?

LO 5.4 12. Mario, a self-employed plumber, makes a maximum contribution to a SEP for his employee, Peach. Peach's compensation is $50,000 for the year. How much is he allowed to contribute to the plan for Peach?

LO 5.4 13. During 2024, Jill, age 39, participated in a 401k plan which provides for maximum employee contributions of 15 percent. Jill's salary was $80,000 for the year. Jill elects to make the maximum contribution. What is Jill's maximum tax-deferred contribution to the plan for the year?

LO 5.4

14. Determine the outcome of each of the following contributions or distributions from a small-business qualified retirement plan:
    a. As an employee of Wumbo Company, Margo is enrolled in the SEP and in 2024, Wumbo provides a contribution of 5 percent of Margo's salary or $2,500. Describe the taxation of the contribution to Margo and Wumbo.
    b. Patrick works at the Krab Shack as a manager. In 2024, the Krab Shack operates a SIMPLE IRA plan and Patrick contributes $10,000 (10 percent of his $100,000 salary). Krab Shack matches the first 3 percent of the employee's annual wages. Describe the tax treatment of Patrick's contribution and the Krab Shack's match to the SIMPLE IRA. Explain whether Patrick has exceeded the maximum contribution allowed to the SIMPLE IRA versus a traditional or Roth IRA in 2024 assuming he is age 45 versus age 55.
    c. As an employee of Undersea Labs, in 2024 Sandy, age 35, elects to defer $6,500 of her salary into the company's Roth 401k plan. Sandy's salary is $160,000 in 2024. Explain how the Roth 401k contribution limitations apply to Sandy.

LO 5.6

15. Linda installed a special pool for the hydrotherapeutic treatment of severe arthritis, as prescribed by her doctor. The cost of installing the pool was $20,000, and her insurance company paid $5,000 toward its cost. The pool increased the value of Linda's house by $7,000, and it has a useful life of 10 years. Determine the amount of the deduction Linda is entitled to and explain why.

LO 5.6

16. In 2024, Margaret and John Murphy (both over age 65) are married taxpayers who file a joint tax return with AGI of $30,000. During the year they incurred the following expenses:

Medical insurance premiums	$1,200
Premiums on an insurance policy that pays $100 per day for each day Margaret is hospitalized	400
Medical care lodging (two people, one night)	160
Hospital bills	2,500
Herbal supplements	75
Dentist bills	250
Prescription drugs and medicines	360
Cosmetic surgery	400

In addition, they drove 124 miles for medical transportation, and their insurance company reimbursed them $500 for the above expenses. Using the Medical and Dental Expenses portion of Schedule A of Form 1040 from Appendix F, calculate the Murphy's medical expense deduction.

LO 5.6

17. Janet needs an elevator seat attached to her stairs since she has a medical condition that makes her unable to climb the stairs in her house. The $10,000 spent on the elevator seat does not increase the value of her house according to a local appraiser. How much of the capital asset is deductible in Janet's tax return as a medical expense?

LO 5.7

18. Lyndon's employer withheld $8,500 in state income taxes from Lyndon's wages in 2024. Lyndon obtained a refund of $1,700 this year for overpayment of state income taxes for 2023. State income taxes were an itemized deduction on his 2023 return. His 2024 liability for state income tax is $8,200. Indicate the amount of Lyndon's deduction for state income taxes on his federal tax return assuming he elects to deduct state income taxes for 2024.

LO 5.7

19. Mike sells his home to Jane on April 2, 2024. Jane pays the property taxes covering the full calendar year in October, which amount to $2,500. How much may Mike and Jane each deduct for property taxes in 2024?

LO 5.7 20. Jaliyah is a single taxpayer living in New Jersey with adjusted gross income for the 2024 tax year of $86,000. Jaliyah's employer withheld $8,666 in state income tax from her salary. In May of 2024, she received a $400 state income tax refund from her prior year's tax return. The real estate taxes paid on her home are $2,143 for 2024, and her personal property taxes, based on the value of the property, amount to $126. Also, she paid $80 for state gasoline taxes for the year. Use the Taxes You Paid portion of Schedule A of Form 1040 from Appendix F to report Jaliyah's 2024 deduction for taxes assuming she chooses to deduct state and local income taxes.

LO 5.7 21. Mary paid $2,000 of state income taxes in 2024. She paid $1,500 of state sales tax on the purchase of goods and she also purchased a car in 2024 and paid sales tax of $3,000. How should Mary treat the taxes paid on her 2024 tax return?

LO 5.8 22. Mary's mother defaults on a home loan and Mary pays $600 in loan payments, including $175 in interest. Mary is not legally obligated on the loan and has no ownership interest in her mother's home.
   a. What amount, if any, may Mary claim as an itemized deduction for the current tax year?
   b. Why?

LO 5.8 23. Matthew borrows $250,000 to invest in bonds. During the current year, his interest on the loan is $30,000. Matthew's taxable interest income from the bonds is $10,000. This is Matthew's only investment income and he has no other investment expenses other than the interest on the loan.
   a. Calculate Matthew's itemized deduction for investment interest expense for this year.
   b. Is Matthew entitled to a deduction in future years? Explain your rationale.

LO 5.8 24. Ken paid the following amounts for interest during 2024:

Qualified interest on home mortgage	$7,268
Auto loan interest	800
"Points" on the mortgage for acquisition of his personal residence	1,100
Home equity loan interest (proceeds used to pay for an addition to his home)	1,344
Mastercard interest	300

The amount of debt secured by Ken's home is less than $700,000. Use the Interest You Paid portion of Schedule A of Form 1040 from Appendix F to report Ken's itemized deduction for interest.

LO 5.8 25. Barbie and Ken purchased their personal dreamhouse residence 15 years ago for $300,000. For the current year, they have an $80,000 first mortgage on their home, on which they paid $6,000 in interest. They also have a home equity loan to pay for the children's college tuition secured by their home with a balance throughout the year of $150,000. They paid interest on the home equity loan of $9,000 for the year.
   a. Calculate the qualified residence acquisition debt interest for the current year.
   b. Calculate the qualified home equity debt interest for the current year.

LO 5.8 26. Inderjeet paid the following amounts of interest during the 2024 tax year:

Mortgage interest on Dallas residence (loan balance $50,000)	$1,688
Automobile loan interest (personal use only)	440
Mortgage interest on Vail residence (loan balance $50,000)	3,079
Student loan interest	775

Calculate the amount of Inderjeet's itemized deduction for interest (after limitations, if any) for 2024.

LO 5.8

27. At the end of 2024, Mark owes $250,000 on the mortgage related to the 2016 purchase of his residence. When his daughter went to college in the fall of 2024, he borrowed $20,000 through a home equity loan on his house to help pay for her education. The interest expense on the main mortgage is $15,000, and the interest expense on the home equity loan is $1,500. How much of the interest is deductible as an itemized deduction and why?

LO 5.9

28. Tabitha donates a painting that she purchased three years ago for $8,000, to a university for display in the president's office. The fair market value of the painting on the date of the gift is $14,000. If Tabitha had sold the painting, the difference between the sales price and her cost would have been a long-term capital gain.
    a. How much is Tabitha's charitable contribution deduction for this donation (before any AGI-based limitations)?
    b. Explain why.

LO 5.9

29. Doran made the following contributions during 2024:

His synagogue (by check)	$4,800
The Republican Party (by check)	400
The American Red Cross (by credit card)	1,200
His fraternal organization for tickets to a holiday party	100
A baseball autographed by hall-of-fame baseball pitcher Sandy Koufax (basis $0) donated to a public charity	6,600

    In addition, Doran donated used furniture to the Salvation Army that he purchased 11 years ago for $10,000 with a fair market value of $2,000. Assuming Doran has adjusted gross income of $25,000, has the necessary written acknowledgments, and itemizes deductions, use the Charitable Contributions Limitations worksheet and the Gifts to Charity portion of Schedule A of Form 1040 from Appendix F to report the itemized deduction for charitable contributions.

LO 5.9

30. Richard donates publicly traded Gold Company stock with a basis of $1,000 and a fair market value of $15,000 to the college he attended, which is considered a public charity. Richard has owned the shares for 10 years. How is this contribution treated on Richard's tax return?

LO 5.9

31. Hartley, a single taxpayer, donates cash of $600 and also provides some gently-used clothing worth $150 to a local church. Hartley does not itemize deductions. What is the nature of any deduction for these items for Hartley in 2024?

LO 5.10

32. On January 3, 2024, Carey discovers his diamond bracelet has been stolen. The bracelet had a fair market value and adjusted basis of $7,500. Assuming Carey had no insurance coverage on the bracelet and his adjusted gross income for 2024 is $45,000, calculate the amount of his theft loss deduction.

LO 5.10

33. Vida's car is totaled in tornado that is declared a federal disaster. The car originally cost $18,000, but is worth $7,500 at the time of the accident. Vida's insurance company gives them a check for $5,000. Vida has $30,000 of adjusted gross income. How much can Vida claim as a casualty loss on their tax return? Please explain.

LO 5.10

34. During the 2024 tax year, Irma incurred the following expenses:

Union dues	$244
Tax return preparation fee	150
Brokerage fees for the purchase of stocks	35
Uniform expenses not reimbursed by her employer	315

    If Irma's adjusted gross income is $23,000, calculate her miscellaneous deductions.

Group 3: Writing Assignment

Ethics

1. While preparing Massie Miller's 2024 Schedule A, you review the following list of possible charitable deductions provided by Massie:

Cash contribution to a family whose house burned down	$1,000
Time while working as a volunteer at Food Bank (five hours @ $50/hour)	250
Cash contribution to United Methodist Church (receipt provided)	800
Cash contribution to Salvation Army *(note from Massie: "I can't remember exactly the amount that I gave and I can't find the receipt. I think it was around $500.")*	500
Total	$2,550

What would you say to Massie regarding her listed deductions? How much of the deduction is allowed for charitable contributions?

Research

2. In 2024, Gale and Cathy Alexander hosted an exchange student, Axel Muller, for nine months. Axel was part of International Student Exchange Programs (a qualified organization). Axel attended tenth grade at the local high school. Gale and Cathy did not claim Axel as a dependent but paid the following items for Axel's well-being:

Food and clothing	$1,500
Medical care	200
Fair market value of lodging	2,700
Entertainment	100
Total	$4,500

Gale and Cathy have asked for your help in determining if any of the $4,500 can be deducted as a charitable contribution.

Required: Go to the IRS website **(www.irs.gov)** and locate Publication 526. Write a letter to Gale and Cathy answering their question. If they can claim a deduction, be sure to include in your letter the amount that can be deducted and any substantiation requirements. (An example of a client letter is available at the website for this textbook located at **www.cengage.com**.)

Group 4:
Comprehensive Problems

1. Anthony Stork (birthdate August 2, 1980) is a single taxpayer. Anthony's earnings and withholdings as the manager of a local casino for 2024 are reported on his Form W-2:

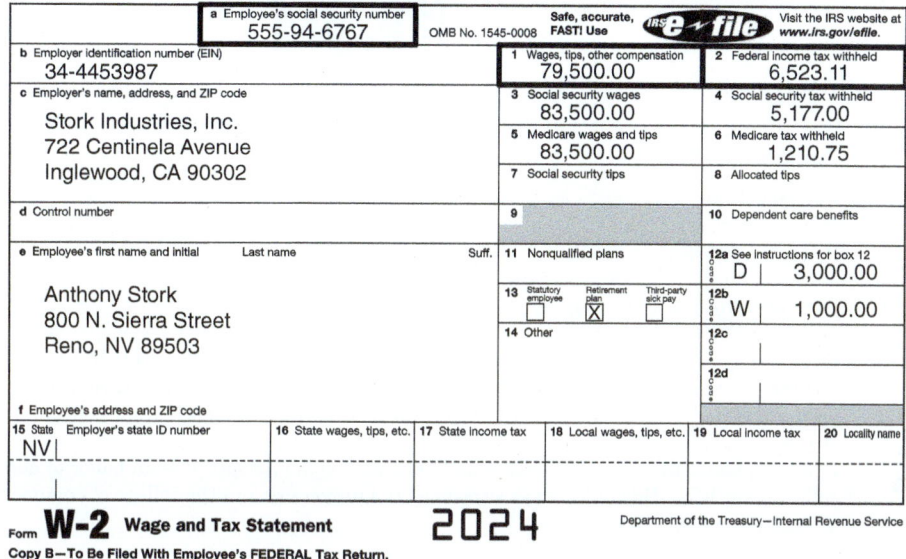

Anthony pays his ex-spouse, Salty Pans, $3,900 per month in accordance with their February 12, 2020 divorce decree. When their 12-year-old child (in the ex-spouse's custody) reaches the age of 18, the payments are reduced to $2,800 per month. His spouse's Social Security number is 554-44-5555.

In 2024, Anthony purchased a new car and so he kept track of his sales tax receipts during the year. His actual sales tax paid was $4,134 for the car and $1,817 for all other purchases.

Anthony participates in a high-deductible health plan and is eligible to contribute to a health savings account. His HSA earned $86 in 2024.

During the year, Anthony paid the following amounts (all of which can be substantiated):

Credit card interest	$1,760
Auto loan interest	2,300
Auto insurance	900
Property taxes on personal residence	3,145
Contributions to HSA	3,150
Income tax preparation fee	900
Charitable contributions (all cash):	
Boy Scouts of America	1,300
St. Matthews Church	3,100
Nevada Democratic Party	250

In 2024, Anthony inherited over $500,000 from his father, Howard, who died in 2024. Although Anthony invested a large portion, he also made a $51,000 cash donation to the Stork School of Engineering at Reno State University.

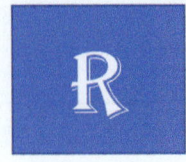

Reno State University

November 15, 2024

Anthony Stork
800 North Sierra Street
Reno, NV 89503

Dear Mr. Stork,

Our hearts are overflowing with gratitude! Thank you for your recent contribution of $51,000 to the newly named Stork School of Engineering at Reno State University. We are very thankful for your commitment to the students, faculty, and staff of the college.

It was an honor knowing your father and with your generous gift, it is an honor to name the college after him. Howard always supported the university and the college of engineering. We miss him every day.

Thanks to donors like you, Reno State University will continue to be a resource for students far into the future. Thank you again for your support.

With extreme gratitude,

Obadiah Stain
President
Reno State University

Donation amount: $51,000.00   Date: November 10, 2024   Designation: Stork College of Engineering

Reno State University is tax-exempt under §501(c)(3) of the U.S. Internal Revenue Code
Tax ID: 95-2119198
No goods or services were exchanged for this donation.

Reno State University
480 Edison Way
Reno, NV 89502
www.renostate.edu

Anthony also received the following Form 1098:

☐ CORRECTED (if checked)

RECIPIENT'S/LENDER'S name, street address, city or town, state or province, country, ZIP or foreign postal code, and telephone no. Reno Savings and Loan 49 Commerce Street Reno, NV 89501	*Caution: The amount shown may not be fully deductible by you. Limits based on the loan amount and the cost and value of the secured property may apply. Also, you may only deduct interest to the extent it was incurred by you, actually paid by you, and not reimbursed by another person.	OMB No. 1545-1380 Form **1098** (Rev. January 2022) For calendar year 20 **24**	**Mortgage Interest Statement**
	1 Mortgage interest received from payer(s)/borrower(s)* $ 9,898.09		Copy B For Payer/ Borrower
RECIPIENT'S/LENDER'S TIN: 33-1234569	PAYER'S/BORROWER'S TIN: 555-94-6767	2 Outstanding mortgage principal $ 353,005.78	3 Mortgage origination date 03/05/2011	The information in boxes 1 through 9 and 11 is important tax information and is being furnished to the IRS. If you are required to file a return, a negligence penalty or other sanction may be imposed on you if the IRS determines that an underpayment of tax results because you overstated a deduction for this mortgage interest or for these points, reported in boxes 1 and 6; or because you didn't report the refund of interest (box 4); or because you claimed a nondeductible item.
		4 Refund of overpaid interest $	5 Mortgage insurance premiums $
PAYER'S/BORROWER'S name Anthony Stork		6 Points paid on purchase of principal residence $
Street address (including apt. no.) 800 N. Sierra Street		7 [X] If address of property securing mortgage is the same as PAYER'S/BORROWER'S address, the box is checked, or the address or description is entered in box 8.
City or town, state or province, country, and ZIP or foreign postal code Reno, NV 89503		8 Address or description of property securing mortgage
9 Number of properties securing the mortgage 1	10 Other		11 Mortgage acquisition date
Account number (see instructions)			

Form **1098** (Rev. 1-2022) (Keep for your records) www.irs.gov/Form1098 Department of the Treasury - Internal Revenue Service

Anthony received the following Form 1099-INT:

2024 Combined Forms 1099

This is important tax information and is being furnished to the IRS (except as indicated). If you are required to file a return, a negligence penalty or other sanction may be imposed on you if this income is taxable and the IRS determines that it has not been reported.

Friar Tuck Investments
38 Wall Street, 8th Floor
New York, NY 10005

Copy B For Recipient
OMB No. 1545-0110

Anthony Stork
800 N. Sierra Street
Reno, NV 89503

Account Number: 3100987765
Tax ID: ***-**-6767
Payer's Federal Tax ID: 33-1357245
Financial Adviser/Phone: Happy Hogan 888-555-1212

Form 1099-INT   **Interest Income**

Box 1 Interest income	Box 2 Early withdrawal penalty	Box 3 Interest on U.S. Savings Bonds and Treasury obligations
3,832.12		
Box 4 Federal income tax withheld	**Box 5 Investment expenses**	**Box 6 Foreign Tax Paid**
Box 7 Foreign country or U.S. possession	**Box 8 Tax-exempt interest**	**Box 9 Specified private activity bond interest**
	1,231.11	
Box 10 Market Discount		**Box 11 Bond Premium**
Box 12 Bond premium on Treasury obligations		**Box 13 Bond premium on tax-exempt bond**

Required: Complete Anthony's federal tax return for 2024. Use Form 1040, Schedule 1, Schedule A, Schedule B, and Form 8889 to complete this tax return. Make realistic assumptions about any missing data.

2A. Bea Krump (birthdate 3/27/1989) moved from Texas to Florida in January 2024 after divorcing her spouse in 2023. She and her daughter, Dee Krump (birthdate 5/30/2014, Social Security number 121-44-6666) live at 654 Ocean Way, Gulfport, FL 33707. Bea provides all of Dee's support. Bea can claim a child tax credit for Dee. Bea's Social Security number is 466-78-6700, and she is single.

Bea owns and operates a shrimping business called Bea Krump's Shrimp. She uses a rented boat to shrimp and has a home office located in their home. The principal business code is 114110. Bea's bookkeeper provided the following income statement from the shrimping business:

Revenues	$50,000
Shrimp boat rental	16,500
Contract labor	6,000
Business taxes	500
Bait and tackle	3,400
Boat fuel	2,500
Shrimping permit	750
Miscellaneous supplies	900
Insurance	800

Bea sells her entire catch at the end of each day and thus, has no inventory. She uses the cash method of accounting and has no depreciation. Bea uses her home office exclusively for conducting business. The office is 160 square feet in her 2,000 square foot home. Other than the interest and taxes reported below, her only other cost is utilities of $1,300. Assume no depreciation. Bea also paid self-employed health insurance premiums of $4,200 associated with her high-deductible plan.

Because the shrimping business is seasonal, Bea also works at a local restaurant as a server. Her 2024 Form W-2 is below:

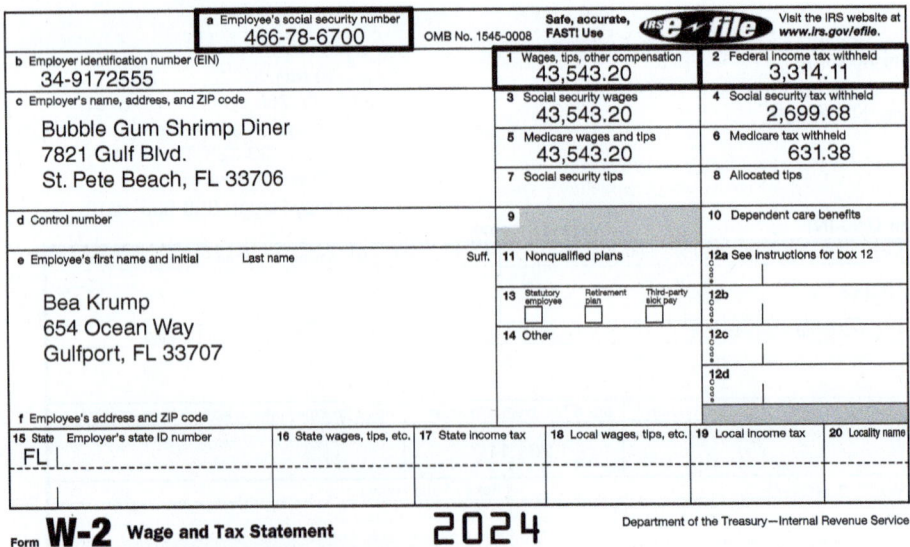

Bea received the following 1099-INT:

Form 1099-INT — Interest Income (Rev. January 2024) — For calendar year 2024

- PAYER'S name, street address: St. Pete Bank of Florida, 958 Pasadena Ave. S., South Pasadena, FL 33707
- PAYER'S TIN: 13-2278912
- RECIPIENT'S TIN: 466-78-6700
- RECIPIENT'S name: Bea Krump
- Street address: 654 Ocean Way
- City, state, ZIP: Gulfport, FL 33707
- Box 1 Interest income: $243.59
- Box 8 Tax-exempt interest: $350.00

Bea also receives $600 per month in alimony from her ex-spouse in accordance with their 2023 divorce decree.

In order to move herself and Dee, Bea spent $800 moving her household goods (trailer rental), $200 on meals and $300 on lodging while traveling between Texas and Florida. The drive was 1,005 miles. Bea purchased her home in Florida on January 15, 2024 for $300,000, with $60,000 of the cost attributed to the land. The property tax payments below reflect only her share. The depreciation percentage for 2024 is 3.485 percent.

After moving to Gulfport, Bea sent Dee to a local private school for the remainder of 5th grade. Bea used $4,100 from Dee's Section 529 plan to pay for private school tuition as reported on the Form 1099-Q. Dee had always attended public schools in Texas.

Form 1099-Q — Payments From Qualified Education Programs (Under Sections 529 and 530) (Rev. November 2024) — For calendar year 2024

- PAYER'S/TRUSTEE'S name, address: Texas College Savings Plan, PO Box 13400, Austin, TX 78711
- PAYER'S/TRUSTEE'S TIN: 22-1456712
- RECIPIENT'S TIN: 121-44-6666
- RECIPIENT'S name: Dee Krump
- Street address: 654 Ocean Way
- City, state, ZIP: Gulfport, FL 33707
- Box 1 Gross distribution: $4,250.00
- Box 2 Earnings: $412.30
- Box 3 Basis: $3,837.70
- Box 5 Distribution is from: Qualified tuition program — State (X)

During 2024, Bea paid the following amounts (all of which can be substantiated):

Home mortgage interest (1098 not shown)	$9,120
Auto loan interest	2,300
Property taxes on personal residence	5,040
Out-of-pocket doctor bills	2,933
Income tax preparation fee	600
Job-hunting expenses	925
Contribution to HSA	4,000
Cash donations to church	$4,600

Bea paid for the out-of-pocket doctor bills with a distribution from her HSA account. Refer to Form 1099-SA below:

[Form 1099-SA]
TRUSTEE'S/PAYER'S: Tampa Health Savings Admin. Inc., 720 N. Franklin Street, Tampa, FL 33602
PAYER'S TIN: 57-8712353
RECIPIENT'S TIN: 466-78-6700
RECIPIENT'S name: Bea Krump
Street address: 654 Ocean Way
City: Gulfport, FL 33707
1 Gross distribution: $2,933.12
3 Distribution code: 1
5 HSA: X
For calendar year 2024

After the divorce, Bea was required to purchase a car (sales taxes of $1,300) and furnish her house. Her actual sales taxes paid (excluding the car) in 2024 totaled $3,200.

Required: Complete Bea's federal tax return for 2024. Use Form 1040, Schedule 1, Schedule 2, Schedule A, Schedule C, Schedule SE, Form 7206, Form 8829, Form 8889 and Form 8995 to complete this tax return. Make realistic assumptions about any missing data.

2B. John Fuji (birthdate June 6, 1984) received the following Form W-2 from his employer related to his job as a manager at a Washington apple-processing plant:

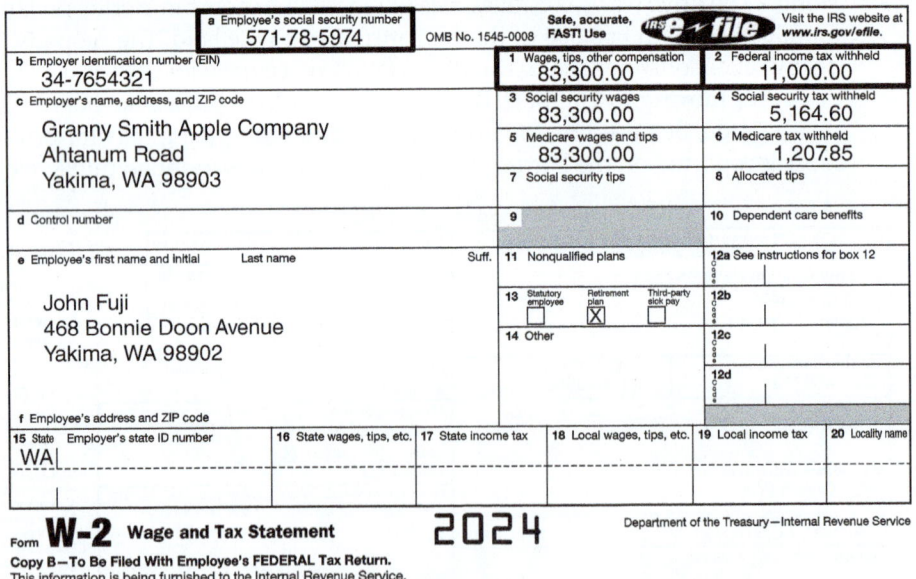

Form W-2 (2024):
- a Employee's social security number: 571-78-5974
- b EIN: 34-7654321
- c Employer: Granny Smith Apple Company, Ahtanum Road, Yakima, WA 98903
- e Employee: John Fuji, 468 Bonnie Doon Avenue, Yakima, WA 98902
- 1 Wages, tips, other compensation: 83,300.00
- 2 Federal income tax withheld: 11,000.00
- 3 Social security wages: 83,300.00
- 4 Social security tax withheld: 5,164.60
- 5 Medicare wages and tips: 83,300.00
- 6 Medicare tax withheld: 1,207.85
- 13 Retirement plan: X
- 15 State: WA

John has income reported to him on a 1099-DIV from his investment in mutual funds:

Form 1099-DIV (Rev. January 2024) — Dividends and Distributions

PAYER'S name, street address, city or town, state or province, country, ZIP or foreign postal code, and telephone no.:
Honeycrisp Equity Fund
900 Western Ave., 12th Floor
Seattle, WA 98104

- 1a Total ordinary dividends: $4,850.00
- 1b Qualified dividends: $4,850.00
- 2a Total capital gain distr.: $1,350.00
- 2b Unrecap. Sec. 1250 gain:
- 2c Section 1202 gain:
- 2d Collectibles (28%) gain:
- 2e Section 897 ordinary dividends:
- 2f Section 897 capital gain:
- 3 Nondividend distributions:
- 4 Federal income tax withheld: $0.00
- 5 Section 199A dividends:
- 6 Investment expenses:
- 7 Foreign tax paid:
- 8 Foreign country or U.S. possession:
- 9 Cash liquidation distributions:
- 10 Noncash liquidation distributions:
- 11 FATCA filing requirement: ☐
- 12 Exempt-interest dividends:
- 13 Specified private activity bond interest dividends:
- 14 State:
- 15 State identification no.:
- 16 State tax withheld:

OMB No. 1545-0110

PAYER'S TIN: 33-9871012
RECIPIENT'S TIN: 571-78-5974

RECIPIENT'S name: John Fuji
Street address: 468 Bonnie Doon Avenue
City: Yakima, WA 98902

Also, in accordance with the January 2016 divorce decree John receives $475 per month alimony from his ex-wife (Dora Fuji, Social Security number 573-79-6075) in 2024.

On December 30, 2024, John sold his primary residence after living there since October 2014. John received the Form 1099-S below from the sale. John paid selling expenses of $35,800. His basis in the home was $292,000. John paid the property taxes on the home for the second half of 2024 of $6,000. The closing statement for the sale indicated that the buyer needed to reimburse John for property taxes of $33.33, which were reflected as an increase in John's gross proceeds.

The entire year's property taxes are reflected on John's 1098.

Form 1099-S (Rev. January 2022) — Proceeds From Real Estate Transactions

FILER'S name, street address, city or town, state or province, country, ZIP or foreign postal code, and telephone number:
Fidelity Title of Washington
113 N 4th St #105
Yakima, WA 98901

- 1 Date of closing: 12/31/2024
- 2 Gross proceeds: $595,033.33
- For calendar year 20 24
- OMB No. 1545-0997

FILER'S TIN: 32-5675671
TRANSFEROR'S TIN: 571-78-5974

- 3 Address: 302 N 27th Ave., Yakima, WA 98902

TRANSFEROR'S name: John Fuji
Street address: 468 Bonnie Doon Ave.
City: Yakima, WA 98902

- 4 Transferor received or will receive property or services as part of the consideration: ☐
- 5 If checked, transferor is a foreign person: ☐
- 6 Buyer's part of real estate tax: $33.33

Form 1098 — Mortgage Interest Statement

CORRECTED (if checked) ☐

RECIPIENT'S/LENDER'S name, street address, city or town, state or province, country, ZIP or foreign postal code, and telephone no.
Braeburn National Bank
1600 W. Nob Hill Blvd.
Yakima, WA 98902

*Caution: The amount shown may not be fully deductible by you. Limits based on the loan amount and the cost and value of the secured property may apply. Also, you may only deduct interest to the extent it was incurred by you, actually paid by you, and not reimbursed by another person.

OMB No. 1545-1380
Form **1098** (Rev. January 2022)
For calendar year 20**24**

Mortgage Interest Statement

1 Mortgage interest received from payer(s)/borrower(s)
$ 3,946.88

RECIPIENT'S/LENDER'S TIN: 54-9019016
PAYER'S/BORROWER'S TIN: 571-78-5974

2 Outstanding mortgage principal: $ 202,403.98
3 Mortgage origination date: 10/01/2014
4 Refund of overpaid interest: $
5 Mortgage insurance premiums: $

PAYER'S/BORROWER'S name: John Fuji
6 Points paid on purchase of principal residence: $

Street address (including apt. no.): 468 Bonnie Doon Avenue
7 ☐ If address of property securing mortgage is the same as PAYER'S/BORROWER'S address, the box is checked, or the address or description is entered in box 8.

City or town, state or province, country, and ZIP or foreign postal code: Yakima, WA 98902

8 Address or description of property securing mortgage:
302 N 27th Ave.
Yakima, WA 98902

9 Number of properties securing the mortgage: 1
10 Other: Prop tax $12,000.00

11 Mortgage acquisition date:

Account number (see instructions):

Copy B For Payer/Borrower

Form **1098** (Rev. 1-2022)

John tried his hand at day trading for one week in February 2024. He received a substitute Form 1099-B from his broker. Because the IRS was provided the acquisition date and basis for all trades and none required any adjustments or codes, these can be entered as a summary entry into Schedule D and no Form 8949 needs to be prepared.

Little John Brokerage Statement
100 Nottingham Street
Sherwood Forest, MA 01233
Substitute Form 1099-B
Tax Year 2024

John Fuji
468 Bonnie Doon Ave.
Yakima, WA 98902
XXX-XX-5974

1a Descrip	1b Shares	1c Date Acq	1d Date Sold	1e Proceeds	Cost Basis	Net Gain or Loss	2 ST/LT
ACM Theatre	44	03/02/24	03/02/24	912.00	688.00	224.00	ST
ACM Theatre	37	03/02/24	03/02/24	740.00	694.88	45.12	ST
ACM Theatre	31	03/02/24	03/02/24	623.00	510.66	112.34	ST
ACM Theatre	28	03/02/24	03/02/24	569.00	424.00	145.00	ST
ACM Theatre	34	03/02/24	03/02/24	683.00	469.55	213.45	ST
ACM Theatre	21	04/02/24	04/02/24	422.00	288.67	133.33	ST
ACM Theatre	40	04/02/24	04/02/24	786.00	778.88	7.12	ST
ACM Theatre	32	04/02/24	04/02/24	646.00	428.66	217.34	ST
ACM Theatre	35	04/02/24	04/02/24	692.00	480.00	212.00	ST
ACM Theatre	30	04/02/24	04/02/24	595.00	478.00	117.00	ST
ACM Theatre	42	05/02/24	05/02/24	847.00	845.88	1.12	ST
ACM Theatre	28	05/02/24	05/02/24	565.00	433.00	132.00	ST
ACM Theatre	33	05/02/24	05/02/24	664.00	421.00	243.00	ST
ACM Theatre	21	05/02/24	05/02/24	422.00	277.00	145.00	ST
ACM Theatre	32	05/02/24	05/02/24	630.00	478.00	152.00	ST
ACM Theatre	39	06/02/24	06/02/24	780.00	663.00	117.00	ST
ACM Theatre	40	06/02/24	06/02/24	796.00	711.00	85.00	ST
ACM Theatre	38	06/02/24	06/02/24	754.00	753.33	0.67	ST
ACM Theatre	34	06/02/24	06/02/24	674.00	672.61	1.39	ST
				12,800.00	10,496.12	2,303.88	

During 2024, John paid the following amounts (all of which can be substantiated):

Auto loan interest	1,575
Credit card interest	655
State sales tax (actual exceeds estimated)	2,677
Doctor bills	5,000
Other deductible medical expenses	1,800
Income tax preparation fee	500
Job-hunting expenses	925
Cash charitable donation to the Jonagold Research Center	3,200
Federal estimated tax payment 12/30/2024	5,000

John's employer offers a retirement plan, but John does not participate. Instead, he made a $7,000 contribution to a Roth IRA.

John owns a condo in Seattle that he lived in years ago and now rents. His rental condo is located at 1012 E Terrace Street Unit 1204, Seattle, WA 98122 and was rented all year to his tenant. The tenant occupied the home on January 1, 2024 and pays rent of $2,000 per month for each month of 2024 (a 12-month lease). John demanded first and last month rent and a security deposit of $500 and all were paid January 1, 2024. Upon the tenant's departure on December 31, John noted damages and is going to retain $300 of the security deposit. John's rental expenses for the year are:

Mortgage interest	$9,700
Real estate taxes	6,700
Insurance	2,000
Depreciation (fully depreciated)	0
Repairs	1,000
Homeowner's association fees	5,600

John actively manages the rental home. He probably spends about seven hours per month on the rental.

Required: Complete John's federal tax return for 2024. Use Form 1040, Schedule 1, Schedule A, Schedule B, Schedule D, Schedule E, Form 8949, Form 8582, and the Qualified Dividends and Capital Gains Tax Worksheet as needed to complete this tax return. Make realistic assumptions about any missing data.

Group 5:
Cumulative Software Problem

1. The following information is available for the Albert and Allison Gaytor family in addition to that provided in Chapters 1–4.

   Albert and Allison received the following form:

   Form 1098 — Mortgage Interest Statement (Rev. January 2022), For calendar year 2024

   RECIPIENT'S/LENDER'S name, address: Jensen Beach Bank, 1000 NE Jensen Beach Blvd, Jensen Beach, FL 34957

   RECIPIENT'S/LENDER'S TIN: 61-7654321
   PAYER'S/BORROWER'S TIN: 266-51-1966
   PAYER'S/BORROWER'S name: Albert and Allison Gaytor
   Street address: 4100 SE Lincoln Street
   City: Stuart, FL 34997

   - Box 1 Mortgage interest received from payer(s)/borrower(s): $10,821.11
   - Box 2 Outstanding mortgage principal: $318,445.12
   - Box 3 Mortgage origination date: 01/10/2024
   - Box 7: [X] If address of property securing mortgage is the same as PAYER'S/BORROWER'S address
   - Box 9 Number of properties securing the mortgage: 1

   Albert and Allison paid the following in 2024 (all by check or can otherwise be substantiated):

Item	Amount
Contributions to St. Anne's Catholic Church	$ 600
Tuition to St. Anne's Catholic School for Crocker (spring 2024)	6,000
Clothes to Salvation Army (10 bags in good condition)	250
Contributions to Marcus Rubius Congressional campaign	250
Psychotherapy for Allison	1,200
Prescription eyeglasses for Crocker	400
Prescription medication and drugs	1,900
Credit card interest	1,345
Actual state sales tax (including sales tax on new auto of $2,000)	3,750
Investment interest expense on stock margin account	300
Auto loan interest reported on Form 1098 (not shown here; auto was paid for by a home equity loan on residence)	860
Auto insurance	1,600
Cosmetic surgery for Albert	3,200
Dave Deduction, CPA, for preparation of last year's tax return	765
Safe-deposit box for storage of stocks and tax data	100
Contribution to an educational savings account for Crocker	1,000
Home property taxes	7,000
Unreimbursed business expense (seminar on dealing with hijacking at sea)	700

Albert received the following Form 1098-E:

Form 1098-E — Student Loan Interest Statement (2024)

- RECIPIENT'S/LENDER'S name: Sallie Mae Loan Servicing Center, 12061 Bluemont Way, V3419, Reston, VA 20190
- RECIPIENT'S TIN: 12-4454123
- BORROWER'S TIN: 266-51-1966
- BORROWER'S name: Albert T. Gaytor
- Street address: 4100 SE Lincoln Street
- City, state, ZIP: Stuart, FL 34997
- Box 1 Student loan interest received by lender: $3,122.45
- Box 2: (not checked)

In August 2024, Crocker was on an out-of-town field trip with the university band and his appendix burst. He required immediate surgery which was considered "out of network" for the Gaytor's health plan, resulting in hospital and doctor's fees of $4,600 not covered by insurance. In addition, Allison drove 320 miles round trip to be with Crocker after the surgery and drove him home after he recovered. She spent two nights in a hotel at a cost of $170 per night.

In June, Albert purchased a new professional digital SLR camera for $7,950. While the Gaytors were on vacation in August, someone broke into their residence and stole the camera. Albert's homeowners' insurance did not reimburse him for any part of the loss since he declined the special premium add-on for high value items required by his policy.

For the 2024 tax year, on April 15, 2025, Albert contributes $7,000 to his traditional IRA and Allison contributes $7,000 to her traditional IRA. Albert is not covered by a qualified retirement plan at work.

Albert managed to gather his gambling loss documentation and can substantiate gambling losses of $5,881 in 2024 (refer back to Chapter 2 for gambling winnings).

As noted in Chapter 4, the Gaytors sold their home in Sebastian, FL in January 2024 and moved to Stuart, FL so that Albert could work for Sport Fishing of Stuart. Stuart and Sebastian are more than 50 miles apart. The Gaytors did not receive any relocation stipend from Albert's new employer and paid $4,300 for the cost of moving household goods. They drove their car 70 miles during the move and incurred no other moving costs.

Required: Combine this new information about the Gaytor family with the information from Chapters 1–4 and complete a revised 2024 tax return for Albert and Allison. Be sure to save your data input files since this case will be expanded with more tax information in each succeeding chapter.

Chapter 6

Accounting Periods and Other Taxes

Learning Objectives

After completing this chapter, you should be able to:

- **LO 6.1** Determine the different accounting periods allowed for tax purposes.
- **LO 6.2** Determine the different accounting methods allowed for tax purposes.
- **LO 6.3** Determine whether parties are considered related for tax purposes, and classify the tax treatment of certain related-party transactions.
- **LO 6.4** Apply the rules for computing tax on the unearned income of minor children and certain students (the "kiddie tax").
- **LO 6.5** Calculate a basic alternative minimum tax.
- **LO 6.6** Apply the special tax and reporting requirements for household employees (the "nanny tax").
- **LO 6.7** Compute the special taxes for high-income taxpayers.
- **LO 6.8** Describe the basic rules surrounding special taxpayer situations such as divorce, deceased taxpayers, nonresident taxpayers, and farmers.
- **LO 6.9** Identify significant differences in the tax law for members of the U.S. Armed Forces.

Overview

Taxpayers operating a business, whether professional, rental, manufacturing, or another activity, should have an understanding of the accounting periods (calendar, fiscal, or short-period tax years) and accounting methods (cash, accrual, or hybrid methods) allowed. Transactions involving related parties often have different rules for inclusion or exclusion of income and deductions. This chapter begins by addressing how and when individual, partnership, and corporate taxpayers should report taxable income.

In addition to the typical income tax, a number of other taxes are also reported through the individual income tax return. On the 2024 Form 1040, Schedule 2 is the primary reporting mechanism for additional taxes. This chapter covers the computation of taxes such as the "kiddie tax," the "nanny tax," the alternative minimum tax, the net investment income tax, and the additional Medicare tax.

6-1 Accounting Periods

Learning Objective 6.1
Determine the different accounting periods allowed for tax purposes.

6-1a Individual Tax Years

Almost all individuals file tax returns using a calendar-year accounting period. Individuals reporting for tax purposes on a fiscal year other than a calendar year are extremely rare since the tax system is set up to accommodate calendar-year taxpayers. However, there are no restrictions on an individual taking a tax year other than a calendar year. The choice to file on a fiscal-year basis must be made with an initial tax return, and books and records must be kept on that basis. An individual may also request IRS approval to change to a fiscal year if certain conditions are met.

6-1b Partnership and Corporation Tax Years

Many individual tax returns include the pass-through of income from partnerships, limited liability companies, S corporations, and personal service corporations. The income or loss from partnerships and S corporations is passed through on Schedule K-1 to the owners and taxed on the owners' personal tax returns. Partnerships and S corporations are not generally taxable entities, only reporting entities. Similarly, wages are passed through to doctors, lawyers, accountants, actuaries, and other professionals from personal service corporations owned by them. Many individuals carry on businesses in partnerships which comprise a large part of the income shown on their tax returns. Other individuals make investments, including the operation of real estate rental activities, in these pass-through entities. Because the pass-through of income and loss from partnerships and S corporations plays a large role in the taxation of many individuals, it is important to understand the rules governing the allowed accounting periods for these entities.

Partnerships and corporations had a great deal of freedom in selecting a tax year in the past. However, Congress decided that this freedom often resulted in an inappropriate deferral of taxable income. For example, if an individual taxpayer has a calendar-tax-year-end and receives income from a partnership with a tax year ending September 30, the taxpayer is able to defer three months of partnership income for an indefinite period of time. Therefore, the tax law was changed to include provisions that specify the required tax year for many partnerships and certain corporations, reducing the opportunities for deferring income.

Corporations have much more flexibility and can generally choose any fiscal year-end for tax purposes. The primary restriction on choosing a fiscal year-end for a corporation is that its books and records must also be maintained on the same fiscal year-end. Fiscal year-ends must always occur on the last day of a month unless the taxpayer adopts a 52–53-week year, which permits the year-end to always fall on the same day of the week. That day of the week must be the one closest to the last day of the month.

Most partnerships, S corporations, and personal service corporations owned by individual taxpayers now conform to the same calendar-year reporting used by almost all individuals. These entities are allowed a September, October, or November year-end if the owners make an annual cash deposit on behalf of the entity or perform other required calculations to assure the IRS that they are not using the fiscal year to defer the payment of federal taxes. The details of the complex requirements which must be met by entities filing non-calendar-tax-year-ends are beyond the scope of this textbook.

6-1c Short-Period Taxable Income

If taxpayers have a short year other than their first or last year of operations, they are required to annualize their taxable income to calculate the tax for the short period. The tax liability is calculated for the annualized period and allocated back to the short period. With the flat 21-percent corporate tax rate, the annualization method is somewhat simplified.

Example Omoto Corporation obtains permission from the IRS to change from a calendar year to a fiscal year ending August 31. For the short period, January 1 through August 31, 2024, the corporation's taxable income was $40,000. Omoto Corporation's tax for the short period is calculated as follows:

Step 1: Annualize the income $40,000 × 12/8 = $60,000
Step 2: Tax on annualized income   21% × $60,000 = $12,600
Step 3: Short period tax $12,600 × 8/12 = $ 8,400

With a flat tax rate, this short-period taxable income calculation is equivalent to $40,000 × 21%. ♦

Self-Study Problem 6.1 *Refer to Appendix E for Solutions to Self-Study Problems*

For the following taxpayers, determine the choice of year-end and place an X in the correct column(s).

Taxpayer	Calendar Year-End	Fiscal Year-End	Fiscal Year-End but Some Restrictions
1. Individual with no separate books and records	___	___	___
2. Partnership for which all the partners are calendar-year-end individuals	___	___	___
3. A corporation that keeps its book and records on a fiscal year ending June 30	___	___	___
4. An S corporation for which all shareholders are calendar-year-end individuals	___	___	___

6-2 Accounting Methods

6.2 Learning Objective
Determine the different accounting methods allowed for tax purposes.

The tax law requires taxpayers to report taxable income using the method of accounting regularly used by the taxpayer in keeping their books, provided the method clearly reflects the taxpayer's income. The cash receipts and disbursements method, the accrual method, and the hybrid method are accounting methods specifically recognized in the tax law.

The cash receipts and disbursements method of accounting (commonly referred to as the cash method or cash basis) is used by most individuals for their overall method of accounting. Generally, wages, interest and dividend income, capital gains, and personal deductions are accounted for on the cash basis for individuals. Individuals may choose to account for a particular business, such as a sole proprietorship reported on Schedule C, using the accrual or hybrid method of accounting. If a taxpayer has two businesses, a different method of accounting may be used for each. The choice of a tax accounting method is a general rule which will be overridden by tax laws for some items of income and expense. For example, individuals reporting on a cash basis may deduct IRAs or pension contributions which are paid in cash in the year following the deduction, the income from savings bonds may be included in taxable income even though it is not received in cash, and prepaid interest may not be allowed as a deduction in the year paid.

The cash method generally results in the recognition of income when it is actually or constructively received. Income is constructively received when it is credited to the taxpayer's account, set apart for the taxpayer, or made available to the taxpayer without restrictions. The taxpayer must be able to draw upon the income at any time or by giving proper notice. Income is not constructively received if the taxpayer's control over the income is substantially limited or restricted.

Example Sybilla operates a small calendar-year-end business on the cash basis of accounting. One of her customer prepays $4,000 on December 28, 2024 for goods that Sybilla will ship on January 2, 2025. Despite having not earned the income, Sybilla will recognize income of $4,000 as she constructively (and actually) received the payment. If Sybilla had shipped the goods on December 28th but not received payment until 2025, she would not recognize the income until 2025. Despite having earned the income, she has neither actually nor constructively received the payment. ♦

Taxpayers on the accrual basis generally recognize income when it is earned and the amount can be reasonably estimated (known as the "all-events test"), regardless of when it is received. If an accrual-based taxpayer receives an advance payment for goods or services not yet provided, the recognition is deferred until such time as the goods or services are provided.

Example If Sybilla's business in the previous example was accounted for under the accrual-method of accounting, the results would differ. Her customer prepays $4,000 on December 28, 2024, for goods that Sybilla will ship on January 2, 2025. Despite having received the payment, Sybilla will not recognize income of $4,000 until 2025 when she earns the income under the all-events test. If Sybilla had shipped the goods on December 28th but not received payment until 2025, she would recognize the income in 2024. Despite having not received the payment, she met the all-events test and earned the income in 2024. ♦

Certain forms of prepaid income do not follow the general rules. For example, prepaid interest and prepaid rent are generally recognized when received regardless of accounting method.

Under the cash method of accounting, deductions are generally recognized in the year of payment, but a cash-basis taxpayer may not use the cash method for all expenses. If the payment creates an asset that is expected to have a benefit that extends beyond the end of the tax year, the item must be capitalized and amortized or depreciated (refer to Chapter 8).

Example Yun-Seo operates a small business on the cash-method of accounting. In 2024, she purchases land for $10,000, equipment for $5,000, and prepays $24,000 for a 24-month lease on a retail building. All three of the expenditures result in the creation of an asset (land, equipment, and prepaid rent) and are not deductible despite being paid for in 2024. ♦

In order to reduce the likelihood of having to create complex prepaid assets and the resulting amortization for small cash-basis taxpayers, the tax rules permit an exception to the prepaid rules for payments for prepaids that last up to 12 months and do not extend beyond the end of the tax year after the year the payment is made.

Example Continuing from the previous example, in 2024, Yun-Seo prepays $24,000 for a 24-month lease on a retail building on December 1, 2024. She also prepays $12,000 for a 12-month lease on a warehouse on December 1, 2024. The warehouse lease is for a period of 12 months or less and the lease period does not extend beyond December 31, 2025 (the end of the tax year after the year the payment is made), and thus, qualifies for the 12-month rule and $12,000 may be deducted when paid in 2024. The retail building lease extends beyond 12 months and also beyond the end of the following tax year and must be amortized over the lease period ($1,000 per month for 24 months). ♦

Accrual-basis taxpayers deduct expenses under the expense version of the all-events test (the good or services have been provided and the amount of the liability can be reasonably estimated) with one additional requirement known as "economic performance." Economic performance means that all activities related to the incurrence of the liability have been performed. For example, economic performance occurs for the purchase of services when the taxpayer uses the services. When a taxpayer leases or rents property, economic performance is deemed to occur over time.

Example Continuing from the previous example, if Yun-Seo is an accrual-basis taxpayer, both leases will be amortized over the lease period ($1,000 per month for each) as economic performance occurs ratably over time. If Yun-Seo pays for $4,000 services that will not be performed until 2025, she may not deduct the $4,000 until the services are provided (economic performance occurs). ♦

Prepaid interest expense is recognized over time rather than when paid.

Example On December 1, 2024, Debbie Dettor pays interest on her loan for the month of December and also prepays interest for all 12 months of 2025. Whether a cash-basis or accrual basis taxpayer, Debbie will recognize the interest expense over time. ♦

There are exceptions to the general rules of the all-events test and economic performance (for example, the recurring item exception) that are beyond the scope of this textbook.

> **Tax Break**
>
> The cash method allows a certain amount of flexibility in tax planning. Payment of business expenses may be accelerated before year-end to generate additional deductions, if desired. In addition, billings for services may be postponed at year-end so payment will not be received and included in income until the following year. Some itemized deductions such as property taxes, state income taxes, and charitable contributions may also be paid before year-end for an immediate deduction.

6-2a Restrictions on the Use of the Cash Method

The tax law contains certain restrictions on the use of the cash method of accounting. Regular corporations, partnerships that have a regular corporation as a partner, and tax-exempt trusts with unrelated business income are generally prohibited from using the cash method. However, this requirement does not apply to farming businesses, qualified personal service corporations, and entities with average annual gross receipts of $30 million or less in 2024.

Example Orange Associates is a manufacturer of light bulbs with average gross receipts of $32 million. Orange would not be allowed to use the cash method of accounting for tax purposes. ♦

6-2b Change in Accounting Method

Accounting methods extend beyond the overall cash versus accrual method. Using the installment method to recognize gains (Chapter 8), choosing LIFO or FIFO to value inventory (Chapter 3), and expensing non-incidental materials when used (Chapter 3) are all types of specific accounting methods that underlie the overall accounting method. In general, for tax purposes, an accounting method is considered elected if that method is used on a tax return. Once elected, that method is required to be applied consistently unless permission is requested to and granted by the IRS to change the accounting method. Taxpayers generally use Form 3115 to request an accounting method change. These rules also apply if the taxpayer uses an *incorrect* method for at least two tax returns.

For expediency, the IRS permits certain accounting changes to be "automatic." Typically, once a year, the IRS releases a large Revenue Procedure that lists which accounting changes may be requested "automatically." The taxpayer is still required to file a Form 3115, but an automatic change requires fewer materials accompany the request.

When a change of accounting method is approved, the taxpayer generally reports a "catch-up" adjustment in the year of change known as a §481 adjustment. The details of a §481 adjustment are beyond the scope of this textbook.

Lastly, correcting an error is not equivalent to an accounting change and generally requires filing an amended tax return (covered later in this chapter).

Example Julio is preparing their 2024 tax return and notes that the 2023 tax return failed to disallow 50 percent of meals costs for $2,300 of meals. This is an error, and an amended 2023 tax return should be filed. ♦

Example Julio also noted that all of the business 7-year property was being depreciated over a 5-year life for the past few years. Although there is an error (the wrong depreciable life was used), this is the incorrect use of an accounting method for more than one year and will require an accounting method change request and approval. ♦

Example Julio also noted that customers are now required to place a deposit on any sales over $10,000 starting in 2024 and that the business is properly accounting for those payments as deposits. This is a change on the underlying facts of the business and does not require an amended return or an accounting method change request. ♦

The latest guidance, Revenue Procedure 2024-23 issued in 2024, is over 400 pages long. Accounting method changes are a technical specialty, even among highly experienced tax advisors. This section is intended to provide only a broad overview.

Self-Study Problem 6.2 Refer to Appendix E for Solutions to Self-Study Problems

a. Eucalyptus, Inc., a calendar-year-end corporation, has the following transactions in 2024:

1. Receives payment of $10,000 for services performed in 2024.
2. Receives payment of $8,000 for services expected to be rendered in 2025.
3. Receives a payment of $5,000 for goods expected to be shipped in 2025.
4. Receives a rental payment of $6,000 ($1,000 per month) for a lease agreement that starts December 1, 2024 and ends May 31, 2025.
5. Prepays interest expense of $12,000 for the period July 1, 2024 through June 30, 2025.
6. Prepays rent expense of $24,000 for a 24-month lease starting December 1, 2024.
7. Prepays rent expense of $6,000 for a 12-month lease starting December 1, 2024.

What is the tax recognition of each item of income or expense if Eucalyptus is a cash-basis taxpayer? What if Eucalyptus is an accrual-basis taxpayer?

> **Self-Study Problem 6.2, continued** *Refer to Appendix E for Solutions to Self-Study Problems*
>
> b. Determine whether or not each of the following entities may use the cash method for tax purposes during 2024.
>   1. A corporation engaged in orange farming.
>   2. A dentist with a personal service corporation.
>   3. A corporate car dealer with sales of $35 million per year.
>   4. A corporation engaged in certified public accounting.

6-3 Related Parties (Section 267)

6.3 Learning Objective
Determine whether parties are considered related for tax purposes, and classify the tax treatment of certain related-party transactions.

When taxpayers who are related to each other engage in transactions, there is potential for abuse of the tax system. To prevent this abuse, the tax law contains provisions that govern related-party transactions. Under these rules, related parties who undertake certain types of transactions may find the timing of income or deduction recognition differs from typical rules.

There are two types of transactions between related parties restricted by Section 267 of the tax law. These transactions are:

1. Sales of property at a loss
2. Unpaid expenses and interest

6-3a Losses

Under the tax law "losses from sale or exchange of property . . . directly or indirectly" are disallowed between related parties. When the property is later sold to an unrelated party, any disallowed loss may be used to offset gain on that transaction.

Example Sauda sells stock with a basis of $10,000 to her son, Jengo, for $8,000, resulting in a disallowed loss of $2,000. Three years later, Jengo sells the stock to an unrelated party for $13,000. Jengo has a gain on the sale of $5,000 ($13,000 − $8,000). However, only $3,000 ($5,000 − $2,000) of the gain is taxable to Jengo since the previously disallowed loss can reduce his gain. ♦

Example Assume the same facts as in the example above, except the stock is sold for $9,500 (instead of $13,000). None of the gain of $1,500 ($9,500 − $8,000) would be taxable, because the disallowed loss would absorb it. $500 of Sauda's disallowed loss is not available to Jengo. ♦

Example Assume the same facts as in the example above, except Jengo sells the stock three years later for $7,000 (instead of $9,500). Jengo now has a $1,000 realized loss, which can be deducted subject to any capital loss limitations. Because there is no gain on this transaction, the tax benefit of Sauda's $2,000 disallowed loss is not available to Jengo. ♦

6-3b Unpaid Expenses and Interest

Under Section 267, related taxpayers are prevented from engaging in tax avoidance schemes in which one taxpayer uses the cash method of accounting and the other taxpayer uses the accrual method.

Example Ficus Corporation, an accrual-basis taxpayer, is owned by Isaiah, an individual who uses the cash method of accounting for tax purposes. On December 31, Ficus Corporation accrues interest expense of $10,000 on a loan from Isaiah, but the interest is not paid to him. Ficus Corporation may not deduct the $10,000 until the tax year in which it is actually paid to Isaiah. This rule also applies to other expenses such as salaries and bonuses. ♦

6-3c Relationships

Section 267 has a complex set of rules to define who is a related party for disallowance purposes. The common related parties under Section 267 include the following:

1. Family members. A taxpayer's family includes brothers and sisters (whole or half), a spouse, ancestors (parents, grandparents, etc.), and lineal descendants (children, grandchildren, etc.).
2. A corporation or an individual who directly or indirectly owns more than 50 percent of the corporation.
3. Two corporations that are members of the same controlled group.
4. Trusts, corporations, and certain charitable organizations. They are subject to a complex set of relationship rules.

Example Kalmia Corporation is owned 70 percent by C.J. and 30 percent by Stephanie. C.J. and Stephanie are unrelated to each other. Since C.J. owns over 50 percent of the corporation, he is deemed to be a related party to the corporation. As a result, if C.J. sells property to the corporation at a loss, the loss will be disallowed. Since Stephanie is not related to the corporation, the rules of Section 267 do not apply to Stephanie. ♦

Related-party rules also consider constructive ownership in determining whether parties are related to each other. Under these rules, taxpayers are deemed to own stock owned by certain relatives and related entities. The common constructive ownership rules are as follows:

1. A taxpayer is deemed to own all the stock owned by their spouse, brothers and sisters (whole or half), ancestors, and lineal descendants.
2. A taxpayer is deemed to own their proportionate share of stock owned by any partnership, corporation, trust, or estate in which they are a partner, shareholder, or beneficiary.
3. A taxpayer is deemed to own any stock owned directly or indirectly by a partner.

Example ABC Corporation is owned 40 percent by Andy, 30 percent by Betty, and 30 percent by Chee. Betty and Chee are married to each other. For purposes of related-party rules, Andy is not a related party to the corporation since he does not own more than 50 percent of the corporation. Betty is a related party because she is a 60-percent shareholder (30 percent directly and 30 percent from her husband, Chee). Using the same rule, Chee is also a related party since he also owns 60 percent (30 percent directly and 30 percent from his wife, Betty). ♦

Example Robert owns 40 percent of R Corporation and 40 percent of T Corporation. T Corporation owns 60 percent of R Corporation. Robert is deemed to own 64 percent of R Corporation; therefore, he is a related party to R Corp. The 64 percent is calculated as 40 percent direct ownership and 24 percent (40% × 60%) constructive ownership. ♦

There are other sets of related-party and constructive ownership rules in the tax law, which differ from the related-party rules discussed in this section and should not be confused with the Section 267 related-party provisions.

> **Self-Study Problem 6.3** Refer to Appendix E for Solutions to Self-Study Problems
>
> EFG Corporation is owned 40 percent by Ed, 20 percent by Frank, 20 percent by Gene, and 20 percent by X Corporation. X Corporation is owned 80 percent by Ed and 20 percent by an unrelated party. Frank and Gene are brothers. Answer each of the following questions about EFG under the constructive ownership rules of Section 267.
>
> 1. What is Ed's percentage ownership?
> 2. What is Frank's percentage ownership?
> 3. What is Gene's percentage ownership?
> 4. If EFG sells property to Ed for a $15,000 loss, what amount of that loss can be recognized for tax purposes?

6-4 Unearned Income of Minor Children and Certain Students

6.4 Learning Objective

Apply the rules for computing tax on the unearned income of minor children and certain students (the "kiddie tax").

A child generally computes their income tax liability the same as any other taxpayer except that the decreased standard deduction is claimed if the child is a dependent. However, many parents have found it beneficial from a tax-planning standpoint to give income-earning assets, such as stocks, bonds, bank certificates of deposit, and mutual funds, to their minor children. Since minor children are generally in a lower income tax bracket, the unearned income from assets such as interest, dividends, and capital gains on stock sales might have been taxed at a lower rate than the parents' rate. However, one of the provisions of the tax law is that certain unearned income can be taxed at their parent's rate, if higher. This is commonly referred to as the "kiddie tax."

A child is subject to the kiddie tax if:

- the child is required to file a tax return
- the child's unearned income is more than $2,600 (in 2024)
- either parent is alive
- the child
  - Is under 18, or
  - Is age 18 and does not provide more than one-half of their own support, or
  - Is age 19–24, a full-time student, and does not provide more than one-half of their own support

Although there is no statutory definition for a parent, the term is generally considered to mean a parent or step-parent of the child. For purposes of determining the child's (or young adult's) income subject to the parental tax rate, net unearned income is never considered to include wages or salary of a minor child and is computed as follows:

Unearned income	$xxxx.xx
Less the greater of:	
1. $1,300 (child's standard deduction), or	
2. The allowable itemized deductions directly connected with the production of the unearned income	(xxx.xx)
	xxxx.xx
Less the 2024 statutory standard deduction	(1,300)
Net unearned income	$xxxx.xx

If the net unearned income is zero or less, the child's tax is calculated using the child's tax rate. However, if the net unearned income amount is positive, the child's tax is calculated by applying the parents' tax rate, if higher, to that amount.

Example Jordan and Ivana are a high-income married couple in the 37-percent tax bracket. Their 11-year-old son, Ayven, generates $5,000 of interest income from investments. The tax on Ayven's income will be computed at his parents' tax rate as follows:

Unearned income	$5,000
Standard deduction	(1,300)
Statutory standard deduction (for 2024)	(1,300)
Net unearned income	2,400
Taxed at parent's rate	37%
Tax	888
Statutory standard deduction	1,300
Taxed at child's rate	10%
Tax	130
Total tax	$1,018

◆

The more precise method of describing the computation of the kiddie tax is to compute the parent's tax without the child's unearned income and recompute the parent's tax with the child's unearned income. If more than one child is subject to the kiddie tax, then a complex allocation of the tax to each child is required. The kiddie tax is reported on Form 8615, as presented on Page 6-12.

The taxation of a child's unearned income is made even more complex in situations where the child's earned income is unusually high (over approximately $70,000) or where the unearned income is subject to preferential rates such as qualified dividends or long-term capital gains. These situations are beyond the scope of this textbook.

ProConnect™ Tax TIP Although the computation of the kiddie tax is complex, having ProConnect Tax compute the kiddie tax requires no extra input on the part of the preparer. If the taxpayer is noted as being claimed as a dependent, fits the age requirements, and unearned income that exceeds the threshold is input (for example, Forms 1099-INT or 1099-DIV), the software will automatically generate and populate the Form 8615 and calculate the kiddie tax.

6-4a Election to Include a Child's Unearned Income on Parents' Return

If certain conditions are met, parents may elect to include a child's gross income on the parents' tax return. The election eliminates the child's return filing requirements and saves the parents from the trouble of filing the special calculation on Form 8615 for the "kiddie tax." To qualify for this election, the following conditions must be met:

1. The child's gross income is from interest and dividends only.
2. The gross income is more than $1,300 and less than $13,000 (or ten times the lower amount).

3. No estimated tax has been paid in the name of the child and the child is not subject to backup withholding.

Example Sam Jackson is 12 years old and has $2,300 of interest from a savings account established for him by his grandparents. This is Sam's only income for the year. Instead of completing Form 8615 and paying the kiddie tax on his $2,300 in income, Sam's parents, Michael and Janet, may elect to include the $2,300 on their tax return, thereby eliminating Sam's filing requirement. ◆

The election to include the income of a minor child on the parents' return is made on Form 8814, as presented on Page 6-13.

Self-Study Problem 6.4   Refer to Appendix E for Solutions to Self-Study Problems

Carl and Soren are a married couple filing jointly in 2024. They have one 12-year-old child, Travon, whose only income in 2024 is $4,500 of interest income. Carl and Soren's AGI in 2024 is $75,000, taxed at ordinary rates. Their only other deduction is the $29,200 standard deduction. Carl and Soren are eligible for a $2,000 child tax credit.

a. Complete Form 8615 (Page 6-12) assuming Carl and Soren do not make the election to include Travon's income on their tax return.

b. Complete Form 8814 (Page 6-13) assuming Carl and Soren make the election to include Travon's income on their tax return.

Self-Study Problem 6.4, Part a

Form 8615
Department of the Treasury
Internal Revenue Service

Tax for Certain Children Who Have Unearned Income

Attach only to the child's Form 1040 or 1040-NR.
Go to www.irs.gov/Form8615 for instructions and the latest information.

OMB No. 1545-0074

2024

Attachment Sequence No. **33**

Child's name shown on return | Child's social security number

A Parent's name (first, initial, and last). **Caution:** See instructions before completing. | **B** Parent's social security number

C Parent's filing status (check one):
☐ Single ☐ Married filing jointly ☐ Married filing separately ☐ Head of household ☐ Qualifying surviving spouse

Part I — Child's Net Unearned Income

1. Enter the child's unearned income. See instructions **1**
2. If the child **did not** itemize deductions on **Schedule A** (Form 1040) or **Schedule A** (Form 1040-NR), enter $2,600. Otherwise, see instructions **2**
3. Subtract line 2 from line 1. If zero or less, **stop**; do not complete the rest of this form but **do** attach it to the child's return **3**
4. Enter the child's **taxable income** from Form 1040 or 1040-NR, line 15. If the child files Form 2555, see the instructions **4**
5. Enter the **smaller** of line 3 or line 4. If zero, **stop**; do not complete the rest of this form but **do** attach it to the child's return **5**

Part II — Tentative Tax Based on the Tax Rate of the Parent

6. Enter the parent's **taxable income** from Form 1040 or 1040-NR, line 15. If zero or less, enter -0-. If the parent files Form 2555, see the instructions **6**
7. Enter the total, if any, from Forms 8615, line 5, of **all other** children of the parent named above. **Do not** include the amount from line 5 above **7**
8. Add lines 5, 6, and 7. See instructions **8**
9. Enter the tax on the amount on line 8 based on the **parent's** filing status above. See instructions. If the Qualified Dividends and Capital Gain Tax Worksheet, Schedule D Tax Worksheet, or Schedule J (Form 1040) is used to figure the tax, check here ☐ **9**
10. Enter the parent's tax from Form 1040 or 1040-NR, line 16, minus any alternative minimum tax. **Do not** include any tax from **Form 4972** or **Form 8814**, or any tax from the recapture of an education credit. If the parent files Form 2555, see the instructions. If the Qualified Dividends and Capital Gain Tax Worksheet, Schedule D Tax Worksheet, or Schedule J (Form 1040) was used to figure the tax, check here ☐ **10**
11. Subtract line 10 from line 9 and enter the result. If line 7 is blank, also enter this amount on line 13 and go to **Part III** **11**
12a. Add lines 5 and 7 . . . . **12a**
  b. Divide line 5 by line 12a. Enter the result as a decimal (rounded to at least three places) . . . . . . **12b** × .
13. Multiply line 11 by line 12b **13**

Part III — Child's Tax—If lines 4 and 5 above are the same, enter -0- on line 15 and go to line 16.

14. Subtract line 5 from line 4 . . . . **14**
15. Enter the tax on the amount on line 14 based on the **child's** filing status. See instructions. If the Qualified Dividends and Capital Gain Tax Worksheet, Schedule D Tax Worksheet, or Schedule J (Form 1040) is used to figure the tax, check here ☐ **15**
16. Add lines 13 and 15 . . . . **16**
17. Enter the tax on the amount on line 4 based on the **child's** filing status. See instructions. If the Qualified Dividends and Capital Gain Tax Worksheet, Schedule D Tax Worksheet, or Schedule J (Form 1040) is used to figure the tax, check here ☐ **17**
18. Enter the **larger** of line 16 or line 17 here and on the **child's** Form 1040 or 1040-NR, line 16. If the child files Form 2555, see the instructions **18**

For Paperwork Reduction Act Notice, see your tax return instructions. Cat. No. 64113U Form **8615** (2024)

Self-Study Problem 6.4, Part b

Form 8814
Department of the Treasury
Internal Revenue Service

Parents' Election To Report Child's Interest and Dividends

Attach to parents' Form 1040, 1040-SR, or 1040-NR.
Go to www.irs.gov/Form8814 for the latest information.

OMB No. 1545-0074
2024
Attachment Sequence No. **40**

Name(s) shown on your return | Your social security number

Caution: The federal income tax on your child's income, including qualified dividends and capital gain distributions, may be less if you file a separate tax return for the child instead of making this election. This is because you cannot take certain tax benefits that your child could take on his or her own return. For details, see *Tax benefits you cannot take* in the instructions.

A Child's name (first, initial, and last) | **B** Child's social security number

C If more than one Form 8814 is attached, check here . . . . ☐

Part I — Child's Interest and Dividends To Report on Your Return

1a Enter your child's **taxable** interest. If this amount is different from the amounts shown on the child's Forms 1099-INT and 1099-OID, see the instructions **1a**

b Enter your child's **tax-exempt** interest. **Do not** include this amount on line 1a **1b**

2a Enter your child's ordinary dividends, including any Alaska Permanent Fund dividends. If your child received any ordinary dividends as a nominee, see the instructions **2a**

b Enter your child's qualified dividends included on line 2a. See the instructions **2b**

3 Enter your child's capital gain distributions. If your child received any capital gain distributions as a nominee, see the instructions **3**

4 Add lines 1a, 2a, and 3. If the total is $2,600 or less, skip lines 5 through 12 and go to line 13. If the total is $13,000 or more, **do not** file this form. Your child **must** file his or her own return to report the income **4**

5 Base amount. Enter $2,600 . . . . **5**

6 Subtract line 5 from line 4 . . . . **6**

If both lines 2b and 3 are zero or blank, skip lines 7 through 10, enter -0- on line 11, and go to line 12. Otherwise, go to line 7.

7 Divide line 2b by line 4. Enter the result as a decimal (rounded to at least three places) **7**

8 Divide line 3 by line 4. Enter the result as a decimal (rounded to at least three places) **8**

9 Multiply line 6 by line 7. Enter the result here. See the instructions for where to report this amount on your return **9**

10 Multiply line 6 by line 8. Enter the result here. See the instructions for where to report this amount on your return **10**

11 Add lines 9 and 10 . . . . **11**

12 Subtract line 11 from line 6. Include this amount in the total on Schedule 1 (Form 1040), line 8z. In the space next to that line, enter "Form 8814" and show the amount. If you checked the box on line C above, see the instructions. Go to line 13 below **12**

Part II — Tax on the First $2,600 of Child's Interest and Dividends

13 Amount not taxed. Enter $1,300 . . . . **13**

14 Subtract line 13 from line 4. If the result is zero or less, enter -0- **14**

15 **Tax.** Is the amount on line 14 less than $1,300?
☐ **No.** Enter $130 here and see the **Note** below.
☐ **Yes.** Multiply line 14 by 10% (0.10). Enter the result here and see the **Note** below. **15**

Note: If you checked the box on line C above, see the instructions. Otherwise, include the amount from line 15 in the tax you enter on Form 1040, 1040-SR, or 1040-NR, line 16. Be sure to check box 1 on Form 1040, 1040-SR, or 1040-NR, line 16.

For Paperwork Reduction Act Notice, see your tax return instructions. Cat. No. 10750J Form **8814** (2024)

6-5 The Individual Alternative Minimum Tax (AMT)

Learning Objective 6.5
Calculate a basic alternative minimum tax.

A small number of individual taxpayers are subject to two parallel tax calculations, the regular tax and the alternative minimum tax (AMT). The AMT was designed in the 1960s to ensure that wealthy taxpayers could not take advantage of special tax write-offs (tax preferences and other adjustments) to avoid paying tax. In general, taxpayers must pay the alternative minimum tax if their AMT tax liability is larger than their regular tax liability.

The AMT is calculated on Form 6251, using the following formula simplified for purposes of this textbook:

 Regular taxable income (before standard deduction)
$\pm$ Plus or minus AMT preferences and adjustments
$=$ Equals alternative minimum taxable income (AMTI)
$-$ Less AMT exemption (phased out to zero as AMTI increases)
$=$ Equals amount subject to AMT
$\times$ Multiplied by the AMT tax rate(s)
$=$ Equals tentative minimum tax
$-$ Less regular tax
$=$ Equals amount of AMT due with tax return, if a positive amount

6-5a Common AMT Adjustments and Preferences

The terms "AMT adjustments" and "AMT preferences" are often used interchangeably, though they have slightly different meanings. In general, adjustments are *timing* differences that arise because of differences in the regular and AMT tax calculations (e.g., depreciation timing differences), while preferences are special provisions for the regular tax that are not allowed for the AMT (e.g., state income taxes). Both terms refer to items which adjust regular taxable income to arrive at income which is subject to alternative minimum tax. There are more than twenty different types of adjustments and preferences used in the calculation of AMT on Form 6251. Some of the common adjustments and preferences are as follows:

- The standard deduction allowed for regular tax is not allowed for AMT.
- The deductions for property tax, state income tax, and other taxes allowed as itemized deductions for regular tax are not allowed for AMT.
- Depreciation is generally calculated over a longer life for AMT, sometimes using a different method.
- Net operating losses are calculated differently for AMT and often result in an adjustment when they are present.
- State income tax refunds are not considered income for AMT since the state income tax deduction is not allowed for AMT.
- Interest from specified private activity bonds is not taxed for regular tax purposes, but is taxable for AMT.
- Other less commonly seen AMT differences include such items as the calculations related to incentive stock options, oil and gas depletion, research and development expenses, gains on asset sales such as rental real estate, passive losses, and the gain exclusion for small business stock and other items.

The actual details of the calculation of several of the AMT tax preferences and adjustments are complex and infrequently seen in practice. For further information, please consult the IRS website or a tax research service.

6-5b AMT Exemption

To reduce the chances of subjecting a greater number of taxpayers to the AMT, an exemption amount is permitted as a deduction against AMT income. The 2024 AMT exemptions and thresholds presented in Table 6.1.

Table 6.1 AMT Exemption and Threshold Amounts by Filing Status

	Married Filing Jointly	Single and Head of Household	Married Filing Separately
Exemption amount	$ 133,300	$ 85,700	$ 66,650
Threshold	1,218,700	609,350	609,350

The exemption amount is phased out (reduced) 25 cents for each dollar by which the taxpayer's alternative minimum taxable income exceeds the threshold amounts.

Example Abby, a single taxpayer, has AMTI of $340,000 in 2024. Her AMT exemption is $85,700 as she has not reached the threshold for phase-out. ◆

Example Alex and Servando are married and file jointly. They have AMTI of $1,284,000 in 2024. Their AMT exemption is $116,975 [$133,300 − (($1,284,000 − $1,218,700) × 25%)]. ◆

The exemption amounts and phase-out thresholds are both indexed for inflation, but the amounts are scheduled to be reduced significantly after 2025.

6-5c Alternative Minimum Tax Rates

For 2024, the alternative minimum tax rates for calculating the tentative minimum tax are 26 percent of the first $232,600 ($116,300 for married taxpayers filing separately), plus 28 percent on amounts above $232,600 (amounts above $116,300 for married filing separately). These rates are applied to the taxpayer's alternative minimum tax base from the formula above. The alternative minimum tax rate for capital gains and dividends is limited to the rate paid for regular tax purposes (e.g., capital gain or qualified dividends taxed at 15 percent for regular tax purposes will also be taxed at a 15 percent alternative minimum tax rate).

Example In 2024, Teddy, a married filing jointly taxpayer, has alternative minimum taxable income after the exemption deduction of $270,000, none of which is from capital gains. His tentative minimum tax is $70,948, which is calculated as (26% × $232,600) + (28% × [$270,000 − $232,600]). ◆

The large AMT exemption amount and exemption phase-out threshold in conjunction with the limitation on the itemized deduction for state and local taxes and the suspension of miscellaneous itemized deduction subject to the 2-percent floor, results in few taxpayers being subject to the AMT.

Chapter 6 • Accounting Periods and Other Taxes

Example Gram and Sally are married taxpayers who file a joint tax return in 2024. Their taxable income and regular tax liability can be calculated as follows:

Adjusted gross income	$200,000
Itemized deductions:	
State income tax	10,000
Home mortgage interest	20,000
Contributions	1,906
Total itemized deductions	(31,906)
Taxable income	$168,094
Tax from rate schedule	$ 27,087

Gram and Sally have $30,000 of private activity bond interest which is taxable for AMT but not for regular tax. The AMT is calculated as follows (same format as shown on Form 6251 presented on Page 6-17):

Taxable income	$168,094
Interest on private activity bonds	30,000
Add back:	
Taxes	10,000
Alternative minimum taxable income	208,094
AMT exemption	(133,300)
AMT Base	$ 74,794
Tentative minimum tax (26%)	$ 19,446
AMT	$ 0

Because the regular tax of $27,087 exceeds the tentative minimum tax of $19,446 in 2024, no AMT is due. ♦

Self-Study Problem 6.5 *Refer to Appendix E for Solutions to Self-Study Problems*

Harold Brown, a single taxpayer, has adjusted gross income of $630,000. He has a deduction for home mortgage interest of $23,000, cash contributions of $11,000, state income taxes of $10,000, and private activity bond interest income of $120,000. Assuming Harold's regular tax liability is $175,475, use page 1 of Form 6251 on Page 6-17 to calculate the amount of Harold's net alternative minimum tax.

Self-Study Problem 6.5

Form 6251
Department of the Treasury
Internal Revenue Service

Alternative Minimum Tax—Individuals

Attach to Form 1040, 1040-SR, or 1040-NR.
Go to www.irs.gov/Form6251 for instructions and the latest information.

OMB No. 1545-0074

2024

Attachment Sequence No. **32**

Name(s) shown on Form 1040, 1040-SR, or 1040-NR | Your social security number

Part I — Alternative Minimum Taxable Income (See instructions for how to complete each line.)

1. Enter the amount from Form 1040 or 1040-SR, line 15, if more than zero. If Form 1040 or 1040-SR, line 15, is zero, subtract line 14 of Form 1040 or 1040-SR from line 11 of Form 1040 or 1040-SR and enter the result here. (If less than zero, enter as a negative amount.) ... **1**

2a. If filing Schedule A (Form 1040), enter the taxes from Schedule A, line 7; otherwise, enter the amount from Form 1040 or 1040-SR, line 12 ... **2a**

b. Tax refund from Schedule 1 (Form 1040), line 1 or line 8z ... **2b** ( )

c. Investment interest expense (difference between regular tax and AMT) ... **2c**

d. Depletion (difference between regular tax and AMT) ... **2d**

e. Net operating loss deduction from Schedule 1 (Form 1040), line 8a. Enter as a positive amount ... **2e**

f. Alternative tax net operating loss deduction ... **2f** ( )

g. Interest from specified private activity bonds exempt from the regular tax ... **2g**

h. Qualified small business stock, see instructions ... **2h**

i. Exercise of incentive stock options (excess of AMT income over regular tax income) ... **2i**

j. Estates and trusts (amount from Schedule K-1 (Form 1041), box 12, code A) ... **2j**

k. Disposition of property (difference between AMT and regular tax gain or loss) ... **2k**

l. Depreciation on assets placed in service after 1986 (difference between regular tax and AMT) ... **2l**

m. Passive activities (difference between AMT and regular tax income or loss) ... **2m**

n. Loss limitations (difference between AMT and regular tax income or loss) ... **2n**

o. Circulation costs (difference between regular tax and AMT) ... **2o**

p. Long-term contracts (difference between AMT and regular tax income) ... **2p**

q. Mining costs (difference between regular tax and AMT) ... **2q**

r. Research and experimental costs (difference between regular tax and AMT) ... **2r**

s. Income from certain installment sales before January 1, 1987 ... **2s** ( )

t. Intangible drilling costs preference ... **2t**

3. Other adjustments, including income-based related adjustments ... **3**

4. **Alternative minimum taxable income.** Combine lines 1 through 3. (If married filing separately and line 4 is more than $875,950, see instructions.) ... **4**

Part II — Alternative Minimum Tax (AMT)

5. Exemption.

IF your filing status is...	AND line 4 is not over...	THEN enter on line 5...
Single or head of household	$609,350	$85,700
Married filing jointly or qualifying surviving spouse	1,218,700	133,300
Married filing separately	609,350	66,650

If line 4 is **over** the amount shown above for your filing status, see instructions. ... **5**

6. Subtract line 5 from line 4. If more than zero, go to line 7. If zero or less, enter -0- here and on lines 7, 9, and 11, and go to line 10. ... **6**

7. • If you are filing Form 2555, see instructions for the amount to enter.
   • If you reported capital gain distributions directly on Form 1040 or 1040-SR, line 7; you reported qualified dividends on Form 1040 or 1040-SR, line 3a; **or** you had a gain on both lines 15 and 16 of Schedule D (Form 1040) (as refigured for the AMT, if necessary), complete Part III on the back and enter the amount from line 40 here.
   • **All others:** If line 6 is $232,600 or less ($116,300 or less if married filing separately), multiply line 6 by 26% (0.26). Otherwise, multiply line 6 by 28% (0.28) and subtract $4,652 ($2,326 if married filing separately) from the result. ... **7**

8. Alternative minimum tax foreign tax credit (see instructions) ... **8**

9. Tentative minimum tax. Subtract line 8 from line 7 ... **9**

10. Add Form 1040 or 1040-SR, line 16 (minus any tax from Form 4972), and Schedule 2 (Form 1040), line 1z. Subtract from the result Schedule 3 (Form 1040), line 1 and any negative amount reported on Form 8978, line 14 (treated as a positive number). If zero or less, enter -0-. If you used Schedule J to figure your tax on Form 1040 or 1040-SR, line 16, refigure that tax without using Schedule J before completing this line. See instructions ... **10**

11. **AMT.** Subtract line 10 from line 9. If zero or less, enter -0-. Enter here and on Schedule 2 (Form 1040), line 2 ... **11**

For Paperwork Reduction Act Notice, see your tax return instructions. Cat. No. 13600G Form **6251** (2024)

Form 6251 (2024)   Page **2**

Part III   Tax Computation Using Maximum Capital Gains Rates

Complete Part III only if you are required to do so by line 7 or by the Foreign Earned Income Tax Worksheet in the instructions.

12	Enter the amount from Form 6251, line 6. If you are filing Form 2555, enter the amount from line 3 of the worksheet in the instructions for line 7	12
13	Enter the amount from line 4 of the Qualified Dividends and Capital Gain Tax Worksheet in the Instructions for Form 1040 or the amount from line 13 of the Schedule D Tax Worksheet in the Instructions for Schedule D (Form 1040), whichever applies (as refigured for the AMT, if necessary). See instructions. If you are filing Form 2555, see instructions for the amount to enter	13
14	Enter the amount from Schedule D (Form 1040), line 19 (as refigured for the AMT, if necessary). See instructions. If you are filing Form 2555, see instructions for the amount to enter	14
15	If you did not complete a Schedule D Tax Worksheet for the regular tax or the AMT, enter the amount from line 13. Otherwise, add lines 13 and 14, and enter the **smaller** of that result or the amount from line 10 of the Schedule D Tax Worksheet (as refigured for the AMT, if necessary). If you are filing Form 2555, see instructions for the amount to enter	15
16	Enter the **smaller** of line 12 or line 15	16
17	Subtract line 16 from line 12	17
18	If line 17 is $232,600 or less ($116,300 or less if married filing separately), multiply line 17 by 26% (0.26). Otherwise, multiply line 17 by 28% (0.28) and subtract $4,652 ($2,326 if married filing separately) from the result	18
19	Enter: • $94,050 if married filing jointly or qualifying surviving spouse, • $47,025 if single or married filing separately, or • $63,000 if head of household.	19
20	Enter the amount from line 5 of the Qualified Dividends and Capital Gain Tax Worksheet or the amount from line 14 of the Schedule D Tax Worksheet, whichever applies (as figured for the regular tax). If you did not complete either worksheet for the regular tax, enter the amount from Form 1040 or 1040-SR, line 15; if zero or less, enter -0-. If you are filing Form 2555, see instructions for the amount to enter	20
21	Subtract line 20 from line 19. If zero or less, enter -0-	21
22	Enter the **smaller** of line 12 or line 13	22
23	Enter the **smaller** of line 21 or line 22. This amount is taxed at 0%	23
24	Subtract line 23 from line 22	24
25	Enter: • $518,900 if single, • $291,850 if married filing separately, • $583,750 if married filing jointly or qualifying surviving spouse, or • $551,350 if head of household.	25
26	Enter the amount from line 21	26
27	Enter the amount from line 5 of the Qualified Dividends and Capital Gain Tax Worksheet or the amount from line 21 of the Schedule D Tax Worksheet, whichever applies (as figured for the regular tax). If you did not complete either worksheet for the regular tax, enter the amount from Form 1040 or 1040-SR, line 15; if zero or less, enter -0-. If you are filing Form 2555, see instructions for the amount to enter	27
28	Add line 26 and line 27	28
29	Subtract line 28 from line 25. If zero or less, enter -0-	29
30	Enter the smaller of line 24 or line 29	30
31	Multiply line 30 by 15% (0.15)	31
32	Add lines 23 and 30	32
	If lines 32 and 12 are the same, skip lines 33 through 37 and go to line 38. Otherwise, go to line 33.	
33	Subtract line 32 from line 22	33
34	Multiply line 33 by 20% (0.20)	34
	If line 14 is zero or blank, skip lines 35 through 37 and go to line 38. Otherwise, go to line 35.	
35	Add lines 17, 32, and 33	35
36	Subtract line 35 from line 12	36
37	Multiply line 36 by 25% (0.25)	37
38	Add lines 18, 31, 34, and 37	38
39	If line 12 is $232,600 or less ($116,300 or less if married filing separately), multiply line 12 by 26% (0.26). Otherwise, multiply line 12 by 28% (0.28) and subtract $4,652 ($2,326 if married filing separately) from the result	39
40	Enter the **smaller** of line 38 or line 39 here and on line 7. If you are filing Form 2555, do not enter this amount on line 7. Instead, enter it on line 4 of the worksheet in the instructions for line 7	40

Form **6251** (2024)

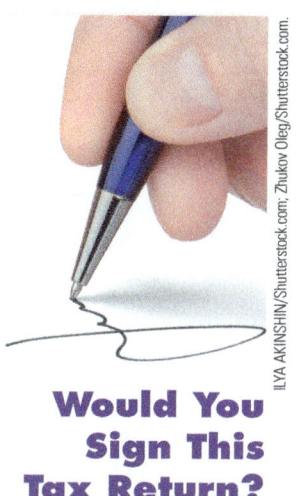

Would You Sign This Tax Return?

Your client, William Warrant, was hired for a management position at an Internet company planning to start a website called "indulgedanimals.com" for dogs, cats, and other pets. When he was hired, William was given an incentive stock option (ISO) worth $500,000, which he exercised during the year. Exercise of the ISO creates a tax preference item for alternative minimum tax (AMT) and causes him to have to pay substantial additional tax when combined with his other tax items for the year. He is livid about the extra tax and refuses to file the AMT Form 6251 with his tax return because the AMT tax is "unfair" and "un-American" according to him. Would you sign this tax return?

6-6 The Nanny Tax

6.6 Learning Objective

Apply the special tax and reporting requirements for household employees (the "nanny tax").

Over the years, the taxation and reporting of household employees' wages has caused many problems for taxpayers and the IRS. The threshold for filing was low ($50 per quarter of wages), and the tax forms to be completed were complex. As a result, many taxpayers ignored the reporting of household workers' wages and taxes. Congress addressed this problem by enacting what are commonly referred to as the "nanny tax" provisions. These provisions simplified the reporting process for employers of domestic household workers.

Household employers are not required to pay FICA taxes on cash payments of less than $2,700 (in 2024) paid to any household employee in a calendar year. If the cash payment to any household employee is $2,700 or more in a calendar year, all the cash payments (including the first $2,700) are subject to FICA taxes (LO 9.2). Household employers must also withhold income taxes if requested by the employee and are required to pay FUTA (Federal Unemployment Tax Act) tax if more than $1,000 in cash wages are paid to household employees during any calendar quarter. The federal unemployment tax rate is 6 percent of an employee's wages up to $7,000.

A taxpayer is a household employer if they hire workers to perform household services in or around the taxpayer's home that are subject to the "will and control" of the taxpayer. Examples of household workers include:

- Babysitters
- Caretakers
- Cooks
- Drivers
- Gardeners
- Housekeepers
- Maids

If the household worker has an employee-employer relationship with the taxpayer, it does not matter if the worker is called something else, such as "independent contractor." Also, it does not matter if the worker is full-time or part-time. The household employer is responsible for the proper reporting, withholding, and payment of any taxes due.

The following workers are not subject to FICA taxes on wages paid for *work in the home*:

- The taxpayer's spouse
- The taxpayer's father or mother
- The taxpayer's children under 21 years of age

- Anyone who is under age 18 during the year, unless providing household services is their principal occupation (being a student is considered an occupation for purposes of this requirement)

Example Allison is a 17-year-old high school student. During the year, she earns $3,000 by babysitting for a neighbor with four children. Any amount she earns is exempt from FICA requirements. However, if Allison is not a student and works full-time as a nanny, she will be subject to the general FICA withholding requirements under the nanny tax rules. ◆

Under the nanny tax provisions, household employers only have to report FICA, federal income tax withholding, and FUTA tax once a year. The taxpayer completes Schedule H and files it with their individual Form 1040. Taxpayers who have nonhousehold worker(s) in addition to household worker(s) can elect to report any FICA taxes and withholding on Forms 941 and 940 with their regular employees. Also, at the close of a tax year, taxpayers must file Form W-2 (Copy A) and Form W-3 with the Social Security Administration for each household employee who earned $2,700 or more in cash wages subject to FICA tax or had federal income taxes withheld from wages. For complete details on reporting the wages of household employees, see IRS Publication 926.

ProConnect™ Tax TIP

Taxes for household employees are input into ProConnect Tax under Taxes. There is a separate subheading for Household Employment Taxes (Schedule H).

Self-Study Problem 6.6 — Refer to Appendix E for Solutions to Self-Study Problems

Susan Green lives in Florida and hires Helen in February 2024 to clean her house for $125 per week. Susan does not withhold income taxes from Helen's wages. Helen's quarterly wages are as follows:

1st quarter	$ 750	($125 × 6 weeks)
2nd quarter	1,625	($125 × 13 weeks)
3rd quarter	1,625	($125 × 13 weeks)
4th quarter	1,625	($125 × 13 weeks)
Total	$5,625	

Assume Susan pays state unemployment tax of $152 to the state of Florida during the year. Complete her 2024 Schedule H (Form 1040) on Pages 6-21 and 6-22, using the above information.

6-6 The Nanny Tax   6-21

Self-Study Problem 6.6

SCHEDULE H
(Form 1040)

Department of the Treasury
Internal Revenue Service

Household Employment Taxes
(For Social Security, Medicare, Withheld Income, and Federal Unemployment (FUTA) Taxes)
Attach to Form 1040, 1040-SR, 1040-SS, 1040-NR, or 1041.
Go to *www.irs.gov/ScheduleH* for instructions and the latest information.

OMB No. 1545-0074

2024

Attachment Sequence No. **44**

Name of employer

Social security number

Employer identification number

Calendar year taxpayers having no household employees in 2024 don't have to complete this form for 2024.

A Did you pay **any one** household employee cash wages of $2,700 or more in 2024? (If any household employee was your spouse, your child under age 21, your parent, or anyone under age 18, see the line A instructions before you answer this question.)

☐ **Yes.** Skip lines B and C and go to line 1.
☐ **No.** Go to line B.

B Did you withhold federal income tax during 2024 for any household employee?

☐ **Yes.** Skip line C and go to line 7.
☐ **No.** Go to line C.

C Did you pay **total** cash wages of $1,000 or more in **any** calendar **quarter** of 2023 or 2024 to **all** household employees? (**Don't** count cash wages paid in 2023 or 2024 to your spouse, your child under age 21, or your parent.)

☐ **No. Stop.** Don't file this schedule.
☐ **Yes.** Skip lines 1–9 and go to line 10.

Part I	Social Security, Medicare, and Federal Income Taxes

1 Total cash wages subject to social security tax **1**

2 Social security tax. Multiply line 1 by 12.4% (0.124) **2**

3 Total cash wages subject to Medicare tax **3**

4 Medicare tax. Multiply line 3 by 2.9% (0.029) **4**

5 Total cash wages subject to Additional Medicare Tax withholding **5**

6 Additional Medicare Tax withholding. Multiply line 5 by 0.9% (0.009) **6**

7 Federal income tax withheld, if any **7**

8 Total social security, Medicare, and federal income taxes. Add lines 2, 4, 6, and 7 . . . . **8**

9 Did you pay **total** cash wages of $1,000 or more in **any** calendar **quarter** of 2023 or 2024 to **all** household employees? (**Don't** count cash wages paid in 2023 or 2024 to your spouse, your child under age 21, or your parent.)

☐ **No. Stop.** Include the amount from line 8 above on Schedule 2 (Form 1040), line 9. If you're not required to file Form 1040, see the line 9 instructions.

☐ **Yes.** Go to line 10.

For Privacy Act and Paperwork Reduction Act Notice, see the separate instructions.   Cat. No. 12187K   Schedule H (Form 1040) 2024

Schedule H (Form 1040) 2024 — Page **2**

Part II Federal Unemployment (FUTA) Tax

		Yes	No
10	Did you pay unemployment contributions to only one state? If you paid contributions to a credit reduction state, see instructions and check "**No**" 10		
11	Did you pay all state unemployment contributions for 2024 by April 15, 2025? Fiscal year filers, see instructions 11		
12	Were all wages that are taxable for FUTA tax also taxable for your state's unemployment tax? 12		

Next: If you checked the "**Yes**" box on **all** the lines above, complete Section A.
If you checked the "**No**" box on **any** of the lines above, skip Section A and complete Section B.

Section A

13	Name of the state where you paid unemployment contributions _____	
14	Contributions paid to your state unemployment fund 14	
15	Total cash wages subject to FUTA tax 15	
16	**FUTA tax.** Multiply line 15 by 0.6% (0.006). Enter the result here, skip Section B, and go to line 25 . . 16	

Section B

17 Complete all columns below that apply (if you need more space, see instructions):

(a) Name of state	(b) Taxable wages (as defined in state act)	(c) State experience rate period From / To	(d) State experience rate	(e) Multiply col. (b) by 0.054	(f) Multiply col. (b) by col. (d)	(g) Subtract col. (f) from col. (e). If zero or less, enter -0-.	(h) Contributions paid to state unemployment fund

18	Totals 18		
19	Add columns (g) and (h) of line 18 19		
20	Total cash wages subject to FUTA tax (see the line 15 instructions) 20		
21	Multiply line 20 by 6.0% (0.06) 21		
22	Multiply line 20 by 5.4% (0.054) 22		
23	Enter the **smaller** of line 19 or line 22 23		
	(If you paid state unemployment contributions late or you're in a credit reduction state, see instructions and check here) . . . . ☐		
24	**FUTA tax.** Subtract line 23 from line 21. Enter the result here and go to line 25 24		

Part III Total Household Employment Taxes

25	Enter the amount from line 8. If you checked the "**Yes**" box on line C of page 1, enter -0- 25	
26	Add line 16 (or line 24) and line 25 26	
27	Are you required to file Form 1040?	
	☐ **Yes. Stop.** Include the amount from line 26 above on Schedule 2 (Form 1040), line 9. **Don't** complete Part IV below.	
	☐ **No.** You may have to complete Part IV. See instructions for details.	

Part IV Address and Signature — Complete this part **only** if required. See the line 27 instructions.

Address (number and street) or P.O. box if mail isn't delivered to street address | Apt., room, or suite no.

City, town or post office, state, and ZIP code

Under penalties of perjury, I declare that I have examined this schedule, including accompanying statements, and to the best of my knowledge and belief, it is true, correct, and complete. No part of any payment made to a state unemployment fund claimed as a credit was, or is to be, deducted from the payments to employees. Declaration of preparer (other than taxpayer) is based on all information of which preparer has any knowledge.

Employer's signature ▶ _____ Date ▶ _____

Paid Preparer Use Only

Print/Type preparer's name	Preparer's signature	Date	Check ☐ if self-employed	PTIN
Firm's name ▶			Firm's EIN ▶	
Firm's address ▶			Phone no.	

Schedule H (Form 1040) 2024

6-7 Special Taxes for High-Income Taxpayers

6.7 Learning Objective
Compute the special taxes for high-income taxpayers.

There are two separate Medicare taxes for certain high-income taxpayers to help cover the cost of the Affordable Care Act (ACA). The first is the 3.8 percent net investment income tax. The second is a 0.9 percent additional Medicare tax on wages and self-employment income.

6-7a The 3.8 Percent Medicare Tax on Net Investment Income

The ACA imposes a 3.8 percent Medicare tax on the net investment income of individuals with modified AGI over $250,000 for joint filers ($125,000 if married filing separate), and $200,000 for single filers (note that these amounts are not adjusted for inflation). Modified AGI is adjusted gross income increased by certain foreign earned income amounts not covered in this textbook. Investment income subject to the additional 3.8 percent tax includes the following:

- Interest and dividends (excluding tax-exempt interest)
- Royalties
- Annuities
- Net rental income, with some exceptions
- Passive activities
- Most gains on the sale of capital and other assets

Income not subject to the 3.8 percent tax includes the following:

- Tax-exempt interest
- Excluded gain on the sale of a principal residence
- Distributions from retirement plans and individual retirement accounts
- Wages and self-employment income (earned income); however, this income may be subject to a 0.9 percent Medicare tax

Deductions allowed in arriving at net investment income subject to tax include:

- State income taxes reasonably allocated to the investment income
- Investment interest expense

The $3,000 net deduction allowed for capital losses in excess of capital gains for regular tax purposes and net operating losses is not allowed to reduce net investment income. Additional rules govern which income and deductions are included in calculating net investment income. The net investment income tax is reported on Form 8960 shown on Page 6-27.

Example Consider each of the following single taxpayers:

Taxpayer	A	B	C
Investment Income	$ 50,000	$ 80,000	$ 80,000
Modified AGI	190,000	220,000	340,000

The 3.8 percent net investment income tax would be calculated in each case as follows:

Taxpayer	A	B	C
Modified AGI	$190,000	$220,000	$340,000
Threshold	200,000	200,000	200,000
Excess over Threshold	n/a	20,000	140,000
Investment Income	50,000	80,000	80,000
Lesser of Excess or Investment Income	n/a	20,000	80,000
Tax Rate	3.8%	3.8%	3.8%
Net Investment Income Tax	$ 0	$ 760	$ 3,040

♦

6-7b The 0.9 Percent Additional Medicare Tax on Earned Income

In addition to the 3.8 percent Medicare tax on net investment income, the ACA imposed a 0.9 percent Medicare tax on high-income taxpayers' earned income such as salaries, wages, and self-employment income. The 0.9 percent tax applies to high-income taxpayers defined as taxpayers with earned income from wages, compensation, and self-employment income over the following thresholds (which are not adjusted for inflation each year):

a. $250,000 for joint filers
b. $125,000 if married filing separately
c. $200,000 for single filers [including head of household and qualifying widow(er)s]

The ordinary Medicare tax is 2.9 percent of earned income with no upper limitation. Employees split the cost of this tax with employers, with the employee paying 1.45 percent through withholding, and the employer paying 1.45 percent directly. Self-employed individuals pay the full 2.9 percent as calculated on Schedule SE with their Form 1040 income tax return. There is no employer match for the 0.9 percent Medicare tax. The 0.9 percent Medicare tax is reported on Form 8959 (refer to Page 6-28).

6-7c Employees

The 0.9 percent Medicare tax must be withheld from each employee with a salary in excess of $200,000, whether single or married. Married couples must combine their earned income and compare the total with the $250,000 threshold for married taxpayers to determine if they owe the 0.9 percent Medicare tax. Depending on the income of each spouse, the couple may owe additional 0.9 percent Medicare tax when computing the 0.9 percent Medicare tax on their Form 1040 to make up for amounts not fully withheld, or they may treat the excess amount withheld as an additional tax payment. The withholding is reported on each individual's Form W-2 along with other Medicare withholding.

Example Page and Genette are married. Page earns $225,000 in 2024 and Genette does not work. They have no other income in 2024. Page's employer must withhold $225 [0.9% × ($225,000 − $200,000)], from wages. Because Page and Genette do not have earned income in their joint return in excess of the $250,000 threshold for joint filers, the $225 withholding will be treated as an additional payment when they file their Form 1040 income tax return for 2024. ♦

Example Fran and Steve are married and each has wages of $150,000. Because they each earn less than $200,000, their employers are not required to withhold the 0.9 percent Medicare tax. However, when they file their 2024 Form 1040, they will be required to pay $450 (0.9% × $50,000) with their tax return since their $300,000 in joint earnings exceeds the $250,000 threshold for married taxpayers filing jointly. ♦

Example Johnny is single and changes jobs during 2024. His wages are $175,000 from each job for a total of $350,000 of wage income. Johnny's employers are not required to withhold any 0.9 percent Medicare tax from his wages since he does not reach the $200,000 threshold in either job. Johnny must pay $1,350 (0.9% × $150,000, the excess of $350,000 over the $200,000 single threshold amount) with his tax return for 2024. ♦

6-7d Self-Employed Taxpayers

Self-employed taxpayers generally report earnings on Schedule C, Schedule F, and Schedule E in the case of earned royalty income and partnership income passed through on Schedule K-1. The 0.9 percent Medicare tax for self-employed taxpayers must be paid with Form 1040. The following additional rules apply to high-income, self-employed taxpayers:

a. The 0.9 percent Medicare tax is not allowed as part of the computation of the deductible self-employment tax adjustment for AGI shown on the front page of Form 1040.
b. A loss from self-employment may offset gains from another self-employment enterprise by the same individual. In the case of married individuals filing jointly, a loss incurred by one spouse may offset the income earned by the other self-employed spouse for purposes of the 0.9 percent Medicare tax. This is not true for the 2.9 percent Medicare tax on self-employment income because the 2.9 percent Medicare tax of each spouse is required to be computed separately.
c. Losses from self-employment are not allowed to offset salary or wages for purposes of the 0.9 percent Medicare tax.

Example In 2024, Barry is single and earns $500,000 from his construction business, and has a loss of $100,000 from his commercial nursery business. Both businesses are reported on Schedule C in his income tax return. His net self-employment earnings of $400,000 exceed the single individual threshold by $200,000. He must pay $1,800 with his 2024 Form 1040 (0.9% × $200,000) to cover his 0.9 percent Medicare tax. None of the $1,800 is allowed as part of the computation of the self-employment tax adjustment included with his deductions for AGI. ♦

Self-Study Problem 6.7

a. Thornton Meloni is single and independently wealthy. His wages come from his job as a vice-president at a local bank (founded by his great-grandfather) and all of his interest, dividends, and capital gains are from his large investment portfolio of publicly-traded stocks and bonds. He also operates a small business in which he actively participates.

His 2024 Form 1040 is almost complete and reports the following amounts:

Line 1a: $200,000 (wages)
Line 2a: $48,000 (tax-exempt interest)
Line 2b: $54,000 (taxable interest)
Line 3a: $45,000 (qualified dividends)
Line 3b: $45,000 (total dividends)
Line 7: $22,000 (capital gains)
Line 8 and Schedule 1, Line 3: $12,000 (business income)
Line 11: $333,000 (AGI)

He has no investment expenses associated with this income, no foreign earnings exclusion, and lives where there is no state income tax. Complete Form 8960 on Page 6-27 to calculate Thornton's 2024 net investment income tax.

b. Meng and Eang Ung are married. Meng is self-employed and generates self-employment income (Schedule SE, line 6) of $130,000. Eang is a physician at a local hospital and her Form W-2 is presented below. Eang and Meng have no other earned or unearned income. Complete Form 8959 on Page 6-28 to determine how much 0.9 percent additional Medicare tax on earned income Meng and Eang must pay with their joint tax return in 2024 and what 0.9 percent additional Medicare tax withholding will they report?

Form W-2 Wage and Tax Statement — 2024

Box	Description	Amount
a	Employee's social security number	490-22-1818
b	Employer identification number (EIN)	35-1209444
c	Employer's name, address, and ZIP code	General Hospital, 104 Rochester Parkway, Port Charles, NY 14098
e	Employee's name and address	Eang Ung, 25 Lake Ontario Avenue, Port Charles, NY 14098
1	Wages, tips, other compensation	266,000.00
2	Federal income tax withheld	75,000.00
3	Social security wages	168,600.00
4	Social security tax withheld	10,453.20
5	Medicare wages and tips	266,000.00
6	Medicare tax withheld	4,451.00
13	Retirement plan	X
15	State / Employer's state ID number	NY / PCGH334012
16	State wages, tips, etc.	266,000.00
17	State income tax	21,280.00

Self-Study Problem 6.7, Part a

Form 8960
Department of the Treasury
Internal Revenue Service

Net Investment Income Tax—Individuals, Estates, and Trusts
Attach to your tax return.
Go to *www.irs.gov/Form8960* for instructions and the latest information.

OMB No. 1545-2227
2024
Attachment Sequence No. **72**

Name(s) shown on your tax return

Your social security number or EIN

Part I Investment Income

☐ Section 6013(g) election (see instructions)
☐ Section 6013(h) election (see instructions)
☐ Regulations section 1.1411-10(g) election (see instructions)

1	Taxable interest (see instructions)	1
2	Ordinary dividends (see instructions)	2
3	Annuities (see instructions)	3
4a	Rental real estate, royalties, partnerships, S corporations, trusts, trades or businesses, etc. (see instructions) 4a	
b	Adjustment for net income or loss derived in the ordinary course of a non-section 1411 trade or business (see instructions) 4b	
c	Combine lines 4a and 4b	4c
5a	Net gain or loss from disposition of property (see instructions) 5a	
b	Net gain or loss from disposition of property that is not subject to net investment income tax (see instructions) 5b	
c	Adjustment from disposition of partnership interest or S corporation stock (see instructions) 5c	
d	Combine lines 5a through 5c	5d
6	Adjustments to investment income for certain CFCs and PFICs (see instructions)	6
7	Other modifications to investment income (see instructions)	7
8	Total investment income. Combine lines 1, 2, 3, 4c, 5d, 6, and 7	8

Part II Investment Expenses Allocable to Investment Income and Modifications

9a	Investment interest expenses (see instructions) 9a	
b	State, local, and foreign income tax (see instructions) . . . 9b	
c	Miscellaneous investment expenses (see instructions) . . . 9c	
d	Add lines 9a, 9b, and 9c	9d
10	Additional modifications (see instructions)	10
11	Total deductions and modifications. Add lines 9d and 10	11

Part III Tax Computation

12	Net investment income. Subtract Part II, line 11, from Part I, line 8. Individuals, complete lines 13–17. Estates and trusts, complete lines 18a–21. If zero or less, enter -0-	12
	Individuals:	
13	Modified adjusted gross income (see instructions) 13	
14	Threshold based on filing status (see instructions) 14	
15	Subtract line 14 from line 13. If zero or less, enter -0- 15	
16	Enter the smaller of line 12 or line 15	16
17	Net investment income tax for individuals. Multiply line 16 by 3.8% (0.038). **Enter here and include on your tax return** (see instructions)	17
	Estates and Trusts:	
18a	Net investment income (line 12 above) 18a	
b	Deductions for distributions of net investment income and charitable deductions (see instructions) 18b	
c	Undistributed net investment income. Subtract line 18b from line 18a (see instructions). If zero or less, enter -0- 18c	
19a	Adjusted gross income (see instructions) 19a	
b	Highest tax bracket for estates and trusts for the year (see instructions) . . 19b	
c	Subtract line 19b from line 19a. If zero or less, enter -0- 19c	
20	Enter the smaller of line 18c or line 19c	20
21	Net investment income tax for estates and trusts. Multiply line 20 by 3.8% (0.038). **Enter here and include on your tax return** (see instructions)	21

For Paperwork Reduction Act Notice, see your tax return instructions.   Cat. No. 59474M   Form **8960** (2024)

Self-Study Problem 6.7, Part b

Form 8959
Department of the Treasury
Internal Revenue Service

Additional Medicare Tax

If any line does not apply to you, leave it blank. See separate instructions.
Attach to Form 1040, 1040-SR, 1040-NR, or 1040-SS.
Go to *www.irs.gov/Form8959* for instructions and the latest information.

OMB No. 1545-0074

2024

Attachment Sequence No. **71**

Name(s) shown on return | Your social security number

Part I Additional Medicare Tax on Medicare Wages

1. Medicare wages and tips from Form W-2, box 5. If you have more than one Form W-2, enter the total of the amounts from box 5 . . . . **1**
2. Unreported tips from Form 4137, line 6 . . . . **2**
3. Wages from Form 8919, line 6 . . . . **3**
4. Add lines 1 through 3 . . . . **4**
5. Enter the following amount for your filing status:
   Married filing jointly $250,000
   Married filing separately $125,000
   Single, Head of household, or Qualifying surviving spouse . . . $200,000 **5**
6. Subtract line 5 from line 4. If zero or less, enter -0- **6**
7. Additional Medicare Tax on Medicare wages. Multiply line 6 by 0.9% (0.009). Enter here and go to Part II **7**

Part II Additional Medicare Tax on Self-Employment Income

8. Self-employment income from Schedule SE (Form 1040), Part I, line 6. If you had a loss, enter -0- **8**
9. Enter the following amount for your filing status:
   Married filing jointly $250,000
   Married filing separately $125,000
   Single, Head of household, or Qualifying surviving spouse . . . $200,000 **9**
10. Enter the amount from line 4 . . . . **10**
11. Subtract line 10 from line 9. If zero or less, enter -0- **11**
12. Subtract line 11 from line 8. If zero or less, enter -0- **12**
13. Additional Medicare Tax on self-employment income. Multiply line 12 by 0.9% (0.009). Enter here and go to Part III **13**

Part III Additional Medicare Tax on Railroad Retirement Tax Act (RRTA) Compensation

14. Railroad retirement (RRTA) compensation and tips from Form(s) W-2, box 14 (see instructions) **14**
15. Enter the following amount for your filing status:
    Married filing jointly $250,000
    Married filing separately $125,000
    Single, Head of household, or Qualifying surviving spouse . . . $200,000 **15**
16. Subtract line 15 from line 14. If zero or less, enter -0- **16**
17. Additional Medicare Tax on railroad retirement (RRTA) compensation. Multiply line 16 by 0.9% (0.009). Enter here and go to Part IV **17**

Part IV Total Additional Medicare Tax

18. Add lines 7, 13, and 17. Also include this amount on Schedule 2 (Form 1040), line 11 (Form 1040-SS filers, see instructions), and go to Part V **18**

Part V Withholding Reconciliation

19. Medicare tax withheld from Form W-2, box 6. If you have more than one Form W-2, enter the total of the amounts from box 6 . . . . **19**
20. Enter the amount from line 1 . . . . **20**
21. Multiply line 20 by 1.45% (0.0145). This is your regular Medicare tax withholding on Medicare wages **21**
22. Subtract line 21 from line 19. If zero or less, enter -0-. This is your Additional Medicare Tax withholding on Medicare wages **22**
23. Additional Medicare Tax withholding on railroad retirement (RRTA) compensation from Form W-2, box 14 (see instructions) **23**
24. **Total Additional Medicare Tax withholding.** Add lines 22 and 23. Also include this amount with federal income tax withholding on Form 1040, 1040-SR, or 1040-NR, line 25c (Form 1040-SS filers, see instructions) **24**

For Paperwork Reduction Act Notice, see your tax return instructions. Cat. No. 59475X Form **8959** (2024)

6-8 Special Taxpayer Situations

This section of the textbook is designed to provide modest exposure to some of the unique situations that tax preparers may encounter. The tax law in these areas tends to be complex and could provide enough content to fill its own textbook. Each of the areas selected were compiled from a review of various state requirements for federal income tax preparation in states which have such requirements (Oregon, California, and Maryland) and from the IRS' annual filing season program.

6.8 Learning Objective

Describe the basic rules surrounding special taxpayer situations such as divorce, deceased taxpayers, nonresident taxpayers, and farmers.

6-8a Tax Return Errors

From time to time, a taxpayer, tax preparer, or an employer will make a mistake in preparing an income tax return or an information-reporting return such as Form W-2. Understanding that mistakes are occasionally made, the IRS has created procedures to address such situations.

W-2 or 1099-R Wrong or Not Received

If a taxpayer does not receive Forms W-2 or 1099-R (the deadline to send these forms is generally January 31 of the following year), the first and obvious step is to contact the employer or payer and request the missing form. If the forms cannot be obtained, the next step is to contact the IRS and provide identification information and if requested, provide the dates of employment. The IRS recommends contacting them at or around the end of February. The IRS will also send a Form 4852 to the taxpayer if needed. If the missing form is not received by the filing deadline, the taxpayer uses Form 4852 as a substitute Form W-2 or 1099-R based on the year-to-date information known (from paystubs or pension statements). Filing a Form 4852 may cause delays in processing a refund payment.

If a taxpayer receives incorrect Forms W-2 or 1099-R, the first step is to contact the payer to get a corrected form. An employer should provide a Form W-2c (a corrected Form W-2). This form reports the original information and the corrected information on the face of the form (refer to excerpt of federal portion in Figure 6.1). A pension recipient will receive a corrected 1099-R, which is the typical Form 1099-R with the Corrected box marked.

For a missing or corrected form, if the taxpayer has already filed a tax return using incorrect data, the taxpayer has a responsibility to file an amended tax return (Form 1040-X) as presented in the next section. Taxpayers wishing to avoid amending a tax return may want to wait as long as possible to file the original return to increase the chance of receiving the corrected information before the deadline, and thus, avoid the need to amend.

Amended Tax Returns

When a taxpayer files an incorrect tax return, the taxpayer is responsible for amending that return and filing a corrected version on Form 1040-X (which can be electronically filed if amending Forms 1040 or 1040-SR). In general, Form 1040-X requires the taxpayer to report the original amount of income, deductions, credits, or payments and the corrected amount of the same items. Refer to Form 1040-X on Pages 6-31 and 6-32.

However, there are a large number of reasons to file a Form 1040-X besides an incorrect amount (for minor math errors, conventional wisdom is to not file an amended return and let the IRS send a correction notice to the taxpayer first).

Additional common reasons to amend include:

- Change in filing status
- Change from resident taxpayer to nonresident
- Incorrect or missing dependent
- Claim a refund due to a casualty loss or net operating loss in a subsequent year being carried back

Figure 6.1 Form W-2c

[Form W-2c image - standard IRS form for Corrected Wage and Tax Statement, OMB No. 1545-0029, showing boxes a-i for employer/employee information and numbered boxes 1-14 with "Previously reported" and "Correct information" columns]

Example Martha paper-filed her original tax return and made a mathematical error when computing her tax liability. She ended up paying too much tax as a result. Martha should consider waiting until the IRS has processed her tax return and sends her a correction notice, rather than file an amended return. ♦

Example Lew filed his tax return and omitted self-employment income. This error is not likely to be identified by the IRS while processing Lew's return and Lew should file an amended return. ♦

When preparing a Form 1040-X, the taxpayer should generally prepare amended versions of forms that are affected.

Example Hayder accidentally failed to report any deductible charitable contributions on his Schedule A. When preparing the Form 1040-X, Hayder should also prepare a revised Schedule A to attach to his Form 1040-X. ♦

Form **1040-X**	Department of the Treasury—Internal Revenue Service		
(Rev. February 2024)	**Amended U.S. Individual Income Tax Return**		OMB No. 1545-0074
	Go to *www.irs.gov/Form1040X* for instructions and the latest information.		

This return is for calendar year (enter year) _____   **or fiscal year** (enter month and year ended) _____

Your first name and middle initial	Last name	Your social security number
If joint return, spouse's first name and middle initial	Last name	Spouse's social security number
Home address (number and street). If you have a P.O. box, see instructions.	Apt. no.	**Presidential Election Campaign**
City, town, or post office. If you have a foreign address, also complete spaces below. State ZIP code		Check here if you, or your spouse if filing jointly, didn't previously want $3 to go to this fund, but now do. Checking a box below will not change your tax or refund.
Foreign country name Foreign province/state/county Foreign postal code		☐ You ☐ Spouse

Amended return filing status. You **must** check one box even if you are not changing your filing status. **Caution:** In general, you can't change your filing status from married filing jointly to married filing separately after the return due date.

☐ Single ☐ Married filing jointly ☐ Married filing separately (MFS) ☐ Head of household (HOH) ☐ Qualifying surviving spouse (QSS)

If you checked the MFS box, enter the name of your spouse unless you are amending a Form 1040-NR. If you checked the HOH or QSS box, enter the child's name if the qualifying person is a child but not your dependent:

	Enter on lines 1 through 23, columns A through C, the amounts for the return year entered above. Use Part II on page 2 to explain any changes.		**A.** Original amount reported or as previously adjusted (see instructions)	**B.** Net change—amount of increase or (decrease)—explain in Part II	**C.** Correct amount
	Income and Deductions				
1	Adjusted gross income. If a net operating loss (NOL) carryback is included, check here ☐	1			
2	Itemized deductions or standard deduction	2			
3	Subtract line 2 from line 1	3			
4a	Reserved for future use	4a			
b	Qualified business income deduction	4b			
5	Taxable income. Subtract line 4b from line 3. If the result for column C is zero or less, enter -0- in column C	5			
	Tax Liability				
6	Tax. Enter method(s) used to figure tax (see instructions): _____	6			
7	Nonrefundable credits. If a general business credit carryback is included, check here ☐	7			
8	Subtract line 7 from line 6. If the result is zero or less, enter -0-	8			
9	Reserved for future use	9			
10	Other taxes	10			
11	Total tax. Add lines 8 and 10	11			
	Payments				
12	Federal income tax withheld and excess social security and tier 1 RRTA tax withheld. (**If changing**, see instructions.)	12			
13	Estimated tax payments, including amount applied from prior year's return	13			
14	Earned income credit (EIC)	14			
15	Refundable credits from: ☐ Schedule 8812 Form(s) ☐ 2439 ☐ 4136 ☐ 8863 ☐ 8885 ☐ 8962 or ☐ other (specify): _____	15			
16	Total amount paid with request for extension of time to file, tax paid with original return, and additional tax paid after return was filed				16
17	Total payments. Add lines 12 through 15, column C, and line 16				17
	Refund or Amount You Owe				
18	Overpayment, if any, as shown on original return or as previously adjusted by the IRS				18
19	Subtract line 18 from line 17. (If less than zero, see instructions.)				19
20	**Amount you owe.** If line 11, column C, is more than line 19, enter the difference				20
21	If line 11, column C, is less than line 19, enter the difference. This is the amount **overpaid** on this return				21
22	Amount of line 21 you want **refunded to you**				22
23	Amount of line 21 you want **applied to your** (enter year): _____ estimated tax	23			

Complete and sign this form on page 2.

For Paperwork Reduction Act Notice, see separate instructions.   Cat. No. 11360L   Form **1040-X** (Rev. 2-2024)

Form 1040-X (Rev. 2-2024) Page **2**

Part I — Dependents

Complete this part to change any information relating to your dependents. This would include a change in the number of dependents. Enter the information for the return year entered at the top of page 1.

		A. Original number of dependents reported or as previously adjusted	**B.** Net change—amount of increase or (decrease)	**C.** Correct number
24	Reserved for future use			
25	Your dependent children who lived with you			
26	Reserved for future use			
27	Other dependents			
28	Reserved for future use			
29	Reserved for future use			

30 List **ALL** dependents (children and others) claimed on this amended return.

Dependents (see instructions):

If more than four dependents, see instructions and check here ☐

(a) First name	Last name	(b) Social security number	(c) Relationship to you	(d) Check the box if qualifies for (see instructions)	
				Child tax credit	Credit for other dependents
				☐	☐
				☐	☐
				☐	☐
				☐	☐

Part II — Explanation of Changes.

In the space provided below, tell us why you are filing Form 1040-X. Attach any supporting documents and new or changed forms and schedules.

Remember to keep a copy of this form for your records.

Under penalties of perjury, I declare that I have filed an original return, and that I have examined this amended return, including accompanying schedules and statements, and to the best of my knowledge and belief, this amended return is true, correct, and complete. Declaration of preparer (other than taxpayer) is based on all information about which the preparer has any knowledge.

Sign Here

Your signature	Date	Your occupation	If the IRS sent you an Identity Protection PIN, enter it here (see inst.)
Spouse's signature. If a joint return, **both** must sign.	Date	Spouse's occupation	If the IRS sent your spouse an Identity Protection PIN, enter it here (see inst.)
Phone no.		Email address	

Paid Preparer Use Only

Preparer's name	Preparer's signature	Date	PTIN	Check if: ☐ Self-employed
Firm's name			Phone no.	
Firm's address			Firm's EIN	

For forms and publications, visit *www.irs.gov/Forms*. Form **1040-X** (Rev. 2-2024)

In some instances, certain items are permitted to be omitted from the Form 1040-X, as discussed in the instructions for Form 1040-X.

Example Louisa accidentally filed a Form 1040 as a resident taxpayer, not realizing she is a nonresident for the current tax year and should have filed Form 1040-NR. The Form 1040-X instructions instruct Louisa to provide her identifying information at the top of page 1 of Form 1040-X but not complete any of the income, deductions, credits or tax information nor any of Parts I or II. Instead, Louisa is instructed to complete a new Form 1040-NR and submit the entire return with her Form 1040-X on which she provides the reason for the amendment in Part III. ♦

With the advent of electronic filing of amended returns, tax preparers should pay careful attention to the Form 1040-X instructions as they provide detailed procedures for a number of special situations and are subject to change.

6-8b Divorce and Separation

Recent data shows that somewhere between 750,000 and 1 million people get divorced in the United States each year and that about one-third of all Americans over the age of 20 have been divorced once. The tax consequences of divorce extend beyond filing status (Chapter 1) and alimony, child support, and property divisions (Chapter 2). This section considers some of the more common tax-related outcomes of divorce.

Divorce is a determination made at the state level. The authority to marry and divorce is vested in states and thus, not all states follow the same rules or even use the same language when discussing the dissolution of a marriage. The tax rules that define "married status" for purposes of determination of filing status indicate that a taxpayer is unmarried if the taxpayer is single (never married) or has obtained a final decree of divorce or separate maintenance by the last day of the tax year and under state law the taxpayer is divorced or legally separated.

In most states, a divorce is considered final when a judge approves or signs the divorce decree or divorce settlement agreement. Unlike a divorce, a separation may have a number of different stages. For example, a trial separation generally does not require any court filings or approval by the state and simply entails the two spouses living apart. In most states, a legal separation is awarded through a court process and approved by a judge. Some states also offer a marriage annulment. An annulment is the state's recognition that a marriage was never legal (and often requires amending prior year returns). If the separation, divorce, or annulment are recognized by the state, the tax rules will generally follow and treat these taxpayers as unmarried (the abandoned spouse exception is covered in Chapter 1).

As covered in Chapter 2, the division of property between ex-spouses is not generally a taxable event. Technically, the transfers that are incident to a divorce are treated as a non-taxable gift if made within one year of the divorce. Special rules apply to property divisions of qualified retirement plan assets such as pensions, 401k, and other similar plans. Typically, distributions from qualified plans are subject to income tax and, if the taxpayer is under age 59½, a 10-percent penalty is assessed. A distribution pursuant to a qualified domestic relations order (QDRO); however, is not generally subject to the tax or penalty. A QDRO is issued by the court and recognizes that some form of retirement assets should also be divided between ex-spouses. The tax treatment that would have applied to the original owner of the retirement assets will apply to the new owner when distributions are made.

Example As part of Brad and Angelina's divorce, the court issues a QDRO providing that one-half of Angelina's 401k balance of $40,000 be transferred to Brad. Angelina and Angelina's employer had made only pre-tax contributions to the 401k account, and thus, Angelina had no basis in the plan assets. Brad will receive a distribution of $20,000 and if he places the transferred funds in a retirement account such as a rollover IRA, he will not be taxed on the transfer. When Brad turns 65 and starts taking distributions from the IRA, he will be taxed just as Angelina would have. ♦

Division of the assets in a health savings account work in the same fashion.

Tax Liability Issues with a Current or Former Spouse

When a married couple files a joint tax return, both partners are liable for the entire tax liability. There are three different ways a spouse can request relief from joint liability:

1. Innocent Spouse Relief
2. Separation of Liability Relief
3. Equitable Relief

As soon as a spouse determines they might be liable for a tax liability that should be attributed to only their spouse or former spouse, a Form 8857 should be filed to claim one of the above three forms of relief.

Innocent spouse relief provides relief from tax liability to a spouse or ex-spouse that was not aware of the liability when they signed the tax return. To qualify for innocent spouse relief, a taxpayer must meet the requirements presented in Figure 6.2 (from IRS Publication 971).

Figure 6.2 Innocent Spouse Relief Decision Tree

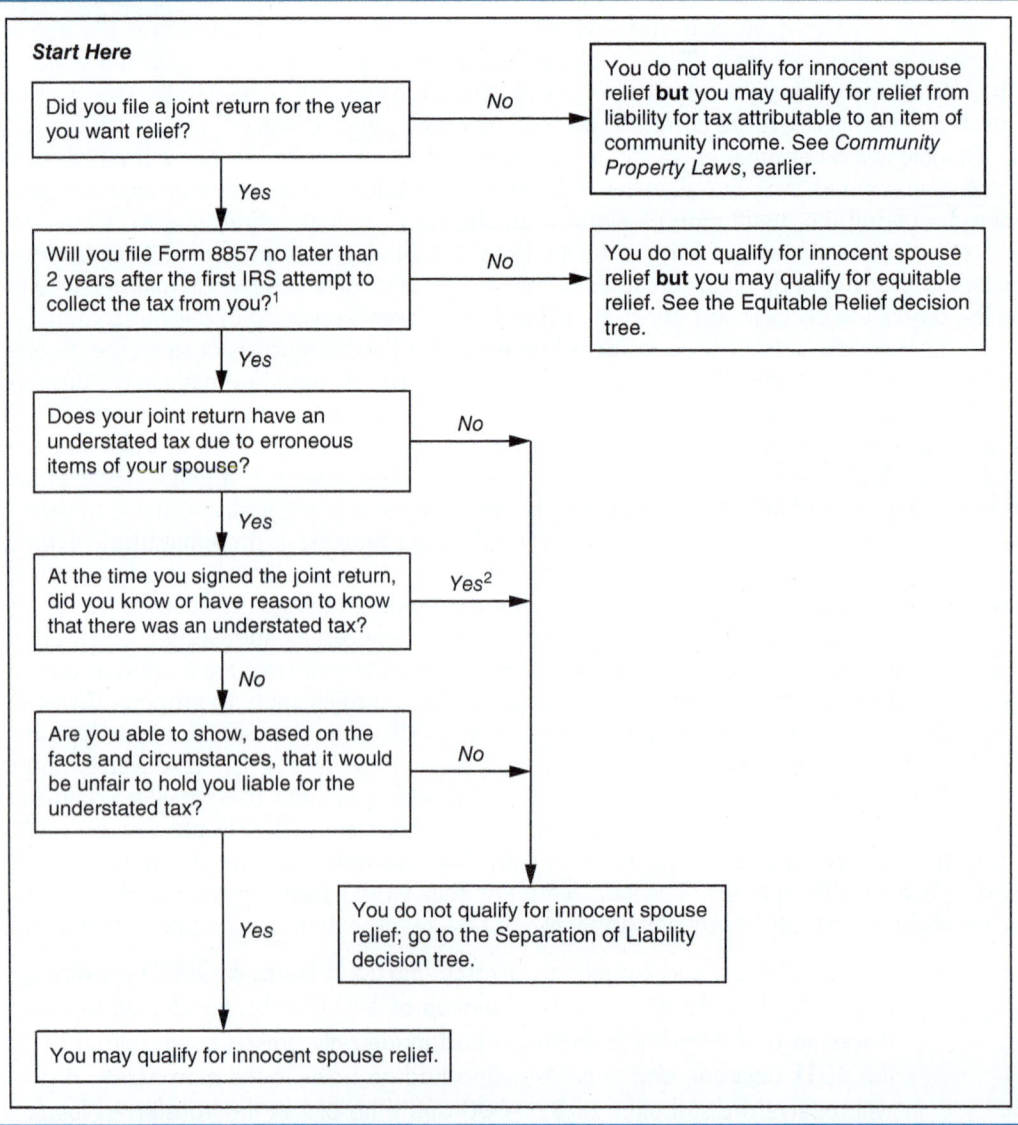

Source: IRS Publication 971

[1] Collection activities that may start the 2-year period are described earlier under *How To Request Relief*.
[2] You may qualify for partial relief if, at the time you filed your return, you knew or had reason to know of only a portion of an erroneous item.

Separation of liability relief pertains to situations in which the ex-spouse wishes to allocate the joint liability on a previously filed return to reflect each spouse's share of liability. Separation of liability relief is available only to taxpayers that have a final divorce decree or a legal separation and do not live in the same household for a 12-month period.

Example Bill and Karen filed a joint return in 2024. Karen reported wages of $50,000 and Bill reported self-employment income of $10,000. Subsequent to Bill and Karen's divorce, it was discovered that Bill should have reported an additional $20,000 of self-employment income. If Karen can demonstrate she qualifies for separation of liability relief, Bill will be separately liable for the tax, penalties, and interest on his understatement of income. ♦

Separation of liability relief requires that the spouse requesting relief have had no actual knowledge of the erroneous information at the time of the filing. There are exceptions to this requirement if the spouse was a victim of domestic violence or spousal abuse. Figure 6.3 on Page 6-36 shows the requirements for separation of liability relief.

Equitable relief is available only if the taxpayer does not qualify for innocent spouse or separation of liability relief. Of the three types of relief, only equitable relief will provide relief from an unpaid tax.

Example Brad and Jennifer's joint return shows that tax owed is $5,000 of which only $2,000 was paid with the return. Jennifer might be able to claim equitable relief from the remaining $3,000 tax to be paid. ♦

The requirements for equitable relief are shown in Figure 6.4 on Page 6-37.

All three claims for relief require that the taxpayer and spouse or former spouse did not transfer assets to one another as part of a fraudulent scheme for the main purpose of avoiding tax or the payment of tax.

Innocent spouse relief should not be confused with injured spouse relief. Injured spouse relief is when a joint return is filed and the refund is used to pay one spouse's past-due federal tax, state income tax, state unemployment compensation debts, child support, spousal support, or federal nontax debt, such as a student loan, resulting in the other spouse being considered an injured spouse. An injured spouse can get back their share of the joint overpayment using Form 8379. To be an injured spouse, the taxpayer must not be legally obligated to pay the past-due amount, and meet *any* of the following conditions: (1) the taxpayer claiming to be an injured spouse made and reported tax payments (such as federal income tax withholding or estimated tax payments), (2) the taxpayer had earned income (such as wages, salaries, or self-employment income) and claimed the earned income credit or the additional child tax credit, or (3) the taxpayer claimed a refundable tax credit, such as the health coverage tax credit or the refundable credit for prior year minimum tax.

Dependents of Divorced Spouses

In most instances, the dependent child of a divorced couple will be claimed by the custodial parent (due to the domicile test in Chapter 1). A child of divorced or separated parents can be a dependent of the noncustodial parent if all the following requirements are met:

- The parents are divorced, legally separated under a maintenance or written agreement or have lived apart for the last six months of the year
- The child received more than half of the support from the parents
- The child is in the custody of one or both the parents for more than one-half of the year
- The custodial parent signs a written declaration (Form 8332) that they will not claim the child that year

Figure 6.3 Separation of Liability Relief Decision Tree

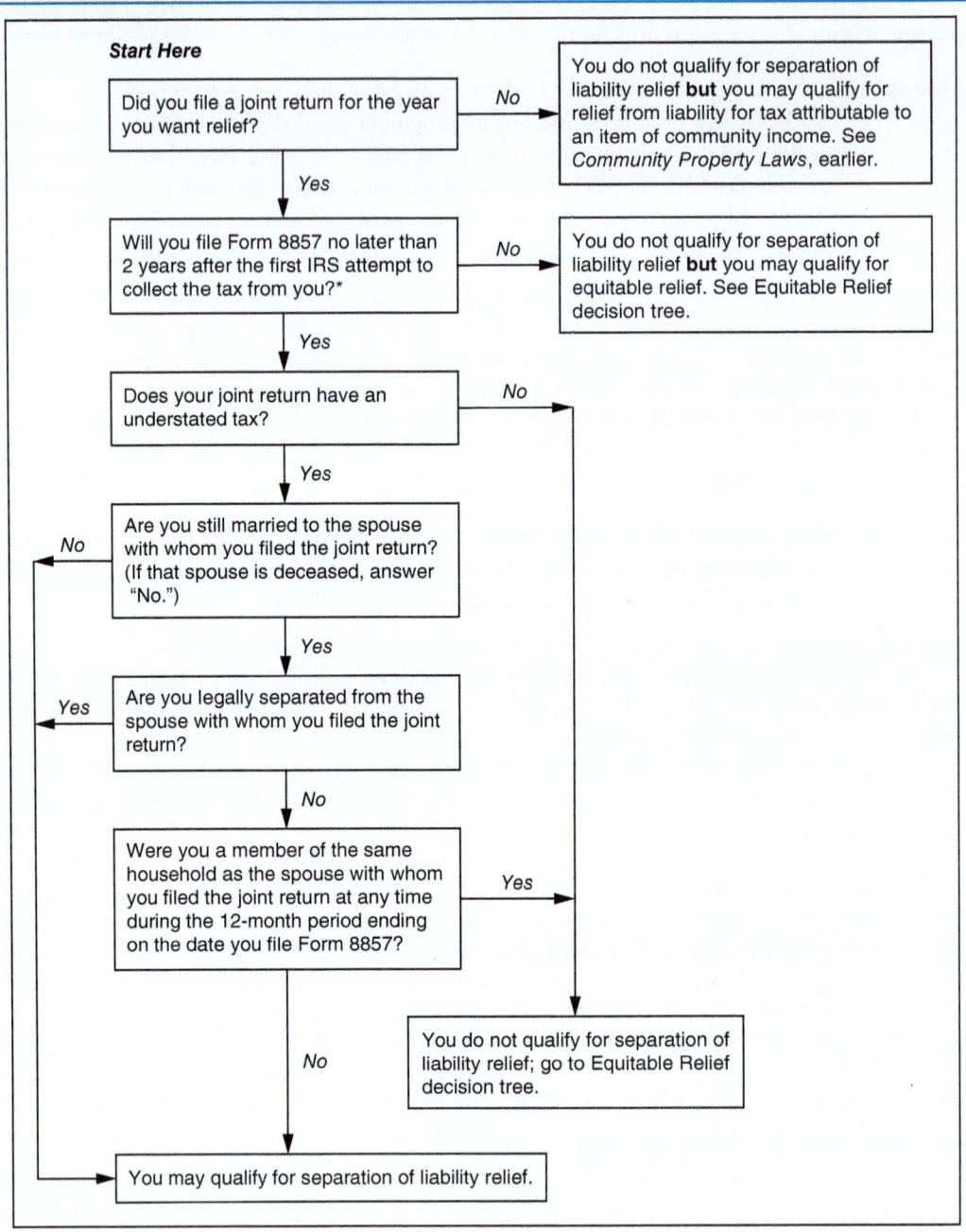

Source: IRS Publication 971

*Collection activities that may start the 2-year period are described earlier under *How To Request Relief*.

In some instances, a child could be claimed by either divorced parent. The tie-breaker rules discussed in Chapter 1 would apply.

Example Brad and Gwyneth, married couple, lived together with their son, Davos through the end of July 2024 at which time they legally separated. Davos moved with Gwyneth after the separation. Although both parents are able to claim Davos, Gwyneth will claim Davos because he lived with her for more of the year. Gwyneth could provide Brad with a Form 8332 showing she will not be claiming Davos, allowing Brad to claim Davos as a dependent. ♦

Figure 6.4 Equitable Relief Decision Tree

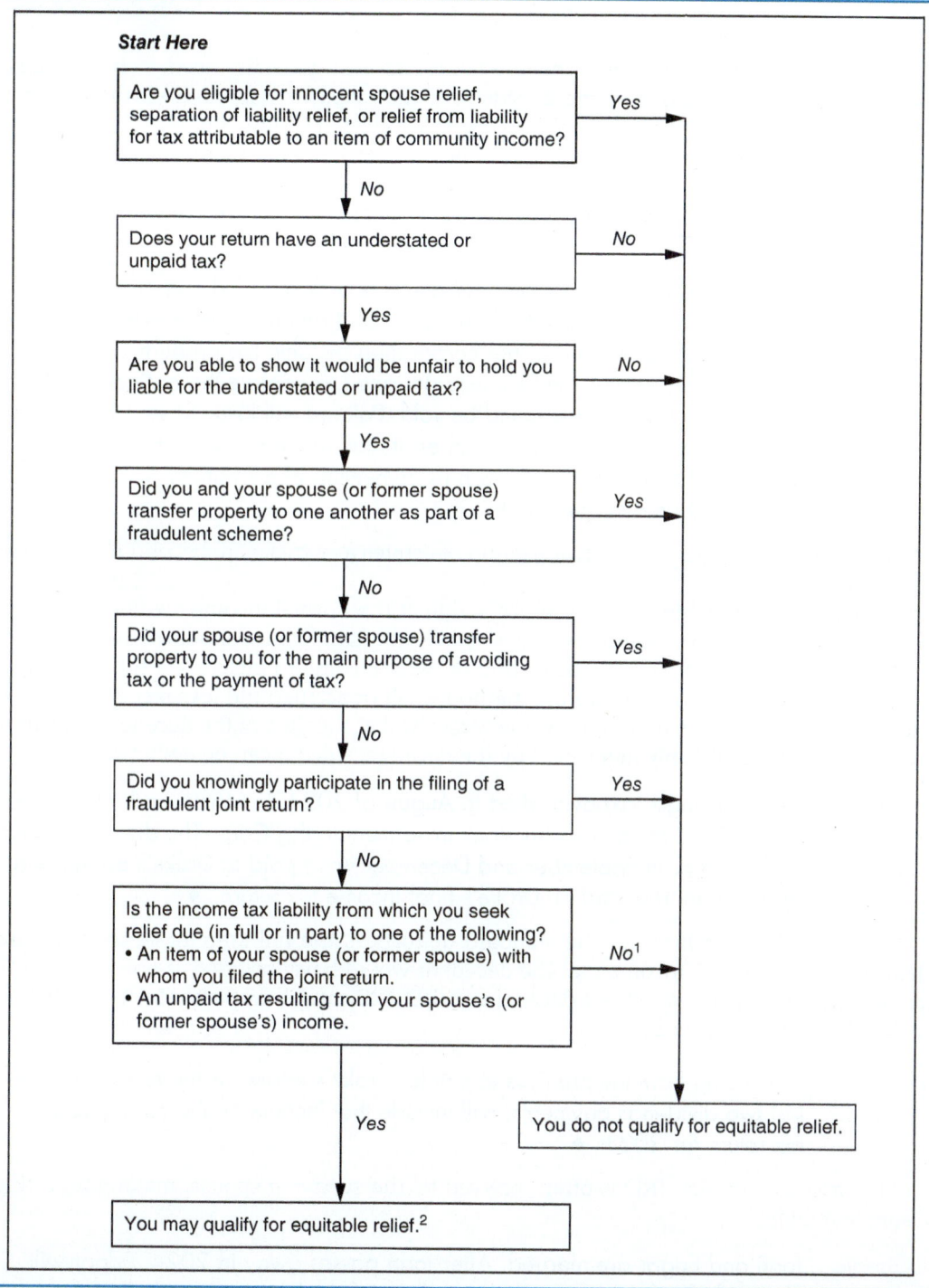

Source: IRS Publication 971

[1] You may qualify for equitable relief if you meet any of the exceptions to condition (7) discussed earlier under *Conditions for Getting Equitable Relief*.

[2] You must file Form 8857 by the filing deadlines explained earlier in *Exception for equitable relief* under *How To Request Relief*.

Nondeductible Divorce Expenses

Legal fees and court costs associated with a divorce are nondeductible. Fees paid to accountants for determining the correct tax, appraisers, actuaries, and other experts are also nondeductible.

6-8c Death of the Taxpayer

In 1789, Benjamin Franklin is purported to have said, "nothing is certain but death and taxes." This section discusses how death and taxes intersect, as even death does not prevent the payment of taxes.

When a taxpayer dies, a final income tax return will generally need to be prepared by a personal representative of the decedent. If the taxpayer was married, the personal representative can be, but is not required to be, the surviving spouse. As covered in Chapter 1, if a spouse dies, the surviving spouse can file married filing jointly for the year of death (and may be eligible for surviving spouse for two years thereafter). A taxpayer's death can introduce many different tax consequences such as estate and gift taxes, and under certain circumstances, an income tax requirement for the decedent's estate.

Example Paloma died in 2024. Among her assets is a closely-held corporation for which she was both the sole shareholder and an employee. Under the provisions of Paloma's will, her corporation became the property of a trust owned by her estate. The trust was designed to operate the business until such time as the business could be sold. Paloma will likely have a final personal income tax return and an estate tax return to report the transfer of her assets. Paloma's trust, through its ownership of a business, will also need to file an income tax return. ♦

Estate and gift taxes and the income taxation of estates and trusts are beyond the scope of this textbook.

The final individual income tax return is due at the normal income tax filing deadline of April 15 (or later if a weekend or holiday) and if not filing jointly, should state "deceased" on the top of the return. The determination of what income to include on the decedent's final return is based on the accounting method (cash or accrual) the taxpayer was using. If the cash method, only income constructively received at the time of the decedent's death is included and generally only items paid by the decedent's death can be deducted.

Example Drake, a single taxpayer, died in August of 2024. In March and June, Drake received dividends from his stock investment in Big Corp. The dividends paid by Big Corp. in September and December were paid to Drake's estate, and thus, are not reported on Drake's final income tax return. ♦

If the final return includes the standard deduction, the full amount of the standard deduction is permitted. Income that the decedent would have included, if not for death, is classified as income in respect of a decedent or IRD. IRD must be reported by the party that received the income after death.

Example Continuing from the previous example, Drake's estate, as the recipient of the last two dividends payments, will include that income on the estate income tax return for 2024. ♦

For married couples, IRD is often received by the surviving spouse, making reporting a simple matter.

Example Joan and Edgar are married. After Joan passes away in 2024, Edgar will file jointly for the tax year. Joan's will transferred ownership of all of the investments to Edgar upon her death. The income that Joan would have earned in 2024 but for her death, is now Edgar's income that he will report on the joint return. ♦

Because certain income will be allocated to the decedent's final tax return and IRD may be allocated to another income tax return, deductions may also need to be allocated between the two income tax returns. Deductions in respect of a decedent are reported on the return of the party that captured the IRD.

Example Gretchen died in 2024. Gretchen was operating a business on the cash basis, and the income of her business after death became the IRD of her estate. The business deductions that were incurred prior to her death but not paid until after her death are deducted on her estate income tax return. ♦

IRD can be included in the estate of the decedent (as part of estate tax) on which estate taxes are paid and the same IRD can also be reported on the estate's income tax return. In this situation, the estate's income tax return may deduct the estate taxes paid that are associated with the IRD.

If the estate of the decedent is terminated and the estate's final return results in unused NOL carryforwards or excess deductions (other than the charitable contributions deduction), the beneficiaries of the estate may claim the deductions on the beneficiary's tax return.

Example Amanda died in 2023. In 2024, her estate is winding up and reports an unused NOL of $10,000. All of Amanda's estate is being transferred to her daughter, Sarah. Sarah may use the estate's NOL on her own income tax return as permitted. ♦

The final tax liability is forgiven in its entirety for an armed forces member killed in combat, by military action, or by terrorist action, and for an astronaut killed in the line of duty.

If the personal representative filing the final income tax return is not a spouse or court appointed representative, Form 1310 must be filed in order to receive a refund.

The estate, trust, and gift tax consequences of the death of a taxpayer are complex. This section of the textbook provides an overview to raise awareness of the issues but does not contemplate a complete analysis of all the possible tax consequences associated with the death of a taxpayer.

6-8e Nonresident and International Issues

Taxpayers that are U.S. citizens, green card holders, or meet the requirements of the substantial presence test are treated as tax residents for income tax purposes. Any other individual that earns U.S. sourced income is treated as a nonresident for tax purposes.

Example Luka, a Croatian citizen, is in the United States for 170 days of 2024 working for his employer's office located in Dallas, TX. Luka is not considered a resident for U.S. tax purposes, but his income is sourced from the United States while in Dallas, and thus, is subject to U.S. income taxation. ♦

Nonresidents have a very different income tax regime in the United States and file a different tax form (Form 1040-NR). A nonresident that is married to a U.S. resident; however, can make an election to file a married filing jointly return. The election applies for the entire year in which it is made.

Example Bao and Hien are married, and both are nonresident aliens at the beginning of the year. In June, Bao became a resident alien and remained a resident alien for the rest of the year. Bao and Hien both elect to be treated as resident aliens. Bao and Hien must file a joint return for the year they make the election, but they can file either joint or separate returns for later years. ♦

The substantial presence test and the many additional differences between a nonresident and resident tax return are outside the scope of this textbook. Additional details can be found in the instructions to Form 1040-NR, IRS Publication 519, and IRS Publication 901.

Form 843

Most nonresidents are not subject to Social Security or Medicare taxes, but many employers will mistakenly withhold these taxes not realizing the exclusion. If a nonresident taxpayer has Social Security or Medicare taxes withheld in error, the taxpayer should contact the employer who withheld the taxes for a refund. If unable to get a full refund of the amount from the employer, the nonresident taxpayer should file a claim for refund with the IRS on Form 843 and attach the following items as appropriate:

- A copy of their Form W-2 to prove the amount of Social Security and Medicare taxes withheld.
- A copy of their visa.
- Form I-94 (or other documentation showing their dates of arrival or departure).
- A statement from the employer indicating the amount of the reimbursement the employer provided and the amount of the credit or refund the employer claimed or was authorized to claim. If this statement cannot be obtained from the employer, this information must be provided on Form 843 explaining why no statement from the employer is attached.
- If the nonresident taxpayer is a F, J, or M type visa holder, attach Form 8316.

Form 843 and attachments are filed at the Department of the Treasury Internal Revenue Service Center Ogden, UT 84201-0038 regardless of where the original tax return was filed.

Reporting Foreign Financial Accounts (FBAR, FinCEN, and Form 8938)

A U.S. person is subject to two separate reporting responsibilities with respect to a financial interest or signatory authority of a foreign financial account:

1. Reporting foreign financial accounts in the U.S. Treasury's Financial Crimes Enforcement Network (FinCEN)
2. Reporting specified foreign financial assets on Form 8938

If an individual has an interest in or authority over foreign financial accounts for which the aggregate value of all accounts exceeds $10,000 (in U.S. dollars or USD) at any time during the year, the individual is required to complete Report 114 in FinCEN's Bank Secrecy Act E-Filing System (**https://bsaefiling.fincen.treas.gov/main.html**), commonly known as FBAR. FinCEN is the same organization that administers beneficial ownership interest (BOI) reporting covered in Chapter 11.

Example Paula is a U.S. citizen. In 2024, Paula's father, who is a citizen and resident of Spain dies, and she inherits his bank account in a Spanish bank that holds the equivalent of USD 12,000. Paula has an FBAR filing requirement in 2024. ♦

Example Heather is a citizen of Nigeria but has been in the United States for three years and files as a United States tax resident starting in 2024. She maintains a joint personal bank account in Nigeria with her parents. If her Nigerian bank account has a value of over USD 10,000 at any time during the year, Heather will have a FBAR filing requirement. ♦

Example Gabe, a U.S. citizen, has signatory authority over three bank accounts in three different countries outside the United States. The bank accounts hold the equivalent of USD 3,000, $4,000, and $8,000 during 2024. Gabe is required to report all three accounts because the aggregate value exceeds USD 10,000. ♦

Form 8938 is used to report specified foreign assets if the value of those assets exceeds a specified reporting threshold. Table 6.2 presents common filing thresholds for individual taxpayers.

Table 6.2 Form 8938 Filing Thresholds

Filing Status	Timing	Living in U.S.	Living Outside U.S.
Married filing jointly	End of year	USD 100,000	USD 400,000
	During year	150,000	600,000
All Others	End of year	50,000	200,000
	During year	75,000	300,000

Example Joe is a single, U.S. citizen that lives in the United States in 2024. He owns specified foreign assets valued at USD 60,000 at the end of the year. Joe is required to file Form 8938 since his assets exceed the USD 50,000 threshold for an unmarried individual living in the United States. ♦

Filing FBAR does not relieve an individual from the requirements to file Form 8938 and vice versa.

Example In the previous example, Joe files Form 8938 with the IRS. Joe is also required to file FBAR since he has more than USD 10,000 in foreign financial assets. ♦

If a taxpayer is found to have willfully failed to report their relationship with foreign accounts, the penalties are the larger of $100,000 or 50 percent of the highest balance in the account. The U.S. courts are consistently ruling that willfulness includes reckless conduct.

6-8f Farmers

According to the U.S. Department of Agriculture, in 2020 there were over 1.7 million family-owned farms. The business of farming is the cultivation, operation, or management of a farm for profit, either as owner or tenant. A farm includes livestock, dairy, poultry, fish, fruit, and truck farms. It also includes plantations, ranches, ranges, and orchards and groves.

Farmers that operate their farms individually or with their spouse (as a qualified joint venture—covered in Chapter 10) report farming income and expenses on Schedule F of Form 1040. The tax law includes a number of special provisions that apply to farmers, making this area of taxation a specialty area that should not be taken on by a tax preparer without considerable additional training. Table 6.3 provides a selection of special tax provisions for farmers.

Table 6.3 Special Tax Provisions for Farmers

Provisions	Overview
Farm-price inventory method	Value at market price less cost to sell
Unit-livestock-price inventory method	Use a standard price for livestock based on age and type
Crop method of accounting	For crops not planted and harvested in the same year
Agricultural program payments	Government payments typically income
Commodity Credit Corporation loans	Treat loan as a sale if production used as collateral
Conservation Reserve Program	Payments generally treated as income
Crop Insurance and Disaster Payments	Generally income but can be deferred
Feed Assistance	Income in year received
Qualified farm debt	Exclude from cancellation of debt income
Income averaging	Use average tax rate from prior three years
Prepaid farm supplies	Cash-basis deduction, can be limited
Prepaid livestock feed	Cash-basis deduction, can be limited
Breeding fees	May need to be capitalized
Forestation and reforestation costs	Election to deduct
Soil and water conservation expenses	May be immediately deductible, but limited
Livestock sales	Can be treated as Section 1231
Farm and nonfarm optional methods of self-employment tax	Can reduce self-employment tax for low-income farmers
Fuel excise tax credit/refund	Credit or refund of excise taxes for fuel used for farming purposes
Estimated taxes	Payment timing can be later, if qualify

Source: Adapted from IRS Publication 225

Self-Study Problem 6.8

Refer to Appendix E for Solutions to Self-Study Problems

Determine whether each statement is true or false.

1. If a taxpayer does not receive a Form W-2, the first step is to contact the IRS.
2. An amended income tax return is filed on Form 1040-C.
3. A married couple in a trial separation should file as unmarried.
4. A division of the assets of a qualified retirement plan incident to divorce is handled by a QDRO.
5. If Mary believes that she should be relieved of the income tax liability that is unpaid at the time of filing, she should file for injured spouse relief.
6. Most individuals are not required to file an income tax return in the year of death.
7. Chamu's employer withheld Social Security and Medicare taxes from her wages even though Chamu is a nonresident and is not liable for employment taxes. Chamu should file a Form 1040-X.
8. A taxpayer that properly files Form 8938 to report foreign assets is not required to also file FBAR since the Form 8938 thresholds to file are higher.
9. Individual farmers file Schedule F to report farm income.

6-9 Military Taxpayers

Learning Objective 6.9

Identify significant differences in the tax law for members of the U.S. Armed Forces.

The tax law provides certain tax advantages to active members of the U.S. Armed Forces. The U.S. Armed Forces includes commissioned officers, warrant officers, and enlisted personnel in all regular and reserve units of the Army, Navy, and Air Force. This designation generally includes the U.S. Coast Guard and some members of the Public Health Service, and the National Oceanic and Atmospheric Administration are also eligible for many of the same benefits. Special benefits are available to individuals serving in combat zones.

6-9a Gross Income Inclusions and Exclusions

As with most employees, members of the armed forces include most forms of compensation in gross income. Living allowances and combat pay are significant forms of military pay that are excluded from gross income.

Basic allowance for housing (BAH) is an allowance to offset the cost of housing when the military taxpayer does not receive government-provided housing. The amount of BAH depends upon location, pay grade and whether a taxpayer has dependents. BAH rates in high-cost areas will be much greater than those in low-cost areas. Basic allowance for subsistence (BAS) is meant to offset costs for a military taxpayer's meals and is based on the tradition in which the military provides room and board (or rations) as part of a member's pay. Other allowances that are excluded include clothing allowance, dislocation allowance (DLA), family separation allowance (FSA), and family supplemental subsistence allowance (FSSA).

Example Mike Metcalf receives basic active duty pay of $30,000, a reenlistment bonus of $2,000, a BAH of $12,000 and a BAS of $6,000 in 2024. Based on this information, $32,000 of taxable compensation will be reported in Box 1 of Mike's Form W-2. The BAH and BAS are both excluded. ♦

The pay earned in the month a military taxpayer is assigned to a combat zone is also generally excluded for enlisted, warrant officers, and commissioned officers (a combat zone tax exclusion or CZTE). A combat zone is designated by the President of the United States by executive order. A list of current designated combat zones can be found at **www.dfas.mil/MilitaryMembers/payentitlements/Pay-Tables/CZ1/**. To be eligible for CZTE, the pay must have been earned in a month in which the taxpayer either serves in combat zone or was hospitalized as a result of a wound, disease or injury while serving in a combat zone. If serving outside a combat zone but the military designates the service in direct support of operations in the combat zone and the service is duty subject to hostile fire or imminent danger, the service is considered eligible for CZTE. Although excluded from taxable income, CTZE pay is considered earned income for purposes of an IRA deduction.

The foreign income exclusion (Chapter 7) is not generally available to members of the U.S. military; however, the exclusion may apply to the income of a spouse working overseas.

Veterans of the military who are discharged due to medical disability may receive a disability severance from the Department of Veterans Administration (VA). If the payments are associated with a combat-related injury or otherwise classified as disability compensation, the amounts are excluded from gross income. In some instances, the VA's decision to classify pension as disability pension will come after the pension payments have been made and the Form 1099-R will not reflect the exclusion. If a retroactive disability determination requires adjustment to reflect only the taxable portion of the pension, the military taxpayer should attach a copy of the VA's determination letter with the tax return (or amended tax return as needed).

Example On October 1, 2023, Sergeant Jordan O'Neal was medically separated from the Army. Beginning in 2024, O'Neal received a $1,000 per month pension. In August 2024, O'Neal received a VA determination letter showing she was entitled to a disability pension of 75 percent. For the last 4 months of 2024, O'Neal received monthly payments of $750 directly from the VA and $250 from her pension. O'Neal will need to adjust her 1099-R to reduce the taxable amount by $6,000 ($750 × 8 months). She should attach a copy of the VA determination letter to her tax return. ♦

As noted in Figure 6.5, a number of different pay classifications are available for military taxpayers. Fortunately, the taxpayer's Form W-2 should reflect the proper classification of pay as excluded or included. Generally, military taxpayers should not adjust the wages as reported on the Form W-2. If information on the W-2 appears incorrect, the taxpayer should contact their finance office to discuss the issue and have a corrected Form W-2c issued as needed.

Figure 6.5 Armed Forces Gross Income

Armed Forces Gross Income

Members of the Armed Forces receive many different types of pay and allowances. Some are included in gross income while others are excluded from gross income. **Table 1** lists included items that are subject to tax and must be reported on your tax return. **Table 2** lists excluded items that are not subject to tax, but may have to be shown on your tax return. See Publication 3, Armed Forces' Tax Guide, for additional information.

To determine taxability at the state level, check with your state's department of revenue.

Table 1—Included Items
These items are included in gross income, unless the pay is for service in a combat zone

Category	Items	Category	Items	Category	Items
Basic pay	• Active duty • Attendance at a designated service school • Back wages • Drills (Inactive Duty Training) • Reserve training • Training Duty	**Special pay (cont.)**	• Hostile fire or imminent danger • Medical and dental officers • Nuclear-qualified officers • Optometry • Other Health Professional Special Pay (for example, nurse, physician assistant, social work, etc.) • Pharmacy • Special compensation for assistance with activities of daily living (SCAADL) • Special duty assignment pay • Veterinarian • Voluntary Separation Incentive	**Incentive pay**	• Submarine • Flight • Hazardous duty • High altitude/Low altitude (HALO)
				Other pay	• Accrued leave • CONUS COLA • High deployment per diem • Personal money allowances paid to high ranking officers • Student loan repayment from programs such as the Department of Defense Educational Loan Repayment Program when year's service (requirement) isn't attributable to a combat zone
Special pay	• Aviation career incentives • Career sea • Diving duty • Foreign duty (outside the 48 contiguous states and the District of Columbia) • Foreign language proficiency • Hardship duty	**Bonus pay**	• Career status • Continuation pay • Enlistment • Officer • Overseas extension • Reenlistment	**In-kind military benefits**	• Personal use of government-provided vehicle

Table 2—Excluded Items
The exclusion for certain items applies whether the item is furnished in-kind or is a reimbursement or allowance. There is no exclusion for the personal use of a government-provided vehicle.

Category	Items	Category	Items	Category	Items
Combat zone and qualified hazardous duty area pay	• Compensation for active service while in a combat zone **Note:** Limited amount for commissioned officers • Leave earned or accrued while performing service in a combat zone	**Family allowances**	• Certain educational expenses for dependents • Emergencies • Evacuation to a place of safety • Separation	**Travel allowances**	• Annual round trip for dependent students • Leave between consecutive overseas tours • Reassignment in a dependent restricted status • Transportation for you or your dependents during ship overhaul or inactivation • Per diem
Other pay	• Certain amounts received under Armed Force Health Professions Scholarship and Financial Assistance Program payments • Disability, including payments received for injuries incurred as a direct result of a terrorist or military action • Disability severance payments • Group-term life insurance • Professional education • ROTC educational and subsistence allowances • State bonus pay for service in a combat zone • Survivor and retirement protection plan premiums • Uniform allowances • Uniforms furnished to enlisted personnel • Certain loan payments made by an employer after March 27, 2020, and before January 1, 2026, of principal or interest on certain qualified education loans.	**Living allowances**	• BAH (Basic Allowance for Housing) • BAS (Basic Allowance for Subsistence) • Housing and cost-of-living allowances abroad paid by the U.S. Government or by a foreign government • OHA (Overseas Housing Allowance)	**In-kind military benefits**	• Dependent-care assistance program • Defense Counsel Services • Legal assistance • Medical/dental care • Commissary/exchange discounts • Space-available travel on government aircraft • Uniforms furnished to enlisted personnel
Death allowances	• Burial services • Death gratuity payments to eligible survivors • Travel of dependents to burial site	**Moving allowances**	• Dislocation • Military base realignment and closure benefit (the exclusion is limited as described above) • Move-in housing • Move household and personal items • Moving trailers or mobile homes • Storage • Temporary lodging and temporary lodging expenses		

6-9b For AGI Deductions

As presented in Chapter 5, the deduction for moving costs (and the exclusion of moving allowances) are currently limited to military taxpayer's permanent change of station (PCS). A permanent change of station includes a move from:

- Home to the area of the first post of duty.
- One permanent post of duty to another.
- The last post of duty to home or to a nearer point in the United States. The armed forces' member must move within one year of ending active duty or within the period allowed under the Joint Travel Regulations.

Example Yana is a newly enlisted member of the U.S. Armed Forces and lives in Miami, FL. She has been assigned her first post of duty in San Diego, CA. Her move is considered a PCS. After seven years in the military, Yana leaves service. Her last station was Honolulu, HI, and she stays in Honolulu for two years after leaving service before returning to her hometown of Miami. Because she waited longer than one year, her move home is not a PCS. ♦

Moving expenses fall into two categories:

1. The cost of moving household goods and personal effects, and
2. Reasonable travel and lodging costs.

Moving household goods and effects includes expenses for hauling a trailer, packing, crating, in-transit storage, and insurance. Expenses for moving furniture or other items purchased on the way from the old home to the new home are not deductible. Storage of household goods within any period of 30 days after the goods are moved from the old home qualify. If the move is to a foreign country (not including U.S. possessions), the storage fees for the time the main job remains in a foreign country are deductible. Travel costs include lodging (but not meals), airline expenses, and car expenses under the mileage method ($0.21 per mile in 2024) or actual out-of-pocket expenses for gas, oil, and other costs (but not repairs or depreciation). Reasonable assumes the route taken was the shortest, most direct route available, from the former home to the new home. Additional expenses for side trips, stopovers, or pre-move house hunting expenses are not deductible as moving expenses. Other nondeductible moving costs include:

- Any part of the purchase price of your new home
- Car tags
- Driver's license
- Expenses of buying or selling a home (including closing costs, mortgage fees, and points)
- Expenses of entering into or breaking a lease
- Home improvements to help sell your home
- Loss on the sale of your home
- Losses from disposing of memberships in clubs
- Mortgage penalties
- Real estate taxes
- Refitting of carpet and draperies
- Return trips to your former residence

Example Helicopter pilot Gordon and his family are moved from a base in Texas to a base in California; the move qualifies as a PCS. Before moving, Gordon's spouse made two trips to the new area to look for a new home. The cost of moving the household goods was $12,000 and included two weeks of storage of their goods in California while the new home was prepared for their arrival. Gordon and family required lodging for one night in their old town after their furniture was moved and spent two additional nights on the road. They ate meals out for three days. The unreimbursed costs for moving the household goods, the storage and all three nights of lodging are deductible moving costs. The house hunting trips and the meals are not deductible. ♦

The U.S. military normally provides a reimbursement allowance for moves. Any costs reimbursed are not deductible. If the military taxpayer moves themselves (a personally procured move or PPM), the allowance provided is often 95 percent of the estimated move cost. The PPM allowance, net of actual expenses, will be included in the taxpayer's Form W-2 as taxable income.

Example Maverick receives orders for a PCS and chooses to move herself. The Air Force estimates the cost of the move as $4,000 and pays Maverick a $3,800 PPM. Maverick's actual qualifying cost to move are $2,000. Maverick's Form W-2 will include $1,800 in Box 1 as taxable compensation. ♦

A moving expense deduction can be claimed only for expenses not reimbursed through the moving allowance. If a military taxpayer has qualifying moving expenses in excess of the reimbursement, those expenses are reported on Form 3903 shown below. Moving expenses that do not qualify include security deposits on new housing, a sales commission on the sale of a former home, and meals while traveling. Nonqualified moving expenses paid by the employer are included in Box 1 of Form W-2. Qualified moving expenses paid to an employee are included in Box 12 under Code P.

Form 3903 — **Moving Expenses**
Department of the Treasury — Internal Revenue Service
Attach to Form 1040, 1040-SR, or 1040-NR.
Go to www.irs.gov/Form3903 for instructions and the latest information.
OMB No. 1545-0074
2024
Attachment Sequence No. 170

Name(s) shown on return | Your social security number

Before you begin: You can deduct moving expenses only if you are a **Member of the Armed Forces** on active duty and, due to a military order, you, your spouse, or your dependents move because of a permanent change of station.
Check here to certify that you meet these requirements. See the instructions . . . . ☐

1. Transportation and storage of household goods and personal effects (see instructions) . . . . . 1 _____
2. Travel (including lodging) from your old home to your new home (see instructions). **Do not** include the cost of meals . . . . . 2 _____
3. Add lines 1 and 2 . . . . . . 3 _____
4. Enter the total amount the government paid you for the expenses listed on lines 1 and 2 that is **not** included in box 1 of your Form W-2 (wages). This amount should be shown in box 12 of your Form W-2 with code **P** . . . . 4 _____
5. Is line 3 **more than** line 4?
   ☐ **No.** You **cannot** deduct your moving expenses. If line 3 is less than line 4, subtract line 3 from line 4 and include the result on Form 1040, 1040-SR, 1040-NR, line 1h.
   ☐ **Yes.** Subtract line 4 from line 3. Enter the result here and on Schedule 1 (Form 1040), line 14. This is your **moving expense deduction** . . . . 5 _____

For Paperwork Reduction Act Notice, see your tax return instructions. Cat. No. 12490K Form **3903** (2024)

If the military taxpayer has qualified moving expenses in excess of reimbursement, the Form 3903 can be completed in the year before or after the reimbursement.

Example In 2023, Petty Officer Rachel Heatherly moves in a qualified PCS. Heatherly incurs $600 in mileage expenses and $1,200 in lodging. She paid $2,000 to ship goods in excess of the allowed weight limit and $400 to ship her pet cat. In 2024, Heatherly files a travel voucher and receives a reimbursement of $1,800 for the mileage and lodging. Heatherly can report the $2,400 in unreimbursed qualifying expenses on Form 3903 in either 2023 or 2024. ♦

Refer to Chapter 5 for a discussion of reservists' travel expenses deduction.

6-9c Other Military Taxpayer Issues

Several additional items specific to military taxpayers are listed below.

Exclusion on Sale of Primary Residence

Exclusion of gain on sale of primary residence requires meeting the same two years test as discussed in Chapter 4; however, a military taxpayer can elect to suspend the five-year window if serving on qualified official extended duty.

Example Tameka Kazansky purchased a home in 2015. She lived in the home for three years before receiving orders to move for six years for qualified official extended duty. She sold the home in 2024. Ordinarily, since Tameka did not live in the home for two of the last five years, she would not be eligible to exclude any gain; however, if she chooses to suspend the six years she was on extended duty, the test applies to the years prior to extended duty and gain exclusion can apply. ♦

The suspension period cannot last more than 10 years and cannot be applied to the same property more than one time. Qualified extended duty is when a taxpayer is ordered to a duty station more than 50 miles from the home or when ordered to live in government quarters and the order is for more than 90 days or for an indefinite time period.

Forgiveness of Tax Liability

If a member of the U.S. Armed Forces dies while in active service in a combat zone, from wounds, disease, or injury received in a combat zone, or from wounds or injury caused in a terrorist or military action, their tax liability can be forgiven.

If death occurs in a combat zone or outside of a combat zone but the taxpayer was in direct support of a military operation in the combat zone and was eligible for special hostile fire or imminent danger military pay, the forgiveness of tax liabilities is extended to the year the taxpayer dies and any earlier or later year ending on or after the first day of service in the combat zone.

Example Rick Neven is ordered to service in a combat zone in 2023. In 2024, he is injured while fighting and passes away from his injuries in 2025. Neven is eligible to forgive his tax liability for tax years 2022 (the year prior to his service in the combat zone), 2023 (when his combat zone service started), 2024 (when hospitalized as a result of injuries sustained while serving in a combat zone), and 2025 (year of death from combat zone injuries). ♦

For death that occurs as part of a terrorist or military action, the forgiveness extends to the year prior to death through the year of death.

If filing a joint return, only the deceased taxpayer's portion of the tax liability is forgiven. Any tax liability associated with IRD (refer to LO 6.8) of the deceased taxpayer is also forgiven.

To file for a claim of forgiveness for those years a tax return has already been filed, the IRS requires a Form 1040-X to be filed for each year in question. The return should identify the conflict or action on the top of page 1 of the return written in bold letters. For example, "Iraqi Freedom – KIA" written on the top of page 1 of Form 1040 of 1040-X as the case may be. If killed in a terrorist action "KITA" should be written on the top of page 1.

If filing jointly, the tax regulations require that the portion of the decedent's joint income tax liability that can be forgiven is calculated by multiplying the joint tax liability by the ratio of the decedent's tax liability based on a separate return, to the total of each spouse's separate return tax liability. This calculation requires the preparation of a married filing separate tax return for each spouse.

Example Continuing from the previous example, if in 2024, the joint tax return reported a total tax liability of $14,000, with Rick's liability calculated separately as $8,000 and his spouse's separate liability as $7,000, the 2024 forgiveness due to Rick's death will be $7,467 ($8,000 ÷ $15,000 × $14,000). ♦

When claiming the forgiveness, a Form 1310 (Statement of Person Claiming Refund Due a Deceased Taxpayer) must accompany the return unless filed by a surviving spouse filing a joint or amended joint return, or a personal representative filing an original Form 1040 for the decedent (with a court certificate noting the appointment attached). In all cases, a copy of the death certificate (most likely Department of Defense Form 1300) must be attached to the return.

Extension to File and Pay Taxes

A military taxpayer inside the United States is subject to the same extension rules as any other taxpayer: An automatic six-month extension is available if a Form 4868 is filed by the original due date. An automatic two-month extension (typically until June 15) will apply if the taxpayer lives outside the United States and Puerto Rico and has a work home or post of duty outside the United States and Puerto Rico, or if the taxpayer has been assigned service outside the United States and Puerto Rico for a period that includes the due date of the return. Under both extensions, taxes should be paid by the original due date (typically April 15) to avoid interest or penalties (Chapter 9).

For military taxpayers serving in a combat zone, the extension provisions provide additional relief and also include some increased complexity. The additional relief is extended due dates for the filing of the tax return (income, estate, gift, and employment tax), the payment of any of these same taxes, and the contribution to an IRA. To qualify for these special extensions, the taxpayer must serve or have served in a combat zone or have qualifying service outside of a combat zone, or while serving on a contingency operation (as designated by the Secretary of Defense). The extension is awarded in two steps. In the first step, the deadline is extended for 180 days after the later of: (A) the last day the taxpayer was in a combat zone or (B) the last day of any continuous hospitalization for injury while serving in the combat zone. In the second step, the deadline is extended by the number of days remaining for the taxpayer to take action with the IRS when they entered the combat zone.

Example Charlotte Blackwood has served in the Air Force since 2019. On December 1, 2022, she entered service in Saudi Arabia (a combat zone) and served there until March 31, 2024, when she departed for the United States. She was not injured and did not return to a combat zone.

- Her 2022 tax return has a deadline of January 10, 2025 (285 days later) calculated as the date of her return (March 31, 2024) plus 180 days plus an additional 105 days (the number of days left in the 3.5 month filing period from January 1, 2023 to April 15, 2023) when she left.
- Her 2023 tax return has a deadline of January 11, 2025, calculated in the same manner same as the 2022 return but considering leap year (180 days plus 106 days from January 1, 2024 to April 15, 2024).
- Her 2024 return is not extended under these special provisions because the extended due date would be January 10, 2025 (same 285 days apply as the 2022 tax year) but this date ends within the normal filing period of the 2024 return (January 1 to April 15, 2025). Charlotte may extend her 2024 return using the previously mentioned automatic extension.

For purposes of this example, the adjustment of the due date due to weekends or holidays (e.g., the 2023 return was actually due April 18, 2024) was ignored for simplicity's sake but these would be considered and reflected in the extension due date. ♦

As a reminder, the special extension to file is accompanied by an extension to pay as well.

If a military taxpayer serving outside of a combat zone notifies the IRS that their ability to pay income tax has been materially affected by military service, the taxpayer can defer collection of income tax due during the member's military service for a period up to 180 days after the taxpayer's termination or release from military service. No interest or penalty for non-payment of tax accrues for the deferment period. If a deferment is granted, the statute of limitations for tax collection is suspended for the member's period of military service plus an additional 270 days. The deferral does not apply to Social Security or Medicare taxes.

Members of the military are encouraged to e-file when possible. A tax return that includes forgiveness of decedent's tax liability must be paper filed and mailed to Internal Revenue Service, 333 W. Pershing Street, Stop 6503, P5, Kansas City, MO 64108. Other members of the military should send the federal tax return to the Internal Revenue Service Center for the place where the individual lives (not necessarily the permanent address). If the military member is overseas and has an APO or FPO address, file the return with the Internal Revenue Service Center listed for an APO or FPO address. The instructions for Form 1040 include all the necessary addresses.

Self-Study Problem 6.9 — Refer to Appendix E for Solutions to Self-Study Problems

1. Classify each of the following type of military pay as either included or excluded from gross income.
   a. Basic active duty pay
   b. Reenlistment bonus pay (if reenlistment occurred outside combat zone)
   c. Basic Allowance for Housing
   d. Reenlistment bonus pay (if reenlistment occurred inside combat zone)
   e. Basic Allowance for Subsistence
   f. Moving allowance in excess of qualified expenses

2. Nick "Goose" Bradshaw receives orders to move to his new station in San Diego, CA from his home in Great Lakes, IL. Goose is provided a $4,300 moving allowance and the entire amount was reported to Goose in Box 12 of his Form W-2 under Code P. His actual moving expenses are:

   - Rental truck to move household goods and personal effects $2,500
   - Gas and tolls for trip   250
   - Lodging for night in Great Lakes after furniture placed in truck   120
   - Lodging for two nights while driving   270
   - Meals while driving   75
   - Cost to ship his personal car to San Diego   1,000
   - Cost to ship his dog   500
   - Cost to store his household goods for 10 days in San Diego until his housing was ready   800
   - Cost of temporary lodging in San Diego   2,000

   Prepare Goose's Form 3903 (found in Appendix F) to report his deductible moving expenses, if any.

Key Terms

accounting periods, 6-2
fiscal year-end, 6-2
short-period taxable income, 6-2
accounting methods, 6-3
cash method, 6-3
constructive receipt, 6-4
accrual method, 6-4
all-events test, 6-4

economic performance, 6-5
related parties, 6-7
constructive ownership, 6-8
"kiddie tax," 6-9
alternative minimum tax (AMT), 6-14
AMT adjustments, 6-14
AMT preferences, 6-14
AMT exemption, 6-15

nanny tax, 6-19
household employee, 6-19
3.8 percent Medicare tax, 6-23
net investment income tax, 6-23
0.9 percent additional Medicare tax, 6-24
Form W-2c, 6-29
Form 1040-X, 6-29

qualified domestic relations order (QDRO), 6-33
innocent spouse relief, 6-34
separation of liability relief, 6-35
equitable relief, 6-35
income in respect of a decedent (IRD), 6-38
tax residents, 6-39
nonresident, 6-39

Form 1040-NR, 6-39
Form 843, 6-39
FinCEN, 6-40
FBAR, 6-40
basic allowance for housing (BAH), 6-42
basic allowance for subsistence (BAS), 6-42
combat pay, 6-43

combat zone tax exclusion (CZTE), 6-43
disability severance, 6-43
permanent change of station (PCS), 6-45
moving expenses, 6-45
forgiveness of tax liability, 6-47

Key Points

Learning Objectives	Key Points
LO 6.1: Determine the different accounting periods allowed for tax purposes.	• Almost all individuals file tax returns using a calendar-year accounting period. • Partnerships and corporations had a great deal of freedom in selecting a tax year in the past. However, Congress set limits on this freedom when a fiscal year-end resulted in an inappropriate deferral of taxable income. • A personal service corporation is a corporation whose shareholder-employees provide personal services (e.g., medical, legal, accounting, actuarial, or consulting services) for the corporation's patients or clients. Personal service corporations generally must adopt a calendar year-end. • If taxpayers have a short year other than their first or last year of operations, they are required to annualize their taxable income to calculate the tax for the short period.
LO 6.2: Determine the different accounting methods allowed for tax purposes.	• The tax law requires taxpayers to report taxable income using the method of accounting regularly used by the taxpayer in keeping their books, provided the method clearly reflects the taxpayer's income. • The cash receipts and disbursements (cash) method, the accrual method, and the hybrid method are accounting methods specifically recognized in the tax law.
LO 6.3: Determine whether parties are considered related for tax purposes, and classify the tax treatment of certain related-party transactions.	• The two types of disallowed related-party transactions are: (1) sales of property at a loss, and (2) unpaid expenses and interest. • Any loss or deduction arising from transactions between related parties are disallowed by Section 267. • The common related parties under Section 267 include brothers and sisters (whole or half), a spouse, ancestors (parents, grandparents, etc.), lineal descendants (children, grandchildren, etc.), and a corporation or an individual shareholder who directly or constructively owns more than 50 percent of the corporation. • Related-party rules also consider constructive ownership in determining whether parties are related to each other (e.g., taxpayers are deemed to own stock owned by certain relatives and related entities).
LO 6.4: Apply the rules for computing tax on the unearned income of minor children and certain students (the "kiddie tax").	• The tax law contains provisions that limit the benefit of shifting income to certain dependent children. • The net unearned income of dependent children may be taxed at the parent's rate, if higher ("kiddie tax"). • The kiddie tax applies to dependent children who are required to file a tax return, are ages 18 or younger, are age 18 and do not provide more than half of their own support, or are students ages 19 through 24, who have at least one living parent, and who have "net unearned income" of more than $2,600 for 2024. • If certain conditions are met, parents may elect to include a child's gross income on the parents' tax return. The election eliminates the child's return filing requirements, including the special calculation on Form 8615 for the kiddie tax.

Key Points

LO 6.5:
Calculate a basic alternative minimum tax.

- The AMT was designed to ensure that wealthy taxpayers could not take advantage of special tax write-offs (tax preferences and other adjustments) to avoid paying tax. In general, taxpayers must pay the AMT if their AMT liability is greater than their regular tax liability.
- Adjustments are timing differences that arise because of differences between the regular and AMT calculations (e.g., depreciation timing differences), while preferences are special provisions for the regular tax that are not allowed for the AMT (e.g., state income taxes).
- For 2024, the AMT exemption allowance is $133,300 for married taxpayers filing joint returns, $85,700 for single and head of household taxpayers, and $66,650 for married taxpayers filing separate returns. The AMT exemption allowance amount is phased out for high-income taxpayers.
- For 2024, for all taxpayers, except married filing separately, the alternative minimum tax rates for calculating the tentative minimum tax are 26 percent of the first $232,600 plus 28 percent on amounts above $232,600, applied to the taxpayer's alternative minimum tax base.
- The increases in the AMT exemptions and thresholds coupled with the limitations or suspension of certain itemized deductions are expected to reduce the number of taxpayers subject to the AMT.

LO 6.6:
Apply the special tax and reporting requirements for household employees (the "nanny tax").

- The "nanny tax" provisions provide a simplified reporting process for employers of household workers.
- Household employers are not required to pay FICA taxes on cash payments of less than $2,700 paid to any household employee in a calendar year.
- If the cash payment to any household employee is $2,700 or more in a calendar year, all the cash payments are subject to Social Security and Medicare taxes.
- If more than $1,000 in cash wages are paid to household employees during any calendar quarter, employers are required to pay FUTA taxes.
- A taxpayer is a household employer if they hire workers to perform household services in or around the taxpayer's home that are subject to the "will and control" of the taxpayer (e.g., babysitters, caretakers, cooks, drivers, gardeners, housekeepers, and maids).
- Certain workers are not subject to Social Security and Medicare taxes on wages paid for work in the home. These workers include the taxpayer's spouse, the taxpayer's father or mother, the taxpayer's children under 21 years of age, and anyone who is under age 18 during the year, unless providing household services is their principal occupation.
- Under the nanny tax provisions, a household employer must report Social Security and Medicare taxes, federal income tax withholding, and FUTA tax once a year by filing Schedule H with their individual Form 1040.
- At the close of the tax year, household employers must also file Form W-2 (copy A) and Form W-3 for each household employee whose income is reflected on Schedule H or had federal income tax withheld from wages.

LO 6.7:
Compute the special taxes for high-income taxpayers.

- The Affordable Care Act (ACA) added a 3.8 percent Medicare tax on net investment income and a 0.9 percent additional Medicare tax on earned income for certain high-income taxpayers.
- The 3.8 percent net investment income tax applies to the net investment income of individuals with modified AGI over $250,000 for joint filers ($125,000 if married filing separate), and $200,000 for single filers.
- The 0.9 percent Medicare tax is imposed on earned income from salaries, wages, and self-employment income of joint filers with earned income over $250,000 ($125,000 if married filing separate) and single taxpayers with earned income over $200,000.
- Employers are required to withhold the 0.9 percent Medicare tax when a taxpayer's salary exceeds $200,000.
- Self-employed taxpayers must pay the tax with their individual income tax returns.

LO 6.8: Describe the basic rules surrounding special taxpayer situations such as divorce, deceased taxpayers, nonresident taxpayers, and farmers.	• Taxpayers should contact payer first if Forms W-2 and 1099-R are missing or incorrect. • Amended tax returns are filed on Form 1040-X. • Divorce and legal separation are determined under state law. • Spouses and ex-spouses can seek relief from tax under innocent spouse, separation of liability, or equitable relief using Form 8857. • Deceased taxpayers may need to file a final tax return. • Income in respect of a decedent (IRD) is income that would have been reported by the taxpayer, if not for death. • A nonresident married to a resident can file a joint resident return. • Tax residents with foreign financial accounts may need to report them in two ways: FBAR and/or Form 8938. • Individual farmers report income on Schedule F and are subject to many special tax provisions.
LO 6.9: Identify significant differences in the tax law for members of the U.S. Armed Forces.	• Members of the U.S. Armed Forces may exclude certain types of pay including basic allowance for housing (BAH), basic allowance for subsistence (BAS), and pay earned while in a CZTE area. • CZTE designation is made by executive order of the President of the United States. • Members of the U.S. Armed Forces may deduct (or exclude) qualified moving costs associated with a permanent change of station (PCS). • Members killed in a combat zone are eligible for forgiveness of tax liability for a certain number of years surrounding the year of death. • Members serving in a combat zone are eligible for additional special extensions to file and pay taxes.

Questions and Problems

Group 1:
Multiple Choice Questions

LO 6.1 1. E Corporation is a subchapter S corporation owned by three individuals with calendar year-ends. The corporation sells a sports drink as its principal product and has similar sales each month. What options does E Corporation have in choosing a tax year?
   a. E Corporation may choose any month-end as its tax year.
   b. Because the owners of E Corporation have tax years ending in December, E Corporation must also choose a December year-end.
   c. E Corporation may choose an October, November, or December tax year-end.
   d. E Corporation may choose a tax year ending in September, October, or November, but only if the corporation also makes an annual cash deposit and adjusts the amount every year depending on the income deferred.

LO 6.1 2. Income and loss from which of the following entities is passed through and taxed on the individual's personal tax returns?
   a. S corporation
   b. Partnership
   c. Sole proprietor
   d. All of the above

LO 6.1   3. Which of the following entities is likely to have the greatest flexibility in choosing a year-end other than a calendar year-end?
     a. Sole proprietor
     b. General partnership
     c. Corporation
     d. S corporation

LO 6.2   4. Which of the following is an acceptable method of accounting under the tax law?
     a. The accrual method
     b. The hybrid method
     c. The cash method
     d. All of the choices are acceptable
     e. None of the choices are acceptable

LO 6.2   5. Which of the following entities is required to report on the accrual basis?
     a. An accounting firm operating as a Personal Service Corporation.
     b. A manufacturing business with $32 million of gross receipts operating as a regular C corporation.
     c. A corporation engaged in tropical fruit farming in Southern California.
     d. A partnership with gross receipts of $13 million and all of the partners are individuals with a December year-end.

LO 6.2   6. A cash-basis taxpayer will recognize gross income when:
     a. earned
     b. actually or constructively received
     c. when reasonably estimable
     d. when shipped for goods and when provided for services

LO 6.2   7. In addition to the liability existing in an estimable amount, an accrual-basis taxpayer cannot deduct an expense without this also occurring:
     a. The expense is paid
     b. An invoice has been received for the expense
     c. Economic performance has occurred
     d. The expense has been paid in cash

LO 6.3   8. Pekoe sold stock to his sister Rose for $12,000, its fair market value. Pekoe bought the stock five years ago for $16,000. Also, Pekoe sold Earl (an unrelated party) stock for $6,500 that he bought three years ago for $8,500. What is Pekoe's recognized gain or loss?
     a. $6,500 loss
     b. $6,000 loss
     c. $3,000 loss
     d. $2,000 loss
     e. $1,000 gain

LO 6.3   9. B Corporation, a calendar year-end, accrual-basis taxpayer, is owned 75 percent by Baylee, a cash-basis taxpayer. On December 31, 2024, the corporation accrues interest of $4,000 on a loan from Baylee and also accrues a $15,000 bonus to Baylee. The bonus is paid to Baylee on February 1, 2025; the interest is not paid until 2026. How much can B Corporation deduct on its 2024 tax return for these two expenses?
     a. $0
     b. $4,000
     c. $15,000
     d. $19,000
     e. $12,000

LO 6.3 10. B Corporation, a calendar year-end, accrual-basis taxpayer, is owned 75 percent by Beata, a cash-basis taxpayer. On December 31, 2024, the corporation accrues interest of $4,000 on a loan from Beata and also accrues a $15,000 bonus to Beata. The bonus is paid to Beata on February 1, 2025; the interest is not paid until 2026. How much can B Corporation deduct on its 2025 tax return for these two expenses?
   a. $0
   b. $4,000
   c. $15,000
   d. $19,000
   e. $12,000

LO 6.3 11. LMJ Corporation is owned 40 percent by Lukas, 30 percent by Machli, and 30 percent by the Julius Partnership. Lukas and Machli are father and son. Machli has a 10 percent interest in Julius Partnership. What is Machli's total direct and constructive ownership of LMJ Corporation under Section 267?
   a. 30 percent
   b. 70 percent
   c. 40 percent
   d. 73 percent
   e. 33 percent

LO 6.4 12. Which of the following is required for a taxpayer to be subject to the tax on unearned income of minors (kiddie tax) in 2024?
   a. Must have no earned income
   b. 21 years of age or younger
   c. Both parents must be living
   d. Net unearned income must exceed $2,600
   e. All of the above are required

LO 6.4 13. Which of the following is an option for a minor with unearned income of $3,500?
   a. Pay tax at trust and estate rates
   b. Pay tax at the parent's rate
   c. Pay $0 tax since the income is unearned
   d. Pay at the minor's individual tax rate

LO 6.5 14. An individual taxpayer will be liable for alternative minimum tax when:
   a. The regular tax liability exceeds the tentative minimum tax
   b. The tentative minimum tax exceeds the regular tax liability
   c. The taxpayer's income is below the filing threshold
   d. The standard deduction or any credit is claimed

LO 6.5 15. Which of the following is an adjustment for AMT purposes?
   a. Itemized deduction for home mortgage interest
   b. Itemized deduction for charitable contributions
   c. State income tax refunds
   d. Itemized deduction for medical expenses in excess of 7.5 percent of AGI

LO 6.5 16. The alternative minimum tax exemption:
   a. Is a direct reduction of the tentative minimum tax
   b. Is a reduction of alternative minimum taxable income for certain taxpayers
   c. Permits certain taxpayers to elect to treat AMT as a reduction of tax
   d. Is subject to carryback and carryforward provisions
   e. Increases the effects of tax preference items

LO 6.5   17. Alternative minimum tax rates for individuals:
   a. Are the same as regular tax rates but on adjusted minimum taxable income
   b. Higher than the highest marginal tax rate for individuals depending on filing status
   c. Are 26 percent and 28 percent
   d. Are 21 percent

LO 6.6   18. Bob employs a maid intermittently to clean his house. He pays her $1,040 during the current year. What is the proper tax treatment of the Social Security and Medicare tax for the maid?
   a. Bob is not required to pay or withhold Social Security and Medicare taxes on the $1,040.
   b. The $1,040 is subject to the Medicare tax, but not the Social Security tax.
   c. $500 is subject to the Social Security and Medicare tax.
   d. Bob is required to withhold Social Security and Medicare taxes on the entire $1,040.

LO 6.6   19. Which of the following employees would *not* be exempt from Social Security and Medicare taxes on wages paid for household work?
   a. The taxpayer's 16-year-old daughter
   b. The taxpayer's wife
   c. The taxpayer's 20-year-old sister
   d. The 14-year-old babysitter from down the street

LO 6.6   20. Individual taxpayers may pay withholding taxes due with their individual income tax returns using Schedule H for each of the following workers *except*:
   a. A nanny hired to watch their children
   b. A maid hired to clean house and cook every day
   c. An attorney with her own business, hired to handle a legal dispute with the taxpayers' neighbor
   d. An unlicensed caregiver for a disabled spouse

LO 6.7   21. The 3.8 percent Medicare tax on net investment income applies to:
   a. Tax-exempt interest income
   b. Interest and dividends
   c. IRA distributions
   d. Wages

LO 6.7   22. Skylar is married, files jointly, and earns $410,000 in salary during 2024. What is the amount of 0.9 percent Medicare tax for high-income taxpayers that his employer must withhold from his wages?
   a. $1,890
   b. $1,800
   c. $1,440
   d. $900

LO 6.7   23. Christine and Vasu are married. In 2024, Christine earns a salary of $250,000 and Vasu earns a salary of $75,000. They have no other income and work for the same employers for all of 2024. How much 0.9 percent Medicare tax for high-income taxpayers will Christine and Vasu have to pay with their 2024 income tax return?
   a. $0
   b. $225
   c. $450
   d. $675

LO 6.8   24. If a taxpayer did not receive a copy of their Form W-2:
   a. They should request a copy from the Social Security Administration.
   b. They should file a tax return and *not* include the income.
   c. They should attach a Form 4852 reporting the missing Form W-2 if a copy cannot be obtained.
   d. They should file a Form 1040-X which is the form used for missing information returns.

LO 6.8 25. If a taxpayer discovers a math error on their tax return in which two lines were added incorrectly:
a. Conventional wisdom is that they simply wait for the IRS to send them a notice addressing the mistake
b. They should immediately file a Form 1040-X
c. They should prepare a new tax return and submit it electronically
d. Prepare the page of the tax return that was wrong and resubmit only that page

LO 6.8 26. Ben and Jennifer get divorced in 2024. Which of the following statements is *true* regarding the tax consequences of the divorce?
a. Ben will be able to deduct any alimony paid to Jennifer in future years.
b. Any property divided between the two will be subject to gain or loss recognition.
c. If a QDRO is issued regarding Ben's qualified retirement plan assets, Jennifer will "step into Ben's shoes" for the plan assets that are transferred to her and will not be taxed on the distribution if rolled over into a new qualified plan.
d. They will file as married filing separately until one of them remarries.

LO 6.8 27. Which of the following is *not* a form of relief from tax liability available to a spouse or ex-spouse?
a. Protective custody relief
b. Innocent spouse relief
c. Separation of liability relief
d. Equitable relief

LO 6.8 28. Reanna was a retired 77-year-old teacher who died in 2024. In 2024, Reanna's pension paid her $45,000 up to her date of death and $13,000 afterward. Which of the following statements best describes Reanna's tax situation for 2024?
a. Her tax liability is reduced to zero due to her death.
b. All of her income will be income in respect of a decedent and will be taxed to her estate.
c. All of her income will be reported on a Form 1040-X which is the form for deceased taxpayers.
d. A final tax return for 2024 is required to be filed that includes her income and deductions up through the date of her death.

LO 6.8 29. If an estate is being terminated but has an NOL carryforward on the final income tax return, which of the following best describes the tax options for the NOL?
a. It expires unused.
b. It can be included on the return of the estate beneficiaries.
c. It can be deducted on the estate's final return and create a refund.
d. It can be used to lower any estate taxes.

LO 6.8 30. Rhianna is a tax resident of the United States and has a bank account in in Switzerland with a balance equivalent to about US $14,000. Which of the following best describes Rhianna's foreign bank account reporting requirements?
a. Rhianna should file FBAR only using the electronic filing system.
b. Rhianna should complete Form 8938 only and file with her tax return.
c. Rhianna should file both FBAR and Form 8938 and submit both with her tax return.
d. Rhianna does not need to report a foreign bank account.

LO 6.9 31. Which of the following forms of compensation to an active member of the U.S Armed Forces is likely to be *excluded* from gross income?
a. Active duty pay
b. Training duty pay
c. Reserve training pay
d. Basic allowance for housing (BAH)
e. None of these are excluded

LO 6.9   32. Which of the following forms of compensation to an active member of the U.S Armed Forces is likely to be **included** in gross income?
  a. Pay earned while in a combat zone
  b. Allowance for qualified moving expenses
  c. Basic allowance for subsistence (BAS)
  d. Enlistment bonus
  e. None of these are included

LO 6.9   33. Which of the following does **not** qualify as a permanent change of station?
  a. The enlisted member is given a first duty post
  b. A move that is less than 100 miles
  c. A move from the final post to a new location that occurs 18 months after the termination of service
  d. A move from one permanent post to another

LO 6.9   34. Which of the following is **not** a qualified moving expense when associated with a permanent change of station?
  a. Cost to pack and ship household goods and personal effects
  b. Cost of a side-trip to visit extended family while driving to new location
  c. Cost to move a family pet to the new location
  d. Lodging costs incurred while moving

LO 6.9   35. Which of the following is **not** a tax benefit offered to members of the U.S Armed Forces?
  a. Forgiveness of tax liability for a member and spouse if the member is killed in a terrorist attack and they file jointly
  b. The exclusion of certain forms of military pay
  c. Extended time to file a tax return when serving in a combat zone
  d. The chance to suspend the 5-year rule for the 2-year ownership and use test

Group 2: Problems

LO 6.1   1. Explain why the tax law prefers flowthrough entities like partnerships and S corporations to have a year-end that matches the year-end of its owners.

LO 6.2   2. Yolanda is a cash-basis taxpayer with the following transactions during the year:

Cash received from sales of products not yet delivered	$70,000
Cash paid for expenses (except rent and interest)	40,000
Rent prepaid on a leased building for 18 months beginning December 1	45,000
Prepaid interest on a bank loan, paid on December 31 for the next 3 months	5,000

Calculate Yolanda's income from her business for this calendar year.

LO 6.2   3. Geraldine is an accrual-basis taxpayer who has the following transactions during the current calendar tax year:

Accrued business income for products shipped (except rent)	$220,000
Cash received in advance for products not yet shipped	10,000
Accrued business expenses (except rent)	170,000
Rental income on a building lease for the next 6 months, received on December 1	21,000
Prepaid rent expense for 6 months, paid on December 1	9,000

Calculate Geraldine's net income from her business for the current year.

LO 6.2

4. Shakura is a calendar-year taxpayer reporting on the cash basis. Please indicate how she should treat the following items for 2024:
    a. She makes a deductible contribution to an IRA on April 15, 2025.
    b. She has made an election to accrue the increase in value of savings bonds even though the increase is not received in cash.
    c. She prepays half a year of interest in advance on her mortgage on the last day of 2024.
    d. She pays all of her outstanding invoices for standard business expenses in the last week of December.
    e. She sends out a big bill to a customer on January 1, 2025, even though she did all of the work in December of 2024.

LO 6.3

5. ZOM Corporation is owned 20 percent by Zhi, 30 percent by Obi, 30 percent by Mumtaz, and 20 percent by Y Corporation. Y Corporation is owned 70 percent by Zhi and 30 percent by an unrelated party. Mumtaz and Obi are siblings. Answer each of the following questions about ZOM under the constructive ownership rules of Section 267:
    a. What is Zhi's percentage ownership?
    b. What is Obi's percentage ownership?
    c. What is Mumtaz's percentage ownership?
    d. If Obi sells property to ZOM for a $6,000 loss, what amount of that loss can be recognized for tax purposes (before any annual limitations)?

LO 6.3

6. You have a problem and need a full-text copy of the Related Party Code Section 267. Go to the Office of the Law Revision Counsel of the United States House of Representatives website (**uscode.house.gov**) and enter Title 26 (the Internal Revenue Code) and Section 267 in the Jump To boxes. What exception to the loss disallowance rule is provided for corporations in Section 267(a)(1)?

LO 6.4

7. Explain the purpose of the provision in the tax law that taxes unearned income of certain minor children at their parents' tax rates.

LO 6.4

8. Goldie and Kurt have a 12-year-old child, Wyatt. For 2024, Goldie and Kurt have taxable income of $101,000, and Wyatt has interest income of $4,700. No election is made to include Wyatt's income on Goldie and Kurt's return.
    a. For purposes of the tax on a child's unearned income, calculate Wyatt's taxable income.
    b. Calculate Wyatt's net unearned income.
    c. Calculate Wyatt's tax for 2024 using tax rate schedules (not the Tax Table).
    d. If there was no kiddie tax and Wyatt were taxed at his own rate, what would the tax on Wyatt's income be?

LO 6.4

9. Explain the two different ways that the tax on unearned income of minor children, or "kiddie tax," can be reported.

LO 6.4

10. Does the tax on unearned income of minor children, or "kiddie tax," apply to wages earned by minors in summer and other jobs?

LO 6.5

11. Rachel and Ross file jointly in 2024 and have alternative minimum taxable income of $1.3 million prior to the AMT exemption. Compute their exemption and AMTI after the exemption.

LO 6.5

12. Otto and Monica are married taxpayers who file a joint tax return. For the current tax year, they have AGI of $80,300. They have excess depreciation on real estate of $67,500, which must be added back to AGI to arrive at AMTI. The amount of their mortgage interest expense for the year was $25,000, and they made charitable contributions of $7,500. If Otto and Monica's taxable income for the current year is $47,800 determine the amount of their AMTI before the exemption.

LO 6.5 13. List two common deductions which are allowed for regular tax purposes but are not deductible for AMT purposes.

LO 6.5 14. What are the two tax rates which are used to calculate AMT, ignoring the special treatment of dividends and capital gains?

LO 6.5 15. Show the simplified formula for calculating AMT. Do not show tax rates or an exemption amount.

LO 6.6 16. Sally hires a maid to work in her home for $500 per month. The maid is 25 years old and not related to Sally. During 2024, the maid worked nine months for Sally.
   a. What is the employer's share of Social Security tax Sally must pay?
   b. What is the employer's share of Medicare tax Sally must pay?
   c. What is the amount of Social Security and Medicare tax which must be withheld from the maid's wages?

LO 6.6 17. Delphia hires a nanny to watch her two children while she works at a local hospital. She pays the 19-year-old nanny $180 per week for 42 weeks during the current year.
   a. What is the employer's portion of Social Security and Medicare tax for the nanny that Delphia should pay when she files her Form 1040 for 2024?
   b. What is the nanny's portion of the Social Security and Medicare tax?

LO 6.7 18. Rachel is single and has wages of $250,000 and dividend income of $90,000. She has no investment expenses. Calculate the amount of the 3.8 percent net investment income tax she must pay.

LO 6.7 19. Married taxpayers Otto and Alma are both self-employed. Otto earns $352,000 of self-employment income and Alma has a self-employment loss of $13,500. How much 0.9 percent Medicare tax for high-income taxpayers will Otto and Alma have to pay with their 2024 income tax return?

LO 6.8 20. Describe the steps a taxpayer should go through if they do not receive a Form W-2?

LO 6.8 21. Define income in respect of a decedent and provide an example of IRD.

LO 6.8 22. Jervis Vision, a single taxpayer under age 65, filed his 2024 tax return in early 2025. He realized after the due date that he failed to rightfully claim his child (Wanda Vision, age 13, Social Security number 444-11-4321) as a dependent and change his status to head of household. His original Form 1040 reported AGI of $54,000 (all wages) and the standard deduction for a single taxpayer resulting in tax liability of $4,499. He had $4,500 income tax withheld from his pay during 2024. Prepare a Form 1040-X (from Appendix F) to report Jervis' change in filing status. Note that Jervis is now eligible for a child tax credit of $2,000. Jervis' Social Security number is 312-21-6890 and he lives at 89 E. 42nd St. Apt. 14F, New York, NY 10001.

LO 6.8 23. Johnny and Amber are married and filed jointly for tax year 2024. Amber was a wage earner and Johnny was self-employed. Johnny prepared their tax return (using Intuit's ProConnect tax preparation software). Amber saw her wages and withholding reported on the tax return before e-filing but did not pay any significant attention to Johnny's Schedule C at the time or the net refund when she authorized the e-filing around April 10, 2025. However, when the refund was directly deposited into their account in May 2025, Amber noticed that the amount was significantly larger than normal. This caused her to take a second, more careful look at a copy of the tax return and she noticed that there was a real possibility that John significantly underreported his income on the tax return. Amber confronted Johnny who denied any such underreporting. Shortly thereafter, Amber and Johnny received a notice from the IRS inquiring about some of the information that was reported on their return.

a. Assuming Amber has filed no additional documents with the IRS, what option(s) does she have with respect to avoiding any personal additional liability for the taxes that may be about to be assessed against her?
b. Assuming that Amber immediately filed a Form 8857 after the first notice of interest in the tax return from the IRS, what option(s) does she have with respect to avoiding any personal additional liability for the taxes that may be about to be assessed against her?
c. Using the original facts provided in part a., and assuming that Amber filed for divorce upon confronting Johnny about the underreporting and also moved out of their home, what option(s) does she have with respect to avoiding any personal additional liability for the taxes that may be about to be assessed against her?

LO 6.8

24. Hugo Rios is a single U.S citizen. His father, Carlos Rios, a Chilean citizen and resident, is becoming quite aged and as a precaution, he added Hugo as a signatory authority to his non-interest bearing Chilean checking (depository) account. During 2024, the account had a maximum value of CLP $64,311,844.45 (USD 67,378). The account balance on December 31, 2024, was CLP $57,461,279.05 (USD 60,200). Both measures were converted at the exchange rate for Chilean pesos using the U.S. Treasury Department's financial management service rate at December 31, 2024 of 954.5 Chilean pesos per USD (see **https://fiscaldata.treasury.gov/currency-exchange-rates-converter/**). The particulars of Hugo and his father are provided below:

	Hugo Rios	Carlos Rios
Social Security number	612-83-1739	n/a
Chilean Tax ID (RUT)	n/a	34.456.789.6
Passport # and country	n/a	P12345509 Chile
Date of birth	09/22/1971	06/01/1941
Address	200 N Ocean Blvd, Palm Beach, FL 33480	Av. Punta Arenas 6711, La Granja, Región Metropolitana, Chile 8930520

The bank account (# 0089122028) is held with Banco Santander Chile located at Av. Concha y Toro 1050, Puente Alto, Región Metropolitana, Chile 8150215.

Using this information, complete a paper version of Parts I and III of FinCEN Report 114 (normally requires e-filing) and the necessary parts of Form 8938 (both forms are located in Appendix F).

LO 6.9

25. List at least three types of military pay that are eligible for exclusion from gross income.

Group 3:
Writing Assignment

Ethics

Charlie's Green Lawn Care is a cash-basis taxpayer. Charlie Adame, the sole proprietor, is considering delaying some of his December 2024 customer billings for lawn care into the next year. In addition, he is thinking about paying some of the bills in late December 2024, which he would ordinarily pay in January 2025. This way, Charlie claims, he will have "less income and more expenses, thereby paying less tax!" Is Charlie's way of thinking acceptable?

Group 4:
Comprehensive Problems

1A. Richard McCarthy (born 2/14/1970; Social Security number 100-10-9090) and Christine McCarthy (born 6/1/1972; Social Security number 101-21-3434) have a 19-year-old son Jack, (born 10/2/2005; Social Security number 555-55-1212), who is a full-time student at the University of Key West. The McCarthys also have a 12-year-old daughter Justine, (born 12/09/2012; Social Security number 444-23-1212), who lives with them. The McCarthys can claim a $2,000 child tax credit for Justine and a $500 other dependent credit for Jack. Richard is the CEO at a paper company. His 2024 Form W-2:

Form W-2 Wage and Tax Statement (2024)

Box	Field	Value
a	Employee's social security number	100-10-9090
b	Employer identification number (EIN)	31-5656567
c	Employer's name, address, and ZIP code	Mufflin-Dunder Paper, 302 Lackawanna Avenue, Scranton, PA 18503
e/f	Employee's name and address	Richard McCarthy, 32 Sleepy Hollow Road, Clarks Summit, PA 18411
1	Wages, tips, other compensation	235,000.00
2	Federal income tax withheld	58,000.00
3	Social security wages	168,600.00
4	Social security tax withheld	10,453.20
5	Medicare wages and tips	258,000.00
6	Medicare tax withheld	4,263.00
12a	D	23,000.00
12b	DD	11,417.33
13	Retirement plan	X
15	State / Employer's state ID	PA / 1PA300906
16	State wages, tips, etc.	235,000.00
17	State income tax	15,600.00

Christine is an optometrist and operates her own practice ("The Eyes of March") in town as a sole proprietor. The shop address is 1030 Morgan Highway, Clarks Summit, PA 18411 and the business code is 621320. Christine keeps her books on the cash basis and her bookkeeper provided the following information:

Gross sales		$291,500
Returns		7,500
Inventory:		
Beginning inventory	$ 25,000	
Purchases	122,000	
Ending inventory	30,000	
Rent		39,000
Insurance		11,500
Professional fees		3,300
Payroll		38,000
Payroll taxes		3,500
Utilities		4,000
Office expenses		2,245
Depreciation on equipment		3,800

Christine paid her rent in 2024 month-to-month, but paid $24,000 in December 2024 for a 12-month lease on her office for all of 2025. One of Christine's customers is a large state prison that purchases special eye glasses for the the inmates that meet prison safety standards. Because the order is large, Christine received a $20,000 advance payment in December 2024 for glasses she delivered in January 2025. The rent and advance payment are included in her financial figures on the previous page.

The McCarthys have a nanny/housekeeper whom they paid $18,000 during 2024. They did not withhold income or FICA taxes. The McCarthys paid Pennsylvania state unemployment tax of $380 in 2024.

Christine received a 2024 Form 1099-INT from the National Bank of Scranton that listed interest income of $23,000. Note that McCarthys reasonably allocate $751 to state income tax expense for purposes of the net investment income tax. Christine's uncle who lives in Scotland, dies in 2024 and left her a checking account at the Royal Bank of Glasgow (account 13308876) located at 167-201 Argyle St, Glasgow G2 8BU, United Kingdom, with a balance of £81,473 or about US $103,000 using an exchange rate of $1 = £0.7912 from the U.S. Treasury's Bureau of the Fiscal Service exchange rate converter. The account did not earn any interest. Christine reported the account on the FinCEN website.

Richard received a Form 1098-E (presented below) reporting the student loan interest he paid.

```
□ CORRECTED (if checked)
RECIPIENT'S/LENDER'S name, street address, city or town, state or    OMB No. 1545-1576
province, country, ZIP or foreign postal code, and telephone number
                                                                              Student
Sallie Mae Loan Servicing Center                          2024           Loan Interest
12061 Bluemont Way, V3419                                                   Statement
Reston, VA 20190                                        Form 1098-E
RECIPIENT'S TIN        BORROWER'S TIN       1 Student loan interest received by lender     Copy B
12-4454123             100-10-9090          $ 2,855.11                                   For Borrower
BORROWER'S name
Richard McCarthy
Street address (including apt. no.)
32 Sleepy Hollow Road
City or town, state or province, country, and ZIP or foreign postal code
Clarks Summit, PA 18411
Account number (see instructions)           2 If checked, box 1 does not include loan origination
                                              fees and/or capitalized interest for loans made before
                                              September 1, 2004                          □
Form 1098-E      (keep for your records)    www.irs.gov/Form1098E   Department of the Treasury - Internal Revenue Service
```

The McCarthys received a Form 1099-G from Pennsylvania that reported a $477 state income tax refund from 2023. The McCarthys filed a Schedule A in 2023 and had $14,223 of state income tax expense that was limited to a $10,000 deduction.

The McCarthys paid the following in 2024:

Home mortgage interest reported on Form 1098 on mortgage of less than $750,000	$17,700
Property taxes	5,767
Estimated state income tax payments	2,500
Estimated Federal income tax payments	4,700
Charitable contributions (all cash)	7,944

Required: Complete the McCarthys' federal tax return for 2024. Use Form 1040, Schedule 1, Schedule 2, Schedule A, Schedule B, Schedule C, Schedule H, Schedule SE, Form 8995, Form 8959, Form 8960, and Form 8938 to complete this tax return. Make realistic assumptions about any missing data and ignore any alternative minimum tax. Do not complete Form 4952, which is used for depreciation.

1B. Complete Problem 1A above before completing Problem 1B. Richard and Christine McCarthy have a 19-year-old son Jack, (born 10/2/2005; Social Security number 555-55-1212), who is a full-time student at the University of Key West. Years ago, the McCarthys shifted a significant amount of investments into Jack's name. In 2024, Jack received Form 1099-INT that reported the following:

Tandy Corporation Bonds interest	$14,500

In addition, Jack works part-time as a waiter in an upscale seafood restaurant in Big Coppitt Key, FL. His 2024 Form W-2 reported:

Wages	$14,100
Federal withholding	1,500

Despite Jack's fairly large income, the McCarthys provide more than 50 percent of his support and claim Jack as a dependent in 2024. Jack's mailing address is 100 Duval Street, Apt. #B12, Key West, FL 33040. Use the parent's information from Problem 1A, Form 1040, Schedule B, and Form 8615, to compute Jack's 2024 income tax.

2A. Warner Robins (born July 4, 1989) and Augustine Robins (born November 11, 1989) have been married for nine years, have no dependents, and file jointly. Warner is the president of Jaystar Corporation located in Macon, Georgia. The Jaystar stock is owned 40 percent by Warner, 40 percent by Augustine, and 20 percent by Warner's father. Warner and Augustine received the following tax documents:

Form W-2 Wage and Tax Statement — 2024

Field	Value
a Employee's social security number	798-09-8526
b Employer identification number (EIN)	43-4321567
c Employer's name, address, and ZIP code	Jaystar Corporation, 1776 Eisenhower Parkway, Macon, GA 32106
e Employee's first name and initial / Last name	Warner Robins
f Employee's address and ZIP code	638 Russell Parkway, Macon, GA 31207
1 Wages, tips, other compensation	135,000.00
2 Federal income tax withheld	8,400.00
3 Social security wages	135,000.00
4 Social security tax withheld	8,370.00
5 Medicare wages and tips	135,000.00
6 Medicare tax withheld	1,957.50
15 State	GA
Employer's state ID number	5643E25
16 State wages, tips, etc.	135,000.00
17 State income tax	3,800.00

Form 1099-INT — Interest Income

☐ CORRECTED (if checked)

PAYER'S name, street address, city or town, state or province, country, ZIP or foreign postal code, and telephone no.
Georgia National Bank
520 Walnut Street
Macon, GA 31201

Payer's RTN (optional):

OMB No. 1545-0112
Form 1099-INT (Rev. January 2024)
For calendar year **2024**

Interest Income — Copy B For Recipient

Box	Description	Amount
1	Interest income	$600.00
2	Early withdrawal penalty	$200.00
3	Interest on U.S. Savings Bonds and Treasury obligations	
4	Federal income tax withheld	
5	Investment expenses	
6	Foreign tax paid	
7	Foreign country or U.S. territory	
8	Tax-exempt interest	
9	Specified private activity bond interest	
10	Market discount	
11	Bond premium	
12	Bond premium on Treasury obligations	
13	Bond premium on tax-exempt bond	
14	Tax-exempt and tax credit bond CUSIP no.	
15	State	
16	State identification no.	
17	State tax withheld	

PAYER'S TIN: 23-8787878
RECIPIENT'S TIN: 445-81-1423

RECIPIENT'S name: Augustine and Warner Robins
Street address: 638 Russell Parkway
City, state, ZIP: Macon, GA 31207

FATCA filing requirement: ☐
Account number (see instructions):

Form 1099-INT (Rev. 1-2024) — (keep for your records) — www.irs.gov/Form1099INT — Department of the Treasury – Internal Revenue Service

---

Form 1098 — Mortgage Interest Statement

☐ CORRECTED (if checked)

RECIPIENT'S/LENDER'S name, street address, city or town, state or province, country, ZIP or foreign postal code, and telephone no.
Georgia National Bank
520 Walnut Street
Macon, GA 31201

Caution: The amount shown may not be fully deductible by you. Limits based on the loan amount and the cost and value of the secured property may apply. Also, you may only deduct interest to the extent it was incurred by you, actually paid by you, and not reimbursed by another person.

OMB No. 1545-1380
Form 1098 (Rev. January 2022)
For calendar year **2024**

Mortgage Interest Statement — Copy B For Payer/Borrower

Box	Description	Amount
1	Mortgage interest received from payer(s)/borrower(s)	$24,700.61
2	Outstanding mortgage principal	$790,000.00
3	Mortgage origination date	10/13/2016
4	Refund of overpaid interest	
5	Mortgage insurance premiums	
6	Points paid on purchase of principal residence	
7	If address of property securing mortgage is the same as PAYER'S/BORROWER'S address, the box is checked	☒
8	Address or description of property securing mortgage	
9	Number of properties securing the mortgage	1
10	Other — Prop. tax	$6,800.00
11	Mortgage acquisition date	

RECIPIENT'S/LENDER'S TIN: 23-8787878
PAYER'S/BORROWER'S TIN: 798-09-8526

PAYER'S/BORROWER'S name: Augustine and Warner Robins
Street address: 638 Russell Parkway
City, state, ZIP: Macon, GA 31207

Account number (see instructions):

Form 1098 (Rev. 1-2022) — (Keep for your records) — www.irs.gov/Form1098 — Department of the Treasury – Internal Revenue Service

---

Form 1099-G — Certain Government Payments

☐ CORRECTED (if checked)

PAYER'S name, street address, city or town, state or province, country, ZIP or foreign postal code, and telephone no.
State of Georgia Treasurer
200 Piedmont Ave. SE Ste 1204
Atlanta, GA 30334

OMB No. 1545-0120
Form 1099-G (Rev. March 2024)
For calendar year **2024**

Certain Government Payments — Copy B For Recipient

Box	Description	Amount
1	Unemployment compensation	
2	State or local income tax refunds, credits, or offsets	$850.00
3	Box 2 amount is for tax year	
4	Federal income tax withheld	
5	RTAA payments	
6	Taxable grants	
7	Agriculture payments	
8	If checked, box 2 is trade or business income	☐
9	Market gain	
10a	State	
10b	State identification no.	
11	State income tax withheld	

PAYER'S TIN: 21-4315123
RECIPIENT'S TIN: 798-09-8526

RECIPIENT'S name: Warner and Augustine Robins
Street address: 638 Russell Parkway
City, state, ZIP: Macon, GA 31207

Account number (see instructions):

Form 1099-G (Rev. 3-2024) — (keep for your records) — www.irs.gov/Form1099G — Department of the Treasury – Internal Revenue Service

Macon Museum of Arts
3231 Vineville Ave.
Macon, GA 31204

November 23, 2024

Mr. and Mrs. Warner and Augustine Robins
638 Russell Parkway
Macon, GA 31207

Dear Mr. and Mrs. Robins:

Thank you for your contribution of the original album cover art for the Almond Sisters Band to the Macon Museum of Arts.

This gift supports the Macon Museum's efforts to bring original and locally-sourced art work to Macon. This continuing support will guarantee our ability to display Almond Sister art work for many years to come.

We have attached a copy of the appraiser's market valuation. Her analysis estimates the value of the painting at $54,000.

Please keep this written acknowledgment of your donation for your tax records. As a token of our appreciation for your support, we have mailed you the Macon Museum tote bag. We estimate the value of the tote bag to be $50. We are required to inform you that your federal income tax deduction for your contribution is the amount of your contribution less the value of the tote bag. Thank you for your continuing support for our important work in this field!

Please retain this letter as proof of your charitable contribution.

Sincerely,

Jack T. Mann
Jack T. Mann
Art Development Officer

Employer Identification Number **22-1234567**
Macon Museum of Arts is a registered 501(c)(3) corporation

The Robins paid the following amounts (all can be substantiated):

General state sales tax	$ 2,203
Auto loan interest	4,800
Medical insurance	11,000
Income tax preparation fee	750
Charitable contributions in cash:	
Church	3,700
Central Georgia Technical University	5,000
Safe-deposit box	200

The Robins had total itemized deductions of $33,567 in 2023 which included a $9,650 state tax deduction.

The tax basis for the donated album cover art is $25,000 and has been owned by Warner and Augustine for five years.

Jaystar does not cover health insurance for its employees. In addition to Warner and Augustine's health insurance premiums shown above, Augustine required surgery which cost $6,500 for which only $3,100 was covered by insurance. In September 2024, Warner had to drive Augustine 126 miles each way to a surgical center.

On January 1, 2024, Warner sold land to Jaystar Corporation for $75,000. He acquired the land five years ago for $160,000. No Form 1099-B was filed for this transaction.

Augustine decided to become a management consultant in late 2024 and provided consulting services to her only client, Jaystar, in 2024 and billed them $7,500 on December 27, 2024. Jaystar is an accrual-based corporation and accrued the consulting expense of $7,500. Jaystar paid Augustine in January 2025 and expects to issue her a 1099-NEC in 2025. This was Augustine's only consulting work in 2024, and she is a cash-based business. She incurred no business-related expenses in 2024.

Jaystar Corporation does not have a qualified pension plan or 401k plan for its employees. Therefore, Warner deposited $14,000 ($7,000 each) into traditional IRA accounts for Augustine and himself (neither are covered by a qualified plan at work).

Required: Complete the Robins' federal tax return for 2024. Use Form 1040, Schedule 1, Schedule A, Schedule D, and Form 8949 to complete this tax return. Make realistic assumptions about any missing data and ignore any alternative minimum tax. Do not complete Form 8283, which is used when large noncash donations are made to charity.

2B. Complete Problem 2A above before starting Problem 2B. The Robins received their income tax refund for 2024 in May 2025. On July 14, 2025, the Robins' primary home in Macon (Bibb County, GA) was hit by the remnants of Hurricane Gator (DR-4690-GA) and suffered damage that decreased the fair market value of their home from $905,000 to $880,000. They originally paid $715,000 for the home. Because Macon is not normally hit by hurricanes, the Robins' had only limited insurance and received $2,500 to cover the cost of repairs. Because this was declared a federal disaster, the Robins wish to amend their 2024 return and obtain an immediate refund. In accordance with IRS guidance, the explanation for the amendment on Form 1040-X should include that the taxpayer is filing an amended return under a Section 165(i) Election and (1) the name or a description of the disaster and date or dates of the disaster which gave rise to the loss, and (2) the address, including the city, town, county, parish, state, and zip code, where the damaged or destroyed property was located at the time of the disaster.

Required: Complete the Robins' 2024 amended federal tax return. Use Form 1040-X, Form 1040, Schedule A, and Form 4684 (including Section D on page 4) to complete this tax return. Make realistic assumptions about any missing data. Note: Because the ProConnect software requires an *actual* federally declared disaster, this problem cannot be completed in the software and must be completed manually.

Group 5:
Cumulative Software Problem

1. The following information is available for the Albert and Allison Gaytor family in addition to that provided in Chapters 1–5.

    Allison discovered a bookkeeping error in her business records. The revenues from Toge Pass should have been $79,800 (not the $64,800 originally recorded).

    Albert owned 1,000 shares of Behemoth Airline stock with a basis of $25 per share. The stock was purchased six years ago on June 16. Albert sells 500 shares of Behemoth stock to his uncle Seth and 500 of the shares to his sister Sara for $5 per share on December 31, 2024. These sales were not reported on Form 1099-B.

Required: Combine this new information about the Gaytor family with the information from Chapters 1–5 and complete a revised 2024 tax return for Albert and Allison. Be sure to save your data input files since this case will be expanded with more tax information in each succeeding chapter.

Chapter 7

Tax Credits

Learning Objectives

After completing this chapter, you should be able to:

- **LO 7.1** Calculate the child tax credit.
- **LO 7.2** Determine the earned income credit (EIC).
- **LO 7.3** Compute the child and dependent care credit for an individual taxpayer.
- **LO 7.4** Calculate the premium tax credit available under the Affordable Care Act.
- **LO 7.5** Apply the special rules applicable to the American Opportunity tax credit (AOTC) and lifetime learning credit.
- **LO 7.6** Compute the foreign income exclusion and tax credit.
- **LO 7.7** Determine the proper use and calculation of the adoption credit.
- **LO 7.8** Recognize other basic individual credits.
- **LO 7.9** Calculate the low-income Retirement Plan Contribution Credit.

Overview

This chapter covers the most common tax credits. Credits differ from deductions. A credit is a direct reduction in tax liability while a deduction decreases taxable income. Credits are used because they target tax relief to certain groups of taxpayers. Because of the progressive rate structure of the income tax, a deduction provides greater benefit to higher-income taxpayers, while a tax credit provides equal benefit, regardless of the taxpayer's income level.

A deduction reduces taxable income by the amount of the deduction and thus results in a tax savings equal to the deduction multiplied by the tax rate. A credit is a dollar-for-dollar reduction of the taxpayer's tax liability. If a taxpayer has a choice between a credit or a deduction of equal amounts, generally the credit will result in greater tax savings.

Many credits exist in the tax law that are not covered here, such as the credit for research and development, the Work Opportunity Tax Credit, and the credit for the elderly and disabled.

Example Vijaya is a single taxpayer. His 2024 taxable income is $60,000 placing him in the 22-percent tax bracket for ordinary income. His income tax liability is $8,259. Not included in the $60,000 of taxable income is a choice between a $1,000 deduction and a $1,000 credit.

	Deduction	Credit
Taxable income	$60,000	$60,000
Deduction	(1,000)	n/a
Revised taxable income	59,000	60,000
Tax on revised income	8,039	8,259
Tax credit	n/a	(1,000)
Tax after credits	8,039	7,259
Original tax	8,259	8,259
Tax savings	$ 220	$ 1,000

Vijaya saves $1,000 (a dollar-for-dollar reduction in tax liability) with the credit. He saves $220 ($1,000 × 22% tax rate) for the deduction. ♦

Most tax credits are limited to the amount of total tax liability that a taxpayer has and thus are "nonrefundable." Certain credits allow taxpayers to claim the credit even when the amount of the credit exceeds their tax liability—these are known as refundable credits since they result in a "refund" of taxes that were never actually paid by the taxpayer.

Example Santana is a taxpayer who files as head of household, with taxable income of $17,000 and a tax liability of $1,712 before any tax credits. Santana has total tax payments (including withholding) of $2,200. Santana is eligible for a tax credit of $2,000. Santana's refund is calculated as follows if the credit is refundable versus nonrefundable:

	Nonrefundable	Refundable
Total tax before credits	$1,712	$1,712
Tax credit	(1,712)	(2,000)
Tax after credits	0	(288)
Tax payments	(2,200)	(2,200)
Total refund	$(2,200)	$(2,488)

The refundable credit increases Santana's refund to an amount in excess of their taxes paid. ♦

7-1 Child Tax Credit

Learning Objective 7.1
Calculate the child tax credit.

The child tax credit permits individual taxpayers to take a tax credit based on the number of their qualifying dependent children. The child tax credit is amidst a temporary expansion. In 2018, the Tax Cuts and Jobs Act (TCJA) made three significant, but temporary, changes to the child tax credit that continue to apply in 2024: (1) increased the credit per child to $2,000, (2) increased the threshold for which the phase-out starts, and (3) increased the refundable amount of the credit for taxpayers whose credit is limited by their pre-credit tax liability. In addition, the TCJA added a new qualifying dependent credit of $500 for certain dependents. All of these provisions are scheduled to expire after 2025.

7-1a Child Tax Credit

To qualify for the child tax credit, the child must be under age 17, a U.S. citizen or U.S. resident alien, claimed as a dependent on the taxpayer's return, and meet the definition of "qualifying child" as covered in Chapter 1. Thus, the child must meet the six tests outlined in Chapter 1: (1) relationship test, (2) domicile test, (3) age test (except in the case of the child tax credit, the child must be under age 17), (4) joint return test, (5) citizenship test, and (6) self-support test. All qualifying children must have a Social Security number at the time of filing.

The maximum credit is $2,000 per qualifying child; however, the available credit begins phasing out when AGI reaches $400,000 for joint filers and $200,000 for all other taxpayers. The credit is phased out by $50 for each $1,000 (or part thereof) of AGI above the threshold amounts. Since the maximum credit available depends on the number of qualifying children, the income level at which the credit is fully phased out also depends on the number of children qualifying for the credit. The phase-out thresholds for the child tax credit are currently not adjusted for cost-of-living increases.

Example Donna and Chris Howser are married and file a joint tax return. They have two children, ages 5 and 7, that are qualifying children under the dependency rules. All members of the family are U.S. citizens with Social Security numbers. In 2024, their AGI was $120,006. In 2024, both children qualify for the child tax credit of $2,000; thus, the maximum credit is $4,000. Because the phase-out for married filing jointly taxpayers in 2024 starts at $400,000, the Howsers are eligible for the maximum credit of $4,000. ♦

Example Fiona and Kris Everest are married and file a joint return. They have one child, age 13. Each member of the Everest family has a Social Security number and their 2024 AGI is $409,100. The maximum child tax credit in 2024 is $2,000 per child; however, the Everest's AGI exceeds the $400,000 threshold. The phase-out amount is $500.

$409,100 − $400,000 = $9,100
$9,100/$1,000 = 9.1 rounded to 10
10 × $50 = $500

The Everest's child tax credit is limited to $1,500 ($2,000 − $500). ♦

The nonrefundable portion of the child tax credit is limited to the amount of tax liability before taking the child tax credit. Because taxpayers may be eligible for other tax credits that also reduce tax liability, the tax law prescribes a "pecking order" to prevent taxpayers from claiming more than one nonrefundable tax credit and creating a refundable credit. The child tax credit comes after the foreign tax credit, the credit for child and dependent care expenses, education credits, and the saver's credit. The Credit Limitation Worksheet A from the Schedule 8812 instructions is used by most taxpayers to compute the nonrefundable portion of the child tax credit.

Example In 2024, Eugene has a tax liability of $2,200 before any tax credits. Eugene has determined he is eligible for an education credit of $400 and a child tax credit of $2,000. Because his two nonrefundable credits exceed his tax liability, Eugene will take a $400 education credit, and his nonrefundable child tax credit will be limited to $1,800 ($2,200 − $400). Eugene's Credit Limitation Worksheet A is presented on the next page. ♦

Credit Limit Worksheet A   *Keep for Your Records*

1. Enter the amount from line 18 of your Form 1040, 1040–SR, or 1040–NR. .... 1. _____ 2,200
2. Add the following amounts (if applicable) from:
   - Schedule 3, line 1 ... foreign tax credit .... + _____
   - Schedule 3, line 2 ... child and dependent care expense credit .... + _____
   - Schedule 3, line 3 ... education credit (AOTC/LLC) .... + _____ 400
   - Schedule 3, line 4 ... retirement savings credit .... + _____
   - Schedule 3, line 5b ... energy efficient home improvement credit ... + _____
   - Schedule 3, line 6d ... elderly credit .... + _____
   - Schedule 3, line 6f ... new clean vehicle credit .... + _____
   - Schedule 3, line 6l ... additional reporting year tax for partner ... + _____
   - Schedule 3, line 6m ... used clean vehicle credit .... + _____

   Enter the total.   2. _____ 400
3. Subtract line 2 from line 1. .... 3. _____ 1,800

   Complete Credit Limit Worksheet B **only** if you meet all the following.
   1. You are claiming one or more of the following credits.
      a. Mortgage interest credit, Form 8396.
      b. Adoption credit, Form 8839.
      c. Residential clean energy credit, Form 5695, Part I.
      d. District of Columbia first-time homebuyer credit, Form 8859.
   2. You are not filing Form 2555.
   3. Line 4 of Schedule 8812 is more than zero.
4. If you are **not** completing Credit Limit Worksheet B, enter -0-; otherwise, enter the amount from Credit Limit Worksheet B. .... 4. _____
5. Subtract line 4 from line 3. Enter here and on Schedule 8812, line 13. .... 5. _____ 1,800

The refundable portion of the child tax credit is the amount of child tax credit that was limited by the taxpayer's tax liability.

Example   Eugene, in the previous example, was eligible for a total child tax credit of $2,000; however, he could only take a credit of $1,800 due to the tax liability limitation. The $200 unclaimed child tax credit *may* be refundable. ♦

If the taxpayer has fewer than three children who are eligible for the child tax credit, the refundable portion of the child tax credit is subject to two additional limitations. The first limitation is that the additional child tax credit cannot exceed $1,700 per child. The second limitation is that the refundable child tax credit cannot exceed 15 percent of the taxpayer's earned income over $2,500. The lower of these two amounts will apply.

Example   In 2024, Tashi and Terry, married filing jointly taxpayers, have two qualifying children, AGI of $72,000 (all earned income) and tax liability before any credits of $1,043. As a result, their child tax credit of $4,000 is limited to $1,043. However, Mike and Laura can claim the refundable portion of child tax credit of $2,957; the lesser of the unclaimed child tax credit $2,957 ($4,000 − $1,043) or 15 percent of earned income over $2,500 [($72,000 − $2,500) × 15% = $10,425], limited to $3,400 ($1,700 per qualifying child). ♦

For taxpayers with three or more qualifying children, the child tax credit amount in excess of tax liability is subject to limitations. The same overall $1,700 limit per child applies. The refundable child tax credit is also limited by the greater of (1) 15 percent of earned income over $2,500 or (2) the amount of Social Security and Medicare taxes paid, up to the unclaimed child tax credit. For purposes of the refundable child tax credit, Social Security and Medicare taxes are the amounts withheld for the employee and 50 percent of self-employment taxes.

Example Molly and Sam are married, file a joint tax return, have five qualifying children, and earned income of $6,000 in 2024. The children are qualifying children for purposes of the child tax credit, but do not qualify under the earned income tax credit. Molly and Sam had $459 of Social Security and Medicare taxes withheld by their employers. Their pre-credit tax liability is $0. Because their pre-credit tax liability is $0, Molly and Sam are not eligible for the $10,000 ($2,000 × 5 children) child tax credit. The refundable portion of the child tax credit is $525, which starts at $10,000 but is first limited to $8,500 ($1,700 × 5) and then further limited to the greater of $459 or $525 [($6,000 − $2,500) × 15%]. ♦

For 2024, the child tax credit is claimed on Schedule 8812 (refer to Pages 7-7 and 7-8). Most taxpayers will complete Part I and those with a limited credit will also complete Part II-A of Schedule 8812. The other portion of the form is for taxpayers with three of more children eligible for the child tax credit.

For dependents that do not qualify for the child tax credit, a $500 "other dependent credit" also exists. For example, a dependent parent or dependent child age 17 or older can still qualify as eligible dependents for the other dependent credit. The qualifying relative test for purposes of the other dependent credit requires the individual must be a U.S. citizen, a U.S. national, or a U.S. resident in order to be eligible for the credit. A Social Security number is not required for the other dependent credit and the credit is nonrefundable. The other dependent credit is also reported on Schedule 8812 in 2024.

Example Alex is a single taxpayer with a 15-year-old child. Alex also takes care of her elderly mother, who qualifies as a dependent. Alex is eligible for a possible $2,000 child tax credit and a $500 other dependent credit for her mother. ♦

Example Demarcus is a single taxpayer with a dependent 21-year-old child who is a full-time student. Demarcus also takes care of his elderly mother who qualifies as a dependent. Demarcus is eligible for a $1,000 other dependent tax credit for his child and his mother. ♦

A taxpayer who erroneously claims the child tax credit due to reckless or intentional disregard of rules or regulations is ineligible to claim the credit for a period of two tax years. If the IRS determines the claim for the credit was fraudulent, the ineligibility window is extended to ten years.

If the IRS rejects a child tax credit for any reason other than a math or clerical error, the taxpayer must complete a Form 8862 in a year after a rejection. Form 8862 is also used for claiming an earned income credit or American Opportunities credit after rejection. Tax preparers that prepare returns on which the child tax credit is claimed are required to complete Form 8867, a due diligence checklist that was also covered in Chapter 1 when the filing status is head of household.

The IRS will not issue refunds for any tax returns that claim a child tax credit (or earned income credit) until February 15 of the year following the tax year. This tax provision is intended to provide the IRS with additional time to review refund claims that stem from refundable credit claims.

ProConnect™ Tax TIP

The child tax credit is handled by ProConnect Tax in an almost seamless fashion. By entering the dependent's birthdate and status (e.g., full-time student) the software will automatically compute the child tax credit, other dependent credit, and additional child tax credit. A number of dropdown boxes are available under the Dependent entry screen that permit overrides and other options for these credits. For this reason, child tax credits or related information will not be found under the Credits input.

Self-Study Problem 7.1   Refer to Appendix E for Solutions to Self-Study Problems

a. Jose and Jane are married and file a joint tax return claiming their three children, ages 4, 5, and 18, as dependents. Their AGI for 2024 is $125,400 and their pre-credit tax liability is $14,000. They are not claiming any other tax credits in 2024. Determine Jose and Jane's child tax credit and other dependent credit, if any for 2024.

b. Herb and Tacey are married and file a joint tax return claiming their three children, ages 4, 5, and 18, as dependents. Their AGI for 2024 is $405,600 and their pre-credit tax liability is about $84,000. What is Herb and Tacey's child tax credit and other dependent credit, if any for 2024?

c. Marie and Pierre Curry are married and file a joint tax return claiming their three children, ages 4, 5, and 16, as dependents. Their AGI for 2024 is $30,000 (all wage income) and their pre-credit tax liability is $230. Marie and Pierre's employers withheld $2,295 in Social Security and Medicare taxes in 2024. They are also claiming a child and dependent care expense credit of $30 but are not claiming any other tax credits. Complete Schedule 8812 and Credit Limit Worksheet A on Pages 7-7 to 7-9 to determine Marie and Pierre's child tax credit and additional refundable child tax credit, if any, for 2024.

Self-Study Problem 7.1, Part c

SCHEDULE 8812
(Form 1040)

Department of the Treasury
Internal Revenue Service

Credits for Qualifying Children and Other Dependents

Attach to Form 1040, 1040-SR, or 1040-NR.
Go to *www.irs.gov/Schedule8812* for instructions and the latest information.

OMB No. 1545-0074

2024

Attachment Sequence No. **47**

Name(s) shown on return

Your social security number

Part I — Child Tax Credit and Credit for Other Dependents

1	Enter the amount from line 11 of your Form 1040, 1040-SR, or 1040-NR		1
2a	Enter income from Puerto Rico that you excluded	2a	
b	Enter the amounts from lines 45 and 50 of your Form 2555	2b	
c	Enter the amount from line 15 of your Form 4563	2c	
d	Add lines 2a through 2c		2d
3	Add lines 1 and 2d		3
4	Number of qualifying children under age 17 with the required social security number	4	
5	Multiply line 4 by $2,000		5
6	Number of other dependents, including any qualifying children who are not under age 17 or who do not have the required social security number	6	
	Caution: Do not include yourself, your spouse, or anyone who is not a U.S. citizen, U.S. national, or U.S. resident alien. Also, do not include anyone you included on line 4.		
7	Multiply line 6 by $500		7
8	Add lines 5 and 7		8
9	Enter the amount shown below for your filing status. • Married filing jointly—$400,000 • All other filing statuses—$200,000		9
10	Subtract line 9 from line 3. • If zero or less, enter -0-. • If more than zero and not a multiple of $1,000, enter the next multiple of $1,000. For example, if the result is $425, enter $1,000; if the result is $1,025, enter $2,000, etc.		10
11	Multiply line 10 by 5% (0.05)		11
12	Is the amount on line 8 more than the amount on line 11?		12
	☐ **No. STOP.** You cannot take the child tax credit, credit for other dependents, or additional child tax credit. Skip Parts II-A and II-B. Enter -0- on lines 14 and 27.		
	☐ **Yes.** Subtract line 11 from line 8. Enter the result.		
13	Enter the amount from **Credit Limit Worksheet A**		13
14	Enter the smaller of line 12 or line 13. **This is your child tax credit and credit for other dependents**. Enter this amount on Form 1040, 1040-SR, or 1040-NR, line 19.		14

If the amount on line 12 is more than the amount on line 14, you may be able to take the **additional child tax credit** on Form 1040, 1040-SR, or 1040-NR, line 28. Complete your Form 1040, 1040-SR, or 1040-NR through line 27 (also complete Schedule 3, line 11) before completing Part II-A.

For Paperwork Reduction Act Notice, see your tax return instructions. Cat. No. 59761M Schedule 8812 (Form 1040) 2024

Schedule 8812 (Form 1040) 2024   Page **2**

Part II-A   Additional Child Tax Credit for All Filers

Caution: If you file Form 2555, you cannot claim the additional child tax credit.

15	Check this box if you **do not** want to claim the additional child tax credit. Skip Parts II-A and II-B. Enter -0- on line 27 . . . . . ▶ ☐	
16a	Subtract line 14 from line 12. If zero, **stop here**; you cannot take the additional child tax credit. Skip Parts II-A and II-B. Enter -0- on line 27	16a
b	Number of qualifying children under age 17 with the required social security number: _____ x $1,700. Enter the result. If zero, **stop here**; you cannot claim the additional child tax credit. Skip Parts II-A and II-B. Enter -0- on line 27	16b
	TIP: The number of children you use for this line is the same as the number of children you used for line 4.	
17	Enter the **smaller** of line 16a or line 16b	17
18a	Earned income (see instructions) 18a	
b	Nontaxable combat pay (see instructions) 18b	
19	Is the amount on line 18a more than $2,500?	
	☐ **No.** Leave line 19 blank and enter -0- on line 20.	
	☐ **Yes.** Subtract $2,500 from the amount on line 18a. Enter the result . . . 19	
20	Multiply the amount on line 19 by 15% (0.15) and enter the result	20
	Next. On line 16b, is the amount $5,100 or more?	
	☐ **No.** If you are a bona fide resident of Puerto Rico, go to line 21. Otherwise, skip Part II-B and enter the **smaller** of line 17 or line 20 on line 27.	
	☐ **Yes.** If line 20 is equal to or more than line 17, skip Part II-B and enter the amount from line 17 on line 27. Otherwise, go to line 21.	

Part II-B   Certain Filers Who Have Three or More Qualifying Children and Bona Fide Residents of Puerto Rico

21	Withheld social security, Medicare, and Additional Medicare taxes from Form(s) W-2, boxes 4 and 6. If married filing jointly, include your spouse's amounts with yours. If your employer withheld or you paid Additional Medicare Tax or tier 1 RRTA taxes, or if you are a bona fide resident of Puerto Rico, see instructions 21	
22	Enter the total of the amounts from Schedule 1 (Form 1040), line 15; Schedule 2 (Form 1040), line 5; Schedule 2 (Form 1040), line 6; and Schedule 2 (Form 1040), line 13 . 22	
23	Add lines 21 and 22	23
24	**1040 and 1040-SR filers:** Enter the total of the amounts from Form 1040 or 1040-SR, line 27, and Schedule 3 (Form 1040), line 11. **1040-NR filers:** Enter the amount from Schedule 3 (Form 1040), line 11. } 24	
25	Subtract line 24 from line 23. If zero or less, enter -0-	25
26	Enter the **larger** of line 20 or line 25	26
	Next, enter the **smaller** of line 17 or line 26 on line 27.	

Part II-C   Additional Child Tax Credit

27	This is your additional child tax credit. Enter this amount on Form 1040, 1040-SR, or 1040-NR, line 28 . .	27

Schedule 8812 (Form 1040) 2024

Self-Study Problem 7.1, Part c, cont.

Credit Limit Worksheet A

Keep for Your Records

1. Enter the amount from line 18 of your Form 1040, 1040–SR, or 1040–NR. .... 1. _____
2. Add the following amounts (if applicable) from:

Schedule 3, line 1	foreign tax credit	+ _____
Schedule 3, line 2	child and dependent care expense credit	+ _____
Schedule 3, line 3	education credit (AOTC/LLC)	+ _____
Schedule 3, line 4	retirement savings credit	+ _____
Schedule 3, line 5b	energy efficient home improvement credit	+ _____
Schedule 3, line 6d	elderly credit	+ _____
Schedule 3, line 6f	new clean vehicle credit	+ _____
Schedule 3, line 6l	additional reporting year tax for partner	+ _____
Schedule 3, line 6m	used clean vehicle credit	+ _____

    Enter the total. 2. _____

3. Subtract line 2 from line 1. .... 3. _____

    Complete Credit Limit Worksheet B **only** if you meet all the following.

    1. You are claiming one or more of the following credits.

        a. Mortgage interest credit, Form 8396.
        b. Adoption credit, Form 8839.
        c. Residential clean energy credit, Form 5695, Part I.
        d. District of Columbia first-time homebuyer credit, Form 8859.

    2. You are not filing Form 2555.

    3. Line 4 of Schedule 8812 is more than zero.

4. If you are **not** completing Credit Limit Worksheet B, enter -0-; otherwise, enter the amount from Credit Limit Worksheet B. .... 4. _____
5. Subtract line 4 from line 3. Enter here and on Schedule 8812, line 13. .... 5. _____

Learning Objective 7.2

Determine the earned income credit (EIC).

7-2 Earned Income Credit

The earned income credit (EIC or sometimes referred to as EITC) is available to qualifying individuals with earned income and AGI below certain levels. The earned income credit is meant to assist the working poor by reducing their tax burden and to supplement wage income through a refundable credit when earnings are less than the taxpayer's maximum income for their filing status. Qualifying taxpayers can receive a refundable EIC even in situations when they have no filing requirement, owe no tax, and had no income tax withheld. Similar to the refundable child tax credit, the refundable EIC can in effect produce a "negative" income tax.

Proper calculation of the EIC requires a taxpayer to answer three important questions:

(1) Does the taxpayer qualify for the EIC?
(2) Does the taxpayer have a qualifying child?
(3) What is the amount of the EIC?

7-2a Does the Taxpayer Qualify?

There are seven rules that all taxpayers must meet in order to claim the EIC and the taxpayer must meet *all seven* rules. Failure to meet just one precludes the taxpayer from claiming the EIC. The seven rules fall into the following categories:

1. AGI limit—AGI limits are indexed for inflation and can change each year. In addition, the AGI limits vary based on filing status and number of qualifying children. The EIC phases out for taxpayers with income over the limits. For 2024, the limits are presented in Table 7.1.

Table 7.1 Earned Income Credit AGI Limits

Qualifying Children	Other Than Joint Filers		Joint Filers	
	Phase-out Begins	Phase-out Ends	Phase-out Begins	Phase-out Ends
None	$10,330	$18,591	$17,250	$25,511
1	22,720	49,084	29,640	56,004
2	22,720	55,768	29,640	62,688
3 or more	22,720	59,899	29,640	66,819

The phase-out percentages vary; however, only the IRS EIC Tables (Appendix B) may be used to calculate the EIC amount.

2. Social Security numbers—The taxpayer (and spouse, if filing jointly) plus any qualifying children, must all have valid Social Security numbers. If a taxpayer's child(ren) does not have a Social Security number, the taxpayer may still claim the EIC for no children if qualified otherwise.
3. Married filing separately not allowed unless one spouse lives with a qualifying child for at least one-half of the year and has not lived in the same abode as the other spouse for the last six months of the year or has a separation decree.
4. U.S. citizenship or resident alien status is required for the entire tax year.
5. Foreign income exclusion not allowed—tax law provides for certain taxpayers to exclude income earned overseas (reported on Form 2555 or Form 2555-EZ). The foreign income exclusion is beyond the scope of this textbook.
6. Investment income limit—generating a certain amount of "disqualified" income ($11,600 in 2024) precludes claiming the EIC. Disqualified income includes most typical forms of investment income such as interest, dividends, net income from rents and royalties and most forms of capital gains.
7. Earned income requirement—Since the design of the EIC is to assist the working poor, an obvious requirement is that the taxpayer (or spouse, if filing jointly) have earned income. Earned income includes wages, salaries, tips, and other taxable employee pay and self-employment income after deducting one-half of self-employment tax. For purposes of the EIC, earned income also includes taxable long-term disability benefits received prior to minimum retirement age (typically reported on Form 1099-R with

distribution code 3) and, if elected by the taxpayer, combat pay (refer to Chapter 6). The earned income limits for 2024 presented in Table 7.2.

Table 7.2 Earned Income Credit Earned Income Limits

Qualifying Children	Other Than Joint Filers		Joint Filers	
	Minimum Earned Income	Maximum Earned Income	Minimum Earned Income	Maximum Earned Income
None	$1	$18,591	$1	$25,511
1	1	49,084	1	56,004
2	1	55,768	1	62,688
3 or more	1	59,899	1	66,819

Example Doug is married but files separately in 2024. Doug has no qualifying children. Doug does not qualify for the EIC in 2024 because he does not meet the specific qualifications for separated spouses. ♦

Example In 2024, Jane has income of $7,000, is single, has a valid Social Security number, and is not a qualifying child of another taxpayer. Her income includes $4,500 of interest on a corporate bond. Jane is eligible for the EIC because her investment income does not exceed $11,600. ♦

Example In 2024, Eddie and Lindsey had a new baby. Their earned income and AGI in 2024 was $12,500, they filed jointly, lived in the United States, and had no investment income. Eddie and Lindsey have Social Security numbers but have not had the time to get a Social Security number for the baby yet. Eddie and Lindsey may claim an EIC in 2024 but only with no qualifying child since the baby does not have a valid Social Security number. They should consider applying for a Social Security number by the filing deadline. ♦

Example In 2024, Jerry earns wages of $22,000 from his job and has no adjustments or other forms of income. He has no qualifying children and no investment income. Even if Jerry meets all the other requirements (Social Security number, U.S. residence, etc.), he will not be eligible for the EIC as his AGI exceeds the threshold amount for an unmarried taxpayer with no qualifying children ($18,591 in 2024). ♦

7-2b Does the Taxpayer Have a Qualifying Child?

Determining whether the taxpayer has a qualifying child is important because the eligibility rules differ based on whether a qualifying child is claimed or not. Because the rules defining a qualifying child for the EIC are similar to the rules for claiming a dependent, a review of the rules in Chapter 1 is suggested.

7-2c Taxpayer with No Qualifying Child

If the taxpayer does not have a qualifying child, the previous seven rules *must* be met along with four additional rules:

1. Taxpayer's age—in 2024, the taxpayer or the spouse (but not both) must be at least 25 years of age by the end of the tax year but less than 65 years of age.
2. Dependency status—the taxpayer (or spouse, if filing jointly) must not be eligible to be claimed as a dependent on another taxpayer's return, whether they are claimed or not.
3. Cannot be a qualifying child—the taxpayer claiming the EIC may not be the qualifying child of another taxpayer. Note the qualifying child definition covered in Chapter 1 applies here with two notable exceptions: (1) the child need not meet the support test, and (2) the child must live in a U.S. home for more than one-half of the year (a slight extension of the domicile test).

4. U.S. home—the taxpayer must have lived in the United States for more than one-half of the tax year.

Example Marco and Llewelyn are married, file jointly with no qualifying children in 2024, and meet the general rules to claim the EIC. Marco turned 66 on December 14, 2024, and Llewelyn turned 65 on April 3, 2024. Due to their age, Marco and Llewelyn do not qualify to claim the 2024 EIC. ♦

Example Monica is a 23-year-old single taxpayer with no qualifying children in 2024. She is a full-time student at State College and generates enough income to live on from her nontaxable scholarships and a job on campus; however, she lets her father claim her as a dependent as the scholarship money is not included in her support test. Even if Monica meets the seven general rules, because she is claimed as a dependent by another taxpayer, she is not eligible to claim the EIC. ♦

7-2d Taxpayer with a Qualifying Child

To claim an EIC with a qualifying child, three additional rules must be considered:

1. Qualifying child tests—the child must meet the qualifying child tests. These are the same tests as covered in Chapter 1 with two notable exceptions: (1) the child need not meet the support test, and (2) the child must live in a U.S. home for more than one-half of the year (a slight extension of the domicile test).
2. Qualifying child cannot be claimed by more than one person–only one taxpayer may claim a qualifying child for the EIC. If the child meets the definition of a qualifying child for more than one taxpayer, tiebreaker rules similar to those covered in Chapter 1 must be applied.
3. Taxpayer cannot be a qualifying child of another taxpayer—refer to rule 3 under taxpayer with no qualifying child in Section 7-2c.

With so many qualification rules, it is no wonder that taxpayers and tax preparers have been known to make numerous errors when determining the EIC. Numerous checklists and aids have been prepared to assist taxpayers with preparing the EIC calculation. IRS Publication 596 contains an EIC Eligibility Checklist provided in Figure 7.1.

In addition to checklists, the IRS has implemented some additional procedural steps to ensure the EIC is not being abused by taxpayers. Similar to the child tax credit rules, taxpayers claiming an earned income credit must have a Social Security number for the taxpayer, spouse (if married), and each qualifying child by the due date (including extensions) of the return.

If the IRS rejects an earned income credit for any reason other than a math or clerical error, the taxpayer must complete a Form 8862 in order to claim the EIC in a future year.

In addition, a taxpayer who erroneously claims the EIC due to reckless or intentional disregard of rules or regulations is ineligible to claim the credit for a period of two tax years. If the IRS determines the claim for the credit was fraudulent, the ineligibility window is extended to ten years.

The IRS will not issue refunds for any tax returns that claim an EIC until February 15th of the following year to provide the IRS with additional time to review refund claims that stem from refundable EIC claims.

To assist tax preparers with the accurate completion of the EIC (and the child tax credit and American Opportunities tax credit), Form 8867 (covered in Chapter 1) must be prepared and filed with the tax return and a copy retained by the tax preparer. If a taxpayer is claiming more than one of the credits covered by Form 8867, only one form is required to be filed. Failure to file Form 8867 could result in a $635 penalty.

7-2e What Is the Amount of the EIC?

Taxpayers are required to have some earned income to qualify for the EIC; however, too much earned income renders the taxpayer ineligible for the EIC. As stated previously, the EIC amount must be derived from the EIC Tables in Appendix B and should not be calculated using the statutory credit percentages to avoid rounding issues. To find the correct amount of EIC in the EIC Tables, the taxpayer must compare the EIC Table amount based on the taxpayer's earned income with the EIC Table amount associated with the taxpayer's AGI. The taxpayer is required to claim the smaller of the two EIC amounts.

Part of the complexity of the EIC is that a number of the thresholds, amounts, and limits change each year. As a result, new EIC tables must be used each year. The EIC is reported on Line 27 of Form 1040. Similar to the child tax credit, a specific form to support the EIC computation is not always required to be prepared and filed. Instead, a series of supporting worksheets found within the instructions to the Form 1040 are available to assist with preparation. Worksheet A is used for taxpayers with wage income only and Worksheet B is used by taxpayers with self-employment income. For taxpayers claiming a qualifying child for the EIC, Schedule EIC must also be filed.

Figure 7.1 2024 EIC Eligibility Checklist

1. Is your AGI less than: ☐ Yes ☐ No
   - $18,591 ($25,511 for married filing jointly) if you do not have a qualifying child,
   - $49,084 ($56,004 for married filing jointly) if you have one qualifying child,
   - $55,768 ($62,688 for married filing jointly) if you have two qualifying children, or
   - $59,899 ($66,819 for married filing jointly) if you have more than two qualifying children?
2. Do you and your spouse each have a valid SSN (by the due date of your return including extensions)? ☐ Yes ☐ No
3. Is your filing status married filing jointly, head of household, surviving spouse, or single? ☐ Yes ☐ No
4. Answer "**Yes**" if you are not filing Form 2555 or Form 2555-EZ. Otherwise, answer "**No**." ☐ Yes ☐ No
5. Is your investment income $11,600 or less? ☐ Yes ☐ No
6. Is your total earned income at least $1 but less than: ☐ Yes ☐ No
   - $18,591 ($25,511 for married filing jointly) if you do not have a qualifying child,
   - $49,084 ($56,004 for married filing jointly) if you have one qualifying child,
   - $55,768 ($62,688 for married filing jointly) if you have two qualifying children, or
   - $59,899 ($66,819 for married filing jointly) if you have more than two qualifying children?
7. Answer "**Yes**" if (a) you are not a qualifying child of another taxpayer or (b) you are filing a joint return. Otherwise, answer "NO." ☐ Yes ☐ No
8. Does your child meet the relationship, age, residency, and joint return tests for a qualifying child and have a Social Security number received by the due date of the tax return (including extensions)? ☐ Yes ☐ No
9. Is your child a qualifying child only for you? Answer "**Yes**" if (a) your qualifying child does not meet the tests to be a qualifying child of any other person or (b) your qualifying child meets the tests to be a qualifying child of another person but you are the person entitled to treat the child as a qualifying child under the tiebreaker rules. Answer "**No**" if the other person is the one entitled to treat the child as a qualifying child under the tiebreaker rules. ☐ Yes ☐ No
10. Were you (or your spouse if filing a joint return) at least age 25 but under age 65 at the end of 2024? ☐ Yes ☐ No
11. Answer "**Yes**" if (a) you cannot be claimed as a dependent on anyone else's return or (b) you are filing a joint return. Otherwise, answer "**No**." ☐ Yes ☐ No
12. Was your main home (and your spouse's if filing a joint return) in the United States for more than half the year? ☐ Yes ☐ No

PERSONS WITH A QUALIFYING CHILD: If you answered "**Yes**" to questions 1 through 9, you can claim the EIC. Remember to fill out Schedule EIC and attach it to your Form 1040. If you answered "**Yes**" to questions 1 through 7 and "**No**" to question 8, answer questions 10 through 12 to see if you can claim the EIC without a qualifying child.

PERSONS WITHOUT A QUALIFYING CHILD: If you answered "**Yes**" to questions 1 through 7, and 10 through 12, you can claim the EIC.

If you answered "No" to any questions that applies to you: You cannot claim the EIC.

Example Ying and Michael are married filing jointly taxpayers with earned income and AGI of $33,200 in 2024. They have two children ages 3 and 5. All members of the family have Social Security numbers, are U.S. citizens, and lived together in the United States all year. Ying had $820 of tax withheld from her wages during the year. Michael did not work. Ying and Michael can claim the EIC as they meet all the tests for taxpayers with a qualifying child. Based on earned income of $33,200, filing jointly with two qualifying children, their EIC per the 2024 table (Appendix B) is $6,205. ♦

Self-Study Problem 7.2 — Refer to Appendix E for Solutions to Self-Study Problems

Dennis and Lynne have a 5-year-old child. Dennis has a salary of $18,000. Lynne is self-employed with a loss of $400 from her business. Dennis and Lynne receive $150 of taxable interest income during the year. Their earned income for the year is $17,600 and their adjusted gross income is $17,750 ($18,000 − $400 + $150).

Use Worksheet A and EIC table in Appendix B to calculate their earned income credit.

ProConnect™ Tax TIP

ProConnect Tax determines whether the earned income credit applies based on the information that the preparer inputs (most importantly, income and dependent information). However, if the earned income credit is not computing and the preparer believes the taxpayer is eligible, the earned income credit worksheets can be produced by ProConnect Tax to allow for review of the calculation. To produce the EIC worksheets, click on the Credits section and on the EIC, Residential Energy, Other Credits screen, expand the Earned Income Credit section and scroll down to the bottom to select the box Force Earned Income Credit Worksheets.

7-3 Child and Dependent Care Credit

Learning Objective 7.3 — Compute the child and dependent care credit for an individual taxpayer.

Congress enacted tax laws to provide benefits to taxpayers with dependents who must be provided with care and supervision while the taxpayers work. Taxpayers are allowed a credit for expenses for the care of their children and certain other dependents. Form 2441 is used to calculate and report the credit for child and dependent care expenses. To be eligible for the child and dependent care credit, the dependent must either be under the age of 13 or be a dependent or spouse of any age who is incapable of self-care. If a child's parents are divorced, the child need not be the dependent of the taxpayer claiming the credit, but the child must live with that parent more than the child lives with the other parent. For example, a divorced mother with custody of a child may be entitled to the credit even though the child is a dependent of the father.

7-3a Qualified Expenses

The expenses that qualify for the credit include amounts paid to enable both the taxpayer and their spouse to be employed. Qualified expenses include amounts paid for in-home care, such as a nanny, as well as out-of-home care, such as a day care center. Overnight camps do not qualify for the credit, nor do activities providing standard education such as kindergarten. Day camps such as soccer camps, music camps, math camps, and dinosaur camps do qualify for the credit since they are not considered standard education. Payments to relatives are eligible for the credit, unless the payments are to a dependent of the taxpayer or to the taxpayer's child who is under the age of 19 at the end of the tax year. To claim the credit, the taxpayer must include on their tax return, the name, address, and taxpayer identification number of the person or organization providing the care. Qualified expenses do not include amounts provided under an employer dependent care assistance program as covered in Chapter 2.

7-3b Allowable Credit

For taxpayers with AGI of less than $15,000, the child and dependent care credit is equal to 35 percent of the qualified expenses. For taxpayers with AGI of $15,000 or more, the applicable percentage of qualified expenses is reduced by 1 percent for each $2,000 (or part thereof) of AGI above $15,000 but not below 20 percent. In determining the credit, the maximum amount of qualified expenses to which the applicable percentage is applied is $3,000 for one dependent and $6,000 for two or more dependents.

Tax Break

The cost of summer camp for dependents often meets the definition of qualified expenses for the child and dependent care credit, even when the camp is centered around sports or fun activities. Overnight camps and summer school; however, do not qualify. Refer to IRS Publication 503 for more details.

Example Heather and Kamal are married filing jointly. They have one child and pay $4,000 for child care expenses during the year. Kamal earns $16,000 and Heather earns $8,500 during the year, resulting in adjusted gross income of $24,500. The 2024 child care credit is calculated as follows:

Maximum qualified expenses for one dependent	$3,000
Credit percentage from Form 2441	× 30%
Credit allowed	$ 900

Example Janie and Bongsik are married filing jointly. They have two children and pay $17,000 for child care expenses during the year. Janie earns $86,000 and Bongsik earns $38,500 during the year, resulting in adjusted gross income of $124,500. The 2024 child care credit is calculated as follows:

Qualified expenses	$17,000
Maximum for more than one dependent	$ 6,000
Credit percentage from Form 2441	× 20%
Credit allowed	$ 1,200

Married taxpayers must generally file a joint return to claim the child and dependent care credit unless legally separated. If the taxpayer is married but files separately, has lived apart from their spouse for the last six months of the tax year, and provided one-half the cost for a principal abode for a qualifying individual, the credit can be claimed. When filing jointly, the qualifying dependent care expenses are limited to the lesser of either spouse's earned income.

Example Jeff and Janie file jointly in 2024. Janie makes $22,000 and Jeff earns $1,500, and they spend $1,900 on child care. The maximum qualifying expenses are $1,500, the lower of earned income from the lowest earning spouse or the qualifying expenses. ♦

A special rule applies when a taxpayer or spouse is a full-time student or disabled. Full-time students or disabled taxpayers with little or no income are deemed to have earned income of $250 per month for one dependent and $500 per month for two or more dependents for purposes of calculating this limitation.

Example Lin and Leon file jointly in 2024. Lin earns $36,000 and Leon is a full-time student for nine months of the year and has no income. The maximum amount of the qualifying expenses for the care of one dependent is $2,250 ($250 per month × 9 months). Lin and Leon's child and dependent care expense credit will be $540 ($2,250 × 24 percent based on their AGI of $36,000). ♦

The child and dependent care expense credit is nonrefundable and is therefore limited to the taxpayer's tax liability reduced by the foreign tax credit.

> **Self-Study Problem 7.3** *Refer to Appendix E for Solutions to Self-Study Problems*
>
> Julie Brown (Social Security number 456-23-6543) has been widowed for five years and has one dependent child, Chuck Brown (Social Security number 123-33-4444). Julie's adjusted gross income and her earned income are $90,000. Julie's employer withheld $5,000 in the dependent care flexible spending account (refer to Chapter 2) that was used toward Chuck's child care. This amount was excluded from her wage income. Assume her taxable income is $46,400, and her regular tax is $5,240 (line 10 on Form 2441). Julie paid child care expenses of $8,500 (including $5,000 from the flexible spending account) to Ivy Childcare (1 Sunflower Street, Terre Haute, IN 47803, EIN 56-7654321) and expenses for the care of her disabled dependent mother, Devona Neuporte (Social Security number 214-55-6666), of $3,400 paid to De Anza Adult Care (13 Fort Harrison Rd., Dewey, IN 47805, EIN 43-1234567). Calculate Julie's child and dependent care credit for 2024 using Form 2441 on Pages 7-18 and 7-19. Make realistic assumptions about any missing data.

ProConnect™ Tax TIP

The child and dependent care credit is a function of two entry points in ProConnect Tax. The first is the input in Dependents as covered in Chapter 1 and in the other credits mentioned earlier in this chapter. The second important input occurs under Credits/Ind Qualifying for Dependent Care Credit. This screen and the Persons and Expenses Qualifying for the Dependent Care Credit are where you identify the dependent for which the expenses were incurred. The provider of the care is entered in the Provider of Dependent Care screen.

Learning Objective 7.4

Calculate the premium tax credit available under the Affordable Care Act.

7-4 The Affordable Care Act

The Affordable Care Act (also called the "ACA" or "Obamacare") contains a number of different provisions that affect a taxpayer's income tax liability and reporting. The net investment income tax of 3.8 percent and 0.9 percent Medicare tax (both covered in Chapter 6) are additional taxes for certain high-income taxpayers.

More recent changes to the tax law now leave only one significant tax provision that relates to individuals from the ACA: health insurance premium tax credits. The individual shared responsibility was repealed starting in 2019.

7-4a Premium Tax Credit

Under the ACA, eligible taxpayers may receive a tax credit intended to lower the cost of health care. To be eligible, a taxpayer must meet all of the following requirements:

- Health insurance is purchased through one of the state exchanges or the federal exchange
- The taxpayer is not eligible for coverage through an employer or government plan
- The taxpayer does not file Married Filing Separately except under very limited conditions
- The taxpayer cannot be claimed as a dependent by another

Calculating the premium tax credit is similar to the EIC in that specific tables are required to compute the allowable credit. The credit is intended to take the form of the lesser of: (1) actual health care premiums paid or (2) benchmark plan premiums, less the amount the taxpayer is expected to contribute to health care. To calculate the premium tax credit, the following steps are required:

Step 1. Calculate modified AGI for all members of the household. This is AGI for all individuals claimed as a dependent (dependent's income is includable if they are required to file a tax return) adjusted for a number of items including tax-exempt interest and nontaxable Social Security benefits.

Step 2. Compare the household income to the previous year's federal poverty line (FPL). Under the ACA, the FPL is set in the *previous* year during open enrollment (around October). The FPL is defined in three ways: (a) the forty-eight contiguous states and the District of Columbia, (b) Alaska, or (c) Hawaii. The FPL selected is based on the household's state of residence as presented in Table 7.3.

Table 7.3 Federal Poverty Line for 48 Contiguous States and DC

Persons in Family/Household	2024 FPL for 48 States and DC
1	$14,580
2	19,720
3	24,860
4	30,000
5	35,140
6	40,280
7	45,420
8	50,560
Each additional person	+ 5,140

The household income is then expressed as a percentage of the FPL.

Step 3. The amount of income deemed appropriately spent on health care premiums is then identified on the 2024 Applicable Figure Table presented on Page 7-20. The applicable figure is designed to represent the maximum percentage of income a household will spend on health care premiums.

Example Ed and Milly are married with two children under the age of 21. Household income is $60,000. Ed and Milly's household income is at 200 percent of the FPL ($60,000 ÷ $30,000 = 2.0 or 200%). For household income of 200 percent of the FPL, the applicable figure is .0200; thus, the intended or deemed amount to be paid for annual health care premiums is $60,000 × 2.00% or $1,200. ♦

Step 4. The amount of the credit is based on comparing the cost of premiums for a designated benchmark plan (the applicable second lowest cost silver plan or SLCSP) in the taxpayer's state with the deemed premium cost calculated above. For example, if the deemed annual premium to be paid by the taxpayer is $1,200 and the SLCSP for that household is $9,000 then the premium tax credit is $7,800 ($9,000 − $1,200). For households that did not have coverage for the entire year, the credit is prorated based on the number of months coverage was maintained. This information is often reported on Form 1095-A.

Step 5. Lastly, the amount calculated in steps 1–4 is compared to the actual premiums paid and the lesser of the two is the premium tax credit (i.e., the credit cannot exceed the actual premiums paid).

Example Thus, to continue with the example above, if Ed and Milly paid annual health care premiums of $5,500, their premium tax credit calculated of $7,800 is limited to $5,500. ♦

Self-Study Problem 7.3

Form 2441
Department of the Treasury
Internal Revenue Service

Child and Dependent Care Expenses

Attach to Form 1040, 1040-SR, or 1040-NR.
Go to www.irs.gov/Form2441 for instructions and the latest information.

OMB No. 1545-0074

2024

Attachment Sequence No. **21**

Name(s) shown on return

Your social security number

A You can't claim a credit for child and dependent care expenses if your filing status is married filing separately unless you meet the requirements listed in the instructions under *Married Persons Filing Separately*. If you meet these requirements, check this box . . ☐

B If you or your spouse was a student or was disabled during 2024 and you're entering deemed income of $250 or $500 a month on Form 2441 based on the income rules listed in the instructions under *If You or Your Spouse Was a Student or Disabled*, check this box . ☐

Part I — Persons or Organizations Who Provided the Care—You must complete this part.

If you have more than three care providers, see the instructions and check this box . . . . ☐

1

(a) Care provider's name	(b) Address (number, street, apt. no., city, state, and ZIP code)	(c) Identifying number (SSN or EIN)	(d) Was the care provider your household employee in 2024? For example, this generally includes nannies but not daycare centers. (see instructions)	(e) Amount paid (see instructions)
			☐ Yes ☐ No	
			☐ Yes ☐ No	
			☐ Yes ☐ No	

Did you receive dependent care benefits?
— **No** — Complete only Part II below.
— **Yes** — Complete Part III on page 2 next.

Caution: If the care provider is your household employee, you may owe employment taxes. For details, see the Instructions for Schedule H (Form 1040). If you incurred care expenses in 2024 but didn't pay them until 2025, or if you prepaid in 2024 for care to be provided in 2025, don't include these expenses in column (d) of line 2 for 2024. See the instructions.

Part II — Credit for Child and Dependent Care Expenses

2 Information about your **qualifying person(s)**. If you have more than three qualifying persons, see the instructions and check this box ☐

(a) Qualifying person's name (First / Last)	(b) Qualifying person's social security number	(c) Check here if the qualifying person was over age 12 and was disabled. (see instructions)	(d) Qualified expenses you incurred and paid in 2024 for the person listed in column (a)
		☐	
		☐	

3 Add the amounts in column (d) of line 2. **Don't** enter more than $3,000 if you had one qualifying person or $6,000 if you had two or more persons. If you completed Part III, enter the amount from line 31 . **3**

4 Enter your **earned income**. See instructions **4**

5 If married filing jointly, enter your spouse's earned income (if you or your spouse was a student or was disabled, see the instructions); **all others**, enter the amount from line 4 . . . . **5**

6 Enter the **smallest** of line 3, 4, or 5 . . . . **6**

7 Enter the amount from Form 1040, 1040-SR, or 1040-NR, line 11 . . . **7**

8 Enter on line 8 the decimal amount shown below that applies to the amount on line 7.

If line 7 is:			If line 7 is:			If line 7 is:		
Over	But not over	Decimal amount is	Over	But not over	Decimal amount is	Over	But not over	Decimal amount is
$0	15,000	.35	$25,000	27,000	.29	$37,000	39,000	.23
15,000	17,000	.34	27,000	29,000	.28	39,000	41,000	.22
17,000	19,000	.33	29,000	31,000	.27	41,000	43,000	.21
19,000	21,000	.32	31,000	33,000	.26	43,000	No limit	.20
21,000	23,000	.31	33,000	35,000	.25			
23,000	25,000	.30	35,000	37,000	.24			

8 X .

9a Multiply line 6 by the decimal amount on line 8 . . . . **9a**

b If you paid 2023 expenses in 2024, complete Worksheet A in the instructions. Enter the amount from line 13 of the worksheet here. Otherwise, enter -0- on line 9b and go to line 9c **9b**

c Add lines 9a and 9b and enter the result **9c**

10 Tax liability limit. Enter the amount from the Credit Limit Worksheet in the instructions **10**

11 **Credit for child and dependent care expenses.** Enter the **smaller** of line 9c or line 10 here and on Schedule 3 (Form 1040), line 2 . . . . **11**

For Paperwork Reduction Act Notice, see your tax return instructions.   Cat. No. 11862M   Form **2441** (2024)

Form 2441 (2024) Page **2**

Part III	Dependent Care Benefits		
12	Enter the total amount of **dependent care benefits** you received in 2024. Amounts you received as an employee should be shown in box 10 of your Form(s) W-2. **Don't** include amounts reported as wages in box 1 of Form(s) W-2. If you were self-employed or a partner, include amounts you received under a dependent care assistance program from your sole proprietorship or partnership	12	
13	Enter the amount, if any, you carried over from 2023 and used in 2024 during the grace period. See instructions	13	
14	If you forfeited or carried over to 2025 any of the amounts reported on line 12 or 13, enter the amount. See instructions	14	( )
15	Combine lines 12 through 14. See instructions	15	
16	Enter the total amount of **qualified expenses** incurred in 2024 for the care of the **qualifying person(s)**	16		
17	Enter the **smaller** of line 15 or 16	17		
18	Enter your **earned income**. See instructions	18		
19	Enter the amount shown below that applies to you. • If married filing jointly, enter your spouse's earned income (if you or your spouse was a student or was disabled, see the instructions for line 5). • If married filing separately, see instructions. • All others, enter the amount from line 18.	19		
20	Enter the **smallest** of line 17, 18, or 19	20		
21	Enter $5,000 ($2,500 if married filing separately **and** you were required to enter your spouse's earned income on line 19). However, don't enter more than the maximum amount allowed under your dependent care plan. See instructions	21		
22	Is any amount on line 12 or 13 from your sole proprietorship or partnership? ☐ **No.** Enter -0-. ☐ **Yes.** Enter the amount here	22		
23	Subtract line 22 from line 15	23		
24	**Deductible benefits.** Enter the **smallest** of line 20, 21, or 22. Also, include this amount on the appropriate line(s) of your return. See instructions	24	
25	**Excluded benefits.** If you checked "No" on line 22, enter the smaller of line 20 or line 21. Otherwise, subtract line 24 from the smaller of line 20 or line 21. If zero or less, enter -0- . .	25	
26	**Taxable benefits.** Subtract line 25 from line 23. If zero or less, enter -0-. Also, enter this amount on Form 1040, 1040-SR, or 1040-NR, line 1e	26	

To claim the child and dependent care credit, complete lines 27 through 31 below.

27	Enter $3,000 ($6,000 if two or more qualifying persons)	27	
28	Add lines 24 and 25	28	
29	Subtract line 28 from line 27. If zero or less, **stop**. You can't take the credit. **Exception.** If you paid 2023 expenses in 2024, see the instructions for line 9b	29	
30	Complete line 2 on page 1 of this form. **Don't** include in column (d) any benefits shown on line 28 above. Then, add the amounts in column (d) and enter the total here	30	
31	Enter the **smaller** of line 29 or 30. Also, enter this amount on line 3 on page 1 of this form and complete lines 4 through 11	31	

Form **2441** (2024)

2024 Applicable Figure Table

> **TIP:** *If the amount on line 5 is 150 or less, your applicable figure is 0.0000. If the amount on line 5 is 400 or more, your applicable figure is 0.0850.*

IF Form 8962, line 5, is...	ENTER on Form 8962, line 7...	IF Form 8962, line 5, is...	ENTER on Form 8962, line 7...	IF Form 8962, line 5, is...	ENTER on Form 8962, line 7...	IF Form 8962, line 5, is...	ENTER on Form 8962, line 7...	IF Form 8962, line 5, is...	ENTER on Form 8962, line 7...
less than 150	0.0000	200	0.0200	251	0.0404	302	0.0605	353	0.0733
150	0.0000	201	0.0204	252	0.0408	303	0.0608	354	0.0735
151	0.0004	202	0.0208	253	0.0412	304	0.0610	355	0.0738
152	0.0008	203	0.0212	254	0.0416	305	0.0613	356	0.0740
153	0.0012	204	0.0216	255	0.0420	306	0.0615	357	0.0743
154	0.0016	205	0.0220	256	0.0424	307	0.0618	358	0.0745
155	0.0020	206	0.0224	257	0.0428	308	0.0620	359	0.0748
156	0.0024	207	0.0228	258	0.0432	309	0.0623	360	0.0750
157	0.0028	208	0.0232	259	0.0436	310	0.0625	361	0.0753
158	0.0032	209	0.0236	260	0.0440	311	0.0628	362	0.0755
159	0.0036	210	0.0240	261	0.0444	312	0.0630	363	0.0758
160	0.0040	211	0.0244	262	0.0448	313	0.0633	364	0.0760
161	0.0044	212	0.0248	263	0.0452	314	0.0635	365	0.0763
162	0.0048	213	0.0252	264	0.0456	315	0.0638	366	0.0765
163	0.0052	214	0.0256	265	0.0460	316	0.0640	367	0.0768
164	0.0056	215	0.0260	266	0.0464	317	0.0643	368	0.0770
165	0.0060	216	0.0264	267	0.0468	318	0.0645	369	0.0773
166	0.0064	217	0.0268	268	0.0472	319	0.0648	370	0.0775
167	0.0068	218	0.0272	269	0.0476	320	0.0650	371	0.0778
168	0.0072	219	0.0276	270	0.0480	321	0.0653	372	0.0780
169	0.0076	220	0.0280	271	0.0484	322	0.0655	373	0.0783
170	0.0080	221	0.0284	272	0.0488	323	0.0658	374	0.0785
171	0.0084	222	0.0288	273	0.0492	324	0.0660	375	0.0788
172	0.0088	223	0.0292	274	0.0496	325	0.0663	376	0.0790
173	0.0092	224	0.0296	275	0.0500	326	0.0665	377	0.0793
174	0.0096	225	0.0300	276	0.0504	327	0.0668	378	0.0795
175	0.0100	226	0.0304	277	0.0508	328	0.0670	379	0.0798
176	0.0104	227	0.0308	278	0.0512	329	0.0673	380	0.0800
177	0.0108	228	0.0312	279	0.0516	330	0.0675	381	0.0803
178	0.0112	229	0.0316	280	0.0520	331	0.0678	382	0.0805
179	0.0116	230	0.0320	281	0.0524	332	0.0680	383	0.0808
180	0.0120	231	0.0324	282	0.0528	333	0.0683	384	0.0810
181	0.0124	232	0.0328	283	0.0532	334	0.0685	385	0.0813
182	0.0128	233	0.0332	284	0.0536	335	0.0688	386	0.0815
183	0.0132	234	0.0336	285	0.0540	336	0.0690	387	0.0818
184	0.0136	235	0.0340	286	0.0544	337	0.0693	388	0.0820
185	0.0140	236	0.0344	287	0.0548	338	0.0695	389	0.0823
186	0.0144	237	0.0348	288	0.0552	339	0.0698	390	0.0825
187	0.0148	238	0.0352	289	0.0556	340	0.0700	391	0.0828
188	0.0152	239	0.0356	290	0.0560	341	0.0703	392	0.0830
189	0.0156	240	0.0360	291	0.0564	342	0.0705	393	0.0833
190	0.0160	241	0.0364	292	0.0568	343	0.0708	394	0.0835
191	0.0164	242	0.0368	293	0.0572	344	0.0710	395	0.0838
192	0.0168	243	0.0372	294	0.0576	345	0.0713	396	0.0840
193	0.0172	244	0.0376	295	0.0580	346	0.0715	397	0.0843
194	0.0176	245	0.0380	296	0.0584	347	0.0718	398	0.0845
195	0.0180	246	0.0384	297	0.0588	348	0.0720	399	0.0848
196	0.0184	247	0.0388	298	0.0592	349	0.0723	400 or more	0.0850
197	0.0188	248	0.0392	299	0.0596	350	0.0725		
198	0.0192	249	0.0396	300	0.0600	351	0.0728		
199	0.0196	250	0.0400	301	0.0603	352	0.0730		

The premium tax credit can be obtained at two different times: (1) in advance (i.e., as a direct reduction in the monthly health care premiums) or (2) at the end of the year when the tax return is filed. If the taxpayer elects to have the credit paid in advance, the exchange will automatically adjust the premiums to reflect an estimated credit based on estimated household income. Since the actual premium tax credit is not known until household income can be computed after the end of the tax year, Form 8962, provided on Pages 7-26 and 7-27, provides a reconciliation of the estimated credit and the actual credit. If the actual credit is greater than the estimated credit, the difference between the two amounts is a refundable credit on the taxpayer's tax return. If the estimated credit taken throughout the year is greater than the actual credit, the difference is treated as additional tax due on the taxpayer's tax return. However, as long as the household income is below 400 percent of the FPL, the repayment amount of the credit is limited as presented in Table 7.4.

Table 7.4 Repayment Limits on Premium Tax Credit

	Single	Taxpayers Other Than Single
Less than 200%	$ 375	$ 750
At least 200% but less than 300%	950	1,900
At least 300% but less than 400%	1,575	3,150
At least 400%	No limit	No limit

Form 1095-A reports the taxpayer's actual premiums paid, the cost of the SLCSP plan, and any advance credits received during the year from the exchange on which they purchased the insurance.

Example Misty and Ryland are married and file jointly in 2024. They purchased health care through their exchange and elected to receive an advance premium tax credit of $4,500 during the year. Misty found new employment at much higher pay in early 2024 and they ended up calculating an actual premium tax credit of only $1,200, a difference of $3,300. If Misty and Ryland's household income is at least 300 percent but less than 400 percent of the federal poverty line, their repayment of the premium tax credit is limited to $3,150. ♦

Coverage and reporting of health care coverage under the ACA is centered around the notion of a "coverage family." The coverage family are the individuals for which health care coverage is purchased through an exchange. The members of the coverage family are not always the same as the members of a "tax family," which is the individuals included on the taxpayer's tax return including dependents.

In general, allocation is required when:

1. The policy covered at least one individual in the tax family and at least one individual in another tax family; and
2. Either:
    a. The taxpayer received a Form 1095-A for the policy that does not accurately represent the members of that taxpayer's tax family who were enrolled in the policy (meaning that it either lists someone who is not in taxpayer's tax family or does not list a member of the taxpayer's tax family who was enrolled in the policy), or
    b. Another tax family received a Form 1095-A for the policy that includes a member of a taxpayer's tax family.

There are many situations when allocation is required including divorce or marriage during the year, married filing separately status, claiming or not claiming a dependent that may be part of the tax family and not the coverage family or vice-versa.

Example Jeff and Mackenzie, a married couple, and their two dependent children, Amy and Zoni, were enrolled in health care through an exchange starting on January 1, 2024. The four of them represent the coverage family. Jeff and Mackenzie divorced on June 30, 2024. Jeff purchased different health care through the exchange for only himself starting July 1 and Mackenzie purchased health care through an exchange for herself, Amy, and Zoni. Jeff claims Amy as a dependent and Mackenzie claims Zoni as a dependent. Jeff and Mackenzie will be required to allocate the premium tax credit because the coverage families and tax families are not the same during the year. ♦

Although many different situations may require allocation, Form 8962 includes schedules to consider four different allocation situations: (1) taxpayers divorced or separated during the year, (2) taxpayers that are married filing separately, (3) the only Form 1095-A issued by the marketplace does not reflect the tax family, and (4) most other situations involving the allocation between two taxpayers. Some situations may call for two allocation methods to be used at different times during the year. Situations that require an allocation among three taxpayers or other complexities are directed to IRS Publication 974.

The instructions for Form 8962 include a three-step inquiry to determine which allocation is appropriate (presented in Figure 7.2).

Figure 7.2 Steps to Determine Allocation Rule

Follow Steps 1–3 below to determine which allocation rule to use in *Part IV*, later, to allocate the policy amounts for each qualified health plan identified in the instructions for line 9. For each policy, if your answer directs you to Part IV, skip directly to the section of the Part IV instructions identified. You do not need to complete the remaining steps below.

STEP 1

IF:
- You divorced or legally separated from a spouse in 2024; and
- For 1 or more months of marriage, the policy covered at least one individual in your tax family **AND** at least one individual in your former spouse's tax family...

THEN allocate using the rules in *Allocation Situation 1* under *Part IV*, later.
Otherwise, continue to Step 2.

STEP 2

IF:
- You were married at the end of 2024 but are filing a separate return from your spouse; and
- The policy covered at least one individual in your tax family **AND** at least one individual in your spouse's tax family...*

THEN allocate using the rules in *Allocation Situation 2* under *Part IV*, later.
Otherwise, continue to Step 3.

* Also follow these instructions if you meet the rules in *Exception 1* or *Exception 2* under Married taxpayers, earlier, and a policy covered at least one individual in your tax family **AND** at least one individual in your spouse's tax family.

STEP 3

IF:
- No APTC was paid for the policy...

THEN allocate using the rules in *Allocation Situation 3* under *Part IV*, later.
Otherwise, allocate using the rules in *Allocation Situation 4* under *Part IV*, later.

The items allocated are the actual premiums paid, the applicable SLCSP premiums, and the advanced credit amount paid to the taxpayer. Except for married taxpayers filing separately, the taxpayer and the other party generally can use whatever allocation percentage they agree to.

Example Christian and Olivia are married on May 1, 2024. Christian has his own health care purchased through an exchange while Olivia was included on her parents' coverage through the marketplace. Neither Christian nor Olivia's parents received an advance premium. Christian's Form 1095-A includes actual premiums and SLCSP premium information for his single plan throughout the year. Olivia's parents' Form 1095-A includes Olivia's cost and SLCSP premiums throughout the year. Using the allocation determination steps in Figure 7.2, because there was no advance premium tax credit paid, Christian and Olivia's parents will use Allocation Situation 3.

Olivia's parents' share a copy of their Form 1095-A with Christian and they agree to allocate 25 percent of the premiums paid and the SLCSP premiums to Olivia for May through December. Part IV of Christian and Olivia's Form 8962 included in their 2024 joint tax return will report the allocation information:

Form 8962 (2024) Page **2**

Part IV Allocation of Policy Amounts

Complete the following information for up to four policy amount allocations. See instructions for allocation details.

Allocation 1

30	(a) Policy Number (Form 1095-A, line 2)	(b) SSN of other taxpayer	(c) Allocation start month	(d) Allocation stop month
	Allocation percentage applied to monthly amounts	(e) Premium Percentage	(f) SLCSP Percentage	(g) Advance Payment of the PTC Percentage

Allocation 2

31	(a) Policy Number (Form 1095-A, line 2)	(b) SSN of other taxpayer	(c) Allocation start month	(d) Allocation stop month
	Allocation percentage applied to monthly amounts	(e) Premium Percentage	(f) SLCSP Percentage	(g) Advance Payment of the PTC Percentage

Allocation 3

32	(a) Policy Number (Form 1095-A, line 2)	(b) SSN of other taxpayer	(c) Allocation start month	(d) Allocation stop month
	CFG100034	111-55-1212	May	December
	Allocation percentage applied to monthly amounts	(e) Premium Percentage	(f) SLCSP Percentage	(g) Advance Payment of the PTC Percentage
		25	25	

Christian's Form 1095-A reported actual premiums of $600 per month and the SLCSP premiums of $575. Olivia's parents' Form 1095-A reported actual premiums of $900 per month and SLCSP premiums of $950 per month. Christian and Olivia's monthly contribution amount is $300 per month. Part II of Christian's Form 8962 will report the following:

Part II — Premium Tax Credit Claim and Reconciliation of Advance Payment of Premium Tax Credit

9 Are you allocating policy amounts with another taxpayer or do you want to use the alternative calculation for year of marriage? See instructions.
☑ **Yes.** Skip to Part IV, Allocation of Policy Amounts, or Part V, Alternative Calculation for Year of Marriage. ☐ **No.** Continue to line 10.

10 See the instructions to determine if you can use line 11 or must complete lines 12 through 23.
☐ **Yes.** Continue to line 11. Compute your annual PTC. Then skip lines 12–23 and continue to line 24.
☑ **No.** Continue to lines 12–23. Compute your monthly PTC and continue to line 24.

Annual Calculation	(a) Annual enrollment premiums (Form(s) 1095-A, line 33A)	(b) Annual applicable SLCSP premium (Form(s) 1095-A, line 33B)	(c) Annual contribution amount (line 8a)	(d) Annual maximum premium assistance (subtract (c) from (b); if zero or less, enter -0-)	(e) Annual PTC allowed (smaller of (a) or (d))	(f) Annual advance payment of PTC (Form(s) 1095-A, line 33C)
11 Annual Totals						

Monthly Calculation	(a) Monthly enrollment premiums (Form(s) 1095-A, lines 21–32, column A)	(b) Monthly applicable SLCSP premium (Form(s) 1095-A, lines 21–32, column B)	(c) Monthly contribution amount (amount from line 8b or alternative marriage monthly calculation)	(d) Monthly maximum premium assistance (subtract (c) from (b); if zero or less, enter -0-)	(e) Monthly PTC allowed (smaller of (a) or (d))	(f) Monthly advance payment of PTC (Form(s) 1095-A, lines 21–32, column C)
12 January	600	575	300	275	275	
13 February	600	575	300	275	275	
14 March	600	575	300	275	275	
15 April	600	575	300	275	275	
16 May	825 (a)	813 (b)	300	513	513	
17 June	825	813	300	513	513	
18 July	825	813	300	513	513	
19 August	825	813	300	513	513	
20 September	825	813	300	513	513	
21 October	825	813	300	513	513	
22 November	825	813	300	513	513	
23 December	825	813	300	513	513	

24 Total PTC. Enter the amount from line 11(e) or add lines 12(e) through 23(e) and enter the total here **24** 5,204

25 Advance payment of PTC. Enter the amount from line 11(f) or add lines 12(f) through 23(f) and enter the total here **25**

(a) $600 + ($900 × 25%)
(b) $575 + ($950 × 25%)

♦

In many situations, the best way for a taxpayer to avoid allocations is to inform the marketplace of changes in circumstances, including the following:

- Changes in household income
- Moving to a different address
- Gaining or losing eligibility for other health care coverage
- Gaining, losing, or other changes to employment
- Birth or adoption
- Marriage or divorce
- Other changes affecting the composition of your tax family

Self-Study Problem 7.4 — Refer to Appendix E for Solutions to Self-Study Problems

Marco and Tracy Brigantine live in California, are married filing jointly, under age 65, and have three children ages 14, 16, and 26. However, the oldest child is not claimed as a dependent and does not live at home. Tracy's adjusted gross income is $52,000 and Marco's is $50,000 and both are self-employed. Tracy and Marco's son Bryan has wages of $4,200 from a part-time job during the summer. They also have $2,000 in interest income from tax-exempt bonds. The Brigantines are enrolled in health insurance for all of 2024 through their state exchange and elected to have the credit paid in advance. Using the Brigantine's 2024 Form 1095-A on Page 7-25, complete Form 8962 on Page 7-26 to determine the following:

1. The actual premium tax credit (Line 24).
2. The net premium tax credit to be claimed on the return, if any (Line 26) or the excess advance payment, if any (Line 27).
3. The repayment amount required, if any (line 29).

Self-Study Problem 7.4

Form 1095-A — Health Insurance Marketplace Statement

Department of the Treasury
Internal Revenue Service

Do not attach to your tax return. Keep for your records.
Go to www.irs.gov/Form1095A for instructions and the latest information.

☐ VOID
☐ CORRECTED

OMB No. 1545-2232

2024

Part I — Recipient Information

#	Field	Value
1	Marketplace identifier	12-3456999
2	Marketplace-assigned policy number	34589A
3	Policy issuer's name	Covered California
4	Recipient's name	Tracy Brigantine
5	Recipient's SSN	123-44-5555
6	Recipient's date of birth	07/01/1972
7	Recipient's spouse's name	Marco Brigantine
8	Recipient's spouse's SSN	124-55-6666
9	Recipient's spouse's date of birth	09/22/1976
10	Policy start date	01/01/2024
11	Policy termination date	12/31/2024
12	Street address (including apartment no.)	3167 Kendra Lane
13	City or town	Poway
14	State or province	CA
15	Country and ZIP or foreign postal code	92064

Part II — Covered Individuals

	A. Covered individual name	B. Covered individual SSN	C. Covered individual date of birth	D. Coverage start date	E. Coverage termination date
16	Tracy Brigantine	123-44-5555	07/01/1972	01/01/2024	12/31/2024
17	Marco Brigantine	124-55-6666	09/22/1976	01/01/2024	12/31/2024
18	Alex Brigantine	503-11-2222	04/28/2010	01/01/2024	12/31/2024
19	Bryan Brigantine	867-53-0922	01/28/2008	01/01/2024	12/31/2024
20					

Part III — Coverage Information

	Month	A. Monthly enrollment premiums	B. Monthly second lowest cost silver plan (SLCSP) premium	C. Monthly advance payment of premium tax credit
21	January	990.00	850.00	487.00
22	February	990.00	850.00	487.00
23	March	990.00	850.00	487.00
24	April	990.00	850.00	487.00
25	May	990.00	850.00	487.00
26	June	990.00	850.00	487.00
27	July	990.00	850.00	487.00
28	August	990.00	850.00	487.00
29	September	990.00	850.00	487.00
30	October	990.00	850.00	487.00
31	November	990.00	850.00	487.00
32	December	990.00	850.00	487.00
33	Annual Totals	11,880.00	10,200.00	5,844.00

For Privacy Act and Paperwork Reduction Act Notice, see separate instructions.   Cat. No. 60703Q   Form **1095-A** (2024)

Self-Study Problem 7.4

Form 8962
Department of the Treasury
Internal Revenue Service

Premium Tax Credit (PTC)

Attach to Form 1040, 1040-SR, or 1040-NR.
Go to www.irs.gov/Form8962 for instructions and the latest information.

OMB No. 1545-0074
2024
Attachment Sequence No. 73

Name shown on your return | Your social security number

A. You cannot take the PTC if your filing status is married filing separately unless you qualify for an exception. See instructions. If you qualify, check the box ☐

Part I — Annual and Monthly Contribution Amount

1. Tax family size. Enter your tax family size. See instructions **1**
2a. Modified AGI. Enter your modified AGI. See instructions **2a**
 b. Enter the total of your dependents' modified AGI. See instructions . . . **2b**
3. Household income. Add the amounts on lines 2a and 2b. See instructions **3**
4. Federal poverty line. Enter the federal poverty line amount from Table 1-1, 1-2, or 1-3. See instructions. Check the appropriate box for the federal poverty table used. **a** ☐ Alaska **b** ☐ Hawaii **c** ☐ Other 48 states and DC . . . **4**
5. Household income as a percentage of federal poverty line (see instructions) . . . . **5** %
6. Reserved for future use
7. Applicable figure. Using your line 5 percentage, locate your "applicable figure" on the table in the instructions . . . **7**
8a. Annual contribution amount. Multiply line 3 by line 7. Round to nearest whole dollar amount **8a** | 8b. Monthly contribution amount. Divide line 8a by 12. Round to nearest whole dollar amount **8b**

Part II — Premium Tax Credit Claim and Reconciliation of Advance Payment of Premium Tax Credit

9. Are you allocating policy amounts with another taxpayer or do you want to use the alternative calculation for year of marriage? See instructions.
   ☐ **Yes.** Skip to Part IV, Allocation of Policy Amounts, or Part V, Alternative Calculation for Year of Marriage.   ☐ **No.** Continue to line 10.
10. See the instructions to determine if you can use line 11 or must complete lines 12 through 23.
   ☐ **Yes.** Continue to line 11. Compute your annual PTC. Then skip lines 12–23 and continue to line 24.   ☐ **No.** Continue to lines 12–23. Compute your monthly PTC and continue to line 24.

	(a) Annual enrollment premiums (Form(s) 1095-A, line 33A)	(b) Annual applicable SLCSP premium (Form(s) 1095-A, line 33B)	(c) Annual contribution amount (line 8a)	(d) Annual maximum premium assistance (subtract (c) from (b); if zero or less, enter -0-)	(e) Annual PTC allowed (smaller of (a) or (d))	(f) Annual advance payment of PTC (Form(s) 1095-A, line 33C)
Annual Calculation						
11 Annual Totals						
Monthly Calculation	(a) Monthly enrollment premiums (Form(s) 1095-A, lines 21–32, column A)	(b) Monthly applicable SLCSP premium (Form(s) 1095-A, lines 21–32, column B)	(c) Monthly contribution amount (amount from line 8b or alternative marriage monthly calculation)	(d) Monthly maximum premium assistance (subtract (c) from (b); if zero or less, enter -0-)	(e) Monthly PTC allowed (smaller of (a) or (d))	(f) Monthly advance payment of PTC (Form(s) 1095-A, lines 21–32, column C)
12 January						
13 February						
14 March						
15 April						
16 May						
17 June						
18 July						
19 August						
20 September						
21 October						
22 November						
23 December						

24. Total PTC. Enter the amount from line 11(e) or add lines 12(e) through 23(e) and enter the total here **24**
25. Advance payment of PTC. Enter the amount from line 11(f) or add lines 12(f) through 23(f) and enter the total here **25**
26. Net PTC. If line 24 is greater than line 25, subtract line 25 from line 24. Enter the difference here and on Schedule 3 (Form 1040), line 9. If line 24 equals line 25, enter -0-. Stop here. If line 25 is greater than line 24, leave this line blank and continue to line 27 . . . . **26**

Part III — Repayment of Excess Advance Payment of the Premium Tax Credit

27. Excess advance payment of PTC. If line 25 is greater than line 24, subtract line 24 from line 25. Enter the difference here **27**
28. Repayment limitation (see instructions) **28**
29. Excess advance PTC repayment. Enter the smaller of line 27 or line 28 here and on Schedule 2 (Form 1040), line 1a **29**

For Paperwork Reduction Act Notice, see your tax return instructions. Cat. No. 37784Z Form **8962** (2024)

Form 8962 (2024) Page **2**

Part IV — Allocation of Policy Amounts

Complete the following information for up to four policy amount allocations. See instructions for allocation details.

Allocation 1

30	(a) Policy Number (Form 1095-A, line 2)	(b) SSN of other taxpayer	(c) Allocation start month	(d) Allocation stop month
	Allocation percentage applied to monthly amounts	(e) Premium Percentage	(f) SLCSP Percentage	(g) Advance Payment of the PTC Percentage

Allocation 2

31	(a) Policy Number (Form 1095-A, line 2)	(b) SSN of other taxpayer	(c) Allocation start month	(d) Allocation stop month
	Allocation percentage applied to monthly amounts	(e) Premium Percentage	(f) SLCSP Percentage	(g) Advance Payment of the PTC Percentage

Allocation 3

32	(a) Policy Number (Form 1095-A, line 2)	(b) SSN of other taxpayer	(c) Allocation start month	(d) Allocation stop month
	Allocation percentage applied to monthly amounts	(e) Premium Percentage	(f) SLCSP Percentage	(g) Advance Payment of the PTC Percentage

Allocation 4

33	(a) Policy Number (Form 1095-A, line 2)	(b) SSN of other taxpayer	(c) Allocation start month	(d) Allocation stop month
	Allocation percentage applied to monthly amounts	(e) Premium Percentage	(f) SLCSP Percentage	(g) Advance Payment of the PTC Percentage

34 Have you completed all policy amount allocations?

☐ **Yes.** Multiply the amounts on Form 1095-A by the allocation percentages entered by policy. Add all allocated policy amounts and non-allocated policy amounts from Forms 1095-A, if any, to compute a combined total for each month. Enter the combined total for each month on lines 12–23, columns (a), (b), and (f). Compute the amounts for lines 12–23, columns (c)–(e), and continue to line 24.

☐ **No.** See the instructions to report additional policy amount allocations.

Part V — Alternative Calculation for Year of Marriage

Complete line(s) 35 and/or 36 to elect the alternative calculation for year of marriage. For eligibility to make the election, see the instructions for line 9. To complete line(s) 35 and/or 36 and compute the amounts for lines 12–23, see the instructions for this Part V.

35	Alternative entries for your SSN	(a) Alternative family size	(b) Alternative monthly contribution amount	(c) Alternative start month	(d) Alternative stop month
36	Alternative entries for your spouse's SSN	(a) Alternative family size	(b) Alternative monthly contribution amount	(c) Alternative start month	(d) Alternative stop month

Form **8962** (2024)

Learning Objective 7.5

Apply the special rules applicable to the American Opportunity tax credit and lifetime learning credit.

7-5 Education Tax Credits

The tax law contains a number of provisions that are intended to reduce the cost of education for taxpayers. Educational credits represent the last of these provisions covered in this textbook. Table 7.5 presents the education tax benefits presented throughout the textbook.

Table 7.5 Education Tax Benefits Textbook Coverage

Educational Tax Benefit	Learning Objective
Exclusion from gross income for scholarships	2.12
Employer-provided education assistance plans	2.5
Tuition reduction for school employees	2.5
Deduction of business educational expenses	3.6
Student loan interest deduction	5.8
Qualified tuition programs (529 plans)	2.14
Coverdell educational savings accounts	2.14
American Opportunity tax credit	7.5
Lifetime learning credit	7.5

7-5a American Opportunity Tax Credit

The American Opportunity tax credit (AOTC) is an education credit available to help qualifying low-income and middle-income individuals defray the cost of higher education.

The AOTC is a credit for students in their first four years of postsecondary education. The AOTC may be claimed for the expenses of students pursuing bachelor's or associate's degrees or vocational training. To be eligible, the student must meet all of the following:

- Pursuing a degree or recognized credential,
- Enrolled at least half-time for one semester, quarter, trimester, etc. starting during the tax year,
- Received a Form 1098-T from the eligible education institution,
- Not have completed the first four years of higher education at the start of the tax year,
- The AOTC has not been claimed for more than four years, and
- Has not been convicted of a felony drug conviction.

Meeting either of the following criteria precludes claiming the AOTC:

- Married filing separate status, or
- Taxpayer is listed as a dependent on another's return.

Example Alice is a single parent filing as head of household. Alice has been taking nursing classes at night to help improve her job performance at the hospital. Alice has a 19-year-old daughter, Melanie, who is a second-year full-time student at Wake Tech Community College pursing her associate degree in accounting. Melanie might go on to pursue a four-year degree at some later date. Alice claims Melanie as a dependent but Melanie files her own tax return to report the income she earns from her part-time job. Alice claimed the AOTC for Melanie last year. As Melanie is enrolled in school at least half-time, is pursuing a degree, and has not claimed the AOTC for more than four years, she is an eligible student for the AOTC. Although Alice's school expense does not qualify for the AOTC, since she is not pursuing a degree or certification, she may qualify for the lifetime learning credit (LLC) covered below. ♦

Like many other education tax benefits, the AOTC depends on an accurate computation of "qualified higher education expenses." Table 7.6 demonstrates how qualified educational expenses can differ across some of the common education benefits.

Qualifying expenses for the AOTC can be paid on behalf of the taxpayer, their spouse, or dependents. As noted previously, expenses paid for room and board, nonacademic fees or for expenses that are not related to the student's course of instruction, do not qualify. Also, expenses for courses that involve sports, games, and hobbies do not qualify for the credit unless the course is part of a degree program. Expenses paid from a gift or inheritance (which is tax-free) do qualify for credits.

Example Trinity's grandmother paid Trinity's $4,000 tuition directly to the university. Assuming Trinity meets the qualifying requirements for the AOTC otherwise, Trinity's parents may include the $4,000 as a qualifying expense when calculating the AOTC. ♦

Table 7.6 Qualified Higher Education Expenses by Tax Benefit Type

Cost	Scholarship	AOTC	Lifetime Learning Credit	Student Loan Interest	Coverdell	QTP (529 Plan)	Employer Provided Education Assistance Plan	Business Deduction for Work-Related Education
Tuition and enrollment fees	X	X	X	X	X	X	X	X
Course-related Books	X	X	Xª	X	X	X	X	X
Course-related supplies and equipment	X	X	Xª	X	X	X	X	X
Room and board				X	X	X		
Transportation				X				X
Certain K-12 education costs					X	X		
Student loan payments						X	X	
Other necessary expenses including special needs services				X	X	X		X

ªOnly if required to be paid to educational institution

Qualifying expenses must be reduced by any tax-free scholarships, grants or other education assistance. Taxpayers claiming the AOTC must have received a Form 1098-T (shown below) and must report the employer identification number of the educational institution on Form 8863.

```
FILER: Wake Tech, 1909 Fayetteville Blvd., Raleigh, NC 27603
Box 1 Payments received for qualified tuition and related expenses: $5,000.00
OMB No. 1545-1574
2024  Form 1098-T  Tuition Statement
FILER'S employer identification no.: 45-3213211
STUDENT'S TIN: 455-22-1234
STUDENT'S name: Melanie Student
Box 5 Scholarships or grants: $1,000.00
Box 8 Checked if at least half-time student: X
Copy B For Student
```

Example Alice's daughter Melanie is an eligible student for the AOTC. Melanie received a 2024 Form 1098-T from Wake Tech as presented above. Additionally, Alice paid $400 for course-related books and materials related to Melanie's school in 2024. Qualified education expenses for the AOTC are $4,400 ($5,000 of tuition and fees less $1,000 of tax-free scholarships plus $400 for books). ♦

The AOTC is calculated as 100 percent of the first $2,000 of qualified expenses paid, and 25 percent of the next $2,000, for a maximum annual credit of $2,500 per student. The AOTC is phased out ratably for joint return filers with income between $160,000 and $180,000 and for single, head of household, or surviving spouse filers with income between $80,000 and $90,000 (these amounts are not adjusted for inflation). The AOTC is 40-percent refundable; thus, up to $1,000 (40 percent of $2,500) may be refunded to the taxpayer if the credit exceeds the taxpayer's tax liability.

Example Jenny graduates from high school in June 2024. In the fall, she enrolls for 12 units at Gwinett University. Gwinett University considers students who take 12 or more units to be full-time students. Jenny's father pays her tuition and fees of $2,300. The American Opportunity tax credit for Jenny's father is $2,075 [(100% × $2,000) + (25% × $300)]. ♦

Example Jason, a single father, has AGI of $85,000 in 2024 and pays $5,000 in qualified tuition for his son, who just started at Alamance University. Without any limitations, Jason would be entitled to a maximum American Opportunity tax credit of $2,500. However, after applying the AGI limitations, Jason's American Opportunity tax credit is reduced by $1,250 [$2,500 × ($90,000 − $85,000)/$10,000], resulting in a credit of $1,250. ♦

Many college students earn income and provide some of their own support. As a result, many parents of college-age students start to consider the consequences of claiming a child as a dependent versus allowing the child to file independently on their own tax return (of course, the support test and others covered in Chapter 1 generally dictate whether a full-time college student can be claimed by their parents). In order to prevent abuse of the AOTC by students attempting to maximize the credit by filing their own tax return, there are special rules related to the refundable portion of the AOTC. A student filing their own tax return will not qualify for the AOTC if 1 (a, b, or c), 2, and 3 apply:

1a. The student is under age 18 at the end of 2024, or
1b. The student is age 18 at the end of 2024 and the student's earned income was less than one-half of their own support, or
1c. The student is over age 18 and under age 24, a full-time student, and the student's earned income was less than one-half of their own support.
2. At least one of the student's parents was alive at the end of 2024.
3. The student is not filing a joint return for 2024.

Example Vance Wilder is a single, 20-year-old full-time student at Harrison College. Vance earned $11,000 from his part-time accounting job and in 2024, provided over one-half of his own support. As a result, his parents no longer claim him as a dependent. Vance meets rules 2 and 3 above but he does not meet 1a, 1b, or 1c because he provided over one-half of his support from his own earned income. Vance is eligible for the refundable portion of the AOTC. ♦

Example Ellie Woods is a 23-year-old single taxpayer who attends college full-time. She has earned income of $4,000, which is not more than one-half of her own support (the remaining support is provided by her parents, who are both alive). Even if Ellie's parents chose not to claim her as a dependent, she would not be eligible for the refundable portion of the AOTC. She meets rules 1c, 2, and 3 above. ♦

Qualifying expenses must be paid during the tax year for education during an academic year beginning within that tax year. If tuition expenses are paid during the tax year for an academic period beginning during the first three months of the following tax year, the expenses may be claimed during the payment year.

Similar to the child tax credit rules, a taxpayer identification number (Social Security number or individual tax identification number) is required for each AOTC qualifying student by the due date of the return (including extensions).

If the IRS rejects an AOTC for any reason other than a math or clerical error, the taxpayer must complete Form 8862 used for claiming certain credits in a year after a rejection.

In addition, a taxpayer who erroneously claims the AOTC due to reckless or intentional disregard of rules or regulations is ineligible to claim the credit for a period of two tax years. If the IRS determines the claim for the credit was fraudulent, the ineligibility window is extended to ten years.

Unlike the child tax credit and EIC, no time restriction was placed on the IRS issuing refunds for any tax returns that claim an AOTC.

Form 8867, a due diligence checklist for tax preparers is required for returns claiming the AOTC. Failure to file Form 8867 could result in a $635 penalty (for returns filed in 2025).

7-5b Lifetime Learning Credit

Taxpayers can elect a nonrefundable tax credit of 20 percent of qualified expenses of up to $10,000, for a maximum credit of $2,000. The lifetime learning credit is available for qualified expenses paid for education of the taxpayer, their spouse, and dependents. The credit is available for undergraduate, graduate, or professional courses at eligible educational institutions. The student can be enrolled in just one course and still get the credit. There is no limit on the number of years a taxpayer can claim the credit. The credit is not subject to felony drug offense restrictions. The purpose of this credit is to encourage taxpayers to take courses at eligible institutions to acquire or improve job skills.

Example In September 2024, Xavier pays $1,200 to take a course to improve his job skills to qualify for a new position at work. His lifetime learning credit for 2024 is $240 (20% × $1,200). ♦

The lifetime learning credit is phased out at the same income levels as the American Opportunity tax credit. Joint return filers with AGI between $160,000 and $180,000 and single, head of household, or surviving spouse filers with income between $80,000 and $90,000, must phase the credit out evenly over the phase-out range.

Example During 2024, Jason, a single father with AGI of $85,000, paid $2,500 of tuition for a master's degree program in fine arts which he has been attending with the hope of eventually becoming a writer. Without any limitations, Jason would be entitled to a maximum lifetime learning credit of $500 (20% × $2,500). However, due to the income phase-out ranges for the lifetime learning credit, his credit is $250 [$500 × (90,000 − $85,000)/$10,000]. ♦

7-5c Using Both Credits

Taxpayers cannot take both the American Opportunity tax credit and the lifetime learning credit for the same student in the same tax year. An American Opportunity tax credit can be claimed for one or more students, and the lifetime learning credit can be claimed for other students in the same tax year. Also, the choice in one year does not bind the taxpayer for future years. For example, a taxpayer can claim the American Opportunity tax credit for a student in one tax year and take the lifetime learning credit for the same

ProConnect™ Tax TIP

Education credits are input under Credits/Education Tuition (1098-T). The typical starting point would be to enter the information obtained from the student's 1098-T.

Self-Study Problem 7.5
Refer to Appendix E for Solutions to Self-Study Problems

a. Judy Estudiante graduates from high school in June 2024. In the fall, she enrolls for twelve units in Southwest University and receives the following Form 1098-T.

Form 1098-T (2024) — Tuition Statement

- FILER'S name and address: Southwest University, 1234 Cleveland Avenue, El Paso, TX 79925
- FILER'S employer identification no.: 12-7652311
- STUDENT'S TIN: 434-11-7812
- STUDENT'S name: Judy Estudiante
- Street address: 12 Fannin Street
- City, state, ZIP: Van Horn, TX 79855
- Box 1 Payments received for qualified tuition and related expenses: $4,411.00
- Box 5 Scholarships or grants: $300.00
- Box 8 Checked if at least half-time student: X

Judy spends $304 on textbooks during the fall semester. Judy's parents, Santiago and Sophia Estudiante, pay her tuition and fees, have AGI of $170,000, have pre-credit tax liability of over $20,000, are claiming no other tax credits, and claim Judy as a dependent. Judy has never been arrested or convicted of any crimes. Complete Form 8863 on Pages 7-33 and 7-34 to determine what is the refundable and nonrefundable American Opportunity tax credit Judy's parents can claim for Judy if they file a joint return.

b. In September 2024, Gene pays $6,800 to take a course to improve their job skills at work. Gene's AGI is $54,000 for 2024. What is Gene's lifetime learning credit for 2024?

Self-Study Problem 7.5a

Form 8863
Department of the Treasury
Internal Revenue Service

Education Credits
(American Opportunity and Lifetime Learning Credits)
Attach to Form 1040 or 1040-SR.
Go to www.irs.gov/Form8863 for instructions and the latest information.

OMB No. 1545-0074
2024
Attachment Sequence No. **50**

Name(s) shown on return

Your social security number

CAUTION: Complete a separate Part III on page 2 for each student for whom you're claiming either credit before you complete Parts I and II.

Part I — Refundable American Opportunity Credit

1. After completing Part III for each student, enter the total of all amounts from all Parts III, line 30 . . . **1**
2. Enter: $180,000 if married filing jointly; $90,000 if single, head of household, or qualifying surviving spouse . . . **2**
3. Enter the amount from Form 1040 or 1040-SR, line 11. But if you're filing Form 2555 or 4563, or you're excluding income from Puerto Rico, see Pub. 970 for the amount to enter instead . . . **3**
4. Subtract line 3 from line 2. If zero or less, **stop**; you can't take any education credit . . . **4**
5. Enter: $20,000 if married filing jointly; $10,000 if single, head of household, or qualifying surviving spouse . . . **5**
6. If line 4 is:
   - Equal to or more than line 5, enter 1.000 on line 6 . . .
   - Less than line 5, divide line 4 by line 5. Enter the result as a decimal (rounded to at least three places) . . . **6**
7. Multiply line 1 by line 6. **Caution:** If you were under age 24 at the end of the year **and** meet the conditions described in the instructions, you **can't** take the refundable American opportunity credit; skip line 8, enter the amount from line 7 on line 9, and check this box ☐ . . . **7**
8. **Refundable American opportunity credit.** Multiply line 7 by 40% (0.40). Enter the amount here and on Form 1040 or 1040-SR, line 29. Then go to line 9 below . . . **8**

Part II — Nonrefundable Education Credits

9. Subtract line 8 from line 7. Enter here and on line 2 of the Credit Limit Worksheet (see instructions) . . . **9**
10. After completing Part III for each student, enter the total of all amounts from all Parts III, line 31. If zero, skip lines 11 through 17, enter -0- on line 18, and go to line 19 . . . **10**
11. Enter the smaller of line 10 or $10,000 . . . **11**
12. Multiply line 11 by 20% (0.20) . . . **12**
13. Enter: $180,000 if married filing jointly; $90,000 if single, head of household, or qualifying surviving spouse . . . **13**
14. Enter the amount from Form 1040 or 1040-SR, line 11. But if you're filing Form 2555 or 4563, or you're excluding income from Puerto Rico, see Pub. 970 for the amount to enter instead . . . **14**
15. Subtract line 14 from line 13. If zero or less, skip lines 16 and 17, enter -0- on line 18, and go to line 19 . . . **15**
16. Enter: $20,000 if married filing jointly; $10,000 if single, head of household, or qualifying surviving spouse . . . **16**
17. If line 15 is:
    - Equal to or more than line 16, enter 1.000 on line 17 and go to line 18
    - Less than line 16, divide line 15 by line 16. Enter the result as a decimal (rounded to at least three places) . . . **17**
18. Multiply line 12 by line 17. Enter here and on line 1 of the Credit Limit Worksheet (see instructions) . **18**
19. **Nonrefundable education credits.** Enter the amount from line 7 of the Credit Limit Worksheet (see instructions) here and on Schedule 3 (Form 1040), line 3 . . . **19**

For Paperwork Reduction Act Notice, see your tax return instructions. Cat. No. 25379M Form **8863** (2024)

Self-Study Problem 7.5a

Form 8863 (2024) Page **2**

Name(s) shown on return | Your social security number

> **CAUTION:** Complete Part III for each student for whom you're claiming either the American opportunity credit or lifetime learning credit. Use additional copies of page 2 as needed for each student.

Part III Student and Educational Institution Information. See instructions.

20 Student name (as shown on page 1 of your tax return)

21 Student social security number (as shown on page 1 of your tax return)

22 Educational institution information (see instructions)

a. Name of first educational institution

b. Name of second educational institution (if any)

(1) Address. Number and street (or P.O. box). City, town or post office, state, and ZIP code. If a foreign address, see instructions.

(1) Address. Number and street (or P.O. box). City, town or post office, state, and ZIP code. If a foreign address, see instructions.

(2) Did the student receive Form 1098-T from this institution for 2024? ☐ Yes ☐ No

(2) Did the student receive Form 1098-T from this institution for 2024? ☐ Yes ☐ No

(3) Did the student receive Form 1098-T from this institution for 2023 with box 7 checked? ☐ Yes ☐ No

(3) Did the student receive Form 1098-T from this institution for 2023 with box 7 checked? ☐ Yes ☐ No

(4) Enter the institution's employer identification number (EIN) if you're claiming the American opportunity credit or if you checked "Yes" in **(2)** or **(3)**. You can get the EIN from Form 1098-T or from the institution.

(4) Enter the institution's employer identification number (EIN) if you're claiming the American opportunity credit or if you checked "Yes" in **(2)** or **(3)**. You can get the EIN from Form 1098-T or from the institution.

23 Has the American opportunity credit been claimed for this student for any 4 prior tax years?
☐ Yes — **Stop!** Go to line 31 for this student.
☐ No — Go to line 24.

24 Was the student enrolled at least half-time for at least one academic period that began or is treated as having begun in 2024 at an eligible educational institution in a program leading towards a postsecondary degree, certificate, or other recognized postsecondary educational credential? See instructions.
☐ Yes — Go to line 25.
☐ No — **Stop!** Go to line 31 for this student.

25 Did the student complete the first 4 years of postsecondary education before 2024? See instructions.
☐ Yes — **Stop!** Go to line 31 for this student.
☐ No — Go to line 26.

26 Was the student convicted, before the end of 2024, of a felony for possession or distribution of a controlled substance?
☐ Yes — **Stop!** Go to line 31 for this student.
☐ No — Complete lines 27 through 30 for this student.

> **CAUTION:** You can't take the American opportunity credit and the lifetime learning credit for the same student in the same year. If you complete lines 27 through 30 for this student, don't complete line 31.

American Opportunity Credit

27 Adjusted qualified education expenses (see instructions). **Don't enter more than $4,000** . . . . . | **27**
28 Subtract $2,000 from line 27. If zero or less, enter -0- . . . . . | **28**
29 Multiply line 28 by 25% (0.25) . . . . . | **29**
30 If line 28 is zero, enter the amount from line 27. Otherwise, add $2,000 to the amount on line 29 and enter the result. Skip line 31. Include the total of all amounts from all Parts III, line 30, on Part I, line 1 . | **30**

Lifetime Learning Credit

31 Adjusted qualified education expenses (see instructions). Include the total of all amounts from all Parts III, line 31, on Part II, line 10 . . . . . | **31**

Form **8863** (2024)

7-6 Foreign Exclusion and Tax Credit

7.6 Learning Objective
Compute the foreign income exclusion and tax credit.

International taxation is one of the most complex areas of the tax law and entire textbooks are devoted to the topic. However, there are two main provisions related to U.S. taxation of international income that apply to individuals: (1) the foreign income exclusion and (2) the foreign tax credit.

7-6a Foreign Income Exclusion

Certain taxpayers working and living outside the United States are eligible to exclude a certain portion of their foreign income from taxable income under the foreign income exclusion. In addition, certain foreign housing can also be excluded or deducted. The foreign income exclusion limit in 2024 is $126,500. The base foreign housing exclusion is limited to 14 percent of the maximum foreign income exclusion amount but can be higher for certain geographic locations.

Example John Adams, a single U.S. citizen, is an employee of a large multinational corporation and works at the company's Mexican subsidiary. He has established a bona fide tax home in Mexico. During the year, John spent 355 days in Mexico and 11 days vacationing in Hawaii. His employer paid him wages of $135,000 in 2024. John excludes $126,500 of his wages from U.S. taxable income. John will not be eligible to claim a foreign tax credit on the wages excluded. ♦

To claim the foreign earned income exclusion and the foreign housing exclusion, or the foreign housing deduction, the following three requirements must be met:

1. The taxpayer's tax home must be in a foreign country, and
2. The taxpayer must have foreign earned income, and
3. The taxpayer must be one of the following:
   a. A U.S. citizen who is a bona fide resident of a foreign country or countries for an uninterrupted period that includes an entire tax year.
   b. A U.S. resident alien who is a citizen or national of a country with which the United States has an income tax treaty in effect and who is a bona fide resident of a foreign country or countries for an uninterrupted period that includes an entire tax year.
   c. A U.S. citizen or a resident alien who is physically present in a foreign country or countries for at least 330 full days during any period of 12 consecutive months.

Tax home (refer to Chapter 3) is the general area of the taxpayer's main place of business, employment, or post of duty, regardless of where the family home is maintained. A tax home is the place where the taxpayer is permanently or indefinitely engaged to work as an employee or self-employed individual.

Example Alan is a salesperson for the U.S. subsidiary of Snyder Electronics, a large electronic components manufacturer based in Paris, France. He lives at 14 Sienna Cir, Warminster, PA 18974 with his spouse (Julie) and two children (Greg and Christine) and works at the Snyder office in Philadelphia, PA. On December 15, 2023, Alan takes a position at the company's headquarters at 35 Rue Joseph Monier, 92500 Rueil-Malmaison, France (just outside Paris) that is expected to last at least three years. Alan keeps ownership of his home outside Philadelphia and his family continues to reside there until the school year finishes in May 2024. Meanwhile, Alan rents a home at 6 Rue Péclet, 75015 Paris, France, establishes a business address in Paris (his email and business cards list Paris as his office), and opens a bank account in Paris. Although Alan arrived in Paris on December 31, 2023, his family moves to Paris in May, bringing most of their furniture and personal belongings. His children enroll in local schools in May 2024. Alan is paid in euros by the Paris office and pays French income tax on his French income. Alan's tax home is Paris and he is a bona fide resident of France for the year 2024. ♦

As an alternative to the bona fide residence test, the physical presence test requires the taxpayer to be present in a foreign country for at least 330 days in any 12-month period. IRS Publication 54 includes a useful flowchart presented in Figure 7.3 to determine qualification for the foreign income and foreign housing exclusion.

Figure 7.3 Flowchart for Foreign Exclusions and Deduction

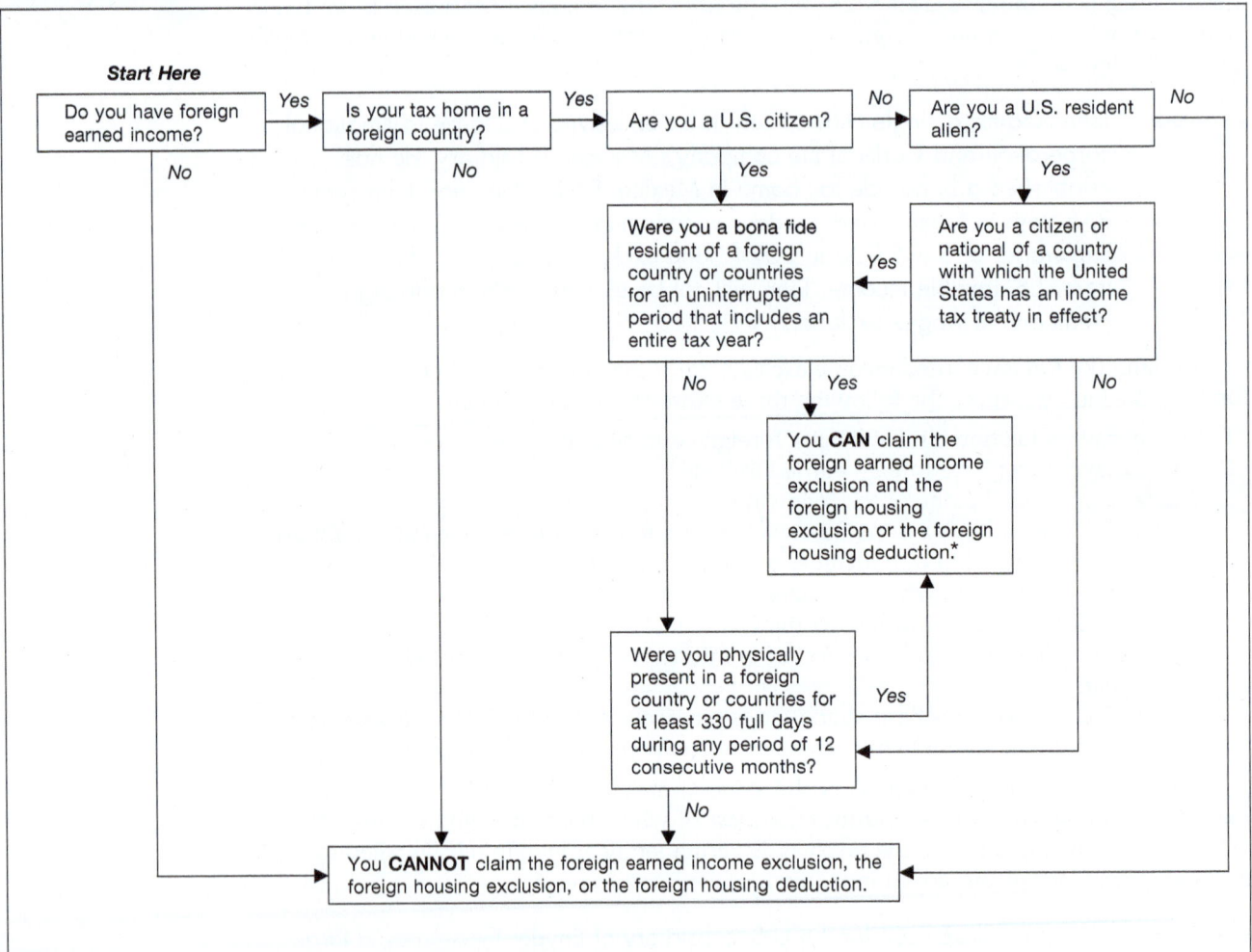

*Foreign housing exclusion applies only to employees. Foreign housing deduction applies only to the self-employed.

Compensation paid in foreign currency must be converted into U.S. dollars (USD) to claim a foreign income or housing exclusion. Typically, the conversion should be based on the exchange rate on the date the income was received. If the foreign income was received evenly throughout the year, and the foreign exchange rate was relatively stable during the year, the taxpayer may use an average rate. There are a number of sources to identify exchange rates including the U.S. Treasury's foreign currency converter (**https://fiscaldata.treasury.gov/currency-exchange-rates-converter/**) and the IRS posts yearly average foreign currency exchange rates for a number of countries each year (**https://www.irs.gov/individuals/international-taxpayers/yearly-average-currency-exchange-rates**).

Taxpayers that meet the exclusion requirements can exclude a certain amount of foreign income and can also elect to exclude an amount of foreign housing costs. The housing exclusion requires establishing the value of qualified housing expenses such as rent, utilities (other than telephone charges), real and personal property insurance, nonrefundable fees paid to obtain a lease, rental of furniture and accessories, residential parking, and household repairs. Qualifying housing expenses are subject to a limit of $37,950 or 30 percent of the foreign income exclusion amount ($126,500 × 30% in 2024). Certain geographic locations have a higher limit as published each year by the IRS. Table 7.7 presents a selection of the cities and the increased limit on qualified housing expenses.

Table 7.7 — 2024 Increased Housing Limits under IRS Notice 2024-31

City	Annual Limit	City	Annual Limit
Buenos Aires, Argentine	$56,500	Milan, Italy	$ 68,300
Sydney, Australia	67,000	Tokyo, Japan	73,100
Montreal, Canada	54,000	Mexico City	47,900
Paris, France	68,600	Doha, Qatar	45,888
Berlin, Germany	41,100	Geneva, Switzerland	107,400
Mumbai, India	67,920	London, UK	67,000

The housing exclusion is based on the actual housing cost (subject to a limit) less an annual base housing cost, which is generally set at 16 percent of the foreign income exclusion amount ($20,240, or $126,500 x 16%). The 30-percent limit less the 16-percent base effectively creates a 14-percent limit.

The foreign housing and income exclusions are claimed on Form 2555.

Example Alan, from the previous example, is paid compensation of €170,000 (which converts to USD 181,818). This amount includes Alan's housing allowance of €14,000. Alan receives no other compensation from his employer in 2024. Snyder, his employer, obtained a French work visa for Alan. Alan rented his home in Paris starting January 1, 2024 through year end for €36,000 (USD 38,503). His family joined him on May 10, 2024. Alan rented their home outside of Philadelphia starting June 1, 2024 to Alex and Servando Morgan, an unrelated couple. Alan and his entire family left France for vacation in the United States from August 1 through August 10. Alan has never claimed the foreign income exclusion before. Alan's Form 2555 claiming a foreign income and housing exclusion is presented on Pages 7-38 to 7-40. ♦

Form 2555 — Foreign Earned Income (2024)

Form 2555
Department of the Treasury
Internal Revenue Service

Foreign Earned Income
Attach to Form 1040 or 1040-SR.
Go to *www.irs.gov/Form2555* for instructions and the latest information.

OMB No. 1545-0074
2024
Attachment Sequence No. 34

For Use by U.S. Citizens and Resident Aliens Only

Name shown on Form 1040 or 1040-SR: **Alan and Julie**
Your social security number:

Part I — General Information

1. Your foreign address (including country): 6 Rue Péclet, 75015 Paris, France
2. Your occupation: Salesperson
3. Employer's name: Snyder Electronics
4. a. Employer's U.S. address: Philadelphia, PA
   b. Employer's foreign address: 35 Rue Joseph Monier, 92500 Rueil-Malmaison, France
5. Employer is (check any that apply):
   - a. ☒ A foreign entity
   - b. ☐ A U.S. company
   - c. ☐ Self
   - d. ☐ A foreign affiliate of a U.S. company
   - e. ☐ Other (specify)
6. a. If you previously filed Form 2555 or Form 2555-EZ, enter the last year you filed the form.
   b. If you didn't previously file Form 2555 or Form 2555-EZ to claim either of the exclusions, check here ☒ and go to line 7.
   c. Have you ever revoked either of the exclusions? ☐ Yes ☐ No
   d. If you answered "Yes," enter the type of exclusion and the tax year for which the revocation was effective.
7. Of what country are you a citizen/national? United States
8. a. Did you maintain a separate foreign residence for your family because of adverse living conditions at your tax home? See *Second foreign household* in the instructions. ☐ Yes ☒ No
   b. If "Yes," enter city and country of the separate foreign residence. Also, enter the number of days during your tax year that you maintained a second household at that address.
9. List your tax home(s) during your tax year and date(s) established. Paris, France 1/1/2024 to 12/31/2024

Next, complete either Part II or Part III. If an item doesn't apply, enter "N/A." If you don't give the information asked for, any exclusion or deduction you claim may be disallowed.

Part II — Taxpayers Qualifying Under Bona Fide Residence Test

Note: Only U.S. citizens and resident aliens who are citizens or nationals of U.S. treaty countries can use this test. See instructions.

10. Date bona fide residence began January 1, 2024, and ended Continues
11. Kind of living quarters in foreign country:
    - a. ☐ Purchased house
    - b. ☒ Rented house or apartment
    - c. ☐ Rented room
    - d. ☐ Quarters furnished by employer
12. a. Did any of your family live with you abroad during any part of the tax year? ☒ Yes ☐ No
    b. If "Yes," who and for what period? Spouse and 2 children. May 11, 2024 through end of year
13. a. Have you submitted a statement to the authorities of the foreign country where you claim bona fide residence that you aren't a resident of that country? See instructions. ☐ Yes ☒ No
    b. Are you required to pay income tax to the country where you claim bona fide residence? See instructions. ☒ Yes ☐ No
    If you answered "Yes" to 13a and "No" to 13b, you don't qualify as a bona fide resident. Don't complete the rest of this part.
14. If you were present in the United States or its territories during the tax year, complete columns (a)–(d) below. **Don't** include the income from column (d) in Part IV, but report it on Form 1040 or 1040-SR.

(a) Date arrived in U.S.	(b) Date left U.S.	(c) Number of days in U.S. on business	(d) Income earned in U.S. on business (attach computation)	(a) Date arrived in U.S.	(b) Date left U.S.	(c) Number of days in U.S. on business	(d) Income earned in U.S. on business (attach computation)
8/1/2024	8/10/2024	0	0				

15. a. List any contractual terms or other conditions relating to the length of your employment abroad. Term of foreign employment expected to last at least 3 years
    b. Enter the type of visa under which you entered the foreign country. Work visa
    c. Did your visa limit the length of your stay or employment in a foreign country? If "Yes," attach explanation. ☐ Yes ☒ No
    d. Did you maintain a home in the United States while living abroad? ☒ Yes ☐ No
    e. If "Yes," enter address of your home, whether it was rented, the names of the occupants, and their relationship to you. 14 Sienna Cir, Warminster, PA 18974 Rented to Alex and Servando Morgan (unrelated)

For Paperwork Reduction Act Notice, see the Instructions for Form 1040. Cat. No. 11900P Form **2555** (2024)

Form 2555 (2024) Page **2**

Part III — Taxpayers Qualifying Under Physical Presence Test

Note: U.S. citizens and all resident aliens can use this test. See instructions.

16. The physical presence test is based on the 12-month period from _____ through _____
17. Enter your principal country of employment during your tax year. _____
18. If you traveled abroad during the 12-month period entered on line 16, complete columns **(a)–(f)** below. Exclude travel between foreign countries that didn't involve travel on or over international waters, or in or over the United States, for 24 hours or more. If you have no travel to report during the period, enter "Physically present in a foreign country or countries for the entire 12-month period." **Don't** include the income from column **(f)** below in Part IV, but report it on Form 1040 or 1040-SR.

(a) Name of country (including U.S.)	(b) Date arrived	(c) Date left	(d) Full days present in country	(e) Number of days in U.S. on business	(f) Income earned in U.S. on business (attach computation)

Part IV — All Taxpayers

Note: Enter on lines 19 through 23 all income, including noncash income, you earned and actually or constructively received during your 2024 tax year for services you performed in a foreign country. If any of the foreign earned income received this tax year was earned in a prior tax year, or will be earned in a later tax year (such as a bonus), see the instructions. **Don't** include income from line 14, column **(d)**, or line 18, column **(f)**. Report amounts in U.S. dollars, using the exchange rates in effect when you actually or constructively received the income.

If you are a cash basis taxpayer, report on Form 1040 or 1040-SR all income you received in 2024, no matter when you performed the service.

2024 Foreign Earned Income		Amount (in U.S. dollars)
19 Total wages, salaries, bonuses, commissions, etc.	19	181,818
20 Allowable share of income for personal services performed (see instructions):		
a In a business (including farming) or profession	20a	
b In a partnership. List partnership's name and address and type of income. _____	20b	
21 Noncash income (market value of property or facilities furnished by employer—attach statement showing how it was determined):		
a Home (lodging)	21a	
b Meals	21b	
c Car	21c	
d Other property or facilities. List type and amount. _____	21d	
22 Allowances, reimbursements, or expenses paid on your behalf for services you performed:		
a Cost of living and overseas differential	22a	
b Family	22b	
c Education	22c	
d Home leave	22d	
e Quarters	22e	
f For any other purpose. List type and amount. _____	22f	
g Add lines 22a through 22f	22g	
23 Other foreign earned income. List type and amount. _____	23	
24 Add lines 19 through 21d, line 22g, and line 23	24	181,818
25 Total amount of meals and lodging included on line 24 that is excludable (see instructions)	25	0
26 Subtract line 25 from line 24. Enter the result here and on line 27 on page 3. This is your **2024 foreign earned income**	26	181,818

Form **2555** (2024)

Form 2555 (2024)   Page **3**

Part V — All Taxpayers

Line	Description		Amount
27	Enter the amount from line 26	27	181,818
	Are you claiming the housing exclusion or housing deduction?		
	☑ **Yes.** Complete Part VI.		
	☐ **No.** Go to Part VII.		

Part VI — Taxpayers Claiming the Housing Exclusion and/or Deduction

Line	Description		Amount
28	Qualified housing expenses for the tax year (see instructions)	28	38,503
29a	Enter location where housing expenses incurred. See instructions. Paris, France		
b	Enter limit on housing expenses. See instructions	29b	68,600 (a)
30	Enter the **smaller** of line 28 or line 29b	30	38,503
31	Number of days in your qualifying period that fall within your 2024 tax year (see instructions) — 31: 366 days		
32	Multiply $55.30 by the number of days on line 31. If 366 is entered on line 31, enter $20,240 here	32	20,240
33	Subtract line 32 from line 30. If the result is zero or less, don't complete the rest of this part or any of Part IX	33	18,263
34	Enter employer-provided amounts. See instructions — 34: 181,818		
35	Divide line 34 by line 27. Enter the result as a decimal (rounded to at least three places), but don't enter more than "1.000"	35	1.00
36	**Housing exclusion.** Multiply line 33 by line 35. Enter the result but don't enter more than the amount on line 34. Also, complete Part VIII	36	18,263

Note: The housing deduction is figured in Part IX. If you choose to claim the foreign earned income exclusion, complete Parts VII and VIII before Part IX.

Part VII — Taxpayers Claiming the Foreign Earned Income Exclusion

Line	Description		Amount
37	Maximum foreign earned income exclusion. Enter $126,500	37	126,500
38	• If you completed Part VI, enter the number from line 31. • All others, enter the number of days in your qualifying period that fall within your 2024 tax year. See the instructions for line 31. — 38: 366 days		
39	• If line 38 and the number of days in your 2024 tax year (usually 366) are the same, enter "1.000." • Otherwise, divide line 38 by the number of days in your 2024 tax year and enter the result as a decimal (rounded to at least three places).	39	1.00
40	Multiply line 37 by line 39	40	126,500
41	Subtract line 36 from line 27	41	163,555
42	**Foreign earned income exclusion.** Enter the **smaller** of line 40 or line 41. Also, complete Part VIII	42	126,500

Part VIII — Taxpayers Claiming the Housing Exclusion, Foreign Earned Income Exclusion, or Both

Line	Description		Amount
43	Add lines 36 and 42	43	144,763
44	Deductions allowed in figuring your adjusted gross income (Form 1040 or 1040-SR, line 11) that are allocable to the excluded income. See instructions and attach computation	44	0
45	Subtract line 44 from line 43. Enter the result here and on Schedule 1 (Form 1040), line 8d. Complete the Foreign Earned Income Tax Worksheet in the Instructions for Form 1040 if you enter an amount on this line	45	144,763

Part IX — Taxpayers Claiming the Housing Deduction

Complete this part only if **(a)** line 33 is more than line 36, and **(b)** line 27 is more than line 43.

Line	Description		Amount
46	Subtract line 36 from line 33	46	
47	Subtract line 43 from line 27	47	
48	Enter the **smaller** of line 46 or line 47	48	

Note: If line 47 is **more than** line 48 and you couldn't deduct all of your 2023 housing deduction because of the 2023 limit, use the Housing Deduction Carryover Worksheet in the instructions to figure the amount to enter on line 49. Otherwise, go to line 50.

Line	Description		Amount
49	Housing deduction carryover from 2023 (from the Housing Deduction Carryover Worksheet in the instructions)	49	
50	**Housing deduction.** Add lines 48 and 49. Enter the total here and on Schedule 1 (Form 1040), line 24j. Complete the Foreign Earned Income Tax Worksheet in the Instructions for Form 1040 if you enter an amount on this line	50	

Form **2555** (2024)

(a) Refer to Table 7.7 for the housing expense limit for Paris, France

If a taxpayer meets the requirements of the foreign income and housing exclusions but is not present in the foreign country for the entire year, the exclusion limit is prorated based on the number of days

Example Assume instead that Alan arrives in Paris on August 14, 2024 and maintains his tax home there until January 31, 2027. The number of qualifying days in 2024 is 140 (August 14 through December 31, 2024). The $126,500 exclusion limit will be prorated by 140/366. ♦

Use of the foreign income exclusion precludes the use of certain credits or deductions (for example, refundable portion of the child tax credit, the EITC, and the foreign tax credit on excluded income). In addition, a number of provisions that require the computation of modified taxable income require the foreign income exclusion to be added back (for example, the limits for a deduction for contributions to an IRA).

Under a process known as the "stacking rule," the tax rate that applies to the taxpayer's income is based on the rates that would apply if no such exclusion existed.

Example Alan elects to exclude $144,763 of foreign income and housing in 2024. The only income Alan and Julie have is his salary of $181,818 and they take no other deductions or credits except the standard deduction. They have $7,855 ($181,818 − $144,763 − $29,200) in other taxable income after deductions. His regular tax liability for 2024 is $1,728 as calculated using the Foreign Income Tax Worksheet from the instruction to Form 1040 as presented below.

Foreign Earned Income Tax Worksheet—Line 16 *Keep for Your Records*

⚠ If Form 1040 or 1040-SR, line 15, is zero, don't complete this worksheet.

1. Enter the amount from Form 1040 or 1040-SR, line 15 .... 1. 7,855
2a. Enter the amount from your (and your spouse's if filing jointly) Form 2555, lines 45 and 50 .... 2a. 144,763
 b. Enter the total amount of any itemized deductions or exclusions you couldn't claim because they are related to excluded income .... b. _____
 c. Subtract line 2b from line 2a. If zero or less, enter -0- .... c. 144,763
3. Add lines 1 and 2c 3. 152,618
4. Figure the tax on the amount on line 3. Use the Tax Table, Tax Computation Worksheet, Qualified Dividends and Capital Gain Tax Worksheet*, Schedule D Tax Worksheet*, or Form 8615, whichever applies. See the instructions for Form 1040 or 1040-SR, line 16, to see which tax computation method applies. (Don't use a second Foreign Earned Income Tax Worksheet to figure the tax on this line.) .... 4. 23,682 (a)
5. Figure the tax on the amount on line 2c. If the amount on line 2c is less than $100,000, use the Tax Table to figure this tax. If the amount on line 2c is $100,000 or more, use the Tax Computation Worksheet .... 5. 21,954 (b)
6. Subtract line 5 from line 4. Enter the result. If zero or less, enter -0-. Also include this amount on the entry space on Form 1040 or 1040-SR, line 16 .... 6. 1,728

(a) $10,852 + [($152,618 − $94,300) × 22%] from Appendix A for taxpayers with income greater than $100,000.
(b) $10,852 + [($144,763 − $94,300) × 22%].

Note that the tax rate that applies to the income is 22 percent ($1,728 ÷ $7,855), which reflects the tax rate that applies to their taxable income if the foreign income exclusion did not apply. ♦

7-6b Foreign Tax Credit

An individual will incur foreign taxes under two typical scenarios: (1) they have engaged in work outside the United States as either an employee or as a self-employed individual (expat), or (2) as a result of foreign investments either directly or through an investment portfolio such as a mutual fund or exchange-traded fund. Although the tax treatment of expats is beyond the scope of this textbook, aside from the benefit available for many expats under the foreign income exclusions described above, an expat may use a foreign tax credit for foreign taxes paid to reduce their U.S. income tax liability. The same is true of an investor whose income is subject to foreign taxes. In both cases, the amount of the credit is limited to the U.S. tax that applies to that income.

Example Tom Jefferson, a single U.S. citizen, works for his employer in France and is not eligible to use the foreign income exclusion. In 2024, Tom paid income taxes in France of $3,500 on his income of $50,000. This was his only income during the year (U.S. or otherwise). Tom claims the standard deduction. Tom's foreign-sourced income is $35,400 ($50,000 less standard deduction of $14,600). His U.S. income for purposes of the foreign tax credit limitation is also $35,400. Tom calculates his U.S. income tax liability before any credits as $4,019. His foreign tax credit limit in this case is:

$$\frac{\text{Net foreign income } \$35,400}{\text{Total taxable income } \$35,400} \times \text{U.S. tax liability } \$4,019 = \$4,019$$

Tom's actual foreign taxes paid are $3,500; thus, his foreign tax credit is not limited and he is eligible for a $3,500 foreign tax credit. ♦

Example Alexander Hamilton held shares in the Federalist International Stock Fund, a mutual fund with extensive foreign holdings. Alexander's earnings of $2,300 from the fund and foreign taxes paid of $632 were reported to him on a Form 1099-DIV. This was Alexander's only portfolio income during the year. Alexander's taxable income was $76,000 and his tax liability before the credit was $11,779 including Alexander's U.S. tax liability associated with dividend income of $345. Alexander's limitation is calculated as

$$\frac{\text{Net foreign income } \$2,300}{\text{Total taxable income } \$76,000} \times \text{U.S. tax liability } \$11,779 = \$356$$

As a result, Alexander's foreign tax credit is limited to $356. The unused credit of $276 ($632 foreign taxes paid less $356 limitation) can be carried back one year or forward for up to 10 years. ♦

A number of simplifications were used in the above examples and the actual computation of the limit can be considerably more complex. Different rules apply to income earned in a U.S. possession. The foreign tax credit is typically claimed on Form 1116 and the rules are explained in the instructions to Form 1116.

A simplified foreign tax credit that does not require the completion of Form 1116 is available if you meet all of the following requirements:

1. All of the foreign-sourced gross income was "passive category income" (which includes most interest and dividends).
2. All the income and any foreign taxes paid on it were reported on a qualified payee statement such as a Form 1099-DIV, Form 1099-INT, Schedule K-1, or similar substitute statements.
3. Total creditable foreign taxes aren't more than $300 ($600, if married filing a joint return).

If the Form 1116 is not used, the foreign tax credit is entered directly on Schedule 3 of Form 1040, Line 1. The foreign tax credit is nonrefundable, and thus, limited to the pre-credit tax amount. Use of the simplified method precludes a carryback of any limited foreign tax credit but the unused credit can be carried forward up to ten years.

As a reminder, this is just an overview of these areas which are, in most instances, extremely complex. Useful publications are IRS Publication 54, Form 1116 and instructions, and Form 2555 and instructions.

> One of the most common ways to pay foreign taxes is through an investment in a mutual fund that happens to hold some international investments and pays foreign taxes at the fund level. The foreign tax payments are generally reported on the taxpayer's Form 1099-DIV and are entered into ProConnect Tax as part of recording the dividend income.

ProConnect™ Tax TIP

Self-Study Problem 7.6 *Refer to Appendix E for Solutions to Self-Study Problems*

Benny Franklin receives a Form 1099-DIV from his investment manager that lists foreign taxes paid of $432 and Benny's foreign investment earnings of $1,500. Benny had no other investment earnings and his total taxable income for the year is $58,000. Benny's tax liability before any foreign taxes is $7,819. Calculate the amount of the foreign tax credit.

7-7 Adoption Expenses

7.7 Learning Objective
Determine the proper use and calculation of the adoption credit.

Taxpayers are allowed two tax breaks for adoption expenses. A tax credit is allowed for qualified adoption expenses paid by taxpayers, and an exclusion from W-2 income is allowed for qualified adoption expenses paid by taxpayers' employers.

7-7a Adoption Credit

Individuals are allowed a nonrefundable income tax credit for qualified adoption expenses. Form 8839 is used to calculate and report the adoption credit. The total expense that can be taken as a credit for all tax years with respect to an adoption of a child is $16,810 for 2024. The credit is the total amount for each adoption and is not an annual amount (i.e., there is only one $16,810 credit per adopted child). The amount of the credit allowable for any tax year is reduced for taxpayers with AGI over $252,150 and is fully phased out when AGI reaches $292,150. The amount of the credit is reduced (but not below zero) by a factor equal to the excess of the taxpayer's AGI over $252,150 divided by $40,000. In some cases, beyond the scope of this textbook, AGI must be modified prior to calculating the adoption credit phase-out. For additional information on calculating modified adjusted gross income (MAGI) with respect to the adoption credit, see the instructions to Form 8839.

Example Ben and Beverly pay $5,000 of qualified adoption expenses in 2024 to adopt a qualified child. Their AGI is $262,150 for 2024, which reduces the adoption credit for 2024 by $1,250 [$5,000 × ($262,150 − $252,150) ÷ $40,000]. Thus, Ben and Beverly's allowable adoption credit for 2024 is $3,750 ($5,000 − $1,250). ◆

The credit is not refundable; however, the unused portion may be carried forward for five years. To claim the credit, married individuals must file jointly, and the taxpayer must include (if known) the name, age, and taxpayer identification number (TIN) of the child on the return.

7-7b Domestic Multiyear Adoptions

In the case of the adoption of an eligible child who is a U.S. citizen or resident of the United States at the time the adoption commenced, the credit for qualified adoption expenses is allowed for the tax year that follows the year during which the expenses are paid or incurred, unless the expenses are paid or incurred in the tax year the adoption becomes final. If the expenses are paid or incurred during the tax year in which the adoption becomes final, the credit is allowed for that year. The full $16,810 credit is allowed in special-needs adoptions regardless of the amount of qualified adoption expenses paid.

Example In connection with the adoption of an eligible child who is a U.S. citizen and is not a child with special needs, a taxpayer pays $7,000 of qualified adoption expenses in 2023 and $10,600 of qualified adoption expenses in 2024. The adoption is not finalized until 2025. The $7,000 of expenses paid or incurred in 2023 would be allowed in 2024, and $9,810 of the $10,600 paid or incurred in 2024 would be allowed in 2025. On the other hand, if the adoption were finalized in 2024, then $16,810 of qualified expenses would be allowed in 2024 (the maximum credit permitted as of 2024). ♦

7-7c Employer-Provided Adoption Assistance

An employee may exclude from W-2 earnings amounts paid or expenses incurred by their employer for qualified adoption expenses connected with the adoption of a child by the employee, if the amounts are furnished under an adoption assistance program. The total amount excludable per child is the same as the adoption credit amount ($16,810). The phase-out is calculated in the same manner as the phase-out for the adoption credit. An individual may claim both a credit and an exclusion in connection with the adoption of an eligible child, but may not claim both a credit and an exclusion for the same expense.

Self-Study Problem 7.7 *Refer to Appendix E for Solutions to Self-Study Problems*

James and Michael Bass finalized the adoption of their daughter, Allison in October 2024, one month after her birth. Allison is a U.S. citizen and is not a child with special needs. Her Social Security number is 466-47-3311. In 2024, James and Michael paid $17,000 in qualified adoption expenses. In addition, Michael's employer paid $4,000 directly to an adoption agency as an employer-provided adoption benefit. The Basses' AGI for 2024 is $259,990 (assume adjusted gross income and modified adjusted gross income are the same for purposes of this problem). The Basses' tax liability is $36,212 and they are not using tax credits except the child tax credit and adoption credit. Use Form 8839 on Pages 7-45 and 7-46 to calculate the Basses' adoption credit and the amount of any employee adoption exclusion.

Self-Study Problem 7.7

Form 8839
Department of the Treasury
Internal Revenue Service

Qualified Adoption Expenses

Attach to Form 1040, 1040-SR, or 1040-NR.
Go to www.irs.gov/Form8839 for instructions and the latest information.

OMB No. 1545-0074

2024

Attachment Sequence No. **38**

Name(s) shown on return

Your social security number

Part I — Information About Your Eligible Child or Children—You **must** complete this part.
See instructions for details, including what to do if you need more space.

1	(a) Child's name (First, Last)	(b) Child's year of birth	(c) born **before 2007** and disabled	(d) a child with special needs	(e) a foreign child	(f) Child's identifying number	(g) Check if adoption became final in 2024 or earlier
Child 1			☐	☐	☐		☐
Child 2			☐	☐	☐		☐
Child 3			☐	☐	☐		☐

Caution: If the child was a foreign child, see **Special rules** in the instructions for line 1, column (e), before you complete Part II or Part III. If you received **employer-provided adoption benefits**, complete Part III on the back next.

Part II — Adoption Credit

			Child 1	Child 2	Child 3
2	Maximum adoption credit per child. Enter $16,810. See instructions.	2			
3	Did you file Form 8839 for a prior year for the same child? ☐ **No.** Enter -0-. ☐ **Yes.** See instructions for the amount to enter	3			
4	Subtract line 3 from line 2	4			
5	**Qualified adoption expenses.** See instructions	5			
	Caution: Your qualified adoption expenses may not be equal to the adoption expenses you paid in 2024.				
6	Enter the **smaller** of line 4 or line 5	6			
7	Enter modified adjusted gross income. See instructions			7	
8	Is line 7 more than $252,150? ☐ **No.** Skip lines 8 and 9, and enter -0- on line 10. ☐ **Yes.** Subtract $252,150 from line 7			8	
9	Divide line 8 by $40,000. Enter the result as a decimal (rounded to at least three places). Do not enter more than 1.000			9	× .
10	Multiply each amount on line 6 by line 9	10			
11	Subtract line 10 from line 6	11			
12	Add the amounts on line 11			12	
13	Credit carryforward, if any, from prior years. See your Adoption Credit Carryforward Worksheet in the 2023 Form 8839 instructions			13	
14	Add lines 12 and 13			14	
15	Enter the amount from line 5 of the Credit Limit Worksheet in the instructions			15	
16	**Adoption credit.** Enter the smaller of line 14 or line 15 here and on Schedule 3 (Form 1040), line 6c. If line 15 is smaller than line 14, you may have a credit carryforward. See instructions			16	

For Paperwork Reduction Act Notice, see your tax return instructions. Cat. No. 22843L Form **8839** (2024)

Form 8839 (2024) Page **2**

Part III Employer-Provided Adoption Benefits

		Child 1	Child 2	Child 3
17	Maximum exclusion per child. Enter $16,810. See instructions			
18	Did you receive employer-provided adoption benefits for a prior year for the same child? ☐ **No.** Enter -0-. ☐ **Yes.** See instructions for the amount to enter			
19	Subtract line 18 from line 17			
20	Employer-provided adoption benefits you received in 2024. This amount should be shown in box 12 of your 2024 Form(s) W-2 with code **T**			
21	Add the amounts on line 20			
22	Enter the **smaller** of line 19 or line 20. But if the child was a child with special needs and the adoption became final in 2024, enter the amount from line 19.			
23	Enter modified adjusted gross income (from the worksheet in the instructions)			
24	Is line 23 more than $252,150? ☐ **No.** Skip lines 24 and 25, and enter -0- on line 26. ☐ **Yes.** Subtract $252,150 from line 23			
25	Divide line 24 by $40,000. Enter the result as a decimal (rounded to at least three places). Do not enter more than 1.000.	× .		
26	Multiply each amount on line 22 by line 25			
27	**Excluded benefits.** Subtract line 26 from line 22			
28	Add the amounts on line 27			
29	**Taxable benefits.** Is line 28 more than line 21? ☐ **No.** Subtract line 28 from line 21. Also, include this amount, if more than zero, on line 1f of Form 1040, 1040-SR, or 1040-NR. ☐ **Yes.** Subtract line 21 from line 28. Enter the result as a negative number. Also, enter the result on line 1f of Form 1040, 1040-SR, or 1040-NR.			

TIP You may be able to claim the adoption credit in Part II on the front of this form if any of the following apply.
- You paid adoption expenses in 2023, those expenses were not fully reimbursed by your employer or otherwise, and the adoption was not final by the end of 2023.
- The total adoption expenses you paid in 2024 were not fully reimbursed by your employer or otherwise, and the adoption became final in 2024 or earlier.
- You adopted a child with special needs and the adoption became final in 2024.

Form **8839** (2024)

7-8 Other Credits

7.8 Learning Objective
Recognize other basic individual credits.

In addition to the credits covered previously in this chapter, there are many other credits that are directed at individuals, businesses in general, and specific types of businesses, especially those involved in renewable energy or energy efficiency products. This list of credits is immense, and many are temporary. Table 7.8 provides a partial list of individual credits that are available and the target taxpayer-type who might benefit from such credits.

Table 7.8 Selected Individual Tax Credits

Credit	Target	Comments
Elderly or disabled credit	Taxpayers 65 or over or disabled	Up to $1,125 depending on filing status. Phases out starting at AGI $7,500 ($10,000 MFJ)
Mortgage interest credit	Individuals with mortgage credit certificate	Credit for certain interest paid up to $2,000 each year
First-time homebuyer credit	Homebuyers before 2011	Credit is in repayment phase

For businesses, there are many unique credits that fit within what is known as the general business credit. Each of the credits are calculated separately but are aggregated into the general business credit on Form 3800 and generally subject to a limitation of 25 percent of the tax liability in excess of $25,000 (the actual limitation is much more nuanced and outside the scope of this textbook). Credits in the general business credit are not refundable. The number of separate credits within the general business credit is immense and constantly subject to change. Part III of Form 3800 lists most of the available credits in any given tax year. Table 7.9 lists a small selection of the over three dozen credits available inside the general business credit in 2024.

Table 7.9 Selected Business Credits

Credit	Comments
Research and experimentation credit	Credit is a given percentage of incremental additional research and experimentation costs
Work opportunity credit	Credit is a percentage of certain wages paid to workers from targeted hard-to-employ groups
Rehabilitation credit	Credit is a percentage of the costs paid to rehabilitate certain historical buildings
Low-income housing credit	Credit for a certain amount of the cost of low-income housing constructed, rehabilitated or acquired
New markets credit	Credit for a certain percentage of business investment in low-income communities

7-8a Energy Credits

Over the past decade, the tax law has included a number of personal tax credits associated with energy-efficient products. These credits have been slowly expiring. By design, many tax credits are temporary additions to the tax law and are designed to create short-term or limited changes in taxpayer behavior as referenced in Chapter 1. The status of many of these credits is presented in Table 7.10.

Table 7.10 Individual Energy Credits

Credit	Code Section	Status
Clean vehicle credit	30D	Extended through 12/31/2032
Energy efficient home improvement credit (formerly nonbusiness energy property credit)	25C	Extended through 12/31/2031
Residential clean energy credit (formerly residential energy efficient property (REEP) credit)	25D	Extended through 12/31/2034
Qualified fuel cell motor vehicle credit	30B	Expired at end of 2021

Because credits are often retroactively extended, be sure and check **www.irs.gov** for any changes.

Three of the more important credits for individual taxpayers are discussed here.

7-8b Clean Vehicle Credit

The clean vehicle credit has three different applications:

1. The personal new clean vehicle credit
2. The personal used clean vehicle credit
3. The commercial clean vehicle credit

The rules vary slightly for all three, but each is claimed using Form 8936 and Schedule A to Form 8936, as needed.

New Clean Vehicle Credit

The new clean vehicle credit has two parts: (1) a $3,750 credit if the critical minerals in the battery are domestically sourced and (2) a $3,750 credit if the battery components are domestically produced. For an individual taxpayer to claim the clean vehicle credit for new vehicles: (1) the vehicle must meet various requirements, and (2) the taxpayer must meet certain requirements. The vehicle requirements include a manufacturer's suggested retail price (MSRP) limit (may not exceed $55,000 or $80,000 if a van, SUV, or pickup truck), the vehicle must have undergone final assembly in the United States, the vehicle's weight may not exceed 14,000 pounds, the manufacturer must agree to report certain information, and the battery must meet critical mineral and component measures. The typical individual consumer may struggle to identify vehicles that qualify without assistance from either the auto dealer or without using the U.S. Department of Energy webpage devoted to electric vehicles (EVs): **https://fueleconomy.gov/feg/tax2023.shtml**. Dealers are required to provide a "time of sale report" (includes information such as dealer name, address, VIN, make, model, placed in service date and maximum credit) to any individual that purchases a credit eligible vehicle.

The clean vehicle credit is not available for taxpayers with AGI above $300,000 for married filing jointly, $225,000 for head of household, and $150,000 for all others. Prior year AGI can be used for this requirement if it is lower. There is no phase-out of the credit if current or prior year AGI exceeds the threshold, the credit is reduced to zero.

Example Belle, a single taxpayer, is considering purchasing a new EV in 2024. She compares the Tesla Model 3, the Honda Prologue, and the Hyundai IONIQ 5. All three vehicles are electric. Using the U.S. Department of Energy website, she determines that only the Tesla and Honda meet the requirements of the clean vehicle credit (the Hyundai does not meet the U.S. assembly requirement, although Hyundai announced in 2024 that manufacturing of the 2025 model year IONIQ Model 5 will begin in the United States in late 2024). The Tesla MSRP is below $55,000 and the Honda's MSRP is below $80,000 (the Prologue qualifies as an SUV). If Belle's 2024 or 2023 AGI is less than $150,000 and she purchases the Tesla or Honda, she can claim a $7,500 nonrefundable credit on her 2024 income tax return. ♦

Both the new clean vehicle credit and the used vehicle credit can be transferred to a qualified dealer. The operation of the transferred credit requires the dealer to reduce the price of the vehicle by the credit amount thus "advancing" the credit to the time of purchase (rather than waiting until the taxpayer files the tax return and claims the credit). The taxpayer is required to file Form 8936 and Schedule A of Form 8936 whether claiming the credit for themselves or transferring to the dealer.

Tax Break

If a taxpayer believes that the nonrefundable clean vehicle credit may be limited by the taxpayer's tax liability, then the credit should be transferred to the dealer. In this way, the full benefit of the credit will be gained in the purchase price reduction.

Used Clean Vehicle Credit

A previously owned (used) clean vehicle credit of 30 percent of the price up to a credit limit of $4,000 is also available. The sales price of the vehicle cannot exceed $25,000 and the vehicle must be at least two years old. The vehicle must be purchased from a qualified dealer. The taxpayer may not claim the used clean vehicle credit if AGI exceeds $150,000 for married filing jointly, $112,500 for head of household, and $75,000 for all others. The used clean vehicle credit may not be claimed more than once every three years.

Example Verner is purchasing a qualifying used electric vehicle in 2024 for $18,000. Verner's income is below the threshold to qualify, and he has not claimed a clean vehicle credit in the last three years. His used clean vehicle credit is $4,000 ($18,000 × 30%, limited to $4,000). Rather than pay $18,000 for the vehicle and then claim the credit on his income taxes, Verner agrees to transfer the credit to the dealer. Verner pays the dealer only $14,000 ($18,000 less the $4,000 clean vehicle credit) at the time of purchase. At year-end Verner prepares Form 8936 but does not claim a credit when filing his 2024 tax return. ♦

Commercial Clean Vehicle Credit

A commercial clean vehicle credit is also available to businesses in 2024. The credit amount varies depending on the gross vehicle weight rating (GVWR):

- Maximum credit of $7,500 for GVWR less than 14,000 pounds (typically cars, vans, trucks, and similar passenger-sized vehicles)
- Maximum credit of $40,000 for GVWR of 14,000 pounds or more (typically larger vehicles like school buses and semi-trucks)

The tentative credit amount is an applicable percentage of the basis (cost of the investment) of the vehicle depending on the engine type:

- 30 percent of basis for a vehicle that is not powered by a gasoline or diesel internal combustion engine, such as an electric vehicle (EV) or fuel cell electric vehicle (FCEV).
- 15 percent of basis for a vehicle that is powered (even partially) by a gasoline or diesel internal combustion engine, such as a plug-in-hybrid electric vehicles (PHEV).

The final amount to consider is the incremental cost of the vehicle (the excess of its purchase price over that of a comparable vehicle powered only by gas or diesel internal combustion). In 2024, to assist taxpayers, the IRS published the Department of Energy's incremental cost for the appropriate class of vehicle:

- $7,000 for compact plug-in hybrid electric vehicles (PHEVs) (includes minicompact and subcompact cars) with a GVWR of less than 14,000 pounds
- $7,500 for all street electric vehicles, other than compact car PHEVs, with a GVWR of less than 14,000 pounds
- $40,000 for all other vehicles with a GVWR of 14,000 pounds or more

The final credit amount is the lesser of the maximum credit, the tentative credit, and the incremental cost.

Example Hubert's Landscaping Company (HLC) purchases two heavy-duty EV trucks for use in the business. Both trucks have a GWVR of 7,500 lbs. and cost $70,000 each. The maximum credit is $7,500, the tentative credit is $21,000 ($70,000 × 30%), and the incremental cost is $7,500. HLC will claim a credit for $7,500 (the least of the three possible credit amounts) for each truck, subject to the overall business credit limitation.

Businesses and tax-exempt organizations qualify for the credit. There is no limit on the number of credits a business can claim but the credits are nonrefundable. The vehicle must be made by a qualified manufacturer (see qualified manufacturers at **https://www.irs.gov/credits-deductions/manufacturers-for-qualified-commercial-clean-vehicle-credit**).

7-8c Energy Efficient Home Improvement Credit

The energy efficient home improvement credit is 30 percent of:

1. Costs paid or incurred for installation of qualified energy efficiency improvements;
2. Qualified residential energy property expenditures, and
3. Amounts paid for home energy audits.

The improvements must have been made to the taxpayer's primary home (located in the United States) and the different expenditure types have different annual limits both individually and in the aggregate. The aggregate annual credit cannot exceed:

- $2,000 in the aggregate for electric or natural gas heat pump water heaters, electric or natural gas heat pumps, and biomass stoves and boilers
- $1,200 in the aggregate for all other qualified expenses

Thus, the total credit claimed by any taxpayer in a single year cannot exceed $3,200. In addition, individual credit limits are:

- $600 for exterior windows and skylights
- $1,200 for qualifying insulation or air sealing materials
- $500 for all exterior doors and $250 for any particular exterior door
- $600 for any item of qualifying property other than electric or natural gas heat pump water heaters, electric or natural gas heat pumps, and biomass stoves and boilers that are subject to the $2,000 aggregate limit
- $150 for home energy audits

As with all nonrefundable credits, the total credit is limited to the taxpayer's pre-credit tax liability adjusted by certain other credits that have priority. The limit for the energy efficient home improvement credit is tax liability reduced by any foreign tax credit, child and dependent care expense credit, elderly and disabled credit, education credits, and the Saver's credit.

Example Kobie is a married filing jointly taxpayer in 2024. His tax liability is $4,399 before any tax credits. Kobie intends to claim a $500 other dependent credit in 2024. Kobie undertakes a significant home renovation project and incurs the following expenses:

- $600 for a home energy audit to identify energy saving opportunities
- Two new exterior doors at a cost of $1,000 each
- New windows and skylights at a cost of $4,200
- A new energy efficient heat pump at a cost of $8,000

Kobie will claim a total energy efficient home improvement credit of $3,200 calculated as follows:

- $500 for the two exterior doors calculated as 30 percent of $1,000 per door ($300) but limited to no more than $250 per door.
- $600 for windows and skylights calculated as 30 percent of $4,200 ($1,260) but limited to no more than $600 for all windows and skylights.
- $150 for the home energy audit calculated as 30 percent of $600 ($180) but limited to no more than $150.

The above three credits total $1,250; however these credits (plus any credits for insulation, electric panels, air conditioners, or gas, oil, or propane water heaters) cannot exceed $1,200 for the year. The credit for the electric heat pump is $2,000 ($8,000 × 30% but limited to $2,000). The total credit is $1,200 plus $2,000 or $3,200. ♦

The energy efficient home improvement credit and the residential clean energy credit (covered below) are both reported on Form 5695.

7-8d Residential Clean Energy Credit

Taxpayers may claim a credit of 30 percent of the amount paid for qualified solar electric property (property which uses solar power to generate electricity in a home), qualified battery storage technology, qualified solar water-heating property, qualified fuel cell property, qualified small wind energy property, and qualified geothermal heat pump property through 2032.

The residential clean energy credit may be claimed for both principal residences and vacation homes. No credit is allowed for installations used to heat swimming pools or hot tubs.

Example Continuing with the previous example, Kobie also installs solar electric panels on his home's roof at a cost of $32,000 and solar pool heater panels at a cost of $8,000. Kobie may claim a nonrefundable residential clean energy credit of $9,600 ($32,000 × 30%) subject to his tax liability. The solar pool heater is not a qualifying expense. ♦

The residential clean energy credit is nonrefundable and thus is limited to the taxpayer's tax liability reduced by any foreign tax credit, child and dependent care expense credit, elderly and disabled credit, education credits, the Saver's credit, the energy efficient home improvement credit, the clean vehicle credit, the child tax credit, and the adoption credit.

Self-Study Problem 7.8
Refer to Appendix E for Solutions to Self-Study Problems

a. Kyra O'Flaherty is a single taxpayer in 2024 with AGI of $67,000 (2023 AGI was $65,000). On October 1, 2024, Kyra purchased a new 2024 Tesla Model 3 (VIN 5YJ3E1EB0RF734523) for $41,000, not including California sales tax of $2,972.50. The dealer's time-of-sale report confirmed that the vehicle is eligible for both parts of the clean vehicle credit in 2024. The vehicle is for personal use and Kyra did not transfer the credit to the dealer. Kyra's pre-credit tax liability is $7,003 and she is not claiming any other credits in 2024. Complete Parts I, II, and III of Schedule A to Form 8936 and Parts I and III of Form 8936 on Pages 7-53 to 7-56 to determine the amount of Kyra's clean vehicle credit.

b. Marquise and Abby Dollkeeper are married and file jointly in 2024. They have two children ages 5 and 8 for which they intend to claim the child tax credit. In 2024, they had a home energy audit performed by their local utility company at a cost of $800. As a result of the audit, they completed an extensive renovation to their main home (located at 300 Bayone Drive, Santa Cruz, CA 95060) that included the following:

- New solar electric panels at a cost of $38,000
- All new energy efficient windows for $7,800
- New insulation that meets the standards to lower heat loss for $3,000
- A fuel-efficient natural gas water heater at a cost of $1,200
- A new front door at a cost of $2,800
- A new electric heat pump at a cost of $5,300
- A new electric subpanel at a cost of $1,800

The Dollkeepers had AGI of $180,000 in 2024 and a tax liability before any credits of $28,344. Use Form 5695 on Pages 7-57 to 7-59 to determine the Dollkeepers' 2024 residential clean energy credit and energy efficient home improvement credit.

Self-Study Problem 7.8, Part a

Form 8936
Department of the Treasury
Internal Revenue Service

Clean Vehicle Credits

Attach to your tax return.
Go to www.irs.gov/Form8936 for instructions and the latest information.

OMB No. 1545-2137
2024
Attachment Sequence No. 69

Name(s) shown on return | Identifying number

Notes:
- Complete a separate Schedule A (Form 8936) for each clean vehicle placed in service during the tax year.
- Individuals who transferred the credit to the dealer at the time of sale must file this form and Schedule A (Form 8936).

Part I — Modified Adjusted Gross Income (MAGI) Amount

1a	Enter the amount from line 11 of your 2024 Form 1040, 1040-SR, or 1040-NR. Estates and trusts, Form 1041, see instructions	1a
b	Enter any income from Puerto Rico you excluded	1b
c	Enter any amount from Form 2555, line 45	1c
d	Enter any amount from Form 2555, line 50	1d
e	Enter any amount from Form 4563, line 15	1e
2	Add lines 1a through 1e	2
3a	Enter the amount from line 11 of your 2023 Form 1040, 1040-SR, or 1040-NR. Estates and trusts, Form 1041, see instructions	3a
b	Enter any income from Puerto Rico you excluded	3b
c	Enter any amount from Form 2555, line 45	3c
d	Enter any amount from Form 2555, line 50	3d
e	Enter any amount from Form 4563, line 15	3e
4	Add lines 3a through 3e	4
5	Enter your 2023 filing status (S, MFS, etc., see chart below)	5

Individuals, estates, or trusts exceeding the following MAGI limits for both 2023 and 2024 can't claim the applicable credit.

Filing Status	Part II/III Limits	Part IV Limits
Single (S)	$150,000	$75,000
Married filing separately (MFS)	$150,000	$75,000
Head of household (HOH)	$225,000	$112,500
Married filing jointly (MFJ)	$300,000	$150,000
Qualifying surviving spouse (QSS)	$300,000	$150,000
Estates and trusts	$150,000	N/A

Part II — Credit for Business/Investment Use Part of New Clean Vehicles

6	Enter the total credit amount figured in Part II of Schedule(s) A (Form 8936)	6
7	New clean vehicle credit from partnerships and S corporations (see instructions)	7
8	**Business/investment use part of credit.** Add lines 6 and 7. Partnerships and S corporations, stop here and report this amount on Schedule K. All others, report this amount on Form 3800, Part III, line 1y	8

Part III — Credit for Personal Use Part of New Clean Vehicles

9	Enter the total credit amount figured in Part III of Schedule(s) A (Form 8936)	9
10	Enter the amount from Form 1040, 1040-SR, or 1040-NR, line 18	10
11	Personal credits from Form 1040, 1040-SR, or 1040-NR (see instructions)	11
12	Subtract line 11 from line 10. If zero or less, enter -0- and stop here. You can't claim the personal use part of the credit	12
13	**Personal use part of credit.** Enter the **smaller** of line 9 or line 12 here and on Schedule 3 (Form 1040), line 6f. If line 12 is smaller than line 9, see instructions	13

Part IV — Credit for Previously Owned Clean Vehicles

14	Enter the total credit amount figured in Part IV of Schedule(s) A (Form 8936)	14
15	Enter the amount from Form 1040, 1040-SR, or 1040-NR, line 18	15
16	Personal credits from Form 1040, 1040-SR, or 1040-NR (see instructions)	16
17	Subtract line 16 from line 15. If zero or less, enter -0- and stop here. You can't claim the Part IV credit	17
18	Enter the **smaller** of line 14 or line 17 here and on Schedule 3 (Form 1040), line 6m. If line 17 is smaller than line 14, see instructions	18

Part V — Credit for Qualified Commercial Clean Vehicles

19	Enter the total credit amount figured in Part V of Schedule(s) A (Form 8936)	19
20	Qualified commercial clean vehicle credit from partnerships and S corporations (see instructions)	20
21	Add lines 19 and 20. Partnerships and S corporations, stop here and report this amount on Schedule K. All others, report this amount on Form 3800, Part III, line 1aa	21

For Paperwork Reduction Act Notice, see separate instructions. Cat. No. 37751E Form **8936** (2024)

Self-Study Problem 7.8, Part a, cont.

SCHEDULE A (Form 8936)
Department of the Treasury
Internal Revenue Service

Clean Vehicle Credit Amount

Attach to your tax return.
Go to www.irs.gov/Form8936 for instructions and the latest information.

OMB No. 1545-2137
2024
Attachment Sequence No. **69A**

Name(s) shown on return _____ Identifying number _____

Notes:
- Complete a separate Schedule A (Form 8936) for each clean vehicle placed in service during the tax year.
- Individuals who transferred the credit to the dealer at the time of sale must file this schedule and Form 8936.

Part I Vehicle Details

1a Year _____
 b Make _____
 c Model _____

2 Vehicle identification number (VIN) (see instructions) . □□□□□□□□□□□□□□□□□

3 Enter date vehicle was placed in service (MM/DD/YYYY) . . . . _____

4a Did you transfer the credit to the dealer at the time of sale?
 ☐ **Yes.** Enter the transferred amount shown on the seller's report _____
 ☐ **No.** Go to line 5.

 b If line 4a is "Yes," complete line 8 or line 13, as applicable, and check here if directed to do so by line 8a, 8d, 13a, or 13c . ☐

5 Does the VIN entered on line 2 belong to a **new clean vehicle** placed in service during the tax year? See instructions for definitions.
 ☐ **Yes.** Go to Part II.
 ☐ **No.** Go to line 6.

6 Does the VIN entered on line 2 belong to a **previously owned clean vehicle** acquired after 2022 and placed in service during the tax year? See instructions for definitions.
 ☐ **Yes.** Go to Part IV.
 ☐ **No.** Go to line 7.

7 Does the VIN entered on line 2 belong to a **qualified commercial clean vehicle** acquired after 2022 and placed in service during the tax year? See instructions for definitions.
 ☐ **Yes.** Go to Part V.
 ☐ **No. Stop here.** You can't use this schedule to figure a credit amount for a vehicle not described on line 5, 6, or 7.

Part II Credit Amount for Business/Investment Use Part of New Clean Vehicle

8a Did you resell the vehicle within 30 days of the placed-in-service date shown on line 3?
 ☐ **Yes. Stop here.** You can't claim a clean vehicle credit for this vehicle. If line 4a is "Yes," check the box on line 4b and report the amount from line 4a on Schedule 2 (Form 1040), line 1b.
 ☐ **No.** Go to line 8b.

8b Are you filing this form with an individual income tax return?
 ☐ **Yes.** Go to line 8c.
 ☐ **No.** Skip lines 8c and 8d and go to line 8e.

8c Complete Form 8936, lines 1 and 2. Is line 2 more than the "Part II/III limits" amount shown on the chart below line 5, Form 8936 for your 2024 filing status?
 ☐ **Yes.** Go to line 8d.
 ☐ **No.** If you transferred the credit amount to the dealer at the time of sale, stop here and see instructions. Otherwise, skip line 8d and go to line 8e.

8d Complete Form 8936, lines 3, 4, and 5. Is line 4 more than the "Part II/III limits" amount shown on the chart below line 5, Form 8936 for your 2023 filing status? See instructions if your 2024 return is a joint return.
 ☐ **Yes. Stop here.** You can't claim a clean vehicle credit for this vehicle. If line 4a is "Yes," check the box on line 4b and report the amount from line 4a on Schedule 2 (Form 1040), line 1b.
 ☐ **No.** If you transferred the credit amount to the dealer at the time of sale, stop here and see instructions. Otherwise, go to line 8e.

For Paperwork Reduction Act Notice, see the Form 8936 instructions. Cat. No. 93602W Schedule A (Form 8936) 2024

Schedule A (Form 8936) 2024 Page **2**

Part II — Credit Amount for Business/Investment Use Part of New Clean Vehicle *(continued)*

8e Did you acquire the vehicle for use or to lease to others, and not for resale? Answer "No" if you are leasing the vehicle from another person.
- ☐ **Yes.**
- ☐ **No. Stop here.** You can't claim a credit amount for a vehicle you didn't acquire for use or to lease to others, or acquired for resale.

9 Tentative credit amount (see instructions)	**9**	
10 Business/investment use percentage (see instructions)	**10**	%
11 Multiply line 9 by line 10. Include this credit amount on line 6 in Part II of Form 8936. If you entered 100% on line 10, stop here. Otherwise, go to Part III below	**11**	

Part III — Credit Amount for Personal Use Part of New Clean Vehicle

12 Subtract line 11 from line 9 in Part II. Stop here and include this credit amount on line 9 in Part III of Form 8936	**12**	

Part IV — Credit Amount for Previously Owned Clean Vehicle

13a Did you resell the vehicle within 30 days of the placed-in-service date shown on line 3?
- ☐ **Yes. Stop here.** You can't claim a clean vehicle credit for this vehicle. If line 4a is "Yes," check the box on line 4b and report the amount from line 4a on Schedule 2 (Form 1040), line 1c.
- ☐ **No.** Go to line 13b.

b Complete Form 8936, lines 1 and 2. Is line 2 more than the "Part IV limits" amount shown on the chart below line 5, Form 8936 for your 2024 filing status?
- ☐ **Yes.** Go to line 13c.
- ☐ **No.** If you transferred the credit amount to the dealer at the time of sale, stop here and see instructions. Otherwise, skip line 13c and go to line 13d.

c Complete Form 8936, lines 3, 4, and 5. Is line 4 more than the "Part IV limits" amount shown on the chart below line 5, Form 8936 for your 2023 filing status? See instructions if your 2024 return is a joint return.
- ☐ **Yes. Stop here.** You can't claim a clean vehicle credit for this vehicle. If line 4a is "Yes," check the box on line 4b and report the amount from line 4a on Schedule 2 (Form 1040), line 1c.
- ☐ **No.** If you transferred the credit amount to the dealer at the time of sale, stop here and see instructions. Otherwise, go to line 13d.

d Have you claimed a previously owned clean vehicle credit for another vehicle purchased in the 3-year period ending on the date you purchased the vehicle identified in Part I? See instructions if you are filing a joint return.
- ☐ **Yes. Stop here.** You can't claim a credit for this vehicle if you have already claimed the previously owned vehicle credit for another vehicle purchased during this 3-year period.
- ☐ **No.** Go to line 13e.

e Is the sales price of the vehicle more than $25,000?
- ☐ **Yes. Stop here.** The vehicle doesn't qualify for the Part IV credit.
- ☐ **No.**

f Did you acquire the vehicle for use and not for resale? Answer "No" if you are leasing the vehicle from another person.
- ☐ **Yes.**
- ☐ **No. Stop here.** You can't claim a credit amount for a vehicle you didn't acquire for use or acquired for resale.

g Can you be claimed as a dependent on another person's tax return, such as your parent's return?
- ☐ **Yes. Stop here.** You can't claim a credit amount if you can be claimed as a dependent.
- ☐ **No.**

14 Enter the sales price of the vehicle	**14**	
15 Multiply line 14 by 30% (0.30)	**15**	
16 Maximum vehicle credit amount	**16**	$4,000
17 Enter the smaller of line 15 or line 16. Stop here and include this credit amount on line 14 in Part IV of Form 8936	**17**	

Schedule A (Form 8936) 2024 Page **3**

Part V — Credit Amount for Qualified Commercial Clean Vehicle

18a If making an elective payment election, enter the IRS-issued registration number for the vehicle _____

  b Is the vehicle of a character subject to the allowance for depreciation? Answer "Yes" if the exception for certain tax-exempt entities discussed in the instructions applies.
- ☐ **Yes.**
- ☐ **No. Stop here.** The vehicle is not a qualified commercial clean vehicle unless the exception applies.

  c Did you acquire the vehicle for use or to lease to others, and not for resale? Answer "No" if you are leasing the vehicle from another person.
- ☐ **Yes.**
- ☐ **No. Stop here.** You can't claim a credit amount for a vehicle you didn't acquire for use or to lease to others, or acquired for resale.

  d Is the vehicle also powered in part by gas or diesel? See instructions.
- ☐ **Yes.**
- ☐ **No.**

  e Enter the vehicle's gross vehicle weight rating (GVWR) . . . . _____

19 Enter the cost or other basis of the vehicle. See instructions . . . . . . | **19** |

20 Section 179 expense deduction (see instructions) . . . . | **20** |

21 Subtract line 20 from line 19 . . . . | **21** |

22 Multiply line 21 by 15% (0.15) (30% (0.30) if the answer on line 18d above is "No") . . | **22** |

23 Enter the incremental cost of the vehicle. See instructions . . . . | **23** |

24 Enter the smaller of line 22 or line 23 . . . . | **24** |

25 **Maximum credit.** Enter $7,500 ($40,000 if the vehicle's gross vehicle weight rating (see line 18e) is 14,000 pounds or more) . . . . | **25** |

26 Enter the smaller of line 24 or line 25. Include this credit amount on line 19 in Part V of Form 8936 . . . . | **26** |

Schedule A (Form 8936) 2024

Self-Study Problem 7.8, Part b

Form 5695
Department of the Treasury
Internal Revenue Service

Residential Energy Credits
Attach to Form 1040, 1040-SR, or 1040-NR.
Go to *www.irs.gov/Form5695* for instructions and the latest information.

OMB No. 1545-0074
2024
Attachment Sequence No. **75**

Name(s) shown on return

Your social security number

Part I — Residential Clean Energy Credit (See instructions before completing this part.)

Note: Skip lines 1 through 11 if you only have a **credit carryforward from 2023**.

Enter the complete address of the home where you installed the property and/or technology associated with lines 1 through 4 and 5b. For more than one home, see instructions.

Number and street	Unit no.	City or town	State	ZIP code

1. Qualified solar electric property costs **1**
2. Qualified solar water heating property costs **2**
3. Qualified small wind energy property costs **3**
4. Qualified geothermal heat pump property costs **4**
5a. Qualified battery storage technology. Does the qualified battery storage technology have a capacity of at least 3 kilowatt hours? (See instructions.) If you checked the "No" box, you cannot claim a credit for qualified battery storage technology .... **5a** ☐ Yes ☐ No
  b. If you checked the "Yes" box, enter the qualified battery technology costs **5b**
6a. Add lines 1 through 5b **6a**
  b. Multiply line 6a by 30% (0.30) **6b**
7a. Qualified fuel cell property. Was qualified fuel cell property installed on, or in connection with, your **main home** located in the United States? (See instructions.) .... **7a** ☐ Yes ☐ No
     If you checked the "No" box, you cannot claim a credit for qualified fuel cell property. Skip lines 7b through 11.
  b. Enter the complete address of the main home where you installed the fuel cell property.

Number and street	Unit no.	City or town	State	ZIP code

  c. If the special rule for joint occupants applies, check here ☐ and attach a statement. (See instructions.)

8. Qualified fuel cell property costs **8**
9. Multiply line 8 by 30% (0.30) **9**
10. Kilowatt capacity of property on line 8 above .... _____ x $1,000 **10**
11. Enter the smaller of line 9 or line 10 .... **11**
12. Credit carryforward from 2023. Enter the amount, if any, from your 2023 Form 5695, line 16 .... **12**
13. Add lines 6b, 11, and 12 .... **13**
14. Limitation based on tax liability. Enter the amount from the Residential Clean Energy Credit Limit Worksheet. (See instructions.) **14**
15. **Residential clean energy credit.** Enter the smaller of line 13 or line 14. Also include this amount on Schedule 3 (Form 1040), line 5a **15**
16. Credit carryforward to 2025. If line 15 is less than line 13, subtract line 15 from line 13 .... **16**

For Paperwork Reduction Act Notice, see your tax return instructions. Cat. No. 13540P Form **5695** (2024)

Form 5695 (2024) Page **2**

Part II Energy Efficient Home Improvement Credit

Section A—Qualified Energy Efficiency Improvements

17a Are the qualified energy efficiency improvements installed in or on your main home located in the United States? (See instructions.) . . . . **17a** ☐ Yes ☐ No

b Are you the original user of the qualified energy efficiency improvements? . . . . **17b** ☐ Yes ☐ No

c Are the components reasonably expected to remain in use for at least 5 years? . . . . **17c** ☐ Yes ☐ No

If you checked the "No" box for line 17a, 17b, or 17c, you cannot claim the energy efficient home improvement credit. Do not complete Part II, Section A.

d Enter the complete address of the main home where you made the qualifying improvements.
Caution: You can only have one main home at a time. (See instructions.)

Number and street	Unit no.	City or town	State	ZIP code

e Were any of these improvements related to the construction of this main home? . . . . . **17e** ☐ Yes ☐ No

If you checked the "Yes" box, you can only claim the energy efficient home improvement credit for qualifying improvements that were not related to the construction of the home. Do not include expenses related to the construction of your main home, even if the improvements were made after you moved into the home.

18 Insulation or air sealing material or system.

a Enter the cost of insulation material or system (include air sealing material or system) specifically and primarily designed to reduce heat loss or gain of your home that meets the criteria established by the IECC. (See instructions.) . . . **18a**

b Multiply line 18a by 30% (0.30). Enter the results. Do **not** enter more than $1,200 . . **18b**

19 Exterior doors that meet the applicable Energy Star requirements.

a Enter the cost of the most expensive door you bought **19a**

b Multiply line 19a by 30% (0.30). Do **not** enter more than $250 **19b**

c Enter the cost of all other qualifying exterior doors **19c**

d Multiply line 19c by 30% (0.30) **19d**

e Add lines 19b and 19d. Do **not** enter more than $500 . . . . **19e**

20 Windows and skylights that meet the Energy Star certification requirements.

a Enter the cost of exterior windows and skylights that meet the Energy Star certification requirements. (See instructions.) **20a**

b Multiply line 20a by 30% (0.30). Enter the results. Do **not** enter more than $600 . . . . . . **20b**

Section B—Residential Energy Property Expenditures

21a Did you incur costs for qualified energy property installed on or in connection with a home located in the United States? . . . . **21a** ☐ Yes ☐ No

b Was the qualified energy property originally placed into service by you? . . . . **21b** ☐ Yes ☐ No

If you checked the "No" box for line 21a or 21b, you cannot claim the credit for your residential energy property costs. Skip lines 22 through 25 and line 29. Go to line 26.

c Enter the complete address of each home where you installed qualified energy property.

Number and street	Unit no.	City or town	State	ZIP code

22 Residential energy property costs (include labor costs for onsite preparation, assembly, and original installation). (See instructions.)

a Enter the cost of central air conditioners **22a**

b Multiply line 22a by 30% (0.30). Enter the results. Do **not** enter more than $600 . . . . . **22b**

23a Enter the cost of natural gas, propane, or oil water heaters **23a**

b Multiply line 23a by 30% (0.30). Enter the results. Do **not** enter more than $600 . . . . . **23b**

24a Enter the cost of natural gas, propane, or oil furnace or hot water boilers . . **24a**

b Multiply line 24a by 30% (0.30). Enter the results. Do **not** enter more than $600 . . . . . **24b**

Form **5695** (2024)

Form 5695 (2024) Page **3**

Section B—Residential Energy Property Expenditures (continued)

25a	Enter the cost of improvements or replacement of panelboards, subpanelboards, branch circuits, or feeders	25a	
b	Multiply line 25a by 30% (0.30). Enter the results. Do **not** enter more than $600 .		25b
26	Home energy audits.		
a	Did you incur costs for a home energy audit that included an inspection of your main home located in the United States and a written report prepared by a certified home energy auditor? (See instructions.)	26a	☐ Yes ☐ No
	If you checked the "No" box, you cannot claim the home energy audit credit. Stop. Go to line 27.		
b	Enter the cost of the home energy audits	26b	
c	Multiply line 26b by 30% (0.30). Enter the results. Do **not** enter more than $150 .		26c
27	Add lines 18b, 19e, 20b, 22b, 23b, 24b, 25b, and 26c	27	
28	Enter the smaller of line 27 or $1,200 .		28
29	Heat pumps and heat pump water heaters; biomass stoves and biomass boilers.		
a	Enter the cost of electric or natural gas heat pumps	29a	
b	Enter the cost of electric or natural gas heat pump water heaters	29b	
c	Enter the cost of biomass stoves and biomass boilers	29c	
d	Add lines 29a, 29b, and 29c .	29d	
e	Multiply line 29d by 30% (0.30). Enter the results. Do **not** enter more than $2,000 .		29e
30	Add lines 28 and 29e		30
31	Limitation based on tax liability. Enter the amount from the Energy Efficient Home Improvement Credit Limit Worksheet. (See instructions.)		31
32	**Energy efficient home improvement credit.** Enter the smaller of line 30 or line 31. Also include this amount on Schedule 3 (Form 1040), line 5b		32
a	If the special rule for joint occupants applies, check here ☐ and attach a statement. (See instructions.)		

Form **5695** (2024)

Learning Objective 7.9

Calculate the low-income Retirement Plan Contribution Credit.

7-9 Low-Income Retirement Plan Contribution Credit

Certain low-income taxpayers may claim a nonrefundable "Low-Income Retirement Plan Contribution Credit," also called the "Saver's Credit," to encourage them to participate in tax-saving retirement plans, including IRAs. The credit rate is 50 percent, 20 percent, or 10 percent depending on the taxpayer's filing status and adjusted gross income. The credit is a direct deduction from income taxes otherwise payable, and the cash saved may be used to make part of the contribution to the plan. Taxpayers receive up to a 50-percent credit for contribution amounts up to $2,000 ($4,000 married filing jointly) or a maximum credit of $1,000 ($2,000 for married filing jointly). The credit phases out for adjusted gross income over certain income limits, as presented in Table 7.11.

Table 7.11 2024 Applicable Percentage Thresholds for Saver's Credit by Filing Status

Filing Status/Adjusted Gross Income for 2024—Saver's Credit				
If AGI is		Filing Status		
		Up to $4,000	Up to $2,000	
Over	But not over	Married Filing Jointly	Head of Household	All Others
$ 0	$23,000	50%	50%	50%
23,000	25,000	50	50	20
25,000	34,500	50	50	10
34,500	37,500	50	20	10
37,500	38,250	50	10	10
38,250	46,000	50	10	0
46,000	50,000	20	10	0
50,000	57,375	10	10	0
57,375	76,500	10	0	0
76,500	—	0	0	0

Example In 2024, Teddy and Sheela file a joint tax return with AGI of $32,000. Teddy contributes $1,500 to a Section 401k plan at work. Teddy and Sheela are entitled to a $750 (50% × $1,500) Retirement Plan Contribution Credit. The credit is in addition to any deduction or exclusion allowed for the contribution. ♦

The Saver's Credit is claimed on Form 8880. Because the Saver's Credit is nonrefundable, the amount of the credit is limited to the income tax liability after reducing by any foreign tax credit, child and dependent care expense credit, education credits, or credit for the elderly and disabled.

Example In 2024, Whitney and Melissa file a joint tax return that reflects AGI of $41,000, income tax liability before any credits of $1,183, and a lifetime learning credit of $240. If Whitney and Melissa contribute $2,100 to an IRA, their Saver's Credit is $943 calculated as the credit amount of $1,050 ($2,100 × 50%), limited to tax liability before the credit of $943 ($1,183 − $240). ♦

Self-Study Problem 7.9 — Refer to Appendix E for Solutions to Self-Study Problems

Steve and Robin Harrington are married filing jointly taxpayers, both 61 years of age and semi-retired. Robin earns wages of $49,000 as a part-time school librarian, and Steve sharpens knives as a hobby, and their 2024 AGI is $55,000. Their tax liability before any credit is $1,183. The Harringtons are not eligible for any other tax credits. Neither Harrington is active in any other income deferral plans. Because the Harringtons have limited financial needs, they also made an IRA contribution of $14,000 ($7,000 each) trying to get ready for retirement. Use the Form 8880 on Pages 7-62 and 7-63 to determine the Harringtons' Saver's Credit.

Starting in 2026, the Saver's Credit is repealed and replaced with a Saver's Match. Under the Saver's Match, instead of receiving an income tax credit, the credit amount will be deposited directly by the IRS into the qualified retirement account of the taxpayer. The amount of the match is a maximum of 50 percent of the contribution amount, which is limited to the first $2,000. The maximum match can be $1,000 per person.

Self-Study Problem 7.9

Form 8880
Department of the Treasury
Internal Revenue Service

Credit for Qualified Retirement Savings Contributions

Attach to Form 1040, 1040-SR, or 1040-NR.
Go to www.irs.gov/Form8880 for the latest information.

OMB No. 1545-0074

2024

Attachment Sequence No. **54**

Name(s) shown on return | Your social security number

CAUTION

You **cannot** take this credit if **either** of the following applies.
- The amount on Form 1040, 1040-SR, or 1040-NR, line 11, is more than $38,250 ($57,375 if head of household; $76,500 if married filing jointly).
- The person(s) who made the qualified contribution or elective deferral **(a)** was born after January 1, 2007; **(b)** is claimed as a dependent on someone else's 2024 tax return; or **(c)** was a **student** (see instructions).

		(a) You	(b) Your spouse
1	Traditional and Roth IRA contributions, and ABLE account contributions by the designated beneficiary for 2024. **Do not** include rollover contributions		
2	Elective deferrals to a 401(k) or other qualified employer plan, voluntary employee contributions, and 501(c)(18)(D) plan contributions for 2024 (see instructions)		
3	Add lines 1 and 2		
4	Certain distributions received **after** 2021 and **before** the due date (including extensions) of your 2024 tax return (see instructions). If married filing jointly, include **both** spouses' amounts in **both** columns. See instructions for an exception		
5	Subtract line 4 from line 3. If zero or less, enter -0-		
6	In each column, enter the **smaller** of line 5 or $2,000		
7	Add the amounts on line 6. If zero, **stop;** you can't take this credit		
8	Enter the amount from Form 1040, 1040-SR, or 1040-NR, line 11* 8		
9	Enter the applicable decimal amount from the table below.		

If line 8 is—		And your filing status is—		
Over—	But not over—	Married filing jointly	Head of household	Single, Married filing separately, or Qualifying surviving spouse
		Enter on line 9—		
---	$23,000	0.5	0.5	0.5
$23,000	$25,000	0.5	0.5	0.2
$25,000	$34,500	0.5	0.5	0.1
$34,500	$37,500	0.5	0.2	0.1
$37,500	$38,250	0.5	0.1	0.1
$38,250	$46,000	0.5	0.1	0.0
$46,000	$50,000	0.2	0.1	0.0
$50,000	$57,375	0.1	0.1	0.0
$57,375	$76,500	0.1	0.0	0.0
$76,500	---	0.0	0.0	0.0

9 | x 0.

Note: If line 9 is zero, **stop;** you can't take this credit.

10	Multiply line 7 by line 9	
11	Limitation based on tax liability. Enter the amount from the Credit Limit Worksheet in the instructions	
12	**Credit for qualified retirement savings contributions.** Enter the **smaller** of line 10 or line 11 here and on Schedule 3 (Form 1040), line 4	

* See Pub. 590-A for the amount to enter if you claim any exclusion or deduction for foreign earned income, foreign housing, or income from Puerto Rico or for bona fide residents of American Samoa.

For Paperwork Reduction Act Notice, see your tax return instructions.   Cat. No. 33394D   Form **8880** (2024)

Section references are to the Internal Revenue Code unless otherwise noted.

Future Developments

For the latest information about developments related to Form 8880 and its instructions, such as legislation enacted after they were published, go to *www.irs.gov/Form8880*.

Reminder

Contributions by a designated beneficiary to an Achieving a Better Life Experience (ABLE) account. A retirement savings contribution credit may be claimed for the amount of contributions you, as the designated beneficiary of an ABLE account, make before January 1, 2026, to the ABLE account. See Pub. 907, Tax Highlights for Persons With Disabilities, for more information.

General Instructions

Purpose of Form

Use Form 8880 to figure the amount, if any, of your retirement savings contributions credit (also known as the saver's credit). The maximum amount of the credit is $1,000 ($2,000 if married filing jointly).

This credit can be claimed in addition to any IRA deduction claimed on Schedule 1 (Form 1040), line 20.

Who Can Take This Credit

You may be able to take this credit if you, or your spouse if filing jointly, made (a) contributions (other than rollover contributions) to a traditional or Roth IRA; (b) elective deferrals to a 401(k), 403(b), governmental 457(b), SEP, SIMPLE, or to the federal Thrift Savings Plan (TSP); (c) voluntary employee contributions to a qualified retirement plan, as defined in section 4974(c) (including the federal TSP); (d) contributions to a 501(c)(18)(D) plan; or (e) contributions, as a designated beneficiary of an ABLE account, to the ABLE account, as defined in section 529A.

However, you can't take the credit if either of the following applies.

- The amount on Form 1040, 1040-SR, or 1040-NR, line 11, is more than $38,250 ($57,375 if head of household; $76,500 if married filing jointly).
- The person(s) who made the qualified contribution or elective deferral (a) was born after January 1, 2007; (b) is claimed as a dependent on someone else's 2024 tax return; or (c) was a student.

You'll need to refigure the amount on Form 1040 or 1040-SR, line 11, if you're filing Form 2555 or Form 4563 or you're excluding income from Puerto Rico. See Pub. 590-A at www.irs.gov/Pub590A for details.

You were a student if during any part of 5 calendar months of 2024 you:

- Were enrolled as a full-time student at a school; or
- Took a full-time, on-farm training course given by a school or a state, county, or local government agency.

A school includes technical, trade, and mechanical schools. It doesn't include on-the-job training courses, correspondence schools, or schools offering courses only through the Internet.

Specific Instructions

Column (b)

Complete column (b) only if you're filing a joint return.

Line 2

Include on line 2 any of the following amounts.

- Elective deferrals (including designated Roth contributions under section 402A, if applicable) to a 401(k), 403(b), governmental 457(b), SEP, SIMPLE, or to the federal TSP.
- Voluntary employee contributions to a qualified retirement plan, as defined in section 4974(c) (including the federal TSP).
- Contributions to a 501(c)(18)(D) plan.

These amounts may be shown in box 12 of your Form(s) W-2 for 2024.

Note: Contributions designated under section 414(h)(2) are treated as employer contributions and, as such, they aren't voluntary contributions made by the employee. They don't qualify for the credit and shouldn't be included on line 2.

Line 4

Enter the total amount of distributions you, and your spouse if filing jointly, received after 2021 and before the due date of your 2024 return (including extensions) from any of the following types of plans.

- Traditional or Roth IRAs, or ABLE accounts.
- 401(k), 403(b), governmental 457(b), 501(c)(18)(D), SEP, SIMPLE, or the federal TSP.
- Qualified retirement plans, as defined in section 4974(c).

Don't include any of the following.

- Distributions not taxable as the result of a rollover or a trustee-to-trustee transfer.
- Distributions that are taxable as the result of an in-plan rollover to your designated Roth account.
- Distributions from your eligible retirement plan (other than a Roth IRA) rolled over or converted to your Roth IRA.
- Loans from a qualified employer plan treated as a distribution.
- Distributions of excess contributions or deferrals (and income allocable to such contributions or deferrals).
- Distributions of contributions made to an IRA during a tax year and returned (with any income allocable to such contributions) on or before the due date (including extensions) for that tax year.
- Distributions of dividends paid on stock held by an employee stock ownership plan under section 404(k).
- Distributions from a military retirement plan (other than the federal TSP).
- Distributions from an inherited IRA by a nonspousal beneficiary.

If you're filing a joint return, include both spouses' amounts in both columns.

Exception. Don't include your spouse's distributions with yours when entering an amount on line 4 if you and your spouse didn't file a joint return for the year the distribution was received.

Example. You received a distribution of $5,000 from a qualified retirement plan in 2024. Your spouse received a distribution of $2,000 from a Roth IRA in 2022. You and your spouse file a joint return in 2024, but didn't file a joint return in 2022. You would include $5,000 in column (a) and $7,000 in column (b).

Line 7

Add the amounts from line 6, columns (a) and (b), and enter the total.

Line 11

Before you complete the following worksheet, figure the amount of any credit for the elderly or the disabled you're claiming on Schedule 3 (Form 1040), line 6d. See Schedule R (Form 1040) to figure the credit.

Credit Limit Worksheet

Complete this worksheet to figure the amount to enter on line 11.

1. Enter the amount from Form 1040, 1040-SR, or 1040-NR, line 18 . . . . 1._____

2. Enter the total of your credits from Schedule 3, lines 1 through 3, 6d, and 6l . . . . . . 2._____

3. Subtract line 2 from line 1. Also enter this amount on Form 8880, line 11. But if zero or less, **stop;** you can't take the credit—don't file this form . 3._____

Key Terms

tax credit, 7-1
nonrefundable credit, 7-2
refundable credit, 7-2
child tax credit, 7-2
Schedule 8812, 7-3
additional (refundable) child tax credit, 7-4
other dependent credit, 7-5
Form 8862, 7-5
earned income credit (EIC), 7-10
qualifying child, 7-12
child and dependent care expense credit, 7-14
Form 2441, 7-14
Affordable Care Act, 7-16

premium tax credit, 7-16
federal poverty line (FPL), 7-17
applicable percentage, 7-17
second lowest cost silver plan (SLCSP), 7-17
Form 1095-A, 7-17
advance premium tax credit, 7-21
Form 8962, 7-21
allocations, 7-21
American Opportunity tax credit, 7-28
qualified higher education expenses, 7-28
Form 1098-T, 7-29
Form 8863, 7-29

lifetime leaning credit, 7-31
foreign income exclusion, 7-35
foreign housing exclusion, 7-35
foreign tax credit, 7-41
adoption credit, 7-43
general business credit, 7-47
new clean vehicle credit, 7-48
used clean vehicle credit, 7-49
commercial clean vehicle credit, 7-49
energy efficient home improvement credit, 7-50
residential clean energy credit, 7-51
low-income retirement plan contribution credit, 7-60
saver's credit, 7-60

Key Points

Learning Objectives	Key Points
LO 7.1: Calculate the child tax credit.	• Credits are a direct reduction in tax liability instead of a deduction from income. • The child tax credit is $2,000 per qualifying child. • All qualifying children must have a Social Security number at the time of filing. • The child tax credit begins phasing out when AGI reaches $400,000 for joint filers and $200,000 for all others. • A portion of the child tax credit is refundable. • The child tax credit also includes an "other dependent credit" of $500 for taxpayers with dependents who do not qualify for the child tax credit.
LO 7.2: Determine the earned income credit (EIC).	• The earned income credit (EIC) is available to qualifying individuals with earned income and AGI below certain levels. • The EIC formula for calculating the credit is based on the AGI of the taxpayer and the number of qualifying children of the taxpayer. • To compute the credit, the taxpayer must fill out a worksheet calculating the credit from the tables based on earned income from wages, salaries, and self-employment income. • To be eligible for the credit with no qualifying children, a worker must be at least 25 years old and under 65 years old and not be claimed as a dependent by another taxpayer.

LO 7.3:
Compute the child and dependent care credit for an individual taxpayer.

- To be eligible for the child and dependent care credit, the dependent must either be under the age of 13 or be a dependent or spouse of any age who is incapable of self-care.
- If a child's parents are divorced, the child need not be the dependent of the taxpayer claiming the credit, but the child must live with that parent more than they live with the other parent.
- The expenses that qualify for the credit include amounts paid to enable both the taxpayer and their spouse to be employed.
- For taxpayers with AGI of less than $15,000, the child and dependent care credit is equal to 35 percent of the qualified expenses. For taxpayers with AGI of $15,000 or more, the credit gradually decreases from 35 percent to 20 percent.
- Full-time students and disabled taxpayers with little or no income are deemed to have earned income of $250 per month for one dependent and $500 per month for two or more dependents for the purpose of calculating this limitation.
- In determining the credit, the maximum amount of qualified expenses to which the applicable percentage is applied is $3,000 for one dependent and $6,000 for two or more dependents.
- Qualified dependent care expenses are limited to the lesser of either spouse's earned income.

LO 7.4:
Calculate the premium tax credit available under the Affordable Care Act.

- Certain lower income taxpayers may be eligible for a premium tax credit to offset some or all of the cost of health care purchased through an exchange.
- The premium tax credit can be received in advance or at the time the tax return is filed.
- The advanced premium tax credit and the actual premium tax credit are reconciled at the time the tax return is prepared. Repayments may be limited.

LO 7.5:
Apply the special rules applicable to the American Opportunity tax credit and lifetime learning credit.

- The partially refundable American Opportunity tax credit is 100 percent of the first $2,000 paid for tuition, fees, books, and course materials paid and 25 percent of the next $2,000, for a total maximum annual credit of $2,500 per student.
- The American Opportunity tax credit is available for the first four years of post-secondary education.
- Taxpayers can elect a nonrefundable lifetime learning credit of 20 percent of the first $10,000 in qualified expenses for education.
- The American Opportunity tax credit and the lifetime learning credit are phased out for joint filers with income between $160,000 and $180,000 and for single, head of household, and surviving spouse filers with income between $80,000 and $90,000.
- Taxpayers cannot take both the American Opportunity tax credit and the lifetime learning credit for the same student in the same tax year.

LO 7.6:
Compute the foreign income exclusion and tax credit.

- The foreign income exclusion limit for 2024 is $126,500.
- U.S. taxpayers are allowed to claim a foreign tax credit on income earned in a foreign country and subject to income taxes in that country.
- Generally, the foreign tax credit is equal to the amount of the taxes paid to foreign governments; however, there is an "overall" limitation on the amount of the credit, which is calculated as the ratio of net foreign income to U.S. taxable income multiplied by the U.S. tax liability.
- Unused foreign tax credits may be carried back 1 year and forward 10 years to reduce any tax liability in those years.

LO 7.7:
Determine the proper use and calculation of the adoption credit.

- Individuals are allowed an income tax credit for qualified adoption expenses. The maximum total expense that can be taken as a credit for all tax years with respect to an adoption of a child is $16,810 for 2024.
- The maximum exclusion from income for benefits under an employer's adoption assistance program is $16,810.
- These amounts are phased out if modified AGI is between $252,150 and $292,150.

Chapter 7 • Tax Credits

LO 7.8: Recognize other basic individual credits.
- A tax credit of up to $7,500 for the purchase of a new clean vehicle is available, subject to AGI limits and car qualifications.
- A tax credit for used and commercial clean energy vehicles is available.
- Taxpayers may claim a 30-percent credit of the amount paid for qualified property such as solar electric property and solar water-heating property subject to aggregate and individual limitations by expenditure.

LO 7.9: Calculate the low-income Retirement Plan Contribution Credit.
- Certain low-income taxpayers may claim a nonrefundable low-income Retirement Plan Contribution Credit, also called the "Saver's Credit," to encourage them to participate in tax-saving retirement plans.

Questions and Problems

Group 1:
Multiple Choice Questions

LO 7.1 1. Which of the following will qualify for the child tax credit of $2,000 in 2024?
   a. A dependent child age 17
   b. A dependent child age 21 and a full-time student
   c. A dependent child age 13
   d. A dependent parent age 67 that lives with the taxpayer

LO 7.1 2. Which of the following best describes the other dependent credit?
   a. A $2,000 credit available to taxpayers with AGI under certain limits and children under age 17.
   b. A $500 credit for a dependent that does not qualify for the child tax credit.
   c. A credit for a percentage of the expenses paid for child or dependent care.
   d. A nonrefundable credit based on a percentage of income.

LO 7.1 3. Russ and Linda are married and file a joint tax return claiming their three children, ages 4, 7, and 18, as dependents. Their adjusted gross income for 2024 is $418,100. What is Russ and Linda's total child and other dependent tax credit for 2024?
   a. $2,000
   b. $3,400
   c. $3,550
   d. $4,500
   e. $9,600

LO 7.1 4. Jennifer is divorced and files a head of household tax return claiming her children, ages 4, 7, and 11, as dependents. Her adjusted gross income for 2024 is $81,200 and her pre-credit tax liability is $6,995. What is Jennifer's total child tax credit for 2024?
   a. $500
   b. $4,500
   c. $6,000
   d. $9,000
   e. $9,600

LO 7.1

5. Hugo and Caroline, a married filing jointly couple, with 2024 AGI of $54,800 all from earned income, have properly calculated their child tax credit as $4,000 (two qualifying children) but have pre-credit tax liability of only $2,605. The total amount of child tax credit that Hugo and Caroline will claim in 2024 is:
   a. Less than $2,605.
   b. Exactly $2,605.
   c. Greater than $2,605.
   d. None of these.

LO 7.2

6. Which of the following is *not* a requirement to claim the earned income credit?
   a. The taxpayer (and spouse if filing jointly) have a valid Social Security number.
   b. The taxpayer's investment income is less than $8,400.
   c. You cannot claim the foreign income exclusion by filing Form 2555.
   d. You have at least $1 of earned income.

LO 7.2

7. Which of the following taxpayers would most likely be eligible to claim an earned income credit with a qualifying child?
   a. Marco is a single parent and files head of household. Marco's child, Rebecca, obtained her Social Security number after the extended filing deadline for the tax year.
   b. Bart, a single parent filing head of household, has two daughters ages 21 and 25. The 25-year-old is not supported by Bart. The 21-year-old is a full-time student that does not provide more than half of her own support and lived with Bart and his ex-spouse (and the daughter's mother) until their divorce in August 2024. After the divorce, Bart and the daughter moved to a new home together.
   c. Julia and Todd take care of Julia's elderly mother and provide all of her support.
   d. Howard and Anne (married filing jointly) have two dependent children under the age of 13. Howard's 2024 earned income is $80,000. Anne does not work.

LO 7.2

8. Assuming they all meet the income requirements, which of the following taxpayers qualify for the earned income credit in 2024?
   a. A married taxpayer who lives with their spouse and who files a separate tax return and has a dependent child
   b. A single taxpayer who waited on tables for three months of the tax year and is claimed as a dependent by her mother
   c. A single taxpayer who is self-employed and has a dependent child
   d. a and c above
   e. None of these taxpayers qualify for the earned income credit

LO 7.3

9. Which of the following payments does *not* qualify as a child care expense for purposes of the child and dependent care credit?
   a. Payments to a day care center
   b. Payments to the taxpayer's sister (21 years old) for daytime babysitting
   c. Payments to a housekeeper who also babysits the child
   d. Payments to the taxpayer's dependent brother (16 years old) for daytime babysitting
   e. All of the payments qualify for the child and dependent care credit

LO 7.3

10. Mabel and Marty are married filing jointly and incurred $8,900 of child care expenses in 2024 for their 6-year-old son. Mabel has earned income of $35,000. Marty is a student and attended classes for eight months in 2024. What is the amount of qualified expenses for which Mabel and Marty will determine the allowable child and dependent care credit?
    a. $0
    b. $2,000
    c. $2,500
    d. $3,000
    e. $8,900

LO 7.3 11. Which of the following individuals is *not* a qualifying individual for purposes of the child and dependent care expense credit?
   a. 14-year old child claimed as a dependent by the taxpayer.
   b. 10-year old child claimed as a dependent by the taxpayer.
   c. A 6-year-old child of divorced parents who lives with the parent/taxpayer for more than one-half of the year but is claimed by the other parent as a dependent.
   d. The disabled parent of the taxpayer.

LO 7.4 12. Which of the following is *not* a requirement to receive the premium tax credit for health care in 2024?
   a. Health care through the employer is not available
   b. Health insurance is purchased through the state or federal exchange
   c. Income must be below 200 percent of the federal poverty line
   d. The taxpayer cannot be claimed as a dependent

LO 7.4 13. For purposes of determining income eligibility for the premium tax credit, household AGI is
   a. AGI for the taxpayer and spouse
   b. AGI for the taxpayer, spouse, and any other household members required to file a tax return
   c. AGI for the taxpayer, spouse, and any other household members required to file a tax return plus any tax-exempt income
   d. AGI for the taxpayer, spouse, and any other household members required to file a tax return plus any tax-exempt income and nontaxable Social Security benefits

LO 7.5 14. The American Opportunity tax credit is 100 percent of the first _____ of tuition and fees paid plus 25 percent of the next _____.
   a. $600; $1,200
   b. $1,100; $550
   c. $2,000; $2,000
   d. $1,100; $5,500
   e. None of these amounts

LO 7.5 15. Jane graduates from high school in June 2024. In the fall, she enrolls for 12 units at Big State University. Big State University considers students who take 12 or more units to be full-time. Jane's father pays her tuition and fees of $2,500 for the fall semester and in December 2024 prepays $2,500 for the spring semester. In 2024, the American Opportunity tax credit for Jane's tuition and fees before any AGI limitation is:
   a. $5,000
   b. $2,500
   c. $2,200
   d. $2,000
   e. Some other amount

LO 7.5 16. Which of the following costs is *not* a qualified education expense for the American Opportunity tax credit?
   a. Tuition
   b. Student loan payments
   c. Course-related books
   d. Lab supplies required by the course

LO 7.5 17. In September 2024, Sam pays $1,375 to take a course to improve his job skills to qualify for a new position at work. Assuming there is no phase-out of the credit, his lifetime learning credit for 2024 is:
   a. $220
   b. $1,100
   c. $275
   d. $1,375
   e. None of these amounts

LO 7.5 18. In November 2024, Simon pays $1,000 to take a course to improve his job skills to qualify for a new position at work. Simon's employer reimbursed him for the cost of the course. For 2024, Simon's lifetime learning credit is:
   a. $0
   b. $200
   c. $1,000
   d. $2,500
   e. None of these amounts

LO 7.5 19. John, a single father, has AGI of $83,000 in 2024. During the year, he pays $4,000 in qualified tuition for his dependent son, who just started attending Small University. What is John's American Opportunity tax credit for 2024?
   a. $0
   b. $1,750
   c. $2,250
   d. $2,500
   e. $4,000

LO 7.5 20. Joan, a single mother, has AGI of $92,000 in 2024. In September 2024, she pays $5,000 in qualified tuition for her dependent son who just started at Big University. What is Joan's American Opportunity tax credit for 2024?
   a. $0
   b. $1,250
   c. $2,125
   d. $2,500
   e. Some other amount

LO 7.5 21. Becky, a college freshman, works part-time and pays $1,650 of her full-time college tuition expenses. Although Becky files her own tax return, her parents claim her as a dependent on their tax return. Becky's parents file jointly and have AGI of $50,000. What is the amount of American Opportunity tax credit her parents can claim on their tax return for the tuition Becky paid?
   a. $0
   b. $413
   c. $1,600
   d. $1,650
   e. Some other amount

LO 7.6 22. Lucas, a single U.S. citizen, works in Denmark for MNC Corp during all of 2024. His MNC salary is $187,000. What amount can Lucas exclude from his gross income?
   a. $0
   b. $108,700
   c. $120,000
   d. $126,500
   e. $187,000

LO 7.6 23. Taxpayer L has income of $55,000 from Norway, which imposes a 40-percent income tax, and income of $45,000 from France, which imposes a 30-percent income tax. L has additional taxable income from U.S. sources of $200,000 and U.S. tax liability before credits of $105,000. What is the amount of the foreign tax credit?
   a. $16,500
   b. $35,000
   c. $35,500
   d. $100,000
   e. $45,000

LO 7.7 24. John and Joan pay $16,500 of qualified adoption expenses in 2024 to finalize the adoption of a qualified child. Their AGI is $199,000 for 2024. What is their adoption credit for 2024?
  a. $0
  b. $16,500
  c. $15,950
  d. $16,810

LO 7.7 25. In connection with the adoption of an eligible child who is a U.S. citizen and who is not a child with special needs, Sean pays $4,000 of qualified adoption expenses in 2023 and $3,000 of qualified adoption expenses in 2024. The adoption is finalized in 2024. There is no phase-out of the adoption credit. What are the adoption credits for both 2023 and 2024, respectively?
  a. $0; $7,000
  b. $4,000; $1,000
  c. $4,000; $3,000
  d. $7,000; $0

LO 7.7 26. If a taxpayer does not have enough tax liability to use all the available adoption credit, the unused portion may be carried forward for how many years?
  a. Two
  b. Three
  c. Five
  d. There is no carryforward

LO 7.8 27. Which of the following would preclude claiming a clean vehicle credit in 2024?
  a. The taxpayer was required to take a loan to purchase the vehicle.
  b. The vehicle was assembled outside the United States.
  c. The taxpayer's income exceeded the purchase price of the vehicle.
  d. The car was assembled in the United States, but by a foreign auto company.
  e. The vehicle is a previously owned (used) vehicle.

LO 7.8 28. Which of the following improvements is *not* eligible for an energy efficient home improvement credit?
  a. A new energy efficient central air conditioner
  b. New energy efficient windows
  c. A new energy efficient refrigerator
  d. An energy efficient exterior door

LO 7.9 29. Virginia and Richard are married taxpayers with adjusted gross income of $33,000 in 2024. If Virginia is able to make a $1,500 contribution to her IRA and Richard makes a $1,500 contribution to his IRA, what is the Saver's Credit Virginia and Richard will be eligible for?
  a. $0
  b. $600
  c. $1,500
  d. $3,000
  e. $4,000

Group 2: Problems

LO 7.1
1. Calculate the total 2024 child and other dependent credit for the following taxpayers. Please show your work.
   a. Jeremy is a single (head of household) father with $80,100 of AGI and has a dependent 8-year-old son.
   b. Jerry and Ann have $100,000 of AGI, file jointly, and claim two dependent preschool (under the age of 6) children.
   c. James and Apple have AGI of $430,300, file jointly, and claim three dependent children (ages 7, 10, and 19).

LO 7.2
2. How does the earned income credit (EIC) produce a "negative" income tax?

LO 7.2
3. List the seven rules that all taxpayers must meet in order to claim the EIC.

LO 7.2
4. List the four rules that apply to taxpayers without a qualifying child in order to claim the EIC.

LO 7.2
5. List the three rules that apply to taxpayers with a qualifying child in order to claim the EIC.

LO 7.2
6. Diane is a single taxpayer who qualifies for the earned income credit. Diane has two qualifying children who are 3 and 5 years old. During 2024, Diane's wages are $23,000 and she receives dividend income of $1,200. Calculate Diane's earned income credit using the EIC table in Appendix B.

LO 7.2
7. Margaret and David Simmons are married and file a joint income tax return. They have two dependent children, Margo, 5 years old (Social Security number 316-31-4890), and Daniel, who was born during the year (Social Security number 316-31-7894). Margaret's wages are $5,000 and David has wages of $15,000. In addition, they receive interest income of $200 during the year. Margaret and David do not have any other items of income and do not have any deductions for adjusted gross income. Assuming the Simmons file Form 1040 for 2024, complete Schedule EIC from Appendix F and the Earned Income Credit Worksheet A from Appendix B (EIC tables are also in Appendix B).

LO 7.2
8. What is the maximum investment income a taxpayer is allowed to have and still be allowed to claim the earned income credit? Please speculate as to why there is an investment income limit in the tax law.

LO 7.3
9. Calculate the amount of the child and dependent care credit allowed before any tax liability limitations or other credits for 2024 in each of the following cases, assuming the taxpayers had no income other than the stated amounts.
   a. William and Carla file a joint tax return. Carla earned $27,500 during the year, while William attended law school full-time for nine months and earned no income. They paid $3,500 for the care of their 3-year-old child, Carl.
   b. Raymond and Michele file a joint tax return. Raymond earned $83,000 during the year, while Michele earned $139,000 for the year from a part-time job. They paid $17,000 for the care of their two children under age 13.

LO 7.2
LO 7.3
10. Clarita is an unmarried taxpayer with two dependent children, ages 10 and 12. Clarita pays $3,000 in qualified child care expenses during the year. If her adjusted gross income (all from wages) for the year is $23,000 and she takes the standard deduction, calculate Clarita's earned income credit and child and dependent care credit for 2024.

LO 7.2
LO 7.3
11. Clarita is an unmarried taxpayer with two dependent children, ages 10 and 12. Clarita pays $3,000 in qualified child care expenses during the year. If her adjusted gross income (all from wages) for the year is $70,000 and she takes the standard deduction, calculate Clarita's earned income credit and child and dependent care credit for 2024.

LO 7.3 12. Mary and John are married and have AGI of $100,000 and two young children. John doesn't work, and they pay $6,000 a year to day care providers so he can shop, clean, and read a little bit in peace. How much child and dependent care credit can Mary and John claim? Why?

LO 7.3 13. Martha has a 3-year-old child and pays $10,000 a year in day care costs. Her salary is $34,000. How much is her 2024 child and dependent care credit?

LO 7.3 14. Raheem and Jean are married and have 4-year-old twins. Jean is going to school full-time for nine months of the year, and Raheem earns $45,000. The twins are in day care so Jean can go to school while Raheem is at work. The cost of day care is $10,000. What is their 2024 child and dependent care credit? Please explain your calculation.

LO 7.4 15. Susan and Stan Collins live in Iowa, are married, and have two children ages 6 and 10. In 2024, Susan's income is $45,000 and Stan's is $23,500 and both are self-employed. They also have $500 in interest income from tax-exempt bonds. The Collinses enrolled in health insurance for all of 2024 through their state exchange but did not elect to have the credit paid in advance. The 2024 Form 1095-A that the Collinses received from the exchange lists the following information:

Annual premiums	$9,800
Annual premium for the designated benchmark plan in the state	$10,800

Compute the Collinses' premium tax credit for 2024.

LO 7.4 16. Using the information in the previous question, assume that the Collinses' Form 1095-A also indicated that the total advance payment of the premium tax credit was $11,792. Calculate the excess advance premium tax credit and the repayment amount for 2024.

LO 7.5 17. What is the reason there are education tax credits in the tax law?

LO 7.5 18. Please explain the difference between the types of education covered by the American Opportunity tax credit and the lifetime learning credit.

LO 7.5 19. Janie graduates from high school in 2024 and enrolls in college in the fall. Her parents pay $4,000 for her tuition and fees.
   a. Assuming Janie's parents have AGI of $172,000, what is the American Opportunity tax credit they can claim for Janie?
   b. Assuming Janie's parents have AGI of $75,000, what is the American Opportunity tax credit they can claim for Janie?

LO 7.5 20. Jasper is single and is a computer software consultant with a college degree. He feels that one of the reasons for his success is that he continually updates his knowledge by taking classes at the local college in various areas related to software design and information technology. This year he spent $2,000 on course tuition and fees.
   a. Assuming Jasper has AGI of $86,000, how much lifetime learning credit can Jasper claim on his tax return?
   b. Would the answer be different if Jasper were married and supporting a spouse who was not working?

LO 7.6 21. Martha and Lew are married taxpayers with $400 of foreign tax withholding from dividends in a mutual fund. They have enough foreign income from the mutual fund to claim the full $400 as a foreign tax credit. Their tax bracket is 24 percent and they itemize deductions. Should they claim the foreign tax credit or a deduction for foreign taxes on their Schedule A? Why?

LO 7.7 22. Carl and Jenny adopt an orphan from the United States. The adoption takes two years and is finalized in 2024. They pay $9,000 in 2023 and $8,500 in 2024 for qualified adoption expenses. In 2024, Carl and Jenny have AGI of $150,000.
   a. What is the adoption credit Carl and Jenny can claim in 2024?
   b. How much credit could they claim if their AGI was $272,150?

LO 7.8 23. Mike bought a solar electric pump to heat his pool at a cost of $2,500 in 2024. What is Mike's residential clean energy credit?

LO 7.8 24. In 2024, Jeff spends $6,000 on solar panels to heat water for his main home. What is Jeff's residential clean energy credit for his 2024 purchase?

LO 7.9 25. George and Amal file a joint return in 2024 and have AGI of $38,200. They each make a $1,600 contribution to their respective IRAs. Assuming that they are not eligible for any other credits, what is the amount of their Saver's Credit?

Group 3:
Writing Assignment

Research

Your supervisor has asked you to research the following situation concerning Scott and Heather Moore. Scott and Heather are married and file a joint return. Scott works full-time as a wildlife biologist, and Heather is a full-time student enrolled at Online University. Scott's earned income for the year is $36,000. Heather does not have a job and concentrates solely on her schoolwork. The university she is enrolled in offers courses only through the Internet. Scott and Heather have one child, Elizabeth (age 8), and pay $3,000 for child care expenses during the year.

Required: Go to the IRS website **(www.irs.gov)**. Locate and review Publication 503. Write a file memorandum stating the amount of child and dependent care credit that Scott and Heather Moore can claim. (An example of a file memorandum is available at the website for this textbook located at **www.cengage.com**.)

Group 4:
Comprehensive Problems

1. Bryce and Kayleigh Young have one child, Jazzy, who is 6 years old (birthdate July 1, 2018). The Youngs reside at 4639 Honeysuckle Lane, Apt. 1201, Los Angeles, CA 90248. Sam's Social Security number is 589-22-1142. Bryce (birthdate May 29, 1991) is a manager at a museum gift store and Kayleigh (birthdate January 31, 1993) is a perfume tester. Their Form W-2s are presented below:

Form W-2 (2024) — Bryce Young

- a. Employee's social security number: 511-77-1133
- b. Employer identification number (EIN): 13-4567123
- c. Employer's name, address, and ZIP code: Rancho Los Cerritos Corporation, 4600 Virginia Rd, Suite 120, Long Beach, CA 90807
- 1. Wages, tips, other compensation: 29,000.00
- 2. Federal income tax withheld: 900.00
- 3. Social security wages: 29,000.00
- 4. Social security tax withheld: 1,798.00
- 5. Medicare wages and tips: 29,000.00
- 6. Medicare tax withheld: 420.50
- e. Employee's name and address: Bryce Young, 4639 Honeysuckle Lane, Apt 1201, Los Angeles, CA 90248
- 15. State: CA; Employer's state ID number: 8002119
- 16. State wages, tips, etc.: 29,000.00
- 17. State income tax: 650.00

Form W-2 (2024) — Kayleigh Young

- a. Employee's social security number: 577-98-1133
- b. Employer identification number (EIN): 13-7899111
- c. Employer's name, address, and ZIP code: Common Scents, 70200 Avalon Blvd # 400, Carson, CA 90746
- 1. Wages, tips, other compensation: 28,000.00
- 2. Federal income tax withheld: 1,100.00
- 3. Social security wages: 28,000.00
- 4. Social security tax withheld: 1,736.00
- 5. Medicare wages and tips: 28,000.00
- 6. Medicare tax withheld: 406.00
- e. Employee's name and address: Kayleigh Young, 4639 Honeysuckle Lane, Apt 1201, Los Angeles, CA 90248
- 15. State: CA; Employer's state ID number: 80003007
- 16. State wages, tips, etc.: 28,000.00
- 17. State income tax: 600.00

Bryce made a $400 contribution to his IRA (he does not have a retirement plan at work). They also received the following 1099-INT from their saving account:

```
☐ CORRECTED (if checked)
PAYER'S name, street address, city or town, state or province, country, ZIP or foreign postal code, and telephone no.
First Bank of Southern California
4440 Atlantic Ave.
Long Beach, CA 90807

Payer's RTN (optional):
OMB No. 1545-0112
Form 1099-INT (Rev. January 2024)
For calendar year 2024
Interest Income — Copy B For Recipient

1 Interest income: $86.33
2 Early withdrawal penalty: $
3 Interest on U.S. Savings Bonds and Treasury obligations: $

PAYER'S TIN: 21-9097081
RECIPIENT'S TIN: 577-98-1133

RECIPIENT'S name: Kayleigh Young
Street address: 4639 Honeysuckle Lane, Apt 1201
City, state, ZIP: Los Angeles, CA 90248

4 Federal income tax withheld: $
5 Investment expenses: $
6 Foreign tax paid: $
7 Foreign country or U.S. territory:
8 Tax-exempt interest: $
9 Specified private activity bond interest: $
10 Market discount: $
11 Bond premium: $
12 Bond premium on Treasury obligations: $
13 Bond premium on tax-exempt bond: $
14 Tax-exempt and tax credit bond CUSIP no.:
15 State:
16 State identification no.:
17 State tax withheld: $
```

Bryce and Kayleigh received the following letter from Jazzy's daycare provider:

KIDDIECARE INC.
10250 Santa Monica Blvd.
Los Angeles, CA 90067
EIN: 13-3345678

January 14, 2025

Bryce and Kayleigh Young
4639 Honeysuckle Lane Unit 1201
Los Angeles, CA 90248

Dear Bryce and Kayleigh,

Thank you for your patronage of our day care center with your child, Jazzy Young, in 2024. This statement serves as a record of the cost of daycare services we provided during calendar year 2024:

Child	Amount	Dates of Service
Jazzy Young	$3,700.00	1/1/2024 – 8/25/2024

Sincerely,

/s/ Marcia Clarke

Marcia Clarke
Director, KiddieCare Inc.

Required: Complete the Youngs' federal tax return for 2024. Use Form 1040, Schedule 1, Schedule 3, Form 2441, Schedule 8812, and Form 8880, as needed. Make realistic assumptions about any missing data.

2A. Steve Jackson (birthdate December 13, 1971) is a single taxpayer living at 3215 Pacific Dr., Apt. B, Pacific Beach, CA 92109. His Social Security number is 465-88-9415. In 2024, Steve's earnings and income tax withholding as laundry attendant of a local hotel are reported on the following Form W-2:

a Employee's social security number			
465-88-9415	OMB No. 1545-0008		
b Employer identification number (EIN)	1 Wages, tips, other compensation	2 Federal income tax withheld	
28-4466771	24,500.00	250.00	
c Employer's name, address, and ZIP code	3 Social security wages	4 Social security tax withheld	
	24,500.00	1,519.00	
Ocean View Motel	5 Medicare wages and tips	6 Medicare tax withheld	
508 Abbott Street	24,500.00	355.25	
San Diego, CA 92107	7 Social security tips	8 Allocated tips	
d Control number	9	10 Dependent care benefits	
e Employee's first name and initial Last name Suff.	11 Nonqualified plans	12a See instructions for box 12	
Steve Jackson	13 Statutory employee Retirement plan Third-party sick pay	12b	
3215 Pacific Drive Apt. B	14 Other	12c	
Pacific Beach, CA 92109		12d	
f Employee's address and ZIP code			
15 State Employer's state ID number	16 State wages, tips, etc.	17 State income tax	18 Local wages, tips, etc. 19 Local income tax 20 Locality name
CA 76661234	24,500.00	100.00	

Form **W-2** Wage and Tax Statement **2024** Department of the Treasury—Internal Revenue Service
Copy B—To Be Filed With Employee's FEDERAL Tax Return.
This information is being furnished to the Internal Revenue Service.

Steve has a daughter, Janet, from a previous marriage. Janet is 11 years old (Social Security number 654-12-6543, birthday June 21, 2013). Steve provides all Janet's support. Also living with Steve is his younger brother, Reggie (Social Security number 667-21-8998, birthday July 17, 1977). Reggie, age 47, is unable to care for himself due to a disability. On a reasonably regular basis, Steve has a caregiver come to the house to help with Reggie. He uses a company called HomeAid, 456 La Jolla Dr., San Diego, CA 92182 (EIN 17-9876543). Steve made payments of $700 to HomeAid in 2024. Janet receives free after-school care provided by the local school district.

Required: Complete Steve's federal tax return for 2024. Use Form 1040, Schedule 3, Form 2441, Schedule 8812, EITC Worksheet A, and Schedule EIC.

2B. David Fleming is a single taxpayer living at 169 Trendie Street, Apartment 6B, La Jolla, CA 92037. His Social Security number is 865-68-9635 and his birthdate is September 18, 1979.

David was employed as a cook for a local pizza restaurant. David's W-2 showed the following:

a Employee's social security number		
865-68-9635		
b Employer identification number (EIN)	1 Wages, tips, other compensation	2 Federal income tax withheld
23-4567321	25,750.00	1,300.00
c Employer's name, address, and ZIP code	3 Social security wages	4 Social security tax withheld
California Pizza Cafe	25,750.00	1,596.50
231 Foodie Street	5 Medicare wages and tips	6 Medicare tax withheld
La Jolla, CA 92037	25,750.00	373.38
e Employee's first name and initial / Last name		
David Fleming		
169 Trendie Street, Apt. 6B		
La Jolla, CA 92037		
15 State: CA	16 State wages, tips, etc.	17 State income tax
Employer's state ID number: D4567221	25,750.00	475.00

Form **W-2** Wage and Tax Statement **2024**

David's only other source of income during the year was a prize he won appearing on a game show. The game show sent David home with a Form 1099-MISC:

PAYER'S name, address		
Price is Accurate Studios		
Studio 44		
Studio City, CA 91604		
	3 Other income	4 Federal income tax withheld
	$ 10,400.00	$ 2,496.00
PAYER'S TIN: 21-8675309	RECIPIENT'S TIN: 865-68-9635	
RECIPIENT'S name: David Fleming		
169 Trendie St. Apt 6B		
La Jolla, CA 92037		

Form **1099-MISC** (Rev. 1-2024)

David attended community college full-time in 2024 as a second-year student. He intends to transfer to a four-year university to complete his degree. David received the following Form 1098-T.

FILER'S name, street address, city or town, state or province, country, ZIP or foreign postal code, and telephone number Windandsea Community College 1300 Genesee Street San Diego, CA 92037	**1 Payments received for qualified tuition and related expenses** $ 1,850.00 **2** OMB No. 1545-1574 **2024** Form **1098-T** **Tuition Statement**
FILER'S employer identification no. 12-7652444	**STUDENT'S TIN** 865-68-9635
STUDENT'S name David Fleming	**3**
Street address (including apt. no.) 169 Trendie Street Apt 6B	**4 Adjustments made for a prior year** $
City or town, state or province, country, and ZIP or foreign postal code La Jolla, CA 92037	**5 Scholarships or grants** $
	6 Adjustments to scholarships or grants for a prior year $
	7 Checked if the amount in box 1 includes amounts for an academic period beginning January–March 2025 ☐
Service Provider/Acct. No. (see instr.)	**8 Checked if at least half-time student** ☒
	9 Checked if a graduate student ☐
	10 Ins. contract reimb./refund $

Copy B For Student — This is important tax information and is being furnished to the IRS. This form must be used to complete Form 8863 to claim education credits. Give it to the tax preparer or use it to prepare the tax return.

Form **1098-T** (keep for your records) www.irs.gov/Form1098T Department of the Treasury - Internal Revenue Service

David's textbooks cost $325. David wishes to claim whatever educational credits he is eligible for. He has not claimed any educational credits in the past and has not been convicted of a felony drug conviction. Unfortunately, David's employer did not provide health care to its employees but David signed up for coverage through his state's health care exchange. The exchange sent him a Form 1095-A as shown on Page 7-79.

Required: Complete David's federal tax return for 2024. Use Form 1040, Schedule 1, Schedule 3, Form 8863, and Form 8962. Make realistic assumptions about any missing data.

Form 1095-A — Health Insurance Marketplace Statement (2024)

Department of the Treasury — Internal Revenue Service
Do not attach to your tax return. Keep for your records.
Go to www.irs.gov/Form1095A for instructions and the latest information.

VOID ☐ CORRECTED ☐
OMB No. 1545-2232

Part I — Recipient Information

#	Field	Value
1	Marketplace identifier	31-9876543
2	Marketplace-assigned policy number	B1234TH
3	Policy issuer's name	Covered California
4	Recipient's name	David Fleming
5	Recipient's SSN	865-68-9635
6	Recipient's date of birth	09/18/1979
7	Recipient's spouse's name	
8	Recipient's spouse's SSN	
9	Recipient's spouse's date of birth	
10	Policy start date	January 1, 2024
11	Policy termination date	December 31, 2024
12	Street address (including apartment no.)	169 Trendie St. Apt 6B
13	City or town	La Jolla
14	State or province	CA
15	Country and ZIP or foreign postal code	92037

Part II — Covered Individuals

	A. Covered individual name	B. Covered individual SSN	C. Covered individual date of birth	D. Coverage start date	E. Coverage termination date
16	David Fleming	865-68-9635	09/18/1979	01/01/2024	12/31/2024
17					
18					
19					
20					

Part III — Coverage Information

	Month	A. Monthly enrollment premiums	B. Monthly second lowest cost silver plan (SLCSP) premium	C. Monthly advance payment of premium tax credit
21	January	325.00	355.00	100.00
22	February	325.00	355.00	100.00
23	March	325.00	355.00	100.00
24	April	325.00	355.00	100.00
25	May	325.00	355.00	100.00
26	June	325.00	355.00	100.00
27	July	325.00	355.00	100.00
28	August	325.00	355.00	100.00
29	September	325.00	355.00	100.00
30	October	325.00	355.00	100.00
31	November	325.00	355.00	100.00
32	December	325.00	355.00	100.00
33	Annual Totals	3,900.00	4,260.00	1,200.00

For Privacy Act and Paperwork Reduction Act Notice, see separate instructions. Cat. No. 60703Q Form **1095-A** (2024)

Group 5:
Cumulative Software Problem

1. The following information is available for the Albert and Allison Gaytor family in addition to that provided in Chapters 1–6.

   The Gaytors paid tuition and fees for both Crocker and Cayman to attend college. Recall that Crocker is a freshman at Tribal River Community College and Cayman is a part-time student in community college. Crocker received a $1,100 scholarship from Tribal River. Crocker's Form 1098-T is shown below. The Gaytors paid tuition and fees of $1,400 for Cayman in 2024.

FILER'S name, address	1 Payments received for qualified tuition and related expenses	OMB No. 1545-1574	
Tribal River Community College 2400 SE Salerno Rd. Stuart, FL 34997	$ 4,280.00	2024 Form 1098-T	Tuition Statement
FILER'S EIN: 44-3421456	STUDENT'S TIN: 261-55-1212	3	Copy B For Student
STUDENT'S name: Crocker Gaytor	4 Adjustments made for a prior year	5 Scholarships or grants $ 1,100.00	
Street address: 4100 SE Lincoln Street	6 Adjustments to scholarships or grants for a prior year	7 Checked if the amount in box 1 includes amounts for an academic period beginning January–March 2025 ☐	
City: Stuart, FL 34997	8 Checked if at least half-time student ☐	9 Checked if a graduate student ☐	10 Ins. contract reimb./refund

   In December 2023, Albert's 82 year-old aunt, Virginia Everglades (Social Security number 699-19-9000), was unable to support and care for herself and moved in with the Gaytors. She lived with them for all of 2024. The Gaytors provided more than one-half of Aunt Virginia's support. Virginia's only source of income is a small annuity that paid her $3,100 in 2024. While Albert and Allison were working, the Gaytors hired a nanny service from time to time to take care of Aunt Virginia. The Gaytors paid $4,400 to Nannys R Us in 2024. Nannys R Us (EIN 34-1234123) is located at 12 SE Central Pkwy #555, Stuart, FL 34994.

   Required: Combine this new information about the Gaytor family with the information from Chapters 1–6 and complete a revised 2024 tax return for Albert and Allison. Be sure to save your data input files since this case will be expanded and completed with more tax information in Chapter 8.

Chapter 8
Depreciation and Sale of Business Property

Learning Objectives

After completing this chapter, you should be able to:

- **LO 8.1** Explain the concept of capitalization and depreciation.
- **LO 8.2** Calculate depreciation expense using the MACRS tables.
- **LO 8.3** Identify when a Section 179 election to expense the cost of property may be used.
- **LO 8.4** Apply the limitations on depreciation of "listed property."
- **LO 8.5** Apply the limitations on depreciation of "luxury automobiles."
- **LO 8.6** Calculate the amortization of goodwill and certain other intangibles.
- **LO 8.7** Classify gains and losses from Section 1231 assets.
- **LO 8.8** Apply the depreciation recapture rules.
- **LO 8.9** Apply the general treatment of casualty gains and losses for business purposes.
- **LO 8.10** Compute the gain on installment sales.
- **LO 8.11** Calculate recognized and deferred gains on like-kind exchanges.
- **LO 8.12** Calculate recognized and deferred gains on involuntary conversions.

Overview

The decision to capitalize an expenditure has significant effects on taxable income. The immediate deduction of a cost versus the slower recovery of a cost over time through depreciation can create a considerable difference in the cash flows of a business. Tax depreciation is largely computed under the Modified Accelerated Cost Recovery System (MACRS) under U.S. tax law. Because the financial impact of depreciation can be significant, lawmakers have frequently created a number of temporary provisions such as bonus depreciation and permanent but limited provisions such as the Section 179 election to expense to accelerate the recovery of costs for property that must be capitalized.

As covered in Chapter 4, realized gains and losses are generally recognized for tax purposes unless there is a tax provision that specifically allows for a different treatment. This chapter focuses on business-related gains and losses. Transactions covered in this chapter include:

- Section 1231 (business) gains and losses
- Depreciation recapture on business assets
- Installment sales
- Like-kind exchanges
- Involuntary conversions

Unlike capital gains and losses which are generally reported on Schedule D, many business asset sale transactions are reported on Form 4797, and installment sales are reported on Form 6252.

8-1 Capitalization and Depreciation

Learning Objective 8.1 — Explain the concept of capitalization and depreciation.

In accounting, capitalization is the process of recording an expenditure for an item that is likely to provide benefits over a long period of time (or at least beyond the end of the year) as an asset on the balance sheet as opposed to an expense on the income statement. In Chapter 4 of Statement of Concepts 8, the Financial Accounting Standards Board defines an asset as "a present right of an entity to an economic benefit." The tax law does not provide as elegant a definition, but rather provides that "no deduction shall be allowed for any amount paid out for new buildings or for permanent improvements or betterments made to increase the value of any property or estate." With so little guidance provided in the statutory law, unsurprisingly, a bevy of administrative and judicial law has been constructed to assist taxpayers with the decision as to whether to deduct or capitalize and depreciate. Many times, the choice to capitalize or deduct is obvious.

Example Caroline purchases an office building and the land on which it sits for $400,000. The cost of the building and land both must be capitalized. ♦

Other times, especially when related to an improvement or repair to property, the choice is less obvious.

Example Tonya owns a building with 22 apartments. The ice maker in the refrigerator of one of the apartments breaks and Tanya has a repairman install a new icemaker for $250. This expenditure could require capitalization or could be deducted as routine maintenance and repairs. ♦

8-1a Capitalization

Generally, an expenditure for property will require capitalization if the expenditure is any of the following:

1. A betterment
2. An adaptation to a new or better use
3. A restoration

A betterment is an amount paid to fix a material condition or defect that existed prior to acquisition or that arose while the property was created. Expenditures for material additions including enlargement, extension, or the addition of a major component are generally treated as a betterment. Expenditures that are expected to increase the productivity, efficiency, strength, quality, or output of the property are considered a betterment.

Example Troy is adding a new extension to their existing factory building. By enlarging the building, they have an expenditure that qualifies as a betterment and should be capitalized. ♦

Example Petro Inc. acquires land that had a leaking underground storage tank. Petro incurs costs to remove the tank and clean up the land. These costs are a betterment as they correct a material defect in the property that existed prior to acquisition. ♦

Example Amon-Ra is renovating the lobby of his office building. The footprint of the building will not be enlarged, and the work does not affect the structure of the building. The work is largely decorative and aesthetic in nature. The existing lobby was fully functional prior to the remodel. This expenditure does not qualify as a betterment. ♦

An adaptation is an expenditure that allows the property to be used in a new or different use.

Example Carpets R Us owns a building in Georgia that is used as a factory to manufacture carpets. When Carpets decides to move its manufacturing facility overseas, the company incurs the cost to convert the factory building into a retail showroom by making modifications to the structure and systems (for example, HVAC and plumbing) of the building. These expenditures represent an adaptation and should be capitalized. ♦

A restoration is the replacement of a major component, a substantial structural part, or combination of parts that make up a substantial component of the property. A restoration also includes amounts paid to return property to its normal operating condition if the property has deteriorated and is no longer functional for its intended use. Amounts paid to rebuild property to return it to a like-new condition after the end of its useful life are also considered a restoration. Lastly, expenditures to replace property for which a gain or loss and associated basis adjustment have been taken are considered restorations.

Example Rexford Soccer Club has a set of bleacher seats that face the northern goal of the soccer field. Because the bleachers have not been maintained, they have fallen into a state of disrepair and cannot be used to seat spectators. Rexford incurs the costs to replace the seats, floors, and railings of the bleachers so that spectators may sit in that section again. Because the bleachers were returned to their normal operating condition, the expenditures are a restoration and should be capitalized. ♦

Example Fiona owns a building that was partially damaged by a hurricane. She recognizes a casualty loss of $10,000 on the building which reduces the building's basis by $10,000. When later Fiona elects to make repairs to the damaged building, the amounts paid to restore the property are considered a restoration and should be capitalized. ♦

If the expenditure does not meet any of the above, the cost can generally be deducted as repairs or maintenance. Costs associated with inventory may require additional analysis that is outside the scope of this textbook.

Although the guidance on the capitalize versus deduct decision is somewhat voluminous, the decision is not always clear and thus, the IRS has created a number of safe harbor provisions that allow taxpayers to treat an item as a deductible repair or maintenance cost if the safe harbor is met.

De Minimis Safe Harbor Election

A taxpayer is permitted to deduct an item of tangible property to the extent that item is deducted on the taxpayer's books and records up to a specific dollar limit. The dollar limit is $5,000 per invoice or item if the taxpayer has applicable financial statements (AFS). For a taxpayer without AFS, the limit is $2,500. AFS are financial statements filed with the Securities and Exchange Commission, audited financial statements with an accompanying CPA report including those prepared for a creditor, reporting to shareholders, or provided to the state or federal government or agency thereof. Taxpayers with AFS must have a written accounting policy that supports the expensing of de minimis items up to the dollar limit. No written policy is required for taxpayers without AFS, but the books and records of the taxpayer must demonstrate that the policy is being consistently followed.

Example Dalvin operates a small business that does not prepare applicable financial statements. Dalvin's accounting policy is to expense any item under $2,000, regardless of the item's useful life. Dalvin may deduct the cost of the same items on his tax return. ♦

Safe Harbor for Routine Maintenance

For property other than buildings, there is an additional safe harbor associated with restoration costs. Under this safe harbor, costs incurred to restore property can be deducted if the restoration is an activity that would be reasonably expected to be performed at least twice during the useful life of the property.

Example Najee takes his business auto to the repair shop. The auto undergoes an oil and filter change, a transmission fluid replacement, a brake pad replacement, and also has a leaky radiator replaced. The recovery period of the auto is five years. Typically, Najee's business autos have the oil and filter changed twice a year and the transmission fluid and brake pads changed every two years. The radiator is not normally replaced during the life of the auto. Najee can elect to deduct the costs of the oil and filter, transmission fluid and brake pads under the safe harbor as all of these activities would be expected to be performed at least twice during the five-year recovery period. The radiator repair does not qualify for the safe harbor and probably should be capitalized. ♦

Building property has a slightly different safe harbor. The cost to perform restoration activities can be deducted if the activity is expected to be performed more than once during a 10-year period starting when the property was placed in service.

Example Cooper Corporation owns a large office building in downtown Metropolis. During the current year, Cooper completed three projects on the building: (1) installed new fiber-optic wiring throughout the building to provide faster connectivity, (2) replaced the plumbing fixtures in a number of the building's restrooms, and (3) replaced the security cameras located on the exterior of the building. The new fiber-optic wiring is not a restoration and should be classified as a betterment and therefore is not eligible for the safe harbor and should be capitalized. The plumbing fixtures are not routinely replaced by Cooper every 10 years. These fixtures are more than 15 years old. As a result, the cost of the plumbing work does not meet the safe harbor and must be capitalized. The security cameras placed on the exterior of the building are subject to weather and Cooper expects to replace them about every four years. Since the cameras are expected to be restored more than once in a 10-year period, the cost to replace them meets the safe harbor and can be deducted. ♦

These safe harbors cannot be applied to inventory costs or betterments.

Small Business Safe Harbor

Lastly, there is a safe harbor for small businesses with annual gross receipts of $10 million or less, and ownership or lease of buildings with an unadjusted basis of $1 million or less.

This safe harbor permits the deduction of costs for work performed on owned or leased buildings if the total amount paid during the year does not exceed the lesser of:

1. 2 percent of the unadjusted basis of building property or
2. $10,000

Example Ja'Marr qualifies as a small business for safe harbor election. His total unadjusted basis of buildings is $400,000 and he spends $5,000 on new exterior siding for the building. Since the cost is below $8,000 (lesser of $10,000 or $400,000 × 2%), Ja'Marr may deduct the $5,000. ♦

8-1b Depreciation

Since many long-lived assets are used in business production over a number of years, accrual-based income is not properly measured if the entire cost of these assets is deducted in the year the assets are purchased. Depreciation is the accounting process of allocating and deducting the cost of an asset over a period of years. The term *depreciation* does not necessarily mean physical deterioration or loss of value of the asset. In fact, in some cases the value of the asset may increase while it is being depreciated. In Accounting Standards Codification 360-10-35-4, depreciation is defined as follows:

> A system of accounting which aims to distribute the cost or other basic value of tangible capital assets, less salvage (if any), over the estimated useful life of the unit (which may be a group of assets) in a systematic and rational manner. It is a process of allocation, not of valuation.

Example Arike operates a small business with two assets: an auto and a building. Although the value of the auto decreases over time and the value of the building increases over time, both will be depreciated for accounting and tax purposes. ♦

Certain assets, such as land, cannot be depreciated for tax purposes. These assets remain on the taxpayer's records at original cost.

Self-Study Problem 8.1 Refer to Appendix E for Solutions to Self-Study Problems

Determine whether each of the following expenditures should be capitalized or deducted or both for tax purposes.

a. Taxpayer pays $12,000 to acquire new tangible personal property (a machine).

b. Taxpayer pays $9,000 to acquire a machine that is not in working condition and spends an additional $3,000 getting the machine ready for use. The taxpayer does not have applicable financial statements or any policies on expensing repairs.

c. Taxpayer incurs cost of $3,000 to perform maintenance on a building system. This maintenance was designed to improve the efficiency of the system.

d. Taxpayer with applicable financial statements and a written policy that calls for expensing all costs under $3,000, purchases 10 computers at a cost of $2,000 each.

e. Taxpayer adds a new wing to his factory to warehouse additional supplies at a cost of $16,000.

Learning Objective 8.2

Calculate depreciation expense using the MACRS tables.

8-2 Modified Accelerated Cost Recovery System (MACRS) and Bonus Depreciation

For tax years after 1980, modifications in the tax law were made to encourage capital investment. As a major part of this tax law change, the Accelerated Cost Recovery System (ACRS) was enacted and later modified in 1986 to become the current tax depreciation system referred to as the Modified Accelerated Cost Recovery System (MACRS). The current MACRS allows taxpayers who invest in capital assets to write off an asset's cost over a period designated in the tax law and to use an accelerated method for depreciation of assets other than real estate. The minimum number of years over which the cost of an asset may be deducted (the recovery period) depends on the type of property and the year in which the property was acquired. The recovery periods are based on asset depreciation ranges (ADRs) as published by the IRS. A schedule of the recovery periods for assets acquired after 1986 is presented in Table 8.1. The recovery period classification for assets acquired after 1980, but before 1987, differs from the recovery period classification presented in Table 8.1.

Table 8.1 Recovery Periods for Assets Placed in Service After 1986

Recovery Period	Recovery Method	Assets
3-year	200% declining balance	ADR midpoint life of 4 years or less, excluding cars and light trucks.
5-year	200% declining balance	ADR midpoint life of more than 4 years but less than 10 years, cars and light trucks, office machinery, certain energy property, R&D property, computers, and certain equipment.
7-year	200% declining balance	ADR midpoint life of 10 years or more but less than 16 years and property without an ADR life (e.g., most business furniture and certain equipment).
10-year	200% declining balance	ADR midpoint life of 16 years or more but less than 20 years, including trees and vines.
15-year	150% declining balance	ADR midpoint life of 20 years or more but less than 25 years, including treatment plants and land improvements (sidewalks, roads, fences, and landscaping).
20-year	150% declining balance	ADR midpoint life of 25 years or more, other than real property with an ADR life of 27.5 years or longer and municipal sewers.
27.5-year	Straight-line	Residential rental real estate.
39-year	Straight-line	Other real property purchased generally on or after May 13, 1993 (previously 31.5-year straight-line).

Under MACRS, taxpayers calculate the depreciation of an asset using a table which contains a percentage depreciation rate for each year of the property's recovery period. The yearly rate is applied to the cost of the asset. The cost of the property to which the rate is applied is not reduced for prior years' depreciation (the unadjusted basis). For personal property (all property except real estate) the depreciation rates in Table 8.2 apply.

Example Assume a taxpayer acquires an asset (5-year class property) in 2024 with a cost basis of $15,000 and uses accelerated depreciation under MACRS. The depreciation expense deduction for each year of the asset's life is calculated (using the depreciation rates in Table 8.2) as follows:

Year	Cost	Depreciation Rate	Deduction
2024	$15,000	20.00	$ 3,000
2025	15,000	32.00	4,800
2026	15,000	19.20	2,880
2027	15,000	11.52	1,728
2028	15,000	11.52	1,728
2029	15,000	5.76	864
Total		100.00%	$15,000

◆

In the above example, note that even though the asset is a 5-year class property, the cost is written off over a period of six tax years. This is due to the convention under MACRS which provides for six months of depreciation during the year the asset is first placed in service and six months of depreciation during the year the asset is fully depreciated, sold, or disposed. This convention is referred to as the *half-year convention* since only one-half of the year of depreciation is allowed in both the year of acquisition and the year of disposition, regardless of the actual acquisition and disposition dates. The half-year convention is built into the depreciation rates in Table 8.2.

Table 8.2 Accelerated Depreciation for Personal Property Assuming Half-Year Convention (For Property Placed in Service after December 31, 1986)

Recovery Year	3-Year (200% DB)	5-Year (200% DB)	7-Year (200% DB)	10-Year (200% DB)	15-Year (150% DB)	20-Year (150% DB)
1	33.33	20.00	14.29	10.00	5.00	3.750
2	44.45	32.00	24.49	18.00	9.50	7.219
3	14.81*	19.20	17.49	14.40	8.55	6.677
4	7.41	11.52*	12.49	11.52	7.70	6.177
5		11.52	8.93*	9.22	6.93	5.713
6		5.76	8.92	7.37	6.23	5.285
7			8.93	6.55*	5.90*	4.888
8			4.46	6.55	5.90	4.522
9				6.56	5.91	4.462*
10				6.55	5.90	4.461
11				3.28	5.91	4.462
12					5.90	4.461
13					5.91	4.462
14					5.90	4.461
15					5.91	4.462
16					2.95	4.461
17						4.462
18						4.461
19						4.462
20						4.461
21						2.231

*Switch to straight-line depreciation.

For property (other than real estate), a taxpayer may elect to use straight-line depreciation instead of the accelerated depreciation rates under MACRS. The taxpayer must use the straight-line MACRS tables for assets for which a straight-line election has been made. The annual depreciation rates to be applied to the cost of an asset for which a straight-line election under MACRS has been made are presented in Table 8.3.

Table 8.3 Straight-Line Depreciation for Personal Property, Assuming Half-Year Convention* (For Property Placed in Service after December 31, 1986)

Recovery Period	Rate First Recovery Year	Other Recovery Years		Last Recovery Years	
		Years	Rate	Year	Rate
3-year	16.67	2–3	33.33	4	16.67
5-year	10.00	2–5	20.00	6	10.00
7-year	7.14	2–7	14.29	8	7.14
10-year	5.00	2–10	10.00	11	5.00
15-year	3.33	2–15	6.67	16	3.33
20-year	2.50	2–20	5.00	21	2.50

*The official table contains a separate row for each year. For ease of presentation, certain years are grouped together in this table. In some instances, this will cause a difference of 0.01 percent for the last digit when compared with the official table.

Example On April 1, 2024, Lori purchased and placed in service a specialized computer for use in her business. The computer costs $18,000 and has a 5-year recovery period. The difference between straight-line depreciation and MACRS depreciation is presented below (the depreciation rates are from Tables 8.2 and 8.3).

Year	Cost	Straight-Line Depreciation Rate	Straight-Line Deduction	MACRS Depreciation Rate	MACRS Deduction
2024	$18,000	10.00	$ 1,800	20.00	$ 3,600
2025	18,000	20.00	3,600	32.00	5,760
2026	18,000	20.00	3,600	19.20	3,456
2027	18,000	20.00	3,600	11.52	2,074
2028	18,000	20.00	3,600	11.52	2,074
2029	18,000	10.00	1,800	5.76	1,036
Total		100.00%	$18,000	100.00%	$18,000

Note that Lori receives a deduction based on six months in the year of purchase (half-year convention), even though the asset was put into service on April 1. If the asset had been placed into service on September 1, Lori still would have received a deduction for six months of depreciation. ♦

Under MACRS, the same method of depreciation (accelerated or straight-line) must be used for all property in a given class placed in service during the tax year.

8-2a Mid-Quarter Convention

When a taxpayer acquires a significant amount of assets during the last quarter of the tax year, the half-year convention, referred to in the above examples, is replaced by the *mid-quarter convention*. The mid-quarter convention must be applied if more than 40 percent of the total cost of a taxpayer's property acquired during the year, other than real property, is placed in service during the last three months of the tax year. The mid-quarter convention treats all property placed in service during any quarter of the tax year as being placed in service on the midpoint of the quarter. The mid-quarter convention, if applied in the year the asset is acquired, also applies upon the disposition of the asset. Assets placed in service and disposed of during the same tax year are not considered in determining

Table 8.4 Accelerated Depreciation for Personal Property Assuming Mid-Quarter Convention* (For Property Placed in Service after December 31, 1986)

Recovery Year	3-Year (200% DB)	5-Year (200% DB)	7-Year (200% DB)
First Quarter			
1	58.33	35.00	25.00
2	27.78	26.00	21.43
3	12.35	15.60	15.31
4	1.54	11.01	10.93
5		11.01	8.75
Second Quarter			
1	41.67	25.00	17.85
2	38.89	30.00	23.47
3	14.14	18.00	16.76
4	5.30	11.37	11.97
5		11.37	8.87
Third Quarter			
1	25.00	15.00	10.71
2	50.00	34.00	25.51
3	16.67	20.40	18.22
4	8.33	12.24	13.02
5		11.30	9.30
Fourth Quarter			
1	8.33	5.00	3.57
2	61.11	38.00	27.55
3	20.37	22.80	19.68
4	10.19	13.68	14.06
5		10.94	10.04

*For ease of presentation, only 3-year, 5-year, and 7-year property and only depreciation rates for the first 5 years are provided. The official table also includes 10-, 15-, and 20-year property. Refer to IRS Publication 946 for the complete table.

whether the taxpayer meets the 40-percent test. An excerpt from the mid-quarter tables can be found in Table 8.4.

Example Jane, a calendar-year taxpayer, purchases the following property during 2024 for use in her business:

Placed in Service	Property	Original Cost	Recovery Period
March 2	Office furniture	$ 3,000	7 years
July 31	Apartment building	200,000	27.5 years
November 1	Automobile	18,000	5 years

Jane does not elect Section 179 and elects out of bonus depreciation. The cost of the automobile acquired during the last three months of the year represents 86 percent of the total cost of assets, other than real property, acquired during the tax year. Since more than 40 percent of Jane's purchases, other than real property, were made during the last three months of the tax year, the mid-quarter convention would apply to all personal property placed in service during this tax year. Depreciation for 2024 on the furniture is $750 ($3,000 × 25%) and on the auto is $900 ($18,000 × 5%). ♦

8-2b Bonus Depreciation

Because the cost recovery of long-lived assets occurs over many years, one way to lower the after-tax cost of capitalized expenditures is through accelerated depreciation. At times, the tax law has provided for "bonus depreciation," which is the immediate deduction of all or some of the cost of otherwise slowly depreciated property. The TCJA increased the bonus depreciation percentage to 100 percent for qualified property acquired and placed in service after September 27, 2017, and through December 31, 2022 (certain long-lived assets have an additional year), but the 100-percent bonus depreciation phases out starting in 2023 as presented in Table 8.5.

Table 8.5 Bonus Depreciation Percentages

Year	Bonus Percentage
2023	80
2024	60
2025	40
2026	20
2027	0

In 2024, the bonus depreciation rules allow taxpayers purchasing property with a MACRS recovery period of 20 years or less (Table 8.1), computer software, and qualified improvement property to directly write off up to 60 percent of the cost of the assets in the year placed in service. Bonus depreciation is presumed to apply unless the taxpayer elects out of the provision. The taxable income limits and thresholds associated with Section 179 (covered in LO 8.3) do not apply to bonus depreciation.

Both new and used property are generally eligible for bonus depreciation.

Example Mary places a new 5-year MACRS-class machine costing $20,000 into service on March 1, 2024. She does not elect out of bonus depreciation on the machine. The bonus depreciation on the machine for 2024 is $12,000 ($20,000 × 60 percent). The remaining basis ($8,000) can be depreciated using typical MACRS. Assuming half-year convention, Mary would deduct another $1,600 ($8,000 × MACRS depreciation factor of 20 percent) in 2024 for total cost recovery in the year placed in service of $13,600. ♦

Between bonus depreciation and the expanded immediate expensing under Section 179, small businesses are not likely to capitalize much of the cost of any non-real property unless they have a net operating loss or anticipate using larger depreciation deductions during higher tax bracket years in the future.

In previous years, certain categories of real property qualified for bonus depreciation. For example, qualified leasehold improvements were eligible for bonus depreciation if placed in service before 2016. Currently, qualified improvement property (QIP) has a 15-year life and is eligible for bonus depreciation. QIP is defined as an internal improvement to nonresidential property, excluding escalators, elevators, internal structural framework, and enlargements to the building.

Example In 2024, Bordeaux decided to upgrade the office building that it owns. The lobby area was completely redesigned to reflect the current standards for security and aesthetics. Also, additional space was added to the rear of the building to provide storage for some high-value goods that need additional security not available in the existing building. The redesign of the lobby (unless changes were made to the structure of the building) is likely to qualify for bonus depreciation, whereas the expansion for additional space will not. ♦

8-2c Real Estate

For real estate acquired after 1986, MACRS requires the property to be depreciated using the straight-line method. The straight-line MACRS realty tables for residential realty (e.g., an apartment building) provide for depreciation over 27.5 years. Nonresidential realty (e.g., an office building) is depreciated over 39 years (31.5 years for realty acquired generally before May 13, 1993). The annual depreciation rates for real estate under MACRS are presented in Table 8.6.

Table 8.6 Straight-Line Depreciation for Real Property Assuming Mid-Month Convention*

27.5-Year Residential Real Property

The applicable annual percentage is (use the column for the month in the first year the property is placed in service):

Recovery Year(s)	1	2	3	4	5	6	7	8	9	10	11	12
1	3.485	3.182	2.879	2.576	2.273	1.970	1.667	1.364	1.061	0.758	0.455	0.152
2–18	3.636	3.636	3.636	3.636	3.636	3.636	3.636	3.636	3.636	3.636	3.636	3.636
19–27	3.637	3.637	3.637	3.637	3.637	3.637	3.637	3.637	3.637	3.637	3.637	3.637
28	1.970	2.273	2.576	2.879	3.182	3.485	3.636	3.636	3.636	3.636	3.636	3.636
29	0.000	0.000	0.000	0.000	0.000	0.000	0.152	0.455	0.758	1.061	1.364	1.667

39-Year Nonresidential Real Property

The applicable annual percentage is (use the column for the month in the first year the property is placed in service):

Recovery Year(s)	1	2	3	4	5	6	7	8	9	10	11	12
1	2.461	2.247	2.033	1.819	1.605	1.391	1.177	0.963	0.749	0.535	0.321	0.107
2–39	2.564	2.564	2.564	2.564	2.564	2.564	2.564	2.564	2.564	2.564	2.564	2.564
40	0.107	0.321	0.535	0.749	0.963	1.177	1.391	1.605	1.819	2.033	2.247	2.461

*The official tables contain a separate row for each year. For ease of presentation, certain years are grouped together in these two tables. In some instances, this will produce a difference of 0.001 percent when compared with the official tables.

Example Carlos purchases a rental house on September 3, 2024, for $90,000 (the land is accounted for separately). The house was immediately rented to a tenant. The annual depreciation expense deduction under MACRS for each of the first four years is illustrated below (the percentages are taken from Table 8.6, 27.5-Year Residential Real Property).

Year	Cost	Depreciation Rate	Deduction
2024	$90,000	1.061	$ 955
2025	90,000	3.636	3,272
2026	90,000	3.636	3,272
2027	90,000	3.636	3,272

Note that the depreciation rates are taken from Table 8.6 under column 9, because the month of acquisition (September) is the ninth month of the year. ♦

Most real property (except QIP) is not eligible for bonus depreciation or Section 179 immediate expensing (refer to LO 8.3).

8-2d Mid-Month Convention

For the depreciation of real property under MACRS, a *mid-month convention* replaces the half-year convention. Real estate is treated as placed in service in the middle of the month the property is placed in service. For example, under the mid-month convention, an asset purchased and placed in service on April 2 is treated as being placed in service on April 15. The mid-month convention is built into the first year's rates in Table 8.6.

8-2e Depreciation Expense in Year of Disposal

The half-year, mid-year, and mid-month conventions apply to the depreciation deduction if depreciable property is disposed of in much the same way as when the property is placed in service. The depreciation tables presented in Tables 8.2, 8.3, 8.4, and 8.6 all consider the convention in the year placed in service (the first year); however, the tables do not consider applying a convention in the year of disposal since that is not known. The calculation of depreciation in a year of disposal requires the application of the applicable convention to the full-year depreciation rate presented in the depreciation tables.

Example On April 1, 2024, Lori purchased and placed in service a specialized computer for use in her business. The computer cost $18,000 and has a 5-year recovery period and Lori elects out of bonus depreciation. This is the only asset placed in service during the year and so Lori applies the half-year convention. Lori disposes of the asset on December 14, 2027. The following table presents Lori's depreciation for the computer using the half-year convention:

Year	Cost	MACRS Depreciation Rate	Full-Year Depreciation	Convention	MACRS Deduction
2024	$18,000	20.00	$3,600	–	$3,600
2025	18,000	32.00	5,760	–	5,760
2026	18,000	19.20	3,456	–	3,456
2027	18,000	11.52	2,074	50%	1,037

The half-year convention is applied in the year of disposal but not necessary for other years as the table considers the convention. ♦

The application of the mid-quarter convention is more difficult. Recall that the mid-quarter convention requires the taxpayer to treat the property as if it had been placed in service in the middle of the quarter in which it was placed in service. The manner in which the mid-quarter convention is applied in the year of disposal is dependent on the quarter in which the property is disposed.

Example From the previous example, assume that instead of the half-year convention, Lori is required to apply the mid-quarter convention. When the computer is disposed of in the fourth quarter of 2027, the mid-quarter convention requires that the disposal be treated as if the computer was taken out of service in the middle of the fourth quarter. Lori is entitled to the first three quarters of depreciation but only one-half of the fourth quarter in 2027. Three and one-half quarters of a full year is 3.5 ÷ 4 or 87.5 percent. The following table presents Lori's depreciation for the computer under the mid-quarter convention:

Year	Cost	MACRS Depreciation Rate	Full-Year Depreciation	Convention	MACRS Deduction
2024	$18,000	25.00	$4,500	–	$4,500
2025	18,000	30.00	5,400	–	5,400
2026	18,000	18.00	3,240	–	3,240
2027	18,000	11.37	2,047	87.5%	1,791

If Lori had disposed of the computer in July (during the third quarter), the mid-quarter convention would require the depreciation to be calculated as if the computer were disposed in the middle of the third quarter. She is entitled to the first two quarters plus one-half of the third quarter or 62.5 percent (2.5 ÷ 4) of the full year amount. ♦

The mid-month convention is applied in much the same way as the mid-quarter convention except that the property is treated as is disposed of in the middle of the month actually disposed.

Example Carlos purchases a rental house on September 3, 2024, for $90,000 (the land is accounted for separately). The house was immediately rented to a tenant. He sells the home on May 25, 2027. Carlos' depreciation in the year of disposal permits a deduction for the first four months (January through April) and one-half of a month for May or 4.5 months out of 12 months or 37.5 percent. The following table presents Carlos' depreciation for the computer using the mid-month convention:

Year	Cost	MACRS Depreciation Rate	Full-Year Depreciation	Convention	MACRS Deduction
2024	$90,000	1.061	$ 955	–	$ 955
2025	90,000	3.636	3,272	–	3,272
2026	90,000	3.636	3,272	–	3,272
2027	90,000	3.636	3,272	37.5%	1,227

If Carlos had disposed of the house in December, he would be entitled to the first eleven months plus one-half of December or 95.8 percent (11.5 ÷ 12) of the full year amount. ♦

8-2f Reporting Depreciation Expense

Depreciation expense is reported on Form 4562, Depreciation and Amortization. Individual taxpayers who have no current year asset additions and who are not reporting depreciation on listed property (refer to LO 8.4) are not required to file Form 4562 with their federal tax return.

> **ProConnect™ Tax TIP**
>
> ProConnect Tax includes a powerful depreciation calculator as part of the software. There are two ways to report depreciation. The first method is to enter the property details into the software. Property can be entered through either a quick entry or detailed input screen, both of which are located under Deductions. The first subheading in the left-hand margin is Depreciation. The property is linked to a business (for example, Schedule C or Schedule E). Based on the type and cost of property placed in service, the software will automatically apply bonus depreciation ("SDA") unless overridden in the detail screen. Section 179 immediate expensing can be input directly. The second method is to compute depreciation outside the ProConnect Tax software and input the deduction as an override. The screens for direct input are located under the normal depreciation screens in the left-hand margin.

Self-Study Problem 8.2
Refer to Appendix E for Solutions to Self-Study Problems

During 2024, Mary Moser purchases the following items for use in her business:

Manufacturing equipment	$ 11,000
(7-year property, placed in service August 1)	
Office furniture	7,000
(7-year property, placed in service December 15)	
Office building, land is accounted for separately	180,000
(placed in service April 30)	

Assume that Mary uses the accelerated depreciation method under MACRS.

a. Use page 1 of Form 4562 on Page 8-15 to report Mary's depreciation deduction for 2024 including bonus depreciation.

b. Calculate Mary's depreciation on each property (but do not complete Form 4562) assuming she elects out of bonus depreciation.

c. Calculate Mary's depreciation deduction on the assets for 2025 (Year 2). Compute amounts assuming bonus depreciation was taken in 2024.

d. Calculate Mary's depreciation deduction on only the manufacturing equipment for 2027 (Year 4) assuming she disposes of the equipment on December 1, 2027. Compute the amount assuming bonus depreciation was taken in 2024.

Self-Study Problems 8.2 and 8.6

Form 4562
Department of the Treasury
Internal Revenue Service

Depreciation and Amortization
(Including Information on Listed Property)
Attach to your tax return.
Go to www.irs.gov/Form4562 for instructions and the latest information.

OMB No. 1545-0172
2024
Attachment Sequence No. **179**

Name(s) shown on return | Business or activity to which this form relates | Identifying number

Part I — Election To Expense Certain Property Under Section 179
Note: If you have any listed property, complete Part V before you complete Part I.

1. Maximum amount (see instructions) **1**
2. Total cost of section 179 property placed in service (see instructions) **2**
3. Threshold cost of section 179 property before reduction in limitation (see instructions) . **3**
4. Reduction in limitation. Subtract line 3 from line 2. If zero or less, enter -0- **4**
5. Dollar limitation for tax year. Subtract line 4 from line 1. If zero or less, enter -0-. If married filing separately, see instructions **5**

6.
(a) Description of property	(b) Cost (business use only)	(c) Elected cost

7. Listed property. Enter the amount from line 29 . . . . **7**
8. Total elected cost of section 179 property. Add amounts in column (c), lines 6 and 7 . . **8**
9. Tentative deduction. Enter the **smaller** of line 5 or line 8 . . . . **9**
10. Carryover of disallowed deduction from line 13 of your 2023 Form 4562 . . . . . . **10**
11. Business income limitation. Enter the smaller of business income (not less than zero) or line 5. See instructions **11**
12. Section 179 expense deduction. Add lines 9 and 10, but don't enter more than line 11 . **12**
13. Carryover of disallowed deduction to 2025. Add lines 9 and 10, less line 12 . . . **13**

Note: Don't use Part II or Part III below for listed property. Instead, use Part V.

Part II — Special Depreciation Allowance and Other Depreciation (Don't include listed property. See instructions.)

14. Special depreciation allowance for qualified property (other than listed property) placed in service during the tax year. See instructions **14**
15. Property subject to section 168(f)(1) election **15**
16. Other depreciation (including ACRS) **16**

Part III — MACRS Depreciation (Don't include listed property. See instructions.)

Section A

17. MACRS deductions for assets placed in service in tax years beginning before 2024 . . **17**
18. If you are electing to group any assets placed in service during the tax year into one or more general asset accounts, check here . . . . ☐

Section B—Assets Placed in Service During 2024 Tax Year Using the General Depreciation System

(a) Classification of property	(b) Month and year placed in service	(c) Basis for depreciation (business/investment use only—see instructions)	(d) Recovery period	(e) Convention	(f) Method	(g) Depreciation deduction
19a 3-year property						
b 5-year property						
c 7-year property						
d 10-year property						
e 15-year property						
f 20-year property						
g 25-year property			25 yrs.		S/L	
h Residential rental property			27.5 yrs.	MM	S/L	
			27.5 yrs.	MM	S/L	
i Nonresidential real property			39 yrs.	MM	S/L	
				MM	S/L	

Section C—Assets Placed in Service During 2024 Tax Year Using the Alternative Depreciation System

20a Class life					S/L	
b 12-year			12 yrs.		S/L	
c 30-year			30 yrs.	MM	S/L	
d 40-year			40 yrs.	MM	S/L	

Part IV — Summary (See instructions.)

21. Listed property. Enter amount from line 28 . . . . **21**
22. **Total.** Add amounts from line 12, lines 14 through 17, lines 19 and 20 in column (g), and line 21. Enter here and on the appropriate lines of your return. Partnerships and S corporations—see instructions . **22**
23. For assets shown above and placed in service during the current year, enter the portion of the basis attributable to section 263A costs **23**

For Paperwork Reduction Act Notice, see separate instructions. Cat. No. 12906N Form **4562** (2024)

Form 4562 (2024) Page **2**

Part V — Listed Property (Include automobiles, certain other vehicles, certain aircraft, and property used for entertainment, recreation, or amusement.)

Note: For any vehicle for which you are using the standard mileage rate or deducting lease expense, complete **only** 24a, 24b, columns (a) through (c) of Section A, all of Section B, and Section C if applicable.

Section A — Depreciation and Other Information (Caution: See the instructions for limits for passenger automobiles.)

24a Do you have evidence to support the business/investment use claimed? ☐ Yes ☐ No   **24b** If "Yes," is the evidence written? ☐ Yes ☐ No

(a) Type of property (list vehicles first)	(b) Date placed in service	(c) Business/ investment use percentage	(d) Cost or other basis	(e) Basis for depreciation (business/investment use only)	(f) Recovery period	(g) Method/ Convention	(h) Depreciation deduction	(i) Elected section 179 cost

25 Special depreciation allowance for qualified listed property placed in service during the tax year and used more than 50% in a qualified business use. See instructions . **25**

26 Property used more than 50% in a qualified business use:

		%						
		%						
		%						

27 Property used 50% or less in a qualified business use:

		%				S/L –		
		%				S/L –		
		%				S/L –		

28 Add amounts in column (h), lines 25 through 27. Enter here and on line 21, page 1 . **28**

29 Add amounts in column (i), line 26. Enter here and on line 7, page 1 . . . . **29**

Section B — Information on Use of Vehicles

Complete this section for vehicles used by a sole proprietor, partner, or other "more than 5% owner," or related person. If you provided vehicles to your employees, first answer the questions in Section C to see if you meet an exception to completing this section for those vehicles.

	(a) Vehicle 1	(b) Vehicle 2	(c) Vehicle 3	(d) Vehicle 4	(e) Vehicle 5	(f) Vehicle 6
30 Total business/investment miles driven during the year (**don't** include commuting miles) .						
31 Total commuting miles driven during the year						
32 Total other personal (noncommuting) miles driven						
33 Total miles driven during the year. Add lines 30 through 32						
	Yes / No	Yes / No	Yes / No	Yes / No	Yes / No	Yes / No
34 Was the vehicle available for personal use during off-duty hours?						
35 Was the vehicle used primarily by a more than 5% owner or related person? . .						
36 Is another vehicle available for personal use?						

Section C — Questions for Employers Who Provide Vehicles for Use by Their Employees

Answer these questions to determine if you meet an exception to completing Section B for vehicles used by employees who **aren't** more than 5% owners or related persons. See instructions.

	Yes	No
37 Do you maintain a written policy statement that prohibits all personal use of vehicles, including commuting, by your employees?		
38 Do you maintain a written policy statement that prohibits personal use of vehicles, except commuting, by your employees? See the instructions for vehicles used by corporate officers, directors, or 1% or more owners . .		
39 Do you treat all use of vehicles by employees as personal use?		
40 Do you provide more than five vehicles to your employees, obtain information from your employees about the use of the vehicles, and retain the information received?		
41 Do you meet the requirements concerning qualified automobile demonstration use? See instructions		

Note: If your answer to 37, 38, 39, 40, or 41 is "Yes," don't complete Section B for the covered vehicles.

Part VI — Amortization

(a) Description of costs	(b) Date amortization begins	(c) Amortizable amount	(d) Code section	(e) Amortization period or percentage	(f) Amortization for this year

42 Amortization of costs that begins during your 2024 tax year (see instructions):

43 Amortization of costs that began before your 2024 tax year **43**

44 Total. Add amounts in column (f). See the instructions for where to report **44**

Form **4562** (2024)

8-3 Election to Expense (Section 179)

8.3 Learning Objective
Identify when a Section 179 election to expense the cost of property may be used.

As part of the landmark Tax Reform Act of 1986, Internal Revenue Code Section 179 was implemented to decrease the cost of investments in business property by permitting small businesses to expense the costs of certain property that would otherwise be capitalized and depreciated over time.

Under Section 179, taxpayers may elect to expense the acquisition cost of certain property, subject to limitations. This cost would otherwise have been deducted over a period of time using the regular cost recovery depreciation rules. Similar to bonus depreciation, the Section 179 deduction applies to both new and used property. Property that qualifies for Section 179 includes personal property (property other than real estate), QIP, and improvements to nonresidential real property that are placed in service after the nonresidential real property was first placed in service, such as roofs; heating, ventilation, and air-conditioning property; fire protection and alarm systems; and security systems.

Section 179 places three limitations on the expensing election: (1) a maximum on the annual amount expensed, (2) a phase-out of the annual amount limit, and (3) the taxable income limit.

Originally, the maximum annual expensing amount was a modest $10,000. Over the years the amount was adjusted for inflation and also increased with economic stimulus in mind. As a result of the financial crisis, the annual maximum was increased to $250,000 in 2008 and then increased again to $500,000 in 2010. Although subject to repeated expiration and extension, the limit had remained at $500,000 until 2015 when it was made permanent and subject to inflation adjustment each year. The maximum annual amount that can be expensed under Section 179 is $1,220,000 in 2024.

The annual maximum expense amount is reduced dollar-for-dollar by the amount of Section 179 property acquired during the year in excess of a threshold amount. Similar to the annual limit, the Section 179 phase-out threshold amount has fluctuated over time. In 2024, the threshold is $3,050,000. As a result, a taxpayer who places in service $4,270,000 or more of Section 179 property during 2024 may not immediately expense in 2024 under Section 179.

Lastly, the amount of acquired qualified property that may be expensed annually is limited to the taxpayer's taxable income, before considering any amount expensed under the Section 179 election, from the trade or business of the taxpayer. Any amount which is limited due to the taxable income limitation may be carried over to succeeding tax years.

Example During 2024, Bob buys used equipment that cost $1,520,000 for his factory. Bob's business generates taxable income of well over $3,000,000 and he elects out of bonus depreciation. Bob's Section 179 property placed in service is below $3,050,000, and thus is not subject to phase-out. With $3 million in taxable income, Bob's Section 179 deduction is not subject to the income limitation. Bob may immediately expense $1,220,000 of his equipment. The remaining $300,000 of equipment cost will be depreciated over the applicable recovery period under MACRS. ♦

Example During 2024, Shuri places in service used manufacturing equipment for use in her business. The machinery cost $2,000,000. Shuri has taxable income (after considering any MACRS depreciation) from her business of $200,000. Under the annual maximum limitation, Shuri can immediately expense up to $1,220,000 and would depreciate the remaining $780,000 under MACRS. However, the maximum amount allowed under the taxable income limitation is only $200,000. The remaining $1,020,000 ($1,220,000 annual maximum less $200,000 permitted under the income limit) is carried forward to succeeding tax years. ♦

Example During 2024, Portia purchased $3,500,000 of new equipment for use in her business. Portia's taxable income before considering immediate expensing is over $4 million. Because the amount of Section 179 property placed in service during the year exceeds the phase-out threshold of $3,050,000, Portia's annual Section 179 expensing limit of $1,220,000 is reduced by the $450,000 phase-out ($3,500,000 − $3,050,000), resulting in a maximum allowable expensing amount of only $770,000 ($1,220,000 − $450,000). ♦

A taxpayer who has made the Section 179 election to expense must reduce the basis of the asset by the amount expensed before calculating regular MACRS depreciation on the remaining cost of the asset. Even if the taxpayer is not able to deduct the full amount expensed in the current year due to the *taxable income limitation*, the basis must be reduced by the full amount of the Section 179 expense election.

When calculating depreciation on an asset, if an election to expense only part of the asset has been made, the amount of the Section 179 election to expense must be decided first. When a taxpayer decides to take only a portion of the cost of the asset as a Section 179 deduction, the rest of the cost of the asset must be depreciated. The depreciation must be deducted from taxable income to determine the income limitation for the Section 179 deduction.

Example On August 1, 2024, Joan purchases a machine for use in her business. It is her only purchase of business property in 2024. The machine cost $1,300,000 and qualifies as 5-year MACRS property. Her business income before any cost recovery is $1,020,000. Joan elects to immediately expense $1,220,000. She elects out of bonus depreciation, thus $80,000 of remaining basis ($1,300,000 − $1,220,000) is subject to MACRS depreciation of $16,000 ($80,000 × 0.20 depreciation factor). As a result of deducting MACRS depreciation of $16,000, Joan's taxable income before Section 179 is reduced to $1,004,000. Joan may only immediately expense $1,004,000 due to the income limit. The excess $216,000 ($1,220,000 − $1,004,000) of Section 179 deduction will be carried forward to 2025. ♦

The effects of bonus depreciation, Section 179 and MACRS depreciation can combine to create substantially accelerated cost recovery. If a taxpayer elects Section 179 immediate expensing and uses bonus depreciation, the cost basis of the property is first reduced by the Section 179 deduction, then by bonus depreciation, and lastly, by typical MACRS depreciation.

Example Hoover Corp. purchases and places in service a machine at a cost of $3,200,000 in 2024 (assume half-year convention and 5-year recovery period). Hoover wishes to maximize cost recovery in the first year and so along with bonus depreciation, Hoover elects the maximum Section 179 expense permitted. Hoover has adequate income to absorb any Section 179 expense. The maximum Section 179 of $1,220,000 must be reduced by $150,000 ($3,200,000 − $3,050,000) since qualifying Section 179 property placed in service exceeds the threshold for 2024. Hoover will reduce its Section 179 election to $1,070,000 ($1,220,000 − $150,000). The remaining adjusted basis of the machine is $2,130,000. Applying the 2024 bonus rate of 60 percent yields bonus depreciation of $1,278,000 ($2,130,000 × 60 percent), leaving a remaining adjusted basis of $852,000 ($3,200,000 − $1,070,000 − $1,278,000) which will be subject to typical MACRS depreciation of $170,400 ($852,000 × 20 percent). Total cost recovery is $2,518,400. ♦

Self-Study Problem 8.3 Refer to Appendix E for Solutions to Self-Study Problems

On June 15, 2024, Chang purchases $3,100,000 of equipment (7-year property) for use in their business. It is their only purchase of business property in 2024. Chang has taxable income from their business of $2.4 million before any cost recovery.

a. Assuming Chang does not elect Section 179 and elects out of bonus depreciation, what is their total 2024 cost recovery?

b. Assuming Chang elects the maximum Section 179 deduction allowable and elects out of bonus depreciation, what is their total 2024 cost recovery?

c. Assuming Chang elects the maximum Section 179 deduction allowable and does not elect out of bonus depreciation, what is their total 2024 cost recovery?

8-4 Listed Property

8.4 Learning Objective

Apply the limitations on depreciation of "listed property."

Congress felt some taxpayers were using the favorable tax incentives of the accelerated cost recovery system and the limited expensing election to claim depreciation deductions on assets used for personal purposes. To curtail this perceived abuse of the tax system, Congress enacted special rules which apply to the depreciation of "listed property." Listed property includes those types of assets which lend themselves to personal use, including the following:

1. Passenger automobiles, defined to include any four-wheeled vehicle manufactured primarily for use on public streets, roads, and highways, rated at 6,000 pounds or less unloaded gross vehicle weight. Specifically excluded from the definition of passenger automobiles are vehicles used directly in the trade or business of transporting persons or property, ambulances and hearses used in a trade or business, and certain trucks and vans not likely to be used more than a de minimis amount for personal purposes, including vehicles which display the company name or advertising.

2. Other property used as a means of transportation (trucks, buses, boats, airplanes, and motorcycles), except vehicles which are not likely to be used for personal purposes,

such as marked police cars, school buses, and tractors, or vehicles used for transporting persons or cargo for compensation.

3. Property generally used for entertainment, recreation, or amusement (video recording equipment, communication equipment, etc.). This category is generally less relevant as entertainment expenses are currently not deductible (Chapter 3).

If listed property is used 50 percent or less in a qualified business, any depreciation deduction must be calculated using the straight-line method of depreciation over an alternate recovery period, and the special election to expense under Section 179 and bonus depreciation are not allowed.

Qualified business use does not include investment use or the use of property owned by an employee in performing services as an employee, unless the use meets the convenience-of-employer and condition-of-employment tests. In addition, the excess depreciation allowed by reason of the property meeting the more-than-50-percent-use test must be included in income if property which meets the test in one year subsequently fails to meet the more-than-50-percent-use test in a succeeding year.

Example Oscar has an automobile he uses 45 percent of the time for personal use and 55 percent of the time in his accounting business. Since Oscar's business-use percentage of 55 percent exceeds 50 percent, Oscar is not required to use the straight-line method in calculating depreciation. The accelerated depreciation method and the election to expense may be used by Oscar on the business-use portion of the auto. ♦

Self-Study Problem 8.4 — Refer to Appendix E for Solutions to Self-Study Problems

a. For each of the following independent situations, indicate if the taxpayer is required to depreciate the property using the straight-line method over the alternate recovery period:

  1. Alvarez uses an automobile 20 percent for his business and 80 percent for personal reasons.
  2. Laura has a truck she uses in her business 55 percent of the time, 15 percent for her real estate investment, and 30 percent for personal use.

b. For each of the scenarios in a. above, assume that the property was placed in service in 2024 at a cost of $40,000, the half-year convention applies, and the luxury auto and taxable income limits do not apply. Compute depreciation in 2024 for each assuming they seek maximum cost recovery in the first year.

Learning Objective 8.5

Apply the limitations on depreciation of "luxury automobiles."

8-5 Limitation on Depreciation of Luxury Automobiles

In addition to the limitations on the depreciation of passenger automobiles imposed by the listed property rules covered in the preceding section, the depreciation of passenger automobiles is subject to an additional limitation, commonly referred to as the "luxury automobile" limitation. Regardless of the method of depreciation used by the taxpayer, accelerated or straight-line, the election to expense, or bonus depreciation, the amount of depreciation expense that may be claimed on a passenger automobile is subject to an annual dollar limitation. The annual dollar limitations that apply to passenger automobiles acquired in 2024 are listed in Table 8.7. Any automobile which would have actual MACRS depreciation exceeding the limits is considered a "luxury automobile" by the IRS for purposes of the depreciation limitation rules.

Table 8.7 Annual Automobile Depreciation Limitations

Year of Use	2024 Limits with Bonus	2024 Limits without Bonus
Year 1	$20,400	$12,400
Year 2	19,800	19,800
Year 3	11,900	11,900
Year 4 (and subsequent years until fully depreciated)	7,160	7,160

Separate higher depreciation limits apply for certain trucks and vans.

Some sport utility vehicles fall outside of the definition of passenger automobiles and can be depreciated or expensed under Section 179 or the bonus depreciation rules without regard to the automobile depreciation limits. To qualify for the exception, the sport utility vehicle must have a gross vehicle weight rating above 6,000 pounds. Vehicles that meet the large sport utility vehicle exception are limited to $30,500 (2024 limit) in Section 179 expensing but may depreciate using the five-year MACRS percentages without the typical auto depreciation limitations.

The annual limitations must be reduced to reflect the actual business-use percentage where business use is less than 100 percent.

Example Lexie purchased a new car for $65,000 in September 2024 which she uses 75 percent for business. Lexie elects out of bonus depreciation. Depreciation on the automobile is calculated as follows:

Total cost	$65,000
	× 0.75
Limited to business use	$48,750
MACRS depreciation (half-year convention) $48,750 × 20% =	$ 9,750
Compared to:	
Maximum luxury automobile depreciation allowed $12,400 × 75% =	$ 9,300

Because the luxury automobile limitation is less than the actual depreciation calculated, Lexie's depreciation deduction is limited to $9,300. ♦

Example In September 2024, Joan purchased a passenger automobile which cost $70,000. The automobile is used 100 percent for business purposes and Joan elects out of bonus depreciation. A comparison of MACRS, with and without the limitation, is as follows:

	Five-Year MACRS	Annual Limit
Year 1	$14,000	$12,400
Year 2	22,400	19,800
Year 3	13,440	11,900
Year 4	8,064	7,160
Year 5	8,064	7,160
Year 6	4,032	7,160
Year 7		4,420

Note that, although the automobile is a 5-year property, it will take seven years to recover the entire cost of the asset because of the annual dollar limits, assuming no election to expense under Section 179 or bonus depreciation. ♦

Would You Believe? Taxpayers hoping to get around the luxury auto depreciation limits by leasing an auto should be aware that there is a rule designed to put them in the same economic position as if they had purchased the auto. The IRS issued tables for computation of an "income inclusion" which must be used to reduce the lease expense deduction for leased autos.

Bonus depreciation on autos is subject to annual depreciation limits also. For years after the first year, the unrecovered basis of the auto is subject to MACRS depreciation but remains limited by the auto limits.

Example Sally purchased a new automobile for $70,000 in September 2024 which she uses 100 percent for business during the life of the auto. Assuming half-year convention, bonus depreciation, and no Section 179 depreciation, Sally's 2024 cost recovery is computed as follows:

Cost basis	$70,000
Bonus depreciation (60 percent)	42,000
Depreciation limit for autos, Year 1	20,400
Basis unrecovered at end of 2024	$49,600

In 2025, MACRS depreciation is $15,872 (unrecovered basis of $49,600 × 32%, which is the depreciation factor for the second year of 5-year property). The second-year limit of $19,800 exceeds the deduction, and thus, does not apply. ◆

Self-Study Problem 8.5 Refer to Appendix E for Solutions to Self-Study Problems

On June 17, 2024, Travis purchased a passenger automobile at a cost of $58,000. The automobile is used 90 percent for qualified business use and 10 percent for personal purposes. Calculate the depreciation expense (with bonus depreciation) for the automobile for 2024, 2025, and 2026, assuming half-year convention and no Section 179 immediate expensing.

Would You Sign This Tax Return?

Duncan Devious (age 52) is a self-employed attorney. Duncan loves to be noticed in public, and therefore, he drives a 7,000-pound, military-type, SUV, the only vehicle he owns. When you are preparing his tax return, you notice that he claims 90 percent of his total auto expenses as a business deduction on his Schedule C and 10 percent as personal use, with total miles driven in 2024 as 10,000. You note from his home and office addresses on his tax return that he lives approximately 15 miles from his office. The total of the expenses (i.e., gas, oil, maintenance, depreciation) he claims is $31,200. He does not have a mileage log to substantiate the business use of the SUV. Would you sign the Paid Preparer's declaration (refer to example above) on this return? Why or why not?

8-6 Intangibles

The current tax guidance provides for two main categories of intangibles: (1) Section 197 intangibles and (2) non-Section 197 intangibles. Section 197 intangibles are those acquired by a taxpayer as part of the acquisition of a trade or business. Section 197 intangibles are amortized over a 15-year period, beginning with the month of acquisition. Amortization is a cost recovery method similar to depreciation in that it spreads the cost recovery over a fixed period of years. It differs from depreciation in that it is applied to intangible assets rather than tangible personal or real property and does not include the half-year or mid-quarter conventions. The 15-year life applies regardless of the actual useful life of the intangible asset. No other amortization or depreciation method may be claimed on Section 197 assets. When acquired as part of a trade or business, the following are defined as qualified Section 197 intangibles:

- Goodwill
- Going-concern value
- Workforce in place
- Information bases, including business books and records and operating systems
- Know-how
- Customer-based intangibles
- License, permit, or right granted by a governmental unit
- Covenant not to compete
- Franchise, trademark, or trade name

> **8.6 Learning Objective**
> Calculate the amortization of goodwill and certain other intangibles.

Example In March 2024, Mary purchases a business from Bill for $250,000. Section 197 goodwill of $36,000 is included in the $250,000 purchase price. Mary amortizes the goodwill over a 15-year period at the rate of $200 per month, starting with the month of purchase. ♦

8-6a Exclusions

Intangible assets that are excluded from the definition of Section 197 intangibles are often referred to as Section 167 intangibles (as they are amortized under the rules of Section 167). Some Section 167 intangibles are not amortizable:

- Interests in a corporation, partnership, trust, or estate
- Interests in land

Other Section 167 intangibles are generally amortizable:

- Computer software readily available for purchase by the general public
- Interests in films, sound recordings, video recordings, and similar property
- Self-created intangible assets

Section 167 intangibles that are separately acquired are generally amortized over their remaining useful life using the straight-line method. For example, a patent could be acquired as part of the purchase of a business (Section 197 intangible) or a patent could be acquired separately (Section 167 intangible). A franchise, trademark, or trade name is treated as a Section 197 intangible whether acquired as part of a business or not.

Example Sam purchases computer software sold to the general public for $20,000. The $20,000 is a Section 167 intangible; and therefore, the amount would be amortized under regular amortization rules (typically 3 years). ♦

Amortization expense is reported on the bottom of page 2 in Part VI of Form 4562.

> **ProConnect™ Tax TIP**
> Amortization is entered into the software in the Depreciation section. Select Non-recovery/Straight-line as the depreciation method. The recovery period (e.g., 15 years for Section 197 intangibles) must be input. An amortization code is available in the detailed input screen.

> **Self-Study Problem 8.6** — Refer to Appendix E for Solutions to Self-Study Problems
>
> a. Determine whether the following items are generally amortizable over 15 years, amortized over their useful life, or not amortized.
>   1. Patent acquired as part of a business
>   2. Separately acquired film rights
>   3. Computer software sold at an office supply store
>   4. Goodwill
>   5. Franchise
>   6. Land
>   7. Trademark
>   8. Interest in a corporation
>
> b. Mary Moser from Self-Study Problem 8.2 acquires the assets of Target Company in a business acquisition for $200,000 on May 23, 2023. The assets acquired are as follows:
>
> | | |
> |---|---:|
> | Machines | $ 30,000 |
> | Building | 90,000 |
> | Land | 10,000 |
> | Customer list (2-year life) | 15,000 |
> | Patent (9-year remaining life) | 20,000 |
> | Total | $165,000 |
>
> The excess purchase price is allocated to goodwill. Mary already owned a business patent with an original 12-year life that was acquired separately at a cost of $25,000. The patent has six years of useful life remaining and is amortized under Section 167.
>
> Use the above information to calculate 2024 amortization for each intangible asset and report on Part VI of Form 4562 found on Pages 8-15 and 8-16.

8-7 Section 1231 Gains and Losses

Learning Objective 8.7

Classify gains and losses from Section 1231 assets.

The first part of this chapter dealt with the acquisition and cost recovery of business property. The remaining sections deal with the sale, exchange, or disposal of business property. The tax rules on capital gains and losses covered in Chapter 4 continue to apply here, but the tax law has been crafted in a way to provide capital treatment for certain business gains and losses and ordinary treatment for others. Unlike much of the tax law covered elsewhere in this textbook, these tax concepts often refer to the Internal Revenue Code section number as the identifying name. For example, Section 1231 is used to describe property used in a trade or business and held for more than one year. Depreciation recapture is commonly referred to as Section 1245 or Section 1250 recapture.

Section 1231 assets are not capital assets (Chapter 4), but they are given special tax treatment. Gains on Section 1231 assets may be treated as long-term capital gains, while losses in some cases may be deducted as ordinary losses. Section 1231 assets include:

1. Depreciable or real property used in a trade or business;
2. Timber, coal, or domestic iron ore;
3. Livestock (not including poultry) held for draft, breeding, dairy, or sporting purposes; and
4. Unharvested crops on land used in a trade or business.

Any property held one year or less, inventory and property held for sale to customers, and copyrights, paintings, government publications, etc., are not Section 1231 property. The calculation of net Section 1231 gains and losses is summarized as follows:

Combine *all* Section 1231 gains and losses to compute *net* Section 1231 gains or losses. If the gains exceed the losses, the excess is a long-term capital gain. When the losses exceed the gains, all gains are treated as ordinary income, and all losses are fully deductible as ordinary losses.

Example Frank Harper had the following business gains and (losses) on the sale of business property during the current year:

Sale of land held for four years	$ 9,500
Sale of truck held for three years	(2,100)
Sale of inventory	6,000

Frank's Section 1231 gains and losses would be calculated as follows:

Gain on land	$ 9,500
Loss on truck	(2,100)
Net Section 1231 gain	$ 7,400

The $7,400 net Section 1231 gain would be treated as a long-term capital gain and would be reported on Form 4797 and transferred to Line 11 of Schedule D of Form 1040. Inventory is not Section 1231 property, and thus, results in ordinary income. ♦

8-7a Section 1231 Lookback

The application of Section 1231 generally favors taxpayers in two ways: (1) net gains are characterized as long-term capital gains and enjoy preferential rates, and (2) net losses are treated as ordinary losses and less likely to be subject to limitation. To prevent taxpayers from abusing the preferred treatment under Section 1231, the tax law includes a lookback provision that requires a taxpayer that has net Section 1231 gains for the current year to recharacterize the current year gain to the extent of Section 1231 losses in the prior five years.

Example Eddie Mahoney operates a small business that started in 2021. His 1231 gains and losses through 2024 are as follows:

Year	Net Section 1231 Gain/(Loss)
2021	0
2022	(4,000)
2023	(2,000)
2024	7,000

In 2024, Eddie will look back over the prior five years and recharacterize $6,000 of the $7,000 Section 1231 gains as ordinary gains under the lookback rule. The remaining $1,000 gain will remain a Section 1231 gain. If Eddie generates a $5,000 Section 1231 gain in 2025, the gain will remain Section 1231 since no unrecharacterized Section 1231 losses exist due to the previous recharacterization in 2024. ♦

Example Roger Nelson generated the following Section 1231 gains and losses:

Year	Net Section 1231 Gain/(Loss)
2021	0
2022	4,000
2023	2,000
2024	(7,000)

In 2024, Roger will not be required to recharacterize his loss. Only Section 1231 *gains* are subject to the lookback rule. Should Roger generate Section 1231 gains through 2029, his 2024 loss would be subject to recharacterization. ♦

Self-Study Problem 8.7 Refer to Appendix E for Solutions to Self-Study Problems

Serena had the following sales of business property during the 2024 tax year:

1. On January 5, 2024, she sold land for $37,000. The original cost of the land was $24,000 when purchased on December 3, 2013. She incurred selling expenses of $500, and there was no depreciation allowable or capital improvements made to the land.
2. Sold a business computer with an adjusted basis of $20,700 that was acquired on April 5, 2023. The original cost was $53,906, and accumulated depreciation was $33,206. The computer was sold on May 2, 2024, for $14,000, resulting in a $6,700 loss.
3. Sold equipment on July 22, 2024 for gross proceeds of $16,000. The equipment was acquired on October 21, 2023 at a cost of $28,177 and accumulated depreciation was $7,477 at the time of the sale. Serena used an equipment broker on this sale and paid a sales commission of $1,600.

Calculate Serena's net gain or loss and determine the character as either capital or ordinary (ignore any depreciation recapture).

8-8 Depreciation Recapture

Learning Objective 8.8

Apply the depreciation recapture rules.

Since long-term capital gains traditionally have been taxed at a lower tax rate than ordinary income, taxpayers have attempted to maximize the amount of income treated as capital gain. Congress enacted depreciation recapture provisions to prevent taxpayers from converting ordinary income into capital gains by claiming maximum depreciation deductions over the life of the asset and then selling the asset and receiving capital gain treatment on the resulting gain at the time of the sale. There are three major depreciation recapture provisions: (1) Section 1245, which generally applies to personal property, (2) Section 1250, which applies to real estate, and (3) "unrecaptured depreciation" previously taken on real estate. The depreciation recapture provisions are extremely complex. Only a brief overview of the general provisions contained in the tax law is presented here.

8-8a Section 1245 Recapture

Under the provisions of Section 1245, any gain recognized on the disposition of a Section 1245 asset will be classified as ordinary income up to an amount equal to the depreciation claimed. Any gain in excess of depreciation taken is classified as a Section 1231 gain. Section 1245 property is:

- Depreciable tangible personal property such as furniture, machines, computers, and automobiles
- Amortizable intangible personal property such as patents, copyrights, leaseholds, and professional sports contracts
- Other tangible property (except buildings) used as an integral part of manufacturing, production or extraction
- Single purpose agricultural or horticultural structures

Section 1245 recapture potential is defined as the total depreciation claimed on Section 1245 property, and is sometimes called "full recapture." The amount of ordinary income recognized upon the sale of an asset under Section 1245 is equal to the lesser of (1) total depreciation claimed on the asset, or (2) the amount of the realized gain on the sale. Any gain recognized in excess of the amount of ordinary income is a Section 1231 gain.

Example On March 1 of the current year, Melvin sells Section 1245 property, which was purchased 4 years ago for $6,000. Melvin had claimed depreciation on the property of $2,500, and sold the property for $5,000. The recapture under Section 1245 is calculated below:

Amount realized	$5,000
Adjusted basis ($6,000 − $2,500)	3,500
Realized gain	$1,500
Total depreciation taken	$2,500

The amount of Section 1245 recapture (the gain characterized as ordinary) is $1,500, which is the lesser of the realized gain ($1,500) or the total depreciation taken ($2,500). ♦

Example Assume the same facts as in the previous example, except that the property is sold for $7,800. The recapture under Section 1245 is calculated below:

Amount realized	$7,800
Adjusted basis ($6,000 − $2,500)	3,500
Realized gain	$4,300
Total depreciation taken	$2,500

The amount of Section 1245 recapture (the gain characterized as ordinary) is $2,500, which is the lesser of the realized gain ($4,300) or the total depreciation taken ($2,500). The residual gain of $1,800 ($4,300 − $2,500) is a Section 1231 gain. ♦

Example Assume the same facts as in the previous example, except that the property is sold for $2,800. Because the property is sold at a loss of $700 ($2,800 − $3,500), Section 1245 recapture does not apply and the loss is treated as a Section 1231 loss. ♦

8-8b Section 1250 Recapture

Section 1250 applies to the gain on the sale of depreciable real property, other than real property included in the definition of Section 1245 property. The amount of Section 1250 recapture potential is equal to the excess of depreciation expense claimed over the life of the asset under an *accelerated* method of depreciation over the amount of depreciation that would have been allowed if the straight-line method of depreciation had been used, and is sometimes known as partial recapture. If property is depreciated using the straight-line method, there is no Section 1250 recapture potential. Since the use of the straight-line method is required for real property acquired after 1986, there will be no Section 1250 recapture on the disposition of such property. In practice, Section 1250 recapture is rarely encountered.

8-8c "Unrecaptured Depreciation" on Real Estate—25 Percent Rate

For non-corporate taxpayers, a special 25-percent tax rate applies to real property gains attributable to depreciation previously taken and not already recaptured under the Section 1245 or Section 1250 rules covered above. Any remaining gain attributable to "unrecaptured depreciation" previously taken, including straight-line depreciation, is taxed at 25 percent rather than the long-term capital gain rate of 15 percent. When the taxpayer's ordinary tax rate is below 25 percent, the depreciation recapture will be taxed at the lower ordinary tax rate to the extent of the remaining amount in the less than 25 percent bracket and then at 25 percent. The application of the 25 percent rate for "unrecaptured depreciation" is frequently seen in practice because it applies to every rental property which is depreciated and then sold at a gain. If the 3.8 percent net investment income tax covered in Chapter 6 applies, the 25 percent rate will be increased to 28.8 percent and the 15 percent rate will be increased to 18.8 percent.

Example Lew, an individual taxpayer, acquired an apartment building in 2014 for $300,000, and sells it in October 2024 for $500,000. The accumulated straight-line depreciation on the building at the time of the sale is $109,000. Lew is in the 35-percent tax bracket for ordinary income. Lew's gain on the sale of the property is $309,000 ($500,000 less adjusted basis of $191,000). Note that $109,000 of the gain is attributable to unrecaptured depreciation and is taxed at 25 percent, while the remaining $200,000 gain is taxed at the 15-percent long-term capital gains rate. Lew may also be subject to the 3.8 percent net investment income tax which is covered in Chapter 6. ♦

The reporting of unrecaptured depreciation on 1250 property gains subject to the 25-percent rate is considerably complex. The amounts from the Form 4797 are reported on Schedule D and the use of the Unrecaptured Section 1250 Gain Worksheet from the Schedule D instructions is also suggested. Amounts from this worksheet are transferred to the Schedule D Tax worksheet (also part of the Schedule D instructions) which is similar to the Qualified Dividends and Capital Gain Tax Worksheet used in earlier chapters of this textbook.

8-8d Section 291 Recapture for Corporations

The tax rules associated with unrecaptured Section 1250 gains are different for corporate taxpayers. Under Section 291, corporations are required to recharacterize 20 percent of unrecaptured depreciation as ordinary and the remaining gain is treated as Section 1231 gain. Losses are not subject to Section 291 recapture.

Example Lewis Corporation acquired an apartment building in 2014 for $300,000, and sells the building in October 2024 for $500,000. The accumulated straight-line depreciation on the building at the time of the sale is $109,000. Lewis Corporation's gain on the sale of the property is $309,000 ($500,000 less adjusted basis of $191,000). Twenty percent of the amount of unrecaptured depreciation ($21,800 = $109,000 × 20%) of the gain will be characterized as ordinary and the remaining $287,200 will remain Section 1231 gain. ♦

Self-Study Problem 8.8   Refer to Appendix E for Solutions to Self-Study Problems

The following information is from Self-Study Problem 8.7:

Serena, an individual taxpayer, had the following sales of business property during the 2024 tax year:

1. On January 5, 2024, she sold land for $37,000. The original cost of the land was $24,000 when purchased on December 3, 2013. She incurred selling expenses of $500, and there was no depreciation allowable or capital improvements made to the asset.

2. Sold a business computer with an adjusted basis of $20,700 that was acquired on April 5, 2023. The original cost was $53,906, and accumulated depreciation was $33,206. The computer was sold on May 2, 2024, for $14,000, resulting in a $6,700 loss.

3. Sold equipment on July 22, 2024, for gross proceeds of $16,000. The equipment was acquired on October 21, 2023, at a cost of $28,177 and accumulated depreciation was $7,477 at the time of the sale. Serena used an equipment broker on this sale and paid a sales commission of $1,600.

Add this new information:

4. Sold a building on October 7, 2024, for $340,000, net of sales commissions of $15,000. Serena acquired the building on December 3, 2013, at a cost of $320,000. Accumulated depreciation has been computed using the straight-line method since acquisition and totaled $126,050 at the time of the sale.

5. Sold furniture on October 7, 2024, for $7,600. The furniture was acquired on December 3, 2013, for $15,000 and accumulated depreciation was $15,000 at the time of the sale.

Serena's employer identification number is 74-8976432. Use Form 4797 on Pages 8-30 and 8-31 to report the above gains and losses (hint: do **not** ignore depreciation recapture and complete Part III first).

ProConnect™ Tax TIP

The sale of business property is entered on the Sale of Asset 4797/6252 screens under deductions.

8-9 Business Casualty Gains and Losses

8.9 Learning Objective
Apply the general treatment of casualty gains and losses for business purposes.

The treatment of casualty gains and losses differs depending on whether the property involved is held for personal use or held for business or investment purposes. Therefore, a taxpayer's business and investment casualty gains and losses are computed separately from personal casualty gains and losses. Deductions for personal casualty losses are restricted to those associated with a federally-declared disaster area. Since the casualty loss is an itemized deduction, the rules for personal casualties are covered in Chapter 5.

The Ninth Circuit Court decided that a man's payment to a woman to keep her from revealing their extramarital affair was not a deductible casualty loss.

Self-Study Problem 8.8

Form 4797 — Sales of Business Property
(Also Involuntary Conversions and Recapture Amounts Under Sections 179 and 280F(b)(2))

OMB No. 1545-0184

2024

Department of the Treasury
Internal Revenue Service

Attach to your tax return.
Go to www.irs.gov/Form4797 for instructions and the latest information.

Attachment Sequence No. **27**

Name(s) shown on return | Identifying number

1a Enter the gross proceeds from sales or exchanges reported to you for 2024 on Form(s) 1099-B or 1099-S (or substitute statement) that you are including on line 2, 10, or 20. See instructions **1a**

b Enter the total amount of gain that you are including on lines 2, 10, and 24 due to the partial dispositions of MACRS assets **1b**

c Enter the total amount of loss that you are including on lines 2 and 10 due to the partial dispositions of MACRS assets **1c**

Part I — Sales or Exchanges of Property Used in a Trade or Business and Involuntary Conversions From Other Than Casualty or Theft—Most Property Held More Than 1 Year (see instructions)

2	(a) Description of property	(b) Date acquired (mo., day, yr.)	(c) Date sold (mo., day, yr.)	(d) Gross sales price	(e) Depreciation allowed or allowable since acquisition	(f) Cost or other basis, plus improvements and expense of sale	(g) Gain or (loss) Subtract (f) from the sum of (d) and (e)

3 Gain, if any, from Form 4684, line 39 . . . . **3**

4 Section 1231 gain from installment sales from Form 6252, line 26 or 37 . . . . **4**

5 Section 1231 gain or (loss) from like-kind exchanges from Form 8824 . . . . **5**

6 Gain, if any, from line 32, from other than casualty or theft **6**

7 Combine lines 2 through 6. Enter the gain or (loss) here and on the appropriate line as follows . **7**

Partnerships and S corporations. Report the gain or (loss) following the instructions for Form 1065, Schedule K, line 10, or Form 1120-S, Schedule K, line 9. Skip lines 8, 9, 11, and 12 below.

Individuals, partners, S corporation shareholders, and all others. If line 7 is zero or a loss, enter the amount from line 7 on line 11 below and skip lines 8 and 9. If line 7 is a gain and you didn't have any prior year section 1231 losses, or they were recaptured in an earlier year, enter the gain from line 7 as a long-term capital gain on the Schedule D filed with your return and skip lines 8, 9, 11, and 12 below.

8 Nonrecaptured net section 1231 losses from prior years. See instructions **8**

9 Subtract line 8 from line 7. If zero or less, enter -0-. If line 9 is zero, enter the gain from line 7 on line 12 below. If line 9 is more than zero, enter the amount from line 8 on line 12 below and enter the gain from line 9 as a long-term capital gain on the Schedule D filed with your return. See instructions **9**

Part II Ordinary Gains and Losses (see instructions)

10 Ordinary gains and losses not included on lines 11 through 16 (include property held 1 year or less):

11 Loss, if any, from line 7 . . . . **11** ( )

12 Gain, if any, from line 7 or amount from line 8, if applicable **12**

13 Gain, if any, from line 31 . . . . **13**

14 Net gain or (loss) from Form 4684, lines 31 and 38a **14**

15 Ordinary gain from installment sales from Form 6252, line 25 or 36 . . . . **15**

16 Ordinary gain or (loss) from like-kind exchanges from Form 8824 . . . . **16**

17 Combine lines 10 through 16 . . . . **17**

18 For all except individual returns, enter the amount from line 17 on the appropriate line of your return and skip lines a and b below. For individual returns, complete lines a and b below.

a If the loss on line 11 includes a loss from Form 4684, line 35, column (b)(ii), enter that part of the loss here. Enter the loss from income-producing property on Schedule A (Form 1040), line 16. (Do not include any loss on property used as an employee.) Identify as from "Form 4797, line 18a." See instructions **18a**

b Redetermine the gain or (loss) on line 17 excluding the loss, if any, on line 18a. Enter here and on Schedule 1 (Form 1040), Part I, line 4 . . . . **18b**

For Paperwork Reduction Act Notice, see separate instructions. Cat. No. 13086I Form **4797** (2024)

Form 4797 (2024) Page **2**

Part III Gain From Disposition of Property Under Sections 1245, 1250, 1252, 1254, and 1255 (see instructions)

19	(a) Description of section 1245, 1250, 1252, 1254, or 1255 property:	(b) Date acquired (mo., day, yr.)	(c) Date sold (mo., day, yr.)
A			
B			
C			
D			

	These columns relate to the properties on lines 19A through 19D.		Property A	Property B	Property C	Property D
20	Gross sales price (**Note:** *See line 1a before completing.*)	20				
21	Cost or other basis plus expense of sale	21				
22	Depreciation (or depletion) allowed or allowable	22				
23	Adjusted basis. Subtract line 22 from line 21	23				
24	Total gain. Subtract line 23 from line 20	24				
25	**If section 1245 property:**					
a	Depreciation allowed or allowable from line 22	25a				
b	Enter the **smaller** of line 24 or 25a	25b				
26	**If section 1250 property:** If straight line depreciation was used, enter -0- on line 26g, except for a corporation subject to section 291.					
a	Additional depreciation after 1975. See instructions	26a				
b	Applicable percentage multiplied by the **smaller** of line 24 or line 26a. See instructions	26b				
c	Subtract line 26a from line 24. If residential rental property **or** line 24 isn't more than line 26a, skip lines 26d and 26e	26c				
d	Additional depreciation after 1969 and before 1976	26d				
e	Enter the **smaller** of line 26c or 26d	26e				
f	Section 291 amount (corporations only)	26f				
g	Add lines 26b, 26e, and 26f	26g				
27	**If section 1252 property:** Skip this section if you didn't dispose of farmland or if this form is being completed for a partnership.					
a	Soil, water, and land clearing expenses	27a				
b	Line 27a multiplied by applicable percentage. See instructions	27b				
c	Enter the **smaller** of line 24 or 27b	27c				
28	**If section 1254 property:**					
a	Intangible drilling and development costs, expenditures for development of mines and other natural deposits, mining exploration costs, and depletion. See instructions	28a				
b	Enter the **smaller** of line 24 or 28a	28b				
29	**If section 1255 property:**					
a	Applicable percentage of payments excluded from income under section 126. See instructions	29a				
b	Enter the **smaller** of line 24 or 29a. See instructions	29b				

Summary of Part III Gains. Complete property columns A through D through line 29b before going to line 30.

30	Total gains for all properties. Add property columns A through D, line 24	30	
31	Add property columns A through D, lines 25b, 26g, 27c, 28b, and 29b. Enter here and on line 13	31	
32	Subtract line 31 from line 30. Enter the portion from casualty or theft on Form 4684, line 33. Enter the portion from other than casualty or theft on Form 4797, line 6	32	

Part IV Recapture Amounts Under Sections 179 and 280F(b)(2) When Business Use Drops to 50% or Less (see instructions)

			(a) Section 179	(b) Section 280F(b)(2)
33	Section 179 expense deduction or depreciation allowable in prior years	33		
34	Recomputed depreciation. See instructions	34		
35	Recapture amount. Subtract line 34 from line 33. See the instructions for where to report	35		

Form **4797** (2024)

The amount of a business casualty or loss depends on whether the property was completely or partially destroyed. If business property is completely destroyed, the loss is the adjusted basis of the property less any insurance reimbursement. If business property is partially destroyed, the loss is calculated as the amount of insurance proceeds reduced by the lesser of (1) the adjusted basis of the property at the time of the casualty, or (2) the decrease in the property's fair market value (FMV) as a result of the casualty event.

Example Joan's business suffered two casualties in the current year. Theft 1: One of Joan's employees stole a business vehicle and ended up abandoning the vehicle. The car was vandalized and damaged. The adjusted basis of the car was $14,000 at the time of the theft and the car was repairable but decreased in value $7,000 because of the damage. Theft 2: A car owned by Joan's business was stolen. The thief was involved in a traffic accident and the car was totally destroyed. The basis of the car was $7,600 at the time of the theft and had a fair market value of $5,000 before the crash. Joan's insurance company reimbursed her $6,000 for the first theft and $4,000 for the second. Theft 1 is a partial destruction and the lesser of the decrease in market value or the adjusted basis is used to compute the loss. Theft 2 is a complete destruction and so the adjusted basis is used to compute the loss.

	Theft 1 Partial Destruction	Theft 2 Complete Destruction
Insurance proceeds	$ 6,000	$ 4,000
Adjusted basis	14,000	7,600
Decrease in FMV	7,000	n/a
Loss	$(1,000)	$(3,600)

Business and investment property must be identified as a capital asset, trade or business property subject to an allowance for depreciation, or ordinary income property. The following rules apply to the treatment of business or investment property:

1. Property held for one year or less—gains from trade or business property (including property used in the production of rental or royalty income) and gains from investment property are netted against losses from trade or business property, and the resulting net gain or loss is treated as ordinary income or loss. Losses from investment property are considered separately.
2. Property held more than one year—gains and losses from trade or business property and investment property are netted.
   a. Net gain—if the result is a net gain, the net gain is included in the calculation of the net Section 1231 gain or loss (the gains and losses are treated as Section 1231 gains and losses).
   b. Net loss—if the result is a net loss, the gains and losses from business and investment property are excluded from Section 1231 treatment.

The tax treatment of the gains and losses depends on whether the property was used in the taxpayer's trade or business or held for investment. Gains and losses from business-use assets are treated as ordinary income and ordinary losses, respectively.

If the taxpayer recognizes a gain as a result of a casualty, and the property involved is depreciable property, the depreciation recapture provisions may cause all or a part of the gain to be treated as ordinary income. A casualty involving business property is included in the definition of an involuntary conversion, so that gain realized may be eligible for deferral under the special involuntary conversion provisions covered in LO 8.12 of this chapter.

The interaction of Section 1231 and casualty gains and losses from business or investment property is complex. Taxpayers should follow the instructions included with Form 4684 and Form 4797. Refer to the IRS website (**www.irs.gov**) for samples of these forms and instructions.

Example Two pieces of manufacturing equipment used by Robert in his business are completely destroyed by fire. One of the pieces of equipment had an adjusted basis of $5,000 ($11,000 original basis less $6,000 accumulated depreciation) and a fair market value of $3,000 on the date of the fire. The other piece of equipment had an adjusted basis of $7,000 ($18,000 original basis less $11,000 of accumulated depreciation) and a fair market value of $10,000. Robert receives $3,000 from his insurance company to compensate him for the loss of the first piece of equipment, and he receives $8,000 for the second piece of equipment. As a result of the casualty, Robert's casualty gain or loss is calculated as follows:

	Item 1	Item 2
Insurance proceeds	$ 3,000	$ 8,000
Adjusted basis of property	(5,000)	(7,000)
(Loss) gain	$(2,000)	$ 1,000

The netting of the business casualty gains and losses results in a net loss of $1,000; thus, the gains and losses are excluded from Section 1231 treatment. Since the loss on Item 1 represents a loss arising from an asset used in the taxpayer's business (not an asset held for investment), the loss is considered an ordinary loss. The $1,000 gain from Item 2 is treated as ordinary income under Section 1245 recapture. ◆

Self-Study Problem 8.9 Refer to Appendix E for Solutions to Self-Study Problems

Jonathan has the following separate casualties during the year:

	Decrease in Fair Market Value	Adjusted Basis	Insurance Reimbursement	Holding Period
Business furniture	$ 4,000	$ 5,000	$ 0	3 years
Business machinery	15,000	14,000	10,000	3 years

The furniture was completely destroyed while the machinery was partially destroyed. Jonathan also sold business land for a Section 1231 gain of $10,000. Calculate the amount and nature of Jonathan's gains and losses as a result of these casualties.

8-10 Installment Sales

8.10 Learning Objective

Compute the gain on installment sales.

Some taxpayers sell property and do not receive payment immediately. Instead, they take a note from the purchaser and receive payments over an extended period of time. Requiring those taxpayers to pay tax on all of the gain on the sale of the property in the year of sale when they may not have received enough cash to cover the taxes could create financial hardship. To provide equity in such situations, Congress passed the installment sale provision. The installment sale provision allows taxpayers to spread the gain (but not a loss) over the tax years in which payments are received. On an installment sale, the taxable gain reported each year is determined as follows:

$$\text{Taxable gain} = \frac{\text{Total gain realized on the sale}}{\text{Contract price}} \times \text{Cash collections during the year}$$

Taxpayers who receive payments over a period of time automatically report gain on the installment method, unless they elect to report all the gain in the year of the sale. An election to report all the gain in the year of sale is made by including all the gain in income for the year of the sale. Taxpayers use Form 6252, Installment Sale Income, to report the installment sale gain on their income tax returns.

Example Arella sells land with an adjusted basis of $20,000 for $50,000. She receives $10,000 in the year of sale, and the balance is payable at $8,000 per year for five years, plus a reasonable amount of interest. If Arella elects not to report under the installment method, the gain in the year of sale would be calculated in the following manner:

Cash	$ 10,000
Note at fair market value	40,000
Amount realized	50,000
Less: the land's basis	(20,000)
Taxable gain	$ 30,000

♦

Example If instead, Arella reports the gain on the installment method, the amount of the taxable gain in the year of sale is $6,000, which is calculated below.

$$\text{Taxable gain} = \frac{\text{Total gain}}{\text{Contract price}} \times \text{Cash collections}$$

$$\text{Taxable gain} = \frac{\$30,000}{\$50,000} \times \$10,000 = \$6,000$$

If $8,000 is collected in the first year after the year of sale, the gain in that year would be $4,800, as illustrated below.

$$\text{Taxable gain} = \frac{\$30,000}{\$50,000} \times \$8,000 = \$4,800$$

Of course, any interest income received on the note is also included in income as portfolio income. ♦

Complex installment sale rules apply to taxpayers who regularly sell real or personal property and to taxpayers who sell certain business or rental real property. For example, any recapture under Section 1245 or Section 1250 must be reported in full in the year of sale, regardless of the taxpayer's use of the installment method. Any remaining gain may be reported under the installment method. Typically, any unrecaptured Section 1250 gain (taxed at 25 percent) is recognized first under the installment method before any typical long-term capital gain. In addition, certain limitations apply where there is an installment sale between related parties.

Example Morena, an individual taxpayer, sells real property for a $100,000 note payable in five equal installments. Morena's initial cost of the property was $70,000 and accumulated depreciation was $30,000 at the time of the sale (adjusted basis $40,000). Morena's realized gain is $60,000 ($100,000 less $40,000) and will be recognized ratably using a gross profit percentage of 60 percent over the next five years. If recognized immediately, $30,000 of the gain is unrecaptured Section 1250 gain and $30,000 is Section

1231 long-term capital gain. The recognition of the gain using the installment sale method is:

Year	1	2	3	4	5	Total
Payment	$20,000	$20,000	$20,000	$20,000	$20,000	$100,000
Gross profit percentage	60%	60%	60%	60%	60%	
Recognized gain	$12,000	$12,000	$12,000	$12,000	$12,000	$60,000
Unrecaptured 1250 gain	$12,000	$12,000	$6,000			$30,000
1231 gain	0	0	6,000	$12,000	$12,000	30,000

The installment method requires that payments be received in a tax year after the year of sale. In a recent decision (*Merchia v. United States IRS*, 565 F. Supp. 3d 26), the court held that the promissory note used to establish the future payment did not provide for any dates for future payments, and therefore, was considered a demand note under applicable state law. Since demand notes are not eligible for installment sale treatment, the entire gain was recognized in the year of sale.

8-10a The Contract Price

The contract price used in calculating the taxable gain is the amount the seller will ultimately collect from the purchaser (other than interest). This amount is usually the sale price of the property. However, the purchaser will occasionally assume the seller's liability on the property, in which case the contract price is computed by subtracting from the selling price any mortgage or notes assumed by the buyer. If the mortgage or notes assumed by the buyer exceed the adjusted basis of the property, the excess is treated as a cash payment received in the year of sale and must be included in the contract price.

Example Floro receives the following for an installment sale of real estate:

Cash	$ 3,000
Floro mortgage assumed by the purchaser	9,000
Note payable to Floro from the purchaser	39,000
Selling price (not including $1,500 of selling expenses)	$51,000

Floro's total gain is computed as follows:

Selling price	$51,000
Less: selling expenses	(1,500)
Amount realized	49,500
Less: Floro's basis in the property	(30,000)
Total gain	$19,500

The contract price is $42,000 ($51,000 − $9,000), and assuming the $3,000 is the only cash received in the year of sale, the taxable gain in the year of sale is $1,393 as shown below:

$$\text{Taxable gain} = \frac{\$19,500}{\$42,000} \times \$3,000 = \$1,393$$

Self-Study Problem 8.10 *Refer to Appendix E for Solutions to Self-Study Problems*

Marius acquired a rental house on January 1, 2008, for a cost of $82,000. Straight-line depreciation on the property of $26,000 has been claimed by Marius. On January 15, 2024, he sells the property for $124,000, receiving $10,000 cash, the buyer's assumption of the remaining $14,000 mortgage on the house, and a note from the buyer for $100,000 at 10-percent interest. The note is payable at $10,000 per year for 10 years, with the first payment to be received one year after the date of sale. Use Form 6252 on Page 8-37 to calculate his taxable gain under the installment method for the year of sale of the rental house. Preparation of Form 4797 is not required.

8-11 Like-Kind Exchanges

Learning Objective 8.11
Calculate recognized and deferred gains on like-kind exchanges.

Although a taxpayer *realizes* a gain or loss on the sale or exchange of property, the *recognition* of the gain or loss may be deferred for tax purposes, such as an installment sale. Another example of such a situation arises when a taxpayer exchanges real property for other real property of a like kind. Under certain circumstances, the transaction may be nontaxable. To qualify as a nontaxable exchange, the property exchanged must be real property, held for productive use in a trade or business, or held for investment. Exchanges of personal or intangible property used in a business or for investment such as machines, cars, trucks, patents, furniture, etc., do not qualify as like-kind. Property held for personal purposes, such as a taxpayer's residence, also does not qualify for a like-kind exchange.

Example Bronny enters into two exchanges during the tax year. In the first exchange, Bronny exchanges his personal use auto for a different auto of the same make and model, but a different year. This exchange does not qualify for like-kind treatment because the property is not held for trade or business or investment and also is not real property. The second exchange involves Bronny giving up five acres of undeveloped land for a one-quarter acre parcel of undeveloped beach front property. Bronny holds the land for investment purposes. The second exchange qualifies for like-kind treatment. ♦

When the exchange involves only qualified like-kind property, no gain or loss is recognized. However, some exchanges include cash or other property in addition to the like-kind property. Even when the exchange is not solely for like-kind assets, the nontaxable treatment usually is not completely lost. Gain is recognized in an amount equal to the lesser of (1) the gain realized or (2) the "boot" received. Boot is money or the fair market value of other property received in addition to the like-kind property. Relief from a liability is treated as boot.

The basis of other property received as boot in an exchange is its fair market value on the date of the exchange. The basis of the like-kind property received is:

> The basis of the like-kind property given up
> + Any boot paid
> − Any boot received
> + Any gain recognized
> = Basis of property received

The holding period for property acquired in a like-kind exchange includes the holding period of the property exchanged. For example, if long-term capital gain property is exchanged today, the new property may be sold immediately, and the gain recognized would be long-term capital gain.

Taxpayers must file Form 8824, Like-Kind Exchanges, to report the exchange of property. This form must be completed even if no gain is recognized.

Self-Study Problem 8.10

Form 6252
Department of the Treasury
Internal Revenue Service

Installment Sale Income
Attach to your tax return.
Use a separate form for each sale or other disposition of property on the installment method.
Go to www.irs.gov/Form6252 for the latest information.

OMB No. 1545-0228

2024
Attachment Sequence No. 67

Name(s) shown on return _____ Identifying number _____

1	Description of property _____
2a	Date acquired (mm/dd/yyyy) _____ **b** Date sold (mm/dd/yyyy) _____
3	Was the property sold to a related party? See instructions. If "Yes," complete Part III for the year of sale and 2 years after the year of the sale unless you received the final payment during the tax year . . . . . ☐ Yes ☐ No
4	Can the total selling price be determined by the close of the tax year in which such sale or other disposition occurs? ☐ Yes ☐ No

Part I — Gross Profit and Contract Price. Complete this part for all years of the installment agreement.

5	Selling price including mortgages and other debts. **Don't** include interest, whether stated or unstated	5	
6	Mortgages, debts, and other liabilities the buyer assumed or took the property subject to (see instructions)	6	
7	Subtract line 6 from line 5	7	
8	Cost or other basis of property sold	8	
9	Depreciation allowed or allowable	9	
10	Adjusted basis. Subtract line 9 from line 8	10	
11	Commissions and other expenses of sale	11	
12	Income recapture from Form 4797, Part III (see instructions)	12	
13	Add lines 10, 11, and 12	13	
14	Subtract line 13 from line 5. If zero or less, **don't** complete the rest of this form. See instructions	14	
15	If the property described on line 1 above was your main home, enter the amount of your excluded gain. See instructions. Otherwise, enter -0-	15	
16	**Gross profit.** Subtract line 15 from line 14	16	
17	Subtract line 13 from line 6. If zero or less, enter -0-	17	
18	**Contract price.** Add line 7 and line 17	18	

Part II — Installment Sale Income. Complete this part for all years of the installment agreement.

19	Gross profit percentage (expressed as a decimal amount). Divide line 16 by line 18. (For years after the year of sale, see instructions.)	19	
20	If this is the year of sale, enter the amount from line 17. Otherwise, enter -0-	20	
21	Payments received during year (see instructions). **Don't** include interest, whether stated or unstated	21	
22	Add lines 20 and 21	22	
23	Payments received in prior years (see instructions). **Don't** include interest, whether stated or unstated	23	
24	**Installment sale income.** Multiply line 22 by line 19. This amount cannot be zero or less. See instructions	24	
25	Enter the part of line 24 that is ordinary income under the recapture rules. See instructions	25	
26	Subtract line 25 from line 24. Enter here and on Schedule D or Form 4797. See instructions	26	

Part III — Related Party Installment Sale Income. Don't complete if you received the final payment this tax year.

27	Name, address, and taxpayer identifying number of related party _____
28	Did the related party resell or dispose of the property ("second disposition") during this tax year? . . . ☐ Yes ☐ No
29	If the answer to question 28 is "Yes," complete lines 30 through 37 below unless one of the following conditions is met. Check the box that applies.
a	☐ The second disposition was more than 2 years after the first disposition (other than dispositions of marketable securities). If this box is checked, enter the date of disposition (mm/dd/yyyy) _____
b	☐ The first disposition was a sale or exchange of stock to the issuing corporation.
c	☐ The second disposition was an involuntary conversion and the threat of conversion occurred after the first disposition.
d	☐ The second disposition occurred after the death of the original seller or buyer.
e	☐ It can be established to the satisfaction of the IRS that tax avoidance wasn't a principal purpose for either of the dispositions. If this box is checked, attach an explanation. See instructions.

30	Selling price of property sold by related party (see instructions)	30	
31	Enter contract price from line 18 for year of first sale	31	
32	Enter the **smaller** of line 30 or line 31	32	
33	Total payments received by the end of this tax year (see instructions)	33	
34	Subtract line 33 from line 32. If zero or less, enter -0-	34	
35	Multiply line 34 by the gross profit percentage on line 19 for year of first sale	35	
36	Enter the part of line 35 that is ordinary income under the recapture rules. See instructions	36	
37	Subtract line 36 from line 35. Enter here and on Schedule D or Form 4797. See instructions	37	

For Paperwork Reduction Act Notice, see page 4. Cat. No. 13601R Form **6252** (2024)

Example Janis and Kevin exchange real estate held as an investment. Janis gives up property with an adjusted basis of $350,000 and a fair market value of $560,000. The property is subject to a mortgage of $105,000 which is assumed by Kevin. In return for this property, Janis receives from Kevin land with a fair market value of $420,000 and cash of $35,000. Kevin's adjusted basis in the property he exchanges is $280,000.

1. Janis recognizes a gain of $140,000, equal to the lesser of the gain realized or the boot received as calculated below.

    Calculation of gain realized:
Fair market value of property received	$ 420,000
Cash received	35,000
Liability assumed by Kevin	105,000
Total amount realized	$ 560,000
Less: the adjusted basis of the property given up	(350,000)
Gain realized	$ 210,000

    Calculation of boot received:
Cash received	$ 35,000
Liability assumed by Kevin	105,000
Total boot received	$ 140,000
Gain recognized: Lesser of gain realized or boot received	$ 140,000

2. The basis of Janis's property is calculated below.

Basis of the property given up	$ 350,000
+ Boot paid	0
− Boot received	(140,000)
+ Gain recognized	140,000
Basis of the like-kind property received	$ 350,000

3. Kevin's recognized gain is equal to the lesser of the gain realized or the boot received. Since he received no boot, the recognized gain is zero.

    Calculation of gain realized:
Fair market value of the property received	$ 560,000
Less: boot paid ($105,000 + $35,000)	(140,000)
Less: adjusted basis of property given up	(280,000)
Gain realized	$ 140,000
Boot received	$ 0
Gain recognized (lesser of gain or boot received)	$ 0

4. The basis of Kevin's new property is calculated below.

Basis of the property given up	$ 280,000
+ Boot paid	140,000
− Boot received	0
+ Gain recognized	0
Basis of the property received	$ 420,000

◆

8-11a Like-Kind Property

The term "like-kind property" does not include inventory, stocks, bonds, or other securities or any personal property such as equipment, cars, trucks, machines, and furniture. Real property is more or less considered to be like-kind with any other real property so long as the original property and the new property are both used in a trade or business or held for investment.

> **Tax Break**
>
> Prior to 2018, the definition of like-kind included certain types of personal property, including automobiles. Because autos generally lose value over time, the trade-in of an auto by a business almost always resulted in a loss that could not be deducted under the like-kind exchange rules. Now that personal property is not eligible for like-kind treatment, the loss has a much greater chance of being deductible.

Self-Study Problem 8.11 *Refer to Appendix E for Solutions to Self-Study Problems*

Ervin James exchanges land used in his business for a new parcel of land. Ervin's basis in the land acquired on February 14, 2017, is $20,000, and the land is subject to a mortgage of $8,000, which is assumed by the other party to the exchange. Ervin receives new land worth $24,000. The exchange agreement and delivery of the title to the land both took place on May 12, 2024. Use Part I and Part III only of Form 8824 on Pages 8-41 and 8-42 to calculate Ervin's recognized gain on the exchange and his basis in the new land.

8-12 Involuntary Conversions

8.12 Learning Objective
Calculate recognized and deferred gains on involuntary conversions.

Occasionally, taxpayers are forced to dispose of property as a result of circumstances beyond their control. At the election of the taxpayer, and provided certain conditions are met, the gain on an involuntary conversion of property may be deferred. The provisions require that the property must be replaced and the basis of the replacement property reduced by the amount of the gain deferred. An involuntary conversion is defined as the destruction of the taxpayer's property in whole or in part, or loss of the property by theft, seizure, requisition, or condemnation. Also, property sold pursuant to reclamation laws, and livestock destroyed by disease or drought, are subject to the involuntary conversion rules. To qualify for nonrecognition of gain, the taxpayer must obtain qualified replacement property. The replacement property must be "similar or related in service or use." This definition is narrower than the like-kind rule; in most cases, the property must be very similar to the property converted. Generally, a taxpayer has two years after the close of the tax year in which a gain was realized to obtain replacement property.

A realized gain on the involuntary conversion of property occurs when the taxpayer receives insurance proceeds or other payments in excess of their adjusted basis in the converted property. Taxpayers need not recognize any gain if they completely reinvest the proceeds or payments in qualified replacement property within the required time period. If they do not reinvest the total amount of the payments received, they must recognize a gain equal to the amount of the payment not reinvested (but limited to the gain realized). The basis of the replacement property is equal to the cost of the replacement property reduced by any gain not recognized on the transaction. The holding period of the replacement property includes the period the original property was held.

Example Tammy's office building, which has an adjusted basis of $600,000, is destroyed by fire in 2024. In the same year, Tammy receives $700,000 of insurance proceeds for the loss. She has until December 31, 2026, (two years after the end of the taxable year in which the gain is realized), to acquire a replacement building. In 2025, Tammy replaces the building with a new building that cost $680,000. Her realized gain on the involuntary conversion is $100,000 ($700,000 − $600,000), and the gain recognized is $20,000, which is the $700,000 of cash received less the amount reinvested ($680,000). The basis of the new building is $600,000 ($680,000 − $80,000), the cost of the new building less the portion of the gain not recognized. ♦

The involuntary conversion provision applies only to gains, not to losses. The provision must be elected by the taxpayer. In contrast, the like-kind exchange provision covered previously applies to both gains and losses and is not elective.

Self-Study Problem 8.12 Refer to Appendix E for Solutions to Self-Study Problems

Sam's store is destroyed in 2024 as a result of a flood. The store has an adjusted basis of $70,000, and Sam receives insurance proceeds of $150,000 on the loss. Sam invests $135,000 in a replacement store in 2025. Calculate Sam's recognized gain, assuming an election under the involuntary conversion provision is made. Calculate Sam's basis in the replacement store.

Self-Study Problem 8.11

Form 8824
Department of the Treasury
Internal Revenue Service

Like-Kind Exchanges
(and section 1043 conflict-of-interest sales)
Attach to your tax return.
Go to *www.irs.gov/Form8824* for instructions and the latest information.

OMB No. 1545-1190

2024

Attachment Sequence No. **109**

Name(s) shown on tax return | Identifying number

Part I — Information on the Like-Kind Exchange

Note: Only real property should be described on lines 1 and 2. If the property described on line 1 or line 2 is real property located outside the United States, indicate the country.

1. Description of like-kind property given up:
   _____
   _____

2. Description of like-kind property received:
   _____
   _____

3. Date like-kind property given up was originally acquired (month, day, year) . . . . **3** MM/DD/YYYY

4. Date you actually transferred your property to the other party (month, day, year) . . . . . . **4** MM/DD/YYYY

5. Date like-kind property you received was identified by written notice to another party (month, day, year). See instructions for 45-day written identification requirement . . . . **5** MM/DD/YYYY

6. Date you actually received the like-kind property from other party (month, day, year). See instructions **6** MM/DD/YYYY

7. Was the exchange of the property given up or received made with a related party, either directly or indirectly (such as through an intermediary)? See instructions. If "Yes," complete Part II. If "No," go to Part III . . ☐ Yes ☐ No

Note: Do not file this form if a related party sold property into the exchange, directly or indirectly (such as through an intermediary); that property became your replacement property; and none of the exceptions on line 11 applies to the exchange. Instead, report the disposition of the property as if the exchange had been a sale. If one of the exceptions on line 11 applies to the exchange, complete Part II.

Part II — Related Party Exchange Information

8. Name of related party | Relationship to you | Related party's identifying number

   Address (no., street, and apt., room, or suite no.; city or town; state; and ZIP code)

9. During this tax year (and before the date that is 2 years after the last transfer of property that was part of the exchange), did the related party sell or dispose of any part of the like-kind property received from you (or an intermediary) in the exchange? . . . . ☐ Yes ☐ No

10. During this tax year (and before the date that is 2 years after the last transfer of property that was part of the exchange), did you sell or dispose of any part of the like-kind property you received? . . . . ☐ Yes ☐ No

If both lines 9 and 10 are "No" and this is the year of the exchange, go to Part III. If both lines 9 and 10 are "No" and this is **not** the year of the exchange, stop here. If either line 9 or line 10 is "Yes," complete Part III and report on this year's tax return the deferred gain or (loss) from line 24 **unless** one of the exceptions on line 11 applies.

11. If one of the exceptions below applies to the disposition, check the applicable box.

   a ☐ The disposition was after the death of either of the related parties.

   b ☐ The disposition was an involuntary conversion, and the threat of conversion occurred after the exchange.

   c ☐ You can establish to the satisfaction of the IRS that neither the exchange nor the disposition had tax avoidance as one of its principal purposes. If this box is checked, attach an explanation. See instructions.

For Paperwork Reduction Act Notice, see the instructions. Cat. No. 12311A Form **8824** (2024)

Form 8824 (2024) Page **2**

Name(s) shown on tax return. Do not enter name and social security number if shown on other side. | Your social security number

Part III — Realized Gain or (Loss), Recognized Gain, and Basis of Like-Kind Property Received

Caution: If you transferred **and** received **(a)** more than one group of like-kind properties, or **(b)** cash or other (not like-kind) property, see *Reporting of multi-asset exchanges* in the instructions.

Note: Complete lines 12 through 14 **only** if you gave up property that was not like-kind. Otherwise, go to line 15.

12   Fair market value (FMV) of other property given up. See instructions . . . . | 12 |
   a   Description of other property given up _____

13   Adjusted basis of other property given up . . . . | 13 |

14   Gain or (loss) recognized on other property given up. Subtract line 13 from line 12. Report the gain or (loss) in the same manner as if the exchange had been a sale . . . . | 14 |

   Caution: If the property given up was used previously or partly as a home, see *Property used as home* in the instructions.

15   Cash received, FMV of other property received, plus net liabilities assumed by other party, reduced (but not below zero) by any exchange expenses you incurred. See instructions . . . . . | 15 |
   a   Description of other property received _____

16   FMV of like-kind property you received . . . . | 16 |
17   Add lines 15 and 16 . . . . | 17 |
18   Adjusted basis of like-kind property you gave up, net amounts paid to other party, plus any exchange expenses **not** used on line 15. See instructions . . . . | 18 |
19   **Realized gain or (loss).** Subtract line 18 from line 17 . . . . | 19 |
20   Enter the smaller of line 15 or line 19, but not less than zero . . . . . . | 20 |
21   Ordinary income under recapture rules. Enter here and on Form 4797, line 16. See instructions | 21 |
22   Subtract line 21 from line 20. If zero or less, enter -0-. If more than zero, enter here and on Schedule D or Form 4797, unless the installment method applies. See instructions . . | 22 |
23   **Recognized gain.** Add lines 21 and 22 . . . . | 23 |
24   Deferred gain or (loss). Subtract line 23 from line 19. If a related party exchange, see instructions . . | 24 |
25   **Basis of like-kind property received.** Subtract line 15 from the sum of lines 18 and 23. See instructions

   Note: Complete lines 25a, 25b, and 25c if you received like-kind section 1250 property, like-kind section 1245 property, or like-kind intangible property in the exchange. | 25 |

   a   Basis of like-kind section 1250 property received . . . . | 25a |
   b   Basis of like-kind section 1245 property received . . . . | 25b |
   c   Basis of like-kind intangible property received . . . . | 25c |

Part IV — Deferral of Gain From Section 1043 Conflict-of-Interest Sales

Note: This part is to be used **only** by officers or employees of the executive branch of the federal government or judicial officers of the federal government (including certain spouses, minor or dependent children, and trustees as described in section 1043) for reporting nonrecognition of gain under section 1043 on the sale of property to comply with the conflict-of-interest requirements. This part can be used **only** if the cost of the replacement property is more than the basis of the divested property.

26   Enter the number from the upper right corner of your certificate of divestiture. (**Do not** attach a copy of your certificate. Keep the certificate with your records.) . . . . | —

27   Description of divested property _____

28   Description of replacement property _____

29   Date divested property was sold (month, day, year) . . . . | 29 | MM/DD/YYYY
30   Sales price of divested property. See instructions . . . . | 30 |
31   Basis of divested property . . . . | 31 |
32   **Realized gain.** Subtract line 31 from line 30 . . . . | 32 |
33   Cost of replacement property purchased within 60 days after date of sale . | 33 |
34   Subtract line 33 from line 30. If zero or less, enter -0- . . . . | 34 |
35   Ordinary income under recapture rules. Enter here and on Form 4797, line 10. See instructions . . | 35 |
36   Subtract line 35 from line 34. If zero or less, enter -0-. If more than zero, enter here and on Schedule D or Form 4797. See instructions . . . . | 36 |
37   **Deferred gain.** Subtract the sum of lines 35 and 36 from line 32 . . . . . | 37 |
38   **Basis of replacement property.** Subtract line 37 from line 33 . . . . . . | 38 |

Form **8824** (2024)

Key Terms

capitalization, 8-2
asset, 8-2
betterment, 8-2
adaptation, 8-3
restoration, 8-3
depreciation, 8-5
Modified Accelerated Cost Recovery System (MACRS), 8-6
recovery period, 8-6
asset depreciation ranges (ADRs), 8-6
half-year convention, 8-7
straight-line depreciation, 8-7
mid-quarter convention, 8-8
bonus depreciation, 8-10

qualified improvement property (QIP), 8-10
mid-month convention, 8-12
Form 4562, 8-14
Section 179, 8-17
election to expense, 8-17
listed property, 8-19
luxury automobile, 8-20
intangibles, 8-23
Section 197 intangibles, 8-23
Section 167 intangibles, 8-23
amortization, 8-23
Section 1231 assets, 8-24
Section 1231 lookback, 8-25
recharacterize, 8-25

depreciation recapture, 8-26
Section 1245 recapture, 8-26
Section 1250 recapture, 8-27
unrecaptured depreciation, 8-28
Section 291 recapture, 8-28
installment sales, 8-33
Form 6252, 8-34
like-kind exchange, 8-36
boot, 8-36
Form 8824, 8-36
like-kind property, 8-39
involuntary conversion, 8-39
qualified replacement property, 8-39

Key Points

Learning Objectives	Key Points
LO 8.1: Explain the concept of capitalization and depreciation.	• Capitalization is the process of recording an expenditure that is likely to provide benefits over a long period of time as an asset on the balance sheet rather than as an expense on the income statement. • Depreciation is the accounting process of allocating and deducting the cost of an asset over a period of years and does not necessarily mean physical deterioration or loss of value of the asset. • Land is not depreciated.
LO 8.2: Calculate depreciation expense using the MACRS tables.	• The Modified Accelerated Cost Recovery System (MACRS) allows taxpayers who invest in capital assets to write off an asset's cost over a period designated in the tax law and to use an accelerated method of depreciation for assets other than real estate. • The minimum number of years over which the cost of an asset may be deducted (the recovery period) depends on the type of property and the year in which the property was acquired. • Under MACRS, taxpayers calculate the depreciation of an asset using a table, which contains a percentage rate for each year of the property's recovery period and includes the half-year convention for personal property and mid-month convention for real property. • The mid-quarter convention must be applied if more than 40 percent of the total cost of a taxpayer's tangible property acquired during the year, other than real property, is placed in service during the last quarter of the tax year. • The bonus depreciation rules allow taxpayers purchasing new or used property with a MACRS recovery period of 20 years or less (Table 8.1), computer software, and certain leasehold improvements to directly write off 60 percent of the cost of the assets placed in service in 2024. Bonus depreciation is presumed to apply unless the taxpayer elects out of the provision. • There are no taxable income limits or thresholds associated with bonus depreciation. • For post-1986 acquired real estate, MACRS uses the straight-line method over 27.5 years for residential realty and 39 years for nonresidential realty (31.5 years for realty acquired generally before May 13, 1993).

LO 8.3: Identify when a Section 179 election to expense the cost of property may be used.	• Qualified Section 179 property is personal property (property other than real estate or assets used in residential real estate rental activities) placed in service during the year and used in a trade or business. • The maximum cost that may be expensed in the year of acquisition under Section 179 is $1,220,000 for 2024. The property may be new or used. • The $1,220,000 maximum is reduced dollar for dollar by the cost of qualifying property placed in service during the year in excess of $3,050,000. • The amount that may be expensed is limited to the taxpayer's taxable income, before considering any amount expensed under this election, from any trade or business of the taxpayer. Any excess amount resulting from the taxable income limitation may be carried forward to succeeding tax years. • Section 179 expensed amounts reduce the basis of the asset before calculating any regular MACRS depreciation on the remaining cost of the asset even when the taxpayer is unable to deduct the full amount expensed due to the taxable income limitation. • If a taxpayer elects Section 179 immediate expensing and uses bonus depreciation, the cost basis of the property is first reduced by the Section 179 deduction, then by bonus depreciation, and lastly, by typical MACRS depreciation.
LO 8.4: Apply the limitations on depreciation of "listed property."	• Special rules apply to the depreciation of listed property. • Listed property includes those types of assets which lend themselves to personal use. • Listed property includes automobiles, certain other vehicles, and property used for entertainment, recreation, or amusement. • If listed property is used 50 percent or less in a qualified business use, any depreciation deduction must be calculated using the straight-line method of depreciation over an alternate recovery period, and the special election to expense under Section 179 and bonus depreciation are not allowed.
LO 8.5: Apply the limitations on depreciation of "luxury automobiles."	• The depreciation of passenger automobiles is subject to an annual dollar limitation, commonly referred to as the luxury automobile limitation. • For automobiles acquired in 2024, the maximum depreciation is $20,400 (including $8,000 bonus) (Year 1), $19,800 (Year 2), $11,900 (Year 3), and $7,160 (Year 4 and subsequent years, until fully depreciated).
LO 8.6: Calculate the amortization of goodwill and certain other intangibles.	• Section 197 intangibles are amortized over a 15-year period, beginning with the month of acquisition. • Qualified Section 197 intangibles include goodwill, going-concern value, workforce in place, information bases, know-how, customer-based intangibles, licenses, permits, rights granted by a governmental unit, covenants not to compete, franchises, trademarks, and trade names. • Examples of Section 197 exclusions are interests in a corporation, partnership, trust, or estate; interests in land; computer software readily available for purchase by the general public; interests in films, sound recordings, and video recordings; and self-created intangible assets.
LO 8.7: Classify gains and losses from Section 1231 assets.	• Section 1231 assets include (1) depreciable or real property used in a trade or business, (2) timber, coal, or domestic iron ore, (3) livestock (not including poultry) held for draft, breeding, dairy, or sporting purposes, and (4) unharvested crops on land used in a trade or business. • If net Section 1231 gains exceed the losses, the excess is a long-term capital gain. When the net Section 1231 losses exceed the gains, all gains are treated as ordinary income, and all losses are fully deductible as ordinary losses. • The tax law includes a lookback provision that requires a taxpayer that has net Section 1231 gains for the current year to recharacterize the current year gain to the extent of Section 1231 losses in the past five years.

LO 8.8:
Apply the depreciation recapture rules.

- Depreciation recapture provisions are meant to prevent taxpayers from converting ordinary income into capital gain by claiming maximum depreciation deductions over the life of the asset and then selling the asset and receiving capital gain treatment on the resulting gain at sale.
- Under Section 1245, any gain recognized on the disposition of a Section 1245 asset (generally personal property) will be classified as ordinary income up to an amount equal to the accumulated depreciation. Any gain in excess of depreciation taken is classified as a Section 1231 gain.
- Section 1250 real property recapture is the excess of depreciation expense claimed, using an accelerated method of depreciation, over what would have been allowed if the straight-line method were used.
- Since the straight-line method is required for real property acquired after 1986, there will be no Section 1250 recapture on the disposition of real property.
- A special 25 or 28.8 percent tax rate applies to real property gains attributable to depreciation previously taken and not already recaptured under Section 1245 or Section 1250.

LO 8.9:
Apply the general treatment of casualty gains and losses for business purposes.

- The amount of a partial casualty loss from business property is insurance proceeds less the decrease in the value of the property or the adjusted basis, whichever is smaller.
- The amount of a casualty loss from a complete destruction of business property is the insurance proceeds less the adjusted basis of the property.
- Gains and losses from business-use assets are generally treated as ordinary income and ordinary losses, respectively.

LO 8.10:
Compute the gain on installment sales.

- On an installment sale, the taxable gain reported each year is determined as follows: taxable gain equals total gain realized on the sale, divided by the contract price, and multiplied by the payment received during the year.

LO 8.11:
Calculate recognized and deferred gains on like-kind exchanges.

- To qualify as a nontaxable like-kind exchange, the property exchanged must be real property, held for use in a trade or business or held for investment, and exchanged for property of a like kind.
- Personal property no longer qualifies for like-kind exchange treatment.
- Like-kind gain is recognized in an amount equal to the lesser of (1) the gain realized or (2) the "boot" received. Boot is money or the fair market value of other property received in addition to the like-kind property. Relief from a liability is the same as receiving cash and is treated as boot.
- If a transaction qualifies as a like-kind exchange, the like-kind exchange provisions must be followed.

LO 8.12:
Calculate recognized and deferred gains on involuntary conversions.

- A realized gain on the involuntary conversion of property occurs when the taxpayer receives proceeds in excess of their adjusted basis.
- Involuntary conversion gain is not recognized if the proceeds or payments are reinvested in qualified replacement property within the required time period and the taxpayer makes the proper election.

Questions and Problems

Group 1:
Multiple Choice Questions

LO 8.1 1. When a taxpayer capitalizes an expenditure:
   a. The taxpayer pays for it with debt or a liability
   b. The amount is expensed immediately in accordance with ordinary and necessary deduction rules
   c. The amount is generally placed on the balance sheet awaiting time or some future event for recognition as an expense
   d. the cost can be recovered only when the item is sold

LO 8.1 2. Which if the following is *not* generally required to be capitalized?
   a. An adaptation to a better use
   b. A betterment by expanding the size of a building
   c. A routinely performed item of maintenance
   d. A restoration of a deteriorated property

LO 8.1 3. Micah's business has four different building projects underway. Select the project that is likely to be immediately deductible.
   a. Micah is installing a new roof on a warehouse. The roof has started to leak due to its age.
   b. Micah is repainting the first-floor restrooms in the showroom. The colors did not match the furniture in the lobby.
   c. Micah is expanding the size of the inventory warehouse. The project will double the size.
   d. Micah is redesigning a machine on the factory floor that is intended to increase the speed of the machine's operation.

LO 8.1 4. Proudfoot, Inc. would like to deduct expenditures for tangible personal property under $4,000 as maintenance and repair costs. To implement this policy, which of the following is *not* required?
   a. A written policy describing a matching treatment for the company's financial statements.
   b. Proudfoot's financial statements are audited and have an accompanying opinion.
   c. Proudfoot must be a small business with gross income below $10 million.
   d. Proudfoot must also deduct expenses under $4,000 in its financial books and records.

LO 8.1 5. Potter Inc. has an accounting policy that calls for expensing items less than $5,000 that is reflected on its audited financial statements. In 2024, Potter purchases four computers at a cost of $4,000 each ($16,000 total) and also acquires two units of a unique inventory for $2,000 each ($4,000 total) that Potter does not sell by year-end. Assuming Potter is an accrual-based taxpayer for tax purposes, Potter will deduct:
   a. $0
   b. $4,000
   c. $5,000
   d. $16,000
   e. $20,000

LO 8.1

6. Hari Corp. uses two machines as part of its manufacturing process. In 2024, machine one requires new belts and a flush and fill of coolant for a cost of $6,000 as part of the machine's typical annual maintenance schedule. Machine two's electric motor fails and is replaced by a newer more energy-efficient motor at a cost of $9,000. Motors are generally expected to last eight years. As an accrual-based taxpayer, how much will Hari deduct for these two activities?
   a. $0
   b. $6,000
   c. $9,000
   d. $15,000

LO 8.2

7. Svana purchases a rental house on June 22, 2024, for a cost of $174,000. Of this amount, $100,000 is considered to be allocable to the cost of the home, with the remaining $74,000 allocable to the cost of the land. What is Svana's maximum depreciation deduction for 2024 using typical MACRS?
   a. $1,970
   b. $1,667
   c. $1,177
   d. $1,061
   e. $3,485

LO 8.2

8. An asset (not an automobile) put in service in June 2024 has a depreciable basis of $30,000 and a recovery period of five years. Assuming half-year convention, no bonus depreciation, and no election to expense is made, what is the maximum amount of cost that can be deducted in 2024?
   a. $4,800
   b. $5,000
   c. $6,000
   d. $30,000
   e. None of the above

LO 8.2

9. An asset (not an automobile) put in service in June 2024 has a depreciable basis of $30,000 and a recovery period of five years. Assuming bonus depreciation is used, half-year convention and no election to expense is made, what is the maximum amount of cost that can be deducted in 2024?
   a. $4,800
   b. $18,000
   c. $30,000
   d. $20,400
   e. $20,160

LO 8.2

10. James purchased a machine for his business. The machine has a depreciable basis of $16,000 and was put in service on June 1, 2024. James decides to elect straight-line depreciation under MACRS for the asset over the minimum number of years (five years), and does not use bonus depreciation or make the election to expense. What is the amount of his depreciation deduction for the equipment for the 2024 tax year?
    a. $9,600
    b. $14,000
    c. $1,142
    d. $1,600
    e. None of the above

LO 8.2 11. Which of the following statements with respect to the depreciation of property under MACRS is *incorrect*?
   a. Under the half-year convention, one-half year of depreciation is allowed in the year the property is placed in service.
   b. If a taxpayer elects to use the straight-line method of depreciation for property in the five-year class, all other five-year class property acquired during the year must also be depreciated using the straight-line method.
   c. In some cases, when a taxpayer places a significant amount of property in service during the last quarter of the year, real property must be depreciated using a mid-quarter convention.
   d. Real property acquired after 1986 must be depreciated using the straight-line method.
   e. The cost of property to which the MACRS rate is applied is not reduced for estimated salvage value.

LO 8.2 12. Which of the following is *true* about the MACRS depreciation system:
   a. A salvage value must be determined before depreciation percentages are applied to depreciable real estate.
   b. Residential rental buildings are depreciated over 39 years straight-line.
   c. Commercial real estate buildings are depreciated over 27.5 years straight-line.
   d. No matter when during the month depreciable real estate is purchased, it is considered to have been placed in service at mid-month for MACRS depreciation purposes.

LO 8.2 13. The bonus percentage in 2024 is:
   a. 100 percent
   b. 80 percent
   c. 60 percent
   d. 40 percent
   e. None of these

LO 8.3 14. On July 20, 2024, Kelli purchases office equipment at a cost of $24,000. Kelli elects out of bonus depreciation but makes the Section 179 election to expense for 2024. She is self-employed as an attorney, and in 2024, her business has a net income of $12,000 before considering this election to expense. What is the maximum amount that Kelli may deduct for 2024 under the election to expense, assuming she elects to expense the entire purchase?
   a. $24,000
   b. $12,000
   c. $6,000
   d. $3,000
   e. $1,000

LO 8.3 15. Which of the following is *not* considered a limit on the immediate expensing election of Section 179 in 2024?
   a. An annual limit of $1,220,000
   b. Total Section 179-eligible property acquired in excess of $3,050,000
   c. The taxable income of the taxpayer considering all income and deductions except for Section 179 immediate expensing
   d. 60 percent of personal property
   e. None of the above

LO 8.4 16. Which of the following is a *true* statement about depreciation on listed property?
   a. All listed property is not depreciable, and any costs are recovered when the property is sold.
   b. Cellphones and computers generally both meet the definition of listed property.
   c. Listed property includes school buses and tractors.
   d. If listed property is used less than 50 percent for business purposes, depreciation must be straight-line.

LO 8.4

17. Sara uses listed property 60 percent for business use in 2023 and takes MACRS depreciation (no bonus or Section 179) as permitted. In 2024, the business use of the listed property falls to 40 percent. To compute depreciation in 2024, Sara will:
    a. Continue to use the MACRS accelerated depreciation rate for the second year to depreciate the business-use portion of the property.
    b. Include the accelerated portion of 2023 depreciation in income for 2024.
    c. Elect Section 179 on the unadjusted basis of the property in 2024.
    d. Stop all depreciation deductions.

LO 8.5

18. In 2024, Haggai purchases and places in service a new auto for his business. The auto costs $67,000 and will be used 60 percent for business. Assuming the half-year convention applies and Haggai elects out of bonus depreciation and Section 179, what will be the depreciation on the auto in 2024?
    a. $11,400
    b. $8,040
    c. $7,440
    d. $6,840
    e. None of the above

LO 8.5

19. In 2024, Haggai purchases and places in service a new auto for his business. The auto costs $67,000 and will be used 100 percent for business. Assuming the half-year convention applies and Haggai does not elect out of bonus depreciation, what will be the depreciation on the auto in 2024?
    a. $67,000
    b. $20,400
    c. $13,400
    d. $20,200
    e. $40,200

LO 8.5

20. Tupper Corp. purchases a new auto in 2024 for $62,000. The auto is used 100 percent for business and the half-year convention applies. Tupper uses bonus depreciation when available. What is the *2025* depreciation for this auto?
    a. $12,400
    b. $13,312
    c. $13,376
    d. $19,200
    e. $20,200

LO 8.6

21. The amortization period for Section 197 intangibles is:
    a. 5 years
    b. 7 years
    c. 10 years
    d. 15 years
    e. 40 years

LO 8.6

22. Which of the following intangibles is defined as a Section 197 intangible asset?
    a. An interest in land
    b. A partnership interest
    c. An interest in a corporation
    d. A covenant not to compete acquired as part of a business
    e. A separately acquired sound recording

LO 8.7

23. Which of the following is Section 1231 property?
    a. Land held for investment purposes
    b. A machine used in a business
    c. Accounts receivable
    d. Inventory
    e. Paintings owned by the artist

24. Which of the following taxpayers would be subject to the Section 1231 lookback rule?
    a. Gun-Joh sold depreciable business property held for more than one year at a gain this year and had Section 1231 losses in the prior year.
    b. Tawny sold business property held for less than one year at a gain.
    c. Hubie sold depreciable business property held for more than one year at a loss this year and has Section 1231 gains in the prior year.
    d. Li sold inventory at a loss in the prior year due to obsolescence but returned to profitable inventory sales in the current year.

25. In 2024, Dearica sells a machine used in her business for $21,000. The machine was purchased on May 1, 2020, at a cost of $24,000. Dearica has deducted depreciation on the machine of $5,000. Dearica has no previous Section 1231 gains or losses. What is the amount and nature of Dearica's gain as a result of the sale of the machine?
    a. $2,000 Section 1231 gain
    b. $2,000 ordinary income under Section 1245
    c. $2,000 ordinary income and $3,000 Section 1231 gain
    d. $3,000 ordinary loss
    e. None of the above

26. In 2024, Carrica sells a machine used in her business for $24,000. The machine was purchased on May 1, 2020, at a cost of $21,000. Carrica has deducted depreciation on the machine of $5,000. Carrica has no previous Section 1231 gains or losses. What is the amount and nature of Carrica's gain as a result of the sale of the machine?
    a. $8,000 Section 1231 gain
    b. $8,000 ordinary income under Section 1245
    c. $5,000 ordinary income and $3,000 Section 1231 gain
    d. $5,000 Section 1231 gain and $3,000 ordinary income under Section 1245
    e. None of the above

27. During 2024, Paul, an individual taxpayer, sells residential rental property for $180,000, which he acquired in 2016 for $160,000. Paul has claimed straight-line depreciation on the building of $50,000. What is the amount and nature of Paul's gain on the sale of the rental property?
    a. $70,000 ordinary income
    b. $10,000 ordinary income and $60,000 ordinary gain
    c. $70,000 Section 1231 gain
    d. $20,000 Section 1231 gain, $50,000 "unrecaptured depreciation"
    e. None of the above

28. Natisha acquired an apartment building in 2017 for $280,000 and sells it for $480,000 in 2024. At the time of sale there is $60,000 of accumulated straight-line depreciation on the apartment building. Assuming Natisha is in the highest tax bracket for ordinary income and the Medicare tax on net investment income applies, how much of her gain is taxed at 28.8 percent?
    a. None
    b. $60,000
    c. $200,000
    d. $280,000
    e. $260,000

29. During 2024, Peters Corporation sells rental real property for $180,000, which was acquired in 2016 for $160,000. Peters has claimed straight-line depreciation on the building of $50,000. What is the amount and nature of Peters' gain on the sale of the real property?
    a. $70,000 ordinary income
    b. $10,000 ordinary income and $60,000 Section 1231 gain
    c. $70,000 Section 1231 gain
    d. $20,000 Section 1231 gain, $50,000 "unrecaptured depreciation"

LO 8.9

30. Sika has business property that is stolen and partially destroyed by the time it was recovered. She receives an insurance reimbursement of $5,000 on property that had a $14,000 adjusted basis and a decrease in market value of $10,000 due to damage caused by the theft. What is the amount of Sika's casualty loss?
   a. $14,000
   b. $5,000
   c. $10,000
   d. $4,000
   e. None of the above

LO 8.9

31. Prashant has business property that is stolen and totally destroyed by the time it was recovered. He receives an insurance reimbursement of $5,000 on property that had a $14,000 basis and a market value of $20,000 before destruction. What is the amount of Prashant's casualty loss?
   a. $14,000
   b. $9,000
   c. $15,000
   d. $20,000
   e. None of the above

LO 8.10

32. Pradhiba sells land for $20,000 cash and a $80,000 four-year note with a reasonable interest rate. If her basis in the property is $30,000 and she receives the $20,000 down payment and the first $20,000 payment on the note in the year of sale, how much is Pradhiba's taxable gain in the year of sale using the installment sales method?
   a. $0
   b. $40,000
   c. $20,000
   d. $28,000
   e. $70,000

LO 8.11

33. Fred and Sarajane exchanged land in a qualifying like-kind exchange. Fred gives up land with an adjusted basis of $11,000 (fair market value of $16,000) in exchange for Sarajane's land with a fair market value of $12,000 plus $4,000 cash. How much gain should Fred recognize on the exchange?
   a. $5,000
   b. $4,000
   c. $1,000
   d. $0
   e. None of the above

LO 8.11

34. Fred and Sarajane exchanged land in a qualifying like-kind exchange. Fred gives up land with an adjusted basis of $11,000 (fair market value of $16,000) in exchange for Sarajane's land with a fair market value of $12,000 plus $4,000 cash. If Sarajane's basis in the land she gave up was $12,000, what is her basis in the land she received?
   a. $0
   b. $12,000
   c. $14,000
   d. $16,000
   e. None of the above

LO 8.12

35. Oscar owns a building that is destroyed in a hurricane. His adjusted basis in the building before the hurricane is $130,000. His insurance company pays him $140,000 and he immediately invests in a new building at a cost of $142,000. What is the amount of recognized gain or loss on the destruction of Oscar's building?
   a. $0
   b. $10,000 gain
   c. $8,000 gain
   d. $12,000 gain
   e. $2,000 loss

LO 8.12

36. Oscar owns a building that is destroyed in a hurricane. His adjusted basis in the building before the hurricane is $130,000. His insurance company pays him $140,000 and he immediately invests in a new building at a cost of $142,000. What is Oscar's basis in his new building?
   a. $130,000
   b. $132,000
   c. $140,000
   d. $142,000

Group 2: Problems

LO 8.1

1. Define each of the following as it relates to the tax rules for capitalization of expenditures:
   a. Betterment
   b. Adaptation
   c. Restoration

LO 8.1

2. Describe the requirements to apply a de minimis safe harbor to tangible property expenditures for a business taxpayer.

LO 8.2

3. Is land allowed to be depreciated? Why or why not?

LO 8.2

4. Is it possible to depreciate a residential rental building when it is actually increasing in value? Why?

LO 8.2

5. On August 8, 2024, Holly purchased a residential apartment building. The cost basis assigned to the building is $400,000. Holly also owns another residential apartment building that she purchased on April 15, 2024, with a cost basis of $650,000.
   a. Calculate Holly's total depreciation deduction for the apartments for 2024 using MACRS and assuming she does not elect out of bonus depreciation.
   b. Calculate Holly's total depreciation deduction for the apartments for 2025 using MACRS.

LO 8.2

6. Give the MACRS depreciation life of the following assets:
   a. An automobile
   b. Business furniture
   c. A computer
   d. Residential real estate
   e. Commercial real estate
   f. Land

LO 8.2

7. Explain the use of the mid-quarter convention for MACRS depreciation:

LO 8.2

8. Calculate the following:
   a. The first year of depreciation on an office building that cost $250,000 purchased on October 2, 2024. This is the only property placed in service this year.
   b. The second year (2025) of depreciation on a computer that cost $5,000 purchased in May 2024, using the half-year convention and accelerated depreciation considering any bonus depreciation taken.
   c. The first year of depreciation on a computer costing $2,800 purchased in May 2024, using the half-year convention and straight-line depreciation with no bonus depreciation.
   d. The third year of depreciation on business furniture costing $10,000 purchased in March 2022, using the half-year convention and accelerated depreciation but no bonus depreciation.

LO 8.2
LO 8.3

9. Mike purchases a new heavy-duty truck (5-year class recovery property) for his delivery service on March 30, 2024. No other assets were purchased during the year. The truck is not considered a passenger automobile for purposes of the listed property and luxury automobile limitations. The truck has a depreciable basis of $60,000 and an estimated useful life of five years. Assume half-year convention for tax.
   a. Calculate the amount of depreciation for 2024 using the straight-line depreciation election, using MACRS tables over the minimum number of years with no bonus depreciation or election to expense.
   b. Calculate the amount of depreciation for 2024, including bonus depreciation but no election to expense, that Mike could deduct using the MACRS tables.
   c. Calculate the amount of depreciation for 2024 including the election to expense and depreciation that Mike could deduct. Assume no income limit on the expense election.

LO 8.2
LO 8.3

10. Tom has a successful business with $100,000 of taxable income before the election to expense in 2024. He purchases one new asset in 2024, a new machine which is seven-year MACRS property and costs $25,000. If you are Tom's tax advisor, how would you advise Tom to treat the purchase for tax purposes in 2024? Why?

LO 8.2
LO 8.4

11. On February 2, 2024, Keiko purchases a personal computer. The computer cost $2,400. Keiko uses the computer 75 percent of the time in her accounting business, and the remaining 25 percent of the time for various personal uses. Calculate Keiko's maximum depreciation deduction for 2024 for the computer, assuming half-year convention and she does not use bonus depreciation or make the election to expense.

LO 8.2
LO 8.3
LO 8.4
LO 8.5

12. During 2024, Khan purchases the following capital assets for use in his catering business:

New passenger automobile (September 30)	$70,000
Baking equipment (June 30)	12,000

Assume that Khan decides to use the election to expense on the baking equipment (and has adequate taxable income to cover the deduction) but not on the automobile, and he also uses the MACRS accelerated method to calculate depreciation but elects out of bonus depreciation. Calculate Khan's maximum depreciation deduction for 2024, assuming he uses the automobile 100 percent in his business.

LO 8.2
LO 8.4
LO 8.5

13. On September 14, 2024, Yun purchased a passenger automobile that is used 75 percent in his business. The automobile has a basis for depreciation purposes of $50,000, and Yun uses the accelerated method under MACRS. Yun does not elect to expense. Calculate Yun's depreciation deduction for 2024 assuming bonus depreciation.

LO 8.2
LO 8.4
LO 8.5

14. During 2024, Pepe Guardio purchases the following property for use in his calendar year-end manufacturing business:

Item	Date Acquired	Cost
Manufacturing equipment (7 year)	June 2	$ 62,000
Office furniture	September 15	11,000
Office computer	November 18	2,000
Passenger automobile (used 90 percent for business)	May 31	55,000
Warehouse	May 9	
Building		180,000
Land		135,000

Pepe uses the accelerated depreciation method under MACRS, if available, and does not make the election to expense and elects out of bonus depreciation. Use Form 4562 in Appendix F to report Pepe's depreciation expense for 2024.

LO 8.2
LO 8.4

15. Complete Problem 13, except assume no election out of bonus depreciation. Use Form 4562 from Appendix F to report Pepe's depreciation expense for 2024.

LO 8.5
LO 8.6

16. Devon purchased a small business from Art on April 30, 2024, and paid the following amounts for the business:

Fixed assets	$180,000
Goodwill	60,000
Covenant not to compete	20,000
Total	$260,000

    a. How much of the $260,000 purchase price is for Section 197 intangible assets?
    b. What amount can Devon deduct on his 2024 tax return as Section 197 intangible amortization?

LO 8.6

17. Annie developed a successful tax practice, sold the practice to her friend Carol for $54,000, and moved to Florida to retire. The tax practice has no assets except intangible benefits such as the goodwill and going-concern value Annie has developed over the years. How should Carol treat the $54,000 cost of the tax practice she has purchased?

LO 8.7
LO 8.8

18. Nadia Shalom has the following transactions during the year:
    - Sale of office equipment on March 15 that cost $19,000 when purchased on July 1, 2022. Nadia has claimed $19,000 in depreciation and sells the asset for $13,500 with no selling costs.
    - Sale of land on April 19 for $118,000. The land cost $125,000 when purchased on February 1, 2013. Nadia's selling costs are $5,000.
    - Sale of an office building on April 19 for $250,000. The building cost $230,000 when purchased on February 1, 2013, and Nadia has claimed $59,000 in depreciation. Nadia pays a sales commission of $12,000.
    - Assume there were no capital improvements on either business asset sold. Nadia's Social Security number is 924-56-5783.

    Complete Form 4797 from Appendix F to report the above gains or losses.

LO 8.2
LO 8.7
LO 8.8

19. In 2020, Abishek purchased depreciable property (7-year recovery period, half-year convention) for $40,000. He disposed of the property in 2024 for $28,000.
    a. Assuming no bonus or Section 179, calculate the depreciation allowed for each year (2020–2024).
    b. Calculate the adjusted basis of the property.
    c. Calculate the realized gain on the sale.
    d. Calculate the amount of ordinary income under Section 1245.
    e. Calculate the Section 1231 gain.

LO 8.9

20. An office machine with a market value of $10,000 used by Pravina in her accounting business was completely destroyed by fire. The adjusted basis of the machine was $8,000 (original basis of $14,000 less accumulated depreciation of $6,000). The machine was not insured. Calculate the amount and nature of Pravina's gain or loss as a result of this casualty.

LO 8.8
LO 8.10

21. Steve Drake sells a rental house on January 1, 2024, and receives $75,000 cash and a note for $55,000 at 7-percent interest. The purchaser also assumes the mortgage on the property of $40,000. Steve's original cost for the house was $180,000 on January 1, 2016, and accumulated depreciation was $38,000 on the date of sale. He collects only the $75,000 down payment in the year of sale.
    a. If Steve elects to recognize the total gain on the property in the year of sale, calculate the taxable gain.
    b. Assuming Steve uses the installment sale method, complete Form 6252 from Appendix F for the year of the sale.
    c. Assuming Steve collects $10,000 (not including interest) of the note principal in the year following the year of sale, calculate the amount of income recognized in that year under the installment sale method.

LO 8.11 22. Carey exchanges land for other land in a qualifying like-kind exchange. Carey's basis in the land given up is $115,000, and the property has a fair market value of $150,000. In exchange for her property, Carey receives land with a fair market value of $100,000 and cash of $10,000. In addition, the other party to the exchange assumes a mortgage loan on Carey's property of $40,000.
a. Calculate Carey's recognized gain, if any, on the exchange.
b. Calculate Carey's basis in the property received.

LO 8.12 23. Teresa's manufacturing plant is destroyed by fire. The plant has an adjusted basis of $270,000, and Teresa receives insurance proceeds of $410,000 for the loss. Teresa reinvests $420,000 in a replacement plant within 2 years of receiving the insurance proceeds.
a. Calculate Teresa's recognized gain if she elects to utilize the involuntary conversion provision.
b. Calculate Teresa's basis in the new plant.

Group 3:
Writing Assignment

Research

1. Your supervisor has asked you to research the following situation concerning Owen and Lisa Cordoncillo. Owen and Lisa are brother and sister. In May 2024, Owen and Lisa exchange land they both held separately for investment. Lisa gives up a two-acre property in Texas with an adjusted basis of $2,000 and a fair market value of $6,000. In return for this property, Lisa receives from Owen a one-acre property in Arkansas with a fair market value of $5,500 and cash of $500. Owen's adjusted basis in the land he exchanges is $2,500. In March 2025, Owen sells the Texas land to a third party for $5,800.

   Required: Go to the IRS website (**www.irs.gov**). Locate and review Publication 544, Chapter 1, Nontaxable Exchanges. Write a file memorandum stating the amount of Owen and Lisa's gain recognition for 2024. Also determine the effect, if any, of the subsequent sale in 2025. (An example of a file memorandum is available at the website for this textbook located at **www.cengage.com**.)

Group 4:
Comprehensive Problems

1. Trish Himple owns Himple Retail, a retail family clothing store. Her store is located at 4321 Heather Drive, Henderson, NV 89002. Her employer identification number is 95-1234321 and her Social Security number is 123-45-6789. Trish keeps her books on the cash basis. The income and expenses for the year are:

Gross sales		$345,000
Returns and allowances		14,000
Expenses:		
Beginning inventory (at cost)	$ 87,000	
Add: purchases	100,000	
Cost of goods available for sale	187,000	
Less: ending inventory (at cost)	72,000	
Cost of goods sold		$115,000
Rent		24,000
Insurance		2,500
Legal and accounting fees		5,000
Payroll		59,000
Payroll taxes		5,000
Utilities		2,000
Office supplies		800
Advertising		6,000

Trish's bookkeeper has provided the following *book-basis* fixed asset rollforward:

Himple Retail
Fixed Asset Rollforward
12/31/2024

BOOK BASIS

ASSET	IN SERVICE	DEPR METHOD	LIFE	COST BASIS	2022 DEPR	2023 DEPR	2024 DEPR	ACCUM DEPR	NET BOOK VALUE
CASH REGISTER	8/15/2022	SL	5	9,500.00	791.67	1,900.00	1,900.00	4,591.67	4,908.33
2022 TOTAL ADDITIONS				9,500.00	791.67	1,900.00	1,900.00	4,591.67	4,908.33
RETAIL FIXTURES	6/21/2023	SL	7	5,500.00		458.33	785.71	1,244.04	4,255.96
FURNITURE	10/12/2023	SL	7	4,200.00		150.00	600.00	750.00	3,450.00
2023 TOTAL ADDITIONS				9,700.00	-	608.33	1,385.71	1,994.04	7,705.96
TOTAL				19,200.00	791.67	2,508.33	3,285.71	6,585.71	12,614.29
DELIVERY TRUCK	6/1/2024	SL	5	38,000.00			4,433.33	4,433.33	33,566.67
DESK AND CABINETRY	6/1/2024	SL	7	11,000.00			916.67	916.67	10,083.33
COMPUTER	6/1/2024	SL	5	3,000.00			350.00	350.00	2,650.00
2024 TOTAL ADDITIONS				52,000.00	-	-	5,700.00	5,700.00	46,300.00
TOTAL				71,200.00	791.67	2,508.33	8,985.71	12,285.71	58,914.29

The truck is not considered a passenger automobile for purposes of the luxury automobile limitations.

Trish also has a qualified home office of 250 sq. ft. Her home is 2,000 sq. ft. Her 2019 purchase price and basis in the home, not including land, is $200,000 (the home's market value is $250,000). She incurred the following costs in 2024 related to the entire home:

Utilities	$3,200
Cleaning	1,200
Insurance	1,800
Property taxes	5,000

Trish also earned wages as express delivery manager in 2024. Her Form W-2 is below.

a Employee's social security number 123-45-6789		
b Employer identification number (EIN) 31-3453457	1 Wages, tips, other compensation 115,000.00	2 Federal income tax withheld 25,000.00
c Employer's name, address, and ZIP code Lightning and Juno Express 100 Didactylus Drive Las Vegas, NV 89032	3 Social security wages 115,000.00	4 Social security tax withheld 7,130.00
	5 Medicare wages and tips 115,000.00	6 Medicare tax withheld 1,667.50
	7 Social security tips	8 Allocated tips
e Employee's first name and initial Last name Trish Himple 350 W. Lake Mead Blvd. North Las Vegas, NV 89032	11 Nonqualified plans	12a
15 State NV	16 State wages, tips, etc.	17 State income tax

Form **W-2** Wage and Tax Statement **2024**

Required: For tax purposes, Trish elected out of bonus depreciation in all years except 2024. She did not elect immediate expensing in any year. The tax lives of the assets are the same as the book lives shown in the fixed asset schedule above. Complete Trish's Schedule C, Form 8829, Form 4562, and Schedule SE. Do not prepare Form 1040 or Schedule 1 for this problem. Make realistic assumptions about any missing data.

2. Tsate Kongai (birthdate 02/14/1958) is an unmarried high school principal. Tsate received the following tax documents:

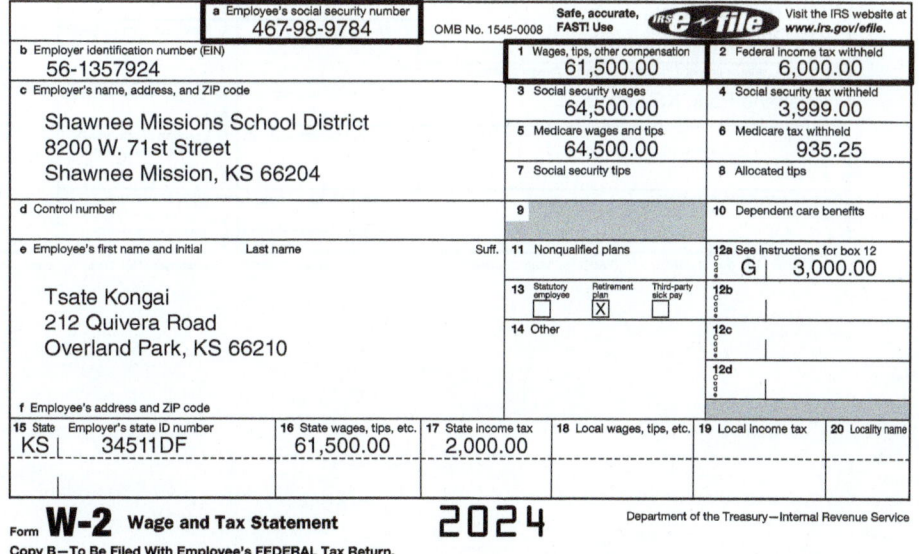

Form 1099-INT

☐ CORRECTED (if checked)

PAYER'S name, street address, city or town, state or province, country, ZIP or foreign postal code, and telephone no.
Olanthe National Bank
1240 E. Santa Fe Street
Olanthe, KS 66061

Payer's RTN (optional)

OMB No. 1545-0112
Form **1099-INT**
(Rev. January 2024)
For calendar year **2024**

Interest Income

1 Interest Income
$ 247.69

2 Early withdrawal penalty
$

Copy B
For Recipient

PAYER'S TIN: 98-7654321
RECIPIENT'S TIN: 467-98-9784

3 Interest on U.S. Savings Bonds and Treasury obligations
$

4 Federal income tax withheld
$

5 Investment expenses
$

RECIPIENT'S name
Tsate Kongai

Street address (including apt. no.)
212 Quivera Road

City or town, state or province, country, and ZIP or foreign postal code
Overland Park, KS 66210

6 Foreign tax paid
$

7 Foreign country or U.S. territory

8 Tax-exempt interest
$

9 Specified private activity bond interest
$

10 Market discount
$

11 Bond premium
$

This is important tax information and is being furnished to the IRS. If you are required to file a return, a negligence penalty or other sanction may be imposed on you if this income is taxable and the IRS determines that it has not been reported.

FATCA filing requirement ☐

12 Bond premium on Treasury obligations
$

13 Bond premium on tax-exempt bond
$

Account number (see instructions)

14 Tax-exempt and tax credit bond CUSIP no.

15 State | **16 State identification no.** | **17 State tax withheld**
$
$

Form **1099-INT** (Rev. 1-2024)   (keep for your records)   www.irs.gov/Form1099INT   Department of the Treasury - Internal Revenue Service

---

Form 1099-DIV

☐ CORRECTED (if checked)

PAYER'S name, street address, city or town, state or province, country, ZIP or foreign postal code, and telephone no.
Johnson Corporation
100 E. 49th Street
New York, NY 10017

1a Total ordinary dividends
$ 4,200.00

OMB No. 1545-0110
Form **1099-DIV**
(Rev. January 2024)

Dividends and Distributions

1b Qualified dividends
$ 4,100.00

For calendar year **2024**

2a Total capital gain distr.
$

2b Unrecap. Sec. 1250 gain
$

Copy B
For Recipient

PAYER'S TIN: 17-2468135
RECIPIENT'S TIN: 467-98-9784

2c Section 1202 gain
$

2d Collectibles (28%) gain
$

2e Section 897 ordinary dividends
$

2f Section 897 capital gain
$

RECIPIENT'S name
Tsate Kongai

3 Nondividend distributions
$

4 Federal income tax withheld
$ 615.00

Street address (including apt. no.)
212 Quivera Rd.

5 Section 199A dividends
$

6 Investment expenses
$

This is important tax information and is being furnished to the IRS. If you are required to file a return, a negligence penalty or other sanction may be imposed on you if this income is taxable and the IRS determines that it has not been reported.

City or town, state or province, country, and ZIP or foreign postal code
Overland Park, KS 66210

7 Foreign tax paid
$

8 Foreign country or U.S. possession

9 Cash liquidation distributions
$

10 Noncash liquidation distributions
$

11 FATCA filing requirement ☐

12 Exempt-interest dividends
$

13 Specified private activity bond interest dividends
$

Account number (see instructions)

14 State | **15 State identification no.** | **16 State tax withheld**
$
$

Form **1099-DIV** (Rev. 1-2024)   (keep for your records)   www.irs.gov/Form1099DIV   Department of the Treasury - Internal Revenue Service

Form 1098 — Mortgage Interest Statement

RECIPIENT'S/LENDER'S name, street address, city or town, state or province, country, ZIP or foreign postal code, and telephone no.
Olanthe National Bank
1240 E. Santa Fe Street
Olanthe, KS 66061

Caution: The amount shown may not be fully deductible by you. Limits based on the loan amount and the cost and value of the secured property may apply. Also, you may only deduct interest to the extent it was incurred by you, actually paid by you, and not reimbursed by another person.

OMB No. 1545-1380
Form **1098** (Rev. January 2022)
For calendar year 20**24**

Mortgage Interest Statement

1 Mortgage interest received from payer(s)/borrower(s): $ 9,611.43

RECIPIENT'S/LENDER'S TIN: 44-1352469
PAYER'S/BORROWER'S TIN: 467-98-9784

2 Outstanding mortgage principal: $ 215,882.21
3 Mortgage origination date: 04/15/2016
4 Refund of overpaid interest: $
5 Mortgage insurance premiums: $

PAYER'S/BORROWER'S name: Tsate Kongai
Street address (including apt. no.): 212 Quivera Road
City or town, state or province, country, and ZIP or foreign postal code: Overland Park, KS 66210

6 Points paid on purchase of principal residence: $
7 [X] If address of property securing mortgage is the same as PAYER'S/BORROWER'S address, the box is checked, or the address or description is entered in box 8.
8 Address or description of property securing mortgage:

9 Number of properties securing the mortgage: 1
10 Other:

11 Mortgage acquisition date:

Copy B For Payer/Borrower

Form **1098** (Rev. 1-2022)

During the year, Tsate paid the following amounts (all of which can be substantiated):

KS state income tax payment for 2023	700
MasterCard interest	550
Life insurance (whole life policy)	750
Property taxes on personal residence	1,300
Out-of-pocket medical expenses	800
Income tax preparation fee	300
Charitable contributions (in cash)	800

Tsate's sole stock transaction was reported on a Form 1099-B:

Form 1099-B — Proceeds From Broker and Barter Exchange Transactions

PAYER'S name, street address, city or town, state or province, country, ZIP or foreign postal code, and telephone no.
Little John Trading
123 Wall Street
New York, NY 10014

Applicable checkbox on Form 8949: A
OMB No. 1545-0715
20**24** Form **1099-B**

1a Description of property: 100 shs. Johnson Corp.
1b Date acquired: 12/31/2023
1c Date sold or disposed: 11/05/2024

PAYER'S TIN: 11-0010011
RECIPIENT'S TIN: 467-98-9784

1d Proceeds: $ 14,500.00
1e Cost or other basis: $ 33,000.00
1f Accrued market discount: $
1g Wash sale loss disallowed: $

RECIPIENT'S name: Tsate Kongai
Street address: 212 Quivera Road
City, state, ZIP: Overland Park, KS 66210

2 Short-term gain or loss [ ]
Long-term gain or loss [ ]
Ordinary [ ]
3 If checked, proceeds from: Collectibles [ ] QOF [ ]
4 Federal income tax withheld: $
5 If checked, noncovered security [ ]
6 Reported to IRS: Gross proceeds [ ] Net proceeds [X]
7 If checked, loss is not allowed based on amount in 1d [ ]

Copy B For Recipient

Form **1099-B**

On January 28, 2024, Tsate sold land for $175,000 (basis to Tsate of $130,000). The land was purchased six years ago as an investment. Tsate received $25,000 as a down payment and the buyer's 10-year note for $150,000. The note is payable at the rate of $15,000 per year plus 3.00 percent interest. On December 31, 2024, Tsate received a payment of $19,500 that included $4,500 of interest.

Tsate also helps support his father, Jay Hawke, who lives in a nearby senior facility. Jay's Social Security number is 433-33-2121 and his date of birth is July 11, 1939. Tsate provides over one-half of Jay's support but Jay also has a pension that paid him income of $4,000 in 2024. Jay's Social Security benefits were $3,200 in 2024.

Required: Complete Tsate's federal tax return for 2024. Use Form 1040-SR, Schedule A, Schedule B, Schedule D, Schedule 8812 and the associated Credit Limit Worksheet A, the Qualified Dividends and Capital Gain Tax Worksheet, and Form 6252, as needed, to complete this tax return. Make realistic assumptions about any missing data.

Group 5:
Cumulative Software Problem

1. The following information is available for the Albert and Allison Gaytor family in addition to that provided in Chapters 1–7.

    On October 14, 2024, Allison purchased the building where her store is located. She paid $400,000 for the building (which includes $100,000 for the land it is located on). Allison's store is the only business in the building. The depreciation on the store needs to be reflected on Schedule C of the business.

Required: Combine this new information about the Gaytor family with the information from Chapters 1 to 7 and complete a revised 2024 tax return for Albert and Allison. This completes the Group 5 multichapter case.

Chapter 9

Employment Taxes, Estimated Payments, and Retirement Plans

Learning Objectives

After completing this chapter, you should be able to:

- **LO 9.1** Determine the classification of workers as employees versus independent contractors.
- **LO 9.2** Compute the income tax withholding from employee wages.
- **LO 9.3** Compute the FICA tax.
- **LO 9.4** Determine taxpayers' quarterly estimated payments.
- **LO 9.5** Apply the federal deposit system to payroll withholding.
- **LO 9.6** Prepare employer payroll reporting.
- **LO 9.7** Compute the amount of FUTA tax for an employer.
- **LO 9.8** Describe the general rules for qualified retirement plans.
- **LO 9.9** Explain the pension plan rollover rules.

Overview

This chapter begins with the classification of an employee versus an independent contractor and then focuses on the payment and reporting of income and other taxes by employers, employees, and self-employed taxpayers. Payroll and other tax topics covered include withholding methods for employees, estimated payments, the FICA tax (Social Security and Medicare taxes), the federal tax deposit system, and employer reporting requirements. In addition, other payroll-related topics such as retirement plans and pensions not covered in Chapter 5 are presented herein.

Much of the collection, payment, and reporting of employment taxes is handled by the employer, not the employee. In most instances, taxpayers are able to rely on the payroll information provided by their employer such as Form W-2. However, understanding how employment taxes are computed remains an important issue for tax advisers and taxpayers.

Learning Objective 9.1

Determine the classification of workers as employees versus independent contractors.

9-1 Employee Versus Independent Contractor

Business owners are required to correctly determine whether the individuals providing services to their businesses are employees or independent contractors. Many taxpayers view this as an option, when in fact, worker classification is a function of law and not a choice on the part of either the employer or employee. Potential employees most often accept the choice made by the employer since attempting to negotiate this classification may prevent obtaining the work. The classification as an employee versus an independent contractor makes a great deal of difference. Generally, an employer must withhold income taxes, withhold and pay Social Security and Medicare taxes, and pay unemployment tax on wages paid to an employee. A business does not generally have to withhold or pay any taxes on payments to independent contractors and will generally only have to provide an informational return such as the Form 1099-NEC. The differences extend beyond just payroll tax liability and processing. For example, employees are far more restricted in deducting employee-related business expenses. Independent contractors are generally not provided benefits and are required to pay self-employment taxes. Because the outcomes differ greatly and the guidance is less well understood, the subject of employee versus independent contractor also tends to be an area of tax controversy.

A potential source of confusion is that the tax code itself does not define employee in any meaningful way. Instead, regulations and court cases have over time congealed into a more-or-less acceptable common law definition that relies heavily on the degree of control and independence between the individual and the business. Characteristics that provide evidence of the degree of control and independence fall into three categories:

1. *Behavioral:* Does the business control or have the right to control what and how the worker does their job?
2. *Financial:* Are the business aspects of the worker's job controlled by the payer (how the worker is paid, whether expenses are reimbursed, who provides tools/supplies, etc.)?
3. *Relationship:* Are there written contracts or employee benefits (i.e. pension plan, insurance, vacation pay, etc.)? Will the relationship continue and is the work performed a key aspect of the business?

Table 9.1 presents the IRS list of twenty factors to consider in classifying a worker as an employee or an independent contractor. The degree of importance for each factor can vary and no single factor is controlling.

Table 9.1 Worker Classification Factors

Behavioral Control Factors	Financial Control Factors	Relationship Factors
1. Instruction: Employees are more likely to be required to comply with when, where, and how the work is to be done.	11. Payment timing: Employees are paid by time period (hour, week, month). Contractors are paid based on project completion.	16. Integration: Employees are more likely to be integrated into business operations.
2. Training: Employees are trained to perform the work.	12. Travel/Business Expenses: Employees' travel and business expenses are controlled and covered by the employer.	17. Multiple Engagements: Contractors work for multiple unrelated businesses.
3. Personally Rendered: Employees must generally perform the work themselves and cannot subcontract the work.	13. Tools and Materials: Furnishing of tools, equipment, or an office indicates employee.	18. Availability of Services: Contractors make their services available to the general public.
4. Hiring, Supervising and Paying Assistants: Independent contractors have the ability to hire, supervise, and pay assistants and are primarily responsible for the end result.		19. Right to Discharge: Employees are subject to firing by the business.
5. Continuing Relationship: Continuing relationships (even at infrequent intervals) are more common with employees.		

Behavioral Control Factors	Financial Control Factors	Relationship Factors
6. Work Hours: Independent contractors are more likely to set their own work hours. 7. Time required: Employees work full-time for an employer. 8. Workplace: Employees are generally required to perform work on premises. 9. Sequence of Work: Employees follow the business entity sequence of work. 10. Reports: Employees will be required to submit regular reports whereas an independent contractor's main goal is to deliver results.	14. Investment: Contractors make a significant investment in the facilities where the work is performed. 15. Profit or loss: Employees generally bear no liability for loss.	20. Right to Quit: Employees can quit without breaching any agreements.

Tax Break

A tax law known as a Section 530 Safe Harbor can provide some protection to a taxpayer that may have classified workers as independent contractors in the past with some uncertainty. Section 530 was passed outside of the Internal Revenue Code and provides relief for possibly mistaken classifications under certain circumstances. To meet the safe harbor, one of the conditions is that the taxpayer must have a reasonable basis for not treating the worker as an employee. A reasonable basis exists if the treatment was based on (1) judicial precedent, published rulings, technical advice to the employer, or a letter ruling to the employer; (2) past examination of the employer by the IRS in which there was no assessment attributable to the treatment for employment tax purposes of individuals holding positions substantially similar to the position held by this individual; or (3) long-standing recognized practice of a significant segment of the industry in which the individual was engaged. The IRS also operates the Voluntary Classification Settlement Program (VCSP) for similar types of worker classification issues.

Example Tabitha works at Pizza Cabana as a cashier. Her manager sets her schedule each week and she was trained by the company's Pizza Cabana University on her job duties and responsibilities. She is naturally expected to perform her role at the restaurant. Tabitha works at Pizza Cabana full time, is paid hourly, and participates in the company's retirement plan. This job is the primary source of Tabitha's income. She can quit at any time but is likely to provide a customary two-week notice. Tabitha appears to be under the behavioral, financial, and relationship control of Pizza Cabana and is classified as an employee. ♦

Example Tracy drives her own vehicle for a number of different shared delivery services. She tends to drive for Flying Food on the weekends because they are connected to restaurants that have more customers during the weekends. She also delivers food for Snax Car and Mobile Munchies. She checks to determine which service seems to have more demand at a particular date or time and logs on to work with that company. Tracy is paid per delivery, by miles driven, and through tips from customers. She only delivers when she feels like it or really needs the money. All the operating expenses, maintenance, and repairs on her vehicle are her costs to bear. Tracy has more of the characteristics associated with an independent contractor. ♦

The classification of a worker from a federal tax perspective has become more complex with the advent of certain states (for example, California) implementing labor laws designed to classify more workers as employees. Technically, these state-level laws would not control federal tax classification, but from a pragmatic perspective, most businesses would generally prefer to classify workers the same for state and federal purposes.

A worker or an employer may request a determination of employer or independent contractor status by filing Form SS-8. If a worker completes the form, after the IRS acknowledges receipt, the IRS will generally send a blank Form SS-8 to the employer for completion as well. The Form SS-8 is five pages and requires that the party making the request address questions related to the three control factors as presented in Table 9.1.

Form SS-8 (Rev. 12-2023)   Page **3**

Part II   Behavioral Control (Provide names and titles of specific individuals, if applicable.) *(continued)*

5   Is the worker required to complete reports? . . . . ☐ Yes   ☐ No
       If "Yes," attach examples.
6a   How frequently does the worker perform services?   ☐ As scheduled   ☐ As needed   ☐ As available
       ☐ Other (specify) _____
 b   Describe the worker's primary services.   ☐ Sales   ☐ Timesheets   ☐ Patient logs
       ☐ Other (specify) _____
7   Where are the services performed? If more than one location, what percentage of the worker's time is spent at each location?
       ☐ Firm premises . . . . _____ %
       ☐ Worker's office or shop . . . . _____ %
       ☐ Customer's location . . . . _____ %
       ☐ Other (specify) _____ _____ %
8a   Is the worker required to attend meetings? . . . . ☐ Yes   ☐ No
       If "Yes," what type of meetings?   ☐ Sales   ☐ Staff   ☐ Other (specify) _____
 b   Is the worker penalized if unable to attend a meeting? . . . . ☐ Yes   ☐ No
       If "Yes," what is the penalty? _____
9   Is the worker required to provide the services personally? . . . . ☐ Yes   ☐ No
10   Can the worker hire substitutes or helpers? . . . . ☐ Yes   ☐ No
11   If the worker hires the substitutes or helpers, is approval required? . . . . ☐ Yes   ☐ No
       If "Yes," who approves the hiring?   ☐ Firm   ☐ Other (specify) _____
12   Does the worker pay substitutes or helpers? . . . . ☐ Yes   ☐ No
       If "Yes," is the worker reimbursed? . . . . ☐ Yes   ☐ No
       If the worker is reimbursed, explain who reimburses them.

Part III   Financial Control (Provide names and titles of specific individuals, if applicable.)

1a   List the supplies, equipment, materials, and property provided by
       The firm: _____
       The worker: _____
 b   Are supplies, equipment, materials, or property provided by another party? . . . . ☐ Yes   ☐ No
       If "Yes," explain. _____

Assuming accurate facts, the IRS is bound by the determination offered.

Self-Study Problem 9.1   Refer to Appendix E for Solutions to Self-Study Problems

Mike performs services for Tatyana. Consider each of the factors and decide whether the factor indicates employee or independent contractor status:

a. Mike works only for Tatyana.
b. Mike sets his own work schedule.
c. Mike obtained his job skills from Tatyana's training program.
d. Mike performs the services at Tatyana's business location.
e. Mike is paid for time worked rather than task performed.
f. Mike works for Tatyana on a continuing basis for the entire year.
g. If Mike's costs exceed his payments, Tatyana will cover the shortfall.
h. If Mike stops working on the project, Tatyana will have no remedy for Mike's breach of contract.

9-2 Income Tax Withholding Methods

9.2 Learning Objective

Compute the income tax withholding from employee wages.

Employers are required to withhold income and employment taxes from amounts paid to employees for wages, including salaries, fees, bonuses, commissions, vacation and retirement pay. Employees complete Form W-4 to provide the information necessary for the employer to withhold income taxes at the prescribed amount. Although most taxpayers' income tax withholding should be adequate to result in an income tax refund at filing time, calculating withholding is more of an art than a science and is subject to the accurate estimation of income and deductions that are ultimately reported for the tax year.

The Form W-4 was redesigned in 2020. In previous years, withholding allowances were tied to the amount of the personal exemptions expected to be claimed by a taxpayer. Since exemptions are suspended from 2018–2025, the latest version of Form W-4 has been adapted and no longer requires an employee to report the number of withholding allowances that they expect to claim. Employees who submitted a Form W-4 in any year before 2020 are not required to submit a new Form W-4. Employers will continue to compute withholding based on the information from the employee's old Form W-4. The withholding tables published by the IRS allow employers to determine withholding based on old and new Forms W-4 under both the percentage and wage bracket methods. All new employees and any existing employees that wish to adjust withholding must use the new Form W-4.

Predicting the outcomes from the scheduled 2025 sunset of the tax provisions associated with the Tax Cuts and Jobs Act of 2017 is a fool's errand at this point. However, should the suspended provisions around exemptions be reinstated, there is some chance that employers would need to consider three different types of Forms W-4.

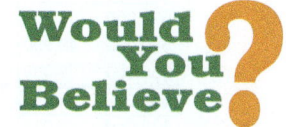

9-2a The Form W-4 After 2019

The new Form W-4 (refer to Pages 9-9 to 9-12) is divided into five steps. Steps 1 and 5 are completed by all taxpayers. Step 1 asks for personal information such as name, address, and filing status. Step 5 is the taxpayer's signature. By design, Steps 1 and 5 are all that most taxpayers would need to complete, and withholding will be based on that taxpayer's wages and filing status only.

For taxpayers with more complex income tax situations—such as those with a working spouse, dependents, or having additional forms of income such as self-employment, investment income—or for taxpayers that itemize, two options for computing additional withholding are provided. The first option is for the taxpayer to use the IRS online withholding estimator (**www.irs.gov/individuals/tax-withholding-estimator**). The online estimator uses information from recent paystubs of the taxpayer and spouse, details from other sources of income, and a previous tax return to estimate any additional withholding needs. Using the online estimator can be a complex process that contemplates a wide variety of taxpayer situations and is similar to approximating a taxpayer's current year tax liability. As a result, the estimator requires the greatest amount of preparation and likely provides the most accurate result.

The second option is to use Steps 2–4 on Form W-4:

- Step 2 is for taxpayers with a working spouse or multiple jobs.
- Step 3 is for taxpayers with dependents.
- Step 4 is for taxpayers that have other forms of income or itemized or other deductions.

Under Step 2, if the taxpayer and the spouse have similar income, the taxpayer can simply check the box on line (c) (the spouse should do the same on their Form W-4) and withholding will be adjusted to reflect a two-income household by halving the standard deduction and tax brackets. Alternatively, the Form W-4 instructions include a multiple jobs worksheet that uses a series of tables to estimate the required additional withholding in situations where the taxpayer has multiple jobs or the spouse's wages differ from the taxpayer.

Example — Dot and Peg expect to file a joint tax return in 2024. Dot and Peg expect to be paid wages of $39,000 and $64,000, respectively. Dot is paid monthly, and Peg is paid every two weeks (26 times a year). Because Dot and Peg's wages are not similar in amount, they should use the Married Filing Jointly table from page 4 of the Form W-4 (presented below). The suggested amount ($3,690) is entered on Line 1 on the Step 2(b) Multiple Jobs Worksheet included on page 3 of Form W-4 (presented on the following page). Because Peg has the higher-paying job, 26 is entered on Line 3 to match the number of payroll periods during the year, and Line 4 of the Multiple Jobs Worksheet is $141.92 ($3,690 ÷ 26). Peg will carry that amount forward to Line 4(c) on page 1 of the Form W-4 as additional withholding for each pay period. ♦

Form W-4 (2024) — Page 4

Married Filing Jointly or Qualifying Surviving Spouse

Higher Paying Job Annual Taxable Wage & Salary	$0 - 9,999	$10,000 - 19,999	$20,000 - 29,999	$30,000 - 39,999	$40,000 - 49,999	$50,000 - 59,999	$60,000 - 69,999	$70,000 - 79,999	$80,000 - 89,999	$90,000 - 99,999	$100,000 - 109,999	$110,000 - 120,000
$0 - 9,999	$0	$0	$780	$850	$940	$1,020	$1,020	$1,020	$1,020	$1,020	$1,020	$1,370
$10,000 - 19,999	0	780	1,780	1,940	2,140	2,220	2,220	2,220	2,220	2,220	2,570	3,570
$20,000 - 29,999	780	1,780	2,870	3,140	3,340	3,420	3,420	3,420	3,420	3,770	4,770	5,770
$30,000 - 39,999	850	1,940	3,140	3,410	3,610	3,690	3,690	3,690	4,040	5,040	6,040	7,040
$40,000 - 49,999	940	2,140	3,340	3,610	3,810	3,890	3,890	4,240	5,240	6,240	7,240	8,240
$50,000 - 59,999	1,020	2,220	3,420	3,690	3,890	3,970	4,320	5,320	6,320	7,320	8,320	9,320
$60,000 - 69,999	1,020	2,220	3,420	3,690	3,890	4,320	5,320	6,320	7,320	8,320	9,320	10,320
$70,000 - 79,999	1,020	2,220	3,420	3,690	4,240	5,320	6,320	7,320	8,320	9,320	10,320	11,320
$80,000 - 99,999	1,020	2,220	3,620	4,890	6,090	7,170	8,170	9,170	10,170	11,170	12,170	13,170
$100,000 - 149,999	1,870	4,070	6,270	7,540	8,740	9,820	10,820	11,820	12,830	14,030	15,230	16,430
$150,000 - 239,999	1,960	4,360	6,760	8,230	9,630	10,910	12,110	13,310	14,510	15,710	16,910	18,110
$240,000 - 259,999	2,040	4,440	6,840	8,310	9,710	10,990	12,190	13,390	14,590	15,790	16,990	18,190
$260,000 - 279,999	2,040	4,440	6,840	8,310	9,710	10,990	12,190	13,390	14,590	15,790	16,990	18,190
$280,000 - 299,999	2,040	4,440	6,840	8,310	9,710	10,990	12,190	13,390	14,590	15,790	16,990	18,380
$300,000 - 319,999	2,040	4,440	6,840	8,310	9,710	10,990	12,190	13,390	14,590	15,980	17,980	19,980
$320,000 - 364,999	2,040	4,440	6,840	8,310	9,710	11,280	13,280	15,280	17,280	19,280	21,280	23,280
$365,000 - 524,999	2,720	6,010	9,510	12,080	14,580	16,950	19,250	21,550	23,850	26,150	28,450	30,750
$525,000 and over	3,140	6,840	10,540	13,310	16,010	18,590	21,090	23,590	26,090	28,590	31,090	33,590

Form W-4 (2024) Page **3**

Step 2(b)—Multiple Jobs Worksheet *(Keep for your records.)*

If you choose the option in Step 2(b) on Form W-4, complete this worksheet (which calculates the total extra tax for all jobs) on **only ONE** Form W-4. Withholding will be most accurate if you complete the worksheet and enter the result on the Form W-4 for the highest paying job. To be accurate, submit a new Form W-4 for all other jobs if you have not updated your withholding since 2019.

Note: If more than one job has annual wages of more than $120,000 or there are more than three jobs, see Pub. 505 for additional tables; or, you can use the online withholding estimator at *www.irs.gov/W4App*.

1. **Two jobs.** If you have two jobs or you're married filing jointly and you and your spouse each have one job, find the amount from the appropriate table on page 4. Using the "Higher Paying Job" row and the "Lower Paying Job" column, find the value at the intersection of the two household salaries and enter that value on line 1. Then, **skip** to line 3 . . . . **1** $ _____3,690_____

2. **Three jobs.** If you and/or your spouse have three jobs at the same time, complete lines 2a, 2b, and 2c below. Otherwise, skip to line 3.

   a. Find the amount from the appropriate table on page 4 using the annual wages from the highest paying job in the "Higher Paying Job" row and the annual wages for your next highest paying job in the "Lower Paying Job" column. Find the value at the intersection of the two household salaries and enter that value on line 2a . . . . **2a** $ _____

   b. Add the annual wages of the two highest paying jobs from line 2a together and use the total as the wages in the "Higher Paying Job" row and use the annual wages for your third job in the "Lower Paying Job" column to find the amount from the appropriate table on page 4 and enter this amount on line 2b . . . . **2b** $ _____

   c. Add the amounts from lines 2a and 2b and enter the result on line 2c . . . . **2c** $ _____3,690_____

3. Enter the number of pay periods per year for the highest paying job. For example, if that job pays weekly, enter 52; if it pays every other week, enter 26; if it pays monthly, enter 12, etc. . . . . . **3** _____26_____

4. **Divide** the annual amount on line 1 or line 2c by the number of pay periods on line 3. Enter this amount here and in **Step 4(c)** of Form W-4 for the highest paying job (along with any other additional amount you want withheld) . . . . **4** $ _____141.92_____

Under Step 3, taxpayers report the impact of the child tax credit and the other dependent credit on tax liability. This amount will be used by the employer to compute withholding.

Example Shirin and Hamed are married filing jointly and have two dependent children ages 13 and 17. Hamed expects his 2024 wages to be $81,000, and Shirin works part-time and expects to earn $46,000. Both are paid monthly. As the higher-paid spouse, Hamed completes a Form W-4 that reflects the additional withholding and dependents. Shirin would not need to reflect this information on her W-4. Using the Multiple Jobs Worksheet, Hamed reports $507.50 ($6,090 ÷ 12) on Line 4(c) of Form W-4. Hamed also reports $2,500 (one child under 17 at $2,000 and one other dependent at $500) on Line 3 under Step 3 (presented below). ♦

Complete Steps 3–4(b) on Form W-4 for only ONE of these jobs. Leave those steps blank for the other jobs. (Your withholding will be most accurate if you complete Steps 3–4(b) on the Form W-4 for the highest paying job.)

Step 3: Claim Dependent and Other Credits	If your total income will be $200,000 or less ($400,000 or less if married filing jointly):		
	Multiply the number of qualifying children under age 17 by $2,000 $	2,000	
	Multiply the number of other dependents by $500 . . . . . . $	500	
	Add the amounts above for qualifying children and other dependents. You may add to this the amount of any other credits. Enter the total here	**3** $	2,500

Step 4 is used when the taxpayer has significant other sources of income (e.g., interest, dividends, retirement) or other deductions such as itemized deductions, deductible IRA contributions, the qualified business income deduction, and student loan interest. Line 4(a) of Form W-4 is where the expected amount of any additional income is reported and Line 4(b) is where any additional deductions are reported. Step 4(b) refers the taxpayer to a simple deduction worksheet included within Form W-4 that ensures the taxpayer compares the total itemized deductions with the standard deduction to capture only the excess amount as an adjustment. A taxpayer that has a two-income household, non-wage income, dependents, and itemizes deductions is effectively estimating their current year taxes in preparing the W-4. Generally, only more sophisticated taxpayers would be required to estimate withholding using this degree of complexity.

Example Fei and Zhi Han are married filing jointly and have three dependent children ages 13, 14, and 18. Zhi's older adult mother is also a dependent. Wage estimates for 2024 are $31,000 and $98,000 for Fei and Zhi, respectively. Both are paid semimonthly (24 times a year). They have an investment portfolio expected to pay $1,400 in interest and $2,400 in qualified dividends. They are not certain if they will have capital gains in 2024, since it depends on the stock market. The Hans own a home and estimate 2024 itemized deductions as $30,100. The Hans expect to make a $7,000 deductible IRA contribution and pay $3,200 in student loan interest. As presented on Pages 9-9 to 9-12, Zhi, as the higher-income spouse, will have a fairly complex Form W-4. Zhi should use the multiple jobs worksheet and will report $203.75 ($4,890 ÷ 24) on Line 4 of the worksheet. In Step 3, Zhi will report two qualifying children under 17 and two other dependents for a total of $5,000 ($2,000 × 2 plus $500 × 2). In Step 4, Zhi will include $3,800 of investment income on Line 4(a) of Form W-4. Zhi will complete the Deductions Worksheet and report $900 ($30,100 − $29,200) on Line 3 and $9,500 ($7,000 IRA deduction and the limit of $2,500 of deductible student loan interest) on Line 4, giving a total of $10,400 in Line 5 of the Deductions Worksheet. As a result, the first page of Zhi's W-4 will report $5,000 on Line 3, $3,800 on Line 4(a), $10,400 on Line 4(b), and $203.75 on Line 4(c). Note that the possible taxation of qualified dividends at a lower 15-percent rate, and the possibility that the student loan interest or the IRA contribution may not be deductible due to income limitations, would need to be considered by Zhi if she wanted to estimate withholding accurately. In this example, Zhi may want to consider using the IRS online withholding estimator. Zhi's completed Form W-4 is presented on Pages 9-9 to 9-12. ♦

The process is considerably more complex if for some reason a Form W-4 is completed during the middle of a year, since the withholding amounts are often associated with annual figures.

The amounts reported on Form W-4 will be used by the employer to make adjustments to the employee's tax withholding based on tables provided by the IRS. A taxpayer that is exempt from withholding should complete Steps 1 [do not check the box in 1(c)] and 5 and write "Exempt" in the space underneath Line 4(c). Employees are eligible to claim exempt if they had no federal tax liability in the prior year *and* expect to have no tax liability in 2024. If the employee completes any part of Form W-4 other than Steps 1(a) and 1(b) and Step 5, the Form W-4 for which exempt is claimed is considered invalid. A Form W-4 claiming exemption from withholding is effective only for that calendar year.

The 2024 version of Form W-4 is published in five different languages other than English: Korean, Spanish, Vietnamese, Russian, and traditional and simplified Chinese. Withholding knows no limits, language or otherwise!

9-2 Income Tax Withholding Methods

Form W-4
Department of the Treasury
Internal Revenue Service

Employee's Withholding Certificate
Complete Form W-4 so that your employer can withhold the correct federal income tax from your pay.
Give Form W-4 to your employer.
Your withholding is subject to review by the IRS.

OMB No. 1545-0074

2024

Step 1: Enter Personal Information

(a) First name and middle initial: **Zhi**   Last name: **Han**

(b) Social security number:

Address:

City or town, state, and ZIP code:

Does your name match the name on your social security card? If not, to ensure you get credit for your earnings, contact SSA at 800-772-1213 or go to www.ssa.gov.

(c)
- [ ] Single or Married filing separately
- [x] Married filing jointly or Qualifying surviving spouse
- [ ] Head of household (Check only if you're unmarried and pay more than half the costs of keeping up a home for yourself and a qualifying individual.)

Complete Steps 2–4 ONLY if they apply to you; otherwise, skip to Step 5. See page 2 for more information on each step, who can claim exemption from withholding, and when to use the estimator at www.irs.gov/W4App.

Step 2: Multiple Jobs or Spouse Works

Complete this step if you (1) hold more than one job at a time, or (2) are married filing jointly and your spouse also works. The correct amount of withholding depends on income earned from all of these jobs.

Do **only one** of the following.

(a) Use the estimator at www.irs.gov/W4App for most accurate withholding for this step (and Steps 3–4). If you or your spouse have self-employment income, use this option; **or**

(b) Use the Multiple Jobs Worksheet on page 3 and enter the result in Step 4(c) below; **or**

(c) If there are only two jobs total, you may check this box. Do the same on Form W-4 for the other job. This option is generally more accurate than (b) if pay at the lower paying job is more than half of the pay at the higher paying job. Otherwise, (b) is more accurate . . . . ☐

Complete Steps 3–4(b) on Form W-4 for only ONE of these jobs. Leave those steps blank for the other jobs. (Your withholding will be most accurate if you complete Steps 3–4(b) on the Form W-4 for the highest paying job.)

Step 3: Claim Dependent and Other Credits

If your total income will be $200,000 or less ($400,000 or less if married filing jointly):

Multiply the number of qualifying children under age 17 by $2,000 $ 4,000

Multiply the number of other dependents by $500 . . . . . $ 1,000

Add the amounts above for qualifying children and other dependents. You may add to this the amount of any other credits. Enter the total here . . . . **3** $ **5,000**

Step 4 (optional): Other Adjustments

(a) **Other income (not from jobs).** If you want tax withheld for other income you expect this year that won't have withholding, enter the amount of other income here. This may include interest, dividends, and retirement income . . . . **4(a)** $ **3,800**

(b) **Deductions.** If you expect to claim deductions other than the standard deduction and want to reduce your withholding, use the Deductions Worksheet on page 3 and enter the result here . . . . **4(b)** $ **10,400**

(c) **Extra withholding.** Enter any additional tax you want withheld each **pay period** . . **4(c)** $ **203.75**

Step 5: Sign Here

Under penalties of perjury, I declare that this certificate, to the best of my knowledge and belief, is true, correct, and complete.

Employee's signature (This form is not valid unless you sign it.)   Date

Employers Only | Employer's name and address | First date of employment | Employer identification number (EIN)

For Privacy Act and Paperwork Reduction Act Notice, see page 3.   Cat. No. 10220Q   Form **W-4** (2024)

Form W-4 (2024) Page **2**

General Instructions

Section references are to the Internal Revenue Code.

Future Developments

For the latest information about developments related to Form W-4, such as legislation enacted after it was published, go to *www.irs.gov/FormW4*.

Purpose of Form

Complete Form W-4 so that your employer can withhold the correct federal income tax from your pay. If too little is withheld, you will generally owe tax when you file your tax return and may owe a penalty. If too much is withheld, you will generally be due a refund. Complete a new Form W-4 when changes to your personal or financial situation would change the entries on the form. For more information on withholding and when you must furnish a new Form W-4, see Pub. 505, Tax Withholding and Estimated Tax.

Exemption from withholding. You may claim exemption from withholding for 2024 if you meet both of the following conditions: you had no federal income tax liability in 2023 **and** you expect to have no federal income tax liability in 2024. You had no federal income tax liability in 2023 if (1) your total tax on line 24 on your 2023 Form 1040 or 1040-SR is zero (or less than the sum of lines 27, 28, and 29), or (2) you were not required to file a return because your income was below the filing threshold for your correct filing status. If you claim exemption, you will have no income tax withheld from your paycheck and may owe taxes and penalties when you file your 2024 tax return. To claim exemption from withholding, certify that you meet both of the conditions above by writing "Exempt" on Form W-4 in the space below Step 4(c). Then, complete Steps 1(a), 1(b), and 5. Do not complete any other steps. You will need to submit a new Form W-4 by February 15, 2025.

Your privacy. Steps 2(c) and 4(a) ask for information regarding income you received from sources other than the job associated with this Form W-4. If you have concerns with providing the information asked for in Step 2(c), you may choose Step 2(b) as an alternative; if you have concerns with providing the information asked for in Step 4(a), you may enter an additional amount you want withheld per pay period in Step 4(c) as an alternative.

When to use the estimator. Consider using the estimator at *www.irs.gov/W4App* if you:

1. Expect to work only part of the year;

2. Receive dividends, capital gains, social security, bonuses, or business income, or are subject to the Additional Medicare Tax or Net Investment Income Tax; or

3. Prefer the most accurate withholding for multiple job situations.

Self-employment. Generally, you will owe both income and self-employment taxes on any self-employment income you receive separate from the wages you receive as an employee. If you want to pay these taxes through withholding from your wages, use the estimator at *www.irs.gov/W4App* to figure the amount to have withheld.

Nonresident alien. If you're a nonresident alien, see Notice 1392, Supplemental Form W-4 Instructions for Nonresident Aliens, before completing this form.

Specific Instructions

Step 1(c). Check your anticipated filing status. This will determine the standard deduction and tax rates used to compute your withholding.

Step 2. Use this step if you (1) have more than one job at the same time, or (2) are married filing jointly and you and your spouse both work.

Option **(a)** most accurately calculates the additional tax you need to have withheld, while option **(b)** does so with a little less accuracy.

Instead, if you (and your spouse) have a total of only two jobs, you may check the box in option **(c)**. The box must also be checked on the Form W-4 for the other job. If the box is checked, the standard deduction and tax brackets will be cut in half for each job to calculate withholding. This option is accurate for jobs with similar pay; otherwise, more tax than necessary may be withheld, and this extra amount will be larger the greater the difference in pay is between the two jobs.

Multiple jobs. Complete Steps 3 through 4(b) on only one Form W-4. Withholding will be most accurate if you do this on the Form W-4 for the highest paying job.

Step 3. This step provides instructions for determining the amount of the child tax credit and the credit for other dependents that you may be able to claim when you file your tax return. To qualify for the child tax credit, the child must be under age 17 as of December 31, must be your dependent who generally lives with you for more than half the year, and must have the required social security number. You may be able to claim a credit for other dependents for whom a child tax credit can't be claimed, such as an older child or a qualifying relative. For additional eligibility requirements for these credits, see Pub. 501, Dependents, Standard Deduction, and Filing Information. You can also include **other tax credits** for which you are eligible in this step, such as the foreign tax credit and the education tax credits. To do so, add an estimate of the amount for the year to your credits for dependents and enter the total amount in Step 3. Including these credits will increase your paycheck and reduce the amount of any refund you may receive when you file your tax return.

Step 4 (optional).

Step 4(a). Enter in this step the total of your other estimated income for the year, if any. You shouldn't include income from any jobs or self-employment. If you complete Step 4(a), you likely won't have to make estimated tax payments for that income. If you prefer to pay estimated tax rather than having tax on other income withheld from your paycheck, see Form 1040-ES, Estimated Tax for Individuals.

Step 4(b). Enter in this step the amount from the Deductions Worksheet, line 5, if you expect to claim deductions other than the basic standard deduction on your 2024 tax return and want to reduce your withholding to account for these deductions. This includes both itemized deductions and other deductions such as for student loan interest and IRAs.

Step 4(c). Enter in this step any additional tax you want withheld from your pay **each pay period**, including any amounts from the Multiple Jobs Worksheet, line 4. Entering an amount here will reduce your paycheck and will either increase your refund or reduce any amount of tax that you owe.

Form W-4 (2024) Page 3

Step 2(b)—Multiple Jobs Worksheet (Keep for your records.)

If you choose the option in Step 2(b) on Form W-4, complete this worksheet (which calculates the total extra tax for all jobs) on **only ONE** Form W-4. Withholding will be most accurate if you complete the worksheet and enter the result on the Form W-4 for the highest paying job. To be accurate, submit a new Form W-4 for all other jobs if you have not updated your withholding since 2019.

Note: If more than one job has annual wages of more than $120,000 or there are more than three jobs, see Pub. 505 for additional tables; or, you can use the online withholding estimator at *www.irs.gov/W4App*.

1. **Two jobs.** If you have two jobs or you're married filing jointly and you and your spouse each have one job, find the amount from the appropriate table on page 4. Using the "Higher Paying Job" row and the "Lower Paying Job" column, find the value at the intersection of the two household salaries and enter that value on line 1. Then, **skip** to line 3 . . . . **1** $ 4,890

2. **Three jobs.** If you and/or your spouse have three jobs at the same time, complete lines 2a, 2b, and 2c below. Otherwise, skip to line 3.

    a. Find the amount from the appropriate table on page 4 using the annual wages from the highest paying job in the "Higher Paying Job" row and the annual wages for your next highest paying job in the "Lower Paying Job" column. Find the value at the intersection of the two household salaries and enter that value on line 2a . . . . **2a** $ _____

    b. Add the annual wages of the two highest paying jobs from line 2a together and use the total as the wages in the "Higher Paying Job" row and use the annual wages for your third job in the "Lower Paying Job" column to find the amount from the appropriate table on page 4 and enter this amount on line 2b . . . . **2b** $ _____

    c. Add the amounts from lines 2a and 2b and enter the result on line 2c . . . . **2c** $ 4,890

3. Enter the number of pay periods per year for the highest paying job. For example, if that job pays weekly, enter 52; if it pays every other week, enter 26; if it pays monthly, enter 12, etc. **3** 24

4. **Divide** the annual amount on line 1 or line 2c by the number of pay periods on line 3. Enter this amount here and in **Step 4(c)** of Form W-4 for the highest paying job (along with any other additional amount you want withheld) . . . . **4** $ 203.75

Step 4(b)—Deductions Worksheet (Keep for your records.)

1. Enter an estimate of your 2024 itemized deductions (from Schedule A (Form 1040)). Such deductions may include qualifying home mortgage interest, charitable contributions, state and local taxes (up to $10,000), and medical expenses in excess of 7.5% of your income . . . . **1** $ 30,100

2. Enter:
   - $29,200 if you're married filing jointly or a qualifying surviving spouse
   - $21,900 if you're head of household
   - $14,600 if you're single or married filing separately
   . . . . . . **2** $ 29,200

3. If line 1 is greater than line 2, subtract line 2 from line 1 and enter the result here. If line 2 is greater than line 1, enter "-0-" . . . . **3** $ 900

4. Enter an estimate of your student loan interest, deductible IRA contributions, and certain other adjustments (from Part II of Schedule 1 (Form 1040)). See Pub. 505 for more information . . . . **4** $ 9,500 (a)

5. **Add** lines 3 and 4. Enter the result here and in **Step 4(b)** of Form W-4 . . . . **5** $ 10,400

Privacy Act and Paperwork Reduction Act Notice. We ask for the information on this form to carry out the Internal Revenue laws of the United States. Internal Revenue Code sections 3402(f)(2) and 6109 and their regulations require you to provide this information; your employer uses it to determine your federal income tax withholding. Failure to provide a properly completed form will result in your being treated as a single person with no other entries on the form; providing fraudulent information may subject you to penalties. Routine uses of this information include giving it to the Department of Justice for civil and criminal litigation; to cities, states, the District of Columbia, and U.S. commonwealths and territories for use in administering their tax laws; and to the Department of Health and Human Services for use in the National Directory of New Hires. We may also disclose this information to other countries under a tax treaty, to federal and state agencies to enforce federal nontax criminal laws, or to federal law enforcement and intelligence agencies to combat terrorism.

You are not required to provide the information requested on a form that is subject to the Paperwork Reduction Act unless the form displays a valid OMB control number. Books or records relating to a form or its instructions must be retained as long as their contents may become material in the administration of any Internal Revenue law. Generally, tax returns and return information are confidential, as required by Code section 6103.

The average time and expenses required to complete and file this form will vary depending on individual circumstances. For estimated averages, see the instructions for your income tax return.

If you have suggestions for making this form simpler, we would be happy to hear from you. See the instructions for your income tax return.

(a) The taxpayer's IRA deduction was $7,000 and the maximum student loan interest deduction was $2,500 in 2024.

Form W-4 (2024) Page 4

Married Filing Jointly or Qualifying Surviving Spouse

Higher Paying Job Annual Taxable Wage & Salary	Lower Paying Job Annual Taxable Wage & Salary										
	$0 - 9,999	$10,000 - 19,999	$20,000 - 29,999	$30,000 - 39,999	$40,000 - 49,999	$50,000 - 59,999	$60,000 - 69,999	$70,000 - 79,999	$80,000 - 89,999	$90,000 - 99,999	$100,000 - 109,999	$110,000 - 120,000
$0 - 9,999	$0	$0	$780	$850	$940	$1,020	$1,020	$1,020	$1,020	$1,020	$1,020	$1,370
$10,000 - 19,999	0	780	1,780	1,940	2,140	2,220	2,220	2,220	2,220	2,220	2,570	3,570
$20,000 - 29,999	780	1,780	2,870	3,140	3,340	3,420	3,420	3,420	3,420	3,770	4,770	5,770
$30,000 - 39,999	850	1,940	3,140	3,410	3,610	3,690	3,690	3,690	4,040	5,040	6,040	7,040
$40,000 - 49,999	940	2,140	3,340	3,610	3,810	3,890	3,890	4,240	5,240	6,240	7,240	8,240
$50,000 - 59,999	1,020	2,220	3,420	3,690	3,890	3,970	4,320	5,320	6,320	7,320	8,320	9,320
$60,000 - 69,999	1,020	2,220	3,420	3,690	3,890	4,320	5,320	6,320	7,320	8,320	9,320	10,320
$70,000 - 79,999	1,020	2,220	3,420	3,690	4,240	5,320	6,320	7,320	8,320	9,320	10,320	11,320
$80,000 - 99,999	1,020	2,220	3,620	4,890	6,090	7,170	8,170	9,170	10,170	11,170	12,170	13,170
$100,000 - 149,999	1,870	4,070	6,270	7,540	8,740	9,820	10,820	11,820	12,830	14,030	15,230	16,430
$150,000 - 239,999	1,960	4,360	6,760	8,230	9,630	10,910	12,110	13,310	14,510	15,710	16,910	18,110
$240,000 - 259,999	2,040	4,440	6,840	8,310	9,710	10,990	12,190	13,390	14,590	15,790	16,990	18,190
$260,000 - 279,999	2,040	4,440	6,840	8,310	9,710	10,990	12,190	13,390	14,590	15,790	16,990	18,190
$280,000 - 299,999	2,040	4,440	6,840	8,310	9,710	10,990	12,190	13,390	14,590	15,790	16,990	18,380
$300,000 - 319,999	2,040	4,440	6,840	8,310	9,710	10,990	12,190	13,390	14,590	15,980	17,980	19,980
$320,000 - 364,999	2,040	4,440	6,840	8,310	9,710	11,280	13,280	15,280	17,280	19,280	21,280	23,280
$365,000 - 524,999	2,720	6,010	9,510	12,080	14,580	16,950	19,250	21,550	23,850	26,150	28,450	30,750
$525,000 and over	3,140	6,840	10,540	13,310	16,010	18,590	21,090	23,590	26,090	28,590	31,090	33,590

Single or Married Filing Separately

Higher Paying Job Annual Taxable Wage & Salary	Lower Paying Job Annual Taxable Wage & Salary										
	$0 - 9,999	$10,000 - 19,999	$20,000 - 29,999	$30,000 - 39,999	$40,000 - 49,999	$50,000 - 59,999	$60,000 - 69,999	$70,000 - 79,999	$80,000 - 89,999	$90,000 - 99,999	$100,000 - 109,999	$110,000 - 120,000
$0 - 9,999	$240	$870	$1,020	$1,020	$1,020	$1,540	$1,870	$1,870	$1,870	$1,870	$1,910	$2,040
$10,000 - 19,999	870	1,680	1,830	1,830	2,350	3,350	3,680	3,680	3,680	3,720	3,920	4,050
$20,000 - 29,999	1,020	1,830	1,980	2,510	3,510	4,510	4,830	4,830	4,870	5,070	5,270	5,400
$30,000 - 39,999	1,020	1,830	2,510	3,510	4,510	5,510	5,830	5,870	6,070	6,270	6,470	6,600
$40,000 - 59,999	1,390	3,200	4,360	5,360	6,360	7,370	7,890	8,090	8,290	8,490	8,690	8,820
$60,000 - 79,999	1,870	3,680	4,830	5,840	7,040	8,240	8,770	8,970	9,170	9,370	9,570	9,700
$80,000 - 99,999	1,870	3,690	5,040	6,240	7,440	8,640	9,170	9,370	9,570	9,770	9,970	10,810
$100,000 - 124,999	2,040	4,050	5,400	6,600	7,800	9,000	9,530	9,730	10,180	11,180	12,180	13,120
$125,000 - 149,999	2,040	4,050	5,400	6,600	7,800	9,000	10,180	11,180	12,180	13,180	14,180	15,310
$150,000 - 174,999	2,040	4,050	5,400	6,860	8,860	10,860	12,180	13,180	14,230	15,530	16,830	18,060
$175,000 - 199,999	2,040	4,710	6,860	8,860	10,860	12,860	14,380	15,680	16,980	18,280	19,580	20,810
$200,000 - 249,999	2,720	5,610	8,060	10,360	12,660	14,960	16,590	17,890	19,190	20,490	21,790	23,020
$250,000 - 399,999	2,970	6,080	8,540	10,840	13,140	15,440	17,060	18,360	19,660	20,960	22,260	23,500
$400,000 - 449,999	2,970	6,080	8,540	10,840	13,140	15,440	17,060	18,360	19,660	20,960	22,260	23,500
$450,000 and over	3,140	6,450	9,110	11,610	14,110	16,610	18,430	19,930	21,430	22,930	24,430	25,870

Head of Household

Higher Paying Job Annual Taxable Wage & Salary	Lower Paying Job Annual Taxable Wage & Salary										
	$0 - 9,999	$10,000 - 19,999	$20,000 - 29,999	$30,000 - 39,999	$40,000 - 49,999	$50,000 - 59,999	$60,000 - 69,999	$70,000 - 79,999	$80,000 - 89,999	$90,000 - 99,999	$100,000 - 109,999	$110,000 - 120,000
$0 - 9,999	$0	$510	$850	$1,020	$1,020	$1,020	$1,020	$1,220	$1,870	$1,870	$1,870	$1,960
$10,000 - 19,999	510	1,510	2,020	2,220	2,220	2,220	2,420	3,420	4,070	4,070	4,160	4,360
$20,000 - 29,999	850	2,020	2,560	2,760	2,760	2,960	3,960	4,960	5,610	5,700	5,900	6,100
$30,000 - 39,999	1,020	2,220	2,760	2,960	3,160	4,160	5,160	6,160	6,900	7,100	7,300	7,500
$40,000 - 59,999	1,020	2,220	2,810	4,010	5,010	6,010	7,070	8,270	9,120	9,320	9,520	9,720
$60,000 - 79,999	1,070	3,270	4,810	6,010	7,070	8,270	9,470	10,670	11,520	11,720	11,920	12,120
$80,000 - 99,999	1,870	4,070	5,670	7,070	8,270	9,470	10,670	11,870	12,720	12,920	13,120	13,450
$100,000 - 124,999	2,020	4,420	6,160	7,560	8,760	9,960	11,160	12,360	13,210	13,880	14,880	15,880
$125,000 - 149,999	2,040	4,440	6,180	7,580	8,780	9,980	11,250	13,250	14,900	15,900	16,900	17,900
$150,000 - 174,999	2,040	4,440	6,180	7,580	9,250	11,250	13,250	15,250	16,900	18,030	19,330	20,630
$175,000 - 199,999	2,040	4,510	7,050	9,250	11,250	13,250	15,250	17,530	19,480	20,780	22,080	23,380
$200,000 - 249,999	2,720	5,920	8,620	11,120	13,420	15,720	18,020	20,320	22,270	23,570	24,870	26,170
$250,000 - 449,999	2,970	6,470	9,310	11,810	14,110	16,410	18,710	21,010	22,960	24,260	25,560	26,860
$450,000 and over	3,140	6,840	9,880	12,580	15,080	17,580	20,080	22,580	24,730	26,230	27,730	29,230

An employer should withhold based on a valid Form W-4 authorized by the employee. If a valid Form W-4 has not been submitted, the employer should withhold based on a single taxpayer with no adjustments. There is no expectation that the employer confirm the information reported by the employee on a Form W-4; however, a Form W-4 is considered invalid if the employee clearly indicates information on Form W-4 is false by an oral or written statement.

An employee who submits a false Form W-4 may be subject to a $500 penalty. Willfully filing a fraudulent Form W-4 or failing to supply information that would increase the amount withheld can result in a fine of up to $1,000 or imprisonment for up to 1 year, or both. Employers must submit copies of Forms W-4 to the IRS only when directed to do so by written notice. Where there is significant underwithholding for a particular employee, the IRS may require the employer to withhold income tax at a higher rate and will notify the employer in writing (known as a "lock-in" letter). Employees are given the right to contest the IRS determination.

Example Brianne is the payroll manager at her company and receives a Form W-4 from her employee, Mike. On his Form W-4, Mike indicated that he is a married employee with five children under age 17. Brianne also noted that Mike did not list a spouse or his children on his application or retirement plan paperwork and earlier mentioned that he was single. Based on both written and oral statements made by Mike, Brianne should ask Mike to prepare a corrected W-4. If he is unwilling to do so, she should withhold as if Mike is a single taxpayer. ♦

Example George works in the payroll department and receives a Form W-4 from a new employee, Beatrice. Beatrice indicates married status and claims $4,000 on Step 3 for dependents on her Form W-4. George notes that her married status is consistent with her other paperwork and Beatrice has provided no oral or written statements that would indicate she is not married and has two children. George is not required to verify the existence of Beatrice's spouse and children. ♦

Although employers are not required to submit Forms W-4 to the Internal Revenue Service, that does not mean that new hires are not reported. In large part designed to assist with the enforcement of child support payments, the Personal Responsibility and Work Opportunity Reconciliation Act of 1996 (PRWORA) was passed requiring states to maintain a database of all new hires. Although many states use a specific form for reporting new hires, states will often also accept a completed Form W-4. The U.S. Department of Health and Human Services offers links to each state's new hire reporting system at https://www.acf.hhs.gov/css/contact-information/state-new-hire-reporting-websites

9-2b The Form W-4 Before 2020

As presented previously, the former version of Form W-4 focused on the concept of "allowances" to determine the amount of income tax withholding. Employees would complete the Personal Allowances Worksheet and carry that information forward to the face of the Form W-4. The number of allowances was adjusted for two-wage earners, additional deductions, and credits. Employees who submitted a Form W-4 in any year before 2020 are not required to submit a new Form W-4. Employers will continue to compute withholding based on the information from the employee's old Form W-4. All new employees and any existing employees that wish to adjust withholding must use the new Form W-4.

Example Using the information from the example of Fei and Zhi Han on Page 9-8, a completed 2019 Form W-4 is presented on Pages 9-14 to 9-17. Note that this example presumes that Zhi completed this form in 2019 and that the employer would continue to use this information for withholding in 2024. ♦

Form W-4 (2019)

Future developments. For the latest information about any future developments related to Form W-4, such as legislation enacted after it was published, go to *www.irs.gov/FormW4*.

Purpose. Complete Form W-4 so that your employer can withhold the correct federal income tax from your pay. Consider completing a new Form W-4 each year and when your personal or financial situation changes.

Exemption from withholding. You may claim exemption from withholding for 2019 if **both** of the following apply.

- For 2018 you had a right to a refund of **all** federal income tax withheld because you had **no** tax liability, **and**
- For 2019 you expect a refund of **all** federal income tax withheld because you expect to have **no** tax liability.

If you're exempt, complete **only** lines 1, 2, 3, 4, and 7 and sign the form to validate it. Your exemption for 2019 expires February 17, 2020. See Pub. 505, Tax Withholding and Estimated Tax, to learn more about whether you qualify for exemption from withholding.

General Instructions

If you aren't exempt, follow the rest of these instructions to determine the number of withholding allowances you should claim for withholding for 2019 and any additional amount of tax to have withheld. For regular wages, withholding must be based on allowances you claimed and may not be a flat amount or percentage of wages.

You can also use the calculator at *www.irs.gov/W4App* to determine your tax withholding more accurately. Consider using this calculator if you have a more complicated tax situation, such as if you have a working spouse, more than one job, or a large amount of nonwage income not subject to withholding outside of your job. After your Form W-4 takes effect, you can also use this calculator to see how the amount of tax you're having withheld compares to your projected total tax for 2019. If you use the calculator, you don't need to complete any of the worksheets for Form W-4.

Note that if you have too much tax withheld, you will receive a refund when you file your tax return. If you have too little tax withheld, you will owe tax when you file your tax return, and you might owe a penalty.

Filers with multiple jobs or working spouses. If you have more than one job at a time, or if you're married filing jointly and your spouse is also working, read all of the instructions including the instructions for the Two-Earners/Multiple Jobs Worksheet before beginning.

Nonwage income. If you have a large amount of nonwage income not subject to withholding, such as interest or dividends, consider making estimated tax payments using Form 1040-ES, Estimated Tax for Individuals. Otherwise, you might owe additional tax. Or, you can use the Deductions, Adjustments, and Additional Income Worksheet on page 3 or the calculator at *www.irs.gov/W4App* to make sure you have enough tax withheld from your paycheck. If you have pension or annuity income, see Pub. 505 or use the calculator at *www.irs.gov/W4App* to find out if you should adjust your withholding on Form W-4 or W-4P.

Nonresident alien. If you're a nonresident alien, see Notice 1392, Supplemental Form W-4 Instructions for Nonresident Aliens, before completing this form.

Specific Instructions

Personal Allowances Worksheet

Complete this worksheet on page 3 first to determine the number of withholding allowances to claim.

Line C. *Head of household please note:* Generally, you may claim head of household filing status on your tax return only if you're unmarried and pay more than 50% of the costs of keeping up a home for yourself and a qualifying individual. See Pub. 501 for more information about filing status.

Line E. Child tax credit. When you file your tax return, you may be eligible to claim a child tax credit for each of your eligible children. To qualify, the child must be under age 17 as of December 31, must be your dependent who lives with you for more than half the year, and must have a valid social security number. To learn more about this credit, see Pub. 972, Child Tax Credit. To reduce the tax withheld from your pay by taking this credit into account, follow the instructions on line E of the worksheet. On the worksheet you will be asked about your total income. For this purpose, total income includes all of your wages and other income, including income earned by a spouse if you are filing a joint return.

Line F. Credit for other dependents. When you file your tax return, you may be eligible to claim a credit for other dependents for whom a child tax credit can't be claimed, such as a qualifying child who doesn't meet the age or social security number requirement for the child tax credit, or a qualifying relative. To learn more about this credit, see Pub. 972. To reduce the tax withheld from your pay by taking this credit into account, follow the instructions on line F of the worksheet. On the worksheet, you will be asked about your total income. For this purpose, total

---

Separate here and give Form W-4 to your employer. Keep the worksheet(s) for your records.

Form W-4
Department of the Treasury
Internal Revenue Service

Employee's Withholding Allowance Certificate

▶ Whether you're entitled to claim a certain number of allowances or exemption from withholding is subject to review by the IRS. Your employer may be required to send a copy of this form to the IRS.

OMB No. 1545-0074

2019

1	Your first name and middle initial: Zhi	Last name: Han	2	Your social security number

Home address (number and street or rural route)

3 ☐ Single ☑ Married ☐ Married, but withhold at higher Single rate.
Note: If married filing separately, check "Married, but withhold at higher Single rate."

City or town, state, and ZIP code

4 If your last name differs from that shown on your social security card, check here. You must call 800-772-1213 for a replacement card. ▶ ☐

5	Total number of allowances you're claiming (from the applicable worksheet on the following pages)	**5**	7
6	Additional amount, if any, you want withheld from each paycheck	**6** $	
7	I claim exemption from withholding for 2019, and I certify that I meet **both** of the following conditions for exemption.		

- Last year I had a right to a refund of **all** federal income tax withheld because I had **no** tax liability, **and**
- This year I expect a refund of **all** federal income tax withheld because I expect to have **no** tax liability.

If you meet both conditions, write "Exempt" here . . . . ▶ | **7** |

Under penalties of perjury, I declare that I have examined this certificate and, to the best of my knowledge and belief, it is true, correct, and complete.

Employee's signature
(This form is not valid unless you sign it.) ▶   **Date ▶**

8	Employer's name and address (**Employer:** Complete boxes 8 and 10 if sending to IRS and complete boxes 8, 9, and 10 if sending to State Directory of New Hires.)	9	First date of employment	10	Employer identification number (EIN)

For Privacy Act and Paperwork Reduction Act Notice, see page 4.   Cat. No. 10220Q   Form **W-4** (2019)

Form W-4 (2019) — Page 2

income includes all of your wages and other income, including income earned by a spouse if you are filing a joint return.

Line G. Other credits. You may be able to reduce the tax withheld from your paycheck if you expect to claim other tax credits, such as tax credits for education (see Pub. 970). If you do so, your paycheck will be larger, but the amount of any refund that you receive when you file your tax return will be smaller. Follow the instructions for Worksheet 1-6 in Pub. 505 if you want to reduce your withholding to take these credits into account. Enter "-0-" on lines E and F if you use Worksheet 1-6.

Deductions, Adjustments, and Additional Income Worksheet

Complete this worksheet to determine if you're able to reduce the tax withheld from your paycheck to account for your itemized deductions and other adjustments to income, such as IRA contributions. If you do so, your refund at the end of the year will be smaller, but your paycheck will be larger. You're not required to complete this worksheet or reduce your withholding if you don't wish to do so.

You can also use this worksheet to figure out how much to increase the tax withheld from your paycheck if you have a large amount of nonwage income not subject to withholding, such as interest or dividends.

Another option is to take these items into account and make your withholding more accurate by using the calculator at *www.irs.gov/W4App*. If you use the calculator, you don't need to complete any of the worksheets for Form W-4.

Two-Earners/Multiple Jobs Worksheet

Complete this worksheet if you have more than one job at a time or are married filing jointly and have a working spouse. If you don't complete this worksheet, you might have too little tax withheld. If so, you will owe tax when you file your tax return and might be subject to a penalty.

Figure the total number of allowances you're entitled to claim and any additional amount of tax to withhold on all jobs using worksheets from only one Form W-4. Claim all allowances on the W-4 that you or your spouse file for the highest paying job in your family and claim zero allowances on Forms W-4 filed for all other jobs. For example, if you earn $60,000 per year and your spouse earns $20,000, you should complete the worksheets to determine what to enter on lines 5 and 6 of your Form W-4, and your spouse should enter zero ("-0-") on lines 5 and 6 of his or her Form W-4. See Pub. 505 for details.

Another option is to use the calculator at *www.irs.gov/W4App* to make your withholding more accurate.

Tip: If you have a working spouse and your incomes are similar, you can check the "Married, but withhold at higher Single rate" box instead of using this worksheet. If you choose this option, then each spouse should fill out the Personal Allowances Worksheet and check the "Married, but withhold at higher Single rate" box on Form W-4, but only one spouse should claim any allowances for credits or fill out the Deductions, Adjustments, and Additional Income Worksheet.

Instructions for Employer

Employees, do not complete box 8, 9, or 10. Your employer will complete these boxes if necessary.

New hire reporting. Employers are required by law to report new employees to a designated State Directory of New Hires. Employers may use Form W-4, boxes 8, 9, and 10 to comply with the new hire reporting requirement for a newly hired employee. A newly hired employee is an employee who hasn't previously been employed by the employer, or who was previously employed by the employer but has been separated from such prior employment for at least 60 consecutive days. Employers should contact the appropriate State Directory of New Hires to find out how to submit a copy of the completed Form W-4. For information and links to each designated State Directory of New Hires (including for U.S. territories), go to *www.acf.hhs.gov/css/employers.*

If an employer is sending a copy of Form W-4 to a designated State Directory of New Hires to comply with the new hire reporting requirement for a newly hired employee, complete boxes 8, 9, and 10 as follows.

Box 8. Enter the employer's name and address. If the employer is sending a copy of this form to a State Directory of New Hires, enter the address where child support agencies should send income withholding orders.

Box 9. If the employer is sending a copy of this form to a State Directory of New Hires, enter the employee's first date of employment, which is the date services for payment were first performed by the employee. If the employer rehired the employee after the employee had been separated from the employer's service for at least 60 days, enter the rehire date.

Box 10. Enter the employer's employer identification number (EIN).

Form W-4 (2019) Page **3**

Personal Allowances Worksheet (Keep for your records.)

A	Enter "1" for yourself	A	1
B	Enter "1" if you will file as married filing jointly	B	1
C	Enter "1" if you will file as head of household	C	
D	Enter "1" if: • You're single, or married filing separately, and have only one job; or • You're married filing jointly, have only one job, and your spouse doesn't work; or • Your wages from a second job or your spouse's wages (or the total of both) are $1,500 or less.	D	
E	**Child tax credit.** See Pub. 972, Child Tax Credit, for more information. • If your total income will be less than $71,201 ($103,351 if married filing jointly), enter "4" for each eligible child. • If your total income will be from $71,201 to $179,050 ($103,351 to $345,850 if married filing jointly), enter "2" for each eligible child. • If your total income will be from $179,051 to $200,000 ($345,851 to $400,000 if married filing jointly), enter "1" for each eligible child. • If your total income will be higher than $200,000 ($400,000 if married filing jointly), enter "-0-"	E	6 (a)
F	**Credit for other dependents.** See Pub. 972, Child Tax Credit, for more information. • If your total income will be less than $71,201 ($103,351 if married filing jointly), enter "1" for each eligible dependent. • If your total income will be from $71,201 to $179,050 ($103,351 to $345,850 if married filing jointly), enter "1" for every two dependents (for example, "-0-" for one dependent, "1" if you have two or three dependents, and "2" if you have four dependents). • If your total income will be higher than $179,050 ($345,850 if married filing jointly), enter "-0-"	F	0
G	**Other credits.** If you have other credits, see Worksheet 1-6 of Pub. 505 and enter the amount from that worksheet here. If you use Worksheet 1-6, enter "-0-" on lines E and F	G	
H	Add lines A through G and enter the total here . . . . ▶	H	8

For accuracy, complete all worksheets that apply.
- If you plan to **itemize** or **claim adjustments to income** and want to reduce your withholding, or if you have a large amount of nonwage income not subject to withholding and want to increase your withholding, see the **Deductions, Adjustments, and Additional Income Worksheet** below.
- If you **have more than one job at a time** or are **married filing jointly and you and your spouse both work**, and the combined earnings from all jobs exceed $53,000 ($24,450 if married filing jointly), see the **Two-Earners/Multiple Jobs Worksheet** on page 4 to avoid having too little tax withheld.
- If **neither** of the above situations applies, **stop here** and enter the number from line H on line 5 of Form W-4 above.

Deductions, Adjustments, and Additional Income Worksheet

Note: Use this worksheet *only* if you plan to itemize deductions, claim certain adjustments to income, or have a large amount of nonwage income not subject to withholding.

1	Enter an estimate of your 2019 itemized deductions. These include qualifying home mortgage interest, charitable contributions, state and local taxes (up to $10,000), and medical expenses in excess of 10% of your income. See Pub. 505 for details	1 $	30,100 (b)
2	Enter: $24,400 if you're married filing jointly or qualifying widow(er) $18,350 if you're head of household $12,200 if you're single or married filing separately	2 $	24,400
3	**Subtract** line 2 from line 1. If zero or less, enter "-0-"	3 $	5,700
4	Enter an estimate of your 2019 adjustments to income, qualified business income deduction, and any additional standard deduction for age or blindness (see Pub. 505 for information about these items) . .	4 $	8,500 (c)
5	**Add** lines 3 and 4 and enter the total	5 $	14,200
6	Enter an estimate of your 2019 nonwage income not subject to withholding (such as dividends or interest) .	6 $	3,800 (b)
7	**Subtract** line 6 from line 5. If zero, enter "-0-". If less than zero, enter the amount in parentheses . . .	7 $	10,400
8	**Divide** the amount on line 7 by $4,200 and enter the result here. If a negative amount, enter in parentheses. Drop any fraction	8	2
9	Enter the number from the **Personal Allowances Worksheet,** line H, above	9	8
10	**Add** lines 8 and 9 and enter the total here. If zero or less, enter "-0-". If you plan to use the **Two-Earners/Multiple Jobs Worksheet,** also enter this total on line 1 of that worksheet on page 4. Otherwise, **stop here** and enter this total on Form W-4, line 5, page 1	10	10

(a) In 2019, the assumed time for filing this Form W-4, all three children would be eligible for the child tax credit.
(b) The current 2024 amounts are assumed to be equal to 2019 amounts.
(c) The maximum IRA deduction was $6,000 and the maximum student loan interest deduction was $2,500 in 2019.

Form W-4 (2019) Page **4**

Two-Earners/Multiple Jobs Worksheet

Note: Use this worksheet *only* if the instructions under line H from the **Personal Allowances Worksheet** direct you here.

1. Enter the number from the **Personal Allowances Worksheet,** line H, page 3 (or, if you used the **Deductions, Adjustments, and Additional Income Worksheet** on page 3, the number from line 10 of that worksheet) . . . . **1** ___10___

2. Find the number in **Table 1** below that applies to the **LOWEST** paying job and enter it here. **However,** if you're married filing jointly and wages from the highest paying job are $75,000 or less and the combined wages for you and your spouse are $107,000 or less, don't enter more than "3" . . . . **2** ___3___

3. If line 1 is **more than or equal to** line 2, subtract line 2 from line 1. Enter the result here (if zero, enter "-0-") and on Form W-4, line 5, page 1. **Do not** use the rest of this worksheet . . . . **3** ___7___

Note: If line 1 is **less than** line 2, enter "-0-" on Form W-4, line 5, page 1. Complete lines 4 through 9 below to figure the additional withholding amount necessary to avoid a year-end tax bill.

4. Enter the number from line 2 of this worksheet . . . . **4** _____
5. Enter the number from line 1 of this worksheet . . . . **5** _____
6. **Subtract** line 5 from line 4 . . . . **6** _____
7. Find the amount in **Table 2** below that applies to the **HIGHEST** paying job and enter it here . . . . . . **7** $_____
8. **Multiply** line 7 by line 6 and enter the result here. This is the additional annual withholding needed . . . **8** $_____
9. **Divide** line 8 by the number of pay periods remaining in 2019. For example, divide by 18 if you're paid every 2 weeks and you complete this form on a date in late April when there are 18 pay periods remaining in 2019. Enter the result here and on Form W-4, line 6, page 1. This is the additional amount to be withheld from each paycheck . . . . **9** $_____

Table 1

Married Filing Jointly		All Others	
If wages from **LOWEST** paying job are—	Enter on line 2 above	If wages from **LOWEST** paying job are—	Enter on line 2 above
$0 - $5,000	0	$0 - $7,000	0
5,001 - 9,500	1	7,001 - 13,000	1
9,501 - 19,500	2	13,001 - 27,500	2
19,501 - 35,000	3	27,501 - 32,000	3
35,001 - 40,000	4	32,001 - 40,000	4
40,001 - 46,000	5	40,001 - 60,000	5
46,001 - 55,000	6	60,001 - 75,000	6
55,001 - 60,000	7	75,001 - 85,000	7
60,001 - 70,000	8	85,001 - 95,000	8
70,001 - 75,000	9	95,001 - 100,000	9
75,001 - 85,000	10	100,001 - 110,000	10
85,001 - 95,000	11	110,001 - 115,000	11
95,001 - 125,000	12	115,001 - 125,000	12
125,001 - 155,000	13	125,001 - 135,000	13
155,001 - 165,000	14	135,001 - 145,000	14
165,001 - 175,000	15	145,001 - 160,000	15
175,001 - 180,000	16	160,001 - 180,000	16
180,001 - 195,000	17	180,001 and over	17
195,001 - 205,000	18		
205,001 and over	19		

Table 2

Married Filing Jointly		All Others	
If wages from **HIGHEST** paying job are—	Enter on line 7 above	If wages from **HIGHEST** paying job are—	Enter on line 7 above
$0 - $24,900	$420	$0 - $7,200	$420
24,901 - 84,450	500	7,201 - 36,975	500
84,451 - 173,900	910	36,976 - 81,700	910
173,901 - 326,950	1,000	81,701 - 158,225	1,000
326,951 - 413,700	1,330	158,226 - 201,600	1,330
413,701 - 617,850	1,450	201,601 - 507,800	1,450
617,851 and over	1,540	507,801 and over	1,540

Privacy Act and Paperwork Reduction Act Notice. We ask for the information on this form to carry out the Internal Revenue laws of the United States. Internal Revenue Code sections 3402(f)(2) and 6109 and their regulations require you to provide this information; your employer uses it to determine your federal income tax withholding. Failure to provide a properly completed form will result in your being treated as a single person who claims no withholding allowances; providing fraudulent information may subject you to penalties. Routine uses of this information include giving it to the Department of Justice for civil and criminal litigation; to cities, states, the District of Columbia, and U.S. commonwealths and possessions for use in administering their tax laws; and to the Department of Health and Human Services for use in the National Directory of New Hires. We may also disclose this information to other countries under a tax treaty, to federal and state agencies to enforce federal nontax criminal laws, or to federal law enforcement and intelligence agencies to combat terrorism.

You aren't required to provide the information requested on a form that's subject to the Paperwork Reduction Act unless the form displays a valid OMB control number. Books or records relating to a form or its instructions must be retained as long as their contents may become material in the administration of any Internal Revenue law. Generally, tax returns and return information are confidential, as required by Code section 6103.

The average time and expenses required to complete and file this form will vary depending on individual circumstances. For estimated averages, see the instructions for your income tax return.

If you have suggestions for making this form simpler, we would be happy to hear from you. See the instructions for your income tax return.

Source: Internal Revenue Service (IRS)

9-2c Computing Income Tax Withholding

The amount of income tax to be withheld by the employer is based on gross taxable wages before deducting FICA (Social Security and Medicare) taxes, pension payments, union dues, insurance, and other deductions. An employer may elect to use any of several methods to determine the amount of the income tax withholding for each individual employee. Most commonly, withholding amounts are determined by use of the percentage method or by use of wage bracket tables.

The withholding tables published by the IRS allow employers to determine withholding based on old and new Forms W-4 under both the percentage and wage bracket methods.

To compute the withholding amount under the percentage method using a post-2019 ("new") Form W-4, the employer should use information from Form W-4 to prepare the adjusted wage amount, the tentative withholding amount, the adjustment for tax credits, and the final withholding. The steps can be summarized as:

1. Adjust the employee's wages for other forms of income [Line 4(a) from the employee's Form W-4] and excess deductions [Line 4(b) from the employee's Form W-4].
2. Determine the tentative withholding amount using the current year percentage method tables (reproduced in Appendix C).
3. Account for tax credits.
4. Add any additional withholding requested to determine the final withholding amount.

IRS Publication 15-T, Federal Income Tax Withholding Methods includes Worksheet 4 for employers to follow in computing withholding under the percentage method for an employee using a post-2019 ("new") Form W-4. When using the new percentage method tables, care should be taken to select the proper tentative withholding amount from the table. There are two tentative withholding amount columns to choose from. The first column is for standard withholding and the second column is for when the taxpayer has checked the box on 2(c) of Form W-4, indicating that the taxpayer's spouse has wages similar to the taxpayer.

Example Using the information presented in the Fei and Zhi Han example from Page 9-8 and the new Form W-4 on Pages 9-9 to 9-12, Worksheet 4 is presented on Page 9-19 for one of Zhi's pay periods in 2024. The amount of withholding under the percentage method is $287.06 ♦

Under the wage bracket method of determining withholding, wage bracket tables are provided for weekly, biweekly, semimonthly, monthly, and daily payroll periods for both married, single, and head of household taxpayers. For a post-2019 Form W-4, the amount of withholding is obtained from the wage bracket method table for the appropriate payroll period and marital status and is based on the adjusted wage amount. The adjusted wage amount can be calculated using Worksheet 2 from Publication 15-T. The wage bracket method semimonthly tables for single and married taxpayers are reproduced in Appendix C. Similar to the percentage method tables, there are two tentative withholding amount columns to choose from. The first column is for standard withholding and the second column is for when the taxpayer has checked the box on 2(c) of Form W-4, indicating that the taxpayer's spouse has wages similar to the taxpayer.

Example Using the information presented in the Fei and Zhi Han example from Page 9-8 and the new Form W-4 on Pages 9-9 to 9-12, Worksheet 2 is presented on Page 9-20 for one of Zhi's pay periods in 2024. The amount of withholding under the wage bracket method is $285.42. ♦

4. Percentage Method Tables for Manual Payroll Systems With Forms W-4 From 2020 or Later

If you compute payroll manually, your employee has submitted a Form W-4 for 2020 or later, and you prefer to use the Percentage Method or you can't use the Wage Bracket Method tables because the employee's annual wages exceed the amount from the last bracket of the table (based on marital status and pay period), use the worksheet below and the Percentage Method tables that follow to figure federal income tax withholding. This method works for any amount of wages.

Worksheet 4. Employer's Withholding Worksheet for Percentage Method Tables for Manual Payroll Systems With Forms W-4 From 2020 or Later

Keep for Your Records

Table 6	Monthly	Semimonthly	Biweekly	Weekly	Daily
	12	24	26	52	260

Step 1. Adjust the employee's wage amount

1a	Enter the employee's total taxable wages this payroll period	1a	$ 4,083.33 (a)
1b	Enter the number of pay periods you have per year (see Table 6)	1b	24
1c	Enter the amount from Step 4(a) of the employee's Form W-4	1c	$ 3,800.00
1d	Divide line 1c by the number on line 1b	1d	$ 158.33
1e	Add lines 1a and 1d	1e	$ 4,241.66
1f	Enter the amount from Step 4(b) of the employee's Form W-4	1f	$ 10,400.00
1g	Divide line 1f by the number on line 1b	1g	$ 433.33
1h	Subtract line 1g from line 1e. If zero or less, enter -0-. This is the **Adjusted Wage Amount**	1h	$ 3,808.33

Step 2. Figure the Tentative Withholding Amount

based on your pay frequency, the employee's Adjusted Wage Amount, filing status (Step 1(c) of Form W-4), and whether the box in Step 2 of Form W-4 is checked.

2a	Find the row in the STANDARD Withholding Rate Schedules (if the box in Step 2 of Form W-4 is NOT checked) or the Form W-4, Step 2, Checkbox, Withholding Rate Schedules (if it HAS been checked) of the Percentage Method tables in this section in which the amount on line 1h is at least the amount in column A but less than the amount in column B, and then enter here the amount from column A of that row	2a	$ 2,183.00 (b)
2b	Enter the amount from column C of that row	2b	$ 96.60
2c	Enter the percentage from column D of that row	2c	12%
2d	Subtract line 2a from line 1h	2d	$ 1,625.33
2e	Multiply the amount on line 2d by the percentage on line 2c	2e	$ 195.04
2f	Add lines 2b and 2e. This is the **Tentative Withholding Amount**	2f	$ 291.64

Step 3. Account for tax credits

3a	Enter the amount from Step 3 of the employee's Form W-4	3a	$ 5,000.00
3b	Divide the amount on line 3a by the number of pay periods on line 1b	3b	$ 208.33
3c	Subtract line 3b from line 2f. If zero or less, enter -0-	3c	$ 83.31

Step 4. Figure the final amount to withhold

4a	Enter the additional amount to withhold from Step 4(c) of the employee's Form W-4	4a	$ 203.75
4b	Add lines 3c and 4a. **This is the amount to withhold from the employee's wages this pay period**	4b	$ 287.06

(a) Zhi's salary of $98,000 ÷ 24 semimonthly pay periods.
(b) Standard Withholding Rate Schedules of the Percentage Method tables are found in Appendix C.

2. Wage Bracket Method Tables for Manual Payroll Systems With Forms W-4 From 2020 or Later

If you compute payroll manually, your employee has submitted a Form W-4 for 2020 or later, and you prefer to use the Wage Bracket Method, use the worksheet below and the Wage Bracket Method tables that follow to figure federal income tax withholding.

These Wage Bracket Method tables cover a limited amount of annual wages (generally, less than $100,000). If you can't use the Wage Bracket Method tables because taxable wages exceed the amount from the last bracket of the table (based on filing status and pay period), use the Percentage Method tables in section 4.

Worksheet 2. Employer's Withholding Worksheet for Wage Bracket Method Tables for Manual Payroll Systems With Forms W-4 From 2020 or Later

Keep for Your Records

Table 5	Monthly	Semimonthly	Biweekly	Weekly	Daily
	12	24	26	52	260

Step 1. Adjust the employee's wage amount

1a	Enter the employee's total taxable wages this payroll period	1a	$ 4,083.33
1b	Enter the number of pay periods you have per year (see Table 5)	1b	24
1c	Enter the amount from Step 4(a) of the employee's Form W-4	1c	$ 3,800.00
1d	Divide the amount on line 1c by the number of pay periods on line 1b	1d	$ 158.33
1e	Add lines 1a and 1d	1e	$ 4,241.66
1f	Enter the amount from Step 4(b) of the employee's Form W-4	1f	$ 10,400.00
1g	Divide the amount on line 1f by the number of pay periods on line 1b	1g	$ 433.33
1h	Subtract line 1g from line 1e. If zero or less, enter -0-. This is the **Adjusted Wage Amount**	1h	$ 3,808.33

Step 2. Figure the Tentative Withholding Amount

2a	Use the amount on line 1h to look up the tentative amount to withhold in the appropriate Wage Bracket Method table in this section for your pay frequency, given the employee's filing status and whether the employee has checked the box in Step 2 of Form W-4. This is the **Tentative Withholding Amount**	2a	$ 290.00 (a)

Step 3. Account for tax credits

3a	Enter the amount from Step 3 of the employee's Form W-4	3a	$ 5,000.00
3b	Divide the amount on line 3a by the number of pay periods on line 1b	3b	$ 208.33
3c	Subtract line 3b from line 2a. If zero or less, enter -0-	3c	$ 81.67

Step 4. Figure the final amount to withhold

4a	Enter the additional amount to withhold from Step 4(c) of the employee's Form W-4	4a	$ 203.75
4b	Add lines 3c and 4a. **This is the amount to withhold from the employee's wages this pay period**	4b	$ 285.42

(a) Standard withholding from the semimonthly wage bracket method tables found in Appendix C.

To compute the withholding amount under the percentage method using an old (before 2020) Form W-4, the employer should:

1. Multiply the number of allowances claimed by the employee (from Form W-4) by the allowance amount;
2. Subtract that amount from the employee's gross taxable wages for the pay period; and
3. Apply the result in Step 2 to the applicable withholding table in Appendix C for the appropriate marital status.

Publication 15-T provides Worksheet 5 to assist employers in calculating withholding under the percentage method for an old Form W-4.

Example Using the information presented in the Fei and Zhi Han example from Page 9-8 and the old Form W-4 on Pages 9-14 to 9-17, Worksheet 5 is presented below for one of Zhi's pay periods in 2024. The amount of withholding under the percentage method is $238.82. ♦

5. Percentage Method Tables for Manual Payroll Systems With Forms W-4 From 2019 or Earlier

If you compute payroll manually and your employee **has not** submitted a Form W-4 for 2020 or later, and you prefer to use the Percentage Method or you can't use the Wage Bracket Method tables because the employee's annual wages exceed the amount from the last bracket of the table (based on marital status and pay period) or the employee claimed more than 10 allowances, use the worksheet below and the Percentage Method tables that follow to figure federal income tax withholding. This method works for any number of withholding allowances claimed and any amount of wages.

Periodic payments of pensions or annuities with a 2021 or earlier Form W-4P. In lieu of Worksheet 1B and the Percentage Method tables in section 1, you may use Worksheet 5 and the Percentage Method tables in this section to figure federal income tax withholding on periodic payments of pensions or annuities with a 2021 or earlier Form W-4P. As an alternative, if you prefer to use the Wage Bracket Method of withholding, you may use Worksheet 3 and the Wage Bracket Method tables in section 3 to figure federal income tax withholding on periodic payments of pensions or annuities with a 2021 or earlier Form W-4P.

Worksheet 5. Employer's Withholding Worksheet for Percentage Method Tables for Manual Payroll Systems With Forms W-4 From 2019 or Earlier

Keep for Your Records

Table 7	Annually	Semiannually	Quarterly	Monthly	Semimonthly	Biweekly	Weekly	Daily
	$4,300	$2,150	$1,075	$358	$179	$165	$83	$17

Step 1. Adjust the employee's wage amount
1a Enter the employee's total taxable wages this payroll period .... 1a $ 4,083.33
1b Enter the number of allowances claimed on the employee's most recent Form W-4 ..... 1b _____7
1c Multiply line 1b by the amount in Table 7 for your pay frequency .... 1c $ 1,253.00
1d Subtract line 1c from line 1a. If zero or less, enter -0-. This is the **Adjusted Wage Amount** .... 1d $ 2,830.33

Step 2. Figure the Tentative Withholding Amount
based on your pay frequency, the employee's Adjusted Wage Amount, and marital status (line 3 of Form W-4).

2a Find the row in the Percentage Method table in this section in which the amount on line 1d is at least the amount in column A but less than the amount in column B, and then enter here the amount from column A of that row .... 2a $ 1,646.00 (a)
2b Enter the amount from column C of that row .... 2b $ 96.70
2c Enter the percentage from column D of that row 2c 12%
2d Subtract line 2a from line 1d .... 2d $ 1,184.33
2e Multiply the amount on line 2d by the percentage on line 2c .... 2e $ 142.12
2f Add lines 2b and 2e. This is the **Tentative Withholding Amount** .... 2f $ 238.82

Step 3. Figure the final amount to withhold
3a Enter the additional amount to withhold from line 6 of the employee's Form W-4 .... 3a $ 0.00
3b Add lines 2f and 3a. **This is the amount to withhold from the employee's wages this pay period** .... 3b $ 238.82

(a) Standard Withholding Rate Schedules of the Percentage Method tables are found in Appendix C.

The wage bracket method for an employee using an old (pre-2020) Form W-4 follows the same steps as a new (post-2019) Form W-4; however, the tentative withholding is determined using Worksheet 3 and the associated wage bracket tables.

Example Using the information presented in the Fei and Zhi Han example from Page 9-8 and the old Form W-4 on Pages 9-14 to 9-17, Worksheet 3 is presented below for one of Zhi's pay periods in 2024. The amount of withholding under the wage bracket method is $238.00. ♦

3. Wage Bracket Method Tables for Manual Payroll Systems With Forms W-4 From 2019 or Earlier

If you compute payroll manually and your employee **has not** submitted a Form W-4 for 2020 or later, use the worksheet below and the Wage Bracket Method tables that follow to figure federal income tax withholding.

These Wage Bracket Method tables cover a limited amount of annual wages (generally, less than $100,000) and up to 10 allowances. If you can't use the Wage Bracket Method tables because taxable wages exceed the amount from the last bracket of the table (based on marital status and pay period) or the employee claimed more than 10 allowances, use the Percentage Method tables in section 5.

Periodic payments of pensions or annuities with a 2021 or earlier Form W-4P. In lieu of Worksheet 1B and the Percentage Method tables in section 1, you may use Worksheet 3 and the Wage Bracket Method tables in this section to figure federal income tax withholding on periodic payments of pensions or annuities with a 2021 or earlier Form W-4P. As an alternative, if you prefer to use the Percentage Method of withholding, you may use Worksheet 5 and the Percentage Method tables in section 5 to figure federal income tax withholding on periodic payments of pensions or annuities with a 2021 or earlier Form W-4P.

Worksheet 3. Employer's Withholding Worksheet for Wage Bracket Method Tables for Manual Payroll Systems With Forms W-4 From 2019 or Earlier

Keep for Your Records

Step 1.	Figure the Tentative Withholding Amount			
	1a Enter the employee's total taxable wages this payroll period	1a	$	4,083.33
	1b Use the amount on line 1a to look up the tentative amount to withhold in the appropriate Wage Bracket Method table in this section for your pay frequency, given the employee's marital status (line 3 of Form W-4) and number of allowances claimed. This is the **Tentative Withholding Amount**	1b	$	238.00 (a)
Step 2.	Figure the final amount to withhold			
	2a Enter the additional amount to withhold from line 6 of the employee's Form W-4	2a	$	0.00
	2b Add lines 1b and 2a. **This is the amount to withhold from the employee's wages this pay period**	2b	$	238.00

(a) Standard Withholding Rate Schedules of the Wage Bracket Method tables are found in Appendix C.

Tax Break The income tax withholding tables are constructed so that taxpayers that have completed their Form W-4 properly will receive an income tax refund during tax filing season. Many taxpayers are satisfied with the resulting refund even though a tax refund represents an interest-free loan to the government. The overpayment of taxes serves as a "forced" savings account which provides the opportunity to purchase a big ticket item in late spring when the refund is received. Taxpayers should also be aware that interest is not charged symmetrically; underpayments of tax may result in penalties and interest (refer to LO 9.4), while overpayments are not usually credited with interest.

9-2d Pension and Deferred Income

Income tax withholding is also required on pension and other deferred income payments based on Form W-4P, Withholding Certificate for Pension or Annuity Payments, as completed and signed by the taxpayer. Financial institutions and corporations must withhold on the taxable part of pension, profit sharing, stock bonus, and individual retirement account payments. The rates used for withholding vary depending on the nature of the payment, as described below:

1. Periodic payments (such as annuities): Rates are based on the taxpayer's Form W-4P or if no W-4P is filed, tax will be withheld as if the taxpayer was single with no adjustments for other income or deductions.
2. Nonperiodic payments: Withholding is deducted at a flat 10-percent rate, except for certain distributions from qualified retirement plans, which have a required 20-percent withholding tax rate. Refer to LO 9.9 for an explanation of withholding on rollover distributions.

Example Adam is a retired college professor and receives a pension of $775 per month. The payor should withhold on the pension, based on Adam's signed W-4P, in the same manner as if it were Adam's salary. ♦

9-2e Tip Reporting

Tips are a significant part of the compensation received by employees in many types of jobs such as the following:

- Barber
- Hairdresser
- Parking attendant
- Porter
- Food and beverage servers
- Busser and others who share restaurant tip pools
- Delivery driver
- Airport skycap
- Bartenders
- Hotel housekeepers
- Manicurists
- Taxi and rideshare drivers

Tips are generally not paid directly by the employer to the employee and as a result, create a unique challenge for tax reporting for both the employee and employer. Additionally, tips are often paid in cash, and capturing tips as income is difficult for the IRS.

To reduce the underreporting of tip income, the IRS requires employees to report tip income to their employers. Historically, employees could use Form 4070 (monthly) or Form 4070A (daily) to report tips; however, both of these forms are no longer supported by the IRS. Currently, most employers in tip-related industries provide a technology-based system for reporting tips such as the POS (point-of-sale) system used to otherwise capture customer payments. An employee may report tips using a simple statement as long as the following information is included:

- The employee's name, address, and social security number.
- The employer's name, address, and business name (if different from employer's name).
- The month (or the dates of any shorter period) in which the employee received tips.
- The total tips required to be reported for that period.

The employer uses the reported tip information to properly withhold employment and income taxes on tip income. To provide some assurance that accurate tip income is being reported by employees in large food or beverage establishments, the employer must compare employee-reported tips to 8 percent of the employer's sales. If the reported tips are less than 8 percent of sales, the employer must allocate the difference to each employee and report this amount on each employee's Form W-2 in Box 8 (Allocated Tips). The allocation of tip income can be accomplished in one of three ways. The employer may allocate the amount based on (1) gross receipts per employee, (2) hours worked by each employee (available only to employers having fewer than the equivalent of twenty-five full-time employees), or (3) a good faith agreement as explained on Form 8027, Employer's Annual Information Return of Tip Income and Allocated Tips. For a detailed explanation of the allocation process, refer to the instructions for Form 8027. With the diversity of businesses and tipping customs, the IRS also permits employers to enter into the Tip Rate Determination/Education Program, in which the employer and the IRS work out a tip rate and reporting system. For more information on tip reporting in general, refer to the IRS website (**www.irs.gov**) or a tax research service.

> **Tax Break**
>
> The IRS has created three programs to help employers in businesses in which employees are compensated with tips: Tip Rate Determination Agreement (TRDA), the Tip Reporting Alternative Commitment (TRAC), and the Gaming Industry Tip Compliance Agreement (GITCA). These programs are designed to help employers and employees more accurately report tip income and simplify the process for reporting tips by employees and employers. The IRS has proposed yet another tip reporting program: Service Industry Tip Compliance Agreement (SITCA) to help service industry employers (except casinos) simplify tip reporting and compliance. IRS Notice 2023-13 has details of the proposal. Once the final regulations are issued, the SITCA program is designed to replace all other tip reporting programs except for GITCA.

9-2f Backup Withholding

In some situations, individuals may be subject to backup withholding on payments such as interest and dividends. The purpose of backup withholding is to ensure that income tax is paid on income reported on many of the different versions of Forms 1099. If backup withholding applies, the payor (e.g., bank or insurance company) must withhold 24 percent of the amount paid to the taxpayer. Payors are required to use backup withholding in the following cases:

1. The taxpayer does not give the payor their taxpayer identification number (e.g., Social Security number),
2. The taxpayer fails to certify that they are not subject to backup withholding,
3. The IRS informs the payor that the taxpayer gave an incorrect identification number, or
4. The IRS informs the payor to start withholding because the taxpayer has not reported the income on their tax return.

Example Kamili earned $2,000 in interest income from Cactus Savings Bank. Kamili failed to certify that she was not subject to backup withholding. As a result, the bank must withhold taxes of $480 (24 percent of $2,000) from the interest payments to Kamili. ♦

Taxpayers who give false information to avoid backup withholding are subject to a $500 civil penalty and criminal penalties, including fines and/or imprisonment.

> **Tax Break**
>
> For students that may work a seasonal or summer job, a part-year withholding method is available for employers to use that will result in less tax being withheld. Typical withholding tables assume the employee is going to work for a full year. The part-year method is for employees expecting to work 245 or fewer days during the year. Details are available in IRS Publication 15-T.

Self-Study Problem 9.2   Refer to Appendix E for Solutions to Self-Study Problems

1. John and Lillian Miles intend to file jointly in 2024. The Miles' address is 456 Peachtree Court, Atlanta, GA 30310. John expects to earn wages of $42,000 in 2024 and Lillian's wages are expected to be very similar at $42,400. They have two dependent children aged 13 and 17. Lillian also has a small business that she expects to generate qualified business income of $6,700 in 2024. She would prefer to increase her withholding rather than make estimated tax payments. They expect to make a $4,700 deductible IRA contribution in 2024 and take the standard deduction. Assuming she is the higher-income earner and is paid monthly, prepare a Form W-4 for Lillian Miles (Social Security number 414-44-1680) including worksheets for steps 2(b) and 4(b), if needed.

2. Assuming that Lillian is paid semimonthly ($1,766.67 per half-month) and using the Form W-4 prepared in part 1, compute Lillian's withholding using (a.) the percentage method and (b.) the wage bracket method. Use the worksheets in Appendix C.

9-3 The FICA Tax

9.3 Learning Objective

Compute the FICA tax.

9-3a FICA Taxes

The Federal Insurance Contributions Act (FICA) imposes Social Security and Medicare taxes. It was passed by Congress in 1935 to provide benefits for qualified retired and disabled workers. If a worker should die, it would also provide the family of the worker with benefits. The Medicare program for older adults is also funded by FICA taxes.

FICA taxes have two parts, Social Security (Old Age, Survivors, and Disability Insurance [OASDI]) and Medicare. Employees and their employers are both required to pay FICA taxes. Employers withhold a specified percentage of each employee's wages up to a maximum base amount, match the amount withheld with an equal amount, and pay the total to the IRS.

The Social Security (OASDI) tax rate is 6.2 percent and the Medicare tax rate is 1.45 percent each for employees and employers in 2024. The maximum wage subject to the Social Security portion of the FICA tax (the "FICA cap") is $168,600 in 2024, and all wages are subject to the Medicare portion of the FICA tax. The maximum wages to which the rates apply have increased over the years as presented in the Table 9.2.

Table 9.2   Maximum Wages Subject to Social Security and Medicare tax

Year	Maximum $ Base for 6.2% (employee and employer)	Maximum $ Base for 1.45% (employee and employer)*
2020	137,700	Unlimited
2021	142,800	Unlimited
2022	147,000	Unlimited
2023	160,200	Unlimited
2024	168,600	Unlimited

*Employees pay a 0.9 percent Medicare tax on wages over $200,000 if single and head of household ($250,000 if married filing jointly). Refer to Chapter 6 for more information.

> **Tax Break**
>
> Taxpayers age 18 and older may request an online statement of Social Security benefits that includes estimates of projected retirement, survivors', and disability benefits. The statement also shows the taxpayer's Social Security earnings history, giving the taxpayer an opportunity to correct any errors or omissions. The personalized online statement is available at **www.ssa.gov/myaccount**. In some cases, the Social Security Administration will provide a paper version of this statement by mail.

Example Katherine earns wages of $21,500 in 2024. The FICA tax on her wages is calculated as follows:

Katherine:	Soc. Sec. (6.2% × $21,500)	$1,333.00
	Medicare (1.45% × $21,500)	311.75
	Total employee FICA tax	$1,644.75
Katherine's employer:	Soc. Sec. (6.2% × $21,500)	$1,333.00
	Medicare (1.45% × $21,500)	311.75
	Total employer FICA tax	$1,644.75
Total FICA tax		$3,289.50

♦

Example Nora is an employee of Serissa Company. Her salary for 2024 is $175,000. Nora's portion of the FICA tax is calculated as follows:

Soc. Sec. (6.2% × $168,600)	$10,453.20
Medicare (1.45% × $175,000)	2,537.50
Total employee FICA tax	$12,990.70

The total combined FICA tax (employee's and employer's share) is $25,981.40. ♦

Example Haley, a single taxpayer, is an employee of Dunphee Company. Hailey's wages in 2024 are $212,000. Haley's Social Security portion of the FICA tax is $168,600 (2024 FICA cap) × 6.2% or $10,453.20. The "regular" Medicare portion withheld will be $3,074.00 ($212,000 × 1.45%); however, Dunphee will also withhold the 0.9 percent additional Medicare tax as described in Chapter 6 on wages over $200,000 or $108.00 ($12,000 × 0.9%). Total withholding will be $13,635.20. Dunphee will pay a matching portion of Social Security ($10,453.20) and regular Medicare ($3,074.00) but is not required to pay the additional 0.9 percent Medicare tax on wages above $200,000. ♦

FICA taxes are paid one-half by employees through withholding and one-half by employers. Since the employer portion of the tax increases the cost of employees, many economists believe that even the employer's share of FICA tax is passed on to employees in the form of lower compensation. Thus, employees, like self-employed individuals, effectively bear both halves of FICA taxes.

9-3b Overpayment of Social Security Taxes

Taxpayers who work for more than one employer during the same tax year may pay more than the maximum amount of Social Security taxes. This occurs when the taxpayer's total wages are more than the FICA cap for the year. When this happens, the taxpayer should compute the excess taxes paid, and report the excess on Line 11 of Schedule 3 of Form 1040 as an additional payment against their tax liability. This way, the taxpayer is refunded the excess Social Security tax. Note that the employer is not entitled to a similar refund for the overpaid matching Social Security tax.

Example Jerry worked for two employers during 2024. The first employer withheld and paid Social Security taxes on $90,000 of salary paid to Jerry, and the second employer withheld and paid Social Security taxes on $81,000 of salary paid to Jerry. The amount of Jerry's excess Social Security taxes paid for 2024 is computed as follows: 6.2% (Social Security rate) × [$90,000 + $81,000 − $168,600 (maximum for Social Security portion of FICA tax)] = $148.80. Jerry receives a credit against the 2024 income tax liability equal to the excess Social Security taxes of $149. No excess Medicare tax has been paid, as there is no upper limit on Medicare wages. ♦

Self-Study Problem 9.3
Refer to Appendix E for Solutions to Self-Study Problems

Hills Scientific Corp. (EIN 33-4434432) has six employees, including founder Juliette Hills. Payroll records indicate the wages paid to the employees during the first and second quarters of 2024:

Employee	Title	Total Q1 Wages	Apr	May	Jun	Total Q2 Wages	Q2 Income Tax Withheld
Juliette	CEO	$ 91,000	$28,000	$28,000	$28,000	$ 84,000	$23,130
Yan	Head Scientist	40,000	13,000	13,000	14,000	40,000	9,999
Sai	Laboratory Manager	20,000	6,700	6,700	6,600	20,000	4,410
Yvette	Sr. Lab Analyst	15,000	5,000	5,000	5,000	15,000	3,150
Juan	Jr. Lab Analyst	9,000	3,000	3,000	3,000	9,000	1,350
Joe	Maintenance & Custodial	6,000	2,000	2,000	2,000	6,000	735
Total		$181,000	$57,700	$57,700	$58,600	$174,000	$42,774

Compute Hills' portion of second quarter employment taxes:
a. Employee's portion Social Security tax
b. Employer's portion Social Security tax
c. Employee's portion Medicare tax
d. Employer's portion Medicare tax

9-4 Estimated Payments

Learning Objective 9.4
Determine taxpayers' quarterly estimated payments.

Self-employed taxpayers are not subject to withholding; however, they must make quarterly estimated tax payments. Taxpayers with large amounts of interest, dividends, and other income not subject to withholding are also generally required to make estimated payments. Payments are made in four installments due April 15, June 15, and September 15 of the tax year, and January 15 of the following year (or the first business day after if the dates fall on a weekend or holiday), based on the taxpayer's estimate of the amount of the tax liability for the year. A taxpayer with self-employment income must begin making payments when they first meet the filing requirements.

> **Tax Break**
>
> Never write out a check to the "IRS." The IRS issues this warning every year, because "IRS" may be easily changed to "MRS" plus an individual's name if the check falls into the wrong hands. Checks must be made payable to the U.S. Treasury, as a reminder that the IRS is merely the collector of revenue for the federal government. Alternatively, individual taxpayers can draft their bank account using Direct Pay or, for a fee, pay using a debit card, credit card, or cash at one of the IRS' retail partners. Information regarding payment methods is available at **www.irs.gov/payments**.

Any individual taxpayer who has estimated tax for the year of $1,000 or more, after subtracting withholding, and whose withholding does not equal or exceed the "required annual payment," must make quarterly estimated payments. The required annual payment is dependent on the taxpayer's prior year income and is presented in Table 9.3:

Table 9.3 Required Annual Payments

Prior Year AGI of $150,000 or Less	Prior Year AGI Greater Than $150,000
Pay the lesser of: • 90 percent of tax shown on current year return • 100 percent of the tax shown on the preceding year's return	Pay the lesser of: • 90 percent of tax shown on current year return • 110 percent of the tax shown on the preceding year's return

Example Judika has AGI of $130,000 and a total tax liability of $25,000 in the prior year. Her current year AGI is $153,000 and tax liability is $28,600. Because Judika's prior year AGI is $150,000 or lower, her required payment is $25,000, the lesser of:

1. $25,740 ($28,600 × 90%)
2. $25,000 ($25,000 × 100%)

Judika is required to make four quarterly payments of $6,250 to avoid penalties.

If Judika's prior year AGI was over $150,000 (assuming same tax liability), her required payment would be $25,740, the lesser of:

1. $25,740 ($28,600 × 90%)
2. $27,500 ($25,000 × 110%)

Judika is required to make four quarterly payments of $6,435 to avoid penalties. ◆

Estimated payments need not be paid if the estimated tax, after subtracting withholding, can reasonably be expected to be less than $1,000. Therefore, employees who also have a modest amount of self-employment income may avoid making estimated payments by filing a new Form W-4 and increasing the amount of their withholding on their regular salary.

Estimating the required annual payment from the current-year tax is more of an art than a science, since it requires estimation of income, deductions, and credits. In addition, when computing the required annual payment, the amount of tax measured is the total of income tax plus any self-employment tax, net investment income tax, and additional Medicare tax (refer to Chapters 4 and 6 for additional explanation). For the prior year tax, these amounts can generally be found on Form 1040. For most taxpayers, the prior year tax is Line 24 from the Form 1040; however, this amount can be reduced by any earned income credit and the refundable portions of the child tax credit, American Opportunities credit, and the premium tax credit, along with some other less common adjustments. To assist taxpayers with estimating the current-year tax, Form 1040-ES, Estimated Tax for Individuals includes a worksheet to assist in the calculation.

Example Colin Procksamite, a single taxpayer with no dependents, operates a small business as a sole proprietor. He expects to report a profit of $82,000 on his 2024 Schedule C, he has no other sources of income or deductions, and expects to take the standard deduction in 2024. Colin's prior year AGI was below $150,000 and his Form 1040 Line 24 reported $15,000 of total tax. Colin's prior year return resulted in a refund of $400, which he applied to the current year estimated tax liability. He did not claim any refundable credits in 2023 or 2024. The worksheet on the following page presents Colin's estimate of his 2024 tax, annual required payment, and first quarter estimated payment. ♦

The IRS imposes a nondeductible penalty on the amounts of any underpayments of estimated tax. The penalty applies when any installment is less than the required annual payment divided by the number of installments that should have been made, which is usually four. Form 2210, Underpayment of Estimated Tax by Individuals, Estates, and Trusts, is used for the calculation of the penalty associated with the underpayment of estimated tax.

Form 2210 calculates the penalties and interest due on underpayments of estimated taxes in two ways:

1. Based on the default assumption that income was earned ratably over the course of the tax year.
2. An annualized method that accounts for income being earned unevenly during the year (e.g., seasonal business).

As presented on pages 9-32 to 9-34, the Form 2210 has three pages. The first page reports the required annual payment and the determination of whether any penalty is owed. The second page uses the default penalty calculation method. The third page calculates any underpayment using the annualized method. The annualized method requires the taxpayer to segregate the income earned into 4 different periods that end on the month-end preceding the date of the required quarterly estimated payment. For example, the second quarter payment is due on June 15 and thus, the income is computed through May 31. If income is earned evenly through the year, the typical calculation and the annualized method should produce very similar penalty amounts. However, if income is earned unevenly, the annualized method can result in smaller penalties. Estimated payments are applied to the earliest quarter's estimated tax.

Example If Colin from the previous example fails to make a second quarter required estimated payment, his third quarter required estimated payment will be applied to the second quarter's tax liability. ♦

Once the underpayments for each quarter are computed, the penalty is calculated based on the number of days before the underpayment was made and the applicable

2024 Estimated Tax Worksheet

Keep for Your Records

Line	Description		Amount	
1	Adjusted gross income you expect in 2024 (see instructions)	1	76,207	(a)
2a	Deductions	2a	14,600	
	• If you plan to itemize deductions, enter the estimated total of your itemized deductions.			
	• If you don't plan to itemize deductions, enter your standard deduction.			
b	If you can take the qualified business income deduction, enter the estimated amount of the deduction	2b	12,321	(b)
c	Add lines 2a and 2b	2c	26,921	
3	Subtract line 2c from line 1	3	49,286	
4	**Tax.** Figure your tax on the amount on line 3 by using the **2024 Tax Rate Schedules**. *Caution:* If you will have qualified dividends or a net capital gain, or expect to exclude or deduct foreign earned income or housing, see Worksheets 2-5 and 2-6 in Pub. 505 to figure the tax	4	5,896	(c)
5	Alternative minimum tax from **Form 6251**	5		
6	Add lines 4 and 5. Add to this amount any other taxes you expect to include in the total on Form 1040 or 1040-SR, line 16	6	5,896	
7	Credits (see instructions). **Do not** include any income tax withholding on this line	7		
8	Subtract line 7 from line 6. If zero or less, enter -0-	8	5,896	
9	Self-employment tax (see instructions)	9	11,586	(d)
10	Other taxes (see instructions)	10		
11a	Add lines 8 through 10	11a	17,482	
b	Earned income credit, additional child tax credit, fuel tax credit, net premium tax credit, refundable American opportunity credit, and section 1341 credit	11b		
c	**Total 2024 estimated tax.** Subtract line 11b from line 11a. If zero or less, enter -0-	11c	17,482	
12a	Multiply line 11c by 90% (66⅔% for farmers and fishermen) . . . **12a** 15,734			
b	Required annual payment based on prior year's tax (see instructions) . . **12b** 15,000			
c	**Required annual payment to avoid a penalty.** Enter the **smaller** of line 12a or 12b	12c	15,000	

Caution: Generally, if you do not prepay (through income tax withholding and estimated tax payments) at least the amount on line 12c, you may owe a penalty for not paying enough estimated tax. To avoid a penalty, make sure your estimate on line 11c is as accurate as possible. Even if you pay the required annual payment, you may still owe tax when you file your return. If you prefer, you can pay the amount shown on line 11c. For details, see chapter 2 of Pub. 505.

Line	Description		Amount	
13	Income tax withheld and estimated to be withheld during 2024 (including income tax withholding on pensions, annuities, certain deferred income, and Additional Medicare Tax withholding)	13	0	
14a	Subtract line 13 from line 12c . . . **14a** 15,000 Is the result zero or less? ☐ **Yes.** Stop here. You are not required to make estimated tax payments. ☑ **No.** Go to line 14b.			
b	Subtract line 13 from line 11c . . . **14b** 17,482 Is the result less than $1,000? ☐ **Yes.** Stop here. You are not required to make estimated tax payments. ☑ **No.** Go to line 15 to figure your required payment.			
15	If the first payment you are required to make is due April 15, 2024, enter ¼ of line 14a (minus any 2023 overpayment that you are applying to this installment) here, and on your estimated tax payment voucher(s) if you are paying by check or money order	15	3,350	(e)

(a) $82,000 − $5,793 (one-half of self-employment tax calculated as $82,000 × 92.35% × 15.3% × 50%).

(b) The QBI deduction before overall limitation is $82,000 − $5,793 (1/2 self-employment tax) × 20% = $15,241. The overall net income limitation is $12,321 [($82,000 − $5,793 − $14,600 standard deduction) × 20%]. Thus, the QBI deduction is limited to $12,321.

(c) $5,426.00 + [($49,286−$47,150) × 22%]. Note that Tax Tables are generally not available at the time of estimate and thus, the Tax Rate Schedules are used even when taxable income is less than $100,000.

(d) $82,000 × 92.35% × 15.3%

(e) ($15,000 × 25%) − $400 prior year refund applied to estimated taxes (first quarter only).

penalty rate for that period. A worksheet is provided in the Form 2210 Instructions and is presented on Page 9-35. Interest and penalties are presented in greater detail in Chapter 12.

The complexities of the calculation of the penalty associated with underpayment of quarterly estimated payments is such that in many instances, the IRS will calculate the penalty for the taxpayer and Form 2210 need not be filed. The top section of page one of Form 2210 provides a flowchart that will determine if the taxpayer should (1) calculate the penalty themselves, and (2) determine what parts, if any, of Form 2210 to file. Most tax preparation software can capably prepare the penalty calculation and the proper portions of Form 2210.

Example Colin, from the previous example, failed to make his second quarter required payment of $3,750 ($15,000 ÷ 4). He did make his third and fourth quarter payments on time and is expected to make any remaining underpayment on April 15 when he files his tax return. Assume Colin's business is seasonal and the $82,000 of income from his sole proprietorship was earned as follows:

1/1–3/31	4/1–5/31	6/1–8/31	9/1–12/31
$12,000	$12,000	$20,000	$38,000

Colin's Form 2210, including the penalty worksheet, is presented on Pages 9-32 to 9-35. Part I of Form 2210 presents the required annual payment based on the actual tax liability for the year; which, in Colin's case, matches his estimate used for Form 1040-ES. Part II confirms the need to prepare an entire or partial Form 2210 using the annualized method. Schedule AI Parts I and II of Form 2210 are used to compute the required payments for each quarter assuming uneven income throughout the year. Part III of Form 2210 is used to report the penalty that is calculated using the supporting Worksheet from the Form 2210 Instructions. Note that if Colin had not used the annualized method, his penalties would have totaled $225 (calculation not provided). ♦

Good tax planning dictates that a taxpayer postpone payment of taxes as long as no penalty is imposed. Unpaid taxes are equivalent to an interest-free loan from the government. Therefore, taxpayers should base their estimated payments on the method which results in the lowest amount of required quarterly or annual payment. For example, a taxpayer who expects their tax liability to increase might base their estimated payments this year on the amount of the tax liability from the prior year. A taxpayer that overpays their tax liability has the option to receive the excess back as a refund or may apply the overpayment to the following year.

Individual taxpayers can pay estimated payments online through a number of different methods. Individual taxpayers with an IRS account can login and make payments through their account (**www.irs.gov/payments/your-online-account**). The IRS website (**www.irs.gov/payments**) provides a number of methods for payment, including Direct Pay (direct debit to your bank account), pay by debit card, credit card, digital wallet (for a fee), and via Electronic Federal Tax Payment System (EFTPS). Taxpayers may also pay estimated taxes using the IRS2Go app for mobile phones. Taxpayers paying online should take care to select the proper type of return (for example, Form 1040) and the proper tax year to increase the probability that the payment is credited to the proper tax type and period. Of course, taxpayers can pay by mail using a check. If paying by check, taxpayers should be certain to include the proper quarterly voucher from Form 1040-ES.

Form 2210

Department of the Treasury
Internal Revenue Service

Underpayment of Estimated Tax by Individuals, Estates, and Trusts

Attach to Form 1040, 1040-SR, 1040-NR, or 1041.
Go to *www.irs.gov/Form2210* for instructions and the latest information.

OMB No. 1545-0140

2024

Attachment Sequence No. **06**

Name(s) shown on tax return: Colin Procksamite

Identifying number:

Do You Have To File Form 2210?

Complete lines 1 through 7 below. Is line 4 or line 7 less than $1,000?
- **Yes** → Don't file Form 2210. You don't owe a penalty.
- **No** → Complete lines 8 and 9 below. Is line 6 equal to or more than line 9?
  - **Yes** → You **don't** owe a penalty. **Don't** file Form 2210 unless box **E** in Part II applies, then file page 1 of Form 2210.
  - **No** → You may owe a penalty. Does any box in Part II below apply?
    - **Yes** → You **must** file Form 2210. Does box **B, C,** or **D** in Part II apply?
      - **No** → You aren't required to figure your penalty because the IRS will figure it and send you a bill for any unpaid amount. If you want to figure it, you may use Part III as a worksheet and enter your penalty amount on your tax return, but **file only page 1 of Form 2210.**
      - **Yes** → You must figure your penalty.
    - **No** → **Don't** file Form 2210. You aren't required to figure your penalty because the IRS will figure it and send you a bill for any unpaid amount. If you want to figure it, you may use Part III as a worksheet and enter your penalty amount on your tax return, but **don't** file Form 2210.

Part I — Required Annual Payment

1	Enter your 2024 tax after credits from Form 1040, 1040-SR, or 1040-NR, line 22. (See the instructions if not filing Form 1040.)	**1** 5,896 (a)
2	Other taxes, including self-employment tax and, if applicable, Additional Medicare Tax and/or Net Investment Income Tax (see instructions)	**2** 11,586 (a)
3	Other payments and refundable credits (see instructions)	**3** ( )
4	Current year tax. Combine lines 1, 2, and 3. If less than $1,000, **stop**; you don't owe a penalty. **Don't** file Form 2210	**4** 17,482 (a)
5	Multiply line 4 by 90% (0.90) . . . **5** 15,734	
6	Withholding taxes. **Don't** include estimated tax payments. See instructions	**6** 0
7	Subtract line 6 from line 4. If less than $1,000, **stop**; you don't owe a penalty. **Don't** file Form 2210	**7** 17,482
8	Maximum required annual payment based on prior year's tax (see instructions)	**8** 15,000 (a)
9	**Required annual payment.** Enter the **smaller** of line 5 or line 8	**9** 15,000

Next: Is line 9 more than line 6?

☐ **No.** You **don't** owe a penalty. **Don't** file Form 2210 unless box **E** below applies.

☒ **Yes.** You may owe a penalty, but **don't** file Form 2210 unless one or more boxes in Part II below applies.
- If box **B, C,** or **D** applies, you must figure your penalty and file Form 2210.
- If box **A** or **E** applies (but not **B, C,** or **D**), file only page 1 of Form 2210. You **aren't** required to figure your penalty; the IRS will figure it and send you a bill for any unpaid amount. If you want to figure your penalty, you may use Part III as a worksheet and enter your penalty on your tax return, but **file only page 1 of Form 2210.**

Part II — Reasons for Filing. Check applicable boxes. If none apply, **don't** file Form 2210.

- **A** ☐ You request a **waiver** (see instructions) of your entire penalty. You must check this box and file page 1 of Form 2210, but you aren't required to figure your penalty.
- **B** ☐ You request a **waiver** (see instructions) of part of your penalty. You must figure your penalty and waiver amount and file Form 2210.
- **C** ☒ Your income varied during the year and your penalty is reduced or eliminated when figured using the **annualized income installment method.** You must figure the penalty using Schedule AI and file Form 2210.
- **D** ☐ Your penalty is lower when figured by treating the federal income tax withheld from your income as paid on the dates it was actually withheld, instead of in equal amounts on the payment due dates. You must figure your penalty and file Form 2210.
- **E** ☐ You filed or are filing a joint return for either 2023 or 2024, but not for both years, and line 8 above is smaller than line 5 above. You must file page 1 of Form 2210, but you **aren't** required to figure your penalty (unless box **B, C,** or **D** applies).

For Paperwork Reduction Act Notice, see separate instructions. Cat. No. 11744P Form **2210**

(a) information taken from the 1040-ES worksheet presented on Page 9-30.

9-4 Estimated Payments   9-33

Form 2210 (2024)   Page **2**

Part III   **Penalty Computation** (See the instructions if you're filing Form 1040-NR.)

Section A—Figure Your Underpayment

		Payment Due Dates			
		(a) 4/15/24	(b) 6/15/24	(c) 9/15/24	(d) 1/15/25
10	**Required installments.** If box C in Part II applies, enter the amounts from Schedule AI, line 27. Otherwise, enter 25% (0.25) of line 9, Form 2210, in each column. For fiscal year filers, see instructions	2,123	3,116	3,927	5,834
11	**Estimated tax paid and tax withheld** (see the instructions). For column (a) only, also enter the amount from line 11 on line 15, column (a). If line 11 is equal to or more than line 10 for all payment periods, stop here; you don't owe a penalty. **Don't file Form 2210 unless you checked a box in Part II**	3,750	0	3,750	3,750
	Complete lines 12 through 18 of one column before going to line 12 of the next column.				
12	Enter the amount, if any, from line 18 in the previous column		1,627	0	0
13	Add lines 11 and 12		1,627	3,750	3,750
14	Add the amounts on lines 16 and 17 in the previous column		0	1,489	1,666
15	Subtract line 14 from line 13. If zero or less, enter -0-. For column (a) only, enter the amount from line 11	3,750	1,627	2,261	2,084
16	If line 15 is zero, subtract line 13 from line 14. Otherwise, enter -0-				
17	**Underpayment.** If line 10 is equal to or more than line 15, subtract line 15 from line 10. Then go to line 12 of the next column. Otherwise, go to line 18		1,489 (b)	1,666 (c)	3,750 (d)
18	**Overpayment.** If line 15 is more than line 10, subtract line 10 from line 15. Then go to line 12 of the next column	1,627 (a)			

Section B—Figure the Penalty (Use the Worksheet for Form 2210, Part III, Section B—Figure the Penalty in the instructions.)

19	**Penalty.** Enter the total penalty from line 14 of the Worksheet for Form 2210, Part III, Section B—Figure the Penalty. Include this amount on Form 1040, 1040-SR, or 1040-NR, line 38; or Form 1041, line 27. **Don't file Form 2210 unless you checked a box in Part II**	148 (e)

Form **2210** (2024)

(a) Colin has an overpayment of $1,627 because his estimated payment was $3,750 but his tax liability under the annualized method was only $2,123 (Line 10).

(b) Under the annualized method, Colin's tax liability at the end of May 31 was $3,116 (Line 10); however, he made no estimated payment but was able to carry forward his overpayment of $1,627 from the first quarter leaving an underpayment of only $1,489.

(c) Colin's third quarter required payment was $3,927 under the annualized method (Line 10). Colin made a payment of $3,750 for the third quarter; however, $1,489 of that payment was applied to his second quarter underpayment. Only $2,261 ($3,750 − $1,489) was left to apply to his third quarter requirement and Colin was underpaid by $1,666 ($3,927 − $2,261).

(d) Colin's fourth quarter required payment was $5,834 (Line 10). He made a fourth quarter payment of $3,750; however, $1,666 of that payment was applied to his third quarter requirement leaving only $2,084 ($3,750 − $1,666) to apply to the fourth quarter and Colin was underpaid by $3,750 ($5,834 − $2,084) for the fourth quarter.

(e) From penalty worksheet on Page 9-35.

Form 2210 (2024) Page **3**

Schedule AI—Annualized Income Installment Method (See the instructions.)

Estates and trusts, **don't** use the period ending dates shown to the right. Instead, use the following: 2/29/24, 4/30/24, 7/31/24, and 11/30/24.

		(a) 1/1/24–3/31/24	(b) 1/1/24–5/31/24	(c) 1/1/24–8/31/24	(d) 1/1/24–12/31/24
Part I	**Annualized Income Installments**				
1	Enter your adjusted gross income for each period. See instructions. (Estates and trusts, enter your taxable income without your exemption for each period.)	11,152	22,304	40,891	76,207 (a)
2	Annualization amounts. (Estates and trusts, see instructions.)	4	2.4	1.5	1
3	Annualized income. Multiply line 1 by line 2	44,608	53,530	61,337	76,207
4	If you itemize, enter itemized deductions for the period shown in each column. All others, enter -0-, and skip to line 7. **Exception:** Estates and trusts, skip to line 9	0	0	0	0
5	Annualization amounts	4	2.4	1.5	1
6	Multiply line 4 by line 5				
7	In each column, enter the amount of your standard deduction from Form 1040 or 1040-SR. (Form 1040-NR filers, enter -0-. **Exception:** Indian students and business apprentices, see instructions.)	14,600	14,600	14,600	14,600
8	Enter the **larger** of line 6 or line 7	14,600	14,600	14,600	14,600
9	Deduction for qualified business income. **Estates and trusts:** Subtract this amount from the amount on line 3, skip line 10, and enter the result on line 11	6,002	7,786	9,347	12,321 (b)
10	Add lines 8 and 9	20,602	22,386	23,947	26,921
11	Subtract line 10 from line 3	24,006	31,144	37,390	49,286
12	Form 1040, 1040-SR, or 1040-NR filers, enter -0- in each column. (Estates and trusts, see instructions.)				
13	Subtract line 12 from line 11. If zero or less, enter -0-	24,006	31,144	37,390	49,286
14	Figure your tax on the amount on line 13. See instructions	2,651	3,503	4,253	5,894 (c)
15	Self-employment tax from line 36 (complete Part II below)	6,783	8,139	9,326	11,586
16	Enter other taxes for each payment period including, if applicable, Additional Medicare Tax and/or Net Investment Income Tax. See instructions				
17	Total tax. Add lines 14, 15, and 16	9,434	11,642	13,579	17,480
18	For each period, enter the same type of credits as allowed on Form 2210, Part I, lines 1 and 3. See instructions				
19	Subtract line 18 from line 17. If zero or less, enter -0-	9,434	11,642	13,579	17,480
20	Applicable percentage	22.5%	45%	67.5%	90%
21	Multiply line 19 by line 20	2,123	5,239	9,166	15,732

Complete lines 22–27 of one column before going to line 22 of the next column.

22	Enter the total of the amounts in all previous columns of line 27		2,123	5,239	9,166
23	Subtract line 22 from line 21. If zero or less, enter -0-	2,123	3,116	3,927	6,566
24	Enter 25% (0.25) of line 9 on page 1 of Form 2210 in each column	3,750	3,750	3,750	3,750
25	Subtract line 27 of the previous column from line 26 of that column		1,627	2,261	2,084
26	Add lines 24 and 25	3,750	5,377	6,011	5,834
27	Enter the **smaller** of line 23 or line 26 here and on Form 2210, Part III, line 10	2,123	3,116	3,927	5,834
Part II	**Annualized Self-Employment Tax** (Form 1040, 1040-SR, or 1040-NR filers only)				
28	Net earnings from self-employment for the period (see instructions)	11,082	22,164	40,634	75,727 (d)
29	Prorated social security tax limit	$42,150	$70,250	$112,400	$168,600
30	Enter actual wages for the period subject to social security tax or the 6.2% portion of the 7.65% railroad retirement (tier 1) tax. **Exception:** If you filed Form 4137 or Form 8919, see instructions				
31	Subtract line 30 from line 29. If zero or less, enter -0-	42,150	70,250	112,400	168,600
32	Annualization amounts	0.496	0.2976	0.186	0.124
33	Multiply line 32 by the **smaller** of line 28 or line 31	5,497	6,596	7,558	9,390
34	Annualization amounts	0.116	0.0696	0.0435	0.029
35	Multiply line 28 by line 34	1,286	1,543	1,768	2,196
36	Add lines 33 and 35. Enter here and on line 15 above	6,783	8,139	9,326	11,586

Form **2210** (2024)

(a) YTD profits less (YTD profits × 92.35% × 15.3% × 50%) to deduct one-half of self-employment taxes.
(b) (line 3 − line 8) × 20%
(c) Calculated using tax rate schedules in Appendix A.
(d) YTD profits × 92.35%

Worksheet for Form 2210, Part III, Section B—Figure the Penalty (Penalty Worksheet)

Keep for Your Records

Complete Rate Period 1 of each column before going to the next column; then go to Rate Periods 2, 3, and 4 in the same manner. If multiple estimated tax payments are applied to the underpayment amount in a column of line 1a, you'll need to make more than one computation for that column.

			Payment Due Dates			
			(a) 04/15/24	(b) 06/15/24	(c) 09/15/24	(d) 01/15/25
1a	Enter your underpayment from Part III, Section A, line 17	1a		1,489	1,666	3,750
1b	Date and amount of each payment applied to the underpayment in the same column. Don't enter more than the underpayment amount on line 1a for each column (see instructions). **Note.** Your payments are applied in the order made first to any underpayment balance in an earlier column until that underpayment is fully paid.	1b		09/15/2024 1,489	01/15/2025 1,666	04/15/2025 3,750
Rate Period 1: April 16, 2024–June 30, 2024						
2	Computation starting dates for this period	2	04/15/24	06/15/24		
3	Number of days **from** the date on line 2 to the date the amount on line 1a was paid **or** 06/30/24, whichever is earlier	3	*Days:*	*Days:* 15		
4	Underpayment on line 1a × (Number of days on line 3)/366 × 0.08	4	$	$ 4.88		
Rate Period 2: July 1, 2024–September 30, 2024						
5	Computation starting dates for this period	5	06/30/24	06/30/24	09/15/24	
6	Number of days **from** the date on line 5 to the date the amount on line 1a was paid **or** 09/30/24, whichever is earlier	6	*Days:*	*Days:* 77	*Days:* 15	
7	Underpayment on line 1a × (Number of days on line 6)/366 × 0.08	7	$	$ 25.06	$ 5.46	
Rate Period 3: October 1, 2024–December 31, 2024						
8	Computation starting dates for this period	8	09/30/24	09/30/24	09/30/24	
9	Number of days **from** the date on line 8 to the date the amount on line 1a was paid **or** 12/31/24, whichever is earlier	9	*Days:*	*Days:*	*Days:* 92	
10	Underpayment on line 1a × (Number of days on line 9)/366 × X.XX	10	$	$	$ 33.50	
Rate Period 4: January 1, 2025–April 15, 2025						
11	Computation starting dates for this period	11	12/31/24	12/31/24	12/31/24	01/15/25
12	Number of days **from** the date on line 11 to the date the amount on line 1a was paid **or** 04/15/25, whichever is earlier	12	*Days:*	*Days:*	*Days:* 15	*Days:* 90
13	Underpayment on line 1a × (Number of days on line 12)/365 × X.XX	13	$	$	$ 5.46	$ 73.97
14	**Penalty.** Add all amounts on lines 4, 7, 10, and 13 in all columns. Enter the total here and on line 19 of Part III, Section B	14				$ 148.33

Instructions for Form 2210 (2024)

Source: Internal Revenue Service (IRS)

Self-Study Problem 9.4 Refer to Appendix E for Solutions to Self-Study Problems

a. Ray Adams, a single taxpayer with no dependents, estimates his 2024 Schedule C net profits as $105,000, one-half of self-employment tax as $7,418, and his QBI deduction as $16,596. In 2023, Ray's AGI was below $150,000 and Line 24 of his 2023 Form 1040 was $22,500. He had no refundable credits last year. Ray's Social Security number is 321-45-9876 and he lives at 1905 Hardin Valley Road, Knoxville, TN 37932. Assuming no other sources of income, deductions, or refundable credits in 2024, calculate Ray's estimated income and required annual payment using the 2024 Estimated Tax Worksheet.

2024 Estimated Tax Worksheet   Keep for Your Records

1	Adjusted gross income you expect in 2024 (see instructions)	1
2a	Deductions • If you plan to itemize deductions, enter the estimated total of your itemized deductions. • If you don't plan to itemize deductions, enter your standard deduction.	2a
b	If you can take the qualified business income deduction, enter the estimated amount of the deduction	2b
c	Add lines 2a and 2b	2c
3	Subtract line 2c from line 1	3
4	**Tax.** Figure your tax on the amount on line 3 by using the **2024 Tax Rate Schedules**. **Caution:** *If you will have qualified dividends or a net capital gain, or expect to exclude or deduct foreign earned income or housing, see Worksheets 2-5 and 2-6 in Pub. 505 to figure the tax*	4
5	Alternative minimum tax from **Form 6251**	5
6	Add lines 4 and 5. Add to this amount any other taxes you expect to include in the total on Form 1040 or 1040-SR, line 16	6
7	Credits (see instructions). **Do not** include any income tax withholding on this line	7
8	Subtract line 7 from line 6. If zero or less, enter -0-	8
9	Self-employment tax (see instructions)	9
10	Other taxes (see instructions)	10
11a	Add lines 8 through 10	11a
b	Earned income credit, additional child tax credit, fuel tax credit, net premium tax credit, refundable American opportunity credit, and section 1341 credit	11b
c	**Total 2024 estimated tax.** Subtract line 11b from line 11a. If zero or less, enter -0-	11c
12a	Multiply line 11c by 90% (66⅔% for farmers and fishermen) 12a	
b	Required annual payment based on prior year's tax (see instructions) . . . 12b	
c	**Required annual payment to avoid a penalty.** Enter the **smaller** of line 12a or 12b	12c
	Caution: *Generally, if you do not prepay (through income tax withholding and estimated tax payments) at least the amount on line 12c, you may owe a penalty for not paying enough estimated tax. To avoid a penalty, make sure your estimate on line 11c is as accurate as possible. Even if you pay the required annual payment, you may still owe tax when you file your return. If you prefer, you can pay the amount shown on line 11c. For details, see chapter 2 of Pub. 505.*	
13	Income tax withheld and estimated to be withheld during 2024 (including income tax withholding on pensions, annuities, certain deferred income, and Additional Medicare Tax withholding)	13
14a	Subtract line 13 from line 12c 14a	
	Is the result zero or less? ☐ **Yes.** Stop here. You are not required to make estimated tax payments. ☐ **No.** Go to line 14b.	
b	Subtract line 13 from line 11c 14b	
	Is the result less than $1,000? ☐ **Yes.** Stop here. You are not required to make estimated tax payments. ☐ **No.** Go to line 15 to figure your required payment.	
15	If the first payment you are required to make is due April 15, 2024, enter ¼ of line 14a (minus any 2023 overpayment that you are applying to this installment) here, and on your estimated tax payment voucher(s) if you are paying by check or money order	15

Self-Study Problem 9.4, continued
Refer to Appendix E for Solutions to Self-Study Problems

b. Continuing from part a, assume that Ray had an overpayment of $475 in 2023 that he received as a refund. Complete the 2024 first quarter voucher for Ray.

Form **1040-ES**	**2024 Estimated Tax**	**Payment Voucher 1**
Department of the Treasury Internal Revenue Service		OMB No. 1545-0074

File only if you are making a payment of estimated tax by check or money order. Mail this voucher with your check or money order payable to "**United States Treasury**." Write your social security number and "2024 Form 1040-ES" on your check or money order. Do not send cash. Enclose, but do not staple or attach, your payment with this voucher.

Calendar year—Due April 15, 2024
Amount of estimated tax you are paying by check or money order.

Pay online at www.irs.gov/etpay
Simple. Fast. Secure.

Print or type:
- Your first name and middle initial | Your last name | Your social security number
- If joint payment, complete for spouse
- Spouse's first name and middle initial | Spouse's last name | Spouse's social security number
- Address (number, street, and apt. no.)
- City, town, or post office. If you have a foreign address, also complete spaces below. | State | ZIP code
- Foreign country name | Foreign province/county | Foreign postal code

For Disclosure, Privacy Act, and Paperwork Reduction Act Notice, see instructions.   Form 1040-ES (2024)

Source: Internal Revenue Service (IRS)

c. Continuing from parts a and b, assume that Ray's 2023 AGI was $155,000 and his current year tax remains the amount calculated in part a. Calculate Ray's 1st quarter estimated payment for 2024.

9-5 Federal Tax Deposit System

9.5 Learning Objective
Apply the federal deposit system to payroll withholding.

Employers must make periodic deposits of the taxes that are withheld from employees' wages. The frequency of the deposits depends on the total income tax withheld and the total FICA taxes for all employees. Employers are either monthly depositors or semiweekly depositors. Prior to the beginning of each calendar year, taxpayers are required to determine which of the two deposit schedules they are required to use.

9-5a Tax Deposits

Monthly or semiweekly deposit status is determined by using a lookback period, consisting of the four quarters beginning July 1 of the second preceding year and ending June 30 of the prior year. If the total income tax withheld from wages and FICA taxes attributable to wages for the four quarters in the lookback period is $50,000 or less, employers are monthly depositors for the current year. Monthly depositors must make deposits of employment taxes and taxes withheld by the fifteenth day of the month following the month of withholding. For new employers, required deposits during the lookback period are deemed to be zero and the employer will default to a monthly depositor.

If the total income tax withheld from wages and FICA attributable to wages for the four quarters in the lookback period is more than $50,000, the employer is a semiweekly depositor for the current year. Taxes on payments made on Wednesday, Thursday, or Friday must be deposited by the following Wednesday; taxes on payments made on the other days of the week must be deposited by the following Friday. If a deposit is scheduled for a day that is not a banking day, the deposit is considered to be made timely if it is made by the close of the next banking day. If income tax withholding and FICA taxes of $100,000 or more are accumulated at any time during the year, the depositor is required to make a deposit on the next business day.

Example Tom runs a small business with 10 employees. During the lookback period for the current year, the total withholding and FICA taxes amounted to $40,000. Since the total taxes are less than $50,000, Tom is a monthly depositor. His payroll tax deposits must be made by the fifteenth day of the month following the month of withholding. ♦

Tax payments (monthly, semiweekly, or daily for large depositors) must be made by Electronic Federal Tax Payment System (EFTPS), or by another electronic transfer method. Generally, employers must file Form 941, Employer's Quarterly Federal Tax Return, which reports the federal income taxes withheld from wages and the total FICA taxes attributable to wages paid during each quarter. Form 941 also reports any payroll taxes not yet deposited for the quarter. A specific deposit rule allows small employers who accumulate less than $2,500 tax liability during a quarter to skip monthly payments and pay the entire amount of their payroll taxes with their quarterly Form 941. Form 941 must be filed by the last day of the month following the end of the quarter. For example, the first quarter Form 941, covering the months of January through March, must be filed by April 30. The Form 941 e-file program allows taxpayers to electronically file Form 941 or Form 944.

Nearly a million very small employers with employment tax liability of $1,000 or less per year are allowed to file employment tax returns just once a year, instead of quarterly; for example, by January 31 of 2025 for 2024 employment taxes. Qualifying small employers receive written notification from the IRS that they should file using a Form 944 instead of the standard Form 941 used by most employers. The Form 944 is due annually, at the end of the month following the taxpayer's year end.

IRS Publications 15 (Circular E) and 15-T cover the rules regarding the calculation and deposit of payroll taxes in detail and are indispensable resources for those working in this complex area.

Tax Break

Many small businesses elect to outsource payroll processing to a third party. The IRS provides guidance to taxpayers on the differences among the four types of third-party arrangements for payroll outsourcing: (1) a payroll service provider, (2) a Reporting Agent, (3) a §3504 Agent, or (4) a Certified Professional Employer Organization. Taxpayers should take heed as to which arrangement they are engaged in since the permissible actions of the third-party and where ultimate liability resides may differ. Refer to **www.irs.gov/businesses/small-businesses-self-employed/third-party-arrangement-chart**.

Self-Study Problem 9.5
Refer to Appendix E for Solutions to Self-Study Problems

1. Using the information from Self-Study Problem 9.3, complete Parts I and II of Form 941 for the Hills Scientific Corp's second quarter on Pages 9-39 and 9-40. Assume that the company made deposits of $68,000 for the second quarter, that income tax withholding was in equal amounts for each month for each employee, and that Hills is a monthly depositor.

Self-Study Problem 9.5

Form 941 for 2024: Employer's QUARTERLY Federal Tax Return
(Rev. March 2024)   Department of the Treasury — Internal Revenue Service

950124
OMB No. 1545-0029

Employer identification number (EIN)

Name *(not your trade name)*

Trade name *(if any)*

Address
Number   Street   Suite or room number
City   State   ZIP code
Foreign country name   Foreign province/county   Foreign postal code

Report for this Quarter of 2024
(Check one.)
☐ 1: January, February, March
☐ 2: April, May, June
☐ 3: July, August, September
☐ 4: October, November, December

Go to *www.irs.gov/Form941* for instructions and the latest information.

Read the separate instructions before you complete Form 941. Type or print within the boxes.

Part 1: Answer these questions for this quarter. Employers in American Samoa, Guam, the Commonwealth of the Northern Mariana Islands, the U.S. Virgin Islands, and Puerto Rico can skip lines 2 and 3, unless you have employees who are subject to U.S. income tax withholding.

1. Number of employees who received wages, tips, or other compensation for the pay period including: *Mar. 12* (Quarter 1), *June 12* (Quarter 2), *Sept. 12* (Quarter 3), or *Dec. 12* (Quarter 4) . . . . 1 _____

2. Wages, tips, and other compensation . . . . 2 _____

3. Federal income tax withheld from wages, tips, and other compensation . . . . 3 _____

4. If no wages, tips, and other compensation are subject to social security or Medicare tax . . . ☐ Check here and go to line 6.

		Column 1		Column 2
5a	Taxable social security wages . .	_____	× 0.124 =	_____
5b	Taxable social security tips . . .	_____	× 0.124 =	_____
5c	Taxable Medicare wages & tips . .	_____	× 0.029 =	_____
5d	Taxable wages & tips subject to Additional Medicare Tax withholding	_____	× 0.009 =	_____

5e. Total social security and Medicare taxes. Add Column 2 from lines 5a, 5b, 5c, and 5d . . . . 5e _____

5f. Section 3121(q) Notice and Demand—Tax due on unreported tips *(see instructions)* . . 5f _____

6. Total taxes before adjustments. Add lines 3, 5e, and 5f . . . . 6 _____

7. Current quarter's adjustment for fractions of cents . . . . 7 _____

8. Current quarter's adjustment for sick pay . . . . 8 _____

9. Current quarter's adjustments for tips and group-term life insurance . . . . 9 _____

10. Total taxes after adjustments. Combine lines 6 through 9 . . . . 10 _____

11. Qualified small business payroll tax credit for increasing research activities. Attach Form 8974 11 _____

12. Total taxes after adjustments and nonrefundable credits. Subtract line 11 from line 10 . . 12 _____

13. Total deposits for this quarter, including overpayment applied from a prior quarter and overpayments applied from Form 941-X, 941-X (PR), or 944-X filed in the current quarter 13 _____

14. Balance due. If line 12 is more than line 13, enter the difference and see instructions . . . 14 _____

15. Overpayment. If line 13 is more than line 12, enter the difference _____ Check one: ☐ Apply to next return. ☐ Send a refund.

You MUST complete both pages of Form 941 and SIGN it.

For Privacy Act and Paperwork Reduction Act Notice, see separate instructions.   Cat. No. 17001Z   Form **941** (Rev. 3-2024)

Name *(not your trade name)*		Employer identification number (EIN)
		950224

Part 2: Tell us about your deposit schedule and tax liability for this quarter.

If you're unsure about whether you're a monthly schedule depositor or a semiweekly schedule depositor, see section 11 of Pub. 15.

16   Check one: ☐   Line 12 on this return is less than $2,500 or line 12 on the return for the prior quarter was less than $2,500, and you didn't incur a $100,000 next-day deposit obligation during the current quarter. If line 12 for the prior quarter was less than $2,500 but line 12 on this return is $100,000 or more, you must provide a record of your federal tax liability. If you're a monthly schedule depositor, complete the deposit schedule below; if you're a semiweekly schedule depositor, attach Schedule B (Form 941). Go to Part 3.

☐   **You were a monthly schedule depositor for the entire quarter.** Enter your tax liability for each month and total liability for the quarter, then go to Part 3.

Tax liability: Month 1   [.   ]

Month 2   [.   ]

Month 3   [.   ]

Total liability for quarter   [.   ]   Total must equal line 12.

☐   **You were a semiweekly schedule depositor for any part of this quarter.** Complete Schedule B (Form 941), Report of Tax Liability for Semiweekly Schedule Depositors, and attach it to Form 941. Go to Part 3.

Part 3: Tell us about your business. If a question does NOT apply to your business, leave it blank.

17   If your business has closed or you stopped paying wages . . . .   ☐ Check here and

enter the final date you paid wages   [/   /   ] ; also attach a statement to your return. See instructions.

18   If you're a seasonal employer and you don't have to file a return for every quarter of the year . . .   ☐ Check here.

Part 4: May we speak with your third-party designee?

Do you want to allow an employee, a paid tax preparer, or another person to discuss this return with the IRS? See the instructions for details.

☐ Yes.   Designee's name and phone number   [   ]   [   ]

Select a 5-digit personal identification number (PIN) to use when talking to the IRS.   [ ][ ][ ][ ][ ]

☐ No.

Part 5: Sign here. You MUST complete both pages of Form 941 and SIGN it.

Under penalties of perjury, I declare that I have examined this return, including accompanying schedules and statements, and to the best of my knowledge and belief, it is true, correct, and complete. Declaration of preparer (other than taxpayer) is based on all information of which preparer has any knowledge.

Sign your name here   [   ]   Print your name here   [   ]

Print your title here   [   ]

Date   [/   /   ]   Best daytime phone   [   ]

Paid Preparer Use Only   Check if you're self-employed   . . . ☐

Preparer's name		PTIN	
Preparer's signature		Date	/ /
Firm's name (or yours if self-employed)		EIN	
Address		Phone	
City		State	ZIP code

Page **2**   Form **941** (Rev. 3-2024)

Source: Internal Revenue Service (IRS)

9-6 Employer Reporting Requirements

9.6 Learning Objective
Prepare employer payroll reporting.

On or before January 31 of the year following the calendar year of payment, an employer must furnish to each employee two copies of the employee's Wage and Tax Statement, Form W-2, for the previous calendar year. If employment is terminated before the end of the year and the employee requests a Form W-2, the employer must furnish the Form W-2 within 30 days after the last wage payment is made or after the employee request, whichever is later. Otherwise, the general rule requiring the W-2 to be furnished to the employee by January 31 applies. The original copy (Copy A) of all Forms W-2 and Form W-3 (Transmittal of Wage and Tax Statements) must be filed by the employer with the Social Security Administration by January 31 of the year following the calendar year of payment. Copy B of Form W-2 is filed with the employee's federal tax return. Employers retain Copy D of Form W-2 for their records. Extra copies of Form W-2 are prepared and provided to the employee to use when filing state and local tax returns. Starting in 2024 (for 2023 Forms W-2), employers that need to file ten or more Forms W-2 must file them electronically.

Form W-2 is used to report wages, tips, and other compensation paid to an employee. Form W-2 also provides the employee with additional supplemental information such as the cost of employer-sponsored health care coverage, employer contributions to a health savings account (HSA), excess group-term life insurance premiums, Roth contributions to an employer plan, and certain reimbursements of travel and other ordinary and necessary expenses. Employers are permitted, but not required, to truncate all but the last four digits of the taxpayer's Social Security number on Form W-2, except for Copy A, which must include all digits. The details of the amounts included on Form W-2 are covered in Chapter 2.

Form W-3 is used to report the totals from all Forms W-2 for a particular employer.

Example Nathan Orkney has two employees that work for his small business. The first employee reports Box 1 wages of $23,000 and the second employee reports Box 1 wages of $20,000. Nathan's Form W-3 will report $43,000 of Box 1 wages along with Copy A of Forms W-2 for both employees. ♦

A Form W-3 must be filed even when only one Form W-2 is being reported, including for household employees.

9-6a Business Expense Reimbursements

Special rules apply to the reimbursement of travel and other ordinary and necessary employee business expenses. If an employee is reimbursed for travel and other ordinary and necessary business expenses, income and employment tax withholding may be required. If a reimbursement payment is considered to have been made under an accountable plan, the amount is excluded from the employee's gross income and consequently is not required to be included on Form W-2, and no withholding is required. Alternatively, reimbursements of travel and other employee business expenses made under a nonaccountable plan must be included as wages on Form W-2, and the amounts are subject to withholding. Payments are considered made under a nonaccountable plan in the following circumstances: (1) the employee receives a reimbursement for expenses under an arrangement which does not require the employee to account adequately to the employer, or the employee receives advances under an arrangement which does not require the employee to return amounts in excess of substantiated expenses; or (2) the employee receives amounts under an arrangement that requires the employee to substantiate reimbursed expenses, but the amounts are not substantiated within a reasonable period of time, or the employee receives amounts under a plan which requires excess reimbursements to be returned to the employer, but the employee does not return such excess amounts within a reasonable period of time. In the first case, the entire amount paid under the expense account plan is considered wages subject to withholding, whereas under the circumstances described in the second situation, only the amounts in excess of the substantiated expenses are subject to withholding.

> **Tax Break**
> The Social Security Administration offers free preparation and filing of up to 50 Forms W-2 and commensurate W-3 at their Business Services Online website (**www.ssa.gov/bso/bsowelcome.htm**).

9-6b Form W-2G

Gambling winnings are reported by gambling establishments on Form W-2G. Amounts that must be reported include certain winnings from horse and dog racing, jai alai, lotteries, state-conducted lotteries, sweepstakes, wagering pools, bingo, keno, and slot machines. In certain cases, withholding of income taxes is required. Forms W-2G must be transmitted to the taxpayer no later than January 31 of the year following the calendar year of payment, and to the IRS along with Form 1096 by March 1 following the calendar year of payment. Requirements to file Form W-2G can differ between the type of wagering or gaming. The due date is March 31 if transmitting electronically to the IRS. More information can be found in the instructions for Form W-2G.

9-6c Information Returns

Taxpayers engaged in a trade or business are required to file Form 1099 for each recipient of certain payments made in the course of their trade or business. Where applicable, federal income tax withheld with respect to the payment is also reported on Form 1099. The common types of payments and the related Forms 1099 are summarized in Table 9.4.

Table 9.4 1099 Forms

Form	Used For
1099-B	Payments of proceeds from brokers
1099-C	Cancellation of debt
1099-DA	Digital assets (starting in 2025)
1099-DIV	Dividend payments
1099-G	Certain government payments (state income tax refund)
1099-INT	Interest payments
1099-K	Merchant card and third-party network transactions
1099-MISC	Miscellaneous payments
1099-NEC	Payments to non-employees
1099-OID	Original issue discount
1099-Q	Payments from qualified education programs
1099-R	Payments of pension, annuity, profit sharing, retirement plan, IRA, insurance contracts, etc.
1099-S	Payments from real estate transactions
1099-SA	Distributions from an HSA

> **Tax Break**
> The IRS now operates an online portal to file Forms 1099 electronically: The Information Return Intake System (IRIS). IRIS is free and allows users to create, upload, edit, view, and download copies of 1099 forms. Users are required to create an online account and will need to request a code ahead of time, perhaps as many as 45 days. Refer to Publication 5717 or go to **www.irs.gov/filing/e-file-information-returns-with-iris** for more information.

Most Forms 1099 must be mailed to the recipients by January 31 of the year following the calendar year of payment. However, payors are allowed until February 15 of the year following the calendar year of payment to provide Forms 1099-B, 1099-S, and certain 1099-MISC forms. A separate Form 1096 must be used to transmit each type of 1099 to the appropriate IRS Campus Processing Site. Different Forms 1099 have different due dates. The IRS publishes a guide titled *General Instructions for Certain Information Returns* each year which has a convenient table of due dates.

For most small businesses, the most commonly used information reporting form is the 1099-MISC. This is used to report payments that total $600 or more to most non-corporate vendors. Taxpayers should use Form 1099-NEC to report nonemployee compensation of $600 or more. Nonemployee compensation generally occurs when an individual who does not qualify as an employee is paid for services provided.

9-6d Form 1099-K Reporting Merchant Card and Third-Party Payments

Banks and online payment networks ("payment settlement entities"), such as PayPal, Venmo, VISA, and MasterCard, are required to use Form 1099-K to report credit card sales and other reportable sales transactions to the IRS and to the businesses making reportable sales. The reporting requirement is triggered for an entity when the total dollar amount of specific transactions for a particular merchant exceeds $600.

Tax Break

If a taxpayer receives a Form 1099, the income reported on that form should generally be included on their tax return. The IRS is going to match the identification number on the Form 1099 to the taxpayer's tax return and likely will notice if that income is missing. A Form 1099 is not usually required to be attached to the taxpayer's return; however, if tax was withheld on the payment reported, the Form 1099 should be attached as necessary if paper filing.

Example Rio sells bags, totes, and purses using an e-commerce website specifically designed for handmade crafts. The website is used as a third-party settlement organization (TPSO) and thus all the sales using credit cards are handled by the e-commerce site. Rio receives a current year 1099-K from the TPSO that reports gross sales of $6,500. Although for many taxpayers, the gross revenue reported may represent accurate gross sales, Rio knows that she sold a couple of personal items on the site for a $200 loss. Rio also compared her records to the gross sales and noticed that the TPSO included the $340 of sales tax collected for Rio's home state as part of the gross revenue as well. When Rio prepares the Schedule C to report business income, the gross sales amount should be adjusted to reflect the personal items and the sales tax. In addition, any sales made outside the TPSO (for example, for cash) should be included in the business gross sales. ♦

9-6e Form W-9 Request for Taxpayer Identification Number

In order to assist in the preparation of information returns, one of the key forms that is often requested of non-employee vendors and others is the Form W-9, Request for Taxpayer Identification Number and Certification.

Form W-9
(Rev. March 2024)
Department of the Treasury
Internal Revenue Service

Request for Taxpayer Identification Number and Certification

Go to *www.irs.gov/FormW9* for instructions and the latest information.

Give form to the requester. Do not send to the IRS.

Before you begin. For guidance related to the purpose of Form W-9, see *Purpose of Form*, below.

1 Name of entity/individual. An entry is required. (For a sole proprietor or disregarded entity, enter the owner's name on line 1, and enter the business/disregarded entity's name on line 2.)

2 Business name/disregarded entity name, if different from above.

3a Check the appropriate box for federal tax classification of the entity/individual whose name is entered on line 1. Check only **one** of the following seven boxes.

☐ Individual/sole proprietor   ☐ C corporation   ☐ S corporation   ☐ Partnership   ☐ Trust/estate

☐ LLC. Enter the tax classification (C = C corporation, S = S corporation, P = Partnership) . . . . . _____

Note: Check the "LLC" box above and, in the entry space, enter the appropriate code (C, S, or P) for the tax classification of the LLC, unless it is a disregarded entity. A disregarded entity should instead check the appropriate box for the tax classification of its owner.

☐ Other (see instructions)

3b If on line 3a you checked "Partnership" or "Trust/estate," or checked "LLC" and entered "P" as its tax classification, and you are providing this form to a partnership, trust, or estate in which you have an ownership interest, check this box if you have any foreign partners, owners, or beneficiaries. See instructions . . . . ☐

4 Exemptions (codes apply only to certain entities, not individuals; see instructions on page 3):

Exempt payee code (if any) _____

Exemption from Foreign Account Tax Compliance Act (FATCA) reporting code (if any) _____

(Applies to accounts maintained outside the United States.)

5 Address (number, street, and apt. or suite no.). See instructions.

Requester's name and address (optional)

6 City, state, and ZIP code

7 List account number(s) here (optional)

Print or type.
See *Specific Instructions* on page 3.

Part I Taxpayer Identification Number (TIN)

Enter your TIN in the appropriate box. The TIN provided must match the name given on line 1 to avoid backup withholding. For individuals, this is generally your social security number (SSN). However, for a resident alien, sole proprietor, or disregarded entity, see the instructions for Part I, later. For other entities, it is your employer identification number (EIN). If you do not have a number, see *How to get a TIN*, later.

Note: If the account is in more than one name, see the instructions for line 1. See also *What Name and Number To Give the Requester* for guidelines on whose number to enter.

Social security number
☐☐☐ – ☐☐ – ☐☐☐☐

or

Employer identification number
☐☐ – ☐☐☐☐☐☐☐

Part II Certification

Under penalties of perjury, I certify that:

1. The number shown on this form is my correct taxpayer identification number (or I am waiting for a number to be issued to me); and
2. I am not subject to backup withholding because (a) I am exempt from backup withholding, or (b) I have not been notified by the Internal Revenue Service (IRS) that I am subject to backup withholding as a result of a failure to report all interest or dividends, or (c) the IRS has notified me that I am no longer subject to backup withholding; and
3. I am a U.S. citizen or other U.S. person (defined below); and
4. The FATCA code(s) entered on this form (if any) indicating that I am exempt from FATCA reporting is correct.

Certification instructions. You must cross out item 2 above if you have been notified by the IRS that you are currently subject to backup withholding because you have failed to report all interest and dividends on your tax return. For real estate transactions, item 2 does not apply. For mortgage interest paid, acquisition or abandonment of secured property, cancellation of debt, contributions to an individual retirement arrangement (IRA), and, generally, payments other than interest and dividends, you are not required to sign the certification, but you must provide your correct TIN. See the instructions for Part II, later.

Sign Here   Signature of U.S. person   Date

Source: Internal Revenue Service (IRS)

In addition to taxpayer name and address, the Form W-9 is used to capture two characteristics of payees: (1) the tax identification number and (2) the type of taxpayer (individual, corporation, etc.). This information is used to prepare the proper type of information reporting.

Example Paola operates a small business and expects to make payments of $3,200 to a new vendor during the current year. Paola will request that the vendor provide a completed Form W-9 as part of the typical vendor set-up process, prior to making any payments to the vendor. The information from the Form W-9 will also be used to determine whether Paola will need to issue any information reporting for this vendor after the end of the year. ♦

Self-Study Problem 9.6 Refer to Appendix E for Solutions to Self-Study Problems

David Flock (PO Box 12344, Melbourne, FL 32901; E.I.N. 95-1234567; telephone 800-555-1212) paid two employees for working for his small business in 2024. David does not offer a retirement plan for his employees. David's payroll records show the following:

Employee	Social Security Number	Hours Worked	Gross Wages	Federal Income Tax Withheld	State Income Tax Withheld	Social Security Withheld	Medicare Withheld	Net Pay
China Jones	398-22-4212	973.50	$17,523.12	$610.00	$0.00	$1,086.43	$254.09	$15,572.60
Lilly Smith	466-19-9001	875.00	14,000.00	235.00	0.00	868.00	203.00	12,694.00
Total			$31,523.12	$845.00	$0.00	$1,954.43	$457.09	$28,266.60

a. China's home address is 2702 Carlson Circle, Apt 2K, Melbourne FL 32901. Complete Copy B of the Form W-2 for China Jones.

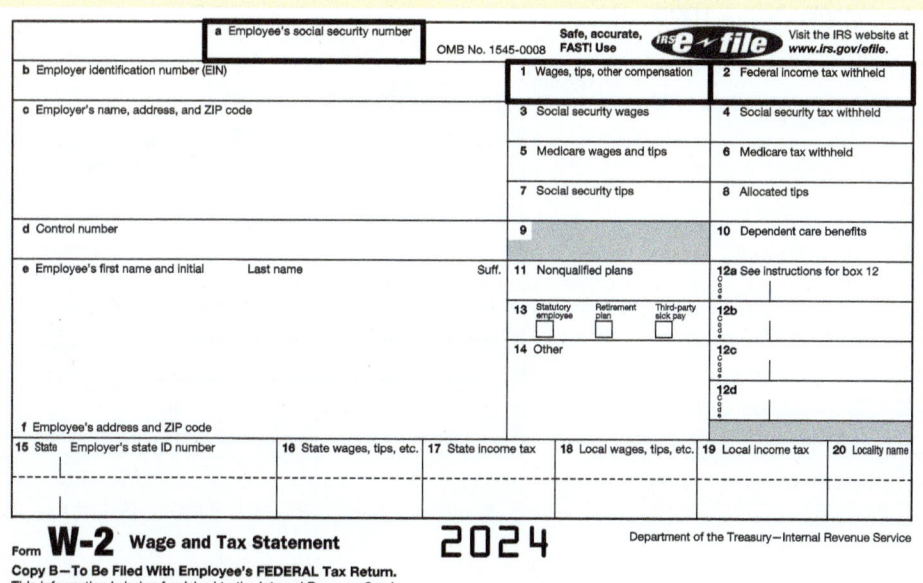

Self-Study Problem 9.6, continued
Refer to Appendix E for Solutions to Self-Study Problems

b. Assume David files a Form 941 to report his taxes. Complete David's Form W-3 for 2024.

c. David also occasionally pays Cielle Harris as a properly classified independent contractor to work for his business. In 2024, David paid Cielle $878.78 for services rendered. No taxes were withheld on payments to Cielle. Cielle lives at 224 Deland Avenue, Indialantic, FL 32903. Her Social Security number is 566-29-9819. Prepare Copy B of Cielle's Form 1099-NEC.

9-7 The FUTA Tax

Please note: Employers in jurisdictions that have not repaid money borrowed from the federal government for unemployment benefits will have a higher FUTA tax than the 0.6 percent illustrated below. In 2023, California and New York were subject to a FUTA credit reduction of 0.6 percent. These same states are expected to be subject to a credit reduction of 0.9 percent in 2024 (official determinations are issued on or around November 10 each year). For purposes of the problems and examples in this textbook, assume that the employer does not reside in one of the jurisdictions where a higher FUTA tax applies.

9.7 Learning Objective

Compute the amount of FUTA tax for an employer.

The Federal Unemployment Tax Act (FUTA) instituted a tax that is not withheld from employees' wages, but instead is paid in full by employers. The federal unemployment tax rate is 6 percent of an employee's wages up to $7,000. In most states, a credit is allowed for state unemployment taxes (SUTA) of 5.4 percent. Therefore, the effective federal unemployment tax rate is only 0.6 percent if the state also assesses an unemployment tax.

Example Karen has two employees in 2024: John, who earned $12,500 this year, and Sue, who earned $15,000. The FUTA tax is calculated as follows:

John's wages, $12,500 (maximum $7,000)	$ 7,000
Sue's wages, $15,000 (maximum $7,000)	7,000
Total FUTA wages	14,000
FUTA tax at 6.0%	840
Credit for SUTA at 5.4%	(756)
FUTA tax at 0.6%	$ 84

♦

Tax Break

One common income-shifting technique is to employ your children as part of your business. This creates an income tax deduction (at a presumably higher rate) and shifts the income to a (presumably) lower-taxed child. If the parent(s) operate(s) a sole proprietorship or a partnership in which both partners are parents of the child, wages paid to the child also escape FICA taxes before age 18 and escape FUTA taxes on the child's wages before age 21.

Employers report their FUTA liability for the year on Form 940, Employer's Annual Federal Unemployment (FUTA) Tax Return. The Form 940 is generally due by January 31st of the following year; however, if all FUTA taxes were deposited when due, the deadline is extended to February 10th (or next business day if a weekend). Like federal income tax withholding and FICA taxes, federal unemployment taxes must be deposited by electronic funds transfer (EFTPS). A deposit is required when the FUTA taxes for the quarter, plus any amount not yet deposited for the prior quarter(s), exceed $500. If required, the deposit must be made by the last day of the month after the end of each quarter.

Example Ti Corporation's federal unemployment tax liability, after reduction by the credit for state unemployment taxes, is $255 for the first quarter of 2024, $200 for the second quarter, $75 for the third quarter, and $25 for the fourth quarter. Ti Corporation must deposit $530, the sum of the first, second, and third quarters' liability, by October 31, 2024. The remaining $25 may be either deposited or paid with Form 940. ♦

Because states administer federal-state unemployment programs, most of the unemployment tax is paid to the state. Employers must pay all state unemployment taxes for the year by the due date of the federal Form 940 to get full credit for the state taxes against FUTA.

Self-Study Problem 9.7

Your client has provided the following annual payroll summary for 2024:

Anatolian Corporation
400 8th Street N
La Crosse, WI 54601
EIN: 94-0001112
December 31, 2024

Employee	Q1	Q2	Q3	Q4	YTD
Nancy Wheeling	14,000	14,000	14,000	14,000	56,000
Dustin Hendrickson	6,000	7,500	8,200	7,800	29,500
John Myers	-	3,200	3,500	-	6,700
Ellie Veen	29,000	26,000	26,000	26,000	107,000
Mike Weeder	-	-	-	8,200	8,200
James Hopps	3,500	3,000	400	-	6,900
William Byars	-	6,800	5,900	-	12,700
Luke Éclair	-	-	3,300	3,500	6,800
Steve Harrison	5,700	5,700	5,700	5,700	22,800
Maxwell Maryfield	4,700	5,100	-	-	9,800
William Hargreaves	5,000	5,000	5,000	5,000	20,000
Joyce Byright	4,000	4,100	4,500	3,800	16,400
	71,900	80,400	76,500	74,000	302,800

Gross Wages ($)

Anatolian pays Wisconsin state unemployment tax and makes the *required* deposits of both federal and state unemployment taxes on a timely basis. There was no overpayment in 2023. Use this information to complete Parts 1–5 of Form 940 on Pages 9-49 and 9-50.

Self-Study Problem 9.7

Form 940 for 2024: Employer's Annual Federal Unemployment (FUTA) Tax Return
Department of the Treasury — Internal Revenue Service

850113
OMB No. 1545-0029

Employer identification number (EIN) [ ][ ] – [ ][ ][ ][ ][ ][ ][ ]

Name (not your trade name)

Trade name (if any)

Address
Number   Street   Suite or room number
City   State   ZIP code
Foreign country name   Foreign province/county   Foreign postal code

Type of Return (Check all that apply.)
☐ a. Amended
☐ b. Successor employer
☐ c. No payments to employees in 2024
☐ d. Final: Business closed or stopped paying wages

Go to www.irs.gov/Form940 for instructions and the latest information.

Read the separate instructions before you complete this form. Please type or print within the boxes.

Part 1: Tell us about your return. If any line does NOT apply, leave it blank. See instructions before completing Part 1.

1a If you had to pay state unemployment tax in one state only, enter the state abbreviation . . . . . . 1a [ ][ ]

1b If you had to pay state unemployment tax in more than one state, you are a multi-state employer . . . . 1b ☐ Check here. Complete Schedule A (Form 940).

2 If you paid wages in a state that is subject to CREDIT REDUCTION . . . . 2 ☐ Check here. Complete Schedule A (Form 940).

Part 2: Determine your FUTA tax before adjustments. If any line does NOT apply, leave it blank.

3 Total payments to all employees . . . . 3 [.]

4 Payments exempt from FUTA tax . . . . 4 [.]

   Check all that apply: 4a ☐ Fringe benefits   4c ☐ Retirement/Pension   4e ☐ Other
                          4b ☐ Group-term life insurance   4d ☐ Dependent care

5 Total of payments made to each employee in excess of $7,000 . . . . 5 [.]

6 Subtotal (line 4 + line 5 = line 6) . . . . 6 [.]

7 Total taxable FUTA wages (line 3 – line 6 = line 7). See instructions . . . . 7 [.]

8 FUTA tax before adjustments (line 7 x 0.006 = line 8) . . . . 8 [.]

Part 3: Determine your adjustments. If any line does NOT apply, leave it blank.

9 If ALL of the taxable FUTA wages you paid were excluded from state unemployment tax, multiply line 7 by 0.054 (line 7 x 0.054 = line 9). Go to line 12 . . . . 9 [.]

10 If SOME of the taxable FUTA wages you paid were excluded from state unemployment tax, OR you paid ANY state unemployment tax late (after the due date for filing Form 940), complete the worksheet in the instructions. Enter the amount from line 7 of the worksheet . . 10 [.]

11 If credit reduction applies, enter the total from Schedule A (Form 940) . . . . 11 [.]

Part 4: Determine your FUTA tax and balance due or overpayment. If any line does NOT apply, leave it blank.

12 Total FUTA tax after adjustments (lines 8 + 9 + 10 + 11 = line 12) . . . . 12 [.]

13 FUTA tax deposited for the year, including any overpayment applied from a prior year . . 13 [.]

14 **Balance due.** If line 12 is more than line 13, enter the excess on line 14.
   • If line 14 is more than $500, you must deposit your tax.
   • If line 14 is $500 or less, you may pay with this return. See instructions . . . . 14 [.]

15 **Overpayment.** If line 13 is more than line 12, enter the excess on line 15 and check a box below 15 [.]

   You **MUST** complete both pages of this form and **SIGN** it.   Check one: ☐ Apply to next return. ☐ Send a refund.

For Privacy Act and Paperwork Reduction Act Notice, see separate instructions.   Cat. No. 11234O   Form **940** (2024)

850212

Name (not your trade name)

Employer identification number (EIN)

Part 5: Report your FUTA tax liability by quarter only if line 12 is more than $500. If not, go to Part 6.

16 Report the amount of your FUTA tax liability for each quarter; do NOT enter the amount you deposited. If you had no liability for a quarter, leave the line blank.

   16a 1st quarter (January 1 – March 31) . . . . 16a ⎵ . ⎵

   16b 2nd quarter (April 1 – June 30) . . . . 16b ⎵ . ⎵

   16c 3rd quarter (July 1 – September 30) . . . . 16c ⎵ . ⎵

   16d 4th quarter (October 1 – December 31) . . . . 16d ⎵ . ⎵

17 Total tax liability for the year (lines 16a + 16b + 16c + 16d = line 17) 17 ⎵ . ⎵   Total must equal line 12.

Part 6: May we speak with your third-party designee?

Do you want to allow an employee, a paid tax preparer, or another person to discuss this return with the IRS? See the instructions for details.

☐ Yes. Designee's name and phone number

Select a 5-digit personal identification number (PIN) to use when talking to the IRS.

☐ No.

Part 7: Sign here. You MUST complete both pages of this form and SIGN it.

Under penalties of perjury, I declare that I have examined this return, including accompanying schedules and statements, and to the best of my knowledge and belief, it is true, correct, and complete, and that no part of any payment made to a state unemployment fund claimed as a credit was, or is to be, deducted from the payments made to employees. Declaration of preparer (other than taxpayer) is based on all information of which preparer has any knowledge.

Sign your name here

Print your name here

Print your title here

Date   /   /

Best daytime phone

Paid Preparer Use Only   Check if you are self-employed ☐

Preparer's name

Preparer's signature

Firm's name (or yours if self-employed)

Address

City   State   ZIP code

PTIN

Date   /   /

EIN

Phone

Form **940** (2024)

Source: Internal Revenue Service (IRS)

9-8 Qualified Retirement Plans

9.8 Learning Objective
Describe the general rules for qualified retirement plans.

The presentation of qualified retirement plans in this chapter is focused on larger employers (refer to Chapter 5 for small business retirement plans). Qualified retirement plans generally offer potential tax savings in two primary ways:

1. Contributions to qualified plans are generally not subject to current income taxation.
2. The income generated by the funds in the plan are not subject to current taxation.

Example In 2024, Gail contributes $2,400 from her $100,000 salary to her employer's qualified profit-sharing plan. Gail's employer contributes $3,600. Gail's wages subject to income tax in 2024 are reduced to $97,600 and the employer contribution of $3,600 is not subject to income taxation currently. ♦

Example Bonnie and her employer have made substantial before-tax contributions to her qualified retirement plan for the past 30 years. In 2024, her retirement account, which is invested in a variety of mutual funds, generated interest income of $4,500, dividend income of $6,000 and capital gains of $14,000. If Bonnie's plan remains qualified and she does not withdraw any distributions from the plan, the earnings in her account are not subject to current income taxation in 2024. ♦

However, as was true with traditional Individual Retirement Accounts (as explained in Chapter 5), because the initial contributions were not subject to income taxation, all of the distributions from the plan are generally subject to income tax.

Example Continuing from the previous example, Bonnie reaches age 60, retires in 2025, and takes a distribution of $30,000 from her retirement account. Although the distribution may be in part from her previous contributions or from the employer's contributions or from the earnings of her account, all of the $30,000 distribution is taxable. ♦

From an income tax planning perspective, the two primary benefits of qualified plans mentioned above create the possibility of three income tax benefits:

1. The deferral of paying income taxes on wages until a later year (taking advantage of the time value of money)
2. The deferral of paying income taxes on the retirement accounts earnings until a later year (also time value of money)
3. The possibility that income, and thus the marginal tax rate on that income, may be lower in a future period when the taxpayer is retired.

Tax planning is explained further in Chapter 12.

9-8a Qualified Plans

For a retirement plan to be a qualified plan for income tax purposes, it must meet the following general requirements:

1. A plan must be created by an employer for the *exclusive benefit* of employees or their beneficiaries.
2. The contributions and benefits under a plan must *not discriminate in* favor of highly-compensated employees.
3. A plan must meet certain *participation and coverage requirements*. The plan must provide that all employees who are at least 21 years old and who have completed at least one year of service with the employer are eligible to participate. If the plan provides for 100-percent vesting of accrued benefits upon commencement of participation in

the plan, the one year of service requirement may be replaced with a requirement that the employee has completed at least two years of service.
4. *Minimum vesting* requirements must be met with respect to both employee and employer contributions.
5. *Uniform minimum distribution* rules must be met.

9-8b Types of Qualified Plans

The tax law provides for several types of qualified plans that are generally designed for larger employers: pension plans, profit-sharing plans, stock bonus plans, Employee Stock Ownership Plans (ESOPs), and Employee Stock Purchase Plans (ESPPs). A pension plan can take one of two forms: a defined contribution plan or a defined benefit plan. Under a defined contribution plan, the amount of contribution for the employee is determined by reference to a formula based on the employee's current compensation. The employee's retirement benefits will be dependent upon the accumulated contributions and earnings in the account at the time of retirement. Under a defined benefit plan, the future retirement benefits of the employee are specified, and a formula is used to determine the contributions necessary to provide for the defined benefit. Defined benefit plans are being used much less frequently by employers.

Example Heather is an employee who earned $30,000 during the current year. Her employer contributed $1,200 (4 percent of Heather's salary) to a qualified retirement plan. This plan is a defined contribution plan. ♦

Example Alan works for an employer whose qualified retirement plan states that Alan will receive a retirement benefit at age 65 equal to 40 percent of his final year's salary. The employer must make adequate contributions to the plan to enable the stated retirement benefit to be paid (a sufficient amount of money must be in the plan upon Alan's retirement to pay for Alan's defined retirement benefit). This plan is a defined benefit plan. ♦

A profit-sharing plan (which requires a plan document and annual reporting) permits discretionary contributions for employers only (no employee contributions). This permits the employer to make contributions in some years and none in others. If a contribution is made, the plan document must contain a set formula by which each employee's account is credited with the contribution. A common formula is the "comp-to-comp" method, which determines each employee's allocation by calculating their share of the total compensation paid to all employees.

Example Spaceman Gears Company operates a profit-sharing plan for its employees and elects to make a $100,000 contribution to the plan in 2024. Jorge, an employee of Spaceman Gears, has compensation of $50,000 in 2024. Total compensation paid to all employees by Spaceman Gears in 2024 is $1.5 million. Jorge's share of the profit-sharing contribution is $3,333.33 ($50,000 ÷ $1.5 million × $100,000). ♦

Profit-sharing plans offer flexible vesting options but must vest at least as quickly as required under tax law which currently permits two methods:

1. Cliff vesting: 100-percent vesting after no more than three years of service.
2. Graded vesting: 20-percent vesting after the second year of service, with 20 percent more each year until 100-percent vesting occurs after the sixth year of service.

Vesting must occur at least this quickly, but the employer has the discretion to vest faster.

Example Chandler Corporation's profit-sharing plan has made the following contributions to Bing, an employee:

Year of contribution	2022	2023	2024
Amount	$3,400	$1,670	$2,355
Vested date	12/31/2024	12/31/2025	12/31/2026

Because the contributions vest at the end of the third year of service, the plan meets the vesting requirements. ♦

Example Green Company's profit-sharing plan has made the following contributions to Rachel, an employee:

Year of contribution	2022	2023	2024
Amount	$3,400	$1,670	$2,355
Vested date and amount			
1/1/2022	$ 0	$ 0	$ 0
1/1/2023	0	0	0
1/1/2024	680	0	0
1/1/2025	680	334	0
1/1/2026	680	334	471
1/1/2027	680	334	471
1/1/2028	680	334	471
1/1/2029	0	334	471
1/1/2030	0	0	471

Because the contributions vest 20 percent per year starting no later than after the second year of service and are fully vested in the year after the sixth year of service, the plan meets the vesting requirements. If Rachel were to leave Green Company in the middle of 2026, she would not vest in any amounts after that date. ♦

Contributions to a profit-sharing plan are limited to the lesser of 100 percent of the employee's compensation or $69,000 (in 2024). As with most qualified plans, eligibility and nondiscrimination requirements must be met to maintain plan status.

A money purchase plan has similar requirements to that of a profit-sharing plan but requires a readily determinable employer contribution each year, typically based on a percentage of each employee's compensation. Unlike a profit-sharing plan, a money purchase plan permits employee elective contributions.

An ESOP is a qualified retirement stock bonus plan designed to allow employees to invest primarily in the employer's securities. The employer contribution limits for an ESOP are 100 percent of the employee's compensation or $69,000 (in 2024), whichever is less. Employee contributions are not permitted. Employer contributions are elective, in that a contribution need not be made each year. Employee vesting rules are the same as profit-sharing plans.

Upon reaching a certain age or years of service, employees may make a non-taxed diversification distribution to diversify their investments. Distributions are taxable at the value of the stock at the time of distribution but can defer taxation by rolling them over into an IRA or other qualified plan (rollovers are explained in LO 9.9).

Because the ESOP is required to purchase shares from the employer, a leveraged ESOP is a commonly used structure in which the ESOP borrows money to purchase shares (which guarantee the loan) and as the employer makes contributions to the ESOP, a portion of the loan is paid off and the shares are allocated to the employees. A leveraged ESOP avoids the upfront use of cash to fund the shares.

An employee stock purchase plan (ESPP) can also be structured as a qualified plan. ESPPs allow employees to purchase their employer's stock that generally reflect a modest price discount. By design, the employee is not taxed until the stock purchased is sold. If the stock is held for at least two years after the option is granted and for at least one year after the option is exercised, any gain or loss from the sale of the stock is treated as a capital gain or loss. Earlier dispositions will result in ordinary gains. No employee may purchase more than $25,000 of employer stock per year.

The tax law allows for qualified plans for governmental and tax-exempt entity plans also. These plans largely function like other qualified plans (require plan documents, annual filing, nondiscrimination testing) and largely differ on what types of entities may offer them. Governmental plans are obviously not used by small businesses, but a small non-profit may wish to institute a version for certain employees.

A 403(b) plan is a qualified plan (sometimes referred to as a tax-sheltered annuity) offered by public schools, colleges, or universities and certain §501(c)(3) tax-exempt organizations. Although traditionally, 403(b) plans invested in annuities, other investment options (e.g., mutual funds) are permitted. Section 403(b) plans have all the typical qualified plan requirements such as employee eligibility, nondiscrimination testing, and a written plan document. Employee elective contributions are equal to those of traditional 401k plans ($23,000 and catch-up of $7,500 in 2024) and total contributions are limited to the lesser of $69,000 or 100 percent of the employee's compensation. For certain 403(b) plans, employees with 15 years of service or more with the same employer, the limitation on catch-up contributions is increased by the lesser of (1) $3,000, (2) $15,000 reduced by any previous catch-up contributions, or (3) $5,000 multiplied by the employee's number of years of service less any previous employee contributions.

A 457(b) plan can differ depending on whether created for a governmental entity or a non-governmental tax-exempt entity (not necessarily a §501(c)(3) entity). A governmental 457(b) plan is established by a state or local government entity (not the federal government) for employees of the agency or department. Both employee and employer contributions are permitted to 457(b) plans and the limits are the same as 403(b) plans ($23,000 in 2024 for employee contributions and lesser of 100% of compensation or $69,000 for total contributions).

457(b) plans may (but are not required to) also offer a special catch-up contribution for employees that have reached the age that is 3 years prior to the age of normal retirement. The special catch-up contribution permits a catch-up contribution of the lesser of twice the basic limit [$46,000 ($23,000 × 2) in 2024] or the current year's limit plus any unused limit from prior years (the "underutilized limit"). The special catch-up contribution calculations are outside the scope of this textbook but can be significant amounts. Taxpayers eligible for a 457(b) plan that are approaching retirement should consider contacting their employer for details.

If established before May 1986, a governmental entity may continue to operate a 401k plan.

9-8c Limitations on Contributions to and Benefits from Qualified Plans

As explained above, employee and employer contributions to qualified plans are subject to certain dollar or percentage limitations. Under a defined contribution plan (including profit-sharing plans), the annual addition to an employee's account is generally not allowed to exceed the lesser of $69,000 (in 2024) or 100 percent of the employee's compensation. Under a defined benefit plan, the annual benefit payable to an employee upon retirement is limited to the lesser of $275,000 (for 2024) or 100 percent of the employee's average compensation for the highest three consecutive years of employment. If an employee is the beneficiary of contributions to both a defined benefit and defined contribution plan, the limit is 25 percent of an employee's compensation or the required funding for the defined benefit plan, whichever is greater. The operational rules for qualified pension plans and the other types of qualified plans are complex and beyond the scope of this textbook.

Self-Study Problem 9.8 Refer to Appendix E for Solutions to Self-Study Problems

a. John works for Continental Company, which has a qualified retirement plan. John's retirement benefit will be based on the amount of the contributions made by John and Continental to his account plus any investment growth up through the date of distribution. Is this a defined benefit or a defined contribution pension plan?

b. Charon is an employee of High Table Inc., which has a qualified retirement plan. This plan does not allow Charon to make any contributions to the plan. Charon's retirement benefit will be based on an applicable percentage based on Charon's years of service with the company multiplied by the average of Charon's three highest years of wages. Is this a defined benefit or a defined contribution pension plan?

c. Perkins has $4,000 of wages deferred from their pay each pay period during the current year and contributed to a qualified retirement plan. In addition, Perkins' employer contributed $3,000 to the qualified plan in the current year. If Perkins' current year wages are $70,000, what is the current year gross income from these two contributions?

d. Winston reaches age 62 and retires during the current year. He takes a distribution of $10,000 from his employer's qualified pension plan. The plan has been funded by pre-tax contributions made by Winston and additional contributions made by his employer. Investment growth over the years has come from interest (30 percent), dividends (20 percent), and capital gains in stocks and bonds (50 percent). What is the amount of gross income from the distribution and what is its character?

e. In 2024, when Viggo's compensation is $50,000, what is the maximum contribution his employer can make to the qualified profit-sharing plan on his behalf?

f. If in the previous question, Viggo's salary was $290,000, what is the maximum contribution?

9-9 Rollovers

9.9 Learning Objective

Explain the pension plan rollover rules.

In many situations, taxpayers need to transfer assets from one retirement plan to another plan of the same or different type. For example, the taxpayer may change jobs, take early retirement, or simply seek a better retirement fund manager. There are two ways this transfer can be accomplished: (1) direct transfer, also known as a trustee-to-trustee transfer, and (2) rollover of the distribution, in whole or in part, to an IRA or other qualified plan. There are potentially different tax treatments for the two types of transfers.

9-9a Direct Transfers

In direct transfers, the taxpayer instructs the trustee of the retirement plan to transfer assets to the trustee of another plan. There are no current-year tax consequences for this transaction. Also, there is no limit to the dollar amount of the transfer or the number of times a taxpayer can do this in a single tax year.

Example Juan has $90,000 in a Section 401(k) plan with his employer. He also has two IRAs, one with ABC Bank ($20,000) and one with XYZ Mutual Fund ($30,000). In March of 20XX, Juan instructs ABC Bank to make a direct transfer to XYZ Mutual Fund of all of his funds ($20,000). In August of 20XX, Juan quits his job and instructs the trustee of the Section 401(k) plan to transfer his $90,000 directly to XYZ Mutual Fund. On December 31, 20XX, Juan has $140,000 in his XYZ Mutual Fund IRA. Since the two transactions were direct transfers, there are no tax consequences to Juan in the current year. ♦

9-9b Distribution Rollovers

In a distribution rollover, the taxpayer receives a distribution of funds from a retirement plan and then transfers part or all of the funds to the new retirement plan trustee. The taxpayer has a maximum of 60 days from the date of the distribution in which to transfer funds to the new plan and avoid taxes and penalties. The 60-day rollover period may be waived in cases of casualty, disaster, and other events beyond the reasonable control of the taxpayer such as death, disability, incarceration, and postal error. The 60-day time limit is extended to 120 days for first-time home buyers.

The major drawback to distribution rollovers is that the trustee must withhold 20 percent of the amount distributed for federal income taxes, giving the taxpayer only 80 percent of the amount in their plan. However, the taxpayer must contribute 100 percent of the amount in the old plan to the new trustee within the required 60-day period to avoid tax on the distribution. Amounts that are not placed in a new plan within the required period are taxable as ordinary income in the current year. Also, if the taxpayer is under 59½ years old, the portion of the retirement plan distribution not transferred will be subject to a 10-percent penalty tax.

The exception to mandatory withholding is a distribution from an IRA; such distributions are not subject to the 20-percent withholding tax. Also, taxpayers are allowed only one distribution rollover each year for transfers from one IRA to another IRA. There are many other complex rules concerning retirement plan rollovers.

Example Bea is 50 years old, has worked for Gold Company for 25 years, and has $200,000 in her retirement plan. This year, Gold Company is purchased by Green Company. As a result of the takeover, Bea was laid off. Bea requests a distribution of her $200,000 from Gold Company's retirement plan. The trustee of Gold's retirement plan must withhold $40,000 (20 percent of $200,000) from the distribution. Bea only receives $160,000 from her retirement plan distribution. If Bea wants to roll her funds into an IRA and avoid taxes, she must contribute $200,000, even though she only received $160,000. If Bea has no other resources and cannot make up the $40,000, the amount not contributed to the IRA will be taxable income to her and subject to a 10-percent penalty. If Bea makes the total rollover contribution of $200,000 within the 60-day timeframe, then the distribution will be nontaxable. The $40,000 will be reported as taxes withheld on her tax return. ♦

If an individual misses the 60-day window to complete a rollover, generally the only way to avoid paying tax on the distribution is to request a private letter ruling from the IRS. The current cost for such a request is $12,500. Luckily, the IRS offers an automatic waiver in a number of circumstances including: (1) a misplaced check that was never cashed, (2) a distribution that was mistakenly placed in an account that was thought to be an eligible retirement account, (3) the taxpayer's home was severely damaged, (4) a family member dies, (5) the taxpayer or a family member was seriously ill, (6) the taxpayer was incarcerated, (7) the post office made an error, and others.

Self-Study Problem 9.9
Refer to Appendix E for Solutions to Self-Study Problems

Carol, age 40, has an IRA with Blue Mutual Fund. Her balance in the fund is $150,000. She has heard good things about the management of Red Mutual Fund, so she opens a Red Fund IRA. Carol requests her balance from the Blue Fund be distributed to her on July 1, 20XX. She opted to have no withholding on the distribution.

a. How much will Carol receive from the Blue Fund IRA?

b. If the funds were distributed from a qualified retirement plan (not an IRA), how much would Carol receive?

c. When is the last day Carol can roll over the amount received into the Red Fund IRA and avoid taxation in the current year?

d. Assuming the funds were distributed from a qualified retirement plan, not from an IRA, how much will Carol have to contribute to the Red Fund IRA to avoid taxable income and any penalties?

Key Terms

employee, 9-2
independent contractor, 9-2
behavioral control factors, 9-2
financial control factors, 9-2
relationship factors, 9-2
Form SS-8, 9-4
income tax withholding, 9-5
Form W-4, 9-5
lock-in-letter, 9-13
allowances, 9-13
percentage method, 9-18
wage bracket method, 9-18
IRS Publication 15-T, 9-18
Form W-4P, 9-23
tip income, 9-23
backup withholding, 9-24
FICA taxes, 9-25
FICA cap, 9-25
Social Security tax, 9-25

Old age, survivors, and disability insurance (OASDI), 9-25
Medicare tax, 9-25
excess Social Security tax, 9-27
estimated payments, 9-28
required annual payment, 9-28
Form 1040-ES, 9-29
Form 2210, 9-29
monthly or semiweekly depositor, 9-37
lookback period, 9-37
Form 941, 9-38
Form 944, 9-38
Form W-2, 9-41
Form W-3, 9-41
accountable plan, 9-41
nonaccountable plan, 9-41
Form W-2G, 9-42
Form 1099, 9-42

Form W-9, 9-44
federal unemployment tax (FUTA), 9-47
Form 940, 9-47
qualified retirement plans, 9-51
defined contribution plan, 9-52
defined benefit plan, 9-52
profit-sharing plan, 9-52
vesting, 9-52
employee stock ownership plan (ESOP), 9-53
employee stock purchase plan (ESPP), 9-54
403(b) plan, 9-54
457(b) plan, 9-54
direct transfer, 9-55
distribution rollover, 9-56

Key Points

Learning Objectives	Key Points
LO 9.1: Determine the classification of workers as employees versus independent contractors.	• The classification of employees and independent contractors is a function of law and each is subject to income and employment taxes differently. • The classification of a worker as an employee or independent contractor depends on the degree of control and independence between the individual and the business. • Factors to consider when classifying a worker are categorized as behavioral, financial, and relationship-based.
LO 9.2: Compute the income tax withholding from employee wages.	• Employers are required to withhold taxes from amounts paid to employees for wages, including salaries, fees, bonuses, commissions, vacation and retirement pay. • Form W-4, showing the filing status and possible adjustments to withholding, is furnished to the employer by the employee. • The percentage method and the wage bracket method of withholding are prescribed for the pre-2020 Form W-4 and post-2019 Form W-4. • Tip income must be reported.
LO 9.3: Compute the FICA tax.	• The Social Security (OASDI) tax rate is 6.2 percent and the Medicare tax rate is 1.45 percent for employers and employees. The maximum wage subject to the Social Security portion of the FICA tax is $168,600 for 2024, and all wages are subject to the Medicare portion of the FICA tax. • Taxpayers working for more than one employer during the same tax year may pay more than the maximum amount of Social Security taxes. If this happens, the taxpayer should compute the excess taxes paid, and report the excess as a payment against their income tax liability.
LO 9.4: Determine taxpayers' quarterly estimated payments.	• Self-employed taxpayers are not subject to withholding; however, they must make quarterly estimated tax payments. • Estimated payments are made in four installments on April 15, June 15, and September 15 of the tax year, and January 15 of the following year. • Any individual taxpayer who has estimated tax for the year of $1,000 or more, after subtracting withholding, and whose withholding does not equal or exceed the "required annual payment," must make quarterly estimated payments. • The required annual payment is the smallest of: (1) 90 percent of the tax shown on the current year's return, or (2) 100 percent (or 110 percent at higher income levels) of the tax shown on the preceding year's return. • Form 2210 is used to calculate the nondeductible penalty associated with the underpayment of estimated tax.
LO 9.5: Apply the federal deposit system to payroll withholding.	• Employers must make periodic deposits of the taxes that are withheld from employees' wages. Deposits must be made electronically. • Employers are either monthly or semiweekly depositors, depending on the total amount of income taxes withheld from wages and FICA taxes attributable to wages. However, if withholding and FICA taxes of $100,000 or more are accumulated at any time during the year, the depositor is subject to a special one-day deposit rule.
LO 9.6: Prepare employer payroll reporting.	• On or before January 31 of the year following the calendar year of payment, an employer must furnish to each employee two copies of Form W-2, the employee's Wage and Tax Statement, for the previous calendar year. • The original copy (Copy A) of all Forms W-2 and Form W-3 (Transmittal of Wage and Tax Statements) must be filed with the Social Security Administration by January 31 of the year following the calendar year of payment. • Most Forms 1099 must be mailed to the recipients by January 31 of the year following the calendar year of payment.

LO 9.7: Compute the amount of FUTA tax for an employer.	• The FUTA (Federal Unemployment Tax Act) tax is not withheld from employees' wages, but instead is paid in full by employers. • The federal unemployment tax rate is 6.0 percent of an employee's wages up to $7,000. A credit of up to 5.4 percent is allowed if state unemployment taxes are paid, resulting in a net effective federal unemployment tax rate of 0.6 percent.
LO 9.8: Describe the general rules for qualified retirement plans.	• In order to be qualified, retirement plans must meet certain requirements related to non-discrimination of lower-compensated employees, participation eligibility, vesting requirements, and distribution rules. • Contributions to qualified retirement plans can be limited to a percentage of compensation or an annual dollar threshold.
LO 9.9: Explain the pension plan rollover rules.	• There are two ways to transfer assets from one retirement plan to another of the same or different type: (1) a direct transfer, also known as a trustee-to-trustee transfer, and (2) a rollover of an actual cash distribution, in whole or in part, to an IRA or other qualified plan. • There are no current-year tax consequences for a direct trustee-to-trustee transfer. • Distribution rollovers are subject to a 60-day time limit for completion and may also be subject to income tax withholding and tax penalties.

Questions and Problems

Group 1:
Multiple Choice Questions

LO 9.1   1. The classification of a worker as an employee or an independent contractor is:
   a. Made by the employer.
   b. Made by the employee.
   c. Based on a negotiation between the employer and employee.
   d. Based on a set of common law factors related to control and independence.

LO 9.1   2. Which of the following is likely to indicate classification of a worker as an employee?
   a. The worker must provide their own tools and equipment.
   b. The worker can provide services at a location they choose.
   c. The worker receives benefits like health care.
   d. The worker makes their services available to the general public.

LO 9.1   3. Which of the following is likely to indicate classification of a worker as an independent contractor?
   a. The worker is likely to be subject to a contractual breach if they quit.
   b. The worker works full-time at a single place of business for greater than one year.
   c. The worker's travel and business expenses are reimbursed by the business.
   d. The tools and office used by the worker are supplied by the business.

LO 9.2   4. Which of the following best describes the purpose of Form W-4?
   a. Report year to date compensation and withholding for a single employee.
   b. Report year to date compensation and withholding for all employees of an employer.
   c. Report the compensation of a non-employee worker.
   d. Report the information necessary for an employer to withhold income tax from an employee's wages.

LO 9.2   5. Abbe, age 56, started a new job in 2024. At Abbe's previous employer, she had filed a Form W-4 with 5 allowances. Abbe's new employer will:
   a. Use a copy of Abbe's previous Form W-4 to calculate income tax withholding.
   b. Permit Abbe to file a new Form W-4 using either the old allowances method or the new method.
   c. Require Abbe to complete a new version of Form W-4.
   d. Require Abbe to withhold as a single taxpayer with no dependents.
   e. Require Abbe to use the IRS on-line withholding estimator.

LO 9.2   6. One of the primary differences between an "old" pre-2020 Form W-4 and a "new" post-2019 Form W-4 is:
   a. The new form does not rely on the number of allowances to determine withholding.
   b. The new form does not account for the possibility of child tax credits in determining the proper withholding.
   c. The old form can only be used for independent contractors.
   d. The new form requires the taxpayer to sign the Form W-4.

LO 9.2   7. Flo is a server at a diner and earns a significant portion of her pay through tips from customers. Some of these tips are paid via credit card and others are paid in cash. Flo is required to do which of the following?
   a. Pay additional tax of 8 percent on all tips.
   b. Report her tips to her employer.
   c. Give a portion of the tip to the diner management.
   d. Keep the cash tips only.

LO 9.2   8. Flo is a server at a diner and earns a significant portion of her pay through tips from customers. Some of these tips are paid via credit card and others are paid in cash. Flo's employer will:
   a. Withhold employment taxes but not income taxes on the tips.
   b. Withhold both employment and income taxes on the cash tips but only employment taxes on the tips paid by credit card.
   c. Withhold both employment and income taxes on all tips.
   d. Not withhold any taxes on cash tips but will withhold both employment and income taxes on credit card tips.

LO 9.2   9. Gloria and Al intend to file jointly in 2024. Gloria's wages are expected to be $90,000 and Al's are expected to be about $39,500. When Gloria is completing a new 2024 Form W-4, the most convenient but reliable way to handle her working spouse is:
   a. Ignore the fact that her spouse has a job.
   b. Check box 2(c) in Step 2: Multiple Jobs or Spouse Works on the new form.
   c. Complete the Multiple Jobs worksheet and use the Higher Paying Job column for her salary in determining the additional withholding required.
   d. Select the Head of Household filing status in Step 1 of Form W-4.

LO 9.3   10. Which of the following is true about FICA taxes?
   a. The FICA tax has two parts, Social Security (Old Age, Survivors, and Disability Insurance) and Medicare tax.
   b. In 2024, the maximum wage base for Social Security tax withholding is $160,200.
   c. Medicare taxes are only charged on wages up to the FICA cap.
   d. When employees work for more than one employer and exceed the maximum wage base for Social Security tax withholding in total, the additional Social Security tax is used to offset any Medicare taxes withheld otherwise.

LO 9.3   11. FICA taxes on employee wages are generally paid as follows:
   a. One-half is withheld from the employee and the other half is paid by the employer.
   b. The entire amount of Social Security is paid by the employee and the employer pays the Medicare portion.

c. The entire amount of Medicare is paid by the employee and the employer pays the Social Security portion.
d. Both portions are paid by the employer and thus, never withheld from an employee's pay.

LO 9.3 12. The rate for the Social Security portion of FICA taxes is:
a. 7.65 percent for the employee and 2.9 percent for the employer.
b. 6.2 percent for the employee and employer (up to the FICA cap).
c. 6.2 percent for the employee and 2.9 percent for the employer.
d. 6 percent but a state credit of 5.4 percent is generally permitted.

LO 9.3 13. The rate for the Medicare portion of FICA taxes for a non-self-employed individual is:
a. 2.9 percent for the employer.
b. 1.45 percent each for the employee and employer (not including any additional 0.9-percent tax for high-income taxpayers).
c. 7.65 percent total for the employee and employer.
d. 6.2 percent each for the employee and employer up to the FICA cap amount.

LO 9.3 14. Carlotta is an employee and generates wages of $170,000 in 2024. Which of the following best describes the rate of tax associated with the Medicare portion of FICA taxes?
a. 7.65 percent payable by Carlotta's employer.
b. 1.45 percent payable by Carlotta and 6.2 percent payable by the employer.
c. 1.45 percent each payable by Carlotta and the employer.
d. 2.9 percent but only up to the current year FICA cap.

LO 9.3 15. Yuzuru is a single employee and generates wages of $205,000 in 2024. Which of the following best describes the rate of tax associated with the Medicare portion of FICA taxes?
a. 1.45 percent each payable by Yuzuru and the employer.
b. 1.45 percent payable by Yuzuru and 2.9 percent payable by the employer.
c. 1.45 percent payable by Yuzuru on the first $200,000 of wages and then 2.35 percent payable by Yuzuru on wages above $200,000 and 1.45 percent payable by the employer on all wages.
d. 1.45 percent each payable by Yuzuru and the employer on the first $200,000 of wages and then 2.35 percent each payable by Yuzuru and the employer on wages above $200,000.

LO 9.3 16. Xinyi worked for two different employers in 2024 and her total wages were $85,000 for one and $87,000 for the other (total $172,000). Which of the following best describes Xinyi's 2024 FICA taxes?
a. Xinyi and the employer will each pay half of Social Security and Medicare taxes on her total wages and both will claim an income tax credit for the portion of each tax in excess of the 2024 FICA cap.
b. Xinyi and the employer will each pay half of Social Security and Medicare taxes on her total wages and only the employer will claim an income tax credit for the portion of each tax in excess of the 2024 FICA cap.
c. Xinyi and the employer will each pay half of Social Security and Medicare taxes on her total wages and only Xinyi will claim an income tax credit for the portion of both Social Security and Medicare tax in excess of the 2024 FICA cap.
d. Xinyi and the employer will each pay half of Social Security and Medicare taxes on her total wages and only Xinyi will claim an income tax credit for the portion of only Social Security tax in excess of the 2024 FICA cap.

LO 9.4 17. Darwin is self-employed in 2024 and expects to make self-employment income of $80,000. What alternative does Darwin have to avoid penalties for failure-to-pay income taxes?
a. Pay all of his income tax liability on January 15th of the following year.
b. Make quarterly estimated payments that are within a few percentage points of his actual income tax liability.

c. Make sure he pays the entire liability on the date he files his tax return on April 15th of the following year.
d. As long as Darwin pays his liability when he files his tax return, there are no penalties.

LO 9.4 18. Typically, estimated payments for individual taxpayers are due on the following dates:
a. Twice a year on April 15 and September 15
b. Four installments on April 15, June 15, September 15, and January 15 of the next year
c. Four times a year on April 15, July 15, September 15, and December 15
d. Twice a year on June 15 and December 15

LO 9.4 19. Amy's prior year adjusted gross income was $170,000. In order to avoid penalties, what is the required annual payment Amy must make in the current year?
a. 110% of the current year tax liability.
b. Any amount that reduces the amount Amy owes for the current year to no less than $5,000.
c. The lesser of 90 percent of the current year tax liability or 100 percent of the prior year tax liability.
d. The lesser of 90 percent of the current year tax liability or 110 percent of the prior year tax liability.

LO 9.4 20. When does the required annual payment for estimated income taxes increase to 110% of the prior year tax liability?
a. When the current year taxable income exceeds $100,000.
b. When prior year adjusted gross income is $150,000 or more.
c. When prior year taxable income exceeds $125,000.
d. When current year tax liability exceeds $20,000.

LO 9.4 21. Yulimar, a single taxpayer, failed to make the required estimated payments of $6,800 in 2024 and owes a penalty. Assuming her income does not vary during the year and she is not requesting a waiver, Yulimar:
a. Must file a Form 2210.
b. Can file a Form 2210 but is not required to as the IRS will figure her penalty.
c. Must file a Form 2210 to report the equal installment method.
d. Will not be subject to penalties because the tax liability is below $10,000.

LO 9.4 22. The annualized income method of calculating required estimated taxes is used to:
a. Determine required payments that vary with income over the year and perhaps lower the amount of penalties for failing to make the required estimated payments.
b. Determine equal allocated required payments.
c. Negotiate a settlement with the IRS on what tax must be paid.
d. Generate interest income for the taxpayer when overpaid.

LO 9.5 23. Employers generally must file a quarterly tax return showing the amount of wages paid and the amount of income tax and FICA tax withholding due. This tax return is filed on:
a. Form 944 or Form 945
b. Schedule H
c. Schedule SE
d. Form 941

LO 9.5 24. Yamin operates a small business with a few part-time employees. The annual employment tax withholding in 2024 is $467.80. Assuming appropriate IRS communications have been received, Yamin should file which employment tax reporting form?
a. Form 944
b. Form 940
c. Form 941
d. Form 9000
e. Form 409

LO 9.5 25. Hugo Inc. is a new business in 2024 with seven employees. What is Hugo's default deposit status for employment taxes and withholding?
   a. Monthly
   b. Semiweekly
   c. Next business day
   d. Annual

LO 9.6 26. Which of the following forms is used to report total wages, tips, and other compensation paid to all employees?
   a. Form W-4
   b. Form W-2G
   c. Form W-2
   d. Form W-3
   e. Form 1099-MISC

LO 9.6 27. Alexandra's nanny comes to work in Alexandra's home each weekday, and Alexandra pays the nanny $27,000 in 2024. Alexandra correctly withholds Social Security and Medicare tax but is not required to withhold income tax. At the end of 2024, Alexandra is required to prepare:
   a. Only a Form W-2 for the nanny.
   b. Only a Form W-3 for the nanny.
   c. A Form W-2 and a Form W-3 for the nanny.
   d. Nothing. Forms W-2 and W-3 are not required for household employees.

LO 9.6 28. Which of the following forms is used to report non-employee compensation?
   a. Form W-2G
   b. Form 1099-MISC
   c. Form 1099-G
   d. Form 1099-NEC
   e. Form 1099-Comp

LO 9.6 29. Griffin Inc. reimburses employees for travel and business expenses using a non-accountable plan. As a result:
   a. Griffin must include all reimbursements as compensation and withhold appropriately.
   b. Griffin must include only meals and entertainment reimbursements as compensation and withhold only FICA taxes on the amount.
   c. Griffin must include all reimbursements as compensation but is only required to withhold income taxes on the amount.
   d. Griffin should not include reimbursements in compensation and no withholding is required.

LO 9.6 30. For what reason is a taxpayer likely to receive a Form W-2G?
   a. Received a state income tax refund
   b. Received wages paid by a government employer
   c. Received unemployment compensation
   d. Earned non-employee compensation in excess of $10,000
   e. Won $6,000 on the slot machines at the casino

LO 9.6 31. Thibodeau Corporation pays Loretta $3,300 for providing services to Thibodeau during the current year. The nature and scope of the relationship between Thibodeau and Loretta is one of employer-employee. Which of the following best describes the income and employment tax requirements for Thibodeau?
   a. Withhold income and employment taxes and issue a timely Form W-2 to Loretta.
   b. Withhold income taxes but not employment taxes and issue a Form 1099-MISC to Loretta.
   c. Withhold no taxes and issue a Form 1099-NEC to Loretta.
   d. Withhold employment taxes but not income taxes and issue a 1099-K to Loretta.

LO 9.7 32. The FUTA tax is:
   a. An unemployment tax with a rate of 2.9 percent on wages up to $168,600 per employee.
   b. A disability tax with a rate of 2.9 percent on wages up to $7,000 per employee.
   c. An unemployment tax with a rate as low as 0.6 percent on wages up to $7,000 per employee.
   d. A disability tax with a rate of 0.6 percent on wages up to $100,000 per employee.

LO 9.7 33. Wei has four employees: Anna, Kenny, Stan, and Seth, who were paid $15,000, $5,000, $16,000, and $3,000, respectively. Assuming a full state credit, Wei's FUTA taxable wages for the year are:
   a. $39,000
   b. $21,000
   c. $28,000
   d. $22,000
   e. $132

LO 9.8 34. Which of the following best describes the typical treatment of contributions in an amount below the annual maximum to a qualified retirement plan?
   a. Employee contributions are currently taxable, but employer contributions are not currently taxable.
   b. Employee contributions are not currently taxable, but employer contributions are currently taxable.
   c. Employee and employer contributions are not currently taxable.
   d. Employee and employer contributions are both currently taxable.

LO 9.8 35. Greta and her employer have both been making contributions to a qualified retirement plan for the last 25 years. Greta is looking forward to her retirement in a few more years and is extremely pleased to have a balance in her retirement account of $480,000 at the start of 2024. During 2024, the account earned interest, dividends, and capital gains and is now worth $500,000. Greta takes no distributions from the plan in 2024. What is the treatment of the $20,000 increase in Greta's retirement account?
   a. The interest, dividends, and realized capital gains (but not losses) are taxable in 2024.
   b. None of the increase is taxable in 2024.
   c. The interest and dividends are taxable in 2024 but the capital gains, both realized and unrealized, are not taxable in 2024.
   d. Only the unrealized capital gains and losses are taxable (if a net increase) in 2024. The other forms of income are not taxable in 2024.

LO 9.8 36. In the current year, Gail's employer contributes $2,000 (5 percent of her $40,000 salary) to a qualified retirement plan for Gail. This pension plan is what kind of plan?
   a. Defined benefit plan
   b. Defined contribution plan
   c. Employee Stock Ownership Plan
   d. Profit-sharing plan
   e. None of the above

LO 9.8 37. Which of the following is a general requirement for a plan to be qualified for tax purposes?
   a. All plan assets are distributed to the employee immediately upon retirement.
   b. Contributions to the plan must not discriminate in favor of highly-compensated employees.
   c. Employees categorized as management or above may not participate.
   d. Contributions to the plan must be taxed currently.

LO 9.8 38. Medal Company uses cliff vesting for contributions to the profit-sharing plan it operates for employees. To be qualified for tax purposes, Medal's contributions must:
   a. Vest immediately to employees.
   b. Vest over the next six years or so.
   c. Vest after no more than three years of service.
   d. Vest by the end of the first year

LO 9.8 39. An employee stock ownership plan (ESOP) is designed to:
   a. Permit employees to purchase employer stock at a deep discount.
   b. Give employees access to employee stock options.
   c. Allow the employer to repurchase stock that was issued to employees previously.
   d. Allow employees to invest primarily in the employer's securities.

LO 9.8 40. Which of the following are retirement plans for a typical government organization?
   a. 403(b) and 457(b) plans
   b. SEP-IRA plans
   c. Employee stock purchase plans (ESPP)
   d. SIMPLE plans

LO 9.9 41. When taxpayers receive distributions from qualified retirement plans, how much time is allowed to roll over the amount received into a new plan to avoid paying taxes on the distribution in the current year, assuming there are no unusual events?
   a. 180 days
   b. 90 days
   c. 60 days
   d. 1 year
   e. There is no time limit

LO 9.9 42. Tom quits his job with $150,000 in his employer's qualified retirement plan. Since he is broke, Tom instructs the plan trustee to pay him the balance in his retirement account. How much will Tom receive when he gets his check from the retirement plan?
   a. $120,000
   b. $100,000
   c. $96,000
   d. $24,000
   e. Some other amount

LO 9.9 43. Betty owns three separate IRA accounts with different banks. She wishes to consolidate her three IRAs into one IRA in 2024. How many distribution rollovers may Betty make in 2024?
   a. One
   b. Two
   c. Four
   d. Ten
   e. There is no limit

LO 9.9 44. Bonnie is getting close to retirement and realizes she has three different IRA accounts at three different financial institutions. To simplify her life, Bonnie wishes to consolidate her three IRAs into a single account in 2024 using trustee-to-trustee direct rollovers. How many rollovers of this type can Bonnie make in 2024?
   a. One
   b. Two
   c. Four
   d. Ten
   e. There is no limit

Group 2: Problems

LO 9.1
1. List four behavioral factors that could be used to classify a worker as either an employee or an independent contractor and provide a brief example.

LO 9.2
2. Phan Mai is single with two dependent children under age 17. Phan estimates her wages for the year will be $58,000 and her itemized deductions will be $20,000. In the previous year, Phan had a small tax liability. Assuming Phan files as head of household, use page 1 of Form W-4 in Appendix F to determine what Phan should report on lines 3, 4(a), 4(b), and 4(c).

LO 9.2
3. Ralph and Kathy Gump are married with one 20-year-old dependent child. Ralph expects to earn $92,500 (paid semimonthly) and estimates their itemized deductions to be $32,000 for the year. Kathy expects to earn wages of $57,000. The Gumps expect to have for AGI deductions of $7,000. Use Form W-4 and worksheet in Appendix F to determine what Ralph should report on lines 3, 4(a), 4(b), and 4(c) of Form W-4.

LO 9.2
4. Sophie is a single taxpayer. For the first payroll period in July 2024, she is paid wages of $1,200 semimonthly. Sophie claims one allowance on her pre-2020 Form W-4. Use the Withholding Tables in Appendix C to answer the following:
   a. Use the percentage method to calculate the amount of Sophie's withholding for a semimonthly pay period.
   b. Use the wage bracket method to determine the amount of Sophie's withholding for the same period.
   c. Use the percentage method assuming Sophie completed a post-2019 Form W-4 and checked only the single box in Step 1(c).
   d. Use the wage bracket method using the same assumptions in part c of this question.

LO 9.2
5. Beckett Rice submitted a new Form W-4 for 2024 as presented on the following page. If Beckett is paid gross wages of $3,100 for the semimonthly period, determine Beckett's income tax withholding using (a) the percentage method and (b) the wage bracket method worksheets and tables from Appendix C.

LO 9.2
6. Cassie works at Capital Bank and is in charge of issuing Forms 1099 to bank customers. Please describe for Cassie the four possible situations that require the bank to implement backup withholding on a customer.

LO 9.3
7. Lamden Company paid its employee, Trudy, wages of $70,000 in 2024. Calculate each of the following: Social Security withheld from Trudy's wages, Medicare withheld from Trudy's wages, Social Security paid by Lamden, and Medicare paid by Lamden.

LO 9.3
8. Lamden Company paid its employee, Chuck, wages of $170,000 in 2024. Calculate each of the following: Social Security withheld from Chuck's wages, Medicare withheld from Chuck's wages, Social Security paid by Lamden, and Medicare paid by Lamden.

LO 9.3
9. Lamden Company paid its employee, William, wages of $270,000 in 2024. Calculate each of the following: Social Security withheld from William's wages, Medicare withheld from William's wages, Social Security paid by Lamden, and Medicare paid by Lamden.

LO 9.3
10. Thuy worked as the assistant manager at Burger Crown through August 2024 and received wages of $93,000. Thuy then worked at Up and Down Burger starting in September of 2024 and received wages of $78,000. Calculate the amount of Thuy's overpayment of Social Security taxes that should be reported on Thuy's 2024 Schedule 3 of Form 1040.

Form W-4 — Employee's Withholding Certificate (2024)

Form W-4
Department of the Treasury
Internal Revenue Service

Complete Form W-4 so that your employer can withhold the correct federal income tax from your pay.
Give Form W-4 to your employer.
Your withholding is subject to review by the IRS.

OMB No. 1545-0074
2024

Step 1: Enter Personal Information

(a) First name and middle initial: Beckett
Last name: Rice
(b) Social security number: 344-56-7890

Address: 6010 Middle Fiskville Road
City or town, state, and ZIP code: Austin, TX 78752

Does your name match the name on your social security card? If not, to ensure you get credit for your earnings, contact SSA at 800-772-1213 or go to www.ssa.gov.

(c)
☐ Single or Married filing separately
☑ Married filing jointly or Qualifying surviving spouse
☐ Head of household (Check only if you're unmarried and pay more than half the costs of keeping up a home for yourself and a qualifying individual.)

Complete Steps 2–4 ONLY if they apply to you; otherwise, skip to Step 5. See page 2 for more information on each step, who can claim exemption from withholding, and when to use the estimator at www.irs.gov/W4App.

Step 2: Multiple Jobs or Spouse Works

Complete this step if you (1) hold more than one job at a time, or (2) are married filing jointly and your spouse also works. The correct amount of withholding depends on income earned from all of these jobs.

Do **only one** of the following.

(a) Use the estimator at www.irs.gov/W4App for most accurate withholding for this step (and Steps 3–4). If you or your spouse have self-employment income, use this option; **or**

(b) Use the Multiple Jobs Worksheet on page 3 and enter the result in Step 4(c) below; **or**

(c) If there are only two jobs total, you may check this box. Do the same on Form W-4 for the other job. This option is generally more accurate than (b) if pay at the lower paying job is more than half of the pay at the higher paying job. Otherwise, (b) is more accurate . . . . ☑

Complete Steps 3–4(b) on Form W-4 for only ONE of these jobs. Leave those steps blank for the other jobs. (Your withholding will be most accurate if you complete Steps 3–4(b) on the Form W-4 for the highest paying job.)

Step 3: Claim Dependent and Other Credits

If your total income will be $200,000 or less ($400,000 or less if married filing jointly):

Multiply the number of qualifying children under age 17 by $2,000 $ 4,000

Multiply the number of other dependents by $500 . . . . . $

Add the amounts above for qualifying children and other dependents. You may add to this the amount of any other credits. Enter the total here . . . . **3** $ 4,000

Step 4 (optional): Other Adjustments

(a) **Other income (not from jobs).** If you want tax withheld for other income you expect this year that won't have withholding, enter the amount of other income here. This may include interest, dividends, and retirement income . . . . **4(a)** $ 5,800

(b) **Deductions.** If you expect to claim deductions other than the standard deduction and want to reduce your withholding, use the Deductions Worksheet on page 3 and enter the result here . . . . **4(b)** $ 3,400

(c) **Extra withholding.** Enter any additional tax you want withheld each **pay period** . . **4(c)** $

LO 9.4

11. Sherina Smith (Social Security number 785-23-9873) lives at 536 West Lapham Street, Milwaukee, WI 53204, and is self-employed for 2024. She estimates her 2024 Schedule C net profit will be $54,000, one-half of self-employment tax will be $3,815, and her qualified business income deduction will be $5,657 in 2024. Sherina has no other forms of income or deductions. She has a dependent child aged 15 and files as head of household. Sherina expects to claim the child tax credit in 2024 but no other credits. Calculate her annual required payment based on 2024 estimates using the 2024 Estimated Tax Worksheet in Appendix F. Complete the worksheet through line 12a only. This question requires the use of the tax rate schedules in Appendix A.

LO 9.4

12. Kana is a single wage earner with no dependents and taxable income of $170,000 in 2024. Her 2023 taxable income was $155,000 and tax liability was $31,050. Calculate Kana's 2024 income tax liability and Kana's 2024 minimum required annual payment necessary to avoid penalty (Note: this question requires the use of the tax rate schedules in Appendix A).

LO 9.5

13. Drew Fogelman operates a small business and his payroll records for the second quarter of 2024 reflect the following:

Employee	Matt D.	Jack F.	Avery F.	Tiffany Y.
Gross wages	$3,100.00	$1,600.00	$2,000.00	$4,100.00
Federal income tax withheld	55.00	27.00	30.00	191.00
FICA taxes withheld	237.15	122.40	153.00	313.65

No employee has year-to-date wages in excess of the FICA cap. Drew's employer identification number is 34-4321321 and his business is located at 732 Nob Hill Blvd. in Yakima, WA 98902. Drew is eligible to pay his withholding at the time he files his quarterly Form 941. Complete pages 1 and 2 of Form 941 located in Appendix F for Drew for the second quarter of 2024.

LO 9.5

14. Each of the three companies below have provided the amount of income taxes withheld plus the FICA taxes attributable to wages paid from their payroll records. Use this information to determine (1) what deposit schedule should each company be on and (2) what form should each company file (i.e., 941 or 944).

a. Pequeño Negocio Inc. has about four employees at any time during the year. The payroll records from 2022 and 2023 report the following:

Q1 2022	Q2 2022	Q3 2022	Q4 2022	Q1 2023	Q2 2023	Q3 2023	Q4 2023
$12,091	$10,138	$10,539	$12,064	$10,849	$12,213	$11,385	$12,782

b. Meniscus Corporation payroll records from 2022 and 2023 report the following:

Q1 2022	Q2 2022	Q3 2022	Q4 2022	Q1 2023	Q2 2023	Q3 2023	Q4 2023
$11,119	$12,023	$11,443	$11,194	$11,853	$13,868	$14,171	$16,782

c. Xochitl operates a small business and takes on part-time employees at certain times of the year. Her payroll records from 2022 and 2023 report the following:

Q1 2022	Q2 2022	Q3 2022	Q4 2022	Q1 2023	Q2 2023	Q3 2023	Q4 2023
$0	$0	$260	$312	$10	$0	$167	$328

LO 9.5

15. Consider each of the following employment tax deposit scenarios:

    a. Based on activity in the lookback period, Hugo Corp is on a semiweekly deposit schedule for income and employment taxes in 2024. In the weekly payroll period ending Sunday, March 10, 2024, Hugo paid executive bonuses that triggered income tax withheld and FICA taxes of $134,649 for that pay period. On what date is Hugo's next required deposit?
    b. Springs Corp. is a semiweekly depositor and processes a payroll on Thursday, September 19, 2024. The resulting tax deposit of income tax withholding and FICA taxes of $7,800 is due on what date?
    c. Rosarita Company is a semiweekly depositor and processes a payroll on Monday, April 8, 2024. The resulting tax deposit of income tax withholding and FICA taxes of $7,800 is due on what date?
    d. Encinitas Inc. is a new company and did not have any employees during the previous quarters. The first payroll is processed on September 20, 2024. The resulting tax deposit of income tax withholding and FICA taxes of $6,700 is due on what date?

LO 9.6

16. For each of the following payments, indicate the form that should be used to report the payment:
    a. Interest of $400 paid by a bank
    b. Payment of $400 in dividends by a corporation to a shareholder
    c. Periodic payments from a retirement plan
    d. Salary as president of the company
    e. Las Vegas keno winnings of $25,000
    f. Payments made to a non-employee

LO 9.6

17. Philcon Corporation created the following 2024 employee payroll report for one of its employees.
    a. Complete the Form W-2 from Appendix F for Louise Alianait from Philcon Corporation.

Philcon Corporation **Employee Payroll Report**
EIN: 12-3456789 2024
PO Box 4563
Anchorage, AK 99508

Emp ID	Name	Wage Type	Date	Period Gross Pay	YTD Gross Pay	401k Contrib	Taxable Wages	YTD Tax Wages	FIT w/h	SS Tax w/h	Med Tax w/h	Net Pay
A1246G	Louise Alianait	Monthly	1/31/2024	14,200.00	14,200.00	568.00	13,632.00	13,632.00	2,399.84	880.40	205.90	10,145.86
A1246G	Louise Alianait	Monthly	2/28/2024	14,200.00	28,400.00	568.00	13,632.00	27,264.00	2,399.84	880.40	205.90	10,145.86
A1246G	Louise Alianait	Bonus	3/15/2024	6,400.00	34,800.00	-	6,400.00	33,664.00	1,408.00	396.80	92.80	4,502.40
A1246G	Louise Alianait	Monthly	3/31/2024	14,200.00	49,000.00	568.00	13,632.00	47,296.00	2,399.84	880.40	205.90	10,145.86
A1246G	Louise Alianait	Monthly	4/30/2024	14,200.00	63,200.00	568.00	13,632.00	60,928.00	2,399.84	880.40	205.90	10,145.86
A1246G	Louise Alianait	Monthly	5/31/2024	14,200.00	77,400.00	568.00	13,632.00	74,560.00	2,399.84	880.40	205.90	10,145.86
A1246G	Louise Alianait	Monthly	6/30/2024	14,200.00	91,600.00	568.00	13,632.00	88,192.00	2,399.84	880.40	205.90	10,145.86
A1246G	Louise Alianait	Monthly	7/31/2024	14,200.00	105,800.00	568.00	13,632.00	101,824.00	2,399.84	880.40	205.90	10,145.86
A1246G	Louise Alianait	Monthly	8/31/2024	14,200.00	120,000.00	568.00	13,632.00	115,456.00	2,399.84	880.40	205.90	10,145.86
A1246G	Louise Alianait	Monthly	9/30/2024	14,200.00	134,200.00	568.00	13,632.00	129,088.00	2,399.84	880.40	205.90	10,145.86
A1246G	Louise Alianait	Monthly	10/31/2024	14,200.00	148,400.00	568.00	13,632.00	142,720.00	2,399.84	880.40	205.90	10,145.86
A1246G	Louise Alianait	Monthly	11/30/2024	14,200.00	162,600.00	568.00	13,632.00	156,352.00	2,399.84	880.40	205.90	10,145.86
A1246G	Louise Alianait	Monthly	12/31/2024	14,200.00	176,800.00	568.00	13,632.00	169,984.00	2,399.84	372.00	205.90	10,654.26
A1246G	Louise Alianait	YTD Total		176,800.00		6,816.00	169,984.00		30,206.08	10,453.20	2,563.60	126,761.12

Employee Mailing Address:
Louise Alianait
5471 East Tudor Road
Anchorage, AK 99508
SSN: 545-64-7745

b. Philcon Corporation also paid $1,200 to Ralph Imiq for presenting a management seminar. Ralph is not a Philcon employee and lives at 1455 Raspberry Road, Anchorage, AK 99508, and his Social Security number is 475-45-3226. Complete the Form 1099-NEC from Appendix F for the payment to Ralph from Philcon Corporation.

LO 9.7

18. Rebecca is an employer with three employees, Theodore, Roy, and Nathan. Theodore's 2024 wages are $46,200, Roy's wages are $6,650, and Nathan's wages are $4,700. The state unemployment tax rate is 5.4 percent. Calculate the following amounts for Rebecca:
    a. FUTA tax before the state tax credit
    b. State unemployment tax
    c. FUTA tax after the state tax credit

LO 9.7

19. Your client has provided the following annual payroll summary for 2024:

    Premium Court Corporation
    1 First Street, NE
    Washington, DC 20543
    EIN: 44-1112223
    December 31, 2024

Employee	Q1	Q2	Q3	Q4	YTD
Samantha Lightning	-	6,500	-	-	6,500
Clark Thomas	7,000	7,000	7,000	7,000	28,000
Rob Johnson	7,100	6,500	-	-	13,600
Jackson Brown	20,000	20,000	20,000	20,000	80,000
Sonya Citimayor	8,000	8,000	8,000	8,000	32,000
Breck Cavendish	2,500	2,500	400	-	5,400
Ellen Caging	-	4,500	-	-	4,500
Neal Orbach	-	2,200	2,200	2,400	6,800
Amy Barry	5,700	5,700	5,700	5,700	22,800
	50,300	62,900	43,300	43,100	199,600

    Premium Court pays District of Columbia (DC) unemployment tax and makes the required deposits of both federal and state unemployment taxes on a timely basis. DC applies a rate of 0.7 percent to the first $9,000 of wages per employee and thus Premium Court paid state unemployment taxes of $477.40 to DC in 2024. DC is not subject to a credit reduction and there was no overpayment of FUTA in 2023. Use this information to complete Parts 1-5 (as necessary) of Form 940 in Appendix F.

LO 9.8

20. In 2024, Kwon Ah Bo is an employee at Sungsam Industries. Kwon is paid wages of $50,000 and is also a participant in the Sungsam 401(k) plan. Kwon contributes 6 percent of her salary to the 401(k) plan and Sungsam matches the first 3 percent of employee contributions.
    a. Describe how Kwon will be taxed on her 6-percent contribution to the 401(k) plan in 2024.
    b. Describe how Kwon will be taxed on the 3-percent match provided by Kwon's employer and contributed to the 401k plan.
    c. Compute the amount of wages subject to (i) income tax and (ii) FICA taxes
    d. Describe how Kwon will be taxed on withdrawals from the 401(k) assuming she reaches the age of 59 and one-half.

LO 9.8

21. Determine the 2024 maximum contributions to a qualified plan for each of the following taxpayers (assume no restrictions for highly-compensated employees):
    a. Vlad Zilinksy is paid wages of $150,000 and may contribute 20 percent of his wages and his employer matches the first 5 percent of employee contributions to the company profit-sharing plan.
    b. Elina Kurlyenko is paid wages of $300,000 and may contribute toward a defined contributions plan through her employer.
    c. Oksana Biel is permitted to contribute up to 10 percent of her $30,000 wage to a qualified defined contribution plan.

LO 9.9

22. Telly, age 38, has a $140,000 IRA with Blue Mutual Fund. They have read good things about the management of Green Mutual Fund, so they open a Green Fund IRA. Telly asked for a distribution rollover and received their balance from the Blue Fund on May 1, 2024. Telly opted to have no withholding on the distribution.
    a. What amount will Telly receive from the Blue Fund IRA?
    b. What amount must Telly contribute to the Green Fund IRA to avoid having taxable income and penalties for early withdrawal?
    c. When is the last day Telly can roll over the amount received into the Green Fund IRA and avoid taxation in the current year, assuming no unusual circumstances?
    d. What amount would Telly receive if the distribution were from their employer's qualified retirement plan?

LO 9.9

23. Allen (age 32) takes a distribution of $20,000 from his traditional IRA account which he plans to deposit into an IRA with a different bank. During the 60-day rollover period, he gambles and loses the entire IRA balance. What income and/or penalties must he show on his tax return related to the failed rollover?

Group 3:
Writing Assignment

Ethics

Eric, your friend, received his Form W-2 from his employer (below) and has asked for your help. Eric's 2024 salary was $180,000 and he does not understand why the amounts in Boxes 1, 3, and 5 are not $180,000? His final paycheck for the year included the following information:

– Eric contributed 5 percent of his salary to the company 401(k) plan on a pre-tax basis.
– Eric is married with two children. He had $5,000 deducted from his wages for a Dependent Care Flexible Spending Account.
– Eric is enrolled in the company-sponsored life insurance program. He has a policy that provides a benefit of $150,000.
– Eric contributed the 2024 maximum amount to the Health Care Flexible Spending Account.

Using the information and Eric's Form W-2, prepare an email to Eric reconciling his salary of $180,000 to the amounts in Boxes 1, 3, and 5.

W-2 Form

a Employee's social security number	791-51-4335
OMB No. 1545-0008	
b Employer identification number (EIN)	12-9456789
c Employer's name, address, and ZIP code	Ivy Technologies, Inc. 436 E. 35 Avenue Gary, IN 46409
1 Wages, tips, other compensation	161,954.00
2 Federal income tax withheld	23,776.42
3 Social security wages	168,600.00
4 Social security tax withheld	10,453.20
5 Medicare wages and tips	170,954.00
6 Medicare tax withheld	2,478.83
7 Social security tips	
8 Allocated tips	
d Control number	
10 Dependent care benefits	5,000.00
e Employee's first name and initial / Last name / Suff.	Eric Hayes 555 E. 81st Street Merrillville, IN 46410
11 Nonqualified plans	
12a	C 104.00
13 Retirement plan	X
12b	D 9,000.00
14 Other	
12c	DD 12,432.17
12d	
15 State	IN
16 State wages, tips, etc.	161,954.00
17 State income tax	6,783.45
18 Local wages, tips, etc.	161,954.00
19 Local income tax	1,893.12
20 Locality name	LAKE

Form **W-2** Wage and Tax Statement **2024** Department of the Treasury—Internal Revenue Service
Copy B—To Be Filed With Employee's FEDERAL Tax Return.
This information is being furnished to the Internal Revenue Service.

Group 4: Problem

Ben Kenofee is a new company accountant for Richmond Industries, a small specialty manufacturing business located in The Woodlands, Texas. Ben is a new employee starting January 1, 2024, expecting to earn wages of $55,920, and will be paid semimonthly. Ben's information is as follows:

- Name and address: Ben Kenofee, 2000 Berrywood Bend Drive, Apartment 3K, Tomball, TX 77375
- Social Security number: 613-27-7730
- Current year filing status: Married filing jointly
- Dependents: One child age 11
- Spouse: Tala Kenofee, is self-employed and expects to earn $33,010 in 2024.
- Tala expects to pay *total* self-employment taxes of $4,664 and her self-employment income is eligible for a 2024 qualified business income deduction of $6,136 and will not be limited by taxable income or other limits.
- Ben and Tala expect to take the standard deduction and do not have any for AGI deductions in 2024.
- Both Ben and Tala are under age 65 and are not blind. They do not expect to claim any credits other than the child tax credit.
- Ben and Tala have a modest investment portfolio and expect to earn interest of $1,200 in 2024.

As the accountant for the company, Ben has access to the Richmond Industries Q4 payroll ledger for 2024 (but some of the information is missing and will need to be calculated):

Richmond Industries
4000 Research Forest Drive, The Woodlands, TX 77381
EIN: 56-8188324
Payroll Report
10-1-2024 to 12-31-2024

Employee	Current Quarter				YTD			
	Gross Wages	FIT W/H	SS W/H	Medicare W/H	Gross Wages	FIT W/H	SS W/H	Medicare W/H
Hannah Richmond 312-49-0025	43,000.00	9,950.00	2,455.20	623.50	172,000.00	39,800.00	10,453.20	2,494.00
Daniel Glover 429-97-7757	7,000.00	700.00	434.00	101.50	28,000.00	2,800.00	1,736.00	406.00
Jeff Proust 192-45-5518	5,800.00	696.00	359.60	84.10	6,430.00	734.00	398.66	93.24
Jane Thor 577-14-6389	-	-	-	-	14,300.00	2,150.00	886.60	207.35
Wilma Wildman 745-45-4641	1,200.00	232.00	74.40	17.40	15,600.00	3,016.00	967.20	226.20
Ben Kenofee 613-27-7730	13,980.00	?	866.76	202.71	55,920.00	?	3,467.04	810.84
Totals	70,980.00	?	4,189.96	1,029.21	292,250.00	?	17,908.70	4,237.63

Note that Ben's information on income tax withholding should be compiled using the answers from part b. Assume that Richmond pays the exact amount of their tax deposits each quarter and thus, does not have overpayments or underpayments from the previous quarter. Richmond does not offer healthcare or a qualified retirement plan to its employees.

Requirements:

a. Prepare Ben's Form W-4 for 2024. Tala will be making estimated payments to cover her share of income taxes, but Ben will reflect the effects of her self-employment income on his W-4 like a second job to reduce the chances that he will be underwithheld. Ignore the for AGI deduction of one-half of Tala's self-employment taxes for purposes of this part.

b. Ben receives his first semimonthly paycheck for gross wages of $2,330.00 on January 15, 2024. Using the W-4 prepared in part a. and the percentage method for withholding, calculate Ben's income tax withholding on his first paycheck. Use Worksheet 4 from Appendix C to assist you.

c. Prepare the 2024 Estimated Tax Worksheet of Form 1040-ES to determine Tala's required annual payment to avoid penalty and the first quarter payment amount. Consider the following when completing this part:

- Line 1: Total AGI will include her expected AGI plus Ben's wages
- Lines 7 and 11b: Do not reflect any child tax credits
- Line 12b: Prior year tax liability was $10,000.
- Assume that withholding for Ben's wages is equal to the withholding calculated in part b above, multiplied by 24 pay periods.
- There were no prior year overpayments applied to this year's first quarter payment.

d. Prepare Part 1 of Form 941 for Richmond Industries for the fourth quarter of 2024. Assume Richmond is a monthly depositor and has made payments of $18,871.91 for the fourth quarter thus far.

e. Prepare parts 1–4 (as needed) of Form 940 for Richmond Industries. Assume Richmond pays state unemployment to only Texas which taxes the first $9,000 of wages at a rate of 1.3%. Texas is not a credit reduction state in 2024.

f. Using the information from the Richmond payroll records and your results from part b., prepare Ben's Form W-2 for 2024 and the Richmond Industries' Form W-3.

g. Assume that Ben's actual 2024 wages are $55,920 and Tala's Schedule C net profits, self-employment tax, and qualified business income deduction are as assumed above. Assume Tala made four equal estimated payments based on the Estimated Tax Worksheet in part c. Compute the Kenofees' tax liability (use tax rate schedules instead of tax tables) and determine the amount of refund or overpayment.

Chapter 10

Partnership Taxation

Learning Objectives

After completing this chapter, you should be able to:

- **LO 10.1** Define a partnership for tax purposes.
- **LO 10.2** Describe the basic tax rules for partnership formation and operation.
- **LO 10.3** Summarize the rules for partnership income reporting.
- **LO 10.4** Describe the tax treatment of partnership distributions.
- **LO 10.5** Determine partnership tax years.
- **LO 10.6** Describe the tax treatment of transactions between partners and their partnerships.
- **LO 10.7** Apply the qualified business income deduction to partners.
- **LO 10.8** Apply the at-risk rule to partnerships.
- **LO 10.9** Describe the tax treatment of limited liability companies (LLCs).

Overview

The partnership form allows taxpayers considerable flexibility in terms of contributions, income and loss allocations, and distributions. One of the primary benefits of the partnership is that partnership income is only taxed at the partner level. Corporate taxpayers (other than S corporations) pay tax at the corporate level and often again at the shareholder level (refer to Chapter 11), which results in corporate double taxation. Since a partnership's income passes through to the partners, there is no federal income tax at the entity level, only at the partner level. Currently, the tax law permits an additional qualified business income deduction for non-corporate owners of pass-through entities like partnerships.

One of the disadvantages of partnerships compared to corporations is the lack of limited liability for partners; whereas, corporate shareholders enjoy protection from liability to third parties (e.g., creditors of the corporation). The advent of the limited liability company (LLC) and the limited liability partnership (LLP) has provided partners this important liability protection. Because LLCs and LLPs can be taxed like partnerships, they are included in this chapter on partnership taxation.

This chapter will provide an understanding of the tax treatment of partnerships and the tax forms (Form 1065 and Schedule K-1) related to reporting partnership income or loss.

10-1 Nature of Partnership Taxation

Learning Objective 10.1 — Define a partnership for tax purposes.

Partnership federal income tax returns (Form 1065 and related Schedule K-1s) are information returns only. Returns show the amount of income by type and the allocation of the income to the partners. Partnership income and other items are passed through to the partners, and each partner is taxed on the individual's distributive share of partnership income. Partnership income is taxable to the partner even if they do not actually receive the income as a cash distribution.

Example Mona is a 50-percent partner in the MAT Partnership. In the current year, MAT generates $10,000 in ordinary income but does not distribute any cash or property to the partners. Mona is allocated $5,000 ($10,000 × 50 percent) of ordinary income and will report this income on her individual income tax return. ♦

Example Mona also owns 50 percent of the stock in AFM Corporation. AFM earns $10,000 of ordinary income in the current year but does not distribute any cash or property to the shareholders. Corporate income is not allocated like partnership income and Mona will not report any of AFM's income on her individual income tax return. Corporations are covered in Chapter 11. ♦

Even though the partnership tax return is only informational, partnerships do have to make various elections and select accounting methods and periods. For example, partnerships must select depreciation and inventory methods. In addition, partnerships are legal entities under civil law, and in most states have rights under the Uniform Partnership Act.

10-1a What Is a Partnership?

The tax law defines a partnership as a syndicate, group, pool, joint venture, or other unincorporated organization through or by means of which any business, financial operation, or venture is carried on, and which is not classified as a corporation, trust, or estate. Entities generally treated as partnerships for tax law purposes include limited partnerships, LLCs, and LLPs. A partnership is required to have more than one owner. The mere co-ownership, rental, and maintenance of real property does not create a partnership for federal income tax purposes; the partners must engage in some type of business or financial activity.

Example Avery and Roberta buy a rental house which they hold jointly. The house is rented and they share the income and expenses for the year. Avery and Roberta have not formed a partnership. However, if they had bought and operated a store together, a partnership would have been formed. Although the ownership of real estate may not rise to the level of a business requiring a partnership return, co-owners of real estate frequently do choose to operate in a partnership, limited partnership, LLP, or LLC form. ♦

Ordinary partnerships, or general partnerships as they are often named, may be formed by a simple verbal agreement or "handshake" between partners. In contrast, the formation of limited partnerships, limited liability companies, limited liability partnerships, and corporations must be documented in writing and the entity must be legally registered in the state in which it is formed. Even though general partnerships may be formed by verbal agreement between partners, partners usually document their agreement in writing with the help of attorneys in the event disagreements arise during the course of operations.

General partners usually take on the risk of legal liability for certain actions of the partnership or debts of the partnership, as specified under state law. To limit some of the liability exposure of operating a joint business, many partnerships are created formally as limited partnerships, LLCs, or LLPs. LLPs are used for licensed professionals such as attorneys and accountants.

Limited partnerships are a type of partnership that has one or more general partners and one or more limited partners. General partners participate in management and have unlimited liability for partnership obligations. Limited partners do not participate in management and have no liability for partnership obligations beyond their capital contributions. Many partnerships are formed as limited partnerships because the limited liability helps to attract passive investors. LLCs and LLPs are legal entities which combine the limited liability of corporations with the tax treatment of partnerships. LLCs and LLPs are covered later in this chapter.

Example The IAW Partnership is a limited partnership with three partners: Monica, who is the general partner, and Polly and Viktor, who are both limited partners. All three invested $5,000 in the partnership. Unfortunately, the partnership fails and has existing debts of $20,000. As limited partners, Polly and Viktor will lose their $5,000 investment but will not be personally responsible for the debts of the partnership while Monica, as the general partner, is personally liable for partnership debts. ♦

Tax Break

For federal tax purposes, an unincorporated business operated by only spouses is considered a partnership. As a result, a business co-run by spouses is generally required to comply with filing and record-keeping requirements for partnerships and partners. Married co-owners wishing to avoid the burden of partnership documentation can form a qualified joint venture. The election to do so is made by simply reporting each spouse's share of income, losses, gains, and deductions on a Schedule C (along with other related forms) in respect of each spouse's interest in the joint venture.

Self-Study Problem 10.1 Refer to Appendix E for Solutions to Self-Study Problems

The YKK entity was formed by two unrelated individual taxpayers, Luis and Bheem, both 50-percent general partners. Each contributed $5,000 to form the entity at the start of the current year. Determine whether the following statements are true or false:

1. If YKK owns a vacation home that Luis and Bheem use personally but do not rent, a partnership for tax purposes has been established.
2. If instead, YKK operates a small business, a partnership for tax purposes has been established.
3. Luis and Bheem are required to create a written partnership agreement for YKK to be taxed as a partnership.
4. In the current year, YKK generated $14,000 of taxable income and made a cash distribution of $1,000 each to the partners (not in excess of their basis). Luis will report $6,000 of partnership income on his individual income tax return.
5. At year-end, the partnership failed and the liabilities of the partnership exceed the assets. Bheem will be liable only for the $5,000 investment he made.

Chapter 10 • Partnership Taxation

Learning Objective 10.2

Describe the basic tax rules for partnership formation and operation.

10-2 Partnership Formation

Generally, there is no gain or loss recognized by a partnership or any of its partners when property is contributed to a partnership in exchange for an interest in the partnership. This rule applies to the formation of a partnership as well as any subsequent contributions to the partnership. However, there are exceptions to the nonrecognition rule. Income may be recognized when a partnership interest is received in exchange for services performed by the partner for the partnership or when a partner transfers to a partnership, property subject to a liability exceeding that partner's basis in the property transferred. In this situation, gain is recognized to the extent that the portion of the liability allocable to the other partners exceeds the basis of the property contributed. If a partner receives money or other property from the partnership, in addition to an interest in the partnership, the transaction may be considered in part a sale or exchange, and a gain or loss may be recognized.

Example Dunn and Church form the Dunn & Church Partnership. Dunn contributes a building with a fair market value of $90,000 and an adjusted basis of $55,000 for a 50-percent interest in the partnership. Dunn does not recognize a gain on the transfer of the building to the partnership. Church performs services for the partnership for his 50-percent interest which is worth $90,000. Church must report $90,000 in ordinary income for the receipt of an interest in the partnership in exchange for services provided to the partnership. ♦

Example Ann and Keith form the A&K Partnership. Ann contributes a building with a fair market value of $200,000 and an adjusted basis of $45,000 for a 50-percent interest in the partnership. The building is subject to a liability of $130,000. Keith contributes cash of $70,000 for a 50-percent interest in the partnership. Ann must recognize a gain on the transfer of the building to the partnership equal to $20,000, the amount by which the liability allocable to Keith, $65,000 (50% × $130,000), exceeds Ann's basis in the building, $45,000. Keith does not recognize a gain on the contribution of cash to the partnership. ♦

A partner's initial basis in a partnership interest (often called outside basis) is equal to the basis of the property transferred plus cash contributed to the partnership. If gain is recognized on the transfer, the partner's basis in the partnership interest is increased by the gain recognized. The basis is reduced by any liabilities of the contributing partner assumed by the other partners through the partnership. For example, if a one-third partner is relieved of a $90,000 liability by the partnership, they would reduce by $60,000 (⅔ of $90,000) their partnership interest basis. After the initial basis in the partnership interest is established, the basis is adjusted for future earnings, losses, contributions to the partnership, and distributions from the partnership.

Example Prentice contributes cash of $50,000 and property with a fair market value of $110,000 (adjusted basis of $30,000) to the P&H Partnership. Prentice's basis in the partnership interest is $80,000 ($50,000 + $30,000). ♦

Example Assume that Prentice, in the example above, also received a partnership interest worth $15,000 for services provided to the partnership. She must recognize $15,000 as ordinary income, and her basis in the partnership interest is $95,000 ($80,000 + $15,000). ♦

Example Referring back to the previous example on the A&K partnership, Keith's basis is $135,000 calculated as $70,000 to reflect the cash he contributed plus $65,000 for the liability for which he is now responsible. Ann's basis is $0 calculated as $45,000 carryover basis from the building plus $20,000 gain (liability for which Ann was relieved in excess of the basis of the property contributed) less the net liability relief of $65,000 ($130,000 total liability less one-half transferred to Keith). ♦

The partner's outside basis changes due to partnership activities. A partner's basis in their partnership interest is increased by the partner's share of (1) additional contributions to the partnership, (2) net ordinary taxable income of the partnership, and (3) capital gains and other income (including tax-exempt income such as municipal bond income) of the partnership. Alternatively, a partner's basis is reduced (but not below zero) by the partner's share of (1) distributions of partnership property, (2) losses from operations of the partnership, and (3) capital losses and other deductions (including disallowed tax deductions such as entertainment expenses) of the partnership. In addition, changes in the partner's share of partnership liabilities affects the basis of a partner's partnership interest.

Example Reid has a 50-percent interest in the Reid Partnership. Her basis in her partnership interest at the beginning of the tax year is $12,000. For the current tax year, the partnership reports ordinary income of $15,000, a capital gain of $3,000, and charitable contributions of $700. The basis of Reid's partnership interest, after considering the above items, would be $20,650 ($12,000 beginning basis + $7,500 share of partnership ordinary income + $1,500 share of partnership capital gain − $350 share of partnership charitable contributions). ♦

As referenced earlier, the partnership's basis in property contributed by a partner (known as "inside basis") is equal to the partner's adjusted basis in the property at the time of the contribution plus any gain recognized by the partner. The transfer of liabilities to the partnership by the partner does not impact the basis of the property to the partnership. The partnership's holding period for the property contributed to the partnership includes the partner's holding period. For example, long-term capital gain property may be transferred to a partnership by a partner and sold immediately, and any gain would be long-term, assuming the property is a capital asset to the partnership.

Example Clark contributes property to the Rose Partnership in exchange for a partnership interest. The property contributed has an adjusted basis to Clark of $45,000 and a fair market value of $75,000 on the date of the contribution. The partnership's basis in the property is $45,000. ♦

Self-Study Problem 10.2
Refer to Appendix E for Solutions to Self-Study Problems

John and Linda form the J&L Partnership. John contributes cash of $36,000 for a 40-percent interest in the partnership. Linda contributes equipment worth $54,000 with an adjusted basis of $17,500 for a 60-percent partnership interest.

1. What is John's recognized gain or loss on the contribution?
2. What is John's basis in his partnership interest?
3. What is Linda's recognized gain or loss on the contribution?
4. What is Linda's basis in her partnership interest?
5. What is J&L Partnership's basis in the equipment received from Linda?

Learning Objective 10.3

Summarize the rules for partnership income reporting.

10-3 Partnership Income Reporting

A partnership is required to report its income and other items on Form 1065, U.S. Return of Partnership Income, even though the partnership entity does not pay federal income tax. The tax return is due on the fifteenth day of the third month following the close of the partnership's tax year. When reporting partnership taxable income, certain transactions must be separated rather than being reported as part of ordinary income. The primary items that must be reported separately are net rental income, interest income, dividend income, capital gains and losses, Section 1231 gains and losses, Section 179 deductions, charitable deductions, tax-exempt income, nondeductible expenses, and most credits. These items are listed as separate income or expenses, since they are often subject to special calculations or limitations on the tax returns of the partners.

Example Nafissatou is a 50-percent general partner in Wix Partnership, which earns $10,000 of ordinary income and $400 of tax-exempt interest from municipal bonds during the current year. If Wix were to report income of $5,200 to Nafissatou, then the partner would over-report taxable income. Instead, Wix reports $5,000 of ordinary income and separately reports $200 of tax-exempt interest to Nafissatou. ♦

After the special items are separated, the partnership reports the remainder of its ordinary income or loss. The ordinary income or loss of a partnership is calculated in the same manner as that of an individual, except the partnership is not allowed to deduct the standard deduction, foreign taxes paid, charitable contributions, net operating losses, or personal itemized deductions. The ordinary business income of the partnership is reported in detail on page one of the Form 1065, lines 1 through 23. The total from line 23 is carried to the first line of Schedule K of Form 1065 and all other separately stated items for the total partnership are reported there as well. Schedule K-1 of Form 1065 presents the allocation of ordinary income or loss, special income and deductions, and gains and losses to each partner. The total of all Schedule K-1s should generally agree to the amounts reported on Schedule K for any particular line.

Example WDL Partnership reports ordinary business income of $1,000. Mikey and Missy are both 50-percent partners in WDL and each receive a Schedule K-1 that reports $500 of ordinary business income on line 1. The ordinary business income reported on line 23 of the first page of Form 1065 and line 1 of Schedule K of the Form 1065 is $1,000. ♦

The Schedule K-1 is also used to report other important information such as self-employment income and qualified business income deduction information, including wages paid and the basis of qualified property related to the QBI deduction. Different codes are used to identify the specific type of additional information. These codes can be found in the instructions to Schedule K-1. The partners report the amounts from their Schedule K-1s on their own individual tax returns.

A partner's deductible loss from a partnership is limited to the basis of the partner's partnership interest at the end of the year in which the loss was incurred. The partner's basis is not affected by the qualified business income deduction. The partner's partnership basis cannot be reduced below zero. Any unused losses may be carried forward and reported in a future year when there is partnership basis available to be reduced by the loss.

Example UKR Partnership is owned equally by Zelly and Lindsay. Zelly's basis before allocating $5,000 of current year partnership losses is $2,000. Zelly may be able to deduct the $2,000 loss to the extent of basis, but the $3,000 loss in excess of basis is "suspended" and carried forward to deduct in a future year when basis is created. Zelly's basis in UKR is $0 at the current year-end. ♦

10-3a Guaranteed Payments

Payments made to a partner for services rendered or for the use of the partner's capital that are made without regard to the income of the partnership are termed guaranteed payments. Such payments are treated by the partnership in the same manner as payments made to a person who is not a partner. The payments are ordinary income to the partner and deductible by the partnership. Guaranteed payments are uniquely treated as both a deduction for ordinary business income and also separately reported on line 4 of Schedule K-1.

Example Alexander and Bryant operate the A&B Partnership. Alexander, a 50-percent partner, receives guaranteed payments of $15,000 for the year. If A&B has net ordinary income (after guaranteed payments) of $53,000, Alexander's total income from A&B is $41,500 ($15,000 + 50% of $53,000). Alexander's Schedule K-1 would report $26,500 on line 1 (ordinary business income) and $15,000 on line 4 (guaranteed payments). ♦

A partnership may show a loss after deducting guaranteed payments. In that case, the receiving partner reports the guaranteed payments as income and reports their share of the partnership loss.

10-3b Self-Employment Income for Partners

Due to their active participation in the management of the partnership, a general partner is subject to self-employment tax on their distributive share of ordinary business income plus any guaranteed payments made to that partner. The treatment as self-employment income is not related to how much time the partner spent on partnership activities. A limited partner treats guaranteed payments as self-employment income but excludes the distributive share of ordinary income. Separately stated items are generally not self-employment income for either type of partner.

Example Yorich is a general partner in the Shakespeare Partnership. His distributive share of ordinary income for the current year is $4,000 and he receives guaranteed payments of $12,000. He is also allocated $1,000 of net rental real estate income and $2,400 of long-term capital gains. Yorich's self-employment income is $16,000 ($4,000 ordinary income and $12,000 guaranteed payments). If Yorich were a limited partner, his self-employment income would be only $12,000 from the guaranteed payments. ♦

Self-employment income is reported on line 14 of Schedule K-1 as an informational item.

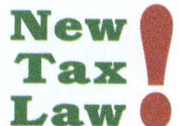

In 2021, the IRS introduced a new Schedule K-2 and Schedule K-3 to provide a specific format to report international information related to pass-through entities. In some instances, a partnership or S corporation with no foreign partners, no assets generating foreign source income, and no foreign taxes paid may still need to report information on Schedules K-2 and K-3. For example, if the partner or shareholder claims the foreign tax credit, the partner generally needs certain information from the partnership on Schedule K-3, Parts II and III, to complete Form 1116. Schedules K-2 and K-3 are outside the scope of this textbook.

Self-Study Problem 10.3

Refer to Appendix E for Solutions to Self-Study Problems

Wita Caddoan and Sapat Illiniwek (SSN 444-14-1414) are equal general partners in the newly formed Cahokia Partnership. Cahokia is located at 40 Rainy Street, Collinsville, IL 62234. Cahokia's employee identification number is 44-4444444. The partnership began operations in 2024 and had the following income and expenses:

Cahokia Parnership Income Statement for the Year Ended December 31, 2024

Gross income from operations	$255,600
Deductions:	
Salaries to employees (includes a $20,000 guaranteed payment to Sapat for services rendered)	$168,000
Rent	12,000
Payroll taxes	6,100
Depreciation	9,250
Charitable contributions (to 50-percent organizations)	1,500
Cash withdrawals ($25,000 for each partner)	50,000

The partnership's balance sheet is as follows:

Cahokia Partnership Balance Sheet as of December 31, 2024

Assets:		
Cash		$ 27,000
Accounts receivable		10,000
Land		115,000
Building	$115,000	
Less: accumulated depreciation	(9,250)	105,750
Total Assets		$257,750
Liabilities and Partners' Capital:		
Accounts payable		$ 29,750
Mortgage payable		187,750
Partners' capital (includes $31,500 originally contributed, $15,750 by each partner)		40,250
Total Liabilities and Partners' Capital		$257,750

Cahokia is a small advertising agency that is classified as business code 541800 and has no inventory. In spite of its small size, Cahokia uses the accrual method. Complete page 1 of Form 1065 on Page 10-9, and Schedules K, L, M-1, and M-2 on Pages 10-13 to 10-14 for Cahokia. Also, complete Schedule K-1 and Statement A related to the QBI deduction on Pages 10-15 and 10-16 for Sapat. Form 4562 for depreciation, Schedule B-1 related to ownership, and Schedules K-2 and K-3 are not required. Cahokia files the tax return online.

Self-Study Problem 10.3

Form 1065 — U.S. Return of Partnership Income
OMB No. 1545-0123
Department of the Treasury
Internal Revenue Service
For calendar year 2024, or tax year beginning _____, 2024, ending _____, 20 ___.
Go to www.irs.gov/Form1065 for instructions and the latest information.
2024

A Principal business activity

B Principal product or service

C Business code number

Type or Print

Name of partnership

Number, street, and room or suite no. If a P.O. box, see instructions.

City or town, state or province, country, and ZIP or foreign postal code

D Employer identification number

E Date business started

F Total assets (see instructions)
$

G Check applicable boxes: (1) ☐ Initial return (2) ☐ Final return (3) ☐ Name change (4) ☐ Address change (5) ☐ Amended return
H Check accounting method: (1) ☐ Cash (2) ☐ Accrual (3) ☐ Other (specify): _____
I Number of Schedules K-1. Attach one for each person who was a partner at any time during the tax year: _____
J Check if Schedules C and M-3 are attached . . . . ☐
K Check if partnership: (1) ☐ Aggregated activities for section 465 at-risk purposes (2) ☐ Grouped activities for section 469 passive activity purposes

Caution: Include **only** trade or business income and expenses on lines 1a through 23 below. See instructions for more information.

Income

1a	Gross receipts or sales	
b	Less returns and allowances	
c	Balance	1c
2	Cost of goods sold (attach Form 1125-A)	2
3	Gross profit. Subtract line 2 from line 1c	3
4	Ordinary income (loss) from other partnerships, estates, and trusts (attach statement)	4
5	Net farm profit (loss) (attach Schedule F (Form 1040))	5
6	Net gain (loss) from Form 4797, Part II, line 17 (attach Form 4797)	6
7	Other income (loss) (attach statement)	7
8	**Total income (loss).** Combine lines 3 through 7	8

Deductions (see instructions for limitations)

9	Salaries and wages (other than to partners) (less employment credits)	9
10	Guaranteed payments to partners	10
11	Repairs and maintenance	11
12	Bad debts	12
13	Rent	13
14	Taxes and licenses	14
15	Interest (see instructions)	15
16a	Depreciation (if required, attach Form 4562)	16a
b	Less depreciation reported on Form 1125-A and elsewhere on return	16b
		16c
17	Depletion (**Do not deduct oil and gas depletion.**)	17
18	Retirement plans, etc.	18
19	Employee benefit programs	19
20	Energy efficient commercial buildings deduction (attach Form 7205)	20
21	Other deductions (attach statement)	21
22	**Total deductions.** Add the amounts shown in the far right column for lines 9 through 21	22
23	**Ordinary business income (loss).** Subtract line 22 from line 8	23

Tax and Payment

24	Interest due under the look-back method—completed long-term contracts (attach Form 8697)	24
25	Interest due under the look-back method—income forecast method (attach Form 8866)	25
26	BBA AAR imputed underpayment (see instructions)	26
27	Other taxes (see instructions)	27
28	**Total balance due.** Add lines 24 through 27	28
29	Elective payment election amount from Form 3800	29
30	Payment (see instructions)	30
31	**Amount owed.** If the sum of line 29 and line 30 is smaller than line 28, enter amount owed	31
32	**Overpayment.** If the sum of line 29 and line 30 is larger than line 28, enter overpayment	32

Sign Here
Under penalties of perjury, I declare that I have examined this return, including accompanying schedules and statements, and to the best of my knowledge and belief, it is true, correct, and complete. Declaration of preparer (other than partner or limited liability company member) is based on all information of which preparer has any knowledge.

Signature of partner or limited liability company member   Date

May the IRS discuss this return with the preparer shown below? See instructions. ☐ Yes ☐ No

Paid Preparer Use Only

Print/Type preparer's name	Preparer's signature	Date	Check ☐ if self-employed	PTIN
Firm's name			Firm's EIN	
Firm's address			Phone no.	

For Paperwork Reduction Act Notice, see separate instructions.   Cat. No. 11390Z   Form **1065** (2024)

Form 1065 (2024) Page **2**

Schedule B — Other Information

		Yes	No
1	What type of entity is filing this return? Check the applicable box:		
a	☐ Domestic general partnership		
b	☐ Domestic limited partnership		
c	☐ Domestic limited liability company		
d	☐ Domestic limited liability partnership		
e	☐ Foreign partnership		
f	☐ Other: _____		
2	At the end of the tax year:		
a	Did any foreign or domestic corporation, partnership (including any entity treated as a partnership), trust, or tax-exempt organization, or any foreign government own, directly or indirectly, an interest of 50% or more in the profit, loss, or capital of the partnership? For rules of constructive ownership, see instructions. If "Yes," attach Schedule B-1, Information on Partners Owning 50% or More of the Partnership		
b	Did any individual or estate own, directly or indirectly, an interest of 50% or more in the profit, loss, or capital of the partnership? For rules of constructive ownership, see instructions. If "Yes," attach Schedule B-1, Information on Partners Owning 50% or More of the Partnership		
3	At the end of the tax year, did the partnership:		
a	Own directly 20% or more, or own, directly or indirectly, 50% or more, of the total voting power of all classes of stock entitled to vote of any foreign or domestic corporation? For rules of constructive ownership, see instructions. If "Yes," complete (i) through (iv) below		

(i) Name of corporation	(ii) Employer identification number (if any)	(iii) Country of incorporation	(iv) Percentage owned in voting stock

b	Own directly an interest of 20% or more, or own, directly or indirectly, an interest of 50% or more in the profit, loss, or capital in any foreign or domestic partnership (including an entity treated as a partnership) or in the beneficial interest of a trust? For rules of constructive ownership, see instructions. If "Yes," complete (i) through (v) below . .

(i) Name of entity	(ii) Employer identification number (if any)	(iii) Type of entity	(iv) Country of organization	(v) Maximum percentage owned in profit, loss, or capital

		Yes	No
4	Does the partnership satisfy **all four** of the following conditions?		
a	The partnership's total receipts for the tax year were less than $250,000.		
b	The partnership's total assets at the end of the tax year were less than $1 million.		
c	Schedules K-1 are filed with the return and furnished to the partners on or before the due date (including extensions) for the partnership return.		
d	The partnership is not filing and is not required to file Schedule M-3 . . . . If "Yes," the partnership is not required to complete Schedules L, M-1, and M-2; item F on page 1 of Form 1065; or item L on Schedule K-1.		
5	Is this partnership a publicly traded partnership, as defined in section 469(k)(2)?		
6	During the tax year, did the partnership have any debt that was canceled, was forgiven, or had the terms modified so as to reduce the principal amount of the debt?		
7	Has this partnership filed, or is it required to file, Form 8918, Material Advisor Disclosure Statement, to provide information on any reportable transaction?		
8	At any time during calendar year 2024, did the partnership have an interest in or a signature or other authority over a financial account in a foreign country (such as a bank account, securities account, or other financial account)? See instructions for exceptions and filing requirements for FinCEN Form 114, Report of Foreign Bank and Financial Accounts (FBAR). If "Yes," enter the name of the foreign country _____		
9	At any time during the tax year, did the partnership receive a distribution from, or was it the grantor of, or transferor to, a foreign trust? If "Yes," the partnership may have to file Form 3520, Annual Return To Report Transactions With Foreign Trusts and Receipt of Certain Foreign Gifts. See instructions		
10a	Is the partnership making, or had it previously made (and not revoked), a section 754 election? If "Yes," enter the effective date of the election _____ See instructions for details regarding a section 754 election.		
b	For this tax year, did the partnership make an optional basis adjustment under section 743(b)? If "Yes," enter the total aggregate net positive amount $ _____ and the total aggregate net negative amount $ (_____) of such section 743(b) adjustments for all partners made in the tax year. The partnership must also attach a statement showing the computation and allocation of each basis adjustment. See instructions		

Form **1065** (2024)

Form 1065 (2024) Page **3**

Schedule B	Other Information *(continued)*	Yes	No

    c For this tax year, did the partnership make an optional basis adjustment under section 734(b)? If "Yes," enter the total aggregate net positive amount $ _____ and the total aggregate net negative amount $ (_____) of such section 734(b) adjustments for all partnership property made in the tax year. The partnership must also attach a statement showing the computation and allocation of each basis adjustment. See instructions . . . .

    d For this tax year, is the partnership required to adjust the basis of partnership property under section 743(b) or 734(b) because of a substantial built-in loss (as defined under section 743(d)) or substantial basis reduction (as defined under section 734(d))? If "Yes," enter the total aggregate amount of such section 743(b) adjustments and/or section 734(b) adjustments for all partners and/or partnership property made in the tax year $ _____ . The partnership must also attach a statement showing the computation and allocation of the basis adjustment. See instructions . . . .

11 Check this box if, during the current or prior tax year, the partnership distributed any property received in a like-kind exchange or contributed such property to another entity (other than disregarded entities wholly owned by the partnership throughout the tax year) . . . . ▶ ☐

12 At any time during the tax year, did the partnership distribute to any partner a tenancy-in-common or other undivided interest in partnership property? . . . .

13 If the partnership is required to file Form 8858, Information Return of U.S. Persons With Respect to Foreign Disregarded Entities (FDEs) and Foreign Branches (FBs), enter the number of Forms 8858 attached. See instructions . . . .

14 Does the partnership have any foreign partners? If "Yes," enter the number of Forms 8805, Foreign Partner's Information Statement of Section 1446 Withholding Tax, filed for this partnership . . . .

15 Enter the number of Forms 8865, Return of U.S. Persons With Respect to Certain Foreign Partnerships, attached to this return . . . .

16a Did you make any payments in 2024 that would require you to file Form(s) 1099? See instructions . . . . .
    b If "Yes," did you or will you file required Form(s) 1099? . . . .

17 Enter the number of Forms 5471, Information Return of U.S. Persons With Respect to Certain Foreign Corporations, attached to this return . . . .

18 Enter the number of partners that are foreign governments under section 892 . . . .

19 During the partnership's tax year, did the partnership make any payments that would require it to file Forms 1042 and 1042-S under chapter 3 (sections 1441 through 1464) or chapter 4 (sections 1471 through 1474)? . . .

20 Was the partnership a specified domestic entity required to file Form 8938 for the tax year? See the Instructions for Form 8938 . . . .

21 Is the partnership a section 721(c) partnership, as defined in Regulations section 1.721(c)-1(b)(14)? . . . . .

22 During the tax year, did the partnership pay or accrue any interest or royalty for which one or more partners are not allowed a deduction under section 267A? See instructions . . . .
    If "Yes," enter the total amount of the disallowed deductions . . . . $ _____

23 Did the partnership have an election under section 163(j) for any real property trade or business or any farming business in effect during the tax year? See instructions . . . .

24 Does the partnership satisfy one or more of the following? See instructions . . . .
    a The partnership owns a pass-through entity with current, or prior year carryover, excess business interest expense.
    b The partnership's aggregate average annual gross receipts (determined under section 448(c)) for the 3 tax years preceding the current tax year are more than $30 million and the partnership has business interest expense.
    c The partnership is a tax shelter (see instructions) and the partnership has business interest expense.
    If "Yes" to any, complete and attach Form 8990.

25 Is the partnership attaching Form 8996 to certify as a Qualified Opportunity Fund? . . . .
    If "Yes," enter the amount from Form 8996, line 15 . . . . $ _____

26 Enter the number of foreign partners subject to section 864(c)(8) as a result of transferring all or a portion of an interest in the partnership or of receiving a distribution from the partnership . . . .
    Complete Schedule K-3 (Form 1065), Part XIII, for each foreign partner subject to section 864(c)(8) on a transfer or distribution.

27 At any time during the tax year, were there any transfers between the partnership and its partners subject to the disclosure requirements of Regulations section 1.707-8? . . . .

28 Since December 22, 2017, did a foreign corporation directly or indirectly acquire substantially all of the properties constituting a trade or business of your partnership, and was the ownership percentage (by vote or value) for purposes of section 7874 greater than 50% (for example, the partners held more than 50% of the stock of the foreign corporation)? If "Yes," list the ownership percentage by vote and by value. See instructions.
    Percentage: By vote: _____   By value: _____

29 Is the partnership required to file Form 7208, Excise Tax on Repurchase of Corporate Stock (see instructions):
    a Under the applicable foreign corporation rules? . . . .

Form **1065** (2024)

Form 1065 (2024) Page **4**

Schedule B	Other Information *(continued)*	Yes	No
b	Under the covered surrogate foreign corporation rules?		
	If "Yes" to either (a) or (b), complete Form 7208. See the Instructions for Form 7208.		
30	At any time during this tax year, did the partnership (a) receive (as a reward, award, or payment for property or services); or (b) sell, exchange, or otherwise dispose of a digital asset (or financial interest in a digital asset)? See instructions		
31	Reserved for future use		
32	Check this box if an election out of subchapter K under section 761 is being made. See instructions . . . ☐		
33	Is the partnership electing out of the centralized partnership audit regime under section 6221(b)? See instructions		
	If "Yes," the partnership must complete Schedule B-2 (Form 1065). Enter the total from Schedule B-2, Part III, line 3 . . . . _____		
	If "No," complete Designation of Partnership Representative below.		

Designation of Partnership Representative *(see instructions)*
Enter below the information for the partnership representative (PR) for the tax year covered by this return.

Name of PR

U.S. address of PR

U.S. phone number of PR

If the PR is an entity, name of the designated individual for the PR

U.S. address of designated individual

U.S. phone number of designated individual

Form **1065** (2024)

Form 1065 (2024) Page **5**

Schedule K — Partners' Distributive Share Items

				Total amount
Income (Loss)	1	Ordinary business income (loss) (page 1, line 23)	1	
	2	Net rental real estate income (loss) (attach Form 8825)	2	
	3a	Other gross rental income (loss) 3a		
	b	Expenses from other rental activities (attach statement) 3b		
	c	Other net rental income (loss). Subtract line 3b from line 3a	3c	
	4	Guaranteed payments: **a** Services 4a **b** Capital 4b		
		c Total. Add lines 4a and 4b	4c	
	5	Interest income	5	
	6	Dividends and dividend equivalents: **a** Ordinary dividends	6a	
		b Qualified dividends 6b **c** Dividend equivalents 6c		
	7	Royalties	7	
	8	Net short-term capital gain (loss) (attach Schedule D (Form 1065))	8	
	9a	Net long-term capital gain (loss) (attach Schedule D (Form 1065))	9a	
	b	Collectibles (28%) gain (loss) 9b		
	c	Unrecaptured section 1250 gain (attach statement) 9c		
	10	Net section 1231 gain (loss) (attach Form 4797)	10	
	11	Other income (loss) (see instructions) Type: _____	11	
Deductions	12	Section 179 deduction (attach Form 4562)	12	
	13a	Cash contributions	13a	
	b	Noncash contributions	13b	
	c	Investment interest expense	13c	
	d	Section 59(e)(2) expenditures: **(1)** Type: _____ **(2)** Amount:	13d(2)	
	e	Other deductions (see instructions) Type: _____	13e	
Self-Employ-ment	14a	Net earnings (loss) from self-employment	14a	
	b	Gross farming or fishing income	14b	
	c	Gross nonfarm income	14c	
Credits	15a	Low-income housing credit (section 42(j)(5))	15a	
	b	Low-income housing credit (other)	15b	
	c	Qualified rehabilitation expenditures (rental real estate) (attach Form 3468, if applicable)	15c	
	d	Other rental real estate credits (see instructions) Type: _____	15d	
	e	Other rental credits (see instructions) Type: _____	15e	
	f	Other credits (see instructions) Type: _____	15f	
International	16	Attach Schedule K-2 (Form 1065), Partners' Distributive Share Items—International, and check this box to indicate that you are reporting items of international tax relevance ☐		
Alternative Minimum Tax (AMT) Items	17a	Post-1986 depreciation adjustment	17a	
	b	Adjusted gain or loss	17b	
	c	Depletion (other than oil and gas)	17c	
	d	Oil, gas, and geothermal properties—gross income	17d	
	e	Oil, gas, and geothermal properties—deductions	17e	
	f	Other AMT items (attach statement)	17f	
Other Information	18a	Tax-exempt interest income	18a	
	b	Other tax-exempt income	18b	
	c	Nondeductible expenses	18c	
	19a	Distributions of cash and marketable securities	19a	
	b	Distributions of other property	19b	
	20a	Investment income	20a	
	b	Investment expenses	20b	
	c	Other items and amounts (attach statement)		
	21	Total foreign taxes paid or accrued	21	

Form **1065** (2024)

Form 1065 (2024) Page **6**

Analysis of Net Income (Loss) per Return

1 Net income (loss). Combine Schedule K, lines 1 through 11. From the result, subtract the sum of Schedule K, lines 12 through 13e, and 21 1

2 Analysis by partner type:	(i) Corporate	(ii) Individual (active)	(iii) Individual (passive)	(iv) Partnership	(v) Exempt organization	(vi) Nominee/Other
a General partners						
b Limited partners						

Schedule L — Balance Sheets per Books

	Assets	Beginning of tax year		End of tax year	
		(a)	(b)	(c)	(d)
1	Cash				
2a	Trade notes and accounts receivable				
b	Less allowance for bad debts				
3	Inventories				
4	U.S. Government obligations				
5	Tax-exempt securities				
6	Other current assets (attach statement) . . .				
7a	Loans to partners (or persons related to partners) .				
b	Mortgage and real estate loans				
8	Other investments (attach statement)				
9a	Buildings and other depreciable assets . . .				
b	Less accumulated depreciation				
10a	Depletable assets				
b	Less accumulated depletion				
11	Land (net of any amortization)				
12a	Intangible assets (amortizable only)				
b	Less accumulated amortization				
13	Other assets (attach statement)				
14	Total assets				
	Liabilities and Capital				
15	Accounts payable				
16	Mortgages, notes, bonds payable in less than 1 year				
17	Other current liabilities (attach statement) . . .				
18	All nonrecourse loans				
19a	Loans from partners (or persons related to partners) .				
b	Mortgages, notes, bonds payable in 1 year or more .				
20	Other liabilities (attach statement)				
21	Partners' capital accounts				
22	Total liabilities and capital				

Schedule M-1 — Reconciliation of Income (Loss) per Books With Analysis of Net Income (Loss) per Return

Note: The partnership may be required to file Schedule M-3. See instructions.

1	Net income (loss) per books		6	Income recorded on books this year not included on Schedule K, lines 1 through 11 (itemize):	
2	Income included on Schedule K, lines 1, 2, 3c, 5, 6a, 7, 8, 9a, 10, and 11, not recorded on books this year (itemize):		a	Tax-exempt interest $ _____	
3	Guaranteed payments (other than health insurance)		7	Deductions included on Schedule K, lines 1 through 13e, and 21, not charged against book income this year (itemize):	
4	Expenses recorded on books this year not included on Schedule K, lines 1 through 13e, and 21 (itemize):		a	Depreciation $ _____	
a	Depreciation $ _____		8	Add lines 6 and 7	
b	Travel and entertainment $ _____		9	Income (loss) (*Analysis of Net Income (Loss) per Return*, line 1). Subtract line 8 from line 5	
5	Add lines 1 through 4				

Schedule M-2 — Analysis of Partners' Capital Accounts

1	Balance at beginning of year . . .		6	Distributions: a Cash	
2	Capital contributed: a Cash . . .			b Property . . .	
	b Property . .		7	Other decreases (itemize): _____	
3	Net income (loss) (see instructions) .				
4	Other increases (itemize): _____		8	Add lines 6 and 7	
5	Add lines 1 through 4		9	Balance at end of year. Subtract line 8 from line 5	

Source: Internal Revenue Service (IRS)

Form **1065** (2024)

Self-Study Problem 10.3

Schedule K-1 (Form 1065) 2024
Department of the Treasury
Internal Revenue Service

For calendar year 2024, or tax year
beginning ___ / ___ / 2024   ending ___ / ___ / ___

Partner's Share of Income, Deductions, Credits, etc. — See separate instructions.

☐ Final K-1   ☐ Amended K-1   OMB No. 1545-0123   651123

Part I — Information About the Partnership

A. Partnership's employer identification number

B. Partnership's name, address, city, state, and ZIP code

C. IRS center where partnership filed return:

D. ☐ Check if this is a publicly traded partnership (PTP)

Part II — Information About the Partner

E. Partner's SSN or TIN (Do not use TIN of a disregarded entity. See instructions.)

F. Name, address, city, state, and ZIP code for partner entered in E. See instructions.

G. ☐ General partner or LLC member-manager ☐ Limited partner or other LLC member

H1. ☐ Domestic partner ☐ Foreign partner

H2. ☐ If the partner is a disregarded entity (DE), enter the partner's:
   TIN _____ Name _____

I1. What type of entity is this partner?

I2. ☐ If this partner is a retirement plan (IRA/SEP/Keogh/etc.), check here

J. Partner's share of profit, loss, and capital (see instructions):

	Beginning	Ending
Profit	___ %	___ %
Loss	___ %	___ %
Capital	___ %	___ %

Check if decrease is due to:
☐ Sale or ☐ Exchange of partnership interest. See instructions.

K1. Partner's share of liabilities:

	Beginning	Ending
Nonrecourse	$ ___	$ ___
Qualified nonrecourse financing	$ ___	$ ___
Recourse	$ ___	$ ___

K2. ☐ Check this box if item K1 includes liability amounts from lower-tier partnerships

K3. ☐ Check if any of the above liability is subject to guarantees or other payment obligations by the partner. See instructions

L. **Partner's Capital Account Analysis**

Beginning capital account . . . . $ _____
Capital contributed during the year . . $ _____
Current year net income (loss) . . . $ _____
Other increase (decrease) (attach explanation) $ _____
Withdrawals and distributions . . . $ (_____)
Ending capital account . . . . $ _____

M. Did the partner contribute property with a built-in gain (loss)?
☐ Yes ☐ No   If "Yes," attach statement. See instructions.

N. Partner's Share of Net Unrecognized Section 704(c) Gain or (Loss)
Beginning . . . . $ _____
Ending . . . . $ _____

Part III — Partner's Share of Current Year Income, Deductions, Credits, and Other Items

1	Ordinary business income (loss)		14	Self-employment earnings (loss)
2	Net rental real estate income (loss)			
3	Other net rental income (loss)		15	Credits
4a	Guaranteed payments for services			
4b	Guaranteed payments for capital		16	Schedule K-3 is attached if checked . . . ☐
4c	Total guaranteed payments		17	Alternative minimum tax (AMT) items
5	Interest income			
6a	Ordinary dividends			
6b	Qualified dividends		18	Tax-exempt income and nondeductible expenses
6c	Dividend equivalents			
7	Royalties			
8	Net short-term capital gain (loss)			
			19	Distributions
9a	Net long-term capital gain (loss)			
9b	Collectibles (28%) gain (loss)		20	Other information
9c	Unrecaptured section 1250 gain			
10	Net section 1231 gain (loss)			
11	Other income (loss)			
12	Section 179 deduction		21	Foreign taxes paid or accrued
13	Other deductions			

22 ☐ More than one activity for at-risk purposes*
23 ☐ More than one activity for passive activity purposes*

*See attached statement for additional information.

For IRS Use Only

For Paperwork Reduction Act Notice, see the Instructions for Form 1065.   www.irs.gov/Form1065   Cat. No. 11394R   Schedule K-1 (Form 1065) 2024

Source: Internal Revenue Service (IRS)

Self-Study Problem 10.3

Statement A—QBI Pass-Through Entity Reporting

Partnership's name:			Partnership's EIN:	
Partner's name:		Partner's identifying number:		

Partner's share of:		Trade or Business 1	Trade or Business 2	Trade or Business 3
		☐ PTP ☐ Aggregated ☐ SSTB	☐ PTP ☐ Aggregated ☐ SSTB	☐ PTP ☐ Aggregated ☐ SSTB
QBI or qualified PTP items subject to partner-specific determinations:				
	Ordinary business income (loss)			
	Rental income (loss)			
	Royalty income (loss)			
	Section 1231 gain (loss)			
	Other income (loss)			
	Section 179 deduction			
	Other deductions			
W-2 wages				
UBIA of qualified property				
Qualified REIT dividends				

Note: The 2024 Statement A was not available when this text went to print. This is a 2023 version of Statement A.

10-4 Current Distributions

10.4 Learning Objective
Describe the tax treatment of partnership distributions.

A partnership may make distributions of money or other property to the partners. A current distribution is defined as one which does not result in the complete termination of the partner's interest in the partnership.

In a current distribution, no gain is recognized by the partner receiving the distribution unless the partner's basis in the partnership has reached zero. In such a case, gain is recognized only to the extent that a distribution of money exceeds the partner's basis in their partnership interest.

The distribution of money or other property reduces the partner's basis in their partnership interest, but not below zero.

Example Calvin is a partner in K&G Interests, and his basis in his partnership interest is $75,000. In the current tax year, Calvin receives a $45,000 cash distribution from the partnership. He does not recognize a gain or loss on the distribution, but his basis in his partnership interest is reduced to $30,000 ($75,000 − $45,000). If the distribution of cash were $80,000 instead of $45,000, Calvin would have a taxable gain of $5,000 ($80,000 − $75,000), and his basis in the partnership interest would be reduced to zero ($75,000 − $80,000 + $5,000). ♦

The basis of property received by a partner in a current distribution will generally be the same as the basis of the property to the partnership immediately prior to the distribution. An overall limitation is imposed, which states that the basis of the assets distributed cannot exceed the partner's basis in the partnership interest, reduced by any money distributed. In some cases, this overall limitation may require that the partner's basis in the partnership interest be allocated among the assets received in the distribution.

Partnership losses, like income, flow through to partners and can be deductible by the partner. When determining the amount of a deductible loss, the partner's outside basis in the partnership is adjusted in a specific order. Outside basis is first increased by any partner contributions to the partnership and then the distributive share of income and income items (including tax-exempt items). Distributions are considered prior to deducting any losses. Any allocated losses in excess of outside basis are suspended and carried forward.

Example Babek has a $5,000 outside basis in his partnership interest. The partnership allocates an ordinary business loss of $10,000 and tax-exempt income of $500 to Babek during the year. To determine the amount of deductible loss, Babek may first increase his outside basis to $5,500 by adding the $500 tax-exempt income. His deductible loss is limited to $5,500 and his basis is reduced to $0. The excess $4,500 loss is suspended and may be carried forward. ♦

Example In the following year, Babek is allocated income of $6,000 and also receives a $6,000 cash distribution from the partnership. Although the income increases Babek's outside basis to $6,000, he must decrease his basis by the $6,000 cash distribution prior to attempting to deduct the loss suspended in the prior year and thus, may not deduct the loss. ♦

Self-Study Problem 10.4
Refer to Appendix E for Solutions to Self-Study Problems

Jiang and Jackson are equal partners in J&J Partnership. Both partners start Year 1 with an outside basis of $10,000 each. Using the following information below, determine (1) the share of allocated income or loss for each partner and (2) the end-of-year outside basis for each partner for each of the three years:

a. Year 1: J&J generates $6,000 of ordinary business income, allocates total municipal bond interest of $300 and allocates nondeductible fines of $100.

b. Year 2: J&J generates a total $20,000 loss that includes a deduction for a guaranteed payment of $2,000 to Jiang. Both Jiang and Jackson receive a cash distribution from the partnership of $7,100 each.

c. Year 3: J&J generates total ordinary business income of $4,000 and long-term capital gains of $1,000. Jiang receives a guaranteed payment of $2,000.

10-5 Tax Years

Learning Objective 10.5
Determine partnership tax years.

The tax law requires that each partner include in gross income for a particular tax year the individual's distributive share of income, including guaranteed payments, from a partnership whose tax year ends with or within that partner's tax year. For example, a calendar-year individual partner should report their income from a partnership with a tax year ending June 30, 2024, on their 2024 tax return. Since a partner reports only income reported by a partnership whose year ends with or within their tax year, it is possible to delay the reporting of partnership income and guaranteed payments for almost an entire year. This would happen, for example, if the partnership's year-end is January 31, and the partner's tax year is a calendar year. To prevent this deferral of income, rigid rules have been established regarding partnership tax years. Under these rules, unless a partnership can establish a business purpose for a fiscal year-end or meet certain tests, it must adopt the same taxable year as that of the majority partners. If such partners do not have the same tax year, then the partnership is required to adopt the tax year of all its principal partners. If neither of these rules can be met, the partnership must adopt a tax year based on the least aggregate deferral method (refer to IRS Publication 538 for more information: **www.irs.gov/forms-pubs/about-publication-538**).

Once established, a partnership will not close its tax year early unless the partnership is terminated. The tax year does not generally close upon the entry of a new partner, or the liquidation, sale, or exchange of an existing partnership interest. A partnership is terminated and will close its tax year if business activity by the partnership ceases.

Self-Study Problem 10.5
Refer to Appendix E for Solutions to Self-Study Problems

R&S Associates is a partnership with a tax year that ends on October 31, 2024. During the partnership's tax year, Robert, a partner, received $1,000 per month as a guaranteed payment, and his share of partnership income after guaranteed payments was $21,000. For November through December of 2024, Robert's guaranteed payment was increased to $1,500 per month. Calculate the amount of income from the partnership that Robert should report for his 2024 calendar tax year.

10-6 Transactions Between Partners and the Partnership

10.6 Learning Objective

Describe the tax treatment of transactions between partners and their partnerships.

When engaging in a transaction with a partnership, a partner is generally regarded as an outside party, and the transaction is reported as it would be if the two parties were unrelated. However, it is recognized that occasionally transactions may lack substance because one party to the transaction exercises significant influence over the other party. Therefore, losses are disallowed for (1) transactions between a partnership and a partner who has a direct or indirect capital or profit interest in the partnership of more than 50 percent, and (2) transactions between two partnerships owned more than 50 percent by the same partners. When a loss is disallowed, the purchaser may reduce a future gain on the disposition of the property by the amount of the disallowed loss.

Example Kyle owns 55 percent of Willow Interests, a partnership. During the current year, Kyle sells property to the partnership for $60,000. Kyle's adjusted basis in the property is $75,000. The $15,000 loss is disallowed, since Kyle is a more than 50-percent partner. If later the partnership sells the property for $80,000, realizing a $20,000 gain ($80,000 − $60,000), only $5,000 of the gain is recognized, since the partnership can use Kyle's disallowed loss to offset $15,000 of the gain. ♦

In a transaction between a partner and a partnership, a gain will be taxed as ordinary income if the partner has more than a 50-percent interest in the partnership and the property sold or transferred is not a capital asset to the transferee.

Example Amy is a 51-percent partner in the A&B Partnership, and her brother, Ben, is the other 49-percent partner. Amy holds land as an investment that has a fair market value of $120,000 and basis of $50,000. Amy sells for land to the partnership which will subdivide the land and sell as single lots. The property qualifies as a long-term capital asset to Amy but is an ordinary asset to the partnership (inventory). Without a rule to recharacterize the gain, Amy would recognize long-term capital gain of $70,000 at preferred tax rates and the partnership would recognize no ordinary income. Because Amy is a greater than 50-percent owner, her gain is deemed to be ordinary income. ♦

The partnership interest may be owned directly or indirectly. For example, a taxpayer indirectly owns the interests owned by their spouse, brothers, sisters, ancestors, and lineal descendants.

Example From the previous example, if instead Ben sold the land to the partnership, the same recharacterization rule applies because Ben is considered a 100-percent partner (49 percent directly and 51 percent indirectly through his sister Amy) ♦

Self-Study Problem 10.6
Refer to Appendix E for Solutions to Self-Study Problems

Maxwell is a 50-percent partner in M&P Associates. Pam, Maxwell's daughter, owns the other 50-percent interest in the partnership. During the current tax year, Maxwell sells ordinary income property to M&P Associates for $70,000. The property's basis to Maxwell is $75,000. Also, Pam sells her personal Mercedes-Benz (a capital asset to Pam), with a basis of $25,000, for $40,000 to M&P Associates for use in the partnership's business (not a capital asset to the partnership).

1. What is the amount of Maxwell's recognized gain or loss on his transaction, and what is the nature of the gain or loss?

2. What is the amount and nature of Pam's gain or loss on her transaction with the partnership?

Learning Objective 10.7

Apply the qualified business income deduction to partners.

10-7 Qualified Business Income Deduction for Partners

The qualified business income deduction is available to individual owners of pass-through businesses such as partnerships and LLCs. The deduction in general is covered in Chapter 4. This section covers some of the items applicable specifically to partnerships.

Qualified business income (QBI) generally includes all items of ordinary business income; however, the tax law specifically excludes certain items including guaranteed payments to partners and payments made to partners by the partnership in situations in which the partner is not acting in their capacity as a partner.

Example Rigby is a 30-percent partner in Regular Partnership. In 2024, Regular has $50,000 of ordinary business income and no other separately stated items. In 2024, Rigby receives guaranteed payments of $10,000 from Regular. Rigby also receives interest income of $1,000 from a loan he makes to the partnership. Regular makes a cash distribution to Rigby of $5,000 and Rigby maintains a positive basis at year-end. The loan is treated as a transaction in which Rigby is not acting in his capacity as a partner; thus, the guaranteed payment and the interest are both excluded from Rigby's QBI. Rigby's QBI is $15,000 ($50,000 × 30%). ♦

Although guaranteed payments and payments to partners not acting as partners are not included in QBI, they are deductible by the partnership in computing ordinary business income (to the extent the items would be deductible otherwise).

For high-income taxpayers, the QBI deduction is limited by W-2 wages or a combination of W-2 wages and qualified property. A partner must be allocated their share of these items in order to properly apply the limitations when applicable.

Example Mordecai is a 50-percent partner in Park Partnership. In 2024, Mordecai's taxable income is high enough to subject his QBI deduction to the wage limitation. Park pays W-2 wages of $70,000 and has qualified property of $300,000 in 2024. If these items are allocated in accordance with the partnership interest, Mordecai will be allocated $35,000 of W-2 wages ($70,000 × 50%) and $150,000 of qualified property ($300,000 × 50%) to compute his limitation on the QBI deduction. ♦

QBI deduction information is reported to partners on Schedule K-1. Informational items are frequently reported on line 20 Other Information of Schedule K-1; however, due to the relative complexity of QBI deduction information, the IRS includes Statement A as part of the instructions for Form 1065 and encourages taxpayers to refer to this statement to report QBI deduction information. The regulations issued by the IRS indicate that failure to report QBI information to partners on the Schedule K-1 or attached Statement A is equivalent to reporting zero for each item.

Statement A—QBI Pass-Through Entity Reporting

Partnership's name:		Partnership's EIN:	
Partner's name:		Partner's identifying number:	
	Trade or Business 1	Trade or Business 2	Trade or Business 3
Partner's share of:	☐ PTP ☐ Aggregated ☐ SSTB	☐ PTP ☐ Aggregated ☐ SSTB	☐ PTP ☐ Aggregated ☐ SSTB
QBI or qualified PTP items subject to partner-specific determinations:			
Ordinary business income (loss)			
Rental income (loss)			
Royalty income (loss)			
Section 1231 gain (loss)			
Other income (loss)			
Section 179 deduction			
Other deductions			
W-2 wages			
UBIA of qualified property			
Qualified REIT dividends			

Note: The 2024 Statement A was not available when this text went to print. This is a 2023 version of Statement A.

ProConnect™ Tax TIP

ProConnect automatically creates Statement A to Schedule K-1 to report qualified business income deduction information. To the extent more than one business is contained within the partnership or there is a need to report the unadjusted basis of qualified property or override wage information, the amounts can be input under Schedule K, Other Schedule K Items, QBI Reporting: Additional Trades or Businesses.

Self-Study Problem 10.7   Refer to Appendix E for Solutions to Self-Study Problems

a. Dr. Marla Cratchitt is a single taxpayer and works as a cardiologist. Marla is an investor in Salem Healthcare LLC, a business that manufactures stents for a variety of cardiovascular issues. Marla's member interest in Salem is 20 percent and the LLC agreement calls for guaranteed payments to Marla of $75,000 per year. In 2024, Marla's ordinary business income allocation from Salem is $200,000. Salem also allocated $5,000 of long-term capital gains to Marla. Salem paid wages to employees of $230,000 and has qualified property of $1,200,000. Marla has taxable income reduced by capital gains of $776,000 for purposes of the QBI limit. Compute Marla's QBI deduction.

b. Assume that same facts as above except that Salem is a service business. Compute Marla's QBI deduction.

Learning Objective 10.8

Apply the at-risk rule to partnerships.

10-8 The At-Risk Rule

The at-risk rule is designed to prevent taxpayers from deducting losses from activities in excess of their investment in those activities. Although the at-risk rule applies to most taxpayers, it is presented here because the rule is commonly applied to investments in partnerships. In general, the at-risk rule limits the losses from a taxpayer's business activities to "amounts at risk" (AAR) in the activity.

To understand the at-risk rule, it is necessary to understand two related terms, "nonrecourse liabilities" and "encumbered property." A nonrecourse liability is a debt for which the borrower is not personally liable. If the debt is not paid, the lender generally can only repossess the property pledged as collateral on the loan. Encumbered property (also referred to as "collateral") is property pledged for the liability. The property is said to be encumbered in the amount of the liability. Taxpayers are at risk in amounts equal to their cash and property contributions to the activities, borrowed amounts to the extent of the property pledged, liabilities for which the taxpayers are personally liable, and retained profits of the activity. For contributions of unencumbered property, the amount considered at risk is the adjusted basis of the property contributed to the activity. For encumbered property, the amount at risk is also the adjusted basis of the property to the taxpayer if they are personally liable for repayment of the debt. If there is no personal liability for the debt, the amount at risk is the difference between the adjusted basis of the property and the amount of the nonrecourse debt on the property.

Example A taxpayer contributes property with an adjusted basis of $100,000, subject to a recourse liability of $25,000 and a nonrecourse liability of $40,000. The taxpayer's AAR is the basis of the property less the amount of the nonrecourse liability, or $60,000 ($100,000 − $40,000). ♦

Under the at-risk rule, taxpayers are allowed a deduction for losses allocable to a business activity to the extent of (1) income received or accrued from the activity without regard to the amount at risk, or (2) the taxpayer's amount at risk at the end of the tax year. Any losses not allowed in the current year may be treated as deductions in succeeding years, with no limit on the number of years the losses may be carried forward. Remember that passive loss rules (presented in Chapter 4) and the basis limitation (presented earlier in this chapter) may also limit the taxpayer's ability to deduct certain losses.

Example A taxpayer contributes $100,000 to an activity. Their amount at risk is $100,000. In the current year, the activity incurs losses of $250,000. For the current year, the taxpayer is allowed a loss of $100,000, the amount at risk. ♦

While real estate acquired before 1987 is not subject to the at-risk rules, the at-risk rules do apply to real estate acquired after 1986. For real estate acquired after 1986, "qualified nonrecourse financing" on real estate is considered to be an amount at risk. Qualified nonrecourse financing is debt that is secured by the real estate and loaned or guaranteed by a governmental agency or borrowed from any person who actively and regularly engages in the lending of money, such as a bank, savings and loan, or insurance company. A taxpayer is not considered at risk for financing obtained from sellers or promoters, including loans from parties related to the sellers or promoters.

Example In the current tax year, Donna buys a real estate investment with a $20,000 cash down payment and $80,000 borrowed from a savings and loan company secured by a mortgage on the property. Donna has $100,000 at risk in this investment. If the mortgage were obtained from the seller, her amount at risk would be limited to her down payment of $20,000. ♦

> **Self-Study Problem 10.8** — Refer to Appendix E for Solutions to Self-Study Problems
>
> During the current tax year, Joe is a partner in a plumbing business. His amount at risk at the beginning of the year is $45,000. During the year, Joe's share of loss is $60,000.
>
> 1. What is the amount of the loss that Joe may deduct for the current tax year?
> 2. If Joe has a profit of $31,000 in the following tax year, how much is taxable?

10-9 Limited Liability Companies

10.9 Learning Objective
Describe the tax treatment of limited liability companies (LLCs).

A limited liability company (LLC) is a hybrid form of business organization having some attributes of a partnership and other attributes of a corporation. Each owner, referred to as a member of an LLC, has limited liability, which may be similar to a stockholder in a corporation. However, an LLC is generally treated as a partnership for tax purposes. Because of this tax treatment, members of LLCs can have the tax advantages of a partnership and still have limited liability similar to a corporation. The benefits of LLCs have made them very popular as an entity choice for small businesses. LLCs are recognized legal entities in all 50 states and the District of Columbia. Many states prohibit certain licensed professionals such as attorneys, architects, and accountants from operating as an LLC but allow the formation of limited liability partnerships (LLPs) if these businesses wish to operate in a partnership form with legal liability protection similar to LLCs.

For the most part, LLCs follow partnership taxation rules. For example, taxable income and losses pass through to members; thereby, the LLC either avoids the corporate tax or allows its members to use the losses. An LLC may elect to be taxed like a corporation rather than a partnership, but very few do. Like partnerships, LLCs' items of income and expense retain their tax attributes (e.g., capital gains and charitable contributions). However, LLCs are not required to have a general partner; unlike a limited partnership, in which there has to be at least one general partner who does not have limited liability. LLC members can participate in the management of the business. Although not entirely settled tax law, the IRS has issued guidance indicating that LLC members actively engaged in the LLC's trade or business will be treated the same as general partners for self-employment tax purposes. Because of the limited liability associated with LLCs, the debt of the LLC is generally treated as nonrecourse. Lastly, LLCs may have a single member, whereas a partnership must have at least two partners. A single-member LLC is treated as a disregarded entity for tax purposes (i.e., the taxable income of the single-member LLC is reported directly on the tax return of its member, not on a separate Form 1065).

Self-Study Problem 10.9

Refer to Appendix E for Solutions to Self-Study Problems

Determine whether the following statements are true or false.

1. A limited liability company is generally treated like a corporation for federal income tax purposes.
2. A general partner is required for a limited liability company.
3. Tax attributes of an LLC transaction pass through to the owners of the LLC.
4. Owners of an LLC can participate in the management of the LLC business.
5. Debt of an LLC is generally treated as recourse debt and thus, included in a member's basis computations.

Key Terms

partnership, 10-2
general partner, 10-3
limited partnership, 10-3
limited partner, 10-3
limited liability partnership (LLP), 10-3
partner's outside basis, 10-4
partnership's inside basis, 10-5

Form 1065, 10-6
separately stated items, 10-6
Schedule K, 10-6
Schedule K-1, 10-6
guaranteed payments, 10-7
partnership distributions, 10-17
current distribution, 10-17
partnership tax year, 10-18

amounts at risk (AAR), 10-22
nonrecourse liabilities, 10-22
encumbered property, 10-22
qualified nonrecourse financing, 10-22
limited liability company (LLC), 10-23

Key Points

Learning Objectives	Key Points
LO 10.1: Define a partnership for tax purposes.	• A partnership is a syndicate, group, pool, joint venture, or other unincorporated organization through or by means of which any business, financial operation, or venture is carried on, and which is not classified as a corporation, trust, or estate. • Partnership federal tax returns are information returns only, which show the amount of income by type and the allocation of the income to the partners. • Partnership income is allocated and generally taxable to the partner even if that individual does not actually receive the income in cash. • Co-ownership of property does not constitute a partnership (e.g., owning investment property); the partners must engage in some type of business or financial activity. • Limited partnerships, limited liability partnerships (LLPs), and limited liability companies (LLCs) are generally treated as partnerships for tax law purposes.

LO 10.2:
Describe the basic tax rules for partnership formation and operation.

- Generally, there is no gain or loss recognized by a partnership or any of its partners when property is contributed to a partnership in exchange for an interest in the partnership.
- When a partner receives a partnership interest in exchange for providing services to the partnership, income is recognized by the partner.
- When a partner transfers property to a partnership in exchange for a partnership interest and that property is subject to a liability exceeding the partner's basis, income may be recognized by the partner.
- A partner's basis is increased by the partner's contributions to the partnership, net ordinary taxable income and capital gains of the partnership, and increases in the partner's share of partnership liabilities.
- A partner's basis is decreased by distributions by the partnership, losses of the partnership, and decreases in the partner's share of partnership liabilities.

LO 10.3:
Summarize the rules for partnership income reporting.

- A partnership is required to report its income and other items on Form 1065, U.S. Return of Partnership Income, even though the partnership entity does not pay federal income tax.
- When reporting partnership taxable income, certain transactions must be separated rather than being reported as part of ordinary income. Separately reported items include net rental income, interest income, dividend income, capital gains and losses, Section 1231 gains and losses, Section 179 deductions, charitable deductions, tax-exempt income, nondeductible expenses, and most credits.
- Schedule K-1 of Form 1065 presents the allocation of ordinary income or loss, special income and deductions, and gains and losses to each partner. The partners report the K-1 amounts on their own individual tax returns.
- Payments made to a partner for services rendered or for the use of the partner's capital that are made without regard to the income of the partnership are termed *guaranteed payments*.
- Guaranteed payments are ordinary income to the partner and deductible by the partnership.
- A partnership may show a loss after deducting guaranteed payments, in which case, the receiving partner reports the guaranteed payments as income and reports their share of the partnership loss.
- Both general and limited partners are subject to self-employment tax on guaranteed payments received. Only general partners are subject to self-employment tax on their distributive share of ordinary business income. Separately stated items are not subject to self-employment tax.

LO 10.4:
Describe the tax treatment of partnership distributions.

- A current distribution (of money or other property) does not result in the complete termination of the partner's interest in the partnership.
- No gain is recognized by the partner receiving a current distribution unless the partner's basis in the partnership has reached zero. In such a case, gain is recognized only to the extent that a distribution of money exceeds the partner's basis in their partnership interest.
- When calculating outside basis, partnership distributions are considered prior to deducting the allocated share of losses.

LO 10.5:
Determine partnership tax years.

- Each partner includes in gross income for a particular tax year their individual distributive share of income, including guaranteed payments, from a partnership whose tax year ends with or within that tax year.
- Unless a partnership can establish a business purpose for a fiscal year-end or meet certain tests, it must adopt the same taxable year as that of the majority partners.
- If the majority partners do not have the same tax year, then the partnership is required to adopt the tax year of all its principal partners; otherwise, the partnership must adopt a tax year based on the least aggregate deferral method.
- The tax year does not generally close upon the entry of a new partner, or upon the liquidation, sale, or exchange of an existing partnership interest.
- A partnership will not close its tax year early unless the partnership is terminated, which occurs when business activity by the partnership ceases.

LO 10.6: Describe the tax treatment of transactions between partners and their partnerships.	• Generally, in a transaction with a partnership, a partner is regarded as an outside party, and the transaction is reported as it would be if the two parties were unrelated. • Losses, however, are disallowed for (1) transactions between a partnership and a partner who has a direct or indirect capital or profit interest in the partnership of more than 50 percent, and (2) transactions between two partnerships owned more than 50 percent by the same partners. • When a loss is disallowed, the purchaser may reduce a future gain on the disposition of the property by the amount of the disallowed loss. • A gain in a transaction between a partner and a partnership will be taxed as ordinary income if the partner has more than a 50-percent interest in the partnership and the property sold or transferred is not a capital asset to the transferee.
LO 10.7: Apply the qualified business income deduction to partners.	• Qualified business income does not include guaranteed payments or payments made to partners by the partnership in situations in which the partner is not acting in their capacity as a partner. • Partners are allocated their share of W-2 wages paid and qualified property of the partnership when computing the QBI deduction.
LO 10.8: Apply the at-risk rule to partnerships.	• In general, the at-risk rule limits the losses from a taxpayer's business activities to "amounts at risk" in the activity. • Taxpayers are at risk in amounts equal to their cash and property contributions to the activities, borrowed amounts to the extent of the property pledged, liabilities for which the taxpayers are personally liable, and retained profits of the activity. • Under the at-risk rule, taxpayers are allowed a deduction for losses allocable to a business activity to the extent of (1) income received or accrued from the activity without regard to the amount at risk, or (2) the taxpayer's amount at risk at the end of the tax year. • Any losses not allowed in the current year may be treated as deductions in succeeding years, with no limit on the number of years the losses may be carried forward.
LO 10.9: Describe the tax treatment of limited liability companies (LLCs).	• A limited liability company (LLC) is a hybrid form of business organization having some attributes of a partnership and other attributes of a corporation. • Each member of an LLC has limited liability similar to that of a stockholder in a corporation and at the same time has the tax advantages of a partnership (e.g., no tax at the entity level, loss pass-through, etc.). • Licensed professionals, such as attorneys, architects, and accountants, most often use a limited liability partnership (LLP) organizational structure, which is similar in many respects to an LLC. • An LLC can have a single member and in such cases, the LLC is treated as a disregarded entity for tax purposes.

Questions and Problems

Group 1:
Multiple Choice Questions

LO 10.1

1. Which of the following may *not* be treated as a partnership for tax purposes?
    a. Arnold and Willis operate a restaurant.
    b. Thelma and Louise establish an LLP to operate an accounting practice.
    c. Lucy and Desi purchase real estate together as a business.
    d. Ana and Ben form a corporation to purchase and operate a hardware store.
    e. All of the above are partnerships.

LO 10.1 2. Which of the following is a partnership for tax purposes?
   a. Monica and Chandler form a corporation to acquire a trucking business.
   b. Jimmy and Stephen both purchase an equal small stock interest in a manufacturing corporation as an investment.
   c. Emeril and Rachel purchase a food truck and sell prepared food dishes at various spots around the city.
   d. Melissa purchases a shoe store and hires her sister, Whitney, to manage the store.
   e. None of the above.

LO 10.1 3. In the current year, Hoffa Partnership allocates ordinary business income of $5,000 to Jimmy, a 40-percent partner. In addition, the partnership makes a cash distribution to Jimmy of $1,000, which is less than his basis in his partnership interest. Ignoring any qualified business income deduction, what is the amount of partnership income Jimmy will need to recognize in the current year?
   a. $0
   b. $3,000
   c. $4,000
   d. $5,000

LO 10.1 4. Jekyll is a limited partner in the JH Partnership. His investment in JH is $10,000. If JH fails and is forced to wind up operations, Jekyll's liability would be:
   a. unlimited
   b. limited to his investment in the partnership
   c. limited to his investment in the partnership plus his allocated share of the partnership liabilities
   d. zero, he has no liability

LO 10.1 5. Theodore has an investment in YYZ Corporation and a different investment in CXB Partnership. He has a 50-percent ownership stake in each. YYZ generates $100,000 of taxable income after paying corporate tax and makes no distribution to Theodore. CXB generates $50,000 of income and makes a $10,000 cash distribution (not in excess of Theodore's basis). Assuming he does not sell either investment and ignoring any qualified business income deduction, what is Theodore's taxable income from these investments in total?
   a. $0
   b. $10,000
   c. $25,000
   d. $35,000
   e. $85,000

LO 10.2 6. A partner's interest in a partnership is increased by:
   a. Capital losses of the partnership
   b. Tax-exempt interest earned by the partnership
   c. Losses of the partnership
   d. Distributions by the partnership
   e. None of the above

LO 10.2 7. A partner's interest in a partnership is decreased by:
   a. Increases in the partner's share of the partnership liabilities
   b. Debt relief that a partner experiences when contributing to the partnership property subject to a liability
   c. The partner's share of tax-exempt income earned by the partnership
   d. Contributions of cash from the partner to the partnership
   e. None of the above

LO 10.2

8. Abigail contributes land with an adjusted basis of $50,000 and a fair market value of $60,000 to Blair and Partners, a partnership. Abigail receives a 50-percent interest in Blair. What is Blair's basis in the land?
   a. $25,000
   b. $30,000
   c. $50,000
   d. $58,000
   e. $60,000

LO 10.2

9. Abigail contributes land with an adjusted basis of $50,000 and a fair market value of $60,000 to Blair and Partners, a partnership. Abigail receives a 50-percent interest in Blair. What is Abigail's basis in her partnership interest?
   a. $25,000
   b. $30,000
   c. $50,000
   d. $58,000
   e. $60,000

LO 10.2

10. Abigail contributes land with an adjusted basis of $50,000 and a fair market value of $60,000 to Blair and Partners, a partnership. Abigail receives a 50-percent interest in Blair. What is Abigail's recognized gain or loss on the contribution?
    a. $0
    b. $10,000 loss
    c. $10,000 gain
    d. $5,000 loss
    e. $5,000 gain

LO 10.2

11. Abigail contributes land with an adjusted basis of $50,000 and a fair market value of $60,000 to Blair and Partners, a partnership. Abigail receives a 50-percent interest in Blair. What is Blair's recognized gain or loss on the contribution?
    a. $0
    b. $10,000 loss
    c. $10,000 gain
    d. $5,000 loss
    e. $5,000 gain

LO 10.2

12. Blake and Ryan form the Poole Partnership. Blake contributes cash of $15,000. Ryan contributes land with an adjusted basis of $1,000 and a fair market value of $21,000. The land is subject to a $6,000 mortgage that Poole assumes. Blake and Ryan both receive a 50-percent interest in Poole. What is Ryan's recognized gain or loss on the contribution?
    a. $2,000
    b. $3,000
    c. $5,000
    d. $20,000
    e. None of the above

LO 10.3

13. Which of the following items do *not* have to be reported separately on a partnership return?
    a. Tax-exempt income
    b. Dividend income
    c. Typical MACRS depreciation expense
    d. Capital gains and losses
    e. Charitable contributions

LO 10.3
14. Which of the following items is generally reported as a separately stated item on a partnership return?
   a. Ordinary income from the operations of the partnership business
   b. Bonus depreciation
   c. Interest expense on business debts
   d. Net rental income
   e. Factory rent expense

LO 10.3
LO 10.7
15. When calculating ordinary income, partnerships are *not* allowed which of the following deductions?
   a. Miscellaneous expenses
   b. Qualified business income deduction
   c. Depreciation
   d. Cost of goods sold
   e. Employee wages

LO 10.3
16. Which of the following forms is used to report *each* partner's share of distributable income, including separately stated items?
   a. Form 1065
   b. Schedule K
   c. Schedule K-1
   d. Schedule P

LO 10.3
17. TYVM Partnership allocates ordinary business income, long-term capital gains, and guaranteed payments of $13,000, $1,000, and $7,000, respectively, to Ariana, a general partner. Based on this information, what is Ariana's self-employment income?
   a. $0
   b. $7,000
   c. $8,000
   d. $20,000
   e. $21,000

LO 10.3
18. Which of the following items is generally reported as a separately stated item on a partnership return?
   a. Sales revenues from business operations
   b. Typical MACRS depreciation
   c. Employee salaries expense
   d. Insurance expense
   e. Guaranteed payments to a partner

LO 10.4
19. Feela is a one-third owner of Alchemy LLC, which is taxed as a partnership. Her basis prior to Alchemy paying Feela an $11,000 cash distribution is $6,000. How much income does Feela recognize from the distribution and what is her basis in her interest in Alchemy after the distribution?
   a. $11,000 income and $6,000 basis
   b. $6,000 income and $5,000 basis
   c. $5,000 income and $0 basis
   d. $0 income and negative $5,000 basis
   e. None of these choices

LO 10.4
20. Khushboo's basis in her 25-percent interest in the Rishi Partnership is $40,000 at the start of the current year. During the current year, Rishi reports ordinary business income of $80,000, after guaranteed payments. Rishi also makes a $10,000 guaranteed payment and $16,000 cash distribution, both to Khushboo. What will Khushboo's basis be at the end of the current year and how much income will Khushboo recognize from these transactions?
   a. Basis of $44,000 and income of $30,000
   b. Basis of $34,000 and income of $80,000
   c. Basis of $34,000 and income of $20,000
   d. Basis of $60,000 and income of $20,000
   e. Basis of $50,000 and income of $16,000

LO 10.4
21. Laura is a non-passive general partner in the Douglass Partnership. At the start of 2024, her outside basis in Douglass is $10,000. During 2024, Douglass allocates loss of $8,000 to Laura and makes a $4,000 cash distribution to Laura. What is Laura's deductible loss for 2024 and what is her basis at year-end?
   a. $0 deductible loss and $0 basis.
   b. $8,000 deductible loss and $0 basis.
   c. $6,000 deductible loss and $4,000 basis.
   d. $6,000 deductible loss and $0 basis.
   e. $8,000 deductible loss and $2,000 basis.

LO 10.5
22. Which of the following circumstances will *not* cause a partnership to close its tax year early?
   a. The partnership terminates by agreement of the partners.
   b. The business activity of the partnership permanently ceases.
   c. All the partners decide to retire, permanently close their stores, and stop conducting business.
   d. A new partner enters the partnership.

LO 10.5
23. Joe, Ben, and Melissa are partners in Collins Partnership. All three use a calendar year-end for their individual taxes. Collins Partnership's year-end is likely to be:
   a. October 31 since that is only three months prior to calendar year-end
   b. The end of any month during the year
   c. January 31 but only if Collins Partnership's accounting year-end is January 31
   d. December 31
   e. None of the above

LO 10.6
24. Kendra is an attorney and owns 60 percent of a law partnership. Kendra sells land to the partnership for $50,000 in the current tax year. She bought the land for $100,000 eight years ago when real estate prices were at their peak. How much gain or loss must Kendra recognize on the land sale to the partnership?
   a. No gain or loss
   b. $30,000 loss
   c. $50,000 loss
   d. $50,000 short-term capital loss, limited to $3,000 allowed per year

LO 10.6
25. A loss from the sale or exchange of property will be disallowed in which of the following situations?
   a. A transaction between a partnership and a partner who owns 40 percent of the partnership capital
   b. A transaction between a partnership and a partner who has a 40-percent profit interest in the partnership
   c. A transaction between two partnerships owned 80 percent by the same partners
   d. A transaction between two partners with investments in the same partnership
   e. None of the above

LO 10.7 26. In 2024, Gloria, a single taxpayer, receives a Schedule K-1 from a partnership in which she is invested. The K-1 reports ordinary business income of $30,000, dividend income of $500, tax-exempt interest of $300, and a guaranteed payment to Gloria of $10,000. Gloria's taxable income before the QBI deduction is $87,000. What is Gloria's 2024 QBI deduction?
   a. $6,160
   b. $6,000
   c. $4,000
   d. $17,400
   e. $8,000

LO 10.7 27. Jay is a 30-percent partner in the Closet Partnership. In 2024, Closet paid W-2 wages of $24,000 and held qualified property of $600,000. In 2024, Jay's QBI deduction is subject to the wage limitation due to his income. If Closet allocates wages and qualified property in the same manner as income (based on percentage ownership), what is Jay's wage and qualified property limit on the QBI deduction?
   a. $12,000
   b. $3,600
   c. $6,300
   d. $4,500

LO 10.7 28. A partnership should disclose qualified business income information on what supplemental form?
   a. Schedule K-2
   b. Statement A to the Schedule K-1
   c. Form 8995
   d. Schedule QBI

LO 10.8 29. Mike, an individual taxpayer, purchases a rental property for $200,000 using cash of $100,000 and borrowing the remaining $100,000 from a lending institution. The loan is considered to be qualified nonrecourse financing. What is Mike's at-risk amount?
   a. $300,000
   b. $200,000
   c. $100,000
   d. $0

LO 10.8 30. Gloria is a 30-percent general partner in the VH Partnership. During the year, VH borrows $40,000 from a bank to fund operations and is able to pay back $10,000 before year-end. VH also borrows $100,000 from Gloria's wealthy retired uncle on a nonrecourse basis using land held by the partnership as the collateral. How much does Gloria's at-risk amount increase or decrease as a result of these transactions?
   a. $9,000 increase
   b. $30,000 decrease
   c. $12,000 increase
   d. $42,000 increase
   e. $42,000 decrease

LO 10.9 31. Which of the following properly describes a difference between a partnership and an LLC?
   a. Partnerships pass income and losses through to the partners while LLCs generally pay an entity level tax and owners pay tax on distributions.
   b. General partners are often personally responsible for the debts of the partnership while LLC members are not liable for LLC debt.
   c. Partnerships may have only one partner but LLCs must have more than one member.
   d. The tax attributes of income in a partnership are retained when included in the partner's income but LLC income is treated as capital income in all cases.

10-32 Chapter 10 • Partnership Taxation

LO 10.9 32. Which of the following generate self-employment income for partners/members?
a. Partnership income allocated to a limited partner
b. Long-term capital gains allocated to an LLC member
c. Income allocated to an LLC member that is actively engaged in the business
d. Tax-exempt income allocated to both general partners and members

Group 2: Problems

LO 10.1 1. Debbie and Alan open an online bookstore together. They have been friends for so long that they start their business on a handshake after discussing how they will share both work and profits or losses from the business. Explain whether Debbie and Alan formed a partnership given that they have signed no written partnership agreement?

LO 10.1 2. Describe how the allocation of a partner's share of income and the distribution of cash to partners differ in triggering the recognition of income by the partner.

LO 10.1 3. Explain the difference in the treatment of liabilities between a general partner and a limited partner.

LO 10.2 4. Nan contributes property with an adjusted basis of $50,000 to a partnership. The property has a fair market value of $60,000 on the date of the contribution. What is the partnership's basis in the property contributed by Nan?

LO 10.2 LO 10.4 5. Elaine's original basis in the Hornbeam Partnership was $40,000. Her share of the taxable income from the partnership since she purchased the interest has been $70,000, and Elaine has received $80,000 in cash distributions from the partnership. Elaine did not recognize any gains as a result of the distributions. In the current year, Hornbeam also allocated $1,000 of tax-exempt interest to Elaine. Calculate Elaine's current basis in her partnership interest.

LO 10.2 6. Juanita contributes property with a fair market value of $30,000 and an adjusted basis of $16,000 to a partnership in exchange for a 10-percent partnership interest.
a. Calculate the amount of gain recognized by Juanita as a result of the transfer of the property to the partnership.
b. Calculate Juanita's basis in her partnership interest immediately following the contribution to the partnership.

LO 10.2 7. Mitchell, Max, and Romeo form a partnership to operate a grocery store. For each of the following contributions by the partners, indicate (1) the amount of income or gain recognized, if any, by the partner, and (2) the partner's basis in the partnership interest immediately after the contribution including the allocation of liabilities.
a. Mitchell contributes property with a basis of $45,000 and subject to a $75,000 liability to the partnership for a one-third partnership interest worth $105,000. The partnership assumes the liability.
b. Max contributes property with a basis of $25,000 and a fair market value of $105,000 to the partnership for a one-third partnership interest.
c. Romeo performs services valued at $105,000 for the partnership for a one-third interest in the partnership.

LO 10.2 8. Kele and Nova wish to form the Sioux Partnership. Kele contributes property with an adjusted basis of $70,000, a fair market value of $200,000 that is subject to an $80,000 liability in exchange for 40 percent of Sioux. Nova receives a 60-percent interest in Sioux in exchange for providing services worth $10,000 and $170,000 cash.
a. What amount of gain or loss must Kele recognize as a result of transferring property to the partnership?

b. What is Kele's basis in the partnership interest immediately after the formation of the partnership including allocation of partnership liabilities?
c. What is the partnership's basis in the property contributed by Kele?
d. What is Nova's basis in the partnership interest immediately after the formation of the partnership including allocation of partnership liabilities?
e. How much income does Nova recognize on the exchange?

LO 10.2
LO 10.4

9. Meredith has a 40-percent interest in the assets and income of the Gantt Partnership, and the basis in her partnership interest is $60,000 at the beginning of 2024. During 2024, the partnership's net loss is $45,000 and Meredith's share of the loss is $18,000. Also, Meredith receives a cash distribution from the partnership of $8,000 on June 30, 2024.
   a. Indicate the amount of income or loss from the partnership that should be reported by Meredith on her 2024 individual income tax return assuming she actively participates in the operations of the partnership.
   b. Calculate Meredith's basis in her partnership interest at the end of 2024.

LO 10.3

10. List five items of income or deductions that are required to be separately stated on Schedule K-1.

LO 10.3

11. K&T Company is a partnership with two equal partners, Kai and Taonga. The partnership has income of $60,000 for the year *before guaranteed payments*. Guaranteed payments of $25,000 are paid to Kai during the year. Calculate the amount of income that should be reported by Kai and Taonga from the partnership for the year.

LO 10.3

12. Georgina receives a Schedule K-1 for her general partner interest in the CCI Partnership that reports the following:

    - Ordinary business income $4,000
    - Net rental real estate income $2,000
    - Short-term capital gains $500
    - Section 1231 loss of $600
    - Guaranteed payments of $1,000
    - Cash distribution of $3,000

    Using the information from her Schedule K-1, compute Georgina's self-employment income:

LO 10.4

13. Elijah and Rona are both 50-percent partners in the Thakkar Partnership. At the start of the current year, Elijah's outside basis in Thakkar is $3,000 and Rona's outside basis in Thakkar is $7,000. During the current year, the distributive share of income for both Elijah and Rona is $500. There are no separately stated items in the current year except for a cash distribution of $5,000 each to Elijah and Rona. Provide an explanation of the computation of Elijah and Rona's income and ending outside basis for the current year.

LO 10.4

14. Walter receives cash of $18,000 and land with a fair market value of $75,000 (adjusted basis of $50,000) in a current distribution. His basis in his partnership interest is $16,000 before the distribution.
    a. What amount of gain must Walter recognize as a result of the current distribution?
    b. What amount of gain must the partnership recognize as a result of the distribution?
    c. What is Walter's basis in his partnership interest immediately after the distribution?

LO 10.5

15. Describe the rules for selecting a partnership year-end.

LO 10.5

16. Kiwi Interests is a partnership with a tax year that ends on September 30, 2024. During that year, Kereru, a partner, received $2,000 per month as a guaranteed payment, and his share of partnership income after guaranteed payments was $14,000. For October through December of 2024, Kereru received guaranteed payments of $3,000 per month. Calculate the amount of income from the partnership that Kereru should report for the tax year ending December 31, 2024.

LO 10.6 17. Louise owns 45 percent of a partnership, and her brother owns the remaining 55 percent interest. During the current tax year, Louise sold a building to the partnership for $160,000 to be used for the partnership's office. She had held the building for three years, and it had an adjusted basis of $120,000 at the time of the sale. What is the amount and nature of Louise's gain on this transaction?

LO 10.6 18. Rhianna owns a two-thirds interest in the ANTI Partnership and a 75-percent interest in the LOUD Partnership. In the current year, ANTI sells property to LOUD at a loss of $10,000. Later in the same year, LOUD sells the same property to an unrelated party for a $2,000 gain. What is the amount of gain or loss recognized by ANTI and LOUD on the sale of this property?

LO 10.7 19. Describe the consequences of not reporting qualified business income information to a partner on the partners' Schedule K-1.

LO 10.7 20. Janie owns a 30-percent interest in Chang Partnership. Chang has W-2 wages of $20,000 and qualified property of $900,000 in 2024.
   a. When computing the W-2 wages limitation, what is the amount of wages that will be allocated to Janie?
   b. What is the amount of qualified property that will be allocated to Janie?

LO 10.8 21. Van makes an investment in a partnership in the current year. Van's capital contributions to the partnership consist of $30,000 cash and a building with an adjusted basis of $70,000, subject to a nonrecourse liability (seller financing) of $20,000.
   a. Calculate the amount that Van has at risk in the partnership immediately after making the capital contributions.
   b. If Van's share of the loss from the partnership is $100,000 in the current year, and assuming that Van has sufficient amounts of passive income, how much of the loss may he deduct in the current year?
   c. What may be done with the nondeductible part of the loss in Part b?

LO 10.8 22. Octavio starts the year with outside basis of $23,000 and an amount at-risk of $23,000 in his 40-percent general partnership interest in Brown Partnership. In the current year, the partnership distributes $5,000 to Octavio. His share of allocated ordinary income is $3,000. The partnership also takes on nonrecourse debt of $20,000 (none of which is qualified nonrecourse financing). Compute Octavio's ending outside basis and amount at-risk.

LO 10.8
LO 10.9 23. Van makes an investment in an LLC in the current year. Van's capital contributions to the LLC consist of $30,000 cash and a building with an adjusted basis of $70,000, subject to a nonrecourse liability (seller financing) of $20,000. Calculate the amount that Van has at risk in the LLC immediately after making the capital contributions.

LO 10.9 24. Describe ways in which LLCs might differ from partnerships.

Group 3:
Comprehensive Problem

Emily Jackson (Social Security number 765-12-4326) and James Stewart (Social Security number 466-74-9932) are partners in a general partnership that owns and operates a barber shop. The partnership's first year of operation is 2024. Emily and James divide income and expenses equally. The partnership name is J&S Barbers, it is located at 1023 Lexington Avenue, New York, NY 10128, and its Federal ID number is 95-6767676. The 2024 financial statements for the partnership are presented below.

J&S Barbers Income Statement
for the Year Ending December 31, 2024

Gross income from operations	$349,000
Interest income	1,000
Deductions:	
Salaries to employees (includes guaranteed payments of $10,000 to Emily)	100,000
Payroll taxes	11,000
Supplies	7,900
Rent	90,000
Depreciation (book)	6,710
Loss	2,000
Nondeductible entertainment	3,000
Charitable contributions	1,000
Net income	$128,390
Partners' withdrawals (each partner)	$ 50,000

J&S Barbers Balance Sheet
as of December 31, 2024

Assets:		
Cash		$ 92,000
Leasehold improvements	$ 3,100	
Equipment	32,000	
Accumulated depreciation	(6,710)	28,390
		$120,390
Liabilities and Capital:		
Recourse long-term debt		$ 52,000
Partners' capital ($20,000 contributed by each partner)		68,390
		$120,390

Emily lives at 456 E. 70th Street, New York, NY 10006, and James lives at 436 E. 63rd Street, New York, NY 10012.

Required: Complete J&S Barbers' 2024 Form 1065, including Schedule D and Form 4562, and Emily and James' Schedule K-1s and Statement A (QBI information), which are expected to be filed electronically. Do not complete Schedule B-1 related to ownership of the partnership. Make realistic assumptions about any missing data.

The equipment is 7-year recovery property placed in service on January 24th by J&S. The leasehold improvements were placed in service on January 21st and are qualified improvement property. J&S wishes to depreciate the equipment and leasehold improvements using the fastest method available.

The partnership received the following Form 1099-B from the sale of some mutual fund shares that were a temporary investment of partners' capital at the start of the year:

Form 1099-B (2024) — Proceeds From Broker and Barter Exchange Transactions

- CORRECTED (if checked): ☐
- PAYER'S name, street address, city or town, state or province, country, ZIP or foreign postal code, and telephone no.:
  J. Rockford Paradise Bond Fund
  29 Cove Road
  Malibu, CA 90265
- Applicable checkbox on Form 8949: A
- OMB No. 1545-0715
- Form 1099-B
- 1a Description of property: 340 Shares Paradise Bond Fund
- 1b Date acquired: 01/05/2024
- 1c Date sold or disposed: 02/13/2024
- PAYER'S TIN: 43-5991923
- RECIPIENT'S TIN: 95-6767676
- 1d Proceeds: $36,000.00
- 1e Cost or other basis: $38,000.00
- 1f Accrued market discount: $
- 1g Wash sale loss disallowed: $
- RECIPIENT'S name: J&S Barbers Partnership
- Street address: 1023 Lexington Avenue
- City, state, ZIP: New York, NY 10128
- 2 Short-term gain or loss: ☒
  Long-term gain or loss: ☐
  Ordinary: ☐
- 3 If checked, proceeds from:
  Collectibles: ☐
  QOF: ☐
- 4 Federal income tax withheld: $
- 5 If checked, noncovered security: ☐
- 6 Reported to IRS:
  Gross proceeds: ☐
  Net proceeds: ☒
- 7 If checked, loss is not allowed based on amount in 1d: ☐
- 8 Profit or (loss) realized in 2024 on closed contracts: $
- 9 Unrealized profit or (loss) on open contracts—12/31/2023: $
- 10 Unrealized profit or (loss) on open contracts—12/31/2024: $
- 11 Aggregate profit or (loss) on contracts: $
- 12 If checked, basis reported to IRS: ☒
- 13 Bartering: $
- Copy B — For Recipient

Chapter 11

The Corporate Income Tax

Learning Objectives

After completing this chapter, you should be able to:

- **LO 11.1** Employ the corporate tax rates to calculate corporate tax liability.
- **LO 11.2** Compute basic gains and losses for corporations.
- **LO 11.3** Apply special corporate deductions to corporate taxable income.
- **LO 11.4** Identify the components of Schedule M-1 and how they are reported to the IRS.
- **LO 11.5** Describe the corporate tax return filing and estimated tax payment requirements.
- **LO 11.6** Explain how an S corporation operates and is taxed.
- **LO 11.7** Describe the basic tax rules for the formation of a corporation.
- **LO 11.8** Describe the rules for the accumulated earnings tax and the personal holding company tax.

Overview

There are many forms of organization which may be used by taxpayers to operate a business. These include the sole proprietorship (Form 1040, Schedule C, covered in Chapter 3); the partnership, LLC, and LLP (Form 1065 covered in Chapter 10); and the regular C corporation and S corporation (covered in this chapter). Regular C corporations are taxed as separate legal taxpaying entities, and S corporations are taxed as flow-through entities similar to partnerships.

This chapter covers corporate tax rates, capital gains and losses, special deductions, the Schedule M-1, filing requirements, corporate formations, and corporate earnings accumulations. Additionally, basic coverage of the S corporation election and operating requirements are presented in this chapter.

This chapter provides a summary of corporate taxation and the tax forms (Form 1120, Form 1120-S, and related schedules) associated with reporting C or S corporation income or loss.

11-1 Corporate Tax Rates

Learning Objective 11.1
Employ the corporate tax rates to calculate corporate tax liability.

Corporations are subject to a flat income tax rate of 21 percent.

Example Jasmine Corporation has taxable income of $175,000 for 2024. The corporation's tax liability for the year is calculated as follows:

Taxable income	$ 175,000
Corporate tax rate	21%
Tax liability	$ 36,750

♦

Unlike the individual alternative minimum tax (AMT), which remains in force, the traditional corporate AMT was repealed for tax years after 2017. Under the prior corporate AMT regime, a corporation subject to AMT may have had unused AMT credits that can be carried over indefinitely to offset regular tax. Due to tax benefits offered during the COVID-19 pandemic, the likelihood of corporations having any remaining AMT credit carryforwards into 2024 is very low.

A new version of a corporate alternative minimum tax (CAMT) was enacted in the Inflation Reduction Act of 2022. Described as a corporate minimum tax on book income, the tax is 15 percent of adjusted financial statement income. The tax generally applies to corporations with a three-year average annual financial statement income of over $1 billion and therefore, applies only to the largest corporations. Additionally, starting in 2023, an excise tax of 1 percent of the value of the stock repurchased applies. The corporate stock repurchase tax applies to any domestic corporation, the stock of which is traded on an established securities market. The details of the CAMT and the stock repurchase excise tax are beyond the scope of this textbook.

Personal service corporations are taxed at the same 21-percent tax rate on all taxable income. A personal service corporation is substantially employee-owned and engages in one of the following activities:

- Health
- Law
- Engineering
- Architecture
- Accounting
- Actuarial science
- Performing arts
- Consulting

Example Elm & Ash, Inc., is a professional service corporation of CPAs. For the current tax year, the corporation has taxable income of $175,000. Elm & Ash will have a 21-percent tax rate like any other corporation and thus, a tax liability of $36,750 (21% × $175,000). ♦

Self-Study Problem 11.1 *Refer to Appendix E for Solutions to Self-Study Problems*

Maple Corporation has taxable income of $335,000 for the current tax year. Calculate the corporation's tax liability, before tax credits.

11-2 Corporate Gains and Losses

Learning Objective 11.2
Compute basic gains and losses for corporations.

If a corporation generates a net capital gain, the net gain is included in ordinary income and the tax is computed at the regular rate except under very rare circumstances. The tax law provides for a maximum rate of 21 percent on corporate capital gains. Thus, Congress intends the ordinary income and capital gains rates to be the same for corporations, so there is no tax rate benefit to having long-term capital gains in a corporation. Net short-term capital gains of a corporation are also taxed as ordinary income.

11-2a Capital Losses

Corporations are not allowed to deduct capital losses against ordinary income. Capital losses may be used only to offset capital gains. If capital losses cannot be used in the year they occur, they may be carried back three years and forward five years to offset capital gains in those years. When a long-term capital loss is carried to another year, it is treated as a short-term capital loss, and may be offset against either long-term or short-term capital gains.

Example In 2024, Eucalyptus Corporation incurs a long-term capital loss of $8,000, none of which may be deducted in that year. The loss is carried back to tax years 2021, 2022, and 2023, in that order. If the loss is not entirely used to offset capital gains in those years, it may be carried forward to 2025, 2026, 2027, 2028, and 2029, in that order. When the long-term loss is carried to another year, it is considered to be short term and may offset against either long-term or short-term capital gains. ♦

11-2b Net Operating Losses

As explained in Chapter 4, corporations—similar to individuals—may also carryforward net operating losses (NOLs) to offset future taxable income. An NOL created before 2018 has a two-year carryback and then a twenty-year carryforward (a taxpayer could elect out of the carryback) and the NOL could be used to offset 100 percent of the future year's taxable income.

Example In 2017, Dez Corporation had a net operating loss of $10,000. Dez elected to forego any carryback and instead carried the NOL forward to 2018. In 2018, Dez generated taxable income of $12,000 eligible to be offset by 100 percent of the 2017 NOL. Dez's 2018 taxable income was $2,000, after the carryforward of the 2017 NOL. ♦

The use of an NOL generated after December 31, 2017 may only be carried forward (indefinitely) and is limited to 80 percent of the current year's taxable income (without regard to the NOL deduction) when used. During the COVID-19 pandemic, the NOL rules were temporarily changed; however, the temporary NOL provisions are unlikely to be relevant at this time.

Example Fez Corporation had a net operating loss of $10,000 in 2024. Fez may only carry the NOL forward. In 2025, Fez generated taxable income of $12,000. Fez may only offset $9,600 ($12,000 × 80%) of its 2025 income which results in taxable income of $2,400. Fez may carryforward the remaining 2024 NOL of $400 to 2026. ♦

Self-Study Problem 11.2 Refer to Appendix E for Solutions to Self-Study Problems

a. During the current tax year, Taxus Corporation has ordinary income of $110,000, a long-term capital loss of $20,000, and a short-term capital loss of $5,000. Calculate Taxus Corporation's tax liability.

b. Maxus Corporation started business in 2022 and generated taxable (loss)/income of ($40,000), $36,000, and 10,000 in 2022, 2023, and 2024, respectively. What is the NOL carryforward to 2025, if any?

11-3 Special Deductions and Limitations

Learning Objective 11.3
Apply special corporate deductions to corporate taxable income.

Corporations are allowed certain "special deductions," including the dividends received deduction and the deduction for organizational expenditures and start-up costs. In addition, the deduction for charitable contributions by a corporation is limited.

11-3a Dividends Received Deduction

When a corporation owns stock in another corporation, income earned by the first corporation could be taxed at least three times in the absence of a special provision. The income would be taxed to the first corporation when earned by the first corporation. Then it would be taxed to the corporation owning the stock in the first corporation when the income is distributed as dividend income. Finally, the income would be taxed to the shareholders of the second corporation when that corporation in turn distributes the earnings to its stockholders as dividends. To mitigate this potential for triple taxation of corporate earnings, corporations are allowed a deduction for all or a portion of dividends received from domestic corporations. Corporations are entitled to a dividends received deduction (DRD) based on their percentage of ownership in the corporation paying the dividend. The deduction percentages are described in Table 11.1

Table 11.1 Dividend Received Deduction Percentages

Percent Ownership	DRD Percentage
Less than 20 percent	50%
20 percent or more, but less than 80 percent	65%
80 percent or more	100%

The dividends received deduction is limited to the applicable deduction percentage times the corporation's taxable income calculated before the dividends received deduction, the net operating loss deduction, and capital loss carrybacks. This taxable income limitation, however, does not apply if the receiving corporation has a net operating loss after reducing taxable income by the dividends received deduction. In other words, there is no taxable income limit if the dividends received deduction creates or increases a net operating loss.

Example The corporations presented below have the following income and expenses during the current year. Each corporation received a $100,000 dividend from a 30-percent-owned corporation.

		Frankberry Corporation	Blueberry Corporation	Chockberry Corporation
Line A	Gross income from operations excluding dividends	$240,000	$190,000	$150,000
Line B	Expenses from operations	(200,000)	(200,000)	(200,000)
Line C	Dividend received from a 30-percent-owned domestic corporation	100,000	100,000	100,000
Line D, (A + B + C)	Pre-DRD taxable income	140,000	90,000	50,000
Line E, (C × 65%)	Calculated full DRD	65,000	65,000	65,000
Line F, (D × 65%)	Taxable income limitation	91,000	58,500	32,500
Line G, (D − E)	Taxable income/(loss) with full DRD	75,000	25,000	(15,000)
Line H, (lesser of E or F, unless a loss is created)	DRD permitted	$65,000	$58,500	$65,000

For Frankberry, the DRD of $65,000 is not limited. For Blueberry, the DRD is limited to 65 percent of pre-DRD income. For Chockberry, the DRD limitation does not apply because the full DRD creates a loss. ♦

11-3b Organizational Expenditures and Start-Up Costs

New businesses may incur organizational expenditures or start-up costs, or both, prior to starting a business. Organizational expenditures are incurred by partnerships, LLCs, and corporations in the process of forming an entity in which to operate a business. Start-up costs may be incurred by any business, including sole proprietorships reported on Schedule C, as well as the entities listed above.

Corporations amortize qualifying *organizational* costs over 180 months, and there is no upper limit to the amount of qualifying costs that can be amortized. Corporations can elect to deduct up to $5,000 of organizational costs in the year they begin business. The $5,000 amount is reduced by each dollar of organizational expenses exceeding $50,000. Costs not expensed as part of the first-year election to expense are amortized ratably over the 180-month period beginning with the month the corporation begins business. Generally, organizational expenditures that qualify for amortization include legal and accounting services incident to organization, expenses of temporary directors and organizational meetings, and fees paid to the state for incorporation. Expenses such as the cost of transferring assets to the corporation and expenses connected with selling the corporation's stock are not organizational expenditures and, therefore, are not subject to amortization.

Example In 2024, Coco Bola Corporation, an accrual-basis, calendar-year taxpayer, incurred $500 in fees to the state for incorporation, legal and accounting fees incident to the incorporation of $1,000, and temporary directors' expenses of $300. Assuming the corporation does not make an election to expense in the first year, the total $1,800 ($500 + $1,000 + $300) may be amortized over 15 years at a rate of $10 per month ($1,800/180 months). If the corporation began operations on June 1, 2024, $70 ($10 per month × 7 months) may be deducted for organizational expenditures for 2024. Alternatively, the corporation could elect to deduct the full $1,800 of organization costs in the first year of business. ♦

The *start-up costs* of a new business are given the same tax treatment as organizational costs, as illustrated in the previous paragraph and example. Start-up costs include both investigatory expenses and preopening costs. Investigatory expenses are expenses to investigate the potential success of a new business before the decision is made to actually pursue the business. Preopening costs are incurred after the taxpayer decides to start a new business but prior to the date the business actually begins. These expenses may include the training of new employees, advertising, and fees paid to consultants and professionals for advisory services.

For an existing business, exploratory (or expansion) costs are not treated the same as start-up costs.

Example Donuts R Us Corp. (DRU) owns a chain of donut shops in the northeast United States. DRU is considering opening new stores in southern California, and DRU's VP of Business Development visits a number of possible locations, meets with lawyers to discuss California regulation of food service and zoning rules, and engages a consulting firm to prepare a market study of the donut market in southern California. Because DRU is already in the donut business, the expenses incurred are considered ordinary and necessary expansion costs and are deductible. ♦

If a taxpayer attempts to expand into a new area of business, the costs are treated as start-up costs, and the resulting deduction is dependent on the type of taxpayer and whether the business is ever started.

Example Donuts R Us Corp. owns a chain of donut shops in the northeast United States. DRU's CEO loves to surf, and so she is considering expanding DRU's operations into the surf shop business in southern California. The DRU VP of Business Development visits a number of locations, meets with lawyers to discuss California regulation of surf shops and zoning rules, and engages a consulting firm to prepare a market study of the surf apparel and surfboard market in Southern California. Because DRU is not in the surf shop business, these expenses are considered pre-operating start-up expenses. If DRU opens a California surf shop business, the expenses incurred are start-up costs and will be expensed or amortized as described previously. If DRU does not end up in the surfshop business, these costs are capitalized until such time as the "failure" occurs and are then deducted as a loss. Note that if DRU is not a corporation, the start-up costs associated with a failed venture are not deductible at all. ♦

11-3c Charitable Contributions

Corporations are allowed a deduction for contributions to qualified charitable organizations. Generally, a deduction is allowed in the year in which a payment is made. If, however, the directors of a corporation which maintains its books on the accrual basis make a pledge before year-end, and the payment is made on or before the fifteenth day of the third month after the close of the tax year, the deduction may be claimed in the year of the pledge.

Typically, a corporation's charitable contributions deduction is limited to 10 percent of taxable income, computed before the deduction for charitable contributions, net operating loss carrybacks, capital loss carrybacks, and the dividends received deduction. Any excess contributions may be carried forward to the five succeeding tax years, but carryforward amounts are subject to the 10-percent annual limitation in the carryover years, with the current year's contributions deducted first.

Example Zircote Corporation had net operating income of $40,000 for the 2024 tax year and made a cash charitable contribution of $16,000 which has not been deducted in arriving at the $40,000 of operating income. Also not included in the operating income were dividends received of $10,000. The corporation's charitable contribution deduction is limited to 10 percent of $50,000 ($40,000 + $10,000), or $5,000. Note that the dividends received deduction is not used in calculating taxable income for purposes of determining the limitation on the charitable contribution deduction. The $11,000 ($16,000 − $5,000) of the charitable contribution that is disallowed in the current year is carried forward for up to five years. ♦

Self-Study Problem 11.3 Refer to Appendix E for Solutions to Self-Study Problems

a. During 2024, Fraxinia Corporation has the following income and expenses:

Gross income from operations, excluding dividends	$ 90,000
Expenses from operations	100,000
Dividends received from a 25-percent-owned domestic corporation	70,000

Calculate the amount of Fraxinia Corporation's dividends received deduction.

Self-Study Problem 11.3, continued
Refer to Appendix E for Solutions to Self-Study Problems

b. Boyce Inc., a calendar-year corporation, incurred organizational costs of $13,000 and start-up costs of $52,000 in 2024. Boyce started business on August 3, 2024. What is the maximum deduction for organizational and start-up costs for Boyce in 2024, and what is Boyce's 2025 deduction for the same costs?

c. Gant Corporation has income in 2024 of $65,000 after a dividends received deduction of $5,000 and a charitable contribution of $25,000. What is the deductible amount of the charitable contribution in 2024?

11-4 Schedule M-1

11.4 Learning Objective: Identify the components of Schedule M-1 and how they are reported to the IRS.

A corporation is required to report its income and other items on Form 1120, U.S. Corporation Income Tax Return. Because of various provisions in the tax law, a corporation's taxable income seldom is the same as its accounting income (commonly referred to as "book income"). The purpose of Schedule M-1 of the Form 1120 corporate tax return is to reconcile a corporation's book income to its taxable income, computed before the net operating loss and special deductions such as the dividends received deduction. On the left side of Schedule M-1 are adjustments that must be added to book income, and on the right side of the schedule are adjustments that must be subtracted from book income to arrive at the amount of taxable income. The amounts that must be added to book income include the amount of federal income tax expense, net capital losses deducted for book purposes, income recorded on the tax return but not on the books, and expenses recorded on the books but not deducted on the tax return. Alternatively, the amounts that must be deducted from book income are income recorded on the books but not included on the tax return, and deductions on the return not deducted on the books.

Example For the current tax year, Wisteria Corporation, an accrual-basis taxpayer, has net income reported on its books of $44,975. Included in this figure are the following items:

- Net capital loss .... $ 5,000
- Interest income on tax-exempt bonds 9,000
- Federal income tax expense 11,025
- Depreciation deducted on the tax return, not deducted on the books 3,500
- Interest deducted on the books, not deductible for tax purposes 4,000

Wisteria Corporation's Schedule M-1, Form 1120, is illustrated as follows:

Schedule M-1	Reconciliation of Income (Loss) per Books With Income per Return			
	Note: The corporation may be required to file Schedule M-3. See instructions.			
1	Net income (loss) per books	44,975	7 Income recorded on books this year not included on this return (itemize): Tax-exempt interest $ 9,000	
2	Federal income tax per books	11,025		
3	Excess of capital losses over capital gains	5,000		
4	Income subject to tax not recorded on books this year (itemize):			9,000
			8 Deductions on this return not charged against book income this year (itemize):	
5	Expenses recorded on books this year not deducted on this return (itemize):		a Depreciation $ 3,500	
a	Depreciation $		b Charitable contributions $	
b	Charitable contributions $			
c	Travel and entertainment $			3,500
	Interest	4,000	9 Add lines 7 and 8	12,500
6	Add lines 1 through 5	65,000	10 Income (page 1, line 28)—line 6 less line 9	52,500

Corporations with total assets of $10 million or more are required to file Schedule M-3. Schedule M-3 has three parts and requires a much greater amount of disclosure than does a Schedule M-1. For example, Part III of Schedule M-3 includes 37 possible reconciling items between book expenses and tax deductions. Schedule M-3 is beyond the scope of this textbook.

Self-Study Problem 11.4 *Refer to Appendix E for Solutions to Self-Study Problems*

Redwood Corporation has net income reported on its books of $115,600. For the current year, the corporation had federal income tax expense of $29,400, a net capital loss of $9,100, and tax-exempt interest income of $4,700. The company deducted depreciation of $17,000 on its tax return and $13,000 on its books. Using Schedule M-1 below, calculate Redwood Corporation's taxable income, before any net operating loss or special deductions, for the current year.

Schedule M-1 Reconciliation of Income (Loss) per Books With Income per Return

Note: The corporation may be required to file Schedule M-3. See instructions.

1. Net income (loss) per books . . . .
2. Federal income tax per books . . . . .
3. Excess of capital losses over capital gains .
4. Income subject to tax not recorded on books this year (itemize): _____
5. Expenses recorded on books this year not deducted on this return (itemize):
   a. Depreciation . . . . $ _____
   b. Charitable contributions . $ _____
   c. Travel and entertainment . $ _____
6. Add lines 1 through 5 . . . .
7. Income recorded on books this year not included on this return (itemize):
   Tax-exempt interest $ _____
8. Deductions on this return not charged against book income this year (itemize):
   a. Depreciation . . . $ _____
   b. Charitable contributions $ _____
9. Add lines 7 and 8 . . . .
10. Income (page 1, line 28)—line 6 less line 9

Learning Objective 11.5

Describe the corporate tax return filing and estimated tax payment requirements.

11-5 Filing Requirements and Estimated Tax

11-5a Filing Requirements and Due Dates

For all tax year-ends except for June 30, the due date for filing a corporate tax return is the fifteenth day of the fourth month after year-end. For June 30 year-end corporations, the filing due date is September 15 (fifteenth day of the third month). An extension provides an additional six months; thus, a calendar year-end corporation has an initial filing deadline of April 15 and an extended deadline of October 15 (six-month extension). However, corporations with tax years ending on June 30 will have an extended filing deadline of April 15 (seven-month extension). When the due date falls on a weekend or holiday, the due date is the next business day. Starting in 2024, corporations with more than ten "returns" (which includes Form 1120, Forms W-2, and Forms 1099) in aggregate over a tax year, are required to file Form 1120 electronically.

To avoid penalties, a corporation must pay any unpaid tax liability by the original due date of the return.

11-5b Estimated Tax Payments

Corporations must make estimated tax payments in a manner similar to those made by self-employed individual taxpayers (Chapter 9). The payments are made in four installments due on the fifteenth day of the fourth, sixth, ninth, and twelfth months of the corporation's tax year.

Example Grew Inc., is a calendar year-end corporation. Estimated payments are due April 15, June 15, September 15, and December 15. If Grew had a September 30 year-end, estimated payments would be due on January 15, March 15, June 15, and September 15. ♦

The penalty for failing to make adequate estimated payments applies when a corporation with an expected tax liability (after credits) of $500 or more fails to pay by the due date either (1) the current year tax liability or (2) an amount equal to the prior year tax liability. For large corporations (those with annual income of $1 million or more in any of the previous three years), use of prior year liability is limited to only the first quarter's estimated payment.

Example Vector Corporation, a calendar year-end corporation that is not a large corporation, had tax liability of $14,000 last year and current year tax liability of $15,000. Vector can avoid penalties by making estimated payments of $14,000. If Vector was a large corporation, estimated payments of $15,000 are required to avoid penalties. ♦

Penalties for underpayment of estimated taxes by a corporation can also be avoided by use of the annualized income method. The annualized income method permits the corporation to estimate income for the four quarters of the year and to determine required estimated payments, rather than wait until the end of the tax year to determine current year tax liability. Note that unlike individuals, a corporation's final quarter's payment is due the fifteenth day of the twelfth month, which is prior to the tax year-end. Under the annualized income method, each payment is designed to be 25 percent of the total tax liability based on estimates of annualized income.

Example Minyon Corporation is a calendar year-end large corporation for purposes of estimated payments. Prior year tax liability was $250,000. Minyon estimates each quarter's *year-to-date income* as follows:

Quarter	Year-to-Date Income
Q1	$ 300,000
Q2	700,000
Q3	950,000
Q4	1,300,000

The step-by-step process to compute the estimated tax payment for the first quarter payment is:

1. Annualize the first quarter's estimated income: $300,000 × 4 = $1,200,000
2. Compute the estimate of tax liability for the year: $1,200,000 × 21% = $252,000
3. Compute the first quarter's estimated payment requirement: $252,000 × 25% = $63,000

The first quarter's estimated payment can be based on either prior year $62,500 ($250,000 × 25%) or the annualized income method. Most corporations will choose to pay the lower amount and conserve cash.

The step-by-step process to compute the estimated tax payment for the second quarter payment is:

1. Annualize the *first* quarter's estimated income: $300,000 × 4 = $1,200,000 (note that the second quarter payment is due June 15 and thus, the second quarter's estimate of income is not yet known).
2. Compute the estimate of tax liability for the year: $1,200,000 × 21% = $252,000.

3. Compute the second quarter's estimated payment requirement: $252,000 × 50% = $126,000 less the previous payment of $62,500 results in a required second quarter estimated payment of $63,500.

Prior year tax liability is not permitted to be used to determine estimated tax payments after the first quarter for a large corporation such as Minyon.

The step-by-step process to compute the estimated tax payment for the third quarter payment is:

1. Annualize the *second* quarter's estimated income: $700,000 × 2 = $1,400,000 (note that the third quarter payment is due September 15 and thus, the third quarter's estimate of income is not yet known).
2. Compute the estimate of tax liability for the year: $1,400,000 × 21% = $294,000.
3. Compute the third quarter's estimate payment requirement: $294,000 × 75% = $220,500 less previous payments of $126,000 results in a required estimated payment of $94,500.

The step-by-step process to compute the estimated tax payment for the fourth quarter payment is:

1. Annualize the *third* quarter's estimated income: $950,000 × 12/9 = $1,266,667 (note that the fourth quarter payment is due December 15 and thus, the fourth quarter's estimate of income is not yet known).
2. Compute the estimate of tax liability for the year: $1,266,667 × 21% = $266,000.
3. Compute the fourth quarter's estimate payment requirement: $266,000 × 100% = $266,000 less previous payments of $220,500 results in a required estimated payment of $45,500. ♦

If estimates of annualized income have been prepared in accordance with regulations, the annualized estimates serve to replace the actual tax liability for the year for purposes of estimated payments. To the extent the actual tax liability exceeds the estimates, any payment is due at the original due date of the return. Overpayments can either be refunded or applied to the subsequent tax year.

Example Minyon Corporation, from the previous example, has actual tax liability of $273,000 ($1,300,000 × 21%). The additional tax due of $7,000 ($273,000 − $266,000) must be paid by April 15 of the following year, the unextended due date of the corporate tax return. ♦

11-5c Beneficial Ownership Information (BOI) Reporting

Starting January 1, 2024, many corporations in the United States must report information about their beneficial owners, the individuals who ultimately own or control the company, to the Financial Crimes Enforcement Network (FinCEN), the same organization referenced in Chapter 6 related to foreign bank account reporting. A beneficial owner is any individual who, directly or indirectly:

- Exercises substantial control over a reporting company; or
- Owns or controls at least 25 percent of the ownership interests of a reporting company.

For companies that existed prior to January 1, 2024, the deadline for reporting is January 1, 2025. For new companies starting in 2024, the deadline to file an initial report is 90 days. After 2024, new companies have 30 days for the initial filing.

The rules permit a number of exemptions as presented in Figure 11.1. None of the exemptions are related to the size of the underlying corporation so even the smallest corporations are expected to comply.

Figure 11.1 BOI Exceptions

Exemption No.	Exemption Short Title
1	Securities reporting issuer
2	Governmental authority
3	Bank
4	Credit union
5	Depository institution holding company
6	Money services business
7	Broker or dealer in securities
8	Securities exchange or clearing agency
9	Other Exchange Act registered entity
10	Investment company or investment adviser
11	Venture capital fund adviser
12	Insurance company
13	State-licensed insurance producer
14	Commodity Exchange Act registered entity
15	Accounting firm
16	Public utility
17	Financial market utility
18	Pooled investment vehicle
19	Tax-exempt entity
20	Entity assisting a tax-exempt entity
21	Large operating company
22	Subsidiary of certain exempt entities
23	Inactive entity

Additional information and filing can be completed at the dedicated FinCEN BOI website (**www.fincen.gov/boi**) at no charge.

A C corporation with less than $250,000 in gross receipts and less than $250,000 in assets is not required to complete Schedule L (balance sheet) or Schedules M-1 and M-2. An S corporation of the same size may also omit these parts of the tax form, except Schedule M-2, which must be completed for all S corporations. The rule allows small businesses to keep records based on their checkbook or cash receipts and disbursements journal. This makes the reporting requirements for a small corporation similar to the reporting requirements for a Schedule C sole proprietorship.

Self-Study Problem 11.5
Refer to Appendix E for Solutions to Self-Study Problems

1. Alberta Corp. is a calendar year-end corporation. In the previous three years, Alberta has reported taxable income of $680,000, $1,100,000 and $925,000. This year Alberta had the following year-to-date estimates of income for each quarter:

   Q1 $225,000
   Q2 $475,000
   Q3 $660,000
   Q4 $920,000

   Alberta's prior year tax liability was $194,250, and they applied an overpayment of $4,500 from the prior year to this year.

   Using this information, calculate the required estimated payment for each quarter.

Self-Study Problem 11.5, continued

Refer to Appendix E for Solutions to Self-Study Problems

2. Aspen Corporation was formed and began operations on January 1, 2024. Aspen is located at 470 Rio Grande Place, Aspen, CO 81611 and the EIN is 92-2222222. Aspen is a boutique retail store specializing in skis, snowboards, and accessories (business code 459110).

Aspen Corporation
Income Statement
for the Year Ended December 31, 2024

Gross income from operations		$ 285,000
Qualified dividends received from a 10-percent- owned domestic corporation		10,000
Total gross income		295,000
Cost of goods sold		(80,000)
Total income		215,000
Other expenses:		
Compensation of officers	$90,000	
Salaries and wages	82,000	
Repairs	8,000	
Depreciation expense for book and tax purposes	5,000	
Payroll taxes	11,000	
Total other expenses		(196,000)
Net income (before federal income tax expense)		$ 19,000

Aspen Corporation
Balance Sheet
as of December 31, 2024

Assets:		
Cash	$ 35,000	
Accounts receivable	10,000	
Land	18,000	
Building	125,000	
Less: accumulated depreciation	(5,000)	
Total assets		$ 183,000
Liabilities and owners' equity:		
Accounts payable	$ 26,940	
Common stock	140,000	
Retained earnings	16,060	
Total liabilities and owners' equity		$ 183,000

Aspen Corporation made estimated tax payments of $3,000.

Based on the above information, complete Form 1120 on Pages 11-13 to 11-18. Assume the corporation's book federal income tax expense is equal to its 2024 federal income tax liability and that any tax overpayment is to be applied to the next year's estimated tax. Schedule UTP, Form 4562, Form 1125-A, and Form 1125-E are not required. Make reasonable assumptions for any missing data.

Self-Study Problem 11.5

Form 1120
Department of the Treasury
Internal Revenue Service

U.S. Corporation Income Tax Return

For calendar year 2024 or tax year beginning _____, 2024, ending _____, 20 ____

Go to *www.irs.gov/Form1120* for instructions and the latest information.

OMB No. 1545-0123

2024

A Check if:
- 1a Consolidated return (attach Form 851) ☐
- b Life/nonlife consolidated return ☐
- 2 Personal holding co. (attach Sch. PH) ☐
- 3 Personal service corp. (see instructions) ☐
- 4 Schedule M-3 attached ☐

TYPE OR PRINT

Name

Number, street, and room or suite no. If a P.O. box, see instructions.

City or town, state or province, country, and ZIP or foreign postal code

B Employer identification number

C Date incorporated

D Total assets (see instructions)
$

E Check if: (1) ☐ Initial return (2) ☐ Final return (3) ☐ Name change (4) ☐ Address change

Income

1a	Gross receipts or sales	1a
b	Returns and allowances	1b
c	Balance. Subtract line 1b from line 1a	1c
2	Cost of goods sold (attach Form 1125-A)	2
3	Gross profit. Subtract line 2 from line 1c	3
4	Dividends and inclusions (Schedule C, line 23)	4
5	Interest	5
6	Gross rents	6
7	Gross royalties	7
8	Capital gain net income (attach Schedule D (Form 1120))	8
9	Net gain or (loss) from Form 4797, Part II, line 17 (attach Form 4797)	9
10	Other income (see instructions—attach statement)	10
11	**Total income.** Add lines 3 through 10	11

Deductions (See instructions for limitations on deductions.)

12	Compensation of officers (see instructions—attach Form 1125-E)	12
13	Salaries and wages (less employment credits)	13
14	Repairs and maintenance	14
15	Bad debts	15
16	Rents	16
17	Taxes and licenses	17
18	Interest (see instructions)	18
19	Charitable contributions	19
20	Depreciation from Form 4562 not claimed on Form 1125-A or elsewhere on return (attach Form 4562)	20
21	Depletion	21
22	Advertising	22
23	Pension, profit-sharing, etc., plans	23
24	Employee benefit programs	24
25	Energy efficient commercial buildings deduction (attach Form 7205)	25
26	Other deductions (attach statement)	26
27	**Total deductions.** Add lines 12 through 26	27
28	Taxable income before net operating loss deduction and special deductions. Subtract line 27 from line 11	28
29a	Net operating loss deduction (see instructions)	29a
b	Special deductions (Schedule C, line 24)	29b
c	Add lines 29a and 29b	29c

Tax, Refundable Credits, and Payments

30	**Taxable income.** Subtract line 29c from line 28. See instructions	30
31	Total tax (Schedule J, line 12)	31
32	Reserved for future use	32
33	Total payments and credits (Schedule J, line 23)	33
34	Estimated tax penalty. See instructions. Check if Form 2220 is attached ☐	34
35	**Amount owed.** If line 33 is smaller than the total of lines 31 and 34, enter amount owed	35
36	**Overpayment.** If line 33 is larger than the total of lines 31 and 34, enter amount overpaid	36
37	Enter amount from line 36 you want: **Credited to 2025 estimated tax** ____ **Refunded**	37

Sign Here
Under penalties of perjury, I declare that I have examined this return, including accompanying schedules and statements, and to the best of my knowledge and belief, it is true, correct, and complete. Declaration of preparer (other than taxpayer) is based on all information of which preparer has any knowledge.

Signature of officer ____ Date ____ Title ____

May the IRS discuss this return with the preparer shown below? See instructions. ☐ Yes ☐ No

Paid Preparer Use Only

Print/Type preparer's name	Preparer's signature	Date	Check ☐ if self-employed	PTIN
Firm's name			Firm's EIN	
Firm's address			Phone no.	

For Paperwork Reduction Act Notice, see separate instructions. Cat. No. 11450Q Form **1120** (2024)

Form 1120 (2024)   Page **2**

Schedule C	Dividends, Inclusions, and Special Deductions (see instructions)	(a) Dividends and inclusions	(b) %	(c) Special deductions (a) × (b)
1	Dividends from less-than-20%-owned domestic corporations (other than debt-financed stock)		50	
2	Dividends from 20%-or-more-owned domestic corporations (other than debt-financed stock)		65	
3	Dividends on certain debt-financed stock of domestic and foreign corporations		See instructions	
4	Dividends on certain preferred stock of less-than-20%-owned public utilities		23.3	
5	Dividends on certain preferred stock of 20%-or-more-owned public utilities		26.7	
6	Dividends from less-than-20%-owned foreign corporations and certain FSCs		50	
7	Dividends from 20%-or-more-owned foreign corporations and certain FSCs		65	
8	Dividends from wholly owned foreign subsidiaries		100	
9	**Subtotal.** Add lines 1 through 8. See instructions for limitations		See instructions	
10	Dividends from domestic corporations received by a small business investment company operating under the Small Business Investment Act of 1958		100	
11	Dividends from affiliated group members		100	
12	Dividends from certain FSCs		100	
13	Foreign-source portion of dividends received from a specified 10%-owned foreign corporation (excluding hybrid dividends) (see instructions)		100	
14	Dividends from foreign corporations not included on line 3, 6, 7, 8, 11, 12, or 13 (including any hybrid dividends)			
15	Reserved for future use			
16a	Subpart F inclusions derived from the sale by a controlled foreign corporation (CFC) of the stock of a lower-tier foreign corporation treated as a dividend (attach Form(s) 5471) (see instructions)		100	
b	Subpart F inclusions derived from hybrid dividends of tiered corporations (attach Form(s) 5471) (see instructions)			
c	Other inclusions from CFCs under subpart F not included on line 16a, 16b, or 17 (attach Form(s) 5471) (see instructions)			
17	Global Intangible Low-Taxed Income (GILTI) (attach Form(s) 5471 and Form 8992)			
18	Gross-up for foreign taxes deemed paid			
19	IC-DISC and former DISC dividends not included on line 1, 2, or 3			
20	Other dividends			
21	Deduction for dividends paid on certain preferred stock of public utilities			
22	Section 250 deduction (attach Form 8993)			
23	**Total dividends and inclusions.** Add column (a), lines 9 through 20. Enter here and on page 1, line 4			
24	**Total special deductions.** Add column (c), lines 9 through 22. Enter here and on page 1, line 29b			

Form **1120** (2024)

Form 1120 (2024) Page **3**

Schedule J	**Tax Computation and Payment** (see instructions)		
1a	Income tax (see instructions)	1a	
b	Tax from Form 1120-L (see instructions)	1b	
c	Section 1291 tax from Form 8621	1c	
d	Tax adjustment from Form 8978	1d	
e	Additional tax under section 197(f)	1e	
f	Base erosion minimum tax from Form 8991	1f	
g	Amount from Form 4255, Part I, line 3, column (q)	1g	
z	Other chapter 1 tax	1z	
2	Total income tax. Add lines 1a through 1z		2
3	Corporate alternative minimum tax from Form 4626, Part II, line 13 (attach Form 4626)		3
4	Add lines 2 and 3		4
5a	Foreign tax credit (attach Form 1118)	5a	
b	Credit from Form 8834 (see instructions)	5b	
c	General business credit (see instructions—attach Form 3800)	5c	
d	Credit for prior year minimum tax (attach Form 8827)	5d	
e	Bond credits from Form 8912	5e	
f	Adjustment from Form 8978	5f	
6	**Total credits.** Add lines 5a through 5f		6
7	Subtract line 6 from line 4		7
8	Personal holding company tax (attach Schedule PH (Form 1120))		8
9a	Amount from Form 4255, Part I, line 3, column (r)	9a	
b	Recapture of low-income housing credit (attach Form 8611)	9b	
c	Completed long-term contract look-back interest due (attach Form 8697)	9c	
d	Interest due under the look-back method—income forecast method (attach Form 8866)	9d	
e	Alternative tax on qualifying shipping activities (attach Form 8902)	9e	
f	Interest/tax due under section 453A(c)	9f	
g	Interest/tax due under section 453(l)	9g	
z	Other (see instructions—attach statement)	9z	
10	**Total.** Add lines 9a through 9z		10
11a	Total tax before deferred taxes. Add lines 7, 8, and 10	11a	
b	Deferred tax on the corporation's share of undistributed earnings of a qualified electing fund	11b	
c	Deferred LIFO recapture tax (section 1363(d))	11c	
12	Total tax. Subtract the sum of lines 11b and 11c from 11a. Enter here and on page 1, line 31		12
13	Preceding year's overpayment credited to the current year		13
14	Current year's estimated tax payments		14
15	Current year's refund applied for on Form 4466		15 ( )
16	Reserved for future use		16
17	Tax deposited with Form 7004		17
18	Withholding (see instructions)		18
19	**Total payments.** Combine lines 13 through 18		19
20	Refundable credits from:		
a	Form 2439	20a	
b	Form 4136	20b	
c	Credit for tax withheld under Chapter 3 or 4 from Form 1042-S, Form 8805, or Form 8288 (attach the applicable form)	20c	
z	Other (attach statement—see instructions)	20z	
21	**Total credits.** Add lines 20a through 20z		21
22	Elective payment election amount from Form 3800		22
23	**Total payments and credits.** Add lines 19, 21, and 22. Enter here and on page 1, line 33		23

Form **1120** (2024)

Form 1120 (2024)   Page **4**

Schedule K   **Other Information** (see instructions)   Yes   No

1. Check accounting method: **a** ☐ Cash   **b** ☐ Accrual   **c** ☐ Other (specify) _____

2. See the instructions and enter the:
   - **a** Business activity code no. _____
   - **b** Business activity _____
   - **c** Product or service _____

3. Is the corporation a subsidiary in an affiliated group or a parent–subsidiary controlled group?
   If "Yes," enter name and EIN of the parent corporation _____

4. At the end of the tax year:
   - **a** Did any foreign or domestic corporation, partnership (including any entity treated as a partnership), trust, or tax-exempt organization own directly 20% or more, or own, directly or indirectly, 50% or more of the total voting power of all classes of the corporation's stock entitled to vote? If "Yes," complete Part I of Schedule G (Form 1120) (attach Schedule G)
   - **b** Did any individual or estate own directly 20% or more, or own, directly or indirectly, 50% or more of the total voting power of all classes of the corporation's stock entitled to vote? If "Yes," complete Part II of Schedule G (Form 1120) (attach Schedule G)

5. At the end of the tax year, did the corporation:
   - **a** Own directly 20% or more, or own, directly or indirectly, 50% or more of the total voting power of all classes of stock entitled to vote of any foreign or domestic corporation not included on **Form 851**, Affiliations Schedule? For rules of constructive ownership, see instructions
   If "Yes," complete (i) through (iv) below.

(i) Name of Corporation	(ii) Employer Identification Number (if any)	(iii) Country of Incorporation	(iv) Percentage Owned in Voting Stock

- **b** Own directly an interest of 20% or more, or own, directly or indirectly, an interest of 50% or more in any foreign or domestic partnership (including an entity treated as a partnership) or in the beneficial interest of a trust? For rules of constructive ownership, see instructions
If "Yes," complete (i) through (iv) below.

(i) Name of Entity	(ii) Employer Identification Number (if any)	(iii) Country of Organization	(iv) Maximum Percentage Owned in Profit, Loss, or Capital

6. During this tax year, did the corporation pay dividends (other than stock dividends and distributions in exchange for stock) in excess of the corporation's current and accumulated earnings and profits? See sections 301 and 316
   If "Yes," file **Form 5452**, Corporate Report of Nondividend Distributions. See the instructions for Form 5452.
   If this is a consolidated return, answer here for the parent corporation and on Form 851 for each subsidiary.

7. At any time during this tax year, did one foreign person own, directly or indirectly, at least 25% of the total voting power of all classes of the corporation's stock entitled to vote or at least 25% of the total value of all classes of the corporation's stock?
   For rules of attribution, see section 318. If "Yes," enter:
   (a) Percentage owned _____ and **(b)** Owner's country _____
   (c) The corporation may have to file **Form 5472**, Information Return of a 25% Foreign-Owned U.S. Corporation or a Foreign Corporation Engaged in a U.S. Trade or Business. Enter the number of Forms 5472 attached _____

8. Check this box if the corporation issued publicly offered debt instruments with original issue discount . . . . ☐
   If checked, the corporation may have to file **Form 8281**, Information Return for Publicly Offered Original Issue Discount Instruments.

9. Enter the amount of tax-exempt interest received or accrued during this tax year $ _____

10. Enter the number of shareholders at the end of the tax year (if 100 or fewer) _____

11. If the corporation has an NOL for the tax year and is electing to forego the carryback period, check here (see instructions) . ☐
    If the corporation is filing a consolidated return, the statement required by Regulations section 1.1502-21(b)(3) must be attached or the election will not be valid.

12. Enter the available NOL carryover from prior tax years (do not reduce it by any deduction reported on page 1, line 29a) $ _____

Form **1120** (2024)

Form 1120 (2024) Page **5**

Schedule K Other Information *(continued from page 4)*

		Yes	No
13	Are the corporation's total receipts (page 1, line 1a, plus lines 4 through 10) for the tax year **and** its total assets at the end of the tax year less than $250,000?		
	If "Yes," the corporation is not required to complete Schedules L, M-1, and M-2. Instead, enter the total amount of cash distributions and the book value of property distributions (other than cash) made during this tax year $ _____		
14	Is the corporation required to file Schedule UTP (Form 1120), Uncertain Tax Position Statement? See instructions . . .		
	If "Yes," complete and attach Schedule UTP.		
15a	Did the corporation make any payments that would require it to file Form(s) 1099?		
b	If "Yes," did or will the corporation file required Form(s) 1099?		
16	During this tax year, did the corporation have an 80%-or-more change in ownership, including a change due to redemption of its own stock?		
17	During or subsequent to this tax year, but before the filing of this return, did the corporation dispose of more than 65% (by value) of its assets in a taxable, non-taxable, or tax deferred transaction?		
18	Did this corporation receive assets in a section 351 transfer in which any of the transferred assets had a fair market basis or fair market value of more than $1 million?		
19	During this corporation's tax year, did the corporation make any payments that would require it to file Forms 1042 and 1042-S under chapter 3 (sections 1441 through 1464) or chapter 4 (sections 1471 through 1474) of the Code?		
20	Is the corporation operating on a cooperative basis?		
21	During this tax year, did the corporation pay or accrue any interest or royalty for which the deduction is not allowed under section 267A? See instructions		
	If "Yes," enter the total amount of the disallowed deductions $ _____		
22	Does this corporation have gross receipts of at least $500 million in any of the 3 preceding tax years? (See sections 59A(e)(2) and (3).)		
	If "Yes," complete and attach Form 8991.		
23	Did the corporation have an election under section 163(j) for any real property trade or business or any farming business in effect during this tax year? See instructions		
24	Does the corporation satisfy one or more of the following? If "Yes," complete and attach Form 8990. See instructions . . .		
a	The corporation owns a pass-through entity with current, or prior year carryover, excess business interest expense.		
b	The corporation's aggregate average annual gross receipts (determined under section 448(c)) for the 3 tax years preceding the current tax year are more than $30 million and the corporation has business interest expense.		
c	The corporation is a tax shelter and the corporation has business interest expense.		
25	Is the corporation attaching Form 8996 to certify as a Qualified Opportunity Fund?		
	If "Yes," enter amount from Form 8996, line 15 . . . . $ _____		
26	Since December 22, 2017, did a foreign corporation directly or indirectly acquire substantially all of the properties held directly or indirectly by the corporation, and was the ownership percentage (by vote or value) for purposes of section 7874 greater than 50% (for example, the shareholders held more than 50% of the stock of the foreign corporation)? If "Yes," list the ownership percentage by vote and by value. See instructions		
	Percentage: By Vote _____ By Value _____		
27	At any time during this tax year, did the corporation (a) receive a digital asset (as a reward, award, or payment for property or services); or (b) sell, exchange, or otherwise dispose of a digital asset (or a financial interest in a digital asset)? See instructions .		
28	Is the corporation a member of a controlled group?		
	If "Yes," attach Schedule O (Form 1120). See instructions.		
29	Corporate Alternative Minimum Tax:		
a	Was the corporation an applicable corporation under section 59(k)(1) in any prior tax year?		
	If "Yes," go to question 29b. If "No," skip to question 29c.		
b	Is the corporation an applicable corporation under section 59(k)(1) in the current tax year because the corporation was an applicable corporation in the prior tax year?		
	If "Yes," complete and attach Form 4626. If "No," continue to question 29c.		
c	Does the corporation meet the requirements of the safe harbor method as provided under section 59(k)(3)(A) for the current tax year? See instructions		
	If "No," complete and attach Form 4626. If "Yes," the corporation is not required to file Form 4626.		
30	Is the corporation required to file Form 7208 relating to the excise tax on repurchase of corporate stock (see instructions):		
a	Under the rules for stock repurchased by a covered corporation (or stock acquired by its specified affiliate)?		
b	Under the applicable foreign corporation rules?		
c	Under the covered surrogate foreign corporation rules?		
	If "Yes" to either 30a, 30b, or 30c, complete Form 7208, Excise Tax on Repurchase of Corporate Stock. See the Instructions for Form 7208.		
31	Is this a consolidated return with gross receipts or sales of $1 billion or more and a subchapter K basis adjustment, as described in the instructions, of $10 million or more?		
	If "Yes," attach a statement. See instructions.		

Form **1120** (2024)

11-18 Chapter 11 • The Corporate Income Tax

Form 1120 (2024) Page **6**

Schedule L	Balance Sheets per Books	Beginning of tax year		End of tax year	
	Assets	(a)	(b)	(c)	(d)
1	Cash				
2a	Trade notes and accounts receivable				
b	Less allowance for bad debts	(	)	(	)
3	Inventories				
4	U.S. government obligations				
5	Tax-exempt securities (see instructions)				
6	Other current assets (attach statement)				
7	Loans to shareholders				
8	Mortgage and real estate loans				
9	Other investments (attach statement)				
10a	Buildings and other depreciable assets				
b	Less accumulated depreciation	(	)	(	)
11a	Depletable assets				
b	Less accumulated depletion	(	)	(	)
12	Land (net of any amortization)				
13a	Intangible assets (amortization only)				
b	Less accumulated amortization	(	)	(	)
14	Other assets (attach statement)				
15	Total assets				
	Liabilities and Shareholders' Equity				
16	Accounts payable				
17	Mortgages, notes, bonds payable in less than 1 year				
18	Other current liabilities (attach statement)				
19	Loans from shareholders				
20	Mortgages, notes, bonds payable in 1 year or more				
21	Other liabilities (attach statement)				
22	Capital stock: a Preferred stock				
	b Common stock				
23	Additional paid-in capital				
24	Retained earnings—Appropriated (attach statement)				
25	Retained earnings—Unappropriated				
26	Adjustments to shareholders' equity (attach statement)				
27	Less cost of treasury stock		(	)	(	)
28	Total liabilities and shareholders' equity				

Schedule M-1	Reconciliation of Income (Loss) per Books With Income per Return
	Note: The corporation may be required to file Schedule M-3. See instructions.

1	Net income (loss) per books		7	Income recorded on books this year not included on this return (itemize):	
2	Federal income tax per books			Tax-exempt interest $ _____	
3	Excess of capital losses over capital gains			_____	
4	Income subject to tax not recorded on books this year (itemize): _____		8	Deductions on this return not charged against book income this year (itemize):	
	_____		a	Depreciation . . $ _____	
5	Expenses recorded on books this year not deducted on this return (itemize):		b	Charitable contributions $ _____	
a	Depreciation $ _____			_____	
b	Charitable contributions $ _____				
c	Travel and entertainment $ _____		9	Add lines 7 and 8	
	_____				
6	Add lines 1 through 5		10	Income (page 1, line 28)—line 6 less line 9	

Schedule M-2	Analysis of Unappropriated Retained Earnings per Books (Schedule L, Line 25)

1	Balance at beginning of year		5	Distributions: a Cash	
2	Net income (loss) per books			b Stock	
3	Other increases (itemize): _____			c Property	
	_____		6	Other decreases (itemize): _____	
			7	Add lines 5 and 6	
4	Add lines 1, 2, and 3		8	Balance at end of year (line 4 less line 7)	

Form **1120** (2024)

Source: Internal Revenue Service (IRS)

11-6 S Corporations

Qualified corporations may elect to be taxed under Subchapter S of the Internal Revenue Code in a manner similar to partnerships. An S corporation does not generally pay tax and each shareholder reports its share of corporate income on their individual tax return. The S corporation election is designed to relieve corporations of certain corporate tax disadvantages, such as the double taxation of income.

To elect S corporation status, a corporation must have the following characteristics:

1. The corporation must be a domestic corporation;
2. The corporation must have 100 or fewer shareholders who are either individuals, estates, certain trusts, certain financial institutions, or certain exempt organizations;
3. The corporation must have only one class of stock; and
4. All shareholders must be U.S. citizens or resident aliens.
5. Not be an ineligible corporation (i.e., certain financial institutions, insurance companies, and domestic international sales corporations).

The S corporation election must be made during the prior year or the first two months and 15 days of the current tax year to obtain the status for the current year. Relief provisions may apply for elections that are filed late.

> **11.6 Learning Objective**
> Explain how an S corporation operates and is taxed.

Example Laurel Corporation is a calendar-year corporation that makes an S corporation election on November 2, 2024. The corporation does not qualify for any of the relief provisions for late S corporation elections for the 2024 tax year. The corporation is not an S corporation until the 2025 tax year; it is a regular C corporation for 2024. ♦

After electing S corporation status, the corporation retains the status until the election is voluntarily revoked or statutorily terminated. If the corporation ceases to qualify as an S corporation (e.g., it has 102 shareholders during the year), the election is statutorily terminated. Also, the election is terminated when a corporation receives 25 percent or more of its gross income from passive investments for three consecutive tax years and the corporation has accumulated earnings and profits at the end of each of those years. If a corporation experiences an involuntary termination of S corporation status, the election is terminated on the day the status changes. For example, the loss of S corporation status on June 1 causes the corporation to be a regular C corporation from that day on.

Upon consent of shareholders owning a majority of the voting stock, an S corporation election can be voluntarily revoked. If the consent to revoke the election is made during the first two months and 15 days of the tax year, the S corporation status will be considered voluntarily terminated effective at the beginning of that year. Shareholders may specify a date on or after the date of the revocation as the effective date for the voluntary termination of the S corporation election. If a prospective revocation date is not specified, and the consent to revoke the election is made after two months and 15 days of the tax year, the earliest that the S corporation status can be terminated is the first day of the following tax year.

Example On January 20, 2024, Juniper Corporation, a calendar-year corporation, files a consent to revoke its S corporation election. No date is specified in the consent as the effective date of the revocation. The corporation is no longer an S corporation effective January 1, 2024. If the election was made after March 15, the corporation would not become a regular C corporation until the 2025 tax year. ♦

11-6a Reporting Income

An S corporation is required to report its income and other items on Form 1120-S, U.S. Income Tax Return for an S Corporation, even though the corporate entity does not pay federal income tax. The tax return is due on the fifteenth day of the third month following the close of the corporation's tax year. S corporations may request a six-month extension for filing its tax return. Each shareholder of an S corporation reports their share of corporate income based on their stock ownership during the year. The taxable income of an S corporation is computed in the same manner as a partnership.

Each shareholder of an S corporation takes into account separately their share of items of income, deductions, and credits on a per share per day basis. Schedule K-1 of Form 1120-S is used to report the allocation of ordinary income or loss, plus all separately stated items of income or loss, to each of the shareholders. Each shareholder's share of these items is included in the shareholder's computation of taxable income for the tax year during which the corporation's year ends. In the case of the death of a shareholder, the shareholder's portion of S corporation items will be taken into account on the shareholder's final tax return.

Example Freda is the sole shareholder of the Freda Corporation, which has an S corporation election in effect. During calendar year 2024, the corporation has ordinary taxable income of $100,000. Freda must report $100,000 on her individual income tax return for 2024 as income from the Freda Corporation. ♦

If an S corporation shareholder disposes of their entire interest in the S corporation, then the S corporation can make a specific accounting election to allocate income or loss based on actual transactions.

Example Pinto Corporation, an S corporation, has two 50-percent shareholders, Jamal and Salim. During the first 6 months of the year, Pinto generates losses of $50,000 and at the end of the first six months, Jamal sells his half of the corporation to Latika. Latika injects capital into Pinto and the corporation generates income of $40,000 in the second half of the year. If income/(loss) were allocated pro rata based on the full year's loss of $10,000:

Shareholder	First half	Second half	Total Year
Jamal	$ (2,500)	$ -	$ (2,500)
Salim	(2,500)	(2,500)	(5,000)
Latika		(2,500)	(2,500)
Total	$ (5,000)	$ (5,000)	$ (10,000)

If a special election is made, the allocation will reflect actual results for each 6-month period:

Shareholder	First half	Second half	Total Year
Jamal	$ (25,000)	$ -	$ (25,000)
Salim	(25,000)	20,000	(5,000)
Latika	-	20,000	20,000
Total	$ (50,000)	$ 40,000	$ (10,000)

♦

11-6b S Corporation Losses

Losses from an S corporation also pass through to the shareholders. However, the amount of loss from an S corporation that a shareholder may report is limited to their adjusted basis in the corporation's stock plus the amount of any loans from the shareholder to the corporation. Any loss in excess of the shareholder's basis in the stock of the corporation plus loans is disallowed and becomes a carryforward loss. If a shareholder was not a shareholder for the entire tax year, losses must be allocated to the shareholder on a daily basis (the seller gets credit for the date of sale). This prevents a shareholder from selling losses late in the year to another taxpayer by selling the stock of an S corporation.

Example Lawson and Mary are equal shareholders in L&M Corporation, an S corporation. On December 1, 2024, Mary sells her interest to Connley for $15,000. Lawson's basis in his L&M Corporation stock is $10,000. For the 2024 tax year, the corporation has a loss of $24,000. Lawson can deduct only $10,000 of his half of the loss ($12,000), since that is the amount of his stock basis. Even though she is not a shareholder at year-end, Mary may deduct $11,014 of the loss, which is 335/365 of $12,000, assuming her basis was at least that amount. Connley may deduct $986, 30/365 of $12,000. In leap years, the amounts would be $11,016 (336/366 × $12,000) and $984 (30/366 × $12,000) for Mary and Connley, respectively. ♦

11-6c Pass-Through Items

Certain items pass through from an S corporation to the shareholders and retain their tax attributes on the shareholders' tax returns. The following are examples of pass-through items that are separately stated on the shareholders' Schedule K-1:

- Capital gains and losses
- Section 1231 gains and losses
- Dividend income
- Charitable contributions
- Tax-exempt interest
- Net rental income
- Section 179 deduction
- Collectibles (28 percent) gains and losses
- Most credits

Unlike partnerships, S corporations do not have guaranteed payments to owners. If an S corporation shareholder provides services to the S corporation, a reasonable wage must be paid and reported on a Form W-2, like any other employee. The S corporation deducts reasonable wages from taxable income.

11-6d Qualified Business Income Deduction

Similar to partnerships, S corporations are flow-through entities that may generate qualified business income (QBI) and individual shareholders may be eligible for the QBI deduction. The same wage and service business limits apply as with other flow-through entities.

S corporations have a unique interaction between wages and qualified business income. The wages paid to an S corporation shareholder are not considered part of qualified business income; however, the wages count toward the wage limit, to the extent one applies to the taxpayer:

Example Hogarth is a single taxpayer and the sole shareholder of Giant Corporation, which is an S corporation for tax purposes. Giant pays reasonable wages to Hogarth, the only employee, of $80,000 and allocates $100,000 of income. Hogarth's total taxable income (including his S corporation wages and allocation of income) is above the threshold for a single taxpayer and he is required to apply the wage limitation to his QBI deduction. Hogarth can include $40,000 ($80,000 × 50%) of wages in computing the wage limit for the QBI deduction but may not consider the $80,000 of wages in the calculation of QBI, only the $100,000 of income allocated. ♦

11-6e Special Taxes

S corporations are not subject to the corporate income tax on their regular taxable income. Under certain circumstances, an S corporation may be liable for tax at the corporate level. An S corporation may be subject to a tax on gains attributable to appreciation in the value of assets held by the corporation prior to the S corporation election, the built-in gains tax. In addition, a tax may be imposed on certain S corporations that have large amounts of passive investment income, such as income from dividends and interest. The rules for the application of these taxes are complex and beyond the scope of this textbook.

Self-Study Problem 11.6 — Refer to Appendix E for Solutions to Self-Study Problems

Assume that Aspen Corporation in Self-Study Problem 11.5 is owned by Ava Mendes, who owns all 100 shares outstanding. Ava lives at 1175 Delaware St., Denver, CO 80204 and her Social Security number is 411-41-4141. Also, assume that the corporation has a valid S corporation election in effect for 2024 and is not subject to any special taxes. Assume no wages are included in Aspen's cost of goods sold. Using the relevant information given in Self-Study Problem 11.5 and assuming the corporation's retained earnings are $19,000, instead of $16,060, accounts payable are $24,000, rather than $26,940, and no estimated tax payments are made, complete Form 1120-S on Pages 11-23 to 11-27 for Aspen Corporation, and complete Schedule K-1 and Statement A (QBI) on Pages 11-28 and 11-29 for Ava. Assume there were no cash distributions to Ava during the year.

11-7 Corporate Formation

Learning Objective 11.7
Describe the basic tax rules for the formation of a corporation.

When a taxpayer incorporates a business and transfers high-value, low-basis property to the corporation in exchange for corporate stock, a substantial gain is realized. This gain is measured at the value of the shares received less the basis of the property transferred. Favorable tax treatment is available in certain cases, which allows many taxpayers to defer the recognition of the realized gain in the year of formation. To defer the gain, the taxpayer must meet certain requirements, including:

1. The taxpayer must transfer property or money to the corporation,
2. The transfer must be solely in exchange for stock of the corporation, and
3. The shareholder(s) qualifying for nonrecognition must own at least 80 percent of the corporation's stock after the transfer.

When the above requirements are met, gains and losses are not recognized on the formation of the corporation.

Example Elaine Muskie forms Nikola Corporation by transferring $10,000 cash, equipment valued at $40,000 and a basis of $12,000, and land worth $20,000 with a basis of $1,000 in exchange for all 100 shares of Nikola stock outstanding. Because Elaine meets the requirements to defer the gain, she is not required to recognize the realized gain of $28,000 on the equipment and $19,000 on the land. ♦

The shareholder must transfer property or cash to the corporation; performing services for corporate stock does not qualify for nonrecognition treatment. The shareholder performing services must recognize income in an amount equal to the value of the stock received. If the shareholder receives other property (boot) in addition to stock of the corporation in exchange for the transfer of cash or other property, the transaction may still qualify for partial nonrecognition treatment, provided the control requirement is met. However, realized gain must be recognized to the extent of the boot received.

Example Geoff Basil and Jackson Dorsal form Amazitter Corporation. Geoff contributes cash of $60,000 and Jackson contributes a building valued at $70,000 (his basis is $30,000). Geoff and Jackson both receive 50 shares in the exchange and Jackson also receives cash of $10,000. Because Jackson receives $10,000 boot, he must recognize $10,000 of his $40,000 gain realized. Geoff will not recognize any gain. ♦

Self-Study Problem 11.6

Form 1120-S
Department of the Treasury
Internal Revenue Service

U.S. Income Tax Return for an S Corporation
Do not file this form unless the corporation has filed or is attaching Form 2553 to elect to be an S corporation.
Go to www.irs.gov/Form1120S for instructions and the latest information.

OMB No. 1545-0123

2024

For calendar year 2024 or tax year beginning _____, 2024, ending _____, 20___

A S election effective date	**Name** (TYPE OR PRINT)	**D** Employer identification number
B Business activity code number (see instructions)	Number, street, and room or suite no. If a P.O. box, see instructions.	**E** Date incorporated
	City or town, state or province, country, and ZIP or foreign postal code	**F** Total assets (see instructions) $
C Check if Sch. M-3 attached ☐		

G Is the corporation electing to be an S corporation beginning with this tax year? See instructions. ☐ Yes ☐ No
H Check if: **(1)** ☐ Final return **(2)** ☐ Name change **(3)** ☐ Address change **(4)** ☐ Amended return **(5)** ☐ S election termination
I Enter the number of shareholders who were shareholders during any part of the tax year
J Check if corporation: **(1)** ☐ Aggregated activities for section 465 at-risk purposes **(2)** ☐ Grouped activities for section 469 passive activity purposes

Caution: Include **only** trade or business income and expenses on lines 1a through 22. See the instructions for more information.

Income

1a	Gross receipts or sales		
b	Less returns and allowances		
c	Balance	1c	
2	Cost of goods sold (attach Form 1125-A)	2	
3	Gross profit. Subtract line 2 from line 1c	3	
4	Net gain (loss) from Form 4797, Part II, line 17 (attach Form 4797)	4	
5	Other income (loss) (see instructions—attach statement)	5	
6	**Total income (loss).** Add lines 3 through 5	6	

Deductions (see instructions for limitations)

7	Compensation of officers (see instructions—attach Form 1125-E)	7	
8	Salaries and wages (less employment credits)	8	
9	Repairs and maintenance	9	
10	Bad debts	10	
11	Rents	11	
12	Taxes and licenses	12	
13	Interest (see instructions)	13	
14	Depreciation from Form 4562 not claimed on Form 1125-A or elsewhere on return (attach Form 4562)	14	
15	Depletion **(do not deduct oil and gas depletion)**	15	
16	Advertising	16	
17	Pension, profit-sharing, etc., plans	17	
18	Employee benefit programs	18	
19	Energy efficient commercial buildings deduction (attach Form 7205)	19	
20	Other deductions (attach statement)	20	
21	**Total deductions.** Add lines 7 through 20	21	
22	**Ordinary business income (loss).** Subtract line 21 from line 6	22	

Tax and Payments

23a	Excess net passive income or LIFO recapture tax (see instructions) . . .	23a		
b	Tax from Schedule D (Form 1120-S)	23b		
c	Add lines 23a and 23b (see instructions for additional taxes)		23c	
24a	Current year's estimated tax payments and preceding year's overpayment credited to the current year	24a		
b	Tax deposited with Form 7004	24b		
c	Credit for federal tax paid on fuels (attach Form 4136)	24c		
d	Elective payment election amount from Form 3800	24d		
z	Add lines 24a through 24d		24z	
25	Estimated tax penalty (see instructions). Check if Form 2220 is attached . . . ☐		25	
26	**Amount owed.** If line 24z is smaller than the total of lines 23c and 25, enter amount owed . . .		26	
27	**Overpayment.** If line 24z is larger than the total of lines 23c and 25, enter amount overpaid . . .		27	
28	Enter amount from line 27: **Credited to 2025 estimated tax** _____ **Refunded**		28	

Sign Here
Under penalties of perjury, I declare that I have examined this return, including accompanying schedules and statements, and to the best of my knowledge and belief, it is true, correct, and complete. Declaration of preparer (other than taxpayer) is based on all information of which preparer has any knowledge.

Signature of officer _____ Date _____ Title _____

May the IRS discuss this return with the preparer shown below? See instructions. ☐ Yes ☐ No

Paid Preparer Use Only

Print/Type preparer's name	Preparer's signature	Date	Check ☐ if self-employed	PTIN
Firm's name			Firm's EIN	
Firm's address			Phone no.	

For Paperwork Reduction Act Notice, see separate instructions. Cat. No. 11510H Form **1120-S** (2024)

Form 1120-S (2024) Page **2**

Schedule B	Other Information (see instructions)	Yes	No

1. Check accounting method: **a** ☐ Cash **b** ☐ Accrual
   c ☐ Other (specify) _____

2. See the instructions and enter the:
   a Business activity _____ **b** Product or service _____

3. At any time during the tax year, was any shareholder of the corporation a disregarded entity, a trust, an estate, or a nominee or similar person? If "Yes," attach Schedule B-1, Information on Certain Shareholders of an S Corporation .

4. At the end of the tax year, did the corporation:
   a Own directly 20% or more, or own, directly or indirectly, 50% or more of the total stock issued and outstanding of any foreign or domestic corporation? For rules of constructive ownership, see instructions. If "Yes," complete (i) through (v) below . . . .

(i) Name of Corporation	(ii) Employer Identification Number (if any)	(iii) Country of Incorporation	(iv) Percentage of Stock Owned	(v) If Percentage in (iv) Is 100%, Enter the Date (if applicable) a Qualified Subchapter S Subsidiary Election Was Made

   b Own directly an interest of 20% or more, or own, directly or indirectly, an interest of 50% or more in the profit, loss, or capital in any foreign or domestic partnership (including an entity treated as a partnership) or in the beneficial interest of a trust? For rules of constructive ownership, see instructions. If "Yes," complete (i) through (v) below . . . . .

(i) Name of Entity	(ii) Employer Identification Number (if any)	(iii) Type of Entity	(iv) Country of Organization	(v) Maximum Percentage Owned in Profit, Loss, or Capital

5a. At the end of the tax year, did the corporation have any outstanding shares of restricted stock? . . . .
   If "Yes," complete lines (i) and (ii) below.
   (i) Total shares of restricted stock . . . . _____
   (ii) Total shares of non-restricted stock . . . . _____

   b At the end of the tax year, did the corporation have any outstanding stock options, warrants, or similar instruments? .
   If "Yes," complete lines (i) and (ii) below.
   (i) Total shares of stock outstanding at the end of the tax year . . _____
   (ii) Total shares of stock outstanding if all instruments were executed _____

6. Has this corporation filed, or is it required to file, **Form 8918**, Material Advisor Disclosure Statement, to provide information on any reportable transaction? . . . .

7. Check this box if the corporation issued publicly offered debt instruments with original issue discount . . . . . ☐
   If checked, the corporation may have to file **Form 8281**, Information Return for Publicly Offered Original Issue Discount Instruments.

8. If the corporation (**a**) was a C corporation before it elected to be an S corporation **or** the corporation acquired an asset with a basis determined by reference to the basis of the asset (or the basis of any other property) in the hands of a C corporation, **and** (**b**) has net unrealized built-in gain in excess of the net recognized built-in gain from prior years, enter the net unrealized built-in gain reduced by net recognized built-in gain from prior years. See instructions . . . . . . $ _____

9. Did the corporation have an election under section 163(j) for any real property trade or business or any farming business in effect during the tax year? See instructions . . . .

10. Does the corporation satisfy one or more of the following? See instructions . . . .
    a The corporation owns a pass-through entity with current, or prior year carryover, excess business interest expense.
    b The corporation's aggregate average annual gross receipts (determined under section 448(c)) for the 3 tax years preceding the current tax year are more than $30 million and the corporation has business interest expense.
    c The corporation is a tax shelter and the corporation has business interest expense.
    If "Yes," complete and attach **Form 8990**, Limitation on Business Interest Expense Under Section 163(j).

11. Does the corporation satisfy **both** of the following conditions? . . . .
    a The corporation's total receipts (see instructions) for the tax year were less than $250,000.
    b The corporation's total assets at the end of the tax year were less than $250,000.
    If "Yes," the corporation is not required to complete Schedules L and M-1.

Form **1120-S** (2024)

Form 1120-S (2024) Page 3

Schedule B	Other Information (see instructions) (continued)	Yes	No
12	During the tax year, did the corporation have any non-shareholder debt that was canceled, was forgiven, or had the terms modified so as to reduce the principal amount of the debt?		
	If "Yes," enter the amount of principal reduction . . . . $		
13	During the tax year, was a qualified subchapter S subsidiary election terminated or revoked? If "Yes," see instructions		
14a	Did the corporation make any payments that would require it to file Form(s) 1099?		
b	If "Yes," did or will the corporation file required Form(s) 1099?		
15	Is the corporation attaching Form 8996 to certify as a Qualified Opportunity Fund?		
	If "Yes," enter the amount from Form 8996, line 15 . . . . $		
16	At any time during the tax year, did the corporation: (a) receive (as a reward, award, or payment for property or services); or (b) sell, exchange, or otherwise dispose of a digital asset (or a financial interest in a digital asset)? See instructions		

Schedule K		Shareholders' Pro Rata Share Items		Total amount
Income (Loss)	1	Ordinary business income (loss) (page 1, line 22)	1	
	2	Net rental real estate income (loss) (attach Form 8825)	2	
	3a	Other gross rental income (loss) . . . 3a		
	b	Expenses from other rental activities (attach statement) 3b		
	c	Other net rental income (loss). Subtract line 3b from line 3a	3c	
	4	Interest income	4	
	5	Dividends: a Ordinary dividends	5a	
		b Qualified dividends . . . 5b		
	6	Royalties	6	
	7	Net short-term capital gain (loss) (attach Schedule D (Form 1120-S))	7	
	8a	Net long-term capital gain (loss) (attach Schedule D (Form 1120-S))	8a	
	b	Collectibles (28%) gain (loss) . . . 8b		
	c	Unrecaptured section 1250 gain (attach statement) 8c		
	9	Net section 1231 gain (loss) (attach Form 4797)	9	
	10	Other income (loss) (see instructions) . . . Type:	10	
Deductions	11	Section 179 deduction (attach Form 4562)	11	
	12a	Cash charitable contributions	12a	
	b	Noncash charitable contributions	12b	
	c	Investment interest expense	12c	
	d	Section 59(e)(2) expenditures . . . Type:	12d	
	e	Other deductions (see instructions) . . . Type:	12e	
Credits	13a	Low-income housing credit (section 42(j)(5))	13a	
	b	Low-income housing credit (other)	13b	
	c	Qualified rehabilitation expenditures (rental real estate) (attach Form 3468, if applicable)	13c	
	d	Other rental real estate credits (see instructions) Type:	13d	
	e	Other rental credits (see instructions) . . . Type:	13e	
	f	Biofuel producer credit (attach Form 6478)	13f	
	g	Other credits (see instructions) . . . Type:	13g	
International	14	Attach Schedule K-2 (Form 1120-S), Shareholders' Pro Rata Share Items—International, and check this box to indicate you are reporting items of international tax relevance . . . ☐		
Alternative Minimum Tax (AMT) Items	15a	Post-1986 depreciation adjustment	15a	
	b	Adjusted gain or loss	15b	
	c	Depletion (other than oil and gas)	15c	
	d	Oil, gas, and geothermal properties—gross income	15d	
	e	Oil, gas, and geothermal properties—deductions	15e	
	f	Other AMT items (attach statement)	15f	
Items Affecting Shareholder Basis	16a	Tax-exempt interest income	16a	
	b	Other tax-exempt income	16b	
	c	Nondeductible expenses	16c	
	d	Distributions (attach statement if required) (see instructions)	16d	
	e	Repayment of loans from shareholders	16e	
	f	Foreign taxes paid or accrued	16f	

Form **1120-S** (2024)

Form 1120-S (2024) Page **4**

Schedule K	Shareholders' Pro Rata Share Items *(continued)*		Total amount
Other Information	17a	Investment income	17a
	b	Investment expenses	17b
	c	Dividend distributions paid from accumulated earnings and profits	17c
	d	Other items and amounts (attach statement)	
Reconciliation	18	**Income (loss) reconciliation.** Combine the total amounts on lines 1 through 10. From the result, subtract the sum of the amounts on lines 11 through 12e and 16f	18

Schedule L	Balance Sheets per Books	Beginning of tax year		End of tax year	
	Assets	(a)	(b)	(c)	(d)
1	Cash				
2a	Trade notes and accounts receivable				
b	Less allowance for bad debts	( )		( )	
3	Inventories				
4	U.S. government obligations				
5	Tax-exempt securities (see instructions)				
6	Other current assets (attach statement)				
7	Loans to shareholders				
8	Mortgage and real estate loans				
9	Other investments (attach statement)				
10a	Buildings and other depreciable assets				
b	Less accumulated depreciation	( )		( )	
11a	Depletable assets				
b	Less accumulated depletion	( )		( )	
12	Land (net of any amortization)				
13a	Intangible assets (amortizable only)				
b	Less accumulated amortization	( )		( )	
14	Other assets (attach statement)				
15	Total assets				
	Liabilities and Shareholders' Equity				
16	Accounts payable				
17	Mortgages, notes, bonds payable in less than 1 year				
18	Other current liabilities (attach statement)				
19	Loans from shareholders				
20	Mortgages, notes, bonds payable in 1 year or more				
21	Other liabilities (attach statement)				
22	Capital stock				
23	Additional paid-in capital				
24	Retained earnings				
25	Adjustments to shareholders' equity (attach statement)				
26	Less cost of treasury stock		( )		( )
27	Total liabilities and shareholders' equity				

Form **1120-S** (2024)

Form 1120-S (2024) Page **5**

Schedule M-1	Reconciliation of Income (Loss) per Books With Income (Loss) per Return

Note: The corporation may be required to file Schedule M-3. See instructions.

1	Net income (loss) per books		5	Income recorded on books this year not included on Schedule K, lines 1 through 10 (itemize):	
2	Income included on Schedule K, lines 1, 2, 3c, 4, 5a, 6, 7, 8a, 9, and 10, not recorded on books this year (itemize): _____ _____		a	Tax-exempt interest $ _____ _____	
3	Expenses recorded on books this year not included on Schedule K, lines 1 through 12e, and 16f (itemize):		6	Deductions included on Schedule K, lines 1 through 12e, and 16f, not charged against book income this year (itemize):	
a	Depreciation $ _____		a	Depreciation $ _____	
b	Travel and entertainment $ _____		7	Add lines 5 and 6	
			8	Income (loss) (Schedule K, line 18). Subtract line 7 from line 4 . . .	
4	Add lines 1 through 3				

Schedule M-2	Analysis of Accumulated Adjustments Account, Shareholders' Undistributed Taxable Income Previously Taxed, Accumulated Earnings and Profits, and Other Adjustments Account (see instructions)

		(a) Accumulated adjustments account	(b) Shareholders' undistributed taxable income previously taxed	(c) Accumulated earnings and profits	(d) Other adjustments account
1	Balance at beginning of tax year				
2	Ordinary income from page 1, line 22 . . .				
3	Other additions				
4	Loss from page 1, line 22	( )			
5	Other reductions	( )			( )
6	Combine lines 1 through 5				
7	Distributions				
8	Balance at end of tax year. Subtract line 7 from line 6				

Form **1120-S** (2024)

Source: Internal Revenue Service (IRS)

Self-Study Problem 11.6

Schedule K-1 (Form 1120-S) 2024

Department of the Treasury
Internal Revenue Service

For calendar year 2024, or tax year beginning ___/___/2024 ending ___/___/___

Shareholder's Share of Income, Deductions, Credits, etc. See separate instructions.

☐ Final K-1 ☐ Amended K-1 OMB No. 1545-0123
671124

Part I — Information About the Corporation

- **A** Corporation's employer identification number
- **B** Corporation's name, address, city, state, and ZIP code
- **C** IRS Center where corporation filed return
- **D** Corporation's total number of shares
  - Beginning of tax year
  - End of tax year

Part II — Information About the Shareholder

- **E** Shareholder's identifying number
- **F1** Shareholder's name, address, city, state, and ZIP code
- **F2** If the shareholder is a disregarded entity, a trust, an estate, or a nominee or similar person, enter the individual or entity responsible for reporting:
  - TIN _____ Name _____
- **F3** What type of entity is this shareholder?
- **G** Current year allocation percentage _____ %
- **H** Shareholder's number of shares
  - Beginning of tax year
  - End of tax year
- **I** Loans from shareholder
  - Beginning of tax year $ _____
  - End of tax year $ _____

Part III — Shareholder's Share of Current Year Income, Deductions, Credits, and Other Items

1	Ordinary business income (loss)	13	Credits
2	Net rental real estate income (loss)		
3	Other net rental income (loss)		
4	Interest income		
5a	Ordinary dividends		
5b	Qualified dividends	14	Schedule K-3 is attached if checked ☐
6	Royalties	15	Alternative minimum tax (AMT) items
7	Net short-term capital gain (loss)		
8a	Net long-term capital gain (loss)		
8b	Collectibles (28%) gain (loss)		
8c	Unrecaptured section 1250 gain		
9	Net section 1231 gain (loss)	16	Items affecting shareholder basis
10	Other income (loss)		
		17	Other information
11	Section 179 deduction		
12	Other deductions		

18 ☐ More than one activity for at-risk purposes*
19 ☐ More than one activity for passive activity purposes*

* See attached statement for additional information.

For Paperwork Reduction Act Notice, see the Instructions for Form 1120-S. www.irs.gov/Form1120S Cat. No. 11520D Schedule K-1 (Form 1120-S) 2024

Source: Internal Revenue Service (IRS)

Self-Study Problem 11.6

Statement A—QBI Pass-Through Entity Reporting

S corporation's name:			S corporation's EIN:	
Shareholder's name:			Shareholder's identifying number:	

Shareholder's share of:		Trade or Business 1	Trade or Business 2	Trade or Business 3
		☐ PTP ☐ Aggregated ☐ SSTB	☐ PTP ☐ Aggregated ☐ SSTB	☐ PTP ☐ Aggregated ☐ SSTB
QBI or qualified PTP items subject to shareholder-specific determinations:				
	Ordinary business income (loss)			
	Rental income (loss)			
	Royalty income (loss)			
	Section 1231 gain (loss)			
	Other income (loss)			
	Section 179 deduction			
	Other deductions			
W-2 wages				
UBIA of qualified property				
Section 199A dividends				

Note: The 2024 Statement A was not available when we went to print. This is a 2023 version of Statement A.

11-7a Liabilities

As a general rule, the assumption of shareholder liabilities by the corporation is not considered boot. For example, if a shareholder transfers land to the corporation for stock and the land is subject to a liability that is assumed by the corporation, no gain would normally be recognized on the transfer. However, if there is no business purpose for transfer of the liability, or tax avoidance appears to be involved, the recognition of any realized gain is required. Also, when the total liabilities transferred to the corporation by a shareholder exceed the total basis of the property transferred by the shareholder, the excess amount is a gain that must be recognized without regard to whether gain is realized.

Example Robusta Corporation is formed by Max, who contributes property with a basis of $12,000 in exchange for 100 percent of the company's stock. On the date of the contribution, the property contributed has a fair market value of $120,000 and is subject to a liability of $20,000. Max must recognize a gain of $8,000 on the transfer of the property to the corporation since the liability transferred to the corporation exceeds his basis in the property transferred. ♦

11-7b Shareholder's Stock Basis

After the transfer, the shareholder's basis in their stock is the basis of the property transferred less any boot received plus any gain recognized on the transfer less any liabilities assumed.

Example Assuming the same facts in the previous example, Max's stock basis is calculated as follows:

Basis of the property transferred	$ 12,000
Less: boot received	0
Plus: gain recognized	8,000
Less: liabilities transferred	(20,000)
Basis in the stock	$ 0

♦

Tax Break

Two special provisions can apply to taxpayers who are the original owners of small business stocks and sell shares. Section 1202 allows shareholders that sell qualifying stock at a gain to exclude 100 percent of the gain (subject to limitations). Section 1244 allows the loss on qualifying small business stock to be characterized as an ordinary loss up to $50,000 ($100,000, if married filing jointly) and avoid capital loss limitations. Refer to IRS Publication 550 for more information on requirements and restrictions.

11-7c Corporation's Basis in Property Contributed

The corporation's basis in the property received from a shareholder in a transaction to which nonrecognition treatment applies is the same as the basis of the property to the shareholder, increased by any gain recognized by the shareholder on the transfer.

Example A, B, and C form Hornbeam Corporation. A contributes property with a basis of $25,000 in exchange for 40 shares of stock worth $40,000. B performs services for the corporation in exchange for 10 shares of stock worth $10,000. C contributes property with a basis of $10,000 in exchange for 45 shares of stock worth $45,000 and $5,000 cash. The stock described above is all of the outstanding stock of the corporation. A and C qualify for complete or partial nonrecognition treatment, since together they own 89 percent (85 of 95 shares) of the stock after the transfer. B's stock is not considered because it was received in exchange for services.

1. A has a realized gain of $15,000 ($40,000 − $25,000), but no recognized gain since no boot was received.
2. B's recognized income is $10,000, since she performed services in exchange for the stock, and stock received for services does not fall within the nonrecognition provisions.
3. C's realized gain is $40,000 ($45,000 + $5,000 − $10,000), but only $5,000 of the gain is recognized, the amount of boot received.
4. A's basis in the stock is $25,000 ($25,000 − $0 + $0 − $0), B's basis in the stock is $10,000 ($0 − $0 + $10,000 − $0), and C's basis in the stock is $10,000 ($10,000 − $5,000 + $5,000 − $0).
5. Hornbeam Corporation's basis in the property contributed by A is $25,000 ($25,000 + $0). The corporation's basis in the property contributed by C is $15,000 ($10,000 + $5,000 gain recognized). ♦

Self-Study Problem 11.7 Refer to Appendix E for Solutions to Self-Study Problems

Tammy has a business which they decide to incorporate. They transfer to the new corporation real estate with a basis of $75,000, subject to a $34,000 mortgage, in exchange for all of its stock. The stock is worth $125,000.

a. What is Tammy's realized gain?
b. What is Tammy's recognized gain?
c. What is Tammy's basis in their stock?
d. What is the corporation's basis in the real estate?

Learning Objective 11.8

Describe the rules for the accumulated earnings tax and the personal holding company tax.

11-8 Corporate Accumulations

In many cases, taxpayers have established corporations to avoid paying income taxes at the shareholder level by allowing earnings to be accumulated by the corporations, rather than paid out as taxable dividends. To prevent that practice, Congress has enacted two special taxes which may be applied to certain corporations: the accumulated earnings tax and the personal holding company tax.

11-8a Accumulated Earnings Tax

The accumulated earnings tax is designed to prevent the shareholders of a corporation from avoiding tax at the shareholder level by retaining earnings in the corporation. The tax is a penalty tax imposed in addition to the regular corporate income tax. The tax is imposed at a rate of 20 percent on amounts that are deemed to be unreasonable accumulations of earnings. For all corporations except service corporations, such as accounting, law, and health care corporations, the first $250,000 in accumulated earnings is exempt from tax. Service corporations will not be taxed on their first $150,000 of accumulated earnings. Even if the accumulated earnings of a corporation exceed the exemption amount, the tax will not be imposed on accumulations that can be demonstrated to be necessary to meet the reasonable needs of the business.

Example Alder Corporation is a manufacturing corporation that has accumulated earnings of $625,000. The corporation can establish reasonable needs for $450,000 of this accumulation. Alder Corporation would be subject to the accumulated earnings tax on $175,000 ($625,000 − $450,000). The amount of the accumulated earnings tax is $35,000 (20% of $175,000). ♦

11-8b Personal Holding Company Tax

Personal holding companies, which are corporations with few shareholders and with income primarily from investments, are subject to a 20-percent tax on their undistributed earnings. The tax is imposed in addition to the regular corporate income tax; however, a corporation cannot be subject to both the accumulated earnings tax and the personal holding company tax in the same year. If both taxes are imposed, the taxpayer pays only the personal holding company tax. The rules for the personal holding company tax are very complex and beyond the scope of this textbook.

Self-Study Problem 11.8 Refer to Appendix E for Solutions to Self-Study Problems

Sugarbush Corporation, an accounting corporation, has accumulated earnings of $340,000, and the corporation cannot establish a reasonable need for any of that amount. Calculate the amount of accumulated earnings tax (if any) that will be imposed on Sugarbush Corporation.

Key Terms

corporate alternative minimum tax (CAMT), 11-2
stock repurchase excise tax, 11-2
personal services corporation, 11-2
corporate capital gains/losses, 11-2
net operating losses (NOLs), 11-3

dividends received deduction (DRD), 11-4
organizational expenditures, 11-5
start-up costs, 11-5
corporate charitable contributions, 11-6

Form 1120, 11-7
book income, 11-7
Schedule M-1, 11-7
corporate estimated tax payments, 11-8
annualized income method, 11-9

Financial Crimes Enforcement Network (FinCEN), 11-10
beneficial ownership interest (BOI), 11-10
S corporation election, 11-19
Form 1120-S, 11-19
boot, 11-22
accumulated earnings tax, 11-32
personal holding company tax, 11-32

Key Points

Learning Objectives	Key Points
LO 11.1: Employ the corporate tax rates to calculate corporate tax liability.	• The U.S. corporate tax rate is a flat 21 percent regardless of income level. • Large corporations may also be subject to a corporate alternative minimum tax on adjusted financial statement income and a tax on the repurchase of corporate shares. • Qualified personal service corporations (health, law, engineering, architecture, accounting, actuarial science, performing arts, and consulting) are taxed at the same 21-percent tax rate on all taxable income.
LO 11.2: Compute basic gains and losses for corporations.	• Corporate ordinary income and capital gains tax rates are the same, so there is no tax rate benefit to having long-term capital gains in a corporation. • Net short-term capital gains of a corporation are taxed as ordinary income. • Capital losses may be used only to offset capital gains. • If capital losses cannot be used in the year they occur, they may be carried back three years and forward five years, to offset capital gains in those years. • When a long-term capital loss is carried to another year, it is treated as a short-term capital loss and may be offset against either long-term or short-term capital gains. • Net operating losses generated after 2017 can be carried forward indefinitely, but are limited to 80 percent of future income.
LO 11.3: Apply special corporate deductions to corporate taxable income.	• Corporations are allowed a dividends received deduction based on their percentage of ownership in the corporation paying the dividend. • The dividends received deduction percentage is 50 percent (for ownership less than 20 percent), 65 percent (for ownership of 20 percent or more, but less than 80 percent), or 100 percent (for ownership of 80 percent or more). • Corporations amortize qualifying organizational costs over 180 months, and there is no upper limit to the amount of qualifying costs that can be amortized. • Corporations can elect to deduct up to $5,000 of organizational costs and $5,000 of start-up costs in the year they begin business. The $5,000 amounts are reduced by each dollar of organizational expenses and start-up costs exceeding $50,000. • A corporation's charitable contribution deduction is limited to 10 percent of taxable income, computed before the deduction for charitable contributions, net operating loss carrybacks, capital loss carrybacks, and the dividends received deduction. • Excess charitable contributions are carried forward to the five succeeding tax years, subject to the 10-percent annual limitation in the carryover years, with the current year's contributions deducted first.
LO 11.4: Identify the components of Schedule M-1 and how they are reported to the IRS.	• The purpose of Schedule M-1 of the corporate tax return is to reconcile a corporation's accounting "book" income to its taxable income. • On the left side of Schedule M-1 are adjustments that must be added to book income, and on the right side of the schedule are adjustments that must be subtracted from book income to arrive at the amount of taxable income. • The additions to book income include the amount of federal income tax expense, net capital losses deducted for book purposes, income recorded on the tax return but not on the books, and expenses recorded on the books but not deducted on the tax return. • The amounts that must be deducted from book income include income recorded on the books but not included on the tax return, and deductions included on the return but not deducted on the books.

LO 11.5:
Describe the corporate tax return filing and estimated tax payment requirements.

- The due date for filing a corporate tax return is the fifteenth day of the fourth month after year-end (fifteenth day of the third month for June 30 year-ends). An extension provides an additional six months; thus a calendar year-end corporation has an initial deadline of April 15 and an extended deadline of October 15. Corporations with a June 30 year-end have a seven-month extended deadline from their initial deadline of September 15 to April 15.
- A corporation must pay any tax liability by the original due date of the return in order to avoid penalties.
- Corporations must make estimated tax payments similar to those made by self-employed individual taxpayers. The payments are due on the fifteenth day of the fourth, sixth, ninth, and twelfth months of the corporation's tax year.
- Most corporations are required to report beneficial ownership interests (BOI) to FinCEN.

LO 11.6:
Explain how an S corporation operates and is taxed.

- Certain qualified corporations may elect to be taxed under Subchapter S of the Internal Revenue Code in a manner similar to partnerships.
- To elect S corporation status, a corporation *must* have the following characteristics: (1) be a domestic corporation; (2) have 100 or fewer shareholders who are either individuals, estates, certain trusts, certain financial institutions, or certain exempt organizations; (3) have only one class of stock; (4) all shareholders must be U.S. citizens or resident aliens; and (5) not be an ineligible corporation.
- Each shareholder of an S corporation reports their share of corporate income based on their stock ownership during the year.
- Schedule K-1 of Form 1120-S is used to report the allocation of ordinary income or loss, and all separately stated items of income or loss, to each of the shareholders.
- Losses from an S corporation pass through to the shareholders, but the loss deduction is limited to the shareholders' adjusted basis in the corporation's stock plus the amount of any loans from the shareholder to the corporation.
- S corporation shareholders are eligible for the qualified business income deduction.

LO 11.7:
Describe the basic tax rules for the formation of a corporation.

- If property is exchanged for stock in a corporation, the shareholders own at least 80 percent (in "control") of the corporation after the transfer, and the shareholders receive no boot, gain on the transfer is not recognized.
- Realized gain is recognized to the extent that the shareholder receives boot.
- The basis of the stock received by the shareholder is equal to the basis of the property transferred plus any gain recognized by the shareholder, less the fair market value of any boot received by the shareholder, less liabilities assumed by the corporation.
- The basis of property received by the corporation is equal to the basis of the transferor plus any gain recognized by the transferor.

LO 11.8:
Describe the rules for the accumulated earnings tax and the personal holding company tax.

- The accumulated earnings tax is a penalty tax, imposed in addition to the regular corporate income tax, at a rate of 20 percent on amounts that are deemed to be unreasonable accumulations of earnings.
- For all corporations, except personal service corporations, the first $250,000 in accumulated earnings is exempt from tax. The first $150,000 in accumulated earnings is exempt for personal service corporations.
- Personal holding companies, which are corporations with few shareholders and income primarily from investments, are subject to a 20 percent tax on undistributed earnings.

Questions and Problems

Group 1:
Multiple Choice Questions

LO 11.1
1. Tayla Corporation generated $500,000 of taxable income in the current year. What is Tayla's corporate tax liability?
   a. $71,400
   b. $84,000
   c. $105,000
   d. $136,000
   e. None of the above

LO 11.1
2. Swifty Engineering Corp. is a personal service corporation and generated $400,000 of taxable income in the current year. Swifty's corporate tax liability is:
   a. $55,678.50 + [($400,000 − $243,725) × 35%]
   b. $400,000 × 37%
   c. $400,000 × 39.6%
   d. $400,000 × 21%

LO 11.1
LO 11.2
3. Ironwood Corporation has ordinary taxable income of $25,000 in the current year, and a short-term capital loss of $15,000. What is the corporation's tax liability for the current year?
   a. $2,100
   b. $5,250
   c. $10,500
   d. $13,650

LO 11.2
4. Which of the following statements is *false* regarding corporate capital losses?
   a. Corporations may deduct $3,000 of net capital loss each year until the loss is used up.
   b. Corporations may carry capital losses back 3 years and forward 5 years to offset capital gains in those years.
   c. Corporations are not allowed to deduct capital losses against ordinary income.
   d. A long-term capital loss carried to another year is treated as a short-term capital loss.

LO 11.2
5. Harrison Corporation generates capital (losses)/gains of ($2,000), $4,000, ($14,000) in 2022, 2023, and 2024, respectively. Harrison started operating in 2022. What is Harrison's capital loss carryforward into 2025?
   a. $0
   b. $10,000
   c. $12,000
   d. $14,000
   e. None of the above

LO 11.2
6. Mask Corporation generated a net operating loss of $24,000 in 2024 and taxable income of $10,000 in 2025. How much NOL can Mask use in 2025 to reduce taxable income?
   a. $8,000
   b. $10,000
   c. $19,200
   d. $24,000

LO 11.2 7. Clarion Corporation generated taxable income of $15,000 in 2023 and a net operating loss of $12,000 in 2024. If Clarion generates taxable income of $5,000 in 2025, what is the NOL carryforward into 2026?
   a. $0
   b. $2,000
   c. $7,000
   d. $8,000

LO 11.3 8. Walnut Corporation owns 26 percent of Teak Corporation, a domestic corporation. During the current year, Walnut Corporation received $20,000 in dividends from Teak Corporation. Assuming that Walnut's taxable income for the current year before the dividends received deduction is $500,000, what is the amount of Walnut's dividends received deduction for the current year?
   a. $10,000
   b. $13,000
   c. $16,000
   d. $20,000
   e. None of the above

LO 11.3 9. Which of the following is *not* a corporate organizational expenditure that may be amortized?
   a. The cost of organizational meetings
   b. Fees paid to the state for incorporation
   c. Accounting fees incident to organization
   d. Legal fees incident to organization
   e. All of the above are organizational expenditures

LO 11.3 10. Charitable contributions by a corporation are limited to what percent of taxable income?
   a. 100 percent
   b. 50 percent
   c. 25 percent
   d. 10 percent

LO 11.3 11. Which of the following statements is *true* regarding the dividends received deduction in the current year?
   a. Dividends from an 80-percent-owned corporation are eligible for a 65-percent dividends received deduction
   b. Dividends from a 20-percent-owned corporation are eligible for a 50-percent dividends received deduction
   c. Dividends from a 100-percent-owned corporation are eligible for a 100-percent dividends received deduction
   d. The dividends received deduction is available to individual taxpayers as well as corporations.

LO 11.4 12. The purpose of Schedule M-1 on the corporate tax return is to:
   a. Reconcile accounting (book) income to taxable income.
   b. Summarize the dividends received deduction calculation.
   c. List the officers of the corporation and their compensation.
   d. Calculate the net operating loss deduction.

LO 11.4 13. Which of the following would *not* generally appear on the M-1 reconciliation?
   a. Federal income tax expense per books
   b. Tax-exempt interest income
   c. Excess tax over book depreciation
   d. Dividends received deduction

LO 11.4 14. Machado Corporation's book earnings of $50,000 includes book depreciation expense of $6,000. Machado's tax depreciation is $9,000. Which of these best describes Machado's M-1 adjustment and taxable income?
   a. A $3,000 adjustment will increase book income to taxable income of $53,000.
   b. A $9,000 adjustment will decrease book income to taxable income of $41,000.
   c. A $3,000 adjustment will decrease book income to taxable income of $47,000.
   d. A $6,000 adjustment will increase book income to taxable income of $56,000.
   e. Depreciation does not impact taxable income and so no adjustment is required.

LO 11.5 15. Which of the following statements is *false* regarding corporate tax return due dates?
   a. Corporate tax returns for 2024 calendar-year corporations are due April 15, 2025.
   b. Corporate tax returns may receive an automatic six-month extension.
   c. Corporate estimated taxes due must be paid no later than the extended due date of the tax return.
   d. When an IRS due date falls on a weekend or holiday, the due date is the next business day.

LO 11.5 16. Mansfield Incorporated, a calendar-year corporation, is expecting to have a current year tax liability of $100,000. Which best describes the tax payments Mansfield should make to avoid penalty?
   a. Make payments at the end of June and December of $40,000 each and $20,000 when filing the return on the original due date.
   b. Make no payments during the year but pay the entire balance on the extended due date.
   c. Make no payments during the year but pay the entire balance on the original due date.
   d. Make quarterly payments totaling $100,000, all during the current year.
   e. None of these will avoid penalty.

LO 11.5 17. Which of the following statements is *true* about estimated tax payments?
   a. The annualized income method uses four quarters of estimated income to determine required estimated payments.
   b. A large corporation (for purposes of estimated payments) is permitted to use the prior year tax liability only when determining the first quarter estimated payment.
   c. Estimated payments of corporate federal income tax are due on the fifteenth of the third, sixth, ninth, and twelfth month of the tax year.
   d. Corporations with an expected tax liability of less than $1,000 are not required to make estimated payments.

LO 11.5 18. Starting in 2024, corporations are required to report what information to FinCEN?
   a. Beneficial ownership interest
   b. Corporate bylaws
   c. Shareholder information, but only if a public company traded on an exchange
   d. Corporate earnings before taxes

LO 11.6 19. Which of the following is *not* required for a corporation to be eligible to make an S corporation election?
   a. The corporation must have 100 or fewer shareholders.
   b. The corporation must be a domestic corporation.
   c. The corporation must have both common and preferred stock.
   d. The shareholders of the corporation must not be nonresident aliens.
   e. All shareholders must be either individuals, estates, certain trusts, or financial institutions.

LO 11.6 20. Which of the following items are passed through and separately stated on Schedule K-1 to shareholders of an S corporation?
   a. Rent expense
   b. Typical MACRS depreciation
   c. Net long-term capital gains
   d. Advertising expense
   e. All of the above retain their character when passed through

Chapter 11 • The Corporate Income Tax

LO 11.6 21. Which of the following is *true* about S corporations?
   a. S corporations pay corporate taxes like other corporations.
   b. S corporations pay the alternative minimum tax for all income.
   c. S corporations cannot issue corporate stock.
   d. The S corporation status may be elected by stockholders only for corporations that meet certain qualifications.
   e. None of the above.

LO 11.6 22. The allocated non-passive loss of an S corporation is deductible:
   a. If the shareholder has adequate sources of other income
   b. Only if the S corporation is engaged in a residential rental business
   c. If the loss does not exceed the shareholder's basis
   d. If the S corporation makes a loss passthrough election

LO 11.6 23. Wages paid by an S corporation to its shareholder:
   a. are not deductible by the S corporation.
   b. are considered part of qualified business income.
   c. are not considered part of qualified business income but are wages for purposes of the wage limitation.
   d. are reported as income to the shareholder on Schedule K-1.

LO 11.7 24. Travis transfers land with a fair market value of $125,000 and basis of $25,000, to a corporation in exchange for 100 percent of the corporation's stock. What amount of gain must Travis recognize as a result of this transaction?
   a. $0
   b. $25,000
   c. $100,000
   d. $125,000
   e. None of the above

LO 11.7 25. Carl transfers land with a fair market value of $120,000 and basis of $30,000, to a new corporation in exchange for 85 percent of the corporation's stock. The land is subject to a $45,000 liability, which the corporation assumes. What amount of gain must Carl recognize as a result of this transaction?
   a. $0
   b. $15,000
   c. $30,000
   d. $45,000
   e. None of the above

LO 11.7 26. What is the shareholder's basis in stock of a corporation received as a result of the transfer of property to the corporation and as a result of which gain was recognized by the stockholder?
   a. The shareholder's basis is equal to the basis of the property transferred less the gain.
   b. The shareholder's basis is equal to the fair market value of the stock received, less any liabilities transferred by the stockholder.
   c. The shareholder's basis is equal to the basis of the property transferred to the corporation, minus any liabilities transferred by the shareholder, plus the gain.
   d. The shareholder's basis is equal to the basis of the property transferred to the corporation, plus any liabilities transferred by the shareholder.
   e. None of the above.

LO 11.8 27. Which of the following statements regarding personal holding companies is *false*?
   a. A personal holding company is one which has few shareholders.
   b. A personal holding company is generally taxed at a 21-percent rate.
   c. A personal holding company operates a business which is a hobby for its owners.
   d. Personal holding companies are subject to a 20-percent tax on income that is left undistributed over a certain threshold amount.

LO 11.8

28. Boyce Industries, a manufacturing corporation, has accumulated earnings of $325,000 and cannot show any reasonable need for the accumulated earnings. What is Boyce's accumulated earnings tax?
   a. $15,000
   b. $0
   c. $13,750
   d. $75,000

Group 2: Problems

LO 11.1

1. Quince Corporation has taxable income of $200,000 for its calendar year-end tax year. Calculate the corporation's income tax liability for 2024 before tax credits.

LO 11.1

2. Ulmus Corporation is an engineering consulting firm and has $1,275,000 in taxable income for the current year. Calculate the corporation's income tax liability.

LO 11.1
LO 11.2

3. For the 2024 tax year, Ilex Corporation has ordinary income of $300,000, a short-term capital loss of $30,000 and a long-term capital gain of $10,000. Calculate Ilex Corporation's tax liability for 2024.

LO 11.2

4. DeMaria Corporation, a calendar-year corporation, generates the following taxable income/(net operating losses) since its inception in 2022:

Year	Taxable result
2022	$40,000
2023	(15,000)
2024	5,000

Assuming DeMaria makes no special elections with regard to NOLs, what is DeMaria's net operating loss carryforward into 2025?

LO 11.3

5. Fisafolia Corporation has gross income from operations of $210,000 and operating expenses of $150,000 for 2024. The corporation also has $30,000 in dividends from publicly-traded domestic corporations in which the ownership percentage was 45 percent.
   a. Calculate the corporation's dividends received deduction for the current year.
   b. Assume that instead of $210,000, Fisafolia Corporation has gross income from operations of $135,000. Calculate the corporation's dividends received deduction for the current year.
   c. Assume that instead of $210,000, Fisafolia Corporation has gross income from operations of $148,000. Calculate the corporation's dividends received deduction for the current year.

LO 11.3

6. Beech Corporation, an accrual-basis, calendar-year taxpayer, was organized and began business in June of the current year. During the year, the corporation incurred the following expenses:

State fees for incorporation	$ 800
Legal and accounting fees incident to organization	4,500
Expenses for the sale of stock	2,500
Organizational meeting expenses	1,000

Assuming that Beech Corporation wishes to deduct organizational expenses as quickly as possible, calculate the corporation's deduction for its current calendar-year-tax year.

LO 11.3 7. Katsura Corporation incurred pre-operating costs:
- Investigatory expenses of $18,000
- New employee training $25,000
- Advertising $10,000
- Land and building for use as a retail store when opened $150,000

Katsura wishes to maximize its deduction for start-up costs. Assuming they open for business on March 27th of the current year, what is the deduction for start-up costs?

LO 11.3 8. Explain the difference in the tax deduction treatment of exploratory or expansion costs and that of start-up costs.

LO 11.3 9. In 2024, Citradoria Corporation is a corporation that contributes $35,000 cash to qualified charitable organizations during the current tax year. The corporation has net operating income of $88,000, before deducting the contributions. Net operating income also excludes a $25,000 dividend received from a less than 20-percent-owned domestic corporation.
   a. What is the amount of Citradoria Corporation's allowable deduction for charitable contributions for 2024?
   b. In 2025, Citradoria contributes $4,000 to charitable organizations. The corporation has net operating income of $250,000 before deducting the contributions, and no dividend income. What is the amount of Citradoria's allowable deduction for charitable contributions in 2025?
   c. If there is any carryover of the charitable contribution deduction from 2025, what year will it expire?

LO 11.4 10. The Loquat Corporation has book net income of $50,000 for the current year. Included in this figure are the following items, which are reported on the corporation's Schedule M-1, Reconciliation of Income (Loss) per Books with Income per Return.

Federal income tax expense	$ 7,500
Depreciation deducted on the books which is not deductible for tax purposes	10,000
Deduction for 50 percent of meals expense which is not allowed for tax purposes	5,500
Deduction for entertainment not allowed for tax purposes	2,000
Tax-exempt interest income included in book income but not in tax income	4,200

Calculate Loquat Corporation's taxable income for the current year based on the information given. Show your calculations.

LO 11.4 11. Caloundra Corporation has book income of $50,000. Included in the book income is $2,000 of tax-exempt interest, $7,500 of federal income tax expense, and a $1,500 non-deductible fine. Also included in book income are $8,000 of dividends Caloundra received from a 15-percent-owned corporation. Using this information and Form 1120 from Appendix F, provide the amounts that go on each line on the form listed below.
   a. Form 1120, Schedule M-1 Line 1
   b. Form 1120, Schedule M-1, Line 10
   c. Form 1120, page 1, Line 28
   d. Form 1120, Schedule C, Line 2, columns (a) and (c)
   e. Form 1120, Schedule C, Line 24
   f. Form 1120, page 1, Line 29b
   g. Form 1120, page 1, Line 30

LO 11.5 12. Mallory Corporation has a calendar year-end and is organized in Kansas. The corporation has paid estimated taxes of $10,000 during 2024 but still owes an additional $5,000 for its 2024 tax year.
   a. When is the 2024 tax return due?
   b. If an automatic extension of time to file is requested, when is the 2024 tax return due?
   c. If an extension of time to file is requested, when is the additional $5,000 of tax for 2024 due?

LO 11.5 13. Cosplay Costumes Corporation (CCC) is an October 31 year-end taxpayer. CCC's prior year tax liability was $42,000. The current year tax liability is $44,000. CCC prepared estimated payments using the annualized income method of $43,000 (four equal payments of $10,750). Using this information, answer the following questions regarding the required payments necessary to avoid penalties associated with underpayment of estimated taxes.
   a. What are the month and day due dates of CCC's four estimated tax payments?
   b. If CCC is not considered a large corporation, what is the smallest amount of tax that could have been paid for the year?
   c. If CCC is a large corporation, what is the smallest amount of tax that could have been paid for the year?
   d. If CCC is a large corporation, what is the smallest amount of tax that could have been paid only for the first quarter?

LO 11.6 14. Cedar Corporation has an S corporation election in effect. During the 2024 calendar tax year, the corporation had ordinary taxable income of $200,000, and on January 15, 2024, the corporation paid dividends to shareholders in the amount of $120,000. How much taxable income, in total, must the shareholders of the corporation report on their 2024 tax returns? Explain your answer.

LO 11.6 15. Bill and Guilda each own 50 percent of the stock of Radiata Corporation, an S corporation. Guilda's basis in her stock is $21,000. On May 26, 2024, Bill sells his stock, with a basis of $40,000, to Loraine for $50,000. For the 2024 tax year, Radiata Corporation has a loss of $104,000.
   a. Calculate the amount of the corporation's loss that may be deducted by Bill on his 2024 tax return.
   b. Calculate the amount of the corporation's loss that may be deducted by Guilda on her 2024 tax return.
   c. Calculate the amount of the corporation's loss that may be deducted by Loraine on her 2024 tax return.

LO 11.6 16. Starlord Corporation is a calendar-year taxpayer with an S corporation election. Quill is the sole shareholder of Starlord for the entire tax year. The year-end financial statements of Starlord report the following (on a tax basis):

Operating revenues	$ 200,000
Cost of sales	(135,000)
Gross margin	65,000
SG&A expenses	(13,500)
Operating income	51,500
Other income/(loss):	
Capital gains	2,000
Section 1231 losses	(3,000)
Interest income	300
Taxable income	$ 50,800
Distributions to owners	$ 30,000

Included in SG&A expenses are wages to the Starlord's sole shareholder of $8,000 and charitable contributions of $500 cash. The capital gains are short-term. Quill has basis in excess of his distributions. Use this information to determine:
   a. The amount of ordinary business income
   b. Each of the separately stated items
   c. From the above information, provide the tax form, line number, and amount that Quill will need to report on his individual income tax return

LO 11.6   17. Helly holds a 100-percent stake in Macro Data Incorporated (MDI), an S corporation operating a qualified trade or business. In the current year, MDI reports $20,000 of ordinary business income (before deducting any wages paid to Helly). Helly can exert influence over the amount of wages she is paid by MDI and although she recognizes that MDI can only deduct a reasonable wage, she is considering some extreme alternatives to judge the possible effects. Determine the following items below, considering Helly could pay herself wages of $1,000 versus wages of $20,000.
  a. The amount of total employment taxes paid by Helly and MDI on the wages (assume Helly's total wages and self-employment income are below the current year FICA cap)?
  b. Assuming Helly has a 25-percent marginal tax rate, the amount of income taxes on her wages?
  c. Assuming Helly has a 25-percent marginal tax rate, the amount of income taxes on her allocation of ordinary business income from MDI (Ignore the deduction MDI can take for employment taxes)?
  d. Explain the primary difference in the tax burden borne jointly by MDI and Helly in the two wage scenarios Helly is considering.

LO 11.7   18. Dylan, Devon, and Ricken form Lemon Corporation in the current year. Dylan contributes $30,000 cash in exchange for 30 shares of Lemon. Devon contributes land with a market value of $50,000 (basis of $15,000) in exchange for 40 shares and $10,000 cash. Ricken provides services to Lemon valued at $30,000 in exchange for 30 shares.
  a. Determine the realized gain or loss on the exchange for each shareholder.
  b. Determine the recognized gain or loss (or income) on the exchange for each shareholder.
  c. Determine the basis of each shareholder's stock
  d. Determine Lemon's basis in the land.

LO 11.7   19. Dylan, Devon, and Ricken form Lemon Corporation in the current year. Dylan contributes $50,000 cash in exchange for 50 shares of Lemon. Devon contributes land with a market value of $50,000 (basis of $15,000) in exchange for 40 shares and $10,000 cash. Ricken provides services to Lemon valued at $10,000 in exchange for 10 shares.
  a. Determine the realized gain or loss on the exchange for each shareholder.
  b. Determine the recognized gain or loss (or income) on the exchange for each shareholder.
  c. Determine the basis of each shareholder's stock
  d. Determine Lemon's basis in the land.

LO 11.7   20. Keri, in forming a new corporation, transfers land to the corporation in exchange for 100 percent of the stock of the corporation. Keri's basis in the land is $280,000, and the corporation assumes a liability on the property in the amount of $300,000. The stock received by Keri has a fair market value of $550,000.
  a. What is the amount of gain or loss that must be recognized by Keri on this transfer?
  b. What is the amount of Keri's basis in the corporation's stock?
  c. What is the amount of the corporation's basis in the land?

LO 11.8   21. Grevilla Corporation is a manufacturing company. The corporation has accumulated earnings of $950,000, and it can establish reasonable needs for $400,000 of that amount. Calculate the amount of the accumulated earnings tax (if any) that Grevilla Corporation is subject to for this year.

Group 3:
Comprehensive Problems

1. New England Candle Corporation (NEC) is a retailer of specialty scented candles (business code 459990). NEC was formed and began operations on January 1, 2024. The corporation is located at 210 N. Main St., Pearisburg, VA 24134 and the EIN is 91-1111111. The corporation's income statement for the year and the balance sheet at year-end are presented below.

The NEC Corporation Income Statement
for the Year Ended December 31, 2024

Gross income from operations		$ 320,000
Qualified dividends received from a 15-percent-		
owned domestic corporation		20,000
Total gross income		340,000
Cost of goods sold		(70,000)
Total income		270,000
Other expenses:		
Compensation of officers	$80,000	
Salaries and wages	20,000	
Bad debts (direct charge-offs)	9,000	
Repairs	3,000	
Depreciation for book (tax depreciation = $90,000)	10,000	
Advertising	3,000	
Payroll taxes	15,000	
Total other expenses		(140,000)
Pretax book income		130,000
Income tax expense		25,200
Net income		$ 104,800

The NEC Corporation Balance Sheet
as of December 31, 2024

Assets:		
Cash	$ 140,600	
Accounts receivable	20,000	
Inventory (at cost)	70,000	
Equipment	90,000	
Less: accumulated depreciation	(10,000)	
Total assets		$310,600
Liabilities and owners' equity:		
Accounts payable	$ 24,000	
Other liabilities	16,800	
Note payable (due in 10 years)	85,000	
Common stock	80,000	
Retained earnings	104,800	
Total liabilities and owners' equity		$310,600

The corporation made estimated tax payments of $9,000. Any tax overpayment is to be applied to the next year's estimated tax. Complete Form 1120 for NEC Corporation. Preparation of Form 1125-A, Form 4562, and Schedule G are not required.

2. Apdroid Corporation is an S corporation started on January 1, 2024, with 50 shares owned by Job Stevens and 50 shares owned by Lee Jaymes. Apdroid is a retailer that sells mobile phones and accessories (business code 449210). The corporation is located at 15620 McMullen Hwy SW, Cumberland, MD 21502 and has EIN 94–8888888. The corporation is not subject to any special taxes and no wages are included in cost of goods sold. The corporation's income statement and balance sheet are presented below.

The Apdroid Corporation Income Statement
for the Year Ended December 31, 2024

Gross income from operations		$ 320,000
Qualified dividends received from a 15-percent-owned domestic corporation		20,000
Total gross income		340,000
Cost of goods sold		(70,000)
Total income		270,000
Other expenses:		
Compensation of officers	$ 80,000	
Salaries and wages	20,000	
Bad debts (direct charge-offs)	9,000	
Repairs	3,000	
Depreciation for book (tax depreciation = $90,000)	10,000	
Advertising	3,000	
Payroll taxes	15,000	
Total other expenses		(140,000)
Net income		$ 130,000

The Apdroid Corporation Balance Sheet
as of December 31, 2024

Assets:		
Cash	$ 109,000	
Accounts receivable	20,000	
Inventory (at cost)	70,000	
Other current assets	40,000	
Equipment	90,000	
Less: accumulated depreciation	(10,000)	
Total assets		$319,000
Liabilities and owners' equity:		
Accounts payable	$ 24,000	
Note payable (due in 10 years)	85,000	
Common stock	80,000	
Retained earnings	130,000	
Total liabilities and owners' equity		$319,000

Using this information, complete Form 1120–S for Apdroid Corporation and Schedule K–1, including Statement A (QBI) for Job (who lives at 12 Bowery St., Frostburg, MD 21532 and has SSN 444-11–5555). Assume there are no cash distributions during the year. Preparation of Form 1125-A, Form 4562, and Schedule G are not required.

Chapter 12
Tax Administration and Tax Planning

Learning Objectives

After completing this chapter, you should be able to:

- **LO 12.1** Identify the organizational structure of the Internal Revenue Service (IRS).
- **LO 12.2** Describe the IRS audit process.
- **LO 12.3** Define the common penalties for taxpayers and apply them to specific situations.
- **LO 12.4** Apply the general rule for the statute of limitations on tax returns and the important exceptions to the general rule.
- **LO 12.5** Describe the rules and penalties that apply to tax practitioners.
- **LO 12.6** Describe the Taxpayer Bill of Rights.
- **LO 12.7** Explain the basic concepts of tax planning.

Overview

Knowing how the Internal Revenue Service (IRS) operates, and how and why the IRS audits certain tax returns, is extremely important to tax practitioners. This chapter covers these topics as well as tax penalties that apply to taxpayers and tax preparers, the statute of limitations on tax liabilities and refund claims, and rules applicable to tax practitioners (i.e., Circular 230). The Taxpayer Bill of Rights, also covered in this chapter, provides taxpayers with significant rights when dealing with the IRS, such as the ability to record an IRS interview.

Arranging one's financial affairs in order to maximize after-tax cash flows is referred to as tax planning. This chapter includes a discussion of basic tax-planning techniques that may be used by individual taxpayers. This final chapter is intended to give an appreciation for the process of dealing with the IRS and several of the many issues involved in conducting a tax practice.

Learning Objective 12.1

Identify the organizational structure of the Internal Revenue Service (IRS).

12-1 The Internal Revenue Service

The tax laws of the United States are administered by the IRS. In administering the tax law, the IRS has the responsibility for determining, assessing, and collecting internal revenue taxes and enforcing other provisions of the tax law. The IRS is a bureau of the Treasury Department. The mission of the IRS is to provide America's taxpayers quality service by helping them understand and meet their tax responsibilities, and enforce the law with integrity and fairness. Congress passes tax laws and requires taxpayers to comply. A taxpayer is expected to understand and meet their tax obligations. The role of the IRS is to help the majority of compliant taxpayers with the tax law, while ensuring that the minority who are unwilling to comply pay their fair share.

The IRS organization currently consists of a national office in Washington, D.C., IRS Campus Processing Sites, and various operational offices throughout the United States. The national office is the headquarters of the commissioner of internal revenue and various deputy and associate commissioners. The commissioner of internal revenue is appointed by the President of the United States with the advice and consent of the Senate. The responsibilities of the commissioner are to establish policy, to supervise the activities of the organization, and to act in an advisory capacity to the Treasury Department on legislative matters. In addition, the commissioner is responsible for the collection of income tax, auditing of tax returns, intelligence operations, and appellate procedures.

12-1a IRS Campus Processing Sites

In addition to the various operational offices presented below, the IRS currently maintains IRS Campus Processing Sites. At these processing sites, the IRS computers process the information from tax documents such as tax returns, payroll tax forms, Forms 1099, and withholding forms.

Paper returns for individuals are processed at the Austin, Kansas City, and Ogden offices while e-filings are processed at many sites. The IRS also maintains a national computer center in Martinsburg, West Virginia, where information from various processing sites is matched with records from other processing sites. This cross-matching of records helps to ensure that taxpayers report all their income and do not file multiple refund claims.

"Tax day is the day that ordinary Americans send their money to Washington, D.C., and wealthy Americans send their money to the Cayman Islands." — Jimmy Kimmel

12-1b The IRS Organizational Structure

The Internal Revenue Service was completely reorganized under the 1998 IRS Restructuring Act (RRA 98), which provided the foundation for the current structure as shown in Figure 12.1.

Figure 12.1

Note: In addition to Figure 12.1 above, more extensive information about the IRS organizational structure is available to the public at **www.irs.gov**.

The Services and Enforcement arm of the IRS, is now responsible for the collection of taxes and the auditing of tax returns, which is accomplished through the offices presented in Table 12.1.

Table 12.1 IRS Divisions and Principal Offices

Division	Responsibility
Small Business/Self-employed (SB/SE)	Small business taxpayers including individuals who file business forms with their tax returns
Large Business and International (LB&I)	Taxpayers with assets of $10 million or more and the Global High Wealth and International Individual Compliance programs
Tax Exempt and Governmental Entities (TE/GE)	Tax exempt and government entities including universities, qualified retirement plans, and tribal governments
Taxpayer Services	Taxpayers whose primary income is derived from wages and investments and who do not file business forms with their tax returns (formerly Wage and Investment)

Office	Responsibility
Criminal Investigation	Law enforcement activities
Office of Professional Responsibility (OPR)	Regulating enrolled agents, attorneys, and CPAs who practice before the IRS
Whistleblower	Handling information that helps uncover tax cheating and providing appropriate rewards to whistleblowers
Return Preparer	Registers and promotes a qualified tax professional community
Online Services	Develops and executes strategies to update and integrate IRS web services
Enterprise Management	Enhance the taxpayer experience by improving business processes and modernizing systems

Of these IRS divisions, the most significant to individual and small business taxpayers are the Small Business/Self-Employed (SB/SE) and the Taxpayer Services offices.

12-1c Small Business/Self-Employed (SB/SE) Division

The SB/SE headquarters are located in Lanham, Maryland, with a mission to serve SB/SE customers by educating and informing them of their tax obligations. The division develops educational products and services and helps the public to understand and comply with applicable laws. The SB/SE Division serves the following taxpayers:

- Individuals filing Forms 1040 and 1040-SR, Schedules C, E, or F, and
- All other businesses with assets under $10 million.

The SB/SE Division serves this taxpayer segment through three organizations:
- Collection (specializing in delinquent taxes and tax returns)
- Examination (specializing in correspondence, office, and field audits)
- Operations Support (provides support to other segments to ensure they are properly equipped)

12-1d Taxpayer Services

The Taxpayer Services Division absorbed the former Wage and Investment Division (W&I). The mission of Taxpayer Services is to help taxpayers understand and comply with applicable tax laws and to protect the public interest by applying the tax law with integrity and fairness to all. Taxpayer Services is headquartered in Atlanta, GA. The taxpayer profile of a typical Taxpayer Services client is:

- Most pay taxes through withholdings,
- More than half prepare their own returns,
- Most interact with the IRS once a year, and
- Most receive refunds.

Organizationally, Taxpayer Services is broken down into several operational administrative centers (offices). The key functional operations of Taxpayer Services include:

- Customer Assistance, Relationships, and Education (CARE)
- Customer Account Services (CAS)
- Return Integrity and Compliance Services (RICS)
- Operations Support (OS)

12-1e Examination of Records

Federal tax law gives the IRS authority to examine a taxpayer's books and records to determine the correct amount of tax due. The IRS also has the right to summon taxpayers and to make them appear before the IRS and produce necessary accounting records. Taxpayers are required by law to maintain accounting records to facilitate an IRS audit.

The IRS may also issue a summons for taxpayer records from third parties such as banks, brokers, and CPAs. A third party may not have the same incentives to protect the privacy of the taxpayers, and thus, the tax rules generally require that a taxpayer be notified prior to the summons being sent to the third party.

Enforcement of summonses is one of the most litigated areas of tax compliance and has been for almost 15 years. An analysis prepared by the Taxpayer Advocates Office shows that the IRS is extremely successful in these cases, winning over 90 percent.

12-1f Collections

Taxpayers have several options when they are unable to pay the money they owe to the IRS as outlined in Publication 594. The IRS wants to help taxpayers move their issues toward resolution, and has tools to help delinquent taxpayers pay the taxes they owe. Taxpayers may ask the IRS for a short-term administrative extension of time and then borrow money or sell assets to pay their tax debt. They may also enter into an installment agreement with the IRS, if their debt is below certain limits, and pay the debt within a two- or three-year time frame. Another option for certain taxpayers is an *offer in compromise* where the IRS accepts a settlement less than the total amount of tax due. Generally, taxpayers who qualify for an offer in compromise are unlikely to ever be able to pay the amount they owe. Alternatively, sometimes the IRS will accept an offer in compromise when the tax liability is disputed, or to avert a costly and time-consuming legal battle.

There are two payment options when making an offer to settle tax debt at an amount that is less than the liability: (1) A lump-sum payment of 20 percent up front and the remainder paid over 5 or fewer installments within 5 months, or (2) periodic payments with the first payment made with the offer, and the remaining payments paid over a period of 6 to 24 months. The IRS has an online tool to establish pre-qualification for an offer-in-compromise at **https://irs.treasury.gov/oic_pre_qualifier/** or IRS Form 656 Booklet at the IRS website.

If a taxpayer does not pay taxes that are due, ignores notices and demands for payment, and fails to make arrangements to pay the amount owed, the IRS will generally start a collection process. This process may include a tax levy that allows the IRS to take a portion of a taxpayer's wages or to seize property such as the taxpayer's house, car, bank account, or other financial accounts. The IRS may also put a tax lien on the taxpayer's property, which is a legal claim to the property. Liens will not be filed unless a taxpayer owes more than $10,000 in taxes. The IRS also has the power to assess significant penalties, some of which are covered later in this chapter.

Self-Study Problem 12.1

Refer to Appendix E for Solutions to Self-Study Problems

Determine whether the following statements are true or false in the current year.

1. The Small Business/Self-Employed Division focuses on individuals that receive a Form W-2.
2. Tax returns are processed at IRS Campus Processing Sites.
3. The commissioner of internal revenue is an elected position.
4. The IRS is part of the U.S. Treasury Department.
5. The IRS has the right to summon a taxpayer's tax records.

12-2 The Audit Process

Learning Objective 12.2 — Describe the IRS audit process.

A primary function of the IRS is to audit taxpayers' tax returns. After the service centers have checked the returns for accuracy, some returns are selected for audit. When a return is selected for examination, it may be subject to an "office audit" or a "field audit." An audit may also be conducted through the mail in what is called a "correspondence audit."

Correspondence audits now account for about 77 percent of the IRS examinations of individual returns each year. Correspondence audits are generally handled entirely by mail. The audit begins when the IRS sends a letter or notice to a taxpayer requesting specific information about their tax return. Usually, the areas covered in correspondence audits relate to questions about Forms W-2 and 1099 that do not agree with the tax return, requests for information supporting charitable contributions, and information related to eligibility for claimed earned income credits. A list of common notices is presented In Table 12.2.

Table 12.2 Common ITS Notices

Notice	General Purpose
CP 11	The IRS has made changes to their return, resulting in a balance due.
CP 12	The IRS found and corrected a mistake(s) on the tax return resulting in a refund or lesser refund amount.
CP 14	The first notice sent by the IRS when a taxpayer has a balance due.
CP 501/CP 503	Reminders if a balance due has not been paid after the CP 14 notice.
CP 2000	The income or payment information the IRS received from third parties, such as employers or financial institutions, does not match the information reported on the tax return. For example, interest income from a Form 1099-INT was not reported or reported at the wrong amount on the tax return.
CP 2501	Like CP 2000; however, this notice is more of an inquiry, asking for additional information or clarification.
LTR 5071C	The IRS needs to verify taxpayer identity.

For assistance on IRS letters and notices, the Taxpayer Advocate maintains a website that allows a taxpayer to input a notice number to determine the nature of the notice and the general purpose (**www.taxpayeradvocate.irs.gov/notices-from-the-irs/**). In addition, common notices are included in the Taxpayer Advocate's Taxpayer Road Map, a fairly complex flowchart that depicts the different stages of filing, assessment, and collection. The road map includes notations to indicate where in the process a particular notice might be issued (**www.taxpayeradvocate.irs.gov/get-help/roadmap/**).

The office audit is conducted in an IRS office and is typically used for individual taxpayers with little or no business activities. In an office audit, the taxpayer takes their records to the IRS office where they are reviewed by a revenue agent. The taxpayer is simply required to substantiate deductions, credits, or income items that appear on their tax return.

In a field audit, the IRS agent reviews a taxpayer's books and records at the taxpayer's place of business or at the office of the taxpayer's accountant. This type of audit is generally used when the accounting records are too extensive to take to the IRS office. Field audits are usually used for taxpayers with substantial trade or business activities. If a taxpayer can present a valid reason, they may have an office audit changed to a field audit.

12-2a Selection of Returns for Audits

The IRS selects returns for audit through a number of different methods:

- Identification of participants in abusive tax avoidance transactions
- Computer scoring (DIF)
- Selection of large corporations
- Information matching
- Related examinations
- Other means

Starting in the 2024 filing season (primarily comprised of 2023 tax returns), the IRS began the Simple Notice Initiative to restructure the look and feel of commonly used IRS notices and letters. Pilot programs demonstrate far fewer follow-up inquiries from taxpayers that received the redesigned notices.

The IRS uses information gleaned from other sources to identify taxpayers involved in abusive tax avoidance transactions. For example, the IRS may identify a promoter of abusive transactions and then use the promoter's records to identify taxpayers that may have engaged in the abusive planning. The IRS also may select a tax return for audit through a related examination. For example, if the IRS selects an entity or taxpayer for examination, they may also select business partners or other investors.

Most large corporations are involved with an IRS audit on a continuous basis and many have set aside permanent office space to house the IRS agents.

For computer scoring, the IRS uses the Discriminant Function System (DIF) and UIDIF (Unreported Income DIF) to select taxpayers for audit. Under the DIF system, the IRS uses mathematical formulas to assign a DIF score to each return. The DIF score represents the potential for discovery of improper treatment of items on the tax return. The higher the DIF score, the more likely the tax return will be selected for audit. The DIF score is designed to identify tax returns likely to contain errors because they contain amounts of income, deductions, or tax credits that fall outside "normal" ranges. For example, a tax return that contains unusually large charitable contributions claimed as a deduction will be assigned a high DIF score, and the chances of it being selected for audit are greater. The UIDIF scores returns for the likelihood of unreported income.

The IRS has operated a random audit selection process for many years under different program names such as the Taxpayer Compliance Measurement Program (TCMP) or, as currently more benignly named, the National Research Program (NRP). These programs are used to assist the IRS in determining which types of taxpayers should be audited and gather data to update the DIF system. These programs have not been without controversy and remain a sensitive issue for the IRS. The National Taxpayer Advocate has suggested providing compensation to taxpayers that are subjected to an NRP audit that results in no change to tax liability.

Other tax returns that are audited are selected due to matching problems between the information forms such as Forms W-2 and 1099 and the related taxpayer's return. As more returns are filed electronically and the IRS information systems have improved, the number of matching notices has increased. For the 2021 tax year, the number of automated underreporting and matching notices greatly exceeds the number of correspondence and field audits by a wide margin. From time to time, the IRS will also target special projects at a local or industry segment. For example, a "random" audit might reveal a tax issue with small auto repair shops. After required approvals from higher positions within the IRS, a number of small auto repair shops may be selected for audit to determine if the issue is pervasive within the industry segment.

Lastly, the IRS can also select returns based on information obtained from other taxing jurisdictions, news sources, or whistleblowers. For example, the IRS and many state departments of revenue share tax information to assist in the identification of returns for examination. Although the IRS has procedures in place to ensure that audits are not targeted at certain groups for political or other motivations, the history of such reported behavior continues to haunt the organization.

According to the IRS, the cost to process an e-filed Form 1040 individual tax return in 2020 was $0.36 per return. The cost to process a paper-filed return of the same type was $15.21. The error rate for paper-filed returns was more than 43 percent in 2020, while the error rate for e-filed returns was less than 5 percent.

12-2b The Appeals Process

After a return is selected for examination, an agent is assigned to perform the audit. There are three possible results arising from the agent's audit. First, the tax return may be found to require no adjustment, in which case the findings are reviewed and the tax return is sent to storage. A second possible outcome of the audit is an agreement between the agent and the taxpayer on a needed change in the tax liability on the tax return. Then, the tax is collected or the refund is paid, and after a review, the return is stored.

The final possible outcome of the audit is a disagreement between the agent and the taxpayer on the amount of the required adjustment to the tax return. In this situation, the appeals procedure begins with the IRS inviting the taxpayer to an informal conference with an appellate agent. If an agreement cannot be reached at the appeals level, then the matter is taken into the federal court system. The Federal Tax Court is open to the public. For tax professionals and tax students, watching the Tax Court in action can be an educational experience. Any group planning a court visit should contact the judge's chambers in advance since the courts are often small and cannot accommodate many spectators. During and subsequent to the COVID-19 pandemic, a select number of Tax Court proceedings are held virtually and open to the public. Refer to the Tax Court website for more information and a calendar of virtual proceedings. Figures 12.2 and 12.3 on Pages 12-9 and 12-10, respectively, illustrate the audit and appeals processes, beginning with the selection of a tax return for audit and ending with a decision of the federal courts.

The IRS considers the appeals function to be highly successful, negotiating and settling 85 to 90 percent of the cases with taxpayers. If this high rate of settlement were not achieved, the number of disputed cases would soon overwhelm the courts hearing tax cases.

Figure 12.2

INCOME TAX AUDIT PROCEDURE OF THE INTERNAL REVENUE SERVICE

Figure 12.3

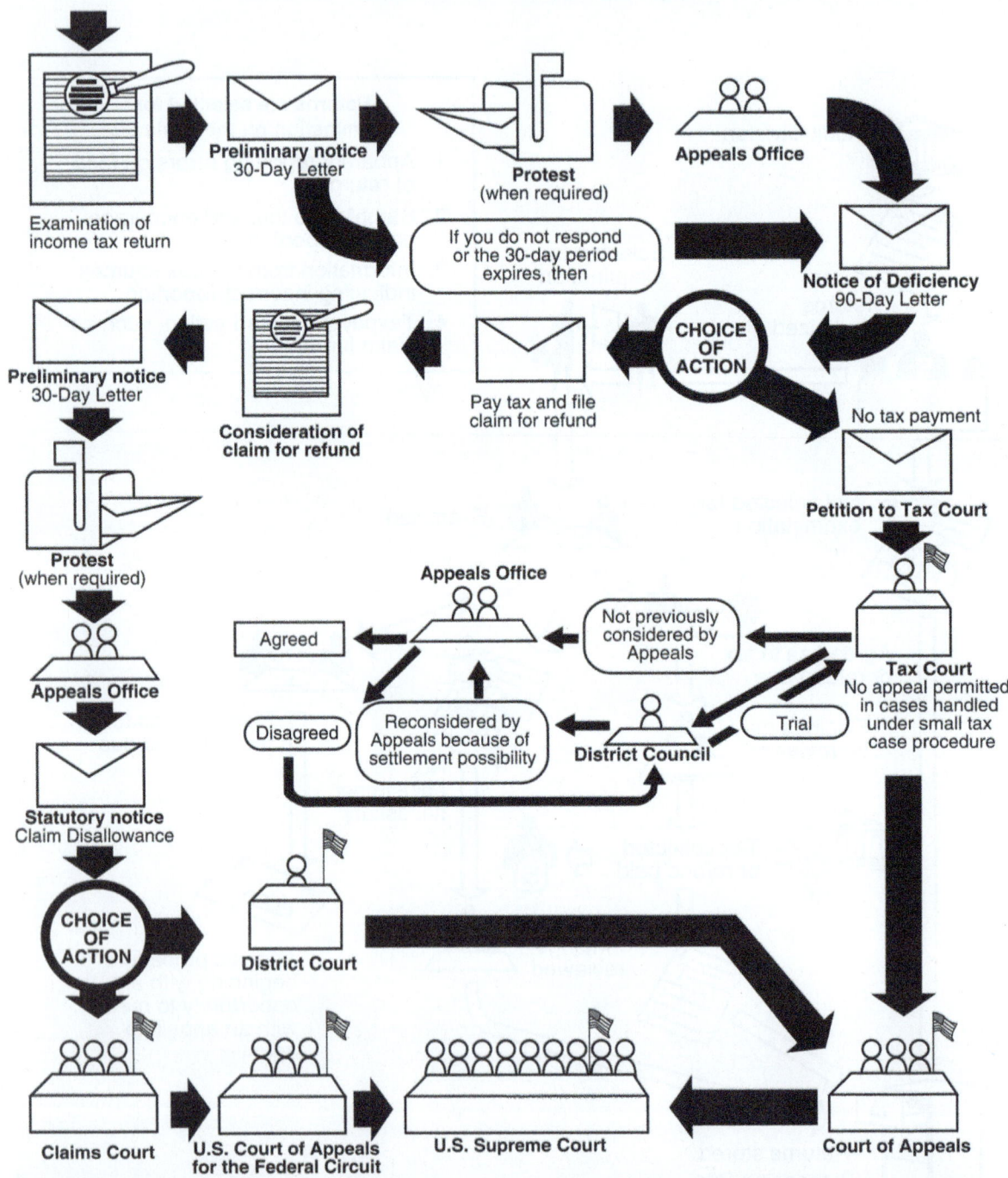

At any stage of procedure:
- You can agree and arrange to pay.
- You can ask the IRS to issue you a notice of deficiency so you can file a petition with the Tax Court.
- You can pay the tax and file a claim for a refund.

Self-Study Problem 12.2

Refer to Appendix E for Solutions to Self-Study Problems

Determine whether the following statements are true or false.

1. The IRS uses computers to select tax returns for audit.
2. A correspondence audit is done at the taxpayer's office.
3. NRP audits are selected randomly.
4. An audit may result in a refund.
5. A taxpayer cannot appeal the results of an IRS audit.

12-3 Interest and Penalties

12.3 Learning Objective

Define the common penalties for taxpayers and apply them to specific situations.

Taxpayers are charged interest on underpayments of taxes, and in some cases the IRS pays interest to taxpayers when they overpay their taxes. Usually, these interest charges or payments result from the settlement of a tax liability for a prior year's tax return. For example, when an IRS audit results in the taxpayer paying additional taxes for a prior tax year, the IRS will charge the taxpayer interest on the amount of additional taxes from the original due date to the date of payment of the tax. If the audit results in a refund, interest will be paid to the taxpayer based on the amount of the refund. The IRS also imposes a nondeductible penalty based on amounts of underpayments of estimated taxes for the current tax year (Refer to Chapter 9), but a taxpayer is not paid interest on a refund arising from an overpayment of estimated taxes during the current tax year.

The interest rate applicable to underpayments and overpayments of taxes is adjusted each quarter based on the short-term federal rate. The rate is equal to the federal short-term rate plus 3 percentage points. Interest is compounded daily except when calculating the penalty for underpayment of estimated taxes by individuals and corporations. In calculating the penalty for underpayment of estimated taxes, the penalty is calculated as simple interest.

The rate of interest for under and overpayments for noncorporate taxpayers for selected recent periods is as follows:

Table 12.3 Interest Rates on Over/Underpayments by Individuals

2024 Quarter	% Rate
1	8
2	8
3	8
4	8

Tables are available from the IRS for performing the actual calculation of interest owed from or due to taxpayers. Interest paid on an underpayment of tax is considered consumer interest; therefore, no deduction is allowed (Chapter 5). The penalty for underpayment of estimated tax is calculated as interest but is a nondeductible penalty. Interest received on an overpayment is income in the year the payment is received. No interest is paid on a current year overpayment, unless the IRS takes more than 45 days to process the return.

Example James pays $2,000 of interest in 2024 for an underpayment of taxes on his 2021 tax return. The $2,000 is not deductible since no deduction is allowed for consumer interest. ♦

Example John receives $700 of interest income on the overpayment of his taxes resulting from an IRS audit on his 2021 tax return. The $700 interest is income in the year it is received by John. ♦

The tax law contains various penalties to ensure taxpayers accurately report and pay their taxes. Penalty payments are considered an addition to the amount of the taxes and therefore, are not deductible. Several of the major taxpayer penalties are described in the following paragraphs.

12-3a The Failure-to-Pay and Failure-to-File Penalties

Taxpayers are subject to a penalty for failure to pay the amount of the taxes due on the due date of their tax return. The penalty for failure to pay is ½ of 1 percent of the amount of taxes due for every month or portion of a month that the payment is late, up to a maximum of 25 percent of the amount of taxes due. The penalty increases to 1 percent per month beginning 10 days after a notice of levy has been given to the taxpayer.

If a taxpayer does not file a tax return on the due date (including extensions), they are subject to a penalty equal to 5 percent of the tax due with the return for every month or portion of a month the return is late. The amount of the penalty for failure to file, however, is limited to a maximum of 25 percent of the amount of taxes due with the tax return. In the event the failure to file is fraudulent, the penalty is increased from 5 percent for each month or portion thereof to 15 percent, and the maximum penalty is increased from 25 percent to 75 percent. Also, if the taxpayer fails to file their tax return within 60 days of its due date, the minimum failure-to-file penalty is the lesser of $510 (for returns required to be filed in 2025) or the total amount of the taxes due with the tax return.

If both the failure-to-file and the failure-to-pay penalties apply, the failure-to-file penalty (5 percent) is reduced by the amount of the failure-to-pay penalty (½ of 1 percent) to 4.5 percent, so the total combined penalty stays at 5 percent. The maximum combined penalty is 25 percent for the first 5 months. After 5 months, the failure-to-pay penalty continues at ½ of 1 percent per month for up to an additional 45 months. Thus, the maximum combined penalty could reach 47.5 percent.

Both the failure-to-file and the failure-to-pay penalties are zero if there is no tax due or if a refund is due from the IRS on the late tax return. The failure-to-file and the failure-to-pay penalty will not be assessed if the taxpayer can demonstrate that they had "reasonable cause" for failing to pay or file the tax return on time.

Example Nancy filed her 2024 tax return 3½ months after the due date, and she had not requested an extension of time to file. The failure to file was not due to fraud. She included with her late return a check for $2,000, which was the balance of the tax she owed. Disregarding interest, her penalties are calculated as follows:

Failure-to-pay penalty		$ 40
(0.5% × $2,000) × 4 months		
Plus:		
Failure-to-file penalty	$400	
(5% × $2,000) × 4 months		
Less: Failure-to-pay penalty	(40)	
Net failure-to-file penalty	360	
Minimum failure-to-file after 60 days	$510	510
Total penalties		$550 ♦

Tax Break The IRS has a first-time penalty abatement program which was meant to allow taxpayers who were assessed penalties for the first time to request a one-time penalty amnesty. The program applies to the failure-to-file and failure-to-pay penalties as well as several others, and can save taxpayers significant amounts of money in certain cases. The penalty abatement waiver must be requested by the taxpayer, but few taxpayers who qualify for the waiver request it or even know the program exists.

12-3b Accuracy-Related Penalty

The tax law imposes a penalty of 20 percent of the applicable underpayment due to (1) negligence of or disregard for rules or regulations, (2) a substantial understatement of income tax, or (3) a substantial valuation overstatement, as well as certain other understatements of income tax. Negligence includes the failure to make a reasonable attempt to comply with the tax law. For example, the penalty could be imposed on a taxpayer who deducts a personal expenditure as a business expense. A substantial understatement of income tax occurs where the required amount of tax exceeds the tax shown on the taxpayer's return by the greater of 10 percent (5 percent if claiming a qualified business income deduction) of the amount of tax that should be shown on the return or $5,000 ($10,000 for corporate taxpayers other than S corporations). A substantial valuation overstatement occurs when the value of property is 150 percent or more of the correct valuation. For example, a taxpayer who inflates the value of depreciable property to generate additional depreciation deductions may be subject to this penalty. The accuracy-related penalty applies only if the taxpayer has filed a return. The tax law also imposes a 20-percent penalty for an "excessive" claim for refund or a credit claim. If the taxpayer can demonstrate that they have reasonable cause for the understatement of tax or claim for refund or credit and that they acted in good faith, the penalty will not be assessed.

Example Kim underpaid her taxes for the current year by $15,000 due to negligence. Kim's penalty for negligence under the accuracy-related penalty is calculated as follows:

Accuracy-related penalty (20% × $15,000) $3,000 ♦

12-3c Fraud Penalty

The tax law also contains provisions for penalties for filing fraudulent tax returns. The fraud penalty is equal to 75 percent of the amount of underpayment of taxes attributable to fraud.

For the IRS to impose the fraud penalty, it must be shown by a "preponderance of evidence" that the taxpayer had an intent to evade taxes; however, once the IRS establishes that any portion of an underpayment of taxes is due to fraud, the entire underpayment is assumed to be attributable to fraud unless the taxpayer establishes otherwise. The tax law does not provide clear rules for what constitutes fraud; however, what is clearly mere negligence by a taxpayer will not cause this penalty to be imposed. When the fraud penalty is applicable, the accuracy-related penalty cannot be imposed. The fraud penalty will be applied only where the taxpayer has actually filed a return. Like the accuracy-related penalty, the fraud penalty will not be assessed if the taxpayer can demonstrate reasonable cause for the underpayment of tax and the taxpayer acted in good faith.

Example Jeff has a $20,000 tax deficiency because of civil fraud. Interest on this underpayment amounts to $8,000. Jeff's total amount due on this underpayment is calculated as follows:

Tax deficiency	$20,000
Fraud penalty (75% × $20,000)	15,000
Interest	8,000
Total due	$43,000

The interest is not deductible due to the disallowance of deductions for consumer interest. The fraud penalty is also not deductible. ♦

According to IRS data, 16 percent of Americans feel that some element of cheating on taxes is acceptable. Experts agree that tax cheating is a significant problem for the IRS, which must enforce the laws, and for honest taxpayers who pay more in taxes than they would otherwise have to. It is generally believed that tax evasion and noncompliance are costing the government more than $630 billion dollars in lost revenue each year.

Would You Sign This Tax Return?

Tim Trying, who is single, purchased a house on the beach in sunny Southern California 35 years ago. He is now retiring and moving to Hawaii for his golden years. Tim sold his house for $1,200,000 this year. Tim has been a client of yours for the past decade. He became a client when he was referred to you by your parents, who lived two houses away from Tim. When asked what his tax basis is in the house, Tim says it is $975,000. Your parents bought their house at about the same time, and you know they paid $100,000 for it. You have seen Tim's house many times and, although the house is well-maintained, you know it does not have any major improvements or betterments. You are reasonably certain that Tim is overstating his tax basis by hundreds of thousands of dollars in order to avoid reporting a taxable gain on the sale. Would you sign the Paid Preparer's declaration (refer to example above) on this return? Why or why not?

12-3d Miscellaneous Penalties

The tax law contains many other penalties applicable to taxpayers. The following are examples of such penalties:

- A civil penalty of $500 and a criminal penalty of up to $1,000 are imposed for filing false withholding information.
- An immediate $5,000 penalty can be assessed against a taxpayer who files a "frivolous" tax return (or document) as a tax protest.
- A tiered penalty system dependent on the timeliness of correction and filing of information returns (including payee information returns) is imposed for failing to file correct information returns. The penalties for information returns filed in 2025 are up to $330 per return, with an annual maximum of $3,987,000 ($1,329,000 for small businesses). If the failure to file is corrected or the information returns are filed closer to the due date, the penalties may be reduced. Exceptions to the information return penalties may be made for reasonable cause.
- Employers are subject to a penalty of 2, 5, or 10 percent of the amount of payroll taxes not deposited on time, depending on the number of days the taxes remain undeposited. A 15-percent penalty may apply where taxes remain undeposited after a delinquency notice has been presented to the taxpayer.
- Taxpayers are subject to a penalty for failure to pay estimated taxes. The penalty is calculated using the interest rates for the period of underpayment (but it is not deductible as interest). Refer to Chapter 9 for more information.
- Taxpayers are subject to a penalty for issuing a "bad" check, unless the taxpayer can demonstrate that the check was issued in good faith. The penalty is equal to 2 percent of the amount of the check. If the check is less than $1,250, then the penalty is the lesser of $25 or the amount of the check.

> **Self-Study Problem 12.3** — Refer to Appendix E for Solutions to Self-Study Problems
>
> a. Linda filed her tax return 43 days late. The tax paid with the return amounts to $3,000. What is Linda's total penalty for failure to file and failure to pay, assuming the failure to file is not fraudulent?
>
> b. Using the same information as above in part a, what is Linda's total penalty if the tax return is 63 days late?
>
> c. Kim underpaid her taxes by $10,000 due to negligence. What is Kim's penalty for negligence?

12-4 Statute of Limitations

12.4 Learning Objective: Apply the general rule for the statute of limitations on tax returns and the important exceptions to the general rule.

The statute of limitations is the time period within which an action may be taken by the IRS and the taxpayer on a tax return. After the statute of limitations has run out on a given tax return, the government cannot assess additional taxes and the taxpayer cannot amend the return to request a refund. In general, the statute of limitations for a tax return runs for three years from the date the tax return was filed or the return due date (without extensions), whichever is later. For taxpayers seeking a refund, the statute of limitations is the later of three years from the time of filing or two years from the date that the taxes were actually paid.

Example Norm files his 2024 tax return on March 19, 2025. Unless an exception presented below applies, the IRS has until April 15, 2028, to assess any additional taxes. ♦

12-4a Exceptions

The tax law contains several exceptions to the general rule of a three-year statute of limitations. Several of these special rules are summarized below:

- If a fraudulent tax return is filed or no return is filed, there is no statute of limitations. The IRS may assess a tax deficiency at any time in the future.
- If a taxpayer omits an amount of gross income in excess of 25 percent of the gross income shown on the return, then the statute of limitations is increased to six years. For example, if a tax return with gross income of $40,000 contains an omission of over $10,000 (25 percent of $40,000) of gross income, the statute of limitations is increased to six years.
- The statute of limitations for the deduction of a bad debt or worthless securities is seven years. This limitation applies only to the bad debt deduction or the worthless security deduction; all other items on the tax return would normally close out after three years.

Besides these exceptions, the statute of limitations may be extended by mutual consent of the IRS and the taxpayer. This extension is for a specific time period and is made by signing the appropriate form in the Form 872 series. An extension is generally used when the statute of limitations is about to lapse and an audit has not been completed.

If a tax deficiency has been assessed by the IRS within the period of the statute of limitations, then the government has 10 years from the date of assessment to collect the tax due.

An IRS study shows that many taxpayers miss out on refunds because they fail to file their returns within the statute of limitations for claiming a refund, which can be either two or three years, depending on the circumstances. The IRS denies millions of dollars in refunds each year which were claimed in delinquent returns.

Self-Study Problem 12.4

Refer to Appendix E for Solutions to Self-Study Problems

Determine whether the following statements are true or false.

1. The general statute of limitations for a tax return is three years.
2. The statute of limitations for a bad debt deduction on a tax return is six years.
3. The statute of limitations for a fraudulent tax return is seven years.
4. The special statute of limitations is six years for a tax return that omits income greater than 25 percent of gross income.
5. For the deduction of worthless securities, the statute of limitations is seven years.

12-5 Preparers, Proof, and Privilege

Learning Objective 12.5
Describe the rules and penalties that apply to tax practitioners.

12-5a Tax Practitioners

Many taxpayers find it desirable or necessary to have their tax returns prepared by a tax practitioner. Tax practitioners include commercial preparers, enrolled agents, attorneys, and certified public accountants (CPAs). Commercial preparers generally prepare non-complex returns of individuals, small corporations, and partnerships. Enrolled agents are individuals who have passed an IRS exam and are allowed to represent clients at IRS proceedings, as well as prepare tax returns. Attorneys and CPAs are individuals who have met education, examination, and experience requirements and are licensed to practice in their respective professions. CPAs and attorneys normally work with complex tax returns of individuals, corporations, partnerships, estates, and trusts. They also provide tax-planning advice to aid their clients in minimizing the amount of their taxes. Preparers that are enrolled agents, CPAs, and attorneys are sometimes referred to as enrolled preparers while other non-credentialed preparers are known as unenrolled preparers.

Tax preparers are regulated in several different ways. For federal income tax returns, the primary regulation comes from Circular 230, which is a Treasury Department regulation. Circular 230 describes the rules for "practice before the IRS," a tax professional's duties and obligations while practicing before the IRS; authorizes specific sanctions for violations of the duties and obligations; and describes the procedures that apply to administrative proceedings for discipline. Circular 230 can be found on the IRS website (www.irs.gov/tax-professionals/office-of-professional-responsibility-and-circular-230). A number of key elements of Circular 230 are:

- Any individual who for compensation prepares or assists with the preparation of all or substantially all of a tax return or claim for refund must have a preparer tax identification number (PTIN). PTINs can be obtained and renewed online from the IRS website for a cost of about $20.

- A practitioner must, on a proper and lawful request by the IRS, promptly submit records or information in any matter before the IRS unless the practitioner believes in good faith and on reasonable grounds that the records or information are privileged.
- Where the requested records or information are not in the possession of the practitioner or the practitioner's client, the practitioner must promptly notify the IRS and the practitioner must provide any information regarding the identity of any person who the practitioner believes may have possession or control of the requested information.
- A practitioner who knows that a client has not complied with the tax law or has made an error in or omission from any return, must advise the client promptly of the fact of such noncompliance, error, or omission. The practitioner must advise the client of the consequences of such noncompliance, error, or omission.

Example Becca prepared Juno's tax return in the prior year. While preparing the current year's tax return, Becca noted an error in the prior year return. Becca has a responsibility to report the error to Juno and explain the consequences if the error is not corrected. Note that Becca is not responsible to report Juno's failure to comply. ♦

- A practitioner must exercise due diligence: (1) in preparing or assisting in the preparation of, approving, and filing tax returns; (2) in determining the correctness of oral or written representations made by the practitioner to the IRS; and (3) in determining the correctness of oral or written representations made by the practitioner to clients.
- A practitioner may not charge an unconscionable fee or contingent fee (except for contingent fees on audits, challenges to interest and penalty assessments, and judicial proceedings).
- A practitioner may not negotiate any refund check by any means into an account owned or controlled by the practitioner.

Circular 230 also provides some best practices for practitioners to follow:

- A practitioner may not willfully, recklessly, or through gross incompetence sign a tax return or claim for refund, or advise a client to take a position on a tax return or claim for refund, or prepare a portion of a tax return or claim for refund containing a position that the practitioner reasonably should know contains a position that (A) lacks a reasonable basis; (B) is an unreasonable position as described in §6694(a)(2); or (C) is a willful attempt by the practitioner to understate the liability for tax or a reckless or intentional disregard of rules or regulations.
- A practitioner may not advise a client to take a position on a document, affidavit or other paper submitted to the IRS unless the position is not frivolous.
- A practitioner must possess the necessary competence to engage in practice before the IRS. Competent practice requires the appropriate level of knowledge, skill, thoroughness, and preparation necessary for the matter for which the practitioner is engaged.

Circular 230 addresses different types of practitioners such as attorneys, CPAs, enrolled agents, registered tax return preparers (RTRPs, note that the RTRP program is no longer operative), and participants in the Annual Filing Season Program. The different practitioners have differing degrees of authority to practice under Circular 230 as shown in Table 12.4.

Table 12.4 Authority to Practice by Practitioner Type

Responsibility	Attorney CPA Enrolled Agent	Annual Filing Season Program (AFSP)	Unenrolled Preparers (non-AFSP)
Practice before IRS	Unlimited	Limited	Limited
Tax preparation	Sign when completed all or substantially all of the return	Sign when completed all or substantially all of the return	Sign when completed all or substantially all of the return
Representation	Before the IRS, during examination and appeals, and for any return or refund	Before IRS revenue agents, customer service, and employees during examination only on returns that were signed by that preparer	Before IRS revenue agents, customer service, and employees during examination only on returns that were signed by that preparer
Advising	Unlimited	Limited to return or refund preparation	Limited to return or refund preparation

Several states also regulate the preparation of income taxes including California, Illinois, Maryland, Nevada, Oregon, New York, and Connecticut. Each state has varying requirements. Iowa has a continuing education requirement but does not require registration.

12-5b Annual Filing Season Program

All paid tax return preparers must sign up with the IRS and obtain a preparer tax identification number (PTIN). Every year, paid tax preparers must sign up or renew their PTIN online.

The IRS operates the Annual Filing Season Program (AFSP), a voluntary tax return preparer program designed to encourage preparers to participate in continuing education courses to help stay abreast of changes in tax law and help reduce the risk of using a preparer without professional credentials. The AFSP requires unenrolled preparers to obtain 18 hours of continuing education from an approved provider, including at least 6 hours of an Annual Federal Tax Refresher (AFTR) course focused on filing season issues and tax updates and two hours of ethics. The AFTR must include a knowledge-based exam administered at the end of the course by the course provider.

In addition to being better prepared for the upcoming filing season, a list of tax preparers meeting the AFSP requirements is published on the IRS website to permit taxpayers to search for qualified tax return preparers. For additional information on the Annual Filing Season Program requirements, refer to the IRS website (**www.irs.gov**).

12-5c Preparer Penalties

Under the tax law, any person who prepares a tax return, including non-income tax returns (e.g., excise tax returns), for compensation is a "tax return preparer." The tax law has various penalty provisions applicable to tax return preparers. These penalties are designed to help the IRS regulate the preparation of tax returns. The more significant penalties are described below:

- $60 for failing to sign a tax return or failing to furnish the preparer's identifying number, $31,500 annual maximum
- $60 for each failure to keep a copy of the prepared return or include the return on a list of taxpayers for whom returns have been prepared, $31,500 annual maximum
- $60 for failing to provide a taxpayer a copy of the tax return prepared, $31,500 annual maximum
- $635 for endorsing or cashing a refund check issued to a taxpayer
- $635 for failure to be diligent in the preparation of eligibility to file as head of household, child tax credit, American Opportunities credit, and earned income credit (Form 8867)
- Greater of $1,000 or 50 percent of the income derived (or to be derived) by the tax return preparer for an undisclosed unrealistic position on a return which does not meet a "substantial authority" standard, and which the preparer knew or reasonably should have known about
- Greater of $5,000 or 75 percent of the income derived (or to be derived) by the tax return preparer for each return in which the preparer willfully attempts to understate the amount of the taxpayer's tax liability, or each return in which an understatement is due to the preparer's reckless or intentional disregard of rules or regulations, reduced by the amount of the $1,000 (or 50 percent) penalty for unrealistic positions (presented above)
- $1,000 ($10,000 for corporate returns) for each return or document filed in aiding or abetting a taxpayer in understating a tax liability
- For each separate activity (sale of an interest, organization of an entity, etc.), the lesser of $1,000 or 100 percent of the gross income derived by the promoter from promoting an "abusive tax shelter"

The tax preparer penalty rules introduce two very important terms: (1) substantial authority and (2) reasonable basis. The understatement penalty can potentially be avoided by the tax preparer if they have substantial authority for the tax position taken or if substantial authority does not exist, a reasonable basis (which is considered a lower standard to meet) for the position exists and such position is disclosed. The substantial authority standard is an objective standard involving an analysis of the law and application of the law to relevant facts and requires that the tax preparer establish that support for the tax position within a set of authoritative guidance:

- Applicable provisions of the Internal Revenue Code and other federal tax law;
- Proposed, temporary, and final regulations;
- Revenue rulings and revenue procedures;
- Tax treaties and regulations thereunder, and Treasury Department and other official explanations of such treaties;
- Court cases;
- Congressional intent as reflected in committee reports, joint explanatory statements of managers included in conference committee reports, and floor statements made prior to enactment by one of a bill's managers;
- General Explanations of tax legislation prepared by the Joint Committee on Taxation (the Blue Book);

- Private letter rulings and technical advice memoranda issued after October 31, 1976;
- Actions on decisions and general counsel memoranda issued after March 12, 1981 (as well as general counsel memoranda published in pre-1955 volumes of the Cumulative Bulletin);
- Internal Revenue Service information or press releases; and
- Notices, announcements and other administrative pronouncements published by the Service in the Internal Revenue Bulletin.

Conclusions reached in treatises, periodicals, newspapers, and textbooks are not considered substantial authority.

A reasonable basis for a position is one that is significantly higher than frivolous or not patently improper. It must be more than merely arguable or a colorable claim. The position is considered reasonable if based on one or more of the authorities that are part of substantial authority. The required disclosure is made on Form 8275.

The longstanding position that erroneous instructions from an IRS employee that result in additional tax do not represent an excuse for taxpayers was tested in the Tax Court again in 2021 and unsurprisingly, maintained. As the Tax Court has stated many times, "the authoritative sources of Federal tax law are in the statutes, regulations, and judicial decisions', not in informal advice or publications."

12-5d Burden of Proof

In most litigation, the party initiating the case has the burden of convincing the court that they are correct with respect to the issue. Historically however, in most civil tax cases, the Internal Revenue Code (the Code) placed the burden of proof on the taxpayer, whether or not they initiated the case, except in cases involving such items as hobby losses, fraud with intent to evade tax, and the accumulated earnings tax.

In the IRS Restructuring and Reform Act of 1998, the tax law was changed to shift the burden of proof to the IRS in many situations. The IRS now has the burden of proof in any court proceeding on an income, gift, estate, or generation-skipping tax liability with respect to factual issues, provided the taxpayer (1) introduces credible evidence of the factual issue, (2) maintains records and substantiates items as presently required under the Code and Regulations, and (3) cooperates with reasonable IRS requests for meetings, interviews, witnesses, information, and documents. For corporations, trusts, and partnerships with net worth exceeding $7 million, the burden of proof remains on the taxpayer.

The burden of proof also automatically shifts to the IRS in two situations:

1. If the IRS uses statistics to reconstruct an individual's income, or
2. If the court proceeding against an individual taxpayer involves a penalty or addition to tax.

12-5e Tax Confidentiality Privilege

The 1998 Act also extended the existing attorney-client privilege of confidentiality in tax matters to nonattorneys authorized to practice before the IRS (e.g., CPAs and enrolled agents). The nonattorney-client privilege may be asserted only in a *noncriminal tax* proceeding before the IRS or federal courts. Also, the nonattorney-client privilege does not extend to written communications between a tax practitioner and a corporation in connection with the promotion of any tax shelter.

CPAs and enrolled agents need to understand the rules regarding tax confidentiality as they have been applied to lawyers to be aware of the tax privilege limits. For example, tax privileged communication usually does not apply to the preparation of tax returns, the giving of accounting or business advice, or to tax accrual workpapers. Also, unlike the general attorney-client privilege, the nonattorney-client privilege does not automatically apply to state tax situations.

Self-Study Problem 12.5
Refer to Appendix E for Solutions to Self-Study Problems

Determine whether the following statements are true or false.

1. Only certified public accountants may represent taxpayers before the IRS.
2. A college degree is required to prepare tax returns for compensation.
3. Only attorneys may prepare corporate tax returns.
4. The tax preparer penalty for filing a document aiding or abetting an individual taxpayer in the understatement of a tax liability is $1,000.
5. The tax preparer penalty for endorsing a taxpayer's refund check is $600.
6. The tax preparer penalty for failing to provide a copy of a tax return to a taxpayer is $60.
7. For audits after 1998, if the IRS uses statistics to reconstruct an individual taxpayer's income, the burden of proof is on the taxpayer.
8. For corporations, trusts, and partnerships with net worth over $7 million, the burden of proof is on the IRS in civil tax matters.
9. CPAs and enrolled agents have tax privileged communication only in noncriminal proceedings before the IRS or federal courts.
10. If an individual taxpayer does not cooperate with reasonable IRS requests for meetings, interviews, witnesses, information, and documents, the burden of proof in a tax matter is on the taxpayer.
11. Commercial tax preparers must have a PTIN.
12. A *Wall Street Journal* article on taxes is substantial authority for purposes of tax preparer penalties.
13. A tax preparer has a reasonable basis for a tax position but lacks substantial authority. If the position is disclosed, the tax preparer can avoid penalty.
14. Circular 230 provides guidance for those that wish to practice before the IRS.

12-6 The Taxpayer Bill of Rights

Learning Objective 12.6
Describe the Taxpayer Bill of Rights.

Over the years, the news media carried many horror stories about taxpayers who claimed they had been abused by the IRS. As a result of this publicity, in 1988 Congress passed a set of provisions referred to as the Taxpayer Bill of Rights. The Taxpayer Bill of Rights has been amended several times since it was originally passed by Congress. This set of provisions requires the IRS to inform taxpayers of their rights in dealing with the IRS, and expands taxpayers' rights and remedies when they are involved in disputes with the IRS. The provisions of the Taxpayer Bill of Rights are summarized in IRS Publication 1, which is reproduced on Pages 12-23 and 12-24. Also note, Publication 1 directs taxpayers to other IRS publications with more details on specific taxpayer rights.

The first part of this publication explains some of the most important rights as a taxpayer. The second part explains the examination, appeal, collection, and refund processes.

Self-Study Problem 12.6
Refer to Appendix E for Solutions to Self-Study Problems

Determine whether the following statements are true or false.

1. Taxpayers have the right to represent themselves or, with proper written authorization, have someone else represent them.
2. The IRS may contact a taxpayer's neighbor or employer to verify information.
3. IRS Publication 594 explains a taxpayer's rights and responsibilities regarding payment of federal taxes.
4. If a taxpayer is audited in the current year for an item that was audited in either of the two previous years and the IRS proposed no change to the tax liability, the taxpayer should contact the IRS as soon as possible to attempt to stop the repeat audit.
5. Generally, both a taxpayer and their spouse are responsible, jointly and individually, for the tax and any interest or penalty due on a joint return.
6. Taxpayers must file a claim for refund within three years of the date they filed their return or two years from the date they paid the tax if they think they paid too much tax.

12-7 Tax Planning

Learning Objective 12.7
Explain the basic concepts of tax planning.

The process of arranging one's financial affairs to maximize one's after-tax wealth is often referred to as tax planning. There is nothing wrong with tax planning to avoid tax, provided legal methods are used. Judge Learned Hand best stated the doctrine of tax planning in 1947 when he wrote:

"Over and over again, courts have said there is nothing sinister in so arranging one's affairs as to keep taxes as low as possible. Everybody does so, rich or poor, and all do right, for nobody owes any public duty to pay more than the law demands: taxes are enforced extractions, not voluntary contributions." *Commissioner v. Newman*, 159 F.2d 848 (CA-2, 1947).

Your Rights as a Taxpayer

Publication 1

This publication explains your rights as a taxpayer and the processes for examination, appeal, collection, and refunds. Also available in Spanish.

The Taxpayer Bill of Rights

1. The Right to Be Informed
Taxpayers have the right to know what they need to do to comply with the tax laws. They are entitled to clear explanations of the laws and IRS procedures in all tax forms, instructions, publications, notices, and correspondence. They have the right to be informed of IRS decisions about their tax accounts and to receive clear explanations of the outcomes.

2. The Right to Quality Service
Taxpayers have the right to receive prompt, courteous, and professional assistance in their dealings with the IRS, to be spoken to in a way they can easily understand, to receive clear and easily understandable communications from the IRS, and to speak to a supervisor about inadequate service.

3. The Right to Pay No More than the Correct Amount of Tax
Taxpayers have the right to pay only the amount of tax legally due, including interest and penalties, and to have the IRS apply all tax payments properly.

4. The Right to Challenge the IRS's Position and Be Heard
Taxpayers have the right to raise objections and provide additional documentation in response to formal IRS actions or proposed actions, to expect that the IRS will consider their timely objections and documentation promptly and fairly, and to receive a response if the IRS does not agree with their position.

5. The Right to Appeal an IRS Decision in an Independent Forum
Taxpayers are entitled to a fair and impartial administrative appeal of most IRS decisions, including many penalties, and have the right to receive a written response regarding the Office of Appeals' decision. Taxpayers generally have the right to take their cases to court.

6. The Right to Finality
Taxpayers have the right to know the maximum amount of time they have to challenge the IRS's position as well as the maximum amount of time the IRS has to audit a particular tax year or collect a tax debt. Taxpayers have the right to know when the IRS has finished an audit.

7. The Right to Privacy
Taxpayers have the right to expect that any IRS inquiry, examination, or enforcement action will comply with the law and be no more intrusive than necessary, and will respect all due process rights, including search and seizure protections, and will provide, where applicable, a collection due process hearing.

8. The Right to Confidentiality
Taxpayers have the right to expect that any information they provide to the IRS will not be disclosed unless authorized by the taxpayer or by law. Taxpayers have the right to expect appropriate action will be taken against employees, return preparers, and others who wrongfully use or disclose taxpayer return information.

9. The Right to Retain Representation
Taxpayers have the right to retain an authorized representative of their choice to represent them in their dealings with the IRS. Taxpayers have the right to seek assistance from a Low Income Taxpayer Clinic if they cannot afford representation.

10. The Right to a Fair and Just Tax System
Taxpayers have the right to expect the tax system to consider facts and circumstances that might affect their underlying liabilities, ability to pay, or ability to provide information timely. Taxpayers have the right to receive assistance from the Taxpayer Advocate Service if they are experiencing financial difficulty or if the IRS has not resolved their tax issues properly and timely through its normal channels.

The IRS Mission | Provide America's taxpayers top-quality service by helping them understand and meet their tax responsibilities and enforce the law with integrity and fairness to all.

Publication 1 (Rev. 9-2017) Catalog Number 64731W Department of the Treasury **Internal Revenue Service** www.irs.gov

Source: Internal Revenue Service (IRS)

Examinations, Appeals, Collections, and Refunds

Examinations (Audits)

We accept most taxpayers' returns as filed. If we inquire about your return or select it for examination, it does not suggest that you are dishonest. The inquiry or examination may or may not result in more tax. We may close your case without change; or, you may receive a refund.

The process of selecting a return for examination usually begins in one of two ways. First, we use computer programs to identify returns that may have incorrect amounts. These programs may be based on information returns, such as Forms 1099 and W-2, on studies of past examinations, or on certain issues identified by compliance projects. Second, we use information from outside sources that indicates that a return may have incorrect amounts. These sources may include newspapers, public records, and individuals. If we determine that the information is accurate and reliable, we may use it to select a return for examination.

Publication 556, Examination of Returns, Appeal Rights, and Claims for Refund, explains the rules and procedures that we follow in examinations. The following sections give an overview of how we conduct examinations.

By Mail

We handle many examinations and inquiries by mail. We will send you a letter with either a request for more information or a reason why we believe a change to your return may be needed. You can respond by mail or you can request a personal interview with an examiner. If you mail us the requested information or provide an explanation, we may or may not agree with you, and we will explain the reasons for any changes. Please do not hesitate to write to us about anything you do not understand.

By Interview

If we notify you that we will conduct your examination through a personal interview, or you request such an interview, you have the right to ask that the examination take place at a reasonable time and place that is convenient for both you and the IRS. If our examiner proposes any changes to your return, he or she will explain the reasons for the changes. If you do not agree with these changes, you can meet with the examiner's supervisor.

Repeat Examinations

If we examined your return for the same items in either of the 2 previous years and proposed no change to your tax liability, please contact us as soon as possible so we can see if we should discontinue the examination.

Appeals

If you do not agree with the examiner's proposed changes, you can appeal them to the Appeals Office of the IRS. Most differences can be settled without expensive and time-consuming court trials. Your appeal rights are explained in detail in both Publication 5, Your Appeal Rights and How To Prepare a Protest If You Don't Agree, and Publication 556, Examination of Returns, Appeal Rights, and Claims for Refund.

If you do not wish to use the Appeals Office or disagree with its findings, you may be able to take your case to the U.S. Tax Court, U.S. Court of Federal Claims, or the U.S. District Court where you live. If you take your case to court, the IRS will have the burden of proving certain facts if you kept adequate records to show your tax liability, cooperated with the IRS, and meet certain other conditions. If the court agrees with you on most issues in your case and finds that our position was largely unjustified, you may be able to recover some of your administrative and litigation costs. You will not be eligible to recover these costs unless you tried to resolve your case administratively, including going through the appeals system, and you gave us the information necessary to resolve the case.

Collections

Publication 594, The IRS Collection Process, explains your rights and responsibilities regarding payment of federal taxes. It describes:

- What to do when you owe taxes. It describes what to do if you get a tax bill and what to do if you think your bill is wrong. It also covers making installment payments, delaying collection action, and submitting an offer in compromise.
- IRS collection actions. It covers liens, releasing a lien, levies, releasing a levy, seizures and sales, and release of property.
- IRS certification to the State Department of a seriously delinquent tax debt, which will generally result in denial of a passport application and may lead to revocation of a passport.

Your collection appeal rights are explained in detail in Publication 1660, Collection Appeal Rights.

Innocent Spouse Relief

Generally, both you and your spouse are each responsible for paying the full amount of tax, interest, and penalties due on your joint return. However, if you qualify for innocent spouse relief, you may be relieved of part or all of the joint liability. To request relief, you must file Form 8857, Request for Innocent Spouse Relief. For more information on innocent spouse relief, see Publication 971, Innocent Spouse Relief, and Form 8857.

Potential Third Party Contacts

Generally, the IRS will deal directly with you or your duly authorized representative. However, we sometimes talk with other persons if we need information that you have been unable to provide, or to verify information we have received. If we do contact other persons, such as a neighbor, bank, employer, or employees, we will generally need to tell them limited information, such as your name. The law prohibits us from disclosing any more information than is necessary to obtain or verify the information we are seeking. Our need to contact other persons may continue as long as there is activity in your case. If we do contact other persons, you have a right to request a list of those contacted. Your request can be made by telephone, in writing, or during a personal interview.

Refunds

You may file a claim for refund if you think you paid too much tax. You must generally file the claim within 3 years from the date you filed your original return or 2 years from the date you paid the tax, whichever is later. The law generally provides for interest on your refund if it is not paid within 45 days of the date you filed your return or claim for refund. Publication 556, Examination of Returns, Appeal Rights, and Claims for Refund, has more information on refunds.

If you were due a refund but you did not file a return, you generally must file your return within 3 years from the date the return was due (including extensions) to get that refund.

Taxpayer Advocate Service

TAS is an *independent* organization within the IRS that can help protect your taxpayer rights. We can offer you help if your tax problem is causing a hardship, or you've tried but haven't been able to resolve your problem with the IRS. If you qualify for our assistance, which is always free, we will do everything possible to help you. Visit www.taxpayeradvocate.irs.gov or call 1-877-777-4778.

Tax Information

The IRS provides the following sources for forms, publications, and additional information.

- *Tax Questions:* 1-800-829-1040 (1-800-829-4059 for TTY/TDD)
- *Forms and Publications:* 1-800-829-3676 (1-800-829-4059 for TTY/TDD)
- *Internet:* www.irs.gov
- *Small Business Ombudsman:* A small business entity can participate in the regulatory process and comment on enforcement actions of the IRS by calling 1-888-REG-FAIR.
- *Treasury Inspector General for Tax Administration:* You can confidentially report misconduct, waste, fraud, or abuse by an IRS employee by calling 1-800-366-4484 (1-800-877-8339 for TTY/TDD). You can remain anonymous.

When illegal methods are used to reduce tax liability, the process can no longer be considered tax planning, but instead becomes tax evasion. Tax evasion can subject the taxpayer and tax practitioner to fines, penalties, and incarceration. Illegal acts are outside the realm of tax-planning services offered by a professional tax practitioner.

Tax planning covers two basic categories of transactions: the "open transaction" and the "closed transaction." In an open transaction, all the events have not yet been completed; therefore, the taxpayer has some degree of control over the tax consequences. In a closed transaction, all material parts of the transaction have been completed. As a result, tax planning involving a closed transaction is limited to presentation of the facts to the IRS in the most favorable, legally acceptable manner possible.

Example Annie enters into an agreement with Erik to exchange real estate held as an investment. Escrow has not closed and the title of the property has not passed between the parties. Since all significant events (title passing) are not complete, the transaction is considered an open transaction. Once the title to the real estate passes, the tax planning involves a closed transaction. ♦

Tax planning cannot be considered in a void. Any tax-planning advice must consider the business goals of the taxpayer. Tax planning for a transaction should not override sound business judgment.

12-7a Tax Rate Terminology

Important to any tax-planning situation is an evaluation of the tax savings arising from increasing deductions or the tax cost of generating additional income. The tax consequences are dependent on the taxpayer's tax rate. The taxpayer's tax rate may be defined in several ways. For tax-planning purposes, the taxpayer needs to understand the difference between the "average" tax rate and the "marginal" tax rate. The average tax rate merely represents the average rate of tax applicable to the taxpayer's income and is calculated as the total tax paid divided by the total income (or sometimes taxable income) of the taxpayer. The marginal tax rate represents the rate at which tax is imposed on the "next" dollar of income.

Example Becky, a single taxpayer, has income of $48,000 during the current year on which she pays tax of $5,619. Her average tax rate is 11.7 percent ($5,619 ÷ $48,000). If Becky's income increases to $58,000, her tax liability will be $7,819. Thus, Becky's marginal rate is 22 percent [($7,819 − $5,619) ÷ ($58,000 − $48,000)]. ♦

When making tax-planning decisions, the taxpayer's marginal tax rate is the most important tax rate. For example, Jason has a 30-percent marginal tax rate and a 20-percent average tax rate and is considering making a tax-deductible expenditure of $2,000. His after-tax cost of the expenditure is calculated using his marginal tax rate, not his average tax rate. Jason's after-tax cost of the expenditure would be $1,400, calculated as follows: [$2,000 − ($2,000 × 30%)]. On the other hand, if Jason is to receive any additional income, he knows that he will pay tax at a rate of 30 percent on the next dollar of income.

12-7b Examples of Tax Planning

Tax planning opportunities can be classified into four categories: (1) timing, (2) jurisdiction, (3) entity, and (4) character. Most tax-planning techniques employ at least one of these characteristics in an attempt to save taxpayers money.

12-7c Timing

In its simplest form, timing implies deferring the payment of taxes to a future year and is generally achieved by either deferring income recognition or accelerating expense deduction.

Example Kara operates a small cash-basis, calendar-year-end business. In order to lower her current year's income, Kara may prepay January's rent in December. She could also delay invoicing her customers in an attempt to defer the recognition of income. ♦

Most simple timing techniques work best when tax rates are not expected to change. If tax rates are expected to change across the periods in which the timing is being changed, a more thorough analysis is going to be required.

Example If in the previous example, Kara expects her tax rate to increase from 24 percent in the current year to 37 percent next year, she may want to consider accelerating the recognition of income into the current year at the lower rate and deferring the deduction of expenses until next year, increasing the value of the deduction. ♦

One disadvantage of using the timing technique is that tax recognition frequently occurs simultaneously with cash transactions. For example, one way to defer income recognition might be to earn no income; however, that generally involves fairly disastrous non-tax consequences.

12-7d Jurisdiction

Using jurisdiction for tax planning involves exploiting differences in tax rates or tax systems to lower tax liabilities.

Example Mark worked for the Lake Tahoe office of the state of California Department of Motor Vehicles for 35 years. In the current year, he starts his well-deserved retirement. Realizing that the individual state tax rate in California can be greater than 10 percent, he moves to nearby Reno, Nevada, knowing that Nevada has no state income tax on individuals. He continues to collect his pension without paying state income tax. ♦

Jurisdiction, although simple in concept, can be difficult to implement for many taxpayers. Most individuals do not have the luxury to simply move to a new state to lower the state income tax rate. Larger businesses may have more flexibility than individuals or small businesses to implement a jurisdictional tax plan.

12-7e Entity

Entity-based tax planning involves making a choice about the type of entity a taxpayer chooses to operate as.

Example Raquel is starting a new small business and expects to operate at a loss for the first few years. In an attempt to take advantage of using the losses to offset her other forms of income, she establishes her new business as a flow-through entity such as an LLC in hopes of passing those losses through to her individual tax return. Perhaps later in the life of her business when it becomes profitable, she will convert to a different entity such as a corporation. ♦

12-7f Character

Using character for tax planning often requires a deeper understanding of tax law than the other tax-planning techniques. Using character means the transaction will be designed to take advantage of the tax law or a taxpayer's current situation.

Example Axel owns stock purchased eleven months ago which has now doubled in value. Although Axel thinks the stock's value has peaked, he wishes to wait one additional month before selling, to convert the short-term capital gain taxed at ordinary tax rates into a long-term capital gain taxed at preferential rates. Although this might also feel like a timing-based plan, the one-month deferral of taxes is not likely to be significant but changing the tax rate from Axel's ordinary rate (as high as 37 percent) to the long-term capital gains rate (as low as 0 percent) is a substantial tax savings. ♦

Example Beck is a single taxpayer with a 24-percent marginal tax rate. Beck is debating between an investment in a taxable bond that pays 5 percent or a tax-exempt bond that pays 4.5 percent. Although the pre-tax return on the taxable bond of 5 percent is higher than the 4.5 percent tax-exempt bond, the after-tax return of the taxable bond is only 3.8 percent [5% × (1 − 0.24 marginal tax rate)]. ♦

Self-Study Problem 12.7
Refer to Appendix E for Solutions to Self-Study Problems

During the current year, K's taxable income is $94,000 and they pay income tax of $10,819. K is married filing jointly, has no dependents, and does not itemize their deductions. J, who files in *exactly* the same manner as K, has taxable income of $95,000 and pays income tax of $11,012.

1. What is K's average tax rate?
2. What is J's average tax rate?
3. If K's income increased to the same amount as J, what would K's marginal tax rate be?

Key Terms

Internal Revenue Service (IRS), 12-2
campus processing sites, 12-2
Small Business/Self-Employed Division, 12-4
Taxpayer Services Division, 12-4
offer in compromise, 12-5
correspondence audit, 12-6
office audit, 12-6
field audit, 12-6

Discriminant Function System (DIF), 12-7
appeals, 12-8
Tax Court, 12-8
failure-to-pay penalty, 12-12
failure-to-file penalty, 12-12
accuracy penalty, 12-13
fraud penalty, 12-13
statute of limitations, 12-15
Circular 230, 12-16

Preparer Tax Identification Number (PTIN), 12-17
Annual Filing Season Program (AFSP), 12-18
preparer penalties, 12-19
substantial authority, 12-19
burden of proof, 12-20
Taxpayer Bill of Rights, 12-22
marginal tax rate, 12-25
average tax rate, 12-25

Key Points

Learning Objectives	Key Points
LO 12.1: Identify the organizational structure of the Internal Revenue Service (IRS).	• The IRS is a bureau of the Treasury Department, tasked with administering the tax laws of the United States. • The national IRS office is the headquarters of the commissioner of internal revenue. The commissioner of internal revenue is appointed by the President of the United States with the advice and consent of the Senate. • The IRS maintains Campus Processing Sites where the IRS computers process the information from tax documents such as tax returns, payroll tax forms, Forms 1099, and withholding forms. • The IRS maintains a national computer center where information from various processing sites is matched with records from other processing sites. • The IRS has the authority to examine a taxpayer's books and records to determine the correct amount of tax due. The IRS also has the right to summon taxpayers to appear before the IRS and produce necessary accounting records.
LO 12.2: Describe the IRS audit process.	• A primary function of the IRS is to audit taxpayers' tax returns. • Correspondence audits are generally handled entirely by mail and account for the majority of the individual tax returns examined each year. • The office audit is conducted in an IRS office and is typically used for individual taxpayers with little or no business activities. • In a field audit, the IRS agent reviews a taxpayer's books and records at the taxpayer's place of business or at the office of the taxpayer's accountant. • For computer scoring, the IRS uses the Discriminant Function System (DIF) to select tax returns for audits of individuals. • Under the DIF system, the IRS uses mathematical formulas to assign a DIF score to each return, which represents the potential for discovery of improper treatment of items on the tax return. • The IRS also selects returns for audit through different methods such as identification of participants in abusive tax avoidance transactions, selection of large corporations, information matching, related examinations, and other means. • If an audit results in a disagreement between the agent and the taxpayer, the appeals procedure begins with the IRS inviting the taxpayer to an informal conference with an appellate agent.
LO 12.3: Define the common penalties for taxpayers and apply them to specific situations.	• Taxpayers are charged interest on underpayments of taxes, and in some cases, the IRS pays interest to taxpayers when they overpay their taxes. • The interest rate applicable to underpayments and overpayments of taxes is adjusted each quarter and is equal to the federal short-term rate plus 3 percentage points. • The penalty for failure to pay is ½ of 1 percent of the amount of taxes due for every month or portion of a month that the payment is late (up to a maximum of 25 percent of the total taxes due). • The failure to file a tax return is subject to a penalty equal to 5 percent of the tax due with the return, for every month or portion of a month the return is late (up to a maximum of 25 percent). If filed more than sixty days from the due date, the minimum failure to file is the lesser of the tax due or $510. • The accuracy-related penalty is 20 percent of the applicable underpayment due to (1) negligence of or disregard for rules or regulations, (2) a substantial understatement of income tax, or (3) a substantial valuation overstatement, as well as certain other understatements of income tax. • When a taxpayer files a fraudulent tax return, there is a fraud penalty equal to 75 percent of the amount of underpayment of taxes attributable to fraud. • The tax law contains many other penalties applicable to taxpayers, including but not limited to a civil penalty of $500 and a criminal penalty of up to $1,000 imposed for filing false withholding information, and there is an immediate $5,000 penalty for filing a "frivolous" tax return (or document) as a tax protest.

LO 12.4: Apply the general rule for the statute of limitations on tax returns and the important exceptions to the general rule.	• In general, the statute of limitations for a tax return runs for three years from the date the tax return was filed or the return due date (without extensions), whichever is later. • If a fraudulent tax return is filed or no return is filed, there is no statute of limitations. • If a taxpayer omits an amount of gross income in excess of 25 percent of the gross income shown on the return, then the statute of limitations is increased to six years. • The statute of limitations for the deduction of a bad debt or worthless securities is seven years (all other items on the tax return would normally be considered closed out after three years). • The statute of limitations may be extended by mutual consent of the IRS and the taxpayer.
LO 12.5: Describe the rules and penalties that apply to tax practitioners.	• Tax practitioners include commercial preparers, enrolled agents, attorneys, and certified public accountants (CPAs). • Circular 230 describes the rules for practice before the IRS. • Unenrolled preparers can currently participate in the Annual Filing Season Program, a voluntary program created to encourage preparers to participate in continuing education. • Tax return preparer penalties include, but are not limited to, (1) $60 for failing to sign a tax return or failing to furnish the preparer's identifying number, (2) $60 for each failure to keep a copy of the prepared return or include the return on a list of taxpayers for whom returns have been prepared, or (3) $60 for failing to provide a taxpayer with a copy of the tax return prepared. • Tax preparers can avoid penalties by ensuring that tax positions have substantial authority or if no such authority exists, a reasonable basis for the position exists and is disclosed to the IRS. • The IRS has the burden of proof in any court proceeding with respect to factual issues, provided the taxpayer (1) introduces credible evidence of the factual issue, (2) maintains records and substantiates items, and (3) cooperates with reasonable IRS requests for meetings, interviews, witnesses, information, and documents. • The tax law extends the attorney-client privilege of confidentiality in noncriminal tax matters to nonattorneys authorized to practice before the IRS (e.g., CPAs and enrolled agents).
LO 12.6: Describe the Taxpayer Bill of Rights.	• The Taxpayer Bill of Rights (IRS Publication 1) requires the IRS to inform taxpayers of their rights in dealing with the IRS, and expands taxpayers' rights and remedies when they are involved in disputes with the IRS.
LO 12.7: Explain the basic concepts of tax planning.	• Tax planning is the process of arranging one's financial affairs to minimize one's overall tax liability. • When illegal methods are used to reduce tax liability, the process can no longer be considered tax planning, but instead becomes tax evasion. • For making tax-planning decisions, the taxpayer's marginal tax rate is the most important tax rate to consider.

Questions and Problems

Group 1:
Multiple Choice Questions

LO 12.1 1. Which of the following is a responsibility of a local office of the IRS?
   a. Advising the Treasury Department on legislation
   b. Intelligence operations
   c. Appellate procedures
   d. Developing IRS rules and regulations
   e. None of the above

LO 12.1 2. The IRS does *not* have the authority to:
   a. Examine a taxpayer's books and records
   b. Summon taxpayers to make them appear before the IRS
   c. Summon third parties for taxpayer records
   d. Place a lien on taxpayer property
   e. None of the above—the IRS has the authority to do all these

LO 12.2 3. Which of the following is the most common type of audit for an individual taxpayer?
   a. Office audit
   b. Correspondence audit
   c. Telephone audit
   d. Field audit
   e. Service center audit

LO 12.2 4. In which of the following ways are tax returns selected for audits?
   a. Through the Discriminant Function System
   b. Through informants
   c. Through news sources
   d. Through information matching
   e. All of the above

LO 12.2 5. When the IRS has completed their examination and the result is an assessment of additional tax, which of the following is *not* a viable option for the taxpayer?
   a. Disagree with the assessment and request an appeal
   b. Agree to the assessment and pay the additional tax
   c. Fail to act and wait for the 90-day letter and either pay the tax and file a claim for a refund or petition the Tax Court
   d. Do not pay the tax and request a District Court hearing

LO 12.2 6. Which of the following is *not* a source of information from which the IRS identifies possible audit targets?
   a. A computer scoring system that identifies possible errors on tax returns
   b. The client records of a particularly abusive tax scheme promoter
   c. News sources
   d. Whistleblowers
   e. All of these items could be sources for IRS audit selection

LO 12.3 7. Which of the following is *not* a penalty that may be imposed by the IRS?
   a. Failure-to-file penalty
   b. Failure-to-pay penalty
   c. Penalty for negligence
   d. Early filing penalty
   e. All of the above may be imposed by the IRS

LO 12.3 8. Martha inadvertently failed to file her 2024 tax return for eleven months. The tax due on the return was $1,000. Her failure to file penalty will be:
   a. $250
   b. $225
   c. $510
   d. $5,000

LO 12.3 9. Which of the following best describes the interest and interest rates for under and overpayments of income tax liability?
   a. The underpayment rate is higher than the overpayment rate.
   b. The interest charged on underpayments is deductible.
   c. The interest paid on overpayments is tax-exempt income.
   d. The overpayment rate and underpayment rate are generally equal and underpayment interest is not deductible and overpayment interest is taxable.

LO 12.3 10. If the IRS owes a taxpayer a refund, the law generally provides that the IRS must pay interest on the refund if it is not paid within _____ days of the date the taxpayer filed their tax return or claim for refund.
   a. 30
   b. 45
   c. 60
   d. 90
   e. None of the above

LO 12.3 11. A taxpayer incorrectly reports income and has a substantial understatement of income tax in the amount of $20,000 (but no fraud). The accuracy-related penalty for this error is:
   a. $20,000
   b. $1,000 (5 percent)
   c. $4,000 (20 percent)
   d. $15,000 (75 percent)

LO 12.3 12. The taxpayer penalty for writing a check to pay for taxes that has insufficient funds is:
   a. The same amount the bank charges the IRS for a returned check
   b. 5 percent of the amount of the total tax liability of the taxpayer
   c. 2 percent of the amount of the check unless the check is for $1,250 or less
   d. Double the check amount

LO 12.4 13. If a taxpayer's 2024 individual income tax return is due on April 15, 2025 and was filed on March 4, 2025, the statute of limitations would normally run out on:
   a. April 15, 2027
   b. March 4, 2026
   c. April 15, 2028
   d. March 4, 2028
   e. None of the above

LO 12.4 14. If a taxpayer's 2024 individual income tax return is due on April 15, 2025 and was filed on June 4, 2025, the statute of limitations would normally run out on:
   a. April 15, 2027
   b. June 4, 2026
   c. April 15, 2028
   d. June 4, 2028
   e. None of the above

LO 12.4 15. Which of the following has a six-year statute of limitations?
   a. Depreciation
   b. Salaries
   c. Travel and entertainment
   d. A return in which the taxpayer omitted gross income in excess of 25 percent of the gross income shown on the return
   e. Worthless securities

LO 12.5 16. Which of the following tax preparers may *not* represent their clients in all IRS proceedings?
   a. An enrolled agent
   b. A certified public accountant
   c. An attorney
   d. All of the above may represent their clients in IRS proceedings

LO 12.5 17. If a tax preparer notes an error on a client's tax return, under Circular 230, the tax preparer should:
   a. Report the mistake to the IRS immediately
   b. Prepare an amended tax return and file such return immediately
   c. Notify the client of the error and the consequences of not correcting it
   d. Contact local authorities and consider whistleblower rewards

LO 12.5 18. Which of the following does *not* result in a minimum $60 fine for an income tax preparer?
   a. Failure to provide a tax preparer identification number
   b. Cashing a refund check for a customer
   c. Failing to keep any record of the returns prepared
   d. Failing to provide a copy of their prepared return to a customer

LO 12.5 19. In which of the following situations does the burden of proof in a tax matter *not* automatically shift to the IRS?
   a. The IRS uses statistics to reconstruct an individual's income.
   b. A court proceeding against an individual taxpayer involves a penalty or addition to tax.
   c. A taxpayer who did not maintain records.
   d. a and b are correct.
   e. a, b, and c are correct.

LO 12.5 20. Which of the following have privileged communication with a client in a noncriminal tax matter?
   a. CPAs
   b. Enrolled agents
   c. Attorneys
   d. a and c
   e. a, b, and c

LO 12.5 21. The burden of proof remains on the taxpayer for corporations, trusts, and partnerships with net worth exceeding:
   a. $1 million
   b. $3 million
   c. $5 million
   d. $7 million
   e. Some other amount

LO 12.6 22. The IRS does *not* have to furnish the taxpayer with information concerning which of the following items?
   a. The way the taxpayer's return was selected for audit
   b. The procedures for appealing an IRS ruling
   c. The refund claims process
   d. The IRS collection process
   e. All of the above must be provided to the taxpayer

LO 12.6 23. Both spouses are responsible, jointly and individually, for paying the full amount of any tax, interest, or penalties due on a joint return. Which of the following is correct in reference to the preceding statement?
   a. This does not apply to spouses who have divorced after the return was filed.
   b. Spouses are responsible jointly but not individually.
   c. Spouses are responsible individually but not jointly.
   d. Innocent spouses may be relieved of the liability for tax, interest, and penalties.
   e. None of the above.

LO 12.6 24. A taxpayer's rights are explained in:
   a. Publication 5
   b. Publication 17
   c. Publication 556
   d. Publication 1
   e. None of the above

LO 12.6 25. Taxpayers have the right to have an IRS examination take place at:
a. The IRS office
b. Any city of the taxpayer's choosing
c. A neutral site
d. A reasonable time and place
e. None of the above

LO 12.6 26. If a U.S. Tax Court agrees with the taxpayer on appeal that the IRS position was largely unjustified, which of the following is correct?
a. The taxpayer must still pay administrative and litigation costs.
b. The taxpayer may recover administrative but not litigation costs.
c. The taxpayer may recover litigation but not administrative costs.
d. To be eligible to recover some of the administrative and litigation costs, the taxpayer must have tried to resolve the case administratively, including going through the appeals process, and must have given the IRS the information necessary to resolve the case.
e. None of the above.

LO 12.7 27. Glen's taxable income is $50,000 and he pays income tax of $6,059. If his income were $60,000, he would pay taxes of $8,259. What is Glen's marginal tax rate?
a. 18.23%
b. 22.00%
c. 12.00%
d. 25.00%
e. Some other amount

LO 12.7 28. Melodie's taxable income is $45,000 and she pays income tax of $5,171. If Melodie's taxable income increases to $49,000, she would pay income taxes of $5,829. What is Melodie's marginal tax rate?
a. 16.45%
b. 22.00%
c. 18.25%
d. 15.05%
e. Some other amount

LO 12.7 29. Jim has a house payment of $2,000 per month of which $1,700 is deductible interest and real estate taxes with the remaining $300 representing a repayment of the principal balance of the note. Jim's marginal tax rate is 30 percent. What is Jim's after-tax cost of his house payment?
a. $510
b. $600
c. $900
d. $1,490
e. Some other amount

Group 2: Problems

LO 12.1
LO 12.2
1. Indicate whether the following statements are true or false:
a. _____ The IRS is a division of the Treasury Department.
b. _____ The IRS has three major divisions.
c. _____ The IRS local offices process most individual tax returns.
d. _____ IRS Campus Processing Sites are the locations that taxpayers should call to obtain tax information.
e. _____ Taxpayers should have their CPAs keep their tax records to prevent the IRS from being able to summon their records.
f. _____ Most IRS audits are conducted through the mail.

LO 12.2
LO 12.3

2. Indicate whether the following statements are true or false:

   a. _____ A field audit by the IRS is an audit conducted at the IRS field office.
   b. _____ A low Discriminant Function System score for a tax return increases the possibility that the return will be selected for audit.
   c. _____ The IRS charges interest on underpayments of taxes, but never pays interest on amounts of overpayments of taxes.
   d. _____ If a taxpayer fails to file a tax return on its due date, they may be subject to a failure-to-file penalty.
   e. _____ The tax law includes a penalty for preparing a tax return in a negligent manner.
   f. _____ If a taxpayer fails to file a tax return, the IRS may impose both the failure-to-file penalty and the fraud penalty.

LO 12.3

3. a. Wilson filed his individual tax return on the original due date, but failed to pay $700 in taxes that were due with the return. If Wilson pays the taxes exactly two months (not over sixty days) late, calculate the amount of his failure-to-pay penalty.
   b. Joan filed her individual income tax return 4½ months after it was due. She did not request an extension of time for filing. Along with her return, Joan remitted a check for $750, which was the balance of the taxes she owed with her return. Disregarding interest, calculate the total penalty that Joan will be required to pay, assuming the failure to file was not fraudulent.
   c. Jack filed his tax return two months and three days late and did not request an extension of time for filing. Jack's return indicated that he is to receive a $50 refund in taxes. Calculate the amount of Jack's penalty for failure to file his tax return on time, assuming the failure to file was not fraudulent.

LO 12.3

4. In the 2024 tax year, Michelle paid the following amounts relating to her 2022 tax return:

Tax deficiency	$5,000
Negligence penalty	1,000
Interest	500
Underpayment of estimated tax penalty	350

   Explain which of the above items may be deducted on Michelle's 2024 individual income tax return.

LO 12.3

5. Linda underpaid her taxes for the current year by $4,000 due to negligence.

   a. Calculate Linda's accuracy-related penalty for negligence.
   b. Assume that the underpayment of taxes by Linda was determined to be fraudulent, and calculate the total amount of Linda's fraud penalty.

LO 12.3

6. For each of the following situations, indicate the nature of the penalty and amount of the penalty that could be imposed, if any.

   a. Larry is a tax protester and files his tax return in the name of "Mickey Mouse."
   b. Anne writes a check for $900 in payment of her taxes that she knows will not clear the bank due to insufficient funds in her account.
   c. Gerald understated his tax liability by $10,000. The total amount of tax that should have been shown on his return was $70,000.

LO 12.3
LO 12.4
LO 12.5
LO 12.6

7. Indicate whether the following statements are true or false:

   a. The tax law includes a penalty for writing a "bad" check in payment of the taxpayer's tax liability.
   b. The statute of limitations for a tax return is normally four years.
   c. If a fraudulent tax return is filed, the IRS may assess a deficiency at any time in the future.
   d. Enrolled agents work for the IRS.
   e. A commercial tax preparer may represent tax clients in any proceeding with the IRS.
   f. The IRS is entitled to choose a place and time for an audit, without regard to the inconvenience to the taxpayer or the reasonableness of the request.

LO 12.4
8. Indicate the date that the statute of limitations would run out on each of the following 2024 individual tax returns with an original due date of April 15, 2025:
   a. A fraudulent tax return that was filed April 15, 2025
   b. A tax return that was filed May 19, 2025
   c. A tax return that was filed February 12, 2025
   d. A tax return that was filed March 1, 2025, and omitted $15,000 in income. The total gross income shown on the tax return was $50,000

LO 12.5
9. For each of the following situations, indicate the amount of the penalty that could be imposed on the tax return preparer:
   a. A tax return preparer understates the taxpayer's tax liability with a frivolous position and does not disclose the position.
   b. A tax return preparer fails to furnish his identifying number.
   c. A tax return preparer aids a taxpayer in understating a tax liability.
   d. A tax return preparer endorses and cashes a client's tax refund check.

LO 12.5
10. Classify each of the following as an enrolled or unenrolled preparer:
    a. Certified public accountant
    b. Enrolled agent
    c. A preparer that has completed the annual filing season program
    d. An attorney

LO 12.6
11. The Taxpayer Bill of Rights lists ten different rights. Name four of those rights.

LO 12.7
12. Indicate whether the following statements are true or false:
    a. _____ Decreasing one's tax liability through legal methods is called tax-planning, while illegally reducing taxes is called tax evasion.
    b. _____ In a "closed" transaction, all tax-significant events have been completed.
    c. _____ The marginal tax rate is computed as the total tax paid divided by the total income of the taxpayer.
    d. _____ The marginal tax rate is the most important rate for decision making in tax-planning situations.
    e. _____ The timing tax-planning technique usually has the objective of deferring the payment of tax until a later year.

Appendix A

Tax Rate Schedules and Tax Table

Contents

2024 Tax Rate Schedules   A-2

2024 Tax Table   A-4

2024 Tax Rate Schedules

 The Tax Rate Schedules are shown so you can see the tax rate that applies to all levels of taxable income. Don't use them to figure your tax. Instead, see the instructions for line 16.

Schedule X—If your filing status is Single

If your taxable income is: Over—	But not over—	The tax is:	of the amount over—
$0	$11,600	.... 10%	$0
11,600	47,150	$1,160.00 + 12%	11,600
47,150	100,525	5,426.00 + 22%	47,150
100,525	191,950	17,168.50 + 24%	100,525
191,950	243,725	39,110.50 + 32%	191,950
243,725	609,350	55,678.50 + 35%	243,725
609,350	....	183,647.25 + 37%	609,350

Schedule Y-1—If your filing status is Married filing jointly or Qualifying surviving spouse

If your taxable income is: Over—	But not over—	The tax is:	of the amount over—
$0	$23,200	.... 10%	$0
23,200	94,300	$2,320.00 + 12%	23,200
94,300	201,050	10,852.00 + 22%	94,300
201,050	383,900	34,337.00 + 24%	201,050
383,900	487,450	78,221.00 + 32%	383,900
487,450	731,200	111,357.00 + 35%	487,450
731,200	....	196,669.50 + 37%	731,200

Schedule Y-2—If your filing status is Married filing separately

If your taxable income is: Over—	But not over—	The tax is:	of the amount over—
$0	$11,600	.... 10%	$0
11,600	47,150	$1,160.00 + 12%	11,600
47,150	100,525	5,426.00 + 22%	47,150
100,525	191,950	17,168.50 + 24%	100,525
191,950	243,725	39,110.50 + 32%	191,950
243,725	365,600	55,678.50 + 35%	243,725
365,600	....	98,334.75 + 37%	365,600

Schedule Z—If your filing status is Head of household

If your taxable income is: Over—	But not over—	The tax is:	of the amount over—
$0	$16,550	.... 10%	$0
16,550	63,100	$1,655.00 + 12%	16,550
63,100	100,500	7,241.00 + 22%	63,100
100,500	191,950	15,469.00 + 24%	100,500
191,950	243,700	37,417.00 + 32%	191,950
243,700	609,350	53,977.00 + 35%	243,700
609,350	....	181,954.50 + 37%	609,350

Note: The tax rate schedules for income of at least $100,000 are presented in the traditional "additive" format on this page and in the somewhat lesser used "deductive" style on Page A-3. Both formats will compute the same tax amounts for taxable income of at least $100,000.

2024 Tax Computation Worksheet—Line 16

See the instructions for line 16 to see if you must use the worksheet below to figure your tax.

Note. If you are required to use this worksheet to figure the tax on an amount from another form or worksheet, such as the Qualified Dividends and Capital Gain Tax Worksheet, the Schedule D Tax Worksheet, Schedule J, Form 8615, or the Foreign Earned Income Tax Worksheet, enter the amount from that form or worksheet in column (a) of the row that applies to the amount you are looking up. Enter the result on the appropriate line of the form or worksheet that you are completing.

Section A—Use if your filing status is **Single**. Complete the row below that applies to you.

Taxable income. If line 15 is—	(a) Enter the amount from line 15	(b) Multiplication amount	(c) Multiply (a) by (b)	(d) Subtraction amount	Tax. Subtract (d) from (c). Enter the result here and on the entry space on line 16.
At least $100,000 but not over $100,525	$	× 22% (0.22)	$	$ 4,947.00	$
Over $100,525 but not over $191,950	$	× 24% (0.24)	$	$ 6,957.50	$
Over $191,950 but not over $243,725	$	× 32% (0.32)	$	$ 22,313.50	$
Over $243,725 but not over $609,350	$	× 35% (0.35)	$	$ 29,625.25	$
Over $609,350	$	× 37% (0.37)	$	$ 41,812.25	$

Section B—Use if your filing status is **Married filing jointly** or **Qualifying surviving spouse**. Complete the row below that applies to you.

Taxable income. If line 15 is—	(a) Enter the amount from line 15	(b) Multiplication amount	(c) Multiply (a) by (b)	(d) Subtraction amount	Tax. Subtract (d) from (c). Enter the result here and on the entry space on line 16.
At least $100,000 but not over $201,050	$	× 22% (0.22)	$	$ 9,894.00	$
Over $201,050 but not over $383,900	$	× 24% (0.24)	$	$ 13,915.00	$
Over $383,900 but not over $487,450	$	× 32% (0.32)	$	$ 44,627.00	$
Over $487,450 but not over $731,200	$	× 35% (0.35)	$	$ 59,250.50	$
Over $731,200	$	× 37% (0.37)	$	$ 73,874.50	$

Section C—Use if your filing status is **Married filing separately**. Complete the row below that applies to you.

Taxable income. If line 15 is—	(a) Enter the amount from line 15	(b) Multiplication amount	(c) Multiply (a) by (b)	(d) Subtraction amount	Tax. Subtract (d) from (c). Enter the result here and on the entry space on line 16.
At least $100,000 but not over $100,525	$	× 22% (0.22)	$	$ 4,947.00	$
Over $100,525 but not over $191,950	$	× 24% (0.24)	$	$ 6,957.50	$
Over $191,950 but not over $243,725	$	× 32% (0.32)	$	$ 22,313.50	$
Over $243,725 but not over $365,600	$	× 35% (0.35)	$	$ 29,625.25	$
Over $365,600	$	× 37% (0.37)	$	$ 36,937.25	$

Section D—Use if your filing status is **Head of household**. Complete the row below that applies to you.

Taxable income. If line 15 is—	(a) Enter the amount from line 15	(b) Multiplication amount	(c) Multiply (a) by (b)	(d) Subtraction amount	Tax. Subtract (d) from (c). Enter the result here and on the entry space on line 16.
At least $100,000 but not over $100,500	$	× 22% (0.22)	$	$ 6,641.00	$
Over $100,500 but not over $191,950	$	× 24% (0.24)	$	$ 8,651.00	$
Over $191,950 but not over $243,700	$	× 32% (0.32)	$	$ 24,007.00	$
Over $243,700 but not over $609,350	$	× 35% (0.35)	$	$ 31,318.00	$
Over $609,350	$	× 37% (0.37)	$	$ 43,505.00	$

2024 Tax Table

See the instructions for line 16 to see if you must use the Tax Table below to figure your tax.

Example. A married couple is filing a joint return. Their taxable income on Form 1040, line 15, is $25,300. First, they find the $25,300-$25,350 taxable income line. Next, they find the column for married filing jointly and read down the column. The amount shown where the taxable income line and filing status column meet is $2,575. This is the tax amount they should enter in the entry space on Form 1040, line 16.

Sample Table

At Least	But Less Than	Single	Married filing jointly*	Married filing separately	Head of a household
			Your tax is—		
25,200	25,250	2,795	2,563	2,795	2,696
25,250	25,300	2,801	2,569	2,801	2,702
25,300	25,350	2,807	(2,575)	2,807	2,708
25,350	25,400	2,813	2,581	2,813	2,714

If line 15 (taxable income) is—		And you are—			
At least	But less than	Single	Married filing jointly *	Married filing separately	Head of a household
			Your tax is—		
0	5	0	0	0	0
5	15	1	1	1	1
15	25	2	2	2	2
25	50	4	4	4	4
50	75	6	6	6	6
75	100	9	9	9	9
100	125	11	11	11	11
125	150	14	14	14	14
150	175	16	16	16	16
175	200	19	19	19	19
200	225	21	21	21	21
225	250	24	24	24	24
250	275	26	26	26	26
275	300	29	29	29	29
300	325	31	31	31	31
325	350	34	34	34	34
350	375	36	36	36	36
375	400	39	39	39	39
400	425	41	41	41	41
425	450	44	44	44	44
450	475	46	46	46	46
475	500	49	49	49	49
500	525	51	51	51	51
525	550	54	54	54	54
550	575	56	56	56	56
575	600	59	59	59	59
600	625	61	61	61	61
625	650	64	64	64	64
650	675	66	66	66	66
675	700	69	69	69	69
700	725	71	71	71	71
725	750	74	74	74	74
750	775	76	76	76	76
775	800	79	79	79	79
800	825	81	81	81	81
825	850	84	84	84	84
850	875	86	86	86	86
875	900	89	89	89	89
900	925	91	91	91	91
925	950	94	94	94	94
950	975	96	96	96	96
975	1,000	99	99	99	99

1,000

At least	But less than	Single	Married filing jointly *	Married filing separately	Head of a household
1,000	1,025	101	101	101	101
1,025	1,050	104	104	104	104
1,050	1,075	106	106	106	106
1,075	1,100	109	109	109	109
1,100	1,125	111	111	111	111
1,125	1,150	114	114	114	114
1,150	1,175	116	116	116	116
1,175	1,200	119	119	119	119
1,200	1,225	121	121	121	121
1,225	1,250	124	124	124	124
1,250	1,275	126	126	126	126
1,275	1,300	129	129	129	129
1,300	1,325	131	131	131	131
1,325	1,350	134	134	134	134
1,350	1,375	136	136	136	136
1,375	1,400	139	139	139	139
1,400	1,425	141	141	141	141
1,425	1,450	144	144	144	144
1,450	1,475	146	146	146	146
1,475	1,500	149	149	149	149
1,500	1,525	151	151	151	151
1,525	1,550	154	154	154	154
1,550	1,575	156	156	156	156
1,575	1,600	159	159	159	159
1,600	1,625	161	161	161	161
1,625	1,650	164	164	164	164
1,650	1,675	166	166	166	166
1,675	1,700	169	169	169	169
1,700	1,725	171	171	171	171
1,725	1,750	174	174	174	174
1,750	1,775	176	176	176	176
1,775	1,800	179	179	179	179
1,800	1,825	181	181	181	181
1,825	1,850	184	184	184	184
1,850	1,875	186	186	186	186
1,875	1,900	189	189	189	189
1,900	1,925	191	191	191	191
1,925	1,950	194	194	194	194
1,950	1,975	196	196	196	196
1,975	2,000	199	199	199	199

2,000

At least	But less than	Single	Married filing jointly *	Married filing separately	Head of a household
2,000	2,025	201	201	201	201
2,025	2,050	204	204	204	204
2,050	2,075	206	206	206	206
2,075	2,100	209	209	209	209
2,100	2,125	211	211	211	211
2,125	2,150	214	214	214	214
2,150	2,175	216	216	216	216
2,175	2,200	219	219	219	219
2,200	2,225	221	221	221	221
2,225	2,250	224	224	224	224
2,250	2,275	226	226	226	226
2,275	2,300	229	229	229	229
2,300	2,325	231	231	231	231
2,325	2,350	234	234	234	234
2,350	2,375	236	236	236	236
2,375	2,400	239	239	239	239
2,400	2,425	241	241	241	241
2,425	2,450	244	244	244	244
2,450	2,475	246	246	246	246
2,475	2,500	249	249	249	249
2,500	2,525	251	251	251	251
2,525	2,550	254	254	254	254
2,550	2,575	256	256	256	256
2,575	2,600	259	259	259	259
2,600	2,625	261	261	261	261
2,625	2,650	264	264	264	264
2,650	2,675	266	266	266	266
2,675	2,700	269	269	269	269
2,700	2,725	271	271	271	271
2,725	2,750	274	274	274	274
2,750	2,775	276	276	276	276
2,775	2,800	279	279	279	279
2,800	2,825	281	281	281	281
2,825	2,850	284	284	284	284
2,850	2,875	286	286	286	286
2,875	2,900	289	289	289	289
2,900	2,925	291	291	291	291
2,925	2,950	294	294	294	294
2,950	2,975	296	296	296	296
2,975	3,000	299	299	299	299

* This column must also be used by a qualifying surviving spouse.

(Continued)

2024 Tax Table — *Continued*

If line 15 (taxable income) is—		And you are—				If line 15 (taxable income) is—		And you are—				If line 15 (taxable income) is—		And you are—			
At least	But less than	Single	Married filing jointly *	Married filing separately	Head of a household	At least	But less than	Single	Married filing jointly *	Married filing separately	Head of a household	At least	But less than	Single	Married filing jointly *	Married filing separately	Head of a household
		Your tax is—						Your tax is—						Your tax is—			
3,000						**6,000**						**9,000**					
3,000	3,050	303	303	303	303	6,000	6,050	603	603	603	603	9,000	9,050	903	903	903	903
3,050	3,100	308	308	308	308	6,050	6,100	608	608	608	608	9,050	9,100	908	908	908	908
3,100	3,150	313	313	313	313	6,100	6,150	613	613	613	613	9,100	9,150	913	913	913	913
3,150	3,200	318	318	318	318	6,150	6,200	618	618	618	618	9,150	9,200	918	918	918	918
3,200	3,250	323	323	323	323	6,200	6,250	623	623	623	623	9,200	9,250	923	923	923	923
3,250	3,300	328	328	328	328	6,250	6,300	628	628	628	628	9,250	9,300	928	928	928	928
3,300	3,350	333	333	333	333	6,300	6,350	633	633	633	633	9,300	9,350	933	933	933	933
3,350	3,400	338	338	338	338	6,350	6,400	638	638	638	638	9,350	9,400	938	938	938	938
3,400	3,450	343	343	343	343	6,400	6,450	643	643	643	643	9,400	9,450	943	943	943	943
3,450	3,500	348	348	348	348	6,450	6,500	648	648	648	648	9,450	9,500	948	948	948	948
3,500	3,550	353	353	353	353	6,500	6,550	653	653	653	653	9,500	9,550	953	953	953	953
3,550	3,600	358	358	358	358	6,550	6,600	658	658	658	658	9,550	9,600	958	958	958	958
3,600	3,650	363	363	363	363	6,600	6,650	663	663	663	663	9,600	9,650	963	963	963	963
3,650	3,700	368	368	368	368	6,650	6,700	668	668	668	668	9,650	9,700	968	968	968	968
3,700	3,750	373	373	373	373	6,700	6,750	673	673	673	673	9,700	9,750	973	973	973	973
3,750	3,800	378	378	378	378	6,750	6,800	678	678	678	678	9,750	9,800	978	978	978	978
3,800	3,850	383	383	383	383	6,800	6,850	683	683	683	683	9,800	9,850	983	983	983	983
3,850	3,900	388	388	388	388	6,850	6,900	688	688	688	688	9,850	9,900	988	988	988	988
3,900	3,950	393	393	393	393	6,900	6,950	693	693	693	693	9,900	9,950	993	993	993	993
3,950	4,000	398	398	398	398	6,950	7,000	698	698	698	698	9,950	10,000	998	998	998	998
4,000						**7,000**						**10,000**					
4,000	4,050	403	403	403	403	7,000	7,050	703	703	703	703	10,000	10,050	1,003	1,003	1,003	1,003
4,050	4,100	408	408	408	408	7,050	7,100	708	708	708	708	10,050	10,100	1,008	1,008	1,008	1,008
4,100	4,150	413	413	413	413	7,100	7,150	713	713	713	713	10,100	10,150	1,013	1,013	1,013	1,013
4,150	4,200	418	418	418	418	7,150	7,200	718	718	718	718	10,150	10,200	1,018	1,018	1,018	1,018
4,200	4,250	423	423	423	423	7,200	7,250	723	723	723	723	10,200	10,250	1,023	1,023	1,023	1,023
4,250	4,300	428	428	428	428	7,250	7,300	728	728	728	728	10,250	10,300	1,028	1,028	1,028	1,028
4,300	4,350	433	433	433	433	7,300	7,350	733	733	733	733	10,300	10,350	1,033	1,033	1,033	1,033
4,350	4,400	438	438	438	438	7,350	7,400	738	738	738	738	10,350	10,400	1,038	1,038	1,038	1,038
4,400	4,450	443	443	443	443	7,400	7,450	743	743	743	743	10,400	10,450	1,043	1,043	1,043	1,043
4,450	4,500	448	448	448	448	7,450	7,500	748	748	748	748	10,450	10,500	1,048	1,048	1,048	1,048
4,500	4,550	453	453	453	453	7,500	7,550	753	753	753	753	10,500	10,550	1,053	1,053	1,053	1,053
4,550	4,600	458	458	458	458	7,550	7,600	758	758	758	758	10,550	10,600	1,058	1,058	1,058	1,058
4,600	4,650	463	463	463	463	7,600	7,650	763	763	763	763	10,600	10,650	1,063	1,063	1,063	1,063
4,650	4,700	468	468	468	468	7,650	7,700	768	768	768	768	10,650	10,700	1,068	1,068	1,068	1,068
4,700	4,750	473	473	473	473	7,700	7,750	773	773	773	773	10,700	10,750	1,073	1,073	1,073	1,073
4,750	4,800	478	478	478	478	7,750	7,800	778	778	778	778	10,750	10,800	1,078	1,078	1,078	1,078
4,800	4,850	483	483	483	483	7,800	7,850	783	783	783	783	10,800	10,850	1,083	1,083	1,083	1,083
4,850	4,900	488	488	488	488	7,850	7,900	788	788	788	788	10,850	10,900	1,088	1,088	1,088	1,088
4,900	4,950	493	493	493	493	7,900	7,950	793	793	793	793	10,900	10,950	1,093	1,093	1,093	1,093
4,950	5,000	498	498	498	498	7,950	8,000	798	798	798	798	10,950	11,000	1,098	1,098	1,098	1,098
5,000						**8,000**						**11,000**					
5,000	5,050	503	503	503	503	8,000	8,050	803	803	803	803	11,000	11,050	1,103	1,103	1,103	1,103
5,050	5,100	508	508	508	508	8,050	8,100	808	808	808	808	11,050	11,100	1,108	1,108	1,108	1,108
5,100	5,150	513	513	513	513	8,100	8,150	813	813	813	813	11,100	11,150	1,113	1,113	1,113	1,113
5,150	5,200	518	518	518	518	8,150	8,200	818	818	818	818	11,150	11,200	1,118	1,118	1,118	1,118
5,200	5,250	523	523	523	523	8,200	8,250	823	823	823	823	11,200	11,250	1,123	1,123	1,123	1,123
5,250	5,300	528	528	528	528	8,250	8,300	828	828	828	828	11,250	11,300	1,128	1,128	1,128	1,128
5,300	5,350	533	533	533	533	8,300	8,350	833	833	833	833	11,300	11,350	1,133	1,133	1,133	1,133
5,350	5,400	538	538	538	538	8,350	8,400	838	838	838	838	11,350	11,400	1,138	1,138	1,138	1,138
5,400	5,450	543	543	543	543	8,400	8,450	843	843	843	843	11,400	11,450	1,143	1,143	1,143	1,143
5,450	5,500	548	548	548	548	8,450	8,500	848	848	848	848	11,450	11,500	1,148	1,148	1,148	1,148
5,500	5,550	553	553	553	553	8,500	8,550	853	853	853	853	11,500	11,550	1,153	1,153	1,153	1,153
5,550	5,600	558	558	558	558	8,550	8,600	858	858	858	858	11,550	11,600	1,158	1,158	1,158	1,158
5,600	5,650	563	563	563	563	8,600	8,650	863	863	863	863	11,600	11,650	1,163	1,163	1,163	1,163
5,650	5,700	568	568	568	568	8,650	8,700	868	868	868	868	11,650	11,700	1,169	1,168	1,169	1,168
5,700	5,750	573	573	573	573	8,700	8,750	873	873	873	873	11,700	11,750	1,175	1,173	1,175	1,173
5,750	5,800	578	578	578	578	8,750	8,800	878	878	878	878	11,750	11,800	1,181	1,178	1,181	1,178
5,800	5,850	583	583	583	583	8,800	8,850	883	883	883	883	11,800	11,850	1,187	1,183	1,187	1,183
5,850	5,900	588	588	588	588	8,850	8,900	888	888	888	888	11,850	11,900	1,193	1,188	1,193	1,188
5,900	5,950	593	593	593	593	8,900	8,950	893	893	893	893	11,900	11,950	1,199	1,193	1,199	1,193
5,950	6,000	598	598	598	598	8,950	9,000	898	898	898	898	11,950	12,000	1,205	1,198	1,205	1,198

(Continued)

* This column must also be used by a qualifying surviving spouse.

2024 Tax Table — *Continued*

If line 15 (taxable income) is—		And you are—				If line 15 (taxable income) is—		And you are—				If line 15 (taxable income) is—		And you are—			
At least	But less than	Single	Married filing jointly *	Married filing separately	Head of a household	At least	But less than	Single	Married filing jointly *	Married filing separately	Head of a household	At least	But less than	Single	Married filing jointly *	Married filing separately	Head of a household
		Your tax is—						Your tax is—						Your tax is—			

12,000

12,000	12,050	1,211	1,203	1,211	1,203
12,050	12,100	1,217	1,208	1,217	1,208
12,100	12,150	1,223	1,213	1,223	1,213
12,150	12,200	1,229	1,218	1,229	1,218
12,200	12,250	1,235	1,223	1,235	1,223
12,250	12,300	1,241	1,228	1,241	1,228
12,300	12,350	1,247	1,233	1,247	1,233
12,350	12,400	1,253	1,238	1,253	1,238
12,400	12,450	1,259	1,243	1,259	1,243
12,450	12,500	1,265	1,248	1,265	1,248
12,500	12,550	1,271	1,253	1,271	1,253
12,550	12,600	1,277	1,258	1,277	1,258
12,600	12,650	1,283	1,263	1,283	1,263
12,650	12,700	1,289	1,268	1,289	1,268
12,700	12,750	1,295	1,273	1,295	1,273
12,750	12,800	1,301	1,278	1,301	1,278
12,800	12,850	1,307	1,283	1,307	1,283
12,850	12,900	1,313	1,288	1,313	1,288
12,900	12,950	1,319	1,293	1,319	1,293
12,950	13,000	1,325	1,298	1,325	1,298

13,000

13,000	13,050	1,331	1,303	1,331	1,303
13,050	13,100	1,337	1,308	1,337	1,308
13,100	13,150	1,343	1,313	1,343	1,313
13,150	13,200	1,349	1,318	1,349	1,318
13,200	13,250	1,355	1,323	1,355	1,323
13,250	13,300	1,361	1,328	1,361	1,328
13,300	13,350	1,367	1,333	1,367	1,333
13,350	13,400	1,373	1,338	1,373	1,338
13,400	13,450	1,379	1,343	1,379	1,343
13,450	13,500	1,385	1,348	1,385	1,348
13,500	13,550	1,391	1,353	1,391	1,353
13,550	13,600	1,397	1,358	1,397	1,358
13,600	13,650	1,403	1,363	1,403	1,363
13,650	13,700	1,409	1,368	1,409	1,368
13,700	13,750	1,415	1,373	1,415	1,373
13,750	13,800	1,421	1,378	1,421	1,378
13,800	13,850	1,427	1,383	1,427	1,383
13,850	13,900	1,433	1,388	1,433	1,388
13,900	13,950	1,439	1,393	1,439	1,393
13,950	14,000	1,445	1,398	1,445	1,398

14,000

14,000	14,050	1,451	1,403	1,451	1,403
14,050	14,100	1,457	1,408	1,457	1,408
14,100	14,150	1,463	1,413	1,463	1,413
14,150	14,200	1,469	1,418	1,469	1,418
14,200	14,250	1,475	1,423	1,475	1,423
14,250	14,300	1,481	1,428	1,481	1,428
14,300	14,350	1,487	1,433	1,487	1,433
14,350	14,400	1,493	1,438	1,493	1,438
14,400	14,450	1,499	1,443	1,499	1,443
14,450	14,500	1,505	1,448	1,505	1,448
14,500	14,550	1,511	1,453	1,511	1,453
14,550	14,600	1,517	1,458	1,517	1,458
14,600	14,650	1,523	1,463	1,523	1,463
14,650	14,700	1,529	1,468	1,529	1,468
14,700	14,750	1,535	1,473	1,535	1,473
14,750	14,800	1,541	1,478	1,541	1,478
14,800	14,850	1,547	1,483	1,547	1,483
14,850	14,900	1,553	1,488	1,553	1,488
14,900	14,950	1,559	1,493	1,559	1,493
14,950	15,000	1,565	1,498	1,565	1,498

15,000

15,000	15,050	1,571	1,503	1,571	1,503
15,050	15,100	1,577	1,508	1,577	1,508
15,100	15,150	1,583	1,513	1,583	1,513
15,150	15,200	1,589	1,518	1,589	1,518
15,200	15,250	1,595	1,523	1,595	1,523
15,250	15,300	1,601	1,528	1,601	1,528
15,300	15,350	1,607	1,533	1,607	1,533
15,350	15,400	1,613	1,538	1,613	1,538
15,400	15,450	1,619	1,543	1,619	1,543
15,450	15,500	1,625	1,548	1,625	1,548
15,500	15,550	1,631	1,553	1,631	1,553
15,550	15,600	1,637	1,558	1,637	1,558
15,600	15,650	1,643	1,563	1,643	1,563
15,650	15,700	1,649	1,568	1,649	1,568
15,700	15,750	1,655	1,573	1,655	1,573
15,750	15,800	1,661	1,578	1,661	1,578
15,800	15,850	1,667	1,583	1,667	1,583
15,850	15,900	1,673	1,588	1,673	1,588
15,900	15,950	1,679	1,593	1,679	1,593
15,950	16,000	1,685	1,598	1,685	1,598

16,000

16,000	16,050	1,691	1,603	1,691	1,603
16,050	16,100	1,697	1,608	1,697	1,608
16,100	16,150	1,703	1,613	1,703	1,613
16,150	16,200	1,709	1,618	1,709	1,618
16,200	16,250	1,715	1,623	1,715	1,623
16,250	16,300	1,721	1,628	1,721	1,628
16,300	16,350	1,727	1,633	1,727	1,633
16,350	16,400	1,733	1,638	1,733	1,638
16,400	16,450	1,739	1,643	1,739	1,643
16,450	16,500	1,745	1,648	1,745	1,648
16,500	16,550	1,751	1,653	1,751	1,653
16,550	16,600	1,757	1,658	1,757	1,658
16,600	16,650	1,763	1,663	1,763	1,664
16,650	16,700	1,769	1,668	1,769	1,670
16,700	16,750	1,775	1,673	1,775	1,676
16,750	16,800	1,781	1,678	1,781	1,682
16,800	16,850	1,787	1,683	1,787	1,688
16,850	16,900	1,793	1,688	1,793	1,694
16,900	16,950	1,799	1,693	1,799	1,700
16,950	17,000	1,805	1,698	1,805	1,706

17,000

17,000	17,050	1,811	1,703	1,811	1,712
17,050	17,100	1,817	1,708	1,817	1,718
17,100	17,150	1,823	1,713	1,823	1,724
17,150	17,200	1,829	1,718	1,829	1,730
17,200	17,250	1,835	1,723	1,835	1,736
17,250	17,300	1,841	1,728	1,841	1,742
17,300	17,350	1,847	1,733	1,847	1,748
17,350	17,400	1,853	1,738	1,853	1,754
17,400	17,450	1,859	1,743	1,859	1,760
17,450	17,500	1,865	1,748	1,865	1,766
17,500	17,550	1,871	1,753	1,871	1,772
17,550	17,600	1,877	1,758	1,877	1,778
17,600	17,650	1,883	1,763	1,883	1,784
17,650	17,700	1,889	1,768	1,889	1,790
17,700	17,750	1,895	1,773	1,895	1,796
17,750	17,800	1,901	1,778	1,901	1,802
17,800	17,850	1,907	1,783	1,907	1,808
17,850	17,900	1,913	1,788	1,913	1,814
17,900	17,950	1,919	1,793	1,919	1,820
17,950	18,000	1,925	1,798	1,925	1,826

18,000

18,000	18,050	1,931	1,803	1,931	1,832
18,050	18,100	1,937	1,808	1,937	1,838
18,100	18,150	1,943	1,813	1,943	1,844
18,150	18,200	1,949	1,818	1,949	1,850
18,200	18,250	1,955	1,823	1,955	1,856
18,250	18,300	1,961	1,828	1,961	1,862
18,300	18,350	1,967	1,833	1,967	1,868
18,350	18,400	1,973	1,838	1,973	1,874
18,400	18,450	1,979	1,843	1,979	1,880
18,450	18,500	1,985	1,848	1,985	1,886
18,500	18,550	1,991	1,853	1,991	1,892
18,550	18,600	1,997	1,858	1,997	1,898
18,600	18,650	2,003	1,863	2,003	1,904
18,650	18,700	2,009	1,868	2,009	1,910
18,700	18,750	2,015	1,873	2,015	1,916
18,750	18,800	2,021	1,878	2,021	1,922
18,800	18,850	2,027	1,883	2,027	1,928
18,850	18,900	2,033	1,888	2,033	1,934
18,900	18,950	2,039	1,893	2,039	1,940
18,950	19,000	2,045	1,898	2,045	1,946

19,000

19,000	19,050	2,051	1,903	2,051	1,952
19,050	19,100	2,057	1,908	2,057	1,958
19,100	19,150	2,063	1,913	2,063	1,964
19,150	19,200	2,069	1,918	2,069	1,970
19,200	19,250	2,075	1,923	2,075	1,976
19,250	19,300	2,081	1,928	2,081	1,982
19,300	19,350	2,087	1,933	2,087	1,988
19,350	19,400	2,093	1,938	2,093	1,994
19,400	19,450	2,099	1,943	2,099	2,000
19,450	19,500	2,105	1,948	2,105	2,006
19,500	19,550	2,111	1,953	2,111	2,012
19,550	19,600	2,117	1,958	2,117	2,018
19,600	19,650	2,123	1,963	2,123	2,024
19,650	19,700	2,129	1,968	2,129	2,030
19,700	19,750	2,135	1,973	2,135	2,036
19,750	19,800	2,141	1,978	2,141	2,042
19,800	19,850	2,147	1,983	2,147	2,048
19,850	19,900	2,153	1,988	2,153	2,054
19,900	19,950	2,159	1,993	2,159	2,060
19,950	20,000	2,165	1,998	2,165	2,066

20,000

20,000	20,050	2,171	2,003	2,171	2,072
20,050	20,100	2,177	2,008	2,177	2,078
20,100	20,150	2,183	2,013	2,183	2,084
20,150	20,200	2,189	2,018	2,189	2,090
20,200	20,250	2,195	2,023	2,195	2,096
20,250	20,300	2,201	2,028	2,201	2,102
20,300	20,350	2,207	2,033	2,207	2,108
20,350	20,400	2,213	2,038	2,213	2,114
20,400	20,450	2,219	2,043	2,219	2,120
20,450	20,500	2,225	2,048	2,225	2,126
20,500	20,550	2,231	2,053	2,231	2,132
20,550	20,600	2,237	2,058	2,237	2,138
20,600	20,650	2,243	2,063	2,243	2,144
20,650	20,700	2,249	2,068	2,249	2,150
20,700	20,750	2,255	2,073	2,255	2,156
20,750	20,800	2,261	2,078	2,261	2,162
20,800	20,850	2,267	2,083	2,267	2,168
20,850	20,900	2,273	2,088	2,273	2,174
20,900	20,950	2,279	2,093	2,279	2,180
20,950	21,000	2,285	2,098	2,285	2,186

* This column must also be used by a qualifying surviving spouse.

(Continued)

2024 Tax Table — Continued

If line 15 (taxable income) is—		And you are—				If line 15 (taxable income) is—		And you are—				If line 15 (taxable income) is—		And you are—			
At least	But less than	Single	Married filing jointly *	Married filing separately	Head of a household	At least	But less than	Single	Married filing jointly *	Married filing separately	Head of a household	At least	But less than	Single	Married filing jointly *	Married filing separately	Head of a household
		Your tax is—						Your tax is—						Your tax is—			
21,000						**24,000**						**27,000**					
21,000	21,050	2,291	2,103	2,291	2,192	24,000	24,050	2,651	2,419	2,651	2,552	27,000	27,050	3,011	2,779	3,011	2,912
21,050	21,100	2,297	2,108	2,297	2,198	24,050	24,100	2,657	2,425	2,657	2,558	27,050	27,100	3,017	2,785	3,017	2,918
21,100	21,150	2,303	2,113	2,303	2,204	24,100	24,150	2,663	2,431	2,663	2,564	27,100	27,150	3,023	2,791	3,023	2,924
21,150	21,200	2,309	2,118	2,309	2,210	24,150	24,200	2,669	2,437	2,669	2,570	27,150	27,200	3,029	2,797	3,029	2,930
21,200	21,250	2,315	2,123	2,315	2,216	24,200	24,250	2,675	2,443	2,675	2,576	27,200	27,250	3,035	2,803	3,035	2,936
21,250	21,300	2,321	2,128	2,321	2,222	24,250	24,300	2,681	2,449	2,681	2,582	27,250	27,300	3,041	2,809	3,041	2,942
21,300	21,350	2,327	2,133	2,327	2,228	24,300	24,350	2,687	2,455	2,687	2,588	27,300	27,350	3,047	2,815	3,047	2,948
21,350	21,400	2,333	2,138	2,333	2,234	24,350	24,400	2,693	2,461	2,693	2,594	27,350	27,400	3,053	2,821	3,053	2,954
21,400	21,450	2,339	2,143	2,339	2,240	24,400	24,450	2,699	2,467	2,699	2,600	27,400	27,450	3,059	2,827	3,059	2,960
21,450	21,500	2,345	2,148	2,345	2,246	24,450	24,500	2,705	2,473	2,705	2,606	27,450	27,500	3,065	2,833	3,065	2,966
21,500	21,550	2,351	2,153	2,351	2,252	24,500	24,550	2,711	2,479	2,711	2,612	27,500	27,550	3,071	2,839	3,071	2,972
21,550	21,600	2,357	2,158	2,357	2,258	24,550	24,600	2,717	2,485	2,717	2,618	27,550	27,600	3,077	2,845	3,077	2,978
21,600	21,650	2,363	2,163	2,363	2,264	24,600	24,650	2,723	2,491	2,723	2,624	27,600	27,650	3,083	2,851	3,083	2,984
21,650	21,700	2,369	2,168	2,369	2,270	24,650	24,700	2,729	2,497	2,729	2,630	27,650	27,700	3,089	2,857	3,089	2,990
21,700	21,750	2,375	2,173	2,375	2,276	24,700	24,750	2,735	2,503	2,735	2,636	27,700	27,750	3,095	2,863	3,095	2,996
21,750	21,800	2,381	2,178	2,381	2,282	24,750	24,800	2,741	2,509	2,741	2,642	27,750	27,800	3,101	2,869	3,101	3,002
21,800	21,850	2,387	2,183	2,387	2,288	24,800	24,850	2,747	2,515	2,747	2,648	27,800	27,850	3,107	2,875	3,107	3,008
21,850	21,900	2,393	2,188	2,393	2,294	24,850	24,900	2,753	2,521	2,753	2,654	27,850	27,900	3,113	2,881	3,113	3,014
21,900	21,950	2,399	2,193	2,399	2,300	24,900	24,950	2,759	2,527	2,759	2,660	27,900	27,950	3,119	2,887	3,119	3,020
21,950	22,000	2,405	2,198	2,405	2,306	24,950	25,000	2,765	2,533	2,765	2,666	27,950	28,000	3,125	2,893	3,125	3,026
22,000						**25,000**						**28,000**					
22,000	22,050	2,411	2,203	2,411	2,312	25,000	25,050	2,771	2,539	2,771	2,672	28,000	28,050	3,131	2,899	3,131	3,032
22,050	22,100	2,417	2,208	2,417	2,318	25,050	25,100	2,777	2,545	2,777	2,678	28,050	28,100	3,137	2,905	3,137	3,038
22,100	22,150	2,423	2,213	2,423	2,324	25,100	25,150	2,783	2,551	2,783	2,684	28,100	28,150	3,143	2,911	3,143	3,044
22,150	22,200	2,429	2,218	2,429	2,330	25,150	25,200	2,789	2,557	2,789	2,690	28,150	28,200	3,149	2,917	3,149	3,050
22,200	22,250	2,435	2,223	2,435	2,336	25,200	25,250	2,795	2,563	2,795	2,696	28,200	28,250	3,155	2,923	3,155	3,056
22,250	22,300	2,441	2,228	2,441	2,342	25,250	25,300	2,801	2,569	2,801	2,702	28,250	28,300	3,161	2,929	3,161	3,062
22,300	22,350	2,447	2,233	2,447	2,348	25,300	25,350	2,807	2,575	2,807	2,708	28,300	28,350	3,167	2,935	3,167	3,068
22,350	22,400	2,453	2,238	2,453	2,354	25,350	25,400	2,813	2,581	2,813	2,714	28,350	28,400	3,173	2,941	3,173	3,074
22,400	22,450	2,459	2,243	2,459	2,360	25,400	25,450	2,819	2,587	2,819	2,720	28,400	28,450	3,179	2,947	3,179	3,080
22,450	22,500	2,465	2,248	2,465	2,366	25,450	25,500	2,825	2,593	2,825	2,726	28,450	28,500	3,185	2,953	3,185	3,086
22,500	22,550	2,471	2,253	2,471	2,372	25,500	25,550	2,831	2,599	2,831	2,732	28,500	28,550	3,191	2,959	3,191	3,092
22,550	22,600	2,477	2,258	2,477	2,378	25,550	25,600	2,837	2,605	2,837	2,738	28,550	28,600	3,197	2,965	3,197	3,098
22,600	22,650	2,483	2,263	2,483	2,384	25,600	25,650	2,843	2,611	2,843	2,744	28,600	28,650	3,203	2,971	3,203	3,104
22,650	22,700	2,489	2,268	2,489	2,390	25,650	25,700	2,849	2,617	2,849	2,750	28,650	28,700	3,209	2,977	3,209	3,110
22,700	22,750	2,495	2,273	2,495	2,396	25,700	25,750	2,855	2,623	2,855	2,756	28,700	28,750	3,215	2,983	3,215	3,116
22,750	22,800	2,501	2,278	2,501	2,402	25,750	25,800	2,861	2,629	2,861	2,762	28,750	28,800	3,221	2,989	3,221	3,122
22,800	22,850	2,507	2,283	2,507	2,408	25,800	25,850	2,867	2,635	2,867	2,768	28,800	28,850	3,227	2,995	3,227	3,128
22,850	22,900	2,513	2,288	2,513	2,414	25,850	25,900	2,873	2,641	2,873	2,774	28,850	28,900	3,233	3,001	3,233	3,134
22,900	22,950	2,519	2,293	2,519	2,420	25,900	25,950	2,879	2,647	2,879	2,780	28,900	28,950	3,239	3,007	3,239	3,140
22,950	23,000	2,525	2,298	2,525	2,426	25,950	26,000	2,885	2,653	2,885	2,786	28,950	29,000	3,245	3,013	3,245	3,146
23,000						**26,000**						**29,000**					
23,000	23,050	2,531	2,303	2,531	2,432	26,000	26,050	2,891	2,659	2,891	2,792	29,000	29,050	3,251	3,019	3,251	3,152
23,050	23,100	2,537	2,308	2,537	2,438	26,050	26,100	2,897	2,665	2,897	2,798	29,050	29,100	3,257	3,025	3,257	3,158
23,100	23,150	2,543	2,313	2,543	2,444	26,100	26,150	2,903	2,671	2,903	2,804	29,100	29,150	3,263	3,031	3,263	3,164
23,150	23,200	2,549	2,318	2,549	2,450	26,150	26,200	2,909	2,677	2,909	2,810	29,150	29,200	3,269	3,037	3,269	3,170
23,200	23,250	2,555	2,323	2,555	2,456	26,200	26,250	2,915	2,683	2,915	2,816	29,200	29,250	3,275	3,043	3,275	3,176
23,250	23,300	2,561	2,329	2,561	2,462	26,250	26,300	2,921	2,689	2,921	2,822	29,250	29,300	3,281	3,049	3,281	3,182
23,300	23,350	2,567	2,335	2,567	2,468	26,300	26,350	2,927	2,695	2,927	2,828	29,300	29,350	3,287	3,055	3,287	3,188
23,350	23,400	2,573	2,341	2,573	2,474	26,350	26,400	2,933	2,701	2,933	2,834	29,350	29,400	3,293	3,061	3,293	3,194
23,400	23,450	2,579	2,347	2,579	2,480	26,400	26,450	2,939	2,707	2,939	2,840	29,400	29,450	3,299	3,067	3,299	3,200
23,450	23,500	2,585	2,353	2,585	2,486	26,450	26,500	2,945	2,713	2,945	2,846	29,450	29,500	3,305	3,073	3,305	3,206
23,500	23,550	2,591	2,359	2,591	2,492	26,500	26,550	2,951	2,719	2,951	2,852	29,500	29,550	3,311	3,079	3,311	3,212
23,550	23,600	2,597	2,365	2,597	2,498	26,550	26,600	2,957	2,725	2,957	2,858	29,550	29,600	3,317	3,085	3,317	3,218
23,600	23,650	2,603	2,371	2,603	2,504	26,600	26,650	2,963	2,731	2,963	2,864	29,600	29,650	3,323	3,091	3,323	3,224
23,650	23,700	2,609	2,377	2,609	2,510	26,650	26,700	2,969	2,737	2,969	2,870	29,650	29,700	3,329	3,097	3,329	3,230
23,700	23,750	2,615	2,383	2,615	2,516	26,700	26,750	2,975	2,743	2,975	2,876	29,700	29,750	3,335	3,103	3,335	3,236
23,750	23,800	2,621	2,389	2,621	2,522	26,750	26,800	2,981	2,749	2,981	2,882	29,750	29,800	3,341	3,109	3,341	3,242
23,800	23,850	2,627	2,395	2,627	2,528	26,800	26,850	2,987	2,755	2,987	2,888	29,800	29,850	3,347	3,115	3,347	3,248
23,850	23,900	2,633	2,401	2,633	2,534	26,850	26,900	2,993	2,761	2,993	2,894	29,850	29,900	3,353	3,121	3,353	3,254
23,900	23,950	2,639	2,407	2,639	2,540	26,900	26,950	2,999	2,767	2,999	2,900	29,900	29,950	3,359	3,127	3,359	3,260
23,950	24,000	2,645	2,413	2,645	2,546	26,950	27,000	3,005	2,773	3,005	2,906	29,950	30,000	3,365	3,133	3,365	3,266

* This column must also be used by a qualifying surviving spouse.

(Continued)

2024 Tax Table — *Continued*

If line 15 (taxable income) is—		And you are—				If line 15 (taxable income) is—		And you are—				If line 15 (taxable income) is—		And you are—			
At least	But less than	Single	Married filing jointly *	Married filing separately	Head of a household	At least	But less than	Single	Married filing jointly *	Married filing separately	Head of a household	At least	But less than	Single	Married filing jointly *	Married filing separately	Head of a household
		Your tax is—						Your tax is—						Your tax is—			
30,000						**33,000**						**36,000**					
30,000	30,050	3,371	3,139	3,371	3,272	33,000	33,050	3,731	3,499	3,731	3,632	36,000	36,050	4,091	3,859	4,091	3,992
30,050	30,100	3,377	3,145	3,377	3,278	33,050	33,100	3,737	3,505	3,737	3,638	36,050	36,100	4,097	3,865	4,097	3,998
30,100	30,150	3,383	3,151	3,383	3,284	33,100	33,150	3,743	3,511	3,743	3,644	36,100	36,150	4,103	3,871	4,103	4,004
30,150	30,200	3,389	3,157	3,389	3,290	33,150	33,200	3,749	3,517	3,749	3,650	36,150	36,200	4,109	3,877	4,109	4,010
30,200	30,250	3,395	3,163	3,395	3,296	33,200	33,250	3,755	3,523	3,755	3,656	36,200	36,250	4,115	3,883	4,115	4,016
30,250	30,300	3,401	3,169	3,401	3,302	33,250	33,300	3,761	3,529	3,761	3,662	36,250	36,300	4,121	3,889	4,121	4,022
30,300	30,350	3,407	3,175	3,407	3,308	33,300	33,350	3,767	3,535	3,767	3,668	36,300	36,350	4,127	3,895	4,127	4,028
30,350	30,400	3,413	3,181	3,413	3,314	33,350	33,400	3,773	3,541	3,773	3,674	36,350	36,400	4,133	3,901	4,133	4,034
30,400	30,450	3,419	3,187	3,419	3,320	33,400	33,450	3,779	3,547	3,779	3,680	36,400	36,450	4,139	3,907	4,139	4,040
30,450	30,500	3,425	3,193	3,425	3,326	33,450	33,500	3,785	3,553	3,785	3,686	36,450	36,500	4,145	3,913	4,145	4,046
30,500	30,550	3,431	3,199	3,431	3,332	33,500	33,550	3,791	3,559	3,791	3,692	36,500	36,550	4,151	3,919	4,151	4,052
30,550	30,600	3,437	3,205	3,437	3,338	33,550	33,600	3,797	3,565	3,797	3,698	36,550	36,600	4,157	3,925	4,157	4,058
30,600	30,650	3,443	3,211	3,443	3,344	33,600	33,650	3,803	3,571	3,803	3,704	36,600	36,650	4,163	3,931	4,163	4,064
30,650	30,700	3,449	3,217	3,449	3,350	33,650	33,700	3,809	3,577	3,809	3,710	36,650	36,700	4,169	3,937	4,169	4,070
30,700	30,750	3,455	3,223	3,455	3,356	33,700	33,750	3,815	3,583	3,815	3,716	36,700	36,750	4,175	3,943	4,175	4,076
30,750	30,800	3,461	3,229	3,461	3,362	33,750	33,800	3,821	3,589	3,821	3,722	36,750	36,800	4,181	3,949	4,181	4,082
30,800	30,850	3,467	3,235	3,467	3,368	33,800	33,850	3,827	3,595	3,827	3,728	36,800	36,850	4,187	3,955	4,187	4,088
30,850	30,900	3,473	3,241	3,473	3,374	33,850	33,900	3,833	3,601	3,833	3,734	36,850	36,900	4,193	3,961	4,193	4,094
30,900	30,950	3,479	3,247	3,479	3,380	33,900	33,950	3,839	3,607	3,839	3,740	36,900	36,950	4,199	3,967	4,199	4,100
30,950	31,000	3,485	3,253	3,485	3,386	33,950	34,000	3,845	3,613	3,845	3,746	36,950	37,000	4,205	3,973	4,205	4,106
31,000						**34,000**						**37,000**					
31,000	31,050	3,491	3,259	3,491	3,392	34,000	34,050	3,851	3,619	3,851	3,752	37,000	37,050	4,211	3,979	4,211	4,112
31,050	31,100	3,497	3,265	3,497	3,398	34,050	34,100	3,857	3,625	3,857	3,758	37,050	37,100	4,217	3,985	4,217	4,118
31,100	31,150	3,503	3,271	3,503	3,404	34,100	34,150	3,863	3,631	3,863	3,764	37,100	37,150	4,223	3,991	4,223	4,124
31,150	31,200	3,509	3,277	3,509	3,410	34,150	34,200	3,869	3,637	3,869	3,770	37,150	37,200	4,229	3,997	4,229	4,130
31,200	31,250	3,515	3,283	3,515	3,416	34,200	34,250	3,875	3,643	3,875	3,776	37,200	37,250	4,235	4,003	4,235	4,136
31,250	31,300	3,521	3,289	3,521	3,422	34,250	34,300	3,881	3,649	3,881	3,782	37,250	37,300	4,241	4,009	4,241	4,142
31,300	31,350	3,527	3,295	3,527	3,428	34,300	34,350	3,887	3,655	3,887	3,788	37,300	37,350	4,247	4,015	4,247	4,148
31,350	31,400	3,533	3,301	3,533	3,434	34,350	34,400	3,893	3,661	3,893	3,794	37,350	37,400	4,253	4,021	4,253	4,154
31,400	31,450	3,539	3,307	3,539	3,440	34,400	34,450	3,899	3,667	3,899	3,800	37,400	37,450	4,259	4,027	4,259	4,160
31,450	31,500	3,545	3,313	3,545	3,446	34,450	34,500	3,905	3,673	3,905	3,806	37,450	37,500	4,265	4,033	4,265	4,166
31,500	31,550	3,551	3,319	3,551	3,452	34,500	34,550	3,911	3,679	3,911	3,812	37,500	37,550	4,271	4,039	4,271	4,172
31,550	31,600	3,557	3,325	3,557	3,458	34,550	34,600	3,917	3,685	3,917	3,818	37,550	37,600	4,277	4,045	4,277	4,178
31,600	31,650	3,563	3,331	3,563	3,464	34,600	34,650	3,923	3,691	3,923	3,824	37,600	37,650	4,283	4,051	4,283	4,184
31,650	31,700	3,569	3,337	3,569	3,470	34,650	34,700	3,929	3,697	3,929	3,830	37,650	37,700	4,289	4,057	4,289	4,190
31,700	31,750	3,575	3,343	3,575	3,476	34,700	34,750	3,935	3,703	3,935	3,836	37,700	37,750	4,295	4,063	4,295	4,196
31,750	31,800	3,581	3,349	3,581	3,482	34,750	34,800	3,941	3,709	3,941	3,842	37,750	37,800	4,301	4,069	4,301	4,202
31,800	31,850	3,587	3,355	3,587	3,488	34,800	34,850	3,947	3,715	3,947	3,848	37,800	37,850	4,307	4,075	4,307	4,208
31,850	31,900	3,593	3,361	3,593	3,494	34,850	34,900	3,953	3,721	3,953	3,854	37,850	37,900	4,313	4,081	4,313	4,214
31,900	31,950	3,599	3,367	3,599	3,500	34,900	34,950	3,959	3,727	3,959	3,860	37,900	37,950	4,319	4,087	4,319	4,220
31,950	32,000	3,605	3,373	3,605	3,506	34,950	35,000	3,965	3,733	3,965	3,866	37,950	38,000	4,325	4,093	4,325	4,226
32,000						**35,000**						**38,000**					
32,000	32,050	3,611	3,379	3,611	3,512	35,000	35,050	3,971	3,739	3,971	3,872	38,000	38,050	4,331	4,099	4,331	4,232
32,050	32,100	3,617	3,385	3,617	3,518	35,050	35,100	3,977	3,745	3,977	3,878	38,050	38,100	4,337	4,105	4,337	4,238
32,100	32,150	3,623	3,391	3,623	3,524	35,100	35,150	3,983	3,751	3,983	3,884	38,100	38,150	4,343	4,111	4,343	4,244
32,150	32,200	3,629	3,397	3,629	3,530	35,150	35,200	3,989	3,757	3,989	3,890	38,150	38,200	4,349	4,117	4,349	4,250
32,200	32,250	3,635	3,403	3,635	3,536	35,200	35,250	3,995	3,763	3,995	3,896	38,200	38,250	4,355	4,123	4,355	4,256
32,250	32,300	3,641	3,409	3,641	3,542	35,250	35,300	4,001	3,769	4,001	3,902	38,250	38,300	4,361	4,129	4,361	4,262
32,300	32,350	3,647	3,415	3,647	3,548	35,300	35,350	4,007	3,775	4,007	3,908	38,300	38,350	4,367	4,135	4,367	4,268
32,350	32,400	3,653	3,421	3,653	3,554	35,350	35,400	4,013	3,781	4,013	3,914	38,350	38,400	4,373	4,141	4,373	4,274
32,400	32,450	3,659	3,427	3,659	3,560	35,400	35,450	4,019	3,787	4,019	3,920	38,400	38,450	4,379	4,147	4,379	4,280
32,450	32,500	3,665	3,433	3,665	3,566	35,450	35,500	4,025	3,793	4,025	3,926	38,450	38,500	4,385	4,153	4,385	4,286
32,500	32,550	3,671	3,439	3,671	3,572	35,500	35,550	4,031	3,799	4,031	3,932	38,500	38,550	4,391	4,159	4,391	4,292
32,550	32,600	3,677	3,445	3,677	3,578	35,550	35,600	4,037	3,805	4,037	3,938	38,550	38,600	4,397	4,165	4,397	4,298
32,600	32,650	3,683	3,451	3,683	3,584	35,600	35,650	4,043	3,811	4,043	3,944	38,600	38,650	4,403	4,171	4,403	4,304
32,650	32,700	3,689	3,457	3,689	3,590	35,650	35,700	4,049	3,817	4,049	3,950	38,650	38,700	4,409	4,177	4,409	4,310
32,700	32,750	3,695	3,463	3,695	3,596	35,700	35,750	4,055	3,823	4,055	3,956	38,700	38,750	4,415	4,183	4,415	4,316
32,750	32,800	3,701	3,469	3,701	3,602	35,750	35,800	4,061	3,829	4,061	3,962	38,750	38,800	4,421	4,189	4,421	4,322
32,800	32,850	3,707	3,475	3,707	3,608	35,800	35,850	4,067	3,835	4,067	3,968	38,800	38,850	4,427	4,195	4,427	4,328
32,850	32,900	3,713	3,481	3,713	3,614	35,850	35,900	4,073	3,841	4,073	3,974	38,850	38,900	4,433	4,201	4,433	4,334
32,900	32,950	3,719	3,487	3,719	3,620	35,900	35,950	4,079	3,847	4,079	3,980	38,900	38,950	4,439	4,207	4,439	4,340
32,950	33,000	3,725	3,493	3,725	3,626	35,950	36,000	4,085	3,853	4,085	3,986	38,950	39,000	4,445	4,213	4,445	4,346

* This column must also be used by a qualifying surviving spouse.

(Continued)

2024 Tax Table — Continued

If line 15 (taxable income) is—		And you are—				If line 15 (taxable income) is—		And you are—				If line 15 (taxable income) is—		And you are—			
At least	But less than	Single	Married filing jointly *	Married filing separately	Head of a household	At least	But less than	Single	Married filing jointly *	Married filing separately	Head of a household	At least	But less than	Single	Married filing jointly *	Married filing separately	Head of a household
		Your tax is—						Your tax is—						Your tax is—			
39,000						**42,000**						**45,000**					
39,000	39,050	4,451	4,219	4,451	4,352	42,000	42,050	4,811	4,579	4,811	4,712	45,000	45,050	5,171	4,939	5,171	5,072
39,050	39,100	4,457	4,225	4,457	4,358	42,050	42,100	4,817	4,585	4,817	4,718	45,050	45,100	5,177	4,945	5,177	5,078
39,100	39,150	4,463	4,231	4,463	4,364	42,100	42,150	4,823	4,591	4,823	4,724	45,100	45,150	5,183	4,951	5,183	5,084
39,150	39,200	4,469	4,237	4,469	4,370	42,150	42,200	4,829	4,597	4,829	4,730	45,150	45,200	5,189	4,957	5,189	5,090
39,200	39,250	4,475	4,243	4,475	4,376	42,200	42,250	4,835	4,603	4,835	4,736	45,200	45,250	5,195	4,963	5,195	5,096
39,250	39,300	4,481	4,249	4,481	4,382	42,250	42,300	4,841	4,609	4,841	4,742	45,250	45,300	5,201	4,969	5,201	5,102
39,300	39,350	4,487	4,255	4,487	4,388	42,300	42,350	4,847	4,615	4,847	4,748	45,300	45,350	5,207	4,975	5,207	5,108
39,350	39,400	4,493	4,261	4,493	4,394	42,350	42,400	4,853	4,621	4,853	4,754	45,350	45,400	5,213	4,981	5,213	5,114
39,400	39,450	4,499	4,267	4,499	4,400	42,400	42,450	4,859	4,627	4,859	4,760	45,400	45,450	5,219	4,987	5,219	5,120
39,450	39,500	4,505	4,273	4,505	4,406	42,450	42,500	4,865	4,633	4,865	4,766	45,450	45,500	5,225	4,993	5,225	5,126
39,500	39,550	4,511	4,279	4,511	4,412	42,500	42,550	4,871	4,639	4,871	4,772	45,500	45,550	5,231	4,999	5,231	5,132
39,550	39,600	4,517	4,285	4,517	4,418	42,550	42,600	4,877	4,645	4,877	4,778	45,550	45,600	5,237	5,005	5,237	5,138
39,600	39,650	4,523	4,291	4,523	4,424	42,600	42,650	4,883	4,651	4,883	4,784	45,600	45,650	5,243	5,011	5,243	5,144
39,650	39,700	4,529	4,297	4,529	4,430	42,650	42,700	4,889	4,657	4,889	4,790	45,650	45,700	5,249	5,017	5,249	5,150
39,700	39,750	4,535	4,303	4,535	4,436	42,700	42,750	4,895	4,663	4,895	4,796	45,700	45,750	5,255	5,023	5,255	5,156
39,750	39,800	4,541	4,309	4,541	4,442	42,750	42,800	4,901	4,669	4,901	4,802	45,750	45,800	5,261	5,029	5,261	5,162
39,800	39,850	4,547	4,315	4,547	4,448	42,800	42,850	4,907	4,675	4,907	4,808	45,800	45,850	5,267	5,035	5,267	5,168
39,850	39,900	4,553	4,321	4,553	4,454	42,850	42,900	4,913	4,681	4,913	4,814	45,850	45,900	5,273	5,041	5,273	5,174
39,900	39,950	4,559	4,327	4,559	4,460	42,900	42,950	4,919	4,687	4,919	4,820	45,900	45,950	5,279	5,047	5,279	5,180
39,950	40,000	4,565	4,333	4,565	4,466	42,950	43,000	4,925	4,693	4,925	4,826	45,950	46,000	5,285	5,053	5,285	5,186
40,000						**43,000**						**46,000**					
40,000	40,050	4,571	4,339	4,571	4,472	43,000	43,050	4,931	4,699	4,931	4,832	46,000	46,050	5,291	5,059	5,291	5,192
40,050	40,100	4,577	4,345	4,577	4,478	43,050	43,100	4,937	4,705	4,937	4,838	46,050	46,100	5,297	5,065	5,297	5,198
40,100	40,150	4,583	4,351	4,583	4,484	43,100	43,150	4,943	4,711	4,943	4,844	46,100	46,150	5,303	5,071	5,303	5,204
40,150	40,200	4,589	4,357	4,589	4,490	43,150	43,200	4,949	4,717	4,949	4,850	46,150	46,200	5,309	5,077	5,309	5,210
40,200	40,250	4,595	4,363	4,595	4,496	43,200	43,250	4,955	4,723	4,955	4,856	46,200	46,250	5,315	5,083	5,315	5,216
40,250	40,300	4,601	4,369	4,601	4,502	43,250	43,300	4,961	4,729	4,961	4,862	46,250	46,300	5,321	5,089	5,321	5,222
40,300	40,350	4,607	4,375	4,607	4,508	43,300	43,350	4,967	4,735	4,967	4,868	46,300	46,350	5,327	5,095	5,327	5,228
40,350	40,400	4,613	4,381	4,613	4,514	43,350	43,400	4,973	4,741	4,973	4,874	46,350	46,400	5,333	5,101	5,333	5,234
40,400	40,450	4,619	4,387	4,619	4,520	43,400	43,450	4,979	4,747	4,979	4,880	46,400	46,450	5,339	5,107	5,339	5,240
40,450	40,500	4,625	4,393	4,625	4,526	43,450	43,500	4,985	4,753	4,985	4,886	46,450	46,500	5,345	5,113	5,345	5,246
40,500	40,550	4,631	4,399	4,631	4,532	43,500	43,550	4,991	4,759	4,991	4,892	46,500	46,550	5,351	5,119	5,351	5,252
40,550	40,600	4,637	4,405	4,637	4,538	43,550	43,600	4,997	4,765	4,997	4,898	46,550	46,600	5,357	5,125	5,357	5,258
40,600	40,650	4,643	4,411	4,643	4,544	43,600	43,650	5,003	4,771	5,003	4,904	46,600	46,650	5,363	5,131	5,363	5,264
40,650	40,700	4,649	4,417	4,649	4,550	43,650	43,700	5,009	4,777	5,009	4,910	46,650	46,700	5,369	5,137	5,369	5,270
40,700	40,750	4,655	4,423	4,655	4,556	43,700	43,750	5,015	4,783	5,015	4,916	46,700	46,750	5,375	5,143	5,375	5,276
40,750	40,800	4,661	4,429	4,661	4,562	43,750	43,800	5,021	4,789	5,021	4,922	46,750	46,800	5,381	5,149	5,381	5,282
40,800	40,850	4,667	4,435	4,667	4,568	43,800	43,850	5,027	4,795	5,027	4,928	46,800	46,850	5,387	5,155	5,387	5,288
40,850	40,900	4,673	4,441	4,673	4,574	43,850	43,900	5,033	4,801	5,033	4,934	46,850	46,900	5,393	5,161	5,393	5,294
40,900	40,950	4,679	4,447	4,679	4,580	43,900	43,950	5,039	4,807	5,039	4,940	46,900	46,950	5,399	5,167	5,399	5,300
40,950	41,000	4,685	4,453	4,685	4,586	43,950	44,000	5,045	4,813	5,045	4,946	46,950	47,000	5,405	5,173	5,405	5,306
41,000						**44,000**						**47,000**					
41,000	41,050	4,691	4,459	4,691	4,592	44,000	44,050	5,051	4,819	5,051	4,952	47,000	47,050	5,411	5,179	5,411	5,312
41,050	41,100	4,697	4,465	4,697	4,598	44,050	44,100	5,057	4,825	5,057	4,958	47,050	47,100	5,417	5,185	5,417	5,318
41,100	41,150	4,703	4,471	4,703	4,604	44,100	44,150	5,063	4,831	5,063	4,964	47,100	47,150	5,423	5,191	5,423	5,324
41,150	41,200	4,709	4,477	4,709	4,610	44,150	44,200	5,069	4,837	5,069	4,970	47,150	47,200	5,432	5,197	5,432	5,330
41,200	41,250	4,715	4,483	4,715	4,616	44,200	44,250	5,075	4,843	5,075	4,976	47,200	47,250	5,443	5,203	5,443	5,336
41,250	41,300	4,721	4,489	4,721	4,622	44,250	44,300	5,081	4,849	5,081	4,982	47,250	47,300	5,454	5,209	5,454	5,342
41,300	41,350	4,727	4,495	4,727	4,628	44,300	44,350	5,087	4,855	5,087	4,988	47,300	47,350	5,465	5,215	5,465	5,348
41,350	41,400	4,733	4,501	4,733	4,634	44,350	44,400	5,093	4,861	5,093	4,994	47,350	47,400	5,476	5,221	5,476	5,354
41,400	41,450	4,739	4,507	4,739	4,640	44,400	44,450	5,099	4,867	5,099	5,000	47,400	47,450	5,487	5,227	5,487	5,360
41,450	41,500	4,745	4,513	4,745	4,646	44,450	44,500	5,105	4,873	5,105	5,006	47,450	47,500	5,498	5,233	5,498	5,366
41,500	41,550	4,751	4,519	4,751	4,652	44,500	44,550	5,111	4,879	5,111	5,012	47,500	47,550	5,509	5,239	5,509	5,372
41,550	41,600	4,757	4,525	4,757	4,658	44,550	44,600	5,117	4,885	5,117	5,018	47,550	47,600	5,520	5,245	5,520	5,378
41,600	41,650	4,763	4,531	4,763	4,664	44,600	44,650	5,123	4,891	5,123	5,024	47,600	47,650	5,531	5,251	5,531	5,384
41,650	41,700	4,769	4,537	4,769	4,670	44,650	44,700	5,129	4,897	5,129	5,030	47,650	47,700	5,542	5,257	5,542	5,390
41,700	41,750	4,775	4,543	4,775	4,676	44,700	44,750	5,135	4,903	5,135	5,036	47,700	47,750	5,553	5,263	5,553	5,396
41,750	41,800	4,781	4,549	4,781	4,682	44,750	44,800	5,141	4,909	5,141	5,042	47,750	47,800	5,564	5,269	5,564	5,402
41,800	41,850	4,787	4,555	4,787	4,688	44,800	44,850	5,147	4,915	5,147	5,048	47,800	47,850	5,575	5,275	5,575	5,408
41,850	41,900	4,793	4,561	4,793	4,694	44,850	44,900	5,153	4,921	5,153	5,054	47,850	47,900	5,586	5,281	5,586	5,414
41,900	41,950	4,799	4,567	4,799	4,700	44,900	44,950	5,159	4,927	5,159	5,060	47,900	47,950	5,597	5,287	5,597	5,420
41,950	42,000	4,805	4,573	4,805	4,706	44,950	45,000	5,165	4,933	5,165	5,066	47,950	48,000	5,608	5,293	5,608	5,426

* This column must also be used by a qualifying surviving spouse.

(Continued)

Tax Rate Schedules and Tax Table A-10

2024 Tax Table — *Continued*

If line 15 (taxable income) is—		And you are—				If line 15 (taxable income) is—		And you are—				If line 15 (taxable income) is—		And you are—			
At least	But less than	Single	Married filing jointly *	Married filing separately	Head of a household	At least	But less than	Single	Married filing jointly *	Married filing separately	Head of a household	At least	But less than	Single	Married filing jointly *	Married filing separately	Head of a household
		Your tax is—						Your tax is—						Your tax is—			
48,000						**51,000**						**54,000**					
48,000	48,050	5,619	5,299	5,619	5,432	51,000	51,050	6,279	5,659	6,279	5,792	54,000	54,050	6,939	6,019	6,939	6,152
48,050	48,100	5,630	5,305	5,630	5,438	51,050	51,100	6,290	5,665	6,290	5,798	54,050	54,100	6,950	6,025	6,950	6,158
48,100	48,150	5,641	5,311	5,641	5,444	51,100	51,150	6,301	5,671	6,301	5,804	54,100	54,150	6,961	6,031	6,961	6,164
48,150	48,200	5,652	5,317	5,652	5,450	51,150	51,200	6,312	5,677	6,312	5,810	54,150	54,200	6,972	6,037	6,972	6,170
48,200	48,250	5,663	5,323	5,663	5,456	51,200	51,250	6,323	5,683	6,323	5,816	54,200	54,250	6,983	6,043	6,983	6,176
48,250	48,300	5,674	5,329	5,674	5,462	51,250	51,300	6,334	5,689	6,334	5,822	54,250	54,300	6,994	6,049	6,994	6,182
48,300	48,350	5,685	5,335	5,685	5,468	51,300	51,350	6,345	5,695	6,345	5,828	54,300	54,350	7,005	6,055	7,005	6,188
48,350	48,400	5,696	5,341	5,696	5,474	51,350	51,400	6,356	5,701	6,356	5,834	54,350	54,400	7,016	6,061	7,016	6,194
48,400	48,450	5,707	5,347	5,707	5,480	51,400	51,450	6,367	5,707	6,367	5,840	54,400	54,450	7,027	6,067	7,027	6,200
48,450	48,500	5,718	5,353	5,718	5,486	51,450	51,500	6,378	5,713	6,378	5,846	54,450	54,500	7,038	6,073	7,038	6,206
48,500	48,550	5,729	5,359	5,729	5,492	51,500	51,550	6,389	5,719	6,389	5,852	54,500	54,550	7,049	6,079	7,049	6,212
48,550	48,600	5,740	5,365	5,740	5,498	51,550	51,600	6,400	5,725	6,400	5,858	54,550	54,600	7,060	6,085	7,060	6,218
48,600	48,650	5,751	5,371	5,751	5,504	51,600	51,650	6,411	5,731	6,411	5,864	54,600	54,650	7,071	6,091	7,071	6,224
48,650	48,700	5,762	5,377	5,762	5,510	51,650	51,700	6,422	5,737	6,422	5,870	54,650	54,700	7,082	6,097	7,082	6,230
48,700	48,750	5,773	5,383	5,773	5,516	51,700	51,750	6,433	5,743	6,433	5,876	54,700	54,750	7,093	6,103	7,093	6,236
48,750	48,800	5,784	5,389	5,784	5,522	51,750	51,800	6,444	5,749	6,444	5,882	54,750	54,800	7,104	6,109	7,104	6,242
48,800	48,850	5,795	5,395	5,795	5,528	51,800	51,850	6,455	5,755	6,455	5,888	54,800	54,850	7,115	6,115	7,115	6,248
48,850	48,900	5,806	5,401	5,806	5,534	51,850	51,900	6,466	5,761	6,466	5,894	54,850	54,900	7,126	6,121	7,126	6,254
48,900	48,950	5,817	5,407	5,817	5,540	51,900	51,950	6,477	5,767	6,477	5,900	54,900	54,950	7,137	6,127	7,137	6,260
48,950	49,000	5,828	5,413	5,828	5,546	51,950	52,000	6,488	5,773	6,488	5,906	54,950	55,000	7,148	6,133	7,148	6,266
49,000						**52,000**						**55,000**					
49,000	49,050	5,839	5,419	5,839	5,552	52,000	52,050	6,499	5,779	6,499	5,912	55,000	55,050	7,159	6,139	7,159	6,272
49,050	49,100	5,850	5,425	5,850	5,558	52,050	52,100	6,510	5,785	6,510	5,918	55,050	55,100	7,170	6,145	7,170	6,278
49,100	49,150	5,861	5,431	5,861	5,564	52,100	52,150	6,521	5,791	6,521	5,924	55,100	55,150	7,181	6,151	7,181	6,284
49,150	49,200	5,872	5,437	5,872	5,570	52,150	52,200	6,532	5,797	6,532	5,930	55,150	55,200	7,192	6,157	7,192	6,290
49,200	49,250	5,883	5,443	5,883	5,576	52,200	52,250	6,543	5,803	6,543	5,936	55,200	55,250	7,203	6,163	7,203	6,296
49,250	49,300	5,894	5,449	5,894	5,582	52,250	52,300	6,554	5,809	6,554	5,942	55,250	55,300	7,214	6,169	7,214	6,302
49,300	49,350	5,905	5,455	5,905	5,588	52,300	52,350	6,565	5,815	6,565	5,948	55,300	55,350	7,225	6,175	7,225	6,308
49,350	49,400	5,916	5,461	5,916	5,594	52,350	52,400	6,576	5,821	6,576	5,954	55,350	55,400	7,236	6,181	7,236	6,314
49,400	49,450	5,927	5,467	5,927	5,600	52,400	52,450	6,587	5,827	6,587	5,960	55,400	55,450	7,247	6,187	7,247	6,320
49,450	49,500	5,938	5,473	5,938	5,606	52,450	52,500	6,598	5,833	6,598	5,966	55,450	55,500	7,258	6,193	7,258	6,326
49,500	49,550	5,949	5,479	5,949	5,612	52,500	52,550	6,609	5,839	6,609	5,972	55,500	55,550	7,269	6,199	7,269	6,332
49,550	49,600	5,960	5,485	5,960	5,618	52,550	52,600	6,620	5,845	6,620	5,978	55,550	55,600	7,280	6,205	7,280	6,338
49,600	49,650	5,971	5,491	5,971	5,624	52,600	52,650	6,631	5,851	6,631	5,984	55,600	55,650	7,291	6,211	7,291	6,344
49,650	49,700	5,982	5,497	5,982	5,630	52,650	52,700	6,642	5,857	6,642	5,990	55,650	55,700	7,302	6,217	7,302	6,350
49,700	49,750	5,993	5,503	5,993	5,636	52,700	52,750	6,653	5,863	6,653	5,996	55,700	55,750	7,313	6,223	7,313	6,356
49,750	49,800	6,004	5,509	6,004	5,642	52,750	52,800	6,664	5,869	6,664	6,002	55,750	55,800	7,324	6,229	7,324	6,362
49,800	49,850	6,015	5,515	6,015	5,648	52,800	52,850	6,675	5,875	6,675	6,008	55,800	55,850	7,335	6,235	7,335	6,368
49,850	49,900	6,026	5,521	6,026	5,654	52,850	52,900	6,686	5,881	6,686	6,014	55,850	55,900	7,346	6,241	7,346	6,374
49,900	49,950	6,037	5,527	6,037	5,660	52,900	52,950	6,697	5,887	6,697	6,020	55,900	55,950	7,357	6,247	7,357	6,380
49,950	50,000	6,048	5,533	6,048	5,666	52,950	53,000	6,708	5,893	6,708	6,026	55,950	56,000	7,368	6,253	7,368	6,386
50,000						**53,000**						**56,000**					
50,000	50,050	6,059	5,539	6,059	5,672	53,000	53,050	6,719	5,899	6,719	6,032	56,000	56,050	7,379	6,259	7,379	6,392
50,050	50,100	6,070	5,545	6,070	5,678	53,050	53,100	6,730	5,905	6,730	6,038	56,050	56,100	7,390	6,265	7,390	6,398
50,100	50,150	6,081	5,551	6,081	5,684	53,100	53,150	6,741	5,911	6,741	6,044	56,100	56,150	7,401	6,271	7,401	6,404
50,150	50,200	6,092	5,557	6,092	5,690	53,150	53,200	6,752	5,917	6,752	6,050	56,150	56,200	7,412	6,277	7,412	6,410
50,200	50,250	6,103	5,563	6,103	5,696	53,200	53,250	6,763	5,923	6,763	6,056	56,200	56,250	7,423	6,283	7,423	6,416
50,250	50,300	6,114	5,569	6,114	5,702	53,250	53,300	6,774	5,929	6,774	6,062	56,250	56,300	7,434	6,289	7,434	6,422
50,300	50,350	6,125	5,575	6,125	5,708	53,300	53,350	6,785	5,935	6,785	6,068	56,300	56,350	7,445	6,295	7,445	6,428
50,350	50,400	6,136	5,581	6,136	5,714	53,350	53,400	6,796	5,941	6,796	6,074	56,350	56,400	7,456	6,301	7,456	6,434
50,400	50,450	6,147	5,587	6,147	5,720	53,400	53,450	6,807	5,947	6,807	6,080	56,400	56,450	7,467	6,307	7,467	6,440
50,450	50,500	6,158	5,593	6,158	5,726	53,450	53,500	6,818	5,953	6,818	6,086	56,450	56,500	7,478	6,313	7,478	6,446
50,500	50,550	6,169	5,599	6,169	5,732	53,500	53,550	6,829	5,959	6,829	6,092	56,500	56,550	7,489	6,319	7,489	6,452
50,550	50,600	6,180	5,605	6,180	5,738	53,550	53,600	6,840	5,965	6,840	6,098	56,550	56,600	7,500	6,325	7,500	6,458
50,600	50,650	6,191	5,611	6,191	5,744	53,600	53,650	6,851	5,971	6,851	6,104	56,600	56,650	7,511	6,331	7,511	6,464
50,650	50,700	6,202	5,617	6,202	5,750	53,650	53,700	6,862	5,977	6,862	6,110	56,650	56,700	7,522	6,337	7,522	6,470
50,700	50,750	6,213	5,623	6,213	5,756	53,700	53,750	6,873	5,983	6,873	6,116	56,700	56,750	7,533	6,343	7,533	6,476
50,750	50,800	6,224	5,629	6,224	5,762	53,750	53,800	6,884	5,989	6,884	6,122	56,750	56,800	7,544	6,349	7,544	6,482
50,800	50,850	6,235	5,635	6,235	5,768	53,800	53,850	6,895	5,995	6,895	6,128	56,800	56,850	7,555	6,355	7,555	6,488
50,850	50,900	6,246	5,641	6,246	5,774	53,850	53,900	6,906	6,001	6,906	6,134	56,850	56,900	7,566	6,361	7,566	6,494
50,900	50,950	6,257	5,647	6,257	5,780	53,900	53,950	6,917	6,007	6,917	6,140	56,900	56,950	7,577	6,367	7,577	6,500
50,950	51,000	6,268	5,653	6,268	5,786	53,950	54,000	6,928	6,013	6,928	6,146	56,950	57,000	7,588	6,373	7,588	6,506

* This column must also be used by a qualifying surviving spouse.

(Continued)

2024 Tax Table — Continued

If line 15 (taxable income) is—		And you are—				If line 15 (taxable income) is—		And you are—				If line 15 (taxable income) is—		And you are—			
At least	But less than	Single	Married filing jointly *	Married filing separately	Head of a household	At least	But less than	Single	Married filing jointly *	Married filing separately	Head of a household	At least	But less than	Single	Married filing jointly *	Married filing separately	Head of a household
		Your tax is—						Your tax is—						Your tax is—			

57,000 | 60,000 | 63,000

At least	But less than	Single	MFJ	MFS	HoH	At least	But less than	Single	MFJ	MFS	HoH	At least	But less than	Single	MFJ	MFS	HoH
57,000	57,050	7,599	6,379	7,599	6,512	60,000	60,050	8,259	6,739	8,259	6,872	63,000	63,050	8,919	7,099	8,919	7,232
57,050	57,100	7,610	6,385	7,610	6,518	60,050	60,100	8,270	6,745	8,270	6,878	63,050	63,100	8,930	7,105	8,930	7,238
57,100	57,150	7,621	6,391	7,621	6,524	60,100	60,150	8,281	6,751	8,281	6,884	63,100	63,150	8,941	7,111	8,941	7,247
57,150	57,200	7,632	6,397	7,632	6,530	60,150	60,200	8,292	6,757	8,292	6,890	63,150	63,200	8,952	7,117	8,952	7,258
57,200	57,250	7,643	6,403	7,643	6,536	60,200	60,250	8,303	6,763	8,303	6,896	63,200	63,250	8,963	7,123	8,963	7,269
57,250	57,300	7,654	6,409	7,654	6,542	60,250	60,300	8,314	6,769	8,314	6,902	63,250	63,300	8,974	7,129	8,974	7,280
57,300	57,350	7,665	6,415	7,665	6,548	60,300	60,350	8,325	6,775	8,325	6,908	63,300	63,350	8,985	7,135	8,985	7,291
57,350	57,400	7,676	6,421	7,676	6,554	60,350	60,400	8,336	6,781	8,336	6,914	63,350	63,400	8,996	7,141	8,996	7,302
57,400	57,450	7,687	6,427	7,687	6,560	60,400	60,450	8,347	6,787	8,347	6,920	63,400	63,450	9,007	7,147	9,007	7,313
57,450	57,500	7,698	6,433	7,698	6,566	60,450	60,500	8,358	6,793	8,358	6,926	63,450	63,500	9,018	7,153	9,018	7,324
57,500	57,550	7,709	6,439	7,709	6,572	60,500	60,550	8,369	6,799	8,369	6,932	63,500	63,550	9,029	7,159	9,029	7,335
57,550	57,600	7,720	6,445	7,720	6,578	60,550	60,600	8,380	6,805	8,380	6,938	63,550	63,600	9,040	7,165	9,040	7,346
57,600	57,650	7,731	6,451	7,731	6,584	60,600	60,650	8,391	6,811	8,391	6,944	63,600	63,650	9,051	7,171	9,051	7,357
57,650	57,700	7,742	6,457	7,742	6,590	60,650	60,700	8,402	6,817	8,402	6,950	63,650	63,700	9,062	7,177	9,062	7,368
57,700	57,750	7,753	6,463	7,753	6,596	60,700	60,750	8,413	6,823	8,413	6,956	63,700	63,750	9,073	7,183	9,073	7,379
57,750	57,800	7,764	6,469	7,764	6,602	60,750	60,800	8,424	6,829	8,424	6,962	63,750	63,800	9,084	7,189	9,084	7,390
57,800	57,850	7,775	6,475	7,775	6,608	60,800	60,850	8,435	6,835	8,435	6,968	63,800	63,850	9,095	7,195	9,095	7,401
57,850	57,900	7,786	6,481	7,786	6,614	60,850	60,900	8,446	6,841	8,446	6,974	63,850	63,900	9,106	7,201	9,106	7,412
57,900	57,950	7,797	6,487	7,797	6,620	60,900	60,950	8,457	6,847	8,457	6,980	63,900	63,950	9,117	7,207	9,117	7,423
57,950	58,000	7,808	6,493	7,808	6,626	60,950	61,000	8,468	6,853	8,468	6,986	63,950	64,000	9,128	7,213	9,128	7,434

58,000 | 61,000 | 64,000

At least	But less than	Single	MFJ	MFS	HoH	At least	But less than	Single	MFJ	MFS	HoH	At least	But less than	Single	MFJ	MFS	HoH
58,000	58,050	7,819	6,499	7,819	6,632	61,000	61,050	8,479	6,859	8,479	6,992	64,000	64,050	9,139	7,219	9,139	7,445
58,050	58,100	7,830	6,505	7,830	6,638	61,050	61,100	8,490	6,865	8,490	6,998	64,050	64,100	9,150	7,225	9,150	7,456
58,100	58,150	7,841	6,511	7,841	6,644	61,100	61,150	8,501	6,871	8,501	7,004	64,100	64,150	9,161	7,231	9,161	7,467
58,150	58,200	7,852	6,517	7,852	6,650	61,150	61,200	8,512	6,877	8,512	7,010	64,150	64,200	9,172	7,237	9,172	7,478
58,200	58,250	7,863	6,523	7,863	6,656	61,200	61,250	8,523	6,883	8,523	7,016	64,200	64,250	9,183	7,243	9,183	7,489
58,250	58,300	7,874	6,529	7,874	6,662	61,250	61,300	8,534	6,889	8,534	7,022	64,250	64,300	9,194	7,249	9,194	7,500
58,300	58,350	7,885	6,535	7,885	6,668	61,300	61,350	8,545	6,895	8,545	7,028	64,300	64,350	9,205	7,255	9,205	7,511
58,350	58,400	7,896	6,541	7,896	6,674	61,350	61,400	8,556	6,901	8,556	7,034	64,350	64,400	9,216	7,261	9,216	7,522
58,400	58,450	7,907	6,547	7,907	6,680	61,400	61,450	8,567	6,907	8,567	7,040	64,400	64,450	9,227	7,267	9,227	7,533
58,450	58,500	7,918	6,553	7,918	6,686	61,450	61,500	8,578	6,913	8,578	7,046	64,450	64,500	9,238	7,273	9,238	7,544
58,500	58,550	7,929	6,559	7,929	6,692	61,500	61,550	8,589	6,919	8,589	7,052	64,500	64,550	9,249	7,279	9,249	7,555
58,550	58,600	7,940	6,565	7,940	6,698	61,550	61,600	8,600	6,925	8,600	7,058	64,550	64,600	9,260	7,285	9,260	7,566
58,600	58,650	7,951	6,571	7,951	6,704	61,600	61,650	8,611	6,931	8,611	7,064	64,600	64,650	9,271	7,291	9,271	7,577
58,650	58,700	7,962	6,577	7,962	6,710	61,650	61,700	8,622	6,937	8,622	7,070	64,650	64,700	9,282	7,297	9,282	7,588
58,700	58,750	7,973	6,583	7,973	6,716	61,700	61,750	8,633	6,943	8,633	7,076	64,700	64,750	9,293	7,303	9,293	7,599
58,750	58,800	7,984	6,589	7,984	6,722	61,750	61,800	8,644	6,949	8,644	7,082	64,750	64,800	9,304	7,309	9,304	7,610
58,800	58,850	7,995	6,595	7,995	6,728	61,800	61,850	8,655	6,955	8,655	7,088	64,800	64,850	9,315	7,315	9,315	7,621
58,850	58,900	8,006	6,601	8,006	6,734	61,850	61,900	8,666	6,961	8,666	7,094	64,850	64,900	9,326	7,321	9,326	7,632
58,900	58,950	8,017	6,607	8,017	6,740	61,900	61,950	8,677	6,967	8,677	7,100	64,900	64,950	9,337	7,327	9,337	7,643
58,950	59,000	8,028	6,613	8,028	6,746	61,950	62,000	8,688	6,973	8,688	7,106	64,950	65,000	9,348	7,333	9,348	7,654

59,000 | 62,000 | 65,000

At least	But less than	Single	MFJ	MFS	HoH	At least	But less than	Single	MFJ	MFS	HoH	At least	But less than	Single	MFJ	MFS	HoH
59,000	59,050	8,039	6,619	8,039	6,752	62,000	62,050	8,699	6,979	8,699	7,112	65,000	65,050	9,359	7,339	9,359	7,665
59,050	59,100	8,050	6,625	8,050	6,758	62,050	62,100	8,710	6,985	8,710	7,118	65,050	65,100	9,370	7,345	9,370	7,676
59,100	59,150	8,061	6,631	8,061	6,764	62,100	62,150	8,721	6,991	8,721	7,124	65,100	65,150	9,381	7,351	9,381	7,687
59,150	59,200	8,072	6,637	8,072	6,770	62,150	62,200	8,732	6,997	8,732	7,130	65,150	65,200	9,392	7,357	9,392	7,698
59,200	59,250	8,083	6,643	8,083	6,776	62,200	62,250	8,743	7,003	8,743	7,136	65,200	65,250	9,403	7,363	9,403	7,709
59,250	59,300	8,094	6,649	8,094	6,782	62,250	62,300	8,754	7,009	8,754	7,142	65,250	65,300	9,414	7,369	9,414	7,720
59,300	59,350	8,105	6,655	8,105	6,788	62,300	62,350	8,765	7,015	8,765	7,148	65,300	65,350	9,425	7,375	9,425	7,731
59,350	59,400	8,116	6,661	8,116	6,794	62,350	62,400	8,776	7,021	8,776	7,154	65,350	65,400	9,436	7,381	9,436	7,742
59,400	59,450	8,127	6,667	8,127	6,800	62,400	62,450	8,787	7,027	8,787	7,160	65,400	65,450	9,447	7,387	9,447	7,753
59,450	59,500	8,138	6,673	8,138	6,806	62,450	62,500	8,798	7,033	8,798	7,166	65,450	65,500	9,458	7,393	9,458	7,764
59,500	59,550	8,149	6,679	8,149	6,812	62,500	62,550	8,809	7,039	8,809	7,172	65,500	65,550	9,469	7,399	9,469	7,775
59,550	59,600	8,160	6,685	8,160	6,818	62,550	62,600	8,820	7,045	8,820	7,178	65,550	65,600	9,480	7,405	9,480	7,786
59,600	59,650	8,171	6,691	8,171	6,824	62,600	62,650	8,831	7,051	8,831	7,184	65,600	65,650	9,491	7,411	9,491	7,797
59,650	59,700	8,182	6,697	8,182	6,830	62,650	62,700	8,842	7,057	8,842	7,190	65,650	65,700	9,502	7,417	9,502	7,808
59,700	59,750	8,193	6,703	8,193	6,836	62,700	62,750	8,853	7,063	8,853	7,196	65,700	65,750	9,513	7,423	9,513	7,819
59,750	59,800	8,204	6,709	8,204	6,842	62,750	62,800	8,864	7,069	8,864	7,202	65,750	65,800	9,524	7,429	9,524	7,830
59,800	59,850	8,215	6,715	8,215	6,848	62,800	62,850	8,875	7,075	8,875	7,208	65,800	65,850	9,535	7,435	9,535	7,841
59,850	59,900	8,226	6,721	8,226	6,854	62,850	62,900	8,886	7,081	8,886	7,214	65,850	65,900	9,546	7,441	9,546	7,852
59,900	59,950	8,237	6,727	8,237	6,860	62,900	62,950	8,897	7,087	8,897	7,220	65,900	65,950	9,557	7,447	9,557	7,863
59,950	60,000	8,248	6,733	8,248	6,866	62,950	63,000	8,908	7,093	8,908	7,226	65,950	66,000	9,568	7,453	9,568	7,874

* This column must also be used by a qualifying surviving spouse.

(Continued)

2024 Tax Table — Continued

If line 15 (taxable income) is—		And you are—				If line 15 (taxable income) is—		And you are—				If line 15 (taxable income) is—		And you are—			
At least	But less than	Single	Married filing jointly *	Married filing separately	Head of a household	At least	But less than	Single	Married filing jointly *	Married filing separately	Head of a household	At least	But less than	Single	Married filing jointly *	Married filing separately	Head of a household
		Your tax is—						Your tax is—						Your tax is—			
66,000						**69,000**						**72,000**					
66,000	66,050	9,579	7,459	9,579	7,885	69,000	69,050	10,239	7,819	10,239	8,545	72,000	72,050	10,899	8,179	10,899	9,205
66,050	66,100	9,590	7,465	9,590	7,896	69,050	69,100	10,250	7,825	10,250	8,556	72,050	72,100	10,910	8,185	10,910	9,216
66,100	66,150	9,601	7,471	9,601	7,907	69,100	69,150	10,261	7,831	10,261	8,567	72,100	72,150	10,921	8,191	10,921	9,227
66,150	66,200	9,612	7,477	9,612	7,918	69,150	69,200	10,272	7,837	10,272	8,578	72,150	72,200	10,932	8,197	10,932	9,238
66,200	66,250	9,623	7,483	9,623	7,929	69,200	69,250	10,283	7,843	10,283	8,589	72,200	72,250	10,943	8,203	10,943	9,249
66,250	66,300	9,634	7,489	9,634	7,940	69,250	69,300	10,294	7,849	10,294	8,600	72,250	72,300	10,954	8,209	10,954	9,260
66,300	66,350	9,645	7,495	9,645	7,951	69,300	69,350	10,305	7,855	10,305	8,611	72,300	72,350	10,965	8,215	10,965	9,271
66,350	66,400	9,656	7,501	9,656	7,962	69,350	69,400	10,316	7,861	10,316	8,622	72,350	72,400	10,976	8,221	10,976	9,282
66,400	66,450	9,667	7,507	9,667	7,973	69,400	69,450	10,327	7,867	10,327	8,633	72,400	72,450	10,987	8,227	10,987	9,293
66,450	66,500	9,678	7,513	9,678	7,984	69,450	69,500	10,338	7,873	10,338	8,644	72,450	72,500	10,998	8,233	10,998	9,304
66,500	66,550	9,689	7,519	9,689	7,995	69,500	69,550	10,349	7,879	10,349	8,655	72,500	72,550	11,009	8,239	11,009	9,315
66,550	66,600	9,700	7,525	9,700	8,006	69,550	69,600	10,360	7,885	10,360	8,666	72,550	72,600	11,020	8,245	11,020	9,326
66,600	66,650	9,711	7,531	9,711	8,017	69,600	69,650	10,371	7,891	10,371	8,677	72,600	72,650	11,031	8,251	11,031	9,337
66,650	66,700	9,722	7,537	9,722	8,028	69,650	69,700	10,382	7,897	10,382	8,688	72,650	72,700	11,042	8,257	11,042	9,348
66,700	66,750	9,733	7,543	9,733	8,039	69,700	69,750	10,393	7,903	10,393	8,699	72,700	72,750	11,053	8,263	11,053	9,359
66,750	66,800	9,744	7,549	9,744	8,050	69,750	69,800	10,404	7,909	10,404	8,710	72,750	72,800	11,064	8,269	11,064	9,370
66,800	66,850	9,755	7,555	9,755	8,061	69,800	69,850	10,415	7,915	10,415	8,721	72,800	72,850	11,075	8,275	11,075	9,381
66,850	66,900	9,766	7,561	9,766	8,072	69,850	69,900	10,426	7,921	10,426	8,732	72,850	72,900	11,086	8,281	11,086	9,392
66,900	66,950	9,777	7,567	9,777	8,083	69,900	69,950	10,437	7,927	10,437	8,743	72,900	72,950	11,097	8,287	11,097	9,403
66,950	67,000	9,788	7,573	9,788	8,094	69,950	70,000	10,448	7,933	10,448	8,754	72,950	73,000	11,108	8,293	11,108	9,414
67,000						**70,000**						**73,000**					
67,000	67,050	9,799	7,579	9,799	8,105	70,000	70,050	10,459	7,939	10,459	8,765	73,000	73,050	11,119	8,299	11,119	9,425
67,050	67,100	9,810	7,585	9,810	8,116	70,050	70,100	10,470	7,945	10,470	8,776	73,050	73,100	11,130	8,305	11,130	9,436
67,100	67,150	9,821	7,591	9,821	8,127	70,100	70,150	10,481	7,951	10,481	8,787	73,100	73,150	11,141	8,311	11,141	9,447
67,150	67,200	9,832	7,597	9,832	8,138	70,150	70,200	10,492	7,957	10,492	8,798	73,150	73,200	11,152	8,317	11,152	9,458
67,200	67,250	9,843	7,603	9,843	8,149	70,200	70,250	10,503	7,963	10,503	8,809	73,200	73,250	11,163	8,323	11,163	9,469
67,250	67,300	9,854	7,609	9,854	8,160	70,250	70,300	10,514	7,969	10,514	8,820	73,250	73,300	11,174	8,329	11,174	9,480
67,300	67,350	9,865	7,615	9,865	8,171	70,300	70,350	10,525	7,975	10,525	8,831	73,300	73,350	11,185	8,335	11,185	9,491
67,350	67,400	9,876	7,621	9,876	8,182	70,350	70,400	10,536	7,981	10,536	8,842	73,350	73,400	11,196	8,341	11,196	9,502
67,400	67,450	9,887	7,627	9,887	8,193	70,400	70,450	10,547	7,987	10,547	8,853	73,400	73,450	11,207	8,347	11,207	9,513
67,450	67,500	9,898	7,633	9,898	8,204	70,450	70,500	10,558	7,993	10,558	8,864	73,450	73,500	11,218	8,353	11,218	9,524
67,500	67,550	9,909	7,639	9,909	8,215	70,500	70,550	10,569	7,999	10,569	8,875	73,500	73,550	11,229	8,359	11,229	9,535
67,550	67,600	9,920	7,645	9,920	8,226	70,550	70,600	10,580	8,005	10,580	8,886	73,550	73,600	11,240	8,365	11,240	9,546
67,600	67,650	9,931	7,651	9,931	8,237	70,600	70,650	10,591	8,011	10,591	8,897	73,600	73,650	11,251	8,371	11,251	9,557
67,650	67,700	9,942	7,657	9,942	8,248	70,650	70,700	10,602	8,017	10,602	8,908	73,650	73,700	11,262	8,377	11,262	9,568
67,700	67,750	9,953	7,663	9,953	8,259	70,700	70,750	10,613	8,023	10,613	8,919	73,700	73,750	11,273	8,383	11,273	9,579
67,750	67,800	9,964	7,669	9,964	8,270	70,750	70,800	10,624	8,029	10,624	8,930	73,750	73,800	11,284	8,389	11,284	9,590
67,800	67,850	9,975	7,675	9,975	8,281	70,800	70,850	10,635	8,035	10,635	8,941	73,800	73,850	11,295	8,395	11,295	9,601
67,850	67,900	9,986	7,681	9,986	8,292	70,850	70,900	10,646	8,041	10,646	8,952	73,850	73,900	11,306	8,401	11,306	9,612
67,900	67,950	9,997	7,687	9,997	8,303	70,900	70,950	10,657	8,047	10,657	8,963	73,900	73,950	11,317	8,407	11,317	9,623
67,950	68,000	10,008	7,693	10,008	8,314	70,950	71,000	10,668	8,053	10,668	8,974	73,950	74,000	11,328	8,413	11,328	9,634
68,000						**71,000**						**74,000**					
68,000	68,050	10,019	7,699	10,019	8,325	71,000	71,050	10,679	8,059	10,679	8,985	74,000	74,050	11,339	8,419	11,339	9,645
68,050	68,100	10,030	7,705	10,030	8,336	71,050	71,100	10,690	8,065	10,690	8,996	74,050	74,100	11,350	8,425	11,350	9,656
68,100	68,150	10,041	7,711	10,041	8,347	71,100	71,150	10,701	8,071	10,701	9,007	74,100	74,150	11,361	8,431	11,361	9,667
68,150	68,200	10,052	7,717	10,052	8,358	71,150	71,200	10,712	8,077	10,712	9,018	74,150	74,200	11,372	8,437	11,372	9,678
68,200	68,250	10,063	7,723	10,063	8,369	71,200	71,250	10,723	8,083	10,723	9,029	74,200	74,250	11,383	8,443	11,383	9,689
68,250	68,300	10,074	7,729	10,074	8,380	71,250	71,300	10,734	8,089	10,734	9,040	74,250	74,300	11,394	8,449	11,394	9,700
68,300	68,350	10,085	7,735	10,085	8,391	71,300	71,350	10,745	8,095	10,745	9,051	74,300	74,350	11,405	8,455	11,405	9,711
68,350	68,400	10,096	7,741	10,096	8,402	71,350	71,400	10,756	8,101	10,756	9,062	74,350	74,400	11,416	8,461	11,416	9,722
68,400	68,450	10,107	7,747	10,107	8,413	71,400	71,450	10,767	8,107	10,767	9,073	74,400	74,450	11,427	8,467	11,427	9,733
68,450	68,500	10,118	7,753	10,118	8,424	71,450	71,500	10,778	8,113	10,778	9,084	74,450	74,500	11,438	8,473	11,438	9,744
68,500	68,550	10,129	7,759	10,129	8,435	71,500	71,550	10,789	8,119	10,789	9,095	74,500	74,550	11,449	8,479	11,449	9,755
68,550	68,600	10,140	7,765	10,140	8,446	71,550	71,600	10,800	8,125	10,800	9,106	74,550	74,600	11,460	8,485	11,460	9,766
68,600	68,650	10,151	7,771	10,151	8,457	71,600	71,650	10,811	8,131	10,811	9,117	74,600	74,650	11,471	8,491	11,471	9,777
68,650	68,700	10,162	7,777	10,162	8,468	71,650	71,700	10,822	8,137	10,822	9,128	74,650	74,700	11,482	8,497	11,482	9,788
68,700	68,750	10,173	7,783	10,173	8,479	71,700	71,750	10,833	8,143	10,833	9,139	74,700	74,750	11,493	8,503	11,493	9,799
68,750	68,800	10,184	7,789	10,184	8,490	71,750	71,800	10,844	8,149	10,844	9,150	74,750	74,800	11,504	8,509	11,504	9,810
68,800	68,850	10,195	7,795	10,195	8,501	71,800	71,850	10,855	8,155	10,855	9,161	74,800	74,850	11,515	8,515	11,515	9,821
68,850	68,900	10,206	7,801	10,206	8,512	71,850	71,900	10,866	8,161	10,866	9,172	74,850	74,900	11,526	8,521	11,526	9,832
68,900	68,950	10,217	7,807	10,217	8,523	71,900	71,950	10,877	8,167	10,877	9,183	74,900	74,950	11,537	8,527	11,537	9,843
68,950	69,000	10,228	7,813	10,228	8,534	71,950	72,000	10,888	8,173	10,888	9,194	74,950	75,000	11,548	8,533	11,548	9,854

* This column must also be used by a qualifying surviving spouse.

(Continued)

2024 Tax Table — *Continued*

If line 15 (taxable income) is—		And you are—				If line 15 (taxable income) is—		And you are—				If line 15 (taxable income) is—		And you are—			
At least	But less than	Single	Married filing jointly *	Married filing separately	Head of a household	At least	But less than	Single	Married filing jointly *	Married filing separately	Head of a household	At least	But less than	Single	Married filing jointly *	Married filing separately	Head of a household
		Your tax is—						Your tax is—						Your tax is—			
75,000						**78,000**						**81,000**					
75,000	75,050	11,559	8,539	11,559	9,865	78,000	78,050	12,219	8,899	12,219	10,525	81,000	81,050	12,879	9,259	12,879	11,185
75,050	75,100	11,570	8,545	11,570	9,876	78,050	78,100	12,230	8,905	12,230	10,536	81,050	81,100	12,890	9,265	12,890	11,196
75,100	75,150	11,581	8,551	11,581	9,887	78,100	78,150	12,241	8,911	12,241	10,547	81,100	81,150	12,901	9,271	12,901	11,207
75,150	75,200	11,592	8,557	11,592	9,898	78,150	78,200	12,252	8,917	12,252	10,558	81,150	81,200	12,912	9,277	12,912	11,218
75,200	75,250	11,603	8,563	11,603	9,909	78,200	78,250	12,263	8,923	12,263	10,569	81,200	81,250	12,923	9,283	12,923	11,229
75,250	75,300	11,614	8,569	11,614	9,920	78,250	78,300	12,274	8,929	12,274	10,580	81,250	81,300	12,934	9,289	12,934	11,240
75,300	75,350	11,625	8,575	11,625	9,931	78,300	78,350	12,285	8,935	12,285	10,591	81,300	81,350	12,945	9,295	12,945	11,251
75,350	75,400	11,636	8,581	11,636	9,942	78,350	78,400	12,296	8,941	12,296	10,602	81,350	81,400	12,956	9,301	12,956	11,262
75,400	75,450	11,647	8,587	11,647	9,953	78,400	78,450	12,307	8,947	12,307	10,613	81,400	81,450	12,967	9,307	12,967	11,273
75,450	75,500	11,658	8,593	11,658	9,964	78,450	78,500	12,318	8,953	12,318	10,624	81,450	81,500	12,978	9,313	12,978	11,284
75,500	75,550	11,669	8,599	11,669	9,975	78,500	78,550	12,329	8,959	12,329	10,635	81,500	81,550	12,989	9,319	12,989	11,295
75,550	75,600	11,680	8,605	11,680	9,986	78,550	78,600	12,340	8,965	12,340	10,646	81,550	81,600	13,000	9,325	13,000	11,306
75,600	75,650	11,691	8,611	11,691	9,997	78,600	78,650	12,351	8,971	12,351	10,657	81,600	81,650	13,011	9,331	13,011	11,317
75,650	75,700	11,702	8,617	11,702	10,008	78,650	78,700	12,362	8,977	12,362	10,668	81,650	81,700	13,022	9,337	13,022	11,328
75,700	75,750	11,713	8,623	11,713	10,019	78,700	78,750	12,373	8,983	12,373	10,679	81,700	81,750	13,033	9,343	13,033	11,339
75,750	75,800	11,724	8,629	11,724	10,030	78,750	78,800	12,384	8,989	12,384	10,690	81,750	81,800	13,044	9,349	13,044	11,350
75,800	75,850	11,735	8,635	11,735	10,041	78,800	78,850	12,395	8,995	12,395	10,701	81,800	81,850	13,055	9,355	13,055	11,361
75,850	75,900	11,746	8,641	11,746	10,052	78,850	78,900	12,406	9,001	12,406	10,712	81,850	81,900	13,066	9,361	13,066	11,372
75,900	75,950	11,757	8,647	11,757	10,063	78,900	78,950	12,417	9,007	12,417	10,723	81,900	81,950	13,077	9,367	13,077	11,383
75,950	76,000	11,768	8,653	11,768	10,074	78,950	79,000	12,428	9,013	12,428	10,734	81,950	82,000	13,088	9,373	13,088	11,394
76,000						**79,000**						**82,000**					
76,000	76,050	11,779	8,659	11,779	10,085	79,000	79,050	12,439	9,019	12,439	10,745	82,000	82,050	13,099	9,379	13,099	11,405
76,050	76,100	11,790	8,665	11,790	10,096	79,050	79,100	12,450	9,025	12,450	10,756	82,050	82,100	13,110	9,385	13,110	11,416
76,100	76,150	11,801	8,671	11,801	10,107	79,100	79,150	12,461	9,031	12,461	10,767	82,100	82,150	13,121	9,391	13,121	11,427
76,150	76,200	11,812	8,677	11,812	10,118	79,150	79,200	12,472	9,037	12,472	10,778	82,150	82,200	13,132	9,397	13,132	11,438
76,200	76,250	11,823	8,683	11,823	10,129	79,200	79,250	12,483	9,043	12,483	10,789	82,200	82,250	13,143	9,403	13,143	11,449
76,250	76,300	11,834	8,689	11,834	10,140	79,250	79,300	12,494	9,049	12,494	10,800	82,250	82,300	13,154	9,409	13,154	11,460
76,300	76,350	11,845	8,695	11,845	10,151	79,300	79,350	12,505	9,055	12,505	10,811	82,300	82,350	13,165	9,415	13,165	11,471
76,350	76,400	11,856	8,701	11,856	10,162	79,350	79,400	12,516	9,061	12,516	10,822	82,350	82,400	13,176	9,421	13,176	11,482
76,400	76,450	11,867	8,707	11,867	10,173	79,400	79,450	12,527	9,067	12,527	10,833	82,400	82,450	13,187	9,427	13,187	11,493
76,450	76,500	11,878	8,713	11,878	10,184	79,450	79,500	12,538	9,073	12,538	10,844	82,450	82,500	13,198	9,433	13,198	11,504
76,500	76,550	11,889	8,719	11,889	10,195	79,500	79,550	12,549	9,079	12,549	10,855	82,500	82,550	13,209	9,439	13,209	11,515
76,550	76,600	11,900	8,725	11,900	10,206	79,550	79,600	12,560	9,085	12,560	10,866	82,550	82,600	13,220	9,445	13,220	11,526
76,600	76,650	11,911	8,731	11,911	10,217	79,600	79,650	12,571	9,091	12,571	10,877	82,600	82,650	13,231	9,451	13,231	11,537
76,650	76,700	11,922	8,737	11,922	10,228	79,650	79,700	12,582	9,097	12,582	10,888	82,650	82,700	13,242	9,457	13,242	11,548
76,700	76,750	11,933	8,743	11,933	10,239	79,700	79,750	12,593	9,103	12,593	10,899	82,700	82,750	13,253	9,463	13,253	11,559
76,750	76,800	11,944	8,749	11,944	10,250	79,750	79,800	12,604	9,109	12,604	10,910	82,750	82,800	13,264	9,469	13,264	11,570
76,800	76,850	11,955	8,755	11,955	10,261	79,800	79,850	12,615	9,115	12,615	10,921	82,800	82,850	13,275	9,475	13,275	11,581
76,850	76,900	11,966	8,761	11,966	10,272	79,850	79,900	12,626	9,121	12,626	10,932	82,850	82,900	13,286	9,481	13,286	11,592
76,900	76,950	11,977	8,767	11,977	10,283	79,900	79,950	12,637	9,127	12,637	10,943	82,900	82,950	13,297	9,487	13,297	11,603
76,950	77,000	11,988	8,773	11,988	10,294	79,950	80,000	12,648	9,133	12,648	10,954	82,950	83,000	13,308	9,493	13,308	11,614
77,000						**80,000**						**83,000**					
77,000	77,050	11,999	8,779	11,999	10,305	80,000	80,050	12,659	9,139	12,659	10,965	83,000	83,050	13,319	9,499	13,319	11,625
77,050	77,100	12,010	8,785	12,010	10,316	80,050	80,100	12,670	9,145	12,670	10,976	83,050	83,100	13,330	9,505	13,330	11,636
77,100	77,150	12,021	8,791	12,021	10,327	80,100	80,150	12,681	9,151	12,681	10,987	83,100	83,150	13,341	9,511	13,341	11,647
77,150	77,200	12,032	8,797	12,032	10,338	80,150	80,200	12,692	9,157	12,692	10,998	83,150	83,200	13,352	9,517	13,352	11,658
77,200	77,250	12,043	8,803	12,043	10,349	80,200	80,250	12,703	9,163	12,703	11,009	83,200	83,250	13,363	9,523	13,363	11,669
77,250	77,300	12,054	8,809	12,054	10,360	80,250	80,300	12,714	9,169	12,714	11,020	83,250	83,300	13,374	9,529	13,374	11,680
77,300	77,350	12,065	8,815	12,065	10,371	80,300	80,350	12,725	9,175	12,725	11,031	83,300	83,350	13,385	9,535	13,385	11,691
77,350	77,400	12,076	8,821	12,076	10,382	80,350	80,400	12,736	9,181	12,736	11,042	83,350	83,400	13,396	9,541	13,396	11,702
77,400	77,450	12,087	8,827	12,087	10,393	80,400	80,450	12,747	9,187	12,747	11,053	83,400	83,450	13,407	9,547	13,407	11,713
77,450	77,500	12,098	8,833	12,098	10,404	80,450	80,500	12,758	9,193	12,758	11,064	83,450	83,500	13,418	9,553	13,418	11,724
77,500	77,550	12,109	8,839	12,109	10,415	80,500	80,550	12,769	9,199	12,769	11,075	83,500	83,550	13,429	9,559	13,429	11,735
77,550	77,600	12,120	8,845	12,120	10,426	80,550	80,600	12,780	9,205	12,780	11,086	83,550	83,600	13,440	9,565	13,440	11,746
77,600	77,650	12,131	8,851	12,131	10,437	80,600	80,650	12,791	9,211	12,791	11,097	83,600	83,650	13,451	9,571	13,451	11,757
77,650	77,700	12,142	8,857	12,142	10,448	80,650	80,700	12,802	9,217	12,802	11,108	83,650	83,700	13,462	9,577	13,462	11,768
77,700	77,750	12,153	8,863	12,153	10,459	80,700	80,750	12,813	9,223	12,813	11,119	83,700	83,750	13,473	9,583	13,473	11,779
77,750	77,800	12,164	8,869	12,164	10,470	80,750	80,800	12,824	9,229	12,824	11,130	83,750	83,800	13,484	9,589	13,484	11,790
77,800	77,850	12,175	8,875	12,175	10,481	80,800	80,850	12,835	9,235	12,835	11,141	83,800	83,850	13,495	9,595	13,495	11,801
77,850	77,900	12,186	8,881	12,186	10,492	80,850	80,900	12,846	9,241	12,846	11,152	83,850	83,900	13,506	9,601	13,506	11,812
77,900	77,950	12,197	8,887	12,197	10,503	80,900	80,950	12,857	9,247	12,857	11,163	83,900	83,950	13,517	9,607	13,517	11,823
77,950	78,000	12,208	8,893	12,208	10,514	80,950	81,000	12,868	9,253	12,868	11,174	83,950	84,000	13,528	9,613	13,528	11,834

(Continued)

* This column must also be used by a qualifying surviving spouse.

2024 Tax Table — *Continued*

If line 15 (taxable income) is—		And you are—				If line 15 (taxable income) is—		And you are—				If line 15 (taxable income) is—		And you are—			
At least	But less than	Single	Married filing jointly *	Married filing separately	Head of a household	At least	But less than	Single	Married filing jointly *	Married filing separately	Head of a household	At least	But less than	Single	Married filing jointly *	Married filing separately	Head of a household
		Your tax is—						Your tax is—						Your tax is—			
84,000						**87,000**						**90,000**					
84,000	84,050	13,539	9,619	13,539	11,845	87,000	87,050	14,199	9,979	14,199	12,505	90,000	90,050	14,859	10,339	14,859	13,165
84,050	84,100	13,550	9,625	13,550	11,856	87,050	87,100	14,210	9,985	14,210	12,516	90,050	90,100	14,870	10,345	14,870	13,176
84,100	84,150	13,561	9,631	13,561	11,867	87,100	87,150	14,221	9,991	14,221	12,527	90,100	90,150	14,881	10,351	14,881	13,187
84,150	84,200	13,572	9,637	13,572	11,878	87,150	87,200	14,232	9,997	14,232	12,538	90,150	90,200	14,892	10,357	14,892	13,198
84,200	84,250	13,583	9,643	13,583	11,889	87,200	87,250	14,243	10,003	14,243	12,549	90,200	90,250	14,903	10,363	14,903	13,209
84,250	84,300	13,594	9,649	13,594	11,900	87,250	87,300	14,254	10,009	14,254	12,560	90,250	90,300	14,914	10,369	14,914	13,220
84,300	84,350	13,605	9,655	13,605	11,911	87,300	87,350	14,265	10,015	14,265	12,571	90,300	90,350	14,925	10,375	14,925	13,231
84,350	84,400	13,616	9,661	13,616	11,922	87,350	87,400	14,276	10,021	14,276	12,582	90,350	90,400	14,936	10,381	14,936	13,242
84,400	84,450	13,627	9,667	13,627	11,933	87,400	87,450	14,287	10,027	14,287	12,593	90,400	90,450	14,947	10,387	14,947	13,253
84,450	84,500	13,638	9,673	13,638	11,944	87,450	87,500	14,298	10,033	14,298	12,604	90,450	90,500	14,958	10,393	14,958	13,264
84,500	84,550	13,649	9,679	13,649	11,955	87,500	87,550	14,309	10,039	14,309	12,615	90,500	90,550	14,969	10,399	14,969	13,275
84,550	84,600	13,660	9,685	13,660	11,966	87,550	87,600	14,320	10,045	14,320	12,626	90,550	90,600	14,980	10,405	14,980	13,286
84,600	84,650	13,671	9,691	13,671	11,977	87,600	87,650	14,331	10,051	14,331	12,637	90,600	90,650	14,991	10,411	14,991	13,297
84,650	84,700	13,682	9,697	13,682	11,988	87,650	87,700	14,342	10,057	14,342	12,648	90,650	90,700	15,002	10,417	15,002	13,308
84,700	84,750	13,693	9,703	13,693	11,999	87,700	87,750	14,353	10,063	14,353	12,659	90,700	90,750	15,013	10,423	15,013	13,319
84,750	84,800	13,704	9,709	13,704	12,010	87,750	87,800	14,364	10,069	14,364	12,670	90,750	90,800	15,024	10,429	15,024	13,330
84,800	84,850	13,715	9,715	13,715	12,021	87,800	87,850	14,375	10,075	14,375	12,681	90,800	90,850	15,035	10,435	15,035	13,341
84,850	84,900	13,726	9,721	13,726	12,032	87,850	87,900	14,386	10,081	14,386	12,692	90,850	90,900	15,046	10,441	15,046	13,352
84,900	84,950	13,737	9,727	13,737	12,043	87,900	87,950	14,397	10,087	14,397	12,703	90,900	90,950	15,057	10,447	15,057	13,363
84,950	85,000	13,748	9,733	13,748	12,054	87,950	88,000	14,408	10,093	14,408	12,714	90,950	91,000	15,068	10,453	15,068	13,374
85,000						**88,000**						**91,000**					
85,000	85,050	13,759	9,739	13,759	12,065	88,000	88,050	14,419	10,099	14,419	12,725	91,000	91,050	15,079	10,459	15,079	13,385
85,050	85,100	13,770	9,745	13,770	12,076	88,050	88,100	14,430	10,105	14,430	12,736	91,050	91,100	15,090	10,465	15,090	13,396
85,100	85,150	13,781	9,751	13,781	12,087	88,100	88,150	14,441	10,111	14,441	12,747	91,100	91,150	15,101	10,471	15,101	13,407
85,150	85,200	13,792	9,757	13,792	12,098	88,150	88,200	14,452	10,117	14,452	12,758	91,150	91,200	15,112	10,477	15,112	13,418
85,200	85,250	13,803	9,763	13,803	12,109	88,200	88,250	14,463	10,123	14,463	12,769	91,200	91,250	15,123	10,483	15,123	13,429
85,250	85,300	13,814	9,769	13,814	12,120	88,250	88,300	14,474	10,129	14,474	12,780	91,250	91,300	15,134	10,489	15,134	13,440
85,300	85,350	13,825	9,775	13,825	12,131	88,300	88,350	14,485	10,135	14,485	12,791	91,300	91,350	15,145	10,495	15,145	13,451
85,350	85,400	13,836	9,781	13,836	12,142	88,350	88,400	14,496	10,141	14,496	12,802	91,350	91,400	15,156	10,501	15,156	13,462
85,400	85,450	13,847	9,787	13,847	12,153	88,400	88,450	14,507	10,147	14,507	12,813	91,400	91,450	15,167	10,507	15,167	13,473
85,450	85,500	13,858	9,793	13,858	12,164	88,450	88,500	14,518	10,153	14,518	12,824	91,450	91,500	15,178	10,513	15,178	13,484
85,500	85,550	13,869	9,799	13,869	12,175	88,500	88,550	14,529	10,159	14,529	12,835	91,500	91,550	15,189	10,519	15,189	13,495
85,550	85,600	13,880	9,805	13,880	12,186	88,550	88,600	14,540	10,165	14,540	12,846	91,550	91,600	15,200	10,525	15,200	13,506
85,600	85,650	13,891	9,811	13,891	12,197	88,600	88,650	14,551	10,171	14,551	12,857	91,600	91,650	15,211	10,531	15,211	13,517
85,650	85,700	13,902	9,817	13,902	12,208	88,650	88,700	14,562	10,177	14,562	12,868	91,650	91,700	15,222	10,537	15,222	13,528
85,700	85,750	13,913	9,823	13,913	12,219	88,700	88,750	14,573	10,183	14,573	12,879	91,700	91,750	15,233	10,543	15,233	13,539
85,750	85,800	13,924	9,829	13,924	12,230	88,750	88,800	14,584	10,189	14,584	12,890	91,750	91,800	15,244	10,549	15,244	13,550
85,800	85,850	13,935	9,835	13,935	12,241	88,800	88,850	14,595	10,195	14,595	12,901	91,800	91,850	15,255	10,555	15,255	13,561
85,850	85,900	13,946	9,841	13,946	12,252	88,850	88,900	14,606	10,201	14,606	12,912	91,850	91,900	15,266	10,561	15,266	13,572
85,900	85,950	13,957	9,847	13,957	12,263	88,900	88,950	14,617	10,207	14,617	12,923	91,900	91,950	15,277	10,567	15,277	13,583
85,950	86,000	13,968	9,853	13,968	12,274	88,950	89,000	14,628	10,213	14,628	12,934	91,950	92,000	15,288	10,573	15,288	13,594
86,000						**89,000**						**92,000**					
86,000	86,050	13,979	9,859	13,979	12,285	89,000	89,050	14,639	10,219	14,639	12,945	92,000	92,050	15,299	10,579	15,299	13,605
86,050	86,100	13,990	9,865	13,990	12,296	89,050	89,100	14,650	10,225	14,650	12,956	92,050	92,100	15,310	10,585	15,310	13,616
86,100	86,150	14,001	9,871	14,001	12,307	89,100	89,150	14,661	10,231	14,661	12,967	92,100	92,150	15,321	10,591	15,321	13,627
86,150	86,200	14,012	9,877	14,012	12,318	89,150	89,200	14,672	10,237	14,672	12,978	92,150	92,200	15,332	10,597	15,332	13,638
86,200	86,250	14,023	9,883	14,023	12,329	89,200	89,250	14,683	10,243	14,683	12,989	92,200	92,250	15,343	10,603	15,343	13,649
86,250	86,300	14,034	9,889	14,034	12,340	89,250	89,300	14,694	10,249	14,694	13,000	92,250	92,300	15,354	10,609	15,354	13,660
86,300	86,350	14,045	9,895	14,045	12,351	89,300	89,350	14,705	10,255	14,705	13,011	92,300	92,350	15,365	10,615	15,365	13,671
86,350	86,400	14,056	9,901	14,056	12,362	89,350	89,400	14,716	10,261	14,716	13,022	92,350	92,400	15,376	10,621	15,376	13,682
86,400	86,450	14,067	9,907	14,067	12,373	89,400	89,450	14,727	10,267	14,727	13,033	92,400	92,450	15,387	10,627	15,387	13,693
86,450	86,500	14,078	9,913	14,078	12,384	89,450	89,500	14,738	10,273	14,738	13,044	92,450	92,500	15,398	10,633	15,398	13,704
86,500	86,550	14,089	9,919	14,089	12,395	89,500	89,550	14,749	10,279	14,749	13,055	92,500	92,550	15,409	10,639	15,409	13,715
86,550	86,600	14,100	9,925	14,100	12,406	89,550	89,600	14,760	10,285	14,760	13,066	92,550	92,600	15,420	10,645	15,420	13,726
86,600	86,650	14,111	9,931	14,111	12,417	89,600	89,650	14,771	10,291	14,771	13,077	92,600	92,650	15,431	10,651	15,431	13,737
86,650	86,700	14,122	9,937	14,122	12,428	89,650	89,700	14,782	10,297	14,782	13,088	92,650	92,700	15,442	10,657	15,442	13,748
86,700	86,750	14,133	9,943	14,133	12,439	89,700	89,750	14,793	10,303	14,793	13,099	92,700	92,750	15,453	10,663	15,453	13,759
86,750	86,800	14,144	9,949	14,144	12,450	89,750	89,800	14,804	10,309	14,804	13,110	92,750	92,800	15,464	10,669	15,464	13,770
86,800	86,850	14,155	9,955	14,155	12,461	89,800	89,850	14,815	10,315	14,815	13,121	92,800	92,850	15,475	10,675	15,475	13,781
86,850	86,900	14,166	9,961	14,166	12,472	89,850	89,900	14,826	10,321	14,826	13,132	92,850	92,900	15,486	10,681	15,486	13,792
86,900	86,950	14,177	9,967	14,177	12,483	89,900	89,950	14,837	10,327	14,837	13,143	92,900	92,950	15,497	10,687	15,497	13,803
86,950	87,000	14,188	9,973	14,188	12,494	89,950	90,000	14,848	10,333	14,848	13,154	92,950	93,000	15,508	10,693	15,508	13,814

* This column must also be used by a qualifying surviving spouse.

(Continued)

2024 Tax Table — *Continued*

If line 15 (taxable income) is—		And you are—			
At least	But less than	Single	Married filing jointly *	Married filing separately	Head of a household
		Your tax is—			

93,000

At least	But less than	Single	MFJ	MFS	HoH
93,000	93,050	15,519	10,699	15,519	13,825
93,050	93,100	15,530	10,705	15,530	13,836
93,100	93,150	15,541	10,711	15,541	13,847
93,150	93,200	15,552	10,717	15,552	13,858
93,200	93,250	15,563	10,723	15,563	13,869
93,250	93,300	15,574	10,729	15,574	13,880
93,300	93,350	15,585	10,735	15,585	13,891
93,350	93,400	15,596	10,741	15,596	13,902
93,400	93,450	15,607	10,747	15,607	13,913
93,450	93,500	15,618	10,753	15,618	13,924
93,500	93,550	15,629	10,759	15,629	13,935
93,550	93,600	15,640	10,765	15,640	13,946
93,600	93,650	15,651	10,771	15,651	13,957
93,650	93,700	15,662	10,777	15,662	13,968
93,700	93,750	15,673	10,783	15,673	13,979
93,750	93,800	15,684	10,789	15,684	13,990
93,800	93,850	15,695	10,795	15,695	14,001
93,850	93,900	15,706	10,801	15,706	14,012
93,900	93,950	15,717	10,807	15,717	14,023
93,950	94,000	15,728	10,813	15,728	14,034

94,000

At least	But less than	Single	MFJ	MFS	HoH
94,000	94,050	15,739	10,819	15,739	14,045
94,050	94,100	15,750	10,825	15,750	14,056
94,100	94,150	15,761	10,831	15,761	14,067
94,150	94,200	15,772	10,837	15,772	14,078
94,200	94,250	15,783	10,843	15,783	14,089
94,250	94,300	15,794	10,849	15,794	14,100
94,300	94,350	15,805	10,858	15,805	14,111
94,350	94,400	15,816	10,869	15,816	14,122
94,400	94,450	15,827	10,880	15,827	14,133
94,450	94,500	15,838	10,891	15,838	14,144
94,500	94,550	15,849	10,902	15,849	14,155
94,550	94,600	15,860	10,913	15,860	14,166
94,600	94,650	15,871	10,924	15,871	14,177
94,650	94,700	15,882	10,935	15,882	14,188
94,700	94,750	15,893	10,946	15,893	14,199
94,750	94,800	15,904	10,957	15,904	14,210
94,800	94,850	15,915	10,968	15,915	14,221
94,850	94,900	15,926	10,979	15,926	14,232
94,900	94,950	15,937	10,990	15,937	14,243
94,950	95,000	15,948	11,001	15,948	14,254

95,000

At least	But less than	Single	MFJ	MFS	HoH
95,000	95,050	15,959	11,012	15,959	14,265
95,050	95,100	15,970	11,023	15,970	14,276
95,100	95,150	15,981	11,034	15,981	14,287
95,150	95,200	15,992	11,045	15,992	14,298
95,200	95,250	16,003	11,056	16,003	14,309
95,250	95,300	16,014	11,067	16,014	14,320
95,300	95,350	16,025	11,078	16,025	14,331
95,350	95,400	16,036	11,089	16,036	14,342
95,400	95,450	16,047	11,100	16,047	14,353
95,450	95,500	16,058	11,111	16,058	14,364
95,500	95,550	16,069	11,122	16,069	14,375
95,550	95,600	16,080	11,133	16,080	14,386
95,600	95,650	16,091	11,144	16,091	14,397
95,650	95,700	16,102	11,155	16,102	14,408
95,700	95,750	16,113	11,166	16,113	14,419
95,750	95,800	16,124	11,177	16,124	14,430
95,800	95,850	16,135	11,188	16,135	14,441
95,850	95,900	16,146	11,199	16,146	14,452
95,900	95,950	16,157	11,210	16,157	14,463
95,950	96,000	16,168	11,221	16,168	14,474

96,000

At least	But less than	Single	MFJ	MFS	HoH
96,000	96,050	16,179	11,232	16,179	14,485
96,050	96,100	16,190	11,243	16,190	14,496
96,100	96,150	16,201	11,254	16,201	14,507
96,150	96,200	16,212	11,265	16,212	14,518
96,200	96,250	16,223	11,276	16,223	14,529
96,250	96,300	16,234	11,287	16,234	14,540
96,300	96,350	16,245	11,298	16,245	14,551
96,350	96,400	16,256	11,309	16,256	14,562
96,400	96,450	16,267	11,320	16,267	14,573
96,450	96,500	16,278	11,331	16,278	14,584
96,500	96,550	16,289	11,342	16,289	14,595
96,550	96,600	16,300	11,353	16,300	14,606
96,600	96,650	16,311	11,364	16,311	14,617
96,650	96,700	16,322	11,375	16,322	14,628
96,700	96,750	16,333	11,386	16,333	14,639
96,750	96,800	16,344	11,397	16,344	14,650
96,800	96,850	16,355	11,408	16,355	14,661
96,850	96,900	16,366	11,419	16,366	14,672
96,900	96,950	16,377	11,430	16,377	14,683
96,950	97,000	16,388	11,441	16,388	14,694

97,000

At least	But less than	Single	MFJ	MFS	HoH
97,000	97,050	16,399	11,452	16,399	14,705
97,050	97,100	16,410	11,463	16,410	14,716
97,100	97,150	16,421	11,474	16,421	14,727
97,150	97,200	16,432	11,485	16,432	14,738
97,200	97,250	16,443	11,496	16,443	14,749
97,250	97,300	16,454	11,507	16,454	14,760
97,300	97,350	16,465	11,518	16,465	14,771
97,350	97,400	16,476	11,529	16,476	14,782
97,400	97,450	16,487	11,540	16,487	14,793
97,450	97,500	16,498	11,551	16,498	14,804
97,500	97,550	16,509	11,562	16,509	14,815
97,550	97,600	16,520	11,573	16,520	14,826
97,600	97,650	16,531	11,584	16,531	14,837
97,650	97,700	16,542	11,595	16,542	14,848
97,700	97,750	16,553	11,606	16,553	14,859
97,750	97,800	16,564	11,617	16,564	14,870
97,800	97,850	16,575	11,628	16,575	14,881
97,850	97,900	16,586	11,639	16,586	14,892
97,900	97,950	16,597	11,650	16,597	14,903
97,950	98,000	16,608	11,661	16,608	14,914

98,000

At least	But less than	Single	MFJ	MFS	HoH
98,000	98,050	16,619	11,672	16,619	14,925
98,050	98,100	16,630	11,683	16,630	14,936
98,100	98,150	16,641	11,694	16,641	14,947
98,150	98,200	16,652	11,705	16,652	14,958
98,200	98,250	16,663	11,716	16,663	14,969
98,250	98,300	16,674	11,727	16,674	14,980
98,300	98,350	16,685	11,738	16,685	14,991
98,350	98,400	16,696	11,749	16,696	15,002
98,400	98,450	16,707	11,760	16,707	15,013
98,450	98,500	16,718	11,771	16,718	15,024
98,500	98,550	16,729	11,782	16,729	15,035
98,550	98,600	16,740	11,793	16,740	15,046
98,600	98,650	16,751	11,804	16,751	15,057
98,650	98,700	16,762	11,815	16,762	15,068
98,700	98,750	16,773	11,826	16,773	15,079
98,750	98,800	16,784	11,837	16,784	15,090
98,800	98,850	16,795	11,848	16,795	15,101
98,850	98,900	16,806	11,859	16,806	15,112
98,900	98,950	16,817	11,870	16,817	15,123
98,950	99,000	16,828	11,881	16,828	15,134

99,000

At least	But less than	Single	MFJ	MFS	HoH
99,000	99,050	16,839	11,892	16,839	15,145
99,050	99,100	16,850	11,903	16,850	15,156
99,100	99,150	16,861	11,914	16,861	15,167
99,150	99,200	16,872	11,925	16,872	15,178
99,200	99,250	16,883	11,936	16,883	15,189
99,250	99,300	16,894	11,947	16,894	15,200
99,300	99,350	16,905	11,958	16,905	15,211
99,350	99,400	16,916	11,969	16,916	15,222
99,400	99,450	16,927	11,980	16,927	15,233
99,450	99,500	16,938	11,991	16,938	15,244
99,500	99,550	16,949	12,002	16,949	15,255
99,550	99,600	16,960	12,013	16,960	15,266
99,600	99,650	16,971	12,024	16,971	15,277
99,650	99,700	16,982	12,035	16,982	15,288
99,700	99,750	16,993	12,046	16,993	15,299
99,750	99,800	17,004	12,057	17,004	15,310
99,800	99,850	17,015	12,068	17,015	15,321
99,850	99,900	17,026	12,079	17,026	15,332
99,900	99,950	17,037	12,090	17,037	15,343
99,950	100,000	17,048	12,101	17,048	15,354

$100,000 or over use the Tax Computation Worksheet

* This column must also be used by a qualifying surviving spouse.

Appendix B

Earned Income Credit Table

Contents

2024 Earned Income Credit Worksheet — B-2

2024 Earned Income Credit Table — B-3

Worksheet A—2024 EIC—Line 27

Keep for Your Records

Before you begin: ✓ Be sure you are using the correct worksheet. Use this worksheet only if you answered "No" to Step 5, question 2. Otherwise, use Worksheet B.

Part 1 — All Filers Using Worksheet A

1. Enter your earned income from Step 5. **1** ☐

2. Look up the amount on line 1 above in the EIC Table (right after Worksheet B) to find the credit. Be sure you use the correct column for your filing status and the number of qualifying children you have who have a valid SSN as defined earlier. Enter the credit here. **2** ☐

   If line 2 is zero, (STOP) You can't take the credit.
   Enter "No" on the dotted line next to Form 1040 or 1040-SR, line 27.

3. Enter the amount from Form 1040 or 1040-SR, line 11. **3** ☐

4. Are the amounts on lines 3 and 1 the same?

   ☐ **Yes.** Skip line 5; enter the amount from line 2 on line 6.

   ☐ **No.** Go to line 5.

Part 2 — Filers Who Answered "No" on Line 4

5. If you have:
   - No qualifying children who have a valid SSN, is the amount on line 3 less than $10,350 ($17,250 if married filing jointly)?
   - 1 or more qualifying children who have a valid SSN, is the amount on line 3 less than $22,750 ($29,650 if married filing jointly)?

   ☐ **Yes.** Leave line 5 blank; enter the amount from line 2 on line 6.

   ☐ **No.** Look up the amount on line 3 in the EIC Table to find the credit. Be sure you use the correct column for your filing status and the number of qualifying children you have who have a valid SSN. Enter the credit here. **5** ☐
   Look at the amounts on lines 5 and 2.
   Then, enter the **smaller** amount on line 6.

Part 3 — Your Earned Income Credit

6. This is your earned income credit. **6** ☐

   Enter this amount on Form 1040 or 1040-SR, line 27.

   Reminder—

   ✓ If you have a qualifying child, complete and attach Schedule EIC.

   ⚠ **CAUTION** *If your EIC for a year after 1996 was reduced or disallowed, see Form 8862, who must file, earlier, to find out if you must file Form 8862 to take the credit for 2024.*

---

*Download the latest version of this worksheet from the Form 1040 Instructions available at www.irs.gov. The 2024 worksheet was not available as we went to print. This worksheet is adapted from the 2023 version.

2024 Earned Income Credit (EIC) Table

Caution. This is **not** a tax table.

1. To find your credit, read down the "At least - But less than" columns and find the line that includes the amount you were told to look up from your EIC Worksheet.

2. Then, go to the column that includes your filing status and the number of qualifying children you have who have valid SSNs as defined earlier. Enter the credit from that column on your EIC Worksheet.

Example. If your filing status is single, you have one qualifying child who has a valid SSN, and the amount you are looking up from your EIC Worksheet is $2,455, you would enter $842.

If the amount you are looking up from the worksheet is—		And your filing status is—							
		Single, head of household, or qualifying surviving spouse and the number of children you have is—							
At least	But less than	0	1	2	3				
2,400	2,450	186	825	970	1,091				
2,450	2,500	189	842	990	1,114				

If the amount you are looking up from the worksheet is—		And your filing status is—									If the amount you are looking up from the worksheet is—		And your filing status is—							
		Single, head of household, or qualifying surviving spouse★ and you have—				Married filing jointly and you have—							Single, head of household, or qualifying surviving spouse★ and you have—				Married filing jointly and you have—			
At least	But less than	0	1	2	3	0	1	2	3		At least	But less than	0	1	2	3	0	1	2	3
1	50	2	9	10	11	2	9	10	11		2,800	2,850	216	961	1,130	1,271	216	961	1,130	1,271
50	100	6	26	30	34	6	26	30	34		2,850	2,900	220	978	1,150	1,294	220	978	1,150	1,294
100	150	10	43	50	56	10	43	50	56		2,900	2,950	224	995	1,170	1,316	224	995	1,170	1,316
150	200	13	60	70	79	13	60	70	79		2,950	3,000	228	1,012	1,190	1,339	228	1,012	1,190	1,339
200	250	17	77	90	101	17	77	90	101		3,000	3,050	231	1,029	1,210	1,361	231	1,029	1,210	1,361
250	300	21	94	110	124	21	94	110	124		3,050	3,100	235	1,046	1,230	1,384	235	1,046	1,230	1,384
300	350	25	111	130	146	25	111	130	146		3,100	3,150	239	1,063	1,250	1,406	239	1,063	1,250	1,406
350	400	29	128	150	169	29	128	150	169		3,150	3,200	243	1,080	1,270	1,429	243	1,080	1,270	1,429
400	450	33	145	170	191	33	145	170	191		3,200	3,250	247	1,097	1,290	1,451	247	1,097	1,290	1,451
450	500	36	162	190	214	36	162	190	214		3,250	3,300	251	1,114	1,310	1,474	251	1,114	1,310	1,474
500	550	40	179	210	236	40	179	210	236		3,300	3,350	254	1,131	1,330	1,496	254	1,131	1,330	1,496
550	600	44	196	230	259	44	196	230	259		3,350	3,400	258	1,148	1,350	1,519	258	1,148	1,350	1,519
600	650	48	213	250	281	48	213	250	281		3,400	3,450	262	1,165	1,370	1,541	262	1,165	1,370	1,541
650	700	52	230	270	304	52	230	270	304		3,450	3,500	266	1,182	1,390	1,564	266	1,182	1,390	1,564
700	750	55	247	290	326	55	247	290	326		3,500	3,550	270	1,199	1,410	1,586	270	1,199	1,410	1,586
750	800	59	264	310	349	59	264	310	349		3,550	3,600	273	1,216	1,430	1,609	273	1,216	1,430	1,609
800	850	63	281	330	371	63	281	330	371		3,600	3,650	277	1,233	1,450	1,631	277	1,233	1,450	1,631
850	900	67	298	350	394	67	298	350	394		3,650	3,700	281	1,250	1,470	1,654	281	1,250	1,470	1,654
900	950	71	315	370	416	71	315	370	416		3,700	3,750	285	1,267	1,490	1,676	285	1,267	1,490	1,676
950	1,000	75	332	390	439	75	332	390	439		3,750	3,800	289	1,284	1,510	1,699	289	1,284	1,510	1,699
1,000	1,050	78	349	410	461	78	349	410	461		3,800	3,850	293	1,301	1,530	1,721	293	1,301	1,530	1,721
1,050	1,100	82	366	430	484	82	366	430	484		3,850	3,900	296	1,318	1,550	1,744	296	1,318	1,550	1,744
1,100	1,150	86	383	450	506	86	383	450	506		3,900	3,950	300	1,335	1,570	1,766	300	1,335	1,570	1,766
1,150	1,200	90	400	470	529	90	400	470	529		3,950	4,000	304	1,352	1,590	1,789	304	1,352	1,590	1,789
1,200	1,250	94	417	490	551	94	417	490	551		4,000	4,050	308	1,369	1,610	1,811	308	1,369	1,610	1,811
1,250	1,300	98	434	510	574	98	434	510	574		4,050	4,100	312	1,386	1,630	1,834	312	1,386	1,630	1,834
1,300	1,350	101	451	530	596	101	451	530	596		4,100	4,150	316	1,403	1,650	1,856	316	1,403	1,650	1,856
1,350	1,400	105	468	550	619	105	468	550	619		4,150	4,200	319	1,420	1,670	1,879	319	1,420	1,670	1,879
1,400	1,450	109	485	570	641	109	485	570	641		4,200	4,250	323	1,437	1,690	1,901	323	1,437	1,690	1,901
1,450	1,500	113	502	590	664	113	502	590	664		4,250	4,300	327	1,454	1,710	1,924	327	1,454	1,710	1,924
1,500	1,550	117	519	610	686	117	519	610	686		4,300	4,350	331	1,471	1,730	1,946	331	1,471	1,730	1,946
1,550	1,600	120	536	630	709	120	536	630	709		4,350	4,400	335	1,488	1,750	1,969	335	1,488	1,750	1,969
1,600	1,650	124	553	650	731	124	553	650	731		4,400	4,450	339	1,505	1,770	1,991	339	1,505	1,770	1,991
1,650	1,700	128	570	670	754	128	570	670	754		4,450	4,500	342	1,522	1,790	2,014	342	1,522	1,790	2,014
1,700	1,750	132	587	690	776	132	587	690	776		4,500	4,550	346	1,539	1,810	2,036	346	1,539	1,810	2,036
1,750	1,800	136	604	710	799	136	604	710	799		4,550	4,600	350	1,556	1,830	2,059	350	1,556	1,830	2,059
1,800	1,850	140	621	730	821	140	621	730	821		4,600	4,650	354	1,573	1,850	2,081	354	1,573	1,850	2,081
1,850	1,900	143	638	750	844	143	638	750	844		4,650	4,700	358	1,590	1,870	2,104	358	1,590	1,870	2,104
1,900	1,950	147	655	770	866	147	655	770	866		4,700	4,750	361	1,607	1,890	2,126	361	1,607	1,890	2,126
1,950	2,000	151	672	790	889	151	672	790	889		4,750	4,800	365	1,624	1,910	2,149	365	1,624	1,910	2,149
2,000	2,050	155	689	810	911	155	689	810	911		4,800	4,850	369	1,641	1,930	2,171	369	1,641	1,930	2,171
2,050	2,100	159	706	830	934	159	706	830	934		4,850	4,900	373	1,658	1,950	2,194	373	1,658	1,950	2,194
2,100	2,150	163	723	850	956	163	723	850	956		4,900	4,950	377	1,675	1,970	2,216	377	1,675	1,970	2,216
2,150	2,200	166	740	870	979	166	740	870	979		4,950	5,000	381	1,692	1,990	2,239	381	1,692	1,990	2,239
2,200	2,250	170	757	890	1,001	170	757	890	1,001		5,000	5,050	384	1,709	2,010	2,261	384	1,709	2,010	2,261
2,250	2,300	174	774	910	1,024	174	774	910	1,024		5,050	5,100	388	1,726	2,030	2,284	388	1,726	2,030	2,284
2,300	2,350	178	791	930	1,046	178	791	930	1,046		5,100	5,150	392	1,743	2,050	2,306	392	1,743	2,050	2,306
2,350	2,400	182	808	950	1,069	182	808	950	1,069		5,150	5,200	396	1,760	2,070	2,329	396	1,760	2,070	2,329
2,400	2,450	186	825	970	1,091	186	825	970	1,091		5,200	5,250	400	1,777	2,090	2,351	400	1,777	2,090	2,351
2,450	2,500	189	842	990	1,114	189	842	990	1,114		5,250	5,300	404	1,794	2,110	2,374	404	1,794	2,110	2,374
2,500	2,550	193	859	1,010	1,136	193	859	1,010	1,136		5,300	5,350	407	1,811	2,130	2,396	407	1,811	2,130	2,396
2,550	2,600	197	876	1,030	1,159	197	876	1,030	1,159		5,350	5,400	411	1,828	2,150	2,419	411	1,828	2,150	2,419
2,600	2,650	201	893	1,050	1,181	201	893	1,050	1,181		5,400	5,450	415	1,845	2,170	2,441	415	1,845	2,170	2,441
2,650	2,700	205	910	1,070	1,204	205	910	1,070	1,204		5,450	5,500	419	1,862	2,190	2,464	419	1,862	2,190	2,464
2,700	2,750	208	927	1,090	1,226	208	927	1,090	1,226		5,500	5,550	423	1,879	2,210	2,486	423	1,879	2,210	2,486
2,750	2,800	212	944	1,110	1,249	212	944	1,110	1,249		5,550	5,600	426	1,896	2,230	2,509	426	1,896	2,230	2,509

★ Use this column if your filing status is married filing separately and you qualify to claim the EIC. See the instructions for line 27.

(Continued)

Earned Income Credit (EIC) Table - Continued

(Caution. This is not a tax table.)

If the amount you are looking up from the worksheet is—		Single, head of household, or qualifying surviving spouse★ and you have—				Married filing jointly and you have—				If the amount you are looking up from the worksheet is—		Single, head of household, or qualifying surviving spouse★ and you have—				Married filing jointly and you have—			
At least	But less than	0	1	2	3	0	1	2	3	At least	But less than	0	1	2	3	0	1	2	3
		Your credit is—				Your credit is—						Your credit is—				Your credit is—			
5,600	5,650	430	1,913	2,250	2,531	430	1,913	2,250	2,531	8,800	8,850	632	3,001	3,530	3,971	632	3,001	3,530	3,971
5,650	5,700	434	1,930	2,270	2,554	434	1,930	2,270	2,554	8,850	8,900	632	3,018	3,550	3,994	632	3,018	3,550	3,994
5,700	5,750	438	1,947	2,290	2,576	438	1,947	2,290	2,576	8,900	8,950	632	3,035	3,570	4,016	632	3,035	3,570	4,016
5,750	5,800	442	1,964	2,310	2,599	442	1,964	2,310	2,599	8,950	9,000	632	3,052	3,590	4,039	632	3,052	3,590	4,039
5,800	5,850	446	1,981	2,330	2,621	446	1,981	2,330	2,621	9,000	9,050	632	3,069	3,610	4,061	632	3,069	3,610	4,061
5,850	5,900	449	1,998	2,350	2,644	449	1,998	2,350	2,644	9,050	9,100	632	3,086	3,630	4,084	632	3,086	3,630	4,084
5,900	5,950	453	2,015	2,370	2,666	453	2,015	2,370	2,666	9,100	9,150	632	3,103	3,650	4,106	632	3,103	3,650	4,106
5,950	6,000	457	2,032	2,390	2,689	457	2,032	2,390	2,689	9,150	9,200	632	3,120	3,670	4,129	632	3,120	3,670	4,129
6,000	6,050	461	2,049	2,410	2,711	461	2,049	2,410	2,711	9,200	9,250	632	3,137	3,690	4,151	632	3,137	3,690	4,151
6,050	6,100	465	2,066	2,430	2,734	465	2,066	2,430	2,734	9,250	9,300	632	3,154	3,710	4,174	632	3,154	3,710	4,174
6,100	6,150	469	2,083	2,450	2,756	469	2,083	2,450	2,756	9,300	9,350	632	3,171	3,730	4,196	632	3,171	3,730	4,196
6,150	6,200	472	2,100	2,470	2,779	472	2,100	2,470	2,779	9,350	9,400	632	3,188	3,750	4,219	632	3,188	3,750	4,219
6,200	6,250	476	2,117	2,490	2,801	476	2,117	2,490	2,801	9,400	9,450	632	3,205	3,770	4,241	632	3,205	3,770	4,241
6,250	6,300	480	2,134	2,510	2,824	480	2,134	2,510	2,824	9,450	9,500	632	3,222	3,790	4,264	632	3,222	3,790	4,264
6,300	6,350	484	2,151	2,530	2,846	484	2,151	2,530	2,846	9,500	9,550	632	3,239	3,810	4,286	632	3,239	3,810	4,286
6,350	6,400	488	2,168	2,550	2,869	488	2,168	2,550	2,869	9,550	9,600	632	3,256	3,830	4,309	632	3,256	3,830	4,309
6,400	6,450	492	2,185	2,570	2,891	492	2,185	2,570	2,891	9,600	9,650	632	3,273	3,850	4,331	632	3,273	3,850	4,331
6,450	6,500	495	2,202	2,590	2,914	495	2,202	2,590	2,914	9,650	9,700	632	3,290	3,870	4,354	632	3,290	3,870	4,354
6,500	6,550	499	2,219	2,610	2,936	499	2,219	2,610	2,936	9,700	9,750	632	3,307	3,890	4,376	632	3,307	3,890	4,376
6,550	6,600	503	2,236	2,630	2,959	503	2,236	2,630	2,959	9,750	9,800	632	3,324	3,910	4,399	632	3,324	3,910	4,399
6,600	6,650	507	2,253	2,650	2,981	507	2,253	2,650	2,981	9,800	9,850	632	3,341	3,930	4,421	632	3,341	3,930	4,421
6,650	6,700	511	2,270	2,670	3,004	511	2,270	2,670	3,004	9,850	9,900	632	3,358	3,950	4,444	632	3,358	3,950	4,444
6,700	6,750	514	2,287	2,690	3,026	514	2,287	2,690	3,026	9,900	9,950	632	3,375	3,970	4,466	632	3,375	3,970	4,466
6,750	6,800	518	2,304	2,710	3,049	518	2,304	2,710	3,049	9,950	10,000	632	3,392	3,990	4,489	632	3,392	3,990	4,489
6,800	6,850	522	2,321	2,730	3,071	522	2,321	2,730	3,071	10,000	10,050	632	3,409	4,010	4,511	632	3,409	4,010	4,511
6,850	6,900	526	2,338	2,750	3,094	526	2,338	2,750	3,094	10,050	10,100	632	3,426	4,030	4,534	632	3,426	4,030	4,534
6,900	6,950	530	2,355	2,770	3,116	530	2,355	2,770	3,116	10,100	10,150	632	3,443	4,050	4,556	632	3,443	4,050	4,556
6,950	7,000	534	2,372	2,790	3,139	534	2,372	2,790	3,139	10,150	10,200	632	3,460	4,070	4,579	632	3,460	4,070	4,579
7,000	7,050	537	2,389	2,810	3,161	537	2,389	2,810	3,161	10,200	10,250	632	3,477	4,090	4,601	632	3,477	4,090	4,601
7,050	7,100	541	2,406	2,830	3,184	541	2,406	2,830	3,184	10,250	10,300	632	3,494	4,110	4,624	632	3,494	4,110	4,624
7,100	7,150	545	2,423	2,850	3,206	545	2,423	2,850	3,206	10,300	10,350	632	3,511	4,130	4,646	632	3,511	4,130	4,646
7,150	7,200	549	2,440	2,870	3,229	549	2,440	2,870	3,229	10,350	10,400	629	3,528	4,150	4,669	632	3,528	4,150	4,669
7,200	7,250	553	2,457	2,890	3,251	553	2,457	2,890	3,251	10,400	10,450	625	3,545	4,170	4,691	632	3,545	4,170	4,691
7,250	7,300	557	2,474	2,910	3,274	557	2,474	2,910	3,274	10,450	10,500	621	3,562	4,190	4,714	632	3,562	4,190	4,714
7,300	7,350	560	2,491	2,930	3,296	560	2,491	2,930	3,296	10,500	10,550	617	3,579	4,210	4,736	632	3,579	4,210	4,736
7,350	7,400	564	2,508	2,950	3,319	564	2,508	2,950	3,319	10,550	10,600	613	3,596	4,230	4,759	632	3,596	4,230	4,759
7,400	7,450	568	2,525	2,970	3,341	568	2,525	2,970	3,341	10,600	10,650	609	3,613	4,250	4,781	632	3,613	4,250	4,781
7,450	7,500	572	2,542	2,990	3,364	572	2,542	2,990	3,364	10,650	10,700	606	3,630	4,270	4,804	632	3,630	4,270	4,804
7,500	7,550	576	2,559	3,010	3,386	576	2,559	3,010	3,386	10,700	10,750	602	3,647	4,290	4,826	632	3,647	4,290	4,826
7,550	7,600	579	2,576	3,030	3,409	579	2,576	3,030	3,409	10,750	10,800	598	3,664	4,310	4,849	632	3,664	4,310	4,849
7,600	7,650	583	2,593	3,050	3,431	583	2,593	3,050	3,431	10,800	10,850	594	3,681	4,330	4,871	632	3,681	4,330	4,871
7,650	7,700	587	2,610	3,070	3,454	587	2,610	3,070	3,454	10,850	10,900	590	3,698	4,350	4,894	632	3,698	4,350	4,894
7,700	7,750	591	2,627	3,090	3,476	591	2,627	3,090	3,476	10,900	10,950	586	3,715	4,370	4,916	632	3,715	4,370	4,916
7,750	7,800	595	2,644	3,110	3,499	595	2,644	3,110	3,499	10,950	11,000	583	3,732	4,390	4,939	632	3,732	4,390	4,939
7,800	7,850	599	2,661	3,130	3,521	599	2,661	3,130	3,521	11,000	11,050	579	3,749	4,410	4,961	632	3,749	4,410	4,961
7,850	7,900	602	2,678	3,150	3,544	602	2,678	3,150	3,544	11,050	11,100	575	3,766	4,430	4,984	632	3,766	4,430	4,984
7,900	7,950	606	2,695	3,170	3,566	606	2,695	3,170	3,566	11,100	11,150	571	3,783	4,450	5,006	632	3,783	4,450	5,006
7,950	8,000	610	2,712	3,190	3,589	610	2,712	3,190	3,589	11,150	11,200	567	3,800	4,470	5,029	632	3,800	4,470	5,029
8,000	8,050	614	2,729	3,210	3,611	614	2,729	3,210	3,611	11,200	11,250	564	3,817	4,490	5,051	632	3,817	4,490	5,051
8,050	8,100	618	2,746	3,230	3,634	618	2,746	3,230	3,634	11,250	11,300	560	3,834	4,510	5,074	632	3,834	4,510	5,074
8,100	8,150	622	2,763	3,250	3,656	622	2,763	3,250	3,656	11,300	11,350	556	3,851	4,530	5,096	632	3,851	4,530	5,096
8,150	8,200	625	2,780	3,270	3,679	625	2,780	3,270	3,679	11,350	11,400	552	3,868	4,550	5,119	632	3,868	4,550	5,119
8,200	8,250	629	2,797	3,290	3,701	629	2,797	3,290	3,701	11,400	11,450	548	3,885	4,570	5,141	632	3,885	4,570	5,141
8,250	8,300	632	2,814	3,310	3,724	632	2,814	3,310	3,724	11,450	11,500	544	3,902	4,590	5,164	632	3,902	4,590	5,164
8,300	8,350	632	2,831	3,330	3,746	632	2,831	3,330	3,746	11,500	11,550	541	3,919	4,610	5,186	632	3,919	4,610	5,186
8,350	8,400	632	2,848	3,350	3,769	632	2,848	3,350	3,769	11,550	11,600	537	3,936	4,630	5,209	632	3,936	4,630	5,209
8,400	8,450	632	2,865	3,370	3,791	632	2,865	3,370	3,791	11,600	11,650	533	3,953	4,650	5,231	632	3,953	4,650	5,231
8,450	8,500	632	2,882	3,390	3,814	632	2,882	3,390	3,814	11,650	11,700	529	3,970	4,670	5,254	632	3,970	4,670	5,254
8,500	8,550	632	2,899	3,410	3,836	632	2,899	3,410	3,836	11,700	11,750	525	3,987	4,690	5,276	632	3,987	4,690	5,276
8,550	8,600	632	2,916	3,430	3,859	632	2,916	3,430	3,859	11,750	11,800	521	4,004	4,710	5,299	632	4,004	4,710	5,299
8,600	8,650	632	2,933	3,450	3,881	632	2,933	3,450	3,881	11,800	11,850	518	4,021	4,730	5,321	632	4,021	4,730	5,321
8,650	8,700	632	2,950	3,470	3,904	632	2,950	3,470	3,904	11,850	11,900	514	4,038	4,750	5,344	632	4,038	4,750	5,344
8,700	8,750	632	2,967	3,490	3,926	632	2,967	3,490	3,926	11,900	11,950	510	4,055	4,770	5,366	632	4,055	4,770	5,366
8,750	8,800	632	2,984	3,510	3,949	632	2,984	3,510	3,949	11,950	12,000	506	4,072	4,790	5,389	632	4,072	4,790	5,389

★ Use this column if your filing status is married filing separately and you qualify to claim the EIC. See the instructions for line 27.

(Continued)

Earned Income Credit Table

Earned Income Credit (EIC) Table - *Continued*

(**Caution.** This is **not** a tax table.)

If the amount you are looking up from the worksheet is–		And your filing status is–								If the amount you are looking up from the worksheet is–		And your filing status is–							
		Single, head of household, or qualifying surviving spouse★ and you have–				Married filing jointly and you have–						Single, head of household, or qualifying surviving spouse★ and you have–				Married filing jointly and you have–			
		0	1	2	3	0	1	2	3			0	1	2	3	0	1	2	3
At least	But less than	Your credit is–				Your credit is–				At least	But less than	Your credit is–				Your credit is–			
12,000	12,050	502	4,089	4,810	5,411	632	4,089	4,810	5,411	15,200	15,250	258	4,213	6,090	6,851	632	4,213	6,090	6,851
12,050	12,100	499	4,106	4,830	5,434	632	4,106	4,830	5,434	15,250	15,300	254	4,213	6,110	6,874	632	4,213	6,110	6,874
12,100	12,150	495	4,123	4,850	5,456	632	4,123	4,850	5,456	15,300	15,350	250	4,213	6,130	6,896	632	4,213	6,130	6,896
12,150	12,200	491	4,140	4,870	5,479	632	4,140	4,870	5,479	15,350	15,400	246	4,213	6,150	6,919	632	4,213	6,150	6,919
12,200	12,250	487	4,157	4,890	5,501	632	4,157	4,890	5,501	15,400	15,450	242	4,213	6,170	6,941	632	4,213	6,170	6,941
12,250	12,300	483	4,174	4,910	5,524	632	4,174	4,910	5,524	15,450	15,500	238	4,213	6,190	6,964	632	4,213	6,190	6,964
12,300	12,350	479	4,191	4,930	5,546	632	4,191	4,930	5,546	15,500	15,550	235	4,213	6,210	6,986	632	4,213	6,210	6,986
12,350	12,400	476	4,213	4,950	5,569	632	4,213	4,950	5,569	15,550	15,600	231	4,213	6,230	7,009	632	4,213	6,230	7,009
12,400	12,450	472	4,213	4,970	5,591	632	4,213	4,970	5,591	15,600	15,650	227	4,213	6,250	7,031	632	4,213	6,250	7,031
12,450	12,500	468	4,213	4,990	5,614	632	4,213	4,990	5,614	15,650	15,700	223	4,213	6,270	7,054	632	4,213	6,270	7,054
12,500	12,550	464	4,213	5,010	5,636	632	4,213	5,010	5,636	15,700	15,750	219	4,213	6,290	7,076	632	4,213	6,290	7,076
12,550	12,600	460	4,213	5,030	5,659	632	4,213	5,030	5,659	15,750	15,800	215	4,213	6,310	7,099	632	4,213	6,310	7,099
12,600	12,650	456	4,213	5,050	5,681	632	4,213	5,050	5,681	15,800	15,850	212	4,213	6,330	7,121	632	4,213	6,330	7,121
12,650	12,700	453	4,213	5,070	5,704	632	4,213	5,070	5,704	15,850	15,900	208	4,213	6,350	7,144	632	4,213	6,350	7,144
12,700	12,750	449	4,213	5,090	5,726	632	4,213	5,090	5,726	15,900	15,950	204	4,213	6,370	7,166	632	4,213	6,370	7,166
12,750	12,800	445	4,213	5,110	5,749	632	4,213	5,110	5,749	15,950	16,000	200	4,213	6,390	7,189	632	4,213	6,390	7,189
12,800	12,850	441	4,213	5,130	5,771	632	4,213	5,130	5,771	16,000	16,050	196	4,213	6,410	7,211	632	4,213	6,410	7,211
12,850	12,900	437	4,213	5,150	5,794	632	4,213	5,150	5,794	16,050	16,100	193	4,213	6,430	7,234	632	4,213	6,430	7,234
12,900	12,950	433	4,213	5,170	5,816	632	4,213	5,170	5,816	16,100	16,150	189	4,213	6,450	7,256	632	4,213	6,450	7,256
12,950	13,000	430	4,213	5,190	5,839	632	4,213	5,190	5,839	16,150	16,200	185	4,213	6,470	7,279	632	4,213	6,470	7,279
13,000	13,050	426	4,213	5,210	5,861	632	4,213	5,210	5,861	16,200	16,250	181	4,213	6,490	7,301	632	4,213	6,490	7,301
13,050	13,100	422	4,213	5,230	5,884	632	4,213	5,230	5,884	16,250	16,300	177	4,213	6,510	7,324	632	4,213	6,510	7,324
13,100	13,150	418	4,213	5,250	5,906	632	4,213	5,250	5,906	16,300	16,350	173	4,213	6,530	7,346	632	4,213	6,530	7,346
13,150	13,200	414	4,213	5,270	5,929	632	4,213	5,270	5,929	16,350	16,400	170	4,213	6,550	7,369	632	4,213	6,550	7,369
13,200	13,250	411	4,213	5,290	5,951	632	4,213	5,290	5,951	16,400	16,450	166	4,213	6,570	7,391	632	4,213	6,570	7,391
13,250	13,300	407	4,213	5,310	5,974	632	4,213	5,310	5,974	16,450	16,500	162	4,213	6,590	7,414	632	4,213	6,590	7,414
13,300	13,350	403	4,213	5,330	5,996	632	4,213	5,330	5,996	16,500	16,550	158	4,213	6,610	7,436	632	4,213	6,610	7,436
13,350	13,400	399	4,213	5,350	6,019	632	4,213	5,350	6,019	16,550	16,600	154	4,213	6,630	7,459	632	4,213	6,630	7,459
13,400	13,450	395	4,213	5,370	6,041	632	4,213	5,370	6,041	16,600	16,650	150	4,213	6,650	7,481	632	4,213	6,650	7,481
13,450	13,500	391	4,213	5,390	6,064	632	4,213	5,390	6,064	16,650	16,700	147	4,213	6,670	7,504	632	4,213	6,670	7,504
13,500	13,550	388	4,213	5,410	6,086	632	4,213	5,410	6,086	16,700	16,750	143	4,213	6,690	7,526	632	4,213	6,690	7,526
13,550	13,600	384	4,213	5,430	6,109	632	4,213	5,430	6,109	16,750	16,800	139	4,213	6,710	7,549	632	4,213	6,710	7,549
13,600	13,650	380	4,213	5,450	6,131	632	4,213	5,450	6,131	16,800	16,850	135	4,213	6,730	7,571	632	4,213	6,730	7,571
13,650	13,700	376	4,213	5,470	6,154	632	4,213	5,470	6,154	16,850	16,900	131	4,213	6,750	7,594	632	4,213	6,750	7,594
13,700	13,750	372	4,213	5,490	6,176	632	4,213	5,490	6,176	16,900	16,950	127	4,213	6,770	7,616	632	4,213	6,770	7,616
13,750	13,800	368	4,213	5,510	6,199	632	4,213	5,510	6,199	16,950	17,000	124	4,213	6,790	7,639	632	4,213	6,790	7,639
13,800	13,850	365	4,213	5,530	6,221	632	4,213	5,530	6,221	17,000	17,050	120	4,213	6,810	7,661	632	4,213	6,810	7,661
13,850	13,900	361	4,213	5,550	6,244	632	4,213	5,550	6,244	17,050	17,100	116	4,213	6,830	7,684	632	4,213	6,830	7,684
13,900	13,950	357	4,213	5,570	6,266	632	4,213	5,570	6,266	17,100	17,150	112	4,213	6,850	7,706	632	4,213	6,850	7,706
13,950	14,000	353	4,213	5,590	6,289	632	4,213	5,590	6,289	17,150	17,200	108	4,213	6,870	7,729	632	4,213	6,870	7,729
14,000	14,050	349	4,213	5,610	6,311	632	4,213	5,610	6,311	17,200	17,250	105	4,213	6,890	7,751	632	4,213	6,890	7,751
14,050	14,100	346	4,213	5,630	6,334	632	4,213	5,630	6,334	17,250	17,300	101	4,213	6,910	7,774	630	4,213	6,910	7,774
14,100	14,150	342	4,213	5,650	6,356	632	4,213	5,650	6,356	17,300	17,350	97	4,213	6,930	7,796	626	4,213	6,930	7,796
14,150	14,200	338	4,213	5,670	6,379	632	4,213	5,670	6,379	17,350	17,400	93	4,213	6,950	7,819	622	4,213	6,950	7,819
14,200	14,250	334	4,213	5,690	6,401	632	4,213	5,690	6,401	17,400	17,450	89	4,213	6,960	7,830	619	4,213	6,960	7,830
14,250	14,300	330	4,213	5,710	6,424	632	4,213	5,710	6,424	17,450	17,500	85	4,213	6,960	7,830	615	4,213	6,960	7,830
14,300	14,350	326	4,213	5,730	6,446	632	4,213	5,730	6,446	17,500	17,550	82	4,213	6,960	7,830	611	4,213	6,960	7,830
14,350	14,400	323	4,213	5,750	6,469	632	4,213	5,750	6,469	17,550	17,600	78	4,213	6,960	7,830	607	4,213	6,960	7,830
14,400	14,450	319	4,213	5,770	6,491	632	4,213	5,770	6,491	17,600	17,650	74	4,213	6,960	7,830	603	4,213	6,960	7,830
14,450	14,500	315	4,213	5,790	6,514	632	4,213	5,790	6,514	17,650	17,700	70	4,213	6,960	7,830	599	4,213	6,960	7,830
14,500	14,550	311	4,213	5,810	6,536	632	4,213	5,810	6,536	17,700	17,750	66	4,213	6,960	7,830	596	4,213	6,960	7,830
14,550	14,600	307	4,213	5,830	6,559	632	4,213	5,830	6,559	17,750	17,800	62	4,213	6,960	7,830	592	4,213	6,960	7,830
14,600	14,650	303	4,213	5,850	6,581	632	4,213	5,850	6,581	17,800	17,850	59	4,213	6,960	7,830	588	4,213	6,960	7,830
14,650	14,700	300	4,213	5,870	6,604	632	4,213	5,870	6,604	17,850	17,900	55	4,213	6,960	7,830	584	4,213	6,960	7,830
14,700	14,750	296	4,213	5,890	6,626	632	4,213	5,890	6,626	17,900	17,950	51	4,213	6,960	7,830	580	4,213	6,960	7,830
14,750	14,800	292	4,213	5,910	6,649	632	4,213	5,910	6,649	17,950	18,000	47	4,213	6,960	7,830	577	4,213	6,960	7,830
14,800	14,850	288	4,213	5,930	6,671	632	4,213	5,930	6,671	18,000	18,050	43	4,213	6,960	7,830	573	4,213	6,960	7,830
14,850	14,900	284	4,213	5,950	6,694	632	4,213	5,950	6,694	18,050	18,100	40	4,213	6,960	7,830	569	4,213	6,960	7,830
14,900	14,950	280	4,213	5,970	6,716	632	4,213	5,970	6,716	18,100	18,150	36	4,213	6,960	7,830	565	4,213	6,960	7,830
14,950	15,000	277	4,213	5,990	6,739	632	4,213	5,990	6,739	18,150	18,200	32	4,213	6,960	7,830	561	4,213	6,960	7,830
15,000	15,050	273	4,213	6,010	6,761	632	4,213	6,010	6,761	18,200	18,250	28	4,213	6,960	7,830	557	4,213	6,960	7,830
15,050	15,100	269	4,213	6,030	6,784	632	4,213	6,030	6,784	18,250	18,300	24	4,213	6,960	7,830	554	4,213	6,960	7,830
15,100	15,150	265	4,213	6,050	6,806	632	4,213	6,050	6,806	18,300	18,350	20	4,213	6,960	7,830	550	4,213	6,960	7,830
15,150	15,200	261	4,213	6,070	6,829	632	4,213	6,070	6,829	18,350	18,400	17	4,213	6,960	7,830	546	4,213	6,960	7,830

★ Use this column if your filing status is married filing separately and you qualify to claim the EIC. See the instructions for line 27.

(Continued)

Earned Income Credit (EIC) Table - Continued

(**Caution.** This is **not** a tax table.)

If the amount you are looking up from the worksheet is—		And your filing status is—								If the amount you are looking up from the worksheet is—		And your filing status is—							
		Single, head of household, or qualifying surviving spouse★ and you have—				Married filing jointly and you have—						Single, head of household, or qualifying surviving spouse★ and you have—				Married filing jointly and you have—			
		0	1	2	3	0	1	2	3			0	1	2	3	0	1	2	3
At least	But less than	Your credit is—				Your credit is—				At least	But less than	Your credit is—				Your credit is—			
18,400	18,450	13	4,213	6,960	7,830	542	4,213	6,960	7,830	21,600	21,650	0	4,213	6,960	7,830	297	4,213	6,960	7,830
18,450	18,500	9	4,213	6,960	7,830	538	4,213	6,960	7,830	21,650	21,700	0	4,213	6,960	7,830	293	4,213	6,960	7,830
18,500	18,550	5	4,213	6,960	7,830	534	4,213	6,960	7,830	21,700	21,750	0	4,213	6,960	7,830	290	4,213	6,960	7,830
18,550	18,600	*	4,213	6,960	7,830	531	4,213	6,960	7,830	21,750	21,800	0	4,213	6,960	7,830	286	4,213	6,960	7,830
18,600	18,650	0	4,213	6,960	7,830	527	4,213	6,960	7,830	21,800	21,850	0	4,213	6,960	7,830	282	4,213	6,960	7,830
18,650	18,700	0	4,213	6,960	7,830	523	4,213	6,960	7,830	21,850	21,900	0	4,213	6,960	7,830	278	4,213	6,960	7,830
18,700	18,750	0	4,213	6,960	7,830	519	4,213	6,960	7,830	21,900	21,950	0	4,213	6,960	7,830	274	4,213	6,960	7,830
18,750	18,800	0	4,213	6,960	7,830	515	4,213	6,960	7,830	21,950	22,000	0	4,213	6,960	7,830	271	4,213	6,960	7,830
18,800	18,850	0	4,213	6,960	7,830	512	4,213	6,960	7,830	22,000	22,050	0	4,213	6,960	7,830	267	4,213	6,960	7,830
18,850	18,900	0	4,213	6,960	7,830	508	4,213	6,960	7,830	22,050	22,100	0	4,213	6,960	7,830	263	4,213	6,960	7,830
18,900	18,950	0	4,213	6,960	7,830	504	4,213	6,960	7,830	22,100	22,150	0	4,213	6,960	7,830	259	4,213	6,960	7,830
18,950	19,000	0	4,213	6,960	7,830	500	4,213	6,960	7,830	22,150	22,200	0	4,213	6,960	7,830	255	4,213	6,960	7,830
19,000	19,050	0	4,213	6,960	7,830	496	4,213	6,960	7,830	22,200	22,250	0	4,213	6,960	7,830	251	4,213	6,960	7,830
19,050	19,100	0	4,213	6,960	7,830	492	4,213	6,960	7,830	22,250	22,300	0	4,213	6,960	7,830	248	4,213	6,960	7,830
19,100	19,150	0	4,213	6,960	7,830	489	4,213	6,960	7,830	22,300	22,350	0	4,213	6,960	7,830	244	4,213	6,960	7,830
19,150	19,200	0	4,213	6,960	7,830	485	4,213	6,960	7,830	22,350	22,400	0	4,213	6,960	7,830	240	4,213	6,960	7,830
19,200	19,250	0	4,213	6,960	7,830	481	4,213	6,960	7,830	22,400	22,450	0	4,213	6,960	7,830	236	4,213	6,960	7,830
19,250	19,300	0	4,213	6,960	7,830	477	4,213	6,960	7,830	22,450	22,500	0	4,213	6,960	7,830	232	4,213	6,960	7,830
19,300	19,350	0	4,213	6,960	7,830	473	4,213	6,960	7,830	22,500	22,550	0	4,213	6,960	7,830	228	4,213	6,960	7,830
19,350	19,400	0	4,213	6,960	7,830	469	4,213	6,960	7,830	22,550	22,600	0	4,213	6,960	7,830	225	4,213	6,960	7,830
19,400	19,450	0	4,213	6,960	7,830	466	4,213	6,960	7,830	22,600	22,650	0	4,213	6,960	7,830	221	4,213	6,960	7,830
19,450	19,500	0	4,213	6,960	7,830	462	4,213	6,960	7,830	22,650	22,700	0	4,213	6,960	7,830	217	4,213	6,960	7,830
19,500	19,550	0	4,213	6,960	7,830	458	4,213	6,960	7,830	22,700	22,750	0	4,213	6,960	7,830	213	4,213	6,960	7,830
19,550	19,600	0	4,213	6,960	7,830	454	4,213	6,960	7,830	22,750	22,800	0	4,204	6,948	7,818	209	4,213	6,960	7,830
19,600	19,650	0	4,213	6,960	7,830	450	4,213	6,960	7,830	22,800	22,850	0	4,196	6,938	7,808	206	4,213	6,960	7,830
19,650	19,700	0	4,213	6,960	7,830	446	4,213	6,960	7,830	22,850	22,900	0	4,188	6,927	7,797	202	4,213	6,960	7,830
19,700	19,750	0	4,213	6,960	7,830	443	4,213	6,960	7,830	22,900	22,950	0	4,180	6,917	7,787	198	4,213	6,960	7,830
19,750	19,800	0	4,213	6,960	7,830	439	4,213	6,960	7,830	22,950	23,000	0	4,172	6,906	7,776	194	4,213	6,960	7,830
19,800	19,850	0	4,213	6,960	7,830	435	4,213	6,960	7,830	23,000	23,050	0	4,164	6,896	7,766	190	4,213	6,960	7,830
19,850	19,900	0	4,213	6,960	7,830	431	4,213	6,960	7,830	23,050	23,100	0	4,156	6,885	7,755	186	4,213	6,960	7,830
19,900	19,950	0	4,213	6,960	7,830	427	4,213	6,960	7,830	23,100	23,150	0	4,148	6,875	7,745	183	4,213	6,960	7,830
19,950	20,000	0	4,213	6,960	7,830	424	4,213	6,960	7,830	23,150	23,200	0	4,140	6,864	7,734	179	4,213	6,960	7,830
20,000	20,050	0	4,213	6,960	7,830	420	4,213	6,960	7,830	23,200	23,250	0	4,132	6,854	7,724	175	4,213	6,960	7,830
20,050	20,100	0	4,213	6,960	7,830	416	4,213	6,960	7,830	23,250	23,300	0	4,124	6,843	7,713	171	4,213	6,960	7,830
20,100	20,150	0	4,213	6,960	7,830	412	4,213	6,960	7,830	23,300	23,350	0	4,116	6,833	7,703	167	4,213	6,960	7,830
20,150	20,200	0	4,213	6,960	7,830	408	4,213	6,960	7,830	23,350	23,400	0	4,108	6,822	7,692	163	4,213	6,960	7,830
20,200	20,250	0	4,213	6,960	7,830	404	4,213	6,960	7,830	23,400	23,450	0	4,100	6,812	7,682	160	4,213	6,960	7,830
20,250	20,300	0	4,213	6,960	7,830	401	4,213	6,960	7,830	23,450	23,500	0	4,092	6,801	7,671	156	4,213	6,960	7,830
20,300	20,350	0	4,213	6,960	7,830	397	4,213	6,960	7,830	23,500	23,550	0	4,084	6,790	7,660	152	4,213	6,960	7,830
20,350	20,400	0	4,213	6,960	7,830	393	4,213	6,960	7,830	23,550	23,600	0	4,076	6,780	7,650	148	4,213	6,960	7,830
20,400	20,450	0	4,213	6,960	7,830	389	4,213	6,960	7,830	23,600	23,650	0	4,068	6,769	7,639	144	4,213	6,960	7,830
20,450	20,500	0	4,213	6,960	7,830	385	4,213	6,960	7,830	23,650	23,700	0	4,060	6,759	7,629	140	4,213	6,960	7,830
20,500	20,550	0	4,213	6,960	7,830	381	4,213	6,960	7,830	23,700	23,750	0	4,052	6,748	7,618	137	4,213	6,960	7,830
20,550	20,600	0	4,213	6,960	7,830	378	4,213	6,960	7,830	23,750	23,800	0	4,044	6,738	7,608	133	4,213	6,960	7,830
20,600	20,650	0	4,213	6,960	7,830	374	4,213	6,960	7,830	23,800	23,850	0	4,036	6,727	7,597	129	4,213	6,960	7,830
20,650	20,700	0	4,213	6,960	7,830	370	4,213	6,960	7,830	23,850	23,900	0	4,028	6,717	7,587	125	4,213	6,960	7,830
20,700	20,750	0	4,213	6,960	7,830	366	4,213	6,960	7,830	23,900	23,950	0	4,020	6,706	7,576	121	4,213	6,960	7,830
20,750	20,800	0	4,213	6,960	7,830	362	4,213	6,960	7,830	23,950	24,000	0	4,012	6,696	7,566	118	4,213	6,960	7,830
20,800	20,850	0	4,213	6,960	7,830	359	4,213	6,960	7,830	24,000	24,050	0	4,004	6,685	7,555	114	4,213	6,960	7,830
20,850	20,900	0	4,213	6,960	7,830	355	4,213	6,960	7,830	24,050	24,100	0	3,996	6,675	7,545	110	4,213	6,960	7,830
20,900	20,950	0	4,213	6,960	7,830	351	4,213	6,960	7,830	24,100	24,150	0	3,988	6,664	7,534	106	4,213	6,960	7,830
20,950	21,000	0	4,213	6,960	7,830	347	4,213	6,960	7,830	24,150	24,200	0	3,980	6,654	7,524	102	4,213	6,960	7,830
21,000	21,050	0	4,213	6,960	7,830	343	4,213	6,960	7,830	24,200	24,250	0	3,973	6,643	7,513	98	4,213	6,960	7,830
21,050	21,100	0	4,213	6,960	7,830	339	4,213	6,960	7,830	24,250	24,300	0	3,965	6,633	7,503	95	4,213	6,960	7,830
21,100	21,150	0	4,213	6,960	7,830	336	4,213	6,960	7,830	24,300	24,350	0	3,957	6,622	7,492	91	4,213	6,960	7,830
21,150	21,200	0	4,213	6,960	7,830	332	4,213	6,960	7,830	24,350	24,400	0	3,949	6,611	7,481	87	4,213	6,960	7,830
21,200	21,250	0	4,213	6,960	7,830	328	4,213	6,960	7,830	24,400	24,450	0	3,941	6,601	7,471	83	4,213	6,960	7,830
21,250	21,300	0	4,213	6,960	7,830	324	4,213	6,960	7,830	24,450	24,500	0	3,933	6,590	7,460	79	4,213	6,960	7,830
21,300	21,350	0	4,213	6,960	7,830	320	4,213	6,960	7,830	24,500	24,550	0	3,925	6,580	7,450	75	4,213	6,960	7,830
21,350	21,400	0	4,213	6,960	7,830	316	4,213	6,960	7,830	24,550	24,600	0	3,917	6,569	7,439	72	4,213	6,960	7,830
21,400	21,450	0	4,213	6,960	7,830	313	4,213	6,960	7,830	24,600	24,650	0	3,909	6,559	7,429	68	4,213	6,960	7,830
21,450	21,500	0	4,213	6,960	7,830	309	4,213	6,960	7,830	24,650	24,700	0	3,901	6,548	7,418	64	4,213	6,960	7,830
21,500	21,550	0	4,213	6,960	7,830	305	4,213	6,960	7,830	24,700	24,750	0	3,893	6,538	7,408	60	4,213	6,960	7,830
21,550	21,600	0	4,213	6,960	7,830	301	4,213	6,960	7,830	24,750	24,800	0	3,885	6,527	7,397	56	4,213	6,960	7,830

★ Use this column if your filing status is married filing separately and you qualify to claim the EIC. See the instructions for line 27.

* If the amount you are looking up from the worksheet is at least $18,550 but less than $18,591, and you have no qualifying children who have valid SSNs, your credit is $2.

If the amount you are looking up from the worksheet is $18,591 or more, and you have no qualifying children who have valid SSNs, you can't take the credit.

(Continued)

Earned Income Credit Table

Earned Income Credit (EIC) Table - Continued

(**Caution.** This is **not** a tax table.)

If the amount you are looking up from the worksheet is-		Single, head of household, or qualifying surviving spouse★ and you have-				Married filing jointly and you have-				If the amount you are looking up from the worksheet is-		Single, head of household, or qualifying surviving spouse★ and you have-				Married filing jointly and you have-			
At least	But less than	0	1	2	3	0	1	2	3	At least	But less than	0	1	2	3	0	1	2	3
		Your credit is-				Your credit is-						Your credit is-				Your credit is-			
24,800	24,850	0	3,877	6,517	7,387	53	4,213	6,960	7,830	28,000	28,050	0	3,365	5,843	6,713	0	4,213	6,960	7,830
24,850	24,900	0	3,869	6,506	7,376	49	4,213	6,960	7,830	28,050	28,100	0	3,357	5,832	6,702	0	4,213	6,960	7,830
24,900	24,950	0	3,861	6,496	7,366	45	4,213	6,960	7,830	28,100	28,150	0	3,349	5,822	6,692	0	4,213	6,960	7,830
24,950	25,000	0	3,853	6,485	7,355	41	4,213	6,960	7,830	28,150	28,200	0	3,341	5,811	6,681	0	4,213	6,960	7,830
25,000	25,050	0	3,845	6,475	7,345	37	4,213	6,960	7,830	28,200	28,250	0	3,333	5,801	6,671	0	4,213	6,960	7,830
25,050	25,100	0	3,837	6,464	7,334	33	4,213	6,960	7,830	28,250	28,300	0	3,325	5,790	6,660	0	4,213	6,960	7,830
25,100	25,150	0	3,829	6,454	7,324	30	4,213	6,960	7,830	28,300	28,350	0	3,317	5,780	6,650	0	4,213	6,960	7,830
25,150	25,200	0	3,821	6,443	7,313	26	4,213	6,960	7,830	28,350	28,400	0	3,309	5,769	6,639	0	4,213	6,960	7,830
25,200	25,250	0	3,813	6,432	7,302	22	4,213	6,960	7,830	28,400	28,450	0	3,301	5,759	6,629	0	4,213	6,960	7,830
25,250	25,300	0	3,805	6,422	7,292	18	4,213	6,960	7,830	28,450	28,500	0	3,293	5,748	6,618	0	4,213	6,960	7,830
25,300	25,350	0	3,797	6,411	7,281	14	4,213	6,960	7,830	28,500	28,550	0	3,285	5,737	6,607	0	4,213	6,960	7,830
25,350	25,400	0	3,789	6,401	7,271	10	4,213	6,960	7,830	28,550	28,600	0	3,277	5,727	6,597	0	4,213	6,960	7,830
25,400	25,450	0	3,781	6,390	7,260	7	4,213	6,960	7,830	28,600	28,650	0	3,269	5,716	6,586	0	4,213	6,960	7,830
25,450	25,500	0	3,773	6,380	7,250	3	4,213	6,960	7,830	28,650	28,700	0	3,261	5,706	6,576	0	4,213	6,960	7,830
25,500	25,550	0	3,765	6,369	7,239	*	4,213	6,960	7,830	28,700	28,750	0	3,253	5,695	6,565	0	4,213	6,960	7,830
25,550	25,600	0	3,757	6,359	7,229	0	4,213	6,960	7,830	28,750	28,800	0	3,245	5,685	6,555	0	4,213	6,960	7,830
25,600	25,650	0	3,749	6,348	7,218	0	4,213	6,960	7,830	28,800	28,850	0	3,237	5,674	6,544	0	4,213	6,960	7,830
25,650	25,700	0	3,741	6,338	7,208	0	4,213	6,960	7,830	28,850	28,900	0	3,229	5,664	6,534	0	4,213	6,960	7,830
25,700	25,750	0	3,733	6,327	7,197	0	4,213	6,960	7,830	28,900	28,950	0	3,221	5,653	6,523	0	4,213	6,960	7,830
25,750	25,800	0	3,725	6,317	7,187	0	4,213	6,960	7,830	28,950	29,000	0	3,213	5,643	6,513	0	4,213	6,960	7,830
25,800	25,850	0	3,717	6,306	7,176	0	4,213	6,960	7,830	29,000	29,050	0	3,205	5,632	6,502	0	4,213	6,960	7,830
25,850	25,900	0	3,709	6,296	7,166	0	4,213	6,960	7,830	29,050	29,100	0	3,197	5,622	6,492	0	4,213	6,960	7,830
25,900	25,950	0	3,701	6,285	7,155	0	4,213	6,960	7,830	29,100	29,150	0	3,189	5,611	6,481	0	4,213	6,960	7,830
25,950	26,000	0	3,693	6,274	7,144	0	4,213	6,960	7,830	29,150	29,200	0	3,181	5,601	6,471	0	4,213	6,960	7,830
26,000	26,050	0	3,685	6,264	7,134	0	4,213	6,960	7,830	29,200	29,250	0	3,174	5,590	6,460	0	4,213	6,960	7,830
26,050	26,100	0	3,677	6,253	7,123	0	4,213	6,960	7,830	29,250	29,300	0	3,166	5,580	6,450	0	4,213	6,960	7,830
26,100	26,150	0	3,669	6,243	7,113	0	4,213	6,960	7,830	29,300	29,350	0	3,158	5,569	6,439	0	4,213	6,960	7,830
26,150	26,200	0	3,661	6,232	7,102	0	4,213	6,960	7,830	29,350	29,400	0	3,150	5,558	6,428	0	4,213	6,960	7,830
26,200	26,250	0	3,653	6,222	7,092	0	4,213	6,960	7,830	29,400	29,450	0	3,142	5,548	6,418	0	4,213	6,960	7,830
26,250	26,300	0	3,645	6,211	7,081	0	4,213	6,960	7,830	29,450	29,500	0	3,134	5,537	6,407	0	4,213	6,960	7,830
26,300	26,350	0	3,637	6,201	7,071	0	4,213	6,960	7,830	29,500	29,550	0	3,126	5,527	6,397	0	4,213	6,960	7,830
26,350	26,400	0	3,629	6,190	7,060	0	4,213	6,960	7,830	29,550	29,600	0	3,118	5,516	6,386	0	4,213	6,960	7,830
26,400	26,450	0	3,621	6,180	7,050	0	4,213	6,960	7,830	29,600	29,650	0	3,110	5,506	6,376	0	4,213	6,960	7,830
26,450	26,500	0	3,613	6,169	7,039	0	4,213	6,960	7,830	29,650	29,700	0	3,102	5,495	6,365	0	4,207	6,953	7,823
26,500	26,550	0	3,605	6,159	7,029	0	4,213	6,960	7,830	29,700	29,750	0	3,094	5,485	6,355	0	4,199	6,942	7,812
26,550	26,600	0	3,597	6,148	7,018	0	4,213	6,960	7,830	29,750	29,800	0	3,086	5,474	6,344	0	4,191	6,932	7,802
26,600	26,650	0	3,589	6,138	7,008	0	4,213	6,960	7,830	29,800	29,850	0	3,078	5,464	6,334	0	4,183	6,921	7,791
26,650	26,700	0	3,581	6,127	6,997	0	4,213	6,960	7,830	29,850	29,900	0	3,070	5,453	6,323	0	4,175	6,911	7,781
26,700	26,750	0	3,573	6,117	6,987	0	4,213	6,960	7,830	29,900	29,950	0	3,062	5,443	6,313	0	4,167	6,900	7,770
26,750	26,800	0	3,565	6,106	6,976	0	4,213	6,960	7,830	29,950	30,000	0	3,054	5,432	6,302	0	4,159	6,889	7,759
26,800	26,850	0	3,557	6,095	6,965	0	4,213	6,960	7,830	30,000	30,050	0	3,046	5,422	6,292	0	4,151	6,879	7,749
26,850	26,900	0	3,549	6,085	6,955	0	4,213	6,960	7,830	30,050	30,100	0	3,038	5,411	6,281	0	4,143	6,868	7,738
26,900	26,950	0	3,541	6,074	6,944	0	4,213	6,960	7,830	30,100	30,150	0	3,030	5,401	6,271	0	4,135	6,858	7,728
26,950	27,000	0	3,533	6,064	6,934	0	4,213	6,960	7,830	30,150	30,200	0	3,022	5,390	6,260	0	4,128	6,847	7,717
27,000	27,050	0	3,525	6,053	6,923	0	4,213	6,960	7,830	30,200	30,250	0	3,014	5,379	6,249	0	4,120	6,837	7,707
27,050	27,100	0	3,517	6,043	6,913	0	4,213	6,960	7,830	30,250	30,300	0	3,006	5,369	6,239	0	4,112	6,826	7,696
27,100	27,150	0	3,509	6,032	6,902	0	4,213	6,960	7,830	30,300	30,350	0	2,998	5,358	6,228	0	4,104	6,816	7,686
27,150	27,200	0	3,501	6,022	6,892	0	4,213	6,960	7,830	30,350	30,400	0	2,990	5,348	6,218	0	4,096	6,805	7,675
27,200	27,250	0	3,493	6,011	6,881	0	4,213	6,960	7,830	30,400	30,450	0	2,982	5,337	6,207	0	4,088	6,795	7,665
27,250	27,300	0	3,485	6,001	6,871	0	4,213	6,960	7,830	30,450	30,500	0	2,974	5,327	6,197	0	4,080	6,784	7,654
27,300	27,350	0	3,477	5,990	6,860	0	4,213	6,960	7,830	30,500	30,550	0	2,966	5,316	6,186	0	4,072	6,774	7,644
27,350	27,400	0	3,469	5,980	6,850	0	4,213	6,960	7,830	30,550	30,600	0	2,958	5,306	6,176	0	4,064	6,763	7,633
27,400	27,450	0	3,461	5,969	6,839	0	4,213	6,960	7,830	30,600	30,650	0	2,950	5,295	6,165	0	4,056	6,753	7,623
27,450	27,500	0	3,453	5,959	6,829	0	4,213	6,960	7,830	30,650	30,700	0	2,942	5,285	6,155	0	4,048	6,742	7,612
27,500	27,550	0	3,445	5,948	6,818	0	4,213	6,960	7,830	30,700	30,750	0	2,934	5,274	6,144	0	4,040	6,731	7,601
27,550	27,600	0	3,437	5,938	6,808	0	4,213	6,960	7,830	30,750	30,800	0	2,926	5,264	6,134	0	4,032	6,721	7,591
27,600	27,650	0	3,429	5,927	6,797	0	4,213	6,960	7,830	30,800	30,850	0	2,918	5,253	6,123	0	4,024	6,710	7,580
27,650	27,700	0	3,421	5,916	6,786	0	4,213	6,960	7,830	30,850	30,900	0	2,910	5,243	6,113	0	4,016	6,700	7,570
27,700	27,750	0	3,413	5,906	6,776	0	4,213	6,960	7,830	30,900	30,950	0	2,902	5,232	6,102	0	4,008	6,689	7,559
27,750	27,800	0	3,405	5,895	6,765	0	4,213	6,960	7,830	30,950	31,000	0	2,894	5,221	6,091	0	4,000	6,679	7,549
27,800	27,850	0	3,397	5,885	6,755	0	4,213	6,960	7,830	31,000	31,050	0	2,886	5,211	6,081	0	3,992	6,668	7,538
27,850	27,900	0	3,389	5,874	6,744	0	4,213	6,960	7,830	31,050	31,100	0	2,878	5,200	6,070	0	3,984	6,658	7,528
27,900	27,950	0	3,381	5,864	6,734	0	4,213	6,960	7,830	31,100	31,150	0	2,870	5,190	6,060	0	3,976	6,647	7,517
27,950	28,000	0	3,373	5,853	6,723	0	4,213	6,960	7,830	31,150	31,200	0	2,862	5,179	6,049	0	3,968	6,637	7,507

★ Use this column if your filing status is married filing separately and you qualify to claim the EIC. See the instructions for line 27.

* If the amount you are looking up from the worksheet is at least $25,500 but less than $25,511, and you have no qualifying children who have valid SSNs, your credit is $0.

If the amount you are looking up from the worksheet is $25,511 or more, and you have no qualifying children who have valid SSNs, you can't take the credit.

(Continued)

Earned Income Credit (EIC) Table - Continued

(Caution. This is **not** a tax table.)

If the amount you are looking up from the worksheet is–		And your filing status is–								If the amount you are looking up from the worksheet is–		And your filing status is–							
		Single, head of household, or qualifying surviving spouse★ and you have–				Married filing jointly and you have–						Single, head of household, or qualifying surviving spouse★ and you have–				Married filing jointly and you have–			
		0	1	2	3	0	1	2	3			0	1	2	3	0	1	2	3
At least	But less than	Your credit is–				Your credit is–				At least	But less than	Your credit is–				Your credit is–			
31,200	31,250	0	2,854	5,169	6,039	0	3,960	6,626	7,496	34,400	34,450	0	2,343	4,495	5,365	0	3,448	5,952	6,822
31,250	31,300	0	2,846	5,158	6,028	0	3,952	6,616	7,486	34,450	34,500	0	2,335	4,484	5,354	0	3,440	5,942	6,812
31,300	31,350	0	2,838	5,148	6,018	0	3,944	6,605	7,475	34,500	34,550	0	2,327	4,474	5,344	0	3,432	5,931	6,801
31,350	31,400	0	2,830	5,137	6,007	0	3,936	6,595	7,465	34,550	34,600	0	2,319	4,463	5,333	0	3,424	5,921	6,791
31,400	31,450	0	2,822	5,127	5,997	0	3,928	6,584	7,454	34,600	34,650	0	2,311	4,453	5,323	0	3,416	5,910	6,780
31,450	31,500	0	2,814	5,116	5,986	0	3,920	6,574	7,444	34,650	34,700	0	2,303	4,442	5,312	0	3,408	5,900	6,770
31,500	31,550	0	2,806	5,106	5,976	0	3,912	6,563	7,433	34,700	34,750	0	2,295	4,432	5,302	0	3,400	5,889	6,759
31,550	31,600	0	2,798	5,095	5,965	0	3,904	6,552	7,422	34,750	34,800	0	2,287	4,421	5,291	0	3,392	5,879	6,749
31,600	31,650	0	2,790	5,085	5,955	0	3,896	6,542	7,412	34,800	34,850	0	2,279	4,411	5,281	0	3,384	5,868	6,738
31,650	31,700	0	2,782	5,074	5,944	0	3,888	6,531	7,401	34,850	34,900	0	2,271	4,400	5,270	0	3,376	5,858	6,728
31,700	31,750	0	2,774	5,064	5,934	0	3,880	6,521	7,391	34,900	34,950	0	2,263	4,390	5,260	0	3,368	5,847	6,717
31,750	31,800	0	2,766	5,053	5,923	0	3,872	6,510	7,380	34,950	35,000	0	2,255	4,379	5,249	0	3,360	5,836	6,706
31,800	31,850	0	2,758	5,042	5,912	0	3,864	6,500	7,370	35,000	35,050	0	2,247	4,369	5,239	0	3,352	5,826	6,696
31,850	31,900	0	2,750	5,032	5,902	0	3,856	6,489	7,359	35,050	35,100	0	2,239	4,358	5,228	0	3,344	5,815	6,685
31,900	31,950	0	2,742	5,021	5,891	0	3,848	6,479	7,349	35,100	35,150	0	2,231	4,348	5,218	0	3,336	5,805	6,675
31,950	32,000	0	2,734	5,011	5,881	0	3,840	6,468	7,338	35,150	35,200	0	2,223	4,337	5,207	0	3,329	5,794	6,664
32,000	32,050	0	2,726	5,000	5,870	0	3,832	6,458	7,328	35,200	35,250	0	2,215	4,326	5,196	0	3,321	5,784	6,654
32,050	32,100	0	2,718	4,990	5,860	0	3,824	6,447	7,317	35,250	35,300	0	2,207	4,316	5,186	0	3,313	5,773	6,643
32,100	32,150	0	2,710	4,979	5,849	0	3,816	6,437	7,307	35,300	35,350	0	2,199	4,305	5,175	0	3,305	5,763	6,633
32,150	32,200	0	2,702	4,969	5,839	0	3,808	6,426	7,296	35,350	35,400	0	2,191	4,295	5,165	0	3,297	5,752	6,622
32,200	32,250	0	2,694	4,958	5,828	0	3,800	6,416	7,286	35,400	35,450	0	2,183	4,284	5,154	0	3,289	5,742	6,612
32,250	32,300	0	2,686	4,948	5,818	0	3,792	6,405	7,275	35,450	35,500	0	2,175	4,274	5,144	0	3,281	5,731	6,601
32,300	32,350	0	2,678	4,937	5,807	0	3,784	6,395	7,265	35,500	35,550	0	2,167	4,263	5,133	0	3,273	5,721	6,591
32,350	32,400	0	2,670	4,927	5,797	0	3,776	6,384	7,254	35,550	35,600	0	2,159	4,253	5,123	0	3,265	5,710	6,580
32,400	32,450	0	2,662	4,916	5,786	0	3,768	6,373	7,243	35,600	35,650	0	2,151	4,242	5,112	0	3,257	5,700	6,570
32,450	32,500	0	2,654	4,906	5,776	0	3,760	6,363	7,233	35,650	35,700	0	2,143	4,232	5,102	0	3,249	5,689	6,559
32,500	32,550	0	2,646	4,895	5,765	0	3,752	6,352	7,222	35,700	35,750	0	2,135	4,221	5,091	0	3,241	5,678	6,548
32,550	32,600	0	2,638	4,885	5,755	0	3,744	6,342	7,212	35,750	35,800	0	2,127	4,211	5,081	0	3,233	5,668	6,538
32,600	32,650	0	2,630	4,874	5,744	0	3,736	6,331	7,201	35,800	35,850	0	2,119	4,200	5,070	0	3,225	5,657	6,527
32,650	32,700	0	2,622	4,863	5,733	0	3,728	6,321	7,191	35,850	35,900	0	2,111	4,190	5,060	0	3,217	5,647	6,517
32,700	32,750	0	2,614	4,853	5,723	0	3,720	6,310	7,180	35,900	35,950	0	2,103	4,179	5,049	0	3,209	5,636	6,506
32,750	32,800	0	2,606	4,842	5,712	0	3,712	6,300	7,170	35,950	36,000	0	2,095	4,168	5,038	0	3,201	5,626	6,496
32,800	32,850	0	2,598	4,832	5,702	0	3,704	6,289	7,159	36,000	36,050	0	2,087	4,158	5,028	0	3,193	5,615	6,485
32,850	32,900	0	2,590	4,821	5,691	0	3,696	6,279	7,149	36,050	36,100	0	2,079	4,147	5,017	0	3,185	5,605	6,475
32,900	32,950	0	2,582	4,811	5,681	0	3,688	6,268	7,138	36,100	36,150	0	2,071	4,137	5,007	0	3,177	5,594	6,464
32,950	33,000	0	2,574	4,800	5,670	0	3,680	6,258	7,128	36,150	36,200	0	2,063	4,126	4,996	0	3,169	5,584	6,454
33,000	33,050	0	2,566	4,790	5,660	0	3,672	6,247	7,117	36,200	36,250	0	2,055	4,116	4,986	0	3,161	5,573	6,443
33,050	33,100	0	2,558	4,779	5,649	0	3,664	6,237	7,107	36,250	36,300	0	2,047	4,105	4,975	0	3,153	5,563	6,433
33,100	33,150	0	2,550	4,769	5,639	0	3,656	6,226	7,096	36,300	36,350	0	2,039	4,095	4,965	0	3,145	5,552	6,422
33,150	33,200	0	2,542	4,758	5,628	0	3,648	6,216	7,086	36,350	36,400	0	2,031	4,084	4,954	0	3,137	5,542	6,412
33,200	33,250	0	2,534	4,748	5,618	0	3,640	6,205	7,075	36,400	36,450	0	2,023	4,074	4,944	0	3,129	5,531	6,401
33,250	33,300	0	2,526	4,737	5,607	0	3,632	6,194	7,064	36,450	36,500	0	2,015	4,063	4,933	0	3,121	5,521	6,391
33,300	33,350	0	2,518	4,727	5,597	0	3,624	6,184	7,054	36,500	36,550	0	2,007	4,053	4,923	0	3,113	5,510	6,380
33,350	33,400	0	2,510	4,716	5,586	0	3,616	6,173	7,043	36,550	36,600	0	1,999	4,042	4,912	0	3,105	5,499	6,369
33,400	33,450	0	2,502	4,706	5,576	0	3,608	6,163	7,033	36,600	36,650	0	1,991	4,032	4,902	0	3,097	5,489	6,359
33,450	33,500	0	2,494	4,695	5,565	0	3,600	6,152	7,022	36,650	36,700	0	1,983	4,021	4,891	0	3,089	5,478	6,348
33,500	33,550	0	2,486	4,684	5,554	0	3,592	6,142	7,012	36,700	36,750	0	1,975	4,011	4,881	0	3,081	5,468	6,338
33,550	33,600	0	2,478	4,674	5,544	0	3,584	6,131	7,001	36,750	36,800	0	1,967	4,000	4,870	0	3,073	5,457	6,327
33,600	33,650	0	2,470	4,663	5,533	0	3,576	6,121	6,991	36,800	36,850	0	1,959	3,989	4,859	0	3,065	5,447	6,317
33,650	33,700	0	2,462	4,653	5,523	0	3,568	6,110	6,980	36,850	36,900	0	1,951	3,979	4,849	0	3,057	5,436	6,306
33,700	33,750	0	2,454	4,642	5,512	0	3,560	6,100	6,970	36,900	36,950	0	1,943	3,968	4,838	0	3,049	5,426	6,296
33,750	33,800	0	2,446	4,632	5,502	0	3,552	6,089	6,959	36,950	37,000	0	1,935	3,958	4,828	0	3,041	5,415	6,285
33,800	33,850	0	2,438	4,621	5,491	0	3,544	6,079	6,949	37,000	37,050	0	1,927	3,947	4,817	0	3,033	5,405	6,275
33,850	33,900	0	2,430	4,611	5,481	0	3,536	6,068	6,938	37,050	37,100	0	1,919	3,937	4,807	0	3,025	5,394	6,264
33,900	33,950	0	2,422	4,600	5,470	0	3,528	6,058	6,928	37,100	37,150	0	1,911	3,926	4,796	0	3,017	5,384	6,254
33,950	34,000	0	2,414	4,590	5,460	0	3,520	6,047	6,917	37,150	37,200	0	1,903	3,916	4,786	0	3,009	5,373	6,243
34,000	34,050	0	2,406	4,579	5,449	0	3,512	6,037	6,907	37,200	37,250	0	1,895	3,905	4,775	0	3,001	5,363	6,233
34,050	34,100	0	2,398	4,569	5,439	0	3,504	6,026	6,896	37,250	37,300	0	1,887	3,895	4,765	0	2,993	5,352	6,222
34,100	34,150	0	2,390	4,558	5,428	0	3,496	6,015	6,885	37,300	37,350	0	1,879	3,884	4,754	0	2,985	5,342	6,212
34,150	34,200	0	2,382	4,548	5,418	0	3,488	6,005	6,875	37,350	37,400	0	1,871	3,874	4,744	0	2,977	5,331	6,201
34,200	34,250	0	2,375	4,537	5,407	0	3,480	5,994	6,864	37,400	37,450	0	1,863	3,863	4,733	0	2,969	5,320	6,190
34,250	34,300	0	2,367	4,527	5,397	0	3,472	5,984	6,854	37,450	37,500	0	1,855	3,853	4,723	0	2,961	5,310	6,180
34,300	34,350	0	2,359	4,516	5,386	0	3,464	5,973	6,843	37,500	37,550	0	1,847	3,842	4,712	0	2,953	5,299	6,169
34,350	34,400	0	2,351	4,505	5,375	0	3,456	5,963	6,833	37,550	37,600	0	1,839	3,832	4,702	0	2,945	5,289	6,159

★ Use this column if your filing status is married filing separately and you qualify to claim the EIC. See the instructions for line 27.

(Continued)

Earned Income Credit (EIC) Table - Continued

(**Caution.** This is **not** a tax table.)

If the amount you are looking up from the worksheet is—		Single, head of household, or qualifying surviving spouse★ and you have—				Married filing jointly and you have—				If the amount you are looking up from the worksheet is—		Single, head of household, or qualifying surviving spouse★ and you have—				Married filing jointly and you have—			
		0	1	2	3	0	1	2	3			0	1	2	3	0	1	2	3
At least	But less than	Your credit is—				Your credit is—				At least	But less than	Your credit is—				Your credit is—			
37,600	37,650	0	1,831	3,821	4,691	0	2,937	5,278	6,148	40,800	40,850	0	1,320	3,147	4,017	0	2,426	4,604	5,474
37,650	37,700	0	1,823	3,810	4,680	0	2,929	5,268	6,138	40,850	40,900	0	1,312	3,137	4,007	0	2,418	4,594	5,464
37,700	37,750	0	1,815	3,800	4,670	0	2,921	5,257	6,127	40,900	40,950	0	1,304	3,126	3,996	0	2,410	4,583	5,453
37,750	37,800	0	1,807	3,789	4,659	0	2,913	5,247	6,117	40,950	41,000	0	1,296	3,115	3,985	0	2,402	4,573	5,443
37,800	37,850	0	1,799	3,779	4,649	0	2,905	5,236	6,106	41,000	41,050	0	1,288	3,105	3,975	0	2,394	4,562	5,432
37,850	37,900	0	1,791	3,768	4,638	0	2,897	5,226	6,096	41,050	41,100	0	1,280	3,094	3,964	0	2,386	4,552	5,422
37,900	37,950	0	1,783	3,758	4,628	0	2,889	5,215	6,085	41,100	41,150	0	1,272	3,084	3,954	0	2,378	4,541	5,411
37,950	38,000	0	1,775	3,747	4,617	0	2,881	5,205	6,075	41,150	41,200	0	1,264	3,073	3,943	0	2,370	4,531	5,401
38,000	38,050	0	1,767	3,737	4,607	0	2,873	5,194	6,064	41,200	41,250	0	1,256	3,063	3,933	0	2,362	4,520	5,390
38,050	38,100	0	1,759	3,726	4,596	0	2,865	5,184	6,054	41,250	41,300	0	1,248	3,052	3,922	0	2,354	4,510	5,380
38,100	38,150	0	1,751	3,716	4,586	0	2,857	5,173	6,043	41,300	41,350	0	1,240	3,042	3,912	0	2,346	4,499	5,369
38,150	38,200	0	1,743	3,705	4,575	0	2,849	5,163	6,033	41,350	41,400	0	1,232	3,031	3,901	0	2,338	4,489	5,359
38,200	38,250	0	1,735	3,695	4,565	0	2,841	5,152	6,022	41,400	41,450	0	1,224	3,021	3,891	0	2,330	4,478	5,348
38,250	38,300	0	1,727	3,684	4,554	0	2,833	5,141	6,011	41,450	41,500	0	1,216	3,010	3,880	0	2,322	4,468	5,338
38,300	38,350	0	1,719	3,674	4,544	0	2,825	5,131	6,001	41,500	41,550	0	1,208	3,000	3,870	0	2,314	4,457	5,327
38,350	38,400	0	1,711	3,663	4,533	0	2,817	5,120	5,990	41,550	41,600	0	1,200	2,989	3,859	0	2,306	4,446	5,316
38,400	38,450	0	1,703	3,653	4,523	0	2,809	5,110	5,980	41,600	41,650	0	1,192	2,979	3,849	0	2,298	4,436	5,306
38,450	38,500	0	1,695	3,642	4,512	0	2,801	5,099	5,969	41,650	41,700	0	1,184	2,968	3,838	0	2,290	4,425	5,295
38,500	38,550	0	1,687	3,631	4,501	0	2,793	5,089	5,959	41,700	41,750	0	1,176	2,958	3,828	0	2,282	4,415	5,285
38,550	38,600	0	1,679	3,621	4,491	0	2,785	5,078	5,948	41,750	41,800	0	1,168	2,947	3,817	0	2,274	4,404	5,274
38,600	38,650	0	1,671	3,610	4,480	0	2,777	5,068	5,938	41,800	41,850	0	1,160	2,936	3,806	0	2,266	4,394	5,264
38,650	38,700	0	1,663	3,600	4,470	0	2,769	5,057	5,927	41,850	41,900	0	1,152	2,926	3,796	0	2,258	4,383	5,253
38,700	38,750	0	1,655	3,589	4,459	0	2,761	5,047	5,917	41,900	41,950	0	1,144	2,915	3,785	0	2,250	4,373	5,243
38,750	38,800	0	1,647	3,579	4,449	0	2,753	5,036	5,906	41,950	42,000	0	1,136	2,905	3,775	0	2,242	4,362	5,232
38,800	38,850	0	1,639	3,568	4,438	0	2,745	5,026	5,896	42,000	42,050	0	1,128	2,894	3,764	0	2,234	4,352	5,222
38,850	38,900	0	1,631	3,558	4,428	0	2,737	5,015	5,885	42,050	42,100	0	1,120	2,884	3,754	0	2,226	4,341	5,211
38,900	38,950	0	1,623	3,547	4,417	0	2,729	5,005	5,875	42,100	42,150	0	1,112	2,873	3,743	0	2,218	4,331	5,201
38,950	39,000	0	1,615	3,537	4,407	0	2,721	4,994	5,864	42,150	42,200	0	1,104	2,863	3,733	0	2,210	4,320	5,190
39,000	39,050	0	1,607	3,526	4,396	0	2,713	4,984	5,854	42,200	42,250	0	1,096	2,852	3,722	0	2,202	4,310	5,180
39,050	39,100	0	1,599	3,516	4,386	0	2,705	4,973	5,843	42,250	42,300	0	1,088	2,842	3,712	0	2,194	4,299	5,169
39,100	39,150	0	1,591	3,505	4,375	0	2,697	4,962	5,832	42,300	42,350	0	1,080	2,831	3,701	0	2,186	4,289	5,159
39,150	39,200	0	1,583	3,495	4,365	0	2,689	4,952	5,822	42,350	42,400	0	1,072	2,821	3,691	0	2,178	4,278	5,148
39,200	39,250	0	1,576	3,484	4,354	0	2,681	4,941	5,811	42,400	42,450	0	1,064	2,810	3,680	0	2,170	4,267	5,137
39,250	39,300	0	1,568	3,474	4,344	0	2,673	4,931	5,801	42,450	42,500	0	1,056	2,800	3,670	0	2,162	4,257	5,127
39,300	39,350	0	1,560	3,463	4,333	0	2,665	4,920	5,790	42,500	42,550	0	1,048	2,789	3,659	0	2,154	4,246	5,116
39,350	39,400	0	1,552	3,452	4,322	0	2,657	4,910	5,780	42,550	42,600	0	1,040	2,779	3,649	0	2,146	4,236	5,106
39,400	39,450	0	1,544	3,442	4,312	0	2,649	4,899	5,769	42,600	42,650	0	1,032	2,768	3,638	0	2,138	4,225	5,095
39,450	39,500	0	1,536	3,431	4,301	0	2,641	4,889	5,759	42,650	42,700	0	1,024	2,757	3,627	0	2,130	4,215	5,085
39,500	39,550	0	1,528	3,421	4,291	0	2,633	4,878	5,748	42,700	42,750	0	1,016	2,747	3,617	0	2,122	4,204	5,074
39,550	39,600	0	1,520	3,410	4,280	0	2,625	4,868	5,738	42,750	42,800	0	1,008	2,736	3,606	0	2,114	4,194	5,064
39,600	39,650	0	1,512	3,400	4,270	0	2,617	4,857	5,727	42,800	42,850	0	1,000	2,726	3,596	0	2,106	4,183	5,053
39,650	39,700	0	1,504	3,389	4,259	0	2,609	4,847	5,717	42,850	42,900	0	992	2,715	3,585	0	2,098	4,173	5,043
39,700	39,750	0	1,496	3,379	4,249	0	2,601	4,836	5,706	42,900	42,950	0	984	2,705	3,575	0	2,090	4,162	5,032
39,750	39,800	0	1,488	3,368	4,238	0	2,593	4,826	5,696	42,950	43,000	0	976	2,694	3,564	0	2,082	4,152	5,022
39,800	39,850	0	1,480	3,358	4,228	0	2,585	4,815	5,685	43,000	43,050	0	968	2,684	3,554	0	2,074	4,141	5,011
39,850	39,900	0	1,472	3,347	4,217	0	2,577	4,805	5,675	43,050	43,100	0	960	2,673	3,543	0	2,066	4,131	5,001
39,900	39,950	0	1,464	3,337	4,207	0	2,569	4,794	5,664	43,100	43,150	0	952	2,663	3,533	0	2,058	4,120	4,990
39,950	40,000	0	1,456	3,326	4,196	0	2,561	4,783	5,653	43,150	43,200	0	944	2,652	3,522	0	2,050	4,110	4,980
40,000	40,050	0	1,448	3,316	4,186	0	2,553	4,773	5,643	43,200	43,250	0	936	2,642	3,512	0	2,042	4,099	4,969
40,050	40,100	0	1,440	3,305	4,175	0	2,545	4,762	5,632	43,250	43,300	0	928	2,631	3,501	0	2,034	4,088	4,958
40,100	40,150	0	1,432	3,295	4,165	0	2,537	4,752	5,622	43,300	43,350	0	920	2,621	3,491	0	2,026	4,078	4,948
40,150	40,200	0	1,424	3,284	4,154	0	2,530	4,741	5,611	43,350	43,400	0	912	2,610	3,480	0	2,018	4,067	4,937
40,200	40,250	0	1,416	3,273	4,143	0	2,522	4,731	5,601	43,400	43,450	0	904	2,600	3,470	0	2,010	4,057	4,927
40,250	40,300	0	1,408	3,263	4,133	0	2,514	4,720	5,590	43,450	43,500	0	896	2,589	3,459	0	2,002	4,046	4,916
40,300	40,350	0	1,400	3,252	4,122	0	2,506	4,710	5,580	43,500	43,550	0	888	2,578	3,448	0	1,994	4,036	4,906
40,350	40,400	0	1,392	3,242	4,112	0	2,498	4,699	5,569	43,550	43,600	0	880	2,568	3,438	0	1,986	4,025	4,895
40,400	40,450	0	1,384	3,231	4,101	0	2,490	4,689	5,559	43,600	43,650	0	872	2,557	3,427	0	1,978	4,015	4,885
40,450	40,500	0	1,376	3,221	4,091	0	2,482	4,678	5,548	43,650	43,700	0	864	2,547	3,417	0	1,970	4,004	4,874
40,500	40,550	0	1,368	3,210	4,080	0	2,474	4,668	5,538	43,700	43,750	0	856	2,536	3,406	0	1,962	3,994	4,864
40,550	40,600	0	1,360	3,200	4,070	0	2,466	4,657	5,527	43,750	43,800	0	848	2,526	3,396	0	1,954	3,983	4,853
40,600	40,650	0	1,352	3,189	4,059	0	2,458	4,647	5,517	43,800	43,850	0	840	2,515	3,385	0	1,946	3,973	4,843
40,650	40,700	0	1,344	3,179	4,049	0	2,450	4,636	5,506	43,850	43,900	0	832	2,505	3,375	0	1,938	3,962	4,832
40,700	40,750	0	1,336	3,168	4,038	0	2,442	4,625	5,495	43,900	43,950	0	824	2,494	3,364	0	1,930	3,952	4,822
40,750	40,800	0	1,328	3,158	4,028	0	2,434	4,615	5,485	43,950	44,000	0	816	2,484	3,354	0	1,922	3,941	4,811

★ Use this column if your filing status is married filing separately and you qualify to claim the EIC. See the instructions for line 27.

(Continued)

Earned Income Credit (EIC) Table - Continued

(Caution. This is **not** a tax table.)

If the amount you are looking up from the worksheet is–		And your filing status is–								If the amount you are looking up from the worksheet is–		And your filing status is–							
		Single, head of household, or qualifying surviving spouse★ and you have–				Married filing jointly and you have–						Single, head of household, or qualifying surviving spouse★ and you have–				Married filing jointly and you have–			
		0	1	2	3	0	1	2	3			0	1	2	3	0	1	2	3
At least	But less than	Your credit is–				Your credit is–				At least	But less than	Your credit is–				Your credit is–			
44,000	44,050	0	808	2,473	3,343	0	1,914	3,931	4,801	47,200	47,250	0	297	1,799	2,669	0	1,403	3,257	4,127
44,050	44,100	0	800	2,463	3,333	0	1,906	3,920	4,790	47,250	47,300	0	289	1,789	2,659	0	1,395	3,246	4,116
44,100	44,150	0	792	2,452	3,322	0	1,898	3,909	4,779	47,300	47,350	0	281	1,778	2,648	0	1,387	3,236	4,106
44,150	44,200	0	784	2,442	3,312	0	1,890	3,899	4,769	47,350	47,400	0	273	1,768	2,638	0	1,379	3,225	4,095
44,200	44,250	0	777	2,431	3,301	0	1,882	3,888	4,758	47,400	47,450	0	265	1,757	2,627	0	1,371	3,214	4,084
44,250	44,300	0	769	2,421	3,291	0	1,874	3,878	4,748	47,450	47,500	0	257	1,747	2,617	0	1,363	3,204	4,074
44,300	44,350	0	761	2,410	3,280	0	1,866	3,867	4,737	47,500	47,550	0	249	1,736	2,606	0	1,355	3,193	4,063
44,350	44,400	0	753	2,399	3,269	0	1,858	3,857	4,727	47,550	47,600	0	241	1,726	2,596	0	1,347	3,183	4,053
44,400	44,450	0	745	2,389	3,259	0	1,850	3,846	4,716	47,600	47,650	0	233	1,715	2,585	0	1,339	3,172	4,042
44,450	44,500	0	737	2,378	3,248	0	1,842	3,836	4,706	47,650	47,700	0	225	1,704	2,574	0	1,331	3,162	4,032
44,500	44,550	0	729	2,368	3,238	0	1,834	3,825	4,695	47,700	47,750	0	217	1,694	2,564	0	1,323	3,151	4,021
44,550	44,600	0	721	2,357	3,227	0	1,826	3,815	4,685	47,750	47,800	0	209	1,683	2,553	0	1,315	3,141	4,011
44,600	44,650	0	713	2,347	3,217	0	1,818	3,804	4,674	47,800	47,850	0	201	1,673	2,543	0	1,307	3,130	4,000
44,650	44,700	0	705	2,336	3,206	0	1,810	3,794	4,664	47,850	47,900	0	193	1,662	2,532	0	1,299	3,120	3,990
44,700	44,750	0	697	2,326	3,196	0	1,802	3,783	4,653	47,900	47,950	0	185	1,652	2,522	0	1,291	3,109	3,979
44,750	44,800	0	689	2,315	3,185	0	1,794	3,773	4,643	47,950	48,000	0	177	1,641	2,511	0	1,283	3,099	3,969
44,800	44,850	0	681	2,305	3,175	0	1,786	3,762	4,632	48,000	48,050	0	169	1,631	2,501	0	1,275	3,088	3,958
44,850	44,900	0	673	2,294	3,164	0	1,778	3,752	4,622	48,050	48,100	0	161	1,620	2,490	0	1,267	3,078	3,948
44,900	44,950	0	665	2,284	3,154	0	1,770	3,741	4,611	48,100	48,150	0	153	1,610	2,480	0	1,259	3,067	3,937
44,950	45,000	0	657	2,273	3,143	0	1,762	3,730	4,600	48,150	48,200	0	145	1,599	2,469	0	1,251	3,057	3,927
45,000	45,050	0	649	2,263	3,133	0	1,754	3,720	4,590	48,200	48,250	0	137	1,589	2,459	0	1,243	3,046	3,916
45,050	45,100	0	641	2,252	3,122	0	1,746	3,709	4,579	48,250	48,300	0	129	1,578	2,448	0	1,235	3,035	3,905
45,100	45,150	0	633	2,242	3,112	0	1,738	3,699	4,569	48,300	48,350	0	121	1,568	2,438	0	1,227	3,025	3,895
45,150	45,200	0	625	2,231	3,101	0	1,731	3,688	4,558	48,350	48,400	0	113	1,557	2,427	0	1,219	3,014	3,884
45,200	45,250	0	617	2,220	3,090	0	1,723	3,678	4,548	48,400	48,450	0	105	1,547	2,417	0	1,211	3,004	3,874
45,250	45,300	0	609	2,210	3,080	0	1,715	3,667	4,537	48,450	48,500	0	97	1,536	2,406	0	1,203	2,993	3,863
45,300	45,350	0	601	2,199	3,069	0	1,707	3,657	4,527	48,500	48,550	0	89	1,525	2,395	0	1,195	2,983	3,853
45,350	45,400	0	593	2,189	3,059	0	1,699	3,646	4,516	48,550	48,600	0	81	1,515	2,385	0	1,187	2,972	3,842
45,400	45,450	0	585	2,178	3,048	0	1,691	3,636	4,506	48,600	48,650	0	73	1,504	2,374	0	1,179	2,962	3,832
45,450	45,500	0	577	2,168	3,038	0	1,683	3,625	4,495	48,650	48,700	0	65	1,494	2,364	0	1,171	2,951	3,821
45,500	45,550	0	569	2,157	3,027	0	1,675	3,615	4,485	48,700	48,750	0	57	1,483	2,353	0	1,163	2,941	3,811
45,550	45,600	0	561	2,147	3,017	0	1,667	3,604	4,474	48,750	48,800	0	49	1,473	2,343	0	1,155	2,930	3,800
45,600	45,650	0	553	2,136	3,006	0	1,659	3,594	4,464	48,800	48,850	0	41	1,462	2,332	0	1,147	2,920	3,790
45,650	45,700	0	545	2,126	2,996	0	1,651	3,583	4,453	48,850	48,900	0	33	1,452	2,322	0	1,139	2,909	3,779
45,700	45,750	0	537	2,115	2,985	0	1,643	3,572	4,442	48,900	48,950	0	25	1,441	2,311	0	1,131	2,899	3,769
45,750	45,800	0	529	2,105	2,975	0	1,635	3,562	4,432	48,950	49,000	0	17	1,431	2,301	0	1,123	2,888	3,758
45,800	45,850	0	521	2,094	2,964	0	1,627	3,551	4,421	49,000	49,050	0	9	1,420	2,290	0	1,115	2,878	3,748
45,850	45,900	0	513	2,084	2,954	0	1,619	3,541	4,411	49,050	49,100	0	*	1,410	2,280	0	1,107	2,867	3,737
45,900	45,950	0	505	2,073	2,943	0	1,611	3,530	4,400	49,100	49,150	0	0	1,399	2,269	0	1,099	2,856	3,726
45,950	46,000	0	497	2,062	2,932	0	1,603	3,520	4,390	49,150	49,200	0	0	1,389	2,259	0	1,091	2,846	3,716
46,000	46,050	0	489	2,052	2,922	0	1,595	3,509	4,379	49,200	49,250	0	0	1,378	2,248	0	1,083	2,835	3,705
46,050	46,100	0	481	2,041	2,911	0	1,587	3,499	4,369	49,250	49,300	0	0	1,368	2,238	0	1,075	2,825	3,695
46,100	46,150	0	473	2,031	2,901	0	1,579	3,488	4,358	49,300	49,350	0	0	1,357	2,227	0	1,067	2,814	3,684
46,150	46,200	0	465	2,020	2,890	0	1,571	3,478	4,348	49,350	49,400	0	0	1,346	2,216	0	1,059	2,804	3,674
46,200	46,250	0	457	2,010	2,880	0	1,563	3,467	4,337	49,400	49,450	0	0	1,336	2,206	0	1,051	2,793	3,663
46,250	46,300	0	449	1,999	2,869	0	1,555	3,457	4,327	49,450	49,500	0	0	1,325	2,195	0	1,043	2,783	3,653
46,300	46,350	0	441	1,989	2,859	0	1,547	3,446	4,316	49,500	49,550	0	0	1,315	2,185	0	1,035	2,772	3,642
46,350	46,400	0	433	1,978	2,848	0	1,539	3,436	4,306	49,550	49,600	0	0	1,304	2,174	0	1,027	2,762	3,632
46,400	46,450	0	425	1,968	2,838	0	1,531	3,425	4,295	49,600	49,650	0	0	1,294	2,164	0	1,019	2,751	3,621
46,450	46,500	0	417	1,957	2,827	0	1,523	3,415	4,285	49,650	49,700	0	0	1,283	2,153	0	1,011	2,741	3,611
46,500	46,550	0	409	1,947	2,817	0	1,515	3,404	4,274	49,700	49,750	0	0	1,273	2,143	0	1,003	2,730	3,600
46,550	46,600	0	401	1,936	2,806	0	1,507	3,393	4,263	49,750	49,800	0	0	1,262	2,132	0	995	2,720	3,590
46,600	46,650	0	393	1,926	2,796	0	1,499	3,383	4,253	49,800	49,850	0	0	1,252	2,122	0	987	2,709	3,579
46,650	46,700	0	385	1,915	2,785	0	1,491	3,372	4,242	49,850	49,900	0	0	1,241	2,111	0	979	2,699	3,569
46,700	46,750	0	377	1,905	2,775	0	1,483	3,362	4,232	49,900	49,950	0	0	1,231	2,101	0	971	2,688	3,558
46,750	46,800	0	369	1,894	2,764	0	1,475	3,351	4,221	49,950	50,000	0	0	1,220	2,090	0	963	2,677	3,547
46,800	46,850	0	361	1,883	2,753	0	1,467	3,341	4,211	50,000	50,050	0	0	1,210	2,080	0	955	2,667	3,537
46,850	46,900	0	353	1,873	2,743	0	1,459	3,330	4,200	50,050	50,100	0	0	1,199	2,069	0	947	2,656	3,526
46,900	46,950	0	345	1,862	2,732	0	1,451	3,320	4,190	50,100	50,150	0	0	1,189	2,059	0	939	2,646	3,516
46,950	47,000	0	337	1,852	2,722	0	1,443	3,309	4,179	50,150	50,200	0	0	1,178	2,048	0	932	2,635	3,505
47,000	47,050	0	329	1,841	2,711	0	1,435	3,299	4,169	50,200	50,250	0	0	1,167	2,037	0	924	2,625	3,495
47,050	47,100	0	321	1,831	2,701	0	1,427	3,288	4,158	50,250	50,300	0	0	1,157	2,027	0	916	2,614	3,484
47,100	47,150	0	313	1,820	2,690	0	1,419	3,278	4,148	50,300	50,350	0	0	1,146	2,016	0	908	2,604	3,474
47,150	47,200	0	305	1,810	2,680	0	1,411	3,267	4,137	50,350	50,400	0	0	1,136	2,006	0	900	2,593	3,463

★ Use this column if your filing status is married filing separately and you qualify to claim the EIC. See the instructions for line 27.

* If the amount you are looking up from the worksheet is at least $49,050 but less than $49,084, and you have one qualifying child who has a valid SSN, your credit is $3.

If the amount you are looking up from the worksheet is $49,084 or more, and you have one qualifying child who has a valid SSN, you can't take the credit.

(Continued)

Earned Income Credit (EIC) Table - Continued

(Caution. This is not a tax table.)

If the amount you are looking up from the worksheet is—		Single, head of household, or qualifying surviving spouse★ and you have—				Married filing jointly and you have—				If the amount you are looking up from the worksheet is—		Single, head of household, or qualifying surviving spouse★ and you have—				Married filing jointly and you have—			
At least	But less than	0	1	2	3	0	1	2	3	At least	But less than	0	1	2	3	0	1	2	3
		Your credit is—				Your credit is—						Your credit is—				Your credit is—			
50,400	50,450	0	0	1,125	1,995	0	892	2,583	3,453	53,200	53,250	0	0	536	1,406	0	444	1,993	2,863
50,450	50,500	0	0	1,115	1,985	0	884	2,572	3,442	53,250	53,300	0	0	525	1,395	0	436	1,982	2,852
50,500	50,550	0	0	1,104	1,974	0	876	2,562	3,432	53,300	53,350	0	0	515	1,385	0	428	1,972	2,842
50,550	50,600	0	0	1,094	1,964	0	868	2,551	3,421	53,350	53,400	0	0	504	1,374	0	420	1,961	2,831
50,600	50,650	0	0	1,083	1,953	0	860	2,541	3,411	53,400	53,450	0	0	494	1,364	0	412	1,951	2,821
50,650	50,700	0	0	1,073	1,943	0	852	2,530	3,400	53,450	53,500	0	0	483	1,353	0	404	1,940	2,810
50,700	50,750	0	0	1,062	1,932	0	844	2,519	3,389	53,500	53,550	0	0	472	1,342	0	396	1,930	2,800
50,750	50,800	0	0	1,052	1,922	0	836	2,509	3,379	53,550	53,600	0	0	462	1,332	0	388	1,919	2,789
50,800	50,850	0	0	1,041	1,911	0	828	2,498	3,368	53,600	53,650	0	0	451	1,321	0	380	1,909	2,779
50,850	50,900	0	0	1,031	1,901	0	820	2,488	3,358	53,650	53,700	0	0	441	1,311	0	372	1,898	2,768
50,900	50,950	0	0	1,020	1,890	0	812	2,477	3,347	53,700	53,750	0	0	430	1,300	0	364	1,888	2,758
50,950	51,000	0	0	1,009	1,879	0	804	2,467	3,337	53,750	53,800	0	0	420	1,290	0	356	1,877	2,747
51,000	51,050	0	0	999	1,869	0	796	2,456	3,326	53,800	53,850	0	0	409	1,279	0	348	1,867	2,737
51,050	51,100	0	0	988	1,858	0	788	2,446	3,316	53,850	53,900	0	0	399	1,269	0	340	1,856	2,726
51,100	51,150	0	0	978	1,848	0	780	2,435	3,305	53,900	53,950	0	0	388	1,258	0	332	1,846	2,716
51,150	51,200	0	0	967	1,837	0	772	2,425	3,295	53,950	54,000	0	0	378	1,248	0	324	1,835	2,705
51,200	51,250	0	0	957	1,827	0	764	2,414	3,284	54,000	54,050	0	0	367	1,237	0	316	1,825	2,695
51,250	51,300	0	0	946	1,816	0	756	2,404	3,274	54,050	54,100	0	0	357	1,227	0	308	1,814	2,684
51,300	51,350	0	0	936	1,806	0	748	2,393	3,263	54,100	54,150	0	0	346	1,216	0	300	1,803	2,673
51,350	51,400	0	0	925	1,795	0	740	2,383	3,253	54,150	54,200	0	0	336	1,206	0	292	1,793	2,663
51,400	51,450	0	0	915	1,785	0	732	2,372	3,242	54,200	54,250	0	0	325	1,195	0	284	1,782	2,652
51,450	51,500	0	0	904	1,774	0	724	2,362	3,232	54,250	54,300	0	0	315	1,185	0	276	1,772	2,642
51,500	51,550	0	0	894	1,764	0	716	2,351	3,221	54,300	54,350	0	0	304	1,174	0	268	1,761	2,631
51,550	51,600	0	0	883	1,753	0	708	2,340	3,210	54,350	54,400	0	0	293	1,163	0	260	1,751	2,621
51,600	51,650	0	0	873	1,743	0	700	2,330	3,200	54,400	54,450	0	0	283	1,153	0	252	1,740	2,610
51,650	51,700	0	0	862	1,732	0	692	2,319	3,189	54,450	54,500	0	0	272	1,142	0	244	1,730	2,600
51,700	51,750	0	0	852	1,722	0	684	2,309	3,179	54,500	54,550	0	0	262	1,132	0	236	1,719	2,589
51,750	51,800	0	0	841	1,711	0	676	2,298	3,168	54,550	54,600	0	0	251	1,121	0	228	1,709	2,579
51,800	51,850	0	0	830	1,700	0	668	2,288	3,158	54,600	54,650	0	0	241	1,111	0	220	1,698	2,568
51,850	51,900	0	0	820	1,690	0	660	2,277	3,147	54,650	54,700	0	0	230	1,100	0	212	1,688	2,558
51,900	51,950	0	0	809	1,679	0	652	2,267	3,137	54,700	54,750	0	0	220	1,090	0	204	1,677	2,547
51,950	52,000	0	0	799	1,669	0	644	2,256	3,126	54,750	54,800	0	0	209	1,079	0	196	1,667	2,537
52,000	52,050	0	0	788	1,658	0	636	2,246	3,116	54,800	54,850	0	0	199	1,069	0	188	1,656	2,526
52,050	52,100	0	0	778	1,648	0	628	2,235	3,105	54,850	54,900	0	0	188	1,058	0	180	1,646	2,516
52,100	52,150	0	0	767	1,637	0	620	2,225	3,095	54,900	54,950	0	0	178	1,048	0	172	1,635	2,505
52,150	52,200	0	0	757	1,627	0	612	2,214	3,084	54,950	55,000	0	0	167	1,037	0	164	1,624	2,494
52,200	52,250	0	0	746	1,616	0	604	2,204	3,074	55,000	55,050	0	0	157	1,027	0	156	1,614	2,484
52,250	52,300	0	0	736	1,606	0	596	2,193	3,063	55,050	55,100	0	0	146	1,016	0	148	1,603	2,473
52,300	52,350	0	0	725	1,595	0	588	2,183	3,053	55,100	55,150	0	0	136	1,006	0	140	1,593	2,463
52,350	52,400	0	0	715	1,585	0	580	2,172	3,042	55,150	55,200	0	0	125	995	0	133	1,582	2,452
52,400	52,450	0	0	704	1,574	0	572	2,161	3,031	55,200	55,250	0	0	114	984	0	125	1,572	2,442
52,450	52,500	0	0	694	1,564	0	564	2,151	3,021	55,250	55,300	0	0	104	974	0	117	1,561	2,431
52,500	52,550	0	0	683	1,553	0	556	2,140	3,010	55,300	55,350	0	0	93	963	0	109	1,551	2,421
52,550	52,600	0	0	673	1,543	0	548	2,130	3,000	55,350	55,400	0	0	83	953	0	101	1,540	2,410
52,600	52,650	0	0	662	1,532	0	540	2,119	2,989	55,400	55,450	0	0	72	942	0	93	1,530	2,400
52,650	52,700	0	0	651	1,521	0	532	2,109	2,979	55,450	55,500	0	0	62	932	0	85	1,519	2,389
52,700	52,750	0	0	641	1,511	0	524	2,098	2,968	55,500	55,550	0	0	51	921	0	77	1,509	2,379
52,750	52,800	0	0	630	1,500	0	516	2,088	2,958	55,550	55,600	0	0	41	911	0	69	1,498	2,368
52,800	52,850	0	0	620	1,490	0	508	2,077	2,947	55,600	55,650	0	0	30	900	0	61	1,488	2,358
52,850	52,900	0	0	609	1,479	0	500	2,067	2,937	55,650	55,700	0	0	20	890	0	53	1,477	2,347
52,900	52,950	0	0	599	1,469	0	492	2,056	2,926	55,700	55,750	0	0	9	879	0	45	1,466	2,336
52,950	53,000	0	0	588	1,458	0	484	2,046	2,916	55,750	55,800	0	0	*	869	0	37	1,456	2,326
53,000	53,050	0	0	578	1,448	0	476	2,035	2,905	55,800	55,850	0	0	0	858	0	29	1,445	2,315
53,050	53,100	0	0	567	1,437	0	468	2,025	2,895	55,850	55,900	0	0	0	848	0	21	1,435	2,305
53,100	53,150	0	0	557	1,427	0	460	2,014	2,884	55,900	55,950	0	0	0	837	0	13	1,424	2,294
53,150	53,200	0	0	546	1,416	0	452	2,004	2,874	55,950	56,000	0	0	0	826	0	5	1,414	2,284

★ Use this column if your filing status is married filing separately and you qualify to claim the EIC. See the instructions for line 27.

* If the amount you are looking up from the worksheet is at least $55,750 but less than $55,768, and you have two qualifying children who have valid SSNs, your credit is $2.

If the amount you are looking up from the worksheet is $55,768 or more, and you have two qualifying children who have valid SSNs, you can't take the credit.

(Continued)

Earned Income Credit (EIC) Table - Continued

(Caution. This is not a tax table.)

If the amount you are looking up from the worksheet is—		Single, head of household, or qualifying surviving spouse★ and you have—				Married filing jointly and you have—				If the amount you are looking up from the worksheet is—		Single, head of household, or qualifying surviving spouse★ and you have—				Married filing jointly and you have—			
At least	But less than	0	1	2	3	0	1	2	3	At least	But less than	0	1	2	3	0	1	2	3
		Your credit is—				Your credit is—						Your credit is—				Your credit is—			
56,000	56,050	0	0	0	816	0	*	1,403	2,273	58,800	58,850	0	0	0	226	0	0	814	1,684
56,050	56,100	0	0	0	805	0	0	1,393	2,263	58,850	58,900	0	0	0	216	0	0	803	1,673
56,100	56,150	0	0	0	795	0	0	1,382	2,252	58,900	58,950	0	0	0	205	0	0	793	1,663
56,150	56,200	0	0	0	784	0	0	1,372	2,242	58,950	59,000	0	0	0	195	0	0	782	1,652
56,200	56,250	0	0	0	774	0	0	1,361	2,231	59,000	59,050	0	0	0	184	0	0	772	1,642
56,250	56,300	0	0	0	763	0	0	1,351	2,221	59,050	59,100	0	0	0	174	0	0	761	1,631
56,300	56,350	0	0	0	753	0	0	1,340	2,210	59,100	59,150	0	0	0	163	0	0	750	1,620
56,350	56,400	0	0	0	742	0	0	1,330	2,200	59,150	59,200	0	0	0	153	0	0	740	1,610
56,400	56,450	0	0	0	732	0	0	1,319	2,189	59,200	59,250	0	0	0	142	0	0	729	1,599
56,450	56,500	0	0	0	721	0	0	1,309	2,179	59,250	59,300	0	0	0	132	0	0	719	1,589
56,500	56,550	0	0	0	711	0	0	1,298	2,168	59,300	59,350	0	0	0	121	0	0	708	1,578
56,550	56,600	0	0	0	700	0	0	1,287	2,157	59,350	59,400	0	0	0	110	0	0	698	1,568
56,600	56,650	0	0	0	690	0	0	1,277	2,147	59,400	59,450	0	0	0	100	0	0	687	1,557
56,650	56,700	0	0	0	679	0	0	1,266	2,136	59,450	59,500	0	0	0	89	0	0	677	1,547
56,700	56,750	0	0	0	669	0	0	1,256	2,126	59,500	59,550	0	0	0	79	0	0	666	1,536
56,750	56,800	0	0	0	658	0	0	1,245	2,115	59,550	59,600	0	0	0	68	0	0	656	1,526
56,800	56,850	0	0	0	647	0	0	1,235	2,105	59,600	59,650	0	0	0	58	0	0	645	1,515
56,850	56,900	0	0	0	637	0	0	1,224	2,094	59,650	59,700	0	0	0	47	0	0	635	1,505
56,900	56,950	0	0	0	626	0	0	1,214	2,084	59,700	59,750	0	0	0	37	0	0	624	1,494
56,950	57,000	0	0	0	616	0	0	1,203	2,073	59,750	59,800	0	0	0	26	0	0	614	1,484
57,000	57,050	0	0	0	605	0	0	1,193	2,063	59,800	59,850	0	0	0	16	0	0	603	1,473
57,050	57,100	0	0	0	595	0	0	1,182	2,052	59,850	59,900	0	0	0	**	0	0	593	1,463
57,100	57,150	0	0	0	584	0	0	1,172	2,042	59,900	59,950	0	0	0	0	0	0	582	1,452
57,150	57,200	0	0	0	574	0	0	1,161	2,031	59,950	60,000	0	0	0	0	0	0	571	1,441
57,200	57,250	0	0	0	563	0	0	1,151	2,021	60,000	60,050	0	0	0	0	0	0	561	1,431
57,250	57,300	0	0	0	553	0	0	1,140	2,010	60,050	60,100	0	0	0	0	0	0	550	1,420
57,300	57,350	0	0	0	542	0	0	1,130	2,000	60,100	60,150	0	0	0	0	0	0	540	1,410
57,350	57,400	0	0	0	532	0	0	1,119	1,989	60,150	60,200	0	0	0	0	0	0	529	1,399
57,400	57,450	0	0	0	521	0	0	1,108	1,978	60,200	60,250	0	0	0	0	0	0	519	1,389
57,450	57,500	0	0	0	511	0	0	1,098	1,968	60,250	60,300	0	0	0	0	0	0	508	1,378
57,500	57,550	0	0	0	500	0	0	1,087	1,957	60,300	60,350	0	0	0	0	0	0	498	1,368
57,550	57,600	0	0	0	490	0	0	1,077	1,947	60,350	60,400	0	0	0	0	0	0	487	1,357
57,600	57,650	0	0	0	479	0	0	1,066	1,936	60,400	60,450	0	0	0	0	0	0	477	1,347
57,650	57,700	0	0	0	468	0	0	1,056	1,926	60,450	60,500	0	0	0	0	0	0	466	1,336
57,700	57,750	0	0	0	458	0	0	1,045	1,915	60,500	60,550	0	0	0	0	0	0	456	1,326
57,750	57,800	0	0	0	447	0	0	1,035	1,905	60,550	60,600	0	0	0	0	0	0	445	1,315
57,800	57,850	0	0	0	437	0	0	1,024	1,894	60,600	60,650	0	0	0	0	0	0	435	1,305
57,850	57,900	0	0	0	426	0	0	1,014	1,884	60,650	60,700	0	0	0	0	0	0	424	1,294
57,900	57,950	0	0	0	416	0	0	1,003	1,873	60,700	60,750	0	0	0	0	0	0	413	1,283
57,950	58,000	0	0	0	405	0	0	993	1,863	60,750	60,800	0	0	0	0	0	0	403	1,273
58,000	58,050	0	0	0	395	0	0	982	1,852	60,800	60,850	0	0	0	0	0	0	392	1,262
58,050	58,100	0	0	0	384	0	0	972	1,842	60,850	60,900	0	0	0	0	0	0	382	1,252
58,100	58,150	0	0	0	374	0	0	961	1,831	60,900	60,950	0	0	0	0	0	0	371	1,241
58,150	58,200	0	0	0	363	0	0	951	1,821	60,950	61,000	0	0	0	0	0	0	361	1,231
58,200	58,250	0	0	0	353	0	0	940	1,810	61,000	61,050	0	0	0	0	0	0	350	1,220
58,250	58,300	0	0	0	342	0	0	929	1,799	61,050	61,100	0	0	0	0	0	0	340	1,210
58,300	58,350	0	0	0	332	0	0	919	1,789	61,100	61,150	0	0	0	0	0	0	329	1,199
58,350	58,400	0	0	0	321	0	0	908	1,778	61,150	61,200	0	0	0	0	0	0	319	1,189
58,400	58,450	0	0	0	311	0	0	898	1,768	61,200	61,250	0	0	0	0	0	0	308	1,178
58,450	58,500	0	0	0	300	0	0	887	1,757	61,250	61,300	0	0	0	0	0	0	298	1,168
58,500	58,550	0	0	0	289	0	0	877	1,747	61,300	61,350	0	0	0	0	0	0	287	1,157
58,550	58,600	0	0	0	279	0	0	866	1,736	61,350	61,400	0	0	0	0	0	0	277	1,147
58,600	58,650	0	0	0	268	0	0	856	1,726	61,400	61,450	0	0	0	0	0	0	266	1,136
58,650	58,700	0	0	0	258	0	0	845	1,715	61,450	61,500	0	0	0	0	0	0	256	1,126
58,700	58,750	0	0	0	247	0	0	835	1,705	61,500	61,550	0	0	0	0	0	0	245	1,115
58,750	58,800	0	0	0	237	0	0	824	1,694	61,550	61,600	0	0	0	0	0	0	234	1,104

★ Use this column if your filing status is married filing separately and you qualify to claim the EIC. See the instructions for line 27.

* If the amount you are looking up from the worksheet is at least $56,000 but less than $56,004, and you have one qualifying child who has a valid SSN, your credit is $0.

If the amount you are looking up from the worksheet is $56,004 or more, and you have one qualifying child who has a valid SSN, you can't take the credit.

** If the amount you are looking up from the worksheet is at least $59,850 but less than $59,899, and you have three qualifying children who have valid SSNs, your credit is $5.

If the amount you are looking up from the worksheet is $59,899 or more, and you have three qualifying children who have valid SSNs, you can't take the credit.

(Continued)

Earned Income Credit (EIC) Table - Continued

(**Caution.** This is **not** a tax table.)

If the amount you are looking up from the worksheet is–		And your filing status is–								If the amount you are looking up from the worksheet is–		And your filing status is–							
		Single, head of household, or qualifying surviving spouse★ and you have–				Married filing jointly and you have–						Single, head of household, or qualifying surviving spouse★ and you have–				Married filing jointly and you have–			
		0	1	2	3	0	1	2	3			0	1	2	3	0	1	2	3
At least	But less than	Your credit is–				Your credit is–				At least	But less than	Your credit is–				Your credit is–			
61,600	61,650	0	0	0	0	0	0	224	1,094	64,400	64,450	0	0	0	0	0	0	0	504
61,650	61,700	0	0	0	0	0	0	213	1,083	64,450	64,500	0	0	0	0	0	0	0	494
61,700	61,750	0	0	0	0	0	0	203	1,073	64,500	64,550	0	0	0	0	0	0	0	483
61,750	61,800	0	0	0	0	0	0	192	1,062	64,550	64,600	0	0	0	0	0	0	0	473
61,800	61,850	0	0	0	0	0	0	182	1,052	64,600	64,650	0	0	0	0	0	0	0	462
61,850	61,900	0	0	0	0	0	0	171	1,041	64,650	64,700	0	0	0	0	0	0	0	452
61,900	61,950	0	0	0	0	0	0	161	1,031	64,700	64,750	0	0	0	0	0	0	0	441
61,950	62,000	0	0	0	0	0	0	150	1,020	64,750	64,800	0	0	0	0	0	0	0	431
62,000	62,050	0	0	0	0	0	0	140	1,010	64,800	64,850	0	0	0	0	0	0	0	420
62,050	62,100	0	0	0	0	0	0	129	999	64,850	64,900	0	0	0	0	0	0	0	410
62,100	62,150	0	0	0	0	0	0	119	989	64,900	64,950	0	0	0	0	0	0	0	399
62,150	62,200	0	0	0	0	0	0	108	978	64,950	65,000	0	0	0	0	0	0	0	388
62,200	62,250	0	0	0	0	0	0	98	968	65,000	65,050	0	0	0	0	0	0	0	378
62,250	62,300	0	0	0	0	0	0	87	957	65,050	65,100	0	0	0	0	0	0	0	367
62,300	62,350	0	0	0	0	0	0	77	947	65,100	65,150	0	0	0	0	0	0	0	357
62,350	62,400	0	0	0	0	0	0	66	936	65,150	65,200	0	0	0	0	0	0	0	346
62,400	62,450	0	0	0	0	0	0	55	925	65,200	65,250	0	0	0	0	0	0	0	336
62,450	62,500	0	0	0	0	0	0	45	915	65,250	65,300	0	0	0	0	0	0	0	325
62,500	62,550	0	0	0	0	0	0	34	904	65,300	65,350	0	0	0	0	0	0	0	315
62,550	62,600	0	0	0	0	0	0	24	894	65,350	65,400	0	0	0	0	0	0	0	304
62,600	62,650	0	0	0	0	0	0	13	883	65,400	65,450	0	0	0	0	0	0	0	294
62,650	62,700	0	0	0	0	0	0	*	873	65,450	65,500	0	0	0	0	0	0	0	283
62,700	62,750	0	0	0	0	0	0	0	862	65,500	65,550	0	0	0	0	0	0	0	273
62,750	62,800	0	0	0	0	0	0	0	852	65,550	65,600	0	0	0	0	0	0	0	262
62,800	62,850	0	0	0	0	0	0	0	841	65,600	65,650	0	0	0	0	0	0	0	252
62,850	62,900	0	0	0	0	0	0	0	831	65,650	65,700	0	0	0	0	0	0	0	241
62,900	62,950	0	0	0	0	0	0	0	820	65,700	65,750	0	0	0	0	0	0	0	230
62,950	63,000	0	0	0	0	0	0	0	810	65,750	65,800	0	0	0	0	0	0	0	220
63,000	63,050	0	0	0	0	0	0	0	799	65,800	65,850	0	0	0	0	0	0	0	209
63,050	63,100	0	0	0	0	0	0	0	789	65,850	65,900	0	0	0	0	0	0	0	199
63,100	63,150	0	0	0	0	0	0	0	778	65,900	65,950	0	0	0	0	0	0	0	188
63,150	63,200	0	0	0	0	0	0	0	768	65,950	66,000	0	0	0	0	0	0	0	178
63,200	63,250	0	0	0	0	0	0	0	757	66,000	66,050	0	0	0	0	0	0	0	167
63,250	63,300	0	0	0	0	0	0	0	746	66,050	66,100	0	0	0	0	0	0	0	157
63,300	63,350	0	0	0	0	0	0	0	736	66,100	66,150	0	0	0	0	0	0	0	146
63,350	63,400	0	0	0	0	0	0	0	725	66,150	66,200	0	0	0	0	0	0	0	136
63,400	63,450	0	0	0	0	0	0	0	715	66,200	66,250	0	0	0	0	0	0	0	125
63,450	63,500	0	0	0	0	0	0	0	704	66,250	66,300	0	0	0	0	0	0	0	115
63,500	63,550	0	0	0	0	0	0	0	694	66,300	66,350	0	0	0	0	0	0	0	104
63,550	63,600	0	0	0	0	0	0	0	683	66,350	66,400	0	0	0	0	0	0	0	94
63,600	63,650	0	0	0	0	0	0	0	673	66,400	66,450	0	0	0	0	0	0	0	83
63,650	63,700	0	0	0	0	0	0	0	662	66,450	66,500	0	0	0	0	0	0	0	73
63,700	63,750	0	0	0	0	0	0	0	652	66,500	66,550	0	0	0	0	0	0	0	62
63,750	63,800	0	0	0	0	0	0	0	641	66,550	66,600	0	0	0	0	0	0	0	51
63,800	63,850	0	0	0	0	0	0	0	631	66,600	66,650	0	0	0	0	0	0	0	41
63,850	63,900	0	0	0	0	0	0	0	620	66,650	66,700	0	0	0	0	0	0	0	30
63,900	63,950	0	0	0	0	0	0	0	610	66,700	66,750	0	0	0	0	0	0	0	20
63,950	64,000	0	0	0	0	0	0	0	599	66,750	66,800	0	0	0	0	0	0	0	9
64,000	64,050	0	0	0	0	0	0	0	589	66,800	66,850	0	0	0	0	0	0	0	**
64,050	64,100	0	0	0	0	0	0	0	578										
64,100	64,150	0	0	0	0	0	0	0	567										
64,150	64,200	0	0	0	0	0	0	0	557										
64,200	64,250	0	0	0	0	0	0	0	546										
64,250	64,300	0	0	0	0	0	0	0	536										
64,300	64,350	0	0	0	0	0	0	0	525										
64,350	64,400	0	0	0	0	0	0	0	515										

★ Use this column if your filing status is married filing separately and you qualify to claim the EIC. See the instructions for line 27.

* If the amount you are looking up from the worksheet is at least $62,650 but less than $62,688, and you have two qualifying children who have valid SSNs, your credit is $4.

If the amount you are looking up from the worksheet is $62,688 or more, and you have two qualifying children who have valid SSNs, you can't take the credit.

** If the amount you are looking up from the worksheet is at least $66,800 but less than $66,819, and you have three qualifying children who have valid SSNs, your credit is $2.

If the amount you are looking up from the worksheet is $66,819 or more, and you have three qualifying children who have valid SSNs, you can't take the credit.

Appendix C

2024 Withholding Tables

Contents

Worksheet 2 and Semimonthly Pay Period Tables for Wage Bracket Method of Withholding (Form W-4 from 2020 or Later) C-2

Worksheet 3 and Semimonthly Pay Period Tables for Wage Bracket Method of Withholding (Form W-4 from 2019 or Earlier) C-6

Worksheet 4 and Tables for Percentage Method of Withholding (Form W-4 from 2020 or Later) C-15

Worksheet 5 and Tables for Percentage Method of Withholding (Form W-4 from 2019 or Earlier) C-17

2. Wage Bracket Method Tables for Manual Payroll Systems With Forms W-4 From 2020 or Later

If you compute payroll manually, your employee has submitted a Form W-4 for 2020 or later, and you prefer to use the Wage Bracket Method, use the worksheet below and the Wage Bracket Method tables that follow to figure federal income tax withholding.

These Wage Bracket Method tables cover a limited amount of annual wages (generally, less than $100,000). If you can't use the Wage Bracket Method tables because taxable wages exceed the amount from the last bracket of the table (based on filing status and pay period), use the Percentage Method tables in section 4.

Worksheet 2. Employer's Withholding Worksheet for Wage Bracket Method Tables for Manual Payroll Systems With Forms W-4 From 2020 or Later

Keep for Your Records

Table 5	Monthly	Semimonthly	Biweekly	Weekly	Daily
	12	24	26	52	260

Step 1. Adjust the employee's wage amount
- 1a Enter the employee's total taxable wages this payroll period .... 1a $ _____
- 1b Enter the number of pay periods you have per year (see Table 5) .... 1b _____
- 1c Enter the amount from Step 4(a) of the employee's Form W-4 .... 1c $ _____
- 1d Divide the amount on line 1c by the number of pay periods on line 1b .... 1d $ _____
- 1e Add lines 1a and 1d .... 1e $ _____
- 1f Enter the amount from Step 4(b) of the employee's Form W-4 .... 1f $ _____
- 1g Divide the amount on line 1f by the number of pay periods on line 1b .... 1g $ _____
- 1h Subtract line 1g from line 1e. If zero or less, enter -0-. This is the **Adjusted Wage Amount** ...... 1h $ _____

Step 2. Figure the Tentative Withholding Amount
- 2a Use the amount on line 1h to look up the tentative amount to withhold in the appropriate Wage Bracket Method table in this section for your pay frequency, given the employee's filing status and whether the employee has checked the box in Step 2 of Form W-4. This is the **Tentative Withholding Amount** .... 2a $ _____

Step 3. Account for tax credits
- 3a Enter the amount from Step 3 of the employee's Form W-4 .... 3a $ _____
- 3b Divide the amount on line 3a by the number of pay periods on line 1b .... 3b $ _____
- 3c Subtract line 3b from line 2a. If zero or less, enter -0- .... 3c $ _____

Step 4. Figure the final amount to withhold
- 4a Enter the additional amount to withhold from Step 4(c) of the employee's Form W-4 .... 4a $ _____
- 4b Add lines 3c and 4a. **This is the amount to withhold from the employee's wages this pay period** .... 4b $ _____

2024 Wage Bracket Method Tables for Manual Payroll Systems with Forms W-4 From 2020 or Later
SEMIMONTHLY Payroll Period

If the Adjusted Wage Amount (line 1h) is		Married Filing Jointly		Head of Household		Single or Married Filing Separately	
		Standard withholding	Form W-4, Step 2, Checkbox withholding	Standard withholding	Form W-4, Step 2, Checkbox withholding	Standard withholding	Form W-4, Step 2, Checkbox withholding
At least	But less than			The Tentative Withholding Amount is:			
$0	$305	$0	$0	$0	$0	$0	$0
$305	$315	$0	$0	$0	$0	$0	$1
$315	$325	$0	$0	$0	$0	$0	$2
$325	$335	$0	$0	$0	$0	$0	$3
$335	$345	$0	$0	$0	$0	$0	$4
$345	$355	$0	$0	$0	$0	$0	$5
$355	$365	$0	$0	$0	$0	$0	$6
$365	$375	$0	$0	$0	$0	$0	$7
$375	$385	$0	$0	$0	$0	$0	$8
$385	$395	$0	$0	$0	$0	$0	$9
$395	$405	$0	$0	$0	$0	$0	$10
$405	$415	$0	$0	$0	$0	$0	$11
$415	$425	$0	$0	$0	$0	$0	$12
$425	$435	$0	$0	$0	$0	$0	$13
$435	$445	$0	$0	$0	$0	$0	$14
$445	$455	$0	$0	$0	$0	$0	$15
$455	$465	$0	$0	$0	$0	$0	$16
$465	$475	$0	$0	$0	$1	$0	$17
$475	$485	$0	$0	$0	$2	$0	$18
$485	$495	$0	$0	$0	$3	$0	$19
$495	$505	$0	$0	$0	$4	$0	$20
$505	$515	$0	$0	$0	$5	$0	$21
$515	$525	$0	$0	$0	$6	$0	$22
$525	$535	$0	$0	$0	$7	$0	$23
$535	$545	$0	$0	$0	$8	$0	$24
$545	$555	$0	$0	$0	$9	$0	$25
$555	$570	$0	$0	$0	$11	$0	$26
$570	$585	$0	$0	$0	$12	$0	$28
$585	$600	$0	$0	$0	$14	$0	$30
$600	$615	$0	$0	$0	$15	$0	$32
$615	$630	$0	$1	$0	$17	$1	$33
$630	$645	$0	$3	$0	$18	$3	$35
$645	$660	$0	$4	$0	$20	$4	$37
$660	$675	$0	$6	$0	$21	$6	$39
$675	$690	$0	$7	$0	$23	$7	$41
$690	$705	$0	$9	$0	$24	$9	$42
$705	$720	$0	$10	$0	$26	$10	$44
$720	$735	$0	$12	$0	$27	$12	$46
$735	$750	$0	$13	$0	$29	$13	$48
$750	$765	$0	$15	$0	$30	$15	$50
$765	$780	$0	$16	$0	$32	$16	$51
$780	$795	$0	$18	$0	$33	$18	$53
$795	$810	$0	$19	$0	$35	$19	$55
$810	$825	$0	$21	$0	$36	$21	$57
$825	$840	$0	$22	$0	$38	$22	$59
$840	$855	$0	$24	$0	$40	$24	$60
$855	$870	$0	$25	$0	$42	$25	$62
$870	$885	$0	$27	$0	$44	$27	$64
$885	$900	$0	$28	$0	$45	$28	$66
$900	$915	$0	$30	$0	$47	$30	$68
$915	$930	$0	$31	$1	$49	$31	$69
$930	$945	$0	$33	$3	$51	$33	$71
$945	$960	$0	$34	$4	$53	$34	$73
$960	$975	$0	$36	$6	$54	$36	$75
$975	$990	$0	$37	$7	$56	$37	$77
$990	$1,005	$0	$39	$9	$58	$39	$78
$1,005	$1,020	$0	$40	$10	$60	$40	$80
$1,020	$1,035	$0	$42	$12	$62	$42	$82
$1,035	$1,050	$0	$43	$13	$63	$43	$84
$1,050	$1,065	$0	$45	$15	$65	$45	$86
$1,065	$1,080	$0	$46	$16	$67	$46	$87
$1,080	$1,095	$0	$48	$18	$69	$48	$89
$1,095	$1,110	$0	$50	$19	$71	$50	$91
$1,110	$1,125	$0	$51	$21	$72	$51	$93

2024 Wage Bracket Method Tables for Manual Payroll Systems with Forms W-4 From 2020 or Later
SEMIMONTHLY Payroll Period

If the Adjusted Wage Amount (line 1h) is		Married Filing Jointly		Head of Household		Single or Married Filing Separately	
At least	But less than	Standard withholding	Form W-4, Step 2, Checkbox withholding	Standard withholding	Form W-4, Step 2, Checkbox withholding	Standard withholding	Form W-4, Step 2, Checkbox withholding
				The Tentative Withholding Amount is:			
$1,125	$1,140	$0	$53	$22	$74	$53	$95
$1,140	$1,155	$0	$55	$24	$76	$55	$96
$1,155	$1,170	$0	$57	$25	$78	$57	$98
$1,170	$1,185	$0	$59	$27	$80	$59	$100
$1,185	$1,200	$0	$60	$28	$81	$60	$102
$1,200	$1,215	$0	$62	$30	$83	$62	$104
$1,215	$1,230	$1	$64	$31	$85	$64	$105
$1,230	$1,245	$2	$66	$33	$87	$66	$107
$1,245	$1,260	$4	$68	$34	$89	$68	$109
$1,260	$1,275	$5	$69	$36	$90	$69	$111
$1,275	$1,290	$7	$71	$37	$92	$71	$113
$1,290	$1,310	$8	$73	$39	$94	$73	$116
$1,310	$1,330	$10	$76	$41	$97	$76	$120
$1,330	$1,350	$12	$78	$43	$99	$78	$125
$1,350	$1,370	$14	$81	$45	$102	$81	$129
$1,370	$1,390	$16	$83	$47	$104	$83	$134
$1,390	$1,410	$18	$85	$49	$106	$85	$138
$1,410	$1,430	$20	$88	$51	$109	$88	$142
$1,430	$1,450	$22	$90	$53	$111	$90	$147
$1,450	$1,470	$24	$93	$55	$114	$93	$151
$1,470	$1,490	$26	$95	$57	$116	$95	$156
$1,490	$1,510	$28	$97	$59	$118	$97	$160
$1,510	$1,530	$30	$100	$61	$121	$100	$164
$1,530	$1,550	$32	$102	$63	$123	$102	$169
$1,550	$1,570	$34	$105	$65	$126	$105	$173
$1,570	$1,590	$36	$107	$67	$128	$107	$178
$1,590	$1,610	$38	$109	$69	$130	$109	$182
$1,610	$1,630	$40	$112	$71	$133	$112	$186
$1,630	$1,650	$42	$114	$74	$135	$114	$191
$1,650	$1,670	$44	$117	$76	$138	$117	$195
$1,670	$1,690	$46	$119	$78	$140	$119	$200
$1,690	$1,710	$48	$121	$81	$142	$121	$204
$1,710	$1,730	$50	$124	$83	$145	$124	$208
$1,730	$1,750	$52	$126	$86	$147	$126	$213
$1,750	$1,770	$54	$129	$88	$150	$129	$217
$1,770	$1,790	$56	$131	$90	$153	$131	$222
$1,790	$1,810	$58	$133	$93	$157	$133	$226
$1,810	$1,830	$60	$136	$95	$162	$136	$230
$1,830	$1,850	$62	$138	$98	$166	$138	$235
$1,850	$1,870	$64	$141	$100	$170	$141	$239
$1,870	$1,890	$66	$143	$102	$175	$143	$244
$1,890	$1,910	$68	$145	$105	$179	$145	$248
$1,910	$1,930	$70	$148	$107	$184	$148	$252
$1,930	$1,950	$72	$150	$110	$188	$150	$257
$1,950	$1,970	$74	$153	$112	$192	$153	$261
$1,970	$1,990	$76	$155	$114	$197	$155	$266
$1,990	$2,010	$78	$157	$117	$201	$157	$270
$2,010	$2,030	$80	$160	$119	$206	$160	$274
$2,030	$2,050	$82	$162	$122	$210	$162	$279
$2,050	$2,070	$84	$165	$124	$214	$165	$283
$2,070	$2,090	$86	$167	$126	$219	$167	$288
$2,090	$2,110	$88	$169	$129	$223	$169	$292
$2,110	$2,130	$90	$172	$131	$228	$172	$296
$2,130	$2,150	$92	$174	$134	$232	$174	$301
$2,150	$2,170	$94	$177	$136	$236	$177	$305
$2,170	$2,190	$96	$179	$138	$241	$179	$310
$2,190	$2,210	$99	$181	$141	$245	$181	$314
$2,210	$2,230	$101	$184	$143	$250	$184	$318
$2,230	$2,250	$103	$186	$146	$254	$186	$323
$2,250	$2,270	$106	$189	$148	$258	$189	$327
$2,270	$2,290	$108	$191	$150	$263	$191	$332
$2,290	$2,310	$111	$193	$153	$267	$193	$336
$2,310	$2,330	$113	$196	$155	$272	$196	$340
$2,330	$2,350	$115	$198	$158	$276	$198	$345
$2,350	$2,370	$118	$201	$160	$280	$201	$349

2024 Wage Bracket Method Tables for Manual Payroll Systems with Forms W-4 From 2020 or Later
SEMIMONTHLY Payroll Period

If the Adjusted Wage Amount (line 1h) is		Married Filing Jointly		Head of Household		Single or Married Filing Separately	
		Standard withholding	Form W-4, Step 2, Checkbox withholding	Standard withholding	Form W-4, Step 2, Checkbox withholding	Standard withholding	Form W-4, Step 2, Checkbox withholding
At least	But less than			The Tentative Withholding Amount is:			
$2,370	$2,390	$120	$203	$162	$285	$203	$354
$2,390	$2,410	$123	$205	$165	$289	$205	$358
$2,410	$2,445	$126	$209	$168	$295	$209	$365
$2,445	$2,480	$130	$213	$172	$303	$213	$373
$2,480	$2,515	$134	$217	$176	$311	$217	$381
$2,515	$2,550	$139	$221	$181	$318	$221	$390
$2,550	$2,585	$143	$225	$185	$326	$225	$398
$2,585	$2,620	$147	$233	$189	$335	$233	$407
$2,620	$2,655	$151	$240	$193	$343	$240	$415
$2,655	$2,690	$155	$248	$197	$352	$248	$423
$2,690	$2,725	$160	$256	$202	$360	$256	$432
$2,725	$2,760	$164	$263	$206	$368	$263	$440
$2,760	$2,795	$168	$271	$210	$377	$271	$449
$2,795	$2,830	$172	$279	$214	$385	$279	$457
$2,830	$2,865	$176	$286	$218	$394	$286	$465
$2,865	$2,900	$181	$294	$223	$402	$294	$474
$2,900	$2,935	$185	$302	$227	$410	$302	$482
$2,935	$2,970	$189	$310	$231	$419	$310	$491
$2,970	$3,005	$193	$317	$235	$427	$317	$499
$3,005	$3,040	$197	$325	$239	$436	$325	$507
$3,040	$3,075	$202	$333	$244	$444	$333	$516
$3,075	$3,110	$206	$340	$248	$452	$340	$524
$3,110	$3,145	$210	$348	$252	$461	$348	$533
$3,145	$3,180	$214	$356	$256	$469	$356	$541
$3,180	$3,215	$218	$363	$260	$478	$363	$549
$3,215	$3,250	$223	$371	$265	$486	$371	$558
$3,250	$3,285	$227	$379	$269	$494	$379	$566
$3,285	$3,320	$231	$387	$273	$503	$387	$575
$3,320	$3,355	$235	$394	$277	$511	$394	$583
$3,355	$3,390	$239	$402	$281	$520	$402	$591
$3,390	$3,425	$244	$410	$286	$528	$410	$600
$3,425	$3,460	$248	$417	$290	$536	$417	$608
$3,460	$3,495	$252	$425	$294	$545	$425	$617
$3,495	$3,530	$256	$433	$298	$553	$433	$625
$3,530	$3,565	$260	$440	$303	$562	$440	$633
$3,565	$3,600	$265	$448	$311	$570	$448	$642
$3,600	$3,635	$269	$456	$318	$578	$456	$650
$3,635	$3,670	$273	$464	$326	$587	$464	$659
$3,670	$3,705	$277	$471	$334	$595	$471	$667
$3,705	$3,740	$281	$479	$341	$604	$479	$675
$3,740	$3,775	$286	$487	$349	$612	$487	$684
$3,775	$3,810	$290	$494	$357	$620	$494	$692
$3,810	$3,845	$294	$502	$365	$629	$502	$701
$3,845	$3,880	$298	$510	$372	$637	$510	$709
$3,880	$3,915	$302	$517	$380	$646	$517	$717
$3,915	$3,950	$307	$525	$388	$654	$525	$726
$3,950	$3,985	$311	$533	$395	$662	$533	$734
$3,985	$4,020	$315	$541	$403	$671	$541	$743
$4,020	$4,055	$319	$548	$411	$679	$548	$751
$4,055	$4,090	$323	$556	$418	$688	$556	$759
$4,090	$4,125	$328	$564	$426	$696	$564	$768
$4,125	$4,160	$332	$571	$434	$704	$571	$776
$4,160	$4,195	$336	$579	$442	$713	$579	$785

3. Wage Bracket Method Tables for Manual Payroll Systems With Forms W-4 From 2019 or Earlier

If you compute payroll manually and your employee **has not** submitted a Form W-4 for 2020 or later, use the worksheet below and the Wage Bracket Method tables that follow to figure federal income tax withholding.

These Wage Bracket Method tables cover a limited amount of annual wages (generally, less than $100,000) and up to 10 allowances. If you can't use the Wage Bracket Method tables because taxable wages exceed the amount from the last bracket of the table (based on marital status and pay period) or the employee claimed more than 10 allowances, use the Percentage Method tables in section 5.

Periodic payments of pensions or annuities with a 2021 or earlier Form W-4P. In lieu of Worksheet 1B and the Percentage Method tables in section 1, you may use Worksheet 3 and the Wage Bracket Method tables in this section to figure federal income tax withholding on periodic payments of pensions or annuities with a 2021 or earlier Form W-4P. As an alternative, if you prefer to use the Percentage Method of withholding, you may use Worksheet 5 and the Percentage Method tables in section 5 to figure federal income tax withholding on periodic payments of pensions or annuities with a 2021 or earlier Form W-4P.

Worksheet 3. Employer's Withholding Worksheet for Wage Bracket Method Tables for Manual Payroll Systems With Forms W-4 From 2019 or Earlier

Keep for Your Records

Step 1.	Figure the Tentative Withholding Amount		
	1a Enter the employee's total taxable wages this payroll period	1a	$ _____
	1b Use the amount on line 1a to look up the tentative amount to withhold in the appropriate Wage Bracket Method table in this section for your pay frequency, given the employee's marital status (line 3 of Form W-4) and number of allowances claimed. This is the **Tentative Withholding Amount**	1b	$ _____
Step 2.	Figure the final amount to withhold		
	2a Enter the additional amount to withhold from line 6 of the employee's Form W-4	2a	$ _____
	2b Add lines 1b and 2a. **This is the amount to withhold from the employee's wages this pay period**	2b	$ _____

2024 Wage Bracket Method Tables for Manual Payroll Systems With Forms W-4 From 2019 or Earlier
SEMIMONTHLY Payroll Period

MARRIED Persons

If the Wage Amount (line 1a) is		And the number of allowances is:										
At least	But less than	0	1	2	3	4	5	6	7	8	9	10
		The Tentative Withholding Amount is:										
$0	$680	$0	$0	$0	$0	$0	$0	$0	$0	$0	$0	$0
$680	$690	$1	$0	$0	$0	$0	$0	$0	$0	$0	$0	$0
$690	$700	$2	$0	$0	$0	$0	$0	$0	$0	$0	$0	$0
$700	$710	$3	$0	$0	$0	$0	$0	$0	$0	$0	$0	$0
$710	$720	$4	$0	$0	$0	$0	$0	$0	$0	$0	$0	$0
$720	$730	$5	$0	$0	$0	$0	$0	$0	$0	$0	$0	$0
$730	$740	$6	$0	$0	$0	$0	$0	$0	$0	$0	$0	$0
$740	$750	$7	$0	$0	$0	$0	$0	$0	$0	$0	$0	$0
$750	$760	$8	$0	$0	$0	$0	$0	$0	$0	$0	$0	$0
$760	$770	$9	$0	$0	$0	$0	$0	$0	$0	$0	$0	$0
$770	$780	$10	$0	$0	$0	$0	$0	$0	$0	$0	$0	$0
$780	$790	$11	$0	$0	$0	$0	$0	$0	$0	$0	$0	$0
$790	$800	$12	$0	$0	$0	$0	$0	$0	$0	$0	$0	$0
$800	$810	$13	$0	$0	$0	$0	$0	$0	$0	$0	$0	$0
$810	$820	$14	$0	$0	$0	$0	$0	$0	$0	$0	$0	$0
$820	$830	$15	$0	$0	$0	$0	$0	$0	$0	$0	$0	$0
$830	$840	$16	$0	$0	$0	$0	$0	$0	$0	$0	$0	$0
$840	$850	$17	$0	$0	$0	$0	$0	$0	$0	$0	$0	$0
$850	$860	$18	$0	$0	$0	$0	$0	$0	$0	$0	$0	$0
$860	$870	$19	$1	$0	$0	$0	$0	$0	$0	$0	$0	$0
$870	$880	$20	$2	$0	$0	$0	$0	$0	$0	$0	$0	$0
$880	$890	$21	$3	$0	$0	$0	$0	$0	$0	$0	$0	$0
$890	$900	$22	$4	$0	$0	$0	$0	$0	$0	$0	$0	$0
$900	$910	$23	$5	$0	$0	$0	$0	$0	$0	$0	$0	$0
$910	$920	$24	$6	$0	$0	$0	$0	$0	$0	$0	$0	$0
$920	$930	$25	$7	$0	$0	$0	$0	$0	$0	$0	$0	$0
$930	$940	$26	$8	$0	$0	$0	$0	$0	$0	$0	$0	$0
$940	$950	$27	$9	$0	$0	$0	$0	$0	$0	$0	$0	$0
$950	$960	$28	$10	$0	$0	$0	$0	$0	$0	$0	$0	$0
$960	$970	$29	$11	$0	$0	$0	$0	$0	$0	$0	$0	$0
$970	$980	$30	$12	$0	$0	$0	$0	$0	$0	$0	$0	$0
$980	$990	$31	$13	$0	$0	$0	$0	$0	$0	$0	$0	$0
$990	$1,000	$32	$14	$0	$0	$0	$0	$0	$0	$0	$0	$0
$1,000	$1,010	$33	$15	$0	$0	$0	$0	$0	$0	$0	$0	$0
$1,010	$1,020	$34	$16	$0	$0	$0	$0	$0	$0	$0	$0	$0
$1,020	$1,030	$35	$17	$0	$0	$0	$0	$0	$0	$0	$0	$0
$1,030	$1,040	$36	$18	$0	$0	$0	$0	$0	$0	$0	$0	$0
$1,040	$1,050	$37	$19	$1	$0	$0	$0	$0	$0	$0	$0	$0
$1,050	$1,060	$38	$20	$2	$0	$0	$0	$0	$0	$0	$0	$0
$1,060	$1,070	$39	$21	$3	$0	$0	$0	$0	$0	$0	$0	$0
$1,070	$1,080	$40	$22	$4	$0	$0	$0	$0	$0	$0	$0	$0
$1,080	$1,090	$41	$23	$5	$0	$0	$0	$0	$0	$0	$0	$0
$1,090	$1,100	$42	$24	$6	$0	$0	$0	$0	$0	$0	$0	$0
$1,100	$1,110	$43	$25	$7	$0	$0	$0	$0	$0	$0	$0	$0
$1,110	$1,120	$44	$26	$8	$0	$0	$0	$0	$0	$0	$0	$0
$1,120	$1,130	$45	$27	$9	$0	$0	$0	$0	$0	$0	$0	$0
$1,130	$1,140	$46	$28	$10	$0	$0	$0	$0	$0	$0	$0	$0
$1,140	$1,150	$47	$29	$11	$0	$0	$0	$0	$0	$0	$0	$0
$1,150	$1,160	$48	$30	$12	$0	$0	$0	$0	$0	$0	$0	$0
$1,160	$1,170	$49	$31	$13	$0	$0	$0	$0	$0	$0	$0	$0
$1,170	$1,180	$50	$32	$14	$0	$0	$0	$0	$0	$0	$0	$0
$1,180	$1,190	$51	$33	$15	$0	$0	$0	$0	$0	$0	$0	$0

2024 Wage Bracket Method Tables for Manual Payroll Systems With Forms W-4 From 2019 or Earlier
SEMIMONTHLY Payroll Period

If the Wage Amount (line 1a) is		MARRIED Persons And the number of allowances is:										
At least	But less than	0	1	2	3	4	5	6	7	8	9	10
		The Tentative Withholding Amount is:										
$1,190	$1,200	$52	$34	$16	$0	$0	$0	$0	$0	$0	$0	$0
$1,200	$1,210	$53	$35	$17	$0	$0	$0	$0	$0	$0	$0	$0
$1,210	$1,220	$54	$36	$18	$0	$0	$0	$0	$0	$0	$0	$0
$1,220	$1,230	$55	$37	$19	$1	$0	$0	$0	$0	$0	$0	$0
$1,230	$1,240	$56	$38	$20	$2	$0	$0	$0	$0	$0	$0	$0
$1,240	$1,250	$57	$39	$21	$3	$0	$0	$0	$0	$0	$0	$0
$1,250	$1,260	$58	$40	$22	$4	$0	$0	$0	$0	$0	$0	$0
$1,260	$1,270	$59	$41	$23	$5	$0	$0	$0	$0	$0	$0	$0
$1,270	$1,280	$60	$42	$24	$6	$0	$0	$0	$0	$0	$0	$0
$1,280	$1,290	$61	$43	$25	$7	$0	$0	$0	$0	$0	$0	$0
$1,290	$1,300	$62	$44	$26	$8	$0	$0	$0	$0	$0	$0	$0
$1,300	$1,310	$63	$45	$27	$9	$0	$0	$0	$0	$0	$0	$0
$1,310	$1,320	$64	$46	$28	$10	$0	$0	$0	$0	$0	$0	$0
$1,320	$1,330	$65	$47	$29	$11	$0	$0	$0	$0	$0	$0	$0
$1,330	$1,340	$66	$48	$30	$12	$0	$0	$0	$0	$0	$0	$0
$1,340	$1,350	$67	$49	$31	$13	$0	$0	$0	$0	$0	$0	$0
$1,350	$1,360	$68	$50	$32	$14	$0	$0	$0	$0	$0	$0	$0
$1,360	$1,370	$69	$51	$33	$15	$0	$0	$0	$0	$0	$0	$0
$1,370	$1,380	$70	$52	$34	$16	$0	$0	$0	$0	$0	$0	$0
$1,380	$1,390	$71	$53	$35	$17	$0	$0	$0	$0	$0	$0	$0
$1,390	$1,400	$72	$54	$36	$18	$0	$0	$0	$0	$0	$0	$0
$1,400	$1,410	$73	$55	$37	$19	$1	$0	$0	$0	$0	$0	$0
$1,410	$1,420	$74	$56	$38	$20	$2	$0	$0	$0	$0	$0	$0
$1,420	$1,430	$75	$57	$39	$21	$3	$0	$0	$0	$0	$0	$0
$1,430	$1,440	$76	$58	$40	$22	$4	$0	$0	$0	$0	$0	$0
$1,440	$1,450	$77	$59	$41	$23	$5	$0	$0	$0	$0	$0	$0
$1,450	$1,460	$78	$60	$42	$24	$6	$0	$0	$0	$0	$0	$0
$1,460	$1,470	$79	$61	$43	$25	$7	$0	$0	$0	$0	$0	$0
$1,470	$1,480	$80	$62	$44	$26	$8	$0	$0	$0	$0	$0	$0
$1,480	$1,490	$81	$63	$45	$27	$9	$0	$0	$0	$0	$0	$0
$1,490	$1,500	$82	$64	$46	$28	$10	$0	$0	$0	$0	$0	$0
$1,500	$1,510	$83	$65	$47	$29	$11	$0	$0	$0	$0	$0	$0
$1,510	$1,520	$84	$66	$48	$30	$12	$0	$0	$0	$0	$0	$0
$1,520	$1,530	$85	$67	$49	$31	$13	$0	$0	$0	$0	$0	$0
$1,530	$1,540	$86	$68	$50	$32	$14	$0	$0	$0	$0	$0	$0
$1,540	$1,550	$87	$69	$51	$33	$15	$0	$0	$0	$0	$0	$0
$1,550	$1,560	$88	$70	$52	$34	$16	$0	$0	$0	$0	$0	$0
$1,560	$1,570	$89	$71	$53	$35	$17	$0	$0	$0	$0	$0	$0
$1,570	$1,580	$90	$72	$54	$36	$18	$0	$0	$0	$0	$0	$0
$1,580	$1,590	$91	$73	$55	$37	$19	$1	$0	$0	$0	$0	$0
$1,590	$1,600	$92	$74	$56	$38	$20	$2	$0	$0	$0	$0	$0
$1,600	$1,610	$93	$75	$57	$39	$21	$3	$0	$0	$0	$0	$0
$1,610	$1,620	$94	$76	$58	$40	$22	$4	$0	$0	$0	$0	$0
$1,620	$1,630	$95	$77	$59	$41	$23	$5	$0	$0	$0	$0	$0
$1,630	$1,640	$96	$78	$60	$42	$24	$6	$0	$0	$0	$0	$0
$1,640	$1,650	$97	$79	$61	$43	$25	$7	$0	$0	$0	$0	$0
$1,650	$1,700	$100	$82	$64	$46	$28	$10	$0	$0	$0	$0	$0
$1,700	$1,750	$106	$87	$69	$51	$33	$15	$0	$0	$0	$0	$0
$1,750	$1,800	$112	$92	$74	$56	$38	$20	$2	$0	$0	$0	$0
$1,800	$1,850	$118	$97	$79	$61	$43	$25	$7	$0	$0	$0	$0
$1,850	$1,900	$124	$103	$84	$66	$48	$30	$12	$0	$0	$0	$0
$1,900	$1,950	$130	$109	$89	$71	$53	$35	$17	$0	$0	$0	$0

2024 Wage Bracket Method Tables for Manual Payroll Systems With Forms W-4 From 2019 or Earlier
SEMIMONTHLY Payroll Period

MARRIED Persons

If the Wage Amount (line 1a) is		And the number of allowances is:									
At least	But less than	0	1	2	3	4	5	6	7	8	9	10
		The Tentative Withholding Amount is:										
$1,950	$2,000	$136	$115	$94	$76	$58	$40	$22	$4	$0	$0	$0
$2,000	$2,050	$142	$121	$99	$81	$63	$45	$27	$9	$0	$0	$0
$2,050	$2,100	$148	$127	$105	$86	$68	$50	$32	$14	$0	$0	$0
$2,100	$2,150	$154	$133	$111	$91	$73	$55	$37	$19	$1	$0	$0
$2,150	$2,200	$160	$139	$117	$96	$78	$60	$42	$24	$6	$0	$0
$2,200	$2,250	$166	$145	$123	$102	$83	$65	$47	$29	$11	$0	$0
$2,250	$2,300	$172	$151	$129	$108	$88	$70	$52	$34	$16	$0	$0
$2,300	$2,350	$178	$157	$135	$114	$93	$75	$57	$39	$21	$3	$0
$2,350	$2,400	$184	$163	$141	$120	$98	$80	$62	$44	$26	$8	$0
$2,400	$2,450	$190	$169	$147	$126	$104	$85	$67	$49	$31	$13	$0
$2,450	$2,500	$196	$175	$153	$132	$110	$90	$72	$54	$36	$18	$0
$2,500	$2,550	$202	$181	$159	$138	$116	$95	$77	$59	$41	$23	$5
$2,550	$2,600	$208	$187	$165	$144	$122	$101	$82	$64	$46	$28	$10
$2,600	$2,650	$214	$193	$171	$150	$128	$107	$87	$69	$51	$33	$15
$2,650	$2,700	$220	$199	$177	$156	$134	$113	$92	$74	$56	$38	$20
$2,700	$2,750	$226	$205	$183	$162	$140	$119	$97	$79	$61	$43	$25
$2,750	$2,800	$232	$211	$189	$168	$146	$125	$103	$84	$66	$48	$30
$2,800	$2,850	$238	$217	$195	$174	$152	$131	$109	$89	$71	$53	$35
$2,850	$2,900	$244	$223	$201	$180	$158	$137	$115	$94	$76	$58	$40
$2,900	$2,950	$250	$229	$207	$186	$164	$143	$121	$100	$81	$63	$45
$2,950	$3,000	$256	$235	$213	$192	$170	$149	$127	$106	$86	$68	$50
$3,000	$3,050	$262	$241	$219	$198	$176	$155	$133	$112	$91	$73	$55
$3,050	$3,100	$268	$247	$225	$204	$182	$161	$139	$118	$96	$78	$60
$3,100	$3,150	$274	$253	$231	$210	$188	$167	$145	$124	$102	$83	$65
$3,150	$3,200	$280	$259	$237	$216	$194	$173	$151	$130	$108	$88	$70
$3,200	$3,250	$286	$265	$243	$222	$200	$179	$157	$136	$114	$93	$75
$3,250	$3,300	$292	$271	$249	$228	$206	$185	$163	$142	$120	$99	$80
$3,300	$3,350	$298	$277	$255	$234	$212	$191	$169	$148	$126	$105	$85
$3,350	$3,400	$304	$283	$261	$240	$218	$197	$175	$154	$132	$111	$90
$3,400	$3,450	$310	$289	$267	$246	$224	$203	$181	$160	$138	$117	$95
$3,450	$3,500	$316	$295	$273	$252	$230	$209	$187	$166	$144	$123	$101
$3,500	$3,550	$322	$301	$279	$258	$236	$215	$193	$172	$150	$129	$107
$3,550	$3,600	$328	$307	$285	$264	$242	$221	$199	$178	$156	$135	$113
$3,600	$3,650	$334	$313	$291	$270	$248	$227	$205	$184	$162	$141	$119
$3,650	$3,700	$340	$319	$297	$276	$254	$233	$211	$190	$168	$147	$125
$3,700	$3,750	$346	$325	$303	$282	$260	$239	$217	$196	$174	$153	$131
$3,750	$3,800	$352	$331	$309	$288	$266	$245	$223	$202	$180	$159	$137
$3,800	$3,850	$358	$337	$315	$294	$272	$251	$229	$208	$186	$165	$143
$3,850	$3,900	$364	$343	$321	$300	$278	$257	$235	$214	$192	$171	$149
$3,900	$3,950	$370	$349	$327	$306	$284	$263	$241	$220	$198	$177	$155
$3,950	$4,000	$376	$355	$333	$312	$290	$269	$247	$226	$204	$183	$161
$4,000	$4,050	$382	$361	$339	$318	$296	$275	$253	$232	$210	$189	$167
$4,050	$4,100	$388	$367	$345	$324	$302	$281	$259	$238	$216	$195	$173
$4,100	$4,150	$394	$373	$351	$330	$308	$287	$265	$244	$222	$201	$179
$4,150	$4,200	$400	$379	$357	$336	$314	$293	$271	$250	$228	$207	$185

2024 Wage Bracket Method Tables for Manual Payroll Systems With Forms W-4 From 2019 or Earlier
SEMIMONTHLY Payroll Period

If the Wage Amount (line 1a) is		SINGLE Persons										
		And the number of allowances is:										
At least	But less than	0	1	2	3	4	5	6	7	8	9	10
		The Tentative Withholding Amount is:										
$0	$250	$0	$0	$0	$0	$0	$0	$0	$0	$0	$0	$0
$250	$260	$1	$0	$0	$0	$0	$0	$0	$0	$0	$0	$0
$260	$270	$2	$0	$0	$0	$0	$0	$0	$0	$0	$0	$0
$270	$280	$3	$0	$0	$0	$0	$0	$0	$0	$0	$0	$0
$280	$290	$4	$0	$0	$0	$0	$0	$0	$0	$0	$0	$0
$290	$300	$5	$0	$0	$0	$0	$0	$0	$0	$0	$0	$0
$300	$310	$6	$0	$0	$0	$0	$0	$0	$0	$0	$0	$0
$310	$320	$7	$0	$0	$0	$0	$0	$0	$0	$0	$0	$0
$320	$330	$8	$0	$0	$0	$0	$0	$0	$0	$0	$0	$0
$330	$340	$9	$0	$0	$0	$0	$0	$0	$0	$0	$0	$0
$340	$350	$10	$0	$0	$0	$0	$0	$0	$0	$0	$0	$0
$350	$360	$11	$0	$0	$0	$0	$0	$0	$0	$0	$0	$0
$360	$370	$12	$0	$0	$0	$0	$0	$0	$0	$0	$0	$0
$370	$380	$13	$0	$0	$0	$0	$0	$0	$0	$0	$0	$0
$380	$390	$14	$0	$0	$0	$0	$0	$0	$0	$0	$0	$0
$390	$400	$15	$0	$0	$0	$0	$0	$0	$0	$0	$0	$0
$400	$410	$16	$0	$0	$0	$0	$0	$0	$0	$0	$0	$0
$410	$420	$17	$0	$0	$0	$0	$0	$0	$0	$0	$0	$0
$420	$430	$18	$0	$0	$0	$0	$0	$0	$0	$0	$0	$0
$430	$440	$19	$1	$0	$0	$0	$0	$0	$0	$0	$0	$0
$440	$450	$20	$2	$0	$0	$0	$0	$0	$0	$0	$0	$0
$450	$460	$21	$3	$0	$0	$0	$0	$0	$0	$0	$0	$0
$460	$470	$22	$4	$0	$0	$0	$0	$0	$0	$0	$0	$0
$470	$480	$23	$5	$0	$0	$0	$0	$0	$0	$0	$0	$0
$480	$490	$24	$6	$0	$0	$0	$0	$0	$0	$0	$0	$0
$490	$500	$25	$7	$0	$0	$0	$0	$0	$0	$0	$0	$0
$500	$510	$26	$8	$0	$0	$0	$0	$0	$0	$0	$0	$0
$510	$520	$27	$9	$0	$0	$0	$0	$0	$0	$0	$0	$0
$520	$530	$28	$10	$0	$0	$0	$0	$0	$0	$0	$0	$0
$530	$540	$29	$11	$0	$0	$0	$0	$0	$0	$0	$0	$0
$540	$550	$30	$12	$0	$0	$0	$0	$0	$0	$0	$0	$0
$550	$560	$31	$13	$0	$0	$0	$0	$0	$0	$0	$0	$0
$560	$570	$32	$14	$0	$0	$0	$0	$0	$0	$0	$0	$0
$570	$580	$33	$15	$0	$0	$0	$0	$0	$0	$0	$0	$0
$580	$590	$34	$16	$0	$0	$0	$0	$0	$0	$0	$0	$0
$590	$600	$35	$17	$0	$0	$0	$0	$0	$0	$0	$0	$0
$600	$610	$36	$18	$0	$0	$0	$0	$0	$0	$0	$0	$0
$610	$620	$37	$19	$1	$0	$0	$0	$0	$0	$0	$0	$0
$620	$630	$38	$20	$2	$0	$0	$0	$0	$0	$0	$0	$0
$630	$640	$39	$21	$3	$0	$0	$0	$0	$0	$0	$0	$0
$640	$650	$40	$22	$4	$0	$0	$0	$0	$0	$0	$0	$0
$650	$660	$41	$23	$5	$0	$0	$0	$0	$0	$0	$0	$0
$660	$670	$42	$24	$6	$0	$0	$0	$0	$0	$0	$0	$0
$670	$680	$43	$25	$7	$0	$0	$0	$0	$0	$0	$0	$0
$680	$690	$44	$26	$8	$0	$0	$0	$0	$0	$0	$0	$0
$690	$700	$45	$27	$9	$0	$0	$0	$0	$0	$0	$0	$0
$700	$710	$46	$28	$10	$0	$0	$0	$0	$0	$0	$0	$0
$710	$720	$47	$29	$11	$0	$0	$0	$0	$0	$0	$0	$0
$720	$730	$48	$30	$12	$0	$0	$0	$0	$0	$0	$0	$0
$730	$780	$51	$33	$15	$0	$0	$0	$0	$0	$0	$0	$0
$780	$830	$57	$38	$20	$2	$0	$0	$0	$0	$0	$0	$0
$830	$880	$63	$43	$25	$7	$0	$0	$0	$0	$0	$0	$0

2024 Wage Bracket Method Tables for Manual Payroll Systems With Forms W-4 From 2019 or Earlier
SEMIMONTHLY Payroll Period

SINGLE Persons

If the Wage Amount (line 1a) is		And the number of allowances is:										
At least	But less than	0	1	2	3	4	5	6	7	8	9	10
		The Tentative Withholding Amount is:										
$880	$930	$69	$48	$30	$12	$0	$0	$0	$0	$0	$0	$0
$930	$980	$75	$53	$35	$17	$0	$0	$0	$0	$0	$0	$0
$980	$1,030	$81	$59	$40	$22	$4	$0	$0	$0	$0	$0	$0
$1,030	$1,080	$87	$65	$45	$27	$9	$0	$0	$0	$0	$0	$0
$1,080	$1,130	$93	$71	$50	$32	$14	$0	$0	$0	$0	$0	$0
$1,130	$1,180	$99	$77	$56	$37	$19	$1	$0	$0	$0	$0	$0
$1,180	$1,230	$105	$83	$62	$42	$24	$6	$0	$0	$0	$0	$0
$1,230	$1,280	$111	$89	$68	$47	$29	$11	$0	$0	$0	$0	$0
$1,280	$1,330	$117	$95	$74	$52	$34	$16	$0	$0	$0	$0	$0
$1,330	$1,380	$123	$101	$80	$58	$39	$21	$3	$0	$0	$0	$0
$1,380	$1,430	$129	$107	$86	$64	$44	$26	$8	$0	$0	$0	$0
$1,430	$1,480	$135	$113	$92	$70	$49	$31	$13	$0	$0	$0	$0
$1,480	$1,530	$141	$119	$98	$76	$55	$36	$18	$0	$0	$0	$0
$1,530	$1,580	$147	$125	$104	$82	$61	$41	$23	$5	$0	$0	$0
$1,580	$1,630	$153	$131	$110	$88	$67	$46	$28	$10	$0	$0	$0
$1,630	$1,680	$159	$137	$116	$94	$73	$51	$33	$15	$0	$0	$0
$1,680	$1,730	$165	$143	$122	$100	$79	$57	$38	$20	$2	$0	$0
$1,730	$1,780	$171	$149	$128	$106	$85	$63	$43	$25	$7	$0	$0
$1,780	$1,830	$177	$155	$134	$112	$91	$69	$48	$30	$12	$0	$0
$1,830	$1,880	$183	$161	$140	$118	$97	$75	$54	$35	$17	$0	$0
$1,880	$1,930	$189	$167	$146	$124	$103	$81	$60	$40	$22	$4	$0
$1,930	$1,980	$195	$173	$152	$130	$109	$87	$66	$45	$27	$9	$0
$1,980	$2,030	$201	$179	$158	$136	$115	$93	$72	$50	$32	$14	$0
$2,030	$2,080	$207	$185	$164	$142	$121	$99	$78	$56	$37	$19	$1
$2,080	$2,130	$213	$191	$170	$148	$127	$105	$84	$62	$42	$24	$6
$2,130	$2,180	$219	$197	$176	$154	$133	$111	$90	$68	$47	$29	$11
$2,180	$2,230	$225	$203	$182	$160	$139	$117	$96	$74	$53	$34	$16
$2,230	$2,270	$234	$209	$187	$166	$144	$123	$101	$80	$58	$39	$21
$2,270	$2,310	$243	$214	$192	$171	$149	$128	$106	$85	$63	$43	$25
$2,310	$2,350	$251	$218	$197	$175	$154	$132	$111	$89	$68	$47	$29
$2,350	$2,390	$260	$223	$202	$180	$159	$137	$116	$94	$73	$51	$33
$2,390	$2,430	$269	$230	$207	$185	$164	$142	$121	$99	$78	$56	$37
$2,430	$2,470	$278	$238	$211	$190	$168	$147	$125	$104	$82	$61	$41
$2,470	$2,510	$287	$247	$216	$195	$173	$152	$130	$109	$87	$66	$45
$2,510	$2,550	$295	$256	$221	$199	$178	$156	$135	$113	$92	$70	$49
$2,550	$2,590	$304	$265	$226	$204	$183	$161	$140	$118	$97	$75	$54
$2,590	$2,630	$313	$274	$234	$209	$188	$166	$145	$123	$102	$80	$59
$2,630	$2,670	$322	$282	$243	$214	$192	$171	$149	$128	$106	$85	$63
$2,670	$2,710	$331	$291	$252	$219	$197	$176	$154	$133	$111	$90	$68
$2,710	$2,750	$339	$300	$261	$223	$202	$180	$159	$137	$116	$94	$73
$2,750	$2,790	$348	$309	$269	$230	$207	$185	$164	$142	$121	$99	$78
$2,790	$2,830	$357	$318	$278	$239	$212	$190	$169	$147	$126	$104	$83
$2,830	$2,870	$366	$326	$287	$248	$216	$195	$173	$152	$130	$109	$87
$2,870	$2,910	$375	$335	$296	$256	$221	$200	$178	$157	$135	$114	$92
$2,910	$2,950	$383	$344	$305	$265	$226	$204	$183	$161	$140	$118	$97
$2,950	$2,990	$392	$353	$313	$274	$235	$209	$188	$166	$145	$123	$102
$2,990	$3,030	$401	$362	$322	$283	$243	$214	$193	$171	$150	$128	$107
$3,030	$3,070	$410	$370	$331	$292	$252	$219	$197	$176	$154	$133	$111
$3,070	$3,110	$419	$379	$340	$300	$261	$224	$202	$181	$159	$138	$116
$3,110	$3,150	$427	$388	$349	$309	$270	$230	$207	$185	$164	$142	$121
$3,150	$3,190	$436	$397	$357	$318	$279	$239	$212	$190	$169	$147	$126
$3,190	$3,230	$445	$406	$366	$327	$287	$248	$217	$195	$174	$152	$131

2024 Wage Bracket Method Tables for Manual Payroll Systems With Forms W-4 From 2019 or Earlier
SEMIMONTHLY Payroll Period

If the Wage Amount (line 1a) is		SINGLE Persons									
		And the number of allowances is:									
At least	But less than	0	1	2	3	4	5	6	7	8	9	10
		The Tentative Withholding Amount is:									
$3,230	$3,270	$454	$414	$375	$336	$296	$257	$221	$200	$178	$157	$135
$3,270	$3,310	$463	$423	$384	$344	$305	$266	$226	$205	$183	$162	$140
$3,310	$3,350	$471	$432	$393	$353	$314	$274	$235	$209	$188	$166	$145
$3,350	$3,390	$480	$441	$401	$362	$323	$283	$244	$214	$193	$171	$150
$3,390	$3,430	$489	$450	$410	$371	$331	$292	$253	$219	$198	$176	$155
$3,430	$3,470	$498	$458	$419	$380	$340	$301	$261	$224	$202	$181	$159
$3,470	$3,510	$507	$467	$428	$388	$349	$310	$270	$231	$207	$186	$164
$3,510	$3,550	$515	$476	$437	$397	$358	$318	$279	$240	$212	$190	$169
$3,550	$3,590	$524	$485	$445	$406	$367	$327	$288	$248	$217	$195	$174
$3,590	$3,630	$533	$494	$454	$415	$375	$336	$297	$257	$222	$200	$179
$3,630	$3,670	$542	$502	$463	$424	$384	$345	$305	$266	$227	$205	$183
$3,670	$3,710	$551	$511	$472	$432	$393	$354	$314	$275	$235	$210	$188
$3,710	$3,750	$559	$520	$481	$441	$402	$362	$323	$284	$244	$214	$193
$3,750	$3,790	$568	$529	$489	$450	$411	$371	$332	$292	$253	$219	$198
$3,790	$3,830	$577	$538	$498	$459	$419	$380	$341	$301	$262	$224	$203
$3,830	$3,870	$586	$546	$507	$468	$428	$389	$349	$310	$271	$231	$207
$3,870	$3,910	$595	$555	$516	$476	$437	$398	$358	$319	$279	$240	$212
$3,910	$3,950	$603	$564	$525	$485	$446	$406	$367	$328	$288	$249	$217
$3,950	$3,990	$612	$573	$533	$494	$455	$415	$376	$336	$297	$258	$222
$3,990	$4,030	$621	$582	$542	$503	$463	$424	$385	$345	$306	$266	$227
$4,030	$4,070	$630	$590	$551	$512	$472	$433	$393	$354	$315	$275	$236
$4,070	$4,110	$639	$599	$560	$520	$481	$442	$402	$363	$323	$284	$245
$4,110	$4,150	$647	$608	$569	$529	$490	$450	$411	$372	$332	$293	$253
$4,150	$4,190	$656	$617	$577	$538	$499	$459	$420	$380	$341	$302	$262

2024 Wage Bracket Method Tables for Manual Payroll Systems With Forms W-4 From 2019 or Earlier
MONTHLY Payroll Period

If the Wage Amount (line 1a) is		MARRIED Persons And the number of allowances is:									
At least	But less than	0	1	2	3	4	5	6	7	8	9	10
		The Tentative Withholding Amount is:										
$0	$1,360	$0	$0	$0	$0	$0	$0	$0	$0	$0	$0	$0
$1,360	$1,400	$2	$0	$0	$0	$0	$0	$0	$0	$0	$0	$0
$1,400	$1,440	$6	$0	$0	$0	$0	$0	$0	$0	$0	$0	$0
$1,440	$1,480	$10	$0	$0	$0	$0	$0	$0	$0	$0	$0	$0
$1,480	$1,520	$14	$0	$0	$0	$0	$0	$0	$0	$0	$0	$0
$1,520	$1,560	$18	$0	$0	$0	$0	$0	$0	$0	$0	$0	$0
$1,560	$1,600	$22	$0	$0	$0	$0	$0	$0	$0	$0	$0	$0
$1,600	$1,640	$26	$0	$0	$0	$0	$0	$0	$0	$0	$0	$0
$1,640	$1,680	$30	$0	$0	$0	$0	$0	$0	$0	$0	$0	$0
$1,680	$1,720	$34	$0	$0	$0	$0	$0	$0	$0	$0	$0	$0
$1,720	$1,760	$38	$2	$0	$0	$0	$0	$0	$0	$0	$0	$0
$1,760	$1,800	$42	$6	$0	$0	$0	$0	$0	$0	$0	$0	$0
$1,800	$1,840	$46	$10	$0	$0	$0	$0	$0	$0	$0	$0	$0
$1,840	$1,880	$50	$14	$0	$0	$0	$0	$0	$0	$0	$0	$0
$1,880	$1,920	$54	$18	$0	$0	$0	$0	$0	$0	$0	$0	$0
$1,920	$1,960	$58	$22	$0	$0	$0	$0	$0	$0	$0	$0	$0
$1,960	$2,000	$62	$26	$0	$0	$0	$0	$0	$0	$0	$0	$0
$2,000	$2,040	$66	$30	$0	$0	$0	$0	$0	$0	$0	$0	$0
$2,040	$2,080	$70	$34	$0	$0	$0	$0	$0	$0	$0	$0	$0
$2,080	$2,120	$74	$38	$3	$0	$0	$0	$0	$0	$0	$0	$0
$2,120	$2,160	$78	$42	$7	$0	$0	$0	$0	$0	$0	$0	$0
$2,160	$2,200	$82	$46	$11	$0	$0	$0	$0	$0	$0	$0	$0
$2,200	$2,240	$86	$50	$15	$0	$0	$0	$0	$0	$0	$0	$0
$2,240	$2,280	$90	$54	$19	$0	$0	$0	$0	$0	$0	$0	$0
$2,280	$2,320	$94	$58	$23	$0	$0	$0	$0	$0	$0	$0	$0
$2,320	$2,360	$98	$62	$27	$0	$0	$0	$0	$0	$0	$0	$0
$2,360	$2,400	$102	$66	$31	$0	$0	$0	$0	$0	$0	$0	$0
$2,400	$2,440	$106	$70	$35	$0	$0	$0	$0	$0	$0	$0	$0
$2,440	$2,480	$110	$74	$39	$3	$0	$0	$0	$0	$0	$0	$0
$2,480	$2,520	$114	$78	$43	$7	$0	$0	$0	$0	$0	$0	$0
$2,520	$2,560	$118	$82	$47	$11	$0	$0	$0	$0	$0	$0	$0
$2,560	$2,600	$122	$86	$51	$15	$0	$0	$0	$0	$0	$0	$0
$2,600	$2,640	$126	$90	$55	$19	$0	$0	$0	$0	$0	$0	$0
$2,640	$2,680	$130	$94	$59	$23	$0	$0	$0	$0	$0	$0	$0
$2,680	$2,720	$134	$98	$63	$27	$0	$0	$0	$0	$0	$0	$0
$2,720	$2,760	$138	$102	$67	$31	$0	$0	$0	$0	$0	$0	$0
$2,760	$2,800	$142	$106	$71	$35	$0	$0	$0	$0	$0	$0	$0
$2,800	$2,840	$146	$110	$75	$39	$3	$0	$0	$0	$0	$0	$0
$2,840	$2,880	$150	$114	$79	$43	$7	$0	$0	$0	$0	$0	$0
$2,880	$2,920	$154	$118	$83	$47	$11	$0	$0	$0	$0	$0	$0
$2,920	$2,960	$158	$122	$87	$51	$15	$0	$0	$0	$0	$0	$0
$2,960	$3,000	$162	$126	$91	$55	$19	$0	$0	$0	$0	$0	$0
$3,000	$3,040	$166	$130	$95	$59	$23	$0	$0	$0	$0	$0	$0
$3,040	$3,080	$170	$134	$99	$63	$27	$0	$0	$0	$0	$0	$0
$3,080	$3,120	$174	$138	$103	$67	$31	$0	$0	$0	$0	$0	$0
$3,120	$3,160	$178	$142	$107	$71	$35	$0	$0	$0	$0	$0	$0
$3,160	$3,200	$182	$146	$111	$75	$39	$3	$0	$0	$0	$0	$0
$3,200	$3,240	$186	$150	$115	$79	$43	$7	$0	$0	$0	$0	$0
$3,240	$3,280	$190	$154	$119	$83	$47	$11	$0	$0	$0	$0	$0
$3,280	$3,320	$194	$158	$123	$87	$51	$15	$0	$0	$0	$0	$0
$3,320	$3,380	$200	$163	$128	$92	$56	$20	$0	$0	$0	$0	$0
$3,380	$3,440	$208	$169	$134	$98	$62	$26	$0	$0	$0	$0	$0

2024 Wage Bracket Method Tables for Manual Payroll Systems With Forms W-4 From 2019 or Earlier
MONTHLY Payroll Period

If the Wage Amount (line 1a) is		MARRIED Persons									
		And the number of allowances is:									
At least	But less than	0	1	2	3	4	5	6	7	8	9	10
		The Tentative Withholding Amount is:									
$3,440	$3,500	$215	$175	$140	$104	$68	$32	$0	$0	$0	$0	$0
$3,500	$3,560	$222	$181	$146	$110	$74	$38	$2	$0	$0	$0	$0
$3,560	$3,620	$229	$187	$152	$116	$80	$44	$8	$0	$0	$0	$0
$3,620	$3,680	$236	$193	$158	$122	$86	$50	$14	$0	$0	$0	$0
$3,680	$3,740	$244	$201	$164	$128	$92	$56	$20	$0	$0	$0	$0
$3,740	$3,800	$251	$208	$170	$134	$98	$62	$26	$0	$0	$0	$0
$3,800	$3,860	$258	$215	$176	$140	$104	$68	$32	$0	$0	$0	$0
$3,860	$3,920	$265	$222	$182	$146	$110	$74	$38	$2	$0	$0	$0
$3,920	$3,980	$272	$229	$188	$152	$116	$80	$44	$8	$0	$0	$0
$3,980	$4,040	$280	$237	$194	$158	$122	$86	$50	$14	$0	$0	$0
$4,040	$4,100	$287	$244	$201	$164	$128	$92	$56	$20	$0	$0	$0
$4,100	$4,160	$294	$251	$208	$170	$134	$98	$62	$26	$0	$0	$0
$4,160	$4,220	$301	$258	$215	$176	$140	$104	$68	$32	$0	$0	$0
$4,220	$4,280	$308	$265	$222	$182	$146	$110	$74	$38	$3	$0	$0
$4,280	$4,340	$316	$273	$230	$188	$152	$116	$80	$44	$9	$0	$0
$4,340	$4,400	$323	$280	$237	$194	$158	$122	$86	$50	$15	$0	$0
$4,400	$4,460	$330	$287	$244	$201	$164	$128	$92	$56	$21	$0	$0
$4,460	$4,520	$337	$294	$251	$208	$170	$134	$98	$62	$27	$0	$0
$4,520	$4,580	$344	$301	$258	$215	$176	$140	$104	$68	$33	$0	$0
$4,580	$4,640	$352	$309	$266	$223	$182	$146	$110	$74	$39	$3	$0
$4,640	$4,700	$359	$316	$273	$230	$188	$152	$116	$80	$45	$9	$0
$4,700	$4,760	$366	$323	$280	$237	$194	$158	$122	$86	$51	$15	$0
$4,760	$4,820	$373	$330	$287	$244	$201	$164	$128	$92	$57	$21	$0
$4,820	$4,880	$380	$337	$294	$251	$208	$170	$134	$98	$63	$27	$0
$4,880	$4,940	$388	$345	$302	$259	$216	$176	$140	$104	$69	$33	$0
$4,940	$5,000	$395	$352	$309	$266	$223	$182	$146	$110	$75	$39	$3
$5,000	$5,060	$402	$359	$316	$273	$230	$188	$152	$116	$81	$45	$9
$5,060	$5,120	$409	$366	$323	$280	$237	$194	$158	$122	$87	$51	$15
$5,120	$5,180	$416	$373	$330	$287	$244	$201	$164	$128	$93	$57	$21
$5,180	$5,240	$424	$381	$338	$295	$252	$209	$170	$134	$99	$63	$27
$5,240	$5,300	$431	$388	$345	$302	$259	$216	$176	$140	$105	$69	$33
$5,300	$5,360	$438	$395	$352	$309	$266	$223	$182	$146	$111	$75	$39
$5,360	$5,420	$445	$402	$359	$316	$273	$230	$188	$152	$117	$81	$45
$5,420	$5,480	$452	$409	$366	$323	$280	$237	$194	$158	$123	$87	$51
$5,480	$5,540	$460	$417	$374	$331	$288	$245	$202	$164	$129	$93	$57
$5,540	$5,600	$467	$424	$381	$338	$295	$252	$209	$170	$135	$99	$63
$5,600	$5,660	$474	$431	$388	$345	$302	$259	$216	$176	$141	$105	$69
$5,660	$5,720	$481	$438	$395	$352	$309	$266	$223	$182	$147	$111	$75
$5,720	$5,780	$488	$445	$402	$359	$316	$273	$230	$188	$153	$117	$81
$5,780	$5,840	$496	$453	$410	$367	$324	$281	$238	$195	$159	$123	$87
$5,840	$5,900	$503	$460	$417	$374	$331	$288	$245	$202	$165	$129	$93
$5,900	$5,960	$510	$467	$424	$381	$338	$295	$252	$209	$171	$135	$99
$5,960	$6,020	$517	$474	$431	$388	$345	$302	$259	$216	$177	$141	$105
$6,020	$6,080	$524	$481	$438	$395	$352	$309	$266	$223	$183	$147	$111
$6,080	$6,140	$532	$489	$446	$403	$360	$317	$274	$231	$189	$153	$117
$6,140	$6,200	$539	$496	$453	$410	$367	$324	$281	$238	$195	$159	$123
$6,200	$6,260	$546	$503	$460	$417	$374	$331	$288	$245	$202	$165	$129
$6,260	$6,320	$553	$510	$467	$424	$381	$338	$295	$252	$209	$171	$135
$6,320	$6,380	$560	$517	$474	$431	$388	$345	$302	$259	$216	$177	$141
$6,380	$6,440	$568	$525	$482	$439	$396	$353	$310	$267	$224	$183	$147
$6,440	$6,500	$575	$532	$489	$446	$403	$360	$317	$274	$231	$189	$153
$6,500	$6,560	$582	$539	$496	$453	$410	$367	$324	$281	$238	$195	$159

4. Percentage Method Tables for Manual Payroll Systems With Forms W-4 From 2020 or Later

If you compute payroll manually, your employee has submitted a Form W-4 for 2020 or later, and you prefer to use the Percentage Method or you can't use the Wage Bracket Method tables because the employee's annual wages exceed the amount from the last bracket of the table (based on marital status and pay period), use the worksheet below and the Percentage Method tables that follow to figure federal income tax withholding. This method works for any amount of wages.

Worksheet 4. Employer's Withholding Worksheet for Percentage Method Tables for Manual Payroll Systems With Forms W-4 From 2020 or Later

Keep for Your Records

Table 6	Monthly	Semimonthly	Biweekly	Weekly	Daily
	12	24	26	52	260

Step 1. Adjust the employee's wage amount
- 1a Enter the employee's total taxable wages this payroll period .... 1a $ _____
- 1b Enter the number of pay periods you have per year (see Table 6) .... 1b _____
- 1c Enter the amount from Step 4(a) of the employee's Form W-4 .... 1c $ _____
- 1d Divide line 1c by the number on line 1b .... 1d $ _____
- 1e Add lines 1a and 1d .... 1e $ _____
- 1f Enter the amount from Step 4(b) of the employee's Form W-4 .... 1f $ _____
- 1g Divide line 1f by the number on line 1b .... 1g $ _____
- 1h Subtract line 1g from line 1e. If zero or less, enter -0-. This is the **Adjusted Wage Amount** ...... 1h $ _____

Step 2. Figure the Tentative Withholding Amount
based on your pay frequency, the employee's Adjusted Wage Amount, filing status (Step 1(c) of Form W-4), and whether the box in Step 2 of Form W-4 is checked.

- 2a Find the row in the STANDARD Withholding Rate Schedules (if the box in Step 2 of Form W-4 is NOT checked) or the Form W-4, Step 2, Checkbox, Withholding Rate Schedules (if it HAS been checked) of the Percentage Method tables in this section in which the amount on line 1h is at least the amount in column A but less than the amount in column B, and then enter here the amount from column A of that row .... 2a $ _____
- 2b Enter the amount from column C of that row .... 2b $ _____
- 2c Enter the percentage from column D of that row .... 2c _____ %
- 2d Subtract line 2a from line 1h .... 2d $ _____
- 2e Multiply the amount on line 2d by the percentage on line 2c .... 2e $ _____
- 2f Add lines 2b and 2e. This is the **Tentative Withholding Amount** .... 2f $ _____

Step 3. Account for tax credits
- 3a Enter the amount from Step 3 of the employee's Form W-4 .... 3a $ _____
- 3b Divide the amount on line 3a by the number of pay periods on line 1b .... 3b $ _____
- 3c Subtract line 3b from line 2f. If zero or less, enter -0- .... 3c $ _____

Step 4. Figure the final amount to withhold
- 4a Enter the additional amount to withhold from Step 4(c) of the employee's Form W-4 .... 4a $ _____
- 4b Add lines 3c and 4a. **This is the amount to withhold from the employee's wages this pay period** .... 4b $ _____

2024 Percentage Method Tables for Manual Payroll Systems With Forms W-4 from 2020 or Later
SEMIMONTHLY Payroll Period

STANDARD Withholding Rate Schedules (Use these if the box in Step 2 of Form W-4 is NOT checked)					Form W-4, Step 2, Checkbox, Withholding Rate Schedules (Use these if the box in Step 2 of Form W-4 IS checked)				
If the Adjusted Wage Amount (line 1h) is:		The tentative amount to withhold is:	Plus this percentage—	of the amount that the Adjusted Wage exceeds—	If the Adjusted Wage Amount (line 1h) is:		The tentative amount to withhold is:	Plus this percentage—	of the amount that the Adjusted Wage exceeds—
At least—	But less than—				At least—	But less than—			
A	B	C	D	E	A	B	C	D	E
Married Filing Jointly					**Married Filing Jointly**				
$0	$1,217	$0.00	0%	$0	$0	$608	$0.00	0%	$0
$1,217	$2,183	$0.00	10%	$1,217	$608	$1,092	$0.00	10%	$608
$2,183	$5,146	$96.60	12%	$2,183	$1,092	$2,573	$48.40	12%	$1,092
$5,146	$9,594	$452.16	22%	$5,146	$2,573	$4,797	$226.12	22%	$2,573
$9,594	$17,213	$1,430.72	24%	$9,594	$4,797	$8,606	$715.40	24%	$4,797
$17,213	$21,527	$3,259.28	32%	$17,213	$8,606	$10,764	$1,629.56	32%	$8,606
$21,527	$31,683	$4,639.76	35%	$21,527	$10,764	$15,842	$2,320.12	35%	$10,764
$31,683		$8,194.36	37%	$31,683	$15,842		$4,097.42	37%	$15,842
Single or Married Filing Separately					**Single or Married Filing Separately**				
$0	$608	$0.00	0%	$0	$0	$304	$0.00	0%	$0
$608	$1,092	$0.00	10%	$608	$304	$546	$0.00	10%	$304
$1,092	$2,573	$48.40	12%	$1,092	$546	$1,286	$24.20	12%	$546
$2,573	$4,797	$226.12	22%	$2,573	$1,286	$2,398	$113.00	22%	$1,286
$4,797	$8,606	$715.40	24%	$4,797	$2,398	$4,303	$357.64	24%	$2,398
$8,606	$10,764	$1,629.56	32%	$8,606	$4,303	$5,382	$814.84	32%	$4,303
$10,764	$25,998	$2,320.12	35%	$10,764	$5,382	$12,999	$1,160.12	35%	$5,382
$25,998		$7,652.02	37%	$25,998	$12,999		$3,826.07	37%	$12,999
Head of Household					**Head of Household**				
$0	$913	$0.00	0%	$0	$0	$456	$0.00	0%	$0
$913	$1,602	$0.00	10%	$913	$456	$801	$0.00	10%	$456
$1,602	$3,542	$68.90	12%	$1,602	$801	$1,771	$34.50	12%	$801
$3,542	$5,100	$301.70	22%	$3,542	$1,771	$2,550	$150.90	22%	$1,771
$5,100	$8,910	$644.46	24%	$5,100	$2,550	$4,455	$322.28	24%	$2,550
$8,910	$11,067	$1,558.86	32%	$8,910	$4,455	$5,533	$779.48	32%	$4,455
$11,067	$26,302	$2,249.10	35%	$11,067	$5,533	$13,151	$1,124.44	35%	$5,533
$26,302		$7,581.35	37%	$26,302	$13,151		$3,790.74	37%	$13,151

5. Percentage Method Tables for Manual Payroll Systems With Forms W-4 From 2019 or Earlier

If you compute payroll manually and your employee **has not** submitted a Form W-4 for 2020 or later, and you prefer to use the Percentage Method or you can't use the Wage Bracket Method tables because the employee's annual wages exceed the amount from the last bracket of the table (based on marital status and pay period) or the employee claimed more than 10 allowances, use the worksheet below and the Percentage Method tables that follow to figure federal income tax withholding. This method works for any number of withholding allowances claimed and any amount of wages.

Periodic payments of pensions or annuities with a 2021 or earlier Form W-4P. In lieu of Worksheet 1B and the Percentage Method tables in section 1, you may use Worksheet 5 and the Percentage Method tables in this section to figure federal income tax withholding on periodic payments of pensions or annuities with a 2021 or earlier Form W-4P. As an alternative, if you prefer to use the Wage Bracket Method of withholding, you may use Worksheet 3 and the Wage Bracket Method tables in section 3 to figure federal income tax withholding on periodic payments of pensions or annuities with a 2021 or earlier Form W-4P.

Worksheet 5. Employer's Withholding Worksheet for Percentage Method Tables for Manual Payroll Systems With Forms W-4 From 2019 or Earlier

Keep for Your Records

Table 7	Annually	Semiannually	Quarterly	Monthly	Semimonthly	Biweekly	Weekly	Daily
	$4,300	$2,150	$1,075	$358	$179	$165	$83	$17

Step 1. Adjust the employee's wage amount
- 1a Enter the employee's total taxable wages this payroll period .... 1a $ _____
- 1b Enter the number of allowances claimed on the employee's most recent Form W-4 .... 1b _____
- 1c Multiply line 1b by the amount in Table 7 for your pay frequency .... 1c $ _____
- 1d Subtract line 1c from line 1a. If zero or less, enter -0-. This is the **Adjusted Wage Amount** .... 1d $ _____

Step 2. Figure the Tentative Withholding Amount
based on your pay frequency, the employee's Adjusted Wage Amount, and marital status (line 3 of Form W-4).

- 2a Find the row in the Percentage Method table in this section in which the amount on line 1d is at least the amount in column A but less than the amount in column B, and then enter here the amount from column A of that row .... 2a $ _____
- 2b Enter the amount from column C of that row .... 2b $ _____
- 2c Enter the percentage from column D of that row .... 2c _____ %
- 2d Subtract line 2a from line 1d .... 2d $ _____
- 2e Multiply the amount on line 2d by the percentage on line 2c .... 2e $ _____
- 2f Add lines 2b and 2e. This is the **Tentative Withholding Amount** .... 2f $ _____

Step 3. Figure the final amount to withhold
- 3a Enter the additional amount to withhold from line 6 of the employee's Form W-4 .... 3a $ _____
- 3b Add lines 2f and 3a. **This is the amount to withhold from the employee's wages this pay period** ...... 3b $ _____

2024 Percentage Method Tables for Manual Payroll Systems With Forms W-4 From 2019 or Earlier

WEEKLY Payroll Period

MARRIED Persons					SINGLE Persons				
If the Adjusted Wage Amount (line 1d) is		The tentative amount to withhold is…	Plus this percentage …	of the amount that the wage exceeds…	If the Adjusted Wage Amount (line 1d) is		The tentative amount to withhold is…	Plus this percentage …	of the amount that the wage exceeds…
at least…	But less than…				at least…	But less than…			
A	B	C	D	E	A	B	C	D	E
$0	$313	$0.00	0%	$0	$0	$115	$0.00	0%	$0
$313	$760	$0.00	10%	$313	$115	$338	$0.00	10%	$115
$760	$2,127	$44.70	12%	$760	$338	$1,022	$22.30	12%	$338
$2,127	$4,180	$208.74	22%	$2,127	$1,022	$2,049	$104.38	22%	$1,022
$4,180	$7,696	$660.40	24%	$4,180	$2,049	$3,807	$330.32	24%	$2,049
$7,696	$9,688	$1,504.24	32%	$7,696	$3,807	$4,802	$752.24	32%	$3,807
$9,688	$14,375	$2,141.68	35%	$9,688	$4,802	$11,834	$1,070.64	35%	$4,802
$14,375		$3,782.13	37%	$14,375	$11,834		$3,531.84	37%	$11,834

BIWEEKLY Payroll Period

MARRIED Persons					SINGLE Persons				
If the Adjusted Wage Amount (line 1d) is		The tentative amount to withhold is…	Plus this percentage …	of the amount that the wage exceeds…	If the Adjusted Wage Amount (line 1d) is		The tentative amount to withhold is…	Plus this percentage …	of the amount that the wage exceeds…
at least…	But less than…				at least…	But less than…			
A	B	C	D	E	A	B	C	D	E
$0	$627	$0.00	0%	$0	$0	$231	$0.00	0%	$0
$627	$1,519	$0.00	10%	$627	$231	$677	$0.00	10%	$231
$1,519	$4,254	$89.20	12%	$1,519	$677	$2,044	$44.60	12%	$677
$4,254	$8,360	$417.40	22%	$4,254	$2,044	$4,097	$208.64	22%	$2,044
$8,360	$15,392	$1,320.72	24%	$8,360	$4,097	$7,613	$660.30	24%	$4,097
$15,392	$19,375	$3,008.40	32%	$15,392	$7,613	$9,605	$1,504.14	32%	$7,613
$19,375	$28,750	$4,282.96	35%	$19,375	$9,605	$23,667	$2,141.58	35%	$9,605
$28,750		$7,564.21	37%	$28,750	$23,667		$7,063.28	37%	$23,667

SEMIMONTHLY Payroll Period

MARRIED Persons					SINGLE Persons				
If the Adjusted Wage Amount (line 1d) is		The tentative amount to withhold is…	Plus this percentage …	of the amount that the wage exceeds…	If the Adjusted Wage Amount (line 1d) is		The tentative amount to withhold is…	Plus this percentage …	of the amount that the wage exceeds…
at least…	But less than…				at least…	But less than…			
A	B	C	D	E	A	B	C	D	E
$0	$679	$0.00	0%	$0	$0	$250	$0.00	0%	$0
$679	$1,646	$0.00	10%	$679	$250	$733	$0.00	10%	$250
$1,646	$4,608	$96.70	12%	$1,646	$733	$2,215	$48.30	12%	$733
$4,608	$9,056	$452.14	22%	$4,608	$2,215	$4,439	$226.14	22%	$2,215
$9,056	$16,675	$1,430.70	24%	$9,056	$4,439	$8,248	$715.42	24%	$4,439
$16,675	$20,990	$3,259.26	32%	$16,675	$8,248	$10,405	$1,629.58	32%	$8,248
$20,990	$31,146	$4,640.06	35%	$20,990	$10,405	$25,640	$2,319.82	35%	$10,405
$31,146		$8,194.66	37%	$31,146	$25,640		$7,652.07	37%	$25,640

MONTHLY Payroll Period

MARRIED Persons					SINGLE Persons				
If the Adjusted Wage Amount (line 1d) is		The tentative amount to withhold is…	Plus this percentage …	of the amount that the wage exceeds…	If the Adjusted Wage Amount (line 1d) is		The tentative amount to withhold is…	Plus this percentage …	of the amount that the wage exceeds…
at least…	But less than…				at least…	But less than…			
A	B	C	D	E	A	B	C	D	E
$0	$1,358	$0.00	0%	$0	$0	$500	$0.00	0%	$0
$1,358	$3,292	$0.00	10%	$1,358	$500	$1,467	$0.00	10%	$500
$3,292	$9,217	$193.40	12%	$3,292	$1,467	$4,429	$96.70	12%	$1,467
$9,217	$18,113	$904.40	22%	$9,217	$4,429	$8,877	$452.14	22%	$4,429
$18,113	$33,350	$2,861.52	24%	$18,113	$8,877	$16,496	$1,430.70	24%	$8,877
$33,350	$41,979	$6,518.40	32%	$33,350	$16,496	$20,810	$3,259.26	32%	$16,496
$41,979	$62,292	$9,279.68	35%	$41,979	$20,810	$51,279	$4,639.74	35%	$20,810
$62,292		$16,389.23	37%	$62,292	$51,279		$15,303.89	37%	$51,279

Appendix D

Additional Comprehensive Tax Return Problems

Contents

Comprehensive Problem One: Noah and
Joan Arc's Tax Return   D-2

Comprehensive Problem Two:
Cab and Charlene Neigh's Tax Return   D-6

Comprehensive Problem One

Noah and Joan Arc's Tax Return

Noah and Joan Arc live with their family in Dayton, OH. Noah's Social Security number is 434-11-3311. Noah was born on February 22, 1989, and Joan was born on July 1, 1990. Both enjoy good health and eyesight. Noah owns and operates a pet store, and Joan is a firefighter for the city of Dayton.

1. The Arcs have two children, a son named Shem (Social Security number 598-01-2345), born on March 21, 2017, and a daughter named Rayder (Social Security number 554-33-2411), born on December 3, 2020.
2. Joan and Noah brought a folder of tax documents located on Pages D-3 to D-5.
3. Noah's pet store is located at 1415 S. Patterson Blvd, Dayton, OH 45409. The name of the store is "The Arc" and its taxpayer identification number is 95-9876556. Since you handle Noah's bookkeeping, you have printed the income statement from your Quickbooks software, shown on Page D-5.
4. Details of The Arc's meals and entertainment:

Meals associated with business travel	$ 550
Arc employee holiday party	400
Overtime meals for employees	150
Season tickets to the Dayton Lizards minor league baseball team	700
	$ 1,800

5. Travel costs represent airfare ($500) and lodging ($200 per night) for Noah's attendance at the Global Pet Expo in Las Vegas, NV. Noah spent two days attending the largest retail pet store conference and three days gambling and attending concerts and shows.
6. Miscellaneous expense is a $300 fine paid to the City of Dayton for failure to post a valid business license.
7. Noah and Joan paid the following amounts during the year:

Contributions to Re-elect Goldie Wilson, Mayor of Dayton	$ 250
Church donations (for which a written acknowledgment was received)	5,400
Real estate taxes on their home	2,600
Medical co-pays for doctor visits	700
Mortgage interest for purchase of home	Refer to Form 1098 (Page D-4)
Tax return preparation fees	350
Credit card interest	220
Automobile insurance premiums	600
Uniforms for Joan	125
Contribution to Noah's individual retirement account (made on April 1, 2025)	7,000

8. Noah has a long-term capital loss carryover from last year of $990.
9. Noah and Joan own a condo and use it as a rental property. The condo is located at 16 Oakwood Ave, Unit A, Dayton, OH 45409. Noah provides the management services for the rental including selection of tenants, maintenance, repairs, rent collection, and other services as needed. On average, Noah spends about two hours per week on the rental activity. The revenue and expenses for the year are as follows:

Rental income received	$16,650
Insurance	900
Interest expense	4,800
Property taxes	2,400
Miscellaneous expenses	550

Rental income includes $1,200 per month for two months under the previous lease (which ended February 28, 2024). The new lease is $1,350 per month for 10 months under the new lease but the tenant paid only $750 in May 2024 because the tenant paid $600 for repairs to the apartment, and with the Arc's permission, reduced May's rent by $600. The new lease also required the tenant to pay last month's $1,350 rent in February 2024. The home was acquired for $100,000 in 2008. On May 12, 2024, the Arcs installed new fixtures (7-year recovery period) at a cost of $4,750. They wish to maximize the cost recovery on the new fixtures but make no elections.

10. The Arcs paid Ohio general sales tax of $1,202 during the year.

    Required: You are to prepare the Arcs' federal income tax return in good form, signing the return as the preparer. Do not complete an Ohio state income tax return. Make realistic assumptions about any missing data that you may need. The following forms and schedules are required:

Form 1040	Schedule E
Schedule 1	Schedule SE
Schedule 2	Form 2441
Schedule 3	Form 4562
Schedule A	Schedule 8812
Schedule B	Form 8995
Schedule C	Qualified Dividends and Capital Gain Tax Worksheet
Schedule D	

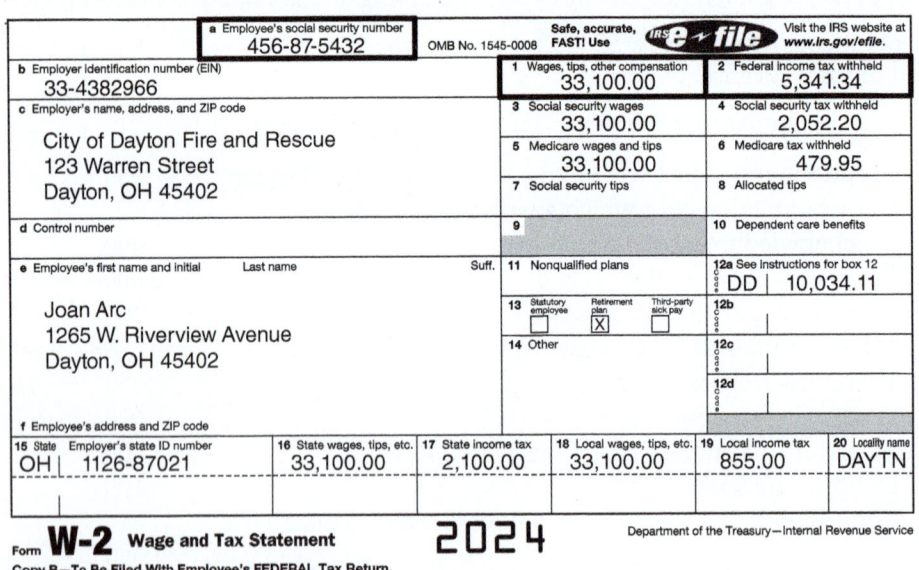

Substitute 1099 Statement

Indiana James Financial Services
123 Wall Street
New York, NY 10005

Joan and Noah Arc
1265 W. Riverview Avenue
Dayton, OH 45402
SSN: 456-87-5432

Date

December 31, 2024

Dividends Payor	Box 1a Ordinary Dividends	Box 1b Qualified Dividends	Box 2a Cap Gain Distrib	Box 4 Federal Income Tax withheld	Box 5 Sec 199A Dividends	Box 7 Foreign Tax Paid
Bellok Industries	310.00	310.00	0.00	0.00	0.00	0.00
Ravenwood Util.	1,200.00	1,200.00	0.00	0.00	0.00	0.00
Sala Growth Fund	580.00	380.00	275.00	0.00	100.00	30.00

Stock Transactions Box 1a Description	Box 1b Date Acq.	Box 1c Date Sold	Box 1d Net Proceeds	Box 1e Basis (reported to IRS)	Box 2 Character
100 shs. Markus Corp.	02/11/2014	08/15/2024	4,750.00	2,600.00	LT
50 shs. Tote Corp.	01/13/2024	06/05/2024	6,075.00	5,600.00	ST
25 shs. Redgie Co.	10/02/2015	10/07/2024	11,400.00	2,050.00	LT

☐ CORRECTED (if checked)

Form 1098 (Rev. January 2022) — For calendar year 20**24**
OMB No. 1545-1380
Mortgage Interest Statement
Copy B For Payer/Borrower

RECIPIENT'S/LENDER'S name, street address, city or town, state or province, country, ZIP or foreign postal code, and telephone no.
Japheth National Bank
3708 N Main Street
Dayton, OH 45405

RECIPIENT'S/LENDER'S TIN: 13-4296127
PAYER'S/BORROWER'S TIN: 434-11-3311

PAYER'S/BORROWER'S name: **Noah and Joan Arc**
Street address: **1265 W. Riverview Avenue**
City, state, ZIP: **Dayton, OH 45402**

1 Mortgage interest received from payer(s)/borrower(s): $ **10,011.22**
2 Outstanding mortgage principal: $ **287,245.66**
3 Mortgage origination date: **03/13/2015**
4 Refund of overpaid interest: $
5 Mortgage insurance premiums: $
6 Points paid on purchase of principal residence: $
7 [X] If address of property securing mortgage is the same as PAYER'S/BORROWER'S address, the box is checked, or the address or description is entered in box 8.
8 Address or description of property securing mortgage:
9 Number of properties securing the mortgage: **1**
10 Other:
11 Mortgage acquisition date:

Account number (see instructions):

Form **1098** (Rev. 1-2022) (Keep for your records) www.irs.gov/Form1098 Department of the Treasury - Internal Revenue Service

ROUNDUP DAY CARE CENTER
555 W THIRD STREET
DAYTON, OH 45402

January 12, 2025

Joan and Noah Arc
1265 W. Riverview Avenue
Dayton, OH 45402

Dear Joan and Noah,

Thank you for a great 2024 at Roundup! We appreciate your patronage during the year and hope to continue to provide excellent service for Rayder in 2025. We have provided the tax information for calendar year 2024 below. Please let us know if you need any additional information.

Sincerely,

Charles F. Antedeluvian

Charles F. Antedeluvian
Executive Director, Roundup Day Care
EIN 54-0983456

Date of service	Amount Paid	Child
January 1, 2024 – December 31, 2024	$7,500.00	Rayder Arc

The Arc
95-9876556
Income Statement
For the Year Ended December 31, 2024

Revenue:		
Gross Sales		$ 150,515.00
Less: Sales Returns and Allowances		2,100.00
Net Sales		148,415.00
Cost of Goods Sold:		
Beginning Inventory	11,000.00	
Add: Purchases	66,500.00	
	77,500.00	
Less: Ending Inventory	10,420.00	
Cost of Goods Sold		67,080.00
Gross Profit (Loss)		81,335.00
Expenses:		
Dues and Subscriptions	-	
Estimated Federal Tax Payments	4,000.00	
Estimated State Tax Payments	3,900.00	
Insurance	4,000.00	
Meals and Entertainment	1,800.00	
Miscellaneous	300.00	
Payroll Taxes	2,100.00	
Professional Fees	1,700.00	
Rent	7,800.00	
Travel	1,500.00	
Utilities	1,500.00	
Vehicle Expenses	-	
Wages	25,000.00	
Total Expenses		53,600.00
Net Operating Income		$ 27,735.00

Comprehensive Problem Two

Cab and Charlene Neigh's Tax Return

Cab R. and Charlene D. Neigh live with their family at the Malbeck House Bed & Breakfast, which Cab operates. The Bed & Breakfast (B&B) is located at 2000 Rose Way, Temecula, CA 92591. Cab (born May 4, 1981) and Charlene (born June 12, 1982) enjoy good health and eyesight.

1. The Neighs have three children:

Child's Name	Social Security Number	Date of Birth	Relationship
Savvy B. Neigh	466-74-1131	04/16/2006	Daughter
Meryl O. Neigh	465-76-8375	12/02/2012	Daughter
Reese L. Neigh	475-23-1426	01/13/2014	Son

All three children live at home and the Neighs provide more than 50 percent of their support.

2. The Malbeck House B&B is operated as a sole proprietorship and had the following income and expenses for the year:

Room rental income	$140,800
Vending machine income	2,200
Advertising expense	4,900
Depreciation for book and tax purposes	18,000
Mortgage interest on the B&B	23,200
Wages of custodial services	17,700
Taxes and licenses	6,500
Supplies consumed	18,800
Business insurance	6,100
Laundry expenses	4,200
Accounting fees	1,800
Office expenses	900
SEP contributions for employees	1,000
Utilities	6,100

All of the above amounts relate to the business portion of the Bed & Breakfast; the personal portion is accounted for separately. The Malbeck House B&B uses the cash method of accounting and has no inventory. The employer tax ID number is 95-1234567.

Form W-2 Wage and Tax Statement — 2024

- a Employee's social security number: 256-43-8819
- OMB No. 1545-0008
- b Employer identification number (EIN): 43-7654321
- c Employer's name, address, and ZIP code:
  Temecula Valley Unified School District
  31350 Rancho Vista Road
  Temecula, CA 92592
- e Employee's first name and initial / Last name:
  Charlene D. Neigh
  2000 Rose Way
  Temecula, CA 92591

Box	Description	Amount
1	Wages, tips, other compensation	19,000.00
2	Federal income tax withheld	1,800.00
3	Social security wages	20,000.00
4	Social security tax withheld	1,240.00
5	Medicare wages and tips	20,000.00
6	Medicare tax withheld	290.00
12a	D	1,000.00
12b	DD	7,824.77
13	Retirement plan	X
15	State / Employer's state ID number	CA / 3990-1832
16	State wages, tips, etc.	19,000.00
17	State income tax	700.00

Copy B—To Be Filed With Employee's FEDERAL Tax Return.
This information is being furnished to the Internal Revenue Service.

3. The Neighs made estimated state income tax payments of $3,000 (all made during 2024).
4. Charlene worked about 1,200 hours as a substitute schoolteacher with the local school district. She also spent $328 out-of-pocket for various supplies for her classroom. For the current year, Charlene's Form W-2 from the school district is presented on the previous page.
5. Cab is retired from the U.S. Navy. His annual statement from the Navy, Form 1099-R, is shown on Page D-10.
6. Cab and Charlene paid (and can substantiate) the following amounts during the year:

Mastercard interest	$1,480
Dental expenses (orthodontics for Savvy)	5,400
California state income tax (for 2023)	2,100
Charitable contributions	900
Life insurance premiums	845
Automobile registration fees (deductible portion)	50
Tax return preparation fee	475
Contributions to the president's re-election campaign	1,000

The Neighs are taking the standard deduction in 2024.

7. Cab and Charlene's investment activity was reported on the Forms 1099 included on Pages D-10 and D-11. Also, Charlene owns Series EE U.S. savings bonds. During the year, the bond redemption value increased by $1,300. Charlene has not elected the accrual method for these bonds. All of the above stocks, bonds, and bank accounts are community property.
8. Cab does all the significant work in the Bed & Breakfast; and therefore, he pays self-employment tax on 100 percent of the earnings from the B&B.
9. During the year, Cab's Uncle Champ died. Champ had a $50,000 life insurance policy that named Cab as the beneficiary. Cab received the check for the benefits payable under the policy on November 30 of the current year. Champ also left Cab a parcel of land with an appraised value of $120,000.
10. Cab is a general partner in a partnership that owns a boutique hotel in northern California and leases the property to a hotel management company. Cab does not materially participate in the partnership activity but the partnership activity does rise to the level of a trade or business. The Schedule K-1 from the partnership is shown on Page D-9.
11. Through her employer, Charlene is eligible for health insurance for the Neigh family.
12. Cab wishes to make the maximum 2024 contribution to his B&B SEP IRA in April 2025 when he files his tax return. Cab wants this amount to be calculated and reported on the 2024 tax return. Cab does not have a retirement plan associated with his partnership interest.
13. On October 4, 2024 the Neighs purchased a 2024 Honda Prologue Touring SUV EV SUV for personal use. The MSRP on the vehicle was $56,550. The total cost including destination fees and sales tax was $61,074. The VIN of the SUV was 3GPKHXRJ1RS506902. They paid $20,000 down and financed the rest with a home equity loan. Interest paid on the home equity loan in 2024 was $700. The Neigh's AGI in 2023 was $65,000.

Required: Cab and Charlene have come to you to prepare their 2024 federal income tax return. Do not complete a California state income tax return. Cab and Charlene have given you several IRS forms (refer to Pages D-9 to D-11). Make realistic assumptions about any missing data that you need. Do not file a federal Form 4952. The following is a list of the forms and schedules that you will need to complete the tax return:

Form 1040	Schedule SE
Schedule 1	Schedule EIC
Schedule 2	Schedule 8812
Schedule 3	Form 8995
Schedule B	Form 8936
Schedule C	Form 8936 Schedule A
Schedule D	Qualified Dividends and Capital Gain Tax Worksheet
Schedule E	

D-9   Appendix D

Schedule K-1 (Form 1065) 2024

OMB No. 1545-0123
651123

☐ Final K-1   ☐ Amended K-1

Department of the Treasury
Internal Revenue Service

For calendar year 2024, or tax year
beginning ___/___/2024 ending ___/___/___

Partner's Share of Income, Deductions, Credits, etc. See separate instructions.

Part I Information About the Partnership

A. Partnership's employer identification number: 11-2343212

B. Partnership's name, address, city, state, and ZIP code
Wine Acres Partners
581 Coombs Street, Napa, CA 94559

C. IRS center where partnership filed return: E-filed

D. ☐ Check if this is a publicly traded partnership (PTP)

Part II Information About the Partner

E. Partner's SSN or TIN (Do not use TIN of a disregarded entity. See instructions.)
543-88-9756

F. Name, address, city, state, and ZIP code for partner entered in E. See instructions.
Cab R. Neigh
2000 Rose Way, Temecula, CA 92591

G. ☒ General partner or LLC member-manager   ☐ Limited partner or other LLC member

H1. ☒ Domestic partner   ☐ Foreign partner

H2. ☐ If the partner is a disregarded entity (DE), enter the partner's:
TIN _____ Name _____

I1. What type of entity is this partner? _____

I2. If this partner is a retirement plan (IRA/SEP/Keogh/etc.), check here ☐

J. Partner's share of profit, loss, and capital (see instructions):

	Beginning	Ending
Profit	2 %	2 %
Loss	2 %	2 %
Capital	2 %	2 %

Check if decrease is due to:
☐ Sale or ☐ Exchange of partnership interest. See instructions.

K1. Partner's share of liabilities:

	Beginning	Ending
Nonrecourse	$ 4,679	$ 4,679
Qualified nonrecourse financing	$	$
Recourse	$	$

K2. ☐ Check this box if item K1 includes liability amounts from lower-tier partnerships

K3. ☐ Check if any of the above liability is subject to guarantees or other payment obligations by the partner. See instructions.

L. **Partner's Capital Account Analysis**

Beginning capital account	$ 13,256
Capital contributed during the year	$
Current year net income (loss)	$ 2,425
Other increase (decrease) (attach explanation)	$
Withdrawals and distributions	$ (400)
Ending capital account	$ 15,281

M. Did the partner contribute property with a built-in gain (loss)?
☐ Yes ☒ No If "Yes," attach statement. See instructions.

N. Partner's Share of Net Unrecognized Section 704(c) Gain or (Loss)
Beginning . . . . $ _____
Ending . . . . . $ _____

Part III Partner's Share of Current Year Income, Deductions, Credits, and Other Items

1	Ordinary business income (loss)		14	Self-employment earnings (loss) 3,200
2	Net rental real estate income (loss) 3,200			
3	Other net rental income (loss)		15	Credits
4a	Guaranteed payments for services			
4b	Guaranteed payments for capital		16	Schedule K-3 is attached if checked ☐
4c	Total guaranteed payments		17	Alternative minimum tax (AMT) items
5	Interest income 25			
6a	Ordinary dividends		18	Tax-exempt income and nondeductible expenses
6b	Qualified dividends			
6c	Dividend equivalents			
7	Royalties			
8	Net short-term capital gain (loss)		19	Distributions A 400
9a	Net long-term capital gain (loss) (800)			
9b	Collectibles (28%) gain (loss)		20	Other information
9c	Unrecaptured section 1250 gain			Z 3,200
10	Net section 1231 gain (loss)			
11	Other income (loss)			
12	Section 179 deduction		21	Foreign taxes paid or accrued
13	Other deductions			

22 ☐ More than one activity for at-risk purposes*
23 ☐ More than one activity for passive activity purposes*
*See attached statement for additional information.

For Paperwork Reduction Act Notice, see the Instructions for Form 1065.   www.irs.gov/Form1065   Cat. No. 11394R   Schedule K-1 (Form 1065) 2024

Additional Comprehensive Tax Return Problems D-10

Form 1099-R (2024) — Distributions From Pensions, Annuities, Retirement or Profit-Sharing Plans, IRAs, Insurance Contracts, etc.

☐ CORRECTED (if checked)

PAYER'S name, street address, city or town, state or province, country, ZIP or foreign postal code, and telephone no.
United States Navy
Retired Benefits Center
Cleveland, OH 43267

OMB No. 1545-0119

Box	Description	Amount
1	Gross distribution	$15,000
2a	Taxable amount	$15,000
2b	Taxable amount not determined / Total distribution	☐ ☐
3	Capital gain (included in box 2a)	
4	Federal income tax withheld	$1,550.00
5	Employee contributions/Designated Roth contributions or insurance premiums	
6	Net unrealized appreciation in employer's securities	
7	Distribution code(s)	7
	IRA/SEP/SIMPLE	☐
8	Other	
9a	Your percentage of total distribution	%
9b	Total employee contributions	
14	State tax withheld	$500.00
15	State/Payer's state no.	CA
16	State distribution	

PAYER'S TIN: 11-4662891
RECIPIENT'S TIN: 543-88-9756

RECIPIENT'S name: Cab R. Neigh
Street address: 2000 Rose Way
City, state, ZIP: Temecula, CA 92591

Form **1099-R**

Form 1099-INT (Rev. January 2024) — Interest Income

☐ CORRECTED (if checked)

PAYER'S name, street address, city or town, state or province, country, ZIP or foreign postal code, and telephone no.
Vintage Bank
6792 Main Street
Temecula, CA 92591

OMB No. 1545-0112
For calendar year 2024

Box	Description	Amount
1	Interest income	$1,462.39
2	Early withdrawal penalty	
3	Interest on U.S. Savings Bonds and Treasury obligations	
4	Federal income tax withheld	
5	Investment expenses	
6	Foreign tax paid	
7	Foreign country or U.S. territory	
8	Tax-exempt interest	
9	Specified private activity bond interest	
10	Market discount	
11	Bond premium	
12	Bond premium on Treasury obligations	
13	Bond premium on tax-exempt bond	
14	Tax-exempt and tax credit bond CUSIP no.	
15	State	
16	State identification no.	
17	State tax withheld	

PAYER'S TIN: 98-8724390
RECIPIENT'S TIN: 543-88-9756

RECIPIENT'S name: Cab R. Neigh
Street address: 2000 Rose Way
City, state, ZIP: Temecula, CA 92591

Form **1099-INT** (Rev. 1-2024) (keep for your records) Department of the Treasury - Internal Revenue Service

2024 Combined Forms 1099

This is important tax information and is being furnished to the IRS (except as indicated). If you are required to file a return, a negligence penalty or other sanction may be imposed on you if this income is taxable and the IRS determines that it has not been reported.

Copy B For Recipient
OMB No. 1545-0110

Friar Tuck Investments
38 Wall Street, 8th Floor
New York, NY 10005

Account Number	Tax ID
56-12232556	***-**-9756
	Payer's Federal Tax ID
	33-1357246
	Financial Adviser/Phone
	888-555-1212
	Ronald Burgundy

Cab and Charlene Neigh
2000 Rose Way
Temecula, CA 92591

Form 1099-B — Proceeds from Broker and Barter Exchange Transactions

Box 6: Gross Proceeds	Box 5: Not checked	Box 3: Basis reported to IRS		Box 2: Type of Gain or Loss: Short Term			
Box 1 Security description (CUSIP)	Quantity sold	Box 1b Date acquired	Box 1c Date sold or disposed	Box 1d Proceeds	Box 1e Cost or other basis	Box 1g Wash sale loss disallowed	Gain/(Loss) amount
Cork Corp	100	12/11/2024	06/19/2024	8,000	3,400	-	4,600
Decanter Inc	50	03/27/2024	09/18/2024	12,000	14,000		(2,000)

Box 6: Gross Proceeds	Box 5: Not checked	Box 3: Basis reported to IRS		Box 2: Type of Gain or Loss: Long Term			
Box 1 Security description (CUSIP)	Quantity sold	Box 1b Date acquired	Box 1c Date sold or disposed	Box 1d Proceeds	Box 1e Cost or other basis	Box 1g Wash sale loss disallowed	Gain/(Loss) amount
Grand Cru Corp	50	10/31/2022	10/23/2024	1,650	2,600	-	(950)

Form 1099-INT — Interest Income

Box 1 Interest income	Box 2 Early withdrawal penalty	Box 3 Interest on U.S. Savings Bonds and Treasury obligations
700.00		

Box 4 Federal income tax withheld	Box 5 Investment expenses	Box 6 Foreign Tax Paid

Box 7 Foreign country or U.S. possession	Box 8 Tax-exempt interest	Box 9 Specified private activity bond interest
	1,500.00	

Form 1099-DIV — Dividend Income

Box 1a Total ordinary dividends	Box 1b Qualified dividends	Box 2a Total capital gain distr.
950.00	950.00	

Box 4 Federal income tax withheld	Box 5 Section 199A dividends	Box 6 Investment expenses

Solutions to Self-Study Problems

Chapter 1 The Individual Income Tax Return

Self-Study Problem 1.1
Answer is d. Answers a, b, and c are goals of the U.S. income tax system.

Self-Study Problem 1.2
1. Schedule B, Forms 1040 and 1040-SR.
2. Schedule D, Forms 1040 and 1040-SR.
3. Schedule 1 and Schedule F, Forms 1040 and 1040-SR.
4. Form 1041 is used to report the income of estates and trusts.
5. Schedule K-1, Form 1065.
6. Form 1040.
7. Schedule 1 and Schedule C, Forms 1040 and 1040-SR.
8. Schedule 1 and Schedule E, Forms 1040 and 1040-SR.
9. Schedule B, Forms 1040 and 1040-SR.
10. Form 1120 or Form 1120-S, if making an S election.
11. Form 1065.
12. Schedule A, Forms 1040 and 1040-SR.
13. Form 1040-SR (may also use Form 1040).

Self-Study Problem 1.3
1. Gross income = $37,000 + $1,500 = $38,500
2. Adjusted gross income = $38,500 − $2,000 = $36,500
3. Standard deduction = $14,600 (exceeds his itemized deduction amount of $9,300)
4. Taxable income = $36,500 − $14,600 = $21,900

Self-Study Problem 1.4
Refer to Figures 1.1, 1.2, and 1.3 in Chapter 1.

1. No Income is below single under 65 threshold. Refer to Figure 1.1.
2. No Income is below MFJ with one spouse 65 or older limit. Refer to Figure 1.1.
3. No Standard deduction is earned income plus $450 up to $14,600 for single dependent. Refer to Figure 1.2.

4. Yes Self-employment income is greater than $400. Refer to Figure 1.3.
5. No   Income is below MFJ threshold; however, the taxpayers should file to obtain a refund. Refer to Figure 1.1.
6. Yes Self-employment income of $400 or more triggers filing requirement. Refer to Figure 1.3.
7. No   Income is below surviving spouse threshold under 65. Refer to Figure 1.1.

Self-Study Problem 1.5
1. B (married filing jointly) is generally preferred but C (married filing separately) is also available.
2. D (head of household) is generally preferred but A (single) is also available, and if the spouse died in the last two years, E (surviving spouse) is also an option.
3. A is the only filing status available.
4. C (married filing separately) is the only likely option since the spouse is unavailable to file jointly.
5. D (head of household) is generally preferred, but A (single) is also an option.
6. E (surviving spouse) would be preferred but D (head of household) and A (single) are also options.

Self-Study Problem 1.6
1. Yes A baby born on or before December 31 qualifies as a dependent for that tax year.
2. No   The brother is not a qualifying child (he is older than Charlie) and fails the gross income test for qualifying relative.
3. Yes The mother is a qualifying relative under the multiple support agreement rules.
4. Yes The son qualifies as a qualifying child and the daughter-in-law is a qualifying relative. The joint return was only filed to claim a refund.
5. Yes The daughter is a full-time student under the age of 24 and Gary provides more than 50 percent of her support. Scholarships are excluded and do not count toward support.
6. Yes The mother is a qualifying relative. Non-taxable Social Security benefits are not counted toward the gross income test.

Self-Study Problem 1.7
1. $14,600. This is the amount for taxpayers filing single under age 65 and not blind.
2. $30,750 = $29,200 + $1,550. $29,200 for married filing jointly and $1,550 for Bill being age 65 or older.
3. $18,500 = $14,600 + $1,950 + $1,950. $14,600 for filing single plus $1,950 for being age 65 or older plus $1,950 for being blind.
4. $21,900. Standard deduction for head of household filing status.
5. $1,300. Because Elizabeth is claimed as a dependent, her standard deduction is limited to the greater of $1,300 or earned income plus $450. The amount is also limited to the typical standard deduction for that filing status.
6. $29,200. Standard deduction for married filing jointly with both taxpayers under age 65 and not blind.

Self-Study Problem 1.8
1. $13,075 = $13,100 − $25
2. $9,000
3. $4,075 = $13,075 − $9,000
4. $4,075 = $13,075 − $9,000
5. Because the stock has been held for more than a year, the gain is a long-term capital gain. The long-term capital gain will be taxed at 0, 15, or 20 percent, depending on the taxpayer's income. A net investment income tax of 3.8 percent may also apply to certain high-income taxpayers.

Self-Study Problem 1.9

1. True
2. True
3. True
4. False Tax Notes Research website offers free access to an extensive library of tax law including tax court cases.

Self-Study Problem 1.10

1. True
2. True
3. True
4. False Taxpayers who e-file may have their refund returned through direct deposit or by check.

Chapter 2   Gross Income and Exclusions

Self-Study Problem 2.1

1. Included
2. Included
3. Excluded
4. Excluded
5. Included
6. Excluded
7. Excluded
8. Excluded
9. Excluded
10. Included
11. Excluded
12. Included
13. Excluded
14. Included
15. Excluded
16. Excluded
17. Excluded
18. Excluded
19. Excluded

Self-Study Problem 2.2

a. Box 1: $53,580
b. Box 2: $3,799
c. Box 12a: $3,420
d. Box 17: $1,816

Self-Study Problem 2.3

None.   Neither the premiums nor the reimbursement are included in gross income.

Self-Study Problem 2.4

1. Excluded
2. Included
3. Excluded
4. Included
5. Excluded

Self-Study Problem 2.5

1. Excluded. No-additional cost service
2. Included (the excess discount over 15%). Employee discount fringe applies but not more than mark-up
3. Excluded. A company party for employees is generally treated as de minimis
4. Excluded. Working condition fringe
5. Included. Personal use does not qualify as a working condition fringe
6. Excluded (up to $5,000)
7. Excluded. Athletic facility fringe

Self-Study Problem 2.6

1. $2,000
2. $10,000 The award was not transferred directly to a charitable organization.
3. $2,500
4. $5,000
5. $0 A service award less than $400 may be excluded from income.

Self-Study Problem 2.7

a. $22,100   The amount excluded from income will be $24,000 × [$47,880 ÷ ($2,400 × 12 months × 21 years)] = $1,900. Therefore, Phil will have taxable income of $22,100 ($24,000 − $1,900).

b.

Simplified Method Worksheet

1. Enter total amount received this year. — 1. $ 24,000
2. Enter cost in the plan at the annuity starting date. — 2. $ 47,880
3. Age at annuity starting date:

	Enter	
55 or under	360	
56–60	310	
61–65	260	3. 260
66–70	210	
71 or older	160	

4. Divide line 2 by line 3. — 4. $ 184
5. Multiply line 4 by the number of monthly payments this year. If the annuity starting date was before 1987, also enter this amount on line 8; and skip lines 6 and 7. Otherwise, go to line 6. — 5. $ 1,840
6. Enter the amount, if any, recovered tax free in prior years. — 6. 0
7. Subtract line 6 from line 2. — 7. $ 47,880
8. Enter the smaller of line 5 or 7. — 8. $ 1,840
9. Taxable amount this year: Subtract line 8 from line 1. Do not enter less than 0. — 9. $ 22,160

Self-Study Problem 2.8

a. Amount received $ 11,250
   Less: 1/10 of $100,000   (10,000)
   Taxable interest $ 1,250

b. $3,436. Proceeds of $12,000 (Form 1099-LS) less Kamala's investment of $8,564 (Form 1099-SB).

Self-Study Problem 2.9

Refer to Schedule B on Page E-5.

Self-Study Problem 2.10

Refer to Schedule B and the Qualifying Dividends and Capital Gain Tax Worksheet on Pages E-5 and E-6.

Self-Study Problem 2.11

a. $40,000   Gifts in a business setting are taxable income, even if there was no obligation to make the payment. This problem is similar to the facts of a court case (*Duberstein*) in which the Supreme Court held that the value of the automobile was income, even where there was no legal obligation to make the gift.

b. $0   Because Napheesa gave the funds with no expectation of future services and from a disinterested generosity, Jahmyr can exclude the gift from his gross income.

Self-Study Problems 2.9 and 2.10

SCHEDULE B (Form 1040)
Department of the Treasury
Internal Revenue Service

Interest and Ordinary Dividends

Attach to Form 1040 or 1040-SR.
Go to www.irs.gov/ScheduleB for instructions and the latest information.

OMB No. 1545-0074
2024
Attachment Sequence No. 08

Name(s) shown on return: Christy and John Harris-Thomas
Your social security number: 313-44-5454

Part I — Interest

(See instructions and the Instructions for Form 1040, line 2b.)

Note: If you received a Form 1099-INT, Form 1099-OID, or substitute statement from a brokerage firm, list the firm's name as the payer and enter the total interest shown on that form.

1. List name of payer. If any interest is from a seller-financed mortgage and the buyer used the property as a personal residence, see the instructions and list this interest first. Also, show that buyer's social security number and address:

Payer	Amount
Lake Osbourne Savings and Loan	1,218
Friar Tuck Investments	365
Friar Tuck US Treasury Bills	700
Accrued interest	(106)

2. Add the amounts on line 1 . . . . **2** 2,177

3. Excludable interest on series EE and I U.S. savings bonds issued after 1989. Attach Form 8815 . . . . **3**

4. Subtract line 3 from line 2. Enter the result here and on Form 1040 or 1040-SR, line 2b . . **4** 2,177

Note: If line 4 is over $1,500, you must complete Part III.

Part II — Ordinary Dividends

(See instructions and the Instructions for Form 1040, line 3b.)

Note: If you received a Form 1099-DIV or substitute statement from a brokerage firm, list the firm's name as the payer and enter the ordinary dividends shown on that form.

5. List name of payer:

Payer	Amount
Tangerine Equity Fund	975
Friar Tuck Investments	1,650

6. Add the amounts on line 5. Enter the total here and on Form 1040 or 1040-SR, line 3b . . **6** 2,625

Note: If line 6 is over $1,500, you must complete Part III.

Part III — Foreign Accounts and Trusts

Caution: If required, failure to file FinCEN Form 114 may result in substantial penalties. Additionally, you may be required to file Form 8938, Statement of Specified Foreign Financial Assets. See instructions.

You must complete this part if you (a) had over $1,500 of taxable interest or ordinary dividends; (b) had a foreign account; or (c) received a distribution from, or were a grantor of, or a transferor to, a foreign trust.

	Yes	No
7a. At any time during 2024, did you have a financial interest in or signature authority over a financial account (such as a bank account, securities account, or brokerage account) located in a foreign country? See instructions		✓
If "Yes," are you required to file FinCEN Form 114, Report of Foreign Bank and Financial Accounts (FBAR), to report that financial interest or signature authority? See FinCEN Form 114 and its instructions for filing requirements and exceptions to those requirements		
b. If you are required to file FinCEN Form 114, list the name(s) of the foreign country(-ies) where the financial account(s) is (are) located: _____		
8. During 2024, did you receive a distribution from, or were you the grantor of, or transferor to, a foreign trust? If "Yes," you may have to file Form 3520. See instructions		✓

For Paperwork Reduction Act Notice, see your tax return instructions. Cat. No. 17146N Schedule B (Form 1040) 2024

Self-Study Problem 2.10

Qualified Dividends and Capital Gain Tax Worksheet—Line 16 *Keep for Your Records*

Before you begin:
- ✓ See the earlier instructions for line 16 to see if you can use this worksheet to figure your tax.
- ✓ Before completing this worksheet, complete Form 1040 or 1040-SR through line 15.
- ✓ If you don't have to file Schedule D and you received capital gain distributions, be sure you checked the box on Form 1040 or 1040-SR, line 7.

1.	Enter the amount from Form 1040 or 1040-SR, line 15. However, if you are filing Form 2555 (relating to foreign earned income), enter the amount from line 3 of the Foreign Earned Income Tax Worksheet	1.	95,000
2.	Enter the amount from Form 1040 or 1040-SR, line 3a*	2.	2,525 (a)
3.	Are you filing Schedule D?* ☐ **Yes.** Enter the **smaller** of line 15 or 16 of Schedule D. If either line 15 or 16 is blank or a loss, enter -0-. ☐ **No.** Enter the amount from Form 1040 or 1040-SR, line 7.	3.	190
4.	Add lines 2 and 3	4.	2,715
5.	Subtract line 4 from line 1. If zero or less, enter -0-	5.	92,285
6.	Enter: $47,025 if single or married filing separately, $94,050 if married filing jointly or qualifying widow(er), $63,000 if head of household.	6.	94,050
7.	Enter the smaller of line 1 or line 6	7.	94,050
8.	Enter the smaller of line 5 or line 7	8.	92,285
9.	Subtract line 8 from line 7. This amount is taxed at 0%	9.	1,765
10.	Enter the smaller of line 1 or line 4	10.	2,715
11.	Enter the amount from line 9	11.	1,765
12.	Subtract line 11 from line 10	12.	950
13.	Enter: $518,900 if single, $291,850 if married filing separately, $583,750 if married filing jointly or qualifying widow(er), $551,350 if head of household.	13.	583,750
14.	Enter the smaller of line 1 or line 13	14.	95,000
15.	Add lines 5 and 9	15.	94,050
16.	Subtract line 15 from line 14. If zero or less, enter -0-	16.	950
17.	Enter the smaller of line 12 or line 16	17.	950
18.	Multiply line 17 by 15% (0.15)	18.	143
19.	Add lines 9 and 17	19.	2,715
20.	Subtract line 19 from line 10	20.	0
21.	Multiply line 20 by 20% (0.20)	21.	0
22.	Figure the tax on the amount on line 5. If the amount on line 5 is less than $100,000, use the Tax Table to figure the tax. If the amount on line 5 is $100,000 or more, use the Tax Computation Worksheet	22.	10,609
23.	Add lines 18, 21, and 22	23.	10,752
24.	Figure the tax on the amount on line 1. If the amount on line 1 is less than $100,000, use the Tax Table to figure the tax. If the amount on line 1 is $100,000 or more, use the Tax Computation Worksheet	24.	11,012
25.	**Tax on all taxable income.** Enter the **smaller** of line 23 or 24. Also include this amount on the entry space on Form 1040 or 1040-SR, line 16. If you are filing Form 2555, don't enter this amount on the entry space on Form 1040 or 1040-SR, line 16. Instead, enter it on line 4 of the Foreign Earned Income Tax Worksheet	25.	10,752

*If you are filing Form 2555, see the footnote in the Foreign Earned Income Tax Worksheet before completing this line.

This worksheet adapted from the 2023 worksheet.

(a) $975 from Tangerine Equity Fund + $1,550 from Friar Tuck Investments

Self-Study Problem 2.12

1. Excluded
2. Included
3. Included
4. Included
5. Included and Excluded. The $7,600 used for qualifying expenses is excluded but the excess scholarship of $2,400 in included in taxable income.
6. Included

Self-Study Problem 2.13

	Deductible by payor	Includable by recipient
a.	$ 0	$ 0
b.	12,000	12,000
c.	0	0

Self-Study Problem 2.14

a. $0. All used for qualified higher education costs.
b. $2,000. Henry's AGI is under $95,000, so there is no phase-out.

Self-Study Problem 2.15

$3,250 Unemployment compensation is fully taxable.

Self-Study Problem 2.16

Simplified Taxable Social Security Worksheet (for most people)

1. Enter the total amount of Social Security income. — 1. $13,000
2. Enter one-half of line 1. — 2. 6,500
3. Enter the total of taxable income items on Form 1040 except Social Security income. — 3. 20,000
4. Enter the amount of tax-exempt interest income. — 4. 30,000
5. Add lines 2, 3, and 4. — 5. 56,500
6. Enter all adjustments for AGI except for student loan interest deduction. — 6. 0
7. Subtract line 6 from line 5. If 0 or less, stop here, none of the Social Security benefits are taxable. — 7. 56,500
8. Enter $25,000 ($32,000 if married filing jointly; $0 if married filing separately and living with spouse at any time during the year). — 8. 32,000
9. Subtract line 8 from line 7. If 0 or less, enter -0-. — 9. 24,500

Note: If line 9 is 0 or less, stop here; none of your benefits are taxable. Otherwise, go on to line 10.

10. Enter $9,000 ($12,000 if married filing jointly; $0 if married filing separately and living with spouse at any time during the year). — 10. 12,000
11. Subtract line 10 from line 9. If 0 or less, enter -0-. — 11. 12,500
12. Enter the **smaller of line 9 or line 10**. — 12. 12,000
13. Enter one-half of line 12. — 13. 6,000
14. Enter the **smaller of line 2 or line 13**. — 14. 6,000
15. Multiply line 11 by 85% (.85). If line 11 is 0, enter -0-. — 15. 10,625
16. Add lines 14 and 15. — 16. 16,625
17. Multiply line 1 by 85% (.85). — 17. 11,050
18. **Taxable benefits. Enter the smaller of line 16 or line 17.** — 18. $11,050

Self-Study Problem 2.17

	Total	a. CA rule	a. CA amount	b. TX rule	b. TX amount
George's salary	40,000	50%	20,000	50%	20,000
Talia's salary	30,000	50%	15,000	50%	15,000
Dividends (George's property)	5,000	0%		50%	2,500
Dividends (Talia's property)	3,000	100%	3,000	50%	1,500
Interest	4,000	50%	2,000	50%	2,000
Total	82,000		40,000		41,000

Self-Study Problem 2.18

a. $0. Bogdan may exclude the cancellation of debt income on the mortgage and student loan.
b. $160,000. The original basis of $200,000 is reduced by the excluded cancellation of debt income of $40,000.

Chapter 3 Business Income and Expenses

Self-Study Problem 3.1
Refer to Schedule C on Pages E-9 and E-10.

Self-Study Problem 3.2

Part III — Cost of Goods Sold (see instructions)

Line	Description	Amount
33	Method(s) used to value closing inventory: **a** ☑ Cost **b** ☐ Lower of cost or market **c** ☐ Other (attach explanation)	
34	Was there any change in determining quantities, costs, or valuations between opening and closing inventory? If "Yes," attach explanation. ☐ Yes ☑ No	
35	Inventory at beginning of year. If different from last year's closing inventory, attach explanation	75,000
36	Purchases less cost of items withdrawn for personal use	200,000
37	Cost of labor. Do not include any amounts paid to yourself	
38	Materials and supplies	
39	Other costs	
40	Add lines 35 through 39	275,000
41	Inventory at end of year	88,000
42	Cost of goods sold. Subtract line 41 from line 40. Enter the result here and on line 4	187,000

Self-Study Problem 3.3

Marc's transportation deduction is the greater of his actual costs or his deduction using the standard mileage method.

Actual Cost Calculation:

Actual cash expenses	$ 4,028
Depreciation	8,000
	12,028
Business percentage (13,000/16,000)	×81.25%
Subtotal	9,773
Parking and tolls	327
Actual costs	$ 10,100

Standard Mileage Calculation:

13,000 miles at 67¢	$ 8,710
Parking and tolls	327
Standard mileage total costs	$ 9,037
Marc's deduction for 2024	$ 10,100

Self-Study Problem 3.1

SCHEDULE C (Form 1040)
Department of the Treasury
Internal Revenue Service

Profit or Loss From Business
(Sole Proprietorship)
Attach to Form 1040, 1040-SR, 1040-SS, 1040-NR, or 1041; partnerships must generally file Form 1065.
Go to www.irs.gov/ScheduleC for instructions and the latest information.

OMB No. 1545-0074
2024
Attachment Sequence No. 09

Name of proprietor: Shelly Wie
Social security number (SSN): 466-47-8833

A. Principal business or profession, including product or service (see instructions): Golf instruction
B. Enter code from instructions: 812990
C. Business name. If no separate business name, leave blank.
D. Employer ID number (EIN) (see instr.)
E. Business address (including suite or room no.): 96-540 Ala'Ike
City, town or post office, state, and ZIP code: Pearl City HI 96782
F. Accounting method: (1) ☑ Cash (2) ☐ Accrual (3) ☐ Other (specify)
G. Did you "materially participate" in the operation of this business during 2024? If "No," see instructions for limit on losses. ☑ Yes ☐ No
H. If you started or acquired this business during 2024, check here ☐
I. Did you make any payments in 2024 that would require you to file Form(s) 1099? See instructions ☐ Yes ☑ No
J. If "Yes," did you or will you file required Form(s) 1099? ☐ Yes ☐ No

Part I — Income

Line	Description	Amount
1	Gross receipts or sales.	48,000
2	Returns and allowances	
3	Subtract line 2 from line 1	48,000
4	Cost of goods sold (from line 42)	
5	Gross profit. Subtract line 4 from line 3	48,000
6	Other income, including federal and state gasoline or fuel tax credit or refund (see instructions)	
7	**Gross income.** Add lines 5 and 6	48,000

Part II — Expenses. Enter expenses for business use of your home **only** on line 30.

Line	Description	Amount	Line	Description	Amount
8	Advertising		18	Office expense (see instructions)	600
9	Car and truck expenses (see instructions)	3,350 (a)	19	Pension and profit-sharing plans	
10	Commissions and fees		20	Rent or lease:	
11	Contract labor (see instructions)		20a	Vehicles, machinery, and equipment	
12	Depletion		20b	Other business property	10,000
13	Depreciation and section 179 expense deduction (not included in Part III) (see instructions)		21	Repairs and maintenance	
			22	Supplies (not included in Part III)	
			23	Taxes and licenses	300
			24	Travel and meals:	
14	Employee benefit programs (other than on line 19)		24a	Travel	1,300
			24b	Deductible meals (see instructions)	700
15	Insurance (other than health)	500	25	Utilities	515
16	Interest (see instructions):		26	Wages (less employment credits)	
16a	Mortgage (paid to banks, etc.)		27a	Other expenses (from line 48)	750
16b	Other		27b	Energy efficient commercial bldgs deduction (attach Form 7205)	
17	Legal and professional services				

28. **Total expenses** before expenses for business use of home. Add lines 8 through 27b. **18,015**
29. Tentative profit or (loss). Subtract line 28 from line 7. **29,985**
30. Expenses for business use of your home. Do not report these expenses elsewhere. Attach Form 8829 unless using the simplified method. See instructions.
Simplified method filers only: Enter the total square footage of (a) your home: _____ and (b) the part of your home used for business: _____. Use the Simplified Method Worksheet in the instructions to figure the amount to enter on line 30.
31. **Net profit or (loss).** Subtract line 30 from line 29. **29,985**
    - If a profit, enter on both **Schedule 1 (Form 1040), line 3**, and on **Schedule SE, line 2**. (If you checked the box on line 1, see instructions.) Estates and trusts, enter on **Form 1041, line 3**.
    - If a loss, you **must** go to line 32.
32. If you have a loss, check the box that describes your investment in this activity. See instructions.
    - 32a ☐ All investment is at risk.
    - 32b ☐ Some investment is not at risk.

(a) 5,000 miles × $0.67 per mile.

Self-Study Problem 3.1

Schedule C (Form 1040) 2024 — Page 2

Part III — Cost of Goods Sold (see instructions)

33 Method(s) used to value closing inventory: a ☐ Cost   b ☐ Lower of cost or market   c ☐ Other (attach explanation)

34 Was there any change in determining quantities, costs, or valuations between opening and closing inventory? If "Yes," attach explanation . . . . ☐ Yes   ☐ No

35 Inventory at beginning of year. If different from last year's closing inventory, attach explanation . . . . . 35 _____

36 Purchases less cost of items withdrawn for personal use . . . . 36 _____

37 Cost of labor. Do not include any amounts paid to yourself . . . . 37 _____

38 Materials and supplies . . . . 38 _____

39 Other costs . . . . 39 _____

40 Add lines 35 through 39 . . . . 40 _____

41 Inventory at end of year . . . . 41 _____

42 **Cost of goods sold.** Subtract line 41 from line 40. Enter the result here and on line 4 . . . . . . 42 _____

Part IV — Information on Your Vehicle.
Complete this part **only** if you are claiming car or truck expenses on line 9 and are not required to file Form 4562 for this business. See the instructions for line 13 to find out if you must file Form 4562.

43 When did you place your vehicle in service for business purposes? (month/day/year)   01/01/2024

44 Of the total number of miles you drove your vehicle during 2024, enter the number of miles you used your vehicle for:

a Business 5,000   b Commuting (see instructions) 1,200   c Other 4,500

45 Was your vehicle available for personal use during off-duty hours? . . . . ☑ Yes ☐ No

46 Do you (or your spouse) have another vehicle available for personal use? . . . . ☐ Yes ☑ No

47a Do you have evidence to support your deduction? . . . . ☑ Yes ☐ No

b If "Yes," is the evidence written? . . . . ☑ Yes ☐ No

Part V — Other Expenses.
List below business expenses not included on lines 8–26, line 27b, or line 30.

Description	Amount
Memberships	750

48 **Total other expenses.** Enter here and on line 27a 48   750

Self-Study Problem 3.4

Deductible expenses:

Airfare (100% since primarily for business)	$ 480
Hotel while working on the audit	825
Meals while working on the audit	168
Laundry	22
Taxi	72
Total travel deduction	$1,567

Self-Study Problem 3.5

Business meals ($500 + $600) × 50% = $550. Entertainment, dues, and personal expenses are not generally deductible.

Self-Study Problem 3.6

Lodging	$1,200
Transportation	350
Snacks and drinks (50% of $30)	15
Restaurant meals (50% of $170)	85
Books	175
Tuition	550
Total deduction	$2,375

The cost of the weekend trip to the Grand Canyon is not deductible.

Self-Study Problem 3.7

1. Deductible. The expense is business-related and incurred by a self-employed individual.
2. Not Deductible. Although business-related, the cost was incurred by an employee. Unreimbursed employee business expenses were previously deductible as a miscellaneous expense subject to the 2-percent floor.
3. Not Deductible. Not business-related.
4. Not Deductible. Expense is incurred by an employee. Union dues were previously deductible as a miscellaneous expense subject to the 2-percent floor.
5. Not Deductible. Not business-related.

Self-Study Problem 3.8

Safety shoes and orange vest	$ 650
Climbing equipment, etc.	275
Total special clothing deduction	$ 925

Self-Study Problem 3.9

1. Mr. Jones		$ 20
2. Mr. Brown		25
3. Mrs. and Mr. Green		25
4. Ms. Gray		0
5. Mr. Edwards		75
6. Various customers		140
Total business gift deduction		$ 285

Self-Study Problem 3.10

1. Business. $16,000 ordinary loss.
2. Nonbusiness. $2,000 short-term capital loss.
3. Nonbusiness. $3,000 (limit on capital losses) short-term capital loss.
4. Business. Ordinary loss of $100,000.
5. Nonbusiness. $3,000 short-term capital loss.

Self-Study Problem 3.11

Part A. Refer to Form 8829 on Page E-13.
Part B. Refer to Form 8829 on Page E-14.

Self-Study Problem 3.12

Income $250. The hobby income must be recognized.
Deduction $0. No deduction is permitted.

Self-Study Problem 3.11, Part a

Form 8829 — Expenses for Business Use of Your Home
Department of the Treasury, Internal Revenue Service
File only with Schedule C (Form 1040). Use a separate Form 8829 for each home you used for business during the year.
Go to www.irs.gov/Form8829 for instructions and the latest information.
OMB No. 1545-0074
2024
Attachment Sequence No. 176

Name(s) of proprietor(s): Terry Cruz
Your social security number: 712-12-9002

Part I — Part of Your Home Used for Business

Line	Description		Amount
1	Area used regularly and exclusively for business, regularly for daycare, or for storage of inventory or product samples (see instructions)	1	150
2	Total area of home	2	1,000
3	Divide line 1 by line 2. Enter the result as a percentage	3	15 %
4	Multiply days used for daycare during year by hours used per day	4	hr.
5	If you started or stopped using your home for daycare during the year, see instructions; otherwise, enter 8,784	5	hr.
6	Divide line 4 by line 5. Enter the result as a decimal amount	6	
7	Business percentage. For daycare facilities not used exclusively for business, multiply line 6 by line 3 (enter the result as a percentage). All others, enter the amount from line 3	7	15 %

Part II — Figure Your Allowable Deduction

Line	Description	(a) Direct expenses	(b) Indirect expenses		Amount
8	Enter the amount from Schedule C, line 29, **plus** any gain derived from the business use of your home, **minus** any loss from the trade or business not derived from the business use of your home. See instructions.			8	46,000
	See instructions for columns (a) and (b) before completing lines 9–22.				
9	Casualty losses (see instructions)				
10	Deductible mortgage interest (see instructions)		7,000		
11	Real estate taxes (see instructions)		(a)		
12	Add lines 9, 10, and 11		7,000		
13	Multiply line 12, column (b), by line 7		1,050		
14	Add line 12, column (a), and line 13			14	1,050
15	Subtract line 14 from line 8. If zero or less, enter -0-			15	44,950
16	Excess mortgage interest (see instructions)				
17	Excess real estate taxes (see instructions)		5,000 (a)		
18	Insurance		3,000		
19	Rent				
20	Repairs and maintenance	200			
21	Utilities		2,000		
22	Other expenses (see instructions)		1,000		
23	Add lines 16 through 22	200	11,000		
24	Multiply line 23, column (b), by line 7		1,650		
25	Carryover of prior year operating expenses (see instructions)				
26	Add line 23, column (a), line 24, and line 25			26	1,850
27	Allowable operating expenses. Enter the **smaller** of line 15 or line 26			27	1,850
28	Limit on excess casualty losses and depreciation. Subtract line 27 from line 15			28	43,100
29	Excess casualty losses (see instructions)				
30	Depreciation of your home from line 42 below		3,054		
31	Carryover of prior year excess casualty losses and depreciation (see instructions)				
32	Add lines 29 through 31			32	3,054
33	Allowable excess casualty losses and depreciation. Enter the **smaller** of line 28 or line 32			33	3,054
34	Add lines 14, 27, and 33			34	5,954
35	Casualty loss portion, if any, from lines 14 and 33. Carry amount to **Form 4684**. See instructions			35	
36	**Allowable expenses for business use of your home.** Subtract line 35 from line 34. Enter here and on Schedule C, line 30. If your home was used for more than one business, see instructions			36	5,954

Part III — Depreciation of Your Home

Line	Description		Amount
37	Enter the **smaller** of your home's adjusted basis or its fair market value. See instructions	37	560,000
38	Value of land included on line 37	38	
39	Basis of building. Subtract line 38 from line 37	39	560,000
40	Business basis of building. Multiply line 39 by line 7	40	84,000
41	Depreciation percentage (see instructions)	41	3.636 %
42	Depreciation allowable (see instructions). Multiply line 40 by line 41. Enter here and on line 30 above	42	3,054

Part IV — Carryover of Unallowed Expenses to 2025

Line	Description		Amount
43	Operating expenses. Subtract line 27 from line 26. If less than zero, enter -0-	43	
44	Excess casualty losses and depreciation. Subtract line 33 from line 32. If less than zero, enter -0-	44	

For Paperwork Reduction Act Notice, see your tax return instructions. Cat. No. 13232M Form **8829** (2024)

(a) Because Terry's state and local tax itemized deduction exceeds $10,000 without considering property taxes on the home office dwelling, the real estate taxes are considered "excess" and are reported on line 17 rather than line 11.

Self-Study Problem 3.11, Part b

Form 8829 — Expenses for Business Use of Your Home
OMB No. 1545-0074
2024
Attachment Sequence No. 176

Department of the Treasury / Internal Revenue Service

File only with Schedule C (Form 1040). Use a separate Form 8829 for each home you used for business during the year.
Go to www.irs.gov/Form8829 for instructions and the latest information.

Name(s) of proprietor(s): Terry Cruz
Your social security number: 712-12-9002

Part I — Part of Your Home Used for Business

Line	Description	Value
1	Area used regularly and exclusively for business, regularly for daycare, or for storage of inventory or product samples (see instructions)	150
2	Total area of home	1,000
3	Divide line 1 by line 2. Enter the result as a percentage	15 %
	For daycare facilities not used exclusively for business, go to line 4. All others, go to line 7.	
4	Multiply days used for daycare during year by hours used per day	hr.
5	If you started or stopped using your home for daycare during the year, see instructions; otherwise, enter 8,784	hr.
6	Divide line 4 by line 5. Enter the result as a decimal amount	
7	Business percentage. For daycare facilities not used exclusively for business, multiply line 6 by line 3 (enter the result as a percentage). All others, enter the amount from line 3	15 %

Part II — Figure Your Allowable Deduction

Line	Description	(a) Direct expenses	(b) Indirect expenses	Total
8	Enter the amount from Schedule C, line 29, **plus** any gain derived from the business use of your home, **minus** any loss from the trade or business not derived from the business use of your home. See instructions.			4,600
9	Casualty losses (see instructions)			
10	Deductible mortgage interest (see instructions)			(a)
11	Real estate taxes (see instructions)			
12	Add lines 9, 10, and 11			
13	Multiply line 12, column (b), by line 7			
14	Add line 12, column (a), and line 13			
15	Subtract line 14 from line 8. If zero or less, enter -0-			4,600
16	Excess mortgage interest (see instructions)		7,000	(a)
17	Excess real estate taxes (see instructions)		5,000	
18	Insurance		3,000	
19	Rent			
20	Repairs and maintenance	200		
21	Utilities		2,000	
22	Other expenses (see instructions)		1,000	
23	Add lines 16 through 22	200	18,000	
24	Multiply line 23, column (b), by line 7			2,700
25	Carryover of prior year operating expenses (see instructions)			
26	Add line 23, column (a), line 24, and line 25			2,900
27	Allowable operating expenses. Enter the **smaller** of line 15 or line 26			2,900
28	Limit on excess casualty losses and depreciation. Subtract line 27 from line 15			1,700
29	Excess casualty losses (see instructions)			
30	Depreciation of your home from line 42 below		3,054	
31	Carryover of prior year excess casualty losses and depreciation (see instructions)			
32	Add lines 29 through 31			3,054
33	Allowable excess casualty losses and depreciation. Enter the **smaller** of line 28 or line 32			1,700
34	Add lines 14, 27, and 33			4,600
35	Casualty loss portion, if any, from lines 14 and 33. Carry amount to **Form 4684**. See instructions			
36	**Allowable expenses for business use of your home.** Subtract line 35 from line 34. Enter here and on Schedule C, line 30. If your home was used for more than one business, see instructions			4,600

Part III — Depreciation of Your Home

Line	Description	Value
37	Enter the **smaller** of your home's adjusted basis or its fair market value. See instructions	560,000
38	Value of land included on line 37	
39	Basis of building. Subtract line 38 from line 37	560,000
40	Business basis of building. Multiply line 39 by line 7	84,000
41	Depreciation percentage (see instructions)	3.636 %
42	Depreciation allowable (see instructions). Multiply line 40 by line 41. Enter here and on line 30 above	3,054

Part IV — Carryover of Unallowed Expenses to 2025

Line	Description	Value
43	Operating expenses. Subtract line 27 from line 26. If less than zero, enter -0-	
44	Excess casualty losses and depreciation. Subtract line 33 from line 32. If less than zero, enter -0-	1,354

For Paperwork Reduction Act Notice, see your tax return instructions. Cat. No. 13232M Form **8829** (2024)

(a) Because Terry does not itemize, all interest and real estate taxes are reported on lines 16 and 17.

Chapter 4 Additional Income and the Qualified Business Income Deduction

Self-Study Problem 4.1

1. No — Inventory is specifically excluded from the definition of a capital asset.
2. Yes
3. No — Property held by the creator is specifically excluded from the definition of a capital asset.
4. No — Accounts receivable are specifically excluded from the definition of a capital asset.
5. Yes — The copyright is not held by the creator.
6. No — Section 1231 assets (depreciable property and real estate used in a trade or business) are specifically excluded from the definition of a capital asset.
7. Yes
8. Yes
9. Yes
10. Yes
11. No — Inventory is specifically excluded from the definition of a capital asset.
12. Yes

Self-Study Problem 4.2

1. Short-term. Held for only about 7.5 months.
2. Long-term. Holding period exceeded 12 months on May 3, 2024.
3. Short-term. Holding period is exactly 12 months but must exceed 12 months for long-term.
4. Long-term. Holding period is over 12 months.

Self-Study Problem 4.3

1. Adjusted basis = $11,000
2. $201,500. $200,000 + $1,000 + $500. The property taxes and mortgage do not affect basis.
3. $6,000 regardless of sales price. Inherited property has a basis of FMV at time of death.
4. $5,400 regardless of sales price. Basis of appreciated gift property is carryover basis.
5. The basis of depreciated gift property can vary based on sales price. When sold for $7,000, which is more than carryover basis, the basis for sale is carryover basis of $6,000. If sold at a loss, the basis is the FMV at the date of the gift ($5,400). If sold for a price in between the FMV and carryover basis, there is no gain or loss and so the basis must be $5,800.

Self-Study Problem 4.4

Net long-term ($12,000 − $4,000) + ($14,000 − $17,500) =	$ 4,500
Net short-term	(1,800)
Net capital gains	2,700
Ordinary income	46,000
Net LT capital gain taxed at 0% ($47,025 − $46,000)	1,025
Net LT capital gain taxed at 15% ($2,700 − $1,025)	1,675
LT capital gains rate	15%
Long-term capital gains tax	$ 251

Self-Study Problem 4.5

Refer to Schedule D, Form 8949, and the Qualified Dividends and Capital Gain Tax Worksheet on Pages E-17 through E-21.

Self-Study Problem 4.6

a. Sales price	$350,000
Basis	(30,000)
Realized gain	320,000
Exclusion	(250,000)
Recognized gain	$ 70,000

b. $0. The $500,000 exclusion for joint filers exceeds the $320,000 realized gain.

c. $25,000 = ($350,000 − $200,000) − (½ × $250,000)

Self-Study Problem 4.7

Refer to Schedule E on Page E-22.

Self-Study Problem 4.8

Part A: Refer to Schedule E and Form 8582 on Pages E-23 to E-26.
Part B: Refer to Schedule E and Form 8582 on Pages E-27 to E-30.

Self-Study Problem 4.9

a. Refer to Form 172 on Page E-31.

b. 2025 taxable income	$12,000
80% limitation	80%
NOL Limit	9,600
NOL carryforward available	10,000
NOL carryforward to 2026	$ 400

Self-Study Problem 4.10

Refer to Schedule SE of Form 1040 on Page E-32.

Self-Study Problem 4.5

SCHEDULE D (Form 1040)
Department of the Treasury
Internal Revenue Service

Capital Gains and Losses
Attach to Form 1040, 1040-SR, or 1040-NR.
Use Form 8949 to list your transactions for lines 1b, 2, 3, 8b, 9, and 10.
Go to www.irs.gov/ScheduleD for instructions and the latest information.

OMB No. 1545-0074

2024
Attachment Sequence No. **12**

Name(s) shown on return: Louis Winthorpe
Your social security number: 123-44-3214

Did you dispose of any investment(s) in a qualified opportunity fund during the tax year? ☐ Yes ☑ No
If "Yes," attach Form 8949 and see its instructions for additional requirements for reporting your gain or loss.

Part I — Short-Term Capital Gains and Losses—Generally Assets Held One Year or Less (see instructions)

See instructions for how to figure the amounts to enter on the lines below.

This form may be easier to complete if you round off cents to whole dollars.

	(d) Proceeds (sales price)	(e) Cost (or other basis)	(g) Adjustments to gain or loss from Form(s) 8949, Part I, line 2, column (g)	(h) Gain or (loss) Subtract column (e) from column (d) and combine the result with column (g)
1a Totals for all short-term transactions reported on Form 1099-B for which basis was reported to the IRS and for which you have no adjustments (see instructions). However, if you choose to report all these transactions on Form 8949, leave this line blank and go to line 1b .				
1b Totals for all transactions reported on Form(s) 8949 with **Box A** checked	15,000	28,200	7,200	(6,000)
2 Totals for all transactions reported on Form(s) 8949 with **Box B** checked				
3 Totals for all transactions reported on Form(s) 8949 with **Box C** checked				
4 Short-term gain from Form 6252 and short-term gain or (loss) from Forms 4684, 6781, and 8824			**4**	
5 Net short-term gain or (loss) from partnerships, S corporations, estates, and trusts from Schedule(s) K-1			**5**	
6 Short-term capital loss carryover. Enter the amount, if any, from line 8 of your **Capital Loss Carryover Worksheet** in the instructions			**6**	( )
7 **Net short-term capital gain or (loss).** Combine lines 1a through 6 in column (h). If you have any long-term capital gains or losses, go to Part II below. Otherwise, go to Part III on the back			**7**	(6,000)

Part II — Long-Term Capital Gains and Losses—Generally Assets Held More Than One Year (see instructions)

	(d) Proceeds (sales price)	(e) Cost (or other basis)	(g) Adjustments to gain or loss from Form(s) 8949, Part II, line 2, column (g)	(h) Gain or (loss) Subtract column (e) from column (d) and combine the result with column (g)
8a Totals for all long-term transactions reported on Form 1099-B for which basis was reported to the IRS and for which you have no adjustments (see instructions). However, if you choose to report all these transactions on Form 8949, leave this line blank and go to line 8b .				
8b Totals for all transactions reported on Form(s) 8949 with **Box D** checked	43,000	33,500		9,500
9 Totals for all transactions reported on Form(s) 8949 with **Box E** checked				
10 Totals for all transactions reported on Form(s) 8949 with **Box F** checked				
11 Gain from Form 4797, Part I; long-term gain from Forms 2439 and 6252; and long-term gain or (loss) from Forms 4684, 6781, and 8824			**11**	
12 Net long-term gain or (loss) from partnerships, S corporations, estates, and trusts from Schedule(s) K-1			**12**	
13 Capital gain distributions. See the instructions			**13**	
14 Long-term capital loss carryover. Enter the amount, if any, from line 13 of your **Capital Loss Carryover Worksheet** in the instructions			**14**	( )
15 **Net long-term capital gain or (loss).** Combine lines 8a through 14 in column (h). Then, go to Part III on the back			**15**	9,500

For Paperwork Reduction Act Notice, see your tax return instructions. Cat. No. 11338H Schedule D (Form 1040) 2024

Self-Study Problem 4.5

Schedule D (Form 1040) 2024 — Page **2**

Part III **Summary**

Line	Description	Amount
16	Combine lines 7 and 15 and enter the result	3,500

- If line 16 is a **gain**, enter the amount from line 16 on Form 1040, 1040-SR, or 1040-NR, line 7. Then, go to line 17 below.
- If line 16 is a **loss**, skip lines 17 through 20 below. Then, go to line 21. Also be sure to complete line 22.
- If line 16 is **zero**, skip lines 17 through 21 below and enter -0- on Form 1040, 1040-SR, or 1040-NR, line 7. Then, go to line 22.

17 Are lines 15 and 16 **both** gains?
☑ **Yes.** Go to line 18.
☐ **No.** Skip lines 18 through 21, and go to line 22.

18 If you are required to complete the **28% Rate Gain Worksheet** (see instructions), enter the amount, if any, from line 7 of that worksheet 18

19 If you are required to complete the **Unrecaptured Section 1250 Gain Worksheet** (see instructions), enter the amount, if any, from line 18 of that worksheet 19

20 Are lines 18 and 19 both zero or blank and you are not filing Form 4952?
☑ **Yes.** Complete the **Qualified Dividends and Capital Gain Tax Worksheet** in the instructions for Form 1040, line 16. **Don't** complete lines 21 and 22 below.

☐ **No.** Complete the **Schedule D Tax Worksheet** in the instructions. **Don't** complete lines 21 and 22 below.

21 If line 16 is a loss, enter here and on Form 1040, 1040-SR, or 1040-NR, line 7, the **smaller** of:
- The loss on line 16; or
- ($3,000), or if married filing separately, ($1,500)

. . . . 21 ( )

Note: When figuring which amount is smaller, treat both amounts as positive numbers.

22 Do you have qualified dividends on Form 1040, 1040-SR, or 1040-NR, line 3a?

☐ **Yes.** Complete the **Qualified Dividends and Capital Gain Tax Worksheet** in the instructions for Form 1040, line 16.

☐ **No.** Complete the rest of Form 1040, 1040-SR, or 1040-NR.

Self-Study Problem 4.5

Form 8949
Department of the Treasury
Internal Revenue Service

Sales and Other Dispositions of Capital Assets

File with your Schedule D to list your transactions for lines 1b, 2, 3, 8b, 9, and 10 of Schedule D.
Go to www.irs.gov/Form8949 for instructions and the latest information.

OMB No. 1545-0074
2024
Attachment Sequence No. 12A

Name(s) shown on return: Louis Winthorpe
Social security number or taxpayer identification number: 123-44-3214

Before you check Box A, B, or C below, see whether you received any Form(s) 1099-B or substitute statement(s) from your broker. A substitute statement will have the same information as Form 1099-B. Either will show whether your basis (usually your cost) was reported to the IRS by your broker and may even tell you which box to check.

Part I **Short-Term.** Transactions involving capital assets you held 1 year or less are generally short-term (see instructions). For long-term transactions, see page 2.

Note: You may aggregate all short-term transactions reported on Form(s) 1099-B showing basis was reported to the IRS and for which no adjustments or codes are required. Enter the totals directly on Schedule D, line 1a; you aren't required to report these transactions on Form 8949 (see instructions).

You **must** check Box **A, B,** or **C** below. Check only one box. If more than one box applies for your short-term transactions, complete a separate Form 8949, page 1, for each applicable box. If you have more short-term transactions than will fit on this page for one or more of the boxes, complete as many forms with the same box checked as you need.

- [x] **(A)** Short-term transactions reported on Form(s) 1099-B showing basis was reported to the IRS (see **Note** above)
- [ ] **(B)** Short-term transactions reported on Form(s) 1099-B showing basis **wasn't** reported to the IRS
- [ ] **(C)** Short-term transactions not reported to you on Form 1099-B

(a) Description of property (Example: 100 sh. XYZ Co.)	(b) Date acquired (Mo., day, yr.)	(c) Date sold or disposed of (Mo., day, yr.)	(d) Proceeds (sales price) (see instructions)	(e) Cost or other basis See the Note below and see Column (e) in the separate instructions.	(f) Code(s) from instructions	(g) Amount of adjustment	(h) Gain or (loss) Subtract column (e) from column (d) and combine the result with column (g).
100 shs. Sargent Corp.	04/18/2024	12/07/2024	12,000	19,200	W	7,200	0
50 shs. Mullin Inc.	05/16/2024	12/16/2024	3,000	9,000			(6,000)
2 Totals. Add the amounts in columns (d), (e), (g), and (h) (subtract negative amounts). Enter each total here and include on your Schedule D, **line 1b** (if **Box A** above is checked), **line 2** (if **Box B** above is checked), or **line 3** (if **Box C** above is checked) . . .			15,000	28,200		7,200	(6,000)

Note: If you checked Box A above but the basis reported to the IRS was incorrect, enter in column (e) the basis as reported to the IRS, and enter an adjustment in column (g) to correct the basis. See *Column (g)* in the separate instructions for how to figure the amount of the adjustment.

For Paperwork Reduction Act Notice, see your tax return instructions. Cat. No. 37768Z Form **8949** (2024)

Self-Study Problem 4.5

Form 8949 (2024) — Attachment Sequence No. **12A** — Page **2**

Name(s) shown on return. Name and SSN or taxpayer identification no. not required if shown on other side | Social security number or taxpayer identification number

Before you check Box D, E, or F below, see whether you received any Form(s) 1099-B or substitute statement(s) from your broker. A substitute statement will have the same information as Form 1099-B. Either will show whether your basis (usually your cost) was reported to the IRS by your broker and may even tell you which box to check.

Part II — **Long-Term.** Transactions involving capital assets you held more than 1 year are generally long-term (see instructions). For short-term transactions, see page 1.

Note: You may aggregate all long-term transactions reported on Form(s) 1099-B showing basis was reported to the IRS and for which no adjustments or codes are required. Enter the totals directly on Schedule D, line 8a; you aren't required to report these transactions on Form 8949 (see instructions).

You *must* check Box D, E, or F below. Check only one box. If more than one box applies for your long-term transactions, complete a separate Form 8949, page 2, for each applicable box. If you have more long-term transactions than will fit on this page for one or more of the boxes, complete as many forms with the same box checked as you need.

- [x] **(D)** Long-term transactions reported on Form(s) 1099-B showing basis was reported to the IRS (see **Note** above)
- [ ] **(E)** Long-term transactions reported on Form(s) 1099-B showing basis **wasn't** reported to the IRS
- [ ] **(F)** Long-term transactions not reported to you on Form 1099-B

1 (a) Description of property (Example: 100 sh. XYZ Co.)	(b) Date acquired (Mo., day, yr.)	(c) Date sold or disposed of (Mo., day, yr.)	(d) Proceeds (sales price) (see instructions)	(e) Cost or other basis See the **Note** below and see *Column (e)* in the separate instructions.	(f) Code(s) from instructions	(g) Amount of adjustment	(h) Gain or (loss) Subtract column (e) from column (d) and combine the result with column (g).
50 shs. Reynolds Corp.	12/18/2015	10/02/2024	25,000	21,000			4,000
100 shs. Second Maid Juice	06/12/2015	08/15/2024	18,000	12,500			5,500
2 Totals. Add the amounts in columns (d), (e), (g), and (h) (subtract negative amounts). Enter each total here and include on your Schedule D, **line 8b** (if **Box D** above is checked), **line 9** (if **Box E** above is checked), or **line 10** (if **Box F** above is checked).			43,000	33,500			9,500

Note: If you checked Box D above but the basis reported to the IRS was incorrect, enter in column (e) the basis as reported to the IRS, and enter an adjustment in column (g) to correct the basis. See *Column (g)* in the separate instructions for how to figure the amount of the adjustment.

Form **8949** (2024)

Self-Study Problem 4.5

Qualified Dividends and Capital Gain Tax Worksheet—Line 16 *Keep for Your Records*

Before you begin:
- ✓ See the earlier instructions for line 16 to see if you can use this worksheet to figure your tax.
- ✓ Before completing this worksheet, complete Form 1040 or 1040-SR through line 15.
- ✓ If you don't have to file Schedule D and you received capital gain distributions, be sure you checked the box on Form 1040 or 1040-SR, line 7.

#	Description		Amount
1.	Enter the amount from Form 1040 or 1040-SR, line 15. However, if you are filing Form 2555 (relating to foreign earned income), enter the amount from line 3 of the Foreign Earned Income Tax Worksheet	1.	50,000
2.	Enter the amount from Form 1040 or 1040-SR, line 3a*	2.	
3.	Are you filing Schedule D?* ☑ **Yes.** Enter the **smaller** of line 15 or 16 of Schedule D. If either line 15 or 16 is blank or a loss, enter -0-. ☐ **No.** Enter the amount from Form 1040 or 1040-SR, line 7.	3.	3,500
4.	Add lines 2 and 3	4.	3,500
5.	Subtract line 4 from line 1. If zero or less, enter -0-	5.	46,500
6.	Enter: $47,025 if single or married filing separately, $94,050 if married filing jointly or qualifying widow(er), $63,000 if head of household.	6.	47,025
7.	Enter the smaller of line 1 or line 6	7.	47,025
8.	Enter the smaller of line 5 or line 7	8.	46,500
9.	Subtract line 8 from line 7. This amount is taxed at 0%	9.	525
10.	Enter the smaller of line 1 or line 4	10.	3,500
11.	Enter the amount from line 9	11.	525
12.	Subtract line 11 from line 10	12.	2,975
13.	Enter: $518,900 if single, $291,850 if married filing separately, $583,750 if married filing jointly or qualifying widow(er), $551,350 if head of household.	13.	518,900
14.	Enter the smaller of line 1 or line 13	14.	50,000
15.	Add lines 5 and 9	15.	47,025
16.	Subtract line 15 from line 14. If zero or less, enter -0-	16.	2,975
17.	Enter the smaller of line 12 or line 16	17.	2,975
18.	Multiply line 17 by 15% (0.15)	18.	446
19.	Add lines 9 and 17	19.	3,500
20.	Subtract line 19 from line 10	20.	0
21.	Multiply line 20 by 20% (0.20)	21.	0
22.	Figure the tax on the amount on line 5. If the amount on line 5 is less than $100,000, use the Tax Table to figure the tax. If the amount on line 5 is $100,000 or more, use the Tax Computation Worksheet	22.	5,351
23.	Add lines 18, 21, and 22	23.	5,797
24.	Figure the tax on the amount on line 1. If the amount on line 1 is less than $100,000, use the Tax Table to figure the tax. If the amount on line 1 is $100,000 or more, use the Tax Computation Worksheet	24.	6,059
25.	**Tax on all taxable income.** Enter the **smaller** of line 23 or 24. Also include this amount on the entry space on Form 1040 or 1040-SR, line 16. If you are filing Form 2555, don't enter this amount on the entry space on Form 1040 or 1040-SR, line 16. Instead, enter it on line 4 of the Foreign Earned Income Tax Worksheet	25.	5,797

If you are filing Form 2555, see the footnote in the Foreign Earned Income Tax Worksheet before completing this line.

This worksheet adapted from the 2023 worksheet.

Self-Study Problem 4.7

SCHEDULE E (Form 1040)
Department of the Treasury
Internal Revenue Service

Supplemental Income and Loss
(From rental real estate, royalties, partnerships, S corporations, estates, trusts, REMICs, etc.)
Attach to Form 1040, 1040-SR, 1040-NR, or 1041.
Go to www.irs.gov/ScheduleE for instructions and the latest information.

OMB No. 1545-0074
2024
Attachment Sequence No. **13**

Name(s) shown on return: Nancy Kapiolani
Your social security number:

Part I — Income or Loss From Rental Real Estate and Royalties

Note: If you are in the business of renting personal property, use **Schedule C**. See instructions. If you are an individual, report farm rental income or loss from **Form 4835** on page 2, line 40.

A Did you make any payments in 2024 that would require you to file Form(s) 1099? See instructions ... ☐ Yes ☑ No
B If "Yes," did you or will you file required Form(s) 1099? ... ☐ Yes ☐ No

1a Physical address of each property (street, city, state, ZIP code)
A 1218 Park Ave S, Tacoma, WA 98447
B
C

1b Type of Property (from list below)	2 For each rental real estate property listed above, report the number of fair rental and personal use days. Check the QJV box only if you meet the requirements to file as a qualified joint venture. See instructions.		Fair Rental Days	Personal Use Days	QJV
A 2		A	365		☐
B		B			☐
C		C			☐

Type of Property:
1 Single Family Residence 3 Vacation/Short-Term Rental 5 Land 7 Self-Rental
2 Multi-Family Residence 4 Commercial 6 Royalties 8 Other (describe) _____

			Properties: A	B	C
Income:					
3	Rents received	3	9,700 (a)		
4	Royalties received	4			
Expenses:					
5	Advertising	5			
6	Auto and travel (see instructions)	6			
7	Cleaning and maintenance	7			
8	Commissions	8			
9	Insurance	9	225		
10	Legal and other professional fees	10			
11	Management fees	11			
12	Mortgage interest paid to banks, etc. (see instructions)	12	1,700		
13	Other interest	13			
14	Repairs	14	400		
15	Supplies	15			
16	Taxes	16	1,100		
17	Utilities	17	900		
18	Depreciation expense or depletion	18	4,364 (b)		
19	Other (list) _____	19			
20	Total expenses. Add lines 5 through 19	20	8,689 (c)		
21	Subtract line 20 from line 3 (rents) and/or 4 (royalties). If result is a (loss), see instructions to find out if you must file **Form 6198**	21	1,011		
22	Deductible rental real estate loss after limitation, if any, on **Form 8582** (see instructions)	22	( )	( )	( )

23a	Total of all amounts reported on line 3 for all rental properties	23a	9,700
b	Total of all amounts reported on line 4 for all royalty properties	23b	
c	Total of all amounts reported on line 12 for all properties	23c	1,700
d	Total of all amounts reported on line 18 for all properties	23d	4,364
e	Total of all amounts reported on line 20 for all properties	23e	8,689
24	**Income.** Add positive amounts shown on line 21. **Do not** include any losses	24	1,011
25	**Losses.** Add royalty losses from line 21 and rental real estate losses from line 22. Enter total losses here	25	( )
26	**Total rental real estate and royalty income or (loss).** Combine lines 24 and 25. Enter the result here. If Parts II, III, and IV, and line 40 on page 2 do not apply to you, also enter this amount on Schedule 1 (Form 1040), line 5. Otherwise, include this amount in the total on line 41 on page 2	26	1,011

For Paperwork Reduction Act Notice, see the separate instructions. Cat. No. 11344L Schedule E (Form 1040) 2024

(a) $2,500 in rent collected from the old tenant plus $200 security deposit kept plus $6,000 monthly rent collected from new tenant plus last month's rent of $1,000.
(b) $120,000 ÷ 27.5 years
(c) Insurance, interest, taxes, and utilities are all 50% of the total since one-half of the duplex is rented.

Self-Study Problem 4.8, Part a

SCHEDULE E (Form 1040)
Department of the Treasury
Internal Revenue Service

Supplemental Income and Loss
(From rental real estate, royalties, partnerships, S corporations, estates, trusts, REMICs, etc.)
Attach to Form 1040, 1040-SR, 1040-NR, or 1041.
Go to www.irs.gov/ScheduleE for instructions and the latest information.

OMB No. 1545-0074
2024
Attachment Sequence No. **13**

Name(s) shown on return: Louise Jefferson
Your social security number: 112-67-1234

Part I — Income or Loss From Rental Real Estate and Royalties

Note: If you are in the business of renting personal property, use **Schedule C**. See instructions. If you are an individual, report farm rental income or loss from **Form 4835** on page 2, line 40.

A Did you make any payments in 2024 that would require you to file Form(s) 1099? See instructions — ☐ Yes ☒ No
B If "Yes," did you or will you file required Form(s) 1099? — ☐ Yes ☐ No

1a Physical address of each property (street, city, state, ZIP code)
  A: 185 E 85th Street, New York, NY 10028
  B:
  C:

1b Type of Property (from list below)
  A: 1
  B:
  C:

2 For each rental real estate property listed above, report the number of fair rental and personal use days. Check the QJV box only if you meet the requirements to file as a qualified joint venture. See instructions.

	Fair Rental Days	Personal Use Days	QJV
A	365		☐
B			☐
C			☐

Type of Property:
1 Single Family Residence   3 Vacation/Short-Term Rental   5 Land   7 Self-Rental
2 Multi-Family Residence   4 Commercial   6 Royalties   8 Other (describe) _____

		Properties: A	B	C
Income:				
3	Rents received	20,000		
4	Royalties received			
Expenses:				
5	Advertising			
6	Auto and travel (see instructions)			
7	Cleaning and maintenance			
8	Commissions			
9	Insurance			
10	Legal and other professional fees			
11	Management fees			
12	Mortgage interest paid to banks, etc. (see instructions)	6,000		
13	Other interest			
14	Repairs			
15	Supplies			
16	Taxes	8,000		
17	Utilities	2,000		
18	Depreciation expense or depletion	9,000		
19	Other (list) _____	4,000		
20	Total expenses. Add lines 5 through 19	29,000		
21	Subtract line 20 from line 3 (rents) and/or 4 (royalties). If result is a (loss), see instructions to find out if you must file **Form 6198**	(9,000)		
22	Deductible rental real estate loss after limitation, if any, on **Form 8582** (see instructions)	(6,000)	( )	( )

23a	Total of all amounts reported on line 3 for all rental properties	20,000
23b	Total of all amounts reported on line 4 for all royalty properties	
23c	Total of all amounts reported on line 12 for all properties	6,000
23d	Total of all amounts reported on line 18 for all properties	9,000
23e	Total of all amounts reported on line 20 for all properties	29,000
24	**Income.** Add positive amounts shown on line 21. **Do not** include any losses	
25	**Losses.** Add royalty losses from line 21 and rental real estate losses from line 22. Enter total losses here	(6,000)
26	**Total rental real estate and royalty income or (loss).** Combine lines 24 and 25. Enter the result here. If Parts II, III, and IV, and line 40 on page 2 do not apply to you, also enter this amount on Schedule 1 (Form 1040), line 5. Otherwise, include this amount in the total on line 41 on page 2	(6,000)

For Paperwork Reduction Act Notice, see the separate instructions.   Cat. No. 11344L   Schedule E (Form 1040) 2024

Self-Study Problem 4.8, Part a

Schedule E (Form 1040) 2024 — Attachment Sequence No. **13** — Page **2**

Name(s) shown on return. Do not enter name and social security number if shown on other side.

Your social security number

Caution: The IRS compares amounts reported on your tax return with amounts shown on Schedule(s) K-1.

Part II — Income or Loss From Partnerships and S Corporations

Note: If you report a loss, receive a distribution, dispose of stock, or receive a loan repayment from an S corporation, you **must** check the box in column **(e)** on line 28 and attach the required basis computation. If you report a loss from an at-risk activity for which **any** amount is **not** at risk, you **must** check the box in column **(f)** on line 28 and attach **Form 6198**. See instructions.

27 Are you reporting any loss not allowed in a prior year due to the at-risk or basis limitations, a prior year unallowed loss from a passive activity (if that loss was not reported on Form 8582), or unreimbursed partnership expenses? If you answered "Yes," see instructions before completing this section. ☐ Yes ☒ No

28

	(a) Name	(b) Enter P for partnership; S for S corporation	(c) Check if foreign partnership	(d) Employer identification number	(e) Check if basis computation is required	(f) Check if any amount is not at risk
A	Bunker Dry Cleaners LP	P	☐	13-3434347	☐	☐
B			☐		☐	☐
C			☐		☐	☐
D			☐		☐	☐

	Passive Income and Loss		Nonpassive Income and Loss		
	(g) Passive loss allowed (attach Form 8582 if required)	(h) Passive income from Schedule K-1	(i) Nonpassive loss allowed (see Schedule K-1)	(j) Section 179 expense deduction from Form 4562	(k) Nonpassive income from Schedule K-1
A	0				
B					
C					
D					

| 29a | Totals | | | | |
| b | Totals | | | | |

30	Add columns (h) and (k) of line 29a	**30**	
31	Add columns (g), (i), and (j) of line 29b	**31**	(0)
32	**Total partnership and S corporation income or (loss).** Combine lines 30 and 31	**32**	0

Part III — Income or Loss From Estates and Trusts

33

	(a) Name	(b) Employer identification number
A		
B		

	Passive Income and Loss		Nonpassive Income and Loss	
	(c) Passive deduction or loss allowed (attach Form 8582 if required)	(d) Passive income from Schedule K-1	(e) Deduction or loss from Schedule K-1	(f) Other income from Schedule K-1
A				
B				

| 34a | Totals | | | |
| b | Totals | | | |

35	Add columns (d) and (f) of line 34a	**35**	
36	Add columns (c) and (e) of line 34b	**36**	( )
37	**Total estate and trust income or (loss).** Combine lines 35 and 36	**37**	

Part IV — Income or Loss From Real Estate Mortgage Investment Conduits (REMICs) — Residual Holder

38

(a) Name	(b) Employer identification number	(c) Excess inclusion from Schedules Q, line 2c (see instructions)	(d) Taxable income (net loss) from Schedules Q, line 1b	(e) Income from Schedules Q, line 3b

| 39 | Combine columns (d) and (e) only. Enter the result here and include in the total on line 41 below | **39** | |

Part V — Summary

40	Net farm rental income or (loss) from **Form 4835**. Also, complete line 42 below	**40**	
41	**Total income or (loss).** Combine lines 26, 32, 37, 39, and 40. Enter the result here and on Schedule 1 (Form 1040), line 5	**41**	(6,000)
42	**Reconciliation of farming and fishing income.** Enter your **gross** farming and fishing income reported on Form 4835, line 7; Schedule K-1 (Form 1065), box 14, code B; Schedule K-1 (Form 1120-S), box 17, code AN; and Schedule K-1 (Form 1041), box 14, code F. See instructions	**42**	
43	**Reconciliation for real estate professionals.** If you were a real estate professional (see instructions), enter the net income or (loss) you reported anywhere on Form 1040, Form 1040-SR, or Form 1040-NR from all rental real estate activities in which you materially participated under the passive activity loss rules	**43**	

Schedule E (Form 1040) 2024

Self-Study Problem 4.8, Part a

Form 8582
Department of the Treasury
Internal Revenue Service

Passive Activity Loss Limitations
See separate instructions.
Attach to Form 1040, 1040-SR, or 1041.
Go to www.irs.gov/Form8582 for instructions and the latest information.

OMB No. 1545-1008
2024
Attachment Sequence No. 858

Name(s) shown on return: Louise Jefferson
Identifying number: 112-67-1234

Part I — 2024 Passive Activity Loss

Caution: Complete Parts IV and V before completing Part I.

Rental Real Estate Activities With Active Participation (For the definition of active participation, see *Special Allowance for Rental Real Estate Activities* in the instructions.)

Line	Description	Amount	Total
1a	Activities with net income (enter the amount from Part IV, column (a))	1a	
1b	Activities with net loss (enter the amount from Part IV, column (b))	1b (9,000)	
1c	Prior years' unallowed losses (enter the amount from Part IV, column (c))	1c ( )	
1d	Combine lines 1a, 1b, and 1c		1d (9,000)

All Other Passive Activities

Line	Description	Amount	Total
2a	Activities with net income (enter the amount from Part V, column (a))	2a	
2b	Activities with net loss (enter the amount from Part V, column (b))	2b 15,000	
2c	Prior years' unallowed losses (enter the amount from Part V, column (c))	2c ( )	
2d	Combine lines 2a, 2b, and 2c		2d (15,000)

3. Combine lines 1d and 2d and subtract any prior year unallowed CRD. See instructions. If this line is zero or more, stop here and include this form with your return; all losses are allowed, including any prior year unallowed losses entered on line 1c or 2c. Report the losses on the forms and schedules normally used ..... **3 (24,000)**

If line 3 is a loss and: • Line 1d is a loss, go to Part II.
• Line 2d is a loss (and line 1d is zero or more), skip Part II and go to line 10.

Caution: If your filing status is married filing separately and you lived with your spouse at any time during the year, **do not** complete Part II. Instead, go to line 10.

Part II — Special Allowance for Rental Real Estate Activities With Active Participation

Note: Enter all numbers in Part II as positive amounts. See instructions for an example.

Line	Description	Amount	Total
4	Enter the **smaller** of the loss on line 1d or the loss on line 3		4 9,000
5	Enter $150,000. If married filing separately, see instructions	5 150,000	
6	Enter modified adjusted gross income, but not less than zero. See instructions	6 138,000	
	Note: If line 6 is greater than or equal to line 5, skip lines 7 and 8 and enter -0- on line 9. Otherwise, go to line 7.		
7	Subtract line 6 from line 5	7 12,000	
8	Multiply line 7 by 50% (0.50). **Do not** enter more than $25,000. If married filing separately, see instructions		8 6,000
9	Enter the **smaller** of line 4 or line 8. If line 3 includes any CRD, see instructions		9 6,000

Part III — Total Losses Allowed

Line	Description	Total
10	Add the income, if any, on lines 1a and 2a and enter the total	10
11	**Total losses allowed from all passive activities for 2024.** Add lines 9 and 10. See instructions to find out how to report the losses on your tax return	11 6,000

Part IV — Complete This Part Before Part I, Lines 1a, 1b, and 1c. See instructions.

Name of activity	Current year (a) Net income (line 1a)	Current year (b) Net loss (line 1b)	Prior years (c) Unallowed loss (line 1c)	Overall gain or loss (d) Gain	Overall gain or loss (e) Loss
Condo		9,000			9,000
Total. Enter on Part I, lines 1a, 1b, and 1c		9,000			

For Paperwork Reduction Act Notice, see instructions. Cat. No. 63704F Form **8582** (2024)

Self-Study Problem 4.8, Part a

Form 8582 (2024) — Page 2

Part V — Complete This Part Before Part I, Lines 2a, 2b, and 2c. See instructions.

Name of activity	Current year (a) Net income (line 2a)	Current year (b) Net loss (line 2b)	Prior years (c) Unallowed loss (line 2c)	Overall gain or loss (d) Gain	Overall gain or loss (e) Loss
Bunker Dry Cleaners LP		15,000			15,000
Total. Enter on Part I, lines 2a, 2b, and 2c		15,000			

Part VI — Use This Part if an Amount Is Shown on Part II, Line 9. See instructions.

Name of activity	Form or schedule and line number to be reported on (see instructions)	(a) Loss	(b) Ratio	(c) Special allowance	(d) Subtract column (c) from column (a).
Condo		9,000	1.00	6,000	3,000
Total		9,000	1.00	6,000	3,000

Part VII — Allocation of Unallowed Losses. See instructions.

Name of activity	Form or schedule and line number to be reported on (see instructions)	(a) Loss	(b) Ratio	(c) Unallowed loss
Condo		3,000	.166667	3,000
Bunker Dry Cleaners LP		15,000	.833333	15,000
Total		18,000	1.00	18,000

Part VIII — Allowed Losses. See instructions.

Name of activity	Form or schedule and line number to be reported on (see instructions)	(a) Loss	(b) Unallowed loss	(c) Allowed loss
Condo		9,000	3,000	6,000
Bunker Dry Cleaners LP		15,000	15,000	0
Total		24,000	18,000	6,000

Form **8582** (2024)

Self-Study Problem 4.8, Part b

SCHEDULE E (Form 1040)
Department of the Treasury
Internal Revenue Service

Supplemental Income and Loss
(From rental real estate, royalties, partnerships, S corporations, estates, trusts, REMICs, etc.)
Attach to Form 1040, 1040-SR, 1040-NR, or 1041.
Go to www.irs.gov/ScheduleE for instructions and the latest information.

OMB No. 1545-0074
2024
Attachment Sequence No. **13**

Name(s) shown on return: Jorge Jefferson
Your social security number: 656-76-4321

Part I — Income or Loss From Rental Real Estate and Royalties

Note: If you are in the business of renting personal property, use **Schedule C**. See instructions. If you are an individual, report farm rental income or loss from **Form 4835** on page 2, line 40.

A. Did you make any payments in 2024 that would require you to file Form(s) 1099? See instructions ☐ Yes ☒ No
B. If "Yes," did you or will you file required Form(s) 1099? ☐ Yes ☐ No

1a Physical address of each property (street, city, state, ZIP code)
A. 186 E 85th Street, New York, NY 10028
B. 8970 Cooper Ave., Queens, NY 11374
C.

1b Type of Property (from list below)	2 For each rental real estate property listed above, report the number of fair rental and personal use days. Check the QJV box only if you meet the requirements to file as a qualified joint venture. See instructions.		Fair Rental Days	Personal Use Days	QJV
A	1	A	365		☐
B	1	B	365		☐
C		C			☐

Type of Property:
1 Single Family Residence 3 Vacation/Short-Term Rental 5 Land 7 Self-Rental
2 Multi-Family Residence 4 Commercial 6 Royalties 8 Other (describe)

			Properties: A	B	C
Income:					
3	Rents received	3	20,000	20,000	
4	Royalties received	4			
Expenses:					
5	Advertising	5			
6	Auto and travel (see instructions)	6			
7	Cleaning and maintenance	7			
8	Commissions	8			
9	Insurance	9			
10	Legal and other professional fees	10			
11	Management fees	11			
12	Mortgage interest paid to banks, etc. (see instructions)	12	6,000	5,000	
13	Other interest	13			
14	Repairs	14			
15	Supplies	15			
16	Taxes	16	8,000	6,000	
17	Utilities	17	2,000	2,000	
18	Depreciation expense or depletion	18	9,000	5,000	
19	Other (list) HOA Fees	19	4,000		
20	Total expenses. Add lines 5 through 19	20	29,000	18,000	
21	Subtract line 20 from line 3 (rents) and/or 4 (royalties). If result is a (loss), see instructions to find out if you must file **Form 6198**	21	(9,000)	2,000	
22	Deductible rental real estate loss after limitation, if any, on **Form 8582** (see instructions)	22	(6,333)	( )	( )

23a	Total of all amounts reported on line 3 for all rental properties	23a	40,000
b	Total of all amounts reported on line 4 for all royalty properties	23b	
c	Total of all amounts reported on line 12 for all properties	23c	11,000
d	Total of all amounts reported on line 18 for all properties	23d	14,000
e	Total of all amounts reported on line 20 for all properties	23e	47,000
24	**Income.** Add positive amounts shown on line 21. **Do not** include any losses	24	2,000
25	**Losses.** Add royalty losses from line 21 and rental real estate losses from line 22. Enter total losses here	25	(6,333)
26	**Total rental real estate and royalty income or (loss).** Combine lines 24 and 25. Enter the result here. If Parts II, III, and IV, and line 40 on page 2 do not apply to you, also enter this amount on Schedule 1 (Form 1040), line 5. Otherwise, include this amount in the total on line 41 on page 2	26	(4,333)

For Paperwork Reduction Act Notice, see the separate instructions. Cat. No. 11344L Schedule E (Form 1040) 2024

Self-Study Problem 4.8, Part b

Schedule E (Form 1040) 2024 — Attachment Sequence No. **13** — Page **2**

Name(s) shown on return. Do not enter name and social security number if shown on other side.

Your social security number:

Caution: The IRS compares amounts reported on your tax return with amounts shown on Schedule(s) K-1.

Part II — Income or Loss From Partnerships and S Corporations

Note: If you report a loss, receive a distribution, dispose of stock, or receive a loan repayment from an S corporation, you **must** check the box in column (e) on line 28 and attach the required basis computation. If you report a loss from an at-risk activity for which **any** amount is **not** at risk, you **must** check the box in column (f) on line 28 and attach **Form 6198**. See instructions.

27 Are you reporting any loss not allowed in a prior year due to the at-risk or basis limitations, a prior year unallowed loss from a passive activity (if that loss was not reported on Form 8582), or unreimbursed partnership expenses? If you answered "Yes," see instructions before completing this section. ☐ Yes ☐ No

28

	(a) Name	(b) Enter P for partnership; S for S corporation	(c) Check if foreign partnership	(d) Employer identification number	(e) Check if basis computation is required	(f) Check if any amount is not at risk
A	Bunker Dry Cleaners LP	P	☐	13-3434347	☐	☐
B			☐		☐	☐
C			☐		☐	☐
D			☐		☐	☐

	Passive Income and Loss		Nonpassive Income and Loss		
	(g) Passive loss allowed (attach Form 8582 if required)	(h) Passive income from Schedule K-1	(i) Nonpassive loss allowed (see Schedule K-1)	(j) Section 179 expense deduction from Form 4562	(k) Nonpassive income from Schedule K-1
A		1,667			
B					
C					
D					
29a Totals					
b Totals		1,667			

30	Add columns (h) and (k) of line 29a	30	
31	Add columns (g), (i), and (j) of line 29b	31	(1,667)
32	**Total partnership and S corporation income or (loss).** Combine lines 30 and 31	32	(1,667)

Part III — Income or Loss From Estates and Trusts

33

	(a) Name	(b) Employer identification number
A		
B		

	Passive Income and Loss		Nonpassive Income and Loss	
	(c) Passive deduction or loss allowed (attach Form 8582 if required)	(d) Passive income from Schedule K-1	(e) Deduction or loss from Schedule K-1	(f) Other income from Schedule K-1
A				
B				
34a Totals				
b Totals				

35	Add columns (d) and (f) of line 34a	35	
36	Add columns (c) and (e) of line 34b	36	( )
37	**Total estate and trust income or (loss).** Combine lines 35 and 36	37	

Part IV — Income or Loss From Real Estate Mortgage Investment Conduits (REMICs)—Residual Holder

38

(a) Name	(b) Employer identification number	(c) Excess inclusion from Schedules Q, line 2c (see instructions)	(d) Taxable income (net loss) from Schedules Q, line 1b	(e) Income from Schedules Q, line 3b

| 39 | Combine columns (d) and (e) only. Enter the result here and include in the total on line 41 below | 39 | |

Part V — Summary

40	Net farm rental income or (loss) from **Form 4835**. Also, complete line 42 below	40	
41	**Total income or (loss).** Combine lines 26, 32, 37, 39, and 40. Enter the result here and on Schedule 1 (Form 1040), line 5	41	(6,000)
42	**Reconciliation of farming and fishing income.** Enter your **gross** farming and fishing income reported on Form 4835, line 7; Schedule K-1 (Form 1065), box 14, code B; Schedule K-1 (Form 1120-S), box 17, code AN; and Schedule K-1 (Form 1041), box 14, code F. See instructions	42	
43	**Reconciliation for real estate professionals.** If you were a real estate professional (see instructions), enter the net income or (loss) you reported anywhere on Form 1040, Form 1040-SR, or Form 1040-NR from all rental real estate activities in which you materially participated under the passive activity loss rules	43	

Schedule E (Form 1040) 2024

Self-Study Problem 4.8, Part b

Form 8582 — Passive Activity Loss Limitations
Department of the Treasury — Internal Revenue Service
See separate instructions.
Attach to Form 1040, 1040-SR, or 1041.
Go to www.irs.gov/Form8582 for instructions and the latest information.
OMB No. 1545-1008
2024
Attachment Sequence No. 858

Name(s) shown on return: Jorge Jefferson
Identifying number: 656-76-4321

Part I — 2024 Passive Activity Loss

Caution: Complete Parts IV and V before completing Part I.

Rental Real Estate Activities With Active Participation (For the definition of active participation, see *Special Allowance for Rental Real Estate Activities* in the instructions.)

1a Activities with net income (enter the amount from Part IV, column (a))	1a	2,000
b Activities with net loss (enter the amount from Part IV, column (b))	1b	(9,000)
c Prior years' unallowed losses (enter the amount from Part IV, column (c))	1c	( )
d Combine lines 1a, 1b, and 1c	1d	(7,000)

All Other Passive Activities

2a Activities with net income (enter the amount from Part V, column (a))	2a	
b Activities with net loss (enter the amount from Part V, column (b))	2b	(15,000)
c Prior years' unallowed losses (enter the amount from Part V, column (c))	2c	( )
d Combine lines 2a, 2b, and 2c	2d	(15,000)

3 Combine lines 1d and 2d and subtract any prior year unallowed CRD. See instructions. If this line is zero or more, stop here and include this form with your return; all losses are allowed, including any prior year unallowed losses entered on line 1c or 2c. Report the losses on the forms and schedules normally used ... **3** (22,000)

If line 3 is a loss and:
- Line 1d is a loss, go to Part II.
- Line 2d is a loss (and line 1d is zero or more), skip Part II and go to line 10.

Caution: If your filing status is married filing separately and you lived with your spouse at any time during the year, **do not** complete Part II. Instead, go to line 10.

Part II — Special Allowance for Rental Real Estate Activities With Active Participation

Note: Enter all numbers in Part II as positive amounts. See instructions for an example.

4	Enter the **smaller** of the loss on line 1d or the loss on line 3	4	7,000
5	Enter $150,000. If married filing separately, see instructions	5	150,000
6	Enter modified adjusted gross income, but not less than zero. See instructions	6	138,000

Note: If line 6 is greater than or equal to line 5, skip lines 7 and 8 and enter -0- on line 9. Otherwise, go to line 7.

7	Subtract line 6 from line 5	7	12,000
8	Multiply line 7 by 50% (0.50). **Do not** enter more than $25,000. If married filing separately, see instructions	8	6,000
9	Enter the **smaller** of line 4 or line 8. If line 3 includes any CRD, see instructions	9	6,000

Part III — Total Losses Allowed

10	Add the income, if any, on lines 1a and 2a and enter the total	10	2,000
11	Total losses allowed from all passive activities for 2024. Add lines 9 and 10. See instructions to find out how to report the losses on your tax return	11	8,000

Part IV — Complete This Part Before Part I, Lines 1a, 1b, and 1c. See instructions.

Name of activity	Current year (a) Net income (line 1a)	Current year (b) Net loss (line 1b)	Prior years (c) Unallowed loss (line 1c)	Overall gain or loss (d) Gain	Overall gain or loss (e) Loss
Condo		9,000			9,000
House	2,000			2,000	
Total. Enter on Part I, lines 1a, 1b, and 1c.	2,000	9,000			

For Paperwork Reduction Act Notice, see instructions. Cat. No. 63704F Form **8582** (2024)

Self-Study Problem 4.8, Part b

Form 8582 (2024)   Page **2**

Part V — Complete This Part Before Part I, Lines 2a, 2b, and 2c. See instructions.

Name of activity	Current year		Prior years	Overall gain or loss	
	(a) Net income (line 2a)	(b) Net loss (line 2b)	(c) Unallowed loss (line 2c)	(d) Gain	(e) Loss
Bunker Dry Cleaners LP		15,000			15,000
Total. Enter on Part I, lines 2a, 2b, and 2c		15,000			

Part VI — Use This Part if an Amount Is Shown on Part II, Line 9. See instructions.

Name of activity	Form or schedule and line number to be reported on (see instructions)	(a) Loss	(b) Ratio	(c) Special allowance	(d) Subtract column (c) from column (a).
Condo		9,000	1.00	6,000	3,000
Total		9,000	1.00	6,000	3,000

Part VII — Allocation of Unallowed Losses. See instructions.

Name of activity	Form or schedule and line number to be reported on (see instructions)	(a) Loss	(b) Ratio	(c) Unallowed loss
Condo		3,000	.166667 (a)	2,667 (b)
Bunker Dry Cleaners LP		15,000	.833333	13,333
Total		18,000	1.00	18,000

Part VIII — Allowed Losses. See instructions.

Name of activity	Form or schedule and line number to be reported on (see instructions)	(a) Loss	(b) Unallowed loss	(c) Allowed loss
Condo		9,000	3,000	6,000
Bunker Dry Cleaners LP		15,000	15,000	0
Total		24,000	18,000	6,000

Form **8582** (2024)

(a) Loss per activity divided by total loss (e.g., $3,000 ÷ 18,000 = 0.166667).
(b) Disallowed loss of $16,000 calculated as $9,000 condo loss plus $15,000 Bunker loss less $6,000 recognized under active management rental exception less $2,000 rental income. The disallowed loss for each activity is the total disallowed loss multiplied by the loss ratio in column (b).

Self-Study Problem 4.9, Part a

Form 172 (January 2025)
Department of the Treasury
Internal Revenue Service

Net Operating Losses (NOLs)
For Individuals, Estates, and Trusts.
Go to www.irs.gov/Form172 for instructions and the latest information.

OMB No. 1545-0074

For calendar year __2024__, or other tax year beginning _____ and ending _____

Name(s) shown on return: Silja Buoy

Social security or employer identification number: _____

Part I — NOL (see instructions)

Line	Description		Amount
1	For individuals, subtract your standard deduction or itemized deductions from your adjusted gross income (AGI) and enter it here. For estates and trusts, enter taxable income increased by the total of the charitable deduction, income distribution deduction, and exemption amount		(28,400) (a)
2	Nonbusiness capital losses before limitation. Enter as a positive number	8,000	
3	Nonbusiness capital gains (without regard to any section 1202 exclusion)	3,000	
4	If line 2 is more than line 3, enter the difference. Otherwise, enter -0-	5,000	
5	If line 3 is more than line 2, enter the difference. Otherwise, enter -0-	0	
6	Nonbusiness deductions (see instructions). Enter as a positive number	14,600	
7	Nonbusiness income other than capital gains (see instructions)	200	
8	Add lines 5 and 7	200	
9	If line 6 is more than line 8, enter the difference. Otherwise, enter -0-		14,400
10	If line 8 is more than line 6, enter the difference. Otherwise, enter -0-. But don't enter more than line 5	0	
11	Business capital losses before limitation. Enter as a positive number	0	
12	Business capital gains (without regard to any section 1202 exclusion)	1,000	
13	Add lines 10 and 12	1,000	
14	Subtract line 13 from line 11. If zero or less, enter -0-	0	
15	Add lines 4 and 14	5,000	
16	Enter, if any, the combined net short-term and long-term capital loss from your Schedule D (Form 1040). Estates and trusts, enter, if any, the total net short-term and long-term loss from Schedule D (Form 1041). Enter as a positive number. If you don't have a loss on that line (and don't have a section 1202 exclusion), skip lines 16 through 21 and enter on line 22 the amount from line 15	4,000	
17	Section 1202 exclusion. Enter as a positive number		0
18	Subtract line 17 from line 16. If zero or less, enter -0-	4,000	
19	If line 16 is a loss, enter, as a positive number, the smaller of: • The loss on line 16; or • $3,000 (If filing Form 1040, $1,500 when married filing separately)	3,000	
20	If line 18 is more than line 19, enter the difference. Otherwise, enter -0-	1,000	
21	If line 19 is more than line 18, enter the difference. Otherwise, enter -0-		0
22	Subtract line 20 from line 15. If zero or less, enter -0-		4,000
23	NOL deduction for losses from other years. Enter as a positive number		0
24	**NOL.** Combine lines 1, 9, 17, and 21 through 23. If the result is less than zero, enter it here. If the result is zero or more, you don't have an NOL		(10,000)

For Paperwork Reduction Act Notice, see the instructions. Cat. No. 16545W Form **172** (1-2025)

(a) $7,000 of wages + $200 interest income − $18,000 business loss − $3,000 net capital loss − $14,600 standard deduction.

Self-Study Problem 4.10

SCHEDULE SE (Form 1040)
Department of the Treasury
Internal Revenue Service

Self-Employment Tax

Attach to Form 1040, 1040-SR, 1040-SS, or 1040-NR.
Go to www.irs.gov/ScheduleSE for instructions and the latest information.

OMB No. 1545-0074

2024

Attachment Sequence No. **17**

Name of person with self-employment income (as shown on Form 1040, 1040-SR, 1040-SS, or 1040-NR): Joanne Plummer

Social security number of person with **self-employment** income:

Part I — Self-Employment Tax

Note: If your only income subject to self-employment tax is **church employee income**, see instructions for how to report your income and the definition of church employee income.

A If you are a minister, member of a religious order, or Christian Science practitioner **and** you filed Form 4361, but you had $400 or more of **other** net earnings from self-employment, check here and continue with Part I ☐

Skip lines 1a and 1b if you use the farm optional method in Part II. See instructions.

Line	Description		Amount
1a	Net farm profit or (loss) from Schedule F, line 34, and farm partnerships, Schedule K-1 (Form 1065), box 14, code A	1a	
1b	If you received social security retirement or disability benefits, enter the amount of Conservation Reserve Program payments included on Schedule F, line 4b, or listed on Schedule K-1 (Form 1065), box 20, code AQ	1b	( )

Skip line 2 if you use the nonfarm optional method in Part II. See instructions.

2	Net profit or (loss) from Schedule C, line 31; and Schedule K-1 (Form 1065), box 14, code A (other than farming). See instructions for other income to report or if you are a minister or member of a religious order	2	172,000
3	Combine lines 1a, 1b, and 2	3	172,000
4a	If line 3 is more than zero, multiply line 3 by 92.35% (0.9235). Otherwise, enter amount from line 3	4a	158,842

Note: If line 4a is less than $400 due to Conservation Reserve Program payments on line 1b, see instructions.

4b	If you elect one or both of the optional methods, enter the total of lines 15 and 17 here	4b	
4c	Combine lines 4a and 4b. If less than $400, **stop**; you don't owe self-employment tax. **Exception:** If less than $400 and you had **church employee income**, enter -0- and continue	4c	158,842
5a	Enter your **church employee income** from Form W-2. See instructions for definition of church employee income — 5a		
5b	Multiply line 5a by 92.35% (0.9235). If less than $100, enter -0-	5b	
6	Add lines 4c and 5b	6	158,842
7	Maximum amount of combined wages and self-employment earnings subject to social security tax or the 6.2% portion of the 7.65% railroad retirement (tier 1) tax for 2024	7	168,600
8a	Total social security wages and tips (total of boxes 3 and 7 on Form(s) W-2) and railroad retirement (tier 1) compensation. If $168,600 or more, skip lines 8b through 10, and go to line 11 — 8a 10,400		
8b	Unreported tips subject to social security tax from Form 4137, line 10 — 8b		
8c	Wages subject to social security tax from Form 8919, line 10 — 8c		
8d	Add lines 8a, 8b, and 8c	8d	10,400
9	Subtract line 8d from line 7. If zero or less, enter -0- here and on line 10 and go to line 11	9	158,200
10	Multiply the **smaller** of line 6 or line 9 by 12.4% (0.124)	10	19,617
11	Multiply line 6 by 2.9% (0.029)	11	4,606
12	**Self-employment tax.** Add lines 10 and 11. Enter here and on **Schedule 2 (Form 1040), line 4**, or Form 1040-SS, Part I, line 3	12	24,223
13	Deduction for one-half of self-employment tax. Multiply line 12 by 50% (0.50). Enter here and on **Schedule 1 (Form 1040), line 15** — 13 12,112		

For Paperwork Reduction Act Notice, see your tax return instructions. Cat. No. 11358Z

Self-Study Problem 4.11

Taxpayer	Eligible for QBI deduction (Y/N)?
a.	Aretha is not eligible for the QBI deduction. Corporations are not eligible for the QBI deduction and Aretha's dividend income from the corporation is not considered QBI income.
b.	Terri is eligible for a $24,000 QBI deduction. Terri's business likely falls into the special services category that would subject her to the wage limitation; however, Terri is not subject to the wage or special service limits because her taxable income is below the $191,950 threshold. Refer to Form 8995 below.
c.	Alice is eligible for a $19,558 QBI deduction. Alice's restaurant business is not subject to the special service limitation; however, her joint taxable income exceeds the $383,900 threshold. As a result, her QBI deduction is subject to the wage limitation. Refer to Form 8995-A on Pages E-34 and E-35.

Self-Study Problem 4.11, Part b

Form 8995 — Qualified Business Income Deduction Simplified Computation

OMB No. 1545-2294

Department of the Treasury
Internal Revenue Service

Attach to your tax return.
Go to www.irs.gov/Form8995 for instructions and the latest information.

2024
Attachment Sequence No. 55

Name(s) shown on return: Terri Jones
Your taxpayer identification number: 317-65-4321

Note: You can claim the qualified business income deduction **only** if you have qualified business income from a qualified trade or business, real estate investment trust dividends, publicly traded partnership income, or a domestic production activities deduction passed through from an agricultural or horticultural cooperative. See instructions.

Use this form if your taxable income, before your qualified business income deduction, is at or below $191,950 ($383,900 if married filing jointly), and you aren't a patron of an agricultural or horticultural cooperative.

1	(a) Trade, business, or aggregation name	(b) Taxpayer identification number	(c) Qualified business income or (loss)
i	The Bee Hive	317-65-4321	120,000
ii			
iii			
iv			
v			

2	Total qualified business income or (loss). Combine lines 1i through 1v, column (c)	2	120,000
3	Qualified business net (loss) carryforward from the prior year	3	( )
4	Total qualified business income. Combine lines 2 and 3. If zero or less, enter -0-	4	120,000
5	Qualified business income component. Multiply line 4 by 20% (0.20)	5	24,000
6	Qualified REIT dividends and publicly traded partnership (PTP) income or (loss) (see instructions)	6	
7	Qualified REIT dividends and qualified PTP (loss) carryforward from the prior year	7	
8	Total qualified REIT dividends and PTP income. Combine lines 6 and 7. If zero or less, enter -0-	8	
9	REIT and PTP component. Multiply line 8 by 20% (0.20)	9	
10	Qualified business income deduction before the income limitation. Add lines 5 and 9	10	24,000
11	Taxable income before qualified business income deduction (see instructions)	11	133,000
12	Enter your net capital gain, if any, increased by any qualified dividends (see instructions)	12	
13	Subtract line 12 from line 11. If zero or less, enter -0-	13	133,000
14	Income limitation. Multiply line 13 by 20% (0.20)	14	26,600
15	Qualified business income deduction. Enter the smaller of line 10 or line 14. Also enter this amount on the applicable line of your return (see instructions)	15	24,000
16	Total qualified business (loss) carryforward. Combine lines 2 and 3. If greater than zero, enter -0-	16	( )
17	Total qualified REIT dividends and PTP (loss) carryforward. Combine lines 6 and 7. If greater than zero, enter -0-	17	( )

For Privacy Act and Paperwork Reduction Act Notice, see instructions. Cat. No. 37806C Form **8995** (2024)

Self-Study Problem 4.11, Part c

Form 8995-A
Department of the Treasury
Internal Revenue Service

Qualified Business Income Deduction

Attach to your tax return.
Go to www.irs.gov/Form8995A for instructions and the latest information.

OMB No. 1545-2294
2024
Attachment Sequence No. 55A

Name(s) shown on return: Alice Delvecchio
Your taxpayer identification number: 565-22-4321

Note: You can claim the qualified business income deduction **only** if you have qualified business income from a qualified trade or business, real estate investment trust dividends, publicly traded partnership income, or a domestic production activities deduction passed through from an agricultural or horticultural cooperative. See instructions.

Use this form if your taxable income, before your qualified business income deduction, is above $191,950 ($383,900 if married filing jointly), or you're a patron of an agricultural or horticultural cooperative.

Part I — Trade, Business, or Aggregation Information

Complete Schedules A, B, and/or C (Form 8995-A), as applicable, before starting Part I. Attach additional worksheets when needed. See instructions.

1	(a) Trade, business, or aggregation name	(b) Check if specified service	(c) Check if aggregation	(d) Taxpayer identification number	(e) Check if patron
A	D's Pizza	☐	☐	565-22-4321	☐
B		☐	☐		☐
C		☐	☐		☐

Part II — Determine Your Adjusted Qualified Business Income

			A	B	C
2	Qualified business income from the trade, business, or aggregation. See instructions	2	100,000		
3	Multiply line 2 by 20% (0.20). If your taxable income is $191,950 or less ($383,900 if married filing jointly), skip lines 4 through 12 and enter the amount from line 3 on line 13	3	20,000		
4	Allocable share of W-2 wages from the trade, business, or aggregation	4	36,000		
5	Multiply line 4 by 50% (0.50)	5	18,000		
6	Multiply line 4 by 25% (0.25)	6	9,000		
7	Allocable share of the unadjusted basis immediately after acquisition (UBIA) of all qualified property	7	67,000		
8	Multiply line 7 by 2.5% (0.025)	8	1,675		
9	Add lines 6 and 8	9	10,675		
10	Enter the greater of line 5 or line 9	10	18,000		
11	W-2 wage and UBIA of qualified property limitation. Enter the smaller of line 3 or line 10	11	18,000		
12	Phased-in reduction. Enter the amount from line 26, if any	12	19,558		
13	Qualified business income deduction before patron reduction. Enter the greater of line 11 or line 12	13	19,558		
14	Patron reduction. Enter the amount from Schedule D (Form 8995-A), line 6, if any. See instructions	14			
15	Qualified business income component. Subtract line 14 from line 13	15	19,558		
16	Total qualified business income component. Add all amounts reported on line 15	16	19,558		

For Privacy Act and Paperwork Reduction Act Notice, see separate instructions. Cat. No. 71661B Form **8995-A** (2024)

Self Study Problem 4.11, Part c

Form 8995-A (2024) Page **2**

Part III Phased-in Reduction

Complete Part III only if your taxable income is more than $191,950 but not $241,950 ($383,900 and $483,900 if married filing jointly) and line 10 is less than line 3. Otherwise, skip Part III.

			A	B	C
17	Enter the amounts from line 3	17	20,000		
18	Enter the amounts from line 10	18	18,000		
19	Subtract line 18 from line 17	19	2,000		
20	Taxable income before qualified business income deduction	20	406,000		
21	Threshold. Enter $191,950 ($383,900 if married filing jointly)	21	383,900		
22	Subtract line 21 from line 20	22	22,100		
23	Phase-in range. Enter $50,000 ($100,000 if married filing jointly)	23	100,000		
24	Phase-in percentage. Divide line 22 by line 23	24	22.1 %		
25	Total phase-in reduction. Multiply line 19 by line 24	25	442		
26	Qualified business income after phase-in reduction. Subtract line 25 from line 17. Enter this amount here and on line 12, for the corresponding trade or business	26	19,558		

Part IV Determine Your Qualified Business Income Deduction

27	Total qualified business income component from all qualified trades, businesses, or aggregations. Enter the amount from line 16	27	19,558		
28	Qualified REIT dividends and publicly traded partnership (PTP) income or (loss). See instructions	28			
29	Qualified REIT dividends and PTP (loss) carryforward from prior years	29	( )		
30	Total qualified REIT dividends and PTP income. Combine lines 28 and 29. If less than zero, enter -0-	30			
31	REIT and PTP component. Multiply line 30 by 20% (0.20)	31			
32	Qualified business income deduction before the income limitation. Add lines 27 and 31			32	19,558
33	Taxable income before qualified business income deduction	33	406,000		
34	Enter your net capital gain, if any, increased by any qualified dividends (see instructions)	34	12,000		
35	Subtract line 34 from line 33. If zero or less, enter -0-			35	394,000
36	Income limitation. Multiply line 35 by 20% (0.20)			36	78,800
37	Qualified business income deduction before the domestic production activities deduction (DPAD) under section 199A(g). Enter the smaller of line 32 or line 36			37	19,558
38	DPAD under section 199A(g) allocated from an agricultural or horticultural cooperative. Don't enter more than line 33 minus line 37			38	
39	Total qualified business income deduction. Add lines 37 and 38			39	19,558
40	Total qualified REIT dividends and PTP (loss) carryforward. Combine lines 28 and 29. If zero or greater, enter -0-			40	( )

Form **8995-A** (2024)

Chapter 5 Deductions for and From AGI

Self-Study Problem 5.1

a. 1. $8,300, which is the limit for a family plan.
    2. $0 A plan with no deductible does not qualify.
    3. $2,000 (the limit is $4,150)
    4. $0 Individuals are not allowed to make contributions to an HSA after age 65 since they qualify for Medicare.

b. HSA Deduction is $4,000 and taxable distribution is $0. Refer to Form 8889 on Page E-37.

Self-Study Problem 5.2
Refer to Form 7206 on Page E-38.

Self-Study Problem 5.3
    a. Refer to Worksheets 1-1 and 1-2 on Pages E-39 to E-40.
    b. Refer to Worksheet 2-2 on Page E-41.
    c. $10,000. Because Kalpana deducted all her contributions, she has no basis in the IRA, and all distributions will be taxable.
    d. $0. Distributions from a Roth IRA to an owner over age 59½ are generally excluded from income.
    e. Refer to Form 5329 on Page E-42.

Self-Study Problem 5.4
    a. $10,000, the lesser of $(0.25 \div 1.25) \times \$50,000$ or $69,000
    b. i. $10,000, lesser of $25\% \times \$40,000$ or $23,000 (annual dollar limit effective for 2024)
       ii. $23,000 (annual dollar limit effective for 2024)
    c. $25,000. Laura has no basis in her contributions as they were all pre-tax. The entire distribution is taxable.
    d. Refer to Form 8881 on Page E-43.

Self-Study Problem 5.5
    a. $175 Professor Hill is not a K-12 educator but may deduct his reimbursed jury duty pay.
    b. $1,100 Jackie worked for two employers, both of which paid her more than $200; her expenses exceeded 10 percent of the gross income from performing artist work ($1,100 > $8,000 × 10%); and her AGI was below $16,000.
    c. $4,500

Self-Study Problem 5.6
Refer to Schedule A on Page E-44.
Line 1 of Schedule A is computed as follows:

Medical insurance	$ 450
Prescription medicines and drugs	375
Hospital bills	2,550
Eyeglasses for Kiran's dependent mother	180
Doctor bills for Kiran's dependent mother	200
Medical transportation in personal vehicle (534 miles * $0.21)	112
Total	3,867
Less reimbursement	(1,100)
Medical and dental expenses	$2,767

Self-Study Problem 5.7
Refer to Schedule A on Page E-44.

Line 5 of Schedule A on Page E-44—The $225 refund is included on line 1 of Schedule 1 of Form 1040 as gross income if included in gross income.

Self-Study Problem 5.1, Part b

Form 8889 — Department of the Treasury, Internal Revenue Service

Health Savings Accounts (HSAs)

Attach to Form 1040, 1040-SR, or 1040-NR.
Go to www.irs.gov/Form8889 for instructions and the latest information.

OMB No. 1545-0074
2024
Attachment Sequence No. 52

Name(s) shown on Form 1040, 1040-SR, or 1040-NR: **Alex Morton**
Social security number of HSA beneficiary. If both spouses have HSAs, see instructions.: **131-13-1313**

Before you begin: Complete Form 8853, Archer MSAs and Long-Term Care Insurance Contracts, if required.

Part I — HSA Contributions and Deduction.
See the instructions before completing this part. If you are filing jointly and both you and your spouse each have separate HSAs, complete a separate Part I for each spouse.

1. Check the box to indicate your coverage under a high-deductible health plan (HDHP) during 2024. See instructions. ☑ Self-only ☐ Family
2. HSA contributions you made for 2024 (or those made on your behalf), including those made by the unextended due date of your tax return that were for 2024. **Do not** include employer contributions, contributions through a cafeteria plan, or rollovers. See instructions .... **2** | 4,000
3. If you were under age 55 at the end of 2024 and, on the first day of **every** month during 2024, you were, or were considered, an eligible individual with the **same** coverage, enter $4,150 ($8,300 for family coverage). **All others**, see the instructions for the amount to enter .... **3** | 4,150
4. Enter the amount you and your employer contributed to your Archer MSAs for 2024 from Form 8853, lines 1 and 2. If you or your spouse had family coverage under an HDHP at any time during 2024, also include any amount contributed to your spouse's Archer MSAs .... **4** |
5. Subtract line 4 from line 3. If zero or less, enter -0- .... **5** | 4,150
6. Enter the amount from line 5. But if you and your spouse each have separate HSAs and had family coverage under an HDHP at any time during 2024, see the instructions for the amount to enter .... **6** | 4,150
7. If you were age 55 or older at the end of 2024, married, and you or your spouse had family coverage under an HDHP at any time during 2024, enter your additional contribution amount. See instructions .... **7** |
8. Add lines 6 and 7 .... **8** | 4,150
9. Employer contributions made to your HSAs for 2024 .... **9** | 150
10. Qualified HSA funding distributions .... **10** |
11. Add lines 9 and 10 .... **11** | 150
12. Subtract line 11 from line 8. If zero or less, enter -0- .... **12** | 4,000
13. **HSA deduction** (see instructions) .... **13** | 4,000 (a)

Part II — HSA Distributions.
If you are filing jointly and both you and your spouse each have separate HSAs, complete a separate Part II for each spouse.

14a. Total distributions you received in 2024 from all HSAs (see instructions) .... **14a** | 1,889
b. Distributions included on line 14a that you rolled over to another HSA. Also include any excess contributions (and the earnings on those excess contributions) included on line 14a that were withdrawn by the due date of your return. See instructions .... **14b** |
c. Subtract line 14b from line 14a .... **14c** | 1,889
15. Qualified medical expenses paid using HSA distributions (see instructions) .... **15** | 1,889 (b)
16. **Taxable HSA distributions.** Subtract line 15 from line 14c. If zero or less, enter -0-. Also, include this amount in the total on Schedule 1 (Form 1040), Part I, line 8f .... **16** | 0
17a. If any of the distributions included on line 16 meet any of the **Exceptions to the Additional 20% Tax** (see instructions), check here ☐
b. **Additional 20% tax** (see instructions). Enter 20% (0.20) of the distributions included on line 16 that are subject to the additional 20% tax. Also, include this amount in the total on Schedule 2 (Form 1040), Part II, line 17c .... **17b** |

Part III — Income and Additional Tax for Failure To Maintain HDHP Coverage.
See the instructions before completing this part. If you are filing jointly and both you and your spouse each have separate HSAs, complete a separate Part III for each spouse.

18. Last-month rule .... **18** |
19. Qualified HSA funding distribution .... **19** |
20. **Total income.** Add lines 18 and 19. Include this amount on Schedule 1 (Form 1040), Part I, line 8f .... **20** |
21. **Additional tax.** Multiply line 20 by 10% (0.10). Include this amount in the total on Schedule 2 (Form 1040), Part II, line 17d .... **21** |

For Paperwork Reduction Act Notice, see your tax return instructions. Cat. No. 37621P Form **8889** (2024)

(a) Generally, enter the smaller of line 2 or line 12 on line 13. However, if the amount on line 2 is more than the amount on line 13, contributions to the HSA exceed the permitted amount an additional tax on the excess contributions may be due.
(b) Medical expenses paid of $2,000 exceeded HSA distributions.

Self-Study Problem 5.2

Form 7206 — Self-Employed Health Insurance Deduction
Department of the Treasury — Internal Revenue Service
Attach to Form 1040, 1040-SR, or 1040-NR.
Go to www.irs.gov/Form7206 for instructions and the latest information.
OMB No. 1545-0074
2024
Attachment Sequence No. 206

Name(s) shown on return: **Gwen Eyeful**
Your taxpayer identification number:

Note: Use a separate Form 7206 for each trade or business under which an insurance plan is established.

1	Enter the total amount paid in 2024 for health insurance coverage established under your business (or the S corporation in which you were a more-than-2% shareholder) for 2024 for you, your spouse, and your dependents. But **don't** include the following. See instructions	1	20,000 (a)
	• Amounts for any month you were eligible to participate in a health plan subsidized by your employer or your spouse's employer or the employer of either your dependent or your child who was under the age of 27 at the end of 2024.		
	• Any amounts paid, not to exceed $3,000, from retirement plan distributions that were **nontaxable** because you are a retired public safety officer. See instructions.		
	• Any payments for qualified long-term care insurance (see line 2).		

2	For coverage under a qualified long-term care insurance contract, enter for each person covered the **smaller** of (a) or (b).
	(a) Total payments made for that person during the year.
	(b) The amount shown below. Use the person's age at the end of the tax year.
	  $470 — if that person is age 40 or younger
	  $880 — if age 41 to 50
	  $1,760 — if age 51 to 60
	  $4,710 — if age 61 to 70
	  $5,880 — if age 71 or older
	Note: The amount of long-term care premiums that can be included as a medical expense is limited by the person's age. **Don't** include payments for any month you were eligible to participate in a long-term care insurance plan subsidized by your employer or your spouse's employer, or the employer of either your dependent or your child who was under the age of 27 at the end of 2024. If more than one person is covered, figure separately the amount to enter for each person. Then enter the total of those amounts
		2	880

3	Add lines 1 and 2	3	20,880
4	Enter your net profit* and any other earned income** from the trade or business under which the insurance plan is established. Don't include Conservation Reserve Program payments exempt from self-employment tax. If the business is an S corporation, skip to line 11	4	90,000
5	Enter the total of all net profits* from Schedule C (Form 1040), line 31; Schedule F (Form 1040), line 34; or Schedule K-1 (Form 1065), box 14, code A, plus any other income allocable to the profitable businesses. Don't include Conservation Reserve Program payments exempt from self-employment tax. See the Instructions for Schedule SE (Form 1040). **Don't** include any net losses shown on these schedules	5	90,000
6	Divide line 4 by line 5	6	1.00
7	Multiply Schedule 1 (Form 1040), line 15, deductible part of self-employment tax, by the percentage on line 6	7	6,358 (b)
8	Subtract line 7 from line 4	8	83,642
9	Enter the amount, if any, from Schedule 1 (Form 1040), line 16, self-employed SEP, SIMPLE, and qualified plans, attributable to the same trade or business in which the insurance plan is established	9	0
10	Subtract line 9 from line 8	10	83,642
11	Enter your Medicare wages (box 5 of Form W-2) from an S corporation in which you are a more-than-2% shareholder and in which the insurance plan is established	11	
12	Enter any amount from Form 2555, line 45, attributable to the amount entered on line 4 or 11 above	12	
13	Subtract line 12 from line 10 or 11, whichever applies	13	83,642
14	**Self-employed health insurance deduction.** Enter the **smaller** of line 3 or line 13 here and on Schedule 1 (Form 1040), line 17. **Don't** include this amount when figuring any medical expense deduction on Schedule A (Form 1040)	14	20,880

*If you used either optional method to figure your net earnings from self-employment from any business, don't enter your net profit from the business. Instead, enter the amount attributable to that business from Schedule SE (Form 1040), Part I, line 4b.

Earned income includes net earnings and gains from the sale, transfer, or licensing of property you created. However, it doesn't include capital gain income.

For Privacy Act and Paperwork Reduction Act Notice, see separate instructions. Cat. No. 56399C Form **7206** (2024)

(a) $15,000 (family) + $2,000 (dental) + $3,000 (son).
(b) $90,000 (Sch. C) × 92.35% × 15.3% ÷ 2.

Self-Study Problem 5.3, Part a

Worksheet 1-1. Figuring Your Modified AGI *Keep for Your Records*

Use this worksheet to figure your modified AGI for traditional IRA purposes.

1.	Enter your adjusted gross income (AGI) from Form 1040, 1040-SR, or Form 1040-NR, line 11, figured without taking into account the amount from Schedule 1 (Form 1040), line 20	1.	81,000 (a)
2.	Enter any student loan interest deduction from Schedule 1 (Form 1040), line 21	2.	
3.	Enter any foreign earned income exclusion and/or housing exclusion from Form 2555, line 45	3.	
4.	Enter any foreign housing deduction from Form 2555, line 50	4.	
5.	Enter any excludable savings bond interest from Form 8815, line 14	5.	
6.	Enter any excluded employer-provided adoption benefits from Form 8839, line 28	6.	
7.	Add lines 1 through 6. This is your **modified AGI** for traditional IRA purposes	7.	81,000

(a) $62,000 + $14,000 + $4,000 + $1,000

Self-Study Problem 5.3, Part a

Worksheet 1-2. Figuring Your Reduced IRA Deduction for 2024

Keep for Your Records

(Use only if you or your spouse are covered by an employer plan and your modified AGI falls between the two amounts shown below for your coverage situation and filing status.)

Note. If you were married and both you and your spouse contributed to IRAs, figure your deduction and your spouse's deduction separately.

IF you...	AND your filing status is...	AND your modified AGI is over...	THEN enter on line 1 below...
are **covered** by an employer plan	single or head of household	$77,000	$87,000
	married filing jointly or qualifying surviving spouse	$123,000	$143,000
	married filing separately	$0	$10,000
aren't covered by an employer plan, but your spouse is **covered**	married filing jointly	$230,000	$240,000
	married filing separately	$0	$10,000

1. Enter applicable amount from table above .... **1.** _87,000_

2. Enter your *modified AGI* (that of both spouses, if married filing jointly) .... **2.** _81,000_

   Note. If line 2 is equal to or more than the amount on line 1, **stop here**. Your IRA contributions aren't deductible. See *Nondeductible Contributions*, earlier.

3. Subtract line 2 from line 1. **If line 3 is $10,000 or more ($20,000 or more if married filing jointly or qualifying surviving spouse and you are covered by an employer plan), stop here.** You can take a full IRA deduction for contributions of up to $7,000 ($8,000 if you are age 50 or older) or 100% of your (and if married filing jointly, your spouse's) compensation, whichever is less .... **3.** _6,000_

4. Multiply line 3 by the percentage below that applies to you. If the result isn't a multiple of $10, round it to the next highest multiple of $10. (For example, $611.40 is rounded to $620.) However, if the result is less than $200, enter $200.
   - Married filing jointly or qualifying surviving spouse **and** you are covered by an employer plan, multiply line 3 by 35% (0.35) (by 40% (0.40) if you are age 50 or older).
   - All others, multiply line 3 by 70% (0.70) (by 80% (0.80) if you are age 50 or older). .... **4.** _4,200_

5. Enter your compensation minus any deductions on Schedule 1 (Form 1040), line 15 (deductible part of self-employment tax), and Schedule 1 (Form 1040), line 16 (self-employed SEP, SIMPLE, and qualified plans). If you are filing a joint return and your compensation is less than your spouse's, include your spouse's compensation reduced by his or her traditional IRA and Roth IRA contributions for this year. If you file Form 1040, 1040-SR, or 1040-NR, don't reduce your compensation by any losses from self-employment .... **5.** _62,000_

6. Enter contributions made, or to be made, to your IRA for 2024, but **don't** enter more than $7,000 ($8,000 if you are age 50 or older). If contributions are more than $7,000 ($8,000 if you are age 50 or older), see *Excess Contributions*, later .... **6.** _7,000_

7. **IRA deduction.** Compare lines 4, 5, and 6. Enter the smallest amount (or a smaller amount if you choose) here and on your Schedule 1 (Form 1040), line 20. If line 6 is more than line 7 and you want to make a nondeductible contribution, go to line 8 .... **7.** _4,200_

8. **Nondeductible contribution.** Subtract line 7 from line 5 or 6, whichever is smaller. Enter the result here and on line 1 of your Form 8606 .... **8.** _____

Self-Study Problem 5.3, Part b
Worksheet 2-2. Determining Your Reduced Roth IRA Contribution Limit

Before using this worksheet, check Table 2-1 to determine whether or not your Roth IRA contribution limit is reduced. If it is, use this worksheet to determine how much it is reduced.

1. Enter your modified AGI for Roth IRA purposes (Worksheet 2-1, line 10) .... **1.**	152,000
2. Enter: • $230,000 if filing a joint return or qualifying surviving spouse, • $-0- if married filing a separate return and you lived with your spouse at any time in 2024, or • $146,000 for all others .... **2.**	146,000
3. Subtract line 2 from line 1 .... **3.**	6,000
4. Enter: • $10,000 if filing a joint return or qualifying surviving spouse or married filing a separate return and you lived with your spouse at any time during the year, or • $15,000 for all others .... **4.**	15,000
5. Divide line 3 by line 4 and enter the result as a decimal (rounded to at least three places). If the result is 1.000 or more, enter 1.000 .... **5.**	0.400
6. Enter the lesser of: • $7,000 ($8,000 if you are age 50 or older), or • Your taxable compensation .... **6.**	8,000
7. Multiply line 5 by line 6 .... **7.**	3,200
8. Subtract line 7 from line 6. Round the result up to the nearest $10. If the result is less than $200, enter $200 .... **8.**	4,800
9. Enter contributions for the year to other IRAs .... **9.**	0
10. Subtract line 9 from line 6 .... **10.**	8,000
11. Enter the lesser of line 8 or line 10. This is your **reduced Roth IRA contribution limit** .... **11.**	4,800

Self-Study Problem 5.3, Part e

Form 5329
Department of the Treasury
Internal Revenue Service

Additional Taxes on Qualified Plans (Including IRAs) and Other Tax-Favored Accounts
Attach to Form 1040, 1040-SR, 1040-NR, or 1041.
Go to www.irs.gov/Form5329 for instructions and the latest information.

OMB No. 1545-0074
2024
Attachment Sequence No. **29**

Name of individual subject to additional tax. If married filing jointly, see instructions.
Tiffani Hicks

Fill in Your Address Only if You Are Filing This Form by Itself and Not With Your Tax Return

Home address (number and street), or P.O. box if mail is not delivered to your home
101 Rolando Drive

City, town or post office, state, and ZIP code. If you have a foreign address, also complete the spaces below. See instructions.
San Diego, CA 92118

If you **only** owe the additional 10% tax on the full amount of the early distributions, you may be able to report this tax directly on Schedule 2 (Form 1040), line 8, without filing Form 5329. See instructions.

Part I — Additional Tax on Early Distributions.
Complete this part if you took a taxable distribution (other than a qualified disaster distribution) before you reached age 59½ from a qualified retirement plan (including an IRA) or modified endowment contract (unless you are reporting this tax directly on Schedule 2 (Form 1040)—see above). You may also have to complete this part to indicate that you qualify for an exception to the additional tax on early distributions or for certain Roth IRA distributions. See instructions.

1	Early distributions includible in income (see instructions). For Roth IRA distributions, see instructions	1	24,000
2	Early distributions included on line 1 that are not subject to the additional tax (see instructions). Enter the appropriate exception number from the instructions: __09__	2	10,000
3	Amount subject to additional tax. Subtract line 2 from line 1	3	14,000
4	**Additional tax.** Enter 10% (0.10) of line 3. Include this amount on Schedule 2 (Form 1040), line 8	4	1,400

Caution: If any part of the amount on line 3 was a distribution from a SIMPLE IRA, you may have to include 25% of that amount on line 4 instead of 10%. See instructions.

Self-Study Problem 5.4, Part d

Form 8881 (Rev. December 2023)
Department of the Treasury
Internal Revenue Service

Credit for Small Employer Pension Plan Startup Costs, Auto-Enrollment, and Military Spouse Participation

Attach to your tax return.
Go to www.irs.gov/Form8881 for instructions and the latest information.

OMB No. 1545-1810
Attachment Sequence No. 130

Name(s) shown on return: Malcolm Company

Identifying number:

Part I — Credit for Small Employer Pension Plan Startup Costs (Including Employer Contributions)

Line	Description	Value
A	Enter the number of qualifying employees. See instructions	70
1	Qualified startup costs incurred during the tax year	7,600
2	Employers with 1-50 employees enter the amount from line 1. Employers with 51-100 employees enter 50% (0.50) of line 1	3,800
3	Enter the number of employees eligible to participate in the pension plan. See instructions. 65 × $250	16,250
4	Enter the greater of $500 or the amount from line 3 (Do not enter more than $5,000)	5,000
5	Enter the smaller of line 2 or line 4	3,800
6a	Enter the number of employees from the preceding tax year. See instructions	0
6b	Enter employer contributions made to the plan, but don't include (i) elective deferrals, (ii) contributions made to employees whose wages paid to the employee were in excess of $100,000 and (iii) any amount of contributions to an employee to whom you made contributions of more than $1,000	52,000
6c	For employees for whom you made matching and nonelective contributions of more than $1,000, (and who are not disqualified because they meet 6b(ii) above), see the instructions for information on how to determine the amount to enter on line 6c. If you did not make this type of contributions, enter -0-	0
6d	Add lines 6b and 6c	52,000

If the number of employees entered on line 6a is 50 or less, enter the amount from line 6d on line 6f. If the number of employees entered on line 6a is 51-100, continue to line 6e(1).

Line	Description	Value
6e(1)	Subtract 50 (50.0) from the number of employees entered on line 6a	
6e(2)	Multiply line 6e(1) by 2% (0.02)	
6e(3)	Multiply line 6e(2) by line 6d	
6e(4)	Subtract line 6e(3) from line 6d	
6f	If you did NOT complete line 6e, enter the amount from line 6d. If you completed line 6e, enter the amount from line 6e(4)	52,000
6g	Applicable percentages. See instructions	52,000

- If this is treated as the first or second year of the plan, enter the amount from line 6f.
- If this is treated as the third year of the plan, multiply line 6f by 75% (0.75).
- If this is treated as the fourth year of the plan, multiply line 6f by 50% (0.50).
- If this is treated as the fifth year of the plan, multiply the amount on line 6f by 25% (0.25).

Line	Description	Value
7	Credit for small employer pension plan startup costs from partnerships and S corporations	
8	Add lines 5, 6g, and 7. Partnerships and S corporations, report this amount on Schedule K. All others, report this amount on Form 3800, Part III, line 1j	55,800

Part II — Small Employer Auto-Enrollment Credit

Line	Description	Value
9	Enter $500 if an auto-enrollment option is provided for retirement savings	500
10	Small employer auto-enrollment credit from partnerships and S corporations	
11	Add lines 9 and 10. Partnerships and S corporations, report this amount on Schedule K. All others, report this amount on Form 3800, Part III, line 1dd	500

Part III — Military Spouse Participation Credit

Caution: You can't claim the credit if you had more than 100 employees in the preceding tax year.

Line	Description	Value
12	Enter the number of military spouse employees participating in an eligible plan. See instructions. ____ × $200	
13	Amount of contributions paid by employer for each eligible military spouse employee. Do not enter more than $300 per employee. See instructions	
14	Credit for small employer military spouse retirement plan from partnerships and S corporations	
15	Add lines 12, 13, and 14. Partnerships and S corporations, report this amount on Schedule K. All others, report this amount on Form 3800, Part III, line 1ee	

For Paperwork Reduction Act Notice, see separate instructions. Cat. No. 33435N Form **8881** (Rev. 12-2023)

Self-Study Problems 5.6, 5.7, 5.8, 5.9, and 5.10

SCHEDULE A (Form 1040)
Department of the Treasury
Internal Revenue Service

Itemized Deductions
Attach to Form 1040 or 1040-SR.
Go to www.irs.gov/ScheduleA for instructions and the latest information.
Caution: If you are claiming a net qualified disaster loss on Form 4684, see the instructions for line 16.

OMB No. 1545-0074
2024
Attachment Sequence No. **07**

Name(s) shown on Form 1040 or 1040-SR | Your social security number

Medical and Dental Expenses	**Caution:** Do not include expenses reimbursed or paid by others.			
	1 Medical and dental expenses (see instructions)	1	2,767	
	2 Enter amount from Form 1040 or 1040-SR, line 11 [2] 26,000			
	3 Multiply line 2 by 7.5% (0.075)	3	1,950	
	4 Subtract line 3 from line 1. If line 3 is more than line 1, enter -0-			4 817
Taxes You Paid	5 State and local taxes.			
	a State and local income taxes or general sales taxes. You may include either income taxes or general sales taxes on line 5a, but not both. If you elect to include general sales taxes instead of income taxes, check this box . ☐	5a	6,600	
	b State and local real estate taxes (see instructions)	5b	3,400	
	c State and local personal property taxes	5c	20	
	d Add lines 5a through 5c	5d	10,020	
	e Enter the smaller of line 5d or $10,000 ($5,000 if married filing separately)	5e	10,000	
	6 Other taxes. List type and amount: _____	6		
	7 Add lines 5e and 6			7 10,000
Interest You Paid **Caution:** Your mortgage interest deduction may be limited. See instructions.	8 Home mortgage interest and points. If you didn't use all of your home mortgage loan(s) to buy, build, or improve your home, see instructions and check this box . ☐			
	a Home mortgage interest and points reported to you on Form 1098. See instructions if limited	8a	9,250	
	b Home mortgage interest not reported to you on Form 1098. See instructions if limited. If paid to the person from whom you bought the home, see instructions and show that person's name, identifying no., and address	8b		
	c Points not reported to you on Form 1098. See instructions for special rules	8c		
	d Reserved for future use	8d		
	e Add lines 8a through 8c	8e	9,250	
	9 Investment interest. Attach Form 4952 if required. See instructions	9	1,000	
	10 Add lines 8e and 9			10 10,250
Gifts to Charity **Caution:** If you made a gift and got a benefit for it, see instructions.	11 Gifts by cash or check. If you made any gift of $250 or more, see instructions	11	10,500	
	12 Other than by cash or check. If you made any gift of $250 or more, see instructions. You **must** attach Form 8283 if over $500	12	12,000	
	13 Carryover from prior year	13		
	14 Add lines 11 through 13			14 22,500
Casualty and Theft Losses	15 Casualty and theft loss(es) from a federally declared disaster (other than net qualified disaster losses). Attach Form 4684 and enter the amount from line 18 of that form. See instructions			15 5,400
Other Itemized Deductions	16 Other—from list in instructions. List type and amount: Gambling losses (limited to gambling winnings) _____			16 1,400
Total Itemized Deductions	17 Add the amounts in the far right column for lines 4 through 16. Also, enter this amount on Form 1040 or 1040-SR, line 12			17
	18 If you elect to itemize deductions even though they are less than your standard deduction, check this box . ☐			

For Paperwork Reduction Act Notice, see the Instructions for Form 1040. Cat. No. 17145C Schedule A (Form 1040) 2024

Self-Study Problem 5.9

Step 1. Enter charitable contributions made during the year

1. Enter contributions of capital gain property to non-50-percent qualified organizations.   1. __1,500__ (a)
2. Enter other contributions to qualified organizations that are non-50-percent organizations. Do not include any contributions entered Line 1   2. __3,200__ (b)
3. Enter contributions of capital gain property to 50-percent-limit organizations deducted at fair market value. Do not include any contributions entered on a previous line.   3. __11,000__ (c)
4. Enter noncash contributions to 50-percent-limit organizations other than capital gain property deducted at fair market value. Be sure to include contributions of capital gain property to 50-percent-limit organizations if electing to deduct at basis. Do not include any contributions entered on a previous line.   4. __1,000__ (d)
5. Enter cash contributions to 50-percent-limit organizations. Do not include any contributions entered on a previous line   5. __8,000__ (e)

Step 2. Figure the deduction for the year (if any result is zero or less, enter -0-)

6. Enter adjusted gross income (AGI)   6. __45,000__

Cash contributions subject to 60% limit (if line 5 is zero, enter -0- on lines 7 through 9)

7. Multiply line 6 by 0.6   7. __27,000__
8. Deductible amount. Enter the smaller of line 5 or line 7   8. __8,000__
9. Carryover. Subtract line 8 from line 5   9. __0__

Noncash contributions subject to 50% limit (if line 4 is zero, enter -0- on lines 10 through 13)

10. Multiply line 6 by 0.5   10. __22,500__
11. Subtract line 8 from line 10   11. __14,500__
12. Deductible amount. Enter the smaller of line 4 or line 11   12. __1,000__
13. Carryover. Subtract line 12 from line 14   13. __0__

Contributions (other than capital gain property) subject to 30% limit (if line 2 is zero, enter -0- on lines 14 through 20)

14. Multiply line 6 by 0.5   14. __22,500__
15. Add lines 3, 4, and 5   15. __20,000__
16. Subtract line 15 from line 14   16. __2,500__
17. Multiply line 6 by 0.3   17. __13,500__
18. Enter line 2   18. __3,200__
19. Deductible amount. Enter the smallest of Line 16, 17, or 18   19. __2,500__
20. Carryover. Subtract line 19 from line 18   20. __700__

Contributions of capital gain property subject to 30% limit (if line 3 is zero, enter -0- on lines 21 through 26)

21. Multiply line 6 by 0.5   21. __22,500__
22. Add lines 4 and 5   22. __9,000__
23. Subtract line 22 from line 21   23. __13,500__
24. Multiply line 6 by 0.3   24. __13,500__
25. Deductible amount. Enter the smallest of Line 3, 23, or 24   25. __11,000__
26. Carryover. Subtract line 25 from line 3   26. __0__

Contributions subject to 20% limit (of line1 is zero, enter -0- on lines 27 through 36)

27. Multiply line 6 by 0.5   27. __22,500__
28. Add lines 8, 12, 19, and 25   28. __22,500__
29. Subtract line 28 from line 27   29. __0__
30. Multiply line 6 by 0.3   30. __13,500__
31. Subtract line 19 from line 30   31. __11,000__
32. Subtract line 25 from line 30   32. __2,500__
33. Multiply line 6 by 0.2   33. __9,000__
34. Enter line 1   34. __1,500__
35. Deductible amount. Enter the smallest of lines 29, 31, 32, 33, or 34   35. __0__
36. Carryover. Subtract line 35 from line 34   36. __1,500__
37. Deduction for the year. Add lines 8, 12, 19, 25, and 35   37. __22,500__

This worksheet has been adapted from Worksheet 2 of IRS Publication 526.

(a) Stock (capital property) donated to non-50-percent organization (item g.)
(b) Cash donated to non-50-percent organization (item e.)
(c) Stock (capital property) donated to a 50-percent organization (item c.)
(d) Clothing (non-cash property) donated to a 50-percent organization (item f.)
(e) Cash donated to a 50-percent organization (item a.)

Self-Study Problem 5.10

Form 4684 — Department of the Treasury, Internal Revenue Service

Casualties and Thefts
Attach to your tax return.
Use a separate Form 4684 for each casualty or theft.
Go to www.irs.gov/Form4684 for instructions and the latest information.

OMB No. 1545-0177
2024
Attachment Sequence No. 26

Name(s) shown on tax return: Roberto

Identifying number:

SECTION A—Personal Use Property (Use this section to report casualties and thefts of property **not** used in a trade or business or for income-producing purposes. For tax years 2018 through 2025, if you are an individual, casualty or theft losses of personal-use property are deductible only if the loss is attributable to a federally declared disaster. You must use a separate Form 4684 (through line 12) for each casualty or theft event involving personal-use property. **If reporting a qualified disaster loss, see the instructions for special rules that apply before completing this section.**)

If the casualty or theft loss is attributable to a federally declared disaster, check here ☑ and enter the DR- **3596** or EM- _____ declaration number assigned by FEMA. (See instructions.)

1. Description of properties (show type, location (city, state, and ZIP code), and date acquired for each property). Use a separate line for each property lost or damaged from the same casualty or theft. If you checked the box and entered the FEMA disaster declaration number above, enter the ZIP code for the property most affected on the line for Property **A**.

	Type of Property	City and State	ZIP Code	Date Acquired
Property A	Automobile	Cedar Key, FL	32625	07/2021
Property B				
Property C				
Property D				

			Properties			
			A	B	C	D
2	Cost or other basis of each property	2	18,500			
3	Insurance or other reimbursement (whether or not you filed a claim) (see instructions). **Note:** If line 2 is **more** than line 3, skip line 4.	3	5,000			
4	Gain from casualty or theft. If line 3 is **more** than line 2, enter the difference here and skip lines 5 through 9 for that column. See instructions if line 3 includes insurance or other reimbursement you did not claim, or you received payment for your loss in a later tax year.	4				
5	Fair market value **before** casualty or theft	5	14,000			
6	Fair market value **after** casualty or theft	6	0			
7	Subtract line 6 from line 5	7	14,000			
8	Enter the **smaller** of line 2 or line 7	8	14,000			
9	Subtract line 3 from line 8. If zero or less, enter -0-	9	9,000			

10	Casualty or theft loss. Add the amounts on line 9 in columns A through D	10	9,000
11	Enter $100 ($500 if qualified disaster loss rules apply; see instructions)	11	100
12	Subtract line 11 from line 10. If zero or less, enter -0-	12	8,900
	Caution: Use only one Form 4684 for lines 13 through 18.		
13	Add the amounts on line 4 of all Forms 4684	13	
14	Add the amounts on line 12 of all Forms 4684. If you have losses not attributable to a federally declared disaster, see the instructions	14	8,900
	Caution: See instructions before completing line 15.		
15	• If line 13 is **more** than line 14, enter the difference here and on Schedule D. **Do not** complete the rest of this section. • If line 13 is **equal** to line 14, enter -0- here. **Do not** complete the rest of this section. • If line 13 is **less** than line 14, and you have no qualified disaster losses subject to the $500 reduction on line 11 on any Form(s) 4684, enter -0- here and go to line 16. If you have qualified disaster losses subject to the $500 reduction, subtract line 13 from line 14 and enter the smaller of this difference or the amount on line 12 of the Form(s) 4684 reporting those losses. Enter that result here and on Schedule A (Form 1040), line 16; or Schedule A (Form 1040-NR), line 7. If you claim the standard deduction, also include on Schedule A (Form 1040), line 16, the amount of your standard deduction (see the Instructions for Form 1040). Do not complete the rest of this section if all of your casualty or theft losses are subject to the $500 reduction.	15	0
16	Add lines 13 and 15. Subtract the result from line 14	16	8,900
17	Enter 10% of your adjusted gross income from Form 1040, 1040-SR, or 1040-NR, line 11. Estates and trusts, see instructions	17	3,500
18	Subtract line 17 from line 16. If zero or less, enter -0-. Also, enter the result on Schedule A (Form 1040), line 15; or Schedule A (Form 1040-NR), line 6. Estates and trusts, enter the result on the "Other deductions" line of your tax return	18	5,400

For Paperwork Reduction Act Notice, see instructions. Cat. No. 12997O Form **4684** (2024)

Self-Study Problem 5.8

Form 4952 — Investment Interest Expense Deduction
Department of the Treasury — Internal Revenue Service
Attach to your tax return.
Go to www.irs.gov/Form4952 for the latest information.
OMB No. 1545-0191
2024
Attachment Sequence No. 51

Name(s) shown on return: Jordin Clapper
Identifying number: 332-17-9111

Part I — Total Investment Interest Expense

Line	Description	Amount
1	Investment interest expense paid or accrued in 2024 (see instructions)	1,600
2	Disallowed investment interest expense from 2023 Form 4952, line 7	
3	**Total investment interest expense.** Add lines 1 and 2	1,600

Part II — Net Investment Income

Line	Description	Sub	Amount
4a	Gross income from property held for investment (excluding any net gain from the disposition of property held for investment)	1,000	
4b	Qualified dividends included on line 4a		
4c	Subtract line 4b from line 4a		1,000
4d	Net gain from the disposition of property held for investment		
4e	Enter the **smaller** of line 4d or your net capital gain from the disposition of property held for investment. See instructions		
4f	Subtract line 4e from line 4d		
4g	Enter the amount from lines 4b and 4e that you elect to include in investment income. See instructions		
4h	Investment income. Add lines 4c, 4f, and 4g		1,000
5	Investment expenses (see instructions)		
6	**Net investment income.** Subtract line 5 from line 4h. If zero or less, enter -0-		1,000

Part III — Investment Interest Expense Deduction

Line	Description	Amount
7	Disallowed investment interest expense to be carried forward to 2025. Subtract line 6 from line 3. If zero or less, enter -0-	600
8	**Investment interest expense deduction.** Enter the **smaller** of line 3 or line 6. See instructions	1,000

For Paperwork Reduction Act Notice, see page 4. Cat. No. 13177Y Form **4952** (2024)

Self-Study Problem 5.8

Refer to Schedule A on Page E-44 for reporting of interest on lines 8 through 10 under Problem 5.8.

	Total	Part a	Part b	Part c
Interest on her home mortgage	$9,250	$9,250	$9,250	$9,250
Service charges on her checking account	48	0	0	0
Credit card interest	168	0	0	0
Auto loan interest	675	0	0	0
Interest from a home equity line of credit (HELOC)	2,300	0	2,300	0
Interest from a loan used to purchase stock (Form 4952 above)	1,600	1,000	1,000	1,000
Credit investigation fee for loan	75	0	0	0
Deductible amount		$10,250	$12,550	$10,250

Jordin's mortgage interest is from qualified mortgage debt (secured by residence, less than $1,000,000) and is deductible in parts a–c. Because Jordin's mortgage originated prior to December 16, 2017, the $1 million threshold continues to apply in 2024. The home equity interest is not deductible in part a in 2024 as generally home equity interest is not deductible under TCJA. In part b, the home equity debt is treated as acquisition debt which continues to qualify as deductible post-TCJA (subject to the $1 million limitation for grandfathered debt). The investment interest remains deductible after TCJA but also remains limited to net investment income ($1,000 in this example). The other forms of interest are nondeductible personal interest.

Self-Study Problem 5.9

Refer to Schedule A on Page E-44
Lines 11 and 12 of Schedule A—Refer to worksheet on Page E-45. The Guayaquil Soup Kitchen is not a qualified organization (non-U.S.) and there is no deduction for sporting tickets.
Line 11: $8,000 + $3,200 − $700 carryover
Line 12: $11,000 + $1,000 + $1,500 − $1,500 carryover

Self-Study Problem 5.10

Refer to Schedule A on Page E-44
Line 15—Refer to Form 4684 on Page E-46.
Line 16 of Schedule A—Gambling losses are deductible subject to the limit of gambling winnings. Miscellaneous deductions subject to the 2 percent of AGI rule are suspended through 2025.

Chapter 6 Accounting Periods and Other Taxes

Self-Study Problem 6.1

Taxpayer	Calendar year-end	Fiscal year-end	Fiscal year-end but some restrictions
1. Individual with no separate books and records	X		
2. Partnership for which all the partners are calendar year-end individuals	X		X
3. A corporation that keeps its book and records on a fiscal year ending June 30		X	
4. An S corporation for which all shareholders are calendar year-end individuals	X		X

Self-Study Problem 6.2

a.

	Cash				Accrual			
	2024	2025	2026	Explanation	2024	2025	2026	Explanation
1	10,000			Constructive receipt	10,000			Meets all-events test
2	8,000			Constructive receipt		8,000		All-events met when earned
3	5,000			Constructive receipt		5,000		All-events met when earned
4	6,000			Constructive receipt	6,000			Prepaid rent when received
5	6,000	6,000		Prepaid interest deducted over time	6,000	6,000		Prepaid interest deducted over time
6	1,000	12,000	11,000	Does not meet 12-month rule	1,000	12,000	11,000	Economic performance occurs over time
7	6,000			Meets 12-month rule	500	5,500		Economic performance occurs over time

b. 1. Yes, the corporation is involved in farming.
2. Yes, personal service corporation.
3. No, annual receipts exceed $30 million.
4. Yes, assuming this is a personal service corporation.

Self-Study Problem 6.3

1. 56%; 40% owned directly and 16% (80% × 20%) through X Corporation.
2. 40%; 20% owned directly plus 20% as Gene's brother.
3. 40%; 20% owned directly plus 20% as Frank's brother.
4. $0; since they are related parties, the loss would be disallowed.

Self-Study Problem 6.4

a. Refer to Form 8615 on Page E-50.
b. Refer to Form 8814 on Page E-51.

Self-Study Problem 6.5

Refer to Form 6251 on Page E-52.

Self-Study Problem 6.6

Refer to Schedule H on Pages E-53 and E-54.

Self-Study Problem 6.7

a. Refer to Form 8960 on Page E-55.
b. Refer to Form 8959 on Page E-56.

Self-Study Problem 6.8

1. F   The first step is to contact the employer or payer and request a copy.
2. F   An amended return is filed on Form 1040-X.
3. F   A trial separation does not typically rise to the level of a legal separation and thus, the taxpayers remain married.
4. T   A qualified domestic relations order is used to divide qualified plan assets.
5. F   Mary should file for equitable relief.
6. F   Taxpayers are generally required to file a final income tax return.
7. F   Chamu should request a correction from her employer and if unable to get one, file Form 843.
8. F   If the individual meets the threshold for both foreign account reporting types, both must be filed.
9. T   Farmers use Schedule F as part of Form 1040.

Self-Study Problem 6.9

1. A. Included
   B. Included
   C. Excluded   Basic allowance for housing (BAH) is excluded.
   D. Excluded   Pay earned while in a combat zone is generally excluded.
   E. Excluded   Basic allowance for substinence (BAS) is excluded.
   F. Included
2. Refer to Form 3903 on Page E-57.

Self-Study Problem 6.4, Part a

Form 8615
Department of the Treasury
Internal Revenue Service

Tax for Certain Children Who Have Unearned Income
Attach only to the child's Form 1040 or 1040-NR.
Go to www.irs.gov/Form8615 for instructions and the latest information.

OMB No. 1545-0074
2024
Attachment Sequence No. **33**

Child's name shown on return: Travon

Child's social security number:

A Parent's name (first, initial, and last). **Caution:** See instructions before completing.
Carl and Soren

B Parent's social security number:

C Parent's filing status (check one):
☐ Single ☒ Married filing jointly ☐ Married filing separately ☐ Head of household ☐ Qualifying surviving spouse

Part I — Child's Net Unearned Income

1	Enter the child's unearned income. See instructions	1	4,500
2	If the child **did not** itemize deductions on **Schedule A** (Form 1040) or **Schedule A** (Form 1040-NR), enter $2,600. Otherwise, see instructions	2	2,600
3	Subtract line 2 from line 1. If zero or less, **stop**; do not complete the rest of this form but **do** attach it to the child's return	3	1,900
4	Enter the child's **taxable income** from Form 1040 or 1040-NR, line 15. If the child files Form 2555, see the instructions	4	3,200 (a)
5	Enter the **smaller** of line 3 or line 4. If zero, **stop**; do not complete the rest of this form but **do** attach it to the child's return	5	1,900

Part II — Tentative Tax Based on the Tax Rate of the Parent

6	Enter the parent's **taxable income** from Form 1040 or 1040-NR, line 15. If zero or less, enter -0-. If the parent files Form 2555, see the instructions	6	45,800 (b)
7	Enter the total, if any, from Forms 8615, line 5, of **all other** children of the parent named above. **Do not** include the amount from line 5 above	7	
8	Add lines 5, 6, and 7. See instructions	8	47,700
9	Enter the tax on the amount on line 8 based on the **parent's** filing status above. See instructions. If the Qualified Dividends and Capital Gain Tax Worksheet, Schedule D Tax Worksheet, or Schedule J (Form 1040) is used to figure the tax, check here ☐	9	5,263 (c)
10	Enter the parent's tax from Form 1040 or 1040-NR, line 16, minus any alternative minimum tax. **Do not** include any tax from **Form 4972** or **Form 8814**, or any tax from the recapture of an education credit. If the parent files Form 2555, see the instructions. If the Qualified Dividends and Capital Gain Tax Worksheet, Schedule D Tax Worksheet, or Schedule J (Form 1040) was used to figure the tax, check here ☐	10	5,035 (c)
11	Subtract line 10 from line 9 and enter the result. If line 7 is blank, also enter this amount on line 13 and go to **Part III**	11	228
12a	Add lines 5 and 7 . . . . 12a		
b	Divide line 5 by line 12a. Enter the result as a decimal (rounded to at least three places)	12b	× .
13	Multiply line 11 by line 12b	13	228

Part III — Child's Tax—If lines 4 and 5 above are the same, enter -0- on line 15 and go to line 16.

14	Subtract line 5 from line 4 . . . . 14 1,300		
15	Enter the tax on the amount on line 14 based on the **child's** filing status. See instructions. If the Qualified Dividends and Capital Gain Tax Worksheet, Schedule D Tax Worksheet, or Schedule J (Form 1040) is used to figure the tax, check here ☐	15	131 (c)
16	Add lines 13 and 15	16	359
17	Enter the tax on the amount on line 4 based on the **child's** filing status. See instructions. If the Qualified Dividends and Capital Gain Tax Worksheet, Schedule D Tax Worksheet, or Schedule J (Form 1040) is used to figure the tax, check here ☐	17	323 (c)
18	Enter the **larger** of line 16 or line 17 here and on the **child's** Form 1040 or 1040-NR, line 16. If the child files Form 2555, see the instructions	18	359

For Paperwork Reduction Act Notice, see your tax return instructions. Cat. No. 64113U Form **8615** (2024)

(a) $4,500 less standard deduction $1,300.
(b) $75,000 less $29,200 standard deduction.
(c) Tax is from tax tables for income less than $100,000 in Appendix A.

Self-Study Problem 6.4, Part b

Form 8814
Department of the Treasury
Internal Revenue Service

Parents' Election To Report Child's Interest and Dividends
Attach to parents' Form 1040, 1040-SR, or 1040-NR.
Go to www.irs.gov/Form8814 for the latest information.

OMB No. 1545-0074
2024
Attachment Sequence No. 40

Name(s) shown on your return: Carl and Soren

Your social security number:

Caution: The federal income tax on your child's income, including qualified dividends and capital gain distributions, may be less if you file a separate tax return for the child instead of making this election. This is because you cannot take certain tax benefits that your child could take on his or her own return. For details, see *Tax benefits you cannot take* in the instructions.

A Child's name (first, initial, and last): Travon
B Child's social security number:

C If more than one Form 8814 is attached, check here . . . . ☐

Part I — Child's Interest and Dividends To Report on Your Return

Line	Description	Value
1a	Enter your child's **taxable** interest. If this amount is different from the amounts shown on the child's Forms 1099-INT and 1099-OID, see the instructions	4,500
1b	Enter your child's **tax-exempt** interest. **Do not** include this amount on line 1a	
2a	Enter your child's ordinary dividends, including any Alaska Permanent Fund dividends. If your child received any ordinary dividends as a nominee, see the instructions	
2b	Enter your child's qualified dividends included on line 2a. See the instructions	
3	Enter your child's capital gain distributions. If your child received any capital gain distributions as a nominee, see the instructions	
4	Add lines 1a, 2a, and 3. If the total is $2,600 or less, skip lines 5 through 12 and go to line 13. If the total is $13,000 or more, **do not** file this form. Your child **must** file his or her own return to report the income	4,500
5	Base amount. Enter $2,600	2,600
6	Subtract line 5 from line 4	1,900

If both lines 2b and 3 are zero or blank, skip lines 7 through 10, enter -0- on line 11, and go to line 12. Otherwise, go to line 7.

Line	Description	Value
7	Divide line 2b by line 4. Enter the result as a decimal (rounded to at least three places)	
8	Divide line 3 by line 4. Enter the result as a decimal (rounded to at least three places)	
9	Multiply line 6 by line 7. Enter the result here. See the instructions for where to report this amount on your return	
10	Multiply line 6 by line 8. Enter the result here. See the instructions for where to report this amount on your return	
11	Add lines 9 and 10	0
12	Subtract line 11 from line 6. Include this amount in the total on Schedule 1 (Form 1040), line 8z. In the space next to that line, enter "Form 8814" and show the amount. If you checked the box on line C above, see the instructions. Go to line 13 below	1,900

Part II — Tax on the First $2,600 of Child's Interest and Dividends

Line	Description	Value
13	Amount not taxed. Enter $1,300	1,300
14	Subtract line 13 from line 4. If the result is zero or less, enter -0-	3,200
15	**Tax.** Is the amount on line 14 less than $1,300? ☒ **No.** Enter $130 here and see the **Note** below. ☐ **Yes.** Multiply line 14 by 10% (0.10). Enter the result here and see the **Note** below.	130

Note: If you checked the box on line C above, see the instructions. Otherwise, include the amount from line 15 in the tax you enter on Form 1040, 1040-SR, or 1040-NR, line 16. Be sure to check box 1 on Form 1040, 1040-SR, or 1040-NR, line 16.

For Paperwork Reduction Act Notice, see your tax return instructions. Cat. No. 10750J Form **8814** (2024)

Self-Study Problem 6.5

Form 6251 — Alternative Minimum Tax—Individuals
Department of the Treasury / Internal Revenue Service
Attach to Form 1040, 1040-SR, or 1040-NR.
Go to www.irs.gov/Form6251 for instructions and the latest information.
OMB No. 1545-0074
2024
Attachment Sequence No. 32

Name(s) shown on Form 1040, 1040-SR, or 1040-NR: **Harold Brown**
Your social security number:

Part I — Alternative Minimum Taxable Income (See instructions for how to complete each line.)

Line	Description	Amount
1	Enter the amount from Form 1040 or 1040-SR, line 15, if more than zero. If Form 1040 or 1040-SR, line 15, is zero, subtract line 14 of Form 1040 or 1040-SR from line 11 of Form 1040 or 1040-SR and enter the result here. (If less than zero, enter as a negative amount.)	586,000 (a)
2a	If filing Schedule A (Form 1040), enter the taxes from Schedule A, line 7; otherwise, enter the amount from Form 1040 or 1040-SR, line 12	10,000
2b	Tax refund from Schedule 1 (Form 1040), line 1 or line 8z	( )
2c	Investment interest expense (difference between regular tax and AMT)	
2d	Depletion (difference between regular tax and AMT)	
2e	Net operating loss deduction from Schedule 1 (Form 1040), line 8a. Enter as a positive amount	
2f	Alternative tax net operating loss deduction	( )
2g	Interest from specified private activity bonds exempt from the regular tax	120,000
2h	Qualified small business stock, see instructions	
2i	Exercise of incentive stock options (excess of AMT income over regular tax income)	
2j	Estates and trusts (amount from Schedule K-1 (Form 1041), box 12, code A)	
2k	Disposition of property (difference between AMT and regular tax gain or loss)	
2l	Depreciation on assets placed in service after 1986 (difference between regular tax and AMT)	
2m	Passive activities (difference between AMT and regular tax income or loss)	
2n	Loss limitations (difference between AMT and regular tax income or loss)	
2o	Circulation costs (difference between regular tax and AMT)	
2p	Long-term contracts (difference between AMT and regular tax income)	
2q	Mining costs (difference between regular tax and AMT)	
2r	Research and experimental costs (difference between regular tax and AMT)	
2s	Income from certain installment sales before January 1, 1987	( )
2t	Intangible drilling costs preference	
3	Other adjustments, including income-based related adjustments	
4	Alternative minimum taxable income. Combine lines 1 through 3. (If married filing separately and line 4 is more than $875,950, see instructions.)	716,000

Part II — Alternative Minimum Tax (AMT)

Line	Description	Amount
5	Exemption. IF your filing status is... Single or head of household, AND line 4 is not over $609,350, THEN enter on line 5 $85,700. Married filing jointly or qualifying surviving spouse, $1,218,700, $133,300. Married filing separately, $609,350, $66,650. If line 4 is **over** the amount shown above for your filing status, see instructions.	59,038 (b)
6	Subtract line 5 from line 4. If more than zero, go to line 7. If zero or less, enter -0- here and on lines 7, 9, and 11, and go to line 10.	656,962
7	• If you are filing Form 2555, see instructions for the amount to enter. • If you reported capital gain distributions directly on Form 1040 or 1040-SR, line 7; you reported qualified dividends on Form 1040 or 1040-SR, line 3a; **or** you had a gain on both lines 15 and 16 of Schedule D (Form 1040) (as refigured for the AMT, if necessary), complete Part III on the back and enter the amount from line 40 here. • **All others:** If line 6 is $232,600 or less ($116,300 or less if married filing separately), multiply line 6 by 26% (0.26). Otherwise, multiply line 6 by 28% (0.28) and subtract $4,652 ($2,326 if married filing separately) from the result.	179,297
8	Alternative minimum tax foreign tax credit (see instructions)	
9	Tentative minimum tax. Subtract line 8 from line 7	179,297
10	Add Form 1040 or 1040-SR, line 16 (minus any tax from Form 4972), and Schedule 2 (Form 1040), line 1z. Subtract from the result Schedule 3 (Form 1040), line 1 and any negative amount reported on Form 8978, line 14 (treated as a positive number). If zero or less, enter -0-. If you used Schedule J to figure your tax on Form 1040 or 1040-SR, line 16, refigure that tax without using Schedule J before completing this line. See instructions	175,475
11	AMT. Subtract line 10 from line 9. If zero or less, enter -0-. Enter here and on Schedule 2 (Form 1040), line 2	3,822

For Paperwork Reduction Act Notice, see your tax return instructions. Cat. No. 13600G Form **6251** (2024)

(a) $630,000 − $23,000 − $11,000 − $10,000
(b) $85,700 − [($716,000 − $609,350) × 25%]

Self-Study Problem 6.6

SCHEDULE H (Form 1040)
Department of the Treasury
Internal Revenue Service

Household Employment Taxes
(For Social Security, Medicare, Withheld Income, and Federal Unemployment (FUTA) Taxes)
Attach to Form 1040, 1040-SR, 1040-SS, 1040-NR, or 1041.
Go to www.irs.gov/ScheduleH for instructions and the latest information.

OMB No. 1545-0074
2024
Attachment Sequence No. 44

Name of employer: Susan Green

Calendar year taxpayers having no household employees in 2024 don't have to complete this form for 2024.

A Did you pay **any one** household employee cash wages of $2,700 or more in 2024? (If any household employee was your spouse, your child under age 21, your parent, or anyone under age 18, see the line A instructions before you answer this question.)

☑ **Yes.** Skip lines B and C and go to line 1.
☐ **No.** Go to line B.

B Did you withhold federal income tax during 2024 for any household employee?

☐ **Yes.** Skip line C and go to line 7.
☐ **No.** Go to line C.

C Did you pay **total** cash wages of $1,000 or more in **any** calendar **quarter** of 2023 or 2024 to **all** household employees? (**Don't** count cash wages paid in 2023 or 2024 to your spouse, your child under age 21, or your parent.)

☐ **No. Stop.** Don't file this schedule.
☐ **Yes.** Skip lines 1–9 and go to line 10.

Part I — Social Security, Medicare, and Federal Income Taxes

Line	Description		Amount
1	Total cash wages subject to social security tax	1 — 5,625	
2	Social security tax. Multiply line 1 by 12.4% (0.124)	2	698
3	Total cash wages subject to Medicare tax	3 — 5,625	
4	Medicare tax. Multiply line 3 by 2.9% (0.029)	4	163
5	Total cash wages subject to Additional Medicare Tax withholding	5	
6	Additional Medicare Tax withholding. Multiply line 5 by 0.9% (0.009)	6	
7	Federal income tax withheld, if any	7	
8	Total social security, Medicare, and federal income taxes. Add lines 2, 4, 6, and 7	8	861

9 Did you pay **total** cash wages of $1,000 or more in **any** calendar **quarter** of 2023 or 2024 to **all** household employees? (**Don't** count cash wages paid in 2023 or 2024 to your spouse, your child under age 21, or your parent.)

☐ **No. Stop.** Include the amount from line 8 above on Schedule 2 (Form 1040), line 9. If you're not required to file Form 1040, see the line 9 instructions.
☑ **Yes.** Go to line 10.

For Privacy Act and Paperwork Reduction Act Notice, see the separate instructions. Cat. No. 12187K Schedule H (Form 1040) 2024

Self-Study Problem 6.6

Schedule H (Form 1040) 2024 — Page **2**

Part II Federal Unemployment (FUTA) Tax

		Yes	No
10	Did you pay unemployment contributions to only one state? If you paid contributions to a credit reduction state, see instructions and check "**No**".	✓	
11	Did you pay all state unemployment contributions for 2024 by April 15, 2025? Fiscal year filers, see instructions	✓	
12	Were all wages that are taxable for FUTA tax also taxable for your state's unemployment tax?	✓	

Next: If you checked the "**Yes**" box on **all** the lines above, complete Section A.
If you checked the "**No**" box on **any** of the lines above, skip Section A and complete Section B.

Section A

13	Name of the state where you paid unemployment contributions	Florida	
14	Contributions paid to your state unemployment fund	**14**	152
15	Total cash wages subject to FUTA tax	**15**	5,625
16	**FUTA tax.** Multiply line 15 by 0.6% (0.006). Enter the result here, skip Section B, and go to line 25	**16**	34

Section B

17 Complete all columns below that apply (if you need more space, see instructions):

(a) Name of state	(b) Taxable wages (as defined in state act)	(c) State experience rate period From	(c) State experience rate period To	(d) State experience rate	(e) Multiply col. (b) by 0.054	(f) Multiply col. (b) by col. (d)	(g) Subtract col. (f) from col. (e). If zero or less, enter -0-.	(h) Contributions paid to state unemployment fund

18	Totals	**18**		
19	Add columns (g) and (h) of line 18	**19**		
20	Total cash wages subject to FUTA tax (see the line 15 instructions)		**20**	
21	Multiply line 20 by 6.0% (0.06)		**21**	
22	Multiply line 20 by 5.4% (0.054)	**22**		
23	Enter the **smaller** of line 19 or line 22. (If you paid state unemployment contributions late or you're in a credit reduction state, see instructions and check here) ☐		**23**	
24	**FUTA tax.** Subtract line 23 from line 21. Enter the result here and go to line 25		**24**	

Part III Total Household Employment Taxes

25	Enter the amount from line 8. If you checked the "**Yes**" box on line C of page 1, enter -0-	**25**	861
26	Add line 16 (or line 24) and line 25	**26**	895
27	Are you required to file Form 1040?		

☑ **Yes. Stop.** Include the amount from line 26 above on Schedule 2 (Form 1040), line 9. **Don't** complete Part IV below.
☐ **No.** You may have to complete Part IV. See instructions for details.

Part IV Address and Signature — Complete this part **only** if required. See the line 27 instructions.

Address (number and street) or P.O. box if mail isn't delivered to street address | Apt., room, or suite no.

City, town or post office, state, and ZIP code

Under penalties of perjury, I declare that I have examined this schedule, including accompanying statements, and to the best of my knowledge and belief, it is true, correct, and complete. No part of any payment made to a state unemployment fund claimed as a credit was, or is to be, deducted from the payments to employees. Declaration of preparer (other than taxpayer) is based on all information of which preparer has any knowledge.

Employer's signature | Date

Paid Preparer Use Only

Print/Type preparer's name	Preparer's signature	Date	Check ☐ if self-employed	PTIN
Firm's name			Firm's EIN	
Firm's address			Phone no.	

Self-Study Problem 6.7, Part a

Form 8960
Department of the Treasury
Internal Revenue Service

Net Investment Income Tax—Individuals, Estates, and Trusts
Attach to your tax return.
Go to www.irs.gov/Form8960 for instructions and the latest information.

OMB No. 1545-2227
2024
Attachment Sequence No. **72**

Name(s) shown on your tax return: Thornton Meloni
Your social security number or EIN:

Part I — Investment Income

☐ Section 6013(g) election (see instructions)
☐ Section 6013(h) election (see instructions)
☐ Regulations section 1.1411-10(g) election (see instructions)

Line	Description		Amount
1	Taxable interest (see instructions)	1	54,000
2	Ordinary dividends (see instructions)	2	45,000
3	Annuities (see instructions)	3	
4a	Rental real estate, royalties, partnerships, S corporations, trusts, trades or businesses, etc. (see instructions)	4a	
4b	Adjustment for net income or loss derived in the ordinary course of a non-section 1411 trade or business (see instructions)	4b	
4c	Combine lines 4a and 4b	4c	
5a	Net gain or loss from disposition of property (see instructions)	5a	22,000
5b	Net gain or loss from disposition of property that is not subject to net investment income tax (see instructions)	5b	
5c	Adjustment from disposition of partnership interest or S corporation stock (see instructions)	5c	
5d	Combine lines 5a through 5c	5d	22,000
6	Adjustments to investment income for certain CFCs and PFICs (see instructions)	6	
7	Other modifications to investment income (see instructions)	7	
8	Total investment income. Combine lines 1, 2, 3, 4c, 5d, 6, and 7	8	121,000

Part II — Investment Expenses Allocable to Investment Income and Modifications

Line	Description		Amount
9a	Investment interest expenses (see instructions)	9a	
9b	State, local, and foreign income tax (see instructions)	9b	
9c	Miscellaneous investment expenses (see instructions)	9c	
9d	Add lines 9a, 9b, and 9c	9d	
10	Additional modifications (see instructions)	10	
11	Total deductions and modifications. Add lines 9d and 10	11	

Part III — Tax Computation

Line	Description		Amount
12	Net investment income. Subtract Part II, line 11, from Part I, line 8. Individuals, complete lines 13–17. Estates and trusts, complete lines 18a–21. If zero or less, enter -0-	12	121,000
Individuals:			
13	Modified adjusted gross income (see instructions)	13	333,000
14	Threshold based on filing status (see instructions)	14	200,000
15	Subtract line 14 from line 13. If zero or less, enter -0-	15	133,000
16	Enter the smaller of line 12 or line 15	16	121,000
17	Net investment income tax for individuals. Multiply line 16 by 3.8% (0.038). Enter here and include on your tax return (see instructions)	17	4,598
Estates and Trusts:			
18a	Net investment income (line 12 above)	18a	
18b	Deductions for distributions of net investment income and charitable deductions (see instructions)	18b	
18c	Undistributed net investment income. Subtract line 18b from line 18a (see instructions). If zero or less, enter -0-	18c	
19a	Adjusted gross income (see instructions)	19a	
19b	Highest tax bracket for estates and trusts for the year (see instructions)	19b	
19c	Subtract line 19b from line 19a. If zero or less, enter -0-	19c	
20	Enter the smaller of line 18c or line 19c	20	
21	Net investment income tax for estates and trusts. Multiply line 20 by 3.8% (0.038). Enter here and include on your tax return (see instructions)	21	

For Paperwork Reduction Act Notice, see your tax return instructions. Cat. No. 59474M Form **8960** (2024)

Self-Study Problem 6.7, Part b

Form 8959
Department of the Treasury
Internal Revenue Service

Additional Medicare Tax

If any line does not apply to you, leave it blank. See separate instructions.
Attach to Form 1040, 1040-SR, 1040-NR, or 1040-SS.
Go to www.irs.gov/Form8959 for instructions and the latest information.

OMB No. 1545-0074
2024
Attachment Sequence No. 71

Name(s) shown on return: Meng and Eang Ung
Your social security number: 490-22-1818

Part I — Additional Medicare Tax on Medicare Wages

Line	Description	Amount
1	Medicare wages and tips from Form W-2, box 5. If you have more than one Form W-2, enter the total of the amounts from box 5	266,000
2	Unreported tips from Form 4137, line 6	
3	Wages from Form 8919, line 6	
4	Add lines 1 through 3	266,000
5	Enter the following amount for your filing status: Married filing jointly $250,000; Married filing separately $125,000; Single, Head of household, or Qualifying surviving spouse $200,000	250,000
6	Subtract line 5 from line 4. If zero or less, enter -0-	16,000
7	Additional Medicare Tax on Medicare wages. Multiply line 6 by 0.9% (0.009). Enter here and go to Part II	144

Part II — Additional Medicare Tax on Self-Employment Income

Line	Description	Amount
8	Self-employment income from Schedule SE (Form 1040), Part I, line 6. If you had a loss, enter -0-	130,000
9	Enter the following amount for your filing status: Married filing jointly $250,000; Married filing separately $125,000; Single, Head of household, or Qualifying surviving spouse $200,000	250,000
10	Enter the amount from line 4	266,000
11	Subtract line 10 from line 9. If zero or less, enter -0-	0
12	Subtract line 11 from line 8. If zero or less, enter -0-	130,000
13	Additional Medicare Tax on self-employment income. Multiply line 12 by 0.9% (0.009). Enter here and go to Part III	1,170

Part III — Additional Medicare Tax on Railroad Retirement Tax Act (RRTA) Compensation

Line	Description	Amount
14	Railroad retirement (RRTA) compensation and tips from Form(s) W-2, box 14 (see instructions)	
15	Enter the following amount for your filing status: Married filing jointly $250,000; Married filing separately $125,000; Single, Head of household, or Qualifying surviving spouse $200,000	
16	Subtract line 15 from line 14. If zero or less, enter -0-	
17	Additional Medicare Tax on railroad retirement (RRTA) compensation. Multiply line 16 by 0.9% (0.009). Enter here and go to Part IV	

Part IV — Total Additional Medicare Tax

Line	Description	Amount
18	Add lines 7, 13, and 17. Also include this amount on Schedule 2 (Form 1040), line 11 (Form 1040-SS filers, see instructions), and go to Part V	1,314

Part V — Withholding Reconciliation

Line	Description	Amount
19	Medicare tax withheld from Form W-2, box 6. If you have more than one Form W-2, enter the total of the amounts from box 6 — 4,451	
20	Enter the amount from line 1 — 266,000	
21	Multiply line 20 by 1.45% (0.0145). This is your regular Medicare tax withholding on Medicare wages — 3,857	
22	Subtract line 21 from line 19. If zero or less, enter -0-. This is your Additional Medicare Tax withholding on Medicare wages	594
23	Additional Medicare Tax withholding on railroad retirement (RRTA) compensation from Form W-2, box 14 (see instructions)	
24	Total Additional Medicare Tax withholding. Add lines 22 and 23. Also include this amount with federal income tax withholding on Form 1040, 1040-SR, or 1040-NR, line 25c (Form 1040-SS filers, see instructions)	594

For Paperwork Reduction Act Notice, see your tax return instructions. Cat. No. 59475X Form **8959** (2024)

Self-Study Problem 6.9

Form 3903 — Moving Expenses (2024)
Department of the Treasury — Internal Revenue Service
OMB No. 1545-0074
Attachment Sequence No. 170

Attach to Form 1040, 1040-SR, or 1040-NR.
Go to www.irs.gov/Form3903 for instructions and the latest information.

Name(s) shown on return: Nick "Goose" Bradshaw

Before you begin: You can deduct moving expenses only if you are a **Member of the Armed Forces** on active duty and, due to a military order, you, your spouse, or your dependents move because of a permanent change of station.
Check here to certify that you meet these requirements. See the instructions . . . ☑

Line	Description	Amount
1	Transportation and storage of household goods and personal effects (see instructions)	4,800 (a)
2	Travel (including lodging) from your old home to your new home (see instructions). **Do not** include the cost of meals	640 (b)
3	Add lines 1 and 2	5,440
4	Enter the total amount the government paid you for the expenses listed on lines 1 and 2 that is **not** included in box 1 of your Form W-2 (wages). This amount should be shown in box 12 of your Form W-2 with code **P**	4,300
5	Is line 3 **more than** line 4? ☐ No. ☑ Yes. Subtract line 4 from line 3. Enter the result here and on Schedule 1 (Form 1040), line 14. This is your **moving expense deduction**	1,140

For Paperwork Reduction Act Notice, see your tax return instructions. Cat. No. 12490K Form **3903** (2024)

(a) $2,500 + $1,000 + $500 + $800
(b) $250 + $120 + $270 (meals and temporary lodging at destination are not qualified moving expenses)

Chapter 7 Tax Credits

Self-Study Problem 7.1

a. $4,500. $2,000 for the children under 17 and $500 for the other dependent child.
b. $4,200. Total possible credit is $4,500. Income of $405,600 exceeds $400,000 threshold by $5,600 which is rounded up to $6,000. $6,000/$1,000 = 6. 6 × $50 = phase out of $300. $4,500 less $300 = $4,200
c. Refer to Schedule 8812 and Credit Limit Worksheet A on Pages E-59 to E-61.

Self-Study Problem 7.2

Presented on Worksheet A—EIC Worksheet on Page E-62.

Self-Study Problem 7.3

Presented on Form 2441 on Pages E-63 and E-64.

Self-Study Problem 7.4

1. $2,764.
2. Excess advance payment of $3,080.
3. Repayment of $3,080.
Refer to Form 8962 on Page E-65.

Self-Study Problem 7.5

a. $500. Refundable American Opportunity tax credit, Line 8 of Form 8863.
$750. Nonrefundable American Opportunity tax credit, Line 19 of Form 8863.
Refer to Form 8863 on Pages E-66 and E-67.
b. $1,360 = 20% × $6,800 ($10,000 maximum)

Self-Study Problem 7.6

Overall limitation:

$$\frac{\$1,500}{\$58,000} \times \$7,819 = \$202$$

The foreign tax credit is limited to $202. The remaining balance of $230 ($432 − $202) can be carried back one year or carried forward 10 years.

Self-Study Problem 7.7

Refer to Form 8839 on Pages E-68 and E-69.

Self-Study Problem 7.8

a. Refer to Form 8936 and Schedule A on Pages E-70 to E-73.
b. $11,400 for the residential clean energy credit and $2,790 for the energy efficient home improvement credit. Refer to Form 5695 on Pages E-74 to E-76.

Self-Study Problem 7.9

$400. Refer to Form 8880 on Page E-77.

Self-Study Problem 7.1, Part c

SCHEDULE 8812 (Form 1040)
Department of the Treasury
Internal Revenue Service

Credits for Qualifying Children and Other Dependents
Attach to Form 1040, 1040-SR, or 1040-NR.
Go to www.irs.gov/Schedule8812 for instructions and the latest information.

OMB No. 1545-0074
2024
Attachment Sequence No. 47

Name(s) shown on return: Marie and Pierre Curry
Your social security number:

Part I — Child Tax Credit and Credit for Other Dependents

Line	Description		Amount
1	Enter the amount from line 11 of your Form 1040, 1040-SR, or 1040-NR	1	30,000
2a	Enter income from Puerto Rico that you excluded	2a	
b	Enter the amounts from lines 45 and 50 of your Form 2555	2b	
c	Enter the amount from line 15 of your Form 4563	2c	
d	Add lines 2a through 2c	2d	
3	Add lines 1 and 2d	3	30,000
4	Number of qualifying children under age 17 with the required social security number	4	3
5	Multiply line 4 by $2,000	5	6,000
6	Number of other dependents, including any qualifying children who are not under age 17 or who do not have the required social security number . . . **Caution:** Do not include yourself, your spouse, or anyone who is not a U.S. citizen, U.S. national, or U.S. resident alien. Also, do not include anyone you included on line 4.	6	
7	Multiply line 6 by $500	7	
8	Add lines 5 and 7	8	6,000
9	Enter the amount shown below for your filing status. • Married filing jointly—$400,000 • All other filing statuses—$200,000	9	400,000
10	Subtract line 9 from line 3. • If zero or less, enter -0-. • If more than zero and not a multiple of $1,000, enter the next multiple of $1,000. For example, if the result is $425, enter $1,000; if the result is $1,025, enter $2,000, etc.	10	0
11	Multiply line 10 by 5% (0.05)	11	0
12	Is the amount on line 8 more than the amount on line 11? ☐ **No. STOP.** You cannot take the child tax credit, credit for other dependents, or additional child tax credit. Skip Parts II-A and II-B. Enter -0- on lines 14 and 27. ☑ **Yes.** Subtract line 11 from line 8. Enter the result.	12	6,000
13	Enter the amount from **Credit Limit Worksheet A**	13	200
14	Enter the smaller of line 12 or line 13. **This is your child tax credit and credit for other dependents** Enter this amount on Form 1040, 1040-SR, or 1040-NR, line 19.	14	200

If the amount on line 12 is more than the amount on line 14, you may be able to take the **additional child tax credit** on Form 1040, 1040-SR, or 1040-NR, line 28. Complete your Form 1040, 1040-SR, or 1040-NR through line 27 (also complete Schedule 3, line 11) before completing Part II-A.

For Paperwork Reduction Act Notice, see your tax return instructions. Cat. No. 59761M Schedule 8812 (Form 1040) 2024

Self-Study Problem 7.1, Part c

Schedule 8812 (Form 1040) 2024 — Page 2

Part II-A Additional Child Tax Credit for All Filers

Caution: If you file Form 2555, you cannot claim the additional child tax credit.

15. Check this box if you **do not** want to claim the additional child tax credit. Skip Parts II-A and II-B. Enter -0- on line 27 . . . . ☐

16a. Subtract line 14 from line 12. If zero, **stop here**; you cannot take the additional child tax credit. Skip Parts II-A and II-B. Enter -0- on line 27 . . . . **16a** 5,800

  b. Number of qualifying children under age 17 with the required social security number: __3__ x $1,700.
  Enter the result. If zero, **stop here**; you cannot claim the additional child tax credit. Skip Parts II-A and II-B. Enter -0- on line 27 . . . . **16b** 5,100
  TIP: The number of children you use for this line is the same as the number of children you used for line 4.

17. Enter the **smaller** of line 16a or line 16b **17** 5,100

18a. Earned income (see instructions) **18a** 30,000
  b. Nontaxable combat pay (see instructions) . . . **18b** ____

19. Is the amount on line 18a more than $2,500?
  ☐ No. Leave line 19 blank and enter -0- on line 20.
  ☒ Yes. Subtract $2,500 from the amount on line 18a. Enter the result . . . **19** 27,500

20. Multiply the amount on line 19 by 15% (0.15) and enter the result **20** 4,125

  Next. On line 16b, is the amount $5,100 or more?
  ☒ No. If you are a bona fide resident of Puerto Rico, go to line 21. Otherwise, skip Part II-B and enter the **smaller** of line 17 or line 20 on line 27.
  ☒ Yes. If line 20 is equal to or more than line 17, skip Part II-B and enter the amount from line 17 on line 27. Otherwise, go to line 21.

Part II-B Certain Filers Who Have Three or More Qualifying Children and Bona Fide Residents of Puerto Rico

21. Withheld social security, Medicare, and Additional Medicare taxes from Form(s) W-2, boxes 4 and 6. If married filing jointly, include your spouse's amounts with yours. If your employer withheld or you paid Additional Medicare Tax or tier 1 RRTA taxes, or if you are a bona fide resident of Puerto Rico, see instructions **21** 2,295

22. Enter the total of the amounts from Schedule 1 (Form 1040), line 15; Schedule 2 (Form 1040), line 5; Schedule 2 (Form 1040), line 6; and Schedule 2 (Form 1040), line 13 . **22** (a)

23. Add lines 21 and 22 . . . . **23** 2,295

24. **1040 and 1040-SR filers:** Enter the total of the amounts from Form 1040 or 1040-SR, line 27, and Schedule 3 (Form 1040), line 11.
  1040-NR filers: Enter the amount from Schedule 3 (Form 1040), line 11. **24** (b)

25. Subtract line 24 from line 23. If zero or less, enter -0- **25** 2,295

26. Enter the **larger** of line 20 or line 25 . . . . **26** 4,125
  Next, enter the **smaller** of line 17 or line 26 on line 27.

Part II-C Additional Child Tax Credit

27. This is your additional child tax credit. Enter this amount on Form 1040, 1040-SR, or 1040-NR, line 28 . **27** 4,125

Schedule 8812 (Form 1040) 2024

(a) This line represents other forms of Social Security and Medicare taxes such as one-half of self-employment taxes and other less common forms (e.g., Social Security and Medicare taxes on unreported tips).
(b) This line reduces the possible refundable child tax credit by any earned income credit or excess Social Security and Medicare taxes withheld.

Self-Study Problem 7.1, Part c

Credit Limit Worksheet A *Keep for Your Records*

1.	Enter the amount from line 18 of your Form 1040, 1040–SR, or 1040–NR.	1. 230
2.	Add the following amounts (if applicable) from:	

Schedule 3, line 1 ... foreign tax credit .... + _____
Schedule 3, line 2 ... child and dependent care expense credit ... + 30
Schedule 3, line 3 ... education credit (AOTC/LLC) .... + _____
Schedule 3, line 4 ... retirement savings credit .... + _____
Schedule 3, line 5b ... energy efficient home improvement credit . + _____
Schedule 3, line 6d ... elderly credit .... + _____
Schedule 3, line 6f ... new clean vehicle credit .... + _____
Schedule 3, line 6l ... additional reporting year tax for partner . + _____
Schedule 3, line 6m ... used clean vehicle credit .... + _____

Enter the total. 2. 30

3. Subtract line 2 from line 1. .... 3. 200

Complete Credit Limit Worksheet B **only** if you meet all the following.

1. You are claiming one or more of the following credits.

    a. Mortgage interest credit, Form 8396.
    b. Adoption credit, Form 8839.
    c. Residential clean energy credit, Form 5695, Part I.
    d. District of Columbia first-time homebuyer credit, Form 8859.

2. You are not filing Form 2555.

3. Line 4 of Schedule 8812 is more than zero.

4. If you are **not** completing Credit Limit Worksheet B, enter -0-; otherwise, enter the amount from Credit Limit Worksheet B. 4. 0

5. Subtract line 4 from line 3. Enter here and on Schedule 8812, line 13. .... 5. 200

E-62 Appendix E

Self-Study Problem 7.2

Worksheet A—2024 EIC—Line 27

Keep for Your Records

Before you begin: √ Be sure you are using the correct worksheet. Use this worksheet only if you answered "No" to Step 5, question 2. Otherwise, use Worksheet B.

Part 1

All Filers Using Worksheet A

1. Enter your earned income from Step 5. — **1** | 17,600

2. Look up the amount on line 1 above in the EIC Table (right after Worksheet B) to find the credit. Be sure you use the correct column for your filing status and the number of qualifying children you have who have a valid SSN as defined earlier. Enter the credit here. — **2** | 4,213

   If line 2 is zero, [STOP] You can't take the credit.
   Enter "No" on the dotted line next to Form 1040 or 1040-SR, line 27.

3. Enter the amount from Form 1040 or 1040-SR, line 11. — **3** | 17,750

4. Are the amounts on lines 3 and 1 the same?

   ☐ **Yes.** Skip line 5; enter the amount from line 2 on line 6.

   ☒ **No.** Go to line 5.

Part 2

Filers Who Answered "No" on Line 4

5. If you have:
   - No qualifying children who have a valid SSN, is the amount on line 3 less than $10,350 ($17,250 if married filing jointly)?
   - 1 or more qualifying children who have a valid SSN, is the amount on line 3 less than $22,750 ($29,650 if married filing jointly)?

   ☒ **Yes.** Leave line 5 blank; enter the amount from line 2 on line 6.

   ☐ **No.** Look up the amount on line 3 in the EIC Table to find the credit. Be sure you use the correct column for your filing status and the number of qualifying children you have who have a valid SSN. Enter the credit here.
   Look at the amounts on lines 5 and 2.
   Then, enter the **smaller** amount on line 6. — **5** |

Part 3

Your Earned Income Credit

6. This is your earned income credit. — **6** | 4,213

   Enter this amount on Form 1040 or 1040-SR, line 27.

   Reminder—
   √ If you have a qualifying child, complete and attach Schedule EIC.

   ⚠ **CAUTION** If your EIC for a year after 1996 was reduced or disallowed, see Form 8862, who must file, earlier, to find out if you must file Form 8862 to take the credit for 2024.

Download the latest version of this worksheet from the Form 1040 Instructions available at **www.irs.gov**. The 2024 worksheet was not available as we went to print. This worksheet is adapted from the 2023 version.

Self-Study Problem 7.3

Form 2441 — Child and Dependent Care Expenses
Department of the Treasury — Internal Revenue Service
Attach to Form 1040, 1040-SR, or 1040-NR.
Go to www.irs.gov/Form2441 for instructions and the latest information.
OMB No. 1545-0074
2024
Attachment Sequence No. 21

Name(s) shown on return: Julie Brown
Your social security number: 456-29-6549

A You can't claim a credit for child and dependent care expenses if your filing status is married filing separately unless you meet the requirements listed in the instructions under *Married Persons Filing Separately*. If you meet these requirements, check this box . ☐

B If you or your spouse was a student or was disabled during 2024 and you're entering deemed income of $250 or $500 a month on Form 2441 based on the income rules listed in the instructions under *If You or Your Spouse Was a Student or Disabled*, check this box . ☐

Part I — Persons or Organizations Who Provided the Care

You **must** complete this part.
If you have more than three care providers, see the instructions and check this box . . . . ☐

1 (a) Care provider's name	(b) Address (number, street, apt. no., city, state, and ZIP code)	(c) Identifying number (SSN or EIN)	(d) Was the care provider your household employee in 2024?	(e) Amount paid (see instructions)
Ivy Childcare	1 Sunflower Street, Terra Haute, IN 47803	56-7654321	☐ Yes ☑ No	8,500
De Anza Adult Care	13 Fort Harrison Rd, Dewey, IN 47805	43-1234567	☐ Yes ☑ No	3,400
			☐ Yes ☐ No	

Did you receive dependent care benefits? — **No** — Complete only Part II below.
— **Yes** — Complete Part III on page 2 next.

Caution: If the care provider is your household employee, you may owe employment taxes. For details, see the Instructions for Schedule H (Form 1040). If you incurred care expenses in 2024 but didn't pay them until 2025, or if you prepaid in 2024 for care to be provided in 2025, don't include these expenses in column (d) of line 2 for 2024. See the instructions.

Part II — Credit for Child and Dependent Care Expenses

2 Information about your **qualifying person(s)**. If you have more than three qualifying persons, see the instructions and check this box ☐

(a) Qualifying person's name (First / Last)	(b) Qualifying person's social security number	(c) Check here if the qualifying person was over age 12 and was disabled. (see instructions)	(d) Qualified expenses you incurred and paid in 2024 for the person listed in column (a)
Chuck Brown	123-33-4444	☐	8,500
Devona Neuporte	214-55-6666	☐	3,400
		☐	

3	Add the amounts in column (d) of line 2. **Don't** enter more than $3,000 if you had one qualifying person or $6,000 if you had two or more persons. If you completed Part III, enter the amount from line 31 .	**3** 1,000
4	Enter your **earned income**. See instructions	**4** 90,000
5	If married filing jointly, enter your spouse's earned income (if you or your spouse was a student or was disabled, see the instructions); **all others**, enter the amount from line 4	**5** 90,000
6	Enter the **smallest** of line 3, 4, or 5	**6** 1,000
7	Enter the amount from Form 1040, 1040-SR, or 1040-NR, line 11 . . . **7** 90,000	
8	Enter on line 8 the decimal amount shown below that applies to the amount on line 7.	

If line 7 is:			If line 7 is:			If line 7 is:		
Over	But not over	Decimal amount is	Over	But not over	Decimal amount is	Over	But not over	Decimal amount is
$0	15,000	.35	$25,000	27,000	.29	$37,000	39,000	.23
15,000	17,000	.34	27,000	29,000	.28	39,000	41,000	.22
17,000	19,000	.33	29,000	31,000	.27	41,000	43,000	.21
19,000	21,000	.32	31,000	33,000	.26	43,000	No limit	.20
21,000	23,000	.31	33,000	35,000	.25			
23,000	25,000	.30	35,000	37,000	.24			

8 X .20

9a	Multiply line 6 by the decimal amount on line 8	**9a** 200
b	If you paid 2023 expenses in 2024, complete Worksheet A in the instructions. Enter the amount from line 13 of the worksheet here. Otherwise, enter -0- on line 9b and go to line 9c	**9b**
c	Add lines 9a and 9b and enter the result	**9c** 200
10	Tax liability limit. Enter the amount from the Credit Limit Worksheet in the instructions **10** 5,240	
11	**Credit for child and dependent care expenses.** Enter the **smaller** of line 9c or line 10 here and on Schedule 3 (Form 1040), line 2	**11** 200

For Paperwork Reduction Act Notice, see your tax return instructions. Cat. No. 11862M Form **2441** (2024)

Self-Study Problem 7.3

Form 2441 (2024) Page **2**

Part III Dependent Care Benefits

Line	Description		Amount
12	Enter the total amount of **dependent care benefits** you received in 2024. Amounts you received as an employee should be shown in box 10 of your Form(s) W-2. **Don't** include amounts reported as wages in box 1 of Form(s) W-2. If you were self-employed or a partner, include amounts you received under a dependent care assistance program from your sole proprietorship or partnership	12	5,000
13	Enter the amount, if any, you carried over from 2023 and used in 2024 during the grace period. See instructions	13	
14	If you forfeited or carried over to 2025 any of the amounts reported on line 12 or 13, enter the amount. See instructions	14 (	)
15	Combine lines 12 through 14. See instructions	15	5,000
16	Enter the total amount of **qualified expenses** incurred in 2024 for the care of the **qualifying person(s)** ... 16	11,900	
17	Enter the **smaller** of line 15 or 16 ... 17	5,000	
18	Enter your **earned income**. See instructions ... 18	90,000	
19	Enter the amount shown below that applies to you. • If married filing jointly, enter your spouse's earned income (if you or your spouse was a student or was disabled, see the instructions for line 5). • If married filing separately, see instructions. • All others, enter the amount from line 18. ... 19	90,000	
20	Enter the **smallest** of line 17, 18, or 19 ... 20	5,000	
21	Enter $5,000 ($2,500 if married filing separately **and** you were required to enter your spouse's earned income on line 19). However, don't enter more than the maximum amount allowed under your dependent care plan. See instructions ... 21	5,000	
22	Is any amount on line 12 or 13 from your sole proprietorship or partnership? ☑ **No.** Enter -0-. ☐ **Yes.** Enter the amount here	22	0
23	Subtract line 22 from line 15 ... 23	5,000	
24	**Deductible benefits.** Enter the **smallest** of line 20, 21, or 22. Also, include this amount on the appropriate line(s) of your return. See instructions	24	0
25	**Excluded benefits.** If you checked "No" on line 22, enter the smaller of line 20 or line 21. Otherwise, subtract line 24 from the smaller of line 20 or line 21. If zero or less, enter -0-	25	5,000
26	**Taxable benefits.** Subtract line 25 from line 23. If zero or less, enter -0-. Also, enter this amount on Form 1040, 1040-SR, or 1040-NR, line 1e	26	0

To claim the child and dependent care credit, complete lines 27 through 31 below.

Line	Description		Amount
27	Enter $3,000 ($6,000 if two or more qualifying persons)	27	6,000
28	Add lines 24 and 25	28	5,000
29	Subtract line 28 from line 27. If zero or less, **stop**. You can't take the credit. **Exception.** If you paid 2023 expenses in 2024, see the instructions for line 9b	29	1,000
30	Complete line 2 on page 1 of this form. **Don't** include in column (d) any benefits shown on line 28 above. Then, add the amounts in column (d) and enter the total here	30	6,900
31	Enter the **smaller** of line 29 or 30. Also, enter this amount on line 3 on page 1 of this form and complete lines 4 through 11	31	1,000

Form **2441** (2024)

Self-Study Problem 7.4

Form 8962 — Premium Tax Credit (PTC)
Department of the Treasury / Internal Revenue Service
Attach to Form 1040, 1040-SR, or 1040-NR.
Go to www.irs.gov/Form8962 for instructions and the latest information.
OMB No. 1545-0074
2024
Attachment Sequence No. 73

Name shown on your return: **Tracy and Marco Brigantine**
Your social security number: **123-44-5555**

A. You cannot take the PTC if your filing status is married filing separately unless you qualify for an exception. See instructions. If you qualify, check the box ☐

Part I — Annual and Monthly Contribution Amount

Line	Description		Value
1	Tax family size. Enter your tax family size.	1	4
2a	Modified AGI. Enter your modified AGI.	2a	104,000 (a)
b	Enter the total of your dependents' modified AGI.	2b	0 (b)
3	Household income. Add the amounts on lines 2a and 2b.	3	104,000
4	Federal poverty line. Enter the federal poverty line amount from Table 1-1, 1-2, or 1-3. Check the appropriate box for the federal poverty table used. a ☐ Alaska b ☐ Hawaii c ☒ Other 48 states and DC	4	30,000
5	Household income as a percentage of federal poverty line	5	346%
6	Reserved for future use		
7	Applicable figure.	7	.0715
8a	Annual contribution amount. Multiply line 3 by line 7.	8a	7,436
8b	Monthly contribution amount. Divide line 8a by 12.	8b	620

Part II — Premium Tax Credit Claim and Reconciliation of Advance Payment of Premium Tax Credit

9. Are you allocating policy amounts with another taxpayer or do you want to use the alternative calculation for year of marriage? ☐ Yes ☒ No. Continue to line 10.
10. See the instructions to determine if you can use line 11 or must complete lines 12 through 23.
   ☒ Yes. Continue to line 11. Compute your annual PTC. Then skip lines 12–23 and continue to line 24.
   ☐ No. Continue to lines 12–23. Compute your monthly PTC and continue to line 24.

Annual Calculation	(a) Annual enrollment premiums (Form(s) 1095-A, line 33A)	(b) Annual applicable SLCSP premium (Form(s) 1095-A, line 33B)	(c) Annual contribution amount (line 8a)	(d) Annual maximum premium assistance (subtract (c) from (b); if zero or less, enter -0-)	(e) Annual PTC allowed (smaller of (a) or (d))	(f) Annual advance payment of PTC (Form(s) 1095-A, line 33C)
11 Annual Totals	11,880	10,200	7,436	2,764	2,764	5,844

Monthly Calculation	(a) Monthly enrollment premiums	(b) Monthly applicable SLCSP premium	(c) Monthly contribution amount	(d) Monthly maximum premium assistance	(e) Monthly PTC allowed	(f) Monthly advance payment of PTC
12 January						
13 February						
14 March						
15 April						
16 May						
17 June						
18 July						
19 August						
20 September						
21 October						
22 November						
23 December						

Line	Description	Value
24	Total PTC. Enter the amount from line 11(e) or add lines 12(e) through 23(e).	2,764
25	Advance payment of PTC. Enter the amount from line 11(f) or add lines 12(f) through 23(f).	5,844
26	Net PTC. If line 24 is greater than line 25, subtract line 25 from line 24. Enter the difference here and on Schedule 3 (Form 1040), line 9. If line 24 equals line 25, enter -0-. Stop here. If line 25 is greater than line 24, leave this line blank and continue to line 27.	

Part III — Repayment of Excess Advance Payment of the Premium Tax Credit

Line	Description	Value
27	Excess advance payment of PTC. If line 25 is greater than line 24, subtract line 24 from line 25.	3,080
28	Repayment limitation (see instructions).	3,150
29	Excess advance PTC repayment. Enter the smaller of line 27 or line 28 here and on Schedule 2 (Form 1040), line 1a.	3,080

For Paperwork Reduction Act Notice, see your tax return instructions. Cat. No. 37784Z Form **8962** (2024)

(a) $52,000 + $50,000 + $2,000
(b) Bryan's income is not included as he is not required to file a tax return (income is below standard deduction amount for a dependent – refer to Chapter 1)

Self-Study Problem 7.5, Part a

Form 8863
Department of the Treasury
Internal Revenue Service

Education Credits
(American Opportunity and Lifetime Learning Credits)
Attach to Form 1040 or 1040-SR.
Go to www.irs.gov/Form8863 for instructions and the latest information.

OMB No. 1545-0074
2024
Attachment Sequence No. **50**

Name(s) shown on return: Santiago and Sophia Estudiante

Your social security number:

⚠ **Caution:** Complete a separate Part III on page 2 for each student for whom you're claiming either credit before you complete Parts I and II.

Part I — Refundable American Opportunity Credit

Line	Description		Amount
1	After completing Part III for each student, enter the total of all amounts from all Parts III, line 30	1	2,500
2	Enter: $180,000 if married filing jointly; $90,000 if single, head of household, or qualifying surviving spouse	2	180,000
3	Enter the amount from Form 1040 or 1040-SR, line 11. But if you're filing Form 2555 or 4563, or you're excluding income from Puerto Rico, see Pub. 970 for the amount to enter instead	3	170,000
4	Subtract line 3 from line 2. If zero or less, **stop**; you can't take any education credit	4	10,000
5	Enter: $20,000 if married filing jointly; $10,000 if single, head of household, or qualifying surviving spouse	5	20,000
6	If line 4 is: • Equal to or more than line 5, enter 1.000 on line 6 • Less than line 5, divide line 4 by line 5. Enter the result as a decimal (rounded to at least three places)	6	.500
7	Multiply line 1 by line 6. **Caution:** If you were under age 24 at the end of the year **and** meet the conditions described in the instructions, you **can't** take the refundable American opportunity credit; skip line 8, enter the amount from line 7 on line 9, and check this box ☐	7	1,250
8	**Refundable American opportunity credit.** Multiply line 7 by 40% (0.40). Enter the amount here and on Form 1040 or 1040-SR, line 29. Then go to line 9 below.	8	500

Part II — Nonrefundable Education Credits

Line	Description		Amount
9	Subtract line 8 from line 7. Enter here and on line 2 of the Credit Limit Worksheet (see instructions)	9	750
10	After completing Part III for each student, enter the total of all amounts from all Parts III, line 31. If zero, skip lines 11 through 17, enter -0- on line 18, and go to line 19	10	
11	Enter the smaller of line 10 or $10,000	11	
12	Multiply line 11 by 20% (0.20)	12	
13	Enter: $180,000 if married filing jointly; $90,000 if single, head of household, or qualifying surviving spouse	13	
14	Enter the amount from Form 1040 or 1040-SR, line 11. But if you're filing Form 2555 or 4563, or you're excluding income from Puerto Rico, see Pub. 970 for the amount to enter instead	14	
15	Subtract line 14 from line 13. If zero or less, skip lines 16 and 17, enter -0- on line 18, and go to line 19	15	
16	Enter: $20,000 if married filing jointly; $10,000 if single, head of household, or qualifying surviving spouse	16	
17	If line 15 is: • Equal to or more than line 16, enter 1.000 on line 17 and go to line 18 • Less than line 16, divide line 15 by line 16. Enter the result as a decimal (rounded to at least three places)	17	.
18	Multiply line 12 by line 17. Enter here and on line 1 of the Credit Limit Worksheet (see instructions)	18	0 (a)
19	**Nonrefundable education credits.** Enter the amount from line 7 of the Credit Limit Worksheet (see instructions) here and on Schedule 3 (Form 1040), line 3	19	750

For Paperwork Reduction Act Notice, see your tax return instructions. Cat. No. 25379M Form **8863** (2024)

(a) The taxpayers have a large tax liability relative to the AOTC. As a result, the nonrefundable AOTC will not be limited.

Self-Study Problem 7.5, Part a

Form 8863 (2024) — Page 2

Name(s) shown on return: Santiago and Sophia Estudiante

Part III Student and Educational Institution Information. See instructions.

20 Student name (as shown on page 1 of your tax return): Judy Estudiante
21 Student social security number (as shown on page 1 of your tax return): 434-11-7812

22 Educational institution information (see instructions)

a. Name of first educational institution: Southwest University

(1) Address: 1234 Cleveland Avenue, El Paso, TX 79925

(2) Did the student receive Form 1098-T from this institution for 2024? ☒ Yes ☐ No

(3) Did the student receive Form 1098-T from this institution for 2023 with box 7 checked? ☐ Yes ☒ No

(4) EIN: 12-7652311

b. Name of second educational institution (if any): —

23 Has the American opportunity credit been claimed for this student for any 4 prior tax years? ☒ No — Go to line 24.

24 Was the student enrolled at least half-time for at least one academic period that began or is treated as having begun in 2024 at an eligible educational institution in a program leading towards a postsecondary degree, certificate, or other recognized postsecondary educational credential? ☒ Yes — Go to line 25.

25 Did the student complete the first 4 years of postsecondary education before 2024? ☒ No — Go to line 26.

26 Was the student convicted, before the end of 2024, of a felony for possession or distribution of a controlled substance? ☒ No — Complete lines 27 through 30 for this student.

American Opportunity Credit

Line	Description	Amount
27	Adjusted qualified education expenses (see instructions). Don't enter more than $4,000	4,000 (a)
28	Subtract $2,000 from line 27. If zero or less, enter -0-	2,000
29	Multiply line 28 by 25% (0.25)	500
30	If line 28 is zero, enter the amount from line 27. Otherwise, add $2,000 to the amount on line 29 and enter the result. Skip line 31. Include the total of all amounts from all Parts III, line 30, on Part I, line 1	2,500

Lifetime Learning Credit

31 Adjusted qualified education expenses (see instructions). Include the total of all amounts from all Parts III, line 31, on Part II, line 10

Form **8863** (2024)

(a) $4,411 less $300 scholarship from 1098-T plus $304 for books, limited to $4,000.

Self-Study Problem 7.7

Form 8839 — Qualified Adoption Expenses
Department of the Treasury — Internal Revenue Service
Attach to Form 1040, 1040-SR, or 1040-NR.
Go to www.irs.gov/Form8839 for instructions and the latest information.
OMB No. 1545-0074
2024
Attachment Sequence No. 38

Name(s) shown on return: James and Michael Bass

Part I — Information About Your Eligible Child or Children

You **must** complete this part. See instructions for details, including what to do if you need more space.

	(a) Child's name (First / Last)	(b) Child's year of birth	(c) born before 2007 and disabled	(d) a child with special needs	(e) a foreign child	(f) Child's identifying number	(g) Check if adoption became final in 2024 or earlier
Child 1	Allison Bass	2024	☐	☐	☐	466-47-3311	☑
Child 2			☐	☐	☐		☐
Child 3			☐	☐	☐		☐

Caution: If the child was a foreign child, see *Special rules* in the instructions for line 1, column (e), before you complete Part II or Part III. If you received **employer-provided adoption benefits**, complete Part III on the back next.

Part II — Adoption Credit

		Child 1	Child 2	Child 3		
2	Maximum adoption credit per child. Enter $16,810. See instructions	16,810				
3	Did you file Form 8839 for a prior year for the same child? ☑ No. Enter -0-. ☐ Yes. See instructions for the amount to enter	0				
4	Subtract line 3 from line 2	16,810				
5	**Qualified adoption expenses.** See instructions. **Caution:** Your qualified adoption expenses may not be equal to the adoption expenses you paid in 2024.	17,000				
6	Enter the **smaller** of line 4 or line 5	16,810				
7	Enter modified adjusted gross income. See instructions				7	259,990
8	Is line 7 more than $252,150? ☐ No. Skip lines 8 and 9, and enter -0- on line 10. ☑ Yes. Subtract $252,150 from line 7				8	7,840
9	Divide line 8 by $40,000. Enter the result as a decimal (rounded to at least three places). Do not enter more than 1.000.				9	× .196
10	Multiply each amount on line 6 by line 9	3,295				
11	Subtract line 10 from line 6	13,515				
12	Add the amounts on line 11				12	13,515
13	Credit carryforward, if any, from prior years. See your Adoption Credit Carryforward Worksheet in the 2023 Form 8839 instructions				13	
14	Add lines 12 and 13				14	13,515
15	Enter the amount from line 5 of the Credit Limit Worksheet in the instructions				15	34,212 (a)
16	**Adoption credit.** Enter the smaller of line 14 or line 15 here and on Schedule 3 (Form 1040), line 6c. If line 15 is smaller than line 14, you may have a credit carryforward. See instructions				16	13,515

For Paperwork Reduction Act Notice, see your tax return instructions. Cat. No. 22843L Form **8839** (2024)

(a) $36,212 less child tax credit of $2,000.

Self-Study Problem 7.7

Form 8839 (2024) Page **2**

Part III Employer-Provided Adoption Benefits

			Child 1	Child 2	Child 3		
17	Maximum exclusion per child. Enter $16,810. See instructions	17	16,810				
18	Did you receive employer-provided adoption benefits for a prior year for the same child? ☑ **No.** Enter -0-. ☐ **Yes.** See instructions for the amount to enter . .	18	0				
19	Subtract line 18 from line 17	19	16,810				
20	Employer-provided adoption benefits you received in 2024. This amount should be shown in box 12 of your 2024 Form(s) W-2 with code **T**	20	4,000				
21	Add the amounts on line 20					21	4,000
22	Enter the **smaller** of line 19 or line 20. But if the child was a child with special needs and the adoption became final in 2024, enter the amount from line 19.	22	4,000				
23	Enter modified adjusted gross income (from the worksheet in the instructions)	23	259,990				
24	Is line 23 more than $252,150? ☐ **No.** Skip lines 24 and 25, and enter -0- on line 26. ☑ **Yes.** Subtract $252,150 from line 23	24	7,840				
25	Divide line 24 by $40,000. Enter the result as a decimal (rounded to at least three places). Do not enter more than 1.000.			25	×	.196		
26	Multiply each amount on line 22 by line 25 . . .	26	784				
27	**Excluded benefits.** Subtract line 26 from line 22 .	27	3,216				
28	Add the amounts on line 27					28	3,216
29	**Taxable benefits.** Is line 28 more than line 21? ☑ **No.** Subtract line 28 from line 21. Also, include this amount, if more than zero, on line 1f of Form 1040, 1040-SR, or 1040-NR. ☐ **Yes.** Subtract line 21 from line 28. Enter the result as a negative number. Also, enter the result on line 1f of Form 1040, 1040-SR, or 1040-NR.					29	784

TIP

You may be able to claim the adoption credit in Part II on the front of this form if any of the following apply.
- You paid adoption expenses in 2023, those expenses were not fully reimbursed by your employer or otherwise, and the adoption was not final by the end of 2023.
- The total adoption expenses you paid in 2024 were not fully reimbursed by your employer or otherwise, and the adoption became final in 2024 or earlier.
- You adopted a child with special needs and the adoption became final in 2024.

Form **8839** (2024)

Self-Study Problem 7.8, Part a

Form 8936
Department of the Treasury
Internal Revenue Service

Clean Vehicle Credits

Attach to your tax return.
Go to www.irs.gov/Form8936 for instructions and the latest information.

OMB No. 1545-2137
2024
Attachment Sequence No. 69

Name(s) shown on return: Kyra O'Flaherty

Identifying number:

Notes:
- Complete a separate Schedule A (Form 8936) for each clean vehicle placed in service during the tax year.
- Individuals who transferred the credit to the dealer at the time of sale must file this form and Schedule A (Form 8936).

Part I — Modified Adjusted Gross Income (MAGI) Amount

Line	Description		Amount
1a	Enter the amount from line 11 of your 2024 Form 1040, 1040-SR, or 1040-NR. Estates and trusts, Form 1041, see instructions	1a	67,000
b	Enter any income from Puerto Rico you excluded	1b	
c	Enter any amount from Form 2555, line 45	1c	
d	Enter any amount from Form 2555, line 50	1d	
e	Enter any amount from Form 4563, line 15	1e	
2	Add lines 1a through 1e	2	67,000
3a	Enter the amount from line 11 of your 2023 Form 1040, 1040-SR, or 1040-NR. Estates and trusts, Form 1041, see instructions	3a	65,000
b	Enter any income from Puerto Rico you excluded	3b	
c	Enter any amount from Form 2555, line 45	3c	
d	Enter any amount from Form 2555, line 50	3d	
e	Enter any amount from Form 4563, line 15	3e	
4	Add lines 3a through 3e	4	65,000
5	Enter your 2023 filing status (S, MFS, etc., see chart below)	5	S

Individuals, estates, or trusts exceeding the following MAGI limits for both 2023 and 2024 can't claim the applicable credit.

Filing Status	Part II/III Limits	Part IV Limits
Single (S)	$150,000	$75,000
Married filing separately (MFS)	$150,000	$75,000
Head of household (HOH)	$225,000	$112,500
Married filing jointly (MFJ)	$300,000	$150,000
Qualifying surviving spouse (QSS)	$300,000	$150,000
Estates and trusts	$150,000	N/A

Part II — Credit for Business/Investment Use Part of New Clean Vehicles

Line	Description		Amount
6	Enter the total credit amount figured in Part II of Schedule(s) A (Form 8936)	6	
7	New clean vehicle credit from partnerships and S corporations (see instructions)	7	
8	**Business/investment use part of credit.** Add lines 6 and 7. Partnerships and S corporations, stop here and report this amount on Schedule K. All others, report this amount on Form 3800, Part III, line 1y	8	

Part III — Credit for Personal Use Part of New Clean Vehicles

Line	Description		Amount
9	Enter the total credit amount figured in Part III of Schedule(s) A (Form 8936)	9	7,500
10	Enter the amount from Form 1040, 1040-SR, or 1040-NR, line 18	10	7,003
11	Personal credits from Form 1040, 1040-SR, or 1040-NR (see instructions)	11	0
12	Subtract line 11 from line 10. If zero or less, enter -0- and stop here. You can't claim the personal use part of the credit	12	7,003
13	**Personal use part of credit.** Enter the **smaller** of line 9 or line 12 here and on Schedule 3 (Form 1040), line 6f. If line 12 is smaller than line 9, see instructions	13	7,003

Part IV — Credit for Previously Owned Clean Vehicles

Line	Description		Amount
14	Enter the total credit amount figured in Part IV of Schedule(s) A (Form 8936)	14	
15	Enter the amount from Form 1040, 1040-SR, or 1040-NR, line 18	15	
16	Personal credits from Form 1040, 1040-SR, or 1040-NR (see instructions)	16	
17	Subtract line 16 from line 15. If zero or less, enter -0- and stop here. You can't claim the Part IV credit	17	
18	Enter the **smaller** of line 14 or line 17 here and on Schedule 3 (Form 1040), line 6m. If line 17 is smaller than line 14, see instructions	18	

Part V — Credit for Qualified Commercial Clean Vehicles

Line	Description		Amount
19	Enter the total credit amount figured in Part V of Schedule(s) A (Form 8936)	19	
20	Qualified commercial clean vehicle credit from partnerships and S corporations (see instructions)	20	
21	Add lines 19 and 20. Partnerships and S corporations, stop here and report this amount on Schedule K. All others, report this amount on Form 3800, Part III, line 1aa	21	

For Paperwork Reduction Act Notice, see separate instructions. Cat. No. 37751E Form **8936** (2024)

Self-Study Problem 7.8, Part a

SCHEDULE A (Form 8936)

Department of the Treasury
Internal Revenue Service

Clean Vehicle Credit Amount

Attach to your tax return.
Go to *www.irs.gov/Form8936* for instructions and the latest information.

OMB No. 1545-2137

2024

Attachment Sequence No. **69A**

Name(s) shown on return: Kyra O'Flaherty

Identifying number:

Notes:
- Complete a separate Schedule A (Form 8936) for each clean vehicle placed in service during the tax year.
- Individuals who transferred the credit to the dealer at the time of sale must file this schedule and Form 8936.

Part I — Vehicle Details

1a Year 2024
b Make . . . . Tesla
c Model . . . . Model 3

2 Vehicle identification number (VIN) (see instructions) . . 5YJ3E1EB0RF734523

3 Enter date vehicle was placed in service (MM/DD/YYYY) 10/01/2024

4a Did you transfer the credit to the dealer at the time of sale?
☐ **Yes.** Enter the transferred amount shown on the seller's report . . . .
☑ **No.** Go to line 5.

b If line 4a is "Yes," complete line 8 or line 13, as applicable, and check here if directed to do so by line 8a, 8d, 13a, or 13c . ☐

5 Does the VIN entered on line 2 belong to a **new clean vehicle** placed in service during the tax year? See instructions for definitions.
☑ **Yes.** Go to Part II.
☐ **No.** Go to line 6.

6 Does the VIN entered on line 2 belong to a **previously owned clean vehicle** acquired after 2022 and placed in service during the tax year? See instructions for definitions.
☐ **Yes.** Go to Part IV.
☐ **No.** Go to line 7.

7 Does the VIN entered on line 2 belong to a **qualified commercial clean vehicle** acquired after 2022 and placed in service during the tax year? See instructions for definitions.
☐ **Yes.** Go to Part V.
☐ **No. Stop here.** You can't use this schedule to figure a credit amount for a vehicle not described on line 5, 6, or 7.

Part II — Credit Amount for Business/Investment Use Part of New Clean Vehicle

8a Did you resell the vehicle within 30 days of the placed-in-service date shown on line 3?
☐ **Yes. Stop here.** You can't claim a clean vehicle credit for this vehicle. If line 4a is "Yes," check the box on line 4b and report the amount from line 4a on Schedule 2 (Form 1040), line 1b.
☑ **No.** Go to line 8b.

8b Are you filing this form with an individual income tax return?
☑ **Yes.** Go to line 8c.
☐ **No.** Skip lines 8c and 8d and go to line 8e.

8c Complete Form 8936, lines 1 and 2. Is line 2 more than the "Part II/III limits" amount shown on the chart below line 5, Form 8936 for your 2024 filing status?
☐ **Yes.** Go to line 8d.
☑ **No.** If you transferred the credit amount to the dealer at the time of sale, stop here and see instructions. Otherwise, skip line 8d and go to line 8e.

8d Complete Form 8936, lines 3, 4, and 5. Is line 4 more than the "Part II/III limits" amount shown on the chart below line 5, Form 8936 for your 2023 filing status? See instructions if your 2024 return is a joint return.
☐ **Yes. Stop here.** You can't claim a clean vehicle credit for this vehicle. If line 4a is "Yes," check the box on line 4b and report the amount from line 4a on Schedule 2 (Form 1040), line 1b.
☐ **No.** If you transferred the credit amount to the dealer at the time of sale, stop here and see instructions. Otherwise, go to line 8e.

For Paperwork Reduction Act Notice, see the Form 8936 instructions. Cat. No. 93602W Schedule A (Form 8936) 2024

Self-Study Problem 7.8, Part a

Schedule A (Form 8936) 2024 Page **2**

Part II Credit Amount for Business/Investment Use Part of New Clean Vehicle *(continued)*

8e Did you acquire the vehicle for use or to lease to others, and not for resale? Answer "No" if you are leasing the vehicle from another person.
☑ **Yes.**
☐ **No. Stop here.** You can't claim a credit amount for a vehicle you didn't acquire for use or to lease to others, or acquired for resale.

9	Tentative credit amount (see instructions)	9	7,500
10	Business/investment use percentage (see instructions)	10	0%
11	Multiply line 9 by line 10. Include this credit amount on line 6 in Part II of Form 8936. If you entered 100% on line 10, stop here. Otherwise, go to Part III below	11	0

Part III Credit Amount for Personal Use Part of New Clean Vehicle

12	Subtract line 11 from line 9 in Part II. Stop here and include this credit amount on line 9 in Part III of Form 8936	12	7,500

Part IV Credit Amount for Previously Owned Clean Vehicle

13a Did you resell the vehicle within 30 days of the placed-in-service date shown on line 3?
☐ **Yes. Stop here.** You can't claim a clean vehicle credit for this vehicle. If line 4a is "Yes," check the box on line 4b and report the amount from line 4a on Schedule 2 (Form 1040), line 1c.
☐ **No.** Go to line 13b.

b Complete Form 8936, lines 1 and 2. Is line 2 more than the "Part IV limits" amount shown on the chart below line 5, Form 8936 for your 2024 filing status?
☐ **Yes.** Go to line 13c.
☐ **No.** If you transferred the credit amount to the dealer at the time of sale, stop here and see instructions. Otherwise, skip line 13c and go to line 13d.

c Complete Form 8936, lines 3, 4, and 5. Is line 4 more than the "Part IV limits" amount shown on the chart below line 5, Form 8936 for your 2023 filing status? See instructions if your 2024 return is a joint return.
☐ **Yes. Stop here.** You can't claim a clean vehicle credit for this vehicle. If line 4a is "Yes," check the box on line 4b and report the amount from line 4a on Schedule 2 (Form 1040), line 1c.
☐ **No.** If you transferred the credit amount to the dealer at the time of sale, stop here and see instructions. Otherwise, go to line 13d.

d Have you claimed a previously owned clean vehicle credit for another vehicle purchased in the 3-year period ending on the date you purchased the vehicle identified in Part I? See instructions if you are filing a joint return.
☐ **Yes. Stop here.** You can't claim a credit for this vehicle if you have already claimed the previously owned vehicle credit for another vehicle purchased during this 3-year period.
☐ **No.** Go to line 13e.

e Is the sales price of the vehicle more than $25,000?
☐ **Yes. Stop here.** The vehicle doesn't qualify for the Part IV credit.
☐ **No.**

f Did you acquire the vehicle for use and not for resale? Answer "No" if you are leasing the vehicle from another person.
☐ **Yes.**
☐ **No. Stop here.** You can't claim a credit amount for a vehicle you didn't acquire for use or acquired for resale.

g Can you be claimed as a dependent on another person's tax return, such as your parent's return?
☐ **Yes. Stop here.** You can't claim a credit amount if you can be claimed as a dependent.
☐ **No.**

14	Enter the sales price of the vehicle	14	
15	Multiply line 14 by 30% (0.30)	15	
16	Maximum vehicle credit amount	16	$4,000
17	Enter the smaller of line 15 or line 16. Stop here and include this credit amount on line 14 in Part IV of Form 8936	17	

Self-Study Problem 7.8, Part a

Schedule A (Form 8936) 2024 — Page **3**

Part V   Credit Amount for Qualified Commercial Clean Vehicle

18a If making an elective payment election, enter the IRS-issued registration number for the vehicle _____

  b Is the vehicle of a character subject to the allowance for depreciation? Answer "Yes" if the exception for certain tax-exempt entities discussed in the instructions applies.
  ☐ **Yes.**
  ☐ **No. Stop here.** The vehicle is not a qualified commercial clean vehicle unless the exception applies.

  c Did you acquire the vehicle for use or to lease to others, and not for resale? Answer "No" if you are leasing the vehicle from another person.
  ☐ **Yes.**
  ☐ **No. Stop here.** You can't claim a credit amount for a vehicle you didn't acquire for use or to lease to others, or acquired for resale.

  d Is the vehicle also powered in part by gas or diesel? See instructions.
  ☐ **Yes.**
  ☐ **No.**

  e Enter the vehicle's gross vehicle weight rating (GVWR) . . . .

19 Enter the cost or other basis of the vehicle. See instructions . . . . | 19 | |

20 Section 179 expense deduction (see instructions) . . . . | 20 | |

21 Subtract line 20 from line 19 . . . . | 21 | |

22 Multiply line 21 by 15% (0.15) (30% (0.30) if the answer on line 18d above is "No") . . . | 22 | |

23 Enter the incremental cost of the vehicle. See instructions . . . . | 23 | |

24 Enter the smaller of line 22 or line 23 . . . . | 24 | |

25 **Maximum credit.** Enter $7,500 ($40,000 if the vehicle's gross vehicle weight rating (see line 18e) is 14,000 pounds or more) . . . . | 25 | |

26 Enter the smaller of line 24 or line 25. Include this credit amount on line 19 in Part V of Form 8936 . . . . | 26 | |

Schedule A (Form 8936) 2024

Self-Study Problem 7.8, Part b

Form 5695
Department of the Treasury
Internal Revenue Service

Residential Energy Credits
Attach to Form 1040, 1040-SR, or 1040-NR.
Go to www.irs.gov/Form5695 for instructions and the latest information.

OMB No. 1545-0074
2024
Attachment Sequence No. 75

Name(s) shown on return: Marquis and Abby Dollkeeper
Your social security number:

Part I — Residential Clean Energy Credit (See instructions before completing this part.)

Note: Skip lines 1 through 11 if you only have a **credit carryforward from 2023**.

Enter the complete address of the home where you installed the property and/or technology associated with lines 1 through 4 and 5b. For more than one home, see instructions.

Number and street: 300 Bayona Drive
Unit no.:
City or town: Santa Cruz
State: CA
ZIP code: 95060

Line	Description	Amount
1	Qualified solar electric property costs	38,000
2	Qualified solar water heating property costs	
3	Qualified small wind energy property costs	
4	Qualified geothermal heat pump property costs	
5a	Qualified battery storage technology. Does the qualified battery storage technology have a capacity of at least 3 kilowatt hours? (See instructions.) If you checked the "No" box, you cannot claim a credit for qualified battery storage technology	☐ Yes ☐ No
b	If you checked the "Yes" box, enter the qualified battery storage costs	
6a	Add lines 1 through 5b	38,000
6b	Multiply line 6a by 30% (0.30)	11,400
7a	Qualified fuel cell property. Was qualified fuel cell property installed on, or in connection with, your **main home** located in the United States? (See instructions.) If you checked the "No" box, you cannot claim a credit for qualified fuel cell property. Skip lines 7b through 11.	☐ Yes ☑ No
b	Enter the complete address of the main home where you installed the fuel cell property.	
c	If the special rule for joint occupants applies, check here ☐ and attach a statement. (See instructions.)	
8	Qualified fuel cell property costs	
9	Multiply line 8 by 30% (0.30)	
10	Kilowatt capacity of property on line 8 above ____ x $1,000	
11	Enter the smaller of line 9 or line 10	
12	Credit carryforward from 2023. Enter the amount, if any, from your 2023 Form 5695, line 16	
13	Add lines 6b, 11, and 12	11,400
14	Limitation based on tax liability. Enter the amount from the Residential Clean Energy Credit Limit Worksheet. (See instructions.)	21,554 (a)
15	**Residential clean energy credit.** Enter the smaller of line 13 or line 14. Also include this amount on Schedule 3 (Form 1040), line 5a	11,400
16	Credit carryforward to 2025. If line 15 is less than line 13, subtract line 15 from line 13	

For Paperwork Reduction Act Notice, see your tax return instructions. Cat. No. 13540P Form **5695** (2024)

(a) $28,344 less $4,000 child tax credit less $2,790 energy efficient home improvement credit.

Self-Study Problem 7.8, Part b

Form 5695 (2024) Page **2**

Part II **Energy Efficient Home Improvement Credit**

Section A—Qualified Energy Efficiency Improvements

17a	Are the qualified energy efficiency improvements installed in or on your main home located in the United States? (See instructions)	17a	☑ Yes	☐ No
b	Are you the original user of the qualified energy efficiency improvements?	17b	☑ Yes	☐ No
c	Are the components reasonably expected to remain in use for at least 5 years?	17c	☑ Yes	☐ No

If you checked the "No" box for line 17a, 17b, or 17c, you cannot claim the energy efficient home improvement credit. Do not complete Part II, Section A.

d Enter the complete address of the main home where you made the qualifying improvements.
Caution: You can only have one main home at a time. (See instructions.)

Number and street	Unit no.	City or town	State	ZIP code
300 Bayone Drive		Santa Cruz	CA	95060

e	Were any of these improvements related to the construction of this main home?	17e	☐ Yes	☑ No

If you checked the "Yes" box, you can only claim the energy efficient home improvement credit for qualifying improvements that were not related to the construction of the home. Do not include expenses related to the construction of your main home, even if the improvements were made after you moved into the home.

18 Insulation or air sealing material or system.

a	Enter the cost of insulation material or system (include air sealing material or system) specifically and primarily designed to reduce heat loss or gain of your home that meets the criteria established by the IECC. (See instructions.) . . .	18a	3,000		
b	Multiply line 18a by 30% (0.30). Enter the results. Do **not** enter more than $1,200			18b	900
19	Exterior doors that meet the applicable Energy Star requirements.				
a	Enter the cost of the most expensive door you bought	19a	2,800		
b	Multiply line 19a by 30% (0.30). Do **not** enter more than $250 .	19b	250		
c	Enter the cost of all other qualifying exterior doors	19c			
d	Multiply line 19c by 30% (0.30)	19d			
e	Add lines 19b and 19d. Do **not** enter more than $500			19e	250
20	Windows and skylights that meet the Energy Star certification requirements.				
a	Enter the cost of exterior windows and skylights that meet the Energy Star certification requirements. (See instructions.)	20a	7,800		
b	Multiply line 20a by 30% (0.30). Enter the results. Do **not** enter more than $600			20b	600

Section B—Residential Energy Property Expenditures

21a	Did you incur costs for qualified energy property installed on or in connection with a home located in the United States?	21a	☑ Yes	☐ No
b	Was the qualified energy property originally placed into service by you?	21b	☑ Yes	☐ No

If you checked the "No" box for line 21a or 21b, you cannot claim the credit for your residential energy property costs. Skip lines 22 through 25 and line 29. Go to line 26.

c Enter the complete address of each home where you installed qualified energy property.

Number and street	Unit no.	City or town	State	ZIP code
300 Bayone Drive		Santa Cruz	CA	95060

22 Residential energy property costs (include labor costs for onsite preparation, assembly, and original installation). (See instructions.)

a	Enter the cost of central air conditioners	22a			
b	Multiply line 22a by 30% (0.30). Enter the results. Do **not** enter more than $600			22b	
23a	Enter the cost of natural gas, propane, or oil water heaters	23a	1,200		
b	Multiply line 23a by 30% (0.30). Enter the results. Do **not** enter more than $600			23b	360
24a	Enter the cost of natural gas, propane, or oil furnace or hot water boilers . .	24a			
b	Multiply line 24a by 30% (0.30). Enter the results. Do **not** enter more than $600			24b	

Form **5695** (2024)

Self-Study Problem 7.8, Part b

Form 5695 (2024) Page **3**

Section B—Residential Energy Property Expenditures *(continued)*

25a	Enter the cost of improvements or replacement of panelboards, subpanelboards, branch circuits, or feeders **25a**	1,800		
b	Multiply line 25a by 30% (0.30). Enter the results. Do **not** enter more than $600		**25b**	540
26	Home energy audits.			
a	Did you incur costs for a home energy audit that included an inspection of your main home located in the United States and a written report prepared by a certified home energy auditor? (See instructions.)		**26a**	☑ Yes ☐ No
	If you checked the "No" box, you cannot claim the home energy audit credit. Stop. Go to line 27.			
b	Enter the cost of the home energy audits **26b**	800		
c	Multiply line 26b by 30% (0.30). Enter the results. Do **not** enter more than $150		**26c**	150
27	Add lines 18b, 19e, 20b, 22b, 23b, 24b, 25b, and 26c **27**	2,800		
28	Enter the smaller of line 27 or $1,200		**28**	1,200
29	Heat pumps and heat pump water heaters; biomass stoves and biomass boilers.			
a	Enter the cost of electric or natural gas heat pumps **29a**	5,300		
b	Enter the cost of electric or natural gas heat pump water heaters ... **29b**			
c	Enter the cost of biomass stoves and biomass boilers **29c**			
d	Add lines 29a, 29b, and 29c **29d**	5,300		
e	Multiply line 29d by 30% (0.30). Enter the results. Do **not** enter more than $2,000		**29e**	1,590
30	Add lines 28 and 29e		**30**	2,790
31	Limitation based on tax liability. Enter the amount from the Energy Efficient Home Improvement Credit Limit Worksheet. (See instructions.)		**31**	24,344 (a)
32	**Energy efficient home improvement credit.** Enter the smaller of line 30 or line 31. Also include this amount on Schedule 3 (Form 1040), line 5b		**32**	
a	If the special rule for joint occupants applies, check here ☐ and attach a statement. (See instructions.)			

Form **5695** (2024)

(a) $28,344 less child tax credit of $4,000 (2 × $2,000).

Self-Study Problem 7.9

Form 8880 — Credit for Qualified Retirement Savings Contributions
Department of the Treasury / Internal Revenue Service
Attach to Form 1040, 1040-SR, or 1040-NR.
Go to www.irs.gov/Form8880 for the latest information.
OMB No. 1545-0074
2024
Attachment Sequence No. 54

Name(s) shown on return: Robin and Steve Harrington
Your social security number:

You cannot take this credit if either of the following applies.
- The amount on Form 1040, 1040-SR, or 1040-NR, line 11, is more than $38,250 ($57,375 if head of household; $76,500 if married filing jointly).
- The person(s) who made the qualified contribution or elective deferral (a) was born after January 1, 2007; (b) is claimed as a dependent on someone else's 2024 tax return; or (c) was a student (see instructions).

		(a) You	(b) Your spouse
1	Traditional and Roth IRA contributions, and ABLE account contributions by the designated beneficiary for 2024. **Do not** include rollover contributions	7,000	7,000
2	Elective deferrals to a 401(k) or other qualified employer plan, voluntary employee contributions, and 501(c)(18)(D) plan contributions for 2024 (see instructions)		
3	Add lines 1 and 2	7,000	7,000
4	Certain distributions received **after** 2021 and **before** the due date (including extensions) of your 2024 tax return (see instructions). If married filing jointly, include **both** spouses' amounts in **both** columns. See instructions for an exception		
5	Subtract line 4 from line 3. If zero or less, enter -0-	7,000	7,000
6	In each column, enter the **smaller** of line 5 or $2,000	2,000	2,000
7	Add the amounts on line 6. If zero, **stop**; you can't take this credit	7	4,000
8	Enter the amount from Form 1040, 1040-SR, or 1040-NR, line 11*	55,000	
9	Enter the applicable decimal amount from the table below.		

If line 8 is—		And your filing status is—		
Over—	But not over—	Married filing jointly	Head of household	Single, Married filing separately, or Qualifying surviving spouse
		Enter on line 9—		
---	$23,000	0.5	0.5	0.5
$23,000	$25,000	0.5	0.5	0.2
$25,000	$34,500	0.5	0.5	0.1
$34,500	$37,500	0.5	0.2	0.1
$37,500	$38,250	0.5	0.1	0.1
$38,250	$46,000	0.5	0.1	0.0
$46,000	$50,000	0.2	0.1	0.0
$50,000	$57,375	0.1	0.1	0.0
$57,375	$76,500	0.1	0.0	0.0
$76,500	---	0.0	0.0	0.0

9 x 0. 10

Note: If line 9 is zero, **stop**; you can't take this credit.

10	Multiply line 7 by line 9	400
11	Limitation based on tax liability. Enter the amount from the Credit Limit Worksheet in the instructions	1,183
12	**Credit for qualified retirement savings contributions.** Enter the **smaller** of line 10 or line 11 here and on Schedule 3 (Form 1040), line 4	400

* See Pub. 590-A for the amount to enter if you claim any exclusion or deduction for foreign earned income, foreign housing, or income from Puerto Rico or for bona fide residents of American Samoa.

For Paperwork Reduction Act Notice, see your tax return instructions. Cat. No. 33394D Form **8880** (2024)

Chapter 8 Depreciation and Sale of Business Property

Self-Study Problem 8.1

a. Capitalize. New property does not meet any safe harbors.
b. Capitalize. Restoration does not meet any safe harbors.
c. Capitalize. Betterment not eligible for safe harbor.
d. Deduct. Acquisition meets safe harbor for company with AFS and a written policy.
e. Capitalize. Betterment is not eligible for safe harbor.

Self-Study Problem 8.2

a. $15,103. Refer to Form 4562 on Page E-80.
b. $5,846
   Equipment: $1,572. MACRS $11,000 × 0.1429
   Furniture: $1,000. MACRS $7,000 × 0.1429
   Total 7-year property: MACRS of $2,572
   Real estate: $3,274. $180,000 × 0.01819
c. $6,379
   Equipment: $1,078. $4,400 × 0.2449
   Furniture: $686. $2,800 × 0.2449
   Real estate: $4,615. $180,000 × 0.02564
d. $275 ($4,400 × 0.1249 × 50%)

Self-Study Problem 8.3

a. $442,990. MACRS of $3,100,000 × 0.1429
b. $1,445,797. $3,100,000 exceeds the §179 threshold of $3,050,000 by $50,000. The maximum §179 is $1,170,000 ($1,220,000 − $50,000). The remaining balance of $1,930,000 ($3,100,000 − $1,170,000) is recovered using MACRS.
   §179 of $1,170,000, plus
   MACRS of $275,797 ($1,930,000 × 0.1429)

c. $2,400,000. The maximum eligible §179 is $1,170,000 as calculated in part b; however, the income limitation applies in this scenario. If the basis of $3,100,000 is reduced by $1,170,000, the adjusted basis for bonus depreciation is $1,930,000. Applying 60-percent bonus rate yields bonus depreciation of $1,158,000. The adjusted basis is now $772,000 ($3,100,000 − $1,170,000 − $1,158,000). Typical MACRS depreciation is $110,319 ($772,000 × 0.1429). The taxable income limit before considering §179 expense is $1,131,681 ($2,400,000 − $1,158,000 − $110,319). Consequently, the maximum allowable §179 deduction is $1,131,681 and the remaining $38,319 ($1,170,000 − $1,131,681) must be carried forward.
   §179 of $1,131,681, plus
   Bonus of $1,158,000, plus
   MACRS of $110,319

Self-Study Problem 8.4

a. 1. Yes Qualified business use is 50 percent or less; therefore, Alvarez must use the straight-line method of depreciation for the auto.
   2. No   Qualified business use is more than 50 percent; therefore, Laura may use the accelerated method of depreciation.

b. $800 for Alavarez. $40,000 cost × 20 percent business use × 10 percent depreciation factor

$26,080 for Laura. The personal use portion (30 percent) is not eligible for depreciation.
Section 179 of $22,000 ($40,000 × 55 percent business use)
Bonus depreciation of $3,600 ($40,000 × 15 percent production of income use × 60 percent bonus factor for 2024)
Typical MACRS of $480. Remaining adjusted basis of $2,400 ($40,000 − $12,000 personal use − $22,000 Section 179 − $3,600 bonus) × 20 percent MACRS depreciation factor

Self-Study Problem 8.5

	2024	2025	2026
Original Cost	$ 58,000	$ 58,000	$ 58,000
Business use percentage	0.90	0.90	0.90
Eligible for depreciation	$ 52,200	$ 52,200	$ 52,200
Adjustment for prior year bonus	n/a	18,360	18,360
Depreciable Basis	52,200	33,840	33,840
Bonus Depreciation (60%)	31,320	n/a	
Depreciation factor	n/a	32%	19.2%
MACRS depreciation	n/a	$ 10,829	$ 6,497
Annual depreciation limit	$ 20,400	$ 19,800	$ 11,900
Business use percentage	0.90	0.90	0.90
Adjusted annual limit	18,360	17,820	10,710
Cost recovery, limited in 2024	$ 18,360	$ 10,829	$ 6,497

Self-Study Problem 8.6

a. 1. 15-year amortization.
    2. Useful life.
    3. Useful life.
    4. 15-year amortization.
    5. 15-year amortization.
    6. Not amortizable.
    7. 15-year amortization.
    8. Not amortizable.

b.
Customer list	$15,000
Patent	20,000
Goodwill	35,000
Total 197 intangibles	$70,000

$70,000/180 months × 8 months = $3,111
Patent $25,000/12 years = $2,083
Refer to Part VI of Form 4652 on Page E-81

Self-Study Problem 8.2, Part a

Form 4562 — Depreciation and Amortization (Including Information on Listed Property)
Department of the Treasury — Internal Revenue Service
Attach to your tax return.
Go to www.irs.gov/Form4562 for instructions and the latest information.
OMB No. 1545-0172
2024
Attachment Sequence No. 179

Name(s) shown on return: Mary Moser
Business or activity to which this form relates:
Identifying number:

Part I — Election To Expense Certain Property Under Section 179
Note: If you have any listed property, complete Part V before you complete Part I.

1. Maximum amount (see instructions) ... **1**
2. Total cost of section 179 property placed in service (see instructions) ... **2**
3. Threshold cost of section 179 property before reduction in limitation (see instructions) ... **3**
4. Reduction in limitation. Subtract line 3 from line 2. If zero or less, enter -0- ... **4**
5. Dollar limitation for tax year. Subtract line 4 from line 1. If zero or less, enter -0-. If married filing separately, see instructions ... **5**

6	(a) Description of property	(b) Cost (business use only)	(c) Elected cost

7. Listed property. Enter the amount from line 29 ... **7**
8. Total elected cost of section 179 property. Add amounts in column (c), lines 6 and 7 ... **8**
9. Tentative deduction. Enter the **smaller** of line 5 or line 8 ... **9**
10. Carryover of disallowed deduction from line 13 of your 2023 Form 4562 ... **10**
11. Business income limitation. Enter the smaller of business income (not less than zero) or line 5. See instructions ... **11**
12. Section 179 expense deduction. Add lines 9 and 10, but don't enter more than line 11 ... **12**
13. Carryover of disallowed deduction to 2025. Add lines 9 and 10, less line 12 ... **13**

Note: Don't use Part II or Part III below for listed property. Instead, use Part V.

Part II — Special Depreciation Allowance and Other Depreciation (Don't include listed property. See instructions.)

14. Special depreciation allowance for qualified property (other than listed property) placed in service during the tax year. See instructions ... **14** 10,800 (a)
15. Property subject to section 168(f)(1) election ... **15**
16. Other depreciation (including ACRS) ... **16**

Part III — MACRS Depreciation (Don't include listed property. See instructions.)

Section A
17. MACRS deductions for assets placed in service in tax years beginning before 2024 ... **17**
18. If you are electing to group any assets placed in service during the tax year into one or more general asset accounts, check here ☐

Section B — Assets Placed in Service During 2024 Tax Year Using the General Depreciation System

(a) Classification of property	(b) Month and year placed in service	(c) Basis for depreciation (business/investment use only—see instructions)	(d) Recovery period	(e) Convention	(f) Method	(g) Depreciation deduction
19a 3-year property						
b 5-year property						
c 7-year property		7,200 (b)	7 yrs.	HY	200 DB	1,029 (c)
d 10-year property						
e 15-year property						
f 20-year property						
g 25-year property			25 yrs.		S/L	
h Residential rental property			27.5 yrs.	MM	S/L	
			27.5 yrs.	MM	S/L	
i Nonresidential real property	04/2024	180,000	39 yrs.	MM	S/L	3,274 (d)
				MM	S/L	

Section C — Assets Placed in Service During 2024 Tax Year Using the Alternative Depreciation System

20a Class life					S/L	
b 12-year			12 yrs.		S/L	
c 30-year			30 yrs.	MM	S/L	
d 40-year			40 yrs.	MM	S/L	

Part IV — Summary (See instructions.)

21. Listed property. Enter amount from line 28 ... **21**
22. **Total.** Add amounts from line 12, lines 14 through 17, lines 19 and 20 in column (g), and line 21. Enter here and on the appropriate lines of your return. Partnerships and S corporations—see instructions ... **22** 15,103
23. For assets shown above and placed in service during the current year, enter the portion of the basis attributable to section 263A costs ... **23**

For Paperwork Reduction Act Notice, see separate instructions. Cat. No. 12906N Form **4562** (2024)

(a) Bonus depreciation calculated as $6,600 (60% × $11,000) + $4,200 (60% × $7,000).
(b) Remaining balance to depreciate after bonus depreciation $4,400 ($11,000 − $6,600) + $2,800 ($7,000 − $4,200).
(c) ($4,400 × 14.29%) + ($2,800 × 14.29%)
(d) $180,000 × 1.819%

Self-Study Problem 8.6, Part b

Form 4562 (2024) — Page 2

Part V Listed Property (Include automobiles, certain other vehicles, certain aircraft, and property used for entertainment, recreation, or amusement.)

Note: For any vehicle for which you are using the standard mileage rate or deducting lease expense, complete **only** 24a, 24b, columns (a) through (c) of Section A, all of Section B, and Section C if applicable.

Section A—Depreciation and Other Information (Caution: See the instructions for limits for passenger automobiles.)

24a Do you have evidence to support the business/investment use claimed? ☐ Yes ☐ No **24b** If "Yes," is the evidence written? ☐ Yes ☐ No

(a) Type of property (list vehicles first)	(b) Date placed in service	(c) Business/investment use percentage	(d) Cost or other basis	(e) Basis for depreciation (business/investment use only)	(f) Recovery period	(g) Method/Convention	(h) Depreciation deduction	(i) Elected section 179 cost

25 Special depreciation allowance for qualified listed property placed in service during the tax year and used more than 50% in a qualified business use. See instructions. **25**

26 Property used more than 50% in a qualified business use:

		%						
		%						
		%						

27 Property used 50% or less in a qualified business use:

		%				S/L –		
		%				S/L –		
		%				S/L –		

28 Add amounts in column (h), lines 25 through 27. Enter here and on line 21, page 1 **28**

29 Add amounts in column (i), line 26. Enter here and on line 7, page 1 **29**

Section B—Information on Use of Vehicles

Complete this section for vehicles used by a sole proprietor, partner, or other "more than 5% owner," or related person. If you provided vehicles to your employees, first answer the questions in Section C to see if you meet an exception to completing this section for those vehicles.

	(a) Vehicle 1	(b) Vehicle 2	(c) Vehicle 3	(d) Vehicle 4	(e) Vehicle 5	(f) Vehicle 6
30 Total business/investment miles driven during the year (**don't** include commuting miles)						
31 Total commuting miles driven during the year						
32 Total other personal (noncommuting) miles driven						
33 Total miles driven during the year. Add lines 30 through 32						
34 Was the vehicle available for personal use during off-duty hours?	Yes No	Yes No	Yes No	Yes No	Yes No	Yes No
35 Was the vehicle used primarily by a more than 5% owner or related person?						
36 Is another vehicle available for personal use?						

Section C—Questions for Employers Who Provide Vehicles for Use by Their Employees

Answer these questions to determine if you meet an exception to completing Section B for vehicles used by employees who **aren't** more than 5% owners or related persons. See instructions.

	Yes	No
37 Do you maintain a written policy statement that prohibits all personal use of vehicles, including commuting, by your employees?		
38 Do you maintain a written policy statement that prohibits personal use of vehicles, except commuting, by your employees? See the instructions for vehicles used by corporate officers, directors, or 1% or more owners		
39 Do you treat all use of vehicles by employees as personal use?		
40 Do you provide more than five vehicles to your employees, obtain information from your employees about the use of the vehicles, and retain the information received?		
41 Do you meet the requirements concerning qualified automobile demonstration use? See instructions		

Note: If your answer to 37, 38, 39, 40, or 41 is "Yes," don't complete Section B for the covered vehicles.

Part VI Amortization

(a) Description of costs	(b) Date amortization begins	(c) Amortizable amount	(d) Code section	(e) Amortization period or percentage	(f) Amortization for this year
42 Amortization of costs that begins during your 2024 tax year (see instructions):					
Acquired intangibles	05/2024	70,000	197	180 mos.	3,111
43 Amortization of costs that began before your 2024 tax year **43**					2,083
44 Total. Add amounts in column (f). See the instructions for where to report **44**					5,914

Form **4562** (2024)

Self-Study Problem 8.7

	Land	Computer	Equipment
Proceeds	$37,000	$14,000	$16,000
Selling Costs	500	0	1,600
Amount Realized	36,500	14,000	14,400
Adjusted Basis:			
Cost	$24,000	$53,906	$28,177
Cost Recovery	0	33,206	7,477
Adjusted Basis	24,000	20,700	20,700
Gain/(Loss)	$12,500	$(6,700)	$(6,300)

The land and the computer are both Section 1231 properties and thus, the gain and loss is netted resulting in a $5,800 net Section 1231 gain. As a result, both the gain on the land and the loss on the computer will be treated as long-term capital gains. The equipment was not held for more than one year, and thus, is an ordinary asset (depreciable business property is not a capital asset—refer to Chapter 4) and the loss will be treated as an ordinary loss.

Self-Study Problem 8.8

Refer to Form 4797 on Pages E-83 and E-84.

Self-Study Problem 8.9

	Furniture (completely destroyed)	Machinery (partially destroyed)
Insurance proceeds	$ 0	$10,000
Adjusted basis	5,000	14,000
Decrease in FMV	n/a	15,000
Loss	$(5,000)	$ (4,000)

Since both result in a casualty loss, the losses are excluded from Section 1231 treatment and are treated as ordinary losses. The gain on the sale of the land would be treated as a Section 1231 long-term capital gain.

Self-Study Problem 8.8

Form 4797 — Sales of Business Property
(Also Involuntary Conversions and Recapture Amounts Under Sections 179 and 280F(b)(2))

Department of the Treasury — Internal Revenue Service
Attach to your tax return.
Go to www.irs.gov/Form4797 for instructions and the latest information.

OMB No. 1545-0184
2024
Attachment Sequence No. 27

Name(s) shown on return: **Serena**
Identifying number: **74-8976432**

1a Enter the gross proceeds from sales or exchanges reported to you for 2024 on Form(s) 1099-B or 1099-S (or substitute statement) that you are including on line 2, 10, or 20. See instructions **1a**

b Enter the total amount of gain that you are including on lines 2, 10, and 24 due to the partial dispositions of MACRS assets **1b**

c Enter the total amount of loss that you are including on lines 2 and 10 due to the partial dispositions of MACRS assets **1c**

Part I — Sales or Exchanges of Property Used in a Trade or Business and Involuntary Conversions From Other Than Casualty or Theft—Most Property Held More Than 1 Year (see instructions)

2 (a) Description of property	(b) Date acquired (mo., day, yr.)	(c) Date sold (mo., day, yr.)	(d) Gross sales price	(e) Depreciation allowed or allowable since acquisition	(f) Cost or other basis, plus improvements and expense of sale	(g) Gain or (loss) Subtract (f) from the sum of (d) and (e)
Land	12/03/2013	12/03/2024	37,000		24,500	12,500
Computer	04/05/2023	05/02/2024	14,000	33,206	53,906	(6,700)

3	Gain, if any, from Form 4684, line 39	**3**
4	Section 1231 gain from installment sales from Form 6252, line 26 or 37	**4**
5	Section 1231 gain or (loss) from like-kind exchanges from Form 8824	**5**
6	Gain, if any, from line 32, from other than casualty or theft	**6** 146,050
7	Combine lines 2 through 6. Enter the gain or (loss) here and on the appropriate line as follows	**7** 151,850

Partnerships and S corporations. Report the gain or (loss) following the instructions for Form 1065, Schedule K, line 10, or Form 1120-S, Schedule K, line 9. Skip lines 8, 9, 11, and 12 below.

Individuals, partners, S corporation shareholders, and all others. If line 7 is zero or a loss, enter the amount from line 7 on line 11 below and skip lines 8 and 9. If line 7 is a gain and you didn't have any prior year section 1231 losses, or they were recaptured in an earlier year, enter the gain from line 7 as a long-term capital gain on the Schedule D filed with your return and skip lines 8, 9, 11, and 12 below.

8	Nonrecaptured net section 1231 losses from prior years. See instructions	**8**
9	Subtract line 8 from line 7. If zero or less, enter -0-. If line 9 is zero, enter the gain from line 7 on line 12 below. If line 9 is more than zero, enter the amount from line 8 on line 12 below and enter the gain from line 9 as a long-term capital gain on the Schedule D filed with your return. See instructions	**9**

Part II — Ordinary Gains and Losses (see instructions)

10 Ordinary gains and losses not included on lines 11 through 16 (include property held 1 year or less):

Description	Date acquired	Date sold	Gross sales price	Depreciation	Cost basis	Gain/(loss)
Equipment	10/21/2023	07/22/2024	16,000	7,477	29,777	(6,300)

11	Loss, if any, from line 7	**11** ( )
12	Gain, if any, from line 7 or amount from line 8, if applicable	**12**
13	Gain, if any, from line 31	**13** 7,600
14	Net gain or (loss) from Form 4684, lines 31 and 38a	**14**
15	Ordinary gain from installment sales from Form 6252, line 25 or 36	**15**
16	Ordinary gain or (loss) from like-kind exchanges from Form 8824	**16**
17	Combine lines 10 through 16	**17** 1,300

18 For all except individual returns, enter the amount from line 17 on the appropriate line of your return and skip lines a and b below. For individual returns, complete lines a and b below.

a If the loss on line 11 includes a loss from Form 4684, line 35, column (b)(ii), enter that part of the loss here. Enter the loss from income-producing property on Schedule A (Form 1040), line 16. (Do not include any loss on property used as an employee). Identify as from "Form 4797, line 18a." See instructions **18a**

b Redetermine the gain or (loss) on line 17 excluding the loss, if any, on line 18a. Enter here and on Schedule 1 (Form 1040), Part I, line 4 ..... **18b** 1,300

For Paperwork Reduction Act Notice, see separate instructions.   Cat. No. 13086I   Form **4797** (2024)

Self-Study Problem 8.8

Form 4797 (2024) Page **2**

Part III — Gain From Disposition of Property Under Sections 1245, 1250, 1252, 1254, and 1255 (see instructions)

19	(a) Description of section 1245, 1250, 1252, 1254, or 1255 property:	(b) Date acquired (mo., day, yr.)	(c) Date sold (mo., day, yr.)
A	Building	12/03/2013	10/07/2024
B	Furniture	12/03/2013	10/07/2024
C			
D			

	These columns relate to the properties on lines 19A through 19D.		Property A	Property B	Property C	Property D
20	Gross sales price (Note: See line 1a before completing.)	20	355,000	7,600		
21	Cost or other basis plus expense of sale	21	335,000	15,000		
22	Depreciation (or depletion) allowed or allowable	22	126,050	15,000		
23	Adjusted basis. Subtract line 22 from line 21	23	208,950	0		
24	Total gain. Subtract line 23 from line 20	24	146,050	7,600		
25	**If section 1245 property:**					
a	Depreciation allowed or allowable from line 22	25a		15,000		
b	Enter the **smaller** of line 24 or 25a	25b		7,600		
26	**If section 1250 property:** If straight line depreciation was used, enter -0- on line 26g, except for a corporation subject to section 291.					
a	Additional depreciation after 1975. See instructions	26a				
b	Applicable percentage multiplied by the **smaller** of line 24 or line 26a. See instructions	26b				
c	Subtract line 26a from line 24. If residential rental property **or** line 24 isn't more than line 26a, skip lines 26d and 26e	26c				
d	Additional depreciation after 1969 and before 1976	26d				
e	Enter the **smaller** of line 26c or 26d	26e				
f	Section 291 amount (corporations only)	26f				
g	Add lines 26b, 26e, and 26f	26g				
27	**If section 1252 property:** Skip this section if you didn't dispose of farmland or if this form is being completed for a partnership.					
a	Soil, water, and land clearing expenses	27a				
b	Line 27a multiplied by applicable percentage. See instructions	27b				
c	Enter the **smaller** of line 24 or 27b	27c				
28	**If section 1254 property:**					
a	Intangible drilling and development costs, expenditures for development of mines and other natural deposits, mining exploration costs, and depletion. See instructions	28a				
b	Enter the **smaller** of line 24 or 28a	28b				
29	**If section 1255 property:**					
a	Applicable percentage of payments excluded from income under section 126. See instructions	29a				
b	Enter the **smaller** of line 24 or 29a. See instructions	29b				

Summary of Part III Gains. Complete property columns A through D through line 29b before going to line 30.

30	Total gains for all properties. Add property columns A through D, line 24	30	153,650
31	Add property columns A through D, lines 25b, 26g, 27c, 28b, and 29b. Enter here and on line 13	31	7,600
32	Subtract line 31 from line 30. Enter the portion from casualty or theft on Form 4684, line 33. Enter the portion from other than casualty or theft on Form 4797, line 6	32	146,050

Part IV — Recapture Amounts Under Sections 179 and 280F(b)(2) When Business Use Drops to 50% or Less (see instructions)

			(a) Section 179	(b) Section 280F(b)(2)
33	Section 179 expense deduction or depreciation allowable in prior years	33		
34	Recomputed depreciation. See instructions	34		
35	Recapture amount. Subtract line 34 from line 33. See the instructions for where to report	35		

Form **4797** (2024)

Self-Study Problem 8.10

Refer to Form 6252 on Page E-86. The 10-percent interest has no impact on the taxable gain but is instead included as interest income each year.

Self-Study Problem 8.11

Refer to Form 8824 on Pages E-87 and E-88.

Self-Study Problem 8.12

1.
Insurance proceeds	$150,000
Less: the adjusted basis of the property	(70,000)
Gain realized	$ 80,000
Insurance proceeds	$150,000
Less: the cost of the replacement store	(135,000)
Proceeds not reinvested	$ 15,000
Gain recognized (the lesser of the gain realized or the proceeds not reinvested)	$ 15,000

2.
Cost of the new store	$135,000
Less: the gain deferred ($80,000 − $15,000)	(65,000)
Basis of the new store	$ 70,000

Self-Study Problem 8.10

Form 6252 — Installment Sale Income
Department of the Treasury / Internal Revenue Service
OMB No. 1545-0228
2024
Attachment Sequence No. 67

Attach to your tax return.
Use a separate form for each sale or other disposition of property on the installment method.
Go to www.irs.gov/Form6252 for the latest information.

Name(s) shown on return: **Marius**
Identifying number:

1. Description of property: **Rental House**
2a. Date acquired (mm/dd/yyyy): **01/01/2008**
2b. Date sold (mm/dd/yyyy): **1/15/2024**
3. Was the property sold to a related party? See instructions. If "Yes," complete Part III for the year of sale and 2 years after the year of the sale unless you received the final payment during the tax year . . . ☐ Yes ☑ No
4. Can the total selling price be determined by the close of the tax year in which such sale or other disposition occurs? ☑ Yes ☐ No

Part I — Gross Profit and Contract Price. Complete this part for all years of the installment agreement.

Line	Description		Amount
5	Selling price including mortgages and other debts. Don't include interest, whether stated or unstated	5	124,000
6	Mortgages, debts, and other liabilities the buyer assumed or took the property subject to (see instructions)	6	14,000
7	Subtract line 6 from line 5	7	110,000
8	Cost or other basis of property sold	8	82,000
9	Depreciation allowed or allowable	9	26,000
10	Adjusted basis. Subtract line 9 from line 8	10	56,000
11	Commissions and other expenses of sale	11	
12	Income recapture from Form 4797, Part III (see instructions)	12	
13	Add lines 10, 11, and 12	13	56,000
14	Subtract line 13 from line 5. If zero or less, don't complete the rest of this form. See instructions	14	68,000
15	If the property described on line 1 above was your main home, enter the amount of your excluded gain. See instructions. Otherwise, enter -0-	15	
16	**Gross profit.** Subtract line 15 from line 14	16	68,000
17	Subtract line 13 from line 6. If zero or less, enter -0-	17	0
18	**Contract price.** Add line 7 and line 17	18	110,000

Part II — Installment Sale Income. Complete this part for all years of the installment agreement.

Line	Description		Amount
19	Gross profit percentage (expressed as a decimal amount). Divide line 16 by line 18. (For years after the year of sale, see instructions.)	19	.61818
20	If this is the year of sale, enter the amount from line 17. Otherwise, enter -0-	20	0
21	Payments received during year (see instructions). Don't include interest, whether stated or unstated	21	10,000
22	Add lines 20 and 21	22	10,000
23	Payments received in prior years (see instructions). Don't include interest, whether stated or unstated	23	
24	**Installment sale income.** Multiply line 22 by line 19. This amount cannot be zero or less. See instructions	24	6,182
25	Enter the part of line 24 that is ordinary income under the recapture rules. See instructions	25	0
26	Subtract line 25 from line 24. Enter here and on Schedule D or Form 4797. See instructions	26	6,182

Part III — Related Party Installment Sale Income. Don't complete if you received the final payment this tax year.

27. Name, address, and taxpayer identifying number of related party

28. Did the related party resell or dispose of the property ("second disposition") during this tax year? . . . ☐ Yes ☐ No
29. If the answer to question 28 is "Yes," complete lines 30 through 37 below unless one of the following conditions is met. Check the box that applies.
    a. ☐ The second disposition was more than 2 years after the first disposition (other than dispositions of marketable securities). If this box is checked, enter the date of disposition (mm/dd/yyyy) . . . _____
    b. ☐ The first disposition was a sale or exchange of stock to the issuing corporation.
    c. ☐ The second disposition was an involuntary conversion and the threat of conversion occurred after the first disposition.
    d. ☐ The second disposition occurred after the death of the original seller or buyer.
    e. ☐ It can be established to the satisfaction of the IRS that tax avoidance wasn't a principal purpose for either of the dispositions. If this box is checked, attach an explanation. See instructions.

30. Selling price of property sold by related party (see instructions)
31. Enter contract price from line 18 for year of first sale
32. Enter the **smaller** of line 30 or line 31
33. Total payments received by the end of this tax year (see instructions)
34. Subtract line 33 from line 32. If zero or less, enter -0-
35. Multiply line 34 by the gross profit percentage on line 19 for year of first sale
36. Enter the part of line 35 that is ordinary income under the recapture rules. See instructions
37. Subtract line 36 from line 35. Enter here and on Schedule D or Form 4797. See instructions

For Paperwork Reduction Act Notice, see page 4. Cat. No. 13601R Form **6252** (2024)

Solutions to Self-Study Problems E-87

Self-Study Problem 8.11

Form 8824
Department of the Treasury
Internal Revenue Service

Like-Kind Exchanges
(and section 1043 conflict-of-interest sales)
Attach to your tax return.
Go to *www.irs.gov/Form8824* for instructions and the latest information.

OMB No. 1545-1190
2024
Attachment Sequence No. **109**

Name(s) shown on tax return: Ervin James

Identifying number:

Part I — Information on the Like-Kind Exchange

Note: Only real property should be described on lines 1 and 2. If the property described on line 1 or line 2 is real property located outside the United States, indicate the country.

1. Description of like-kind property given up:
   Land

2. Description of like-kind property received:
   Land

3. Date like-kind property given up was originally acquired (month, day, year) **3** 02/14/2017

4. Date you actually transferred your property to the other party (month, day, year) **4** 05/12/2024

5. Date like-kind property you received was identified by written notice to another party (month, day, year). See instructions for 45-day written identification requirement **5** 05/12/2024

6. Date you actually received the like-kind property from other party (month, day, year). See instructions **6** 05/12/2024

7. Was the exchange of the property given up or received made with a related party, either directly or indirectly (such as through an intermediary)? See instructions. If "Yes," complete Part II. If "No," go to Part III ..... ☐ Yes ☒ No

Note: Do not file this form if a related party sold property into the exchange, directly or indirectly (such as through an intermediary); that property became your replacement property; and none of the exceptions on line 11 applies to the exchange. Instead, report the disposition of the property as if the exchange had been a sale. If one of the exceptions on line 11 applies to the exchange, complete Part II.

Part II — Related Party Exchange Information

8. Name of related party | Relationship to you | Related party's identifying number

   Address (no., street, and apt., room, or suite no.; city or town; state; and ZIP code)

9. During this tax year (and before the date that is 2 years after the last transfer of property that was part of the exchange), did the related party sell or dispose of any part of the like-kind property received from you (or an intermediary) in the exchange? ..... ☐ Yes ☐ No

10. During this tax year (and before the date that is 2 years after the last transfer of property that was part of the exchange), did you sell or dispose of any part of the like-kind property you received? ..... ☐ Yes ☐ No

If both lines 9 and 10 are "No" and this is the year of the exchange, go to Part III. If both lines 9 and 10 are "No" and this is **not** the year of the exchange, stop here. If either line 9 or line 10 is "Yes," complete Part III and report on this year's tax return the deferred gain or (loss) from line 24 **unless** one of the exceptions on line 11 applies.

11. If one of the exceptions below applies to the disposition, check the applicable box.

    a ☐ The disposition was after the death of either of the related parties.

    b ☐ The disposition was an involuntary conversion, and the threat of conversion occurred after the exchange.

    c ☐ You can establish to the satisfaction of the IRS that neither the exchange nor the disposition had tax avoidance as one of its principal purposes. If this box is checked, attach an explanation. See instructions.

For Paperwork Reduction Act Notice, see the instructions. Cat. No. 12311A Form **8824** (2024)

Self-Study Problem 8.11

Form 8824 (2024) Page **2**

Name(s) shown on tax return. Do not enter name and social security number if shown on other side.
Ervin James

Your social security number

Part III — Realized Gain or (Loss), Recognized Gain, and Basis of Like-Kind Property Received

Caution: If you transferred **and** received **(a)** more than one group of like-kind properties, or **(b)** cash or other (not like-kind) property, see *Reporting of multi-asset exchanges* in the instructions.

Note: Complete lines 12 through 14 **only** if you gave up property that was not like-kind. Otherwise, go to line 15.

Line	Description	Amount
12	Fair market value (FMV) of other property given up. See instructions	
12a	Description of other property given up	
13	Adjusted basis of other property given up	
14	Gain or (loss) recognized on other property given up. Subtract line 13 from line 12. Report the gain or (loss) in the same manner as if the exchange had been a sale	
	Caution: If the property given up was used previously or partly as a home, see *Property used as home* in the instructions.	
15	Cash received, FMV of other property received, plus net liabilities assumed by other party, reduced (but not below zero) by any exchange expenses you incurred. See instructions	8,000
15a	Description of other property received Land	
16	FMV of like-kind property you received	24,000
17	Add lines 15 and 16	32,000
18	Adjusted basis of like-kind property you gave up, net amounts paid to other party, plus any exchange expenses **not** used on line 15. See instructions	20,000
19	**Realized gain or (loss).** Subtract line 18 from line 17	12,000
20	Enter the smaller of line 15 or line 19, but not less than zero	8,000
21	Ordinary income under recapture rules. Enter here and on Form 4797, line 16. See instructions	
22	Subtract line 21 from line 20. If zero or less, enter -0-. If more than zero, enter here and on Schedule D or Form 4797, unless the installment method applies. See instructions	8,000
23	**Recognized gain.** Add lines 21 and 22	8,000
24	Deferred gain or (loss). Subtract line 23 from line 19. If a related party exchange, see instructions	4,000
25	**Basis of like-kind property received.** Subtract line 15 from the sum of lines 18 and 23. See instructions	20,000
	Note: Complete lines 25a, 25b, and 25c if you received like-kind section 1250 property, like-kind section 1245 property, or like-kind intangible property in the exchange.	
25a	Basis of like-kind section 1250 property received	
25b	Basis of like-kind section 1245 property received	
25c	Basis of like-kind intangible property received	

Part IV — Deferral of Gain From Section 1043 Conflict-of-Interest Sales

Note: This part is to be used **only** by officers or employees of the executive branch of the federal government or judicial officers of the federal government (including certain spouses, minor or dependent children, and trustees as described in section 1043) for reporting nonrecognition of gain under section 1043 on the sale of property to comply with the conflict-of-interest requirements. This part can be used **only** if the cost of the replacement property is more than the basis of the divested property.

Line	Description	Amount
26	Enter the number from the upper right corner of your certificate of divestiture. (**Do not** attach a copy of your certificate. Keep the certificate with your records.)	—
27	Description of divested property	
28	Description of replacement property	
29	Date divested property was sold (month, day, year)	MM/DD/YYYY
30	Sales price of divested property. See instructions	
31	Basis of divested property	
32	**Realized gain.** Subtract line 31 from line 30	
33	Cost of replacement property purchased within 60 days after date of sale	
34	Subtract line 33 from line 30. If zero or less, enter -0-	
35	Ordinary income under recapture rules. Enter here and on Form 4797, line 10. See instructions	
36	Subtract line 35 from line 34. If zero or less, enter -0-. If more than zero, enter here and on Schedule D or Form 4797. See instructions	
37	**Deferred gain.** Subtract the sum of lines 35 and 36 from line 32	
38	**Basis of replacement property.** Subtract line 37 from line 33	

Form **8824** (2024)

Chapter 9 Employment Taxes, Estimated Payments, and Retirement Plans

Self-Study Problem 9.1

a. Employee. Independent contractors are more likely to work for multiple businesses.
b. Independent contractor. Employees are more likely to be required to comply with when work is performed.
c. Employee. Employees are generally trained by the hiring party.
d. Employee. Employees are generally required to perform work on premises.
e. Employee. Independent contactors are more likely to be paid based on project completion.
f. Employee. Continuing relationships are more common with employees.
g. Employee. Independent contractors generally bear the risk of a loss.
h. Employee. Employees can quit without breaching contracts.

Self-Study Problem 9.2

1. Refer to Form W-4 on Pages E-90 and E-91.
2. a. Percentage Method: $28.49. Refer to Worksheet 4 on Page E-92.
   b. Wage Bracket Method: $28.83. Refer to Worksheet 2 on Page E-93.

Self-Study Problem 9.3

1. a. Employee's portion: Social Security tax $10,391.20 [$174,000 − ($175,000 − $168,600)] × 6.2%. Note that Juliette's year-to-date pay exceeds the 2024 FICA cap of $168,600.
   b. Employer's portion: Social Security tax $10,391.20 [$174,000 − ($175,000 − $168,600)] × 6.2%
   c. Employee's portion: Medicare tax $2,523.00 ($174,000 × 1.45%)
   d. Employer's portion: Medicare tax $2,523.00 ($174,000 × 1.45%)

Self-Study Problem 9.4

a. The required annual payment is $22,045. Refer to 2024 Estimated Tax Worksheet on Page E-94.
b. Refer to Form 1040-ES voucher on Page E-95.
c. $5,511. Since Ray's prior year AGI exceeds $150,000, the annual required payment is the lesser of 90% of the current year or 110% of the prior year. 110% of the prior year tax of $22,500 is $24,750. 90% of his current year tax is $22,045, as calculated in part a. Thus, Ray's annual required payment is $22,045, and his 1st quarter estimated payment for 2024 remains the same at $5,511, as shown in part b.

Self-Study Problem 9.5

Refer to pages 1 and 2 of Form 941 on Pages E-96 and E-97.

Self-Study Problem 9.2, Part 1

Form W-4
Department of the Treasury
Internal Revenue Service

Employee's Withholding Certificate
Complete Form W-4 so that your employer can withhold the correct federal income tax from your pay.
Give Form W-4 to your employer.
Your withholding is subject to review by the IRS.

OMB No. 1545-0074

2024

Step 1: Enter Personal Information

(a) First name and middle initial: **Lillian** Last name: **Miles**

Address: **456 Peachtree Court**

City or town, state, and ZIP code: **Atlanta, GA 30310**

(b) Social security number: **414-44-1680**

Does your name match the name on your social security card? If not, to ensure you get credit for your earnings, contact SSA at 800-772-1213 or go to www.ssa.gov.

(c)
- [ ] Single or Married filing separately
- [x] Married filing jointly or Qualifying surviving spouse
- [ ] Head of household (Check only if you're unmarried and pay more than half the costs of keeping up a home for yourself and a qualifying individual.)

Complete Steps 2–4 ONLY if they apply to you; otherwise, skip to Step 5. See page 2 for more information on each step, who can claim exemption from withholding, and when to use the estimator at www.irs.gov/W4App.

Step 2: Multiple Jobs or Spouse Works

Complete this step if you (1) hold more than one job at a time, or (2) are married filing jointly and your spouse also works. The correct amount of withholding depends on income earned from all of these jobs.

Do **only one** of the following.

(a) Use the estimator at www.irs.gov/W4App for most accurate withholding for this step (and Steps 3–4). If you or your spouse have self-employment income, use this option; **or**

(b) Use the Multiple Jobs Worksheet on page 3 and enter the result in Step 4(c) below; **or**

(c) If there are only two jobs total, you may check this box. Do the same on Form W-4 for the other job. This option is generally more accurate than (b) if pay at the lower paying job is more than half of the pay at the higher paying job. Otherwise, (b) is more accurate . . . . [x]

Complete Steps 3–4(b) on Form W-4 for only ONE of these jobs. Leave those steps blank for the other jobs. (Your withholding will be most accurate if you complete Steps 3–4(b) on the Form W-4 for the highest paying job.)

Step 3: Claim Dependent and Other Credits

If your total income will be $200,000 or less ($400,000 or less if married filing jointly):

Multiply the number of qualifying children under age 17 by $2,000 $ **2,000**

Multiply the number of other dependents by $500 . . . . . $ **500**

Add the amounts above for qualifying children and other dependents. You may add to this the amount of any other credits. Enter the total here . . . . **3** $ **2,500**

Step 4 (optional): Other Adjustments

(a) **Other income (not from jobs).** If you want tax withheld for other income you expect this year that won't have withholding, enter the amount of other income here. This may include interest, dividends, and retirement income . . . . **4(a)** $ **6,700**

(b) **Deductions.** If you expect to claim deductions other than the standard deduction and want to reduce your withholding, use the Deductions Worksheet on page 3 and enter the result here . . . . **4(b)** $ **6,040**

(c) **Extra withholding.** Enter any additional tax you want withheld each **pay period** . . **4(c)** $

Step 5: Sign Here

Under penalties of perjury, I declare that this certificate, to the best of my knowledge and belief, is true, correct, and complete.

Employee's signature (This form is not valid unless you sign it.)   Date

Employers Only | Employer's name and address | First date of employment | Employer identification number (EIN)

For Privacy Act and Paperwork Reduction Act Notice, see page 3.   Cat. No. 10220Q   Form **W-4** (2024)

Self-Study Problem 9.2, Part 1

Note: Lillian will not complete the Multiple Jobs Worksheet because her wages and John's wages are similar. Instead, she will check the box at Step 2(c) on page 1 of the Form W-4.

Form W-4 (2024)   Page **3**

Step 2(b)—Multiple Jobs Worksheet *(Keep for your records.)*

If you choose the option in Step 2(b) on Form W-4, complete this worksheet (which calculates the total extra tax for all jobs) on **only ONE** Form W-4. Withholding will be most accurate if you complete the worksheet and enter the result on the Form W-4 for the highest paying job. To be accurate, submit a new Form W-4 for all other jobs if you have not updated your withholding since 2019.

Note: If more than one job has annual wages of more than $120,000 or there are more than three jobs, see Pub. 505 for additional tables; or, you can use the online withholding estimator at *www.irs.gov/W4App*.

1 **Two jobs.** If you have two jobs or you're married filing jointly and you and your spouse each have one job, find the amount from the appropriate table on page 4. Using the "Higher Paying Job" row and the "Lower Paying Job" column, find the value at the intersection of the two household salaries and enter that value on line 1. Then, **skip** to line 3 . . . . **1** $ _____

2 **Three jobs.** If you and/or your spouse have three jobs at the same time, complete lines 2a, 2b, and 2c below. Otherwise, skip to line 3.

    a Find the amount from the appropriate table on page 4 using the annual wages from the highest paying job in the "Higher Paying Job" row and the annual wages for your next highest paying job in the "Lower Paying Job" column. Find the value at the intersection of the two household salaries and enter that value on line 2a . . . . **2a** $ _____

    b Add the annual wages of the two highest paying jobs from line 2a together and use the total as the wages in the "Higher Paying Job" row and use the annual wages for your third job in the "Lower Paying Job" column to find the amount from the appropriate table on page 4 and enter this amount on line 2b . . . . **2b** $ _____

    c Add the amounts from lines 2a and 2b and enter the result on line 2c . . . . **2c** $ _____

3 Enter the number of pay periods per year for the highest paying job. For example, if that job pays weekly, enter 52; if it pays every other week, enter 26; if it pays monthly, enter 12, etc. . . . . . . **3** _____

4 **Divide** the annual amount on line 1 or line 2c by the number of pay periods on line 3. Enter this amount here and in **Step 4(c)** of Form W-4 for the highest paying job (along with any other additional amount you want withheld) . . . . **4** $ _____

Step 4(b)—Deductions Worksheet *(Keep for your records.)*

1 Enter an estimate of your 2024 itemized deductions (from Schedule A (Form 1040)). Such deductions may include qualifying home mortgage interest, charitable contributions, state and local taxes (up to $10,000), and medical expenses in excess of 7.5% of your income . . . . **1** $ _____

2 Enter:
   • $29,200 if you're married filing jointly or a qualifying surviving spouse
   • $21,900 if you're head of household
   • $14,600 if you're single or married filing separately   **2** $ _____

3 If line 1 is greater than line 2, subtract line 2 from line 1 and enter the result here. If line 2 is greater than line 1, enter "-0-" . . . . **3** $ _____

4 Enter an estimate of your student loan interest, deductible IRA contributions, and certain other adjustments (from Part II of Schedule 1 (Form 1040)). See Pub. 505 for more information . . . . **4** $ 6,040 (a)

5 **Add** lines 3 and 4. Enter the result here and in **Step 4(b)** of Form W-4 . . . . **5** $ 6,040

Privacy Act and Paperwork Reduction Act Notice. We ask for the information on this form to carry out the Internal Revenue laws of the United States. Internal Revenue Code sections 3402(f)(2) and 6109 and their regulations require you to provide this information; your employer uses it to determine your federal income tax withholding. Failure to provide a properly completed form will result in your being treated as a single person with no other entries on the form; providing fraudulent information may subject you to penalties. Routine uses of this information include giving it to the Department of Justice for civil and criminal litigation; to cities, states, the District of Columbia, and U.S. commonwealths and territories for use in administering their tax laws; and to the Department of Health and Human Services for use in the National Directory of New Hires. We may also disclose this information to other countries under a tax treaty, to federal and state agencies to enforce federal nontax criminal laws, or to federal law enforcement and intelligence agencies to combat terrorism.

You are not required to provide the information requested on a form that is subject to the Paperwork Reduction Act unless the form displays a valid OMB control number. Books or records relating to a form or its instructions must be retained as long as their contents may become material in the administration of any Internal Revenue law. Generally, tax returns and return information are confidential, as required by Code section 6103.

The average time and expenses required to complete and file this form will vary depending on individual circumstances. For estimated averages, see the instructions for your income tax return.

If you have suggestions for making this form simpler, we would be happy to hear from you. See the instructions for your income tax return.

(a) $4,700 IRA deduction + $1,340 ($6,700 × 20%) QBI deduction

Self-Study Problem 9.2, Part 2 a.

4. Percentage Method Tables for Manual Payroll Systems With Forms W-4 From 2020 or Later

If you compute payroll manually, your employee has submitted a Form W-4 for 2020 or later, and you prefer to use the Percentage Method or you can't use the Wage Bracket Method tables because the employee's annual wages exceed the amount from the last bracket of the table (based on marital status and pay period), use the worksheet below and the Percentage Method tables that follow to figure federal income tax withholding. This method works for any amount of wages.

Worksheet 4. Employer's Withholding Worksheet for Percentage Method Tables for Manual Payroll Systems With Forms W-4 From 2020 or Later

Keep for Your Records

Table 6	Monthly	Semimonthly	Biweekly	Weekly	Daily
	12	24	26	52	260

Step 1. Adjust the employee's wage amount

1a	Enter the employee's total taxable wages this payroll period	1a	$ 1,766.67
1b	Enter the number of pay periods you have per year (see Table 6)	1b	24
1c	Enter the amount from Step 4(a) of the employee's Form W-4	1c	$ 6,700.00
1d	Divide line 1c by the number on line 1b	1d	$ 279.17
1e	Add lines 1a and 1d	1e	$ 2,045.84
1f	Enter the amount from Step 4(b) of the employee's Form W-4	1f	$ 6,040.00
1g	Divide line 1f by the number on line 1b	1g	251.67
1h	Subtract line 1g from line 1e. If zero or less, enter -0-. This is the **Adjusted Wage Amount**	1h	$ 1,794.17

Step 2. Figure the Tentative Withholding Amount

based on your pay frequency, the employee's Adjusted Wage Amount, filing status (Step 1(c) of Form W-4), and whether the box in Step 2 of Form W-4 is checked.

2a	Find the row in the STANDARD Withholding Rate Schedules (if the box in Step 2 of Form W-4 is NOT checked) or the Form W-4, Step 2, Checkbox, Withholding Rate Schedules (if it HAS been checked) of the Percentage Method tables in this section in which the amount on line 1h is at least the amount in column A but less than the amount in column B, and then enter here the amount from column A of that row	2a	$ 1,092.00
2b	Enter the amount from column C of that row	2b	$ 48.40
2c	Enter the percentage from column D of that row	2c	12%
2d	Subtract line 2a from line 1h	2d	$ 702.17
2e	Multiply the amount on line 2d by the percentage on line 2c	2e	84.26
2f	Add lines 2b and 2e. This is the **Tentative Withholding Amount**	2f	$ 132.66

Step 3. Account for tax credits

3a	Enter the amount from Step 3 of the employee's Form W-4	3a	$ 2,500.00
3b	Divide the amount on line 3a by the number of pay periods on line 1b	3b	$ 104.17
3c	Subtract line 3b from line 2f. If zero or less, enter -0-	3c	$ 28.49

Step 4. Figure the final amount to withhold

4a	Enter the additional amount to withhold from Step 4(c) of the employee's Form W-4	4a	$ 0.00
4b	Add lines 3c and 4a. **This is the amount to withhold from the employee's wages this pay period**	4b	$ 28.49

Self-Study Problem 9.2, Part 2 b.

2. Wage Bracket Method Tables for Manual Payroll Systems With Forms W-4 From 2020 or Later

If you compute payroll manually, your employee has submitted a Form W-4 for 2020 or later, and you prefer to use the Wage Bracket Method, use the worksheet below and the Wage Bracket Method tables that follow to figure federal income tax withholding.

These Wage Bracket Method tables cover a limited amount of annual wages (generally, less than $100,000). If you can't use the Wage Bracket Method tables because taxable wages exceed the amount from the last bracket of the table (based on filing status and pay period), use the Percentage Method tables in section 4.

Worksheet 2. Employer's Withholding Worksheet for Wage Bracket Method Tables for Manual Payroll Systems With Forms W-4 From 2020 or Later

Keep for Your Records

Table 5	Monthly	Semimonthly	Biweekly	Weekly	Daily
	12	24	26	52	260

Step 1. Adjust the employee's wage amount

1a	Enter the employee's total taxable wages this payroll period	1a $	1,766.67
1b	Enter the number of pay periods you have per year (see Table 5)	1b	24
1c	Enter the amount from Step 4(a) of the employee's Form W-4	1c $	6,700.00
1d	Divide the amount on line 1c by the number of pay periods on line 1b	1d $	279.17
1e	Add lines 1a and 1d	1e $	2,045.84
1f	Enter the amount from Step 4(b) of the employee's Form W-4	1f $	6,040.00
1g	Divide the amount on line 1f by the number of pay periods on line 1b	1g $	251.67
1h	Subtract line 1g from line 1e. If zero or less, enter -0-. This is the **Adjusted Wage Amount**	1h $	1,794.17

Step 2. Figure the Tentative Withholding Amount

2a	Use the amount on line 1h to look up the tentative amount to withhold in the appropriate Wage Bracket Method table in this section for your pay frequency, given the employee's filing status and whether the employee has checked the box in Step 2 of Form W-4. This is the **Tentative Withholding Amount**	2a $	133.00

Step 3. Account for tax credits

3a	Enter the amount from Step 3 of the employee's Form W-4	3a $	2,500.00
3b	Divide the amount on line 3a by the number of pay periods on line 1b	3b $	104.17
3c	Subtract line 3b from line 2a. If zero or less, enter -0-	3c $	28.83

Step 4. Figure the final amount to withhold

4a	Enter the additional amount to withhold from Step 4(c) of the employee's Form W-4	4a $	0.00
4b	Add lines 3c and 4a. **This is the amount to withhold from the employee's wages this pay period**	4b $	28.83

Self-Study Problem 9.4, Part a

2024 Estimated Tax Worksheet
Keep for Your Records

Line	Description		Amount	
1	Adjusted gross income you expect in 2024 (see instructions)	1	97,582	(a)
2a	Deductions	2a	14,600	
	• If you plan to itemize deductions, enter the estimated total of your itemized deductions.			
	• If you don't plan to itemize deductions, enter your standard deduction.			
b	If you can take the qualified business income deduction, enter the estimated amount of the deduction	2b	16,596	(b)
c	Add lines 2a and 2b	2c	31,196	
3	Subtract line 2c from line 1	3	66,386	
4	**Tax.** Figure your tax on the amount on line 3 by using the **2024 Tax Rate Schedules**. **Caution:** *If you will have qualified dividends or a net capital gain, or expect to exclude or deduct foreign earned income or housing, see Worksheets 2-5 and 2-6 in Pub. 505 to figure the tax*	4	9,658	(c)
5	Alternative minimum tax from **Form 6251**	5		
6	Add lines 4 and 5. Add to this amount any other taxes you expect to include in the total on Form 1040 or 1040-SR, line 16	6	9,658	
7	Credits (see instructions). **Do not** include any income tax withholding on this line	7		
8	Subtract line 7 from line 6. If zero or less, enter -0-	8	9,658	
9	Self-employment tax (see instructions)	9	14,836	
10	Other taxes (see instructions)	10		
11a	Add lines 8 through 10	11a	24,494	
b	Earned income credit, additional child tax credit, fuel tax credit, net premium tax credit, refundable American opportunity credit, and section 1341 credit	11b		
c	**Total 2024 estimated tax.** Subtract line 11b from line 11a. If zero or less, enter -0-	11c	24,494	
12a	Multiply line 11c by 90% (66⅔% for farmers and fishermen) — 12a 22,045			
b	Required annual payment based on prior year's tax (see instructions) — 12b 22,500			
c	**Required annual payment to avoid a penalty.** Enter the **smaller** of line 12a or 12b	12c	22,045	
	Caution: *Generally, if you do not prepay (through income tax withholding and estimated tax payments) at least the amount on line 12c, you may owe a penalty for not paying enough estimated tax. To avoid a penalty, make sure your estimate on line 11c is as accurate as possible. Even if you pay the required annual payment, you may still owe tax when you file your return. If you prefer, you can pay the amount shown on line 11c. For details, see chapter 2 of Pub. 505.*			
13	Income tax withheld and estimated to be withheld during 2024 (including income tax withholding on pensions, annuities, certain deferred income, and Additional Medicare Tax withholding)	13	0	
14a	Subtract line 13 from line 12c — 14a 22,045 Is the result zero or less? ☐ **Yes.** Stop here. You are not required to make estimated tax payments. ☒ **No.** Go to line 14b.			
b	Subtract line 13 from line 11c — 14b 24,494 Is the result less than $1,000? ☐ **Yes.** Stop here. You are not required to make estimated tax payments. ☒ **No.** Go to line 15 to figure your required payment.			
15	If the first payment you are required to make is due April 15, 2024, enter ¼ of line 14a (minus any 2023 overpayment that you are applying to this installment) here, and on your estimated tax payment voucher(s) if you are paying by check or money order	15	5,511	(d)

(a) $105,000 − $7,418 (one-half of self-employment tax).
(b) The QBI deduction before overall limitation is $105,000 − $7,418 (one-half self-employment tax) × 20% = $19,516. The overall net income limitation is $16,596 [($105,000 − $7,418 − $14,600 standard deduction) × 20%]. Thus, the QBI deduction is limited to $16,596.
(c) $5,426.00 + [($66,386 − $47,150) × 22%]. Note that Tax Tables are generally not available at the time of estimate and; thus, the tax rate schedules are used even when taxable income is less than $100,000.
(d) Since the prior year overpayment was received as a refund, no overpayment is applied to the first quarter payment.

Self-Study Problem 9.4, Part b

Form 1040-ES
Department of the Treasury
Internal Revenue Service

2024 Estimated Tax

Payment Voucher 1

OMB No. 1545-0074

File only if you are making a payment of estimated tax by check or money order. Mail this voucher with your check or money order payable to "**United States Treasury**." Write your social security number and "2024 Form 1040-ES" on your check or money order. Do not send cash. Enclose, but do not staple or attach, your payment with this voucher.

Calendar year—Due April 15, 2024

Amount of estimated tax you are paying by check or money order. **5,511.00**

Pay online at www.irs.gov/etpay

Simple. Fast. Secure.

Your first name and middle initial	Ray
Your last name	Adams
Your social security number	321-45-9876
Spouse's first name and middle initial	
Spouse's last name	
Spouse's social security number	
Address (number, street, and apt. no.)	1905 Hardin Valley Road
City, town, or post office	Knoxville
State	TN
ZIP code	37932

For Disclosure, Privacy Act, and Paperwork Reduction Act Notice, see instructions.

Form 1040-ES (2024)

E-96 Appendix E

Self-Study Problem 9.5

Form 941 for 2024: Employer's QUARTERLY Federal Tax Return
(Rev. March 2024) — Department of the Treasury — Internal Revenue Service

950124
OMB No. 1545-0029

Employer identification number (EIN): 33-4434432

Name (not your trade name): Hills Scientific Corp.

Trade name (if any):

Address:

Report for this Quarter of 2024 (Check one.)
- [ ] 1: January, February, March
- [X] 2: April, May, June
- [ ] 3: July, August, September
- [ ] 4: October, November, December

Go to www.irs.gov/Form941 for instructions and the latest information.

Read the separate instructions before you complete Form 941. Type or print within the boxes.

Part 1: Answer these questions for this quarter. Employers in American Samoa, Guam, the Commonwealth of the Northern Mariana Islands, the U.S. Virgin Islands, and Puerto Rico can skip lines 2 and 3, unless you have employees who are subject to U.S. income tax withholding.

Line	Description		Value
1	Number of employees who received wages, tips, or other compensation for the pay period including: Mar. 12 (Quarter 1), June 12 (Quarter 2), Sept. 12 (Quarter 3), or Dec. 12 (Quarter 4)	1	6
2	Wages, tips, and other compensation	2	174,000.00
3	Federal income tax withheld from wages, tips, and other compensation	3	42,774.00
4	If no wages, tips, and other compensation are subject to social security or Medicare tax		[ ] Check here and go to line 6.

		Column 1		Column 2	
5a	Taxable social security wages	167,600.00	× 0.124 =	20,782.40	(a)
5b	Taxable social security tips		× 0.124 =		
5c	Taxable Medicare wages & tips	174,000.00	× 0.029 =	5,046.00	
5d	Taxable wages & tips subject to Additional Medicare Tax withholding		× 0.009 =		

Line	Description		Value
5e	Total social security and Medicare taxes. Add Column 2 from lines 5a, 5b, 5c, and 5d	5e	25,828.40
5f	Section 3121(q) Notice and Demand—Tax due on unreported tips (see instructions)	5f	.
6	Total taxes before adjustments. Add lines 3, 5e, and 5f	6	68,602.40
7	Current quarter's adjustment for fractions of cents	7	.
8	Current quarter's adjustment for sick pay	8	.
9	Current quarter's adjustments for tips and group-term life insurance	9	.
10	Total taxes after adjustments. Combine lines 6 through 9	10	68,602.40
11	Qualified small business payroll tax credit for increasing research activities. Attach Form 8974	11	.
12	Total taxes after adjustments and nonrefundable credits. Subtract line 11 from line 10	12	68,602.40
13	Total deposits for this quarter, including overpayment applied from a prior quarter and overpayments applied from Form 941-X, 941-X (PR), or 944-X filed in the current quarter	13	68,000.00
14	Balance due. If line 12 is more than line 13, enter the difference and see instructions	14	602.40
15	Overpayment. If line 13 is more than line 12, enter the difference		. Check one: [ ] Apply to next return. [ ] Send a refund.

You MUST complete both pages of Form 941 and SIGN it.

For Privacy Act and Paperwork Reduction Act Notice, see separate instructions. Cat. No. 17001Z Form **941** (Rev. 3-2024)

(a) Total second quarter payroll subject to Social Security tax due to Juliette's YTD pay of $175,000 exceeding the 2024 FICA cap of $168,600 in the second quarter. Second quarter payroll of $174,000 − ($175,000 − $168,600).

Self-Study Problem 9.5

Name (not your trade name): Hills Scientific Corp.
Employer identification number (EIN): 33-4434432

950224

Part 2: Tell us about your deposit schedule and tax liability for this quarter.

If you're unsure about whether you're a monthly schedule depositor or a semiweekly schedule depositor, see section 11 of Pub. 15.

16 Check one:

☐ Line 12 on this return is less than $2,500 or line 12 on the return for the prior quarter was less than $2,500, and you didn't incur a $100,000 next-day deposit obligation during the current quarter. If line 12 for the prior quarter was less than $2,500 but line 12 on this return is $100,000 or more, you must provide a record of your federal tax liability. If you're a monthly schedule depositor, complete the deposit schedule below; if you're a semiweekly schedule depositor, attach Schedule B (Form 941). Go to Part 3.

☒ **You were a monthly schedule depositor for the entire quarter.** Enter your tax liability for each month and total liability for the quarter, then go to Part 3.

Tax liability:		
Month 1	23,086.10	(a)
Month 2	23,086.10	(a)
Month 3	22,430.20	(b)
Total liability for quarter	68,602.40	Total must equal line 12.

☐ **You were a semiweekly schedule depositor for any part of this quarter.** Complete Schedule B (Form 941), Report of Tax Liability for Semiweekly Schedule Depositors, and attach it to Form 941. Go to Part 3.

Part 3: Tell us about your business. If a question does NOT apply to your business, leave it blank.

17 If your business has closed or you stopped paying wages . . . . ☐ Check here and
enter the final date you paid wages __/__/__ ; also attach a statement to your return. See instructions.

18 If you're a seasonal employer and you don't have to file a return for every quarter of the year . . . ☐ Check here.

Part 4: May we speak with your third-party designee?

Do you want to allow an employee, a paid tax preparer, or another person to discuss this return with the IRS? See the instructions for details.

☐ Yes. Designee's name and phone number

Select a 5-digit personal identification number (PIN) to use when talking to the IRS.

☐ No.

Part 5: Sign here. You MUST complete both pages of Form 941 and SIGN it.

Under penalties of perjury, I declare that I have examined this return, including accompanying schedules and statements, and to the best of my knowledge and belief, it is true, correct, and complete. Declaration of preparer (other than taxpayer) is based on all information of which preparer has any knowledge.

Sign your name here

Print your name here
Print your title here

Date __/__/__
Best daytime phone

Paid Preparer Use Only Check if you're self-employed . . . ☐

Preparer's name		PTIN	
Preparer's signature		Date	__/__/__
Firm's name (or yours if self-employed)		EIN	
Address		Phone	
City		State		ZIP code	

Page **2** Form **941** (Rev. 3-2024)

(a) Monthly payroll of $57,700 × 15.3% plus income tax withheld of $14,258 ($42,774 ÷ 3).
(b) $58,600 (monthly payroll) − $6,400 (Juliette's wages over FICA cap) × 12.4% and $58,600 × 2.9% and income tax withheld of $14,258.

Self-Study Problem 9.6, Part a

Form W-2 Wage and Tax Statement — 2024
Copy B—To Be Filed With Employee's FEDERAL Tax Return.
This information is being furnished to the Internal Revenue Service.

Box	Field	Value
a	Employee's social security number	398-22-4212
b	Employer identification number (EIN)	95-1234567
c	Employer's name, address, and ZIP code	David Flock, PO Box 12344, Melbourne, FL 32901
d	Control number	
e/f	Employee's name and address	China Jones, 2702 Carlson Circle, Apt 2K, Melbourne, FL 32901
1	Wages, tips, other compensation	17,523.12
2	Federal income tax withheld	610.00
3	Social security wages	17,523.12
4	Social security tax withheld	1,086.43
5	Medicare wages and tips	17,523.12
6	Medicare tax withheld	254.09
15	State	FL

OMB No. 1545-0008

Self-Study Problem 9.6, Part b

Form W-3 Transmittal of Wage and Tax Statements — 2024
DO NOT STAPLE
OMB No. 1545-0008

Box	Field	Value
a	Control number	33333
b	Kind of Payer	941 (X)
b	Kind of Employer	None apply (X)
c	Total number of Forms W-2	2
e	Employer identification number (EIN)	95-1234567
f	Employer's name	David Flock
g	Employer's address and ZIP code	PO Box 12344, Melbourne, FL 32901
1	Wages, tips, other compensation	31,523.12
2	Federal income tax withheld	845.00
3	Social security wages	31,523.12
4	Social security tax withheld	1,954.43
5	Medicare wages and tips	31,523.12
6	Medicare tax withheld	457.09
	Employer's contact person	David Flock
	Employer's telephone number	800-555-1212

Self-Study Problem 9.6, Part c

☐ CORRECTED (if checked)

PAYER'S name, street address, city or town, state or province, country, ZIP or foreign postal code, and telephone no. David Flock PO Box 12344 Melbourne, FL 32901		OMB No. 1545-0116 Form **1099-NEC** (Rev. January 2024) For calendar year **2024**	**Nonemployee Compensation**
PAYER'S TIN 95-1234567	RECIPIENT'S TIN 566-29-9819	1 Nonemployee compensation $ 878.78	Copy B **For Recipient**
RECIPIENT'S name Cielle Harris		2 Payer made direct sales totaling $5,000 or more of consumer products to recipient for resale ☐	This is important tax information and is being furnished to the IRS. If you are required to file a return, a negligence penalty or other sanction may be imposed on you if this income is taxable and the IRS determines that it has not been reported.
Street address (including apt. no.) 224 Deland Ave.		3	
City or town, state or province, country, and ZIP or foreign postal code Indialantic, FL 32903		4 Federal income tax withheld $	
Account number (see instructions)		5 State tax withheld $ $	6 State/Payer's state no.	7 State income $ $

Form **1099-NEC** (Rev. 1-2024)   (keep for your records)   www.irs.gov/Form1099NEC   Department of the Treasury - Internal Revenue Service

Self-Study Problem 9.7

Refer to Form 940 on Pages E-100 and E-101.

Self-Study Problem 9.7

Form 940 for 2024: Employer's Annual Federal Unemployment (FUTA) Tax Return
Department of the Treasury — Internal Revenue Service

850113
OMB No. 1545-0029

Employer identification number (EIN): 94-0001112
Name (not your trade name): Anatolian Corporation
Trade name (if any):
Address: 400 8th Street N, La Crosse, WI 54601

Type of Return (Check all that apply.)
- a. Amended
- b. Successor employer
- c. No payments to employees in 2024
- d. Final: Business closed or stopped paying wages

Go to www.irs.gov/Form940 for instructions and the latest information.

Part 1: Tell us about your return.

- **1a** If you had to pay state unemployment tax in one state only, enter the state abbreviation. **1a** WI
- **1b** If you had to pay state unemployment tax in more than one state, you are a multi-state employer. **1b** ☐
- **2** If you paid wages in a state that is subject to CREDIT REDUCTION. **2** ☐

Part 2: Determine your FUTA tax before adjustments.

Line	Description	Amount
3	Total payments to all employees	302,800.00
4	Payments exempt from FUTA tax	
5	Total of payments made to each employee in excess of $7,000	219,400.00 (a)
6	Subtotal (line 4 + line 5 = line 6)	219,400.00
7	Total taxable FUTA wages (line 3 – line 6 = line 7)	83,400.00
8	FUTA tax before adjustments (line 7 × 0.006 = line 8)	500.40

Part 3: Determine your adjustments.

Line	Description	Amount
9	If ALL of the taxable FUTA wages you paid were excluded from state unemployment tax, multiply line 7 by 0.054	.
10	If SOME of the taxable FUTA wages you paid were excluded from state unemployment tax, OR you paid ANY state unemployment tax late	.
11	If credit reduction applies, enter the total from Schedule A (Form 940)	.

Part 4: Determine your FUTA tax and balance due or overpayment.

Line	Description	Amount
12	Total FUTA tax after adjustments (lines 8 + 9 + 10 + 11 = line 12)	500.40
13	FUTA tax deposited for the year, including any overpayment applied from a prior year	0.00
14	Balance due. If line 12 is more than line 13, enter the excess on line 14.	500.40
15	Overpayment. If line 13 is more than line 12, enter the excess on line 15 and check a box below	.

You MUST complete both pages of this form and SIGN it. Check one: ☐ Apply to next return. ☐ Send a refund.

For Privacy Act and Paperwork Reduction Act Notice, see separate instructions. Cat. No. 11234O Form **940** (2024)

(a) Wages in excess of $7,000 for all employees except those paid less than $7,000 (Myers, Hopps, and Eclair).

Self-Study Problem 9.7

Name (not your trade name)
Anatolian Corporation

Employer identification number (EIN)
94-0001112

850212

Part 5: Report your FUTA tax liability by quarter only if line 12 is more than $500. If not, go to Part 6.

16 Report the amount of your FUTA tax liability for each quarter; do NOT enter the amount you deposited. If you had no liability for a quarter, leave the line blank.

Line	Quarter	Amount
16a	1st quarter (January 1 – March 31)	257.40 (a)
16b	2nd quarter (April 1 – June 30)	135.60
16c	3rd quarter (July 1 – September 30)	44.40
16d	4th quarter (October 1 – December 31)	63.00
17	Total tax liability for the year (lines 16a + 16b + 16c + 16d = line 17)	500.40

Total must equal line 12.

Part 6: May we speak with your third-party designee?

Do you want to allow an employee, a paid tax preparer, or another person to discuss this return with the IRS? See the instructions for details.

☐ Yes. Designee's name and phone number

Select a 5-digit personal identification number (PIN) to use when talking to the IRS.

☐ No.

Part 7: Sign here. You MUST complete both pages of this form and SIGN it.

Under penalties of perjury, I declare that I have examined this return, including accompanying schedules and statements, and to the best of my knowledge and belief, it is true, correct, and complete, and that no part of any payment made to a state unemployment fund claimed as a credit was, or is to be, deducted from the payments made to employees. Declaration of preparer (other than taxpayer) is based on all information of which preparer has any knowledge.

Sign your name here

Print your name here

Print your title here

Date / /

Best daytime phone

Paid Preparer Use Only

Check if you are self-employed ☐

Preparer's name

PTIN

Preparer's signature

Date / /

Firm's name (or yours if self-employed)

EIN

Address

Phone

City

State

ZIP code

Page **2**

Form **940** (2024)

(a) Each quarter FUTA wages is calculated as cumulative year-to-date wages up to $7,000 per employee.

Self-Study Problem 9.8

a. This describes a defined contribution plan. The benefit is based on the contributions made to the plan plus any earnings.
b. This describes a defined benefit plan. The benefit is based on a formula and requires the employer to make contributions adequate to fund the benefit.
c. $0. Both contributions are below any maximum contribution thresholds and are excluded from current year gross income.
d. $10,000, all of which will be treated as ordinary income. Because the contributions were previously pre-tax, the distribution is fully taxable whether from contributions or earnings. Additionally, distributions are taxed as ordinary income regardless of the nature of the underlying earnings.
e. $50,000, lesser of 100% × $50,000 or $69,000 (annual limit for 2024)
f. $69,000, lesser of 100% × $290,000 or $69,000 (annual limit for 2024)

Self-Study Problem 9.9

a. $150,000
b. $120,000, [$150,000 − (20% × $150,000)]
c. August 30, 20XX, which is the 60th day after the day the distribution was received, unless the hardship waiver provisions apply.
d. $150,000, the full balance from the Blue Mutual Fund.

Chapter 10 Partnership Taxation

Self-Study Problem 10.1

1. False — The mere joint ownership of property does not constitute a partnership; the owners must engage in some type of business activity.
2. True — A trade or business with more than one owner has been formed as a partnership.
3. False — Although generally very useful, a written partnership agreement is not required to form a general partnership for tax purposes.
4. False — Luis will recognize $7,000 ($14,000 × his 50% interest). A cash distribution does not generally increase or decrease income recognized.
5. False — It would appear that Luis and Bheem are both general partners and both are liable for any partnership liabilities, even in excess of their investment.

Self-Study Problem 10.2

1. $0
2. $36,000 The amount of cash contributed.
3. $0
4. $17,500 The same as Linda's basis in the equipment contributed to the partnership.
5. $17,500 The same as Linda's basis in the equipment contributed.

Self-Study Problem 10.3

Refer to Form 1065, Schedule K-1, and Statement A on Pages E-103 to E-110.

Self-Study Problem 10.3

Form 1065 — U.S. Return of Partnership Income — 2024
OMB No. 1545-0123

For calendar year 2024, or tax year beginning _____, 2024, ending _____, 20 ____.

Department of the Treasury / Internal Revenue Service
Go to www.irs.gov/Form1065 for instructions and the latest information.

- **A** Principal business activity: Advertising
- **B** Principal product or service: Advertising Services
- **C** Business code number: 541800
- Name of partnership: Cahokia Partnership
- Number, street, and room or suite no.: 40 Rainy Street
- City, state, ZIP: Collinsville, IL 62234
- **D** Employer identification number: 44-4444444
- **E** Date business started: 01/01/2024
- **F** Total assets: $257,750

G Check applicable boxes: (1) ☑ Initial return
H Check accounting method: (2) ☑ Accrual
I Number of Schedules K-1: 2

Income

Line	Description	Amount
1a	Gross receipts or sales	255,600
1c	Balance	255,600
3	Gross profit	255,600
8	Total income (loss)	255,600

Deductions

Line	Description	Amount
9	Salaries and wages	148,000
10	Guaranteed payments to partners	20,000
13	Rent	12,000
14	Taxes and licenses	6,100
16a	Depreciation	9,250
16c		9,250
22	Total deductions	195,350
23	Ordinary business income (loss)	60,250

Self-Study Problem 10.3

Note: This page for illustrative purposes only. Self-Study Problem 10.3 did not require completion of this page.

Form 1065 (2024) Page **2**

Schedule B — Other Information

		Yes	No
1	What type of entity is filing this return? Check the applicable box:		
a	☑ Domestic general partnership **b** ☐ Domestic limited partnership		
c	☐ Domestic limited liability company **d** ☐ Domestic limited liability partnership		
e	☐ Foreign partnership **f** ☐ Other:		
2	At the end of the tax year:		
a	Did any foreign or domestic corporation, partnership (including any entity treated as a partnership), trust, or tax-exempt organization, or any foreign government own, directly or indirectly, an interest of 50% or more in the profit, loss, or capital of the partnership? For rules of constructive ownership, see instructions. If "Yes," attach Schedule B-1, Information on Partners Owning 50% or More of the Partnership		✓
b	Did any individual or estate own, directly or indirectly, an interest of 50% or more in the profit, loss, or capital of the partnership? For rules of constructive ownership, see instructions. If "Yes," attach Schedule B-1, Information on Partners Owning 50% or More of the Partnership	✓	
3	At the end of the tax year, did the partnership:		
a	Own directly 20% or more, or own, directly or indirectly, 50% or more, of the total voting power of all classes of stock entitled to vote of any foreign or domestic corporation? For rules of constructive ownership, see instructions. If "Yes," complete (i) through (iv) below		✓

(i) Name of corporation	(ii) Employer identification number (if any)	(iii) Country of incorporation	(iv) Percentage owned in voting stock

b	Own directly an interest of 20% or more, or own, directly or indirectly, an interest of 50% or more in the profit, loss, or capital in any foreign or domestic partnership (including an entity treated as a partnership) or in the beneficial interest of a trust? For rules of constructive ownership, see instructions. If "Yes," complete (i) through (v) below . .		✓

(i) Name of entity	(ii) Employer identification number (if any)	(iii) Type of entity	(iv) Country of organization	(v) Maximum percentage owned in profit, loss, or capital

		Yes	No
4	Does the partnership satisfy **all four** of the following conditions?		
a	The partnership's total receipts for the tax year were less than $250,000.		
b	The partnership's total assets at the end of the tax year were less than $1 million.		
c	Schedules K-1 are filed with the return and furnished to the partners on or before the due date (including extensions) for the partnership return.		
d	The partnership is not filing and is not required to file Schedule M-3		✓
	If "Yes," the partnership is not required to complete Schedules L, M-1, and M-2; item F on page 1 of Form 1065; or item L on Schedule K-1.		
5	Is this partnership a publicly traded partnership, as defined in section 469(k)(2)?		✓
6	During the tax year, did the partnership have any debt that was canceled, was forgiven, or had the terms modified so as to reduce the principal amount of the debt?		✓
7	Has this partnership filed, or is it required to file, Form 8918, Material Advisor Disclosure Statement, to provide information on any reportable transaction?		✓
8	At any time during calendar year 2024, did the partnership have an interest in or a signature or other authority over a financial account in a foreign country (such as a bank account, securities account, or other financial account)? See instructions for exceptions and filing requirements for FinCEN Form 114, Report of Foreign Bank and Financial Accounts (FBAR). If "Yes," enter the name of the foreign country		✓
9	At any time during the tax year, did the partnership receive a distribution from, or was it the grantor of, or transferor to, a foreign trust? If "Yes," the partnership may have to file Form 3520, Annual Return To Report Transactions With Foreign Trusts and Receipt of Certain Foreign Gifts. See instructions		✓
10a	Is the partnership making, or had it previously made (and not revoked), a section 754 election? If "Yes," enter the effective date of the election		✓
	See instructions for details regarding a section 754 election.		
b	For this tax year, did the partnership make an optional basis adjustment under section 743(b)? If "Yes," enter the total aggregate net positive amount $ _____ and the total aggregate net negative amount $ (_____) of such section 743(b) adjustments for all partners made in the tax year. The partnership must also attach a statement showing the computation and allocation of each basis adjustment. See instructions		✓

Form **1065** (2024)

Self-Study Problem 10.3

Note: This page for illustrative purposes only. Self-Study Problem 10.3 did not require completion of this page.

Form 1065 (2024) Page **3**

Schedule B	Other Information *(continued)*	Yes	No
c	For this tax year, did the partnership make an optional basis adjustment under section 734(b)? If "Yes," enter the total aggregate net positive amount $ _____ and the total aggregate net negative amount $ (_____) of such section 734(b) adjustments for all partnership property made in the tax year. The partnership must also attach a statement showing the computation and allocation of each basis adjustment. See instructions		✓
d	For this tax year, is the partnership required to adjust the basis of partnership property under section 743(b) or 734(b) because of a substantial built-in loss (as defined under section 743(d)) or substantial basis reduction (as defined under section 734(d))? If "Yes," enter the total aggregate amount of such section 743(b) adjustments and/or section 734(b) adjustments for all partners and/or partnership property made in the tax year $ _____. The partnership must also attach a statement showing the computation and allocation of the basis adjustment. See instructions . . .		✓
11	Check this box if, during the current or prior tax year, the partnership distributed any property received in a like-kind exchange or contributed such property to another entity (other than disregarded entities wholly owned by the partnership throughout the tax year) . . . . ☐		
12	At any time during the tax year, did the partnership distribute to any partner a tenancy-in-common or other undivided interest in partnership property?		✓
13	If the partnership is required to file Form 8858, Information Return of U.S. Persons With Respect to Foreign Disregarded Entities (FDEs) and Foreign Branches (FBs), enter the number of Forms 8858 attached. See instructions . . . . _____		
14	Does the partnership have any foreign partners? If "Yes," enter the number of Forms 8805, Foreign Partner's Information Statement of Section 1446 Withholding Tax, filed for this partnership _____		✓
15	Enter the number of Forms 8865, Return of U.S. Persons With Respect to Certain Foreign Partnerships, attached to this return . . . . _____		
16a	Did you make any payments in 2024 that would require you to file Form(s) 1099? See instructions	✓	
b	If "Yes," did you or will you file required Form(s) 1099?	✓	
17	Enter the number of Forms 5471, Information Return of U.S. Persons With Respect to Certain Foreign Corporations, attached to this return . . . . _____		
18	Enter the number of partners that are foreign governments under section 892 . . . . _____		
19	During the partnership's tax year, did the partnership make any payments that would require it to file Forms 1042 and 1042-S under chapter 3 (sections 1441 through 1464) or chapter 4 (sections 1471 through 1474)?		✓
20	Was the partnership a specified domestic entity required to file Form 8938 for the tax year? See the Instructions for Form 8938		✓
21	Is the partnership a section 721(c) partnership, as defined in Regulations section 1.721(c)-1(b)(14)? . . .		✓
22	During the tax year, did the partnership pay or accrue any interest or royalty for which one or more partners are not allowed a deduction under section 267A? See instructions . . . . If "Yes," enter the total amount of the disallowed deductions . . . . $ _____		✓
23	Did the partnership have an election under section 163(j) for any real property trade or business or any farming business in effect during the tax year? See instructions		✓
24	Does the partnership satisfy one or more of the following? See instructions		✓
a	The partnership owns a pass-through entity with current, or prior year carryover, excess business interest expense.		
b	The partnership's aggregate average annual gross receipts (determined under section 448(c)) for the 3 tax years preceding the current tax year are more than $30 million and the partnership has business interest expense.		
c	The partnership is a tax shelter (see instructions) and the partnership has business interest expense. If "Yes" to any, complete and attach Form 8990.		
25	Is the partnership attaching Form 8996 to certify as a Qualified Opportunity Fund? . . . . If "Yes," enter the amount from Form 8996, line 15 . . . . $ _____		✓
26	Enter the number of foreign partners subject to section 864(c)(8) as a result of transferring all or a portion of an interest in the partnership or of receiving a distribution from the partnership . . . . _____ Complete Schedule K-3 (Form 1065), Part XIII, for each foreign partner subject to section 864(c)(8) on a transfer or distribution.		
27	At any time during the tax year, were there any transfers between the partnership and its partners subject to the disclosure requirements of Regulations section 1.707-8?		✓
28	Since December 22, 2017, did a foreign corporation directly or indirectly acquire substantially all of the properties constituting a trade or business of your partnership, and was the ownership percentage (by vote or value) for purposes of section 7874 greater than 50% (for example, the partners held more than 50% of the stock of the foreign corporation)? If "Yes," list the ownership percentage by vote and by value. See instructions. Percentage: By vote: _____ By value: _____		✓
29	Is the partnership required to file Form 7208, Excise Tax on Repurchase of Corporate Stock (see instructions):		
a	Under the applicable foreign corporation rules?		✓

Form **1065** (2024)

Self-Study Problem 10.3

Note: This page for illustrative purposes only. Self-Study Problem 10.3 did not require completion of this page.

Form 1065 (2024) Page **4**

Schedule B	Other Information *(continued)*	Yes	No
b	Under the covered surrogate foreign corporation rules?		✓
	If "Yes" to either (a) or (b), complete Form 7208. See the Instructions for Form 7208.		
30	At any time during this tax year, did the partnership (a) receive (as a reward, award, or payment for property or services); or (b) sell, exchange, or otherwise dispose of a digital asset (or financial interest in a digital asset)? See instructions		✓
31	Reserved for future use		
32	Check this box if an election out of subchapter K under section 761 is being made. See instructions ☐		
33	Is the partnership electing out of the centralized partnership audit regime under section 6221(b)? See instructions		✓
	If "Yes," the partnership must complete Schedule B-2 (Form 1065). Enter the total from Schedule B-2, Part III, line 3		
	If "No," complete Designation of Partnership Representative below.		

Designation of Partnership Representative (see instructions)
Enter below the information for the partnership representative (PR) for the tax year covered by this return.

Name of PR	Sapat Illiniwek		
U.S. address of PR	123 Main Street Collinsville, IL 62269	U.S. phone number of PR	618-555-1212

If the PR is an entity, name of the designated individual for the PR

U.S. address of designated individual		U.S. phone number of designated individual	

Form **1065** (2024)

Self-Study Problem 10.3

Form 1065 (2024) — Page 5

Schedule K — Partners' Distributive Share Items

Line	Description		Total amount
Income (Loss)			
1	Ordinary business income (loss) (page 1, line 23)	1	60,250
2	Net rental real estate income (loss) (attach Form 8825)	2	
3a	Other gross rental income (loss)	3a	
b	Expenses from other rental activities (attach statement)	3b	
c	Other net rental income (loss). Subtract line 3b from line 3a	3c	
4	Guaranteed payments: **a** Services 20,000 **b** Capital		
c	Total. Add lines 4a and 4b	4c	20,000
5	Interest income	5	
6	Dividends and dividend equivalents: **a** Ordinary dividends	6a	
b	Qualified dividends **c** Dividend equivalents		
7	Royalties	7	
8	Net short-term capital gain (loss) (attach Schedule D (Form 1065))	8	
9a	Net long-term capital gain (loss) (attach Schedule D (Form 1065))	9a	
b	Collectibles (28%) gain (loss)		
c	Unrecaptured section 1250 gain (attach statement)		
10	Net section 1231 gain (loss) (attach Form 4797)	10	
11	Other income (loss) (see instructions) Type:	11	
Deductions			
12	Section 179 deduction (attach Form 4562)	12	
13a	Cash contributions	13a	1,500
b	Noncash contributions	13b	
c	Investment interest expense	13c	
d	Section 59(e)(2) expenditures: (1) Type: (2) Amount:	13d(2)	
e	Other deductions (see instructions) Type:	13e	
Self-Employment			
14a	Net earnings (loss) from self-employment	14a	80,250 (a)
b	Gross farming or fishing income	14b	
c	Gross nonfarm income	14c	
Credits			
15a	Low-income housing credit (section 42(j)(5))	15a	
b	Low-income housing credit (other)	15b	
c	Qualified rehabilitation expenditures (rental real estate) (attach Form 3468, if applicable)	15c	
d	Other rental real estate credits (see instructions) Type:	15d	
e	Other rental credits (see instructions) Type:	15e	
f	Other credits (see instructions) Type:	15f	
International			
16	Attach Schedule K-2 (Form 1065), Partners' Distributive Share Items—International, and check this box to indicate that you are reporting items of international tax relevance		
Alternative Minimum Tax (AMT) Items			
17a	Post-1986 depreciation adjustment	17a	
b	Adjusted gain or loss	17b	
c	Depletion (other than oil and gas)	17c	
d	Oil, gas, and geothermal properties—gross income	17d	
e	Oil, gas, and geothermal properties—deductions	17e	
f	Other AMT items (attach statement)	17f	
Other Information			
18a	Tax-exempt interest income	18a	
b	Other tax-exempt income	18b	
c	Nondeductible expenses	18c	
19a	Distributions of cash and marketable securities	19a	50,000
b	Distributions of other property	19b	
20a	Investment income	20a	
b	Investment expenses	20b	
c	Other items and amounts (attach statement)		
21	Total foreign taxes paid or accrued	21	

(a) Ordinary business income ($60,250) plus guaranteed payments ($20,000).

Self-Study Problem 10.3

Form 1065 (2024)   Page **6**

Analysis of Net Income (Loss) per Return

1	Net income (loss). Combine Schedule K, lines 1 through 11. From the result, subtract the sum of Schedule K, lines 12 through 13e, and 21 . . . . **1**					78,750
2	Analysis by partner type:	**(i)** Corporate	**(ii)** Individual (active)	**(iii)** Individual (passive)	**(iv)** Partnership	**(v)** Exempt organization	**(vi)** Nominee/Other
a	General partners		78,750				
b	Limited partners						

Schedule L — Balance Sheets per Books

		Beginning of tax year		End of tax year	
	Assets	(a)	(b)	(c)	(d)
1	Cash		Initial Return		27,000
2a	Trade notes and accounts receivable			10,000	
b	Less allowance for bad debts				10,000
3	Inventories				
4	U.S. Government obligations				
5	Tax-exempt securities				
6	Other current assets (attach statement) . . .				
7a	Loans to partners (or persons related to partners)				
b	Mortgage and real estate loans				
8	Other investments (attach statement)				
9a	Buildings and other depreciable assets . . .			115,000	
b	Less accumulated depreciation			9,250	105,750
10a	Depletable assets				
b	Less accumulated depletion				
11	Land (net of any amortization)				115,000
12a	Intangible assets (amortizable only)				
b	Less accumulated amortization				
13	Other assets (attach statement)				
14	Total assets				257,750
	Liabilities and Capital				
15	Accounts payable				29,750
16	Mortgages, notes, bonds payable in less than 1 year				
17	Other current liabilities (attach statement) . .				
18	All nonrecourse loans				
19a	Loans from partners (or persons related to partners)				
b	Mortgages, notes, bonds payable in 1 year or more .				187,750
20	Other liabilities (attach statement)				
21	Partners' capital accounts				40,250
22	Total liabilities and capital				257,750

Schedule M-1 — Reconciliation of Income (Loss) per Books With Analysis of Net Income (Loss) per Return

Note: The partnership may be required to file Schedule M-3. See instructions.

1	Net income (loss) per books	58,750	6	Income recorded on books this year not included on Schedule K, lines 1 through 11 (itemize):		
2	Income included on Schedule K, lines 1, 2, 3c, 5, 6a, 7, 8, 9a, 10, and 11, not recorded on books this year (itemize):		a	Tax-exempt interest $ _____		
3	Guaranteed payments (other than health insurance)	20,000	7	Deductions included on Schedule K, lines 1 through 13e, and 21, not charged against book income this year (itemize):		
4	Expenses recorded on books this year not included on Schedule K, lines 1 through 13e, and 21 (itemize):		a	Depreciation $ _____		
a	Depreciation $ _____		8	Add lines 6 and 7		
b	Travel and entertainment $ _____		9	Income (loss) (Analysis of Net Income (Loss) per Return, line 1). Subtract line 8 from line 5		78,750
5	Add lines 1 through 4	78,750				

Schedule M-2 — Analysis of Partners' Capital Accounts

1	Balance at beginning of year . . .	0	6	Distributions: **a** Cash		50,000
2	Capital contributed: **a** Cash . . .	31,500		**b** Property . . .		
	b Property . .		7	Other decreases (itemize): _____		
3	Net income (loss) (see instructions) .	78,750		Guaranteed payments		20,000
4	Other increases (itemize): _____		8	Add lines 6 and 7		70,000
5	Add lines 1 through 4	110,250	9	Balance at end of year. Subtract line 8 from line 5		40,250

Form **1065** (2024)

Self-Study Problem 10.3

Schedule K-1 (Form 1065) 2024

OMB No. 1545-0123

☐ Final K-1   ☐ Amended K-1   651123

For calendar year 2024, or tax year beginning __/__/2024 ending __/__/__

Partner's Share of Income, Deductions, Credits, etc. See separate instructions.

Part I — Information About the Partnership

- **A** Partnership's employer identification number: 44-4444444
- **B** Partnership's name, address, city, state, and ZIP code:
  Cahokia Partnership
  40 Rainy Street, Collinsville, IL 62234
- **C** IRS center where partnership filed return: e-file
- **D** ☐ Check if this is a publicly traded partnership (PTP)

Part II — Information About the Partner

- **E** Partner's SSN or TIN: 444-14-1414
- **F** Name, address, city, state, and ZIP code for partner entered in E:
  Sapat Illiniwek
- **G** ☒ General partner or LLC member-manager   ☐ Limited partner or other LLC member
- **H1** ☒ Domestic partner   ☐ Foreign partner
- **H2** ☐ If the partner is a disregarded entity (DE), enter the partner's: TIN __ Name __
- **I1** What type of entity is this partner? Individual
- **I2** ☐ If this partner is a retirement plan (IRA/SEP/Keogh/etc.), check here
- **J** Partner's share of profit, loss, and capital (see instructions):

	Beginning	Ending
Profit	%	50 %
Loss	%	50 %
Capital	%	50 %

Check if decrease is due to: ☐ Sale or ☐ Exchange of partnership interest.

- **K1** Partner's share of liabilities:

	Beginning	Ending
Nonrecourse	$	$
Qualified nonrecourse financing	$	$
Recourse	$	$ 108,750

- **K2** ☐ Check this box if item K1 includes liability amounts from lower-tier partnerships
- **K3** ☐ Check if any of the above liability is subject to guarantees or other payment obligations by the partner.

L — Partner's Capital Account Analysis

Beginning capital account	$ 0
Capital contributed during the year	$ 15,750
Current year net income (loss)	$ 29,375
Other increase (decrease) (attach explanation)	$
Withdrawals and distributions	$(25,000)
Ending capital account	$ 20,125

- **M** Did the partner contribute property with a built-in gain (loss)? ☐ Yes ☒ No
- **N** Partner's Share of Net Unrecognized Section 704(c) Gain or (Loss):
  Beginning $ __   Ending $ __

Part III — Partner's Share of Current Year Income, Deductions, Credits, and Other Items

Line	Description	Amount
1	Ordinary business income (loss)	30,125
2	Net rental real estate income (loss)	
3	Other net rental income (loss)	
4a	Guaranteed payments for services	20,000
4b	Guaranteed payments for capital	
4c	Total guaranteed payments	20,000
5	Interest income	
6a	Ordinary dividends	
6b	Qualified dividends	
6c	Dividend equivalents	
7	Royalties	
8	Net short-term capital gain (loss)	
9a	Net long-term capital gain (loss)	
9b	Collectibles (28%) gain (loss)	
9c	Unrecaptured section 1250 gain	
10	Net section 1231 gain (loss)	
11	Other income (loss)	
12	Section 179 deduction	
13	Other deductions — A	750
14	Self-employment earnings (loss) — A	50,125
15	Credits	
16	Schedule K-3 is attached if checked ☐	
17	Alternative minimum tax (AMT) items	
18	Tax-exempt income and nondeductible expenses	
19	Distributions — A	25,000
20	Other information — Z See statement; AJ Refer to note below	
21	Foreign taxes paid or accrued	

- **22** ☐ More than one activity for at-risk purposes*
- **23** ☐ More than one activity for passive activity purposes*

*See attached statement for additional information.

Line 20, Code AJ is used for disclosure of gross income and gross deductions from a business activity for purposes of the overall business loss limitation (Chapter 4). Gross income is $127,800 ($255,600 × 50%) and gross deductions are $97,675 ($195,350 × 50%).

Self-Study Problem 10.3

Statement A—QBI Pass-Through Entity Reporting

Partnership's name: Cahokia Partnership		Partnership's EIN: 44-4444444	
Partner's name: Sapat Illiniwek		Partner's identifying number: 444-14-1414	

Partner's share of:		Trade or Business 1	Trade or Business 2	Trade or Business 3
		☐ PTP ☐ Aggregated ☒ SSTB	☐ PTP ☐ Aggregated ☐ SSTB	☐ PTP ☐ Aggregated ☐ SSTB
QBI or qualified PTP items subject to partner-specific determinations:				
	Ordinary business income (loss)	30,125		
	Rental income (loss)			
	Royalty income (loss)			
	Section 1231 gain (loss)			
	Other income (loss)			
	Section 179 deduction			
	Other deductions			
W-2 wages		74,000		
UBIA of qualified property		57,500		
Qualified REIT dividends				

Note: The 2024 Statement A was not available when this text went to print. This is a 2023 version of Statement A.

Self-Study Problem 10.4

a. Year 1: Jiang and Jackson both recognize ordinary business income of $3,000. The tax-exempt income and nondeductible expenses do not affect taxable income (although the tax-exempt income will be reported by each partner). Each partner has a basis of $13,100 calculated as follows:

Beginning balance	$10,000
Income allocated	3,000
Tax-exempt income allocated	150
Nondeductible expenses	(50)
Ending balance	$13,100

b. Year 2: Each partner has an outside basis of $0 at year end:

Beginning balance	$13,100
Cash distribution	(7,100)
Basis prior to loss	6,000
Loss allocated and deducted	(6,000)
Ending balance	$ 0

A loss of $10,000 is allocated to each partner; however, the deductible loss amount is limited to basis of $6,000. Each partner has a suspended loss of $4,000. Jiang will also report income of $2,000 from guaranteed payments. Note that guaranteed payments do not directly affect outside basis.

c. Year 3: Each partner has an outside basis of $0 at year end:

Beginning balance	$ 0
Income allocated	2,000
LT capital gain allocated	500
Basis prior to loss	2,500
Suspended loss deducted	(2,500)
Ending balance	$ 0

Both partners will be able to deduct $2,500 of the $4,000 loss suspended in the previous year and will have remaining suspended losses of $1,500. Jiang will also report income of $2,000 from guaranteed payments.

Self-Study Problem 10.5

12 months × $1,000 per month guaranteed payment	$12,000
Add: Robert's distributive share of income	21,000
Total income	$33,000

The $1,500 per month received in November and December of 2024 will be reported on Robert's 2025 income tax return. The guaranteed payments received are reported for the partnership tax year that ends with or within the partner's tax year, in the same manner as a distributive share of the partnership income.

Self-Study Problem 10.6

1. Maxwell has a $5,000 realized loss ($70,000 − $75,000), but the loss is not recognized since he is a more-than-50 percent partner, 50 percent directly and 50 percent indirectly with his daughter.

   Note: *if the partnership later sells the property at a gain, the partnership may be able to offset some or all of the $5,000 disallowed loss against the gain.*

2. The daughter has a $15,000 gain ($40,000 − $25,000). Since she is a more-than-50 percent partner (50 percent directly and 50 percent indirectly), and the car is not a capital asset to the partnership, the gain is ordinary income. If the car was a capital asset to the partnership, the gain would still be considered ordinary since Pam is a more-than-50 percent partner.

Self-Study Problem 10.7

a. Marla's QBI deduction with no limitation is $200,000 × 20% = $40,000. The guaranteed payments and the capital gains are not part of QBI income. Because Marla's income exceeds the phase-out range for taxable income (starts at $191,950 and is completely phased out by $241,950 in 2024), the W-2 wage limitation applies.

   W-2 wages allocated to Marla are $46,000 ($230,000 × 20% interest). Qualified property allocated to Marla is $240,000 ($1,200,000 × 20%). The limit is the greater of:
   i. $46,000 × 50% = $23,000
   ii. ($46,000 × 25%) + ($240,000 × 2.5%) = $17,500

   The W-2 wages limit of $23,000 is less than $40,000; thus, the QBI deduction is $23,000 (note that the taxable income limit of $155,200 ($776,000 × 20%) exceeds the QBI deduction).

b. $0. If Salem is a service business, because Marla's income exceeds the phase-out range for taxable income (starts at $191,950 and completely phased out by $241,950 in 2024), she is ineligible for a QBI deduction.

Self-Study Problem 10.8

1. $45,000, his amount at risk in the activity.
2.
Profit	$ 31,000
Less: carryover of disallowed loss from the prior year ($60,000 − $45,000)	(15,000)
Taxable income for next year	$ 16,000

Self-Study Problem 10.9

1. False — An election must be made to be treated like a corporation for tax purposes.
2. False — LLCs are not required to have a general partner. Also, the owners of LLCs are members, not partners.
3. True
4. True
5. False — Debt of an LLC is generally treated as nonrecourse debt due to the limited liability of the LLC members.

Chapter 11 The Corporate Income Tax

Self-Study Problem 11.1

$335,000 × 21% = $70,350

Self-Study Problem 11.2

a. $110,000 × 21% = $23,100
Neither of the capital losses may be used to offset current year ordinary income. The capital losses may be carried back 3 years and forward 5 years to offset capital gains, if any, recognized during those years.

b. The 2022 loss of $40,000 can be used to offset a maximum of $28,800 of 2023 income (80 percent × $36,000). The remaining 2022 NOL of $11,200 is carried forward into 2024 and can be used to offset $8,000 ($10,000 × 80%) of the 2024 income. The remaining $3,200 NOL is carried forward to 2025.

Self-Study Problem 11.3

a. The dividends received deduction is equal to the lesser of $45,500 = 65% × $70,000; or $39,000 = 65% × $60,000 ($90,000 + $70,000 − $100,000). $39,000 is the amount of the deduction.

b. Organization costs of $5,222.22 can be deducted in 2024. Boyce is eligible to expense $5,000 organization costs. The balance of $8,000 ($13,000 − $5,000) is amortized over 180 months for 5 months of 2024 for a deduction of $222.22 ($8,000 ÷ 180 × 5 months). In 2025, Boyce will deduct $533.33 ($8,000 ÷ 180 × 12 months).

Start-up costs exceed $50,000, thus, Boyce is not eligible to deduct the entire $5,000 of start-up costs. The $5,000 is reduced by $2,000 (the start-up costs in excess of $50,000) to $3,000. The remaining balance of $49,000 ($52,000 − $3,000) is amortized over 180 months × 5 months in 2024 or $1,361.11 for a total 2024 deduction of $4,361.11. In 2025, Boyce will deduct $3,266.67 ($49,000 ÷ 180 × 12 months).

c. Gant's modified taxable income for purposes of the charitable contribution deduction limit of 10% is $95,000 ($65,000 + $5,000 + $25,000). Thus the charitable contribution limit and deductible amount is $9,500 ($95,000 × 10%). The remaining nondeductible charitable contribution of $15,500 can be carried forward for up to 5 years.

Self-Study Problem 11.4

Schedule M-1 Reconciliation of Income (Loss) per Books With Income per Return

Note: The corporation may be required to file Schedule M-3. See instructions.

1	Net income (loss) per books	115,600	7	Income recorded on books this year not included on this return (itemize):	
2	Federal income tax per books	29,400		Tax-exempt interest $ 4,700	
3	Excess of capital losses over capital gains	9,100			
4	Income subject to tax not recorded on books this year (itemize):				4,700
			8	Deductions on this return not charged against book income this year (itemize):	
5	Expenses recorded on books this year not deducted on this return (itemize):		a	Depreciation $ 4,000	
a	Depreciation $		b	Charitable contributions $	
b	Charitable contributions $				
c	Travel and entertainment $				4,000
			9	Add lines 7 and 8	8,700
6	Add lines 1 through 5	154,100	10	Income (page 1, line 28)—line 6 less line 9	145,400

Self-Study Problem 11.5

1.

Quarter	YTD Estimate	Annuali-zation Factor	Annualized	Tax Rate	Annual Taxes	Portion Due	Estimated Amount
Q1	$225,000	4	$900,000	21%	$189,000	25%	$47,250
Q2	225,000	4	900,000	21%	189,000	50%	94,500
Q3	475,000	2	950,000	21%	199,500	75%	149,625
Q4	660,000	12/9	880,000	21%	184,800	100%	184,800

Since taxable income in one of the three preceding years exceeds $1 million, Alberta is considered a large corporation and thus, may use the prior year liability only during the first quarter.

Q1: $42,750. Prior year liability was $194,250 × 25% = $48,562.50 which is greater than the estimated Q1 payment above; thus, Alberta's Q1 payment will be $42,750 ($47,250 less prior year overpayment applied of $4,500)
Q2: $47,250 ($94,500 less amounts previously paid of $42,750 + $4,500)
Q3: $55,125 ($149,625 less amounts previously paid of $94,500)
Q4: $35,175 ($184,800 less amounts previously paid of $149,625)

2. Refer to Form 1120 on Pages E-115 to E-120. The calculation of tax for Aspen Corporation is as follows: 21% × $14,000 = $2,940. Net income per the books is equal to $16,060 ($19,000 net income before income tax expense − $2,940 income tax expense).

Self-Study Problem 11.6

Refer to Form 1120-S, Schedule K-1, and Statement A on Pages E-121 to E-127.

Self-Study Problem 11.7

a. Tammy's realized gain is $125,000 + $34,000 − $75,000 = $84,000.
b. Tammy's recognized gain is $0.
c. Tammy's basis in her stock is $75,000 − $0 + $0 − $34,000 = $41,000.
d. The corporation's basis in the real estate is $75,000 + $0 = $75,000.

Self-Study Problem 11.8

Only $190,000 ($340,000 − $150,000) is subject to the accumulated earnings tax.
20% × $190,000 = $38,000

Self-Study Problem 11.5

Form 1120 — U.S. Corporation Income Tax Return
Department of the Treasury / Internal Revenue Service
For calendar year 2024 or tax year beginning _____, 2024, ending _____, 20 ___
OMB No. 1545-0123
2024

A Check if:
1a Consolidated return (attach Form 851) ☐
b Life/nonlife consolidated return ☐
2 Personal holding co. (attach Sch. PH) ☐
3 Personal service corp. (see instructions) ☐
4 Schedule M-3 attached ☐

Name: Aspen Corporation
Number, street, and room or suite no.: 470 Rio Grande Place
City or town, state, ZIP: Aspen, CO 81611

B Employer identification number: 92-2222222
C Date incorporated: 01/01/2024
D Total assets: $183,000

E Check if: (1) ☑ Initial return (2) ☐ Final return (3) ☐ Name change (4) ☐ Address change

Income

Line	Description	Amount
1a	Gross receipts or sales	285,000
1b	Returns and allowances	
1c	Balance. Subtract line 1b from line 1a	285,000
2	Cost of goods sold (attach Form 1125-A)	80,000
3	Gross profit. Subtract line 2 from line 1c	205,000
4	Dividends and inclusions (Schedule C, line 23)	10,000
5	Interest	
6	Gross rents	
7	Gross royalties	
8	Capital gain net income (attach Schedule D (Form 1120))	
9	Net gain or (loss) from Form 4797, Part II, line 17 (attach Form 4797)	
10	Other income (see instructions—attach statement)	
11	**Total income.** Add lines 3 through 10	215,000

Deductions

Line	Description	Amount
12	Compensation of officers (see instructions—attach Form 1125-E)	90,000
13	Salaries and wages (less employment credits)	82,000
14	Repairs and maintenance	8,000
15	Bad debts	
16	Rents	
17	Taxes and licenses	11,000
18	Interest (see instructions)	
19	Charitable contributions	
20	Depreciation from Form 4562 not claimed on Form 1125-A or elsewhere on return (attach Form 4562)	5,000
21	Depletion	
22	Advertising	
23	Pension, profit-sharing, etc., plans	
24	Employee benefit programs	
25	Energy efficient commercial buildings deduction (attach Form 7205)	
26	Other deductions (attach statement)	
27	**Total deductions.** Add lines 12 through 26	196,000
28	Taxable income before net operating loss deduction and special deductions. Subtract line 27 from line 11	19,000
29a	Net operating loss deduction (see instructions)	
29b	Special deductions (Schedule C, line 24)	5,000
29c	Add lines 29a and 29b	5,000

Tax, Refundable Credits, and Payments

Line	Description	Amount
30	**Taxable income.** Subtract line 29c from line 28. See instructions	14,000
31	Total tax (Schedule J, line 12)	2,940
32	Reserved for future use	
33	Total payments and credits (Schedule J, line 23)	3,000
34	Estimated tax penalty. See instructions. Check if Form 2220 is attached ☐	
35	Amount owed. If line 33 is smaller than the total of lines 31 and 34, enter amount owed	
36	Overpayment. If line 33 is larger than the total of lines 31 and 34, enter amount overpaid	60
37	Enter amount from line 36 you want: Credited to 2025 estimated tax 60 / Refunded	

For Paperwork Reduction Act Notice, see separate instructions. Cat. No. 11450Q Form **1120** (2024)

Self-Study Problem 11.5

Form 1120 (2024)   Page **2**

Schedule C	Dividends, Inclusions, and Special Deductions (see instructions)	(a) Dividends and inclusions	(b) %	(c) Special deductions (a) × (b)
1	Dividends from less-than-20%-owned domestic corporations (other than debt-financed stock)	10,000	50	5,000
2	Dividends from 20%-or-more-owned domestic corporations (other than debt-financed stock)		65	
3	Dividends on certain debt-financed stock of domestic and foreign corporations		See instructions	
4	Dividends on certain preferred stock of less-than-20%-owned public utilities		23.3	
5	Dividends on certain preferred stock of 20%-or-more-owned public utilities		26.7	
6	Dividends from less-than-20%-owned foreign corporations and certain FSCs		50	
7	Dividends from 20%-or-more-owned foreign corporations and certain FSCs		65	
8	Dividends from wholly owned foreign subsidiaries		100	
9	**Subtotal.** Add lines 1 through 8. See instructions for limitations	10,000	See instructions	5,000
10	Dividends from domestic corporations received by a small business investment company operating under the Small Business Investment Act of 1958		100	
11	Dividends from affiliated group members		100	
12	Dividends from certain FSCs		100	
13	Foreign-source portion of dividends received from a specified 10%-owned foreign corporation (excluding hybrid dividends) (see instructions)		100	
14	Dividends from foreign corporations not included on line 3, 6, 7, 8, 11, 12, or 13 (including any hybrid dividends)			
15	Reserved for future use			
16a	Subpart F inclusions derived from the sale by a controlled foreign corporation (CFC) of the stock of a lower-tier foreign corporation treated as a dividend (attach Form(s) 5471) (see instructions)		100	
b	Subpart F inclusions derived from hybrid dividends of tiered corporations (attach Form(s) 5471) (see instructions)			
c	Other inclusions from CFCs under subpart F not included on line 16a, 16b, or 17 (attach Form(s) 5471) (see instructions)			
17	Global Intangible Low-Taxed Income (GILTI) (attach Form(s) 5471 and Form 8992)			
18	Gross-up for foreign taxes deemed paid			
19	IC-DISC and former DISC dividends not included on line 1, 2, or 3			
20	Other dividends			
21	Deduction for dividends paid on certain preferred stock of public utilities			
22	Section 250 deduction (attach Form 8993)			
23	**Total dividends and inclusions.** Add column (a), lines 9 through 20. Enter here and on page 1, line 4	10,000		
24	**Total special deductions.** Add column (c), lines 9 through 22. Enter here and on page 1, line 29b			5,000

Form **1120** (2024)

Self-Study Problem 11.5

Form 1120 (2024) Page **3**

Schedule J — Tax Computation and Payment (see instructions)

1a	Income tax (see instructions)	**1a**	2,940
b	Tax from Form 1120-L (see instructions)	**1b**	
c	Section 1291 tax from Form 8621	**1c**	
d	Tax adjustment from Form 8978	**1d**	
e	Additional tax under section 197(f)	**1e**	
f	Base erosion minimum tax from Form 8991	**1f**	
g	Amount from Form 4255, Part I, line 3, column (q)	**1g**	
z	Other chapter 1 tax	**1z**	
2	Total income tax. Add lines 1a through 1z	**2**	2,940
3	Corporate alternative minimum tax from Form 4626, Part II, line 13 (attach Form 4626)	**3**	
4	Add lines 2 and 3	**4**	2,940
5a	Foreign tax credit (attach Form 1118)	**5a**	
b	Credit from Form 8834 (see instructions)	**5b**	
c	General business credit (see instructions—attach Form 3800)	**5c**	
d	Credit for prior year minimum tax (attach Form 8827)	**5d**	
e	Bond credits from Form 8912	**5e**	
f	Adjustment from Form 8978	**5f**	
6	**Total credits.** Add lines 5a through 5f	**6**	
7	Subtract line 6 from line 4	**7**	2,940
8	Personal holding company tax (attach Schedule PH (Form 1120))	**8**	
9a	Amount from Form 4255, Part I, line 3, column (r)	**9a**	
b	Recapture of low-income housing credit (attach Form 8611)	**9b**	
c	Completed long-term contract look-back interest due (attach Form 8697)	**9c**	
d	Interest due under the look-back method—income forecast method (attach Form 8866)	**9d**	
e	Alternative tax on qualifying shipping activities (attach Form 8902)	**9e**	
f	Interest/tax due under section 453A(c)	**9f**	
g	Interest/tax due under section 453(l)	**9g**	
z	Other (see instructions—attach statement)	**9z**	
10	**Total.** Add lines 9a through 9z	**10**	
11a	Total tax before deferred taxes. Add lines 7, 8, and 10	**11a**	2,940
b	Deferred tax on the corporation's share of undistributed earnings of a qualified electing fund	**11b**	
c	Deferred LIFO recapture tax (section 1363(d))	**11c**	
12	Total tax. Subtract the sum of lines 11b and 11c from 11a. Enter here and on page 1, line 31	**12**	2,940
13	Preceding year's overpayment credited to the current year	**13**	
14	Current year's estimated tax payments	**14**	3,000
15	Current year's refund applied for on Form 4466	**15**	( )
16	Reserved for future use	**16**	
17	Tax deposited with Form 7004	**17**	
18	Withholding (see instructions)	**18**	
19	**Total payments.** Combine lines 13 through 18	**19**	3,000
20	Refundable credits from:		
a	Form 2439	**20a**	
b	Form 4136	**20b**	
c	Credit for tax withheld under Chapter 3 or 4 from Form 1042-S, Form 8805, or Form 8288 (attach the applicable form)	**20c**	
z	Other (attach statement—see instructions)	**20z**	
21	**Total credits.** Add lines 20a through 20z	**21**	
22	Elective payment election amount from Form 3800	**22**	
23	**Total payments and credits.** Add lines 19, 21, and 22. Enter here and on page 1, line 33	**23**	3,000

Form **1120** (2024)

Self-Study Problem 11.5

Form 1120 (2024)   Page **4**

Schedule K   Other Information (see instructions)

		Yes	No
1	Check accounting method: **a** ☐ Cash **b** ☑ Accrual **c** ☐ Other (specify) _____		
2	See the instructions and enter the:		
a	Business activity code no. 459110		
b	Business activity _Sporting goods retailer_		
c	Product or service _Ski and snowboard retailer_		
3	Is the corporation a subsidiary in an affiliated group or a parent–subsidiary controlled group?		✓
	If "Yes," enter name and EIN of the parent corporation		
4	At the end of the tax year:		
a	Did any foreign or domestic corporation, partnership (including any entity treated as a partnership), trust, or tax-exempt organization own directly 20% or more, or own, directly or indirectly, 50% or more of the total voting power of all classes of the corporation's stock entitled to vote? If "Yes," complete Part I of Schedule G (Form 1120) (attach Schedule G)		✓
b	Did any individual or estate own directly 20% or more, or own, directly or indirectly, 50% or more of the total voting power of all classes of the corporation's stock entitled to vote? If "Yes," complete Part II of Schedule G (Form 1120) (attach Schedule G)		✓
5	At the end of the tax year, did the corporation:		
a	Own directly 20% or more, or own, directly or indirectly, 50% or more of the total voting power of all classes of stock entitled to vote of any foreign or domestic corporation not included on **Form 851**, Affiliations Schedule? For rules of constructive ownership, see instructions. If "Yes," complete (i) through (iv) below.		✓

(i) Name of Corporation	(ii) Employer Identification Number (if any)	(iii) Country of Incorporation	(iv) Percentage Owned in Voting Stock

		Yes	No
b	Own directly an interest of 20% or more, or own, directly or indirectly, an interest of 50% or more in any foreign or domestic partnership (including an entity treated as a partnership) or in the beneficial interest of a trust? For rules of constructive ownership, see instructions. If "Yes," complete (i) through (iv) below.		✓

(i) Name of Entity	(ii) Employer Identification Number (if any)	(iii) Country of Organization	(iv) Maximum Percentage Owned in Profit, Loss, or Capital

		Yes	No
6	During this tax year, did the corporation pay dividends (other than stock dividends and distributions in exchange for stock) in excess of the corporation's current and accumulated earnings and profits? See sections 301 and 316. If "Yes," file **Form 5452**, Corporate Report of Nondividend Distributions. See the instructions for Form 5452. If this is a consolidated return, answer here for the parent corporation and on Form 851 for each subsidiary.		✓
7	At any time during this tax year, did one foreign person own, directly or indirectly, at least 25% of the total voting power of all classes of the corporation's stock entitled to vote or at least 25% of the total value of all classes of the corporation's stock? For rules of attribution, see section 318. If "Yes," enter: **(a)** Percentage owned _____ and **(b)** Owner's country _____ **(c)** The corporation may have to file **Form 5472**, Information Return of a 25% Foreign-Owned U.S. Corporation or a Foreign Corporation Engaged in a U.S. Trade or Business. Enter the number of Forms 5472 attached _____		✓
8	Check this box if the corporation issued publicly offered debt instruments with original issue discount . . . . ☐ If checked, the corporation may have to file **Form 8281**, Information Return for Publicly Offered Original Issue Discount Instruments.		
9	Enter the amount of tax-exempt interest received or accrued during this tax year $ _____		
10	Enter the number of shareholders at the end of the tax year (if 100 or fewer) _____		
11	If the corporation has an NOL for the tax year and is electing to forego the carryback period, check here (see instructions) . ☐ If the corporation is filing a consolidated return, the statement required by Regulations section 1.1502-21(b)(3) must be attached or the election will not be valid.		
12	Enter the available NOL carryover from prior tax years (do not reduce it by any deduction reported on page 1, line 29a) $ _____		

Form **1120** (2024)

Self-Study Problem 11.5

Form 1120 (2024) Page **5**

Schedule K Other Information *(continued from page 4)*

		Yes	No
13	Are the corporation's total receipts (page 1, line 1a, plus lines 4 through 10) for the tax year **and** its total assets at the end of the tax year less than $250,000?		✓
	If "Yes," the corporation is not required to complete Schedules L, M-1, and M-2. Instead, enter the total amount of cash distributions and the book value of property distributions (other than cash) made during this tax year $ _____		
14	Is the corporation required to file Schedule UTP (Form 1120), Uncertain Tax Position Statement? See instructions		✓
	If "Yes," complete and attach Schedule UTP.		
15a	Did the corporation make any payments that would require it to file Form(s) 1099?	✓	
b	If "Yes," did or will the corporation file required Form(s) 1099?	✓	
16	During this tax year, did the corporation have an 80%-or-more change in ownership, including a change due to redemption of its own stock?		✓
17	During or subsequent to this tax year, but before the filing of this return, did the corporation dispose of more than 65% (by value) of its assets in a taxable, non-taxable, or tax deferred transaction?		✓
18	Did this corporation receive assets in a section 351 transfer in which any of the transferred assets had a fair market basis or fair market value of more than $1 million?		✓
19	During this corporation's tax year, did the corporation make any payments that would require it to file Forms 1042 and 1042-S under chapter 3 (sections 1441 through 1464) or chapter 4 (sections 1471 through 1474) of the Code?		✓
20	Is the corporation operating on a cooperative basis?		✓
21	During this tax year, did the corporation pay or accrue any interest or royalty for which the deduction is not allowed under section 267A? See instructions		✓
	If "Yes," enter the total amount of the disallowed deductions $ _____		
22	Does this corporation have gross receipts of at least $500 million in any of the 3 preceding tax years? (See sections 59A(e)(2) and (3).)		✓
	If "Yes," complete and attach Form 8991.		
23	Did the corporation have an election under section 163(j) for any real property trade or business or any farming business in effect during this tax year? See instructions		✓
24	Does the corporation satisfy one or more of the following? If "Yes," complete and attach Form 8990. See instructions		✓
a	The corporation owns a pass-through entity with current, or prior year carryover, excess business interest expense.		
b	The corporation's aggregate average annual gross receipts (determined under section 448(c)) for the 3 tax years preceding the current tax year are more than $30 million and the corporation has business interest expense.		
c	The corporation is a tax shelter and the corporation has business interest expense.		
25	Is the corporation attaching Form 8996 to certify as a Qualified Opportunity Fund?		✓
	If "Yes," enter amount from Form 8996, line 15 . . . . $ _____		
26	Since December 22, 2017, did a foreign corporation directly or indirectly acquire substantially all of the properties held directly or indirectly by the corporation, and was the ownership percentage (by vote or value) for purposes of section 7874 greater than 50% (for example, the shareholders held more than 50% of the stock of the foreign corporation)? If "Yes," list the ownership percentage by vote and by value. See instructions		✓
	Percentage: By Vote _____ By Value _____		
27	At any time during this tax year, did the corporation (a) receive a digital asset (as a reward, award, or payment for property or services); or (b) sell, exchange, or otherwise dispose of a digital asset (or a financial interest in a digital asset)? See instructions		✓
28	Is the corporation a member of a controlled group?		✓
	If "Yes," attach Schedule O (Form 1120). See instructions.		
29	Corporate Alternative Minimum Tax:		
a	Was the corporation an applicable corporation under section 59(k)(1) in any prior tax year?		✓
	If "Yes," go to question 29b. If "No," skip to question 29c.		
b	Is the corporation an applicable corporation under section 59(k)(1) in the current tax year because the corporation was an applicable corporation in the prior tax year?		✓
	If "Yes," complete and attach Form 4626. If "No," continue to question 29c.		
c	Does the corporation meet the requirements of the safe harbor method as provided under section 59(k)(3)(A) for the current tax year? See instructions		✓
	If "No," complete and attach Form 4626. If "Yes," the corporation is not required to file Form 4626.		
30	Is the corporation required to file Form 7208 relating to the excise tax on repurchase of corporate stock (see instructions):		
a	Under the rules for stock repurchased by a covered corporation (or stock acquired by its specified affiliate)?		✓
b	Under the applicable foreign corporation rules?		✓
c	Under the covered surrogate foreign corporation rules?		✓
	If "Yes" to either 30a, 30b, or 30c, complete Form 7208, Excise Tax on Repurchase of Corporate Stock. See the Instructions for Form 7208.		
31	Is this a consolidated return with gross receipts or sales of $1 billion or more and a subchapter K basis adjustment, as described in the instructions, of $10 million or more?		✓
	If "Yes," attach a statement. See instructions.		

Form **1120** (2024)

Self-Study Problem 11.5

Form 1120 (2024) — Page 6

Schedule L — Balance Sheets per Books

	Assets	Beginning of tax year (a)	(b)	End of tax year (c)	(d)
1	Cash		Initial return		35,000
2a	Trade notes and accounts receivable			10,000	
b	Less allowance for bad debts	(	)	( )	10,000
3	Inventories				
4	U.S. government obligations				
5	Tax-exempt securities (see instructions)				
6	Other current assets (attach statement)				
7	Loans to shareholders				
8	Mortgage and real estate loans				
9	Other investments (attach statement)				
10a	Buildings and other depreciable assets			125,000	
b	Less accumulated depreciation	(	)	(5,000)	120,000
11a	Depletable assets				
b	Less accumulated depletion	(	)	( )	
12	Land (net of any amortization)				18,000
13a	Intangible assets (amortizable only)				
b	Less accumulated amortization	(	)	( )	
14	Other assets (attach statement)				
15	Total assets				183,000

Liabilities and Shareholders' Equity

		(a)	(b)	(c)	(d)
16	Accounts payable				26,940
17	Mortgages, notes, bonds payable in less than 1 year				
18	Other current liabilities (attach statement)				
19	Loans from shareholders				
20	Mortgages, notes, bonds payable in 1 year or more				
21	Other liabilities (attach statement)				
22	Capital stock: a Preferred stock				
	b Common stock			140,000	140,000
23	Additional paid-in capital				
24	Retained earnings—Appropriated (attach statement)				
25	Retained earnings—Unappropriated				16,060
26	Adjustments to shareholders' equity (attach statement)				
27	Less cost of treasury stock		( )		( )
28	Total liabilities and shareholders' equity				183,000

Schedule M-1 — Reconciliation of Income (Loss) per Books With Income per Return

Note: The corporation may be required to file Schedule M-3. See instructions.

1	Net income (loss) per books	16,060	7	Income recorded on books this year not included on this return (itemize): Tax-exempt interest $ _____		
2	Federal income tax per books	2,940				
3	Excess of capital losses over capital gains					
4	Income subject to tax not recorded on books this year (itemize): _____		8	Deductions on this return not charged against book income this year (itemize):		
			a	Depreciation $ _____		
5	Expenses recorded on books this year not deducted on this return (itemize):		b	Charitable contributions $ _____		
a	Depreciation $ _____					
b	Charitable contributions $ _____					
c	Travel and entertainment $ _____		9	Add lines 7 and 8		0
6	Add lines 1 through 5	19,000	10	Income (page 1, line 28)—line 6 less line 9		19,000

Schedule M-2 — Analysis of Unappropriated Retained Earnings per Books (Schedule L, Line 25)

1	Balance at beginning of year	0	5	Distributions: a Cash	
2	Net income (loss) per books	16,060		b Stock	
3	Other increases (itemize): _____			c Property	
			6	Other decreases (itemize): _____	
			7	Add lines 5 and 6	0
4	Add lines 1, 2, and 3	16,060	8	Balance at end of year (line 4 less line 7)	16,060

Form **1120** (2024)

Self-Study Problem 11.6

Form 1120-S — U.S. Income Tax Return for an S Corporation — OMB No. 1545-0123 — 2024

Department of the Treasury, Internal Revenue Service

Do not file this form unless the corporation has filed or is attaching Form 2553 to elect to be an S corporation.
Go to www.irs.gov/Form1120S for instructions and the latest information.

For calendar year 2024 or tax year beginning _____, 2024, ending _____, 20 ___

- **A** S election effective date: 01/01/2024
- **B** Business activity code number (see instructions): 459110
- **C** Check if Sch. M-3 attached: ☐
- **Name:** Aspen Corporation
- **Number, street, and room or suite no.:** 470 Rio Grande Place
- **City or town, state, ZIP:** Aspen, CO 81611
- **D** Employer identification number: 92-2222222
- **E** Date incorporated: 01/01/2024
- **F** Total assets: $183,000
- **G** Is the corporation electing to be an S corporation beginning with this tax year? ☒ Yes ☐ No
- **H** Check if: (1) ☐ Final return (2) ☐ Name change (3) ☐ Address change (4) ☐ Amended return (5) ☐ S election termination
- **I** Number of shareholders during any part of the tax year: 1
- **J** Check if corporation: (1) ☐ Aggregated activities for section 465 at-risk purposes (2) ☐ Grouped activities for section 469 passive activity purposes

Caution: Include only trade or business income and expenses on lines 1a through 22. See the instructions for more information.

Income

Line	Description	Amount
1a	Gross receipts or sales	285,000
1b	Less returns and allowances	
1c	Balance	285,000
2	Cost of goods sold (attach Form 1125-A)	80,000
3	Gross profit. Subtract line 2 from line 1c	205,000
4	Net gain (loss) from Form 4797, Part II, line 17	
5	Other income (loss)	
6	**Total income (loss).** Add lines 3 through 5	205,000

Deductions

Line	Description	Amount
7	Compensation of officers	90,000
8	Salaries and wages (less employment credits)	82,000
9	Repairs and maintenance	8,000
10	Bad debts	
11	Rents	
12	Taxes and licenses	11,000
13	Interest	
14	Depreciation from Form 4562 not claimed on Form 1125-A or elsewhere (attach Form 4562)	5,000
15	Depletion (do not deduct oil and gas depletion)	
16	Advertising	
17	Pension, profit-sharing, etc., plans	
18	Employee benefit programs	
19	Energy efficient commercial buildings deduction (attach Form 7205)	
20	Other deductions (attach statement)	
21	**Total deductions.** Add lines 7 through 20	196,000
22	**Ordinary business income (loss).** Subtract line 21 from line 6	9,000

Tax and Payments

Line	Description	Amount
23a	Excess net passive income or LIFO recapture tax	
23b	Tax from Schedule D (Form 1120-S)	
23c	Add lines 23a and 23b	0
24a	Current year's estimated tax payments and preceding year's overpayment credited to the current year	
24b	Tax deposited with Form 7004	
24c	Credit for federal tax paid on fuels (attach Form 4136)	
24d	Elective payment election amount from Form 3800	
24z	Add lines 24a through 24d	0
25	Estimated tax penalty. Check if Form 2220 is attached ☐	
26	Amount owed	
27	Overpayment	0
28	Amount from line 27 credited to 2025 estimated tax / Refunded	

Sign Here — Under penalties of perjury...

Paid Preparer Use Only

For Paperwork Reduction Act Notice, see separate instructions. Cat. No. 11510H — Form **1120-S** (2024)

Self-Study Problem 11.6

Form 1120-S (2024) Page **2**

Schedule B — Other Information (see instructions)

		Yes	No
1	Check accounting method: **a** ☐ Cash **b** ☑ Accrual **c** ☐ Other (specify) _____		
2	See the instructions and enter the: **a** Business activity _Sporting goods retailer_ **b** Product or service _Ski and snowboard retail_		
3	At any time during the tax year, was any shareholder of the corporation a disregarded entity, a trust, an estate, or a nominee or similar person? If "Yes," attach Schedule B-1, Information on Certain Shareholders of an S Corporation		✓
4	At the end of the tax year, did the corporation:		
a	Own directly 20% or more, or own, directly or indirectly, 50% or more of the total stock issued and outstanding of any foreign or domestic corporation? For rules of constructive ownership, see instructions. If "Yes," complete (i) through (v) below		✓

(i) Name of Corporation	(ii) Employer Identification Number (if any)	(iii) Country of Incorporation	(iv) Percentage of Stock Owned	(v) If Percentage in (iv) Is 100%, Enter the Date (if applicable) a Qualified Subchapter S Subsidiary Election Was Made

		Yes	No
b	Own directly an interest of 20% or more, or own, directly or indirectly, an interest of 50% or more in the profit, loss, or capital in any foreign or domestic partnership (including an entity treated as a partnership) or in the beneficial interest of a trust? For rules of constructive ownership, see instructions. If "Yes," complete (i) through (v) below		✓

(i) Name of Entity	(ii) Employer Identification Number (if any)	(iii) Type of Entity	(iv) Country of Organization	(v) Maximum Percentage Owned in Profit, Loss, or Capital

		Yes	No
5a	At the end of the tax year, did the corporation have any outstanding shares of restricted stock?		✓
	If "Yes," complete lines (i) and (ii) below. (i) Total shares of restricted stock _____ (ii) Total shares of non-restricted stock _____		
b	At the end of the tax year, did the corporation have any outstanding stock options, warrants, or similar instruments?		✓
	If "Yes," complete lines (i) and (ii) below. (i) Total shares of stock outstanding at the end of the tax year _____ (ii) Total shares of stock outstanding if all instruments were executed _____		
6	Has this corporation filed, or is it required to file, **Form 8918**, Material Advisor Disclosure Statement, to provide information on any reportable transaction?		✓
7	Check this box if the corporation issued publicly offered debt instruments with original issue discount ☐ If checked, the corporation may have to file **Form 8281**, Information Return for Publicly Offered Original Issue Discount Instruments.		
8	If the corporation (**a**) was a C corporation before it elected to be an S corporation **or** the corporation acquired an asset with a basis determined by reference to the basis of the asset (or the basis of any other property) in the hands of a C corporation, **and** (**b**) has net unrealized built-in gain in excess of the net recognized built-in gain from prior years, enter the net unrealized built-in gain reduced by net recognized built-in gain from prior years. See instructions . . . . . . $ _____		
9	Did the corporation have an election under section 163(j) for any real property trade or business or any farming business in effect during the tax year? See instructions		✓
10	Does the corporation satisfy one or more of the following? See instructions		✓
a	The corporation owns a pass-through entity with current, or prior year carryover, excess business interest expense.		
b	The corporation's aggregate average annual gross receipts (determined under section 448(c)) for the 3 tax years preceding the current tax year are more than $30 million and the corporation has business interest expense.		
c	The corporation is a tax shelter and the corporation has business interest expense. If "Yes," complete and attach **Form 8990**, Limitation on Business Interest Expense Under Section 163(j).		
11	Does the corporation satisfy **both** of the following conditions?		✓
a	The corporation's total receipts (see instructions) for the tax year were less than $250,000.		
b	The corporation's total assets at the end of the tax year were less than $250,000. If "Yes," the corporation is not required to complete Schedules L and M-1.		

Form **1120-S** (2024)

Self-Study Problem 11.6

Form 1120-S (2024) — Page 3

Schedule B — Other Information (see instructions) (continued)

		Yes	No
12	During the tax year, did the corporation have any non-shareholder debt that was canceled, was forgiven, or had the terms modified so as to reduce the principal amount of the debt?		✓
	If "Yes," enter the amount of principal reduction . . . $ _____		
13	During the tax year, was a qualified subchapter S subsidiary election terminated or revoked? If "Yes," see instructions		✓
14a	Did the corporation make any payments that would require it to file Form(s) 1099?	✓	
b	If "Yes," did or will the corporation file required Form(s) 1099?	✓	
15	Is the corporation attaching Form 8996 to certify as a Qualified Opportunity Fund?		✓
	If "Yes," enter the amount from Form 8996, line 15 . . . $ _____		
16	At any time during the tax year, did the corporation: (a) receive (as a reward, award, or payment for property or services); or (b) sell, exchange, or otherwise dispose of a digital asset (or a financial interest in a digital asset)? See instructions		✓

Schedule K — Shareholders' Pro Rata Share Items

			Total amount
Income (Loss)	1	Ordinary business income (loss) (page 1, line 22)	9,000
	2	Net rental real estate income (loss) (attach Form 8825)	
	3a	Other gross rental income (loss)	
	b	Expenses from other rental activities (attach statement)	
	c	Other net rental income (loss). Subtract line 3b from line 3a	
	4	Interest income	
	5	Dividends: a Ordinary dividends	10,000
		b Qualified dividends — 5b 10,000	
	6	Royalties	
	7	Net short-term capital gain (loss) (attach Schedule D (Form 1120-S))	
	8a	Net long-term capital gain (loss) (attach Schedule D (Form 1120-S))	
	b	Collectibles (28%) gain (loss) — 8b	
	c	Unrecaptured section 1250 gain (attach statement) — 8c	
	9	Net section 1231 gain (loss) (attach Form 4797)	
	10	Other income (loss) (see instructions) Type:	
Deductions	11	Section 179 deduction (attach Form 4562)	
	12a	Cash charitable contributions	
	b	Noncash charitable contributions	
	c	Investment interest expense	
	d	Section 59(e)(2) expenditures Type:	
	e	Other deductions (see instructions) Type:	
Credits	13a	Low-income housing credit (section 42(j)(5))	
	b	Low-income housing credit (other)	
	c	Qualified rehabilitation expenditures (rental real estate) (attach Form 3468, if applicable)	
	d	Other rental real estate credits (see instructions) Type:	
	e	Other rental credits (see instructions) Type:	
	f	Biofuel producer credit (attach Form 6478)	
	g	Other credits (see instructions) Type:	
International	14	Attach Schedule K-2 (Form 1120-S), Shareholders' Pro Rata Share Items—International, and check this box to indicate you are reporting items of international tax relevance ☐	
Alternative Minimum Tax (AMT) Items	15a	Post-1986 depreciation adjustment	
	b	Adjusted gain or loss	
	c	Depletion (other than oil and gas)	
	d	Oil, gas, and geothermal properties—gross income	
	e	Oil, gas, and geothermal properties—deductions	
	f	Other AMT items (attach statement)	
Items Affecting Shareholder Basis	16a	Tax-exempt interest income	
	b	Other tax-exempt income	
	c	Nondeductible expenses	
	d	Distributions (attach statement if required) (see instructions)	
	e	Repayment of loans from shareholders	
	f	Foreign taxes paid or accrued	

Form **1120-S** (2024)

Self-Study Problem 11.6

Form 1120-S (2024) Page **4**

Schedule K	Shareholders' Pro Rata Share Items *(continued)*		Total amount
Other Information 17a	Investment income	17a	10,000
b	Investment expenses	17b	
c	Dividend distributions paid from accumulated earnings and profits	17c	
d	Other items and amounts (attach statement)		
Reconciliation 18	**Income (loss) reconciliation.** Combine the total amounts on lines 1 through 10. From the result, subtract the sum of the amounts on lines 11 through 12e and 16f	18	19,000

Schedule L	Balance Sheets per Books	Beginning of tax year		End of tax year	
	Assets	(a)	(b)	(c)	(d)
1	Cash				35,000
2a	Trade notes and accounts receivable			10,000	
b	Less allowance for bad debts	(	)	(	) 10,000
3	Inventories				
4	U.S. government obligations				
5	Tax-exempt securities (see instructions)				
6	Other current assets (attach statement)				
7	Loans to shareholders				
8	Mortgage and real estate loans				
9	Other investments (attach statement)				
10a	Buildings and other depreciable assets			125,000	
b	Less accumulated depreciation	(	)	(5,000	) 120,000
11a	Depletable assets				
b	Less accumulated depletion	(	)	(	)
12	Land (net of any amortization)				18,000
13a	Intangible assets (amortizable only)				
b	Less accumulated amortization	(	)	(	)
14	Other assets (attach statement)				
15	Total assets				183,000
	Liabilities and Shareholders' Equity				
16	Accounts payable				24,000
17	Mortgages, notes, bonds payable in less than 1 year				
18	Other current liabilities (attach statement)				
19	Loans from shareholders				
20	Mortgages, notes, bonds payable in 1 year or more				
21	Other liabilities (attach statement)				
22	Capital stock				140,000
23	Additional paid-in capital				
24	Retained earnings				19,000
25	Adjustments to shareholders' equity (attach statement)				
26	Less cost of treasury stock		(	)	( )
27	Total liabilities and shareholders' equity				183,000

Form **1120-S** (2024)

Self-Study Problem 11.6

Form 1120-S (2024) — Page 5

Schedule M-1 — Reconciliation of Income (Loss) per Books With Income (Loss) per Return

Note: The corporation may be required to file Schedule M-3. See instructions.

Line	Description	Amount	Line	Description	Amount
1	Net income (loss) per books	19,000	5	Income recorded on books this year not included on Schedule K, lines 1 through 10 (itemize):	
2	Income included on Schedule K, lines 1, 2, 3c, 4, 5a, 6, 7, 8a, 9, and 10, not recorded on books this year (itemize):		a	Tax-exempt interest $	
3	Expenses recorded on books this year not included on Schedule K, lines 1 through 12e, and 16f (itemize):		6	Deductions included on Schedule K, lines 1 through 12e, and 16f, not charged against book income this year (itemize):	
a	Depreciation $		a	Depreciation $	
b	Travel and entertainment $		7	Add lines 5 and 6	
			8	Income (loss) (Schedule K, line 18). Subtract line 7 from line 4	19,000
4	Add lines 1 through 3	19,000			

Schedule M-2 — Analysis of Accumulated Adjustments Account, Shareholders' Undistributed Taxable Income Previously Taxed, Accumulated Earnings and Profits, and Other Adjustments Account (see instructions)

		(a) Accumulated adjustments account	(b) Shareholders' undistributed taxable income previously taxed	(c) Accumulated earnings and profits	(d) Other adjustments account
1	Balance at beginning of tax year	0			
2	Ordinary income from page 1, line 22	9,000			
3	Other additions	10,000			
4	Loss from page 1, line 22	( )			
5	Other reductions	( )			( )
6	Combine lines 1 through 5	19,000			
7	Distributions				
8	Balance at end of tax year. Subtract line 7 from line 6	19,000			

Form **1120-S** (2024)

Self-Study Problem 11.6

Schedule K-1 (Form 1120-S) 2024

671124
OMB No. 1545-0123

☐ Final K-1   ☐ Amended K-1

Part I — Information About the Corporation

A Corporation's employer identification number: 92-2222222

B Corporation's name, address, city, state, and ZIP code:
Aspen Corporation
470 Rio Grande Place
Aspen, CO 81611

C IRS Center where corporation filed return: Ogden, UT

D Corporation's total number of shares
- Beginning of tax year:
- End of tax year: 100

Part II — Information About the Shareholder

E Shareholder's identifying number: 411-41-4141

F1 Shareholder's name, address, city, state, and ZIP code:
Ava Mendes
1175 Delaware Street
Denver, CO 80204

F2 If the shareholder is a disregarded entity, a trust, an estate, or a nominee or similar person, enter the individual or entity responsible for reporting:
TIN _____ Name _____

F3 What type of entity is this shareholder? Individual

G Current year allocation percentage: 100%

H Shareholder's number of shares
- Beginning of tax year:
- End of tax year: 100

I Loans from shareholder
- Beginning of tax year: $
- End of tax year: $

Part III — Shareholder's Share of Current Year Income, Deductions, Credits, and Other Items

Line	Item	Amount
1	Ordinary business income (loss)	9,000
2	Net rental real estate income (loss)	
3	Other net rental income (loss)	
4	Interest income	
5a	Ordinary dividends	10,000
5b	Qualified dividends	10,000
6	Royalties	
7	Net short-term capital gain (loss)	
8a	Net long-term capital gain (loss)	
8b	Collectibles (28%) gain (loss)	
8c	Unrecaptured section 1250 gain	
9	Net section 1231 gain (loss)	
10	Other income (loss)	
11	Section 179 deduction	
12	Other deductions	
13	Credits	
14	Schedule K-3 is attached if checked ☐	
15	Alternative minimum tax (AMT) items	
16	Items affecting shareholder basis	
17	Other information	
	A	10,000
	V	See statement
	AJ	Refer to note below

18 ☐ More than one activity for at-risk purposes*
19 ☐ More than one activity for passive activity purposes*

* See attached statement for additional information.

Line 17, Code AJ is used for disclosure of gross income and gross deductions from a business activity for purposes of the overall business loss limitation (Chapter 4). Gross income is $205,000 and gross deductions are $196,000.

Self-Study Problem 11.6

Statement A—QBI Pass-Through Entity Reporting

S corporation's name: Aspen Corporation		S corporation's EIN: 92-2222222	
Shareholder's name: Ava Mendes		Shareholder's identifying number: 411-41-4141	

Shareholder's share of:		Trade or Business 1	Trade or Business 2	Trade or Business 3
		☐ PTP ☐ Aggregated ☐ SSTB	☐ PTP ☐ Aggregated ☐ SSTB	☐ PTP ☐ Aggregated ☐ SSTB
QBI or qualified PTP items subject to shareholder-specific determinations:				
	Ordinary business income (loss)	9,000		
	Rental income (loss)			
	Royalty income (loss)			
	Section 1231 gain (loss)			
	Other income (loss)			
	Section 179 deduction			
	Other deductions			
W-2 wages		172,000		
UBIA of qualified property		125,000		
Section 199A dividends				

Note: The 2024 Statement A was not available when we went to print. This is a 2023 version of Statement A.

Chapter 12 Tax Administration and Tax Planning

Self-Study Problem 12.1

1. False — The Taxpayer Services Divisions handles primarily W-2 employee taxpayers.
2. True
3. False — The commissioner of internal revenue is appointed by the President of the United States.
4. True
5. True

Self-Study Problem 12.2

1. True
2. False — A correspondence audit is handled via mail.
3. True
4. True
5. False — Audits can be appealed to an appellate agent.

Self-Study Problem 12.3

Part a.

Failure-to-pay penalty:		
$3,000 × 0.5% × 2 months		$ 30
Failure-to-file penalty:		
$3,000 × 5% × 2 months	$ 300	
Less: failure-to-pay penalty	(30)	
		270
Total		$300

The minimum failure-to-file penalty does not apply since the return was filed within 60 days of the due date.

Part b.

Failure-to-pay penalty:		
$3,000 × 0.5% × 3 months		$ 45
Failure-to-file penalty:		
$3,000 × 5% × 3 months	$ 450	
Less: failure-to-pay penalty	(45)	
	405	
Minimum failure-to-file penalty		510
Total		$555

Part c. 20% × $10,000 $2,000

Self-Study Problem 12.4

1. True
2. False — For bad debts, the statute of limitations is 7 years.
3. False — There is no statute of limitations for fraudulent returns.
4. True
5. True

Self-Study Problem 12.5

1. False — Lawyers and enrolled agents may also represent taxpayers before the IRS.
2. False — A college degree is not required.
3. False — Anyone may prepare corporate tax returns.
4. True
5. False — The penalty is $635 for tax returns filed in 2025.
6. True
7. False — The burden of proof is on the IRS.
8. False — The burden of proof remains on the taxpayer.
9. True
10. True
11. True
12. False — Periodicals and newspapers are not substantial authority.
13. True
14. True

Self-Study Problem 12.6

1. True
2. True — Reasonable notice must be given to the taxpayer.
3. True — Publication 1 directs the reader to Publication 594.
4. True
5. True
6. True

Self-Study Problem 12.7

1. 11.51% = $10,819 / $94,000
2. 11.59% = $11,012 / $95,000
3. 19.3% = ($11,012 − $10,819) / ($95,000 − $94,000)

K's $1,000 increase in income is subject to tax in two different taxpayer rate brackets. The first $300 ($94,300 − $94,000) is taxed at 12% while the remaining $700 is taxed at 22%.

Appendix F

A reminder for students and instructors:

Appendix F (draft tax forms) is found online at the instructor and student sites at cengage.com under the text ISBN for Income Tax Fundamentals 43e.

All Group 2, Group 4, and Appendix D draft tax forms are found in Appendix F. Final forms can be found at www.irs.gov/forms-instructions.

Glossary of Tax Terms

Note: The words and phrases appearing below have been defined to reflect their conventional use in the field of taxation. Such definitions may therefore, be incomplete for other purposes.

20-percent limitation
Taxpayers may not deduct donations of capital gain property in excess of 20 percent of the taxpayer's adjusted gross income (AGI) to a non-50-percent charitable organization.

30-percent limitation
The 30-percent limit of AGI applies to capital gain property donated to a 50-percent organization and also to cash donations made to a non-50-percent organization.

50-percent limitation
Taxpayers may not deduct certain charitable contributions in excess of 50 percent of the taxpayer's gross income.

50-percent organization
Defined by the Internal Revenue Service (IRS) as specific organizations such as public charities, churches, most educational institutions, hospitals, the United States or any state or local government, all private operating foundations, and private nonoperating foundations if they distribute their contributions to public charities within a specific time period. All other qualified organizations are non-50-percent organizations.

60-percent limitation
Taxpayers may not deduct donations for cash contributions to 50-percent organizations in excess of 60 percent of the taxpayer's AGI for tax years 2022 to 2025.

Abandoned spouse
In order to qualify to file as an abandoned spouse, a person must file a separate tax return; must pay more than half the costs of maintaining a home in a year, and must not have a spouse living with them at any time in the last 6 months of the year.

Accelerated death benefits
Early payouts of life insurance, also called accelerated death benefits or viatical settlements, are excluded from gross income for certain terminally or chronically ill taxpayers. The taxpayer may either collect an early payout from the insurance company or sell or assign the policy to a viatical settlement provider. Refer to *Viatical settlements*.

Accelerated depreciation
The depreciation of fixed assets at a faster rate early in their useful lives.

Accident and health benefits
Employee fringe benefits provided by employers through the payment of health and accident insurance premiums, or the establishment of employer-funded medical reimbursement plans. Employers generally are entitled to a deduction for such payments, whereas employees generally exclude the fringe benefits from gross income.

Accounting methods
The two main accounting methods are cash and accrual-basis accounting.

Accounting periods
The timeframe reflected in a business's financial statements and reports to stakeholders.

Accrual method
A method of accounting that reflects expenses incurred and income earned for any one tax year. In contrast to the cash basis of accounting, expenses do not have to be paid to be deductible, nor does income have to be received to be taxable.

Accumulated earnings tax
A tax imposed by the federal government on companies with retained earnings determined to be in excess of what is considered ordinary and necessary.

Accuracy-related penalty
A penalty imposed by the Internal Revenue Service on a taxpayer when a significant amount of taxable income is not reported on a return.

Actual cost method
The IRS-approved method for calculating and claiming expenses related to automobile use for business.

Adaptation
An amount paid to allow the property or facility to be used in a new or different use.

Adjusted basis
The cost or other basis of property reduced by depreciation allowed or allowable and increased by capital improvements. Refer to *Basis*.

Adjusted gross income (AGI)
A determination unique to individual taxpayers used as the basis to calculate limitations on the amount of certain expenses which may be deductible, including medical expenses, charitable contributions, certain personal casualty losses, and certain other itemized deductions. Generally, AGI represents gross income minus specific deductions such as certain trade or business expenses (deductions *for* AGI) but before itemized deductions or the standard deduction (deductions *from* AGI).

Adoption credit
The nonrefundable income tax credit allowed for qualified adoption expenses of an individual.

Adoption expenses
Adoption fees, court costs, attorney fees, and other expenses directly related to the legal adoption of an eligible child.

Affordable Care Act (ACA)
Also referred to as Obamacare, ACA is a federal law providing for a fundamental reform of the U.S. healthcare and health insurance system, signed by President Barack Obama in 2010.

Alimony payments
Payments from one spouse or former spouse, to the other, required as a result of a divorce or separation agreement, which meet certain statutory requirements. Alimony and separate maintenance payments, but not child support payments, are included in the gross income of the recipient and are deducted by the payor for divorces occurring before 2019. The Tax Cuts and Jobs Act (TCJA) has repealed both the deduction of and inclusion of alimony for tax years beginning in 2019. Refer to also Child support payments.

Alternative minimum tax (AMT)
The AMT is a tax calculation that ensures that wealthy taxpayers cannot take advantage of special tax write-offs to avoid paying tax.

American Opportunity tax credit (AOTC)
Previously referred to as the Hope credit, the AOTC is a tax credit available for the first 4 years of postsecondary education expenses for students who meet specific requirements.

Glossary

Amortization
The allocation (and charge to expense) of the cost or other basis of an intangible asset over its estimated useful life. Examples of amortizable intangibles include patents and copyrights.

Amount realized
The amount received by a taxpayer on the sale or exchange of property less the cost incurred to transfer the property. The measure of the amount received is the sum of the cash and the fair market value of any property or services plus any relieved liability of the taxpayer. Determining the amount realized is the starting point for arriving at a realized gain or loss.

AMT adjustments
Timing differences that arise when there are differences between regular and AMT tax calculations (e.g., depreciation timing differences).

AMT exemption allowance
Statutory deduction reducing AMT income for taxpayers based on their filing status.

AMT preferences
Items excluded from the computation of regular taxable income but required to be added to compute alternative minimum taxable income.

Annual contribution limits
The cap on total contributions individuals may make to retirement plans, traditional IRAs, and Roth IRAs in a given tax year.

Annual Federal Tax Refresher (AFTR)
The continuing education course required to be taken by all paid tax return preparers; focusing on the upcoming tax filing season issues and tax updates.

Annual Filing Season Program (AFSP)
A voluntary program that encourages paid tax return preparers to participate in continuing education on tax law changes.

Annualized period
A given period that is less than one year but is computed as if the period was for a full year.

Annuity
A fixed sum payable at specified intervals for a specific period of time or for life. Payments represent a partial return of capital and a return (e.g., interest income) on the capital investment. An exclusion ratio is generally used to compute the amounts of nontaxable and taxable income.

Appeals process of IRS
When a disagreement arises between a taxpayer and the IRS over the outcome of a tax audit, an appeals process is available. If agreement cannot be reached at an informal appeals conference, the process moves to a formal appeals process in the Federal Tax Court.

Asset depreciation range (ADR)
An accounting method established by the IRS to determine the useful life of specific classes of depreciable assets.

At-risk rule
Prevents taxpayers from deducting losses from activities in excess of the investment in the activities. Most commonly related to investments in partnerships.

Audit procedure of IRS
A primary function of the IRS, the process involves selecting some returns for examination in a correspondence audit, an office audit, or a field audit.

Automobile expenses
Automobile expenses are generally deductible only to the extent the automobile is used in business or for the production of income. Personal commuting expenses are not deductible. When calculating the deductible automobile expenses, the taxpayer may deduct actual expenses (including depreciation and insurance), or choose to use the standard mileage rate.

Average tax rate
The tax rate representing the average rate of tax applicable to the taxpayer's income; calculated as the total tax paid divided by the total income of the taxpayer.

Backup withholding
Certain situations in which the issuer of payments such as dividends or interest is required to withhold income tax at the time of payment. Designed to ensure that income tax is collected on income from certain taxpayers (generally, non-U.S. tax residents).

Bad debts
An ordinary deduction is permitted if a business debt, such as an account receivable, subsequently becomes worthless (uncollectible), provided the income arising from the debt was previously included in taxable income. The deduction is allowed only in the year of worthlessness. A nonbusiness bad debt deduction is allowed as a short-term capital loss when a debt which did not arise in connection with the creditor's trade or business activities becomes worthless.

Barter
An exchange of goods or services for other goods or services without using money. The fair market value of bartered goods must be included in reporting gross income for taxation.

Basis
The amount assigned to an asset for income tax purposes. For assets acquired by purchase, the basis would be the cost of the asset plus any direct costs incidental to the purchase. Special rules govern the basis of property received as a result of another's death or by gift. Refer also to *Adjusted basis*.

Beneficial Owner
Any individual who directly or indirectly: (a) exercises substantial control over a reporting company, or (b) owns or controls at least 25 percent of the ownership interests of a reporting company.

Betterment
An amount paid to improve and increase the productivity, efficiency, strength, quality, or output of the property or facility.

Bona fide
Authentic and genuine. In the context of tax law, serving a specific business purpose.

Bonus depreciation
The immediate deduction of all or some of the cost of otherwise depreciated property.

Book income
Another term for a corporation's financial accounting income. Schedule M-1 of the Form 1120 reconciles a corporation's book income to its taxable income, computed before any net operating loss and dividends are deducted.

Boot
Cash or property of a type other than that permitted to be received tax-free in a nontaxable like-kind exchange. The receipt of boot will cause an otherwise tax-free transfer to become taxable to the extent of the lesser of the fair market value of such boot or the realized gain on the transfer.

Built-in gains tax
An S corporation may be subject to a tax on gains attributable to appreciation in the value of assets held by the corporation prior to the S corporation election, referred to as the built-in gains tax.

Business and nonbusiness bad debts
When a taxpayer sells goods or services on credit and the accounts receivable become uncollectible, a bad debt is incurred. Similarly, when a taxpayer makes a personal loan that becomes uncollectible, a nonbusiness bad debt is incurred.

Business gifts
Business gifts are deductible only to the extent that each gift does not exceed $25 per person per year. Exceptions are made for promotional gifts and for certain employee awards.

Cancellation of debt income
Also referred to as forgiveness of debt income. When a lender forgives or cancels all or some of the taxpayer's outstanding loans or other credit account. In general, the amount of debt that has been forgiven is considered taxable income unless specifically excluded.

Capital asset
All assets are capital assets except those specifically excluded by the tax law. Major categories of noncapital assets include property held for sale in the normal course of business (i.e., inventory), trade accounts and notes receivable, depreciable property, and real estate used in a trade or business.

Capital expenditure
An expenditure, the amount of which should be added to the basis of the property improved. For income tax purposes, this generally precludes a deduction for the full amount of the expenditure in the year paid or incurred. Any tax deduction has to come in the form of cost recovery or depreciation.

Capital gain
The gain from the sale or exchange of a capital asset. Gain from property held 12 months or less is deemed to be a short-term capital gain. If the property is held more than 12 months, the gain is deemed to be long-term. Refer to *Capital asset* and *Holding period*.

Capital improvements
Major expenditures for permanent improvements to or restoration of a taxpayer's property.

Capital loss
The loss from the sale or exchange of a capital asset. A loss from property held 12 months or less is deemed to be a short-term capital loss. If the property is held more than 12 months, the loss is deemed to be long-term. Refer to *Capital asset* and *Holding period*.

Capital loss carryovers
A net capital loss that is not deducted in the current tax year but is eligible to be carried forward into future taxable years.

Cash basis
A method of accounting under which income is reported when received and expenses are deductible when paid by the taxpayer. Prepaid rent and prepaid interest must be deducted using the accrual method.

Cash method
The cash method utilizes the cash-basis of accounting whereby income is not counted until payment is actually received, and expenses are not counted until they are actually paid. The cash method is the more commonly used method of accounting by small businesses.

Casualty loss
A casualty is defined as the complete or partial destruction of property resulting from an identifiable event of a sudden, unexpected or unusual nature (e.g., floods, shipwrecks, storms, fires, automobile accidents). Beginning in 2018, personal casualty losses are only eligible for deduction when resulting from a federally declared disaster area. Personal casualty losses are deductible as itemized deductions subject to a $100 nondeductible floor and only to the extent that the taxpayer's total losses from personal-use property (net of the $100 floor) exceed 10 percent of adjusted gross income. Special rules are provided for the combining (netting) of certain casualty gains and losses.

"Catch-up" contribution
A type of retirement savings contribution that allows people 50 or older to make additional contributions to 401k, 403(b), and 457(b) accounts and individual retirement accounts (IRAs).

Certified Public Accountant (CPA)
A designation provided by a state's Board of Accounting to an individual who has passed the Uniform Certified Public Accountant Examination and met the required amount of accounting-related experience.

Charitable contributions
Contributions may be deductible (subject to various restrictions and ceiling limitations) if made to qualified charitable organizations. A cash-basis taxpayer is entitled to a deduction in the year of payment. Accrual-basis corporations may accrue contributions at year-end under certain circumstances.

Child and dependent care credit
This credit is available to individuals who are employed on a full-time basis and maintain a household for a dependent child or disabled spouse or dependent. The amount of the credit is equal to a percentage of the cost of employment-related child and dependent care expenses, up to a stated maximum amount.

Child support payments
Payments for child support do not constitute alimony, and are, therefore, not included in gross income by the recipient or deducted as alimony by the payor to the extent permitted otherwise. Refer also to *Alimony payments*.

Child tax credit
Certain individual taxpayers may take a tax credit based on the number of their dependent children, subject to limitations.

Clean vehicle credit
A tax credit worth up to $7,500 for new or up to $4,000 for used, electric cars and light trucks. Requirements include final assembly of the vehicles must occur in North America. Certain income limits apply to taxpayers.

Closed transaction
A transaction in which all material parts of the transaction have been completed.

Community property
Community property is all property, other than separate property, owned by a married couple. The income from community property is generally split equally between spouses. The classification of property as community property is important in determining the separate taxable income of married taxpayers.

Commuting
Daily transportation traveling from home to one or more regular places of business.

Constructive ownership
A close relationship with an owner, e.g., a spouse; the person in question is treated as an owner.

Constructive receipt
Income is made available so that the taxpayer could actually receive it at any time if notice of intention to receive it has been given and no substantial limitations prevents access.

Consumer interest
Not deductible for tax purposes, consumer interest is interest expense generated from personal loans, credit cards, or other debt used for personal purposes.

Corporate alternative minimum tax
The corporate AMT was repealed for tax years after 2017 by the TCJA.

Corporate tax rate
Since 2018, corporations have been subject to a flat income tax rate of 21 percent.

Correspondence audit
A tax audit conducted by the IRS via written or electronic correspondence without in-person meetings.

Cost of goods sold
The amount equal to the cost of inventory sold during the period. Generally computed as beginning inventory plus purchases of inventory (or the cost to create inventory) less ending inventory. Cost of goods sold is deducted from gross receipts on Schedule C.

Coverdell Education Savings Accounts
Educational savings accounts that allow taxpayers to pay for qualified education expenses, with a maximum contribution allowed of $2,000 annually.

De minimis fringe benefits
A de minimis fringe benefit is one which, considering its value and the frequency with which it is provided, is so small as to make accounting for it unreasonable or impractical. De minimis fringe benefits are excluded under Internal Revenue Code section 132(a)(4) and include items which are not specifically excluded under other sections of the Code.

Deferred compensation
Compensation which will be taxed when received or upon the removal of certain restrictions, not when earned. An example would be contributions by an employer to a qualified pension or profit-sharing plan on behalf of an employee. Such contributions will not be taxed to the employee until the funds are made available or distributed to the employee (e.g., upon retirement). Refer to *Qualified pension or profit-sharing plan*.

Defined benefit plan
A type of pension plan in which the plan specifies the pension payment amounts payable to an employee upon retirement, based on the employee's earnings' history, tenure of service, and age.

Defined contribution plan
A type of pension plan in which the plan specifies the regular contributions made by the employer and employee in which the pension benefits are based on the contribution amounts and the returns of the plan's investments.

Dependent
A child or relative whose characteristics and relationship to a taxpayer allow the taxpayer to claim certain tax deductions and credits, such as from the head of household filing status, the Child Tax Credit, the Earned Income Tax Credit, or the Child and Dependent Care Credit.

Dependent care flexible spending account
A pre-tax benefit account used to pay for eligible dependent care services, such as preschool, summer day camp, before or after school programs, and child or adult daycare.

Depreciation
The reduction in the value of an asset or assets, depreciation decreases the amount of taxes a company or business pays via tax deductions.

Depreciation recapture
The recharacterizing of gain on the sale of certain property used in a trade or business to ordinary income to the extent of depreciation previously allowed.

Discriminant Function System (DIF)
One process by which the IRS selects tax returns for audits. The DIF is a computerized statistical sampling technique.

Dividend
A distribution made by a corporation out of its earnings and profits.

Dividends received deduction
A special deduction for corporations that receive dividend income distributions from a domestic corporation of which it has an ownership interest. Generally designed to prevent double taxation of corporate dividends paid by a corporate subsidiary to its corporate owner(s).

Earned income
Income from personal services as distinguished from income generated by property.

Earned income credit
The earned income credit is a refundable credit available to qualifying individuals with income and AGI below certain levels.

Economic performance
All activities related to the incurrence of a liability have been performed.

Education assistance plans
Under an educational assistance plan, employers may provide up to $5,250 of excludable annual tuition assistance.

Education expenses
Employees may deduct education expenses if such items are incurred either (1) to maintain or improve existing job-related skills or (2) to meet the express requirements of the employer or the requirements imposed by law to retain employment status. Such expenses are not deductible if the education is required to meet the minimum educational requirements for the taxpayer's job or the education qualifies the individual for a new trade or business.

Educational savings account
Refer to Coverdell Education Savings Accounts.

E-filing
The process of transmitting federal income tax return information to the IRS Service Center using a device with Internet access.

EFTPS
The Electronic Federal Tax Payment System, a free service of the U.S. Department of the Treasury.

Election to expense (Section 179)
The tax code Section 179 allows a taxpayer to elect to immediately expense and deduct the cost of certain property when placed in service, up to a certain limit, rather than capitalizing and depreciating such property.

Elective contributions
An employee may elect to defer a portion of their salary to be withheld and transferred directly into an employer-sponsored retirement savings plan (such as 401k plans). Elective deferrals are generally limited in amounts that vary by plan type.

Employee
Under common-law rules, a worker who performs services for another party is an employee if that party can control what will be done and how it will be done.

Employee annuities
Retirement plans organized by employers, who make periodic payments into the plans on behalf of the employees.

Employee fringe benefits
Non-wage benefits or perquisites (perks) provided to employees in addition to their normal wages and salaries. Most fringe benefits are required to be included in the employee's gross income; however, certain *qualified* fringe benefits such as employee-paid health insurance premiums may be excluded from the employee's gross income but remain deductible by the business.

Employee Stock Ownership Plan (ESOP)
A type of defined contribution pension plan in which employers provide their employees with ownership in the employer's stock.

Encumbered property
Also known as collateral, this is property pledged for a liability in the amount of the liability.

Energy credit
Tax law in the past decade included personal tax credits associated with energy-efficient products. Many have been extended or expired but the IRS website maintains updated information.

Energy efficient home improvement credit
An individual nonrefundable tax credit for the purchase of qualifying equipment, home improvements, and energy audits associated with an individual taxpayer's primary residence. The credit is limited by category and in the aggregate.

Entertainment expenses
Starting in 2018, the TCJA has disallowed the deductibility of entertainment expenses.

Estimated payments
Self-employed taxpayers are not subject to income tax withholding but must make quarterly estimated tax payments in four installments in a tax year.

Exclusions—gross income
Certain types of income are specifically excluded from gross income. These may be referred to as exempt income, exclusions, or tax exemptions.

Exclusion ratio
The percentage of an investor's return that is not subject to taxes.

Failure-to-file penalty
A penalty charged on tax returns filed after the due date or extended due date, absent a reasonable cause for filing late. The failure-to-file penalty is 5 percent of the unpaid taxes for each month or part of a month that a tax return is late; not to exceed 25 percent of unpaid taxes.

Failure-to-pay penalty
A penalty charged for failing to pay tax by its due date. The late payment penalty is 0.5 percent of the tax owed after the due date, for each month or part of a month the tax remains unpaid, up to 25 percent.

Fair market value
The amount at which property would change hands between a willing buyer and a willing seller, neither being under any compulsion to buy or sell, and both having reasonable knowledge of the relevant facts.

Federal Insurance Contributions Act (FICA)
FICA imposes social taxes on forms of earned income to provide benefits for retired and disabled workers. Referred to as FICA taxes, Social Security and Medicare taxes are withheld using a specific percentage from an employee's wages. The employer, the employee, and the self-employed are responsible for the payment of FICA taxes. Refer to *FICA cap, OASDI, and Social Security tax*.

Federal poverty line (FPL)
A measure of income issued annually by the Department of Health and Human Services (HHS). FPLs are used to determine eligibility for certain programs and benefits.

Federal Tax Court
A federal trial court of record established by the U.S. Congress which specializes in adjudicating disputes over federal income tax, generally prior to the time at which formal tax assessments are made by the Internal Revenue Service.

FICA cap
The amount of earnings subject to Old-Age, Survivors, and Disability Insurance taxation (Social Security tax) for a given year. Refer to *Federal Insurance Contributions Act (FICA), OASDI, and Social Security tax*.

Field audit
One of three types of tax return audits conducted by the IRS; this audit is conducted at either a taxpayer's home, place of business, or accountant's office.

First in, first out (FIFO)
An accounting method for determining the cost of inventories. Under the FIFO method, the first merchandise acquired is the first to be sold. Thus, the cost of inventory on hand is deemed to be the cost of the most recently acquired merchandise (goods).

Fiscal year
A fiscal year is a one-year (12-month) period that companies and governments use for financial reporting and budgeting that ends on a month-end other than December.

Fiscal year-end
An annual accounting period which does not end on December 31, a calendar year-end. An example of a fiscal year is July 1 through June 30.

Flexible spending account
A pre-tax benefit account used to pay for eligible out-of-pocket healthcare costs.

Foreign housing exclusion
An exclusion or a deduction from gross income for a foreign housing amount if a qualifying taxpayer's tax home is in a foreign country.

Foreign income exclusion
The foreign earned income exclusion is intended to prevent double taxation by excluding income from U.S. taxation that has been earned in another country if a qualifying taxpayer's tax home is in a foreign country.

Foreign tax credit or deduction
Both U.S. individual taxpayers and U.S. corporations may claim a foreign tax credit on income earned and subject to tax in a foreign country or U.S. possession. As an alternative to the credit, a deduction may be taken for the foreign taxes paid. The purpose of this credit is to eliminate double taxation on income earned in a foreign country.

Forgiveness of debt
Refer to *Cancellation of debt income*.

Fraud penalty
Under the IRS Code, "if any part of an underpayment of tax required to be shown on a return is due to fraud, there shall be added to the tax an amount equal to 75 percent of the portion of the underpayment which is attributable to fraud." Criminal charges are also possible in some cases.

FUTA
The Federal Unemployment Tax Act (FUTA) along with state unemployment systems provides for payments of unemployment compensation to workers who have lost their jobs. Most employers pay both a federal and a state unemployment tax.

General (ordinary) partnerships
A basic form of partnership that is a business arrangement between two or more parties and may be formed by a simple verbal agreement. The partners agree to unlimited liability and share in all assets, profits, and financial and legal liabilities.

Gift
A transfer of property for less than adequate consideration. Gifts usually occur in a personal setting (such as between members of the same family) and are generally excluded from taxable income. Business gifts are subject to dollar limitations in order to be tax deductible. Refer to *qualified plan award*.

Goodwill
The ability of a business to generate income in excess of a normal rate on assets due to superior managerial skills, market position, new product technology, etc. In the purchase of a business, goodwill is the difference between the purchase price and the value of the net assets. Goodwill is an intangible asset which possesses an indefinite life; however, it is amortized over a 15-year period for federal income tax purposes.

Gross income
All income from whatever source derived except that which is specifically excluded by tax law. Gross income does not include income such as interest on municipal bonds. In the case of a manufacturing or merchandising business, gross income means gross profit (i.e., gross sales or gross receipts less cost of goods sold).

Glossary

Guaranteed payments

Payments made to a partner for services rendered or for use of the partner's capital, that are made without regard to the income of the partnership (similar to wages). The payments are generally ordinary income to the partner and deductible by the partnership.

Half-year convention

The half-year convention is a depreciation tax rule that assumes the asset is obtained and disposed of halfway through the acquisition and disposal year.

Head of household

An unmarried individual who maintains a household for another and satisfies certain conditions. Such status enables the taxpayer to use income tax rates lower than those applicable to other unmarried individuals (single) but higher than those applicable to surviving spouses [widow(er)] and married persons filing a joint return.

Health savings accounts (HSA)

A type of savings account established by an employer to pay unreimbursed medical expenses by taxpayers with certain high-deductible medical insurance. Contributions to HSAs are deductible for AGI and are subject to limitations.

Healthcare flexible spending accounts

(Refer to *Flexible Spending Account*).

High-low method

A simplified way of computing the federal per diem rate for travel within the United States.

Hobby loss

A nondeductible loss arising from a personal hobby as contrasted with an activity engaged in for profit. Generally, the law provides a presumption that an activity is engaged in for profit if profits are earned during any 3 or more years in a 5-year period.

Household workers

Employees hired to work at specific tasks within a household, including child care, cleaning, meal preparation, and household administration. The payment of household workers generally subjects the taxpayer to a requirement to withhold or pay related payroll taxes. Refer to *Nanny tax*.

Holding period

The period of time that property has been held by a taxpayer. The holding period is of significance in determining whether gains or losses from the sale or exchange of capital assets are classified as long-term or short-term. Refer to *Capital asset*, *Capital gain*, and *Capital loss*.

Hybrid method

A method of accounting that involves the use of both the cash and accrual methods of accounting. The tax law permits the use of a hybrid method, provided the taxpayer's income is clearly reflected by the method.

Independent contractor

Under common-law rules, a worker who performs services for another party and does not meet the definition of employee.

Inflation Reduction Act

Signed into law in 2022, its tax provisions impacted energy-related tax credits and brought back a form of the corporate alternative minimum tax to a limited number of very large corporations.

Installment method

A method of accounting enabling a taxpayer to spread the recognition of gain on the sale of property over the payment period. Under this procedure, the seller computes the gross profit percentage from the sale (i.e., the gain divided by the contract price) and applies the percentage to each payment received to arrive at the gain recognized for each accounting period.

Installment sales

A sale in which part of the proceeds will be received in a tax year or years following the year of sale resulting in the partial deferral of gain to future tax years. Refer to *Installment method*.

Intangible assets

An asset that does not have a physical presence but has value. Some examples of intangible assets include copyrights, goodwill, patents, trademarks, etc.

Interest

The amount paid for the use of borrowed funds.

Internal Revenue Code

Sometimes referred to as the Tax Code or the Code, the comprehensive set of tax laws enacted as Title 26 of the United States Code of Congress. The Code is organized according to topic, and covers all relevant rules pertaining to income, gift, estate sales, payroll, and excise taxes. The IRS is the implementing agency of the Internal Revenue Code.

Internal Revenue Service (IRS)

A United States government agency that is responsible for the enforcement of the Internal Revenue Code and collection of taxes. The IRS was established in 1862 by President Lincoln and operates under the authority of the United States Department of the Treasury.

Inventory

The goods and raw materials used to produce goods, held for sale by a business, to be sold to produce a profit.

Involuntary conversion

The loss or destruction of property through theft, casualty, or condemnation. If the owner reinvests any proceeds received within a prescribed period of time in property that is similar or related in service or use, any gain realized on an involuntary conversion can, at the taxpayer's election, be deferred for federal income tax purposes.

IRS Campus Processing Sites

Sites at which IRS computers process information from tax documents such as tax returns, payroll tax forms, Form 1099s, and withholding forms.

IRS online withholding estimator

An online estimator that uses information from recent paystubs of a taxpayer and spouse, details from other sources of income, and a previous tax return to estimate additional withholding needs.

Itemized deductions

Tax deductions taken for various personal expenses incurred during the tax year that decrease taxable income. Itemized deductions are generally used by the taxpayer when the total exceeds the standard deduction. Refer to *Standard deduction*.

Kiddie tax

The amount of tax on the unearned income of certain dependent children.

Last in, first out (LIFO)

An accounting method for determining the cost of inventories. Under the LIFO method, the most recently acquired goods are sold first and the cost of inventory on hand is deemed to consist of the earliest purchased merchandise (goods).

Life insurance proceeds

Generally, life insurance proceeds paid to a beneficiary upon the death of the insured are exempt from federal income tax. An exception exists when a life insurance contract has been transferred for valuable consideration to another individual who assumes ownership rights. In such a case, the proceeds are income to the assignee to the extent that the proceeds exceed the amount paid for the policy (cash surrender value at the time of transfer) plus any subsequent premiums paid.

Lifetime learning credit

The lifetime learning credit may be used in any tax year the American Opportunity tax credit is not used for expenses paid for education. Unlike the American Opportunity tax credit, the lifetime learning credit may be claimed for an unlimited number of tax years.

Like-kind exchange

An exchange of property held for productive use in a trade or business or for investment (except inventory and stocks and bonds) for property of the same type.

Unless different property is received (i.e., "boot"), the exchange will be nontaxable.

Like-kind property
Refer to *Like-kind exchange*.

Limited Liability Company (LLC)
Business organizations usually treated as partnerships for tax purposes but offering the limited liability of a corporate stockholder to all members.

Limited liability partnerships (LLPs)
A partnership structure where each partner's liability is limited to the amount contributed to the business.

Low-income Retirement Plan Contribution Credit
Certain low-income taxpayers may claim a nonrefundable "Low-Income Retirement Plan Contribution Credit," also called the "Saver's Credit," to encourage participation in tax-saving retirement plans, including IRAs.

Marginal tax rate
The amount of additional tax paid for every additional dollar earned as income.

Market discount
The excess of an bond's stated redemption price over its lower trading price in the secondary market.

Market premium
The excess of a bond's trading price on the secondary market over its lower stated redemption price.

Married filing jointly
A filing status for married couples that have wed before the end of the tax year.

Married filing separately
A tax status used by married couples who choose to record their incomes, exemptions, and deductions on separate tax returns.

Medical expenses
Medical expenses of an individual, spouse, and dependents may be allowed as an itemized deduction to the extent that total medical expenses, less insurance reimbursements, exceed limitations based on the taxpayer's AGI.

Medical flexible spending account (FSA)
A medical flexible spending account is a fringe benefit that allows employees to be reimbursed for medical expenses tax-free up to a certain dollar limit when incurred and claimed within a specific time period. FSAs are usually funded through an employee's voluntary salary reduction agreement with their employer.

Medicare tax
After 2012, the Affordable Care Act (ACA) imposed an additional Medicare tax on high-income taxpayers, at a rate of 0.9 percent applicable to wages, compensation, and self-employment income above an annual threshold amount.

Mid-month convention
The mid-month convention states that all fixed asset acquisitions are assumed to have been purchased in the middle of the month for depreciation purposes.

Mid-quarter convention
The mid-quarter convention states that a business acquiring fixed assets in a reporting quarter should account for them as though they were acquired at the mid-point of the quarter.

Medicare
Federal health insurance provided by the government for persons 65 and over in the United States.

Modified Accelerated Cost Recovery System (MACRS)
The current tax depreciation system in the United States.

Modified adjusted gross income (MAGI)
A household's adjusted gross income with any tax-exempt interest income and certain deductions added back.

Moving expenses
A deduction in arriving at adjusted gross income available to employees and self-employed individuals provided certain tests are met (e.g., the taxpayer's new job must be at least 50 miles farther from the former residence than the former residence was from the former place of work). However, the TCJA has suspended the deduction of moving expenses for all taxpayers except members of the U.S. Armed Services beginning in the 2018 tax year and ending in 2025.

Municipal bond interest
Interest income that is generally exempt from federal tax.

Nanny tax
Payroll taxes paid by a taxpayer that employs certain household workers. Refer to *Household workers*.

Necessary
Appropriate and helpful in furthering the taxpayer's business or income-producing activity. Refer to *Ordinary*.

Net capital gains
The amount by which net long-term capital gains are more than net short-term capital losses.

Net capital losses
The amount by which total capital losses exceed total capital gains.

Nonelective contributions
A mandatory contribution made by an employer to a qualified retirement plan for a particular tax year. Nonelective contributions are generally excluded from the employees' gross income.

Net investment income
Income such as dividends and interest from investment assets such as stocks, bonds, mutual funds and other investment assets, less investment expenses other than interest expense.

Net investment income tax
The ACA imposed a 3.8 percent Medicare tax on certain net investment income of individuals that have net investment income or modified adjusted gross income above the annual statutory threshold amounts.

Net operating loss (NOL)
When a business's allowable deductions exceed its taxable income within a tax period, a NOL is generated. The NOL can generally be used to offset a business's taxable income, subject to annual limitations.

Non-50-percent organization
Refer to *50-percent organization*.

Nonattorney-client privilege
The extension of attorney-client privilege of confidentiality in tax matters to nonattorneys authorized to practice before the IRS. This privilege may be asserted only in noncriminal tax proceedings before the IRS or federal courts.

Nonbusiness bad debts
A bad debt loss not incurred in connection with a taxpayer's trade or business. Such loss is deductible subject to annual limitations, as a short-term capital loss, and will only be allowed in the year the debt becomes entirely worthless. Many investor losses fall into the classification of nonbusiness bad debts.

Nondeductible penalty
Taxpayers are not allowed to deduct penalties assessed by the IRS.

Nondeductible traditional IRA
A retirement plan funded with after-tax dollars.

Nonqualified recipients

Charitable contributions made to nonqualified recipients are not tax deductible. These include needy individuals, social clubs, labor unions, international organizations, and political parties.

Nonrecourse debt

An obligation for which the endorser is not personally liable. An example of a nonrecourse debt is a mortgage on real estate acquired by a partnership without the assumption of any liability on the mortgage by the partnership or any of the partners. The acquired property generally is pledged as collateral for the loan.

OASDI

A component of the FICA tax. Old age, survivors, and disability insurance tax; the money that an employer collects goes to the federal government in order to fund the Social Security program. Refer to *Federal Insurance Contributions Act (FICA)* and *Social security tax.*

Offer in compromise

The IRS may make an offer in compromise that allows a taxpayer to settle tax debt for less than the full amount owed. It may be a legitimate option if someone can't pay their full tax liability, or if doing so creates a financial hardship.

Office audit

A type of tax return audit conducted by the IRS at one of their offices.

Open transaction

Transaction in which not all of the tax events have been completed, therefore providing an opportunity to make modifications and influence the tax result.

Ordinary

Common, accepted, and legitimate in the general industry or type of activity in which the taxpayer is engaged. It comprises one of the tests for the deductibility of expenses incurred or paid in connection with a trade or business: for the production or collection of income; for the management, conservation, or maintenance of property held for the production of income; or in connection with the determination, collection, or refund of any tax. Refer to *Necessary.*

Ordinary gains and losses

Gains and losses that are realized in the course of doing business and from the sale of noncapital assets are typically ordinary.

Organizational expenses/expenditures

Organizational expenses (also known as organizational costs) are associated with the formation of a business prior to the beginning of operation. A corporation may amortize organizational expenses over a period of 180 months. Certain expenses related to starting a company do not qualify for amortization (e.g., expenses connected with issuing or selling stock or other securities).

Original Issue Discount (OID)

The difference between a bond's original redemption value and the lower issuance price of the bond.

Partnerships

Partnerships are conduit, reporting entities that engage in some type of business or financial activity, and are not subject to taxation. Various items of partnership income, expenses, gains, and losses flow through to the partners and are reported on the partners' respective individual income tax returns.

Pass-through Entity Tax (PTE)

A state tax provision that allows certain pass-through businesses such as partnerships, to pay an entity-level income tax at the state level and claim an offsetting state income tax credit.

Passive activity

A trade or business in which the taxpayer does not materially participate. Passive activities include most rental real estate activity.

Passive losses

Passive losses are deductible only to the extent of passive income. Losses from actively managed rental real estate may be deducted up to $25,000 annually. Unused passive losses carry forward indefinitely (or until the activity which generated the losses is disposed of) and can be used by taxpayers to offset passive income in future years.

Patents

A patent is an intangible asset which may be amortized over its life. The sale of a patent usually results in long-term capital gain treatment.

Payroll Deduction IRA

Under a Payroll Deduction IRA, employees establish an IRA (either a Traditional or Roth IRA) with a financial institution and authorize a payroll deduction amount for it.

Pension plans

A pension plan is a type of retirement plan where employers promise to pay a defined benefit to employees for life after they retire.

Per diem

An alternative to reporting actual expenses, a per diem allows for a daily allowance for travel expenses including lodging, meals, and incidentals to be reimbursed to employees. Per diem reporting is designed to eliminate the record keeping usually associated with travel expenses.

Percentage method of withholding

A method of calculating employees' federal tax withholdings; this method has no wage or allowance limits and can be used if the employee's wages exceed the wage bracket's limit.

Personal expenses

Expenses of an individual incurred for personal reasons which are not deductible unless specifically allowed under the tax law.

Personal holding company tax

Personal holding companies are subject to a 20-percent tax on their undistributed earnings.

Personal property

Generally, all property other than real estate. Personal property is sometimes designated as "personalty" while real estate is termed "realty." Personal property can also refer to property not used in a taxpayer's trade or business or held for the production or collection of income. When used in this sense, personal property could include both realty (e.g., a personal residence) and personalty (e.g., personal effects such as clothing and furniture).

Personal residence

The sale of a personal residence may result in the recognition of capital gain (but not loss). Taxpayers may permanently exclude $250,000 ($500,000 if married) of gain on the sale of their personal residence from income provided certain requirements are met, but generally not more than once every two years.

Points

Loan origination fees paid that are generally deductible as interest expense by a buyer of property.

Portfolio income

Portfolio income includes dividends, interest, royalties, annuities, and realized gains or losses on the sale of assets producing portfolio income.

Premium tax credit

A refundable credit that helps eligible individual taxpayers and families cover the premiums for health insurance purchased through the Health Insurance Marketplace.

Prepaid interest

Prepaid interest is the interest a borrower pays on a loan before the first scheduled debt repayment.

Preparer tax identification number (PTIN)

A PTIN is a number issued by the IRS to paid tax return preparers. It is used as the tax return preparer's identification number and, when applicable, must be placed in the Paid Preparer section of a tax return that the tax return preparer prepared for compensation.

Private mortgage insurance (PMI)
Private mortgage insurance is an additional expense charged to a borrower that is often required when the borrower makes only a small investment (down payment) on their home at time of purchase.

Prizes and awards
The fair market value of a prize or award generally is included in gross income.

Property transfers
A property transfer occurs when money or the ownership title on a piece of property, such as a house or parcel of land, changes hands. The majority of property transfers occur on someone's death, where the will stipulates who will inherit the deceased's property.

Public Safety Officer health insurance exclusion
An exclusion from income distributions made from an eligible retired public safety officer's retirement plan used to pay the premiums for coverage by an accident or health plan or a long-term-care insurance contract.

Qualified business income (QBI)
The income attributed to individual taxpayers by a pass-through entity such as a sole proprietorship, partnership, or S corporation that excludes capital gains, most dividends, interest, and other nonbusiness income.

Qualified business income (QBI) deduction
A deduction in the amount of 20 percent of the QBI, subject to certain limitations such as the taxable income limit, the wage limitation, and the specified service business limitation. The limitations are computed before considering the QBI deduction.

Qualified business property
Tangible property subject to depreciation (i.e., not inventory or land) for which the depreciable period has not ended before the close of the taxable year, held by the business at year-end, and used at any point during the year in the production of QBI. Qualified business property is an element of the wage and capital limitation, which is a component of the wage limitation, used in the calculation of the QBI deduction.

"Qualified" federal disasters
Disasters such as hurricanes and wildfires, which may be termed "qualified" by the U.S. government and eligible for federal relief.

Qualified higher education expenses
These include tuition, fees, books, supplies, and equipment required for the enrollment or attendance at an eligible educational institution.

Qualified improvement property (QIP)
Any improvement to a building's interior with the exception of improvements relating to enlarging the building, any elevator or escalator, or the internal structural framework of the building.

Qualified nonrecourse financing
Debt secured by real estate and loaned or guaranteed by a governmental agency or borrowed from any person who actively and regularly engages in the lending of money (bank, insurance company).

Qualified pension or profit-sharing plan
An employer-sponsored plan that meets certain requirements. If these requirements are met, none of the employer's contributions to the plan will be taxed to the employee until distributed to them. The employer will be allowed a deduction in the year the contributions are made.

Qualified plan
A retirement plan that meets requirements that allow tax benefits to be extended to it.

Qualified plan award
An employee achievement award in the form of tangible personal property that has a maximum exclusion of $1,600.

Qualified recipient
An individual, group, or organization eligible for tax deductible charitable contributions, having met appropriate tax law criteria.

Qualified replacement property
Replacement property that must be "similar or related in service or use," as defined by tax law.

Qualified residence acquisition debt
Debt secured by the taxpayer's primary or secondary residence in acquiring, constructing, or substantially improving that residence.

Qualified tuition program
Refer to *Section 529 tuition plan*.

Qualified trade or business
Any trade or business other than a specified service trade or business, or the trade or business of performing services as an employee.

Qualifying child
A dependent child who has met the tests set forth by the IRS: relationship, domicile, age, joint return, citizenship, and self-support.

Qualifying person
A dependent that meets the qualifications to permit a taxpayer to claim head of household status.

Qualifying relative
An individual that is not a qualifying child but meets the tests to be claimed as a dependent.

Qualifying widow(er)
Refer to *Surviving spouse*.

Realized gain or loss
The difference between the amount realized upon the sale or other disposition of property and the adjusted basis of such property.

Recognized gain or loss
The portion of realized gain or loss that is subject to income taxation. Refer to *Realized gain or loss*.

Recovery period
The amount of time in which a business asset is depreciated and thereby creating a tax deduction, under the useful life requirements established by the IRS.

Related parties
IRS rules define related parties for disallowance purposes. Common related parties include defined family members; a corporation or individual who owns more than 50 percent of the corporation; two corporations that are members of the same controlled group; and trust, corporations, and certain charitable organizations.

Required minimum distributions (RMDs)
The minimum amount of money that must be withdrawn each year from a traditional IRA, SEP, or SIMPLE IRA by owners and qualified retirement plan participants of retirement age. The retiree must withdraw the RMD amount annually, starting in the year the retiree turns age 72 (70½ years old before January 1, 2021). Roth IRAs do not require withdrawals until after the death of the owner.

Resident
An individual taxpayer that is a citizen of the Unites States, a green card holder, or meets the substantial presence test.

Residential clean energy credit
A nonrefundable 30-percent tax credit for individuals related to renewable energy and energy efficient home improvements such as solar, wind, geothermal, and fuel-cell technology.

Rollover
Transfer of pension funds from one plan or trustee to another. The transfer may be a direct transfer or a rollover distribution.

Roth 401k
A Roth 401k is an employer-sponsored investment savings account that is funded with after-tax dollars up to the plan's contribution limit.

Roth IRA
The Roth individual retirement account (IRA) allows nondeductible contributions. Although the contributions to a Roth IRA are not deductible, earnings accumulate tax-free, and qualified distributions are generally not included in income when received.

Roth IRA conversion
A transfer of retirement assets from a Traditional, SEP, or SIMPLE IRA into a Roth IRA, which creates a taxable event.

S corporation
A small business corporation whose shareholders have filed an election permitting the corporation to be treated in a manner similar to partnerships for income tax purposes. Of major significance are the facts that S corporations usually avoid the corporate income tax and that corporate losses can be claimed by the shareholders, limited to individual shareholder's adjusted basis.

Safe harbor 401k
A type of tax-deductible 401k plan that ensures all employees at a company have some set of minimum contributions made to their individual 401k plans, regardless of their title, compensation, or length of service. It is not subject to the complex annual nondiscrimination tests that apply to traditional 401k plans.

Sale or exchange
A sale generally requires the receipt of money or the relief from liabilities in exchange for property; an exchange is the transfer of ownership of one property for another property.

Saver's Credit
A tax credit designed to give low-to-moderate-income taxpayers a tax credit for part of a contribution to a qualified retirement plan.

Scholarships
Scholarships are generally taxable income to the recipient except for amounts received for tuition, fees, books, and course-required supplies and equipment.

Section 179
Refer to *Election to expense (Section 179)*.

Section 197 intangibles
The category of intangibles that consists of those acquired by a taxpayer as part of the acquisition of a trade or business. They are amortized over a 15-year period, beginning with the month of acquisition.

Section 199A dividend
Qualified real estate investment trust (REIT) dividends that are eligible for the qualified business income deduction.

Section 401k plan
A Section 401k plan is a qualified retirement plan which grants employee participants a deferral of income for employer contributions to the plan. The plan allows taxpayers to elect to contribute compensation or to have the employer make a contribution to the retirement plan. The plan may be structured as a salary reduction plan. There is a maximum annual dollar limitation, as well as a limitation based on the employee's compensation. Some employers match employee contributions up to a certain limit in order to encourage participation.

Section 403(b) plan
A qualified retirement plan offered to certain employees of public schools, state colleges, universities, and other tax-exempt organizations that operates in a manner similar to 401k plans used by private-sector employees.

Section 457(b) plan
A qualified retirement plan offered to state and local government employees and operates in a similar manner to a 401k plan used by private-sector employees.

Section 529 tuition plan
Also known as a Qualified Tuition Program; allows taxpayers to buy in-kind tuition credits or certificates for qualified higher education expenses (a prepaid plan); or to contribute to an account established to meet qualified higher education expenses (a savings plan).

Section 1202 stock
Qualified small business stock for which an exclusion is permitted for the gain at the time of sale.

Section 1231 assets
Section 1231 assets include depreciable assets and real estate used in a trade or business, held for the long-term holding period. Under certain circumstances, the classification also includes timber, coal, domestic iron ore, livestock (held for draft, breeding, dairy, or sporting purposes), and unharvested crops. Gains may be treated as long-term capital gains while losses in some cases may be deducted as ordinary losses.

Section 1244 stock
Qualified small business stock for which an ordinary loss is permitted when sold up to certain thresholds.

Section 1245 recapture
Refer to *Depreciation recapture*.

Section 1250 recapture
Refer to *Depreciation recapture*.

Self-employment income
Self-employment income is the taxpayer's net earnings from self-employment, which includes gross income from a taxpayer's trade or business, less trade or business deductions. Self-employment income also includes the taxpayer's share of income from a partnership trade or business.

Self-employment tax
Tax required to be paid by self-employed taxpayers, sole proprietors, and independent contractors with net earnings of $400 or more annually.

Simplified Employee Pension (SEP)
A retirement plan that any employer or self-employed individual can establish. SEPs are simple to establish and have flexible funding arrangements with contributions that are limited on an annual basis.

Separate property
Separate property is property, other than community property, acquired by a spouse before marriage or after marriage as a gift or inheritance.

Short-period taxable income
When taxpayers have a short year other than their first or last year of operations, they are required to annualize their taxable income to calculate the tax for the short period.

SIMPLE 401k
A SIMPLE 401k plan is a retirement plan offered by small business employers with 100 or fewer employees that operates in a fashion similar to a typical 401k plan. Refer to *Section 401k plan*.

SIMPLE IRA
A form of qualified retirement plan for small businesses with 100 or fewer employees. Unlike a SEP, employers are required to make certain contributions.

Simplified Employee Pension (SEP) IRA
A form of qualified retirement plan for certain small businesses. Refer to *SEP*.

Simplified method
A specific calculation used by individual taxpayers to calculate the taxable amount of a payment from an annuity after November 18, 1996.

Single filing status
A taxpayer who does not meet the definition of married, surviving spouse, or head of household status must file as single.

Social Security
The U.S. social insurance program consisting of retirement, disability, and survivor benefits.

Social Security number

A unique 9-digit number provided by the U.S. Social Security Administration to identify each person and track Social Security benefits. Most taxpayers use the Social Security number as their taxpayer identification number. Refer to *Taxpayer identification number*.

Social Security tax

A component of FICA (refer to *Federal Insurance Contributions Act [FICA]*), Social Security taxes refer to Old Age, Survivors, and Disability Insurance (OASDI) and is applied to all wages, up to an annual limitation (refer to *FICA cap*). Refer to *OASDI*.

Specified service trade or business

Used in the context of qualified business income as being excluded from a qualified trade or business, it involves the performance of services where the principal asset of such trade or business is based on the reputation or skill of one or more of its employees, such as accounting, actuarial science, consulting, financial and brokerage services, health, law, performing arts, and professional athletes.

Standard deduction

Taxpayers can deduct the larger of the standard deduction or their itemized deductions in calculating taxable income. An extra standard deduction amount is allowed for elderly and blind taxpayers. The standard deduction amounts are set by the IRS and may change annually. Refer to *"Catch up" contribution* and *Itemized deductions*.

Standard mileage method

Using a rate determined annually by the IRS, some taxpayers are entitled to calculate deductions for transportation costs.

Standard mileage rate

The rate announced annually by the IRS for use in calculating a standard mileage deduction.

Start-up costs

New business start-up costs include investigatory and preopening costs.

Statute of limitations

A time period within which an action may be taken by the IRS or a taxpayer on a tax return. In general, the statute of limitations for a tax return runs for 3 years from the date the tax return was filed or the return extended due date, whichever is later.

Stock bonus plan

Under tax law, a stock bonus plan is one of several qualified retirement plans. Employer contributions on behalf of an employee consisted of stock of the employer company.

Straight-line depreciation

The simplest method of depreciation, it results in an equal portion of cost being deducted in each period of an asset's life.

Support

Expenditures for food, clothing, shelter, education, medical and dental care, recreation, and transportation.

Surviving spouse

Also referred to as a qualifying widow(er), a tax filing status available to widows or widowers for two years after their spouse's death. To claim this status, the taxpayer must also have a dependent child who lives in the household for whom the taxpayer pays over half the cost of maintaining the household.

Tangible personal property

Property that can be moved or touched, and commonly includes items such as business equipment, furniture, and automobiles. This is contrasted with intangible personal property, which includes stocks, bonds, and intellectual property like copyrights and patents.

Tax

A tax is imposed by a government to raise revenue for general public purposes.

Tax credit

An amount of money that can be offset directly against a tax liability. Tax credits can be refundable (may exceed the tax liability) or nonrefundable (limited to the tax liability and any excess is lost).

Tax Cuts and Jobs Act (TCJA)

The TCJA was signed into law in 2017 representing the most dramatic change to the tax code since 1986. Significant changes include reforms to the itemized deductions and alternative minimum tax, an expanded standard deduction and child tax credit, and lower marginal tax rates across brackets. Some of the individual income tax changes are scheduled to expire after December 31, 2025.

Tax evasion

Failing to pay taxes, failing to file taxes, inaccurate information on taxes, and fraud are all considered part of tax evasion and noncompliance, which may cost the government $1 trillion annually.

Tax Exempt Organization Search

An online search tool of the IRS that provides information about the deductibility of a charitable contribution to a specific organization.

Tax home

Since travel expenses of a taxpayer are deductible only if the taxpayer is away from home, the deductibility of such expenses rests upon the definition of "tax home." The IRS position is that the "tax home" is the business location, post, or station of the taxpayer. If the taxpayer is temporarily reassigned to a new post for a period of one year or less, the taxpayer's home should be his or her personal residence and the travel expenses should be deductible.

Tax planning

The process of arranging one's financial affairs to maximize one's after-tax wealth.

Tax practitioner

Commercial tax preparers, enrolled agents, attorneys, and CPAs are all considered to be tax practitioners.

Tax Rate Schedule

Formulas issued by the IRS annually to calculate individual income tax liability for taxpayers with taxable income of $100,000 or more.

Tax return preparer

Any person who prepares a tax return for compensation.

Tax Table

Amounts issued by the IRS annually to report individual income tax liability for taxpayers with taxable income below $100,000.

Taxpayer Bill of Rights

Passed by Congress in 1988 and amended several times, this set of provisions requires that the IRS informs taxpayers of their rights when dealing with the IRS and it expands taxpayers' rights and remedies when involved in disputes with the IRS. The provisions of the Taxpayer Bill of Rights are summarized in IRS Publication 1.

Taxpayer identification number

A unique number of a taxpayer used by the IRS in the administration of tax laws. For individuals, it is generally a Social Security number, but can also be an Individual Taxpayer Identification Number (ITIN) which is issued by the IRS to individuals who are not eligible to receive a Social Security number. For employers, it is an IRS-issued number known as an Employer Identification Number (EIN). Refer to *Social Security number*.

Trade or business expenses

Deductions for AGI which are attributable to a taxpayer's business or profession. The expenses must be ordinary and necessary to that business. Refer to *Ordinary* and *Necessary*.

Traditional IRA

An individual retirement account (IRA) for taxpayers. The traditional IRA generally permits a deduction for contributions and deferred taxation of earnings until withdrawals.

Transportation expenses

Transportation expenses for a taxpayer include only the costs of transportation (taxi fares, automobile expenses, etc.) in the course of employment where the taxpayer is not "away from home" in a travel status. Commuting expenses are not deductible.

Travel expenses

Travel expenses include meals (50-percent deductible in 2023), lodging, and transportation expenses while away from home in the pursuit of a trade or business (including that as an employee).

Trustee-to-trustee transfer

When a trustee of a retirement plan transfers assets to the trustee of a different retirement plan, upon instruction from the taxpayer. There are no tax implications nor are there any restrictions on amounts or number of transfer occurrences in a given year.

Unearned income

For tax purposes, unearned income (e.g., rent) is taxable in the year of receipt. In certain cases involving advance payments for goods and services, income may be deferred.

U.S. savings bond

The U.S. government issues the following basic types of savings bonds to individuals: Series EE and Series I, which do not pay interest until maturity.

Unreported Income DIF (UIDIF)

One of two systems used by the IRS to select taxpayers for audit.

Vacation home

The Internal Revenue Code places restrictions upon taxpayers who rent their residence or vacation home for part of the tax year. The restrictions may result in the limitation of certain expenses related to the vacation home.

Viatical settlements

An early payout resulting from the sale of a life insurance policy often due to the insured being terminally or chronically ill. A viatical settlement is a way to extract value from the policy while the policy holder is still alive. Refer to *Accelerated death benefits*.

Wage and capital limitation

A limitation on the qualified business income deduction of 25 percent of wages and 2.5 percent of qualified business property, used in the calculation of the QBI deduction.

Wage and Investment (W&I) Division

A division of the IRS that helps taxpayers understand and comply with applicable tax laws and to protect the public interest by applying the tax law with integrity and fairness.

Wage bracket method

A method for determining tax withholding in which wage bracket tables are provided each year by the IRS for weekly, biweekly, semi-monthly, monthly, and daily payroll periods.

Wage limitation

A limitation on the qualified business income deduction of 50 percent of wages, used in the calculation of the QBI deduction.

Wash Sale

The purchase of a substantially identical security within 30 days before or after the sale of a security at a loss.

Withholding

The amount of tax deducted (withheld) by a payer and ultimately remitted to the tax authority as a tax payment on behalf of the payment recipient. For example, income taxes are often withheld from an employee's wages and then remitted on behalf of the employee as a tax payment to the IRS.

Index

A

AAR (amounts at risk), 10-22
Abandoned spouse, 1-11
Abode test, 1-18, 1-21 to 1-22
ACA. *See* Affordable Care Act (ACA)
Accelerated cost recovery system (ACRS), 8-6
Accelerated death benefits, 2-23
Accelerated depreciation, 8-9, 8-10
Accident and health insurance, 2-7 to 2-8
Accounting methods, 6-3 to 6-6
Accrual method of accounting, 6-3 to 6-4
Accumulated earnings tax, 11-32
Accuracy-related penalty, 12-13
Achievement awards, 2-18
ACRS (Accelerated cost recovery system), 8-6
Active income, 4-31
Active management exception, 4-33
Actual cost method, 3-14
Additional comprehensive tax return problems, D-1 to D-11
Additional Medicare Tax (Form 8959), 6-24, 6-28
Adjusted basis, 1-30, 4-5 to 4-8
Adjusted gross income (AGI), 1-6
Adjusted gross income deduction, 1-5 to 1-6
Adoption credit, 7-43, 7-45 to 7-46
Adoption expenses, 7-43 to 7-46
ADR (Asset depreciation range), 8-6
Affordable Care Act (ACA)
   0.9 percent additional Medicare tax, 6-24
   3.8 percent Medicare tax on net investment income, 6-23
   health savings account (HSA), 5-3
   premium tax credit (PTC), 7-16 to 7-27
AFS (applicable financial statements), 3-10
AFSP (Annual Filing Season Program), 12-18
After-tax, 2-19
AFTR (Annual Federal Tax Refresher), 12-18
Age test, 1-18
AGI (adjusted gross income), 1-6
AI (artificial intelligence), 1-34 to 1-35
Airport skycaps, 9-23
Alimony
   child support, 2-40 to 2-41
   ProConnect, 2-41
   property transfers, 2-40
   qualifying requirements, 2-39 to 2-40
Allocable rental expenses, 4-29
Alternative minimum tax (AMT)
   individuals, 6-17 to 6-18 (*See also* Individual alternative minimum tax)
Amended Tax Returns, 6-29 to 6-33
American Institute of Certified Public Accountants (AICPA), 3-22
American Opportunity tax credit (AOTC), 7-28 to 7-31
Amortization, 8-23
Amount realized, 1-30, 4-4
Amounts at risk (AAR), 10-22
AMT. *See* Alternative minimum tax (AMT)
Annual Federal Tax Refresher (AFTR), 12-18
Annual Filing Season Program (AFSP), 12-18
Annualized income method, 11-9
Annualized period, 6-2

Annuity, 2-18 to 2-23
   defined, 2-18
   exclusion for public safety officers, 2-22
   general rule, 2-21
   nonqualified plan, 2-19
   reporting, 2-21 to 2-22
   simplified method, 2-19 to 2-21
   standard mortality tables, 2-19
Appeals process, 12-8, 12-10, 12-24. *See also* Tax litigation
Applicable financial statements (AFS), 3-10
Archer MSA, 5-2
Architect fees, 4-5
Artificial intelligence (AI), 1-34 to 1-35
Asset depreciation range (ADR), 8-6
At-risk rule, 10-22 to 10-23
Attorney-client privilege, 12-20
Attorneys, 12-16
Audit process
   appeals process, 12-8, 12-10, 12-24
   correspondence audit, 12-6
   DIF score, 12-7
   field audit, 12-6
   matching problems, 12-8
   NRP audit, 12-7 to 12-8
   office audit, 12-6
   overview (flowchart), 12-9
   selection of returns for audits, 12-7 to 12-8
   TCMP audit, 12-7
   UIDIF score, 12-7
Auto enrollment of employees, 5-26
Automobiles, 8-19 to 8-22
Average tax rate, 12-25
Awards and prizes, 2-17 to 2-18

B

Backup withholding, 9-24
"Bad" check, 12-14
Bad debts, 3-25 to 3-26
Banks, 9-43
Barbers, 9-23
Bartenders, 9-23
Barter, 2-2
Basic allowance for housing (BAH), 6-42
Basic allowance for subsistence (BAS), 6-42
Before-tax, 2-19
Behavioral factors, 9-2 to 9-3
Below market loans, 2-30
Beneficial ownership information (BOI), 11-10 to 11-11
Bicycle commuting, 2-12
Bill of Rights (taxpayers), 12-22
Bingo, 9-42
Blindness, 1-28
Bond discount and premium, 2-29 to 2-30
Bond interest, 2-27 to 2-30
Bonus depreciation, 8-10 to 8-11
Book income, 11-7
Boot, 8-36, 11-22
Bribes and kickbacks, 3-3
Built-in gains tax, 11-21
Business and pleasure trip combined, 3-16
Business bad debts, 3-25 to 3-26

Business casualty gains and losses, 8-29 to 8-33
Business education expenses, 3-20 to 3-22
Business expense reimbursements, 9-41
Business gifts, 3-24
Business income and expenses
   bad debts, 3-25 to 3-26
   business gifts, 3-24
   dues, subscriptions, and publications, 3-22 to 3-23
   education expenses, 3-20 to 3-22
   hobby losses, 3-32 to 3-33
   inventories (*See* Inventory)
   meals and entertainment, 3-19, 3-24
   office in the home (*See* Home office deduction)
   per diem allowances, 3-17
   special clothing and uniforms, 3-23
   tests for deductibility, 3-2 to 3-3
   trade or business, 3-2
   transportation expenses, 3-13 to 3-15
   travel expenses (*See* Travel expenses)
Business purpose test, 3-2 to 3-3

C

Cafeteria plan, 2-10
California Poly Academy (CPA), 1-27
California wildfires, 5-59
CAMT (corporate alternative minimum tax), 11-2
Cancellation of debt income, 2-53 to 2-55
Capital asset, 1-31, 4-2
Capital gain distributions, 2-34
Capital gains and losses
   adjusted basis, 4-5 to 4-8
   amount realized, 4-4
   calculation of gain or loss, 4-4 to 4-8
   capital asset, 1-31, 4-2
   capital gains and losses, 1-30 to 1-31
   capital improvements, 4-5
   capital loss carryover, 4-12
   Form 8949 (sales and other dispositions of capital assets), 4-20 to 4-21
   formula to calculate gain or loss, 1-30
   holding period, 4-3
   long-term capital gains, 1-31, 4-3
   long-term collectibles gains, 4-10
   net capital gains, 4-9 to 4-11
   net capital loss, 1-31, 4-12 to 4-13
   net long-term capital gain, 4-11
   ordering rules for capital gains, 4-11
   ordering rules for capital losses, 4-13
   ordinary gains and losses, 1-30
   original basis, 4-5
   overview, 1-30 to 1-32
   personal capital losses, 4-13
   sale or exchange, 4-4
   Schedule D, 4-14 to 4-15
   settlement fees or closing costs, 4-5
   short-term capital gains, 1-31, 4-3
   special rules for small company stock, 4-14
   tax rates, 4-9 to 4-10
   unrecaptured section 1250 gain, 4-11
   wash sales, 4-13 to 4-14
Capital improvements, 4-5
Capitalization, 8-2 to 8-5
Capital loss carryover, 4-12

Index

Cash donation, 5-53, 5-55
Cash method of accounting, 6-3 to 6-6
Casualty and theft losses, 5-57, 5-61
    California wildfires, 5-59
    casualty, defined, 5-57
    deductible losses, 5-57
    deduction limitations, 5-58 to 5-59
    disasters/acts of god, 5-58 to 5-59
    embezzlement, 5-57
    Form 4684, 5-59, 5-61
    general rule, 5-57
    hurricanes, 5-59
    indirect losses, 5-57
    measuring the loss, 5-57 to 5-58
    qualified federal disasters, 5-59
    Rule A, 5-57
    Rule B, 5-57
    TCJA, 5-60
    termite damage, 5-57
Celebratory meals, 3-19
Cell phones, 2-15
Certified public accountant (CPA), 12-16
Chambers of Commerce, 3-19
Character, 1-15
Charitable contributions, 5-50 to 5-56
    cash donation, 5-53, 5-55
    clothing and household items, 5-55
    contribution carryovers, 5-54
    corporation, 11-6
    credit card contributions, 5-55
    deductibility, 5-50
    donated property, 5-50
    false written acknowledgment penalty, 5-56
    IRS online search tool, 5-50
    non-deductibility, 5-50
    nonqualified recipient, 5-50
    percentage limitations, 5-51 to 5-55
    20-percent limitation, 5-54 to 5-55
    30-percent limitation, 5-53 to 5-54
    50-percent limitation, 5-51 to 5-52
    60-percent limitation, 5-51
    qualified recipient, 5-50
    quid pro quo contributions, 5-56
    rules on, 5-51 to 5-55
    sub-$250 cash donations, 5-55 to 5-56
    substantiation rules, 5-55 to 5-56
    used vehicles, 5-56
ChatGPT, 1-34 to 1-35
Cheating on taxes, 12-13
Child and dependent care credit, 7-14 to 7-16
Child and Dependent Care Expenses, 7-16
Children
    child and dependent care credit, 7-14 to 7-16
    child tax credit (See Child tax credit)
    gift to Roth IRA for child, 5-18
    qualifying child, 1-17 to 1-20
    unearned income (See Kiddie tax)
Child support, 2-40 to 2-41, 9-13
Child tax credit, 1-25 to 1-26, 7-2 to 7-6
    credits for qualifying children and other dependents, 7-7 to 7-8
    due diligence checklist, 7-5
    erroneous claims (ineligibility window), 7-5
    Form 8862, 7-5
    limitations, 7-4 to 7-5
    other dependent credit, 7-5
    pecking order (refundable/nonrefundable credits), 7-3
    phasing out, 7-3
    qualifying tests, 7-3
    refund claims, 7-5
    Schedule 8812, 7-5, 7-7 to 7-8
Circular 230, 12-1, 12-16 to 12-18

Clean vehicle credit, 7-48 to 7-50, 7-53 to 7-56
Client meals, 3-19
Closed transaction, 12-25
Club dues, 3-19
Collateral, 10-22
Collectibles, 4-11
Combat pay, 6-42
Combat zone tax exclusion (CZTE), 6-43
Combined business and pleasure trip, 3-16
Commercial clean vehicle credit, 7-49 to 7-50
Commissioner of internal revenue, 12-2
Commissioner v. Newman, 12-22
Community property, 2-51 to 2-53
    spouses living apart, 2-52 to 2-53
Community property states, 2-52
Commuting, 2-12, 3-13
Company picnic, 3-19
Constructive ownership rules, 6-9
Consumer interest, 5-44
Consumer price index inflation calculator, 2-47
Contest winnings, 2-17
Continuing education expenses, 3-20
Contract price, 8-35
Convenience of employer, 2-8
Co-ownership of property, 10-2
Corporate alternative minimum tax (CAMT), 11-2
Corporate bonds, 2-28
Corporate capital gains/losses, 11-2 to 11-3
Corporation, 1-4
    accumulated earnings tax, 11-32
    assumption of shareholder liabilities by corporation, 11-30
    boot, 11-22
    capital losses, 11-3
    charitable contributions, 11-6
    corporation's basis in property contributed, 11-30 to 11-31
    dividends received deduction, 11-4
    estimated tax payments, 11-8 to 11-10
    filing deadline, 11-8
    fiscal year, 6-2
    Form 1120, 11-13 to 11-18
    formation, 11-22
    investigatory expenses, 11-5
    June 30 year-end corporation, 11-8
    net operating loss (NOL), 11-3
    nonrecognition rule, 11-22, 11-30 to 11-31
    organizational expenditures, 11-5 to 11-6
    personal holding company tax, 11-32
    personal service, 11-2
    preopening costs, 11-5
    quarterly estimated tax payments, 11-9
    S (See S corporation)
    Schedule K-1, 11-20, 11-28 to 11-29
    Schedule L (balance sheet), 11-11, 11-18
    Schedule M-1, 11-7 to 11-8, 11-11, 11-18
    service, 11-32
    shareholder's stock basis, 11-30
    small, 11-11
    special deductions and limitations, 11-4 to 11-7
    start-up costs, 11-5 to 11-6
    taxable income *vs.* book income, 11-7
    tax rate, 11-2
    tax year, 6-2
Correspondence audit, 12-6
Cost of goods sold, 3-5 to 3-6, 3-10, 3-11
Covenant not to compete, 8-23
Coverdell education savings account, 2-44
COVID-19 pandemic, 11-2 to 11-3
    virtual proceedings during, 12-8
CPA (Certified public accountant), 12-16
Credit card charitable contributions, 5-55
Credit card sales, 9-43

Credit for Qualified Retirement Savings Contributions (Form 8880), 7-60 to 7-63
Credits. *See* Tax credits
Criminal Investigation Office, 12-4
Cross-matching of records, 12-2
Cryptocurrency, 4-2 to 4-3

D

Deductions. *See* Tax deductions
Deductions, Adjustments, and Additional Income Worksheet, 9-16
Defined benefit plan, 9-52
Defined contribution plan, 9-52
Degree of control and independence, 9-2 to 9-3
Delivery drivers, 9-23
De Minimis financial incentives, 5-58
De minimis fringe benefits, 2-15
De minimis meals, 2-9
De Minimis Safe Harbor Election, 8-3 to 8-4
De minimis transportation benefits, 2-11
Dependent
    credits for children and other, 1-25 to 1-26
    defined, 1-17
    filing requirements, 1-7
    qualifying child, 1-17 to 1-20
    qualifying relative, 1-21 to 1-23
    Social Security number, 1-17
    standard deduction, 1-28 to 1-29
    tiebreaker rules, 1-20 to 1-21
Dependent care assistance programs, 2-12
Dependent care flexible spending account, 2-11
Depreciation, 8-5
Depreciation and Amortization (Form 4562), 8-14 to 8-16
Depreciation and sale of business property
    accelerated depreciation, 8-9 to 8-10
    automobiles, 8-19 to 8-22
    bonus depreciation, 8-10 to 8-11
    business casualty gains and losses, 8-29 to 8-33
    capitalization and depreciation, 8-2 to 8-5
    depreciation calculator, 8-14
    depreciation expense in year of disposal, 8-12 to 8-13
    depreciation expense, reporting, 8-14
    depreciation recapture, 8-26 to 8-28
    election to expense (section 179), 8-17 to 8-19
    Form 4562, 8-14 to 8-16
    Form 4797, 8-30 to 8-31
    Form 6252, 8-34, 8-37
    half-year convention, 8-8
    installment sales, 8-33 to 8-35
    intangibles, 8-23
    involuntary conversion, 8-39 to 8-40
    like-kind exchanges, 8-36 to 8-38
    listed property, 8-19 to 8-20
    luxury automobiles, 8-20 to 8-22
    MACRS, 8-6 to 8-14
    MACRS realty tables, 8-11
    mid-month convention, 8-12
    mid-quarter convention, 8-8 to 8-10
    passenger automobiles, 8-19 to 8-22
    recovery periods, 8-6
    Section 179 election to expense, 8-17 to 8-19
    Section 1231 gains and losses, 8-24 to 8-26
    Section 197 intangibles, 8-23
    Section 1231 lookback, 8-25 to 8-26
    Section 1245 recapture, 8-26 to 8-28
    Section 1250 recapture, 8-27 to 8-28
    Section 291 Recapture for Corporations, 8-28
    special 15 or 18.8-percent tax rate, 8-28
    special 25 or 28.8-percent tax rate, 8-28, 8-39 to 8-40
    straight-line depreciation, 8-7 to 8-8
    taxable income limitation, 8-18

unrecaptured depreciation, 8-28
39-year nonresidential property, 8-11
27.5-year residential real property, 8-11
Depreciation calculator, 8-14
Depreciation expense in year of disposal, 8-12 to 8-13
Depreciation expense, reporting, 8-14
Depreciation recapture, 3-31, 8-26 to 8-28
DIF (Discriminant function system) score, 12-7
Direct transfer, 9-56
Disability severance, 6-43
Disasters, 5-59
Discharge of debt income, 2-53 to 2-55
Discriminant function system (DIF) score, 12-7
Distribution rollover, 9-56
Dividend income. *See* Interest and dividend income
Dividends received deduction (DRD), 11-4
Divorce and separation, 6-33 to 6-37
Divorced Spouses, 6-35 to 6-37
Divorcing couples
   alimony, 2-39 to 2-40
   child support, 2-41
   tax savings, 1-12
   transfer of property in settlement of divorce, 2-41
Dog racing, 9-42
Domestic multiyear adoptions, 7-43 to 7-44
Domicile test, 1-18, 1-21 to 1-22
Donations. *See* Charitable contributions
Door prizes, 2-17
Due diligence checklist, 7-5, 7-31
Dues, subscriptions, and publications, 3-22 to 3-23

E

Earned income credit (EIC)
   AGI limit, 7-10
   earned income requirement, 7-10 to 7-11
   EIC table, B-3
   eligibility checklist, 7-13
   eligibility qualifications, 7-11
   investment income limit, 7-11
   "negative" income tax, 7-11
   qualifying child, 7-11 to 7-12
   questions to ask, 7-10
   reporting requirements, 7-12 to 7-13
   Schedule EIC, 7-13
   where taxpayer has no qualifying child, 7-11 to 7-12
   worksheets, 7-13, B-2 to B-13
Economic performance, 6-5
Educational expenses, 3-20 to 3-22
   education required by employer or law, 3-21
   expenses of travel for educational purposes, 3-21 to 3-22
   maintaining or improving existing skills, 3-21
   "travel as a form of education," 3-22
Educational incentives, 2-42 to 2-46
   educational savings accounts, 2-44 to 2-45
   Qualified Tuition Programs (QTP), 2-42 to 2-44
Educational savings accounts, 2-44 to 2-45
Education assistance plan, 2-13
Education tax credits, 7-28 to 7-34
Educator expenses, 5-32
e-filing, 1-36
EFTPS (Electronic Federal Tax Payment System), 9-31, 9-39, 9-47
Eggers, Roscoe, 1-4
EIC. *See* Earned income credit (EIC)
EIC eligibility checklist, 7-13
80-percent income limitation rule (NOL), 11-3
EITC, 7-10. *See also* Earned income credit (EIC)
Elderly or disabled credit, 7-47

Election to expense (section 179), 8-17 to 8-19
Electronic Federal Tax Payment System (EFTPS), 9-31, 9-39, 9-47
Electronic filing (e-filing), 1-36
Electronic funds transfer, 9-47
Emancipation Day, 1-7
Embezzlement, 5-57
Employee
   athletic facilities, 2-15
   auto enrollment, 5-26
   cell phones, 2-15
   foreign housing exclusion, 7-35
   home office deduction, 3-31
   independent contractor, distinguished, 9-2 to 9-4
   new hires, 9-13
   0.9 percent Medicare tax, 6-24
   retirement planning fringe benefit, 2-15
   tuition reduction, 2-13
   unreimbursed employee expenses, 5-59
Employee discounts, 2-13 to 2-14
Employee fringe benefits
   bicycle commuting, 2-12
   de minimis fringe benefits, 2-15
   education assistance plan, 2-13
   and eligibility, 2-15 to 2-17
   employee discounts, 2-13 to 2-14
   flexible spending account (FSA), 2-10 to 2-11
   no-additional-cost services, 2-13 to 2-14
   parking at work, 2-11
   public transportation, 2-11
   working condition fringe benefits, 2-14
Employee Stock Ownership Plan (ESOP), 9-52 to 9-53
Employee's Withholding Certificate, 9-9 to 9-12
Employer
   household, 6-19
   information returns, 9-42 to 9-43
   payroll reporting requirements, 9-41 to 9-46
   quarterly federal tax return (Form 941), 9-38 to 9-40
   small, 9-38
Employer payroll reporting requirements, 9-41 to 9-46
Employer-provided adoption assistance, 7-44
Employer-provided cell phones, 2-15
Employer's Annual Federal Unemployment (FUTA) Tax Return (Form 940), 9-47, 9-49 to 9-50
Employer's Annual Information Return of Tip Income and Allocated Tips, 9-24
Employer's QUARTERLY Federal Tax Return (Form 941), 9-38 to 9-40
Employer's Report of Tips to Employer, 9-23
Employer's Withholding Allowance Certificate, 9-14 to 9-15, 9-67
Encumbered property, 10-22
Ending inventory, 3-10
Energy credits, 7-47 to 7-48
Energy efficient home improvement credit, 7-48, 7-50 to 7-51
Enrolled agents, 12-16
Entertainment costs, 3-19
Entertainment-related club dues, 3-19
Entertainment-related meal, 3-19
Entity-based tax planning, 12-26
Equitable Relief, 6-35, 6-37
ESOP. *See* Employee stock ownership plan (ESOP)
Estimated payments (quarterly estimated tax payments), 9-28 to 9-31, 11-8 to 11-10
Exclusion for public safety officers, 2-22
Exclusions, 2-2 to 2-3
Exemption, 1-6, 2-2
Expenses for Business Use of Your Home (Form 8829), 3-4 to 3-5, 3-29
Expensing election (section 179), 8-17 to 8-19

F

Failure-to-file penalty, 12-12
Failure-to-pay penalty, 12-12
Fantasy sports, 2-17
Farmers, 6-41 to 6-42
   Special Tax Provisions For, 6-41
Federal Income Tax Withholding Methods (IRS Pub 15-T), 9-18, 9-38
Federal Insurance Contributions Act (FICA), 4-44 to 4-46, 6-19 to 6-20. *See also* FICA tax
Federal poverty line (FPL), 7-17
Federal Tax Court, 12-8
Federal tax deposit system
   lookback period, 9-37
   small employers, 9-38
   typical tax deposits, 9-37 to 9-38
Federal Unemployment Tax Act (FUTA), 9-47
Fee, 5-37
Fee-basis government officials, 5-32
FICA tax, 9-25 to 9-26
   employer portion of the tax, 9-26
   Medicare tax, 9-26
   overpayment of Social Security taxes, 9-27
   Social Security tax, 9-27
Field audit, 12-6
FIFO (First in, first out), 3-10
50-percent organization, 5-51
Filing deadline. *See also* Filing requirements
   children and other dependents, 1-9
   corporation, 11-8
   e-filing, 1-36
   extension of time to file, 1-8
   filing status (*See* Filing status)
   individuals, 1-7 to 1-9
   other situations when you must file, 1-9
   refunds, 1-7
   S corporation, 11-19
   who must file?, 1-7 to 1-9
Filing requirements, 1-7
Filing status
   head of household, 1-12
   married filing jointly, 1-10 to 1-11
   married filing separately, 1-11
   single filing status, 1-10
   surviving spouse, 1-12
Fillable forms program, 1-36
Financial control factors, 9-2 to 9-3
Financial Crimes Enforcement Network (FinCEN), 11-10
Fines and penalties, 3-3
First in, first out (FIFO), 3-11 to 3-12
First-time homebuyer credit, 7-47
First-time penalty abatement program, 12-12
Fixing-up expenses, 4-25
Flexible spending account (FSA), 2-10 to 2-11
Food and beverage servers, 9-23
"Forced" savings (overpayment of taxes), 9-22
Foreign exclusions and deduction, 7-36
Foreign Financial Accounts (FBAR), 6-40 to 6-41
Foreign housing exclusion, 7-35
Foreign income exclusion, 7-35 to 7-41
Foreign tax credit, 7-41 to 7-42
Forgiveness of tax liability, 6-47 to 6-48
Form 172, 4-45
Form 461, 4-43
Form 843, 6-39 to 6-40
Form 940, 9-47, 9-49 to 9-50
Form 941, 9-38 to 9-40
Form 944, 9-38
Form 1040, 1-3 to 1-4, 2-32 to 2-34, 4-48
Form 1041, 1-4
Form 1065, 1-4, 10-6, 10-9 to 10-14
Form 1098, 7-28

Index

Form 1116, 7-42
Form 1120, 1-4, 11-13 to 11-18
Form 1310, 6-39
Form 2106, 3-15
Form 2210, 9-31
Form 2441, 7-16
Form 2555, 7-37 to 7-40, 7-42
Form 4070, 9-23
Form 4562, 8-14 to 8-16
Form 4684, 5-59, 5-61
Form 4797, 8-30 to 8-31
Form 4868, 1-8
Form 4952, 5-48
Form 5329, 5-19
Form 5695, 7-51, 7-57 to 7-59
Form 6251, 6-14, 6-17
Form 6252, 8-34, 8-37
Form 7206, 5-8
Form 8027, 9-24
Form 8283, 5-55
Form 8582, 4-34, 4-39 to 4-40
Form 8615, 6-10 to 6-12
Form 8814, 6-11, 6-13
Form 8815, 2-27
Form 8824, 8-36, 8-41 to 8-42
Form 8829, 3-4 to 3-5, 3-29
Form 8839, 7-43, 7-45
Form 8857, 6-34
Form 8862, 7-5
Form 8863, 7-29, 7-33 to 7-34
Form 8867, 1-12 to 1-14, 7-5, 7-12, 7-31
Form 8880, 7-60 to 7-63
Form 8889, 5-3, 5-5
Form 8936, 7-53 to 7-56
Form 8938, 6-40 to 6-41
Form 8949, 4-20 to 4-21
Form 8959, 6-24, 6-28
Form 8960, 6-23, 6-27
Form 8962, 7-21, 7-22, 7-26 to 7-27
Form 8995, 4-55 to 4-57
Form 1095-A, 7-21 to 7-22, 7-25, 7-29
Form 8995-A, 4-56 to 4-57
Form 1099-B, 4-15, 9-42
Form 1098-C, 5-56
Form 1099-C, 9-42
Form 1099-DIV, 2-37, 2-54, 9-42
Form 1040-ES, 9-29, 9-31, 9-37
Form 1099-G, 9-42
Form 1099-INT, 2-38, 9-42
Form 1099-K, 9-42
Form 1099-MISC, 9-42
Form 1099-NEC, 9-42
Form 1040-NR, 6-33, 6-39
Form 1099-OID, 9-42
Form 1099-Q, 9-42
Form 1099-R, 2-22, 9-42
Form 1099-S, 4-24, 9-42
Form 1120-S, 1-4, 11-23 to 11-27
Form 1099-SA, 5-3, 9-42
Forms and Publications search function, 1-33
Form 1040-SR, 1-3
Form SSA-1099, 2-47
Form 1098-T, 2-39
Form W-2, 2-5 to 2-8, 6-43, 9-41
Form W-3, 9-41
Form W-4 after 2019, 9-5 to 9-13
Form W-4 before 2020, 9-13 to 9-17
Form W-2G, 9-42
Form W-4P, 9-23
Form W-9 Request for Taxpayer Identification Number, 9-44 to 9-45
Form 1040-X, 6-31 to 6-32
457(c) plan, 5-21
401(k)-based plans, 5-24 to 5-26

403(b) plan, 5-21
FPL (Federal poverty line), 7-17
Franchise, 8-23
Fraud penalty, 12-13
Fringe benefits. *See* Employee fringe benefits
Frivolous tax return, 12-14
FSA (Flexible spending account), 2-10 to 2-11
Funeral, 2-13
FUTA tax, 9-47

G

Gambling losses, 5-60
Gambling winnings, 9-42
General business credit, 7-47
General Instructions for Certain Information Returns, 9-43
General partner, 10-3
General partnership, 10-2 to 10-3
General Services Administration (GSA), 3-18
Gift loans, 2-30
Gifts, 2-38, 3-24
Going-concern value, 8-23
Good faith defense, 12-13 to 12-14
Goodwill, 8-23
Gross income, 1-5
  accident and health insurance, 2-7 to 2-8
  alimony, 2-39 to 2-40
  annuity, 2-18 to 2-23
  cancellation of debt income, 2-53 to 2-55
  community property, 2-51 to 2-53
  Coverdell education savings account, 2-44
  defined, 2-2
  educational incentives, 2-42 to 2-46
  fringe benefits (*See* Employee fringe benefits)
  gifts and inheritances, 2-38
  inclusions/exclusions, 2-2, 6-42 to 6-44
  interest and dividends (*See* Interest and dividend income)
  life insurance, 2-23 to 2-25
  meals and lodging, 2-8 to 2-10
  prizes and awards, 2-17 to 2-18
  Qualified Tuition Program (QTP), 2-42 to 2-44
  refund of taxes, 5-39
  salary and wages, 2-4 to 2-7
  scholarships, 2-39
  Social Security benefits, 2-46 to 2-49
  unemployment compensation, 2-46
Gross income test, 1-22
Gross tax liability, 1-6
Gross vehicle weight rating (GVWR), 7-49
Group term life insurance, 2-12 to 2-13
GSA (General Services Administration), 3-18
Guaranteed payments, 10-7, 10-20

H

Hairdressers, 9-23
Half-year convention, 8-8
Head of household, 1-12
Health care flexible spending account, 2-10 to 2-11
Health insurance
  health savings account (HSA), 5-2 to 5-4
  medical expenses, 5-34 to 5-36
  self-employed health insurance deduction, 5-6 to 5-7
Health Insurance Marketplace Statement, 7-25
Health insurance premium tax credits, 7-16 to 7-24
Health reimbursement arrangement (HRA), 5-2
Health savings account (HSA), 5-2 to 5-4
  catch-up contributions, 5-3
  contribution limits, 5-3
  Form 8889, 5-3, 5-5
  Form 1099-SA, 5-3
  guidance (IRS Publication 969), 5-4

Higher education student loan, 5-29
High-income taxpayers
  defined, 6-23
  employees, 6-24
  0.9 percent additional Medicare tax, 6-24
  3.8 percent Medicare tax on net investment income, 6-23
  phase-out of itemized deductions, 5-60
  self-employed taxpayers, 6-25 to 6-26
  special taxes, 6-23 to 6-28
High-low method, 3-18
Hobby income, 3-32
Hobby losses, 3-32 to 3-33
Holding period, 4-3
Holiday parties, 3-19
Home
  defined, 5-45
  mortgage interest, 5-44 to 5-46
  office in the home, 3-27 to 3-31
  part-year rental property (vacation home), 4-28 to 4-30
  principal residence (*See* Personal residence exclusion laws)
Home equity debt, 5-45
Home mortgage interest deduction, 5-45
Home office deduction
  depreciation expense, 3-28
  employees, 3-31
  exceptions to general rule, 3-27
  home office allocation, 3-28 to 3-30
  income limitation, 3-28
  optional safe harbor method, 3-30
  self-employed taxpayers, 3-27, 3-29
  simplified method, 3-30
Horse racing, 9-42
Hotel housekeepers, 9-23
Household employers, 6-19. *See also* Nanny tax
Household Employment Taxes (Sch. H), 6-20 to 6-22
HRA (Health reimbursement arrangement), 5-2
HSA. *See* Health savings account (HSA)
Hurricanes, 5-59
Hybrid method of accounting, 6-3

I

Illegal drugs-related expenditures, 3-3
Income taxes, 5-39 to 5-42
Income tax withholding. *See* Withholding and payroll taxes
Independent contractor, 9-2 to 9-4
Individual
  AMT (*See* Individual alternative minimum tax)
  filing deadline, 1-7 to 1-9
  filing status (*See* Filing status)
  Form 1040, 1-3 to 1-4
  international income, 7-35
  seniors (*See* Seniors)
  Social Security earnings history, 9-26
  standard deduction (*See* Standard deduction)
  taxable entity, as, 1-3
  tax formula (*See* Tax formula for individuals)
  tax rates, 1-15
  tax year, 6-2
  volunteer income tax assistance (VITA) program, 1-32
Individual alternative minimum tax
  AMT adjustments and preferences, 6-14 to 6-15
  AMT exemptions and thresholds, 6-15
  calculating the tax, 6-14
  Form 6251, 6-14, 6-17
  tax rates, 6-15 to 6-16
Individual retirement account (IRA), 5-9 to 5-17
  catch-up contributions, 5-9
  contribution limits, 5-9

Index I-5

distribution rollover, 9-56 to 9-57
general rule, 5-9
gift to Roth IRA for child, 5-18
inherited IRAs, 5-16 to 5-17
nondeductible traditional IRA contribution, 5-10 to 5-13
payroll deduction IRA, 5-21
penalty for early withdrawals, 5-13
penalty-free withdrawals, 5-13
phase-out ranges, 5-10
prohibited transactions, 5-17
required minimum distributions (RMDs), 5-15 to 5-16
Roth IRA conversions, 5-13
Roth IRA distributions, 5-13 to 5-14
SIMPLE IRA, 5-22 to 5-24
traditional IRA distributions, 5-13
Information returns, 9-42 to 9-43
Inheritances, 2-38
Inherited IRAs, 5-16 to 5-17
Innocent spouse relief, 6-34, 12-24
Installment Sale Income (Form 6252), 8-34, 8-37
Installment sales, 8-33 to 8-35
Insurance
  accident and health, 2-7 to 2-8
  life, 2-23 to 2-25
Intangibles, 8-23
Interest, 5-44
Interest and dividend income
  below market loans, 2-30
  bond interest, 2-27 to 2-30
  capital gain distributions, 2-34
  nontaxable distributions, 2-34
  ordinary dividends, 2-34
  ProConnect, 2-38
  reporting requirements, 2-30
  section 199A dividends, 2-36
  tax rates for dividends, 2-34 to 2-36
  U.S. savings bonds, 2-25 to 2-27
Interest and Ordinary Dividends (Sch. B), 2-37
Interest and penalties
  accuracy-related penalty, 12-13
  "bad" check, 12-14
  failure-to-file penalty, 12-12
  failure-to-pay penalty, 12-12
  first-time penalty abatement program, 12-12
  fraud penalty, 12-13
  frivolous tax return, 12-14
  good faith defense, 12-13 to 12-14
  miscellaneous penalties, 12-14
  negligence/disregard for rules, 12-13
  nondeductible penalty, 12-11
  overpayment of tax, 12-11
  preparer penalties, 12-19 to 12-20
  substantial understatement of income, 12-13
  substantial valuation overstatement, 12-13
  underpayment of tax, 12-11
Interest deduction, 5-44 to 5-48
  consumer interest, 5-44
  deductible/non-deductible items, 5-44
  home equity debt, 5-45
  interest, defined, 5-44
  investment interest, 5-47
  prepaid interest, 5-44 to 5-45
  private mortgage insurance (PMI), 5-44
  qualified mortgage debt, 5-45
  qualified residence interest, 5-45 to 5-46
  student loan interest, 5-46 to 5-47
  taxpayer's obligation, 5-44
Internal Revenue Service (IRS)
  Annual Filing Season Program (AFSP), 12-18
  assistance for taxpayers, 1-33
  audit (See Audit process)

  collections, 12-5 to 12-6, 12-24
  commissioner of internal revenue, 12-2
  cross-matching of records, 12-2
  divisions and principal offices, 12-4
  examination of records, 12-5
  fillable forms program, 1-36
  Forms and Publications search function, 1-33
  information returns, 9-42 to 9-43
  interest and penalties (See Interest and penalties)
  LB&I Division, 12-4
  lock-in letter, 9-13
  mission, 12-2, 12-23
  national computer center, 12-2
  national office, 12-2
  news feeds, 1-33
  number of returns audited by, 12-7
  offer in compromise, 12-5
  1099 forms, 9-42
  online sales tax deduction calculator, 5-40
  online withholding estimator, 9-6
  organizational structure, 12-3 to 12-4
  role, 12-2
  SB/SE Division, 12-4
  sources of further information, 12-24
  summons, 12-5
  Tax Exempt Organization Search, 5-50
  taxpayer appeals (See Tax litigation)
  taxpayer services, 12-4 to 12-5
  tax preparation and e-filing software, 1-36
  TE/GE Division, 12-4
  third-party summons, 12-5
  tip reporting, 9-23 to 9-24
  underpayments of estimated tax, 9-29
  website, 1-33, 1-36
  W&I Division, 12-4
  writing out a check to "IRS," 9-28
  YouTube channel, 1-33
Internet
  ChatGPT, 1-34 to 1-35
  Intuit's ProConnect Tax Online, 1-34
  IRS website, 1-33, 1-36
  online payment networks, 9-43
  online sales tax deduction calculator, 5-40
  online search tool for charitable organizations, 5-50
  online statement of Social Security benefits, 9-26
  online withholding estimator, 9-6
  Tax Notes, 1-34
Inventory
  applicable financial statements (AFS), 3-10
  cash method accounting, 3-10
  cost of goods sold, 3-10 to 3-12
  defined, 3-10
  ending, 3-10
  first in, first out (FIFO), 3-11 to 3-12
  inventory flow method, 3-10
  last in, first out (LIFO), 3-11 to 3-12
  non-incidental materials and supplies (NIMS), 3-10
  physical, 3-10
  UNICAP rules, 3-11
  using same accounting method as normally used in the business, 3-10
Inventory flow method, 3-10 to 3-12
Investigatory expenses, 11-5
Investment interest deduction, 5-47
Involuntary conversion, 8-39 to 8-40
IRA. See Individual retirement account (IRA)
IRS. See Internal Revenue Service (IRS)
IRS Campus Processing Sites, 12-2
IRS2GO, 1-33
@IRSnews, 1-33
IRS Publication 1, 12-22

IRS Publication 54, 7-42
IRS Publication 463, 3-17
IRS Publication 538, 10-18
IRS Publication 556, 12-24
IRS Publication 594, 12-5
IRS Publication 596, 7-12
IRS Publication 926, 6-20
IRS Publication 946, 8-9
IRS Publication 969, 5-4
IRS Publication 15-T, 9-18, 9-38
IRS Restructuring and Reform Act (1998), 12-20
Itemized deductions, 1-6
Itemized deductions (Sch. A), 5-2, 5-37, 5-38. See also Tax deductions

J

Jai alai, 9-42
June 30 year-end corporation, 11-8

K

Keno, 9-42
Kickbacks, 3-3
Kiddie tax
  children subject to the tax, 6-9
  computation of the tax, 6-10
  election to include child's income on parents' return (Form 8814), 6-10, 6-13
  net unearned income, 6-9
  parent, defined, 6-9
  ProConnect, 6-10
  reporting the tax (Form 8615), 6-10
Kimmel, Jimmy, 12-2
Kiwanis, 3-19

L

Lacerte, 1-34
Large Business and International (LB&I) Division, 12-4
Last in, first out (LIFO), 3-10
LB&I (Large Business and International) Division, 12-4
Life insurance, 2-23 to 2-25
Lifetime learning credit, 7-31
LIFO (Last in, first out), 3-10
Like-kind exchanges, 8-36 to 8-38
Like-kind property, 8-39
Limited liability company (LLC), 10-23
Limited liability partnership (LLP), 10-23
Limited partnership, 10-2 to 10-3
Listed property, 8-19 to 8-20
LLC (limited liability company), 10-23
LLP (limited liability partnership), 10-23
Lobbying and political expenditures, 3-3
Lock-in letter, 9-13
Lodging, 2-8 to 2-10
Long-term capital gains, 1-31, 4-3
Long-term collectibles gains, 4-11
Long-term holding period requirement, 4-3
Lookback period, 9-37
Loss harvesting, 4-13 to 4-14
Lotteries, 2-17, 9-42
Low-income housing, 4-34
Low-income housing credit, 7-47
Low-income retirement plan contribution credit, 7-60 to 7-61
Lump-sum payment, 12-5
Luxury automobiles, 8-20 to 8-22

M

MACRS (modified accelerated cost recovery system), 8-6 to 8-14

MACRS realty tables, 8-11
MAGI (modified adjusted gross income), 2-46
Magic line, 1-6
Manicurists, 9-23
Marginal tax rate, 12-25
Market discount and premium, 2-29
Married filing jointly, 1-10 to 1-11
Married filing separately, 1-11
Married status, 6-33
Married taxpayers
   child and dependent care credit, 7-16
   community property (spouses living apart), 2-52
   filing status, 1-10 to 1-11
   innocent spouse relief, 12-24
   IRS recommendations, 1-36, 6-25
   lifetime learning credit, 7-31
   passive loss limitations, 4-31 to 4-33
   sale of personal residence, 4-23 to 4-24
   unincorporated business operated by spouses, 10-3
Mastercard, 9-43
Meals and entertainment, 3-19, 3-24
Meals and incidental expenses (M&IE), 3-18
Meals and lodging, 2-8 to 2-10
Medical expenses, 2-10, 5-34 to 5-36
   calculating the deduction, 5-34
   capital expenditures, 5-36
   lodging for medical care, 5-36
   medical insurance, 5-35
   medicine and drugs, 5-36
   transportation, 5-36
   what qualifies?, 5-34 to 5-35
Medical insurance, 5-35
Medical savings account (MSA), 5-2
Medicare tax
   0.9 additional tax on earned income, 6-24
   FICA tax, 9-25
   3.8 percent net investment income tax, 6-23
Medicine and drugs, 5-36
Merchant card and third-party payments, 9-43
Mid-month convention, 8-12
Mid-quarter convention, 8-8 to 8-10
M&IE allowance. *See* Meals and incidental expenses (M&IE)
Military taxpayers, 6-42 to 6-49
   AGI deductions, 6-45 to 6-46
   exclusion on sale of primary residence, 6-47
   extension to file and pay taxes, 6-48 to 6-49
   forgiveness of tax liability, 6-47 to 6-48
   gross income inclusions and exclusions, 6-42 to 6-44
Miscellaneous expenses, 5-59 to 5-60
Modified accelerated cost recovery system (MACRS), 8-6 to 8-14
Modified adjusted gross income (MAGI), 2-46
Money purchase plan, 5-21
Monthly or semiweekly depositors, 9-37
More-than-50-percent-use test, 8-20
Mortage interest credit, 7-47
Mortgage interest, 5-44 to 5-46
Moving expenses, 5-33
MSA (Medical savings account), 5-2
Multiple jobs worksheet, 9-6

N

Nanny tax
   guidance (IRS Publication 926), 6-20
   household employer, defined, 6-19
   ProConnect, 6-20
   reporting requirements, 6-20
   Schedule H, 6-20 to 6-22
National Guard members, 5-32

National Research Program (NRP) audit, 12-7 to 12-8
Negligence/disregard for rules, 12-13
Net capital gains, 4-9 to 4-11
Net capital loss, 1-31, 4-12 to 4-13
Net investment income, 5-47
Net Investment Income Tax—Individuals, Estates and Trusts (Form 8960), 6-23, 6-27
Net long-term capital gain, 4-11
Net operating loss (NOL)
   carryforward and carryback, 4-42
   corporation, 11-3
   excess business loss limitation, 4-42 to 4-43
   ProConnect, 4-43
   purpose of NOL provision, 4-36
   tax items to be considered, 4-36
New clean vehicle credit, 7-48 to 7-49
New markets credit, 7-47
NIMS (non-incidental materials and supplies), 3-10
No-additional-cost services, 2-13 to 2-14
Nobel prize, 2-18
NOL. *See* Net operating loss (NOL)
NOL carryback/carryforward, 11-3
Nonattorney-client privilege, 12-20
Nonbusiness bad debts, 3-25 to 3-26
Nondeductible divorce expenses, 6-37
Nondeductible traditional IRA contribution, 5-10 to 5-13
Non-incidental materials and supplies (NIMS), 3-10
Nonqualified plan annuity, 2-19
Nonqualified recipient, 5-50
Nonrecourse liability, 10-22
Nonrefundable credits, 7-2
Nonresident and International Issue, 6-39 to 6-41
Non-Section 197 intangibles, 8-23
Nontaxable distributions, 2-34
NRP (National Research Program) audit, 12-7 to 12-8

O

OASDI (Old Age, Survivors, and Disability Insurance), 9-25
Obamacare, 7-16. *See also* Affordable Care Act (ACA)
Offer in compromise, 12-5
Office audit, 12-6
Office of Online Services, 12-4
Office of Professional Responsibility (OPR), 12-4
Oil and gas investments, 4-34
Old Age, Survivors, and Disability Insurance (OASDI), 4-44, 9-25
1099 Forms, 9-42
Online activities. *See* Internet
Online payment networks, 9-43
Open transaction, 12-25
OPR (Office of Professional Responsibility), 12-4
Ordinary and necessary test, 3-2
Ordinary dividends, 2-34
Ordinary gains and losses, 1-30
Ordinary partnership, 10-2 to 10-3
Ordinary repairs and maintenance expenditures, 4-5, 4-8
Organizational expenditures, 11-5 to 11-6
Original basis, 4-5
Original issue discount (OID), 2-28
Other dependent credit, 1-26, 7-5
"Overnight," 3-15
Owned (used) clean vehicle credit, 7-49

P

Paid Preparer's Due Diligence Checklist, 7-5, 7-31

Parents' Election to Report Child's Interest and Dividends (Form 8814), 6-10 to 6-11, 6-13
Parking attendants, 9-23
Parking at work, 2-11
Partnership
   at-risk rule, 10-22 to 10-23
   co-ownership of property, 10-2
   current distributions, 10-17
   Form 1065, 10-6, 10-9 to 10-14
   formation, 10-4 to 10-5
   general, 10-2 to 10-3
   guaranteed payments, 10-7, 10-20
   income reporting, 10-6
   legal entity, 10-2
   limited, 10-2
   nonrecognition rule, 10-4
   partner's deductible loss, 10-6
   partner's initial basis, 10-4
   pass-through entity, 10-7
   qualified business income (QBI) deduction, 10-20 to 10-21
   reporting entity, not a taxable entity, 1-4
   Schedule K-1, 10-6, 10-15
   self-employment income for partners, 10-7
   tax year, 6-2, 10-18
   transactions between partners and partnership, 10-19
   Uniform Partnership Act, 10-2
   unincorporated business operated byspouses, 10-3
Partnership income reporting, 10-6
Part-year rental property (vacation home), 4-28 to 4-30
Part-year withholding method, 9-24
Passenger automobiles, 8-19 to 8-22
Passive activity, 4-31
Passive Activity Loss Limitations, 4-39 to 4-40
Passive category income, 7-42
Passive income and losses, 4-31
Passive loss/credit carryover, 4-31
Passive loss limitations
   categories of income, 4-31
   complexity of legislation, 4-34
   Form 8582, 4-34, 4-39 to 4-40
   married taxpayers, 4-31 to 4-33
   passive activity, 4-31
   passive loss/credit carryover, 4-31
   real estate rental as trade or business, 4-33 to 4-34
Patent, 8-23
Patriots' Day, 1-7
Payment methods, 12-5
Payment settlement entities, 9-43
PayPal, 9-43
Payroll deduction IRA, 5-21
Payroll taxes. *See* Withholding and payroll taxes
Pease phase-out, 5-57, 5-60
Penalties. *See* Interest and penalties
Pension and deferred income, 9-23
Pension plan, 9-52
Pension plan rollovers, 9-55 to 9-57
Percentage method of determining withholding, 9-18 to 9-19, 9-21, C-15 to C-18
Per diem allowances, 3-17
Performing artists, 5-32 to 5-33
Periodic payments, 12-5
Permanent change of station (PCS), 6-45
Personal Allowances Worksheet, 9-13, 9-16
Personal capital losses, 4-13
Personal holding company tax, 11-32
Personal property taxes, 5-43
Personal residence exclusion laws
   exclusion amount, 4-23

fixing-up expenses, 4-25
married taxpayers, 4-23 to 4-24
ownership and use requirements, 4-23
personal residence, defined, 4-23
post May 6/97 sales, 4-23
pre/May 7/97 sales, 4-25 to 4-26
reporting the sale, 4-24
"rollover basis," 4-25 to 4-26
unforeseen circumstances, 4-23
Personal Responsibility and Work Opportunity Act (PRWORA), 9-13
Personal service corporation, 11-2
Physical inventory, 3-10
PMI (Private mortgage insurance), 5-44
Political expenditures and lobbying, 3-3
Porters, 9-23
Portfolio income, 4-31
Premium tax credit (PTC)
  calculating the credit, 7-16 to 7-24
  credit paid in advance, 7-21, 7-25
  federal poverty line (FPL), 7-17
  Form 8962, 7-21, 7-26 to 7-27
  Form 1095-A, 7-21, 7-25
Preopening costs, 11-5
Prepaid interest, 5-44 to 5-45
Preparer penalties, 12-19 to 12-20
Preparers. *See* Tax practitioners
Preparer tax identification (PTIN), 12-17 to 12-18
Principal place of business, 3-15
Principal residence. *See* Personal residence exclusion laws
Private mortgage insurance (PMI), 5-44
Prizes and awards, 2-17 to 2-18
ProConnect
  alimony, 2-41
  bad debts, 3-26
  casualty, 5-59
  child and dependent care credit, 7-16
  child tax credit, 1-25 to 1-26, 7-6
  dependents, 1-25
  dependent window, 1-26
  depreciation calculator, 8-14
  earned income credit, 1-25, 7-14
  education credits, 7-32
  filing status, 1-16
  foreign taxes, 7-43
  Form W-2, 2-7
  health savings account (HSA), 5-3
  home office deduction, 3-31
  interest and dividends, 2-38
  itemized deductions, 5-37
  kiddie tax, 6-10
  nanny tax, 6-20
  net operating loss (NOL), 4-43
  profits from sole proprietorship, 3-7
  real estate professional exception to passive loss rules, 4-33
  rental activity, 4-30
  sale of business property, 8-29
  self-employed health insurance, 5-7
  Social Security benefits, 2-49
  state sales tax calculator, 5-40
  state tax deduction information, 5-40
  vehicle expenses, 3-15
  wages, salaries, tips, 2-7
Profit or Loss from Business (Sch. C), 3-8 to 3-9
Profit sharing plan, 9-52
Property taxes, 5-42
PRWORA (Personal Responsibility and Work Opportunity Act), 9-13
PTC. *See* Premium tax credit (PTC)
Public safety officers, 2-22
Public transportation, 2-11
Puerto Rico bonds, 2-28

Q

Qalified business income (QBI) deduction, 1-6
QBI deduction. *See* Qualified business income (QBI) deduction
QIP (qualified improvement property), 8-10
QTP (Qualified Tuition Program), 2-42 to 2-44
Qualified Adoption Expenses, 7-43 to
Qualified business income (QBI) deduction
  "below the line" deduction, 4-49
  defined, 4-49 to 4-50
  excess amount, 4-52
  exclusions, 4-49
  Form 8995, 4-55 to 4-57
  Form 8995-A, 4-56 to 4-57
  partnership, 10-20 to 10-21
  qualified business property, 4-51
  qualified trade or business, 4-49
  reporting requirements, 4-54
  safe harbor, 4-49
  S corporation, 11-21
  simplified computation (Form 8995), 4-55 to 4-57
  specified service business limitation, 4-52 to 4-54
  taxable income limitation, 4-50
  wage limitation, 4-50 to 4-52
Qualified Business Income Deduction Simplified Computation (Form 8995), 4-55 to 4-57
Qualified business property (QBI deduction), 4-51
Qualified Dividends and Capital Gain Tax Worksheet, 2-33, 2-36, 8-28
Qualified domestic relations order (QDRO), 6-33
Qualified education expenses, 2-44 to 2-45
Qualified employee discounts, 2-13 to 2-14
Qualified federal disasters, 5-59
Qualified fuel cell motor vehicle credit, 7-48
Qualified higher education expenses, 2-42, 5-46, 7-28
Qualified improvement property (QIP), 8-10
Qualified mortgage debt, 5-45
Qualified moving expenses, 6-46
Qualified nonrecourse financing debt, 10-22
Qualified plan, 5-15, 9-52. *See also* Qualified retirement plans; Small business and self-employed retirement plans
Qualified plan award, 2-18
Qualified principal residence exception, 2-54
Qualified recipient, 5-50
Qualified replacement property, 8-39
Qualified residence acquisition debt, 5-45 to 5-46
Qualified residence interest, 5-45 to 5-46
Qualified retirement plans
  eligibility requirements, 9-51 to 9-52
  limitations on contributions to/benefits from plan, 9-54 to 9-55
  rollovers, 9-55 to 9-57
  small business (*See* Small business and self-employed retirement plans)
  types of qualified plans, 9-52 to 9-54
  uniform minimum distribution rules, 9-52
  vesting requirements, 9-52
Qualified Section 197 intangibles, 8-23
Qualified trade or business (QBI deduction), 4-49
Qualified transportation benefits, 2-11
Qualified Tuition Program (QTP), 2-42 to 2-44
Qualifying child, 1-17 to 1-20
Qualifying dependent, 1-17 to 1-26. *See also* Dependent
Qualifying person, 1-23, 1-25 to 1-26
Qualifying relative, 1-21 to 1-23
Qualifying widow(er), 1-12
Quarterly estimated tax payments, 9-28 to 9-31, 11-9
Quid pro quo contributions, 5-56

R

Race horses, 3-32
Radio game show prizes, 2-17
Real estate professional exception to passive loss rules, 4-33
Reasonableness test, 3-3
Recovery periods, 8-6
REEP credit, 7-48
Refinanced debt, 5-45
Refundable credits, 7-2
Refunds of taxes, 1-7, 5-39, 12-12, 12-16, 12-24
Rehabilitation credit, 7-47
Related parties, 6-7 to 6-9. *See also* Section 267 related-party provisions
Relationship factors, 9-2 to 9-3
Relationship test, 1-17 to 1-18, 1-21
Rental income and expenses, 4-27 to 4-30
Required annual payment, 9-28
Required minimum distributions (RMDs), 5-15 to 5-16
Research and experimentation credit, 7-47
Residential clean energy credit, 7-51 to 7-52
Residential energy-efficient property (REEP) credit, 7-48
Restaurant servers, 9-23
Retirement plan rollovers, 9-55 to 9-57
Retirement plans
  qualified (*See* Qualified retirement plans)
  small businesses (*See* Small business and self-employed retirement plans)
Return Preparer Office, 12-4
RMDs (required minimum distributions), 5-15 to 5-16
Rollovers, 9-55 to 9-57
Rotary Club, 3-19
Roth IRA, 5-13. *See also* Individual retirement account (IRA)
Roth IRA contributions, 5-21
Roth IRA conversions, 5-13
Roth IRA distributions, 5-13 to 5-14
Roth 401(k) plan, 5-26
Rule A, 5-57
Rule B, 5-57

S

Safe Harbor for Routine Maintenance, 8-4
Safe harbor 401(k) plan, 5-25 to 5-26
Salary and wages, 2-4 to 2-7
Sale of personal residence. *See* Personal residence exclusion laws
Sale or exchange, 4-4
Sales and Other Dispositions of Capital Assets (Form 8949), 4-20 to 4-21
Sales of Business Property (Form 4797), 8-30 to 8-31
Sales tax, 5-39 to 5-42
Sales tax estimation table, 5-40
Saver's credit, 7-60
Savings bonds, 2-25 to 2-27
SB/SE (Small Business/Self-Employed) Division, 12-4
Schedule 1, 1-4
Schedule 2, 1-4
Schedule 3, 1-4
Schedule 8812, 7-5, 7-7 to 7-8
Schedule A, 1-4, 5-38
Schedule B, 1-4, 2-25, 2-30 to 2-31
Schedule C, 1-4, 3-2, 3-14, 4-27
  cost of goods sold, 3-5 to 3-6
  expenses (Part II), 3-4 to 3-5

Schedule C (*Continued*)
  form (Profit or Loss from Business), 3-8 to 3-9
  income (Part I), 3-4
  other expenses, 3-7
  principal business or professional activity code, 3-3 to 3-4
  use, 3-3
  vehicle information, 3-5 to 3-6
Schedule D, 1-4, 2-34, 2-36
Schedule D Tax worksheet, 8-28
Schedule E, 1-4, 4-27, 4-30, 4-37 to 4-38
Schedule EIC, 7-13
Schedule F, 1-4, 3-2, 3-14
Schedule H, 6-20 to 6-22
Schedule K-1, 1-4, 10-6, 10-15, 11-20, 11-28 to 11-29
Schedule K-2, 10-7
Schedule K-3, 10-7
Schedule L (balance sheet), 11-11, 11-18
Schedule M-1, 11-7 to 11-8, 11-11, 11-18
Schedule M-2, 11-11, 11-18
Schedule SE, 3-7, 4-48, 6-24
Scholarships, 2-39
S corporation, 1-4
  built-in gains tax, 11-21
  death of shareholder, 11-20
  electing S corporation status, 11-19
  filing deadline, 11-19
  Form 1120-S, 11-23 to 11-27
  involuntary termination, 11-19
  losses, 11-20
  pass-through items, 11-21
  qualified business income (QBI) deduction, 11-21
  reporting income, 11-19 to 11-20
  Schedule K-1, 11-20
  statutory termination, 11-19
  voluntary revocation, 11-19
Second lowest cost silver plan (SLCSP), 7-17, 7-21 to 7-22
Section 199A deduction, 4-49. *See also* Qualified business income (QBI) deduction
Section 199A dividends, 2-36
Section 179 election to expense, 8-17 to 8-19
Section 1231 gains and losses, 8-24 to 8-26
Section 197 intangibles, 8-23
Section 1231 lookback, 8-25 to 8-26
Section 401(k) plan, 5-24 to 5-26
Section 1245 property, 8-26 to 8-27
Section 1245 recapture, 8-26 to 8-27
Section 1250 recapture, 8-27 to 8-28
Section 291 Recapture for Corporations, 8-28
Section 1245 recapture potential, 8-27
Section 267 related-party provisions
  common related parties, 6-8
  constructive ownership rules, 6-9
  losses, 6-7
  unpaid expenses and interest, 6-7 to 6-8
Section 530 Safe Harbor, 9-3
Section 1202 stock, 4-14
Section 1244 stock, 4-14
Section 529 tuition plan, 2-42
Self-employed 401(k), 5-26
Self-employed taxpayers
  automobile loans, 3-14
  continuing education expenses, 3-20
  dues and subscriptions, 3-22
  foreign housing exclusion, 7-35
  health insurance deduction, 5-6 to 5-7
  high-income taxpayers, 6-24 to 6-26
  home office deduction, 3-27, 3-29
  0.9 percent Medicare tax, 6-24
  quarterly estimated tax payments, 9-28 to 9-31

retirement plans (*See* Small business and self-employed retirement plans)
  self-employment tax (*See* Self-employment tax)
  special clothing and uniforms, 3-23
  transportation expenses, 3-14
Self-employment tax, 3-7, 4-44 to 4-48
  Schedule SE, 6-24
Self-Employment Tax (Sch. SE), 6-24
Self-study questions, solutions, E-1 to E-129
Self-support test, 1-18 to 1-19
Seniors
  Form 1040-SR, 1-3
  standard deduction, 1-28
SEP, 5-21 to 5-22
Separate property, 2-52
Separation of Liability Relief, 6-35
SEP IRA, 5-21 to 5-22
Series EE bonds, 2-25 to 2-26
Series HH bonds, 2-25
Series I bonds, 2-25 to 2-26
Service corporation, 11-32
Settlement fees or closing costs, 4-5
Settlement Statement (HUD-1), 4-6 to 4-7
Sex abuse or harassment-related expenses, 3-3
Short-period taxable income, 6-2 to 6-3
"Similar or related in service or use," 8-39
SIMPLE IRA, 5-22 to 5-24
SIMPLE IRA plan, 5-26
SIMPLE 401k plan, 5-25
Simplified employee pension (SEP), 5-21 to 5-22
Single filing status, 1-10
Single-member LLC, 10-23
Slot machines, 9-42
Small business and self-employed retirement plans, 5-20 to 5-31
  early withdrawals, 5-20
  fiduciary responsibility, 5-20
  401(k)-based plans, 5-24 to 5-26
  general rule, 5-20
  payroll deduction IRA, 5-21
  qualified plan contributions and distributions, 5-29 to 5-30
  qualified plans (*See* Qualified retirement plans)
  qualified student loan payments, 5-29
  Roth 401(k) plan, 5-26
  safe harbor 401(k) plan, 5-25 to 5-26
  self-employed 401(k), 5-26
  SEP IRA, 5-21 to 5-22
  SIMPLE IRA, 5-22 to 5-24
  small employer automatic enrollment credit, 5-26
  small employer pension plan startup costs credit, 5-26 to 5-28
  solo 401(k) plan, 5-26
  traditional 401(k) plan, 5-24 to 5-25
  vesting requirements, 5-20
Small Business Safe Harbor, 8-4 to 8-5
Small Business/Self-Employed (SB/SE) Division, 12-4
Small corporations, 11-11
Small Employer Automatic Enrollment credit, 5-26
Small employers, 9-38
Social Security Administration (SSA), 9-42
Social Security benefits, 2-46 to 2-49, 9-26
Social Security earnings history, 9-26
Social Security income inclusion formulas, 2-49
Social Security number, 1-17
Social Security tax, 3-7, 9-27
Solo 401(k) plan, 5-24 to 5-26
Solutions to self-study questions, E-1 to E-129
Special clothing and uniforms, 3-23
Special 15 or 18.8-percent tax rate, 8-28
Special 25 or 28.8-percent tax rate, 8-28
Specific charge-off method, 3-25

Specified service trade or business, 4-52 to 4-54
Standard deduction
  amounts (2024), 1-6, 1-28
  blindness, 1-28
  non-eligible individuals, 1-28 to 1-29
  old age, 1-28
  special limitations for dependents, 1-29
  tax rates, 1-6
Standard federal rate method, 3-18
Standard mileage method, 3-14
Start-up costs, 11-5 to 11-6
Start-up costs credit, 5-26 to 5-28
State and local bonds, 2-28
State unemployment taxes, 9-47
Statute of limitations, 12-15 to 12-16
Stock bonus plan, 9-52
stock repurchase excise tax, 11-2
Straight-line depreciation, 8-7 to 8-8
Student loan interest, 5-46 to 5-47
Student loans, 2-54
Students
  American Opportunity tax credit (AOTC), 7-28 to 7-31
  educational savings accounts, 2-44 to 2-45
  lifetime learning credit, 7-31
  Qualified Tuition Program (QTP), 2-42 to 2-44
  scholarships, 2-39
  student loans, 2-54
  unearned income (*See* Kiddie tax)
Subscriptions and publications, 3-22 to 3-23
Substantial authority, 12-19 to 12-20
Substantial understatement of income, 12-13
Substantial valuation overstatement, 12-13
Supplemental Income and Loss (Sch. E), 4-32, 4-37 to 4-38
Support, 1-18
Support test, 1-22 to 1-23
Surviving spouse, 1-12
Sweepstakes, 9-42

T

TAS (Taxpayer Advocate Service), 12-24
Tax, 5-37. *See also* Taxes
Taxable income limitation, 8-18
  QBI deduction, 4-50
  Section 179 election to expense, 8-18
Taxable social security worksheet, 2-47 to 2-49
Tax accounting methods, 6-3 to 6-6
Tax administration. *See* Internal Revenue Service (IRS)
Tax brackets, 1-15. *See also* Tax rates
Tax cheating, 12-13
Tax computation. *See also* Tax payments
  tax brackets, 1-15
  tax computation worksheet, A-3
  tax rates (*See* Tax rates)
  2024 tax table, A-4 to A-15
Tax confidentiality privilege, 12-20 to 12-21
Tax credits, 1-25 to 1-26
  adoption credit, 7-43, 7-45 to 7-46
  adoption expenses, 7-43 to 7-44
  American Opportunity tax credit (AOTC), 7-28 to 7-31
  child and dependent care credit, 7-14 to 7-16
  child tax credit (*See* Child tax credit)
  clean vehicle credit, 7-48 to 7-50, 7-53 to 7-56
  defined, 7-1
  dependents, 1-25 to 1-26
  education tax credits, 7-28 to 7-34
  EIC (*See* Earned income credit (EIC))
  elderly or disabled credit, 7-47
  energy credits, 7-47 to 7-48

Index I-9

energy efficient home improvement credit, 7-48, 7-50 to 7-51
first-time homebuyer credit, 7-47
foreign income exclusion, 7-35
foreign tax credit, 7-41 to 7-42
general business credit, 7-47
lifetime learning credit, 7-31
low-income housing credit, 7-47
low-income retirement plan contribution credit, 7-60 to 7-61
mortage interest credit, 7-47
new markets credit, 7-47
premium tax credit (PTC), 7-16 to 7-24
REEP credit, 7-48
rehabilitation credit, 7-47
research and experimentation credit, 7-47
residential clean energy credit, 7-51 to 7-52
saver's credit, 7-60
tax deduction, compared, 1-25 to 1-26, 7-1
work opportunity credit, 7-47
Tax Cuts and Jobs Act (TCJA)
bonus depreciation, 8-10 to 8-11
child tax credit, 7-2
elimination of personal and dependency exemptions, 1-17
moving expenses, 5-33
2 percent of AGI rule, 3-32 to 3-33, 5-59
personal casualty losses, 5-58
qualified mortgage debt, 5-45
taxes as deductions, 5-37
Tax deductions
business deductions (*See* Business income and expenses)
casualty and theft (*See* Casualty and theft losses)
charitable contributions (*See* Charitable contributions)
defined, 1-26, 7-1
educator expenses, 5-32
fee-based government officials, 5-32
gambling losses, 5-60
interest (*See* Interest deduction)
IRA (*See* Individual retirement account (IRA))
jury duty, 5-33
medical expenses, 5-34 to 5-36
miscellaneous expenses, 5-59 to 5-60
moving expenses, 5-33
National Guard members, 5-32
2 percent of AGI rule, 3-32 to 3-33, 5-59
performing artists, 5-32 to 5-33
phase-out of itemized deductions, 5-60
refundable/nonrefundable credits, 7-2
reserved members of armed forces, 5-32
Schedule A (Itemized Deductions), 5-38
self-employed health insurance deduction, 5-6 to 5-7
tax credits, compared, 1-25 to 1-26, 7-1
taxes (*See* Taxes)
unreimbursed employee expenses, 5-59
Tax drivers, 9-23
Taxes, 5-37 to 5-43
$10,000 aggregate limitation rule, 5-37
general sales tax deduction worksheet, 5-41
income, 5-39 to 5-42
non-deductible, 5-39
personal property, 5-42
pre-TCJA law, 5-37
property, 5-42
refunds, 1-6 to 1-7, 5-39
sales, 5-39 to 5-42
tax/fee, compared, 5-37
Taxes owing. *See* Tax computation
Tax evasion, 12-13
Tax Exempt & Government Entities (TE/GE) Division, 12-4

Tax-exempt income-related expenses, 3-3
Tax Exempt Organization Search, 5-50
Tax-favored medical spending plans, 5-2
Tax for Certain Children Who Have Unearned Income (Form 8615), 6-10 to 6-12
Tax formula for individuals
adjusted gross income (AGI), 1-6
basic formula, 1-5
deductions for adjusted gross income, 1-5 to 1-6
exemptions, 1-6
gross income, 1-5
gross tax liability, 1-6
qualified business income deduction, 1-6
standard deduction for itemized deductions, 1-6
Tax home, 3-15
Tax law
history and objectives, 1-2
origins of U.S. income tax, 1-2
Tax liability issues, 6-34 to 6-35, 6-37
Tax litigation
appeals process, 12-8, 12-10, 12-24
attorney-client privilege, 12-20
burden of proof, 12-20
interest and penalties (*See* Interest and penalties)
nonattorney-client privilege, 12-20
statute of limitations, 12-15 to 12-16
tax confidentiality privilege, 12-20 to 12-21
Tax Notes, 1-34
Taxpayer Advocate Service (TAS), 12-24
Taxpayer Bill of Rights, 12-22
Taxpayer Compliance Measurement Program (TCMP) audit, 12-7
Taxpayers, 3-20
death of the, 6-38 to 6-39
Taxpayer services, 12-4 to 12-5
Taxpayer Services Division, 12-4
Tax payments. *See also* Tax computation
payment of balance due, 1-6
quarterly estimated tax payments, 9-28 to 9-31, 11-9
tax computation (*See* Tax computation)
withholdings (*See* Withholding and payroll taxes)
Tax planning
average tax rate, 12-25
cash-basis taxpayers, 6-4
character, 12-26 to 12-27
closed transaction, 12-25
entity, 12-26
jurisdiction, 12-26
Learned Hand's comments, 12-22
marginal tax rate, 12-25
open transaction, 12-25
quarterly estimated tax payments, 9-31
tax evasion, compared, 12-25
timing, 12-25 to 12-26
Tax practitioners
Annual Filing Season Program (AFSP), 12-18
due diligence checklist, 7-5, 7-31
preparer penalties, 12-19 to 12-20
preparer tax identification (PTIN), 12-16 to 12-17
types, 12-17 to 12-18
Tax preparation. *See* ProConnect
Tax preparers. *See* Tax practitioners
Tax protestors, 1-8
Tax rates
alternative minimum tax (AMT), 6-15 to 6-16
capital gains and losses, 4-9 to 4-10
corporation, 11-2
dividends, 2-34 to 2-36
individual alternative minimum tax, 6-15 to 6-16
single tax rate schedule, 1-15
tax rate schedules, A-2
2024 tax table, A-4 to A-15

Tax rate schedule, 1-15
Tax refund, 1-6 to 1-7, 5-39
Tax return errors, 6-29 to 6-33
Tax return preparer. *See* Tax practitioners
Tax return problems, comprehensive, D-1 to D-11
Tax table, 1-15
Tax withholding. *See* Withholding and payroll taxes
Tax year
corporation, 6-2
individuals, 6-2
partnership, 6-2, 10-18
TCJA. *See* Tax Cuts and Jobs Act (TCJA)
TCMP (Taxpayer Compliance Measurement Program) audit, 12-7
TE/GE (Tax Exempt & Government Entities) Division, 12-4
Television game show prizes, 2-17
$10,000 aggregate limitation rule, 5-37
Tentative credit, 7-49 to 7-50
Termite damage, 5-57
Theft. *See* Casualty and theft losses
Third-party summons, 12-5
39-year nonresidential property, 8-11
3.8 percent Medicare tax on net investment income, 6-23
Tiebreaker rules, 1-20 to 1-21
Tip rate determination agreement (TRDA), 9-24
Tip reporting alternative agreement (TRAC), 9-24
Tips, 2-6 to 2-7, 9-23 to 9-24
Toll fees, 3-14
Total tax, 1-7
TRAC (Tip reporting alternative agreement), 9-24
Trademark, 8-23
Trade name, 8-23
Trade or business, 3-2
Traditional 401(k) plan, 5-24 to 5-25
Transportation (commuting) benefits, 2-11
Transportation expenses, 3-13 to 3-15, 5-36
"Travel as a form of education," 3-22
Travel expenses
combined business and pleasure trip, 3-16
defined, 3-15
employer payroll reporting requirements, 9-41 to 9-46
included expenses, 3-15
meals, 3-15
"overnight," 3-15
per diem substantiation, 3-17 to 3-18
principal place of business, 3-15
recordkeeping requirements, 3-18
tax home, 3-15
temporary assignment, 3-16
travelling outside the United States, 3-16
TRDA (Tip rate determination agreement), 9-24
Treasury bills, 2-27 to 2-28
Treasury bonds, 2-27 to 2-28
Treasury notes, 2-27 to 2-28
Trustee-to-trustee transfer, 9-55
Tuition, 2-42 to 2-44
Tuition reduction, 2-13
Turbo Tax, 1-34
27.5-year residential real property, 8-11
2020 Tax Complexity Index, 1-2
Two-Earners/Multiple Jobs Worksheet, 9-17
Two-income household, 9-6

U

UIDIF (Unreported income DIF) score, 12-7
Unadjusted basis immediately after acquisition (UBIA), 4-50
Uncollectible debts, 3-25
Underpayment of Estimated Tax by Individuals, Estates, and Trusts, 9-29

Index

Unearned income. *See* Kiddie tax
Unemployment compensation, 2-46
Unemployment tax, 9-47
Unforeseen circumstances, 4-23
UNICAP rules, 3-11
Uniform minimum distribution rules, 9-52
Uniform Partnership Act, 10-2
Uniforms, 3-23
United States, 3-16 to 3-17, 6-33
United States (U.S.) tax law, 1-2
Unrecaptured depreciation, 8-28
Unrecaptured Section 1250 Gain Worksheet, 8-28
Unreimbursed employee expenses, 5-59
Unreported income DIF (UIDIF) score, 12-7
U.S. Armed Forces gross income, 6-42 to 6-44
U.S. savings bonds, 2-25 to 2-27
U.S. Treasury Bills, 2-27 to 2-28

V

Vacation home
  allocable rental expenses, 4-29
  defined, 4-28
  general rule, 4-28
  primarily personal use, 4-28
  primarily rental use, 4-28 to 4-29
  rental/personal use, 4-29 to 4-30
VCSP (Voluntary Classification Settlement Program), 9-3
Vehicle/Employee Business Expense, 3-15
Vehicle expenses, 3-15
Vehicle information, 3-5 to 3-6
Venmo, 9-43
Vesting requirements, 5-20, 9-52
Viatical settlements, 2-23
Virtual currency, 4-2 to 4-3

VISA, 9-43
Voluntary Classification Settlement Program (VCSP), 9-3
Volunteer income tax assistance (VITA) program, 1-32

W

Wage and capital limit, 4-50
Wage and Investment (W&I) Division, 12-4
Wage bracket method of determining withholding, 9-18, 9-20, 9-22, C-2 to C-14
Wage limit, 4-50 to 4-52
Wagering pools, 9-42
Wages, 2-4 to 2-7
Wash sales, 4-13 to 4-14
Whistleblower Office (WO), 12-4
W&I (Wage and Investment) Division, 12-4
Withholding and payroll taxes
  backup withholding, 9-24
  claiming exemption from withholding, 9-8
  computing income tax withholding, 9-18 to 9-21
  credit card sales, 9-43
  employer reporting requirements, 9-41 to 9-46
  estimated payments, 9-28 to 9-31
  false Form W-4, 9-13
  federal tax deposit system (*See* Federal tax deposit system)
  FICA tax (*See* FICA tax)
  "forced" savings (overpayment of taxes), 9-22
  Form W-4 after 2019, 9-5 to 9-13
  Form W-4 before 2020, 9-13 to 9-17
  Form W-9 Request for Taxpayer Identification Number, 9-44 to 9-45
  gambling winnings, 9-42
  information returns, 9-42 to 9-43

  IRS online withholding estimator, 9-6
  IRS Publication 15-T, 9-18, 9-38
  lock-in letter, 9-13
  lookback period, 9-37
  merchant card and third-party payments, 9-43
  monthly or semiweekly depositors, 9-37
  multiple jobs worksheet, 9-6
  new employees, 9-13
  1099 Forms, 9-42
  pension and deferred income, 9-23
  percentage method, 9-18, C-15 to C-18
  required annual payment, 9-28 to 9-29
  tip reporting, 9-23 to 9-24
  two-income household, 9-6
  wage bracket method, 9-18, 9-20, 9-22, C-2 to C-14
  withholding tables, 9-18
  Worksheet 4 (income tax withholding methods), 9-18
Withholding Certificate for Pension or Annuity Payments, 9-23
WO (Whistleblower Office), 12-4
W-2 or 1099-R Wrong or Not Received, 6-29
Worker classification factors, 9-2 to 9-3
Working condition fringe benefits, 2-14
Work opportunity credit, 7-47
Worksheet 4 (income tax withholding methods), 9-18
W-2 Wages, 4-50

Y

YouTube channel, 1-33